T0305305

INVESTMENT PERFORMANCE MEASUREMENT

CFA Institute Investment Perspectives Series is a thematically organized compilation of high-quality content developed to address the needs of serious investment professionals. The content builds on issues accepted by the profession in the CFA Institute Global Body of Investment Knowledge and explores less established concepts on the frontiers of investment knowledge. These books tap into a vast store of knowledge of prominent thought leaders who have focused their energies on solving complex problems facing the financial community.

CFA Institute is the global association for investment professionals. It administers the CFA® and CIPM curriculum and exam programs worldwide; publishes research; conducts professional development programs; and sets voluntary, ethics-based professional and performance-reporting standards for the investment industry. CFA Institute has more than 95,000 members, who include the world's 82,000 CFA charterholders, in 134 countries and territories, as well as 135 affiliated professional societies in 56 countries and territories.

www.cfainstitute.org

Research Foundation of CFA Institute is a not-for-profit organization established to promote the development and dissemination of relevant research for investment practitioners worldwide. Since 1965, the Research Foundation has emphasized research of practical value to investment professionals, while exploring new and challenging topics that provide a unique perspective in the rapidly evolving profession of investment management.

To carry out its work, the Research Foundation funds and publishes new research, supports the creation of literature reviews, sponsors workshops an seminars, and delivers online webcasts and audiocasts. Recent efforts from the Research Foundation have addressed a wide array of topics, ranging from private wealth management to quantitative tools for portfolio management.

www.cfainstitute.org/foundation

INVESTMENT PERFORMANCE MEASUREMENT

Evaluating and Presenting Results

Philip Lawton, CFA, CIPM
Todd Jankowski, CFA

WILEY

John Wiley & Sons, Inc.

Published by John Wiley & Sons, Inc., Hoboken, New Jersey.
Published simultaneously in Canada.

For general information on our other products and services or for technical support, please contact our Customer Care Department within the United States at (800) 762-2974, outside the United States at (317) 572-3993 or fax (317) 572-4002.

Wiley also publishes its books in a variety of electronic formats. Some content that appears in print may not be available in electronic books. For more information about Wiley products, visit our web site at www.wiley.com.

Library of Congress Cataloging-in-Publication Data:
  Investment performance measurement : evaluating and presenting results/Philip Lawton, Todd Jankowski.
    p. cm.
  Includes index.
    ISBN 978-0-470-39502-8 (cloth)
      1. Investment analysis. 2. Investments. I. Lawton, Philip (John Philip) II. Jankowski, Todd.
  HG4529.I5745 2009
  332.63'2042—dc22
                                                                                    2009004092

Printed in the United States of America.

10 9 8 7 6 5 4 3 2 1

CONTENTS

FOREWORD

Investment management firms and their relationship managers need to be able to communicate their results to clients clearly and fairly. Investors, portfolio managers, advisers, and consultants need to be able to evaluate these results and ascertain to what extent performance was attributable to asset allocation, security selection, or other decisions. Technology staff, accountants, and compliance officers also need to understand performance measurement to design and audit systems that generate these results.

The field of performance measurement has made great strides since Gray P. Brinson, L. Randolph Hood, and Gilbert L. Beebower published their pioneering work on attribution analysis in 1986 and the Committee for Performance Reporting Standards of the Financial Analysts Federation (a predecessor of CFA Institute) proposed the development of performance presentation standards in 1987. These Standards have developed progressively over the last 20 years through the work of CFA Institute and almost 30 country sponsors. Today, the Global Investment Performance Standards (GIPS®) articulate a set of industrywide ethical principles that provide investment firms with guidance on how to calculate and report their investment results. Furthermore, a professional designation program has developed for professionals desiring to specialize in this area: the Certificate in Investment Performance Measurement (CIPM®).

This volume provides the reader with the tools necessary to measure, present, and evaluate investment performance results. It is a compilation of some of the best writings on presenting and evaluating investment performance. These include articles from the Research Foundation of CFA Institute, the *Financial Analysts Journal, CFA Institute Conference Proceedings Quarterly, CFA Magazine,* and the CIPM program. We are grateful to the distinguished team of authors for sharing their knowledge with investors and investment professionals through CFA Institute.

The 41 papers included here are organized in five sections beginning with an overview and followed by sections on performance measurement (what happened), performance attribution (why it happened), performance appraisal (how the investment manager did), and the Global Investment Performance Standards (how results should be presented).

CFA Institute is pleased to present *Investment Performance Measurement: Evaluating and Presenting Results,* the second in our CFA Institute Investment Perspectives series. We hope you will find it a useful guide and resource in performance measurement.

Robert R. Johnson, CFA
Deputy CEO
CFA Institute

INTRODUCTION

Evaluating performance insightfully and presenting it fairly are crucial to the vitality of an investment firm. Security analysts and portfolio managers make decisions under conditions of uncertainty about the relative attractiveness of market sectors and individual investments; the role of performance analysts is to explain the outcome of those decisions. At its best, the intelligent feedback provided by trained, experienced performance analysts can help the firm improve its decision process and refine its investment strategies, and the performance presentations they prepare can contribute to the firm's success in expanding client relationships and winning new business. Whether markets are rising or falling, resilient investment organizations value highly qualified performance professionals. Indeed, there is a curious countercyclicality to the demand for their expertise: It is when results are most disappointing that cogent explanations are most urgently needed.

In the chapter that opens this volume in the CFA Institute Investment Perspectives series, authors Jeffery V. Bailey, Thomas M. Richards, and David E. Tierney state that three questions arise in the process of evaluating the performance of an account—that is, a portfolio or a group of portfolios:

1. What was the account's performance?
2. Why did the account produce the observed performance?
3. Is the account's performance a result of luck or skill?

The first question falls in the domain of performance measurement, more narrowly defined in this context than in common usage. It is answered by calculating the account's rate of return over the evaluation period. Rate-of-return calculations are relatively straightforward in the case of traditional, long-only equity portfolios holding assets denominated in a single currency, but they are appreciably thornier for portfolios with more esoteric strategies. Once the return of the portfolio has been determined, it remains to judge whether the results meet the client's expectations, usually by comparing the portfolio's return with the return of a valid benchmark. Bailey, Richards, and Tierney set forth widely accepted criteria of benchmark validity and useful tests of benchmark quality.

The second question belongs to the realm of performance attribution. It is answered by applying quantitative techniques to establish the sources of the portfolio's return relative to the benchmark (i.e., to determine which investment decisions added value and, of course, which ones did not). Here, too, the mathematics of attribution analysis is fairly easy to grasp in the case of single-currency, long-only equity portfolios considered over a single evaluation period, but it is more challenging for portfolios holding both long and short positions, measured over multiple periods, or invested in fixed-income securities, derivatives, and assets denominated in multiple currencies. Attribution analysis, often accompanied by portfolio characteristics analysis, enables proficient performance professionals to discern what the firm does well and not so well. It also facilitates productive dialogue with clients who may be reassured to find that the firm is investing as expected, following its mandate and adhering to its discipline even when the agreed-upon strategy is out of favor in the marketplace.

The third, and the most difficult and consequential, question pertains to performance appraisal. When conducting manager searches and monitoring managers' performance, institutional investors and their consultants seek to identify the investment firms most likely to produce consistently favorable results—firms whose track records arise not merely from fortunate timing but from the competent, disciplined execution of coherent, evidence-based investment strategies. Luck may change at any moment, whereas in stable organizations, skillfulness may reasonably be expected to persist. Because it is costly to terminate an advisory relationship and transfer assets to a new manager, investors must select managers prudently, and if portfolio returns prove disappointing, as they sometimes will, investors must attempt to distinguish between a simple run of bad luck and a much more serious lack, or loss, of skill. It is generally acknowledged, however, that investors cannot definitively establish, in a realistic timeframe, whether investment results are because of the manager's skill or dumb luck. In practice, therefore, performance appraisal commonly focuses on related and somewhat more decidable issues, to wit, determining whether the manager has taken acceptable risks and whether, over time, the investor has been adequately compensated for them.

In addition to evaluating decisions made on behalf of existing clients, performance professionals employed by investment firms are responsible for preparing presentations for the use of prospective clients. Working in close collaboration with numerous other organizations over the last two decades, CFA Institute has been a leader in developing voluntary performance presentation standards that protect the interests of prospective clients. The Global Investment Performance Standards (GIPS®) advance the ethical ideals of presenting investment results fairly and disclosing them fully. The Standards set forth minimum requirements and recommend best practices related to input data, calculation methodology, composite construction, disclosures, and the presentation and reporting of investment performance—all intended to ensure that a firm claiming compliance gives prospective clients complete and accurate information about its historical results. Now widely endorsed (and still evolving), the GIPS standards are a signal contribution to the investment industry, benefiting investors and investment firms around the world. It behooves anyone with an interest in performance measurement to become familiar with them.

The foregoing survey of the field of investment performance measurement accounts for the way in which we have organized the papers selected for this specialized collection from the wealth of CFA Institute publications. Participants in the Certificate in Investment Performance Measurement (CIPM®) program will recognize some papers from their study of the curriculum; this volume contains most of the Principles-level readings and several Expert-level readings.[1]

OVERVIEW

The "Overview" section contains the outstanding essay, previously mentioned, by Jeffery V. Bailey, Thomas M. Richards, and David E. Tierney. "Evaluating Portfolio Performance" is a masterful introduction to performance measurement, attribution, and appraisal. The authors explain the algebra of time-weighted and money-weighted rates of return, evaluate various types of benchmarks (notably including custom security-based benchmarks), present a widely used method of attribution analysis for individual portfolios and a systematic approach to attribution analysis at the total fund level, and give a well-considered account of the

---

[1]The CIPM program is described at www.cfainstitute.org/cipm.

objectives and techniques of performance appraisal, including *ex post* risk measures, quality control charts, and manager continuation policies. To those who are exploring the field for the first time, the value of this paper is inestimable; however, we recommend it no less enthusiastically to readers long acquainted with the challenges of performance evaluation.

PERFORMANCE MEASUREMENT

The section of this book devoted to performance measurement includes only one paper on rate-of-return calculations. In his important treatment of after-tax performance evaluation, James M. Poterba argues that the return calculation methodology should capture the contingent tax liability associated with unrealized gains held in the portfolio at the end of an evaluation period. For the rest, this section centers on issues surrounding the construction and selection of performance benchmarks.

Re-published here in full, Laurence B. Siegel's monograph "Benchmarks and Investment Management" recounts the historical development of benchmarking in the context of modern portfolio theory and judiciously addresses a range of fundamental and often contentious issues. By comparing the philosophies and methodologies of two major index providers, Christopher G. Luck illustrates how the choice of a benchmark can affect the behavior of active portfolio managers. Lee N. Price describes three progressively accurate techniques for approximating the after-tax return of a pre-tax benchmark. Arguing that generic, capitalization-weighted bond indices do not represent the true opportunity set for most fixed-income portfolios, William L. Nemerever suggests using derivative securities to construct alternative benchmarks. Brent Ambrose and Arthur Warga demonstrate that dollar-duration weighting results in significantly more reliable estimates of fixed-income portfolio yields than the conventional market-value-weighted approach. Finally, Crystal Detamore-Rodman presents the views of several thought leaders on selecting appropriate benchmarks, isolating pure alpha (i.e., the risk-adjusted excess return due not to market exposures but to the portfolio manager's active decisions), and constructing synthetic universes representing the portfolios that might have been formed from the benchmark's constituent securities. In their diversity, the articles assembled in this section will give thoughtful readers a solid understanding of the theoretical grounds for benchmarking and the trade-offs encountered in practice.

PERFORMANCE ATTRIBUTION

The section devoted to performance attribution analysis opens with a groundbreaking piece that first appeared almost a quarter century ago, followed by an update published in 1991 and a letter to the *Financial Analysts Journal* written by one of the authors in 2005. In their short, powerful 1986 article "Determinants of Portfolio Performance," Gary P. Brinson, L. Randolph Hood, and Gilbert L. Beebower famously presented their finding that, at the total fund level, investment policy—an investor's decisions about which asset classes to include and what normal weights to assign them—contributes far more to the variation of returns than does active management in the form of market timing and security (or manager) selection. From a performance analyst's point of view, the decisive importance of this empirical result is matched by the lasting impact of the authors' conceptual framework for decomposing returns. In "Determinants of Portfolio Performance II: An Update," Brian D. Singer joins Brinson and Beebower in presenting further, confirmatory research on the total return contributions from policy and active management decisions and in extending the analytical method to capture the effect of internal risk positioning, for instance, by using futures, carrying cash, or hedging currency exposures. In "Determinants of Portfolio Performance—20 Years Later," L. Randolph Hood reflects on the debate that followed the appearance of the original article. "The consensus," he writes, ". . . appears to have settled in to agree with us that investment policy will be very important in subsequent results and in describing those results."

Philip Lawton and Stephen C. Gaudette explain how equity portfolio characteristics analysis can help performance practitioners discern shifts in strategy, evaluate investment style, and determine the return effects of factor exposures. Taking into account the costs of acquiring and trading on information, Daniel C. Indro, Christine X. Jiang, Michael Y. Hu, and Wayne Y. Lee investigate the relationship between mutual fund size and performance.

"Multiperiod Arithmetic Attribution" is the first of three articles by José Menchero included in this collection. The accuracy of widely used arithmetic attribution methodologies, such as the Brinson model, decays when they are applied to extended reporting periods over which portfolios are rebalanced. In light of desirable qualitative characteristics and quantitative properties, Menchero classifies and evaluates competing algorithms designed to eliminate unexplained residuals in multiperiod arithmetic attribution analyses. In "Optimized Geometric Attribution," he presents a metric-preserving method for distributing the residuals that are generated in the process of geometric buy-and-hold attribution analysis so as to minimize the distortion of sector effects. In "Custom Factor Attribution," Menchero collaborates with Vijay Poduri in presenting a framework for explaining the sources of risk-adjusted performance by attributing the information ratio (defined as active return divided by the tracking error) to custom factors that reflect the actual investment strategy and decision-making process. The method proposed by Menchero and Poduri may represent a step forward in realizing the promise of performance attribution analysis by aligning it with controllable aspects of the firm's portfolio management and risk modeling processes. In an article entitled "Return, Risk, and Performance Attribution," Kevin Terhaar illustrates the need for such consistency by describing cases where attribution analyses that disregard the firm's investment process, strategy, and risk factors can lead to erroneous results.

Managing portfolios that hold assets issued in foreign markets and denominated in foreign currencies entails making decisions that are not contemplated in domestic investing. We are pleased to republish in its entirety a seminal monograph, "Global Asset Management and Performance Attribution," in which Denis S. Karnosky and Brian D. Singer develop an analytical framework for evaluating global markets and construct a performance attribution system that isolates the effects of market allocation, currency management, and security selection on portfolio returns. Performance analysts who are familiar with the Karnosky–Singer method from formula-centered summaries in secondary sources, or indeed use it in their work, will likely find that grasping its theoretical basis contributes immeasurably to their understanding of global investment management. In "Currency Overlay in Performance Evaluation," Cornelia Paape critiques the Karnosky–Singer approach and presents a performance measurement system whose attribution variables separate the effects of active management decisions into market allocation, security selection, currency allocation, and currency selection.

PERFORMANCE APPRAISAL

The section of this book devoted to performance appraisal opens with four articles about hedge fund risks and returns. Bing Liang introduces the topic by describing salient features of hedge funds and reporting the results of a study conducted during a period of strong performance (1992–1996). Stan Beckers focuses on the risk-adjusted returns achieved by funds of hedge funds over the 10-year period 1997–2006 and cautions that "buying beta disguised as alpha is an expensive proposition." Cynthia Harrington discusses measures investors can take to counteract hedge funds' characteristic lack of transparency and surveys commonly used risk measures.

Performance analysts may evaluate portfolio managers' track records in "up" and "down" markets, but they typically do not take the state of the economy into account. Conditional performance evaluation, however, compares a fund's returns with the returns of a dynamic strategy that matches the fund's time-varying risk exposures. In "Conditional Performance Evaluation, Revisited," a Research Foundation of CFA Institute monograph, Wayne E. Ferson and Meijun Qian review the main empirical results of previous studies, expand the list of state variables, present an analysis of mutual funds' conditional performance at the level of broadly defined style groups, and examine evidence of market-timing ability. By helping to distinguish between luck and skill, conditional performance evaluation may guide investors and consultants toward better decisions about investment managers. Conditional performance evaluation is also presented in a shorter, earlier article by Ferson and Vincent A. Warther that appears further along in this volume.

In his article "Distinguishing True Alpha from Beta," Laurence B. Siegel describes the dimensions of active management; differentiates active, or alpha, risk from policy, or beta, risk; applies those concepts to hedge funds; and draws out their policy implications for pension funds and other investors.

The Sharpe ratio, as traditionally defined, compares a portfolio's excess return (that is, its return in excess of the risk-free rate) with the total risk of the portfolio, represented by the standard deviation of returns. It is well known, however, that the theoretical foundation for the Sharpe ratio does not apply when excess returns are not normally distributed. Michael Stutzer reviews three approaches to overcoming this limitation and proposes an alternative performance index that reflects investors' preference for positive skewness. Angelo Lobosco and Dan DiBartolomeo provide a primer on returns-based style analysis—a form of constrained regression used to determine the weighted combination of market indices that most closely matches the historical return pattern of the portfolio being analyzed—and define a method for establishing confidence intervals around the weights. Andrew W. Lo investigates the statistical properties of the Sharpe ratio and reaches conclusions of considerable practical importance about, for instance, the distorting impact of serial correlation in hedge funds' monthly returns. In an updated version of "Risk-Adjusted Performance: The Correlation Correction," Arun S. Muralidhar argues that current measures of risk-adjusted performance, including the Sharpe ratio and the M^2 measure, are insufficient bases for ranking mutual funds or constructing portfolios that are likely to earn the highest alpha for a given tracking error. He proposes a new measure, M-3, as a more comprehensive alternative that incorporates the correlation between mutual fund returns and benchmark returns. Muralidhar modestly revised this paper for the present volume, making note of related research into further applications of the M-3 measure in the domain of manager selection.

The "reconstitution effect" is one of the ways in which benchmarking affects markets and institutions. Honghui Chen, Gregory Noronha, and Vijay Singal estimate that investors in funds linked to the S&P 500 Index and the Russell 2000 Index may lose more than US$2 billion a year because of arbitrage around the time of index changes. They describe the arbitrage opportunity as an unintended consequence of the widespread evaluation of index fund managers on the basis of tracking error. Indexers rebalance their portfolios on the effective date in order to minimize tracking error; arbitrageurs buy the stocks to be added to the index when the addition is announced and sell the stocks to the indexers at a higher price on the effective date. In addition to suggesting that tracking error targets are inappropriate, the authors recommend policies that indexing firms might adopt to limit arbitrageurs' front running of index funds.

Two papers center on calculating and interpreting the information ratio, a fundamentally important measure of risk-adjusted performance that compares the benchmark-relative excess return of an investment strategy with its excess risk. Neil Constable and Jeremy Armitage consider the interaction of information ratios with "batting averages," another frequently quoted measure of success defined as the percentage of investment decisions that led to a profit. The information ratio does not describe the series of successes and failures that led to the outcome it expresses, whereas the batting average contains only directional information. Constable and Armitage demonstrate that the two measures can be usefully combined to give investors a more comprehensive view of their choices. Thomas H. Goodwin rigorously sets forth how the information ratio is defined, annualized, and interpreted, including helpful accounts of its relationship to the Sharpe ratio and the t-statistic.

Roger G. Ibbotson and Paul D. Kaplan reprise the question raised by Brinson et al., namely, how much of the variability of returns across time is explained by policy (about 90 percent in the sample and over the period the authors studied), and additionally ask how much of the variation in returns among funds is explained by differences in policy (about 40 percent) and what portion of the return level is explained by policy return (on average about 100 percent).

Institutional investors, such as pension plans and charitable foundations, engage managers for specific roles within diversified, multiple-asset-class, multiple-manager investment programs, and they expect the managers to invest in accordance with their mandates. Several papers selected for this volume address key aspects of manager selection and monitoring. John G. Gallo and Larry J. Lockwood present the results of an empirical study of mutual funds that underwent management changes during the 1983–1991 period. They find significant differences in performance, risk, and investment style after the management changes. Louisa Wright Sellers describes how her organization, a well-established family office, selects and monitors hedge funds and other external managers and explains what she considers catalysts for changing managers. Philip Halpern, Nancy Calkins, and Tom Ruggels share lessons derived from their own experience and comment on three possible reasons why it is so difficult for institutional investors to succeed in selecting consistently outperforming managers: The evaluation criteria are inappropriate, the search process is flawed, or the number of truly skillful managers is so small that still greater effort is required to find them. In a paper that deserves to be recognized as a classic, Ronald N. Kahn and Andrew Rudd examine in-sample and out-of-sample track records of equity and fixed-income mutual funds for evidence of persistent performance. They find evidence of persistence of selection returns among fixed-income funds but no such evidence for equity funds, and they consider the investment implications of these findings. Kahn and Rudd advocate basing active manager selections on information that goes beyond historical performance.

John P. Meier focuses on determining whether managers are doing what is expected of them. Written from the total fund perspective, his paper "Investment Performance Appraisal" is an integrative case study proficiently demonstrating the application of analytical approaches and the exercise of professional judgment in monitoring and evaluating an investment manager.

Susan Trammell's informative, nontechnical report on developments in the risk management industry closes the performance appraisal section of this work.

GLOBAL INVESTMENT PERFORMANCE STANDARDS

Presenting investment results is, as we previously observed, one of the ways in which performance professionals contribute to their firms' growth. In an industry that is based upon credibility and trust, however, the quality of performance presentations has implications greater than the fortunes of any one firm. Founded on the ideals of fair representation and full disclosure of an investment management firm's performance history, the voluntary Global Investment Performance Standards contain provisions requiring certain practices and recommending others in such areas as input data, rate-of-return calculation methodologies, and performance presentations. Philip Lawton and W. Bruce Remington recount the history and explain the provisions of the GIPS standards, with attention to many practical issues that arise in the course of firmwide implementation. (The official text of the Standards in effect as of this writing is also included as an appendix in this volume.) The development of the GIPS standards continues apace as the GIPS Executive Committee and its technical subcommittees address outstanding and emerging issues, and we encourage readers seeking the most up-to-date guidance to visit the website at www.gipsstandards.org.

SUMMARY

This volume contains the insights of 56 contributors who have spent a great deal of their professional lives focusing on performance evaluation. And as a result, the material presented here is diverse, in depth, and of great practical value. We are delighted to present this resource to the performance measurement community. We hope it serves as a foundation for future innovation in analytical frameworks that address the growing needs of asset management firms and their clients for accurate, useful information about investment results.

Philip Lawton, CFA, CIPM
Todd Jankowski, CFA

PART I

OVERVIEW OF PERFORMANCE EVALUATION

CHAPTER 1

EVALUATING PORTFOLIO PERFORMANCE

Jeffery V. Bailey, CFA

Thomas M. Richards, CFA

David E. Tierney

The *ex post* analysis of investment performance stands as a prominent and ubiquitous feature of modern investment management practice. Investing involves making decisions that have readily quantifiable consequences and that, at least on the surface, lend themselves to elaborate dissection and review. We broadly refer to the measurement and assessment of the outcomes of these investment management decisions as **performance evaluation.** At the institutional investor level, and to a lesser (but growing) extent on the individual investor level, a large industry has developed to satisfy the demand for performance evaluation services. Although some observers contend that performance evaluation is misguided, frequently misapplied, or simply unattainable with any reasonable degree of statistical confidence, we believe that analytic techniques representing best practices can lead to valid insights about the sources of past returns, and such insights can be useful inputs for managing an investment program.

The purpose of this chapter is to provide an overview of current performance evaluation concepts and techniques. Our focus will be on how institutional investors—both fund sponsors and investment managers—conduct performance evaluation. Individual investors tend to use variations of the performance evaluation techniques employed by institutional investors. We define fund sponsors to be owners of large pools of investable assets, such as corporate and public pension funds, endowments, and foundations. These organizations typically retain multiple investment management firms deployed across a range of asset categories. Fund sponsors have the challenge of evaluating not only the performance of the individual managers, but also the investment results within the asset categories and for their total investment programs.

Reprinted from *Managing Investment Portfolios: A Dynamic Process*, 3rd Edition (John Wiley & Sons, 2007):717–780.

In the section titled The Importance of Performance Evaluation, we distinguish between the perspectives of the fund sponsor and the investment manager. In The Three Components of Performance Evaluation, we divide the broad subject of performance evaluation into three components: **performance measurement, performance attribution**, and **performance appraisal**. Under the topic of performance measurement, we discuss several methods of calculating portfolio performance. The next section introduces the concept of performance benchmarks. Turning to performance attribution, we consider the process of analyzing the sources of returns relative to a designated benchmark both from the total fund (fund sponsor) level and from the individual portfolio (investment manager) level. This is followed by performance appraisal, which deals with assessing investment skill. The chapter ends by addressing key issues in the practice of performance evaluation.

THE IMPORTANCE OF PERFORMANCE EVALUATION

Performance evaluation is important from the perspectives of both the fund sponsor and the investment manager.

The Fund Sponsor's Perspective

A typical fund sponsor would consider its investment program incomplete without a thorough and regular evaluation of the fund's performance relative to its investment objectives. Applied in a comprehensive manner, performance evaluation is more than a simple exercise in calculating rates of return. Rather, it provides an exhaustive "quality control" check, emphasizing not only the performance of the fund and its constituent parts relative to objectives, but the sources of that relative performance as well.

Performance evaluation is part of the feedback step of the investment management process. As such, it should be an integral part of a fund's investment policy and documented in its investment policy statement. As discussed in Ambachtsheer (1986) and Ellis (1985), investment policy itself is a combination of philosophy and planning. On the one hand, it expresses the fund sponsor's attitudes toward a number of important investment management issues, such as the fund's mission, the fund sponsor's risk tolerance, the fund's investment objectives, and so on. On the other hand, investment policy is a form of long-term strategic planning. It defines the specific goals that the fund sponsor expects the fund to accomplish, and it describes how the fund sponsor foresees the realization of those goals.

Investment policy gives an investment program a sense of direction and discipline. Performance evaluation enhances the effectiveness of a fund's investment policy by acting as a feedback and control mechanism. It identifies an investment program's strengths and weaknesses and attributes the fund's investment results to various key decisions. It assists the fund sponsor in reaffirming a commitment to successful investment strategies, and it helps to focus attention on poorly performing operations. Moreover, it provides evidence to fund trustees, who ultimately bear fiduciary responsibility for the fund's viability, that the investment program is being conducted in an appropriate and effective manner.

Fund sponsors are venturing into nontraditional asset categories and hiring a larger assortment of managers exhibiting unique investment styles, with the addition of hedge fund managers representing the latest and perhaps most complex example of this trend. Some fund sponsors are taking more investment decisions into their own hands, such as tactical asset allocation and style timing. Others are taking a quite different direction, giving their managers broad discretion to make asset allocation and security selection decisions. As a consequence of these developments, alert trustee boards are demanding more information from their investment staffs. The staffs, in turn, are seeking to better understand the extent of their own contributions and those of the funds' investment managers to the funds' investment results. The increased complexity of institutional investment management has brought a correspondingly greater need for sophisticated performance evaluation from the fund sponsor's perspective.

The Investment Manager's Perspective

Investment managers have various incentives to evaluate the performance of the portfolios that they manage for their clients. Virtually all fund sponsors insist that their managers offer some type of accounting of portfolio investment results. In many cases, performance evaluation conducted by the investment manager simply takes the form of reporting investment returns, perhaps presented alongside the returns of some designated benchmark. Other clients may insist on more sophisticated analyses, which the managers may produce in-house or acquire from a third party.

Some investment managers may seriously wish to investigate the effectiveness of various elements of their investment processes and examine the relative contributions of those elements. Managing investment portfolios involves a complex set of decision-making procedures. For example, an equity manager must make decisions about which stocks to hold, when to transact in those stocks, how much to allocate to various economic sectors, and how to allocate funds between stocks and cash. Numerous analysts and portfolio managers may be involved in determining a portfolio's composition. Just as in the case of the fund sponsor, performance evaluation can serve as a feedback and control loop, helping to monitor the proficiency of various aspects of the portfolio construction process.

THE THREE COMPONENTS OF PERFORMANCE EVALUATION

In light of the subject's importance to fund sponsors and investment managers alike, we want to consider the primary questions that performance evaluation seeks to address. In discussing performance evaluation we shall use the term *account* to refer generically to one or more portfolios of securities, managed by one or more investment management organizations. Thus, at one end of the spectrum, an account might indicate a single portfolio invested by a single manager. At the other end, an account could mean a fund sponsor's total fund, which might involve numerous portfolios invested by many different managers across multiple asset categories. In between, it might include all of a fund sponsor's assets in a particular asset category or the aggregate of all of the portfolios managed by an investment manager according to a particular mandate. The basic performance evaluation concepts are the same, regardless of the account's composition.

With the definition of an account in mind, three questions naturally arise in examining the investment performance of an account:

1. What was the account's performance?
2. Why did the account produce the observed performance?
3. Is the account's performance due to luck or skill?

In somewhat simplistic terms, these questions constitute the three primary issues of performance evaluation. The first issue is addressed by performance measurement, which calculates rates of return based on investment-related changes in an account's value over specified time periods. Performance attribution deals with the second issue. It extends the results of performance measurement to investigate both the sources of the account's performance relative to a specific investment benchmark and the importance of those sources. Finally, performance appraisal tackles the third question. It attempts to draw conclusions concerning the quality (that is, the magnitude and consistency) of the account's relative performance.

PERFORMANCE MEASUREMENT

To many investors, performance measurement and performance evaluation are synonymous. However, according to our classification, performance measurement is a component of performance evaluation. Performance measurement is the relatively simple procedure of calculating returns for an account. Performance evaluation, on the other hand, encompasses the broader and much more complex task of placing those investment results in the context of the account's investment objectives.

Performance measurement is the first step in the performance evaluation process. Yet it is a critical step, because to be of value, performance evaluation requires accurate and timely rate-of-return information. Therefore, we must fully understand how to compute an account's returns before advancing to more involved performance evaluation issues.

Performance Measurement without Intraperiod External Cash Flows

The rate of return on an account is the percentage change in the account's market value over some defined period of time (the evaluation period), after accounting for all external cash flows.[1] (External cash flows refer to contributions and withdrawals made to and from an account, as opposed to internal cash flows such as dividends and interest payments.) Therefore, a rate of return measures the relative change in the account's value due solely to investment-related sources, namely capital appreciation or depreciation and income. The mere addition or subtraction of assets to or from the account by the account's owner should not affect the rate of return. Of course, in the simplest case, the account would experience no external cash flows. In that situation, the account's rate of return during evaluation period t equals the market value (MV_1) at the end of the period less the market value at the beginning of the period (MV_0), divided by the beginning market value.[2] That is,

$$r_t = \frac{MV_1 - MV_0}{MV_0} \tag{1.1}$$

Example 1.1 illustrates the use of Equation 1.1.

EXAMPLE 1.1   Rate-of-Return Calculations When There Are No External Cash Flows

---

Winter Asset Management manages institutional and individual accounts, including the account of the Mientkiewicz family. The Mientkiewicz account was initially valued at $1,000,000. One month later it was worth $1,080,000. Assuming no external cash flows and the reinvestment of all income, applying Equation 1.1, the return on the Mientkiewicz account for the month is

$$r_t = \frac{\$1,080,000 - \$1,000,000}{\$1,000,000} = 8.0\%$$

Fund sponsors occasionally (and in some cases frequently) add and subtract cash to and from their managers' accounts. These external cash flows complicate rate-of-return calculations. The rate-of-return algorithm must deal not only with the investment earnings on the initial assets in the account, but also with the earnings on any additional assets added to or subtracted from the account during the evaluation period. At the same time, the algorithm must exclude the direct impact of the external cash flows on the account's value.

An account's rate of return may still be computed in a straightforward fashion if the external cash flows occur at the beginning or the end of the measurement period when the account is valued. If a contribution is received at the start of the period, it should be added to (or, in the case of a withdrawal, subtracted from) the account's beginning value when calculating the account's rate of return for that period. The external cash flow will be invested alongside the rest of the account for the full length of the evaluation period and will have the same investment-related impact on the account's ending market value and, hence, should receive a full weighting. Thus, the account's return in the presence of an external cash flow at the beginning of the evaluation period should be calculated as

$$r_t = \frac{MV_1 - (MV_0 + CF)}{MV_0 + CF} \tag{1.2}$$

If a contribution is received at the end of the evaluation period, it should be subtracted from (or, in the case of a withdrawal, added to) the account's ending value. The external cash flow had no opportunity to affect the investment-related value of the account, and hence it should be ignored.

$$r_t = \frac{(MV_1 - CF) - MV_0}{MV_0} \tag{1.3}$$

EXAMPLE 1.2   Rate-of-Return Calculations When External Cash Flows Occur at the Beginning or End of an Evaluation Period

Returning to the example of the Mientkiewicz account, assume that the account received a $50,000 contribution at the beginning of the month. Further, the account's ending and beginning market values equal the same amounts previously stated, $1,080,000 and $1,000,000, respectively. Applying Equation 1.2, the rate of return for the month is therefore

$$r_t = \frac{\$1,080,000 - (\$1,000,000 + \$50,000)}{\$1,000,000 + \$50,000} = 2.86\%$$

If the contribution had occurred at month-end, using Equation 1.3, the account's return would be

$$r_t = \frac{(\$1,080,000 - \$50,000) - \$1,000,000}{\$1,000,000} = 3.00\%$$

Both returns are less than the 8 percent return reported when no external cash flows took place because we are holding the ending account value fixed at $1,080,000. In the case of the beginning-of-period contribution, the account achieves an ending value of $1,080,000 on a beginning value that is higher than in Example 1.1, so its return must be less than 8 percent. In the case of the end-of-period contribution, the return is lower than 8 percent because the ending value of $1,080,000 is assumed to reflect an end-of-period contribution that is removed in calculating the return. In both instances, a portion of the account's change in value from $1,000,000 to $1,080,000 resulted from the contribution; in Example 1.1, by contrast, the change in value resulted entirely from positive investment performance by the account.[3]

The ease and accuracy of calculating returns when external cash flows occur, if those flows take place at the beginning or end of an evaluation period, lead to an important practical recommendation: Whenever possible, a fund sponsor should make contributions to, or withdrawals from, an account at the end of an evaluation period (or equivalently, the beginning of the next evaluation period) when the account is valued. In the case of accounts that are valued on a daily basis, the issue is trivial. However, despite the increasing prevalence of daily valued accounts, many accounts are still valued on an audited basis once a month (or possibly less frequently), and the owners of those accounts should be aware of the potential for rate-of-return distortions caused by intraperiod external cash flows.

What does happen when external cash flows occur between the beginning and the end of an evaluation period? The simple comparison of the account's value relative to the account's beginning value must be abandoned in favor of more intricate methods.

Total Rate of Return

Interestingly, widely accepted solutions to the problem of measuring returns in the presence of intraperiod external cash flows are relatively recent developments. Prior to the 1960s, the issue received little attention, largely because the prevailing performance measures were unaffected by such flows. Performance was typically measured on an income-only basis, thus excluding the impact of capital appreciation. For example, current yield (income-to-price) and yield-to-maturity were commonly quoted return measures.

The emphasis on income-related return measures was due to several factors:

- **Portfolio management emphasis on fixed-income assets.** Particularly in the low-volatility interest rate environment that existed prior to the late 1970s, bond prices tended to be stable. Generally high allocations to fixed-income assets made income the primary source of investment-related wealth production for many investors.
- **Limited computing power.** Accurately accounting for external cash flows when calculating rates of return that include capital appreciation requires the use of computers. Access to the necessary computing resources was not readily available. The income-related return measures were simpler and could be performed by hand.
- **Less competitive investment environment.** Investors, as a whole, were less sophisticated and less demanding of accurate performance measures.

As portfolio allocations to equity securities increased, as computing costs declined, and as investors (particularly larger institutional investors) came to focus more intently on the performance of their portfolios, the demand grew for rate-of-return measures that correctly incorporated all aspects of an account's investment-related increase in wealth. This demand led to the adoption of total rate of return as the generally accepted measure of investment performance.

Total rate of return measures the increase in the investor's wealth due to both investment income (for example, dividends and interest) and capital gains (both realized and unrealized). The total rate of return implies that a dollar of wealth is equally meaningful to the investor whether that wealth is generated by the secure income from a 90-day Treasury bill or by the unrealized appreciation in the price of a share of common stock.

Acceptance of the total rate of return as the primary measure of investment performance was assured by a seminal study performed in 1968 by the Bank Administration Institute (BAI). The BAI study (which we refer to again shortly) was the first comprehensive research conducted on the issue of performance measurement. Among its many important contributions, the study strongly endorsed the use of the total rate of return as the only valid measure of investment performance. For our purposes, henceforth, it will be assumed that rate of return refers to the total rate of return, unless otherwise specified.

The Time-Weighted Rate of Return

We now return to considering the calculation of rates of return in the context of intraperiod external cash flows. To fully appreciate the issue at hand, we must think clearly about the meaning of "rate of return." In essence, the rate of return on an account is the investment-related growth rate in the account's value over the evaluation period. However, we can envision this growth rate being applied to a single dollar invested in the account at the start of the evaluation period or to an "average" amount of dollars invested in the account over the evaluation period. This subtle but important distinction leads to two different measures: the time-weighted and the money-weighted rates of return.

The **time-weighted rate of return** (TWR) reflects the compound rate of growth over a stated evaluation period of one unit of money initially invested in the account. Its calculation requires that the account be valued every time an external cash flow occurs. If no such flows take place, then the calculation of the TWR is trivial; it is simply the application of Equation 1.1, in which the change in the account's value is expressed relative to its beginning value. If external cash flows do occur, then the TWR requires computing a set of subperiod returns (with the number of subperiods equaling one plus the number of dates on which external cash flows occur). These subperiod returns must then be linked together in computing the TWR for the entire evaluation period.

EXAMPLE 1.3   Calculating Subperiod Rates of Return

Returning again to the Mientkiewicz account, let us assume that the account received two cash flows during month t: a contribution of $30,000 on day 5 and a contribution of $20,000 on day 16. Further, assume that we use a daily pricing system that provides us with values of the Mientkiewicz account (inclusive of the contributions) of $1,045,000 and $1,060,000 on days 5 and 16 of the month, respectively. We can then calculate three separate subperiod returns using the rate-of-return computation applicable to situations when external cash flows occur at the end of an evaluation period, as given by Equation 1.3:

$$\text{Subperiod } 1 = \text{Days } 1-5$$

$$\text{Subperiod } 2 = \text{Days } 6-16$$

$$\text{Subperiod } 3 = \text{Days } 17-30$$

For subperiod 1:

$$r_{t,1} = [(\$1,045,000 - \$30,000) - \$1,000,000]/\$1,000,000$$

$$= 0.0150$$

$$= 1.50\%$$

For subperiod 2:

$$r_{t,2} = [(\$1,060,000 - \$20,000) - \$1,045,000]/\$1,045,000$$

$$= -0.0048$$

$$= -0.48\%$$

For subperiod 3:

$$r_{t,3} = (\$1,080,000 - \$1,060,000)/\$1,060,000$$

$$= 0.0189$$

$$= 1.89\%$$

The subperiod returns can be combined through a process called **chain-linking**. Chain-linking involves first adding 1 to the (decimal) rate of return for each subperiod to create a set of wealth relatives. A **wealth relative** can be thought of as the ending value of one unit of money (for example, one dollar) invested at each subperiod's rate of return. Next, the wealth relatives are multiplied together to produce a cumulative wealth relative for the full period, and 1 is subtracted from the result to obtain the TWR. Note that this process of chain-linking implicitly assumes that the initially invested dollar and earnings on that dollar are reinvested (or compounded) from one subperiod to the next. The cumulative wealth relative from the chain-linking of the subperiod wealth relatives can be interpreted as the ending value of one dollar invested in the account at the beginning of the evaluation period. Subtracting 1 from this wealth relative produces the TWR for the account:

$$r_{twr} = (1 + r_{t,1}) \times (1 + r_{t,2}) \times \cdots \times (1 + r_{t,n}) - 1 \qquad (1.4)$$

Note that unless the subperiods constitute a year, the time-weighted rate of return will not be expressed as an annual rate. Example 1.4 illustrates the calculation of a time-weighted rate of return.

EXAMPLE 1.4   Calculating the TWR

Continuing with the Mientkiewicz account, its TWR is

$$r_{twr} = (1 + 0.0150) \times (1 + -0.0048) \times (1 + 0.0189) - 1$$

$$= 0.0292$$

$$= 2.92\%$$

The TWR derives its name from the fact that each subperiod return within the full evaluation period receives a weight proportional to the length of the subperiod relative to the length of the full evaluation period. That relationship becomes apparent if each subperiod return is expressed as the cumulative return over smaller time units. In the Mientkiewicz account example, the return in the first subperiod is 0.015 over five days. On a daily compounded basis that return is $0.0030[=(1 + 0.015)^{1/5} - 1]$. Performing the same calculation for the other two subperiods yields the following:

$$r_{twr} = (1 + 0.0030)^5 \times (1 + -0.0004)^{11} \times (1 + 0.0013)^{14} - 1$$

$$= 0.0292 = 2.92\% \text{ (allowing for rounding)}$$

From this expression for the TWR, we can see that the subperiods 1, 2, and 3 receive compounding "weights" of 5/30, 11/30, and 14/30, respectively.

The Money-Weighted Rate of Return

The **money-weighted rate of return** (MWR) measures the compound growth rate in the value of all funds invested in the account over the evaluation period. In the corporate finance literature, the MWR goes by the name **internal rate of return,** or IRR. Of importance for performance measurement, the MWR is the growth rate that will link the ending value of the account to its beginning value plus all intermediate cash flows. With MV_1 and MV_0 the values of the account at the end and beginning of the evaluation period, respectively, in equation form the MWR is the growth rate R that solves

$$MV_1 = MV_0(1 + R)^m + CF_1(1 + R)^{m-L(1)} + \cdots + CF_n(1 + R)^{m-L(n)} \qquad (1.5)$$

where

m = number of time units in the evaluation period (for example, the number of days in the month)

CF_i = the ith cash flow

$L(i)$ = number of time units by which the ith cash flow is separated from the beginning of the evaluation period

Note that R is expressed as the return per unit of time composing the evaluation period. For example, in the case of monthly performance measurement, where the constituent time unit is one day, R would be the daily MWR of the account. Extending this thought, $[(1 + R)^m - 1]$ can be seen to be the account's MWR for the entire evaluation period, as $(1 + R)^m = (1 + r_{mwr})$. Therefore, in the case of no external cash flows, with some algebraic manipulation Equation 1.4 reduces to Equation 1.1, the simple expression for rate of return:

$$MV_1 = MV_0(1 + R)^m + 0$$

$$(1 + R)^m = MV_1/MV_0$$

$$(1 + r_{mwr}) = MV_1/MV_0$$

$$r_{mwr} = (MV_1 - MV_0)/MV_0$$

$$= r_t$$

EXAMPLE 1.5   Calculating the MWR

Consider the Mientkiewicz account again. Its MWR is found by solving the following equation for R:

$$\$1,080,000 = \$1,000,000(1 + R)^{30} + \$30,000(1 + R)^{30-5} + \$20,000(1 + R)^{30-16}$$

There exists no closed-form solution for R. That is, Equation 1.4 cannot be manipulated to isolate R on the left-hand side. Consequently, R must be solved iteratively through a trial-and-error process. In our example, we begin with an initial guess of $R = 0.001$. The right-hand side of the equation becomes $\$1,081,480$. Thus our initial guess is too high and must be lowered. Next, try a value $R = 0.0007$. In this case the right-hand side now equals $\$1,071,941$. Therefore, our second guess is too low.

We can continue this process. Eventually, we will arrive at the correct value for R, which for the Mientkiewicz account is 0.0009536. Remember that this value is the Mientkiewicz account's daily rate of return during the month. Expressed on a monthly basis, the MWR is 0.0290 $[-(1 + 0.0009536)^{30} - 1]$, or 2.90%.

As one might expect, a computer is best suited to perform the repetitious task of calculating the MWR. Spreadsheet software to perform these computations is readily available.

TWR versus MWR

The MWR represents the average growth rate of all money invested in an account, while the TWR represents the growth of a single unit of money invested in the account. Consequently, the MWR is sensitive to the size and timing of external cash flows to and from the account, while the TWR is unaffected by these flows. Under "normal" conditions, these two return measures will produce similar results. In the example of the Mientkiewicz account, the MWR was 2.90 percent for the month and the TWR was 2.92 percent.

However, when external cash flows occur that are large relative to the account's value and the account's performance is fluctuating significantly during the measurement period, then the MWR and the TWR can differ materially.

EXAMPLE 1.6   When TWR and MWR Differ

Consider the Charlton account, worth $800,000 at the beginning of the month. On day 10 it is valued at $1.8 million after receiving a $1 million contribution. At the end of the month, the account is worth $3 million. As a result, the Charlton account's MWR is 87.5 percent, while its TWR is only 66.7 percent.

For subperiod 1:

$$r_{t,1} = [(\$1,800,000 - \$1,000,000) - \$800,000]/\$800,000$$
$$= 0.0 \text{ or } 0\%$$

For subperiod 2:

$$r_{t,2} = (\$3,000,000 - \$1,800,000)/\$1,800,000$$
$$= 0.6667 \text{ or } 66.7\%$$

Then

$$r_{twr} = (1 + 0) \times (1 + 0.667) - 1$$
$$= 0.667 \text{ or } 66.7\%$$

For MWR, we need to solve:

$$\$3,000,000 = \$800,000(1 + R)^{30} + \$1,000,000(1 + R)^{30-10}$$

By trial and error, R comes out to be 0.020896. Expressed on a monthly basis, MWR is 0.859709 or 86.0%[$= (1 + 0.020896)^{30} - 1$].

If funds are contributed to an account prior to a period of strong performance (as in the case of the Charlton account in Example 1.6), then the MWR will be positively affected compared to the TWR, as a relatively large sum is invested at a high growth rate. That is, in the case of the Charlton account, a contribution was made just prior to a subperiod in which a dollar invested in the account earned 66.7 percent. In the prior subperiod, the account earned 0.0 percent. Thus, on average, the account had more dollars invested earning

66.7 percent than it had dollars earning 0.0 percent, resulting in an MWR greater than the TWR. Conversely, if funds are withdrawn from the account prior to the strong performance, then the MWR will be adversely affected relative to the TWR. (The opposite conclusions hold if the external cash flow occurred prior to a period of weak performance.)

As noted, the TWR is unaffected by external cash flow activity. Valuing the account at the time of each external cash flow effectively removes the impact of those flows on the TWR. Consequently, the TWR accurately reflects how an investor would have fared over the evaluation period if he or she had placed funds in the account at the beginning of the period.

In most situations, an investment manager has little or no control over the size and timing of external cash flows into or out of his or her accounts. Therefore, practitioners generally prefer a rate-of-return measure that is not sensitive to cash flows if they want to evaluate how a manager's investment actions have affected an account's value. This consideration led the authors of the Bank Administration Institute study to recommend that the TWR be adopted as the appropriate measure of account performance. That recommendation has received almost universal acceptance since the study's publication. (Note that the Global Investment Performance Standards [GIPS®] generally require a TWR methodology.)

However, one can readily conceive of situations in which the MWR may prove useful in evaluating the returns achieved by an investment manager. The most obvious examples are those situations in which the investment manager maintains control over the timing and amount of cash flows into the account. Managers of various types of private equity investments typically operate under arrangements that permit them to call capital from their investors at the managers' discretion and ultimately to determine when the original capital, and any earnings on that capital, will be returned to investors. In these "opportunistic" situations, it is generally agreed that the MWR is the more appropriate measure of account returns.[4]

The Linked Internal Rate of Return

Despite its useful characteristics, the TWR does have an important disadvantage: It requires account valuations on every date that an external cash flow takes place. Thus, calculation of the TWR typically necessitates the ability to price a portfolio of securities on a daily basis. Although daily pricing services are becoming more common, marking an account to market daily is administratively more expensive and cumbersome, and potentially more error-prone, than traditional monthly accounting procedures. For these reasons, use of pure TWR is not yet standard practice, with the prominent exception of the mutual fund industry.[5] The MWR, on the other hand, despite its sensitivity to the size and timing of external cash flows, requires only that an account be valued at the beginning and end of the evaluation period and that the amounts and dates of any external cash flows be recorded.

The complementary advantages and disadvantages of the TWR and the MWR led the authors of the BAI study to make an important recommendation: The TWR should be approximated by calculating the MWR over reasonably frequent time intervals and then chain-linking those returns over the entire evaluation period. This process is referred to as the Linked Internal Rate of Return (LIRR) method and originally was developed by Peter Dietz (1966). The BAI study estimated that if the LIRR method were applied to an account experiencing "normal" cash flow activity, then using monthly valuations and daily dating of external cash flows, the calculated rate of return on average would fall within 4 basis points per year of the true TWR.[6] Given the inaccuracies inherent in the pricing of even the most liquid portfolios, this slight difference appears immaterial.

EXAMPLE 1.7   An Example of LIRR

Suppose, in a given month, the Mientkiewicz account's MWR is calculated each week. These MWRs are 0.021 in week 1, 0.0016 in week 2, -0.014 in week 3, and 0.018 in week 4. The LIRR is obtained by linking these rates:

$$R_{LIRR} = (1 + 0.021) \times (1 + 0.0016) \times (1 + -0.014) \times (1 + 0.018) -1$$
$$= 0.0265 \text{ or } 2.65\%$$

The BAI study concluded that only under unusual circumstances would the LIRR fail to provide an acceptable representation of the TWR. Specifically, the LIRR would fail if both large external cash flows (generally over 10 percent of the account's value) and volatile swings in subperiod performance occurred during the evaluation period. With an evaluation period as short as one month, the chances of such a joint event occurring for an account are low. Nevertheless, if it should happen, the BAI study recommended valuing the account on the date of the intramonth cash flow.

Annualized Return

For comparison purposes, rates of return are typically reported on an annualized basis. As defined here, the annualized return represents the compound average annual return earned by the account over the evaluation period. The calculation is also known as the compound growth rate or geometric mean return. An annualized return is computed by employing the same chain-linking method used to calculate linked internal rates of return, except that the product of the linking is raised to the reciprocal of the number of years covering the evaluation period (or equivalently, taking the appropriate root of the linked product, where the root is the number of years in the measurement period).

EXAMPLE 1.8   Annualized Return

If in years 1, 2, and 3 of a three-year evaluation period an account earned 2.0 percent, 9.5 percent, and -4.7 percent, respectively, then the annualized return for the evaluation period would be:

$$r_a = [(1 + 0.02) \times (1 + 0.095) \times (1 - 0.047)]^{1/3} - 1$$
$$= 0.021 \text{ or } 2.1\%$$

If 12 quarterly returns had been available for the account instead of three yearly returns, then those quarterly returns would have been similarly linked and the cube root of the product would have been calculated to produce the account's annualized return over the three-year period.

In general, with measurement periods shorter than a full year, it is inadvisable to calculate annualized returns. Essentially, the person calculating returns is extrapolating the account's returns over a sample period to the full year. Particularly for equity accounts, returns can fluctuate significantly during the remaining time in the evaluation period, making the annualized return a potentially unrealistic estimate of the account's actual return over the full year.

Data Quality Issues

The performance measurement process is only as accurate as the inputs to the process. Often performance report users fail to distinguish between rates of return of high and low reliability. In the case of accounts invested in liquid and transparently priced securities and experiencing little external cash flow activity, the reported rates of return are likely to be highly reliable performance indicators. They will accurately reflect the experience of an investor who entered such an account at the beginning of the evaluation period and liquidated his or her investment at the end of the period. Conversely, for accounts invested in illiquid and infrequently priced assets, the underlying valuations may be suspect, thereby invalidating the reported rates of return. For example, due to the inaccuracy inherent in estimation techniques, quarterly valuations of venture capital funds typically have limited economic content. An investor may not be able to enter or leave the account at a value anywhere near the reported valuations. As a result, monthly or even annual performance measurement of such funds should be viewed with caution.

Various services exist that collect data on recent market transactions for a wide range of fixed-income and equity securities. Particularly for many thinly traded fixed-income securities, a current market price may not always be available. In that case, estimated prices may be derived based on dealer-quoted prices for securities with similar attributes (for example, a security with a similar credit rating, maturity, and economic sector). This approach is referred to as **matrix pricing.** For highly illiquid securities, reasonable estimates of market prices may be difficult or impossible to obtain. Investment managers may carry these securities at cost or the price of the last trade in those securities. It is outside the scope of this discussion to address in detail the subject of account valuation. Suffice it to say that *caveat emptor*—"let the buyer beware"—should be the motto of any user of performance measurement reports who deals with securities other than liquid stocks and bonds.

In addition to obtaining accurate account valuations and external cash flow recognition, reliable performance measurement requires appropriate data collection procedures. For example, account valuations should be reported on a trade-date, fully accrued basis. That is, the stated value of the account should reflect the impact of any unsettled trades and any income owed by or to the account but not yet paid. Such a valuation process correctly represents the best available statement of the account's position at a point in time. Other methods, such as settlement date accounting and the exclusion of accrued income, incorrectly reflect the account's market value.

BENCHMARKS

Performance evaluation cannot be conducted in a vacuum. By its nature, performance evaluation is a relative concept. Absolute performance numbers mean little. Even so-called "absolute return" managers should provide some sense of how alternative uses of their clients' money would have performed if exposed to similar risks. Consider how one interprets a 7 percent return on a well-diversified common stock portfolio during a given month. If you knew that the broad stock market had declined 15 percent during the month, you might be impressed. Conversely, if the market had advanced 25 percent, you might be disappointed. If we are to conduct meaningful performance evaluation, then we must develop an appropriate benchmark against which an account's performance can be compared.

Concept of a Benchmark

The *Merriam-Webster Dictionary* defines a benchmark as a "standard or point of reference in measuring or judging quality, value, etc." Applying this general definition to investment management, a benchmark is a collection of securities or risk factors and associated weights that represents the persistent and prominent investment characteristics of an asset category or manager's investment process. At the asset category level, we can think of a benchmark as the collection of securities that the fund sponsor would own if the fund sponsor were required to place all of its investments within the asset category in a single, passively managed portfolio. (In other words, the benchmark is the fund sponsor's preferred index fund for the asset category.) At the manager level, we can think of a benchmark as a passive representation of the manager's investment style, incorporating the salient investment features (such as significant exposures to particular sources of systematic risk) that consistently appear in the manager's portfolios. More metaphorically, a manager's benchmark encompasses the manager's "area" of expertise. Just as an angler has a favorite fishing hole, an investment manager also has distinct preferences for certain types of securities and risk exposures. The opportunity set that represents the manager's area of expertise may be broad or narrow, reflecting the resources and investment processes that the manager brings to bear on the portfolio selection problem.

A little algebra succinctly conveys these concepts. Begin with the simple identity of an investment manager's portfolio; that is, any portfolio is equal to itself:[7]

$$P = P$$

Now, consider an appropriately selected benchmark B. If we add and subtract B from the right-hand side of this identity, effectively adding a zero to the relationship, the result is

$$P = B + (P - B)$$

Additionally, if we define the manager's active investment judgments as being the difference between the manager's portfolio P and the benchmark B so that $A = (P - B)$, then the equation just given becomes

$$P = B + A \tag{1.6}$$

Thus, the managed portfolio P can be viewed as a combination of (1) the benchmark B and (2) active management decisions A composed of a set of over- and underweighted positions in securities relative to the benchmark. We can extend this relationship by introducing a market index M. Adding and subtracting M from the right-hand side of Equation 1.6 gives

$$P = M + (B - M) + A$$

The difference between the manager's benchmark portfolio and the market index $(B - M)$ can be defined as the manager's investment style S. If we let $S = (B - M)$, then the equation just given becomes

$$P = M + S + A \qquad (1.7)$$

Equation 1.7 states that a portfolio has three components: market, style, and active management.

There are several interesting applications of Equation 1.7. First, note that if the portfolio is a broad market index fund, then $S = (B - M) = 0$ (that is, no style biases) and $A = (P - B) = 0$ (that is, no active management). Consequently, Equation 1.7 reduces to $P = M$; the portfolio is equivalent to the market index.

Second, if we define the benchmark as the market index [that is, $S = (B - M) = 0$, or no style], then Equation 1.7 reduces to Equation 1.6 and substituting M for B gives

$$P = M + A$$

Because many managers and fund sponsors have been willing to define a manager's benchmark as a broad market index (for example, the S&P 500 in the case of U.S. common stock managers), both parties are implicitly stating that they believe that the manager has no distinct investment style. However, most practitioners would agree that the vast majority of managers pursue specific investment styles. Specialization has become the hallmark of our postindustrial society, and it should not be surprising that, with respect to a subject as complex as portfolio management, many managers have chosen to focus their skills on certain segments of that subject.

EXAMPLE 1.9   Returns Due to Style and Active Management

Suppose the Mientkiewicz account earns a total return of 3.6 percent in a given month, during which the portfolio benchmark has a return of 3.8 percent and the market index has a return of 2.8 percent. Then the return due to the portfolio manager's style is

$$S = B - M = 3.8\% - 2.8\% = 1\%$$

and the return due to active management is

$$A = P - B = 3.6\% - 3.8\% = -0.2\%$$

Properties of a Valid Benchmark

Although in practice an acceptable benchmark is simply one that both the manager and the fund sponsor agree fairly represents the manager's investment process, to function effectively in performance evaluation, a benchmark should possess certain basic properties. A valid benchmark is

- **Unambiguous.** The identities and weights of securities or factor exposures constituting the benchmark are clearly defined.
- **Investable.** It is possible to forgo active management and simply hold the benchmark.
- **Measurable.** The benchmark's return is readily calculable on a reasonably frequent basis.
- **Appropriate.** The benchmark is consistent with the manager's investment style or area of expertise.
- **Reflective of current investment opinions.** The manager has current investment knowledge (be it positive, negative, or neutral) of the securities or factor exposures within the benchmark.
- **Specified in advance.** The benchmark is specified prior to the start of an evaluation period and known to all interested parties.
- **Owned.** The investment manager should be aware of and accept accountability for the constituents and performance of the benchmark. It is encouraged that the benchmark be embedded in and integral to the investment process and procedures of the investment manager.

The failure of a benchmark to possess these properties compromises its utility as an effective investment management tool. A benchmark represents an equivalent risk opportunity cost to the fund sponsor. The properties listed merely formalize intuitive notions of what constitutes a fair and relevant performance comparison. It is interesting to observe that a number of commonly used benchmarks fail to satisfy these properties.

Types of Benchmarks

At the investment manager level, a benchmark forms the basis of a covenant between the manager and the fund sponsor. It reflects the investment style that the fund sponsor expects the manager to pursue, and it becomes the basis for evaluating the success of the manager's investment management efforts. Many different benchmarks may satisfy the criteria for an acceptable benchmark and, if agreed upon by both parties, could be implemented. In general, there are seven primary types of benchmarks in use.

1. *Absolute.* An absolute return can be a return objective. Examples include an actuarial rate-of-return assumption or a minimum return target that the fund strives to exceed. Unfortunately, absolute return objectives are not investable alternatives and do not satisfy the benchmark validity criteria.[8]
2. *Manager universes.* Consultants and fund sponsors frequently use the median manager or fund from a broad universe of managers or funds as a performance evaluation benchmark. As discussed in more detail later, a median manager benchmark fails all the tests of benchmark validity except for being measurable.
3. *Broad market indexes.* Many managers and fund sponsors use **broad market indexes** as benchmarks. Prominent examples of broad market indexes used by U.S. investors include the S&P 500, Wilshire 5000, and Russell 3000 indexes for U.S. common stocks; the Lehman Aggregate and the Citigroup Broad Investment-Grade (U.S. BIG) Bond Indexes for U.S. investment-grade debt; and the Morgan Stanley Capital International (MSCI)

Europe, Australasia, and Far East (EAFE) Index for non-U.S. developed-market common stocks. Market indexes are well recognized, easy to understand, and widely available, and satisfy several properties of valid benchmarks. They are unambiguous, generally investable, and measurable, and they may be specified in advance. In certain situations, market indexes are perfectly acceptable as benchmarks, particularly as benchmarks for asset category performance or for "core" type investment approaches in which the manager selects from a universe of securities similar in composition to the benchmark. However, in other circumstances, the manager's style may deviate considerably from the style reflected in a market index. For example, assigning a micro-capitalization U.S. growth stock manager an S&P 500 benchmark clearly violates the appropriateness criterion.

4. *Style indexes.* Broad market indexes have been increasingly partitioned to create **investment style indexes** that represent specific portions of an asset category: for example, subgroups within the U.S. common stock asset category. Four popular U.S. common stock style indexes are (1) large-capitalization growth, (2) large-capitalization value, (3) small-capitalization growth, and (4) small-capitalization value. (Mid-capitalization growth and value common stock indexes are also available.) The Frank Russell Company, Standard & Poor's, and Morgan Stanley Capital International produce the most widely used U.S. common stock style indexes. International common stock style indexes are more recent developments.

Fixed-income style indexes are produced in a similar manner. In many ways, investment-grade bonds are a more convenient asset category for developing style indexes because the broad market indexes are easily segregated into various types of securities. For example, broad bond market indexes, such as the Lehman Aggregate for U.S. debt, can be broken up into their constituent parts, such as the Lehman Government/Credit Index, the Lehman Mortgage Index, and so on. The Lehman Aggregate can also be decomposed along the lines of maturity (or duration) and quality.

Similar to broad market indexes, investment style indexes are often well known, easy to understand, and widely available. However, their ability to pass tests of benchmark validity can be problematic. Some style indexes contain weightings in certain securities and economic sectors that are much larger than what many managers consider prudent. Further, the definition of investment style implied in the benchmark may be ambiguous or inconsistent with the investment process of the manager being evaluated. Differing definitions of investment style at times can produce rather extreme return differentials. In 1999, the S&P Large Value Index had a return of 12.72 percent, and the Russell Large Value Index had a return of 7.35 percent. These large return differences among indexes presumably designed to represent the results of the same investment style are disconcerting. Users of style indexes should closely examine how the indexes are constructed and assess their applicability to specific managers.

5. *Factor model based.* Factor models provide a means of relating one or more systematic sources of return to the returns on an account.[9] As a result, a specified set of factor exposures could potentially be used as a **factor model–based benchmark.** The simplest form of factor model is a one-factor model, such as the familiar **market model.** In that relationship, the return on a security, or a portfolio of securities, is expressed as a linear function of the return on a broad market index, established over a suitably long period (for example, 60 months):

$$R_p = a_p + \beta_p R_I + \varepsilon_p \qquad (1.8)$$

where R_p represents the periodic return on an account and R_I represents the periodic return on the market index.[10] The market index is used as a proxy for the underlying systematic return factor (or factors). The term ε_p is the residual, or nonsystematic, element of the relationship. The term β_p measures the sensitivity of the returns on the account to the returns on the market index; it is typically estimated by regressing the account's returns on those of the market index. The sensitivity term is called the beta of the account. Finally, the intercept a_p is the "zero factor" term, representing the expected value of R_p if the factor value was zero.

EXAMPLE 1.10   Returns from a Market Model

Consider an account with a zero-factor value of 2.0 percent and a beta of 1.5. Applying Equation 1.8, a return of 8 percent for the market index generates an expected return on the account of 14% (= 2.0% + 1.5 × 8%).

Some managers hold accounts that persistently display a beta greater than 1.0, while other managers hold accounts with betas persistently less than 1.0. Out of these patterns arises the concept of a benchmark with a "normal beta" consistent with these observed tendencies. For example, suppose that an analysis of past account returns, combined with discussions with the manager, suggests a normal beta of 1.2. This normal beta becomes the basis for the benchmark that specifies the level of return that the account would be expected to generate in the absence of any value added by active management on the part of the manager.

Incorporating multiple sources of systematic risk can enhance the richness of the factor model approach. That is, Equation 1.8 can be extended to include more than one factor. For example, a company's size, industry, growth characteristics, financial strength, and other factors may have a systematic impact on a portfolio's performance. Generalizing Equation 1.8 produces

$$R_p = a_p + b_1 F_1 + b_2 F_2 + \cdots + b_K F_K + \varepsilon_p$$

where $F_1, F_2, \ldots F_K$ represent the values of factors 1 through K, respectively. Numerous commercially available multifactor risk models have been produced. Rosenberg and Marathe (1975) pioneered the development of these models, and their work was extended to create performance evaluation benchmarks. The concept of a "normal beta" in a multifactor context leads to the concept of a normal portfolio. A **normal portfolio** is a portfolio with exposures to sources of systematic risk that are typical for a manager, using the manager's past portfolios as a guide.

Benchmarks based on factor exposures can be useful in performance evaluation. Because they capture the systematic sources of return that affect an account's performance, they help managers and fund sponsors better understand a manager's investment style. However, they are not always intuitive to the fund sponsor and particularly to the investment managers (who rarely think in terms of factor exposures when designing investment strategies), are not always easy to obtain, and are potentially expensive to use.

In addition, they are ambiguous. We can build multiple benchmarks with the same factor exposures, but each benchmark can earn different returns. For example, we can construct two different portfolios, each with a beta of 1.2 ("normal beta"), but the portfolios can have materially different returns. Also, because the composition of a factor-based benchmark is not specified with respect to the constituent securities and their weights, we cannot verify all the validity criteria (the benchmark may not be investable, for example).

6. *Returns based.* Sharpe (1988, 1992) introduced the concept of **returns-based benchmarks.** These benchmarks are constructed using (1) the series of a manager's account returns (ideally, monthly returns going back in time as long as the investment process has been in place) and (2) the series of returns on several investment style indexes over the same period. These return series are then submitted to an allocation algorithm that solves for the combination of investment style indexes that most closely track the account's returns.[11]

For example, assume that we have 10 years of monthly returns of a U.S. equity mutual fund. Also, assume that we have the monthly returns of four U.S. equity style indexes—(1) large-cap growth, (2) large-cap value, (3) small-cap growth, and (4) small-cap value—over the same time period. If we submit these return series to a properly constructed allocation algorithm, we can solve for a particular set of allocation weights for the four style indexes that will track most closely the return series of the manager's actual portfolio. The returns-based benchmark is represented by these allocation weights.

Returns-based benchmarks are generally easy to use and are intuitively appealing. They satisfy most benchmark validity criteria, including those of being unambiguous, measurable, investable, and specified in advance. Returns-based benchmarks are particularly useful in situations where the only information available is account returns. One disadvantage of returns-based benchmarks is that, like the style indexes that underlie the benchmarks, they may hold positions in securities and economic sectors that a manager might find unacceptable. Further, they require many months of observation to establish a statistically reliable pattern of style exposures. In the case of managers who rotate among style exposures, such a pattern may be impossible to discern.

7. *Custom security based.* An investment manager will typically follow an investment philosophy that causes the manager to focus its research activities on certain types of securities. The manager will select those securities that represent the most attractive investment opportunities that the research process has identified. As the financial and investment characteristics of securities will change over time, a manager's research universe will similarly evolve.

A **custom security-based benchmark** is simply a manager's research universe weighted in a particular fashion. Most managers do not use a security weighting scheme that is exactly an equal weighting across all securities or one that exactly assigns weights according to market capitalization. Consequently, a custom benchmark reflecting a particular manager's unique weighting approach can be more suitable than a published index for a fair and accurate appraisal of that manager's performance.

The overwhelming advantage of a custom security-based benchmark is that it meets all of the required benchmark properties and satisfies all of the benchmark validity criteria, making it arguably the most appropriate benchmark for performance evaluation purposes. In addition, it is a valuable tool for managers to monitor and control their investment processes and for fund sponsors to effectively allocate or budget risk across teams of investment managers. One major disadvantage is that custom security-based benchmarks are expensive to construct and maintain. In addition, as they are not composed of published indexes, the perception of a lack of transparency can be of concern.

Building Custom Security-Based Benchmarks

A valid custom security-based benchmark is the product of discussions between the client or the client's consultant and the manager and of a detailed analysis of the manager's past security holdings. The construction of such a benchmark involves the following steps:

1. Identify prominent aspects of the manager's investment process.
2. Select securities consistent with that investment process.
3. Devise a weighting scheme for the benchmark securities, including a cash position.
4. Review the preliminary benchmark and make modifications.
5. Rebalance the benchmark portfolio on a predetermined schedule.

For the purpose of custom benchmark construction, an analysis of the manager's past portfolios will identify prominent aspects of the manager's investment process. The selection of benchmark portfolio securities requires both a broad universe of potential candidates and a set of screening criteria consistent with the manager's investment process. Weighting schemes may include aspects of equal weighting and capitalization weighting, depending on the manager's investment process and client restrictions. Following these steps, a preliminary benchmark portfolio is selected. At this point, the benchmark's composition is reviewed and final modifications are made. Ultimately, keeping the benchmark portfolio current with the manager's investment process necessitates rebalancing the portfolio at regularly scheduled intervals.

These steps, though simple in appearance, constitute a complex task. A proper benchmark must make a fine distinction between the manager's "normal" or policy investment decisions and the manager's active investment judgments. Considerable resources are required, including a comprehensive security database, an efficient computer screening capability, a flexible security weighting system, and a means of maintaining the integrity of the benchmark over time.

Critique of Manager Universes as Benchmarks

Fund sponsors have a natural interest in knowing how their investment results compare to those achieved by similar institutions and how the returns earned by the managers they have selected compare to those earned by managers they might have engaged. To facilitate peer group comparisons, some consulting firms and custodial banks have developed databases or "universes" of account returns ranked in descending order. Fund sponsors often use the median account in a particular peer group as a return benchmark. For instance, the investment policy statement of a public fund might specify that the fund's objective is to perform in the top half of a certain universe of public funds, and the guidelines for a domestic large-cap equity account might state that the manager's results are expected to exceed those of the median account in a certain universe consisting of portfolios with large-cap value mandates or characteristics.

With the exception of being measurable, the median account in a typical commercially available universe does not have the properties of a valid benchmark described above. One of the most significant deficiencies is that, although the universe can be named, the median account cannot be *specified in advance*. Universe compilers can only establish the median account on an *ex post* basis, after the returns earned by all accounts have been calculated and ranked. Prior to the start of an evaluation period, neither the manager nor the fund sponsor has any knowledge of who the median manager will be at period end. In addition, different accounts will fall at the median from one evaluation period to another. For these reasons, the benchmark is not *investable* and cannot serve as a passive alternative to holding the account that is under analysis. Even after the evaluation period concludes, the identity of the median manager typically remains unknown, preventing the benchmark from satisfying the *unambiguous* property. The ambiguity of the median manager benchmark makes it impossible to verify its *appropriateness* by examining whether the investment style it represents adequately corresponds to the account being evaluated. The fund sponsor who chooses to employ universes for peer group comparisons can only rely on the compiler's representations that accounts have been rigorously screened against well-defined criteria for inclusion, the integrity of the input data is scrupulously monitored, and a uniform return calculation methodology has been used for all accounts in all periods.

One other disadvantage merits attention. Because fund sponsors terminate underperforming managers, universes are unavoidably subject to "survivor bias." Consider the hypothetical universe represented in Table 1.1, where a shaded cell indicates that a particular account existed for a given year and an X indicates that a rate of return can be calculated for the referenced evaluation period.

In this example, there were six accounts in the universe at the end of year 1, and there were six at the end of year 7. They were not all the same accounts, however; in fact, only two have survived for the full period to achieve seven-year returns. The other four in the year 1 cohort were no longer present because the sponsors reallocated funds or possibly because the managers' performance was unsatisfactory. In any event, it is likely that the two survivors were among the best-performing in the group of accounts that existed in year 1; sponsors are naturally reluctant to dismiss strong performing managers. Because the survivors' returns were presumably high, the actual median seven-year return for this universe will be higher than the median of a hypothetical return distribution from which no accounts were removed.

Why are these deficiencies of the median manager benchmark of concern? From the perspective of performance evaluation, the question becomes, "To what is the manager expected

TABLE 1.1   Survivor Bias in a Manager Universe

	YEAR 1	YEAR 2	YEAR 3	YEAR 4	YEAR 5	YEAR 6	YEAR 7	ANNUALIZED RETURNS AT END OF YEAR 7			
								1 YEAR	3 YEARS	5 YEARS	7 YEARS
Manager 1											
Manager 2								X	X	X	X
Manager 3								X			
Manager 4								X	X		
Manager 5											
Manager 6											
Manager 7								X	X	X	X
Manager 8								X	X	X	
Manager 9								X			
Manager 10											
Observations	6	6	7	7	7	5	6	6	4	3	2

to add value?" Without a valid reference point, superior performance remains an elusive notion. Placing above the median of a universe of investment managers or funds may be a reasonable investment *objective*, but the performance of a particular manager or fund is not a suitable performance benchmark that can be used to assess investment skill.[12]

Tests of Benchmark Quality

In many organizations, benchmarks have become an important element of the investment management process. Moreover, benchmark use has expanded beyond performance evaluation. Benchmarks are now an integral part of risk management, at both the investment manager and fund sponsor levels. Most forms of risk budgeting use benchmarks to estimate the risks to which a fund sponsor's investment program is exposed at the asset category and investment manager levels.

Given the important uses of benchmarks, it is in the interests of all parties involved (fund sponsors, consultants, and managers) to identify good benchmarks and to improve or replace poor benchmarks. Good benchmarks increase the proficiency of performance evaluation, highlighting the contributions of skillful managers. Poor benchmarks obscure manager skills. Good benchmarks enhance the capability to manage investment risk. Poor benchmarks promote inefficient manager allocations and ineffective risk management. They also increase the likelihood of unpleasant surprises, which can lead to counterproductive actions and unnecessary expense on the part of the fund sponsor.

Bailey (1992b) presents a heuristic set of benchmark quality criteria designed to distinguish good benchmarks from poor benchmarks. These criteria are based on the fundamental properties of valid benchmarks discussed previously and on a logical extension of the purposes for which benchmarks are used. Although none of the criteria alone provides a definitive indicator of benchmark quality, taken together they provide a means for evaluating alternative benchmarks.

- **Systematic biases.** Over time, there should be minimal systematic biases or risks in the benchmark relative to the account. One way to measure this criterion is to calculate the historical beta of the account relative to the benchmark; on average, it should be close to 1.0.[13]

    Potential systematic bias can also be identified through a set of correlation statistics. Consider the correlation between $A = (P - B)$ and $S = (B - M)$. The contention is that a manager's ability to identify attractive and unattractive investment opportunities should be uncorrelated with whether the manager's style is in or out of favor relative to the overall market. Accordingly, a good benchmark will display a correlation between A and S that is not statistically different from zero.

    Similarly, let us define the difference between the account and the market index as $E = (P - M)$. When a manager's style (S) is in favor (out of favor) relative to the market, we expect both the benchmark and the account to outperform (underperform) the market. Therefore, a good benchmark will have a statistically significant positive correlation coefficient between S and E.

- **Tracking error.** We define tracking error as the volatility of A or $(P - B)$. A good benchmark should reduce the "noise" in the performance evaluation process. Thus, the volatility (standard deviation) of an account's returns relative to a good benchmark should be less than the volatility of the account's returns versus a market index or other alternative benchmarks. Such a result indicates that the benchmark is capturing important aspects of the manager's investment style.

- **Risk characteristics.** An account's exposure to systematic sources of risk should be similar to those of the benchmark over time.[14] The objective of a good benchmark is to reflect but not to replicate the manager's investment process. Because an active manager is constantly making bets against the benchmark, a good benchmark will exhibit risk exposures at times greater than those of the managed portfolio and at times smaller. Nevertheless, if the account's risk characteristics are always greater or always smaller than those of the benchmark, a systematic bias exists.
- **Coverage.** Benchmark coverage is defined as the proportion of a portfolio's market value that is contained in the benchmark. For example, at a point in time, all of the securities and their respective weights that are contained in the account and the benchmark can be examined. The market value of the jointly held securities as a percentage of the total market value of the portfolio is termed the *coverage ratio*. High coverage indicates a strong correspondence between the manager's universe of potential securities and the benchmark. Low coverage indicates that the benchmark has little relationship, on a security level, with the opportunity set generated by the manager's investment process.
- **Turnover.** Benchmark turnover is the proportion of the benchmark's market value allocated to purchases during a periodic rebalancing of the benchmark. Because the benchmark should be an investable alternative to holding the manager's actual portfolio, the benchmark turnover should not be so excessive as to preclude the successful implementation of a passively managed portfolio.
- **Positive active positions.** An active position is an account's allocation to a security minus the corresponding weight of the same security in the benchmark. For example, assume an account has a 3 percent weighting in General Electric (GE). If the benchmark has a 2 percent weighting in GE, then the active position is 1 percent (3% − 2%). Thus, the manager will receive positive credit if GE performs well. Actively managed accounts whose investment mandates permit only long positions contain primarily securities that a manager considers to be attractive. When a good custom security-based benchmark has been built, the manager should be expected to hold largely positive active positions for actively managed long-only accounts.[15] Note that when an account is benchmarked to a published index containing securities for which a long-only manager has no investment opinion and which the manager does not own, negative active positions will arise. A high proportion of negative active positions is indicative of a benchmark that is poorly representative of the manager's investment approach.

Hedge Funds and Hedge Fund Benchmarks

Hedge funds have become increasingly popular among institutional and high-net-worth investors in recent years. Although the term *hedge fund* covers a wide range of investment strategies, there are some common threads that link these strategies. In general, **hedge funds** attempt to expose investors to a particular investment opportunity while minimizing (or hedging) other investment risks that could impact the outcome. In most cases, hedging involves both long and short investment positions.

The term *hedge fund* is believed to have originated as a description of an investment strategy developed by Alfred Winslow Jones.[16] The basic strategy involved shorting stocks that managers considered to be overvalued and using the proceeds to invest in stocks that were deemed to be undervalued. In addition, an incentive fee was established, and Jones committed his own capital to assure investors that his interests were aligned with their interests.

In essence, the Jones strategy is the same as the standard long-only strategy in that, relative to the benchmark, a long-only manager will overweight undervalued securities and underweight overvalued securities. The difference is that the long-only manager is limited to a minimum investment of zero in any security. As a result, the maximum "negative bet" that a long-only manager can place on a security that is rated as overvalued is not to hold it (a weight of zero). For example, because approximately 450 companies in the S&P 500 have weights less than 0.5 percent, a long-only manager with an S&P 500 benchmark and a negative opinion on any of these stocks would be limited to, at most, a −0.5 percent active position. By removing the zero weight constraint (that is, allowing shorting), a manager can further exploit overvalued stocks.

There are, however, performance measurement issues as well as numerous administrative and compliance issues that are created when there are short positions in an account. Recall that earlier in the chapter (Equation 1.1), we stated that an account's rate of return is equal to its market value (MV_1) at the end of a period less its market value at the beginning of the period (MV_0), divided by the beginning market value:

$$r_t = \frac{MV_1 - MV_0}{MV_0}$$

In theory, the net assets of a long-short portfolio could be zero; the value of the portfolio's long positions equal the value of the portfolio's short positions. In this case, the beginning market value, MV_0, would be zero and the account's rate of return would be either positive infinity or negative infinity. In the real world of long-short investing, an account will typically have a positive net asset value due to various margin and administrative requirements. However, as the net asset value gets smaller and approaches zero, the account's return will become nonsensically extreme (large positive or large negative).

To address this problem, we need to revise our performance measurement methodology. One approach would be to think in terms of performance impact, which is discussed in more detail later in the chapter. That is,

$$r_v = r_p - r_B \tag{1.9}$$

where

r_v = value-added return
r_p = portfolio return
r_B = benchmark return

Here, the term r_v is the value-added return on a long-short portfolio where the active weights sum to zero, which is the same situation as a zero-net asset hedge fund. Although the active weights sum to zero, a return can be determined by summing the performance impacts of the n individual security positions (both long and short).

$$\sum_{i=1}^{n} w_{vi} = \left(\sum_{i=1}^{n} w_{pi} - \sum_{i=1}^{n} w_{Bi} \right) = 0; \text{ and}$$

$$r_v = \sum_{i=1}^{n} [w_{vi} \times r_i] = \sum_{i=1}^{n} [(w_{pi} - w_{Bi}) \times r_i] = \sum_{i=1}^{n} (w_{pi} \times r_i) - \sum_{i=1}^{n} (w_{Bi} \times r_i) = r_p - r_B$$

where w_{vi}, w_{pi}, and w_{Bi} are, respectively, the *active* weight of security i in the portfolio, the weight of security i in the portfolio, and the weight of security i in the benchmark. A return could be calculated for the period during which the individual security positions were maintained. Once an individual security position changed, the return period would end and a new return period would start.[17]

The application of benchmarks to long-only portfolios has reached a mature status. Issues regarding the quality of various benchmark designs and the concerns of overly constraining active management strategies by somehow tying performance too closely to benchmarks remain contentious issues. (For example, see Bernstein 2003.) Nevertheless, it is the rare fund sponsor or investment manager who does not make reference to account performance relative to some benchmark. The advent of hedge funds, however, added a new dynamic to the discussion of the use and design of benchmarks. Some practitioners eschew the use of benchmarks entirely for hedge fund managers, contending that the "absolute return" mandate associated with hedge funds implies that relative performance comparisons are meaningless.

The discussion of hedge fund benchmarks is confounded by the vagueness of the definition of hedge funds. A wide variety of active investment strategies fall under the category of hedge funds. The implications of that diversity for benchmark design are considerable. Underlying all long-only benchmark designs are references to the opportunity set available to the manager. Some hedge fund managers have very clearly definable investment universes composed of highly liquid, daily priced securities. For example, many long-short equity managers also manage long-only portfolios. The universe of securities from which they select on the short side often closely resembles the universe of securities from which they select on the long side. Given information regarding the historical returns and holdings of a long-short equity manager's long and short portfolios, we could use either returns-based or security-based benchmark building approaches to construct separate long and short benchmarks for the manager. These benchmarks could be combined in appropriate proportions to create a valid benchmark. Other hedge fund managers, such as macro hedge fund managers, take rapidly changing long-short leveraged positions in an array of asset categories ranging from equities to commodities, which present significant benchmark building challenges.

The ambiguity of hedge fund manager opportunity sets has led to the widespread use of the Sharpe ratio to evaluate hedge fund manager performance. As discussed later in this chapter, the traditional Sharpe ratio is a measure of excess returns (over a risk-free return) relative to the volatility of returns; notably, it can be calculated without reference to the manager's underlying investment universe. Typically, a hedge fund's Sharpe ratio is compared to that of a universe of other hedge funds that have investment mandates assumed to resemble those of the hedge fund under evaluation. Unfortunately, this approach is exposed to the same benchmark validity criticisms leveled against standard manager universe comparisons. Further, the standard deviation as a measure of risk (the denominator of the Sharpe ratio) is questionable when an investment strategy incorporates a high degree of optionality (skewness), as is the case for the strategies of many hedge funds.

PERFORMANCE ATTRIBUTION

We now move to the second phase of performance evaluation, performance attribution. Fama (1972) proposed the first approach to analyzing the sources of an account's returns.

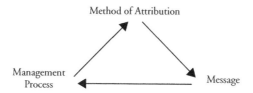

Practitioners use various forms of performance attribution, but the basic concept remains the same: a comparison of an account's performance with that of a designated benchmark and the identification and quantification of sources of differential returns. Further, a unifying mathematical relationship underlies all performance attribution approaches: Impact equals weight times return. We will return to that relationship shortly.

Performance attribution provides an informed look at the past. It identifies the sources of different-from-benchmark returns (**differential returns**) and their impacts on an account's performance. Presuming that one of the objectives of performance attribution is to gain insights helpful for improving the portfolio management process, that process should dictate the method of attribution. The result will be information or a message that will directly relate to the inputs that have gone into the portfolio management process.

When performance attribution is conducted in this manner, the message will either (1) *reinforce* the effectiveness of the management process or (2) cause a *rethinking* of that process.

Effective performance attribution requires an appropriate analytical framework for decomposing an account's returns relative to those of the benchmark. There is no single correct approach. The appropriate framework will depend on the context of the analysis. In particular, the appropriate framework should reflect the decision-making processes of the organizations involved.

We will consider two basic forms of performance attribution from the standpoints of the fund sponsor and the investment manager. Each form seeks to explain the sources of differential returns. We refer to the performance attribution conducted on the fund sponsor level as **macro attribution.** Performance attribution carried out on the investment manager level we call **micro attribution.** The distinction relates to the specific decision variables involved, as opposed to which organization is actually conducting the performance attribution. While it is unlikely that an investment manager would be in a position to carry out macro attribution, one can easily envision situations in which a fund sponsor may wish to conduct both macro and micro attribution.

Impact Equals Weight Times Return

A manager can have a positive impact on an account's return relative to a benchmark through two basic avenues: (1) selecting superior (or avoiding inferior) performing assets and (2) owning the superior (inferior) performing assets in greater (lesser) proportions than are held in the benchmark. This simple concept underlies all types of performance attribution. The assets themselves may be divided or combined into all sorts of categories, be they economic sectors, financial factors, or investment strategies. In the end, however, the fundamental rule prevails that impact equals (active) weight times return.

The nature of this concept is illustrated through Example 1.11.

EXAMPLE 1.11   An Analogy to the Expression for Revenue

Consider a business that sells widgets. Its total revenue is determined by the formula

$$\text{Revenue} = \text{Price} \times \text{Quantity sold}$$

This year, revenue has risen. The company wants to know why. Based on the above formula, the increase in revenues can be attributed to changes in the unit prices or quantity sold or both (perhaps offsetting to a degree). Figure 1.1 displays the situation in which both price and quantity sold have risen. The old revenue was equal to $P_1 \times Q_1$. The new revenue is equal to $P_2 \times Q_2$. The difference in revenues is a bit more complicated, however. It is due in part to an increase in price [$(P_2 - P_1) \times Q_1$; Area 1], in part to an increase in quantity sold [$(Q_2 - Q_1) \times P_1$; Area 2], and in part to the interaction of both variables [$(P_2 - P_1) \times (Q_2 - Q_1)$; Area 3]. Making the connection to performance attribution, the change in quantity is roughly analogous to a difference in weights between securities held in the account and the benchmark, while the change in price represents the difference in returns between securities held in the account and the benchmark.

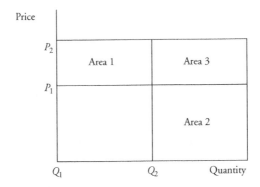

FIGURE 1.1   A Price–Quantity Analogy

Macro Attribution Overview

Let us assume for the moment that for a fund sponsor the term account refers to a total fund consisting of investments in various asset categories (for example, domestic stocks, international stocks, domestic fixed income, and so on) and that the investments are managed by various investment managers. For ease of exposition, we will call this particular account the "Fund." The fund sponsor controls a number of variables that have an impact on the performance of the Fund. For example, the fund sponsor determines the broad allocation of assets to stocks, bonds, and other types of securities. Further, because the fund sponsor retains multiple investment managers to invest the assets of the Fund, decisions must be made regarding allocations across the various investment styles offered by the managers and allocations to the individual managers themselves.

Macro attribution can be carried out solely in a rate-of-return metric. That is, the results of the analysis can be presented in terms of the effects of decision-making variables on the differential return. Most forms of macro attribution follow that approach. The analysis can be enriched by considering the impacts of the decision-making variables on the differential returns in monetary terms. Consider that it is one thing to report that a fund sponsor's active managers added, say, 0.30 percent to the Fund's performance last month. It is quite another thing to state that the 30 basis points of positive active management added US$5 million to the value of the Fund. Performance attribution expressed in a value metric (as opposed to a return metric) can make the subject more accessible not only to investment professionals, but particularly to persons not regularly exposed to the subtle issues of performance attribution. We will present examples of both approaches.

Macro Attribution Inputs

Three sets of inputs constitute the foundation of the macro attribution approach:

1. Policy allocations
2. Benchmark portfolio returns
3. Fund returns, valuations, and external cash flows

With these inputs in hand we can decompose the Fund's performance from a macro perspective.

In the following, we illustrate each concept with data for a hypothetical fund sponsor, the Michigan Endowment for the Performing Arts (MEPA). We use the data for MEPA in the subsequent section to illustrate a macro performance attribution analysis.

Policy Allocations

As part of any effective investment program, fund sponsors should determine normal weightings (that is, policy allocations) to the asset categories within the Fund and to individual managers within the asset categories. By "normal" we mean a neutral position that the fund sponsor would hold in order to satisfy long-term investment objectives and constraints. Policy allocations are a function of the fund sponsor's risk tolerance, the fund sponsor's long-term expectations regarding the investment risks and rewards offered by various asset categories and money managers, and the liabilities that the Fund is eventually expected to satisfy.

Table 1.2 displays the policy allocations of MEPA. It has divided the Fund's assets between two asset categories, with 75 percent assigned to domestic equities and 25 percent assigned to domestic fixed income. Within each asset category, MEPA has retained two active managers. It has allocated 65 percent of the domestic equities to Equity Manager 1 and the remaining 35 percent to Equity Manager 2. Similarly, the fund sponsor has assigned 55 percent of the domestic fixed income to Fixed-Income Manager 1 and 45 percent to Fixed-Income Manager 2.

Benchmark Portfolio Returns

We defined benchmarks earlier. Table 1.3 presents the benchmarks that MEPA has selected for its two asset categories and the managers within those asset categories. The fund sponsor uses broad market indexes as the benchmarks for asset categories, while it uses more narrowly focused indexes to represent the managers' investment styles.[18]

TABLE 1.2   Michigan Endowment for the
Performing Arts Investment Policy Allocations

Asset Category	Policy Allocations
Domestic Equities	75.0%
Equity Manager 1	65.0
Equity Manager 2	35.0
Domestic Fixed Income	25.0
Fixed-Income Manager 1	55.0
Fixed-Income Manager 2	45.0
Total Fund	100.0%

TABLE 1.3   Michigan Endowment for the Performing Arts
Benchmark Assignments

Asset Category	Benchmark
Domestic Equities	S&P 500
Equity Manager 1	Large-Cap Growth Index
Equity Manager 2	Large-Cap Value Index
Domestic Fixed Income	Lehman Govt/Credit Index
Fixed-Income Manager 1	Lehman Int Govt/Credit Index
Fixed-Income Manager 2	Lehman Treasury Index

Returns, Valuations, and External Cash Flows

Macro attribution in a return-only metric requires fund returns. These returns must be computed at the level of the individual manager to allow an analysis of the fund sponsor's decisions regarding manager selection. If macro attribution is extended to include a value-metric approach, then account valuation and external cash flow data are needed not only to calculate accurate rates of return, but also to correctly compute the value impacts of the fund sponsor's investment policy decision making.

For the month of June 20XX, Table 1.4 shows the beginning and ending values, external cash flows, and the actual and benchmark returns for MEPA's total fund, asset categories, and investment managers.

With the inputs for our hypothetical fund sponsor in hand, we turn to an example of a macro performance attribution analysis in the next section.

Conducting a Macro Attribution Analysis

One can envision a number of different variables of interest when evaluating the fund sponsor's decision-making process. Below, we present six levels or components of investment

TABLE 1.4   Michigan Endowment for the Performing Arts Account Valuations, Cash Flows, and Returns: June 20XX

Asset Category	Beginning Value	Ending Value	Net Cash Flows	Actual Return	Benchmark Return
Domestic Equities	$143,295,254	$148,747,228	$(1,050,000)	4.55%	4.04%
Equity Mgr 1	93,045,008	99,512,122	1,950,000	4.76	4.61
Equity Mgr 2	50,250,246	49,235,106	(3,000,000)	4.13	4.31
Domestic Fixed Income	43,124,151	46,069,371	2,000,000	2.16	2.56
Fixed-Income Mgr 1	24,900,250	25,298,754	0	1.60	1.99
Fixed-Income Mgr 2	18,223,900	20,770,617	2,000,000	2.91	2.55
Total Fund	$186,419,405	$194,816,599	$950,000	3.99%	3.94%

policy decision making into which the Fund's performance might be analyzed. We do not imply that these are the only correct variables—they are simply logical extensions of a typical fund sponsor's decision-making process.

Specifically, those levels (which we later refer to as *investment strategies* for reasons to become apparent shortly) are:

1. Net contributions
2. Risk-free asset
3. Asset categories
4. Benchmarks
5. Investment managers
6. Allocation effects

Macro attribution analysis starts with the Fund's beginning-of-period and end-of-period values. Simply put, the question under consideration is: How much did each of the decision-making levels contribute, in either a return or a value metric, to the Fund's change in value over an evaluation period? Macro attribution takes an incremental approach to answering this question. Each decision-making level in the hierarchy is treated as an investment strategy, and its investment results are compared to the cumulative results of the previous levels. That is, each decision-making level represents an unambiguous, appropriate, and specified-in-advance investment alternative: in other words, a valid benchmark. The fund sponsor has the option to place all of the Fund's assets in any of the investment strategies. The strategies are ordered in terms of increasing volatility and complexity. Presumably, the fund sponsor will move to a more aggressive strategy only if it expects to earn positive incremental returns. Macro attribution calculates the incremental contribution that the choice to move to the next strategy produces.

In the previous section, we gave the inputs necessary to conduct a macro performance attribution analysis for a hypothetical fund sponsor, MEPA, for the month of June 20XX. We apply the macro attribution framework just outlined to MEPA in the following discussion. Table 1.5 summarizes the results.

TABLE 1.5   Michigan Endowment for the Performing Arts Monthly Performance
Attribution: June 20XX

Decision-Making Level (Investment Alternative)	Fund Value	Incremental Return Contribution	Incremental Value Contribution
Beginning value	$186,419,405	—	—
Net contributions	187,369,405	0.00%	$950,000
Risk-free asset	187,944,879	0.31	575,474
Asset category	194,217,537	3.36	6,272,658
Benchmarks	194,720,526	0.27	502,989
Investment managers	194,746,106	0.01	25,580
Allocation effects	194,816,599	0.04	70,494
Total Fund	194,816,599	3.99	8,397,194

We now examine each of the six levels in turn.

Net Contributions

Table 1.5 indicates that the starting point of the analysis is the Fund's beginning market value. In our example, at the beginning of June 20XX, the market value of the Fund was $186,419,405. During a given month, the Fund may experience contributions and/or withdrawals. The Net Contributions investment strategy specifies that the net inflows are invested at a zero rate of return and, therefore, the Fund's value changes simply by the total amount of these flows. During June 20XX, net contributions to the Fund were a positive $950,000. Adding this amount to the Fund's beginning value produces a value of $187,369,405 for the Fund under the Net Contributions investment strategy. Although no fund sponsor would deliberately follow this investment strategy, it provides a useful baseline to begin the analysis.

Risk-Free Asset

One highly conservative (but certainly reasonable) investment strategy open to a fund sponsor is to invest all of the Fund's assets in a risk-free asset, such as 90-day Treasury bills.[19] Assuming that the Fund's beginning value and its net external cash inflows (accounting for the dates on which those flows occur) are invested at the risk-free rate, the Fund's value will increase by an additional amount over the value achieved under the Net Contributions investment strategy with its zero rate of return. The Risk-Free Asset investment strategy, using a risk-free rate during June 20XX of 0.31 percent, produces an incremental increase in value of $575,474 (=$187,944,879 − 187,369,405) over the results of the Net Contributions investment strategy, for a total fund value of $187,944,879.[20]

Asset Category

Most fund sponsors view the Risk-Free Asset investment strategy as too risk-averse and therefore overly expensive. Instead, they choose to invest in risky assets, based on the widely held belief that, over the long run, the market rewards investors who bear systematic risk. The

Asset Category investment strategy assumes that the Fund's beginning value and external cash flows are invested passively in a combination of the designated asset category benchmarks, with the specific allocation to each benchmark based on the fund sponsor's policy allocations to those asset categories.

In essence, this approach is a pure index fund approach. The Fund's value under this investment strategy will exceed or fall below the value achieved under the Risk-Free Asset investment strategy depending on whether the capital markets fulfill the expectation that risk-taking investors are rewarded. From a return-metric perspective, the incremental return contribution is

$$r_{AC} = \sum_{i=1}^{A} w_i \times (r_{Ci} - r_f) \qquad (1.10)$$

where r_{AC} is the incremental return contribution of the Asset Category investment strategy, r_{Ci} is the return on the ith asset category, r_f is the risk-free return, w_i is the policy weight assigned to asset category i, and A is the number of asset categories. From a value-metric perspective, the incremental contribution of the Asset Category investment strategy is found by investing each asset category's policy proportion of the Fund's beginning value and all net external cash inflows at the differential rate between the asset category's benchmark rate of return and the risk-free rate, and then summing across all asset categories.

In the Fund's case, investing 75 percent of the Fund's beginning value and net external cash inflows in the S&P 500 and 25 percent in the Lehman Brothers Government/Credit Bond Index (for a combined return of 3.67 percent in the month, or 3.36 percent above the risk-free rate) increases the Fund's market value by $6,272,658 (= $194,217,537 − $187,944,879) over the value produced by the Risk-Free Asset investment strategy. As a result, the Fund's value totals $194,217,537 under the Asset Category investment strategy.

It would be entirely appropriate for a fund sponsor to stop at the Asset Category investment strategy. In fact, an efficient markets proponent might view this all-passive approach as the most appropriate course of action. Nevertheless, fund sponsors typically choose to allocate their funds within an asset category among a number of active managers, most of whom pursue distinctly different investment styles. Importantly for macro attribution, when fund sponsors hire active managers, they are actually exposing their assets to two additional sources of investment returns (and risks): investment style and active management skill.

An investment manager's performance versus the broad markets is dominated by the manager's investment style. With respect to U.S. common stocks, for example, active managers cannot realistically hope to consistently add more than 2–3 percentage points (if that much) annually to their investment styles, as represented by appropriate benchmarks. Conversely, the difference in performance between investment styles can easily range from 15 to 30 percentage points per year.

Benchmarks

The macro attribution analysis can be designed to separate the impact of the managers' investment styles (as represented by the managers' benchmarks) on the Fund's value from the effect of the managers' active management decisions. In this case, the next level of analysis assumes that the Fund's beginning value and net external cash inflows are passively invested in the aggregate of the managers' respective benchmarks. An aggregate manager benchmark return is calculated as a weighted average of the individual managers' benchmark returns.

The weights used to compute the aggregate manager benchmark return are based on the fund sponsor's policy allocations to the managers. From a return-metric perspective,

$$r_{IS} = \sum_{i=1}^{A} \sum_{j=1}^{M} w_i \times w_{ij} \times (r_{Bij} - r_{Ci}) \tag{1.11}$$

where r_{IS} is the incremental return contribution of the Benchmarks strategy, r_{Bij} is the return for the jth manager's benchmark in asset category i, r_{Ci} is the return on the ith asset category, w_i is the policy weight assigned to the ith asset category, w_{ij} is the policy weight assigned to the jth manager in asset category i, and A and M are the number of asset categories and managers, respectively.[21] (Note that summed across all managers and asset categories, $w_i \times w_{ij} \times r_{Bij}$ is the aggregate manager benchmark return.) From a value-metric perspective, the incremental contribution of the Benchmarks strategy is calculated by multiplying each manager's policy proportion of the total fund's beginning value and net external cash inflows by the difference between the manager's benchmark return and the return of the manager's asset category, and then summing across all managers.

In the case of the Fund, the aggregate manager benchmark return was 3.94 percent in June 20XX. Investing the Fund's beginning value and net external cash inflows at this aggregate manager benchmark return produces an incremental gain of $502,989 (= $194,720,526 − $194,217,537) over the Fund's value achieved under the Asset Category investment strategy. As a result, under the Investment Style investment strategy, the Fund's value grows to $194,720,526.

Paralleling the Asset Category investment strategy, the Benchmarks strategy is essentially a passively managed investment in the benchmarks of the Fund's managers. The difference in performance between the aggregate of the managers' benchmarks and the aggregate of the asset category benchmarks is termed *misfit return* or, less formally, *style bias*. In June 20XX, the Fund's misfit return was (3.94% − 3.67%), or a positive 0.27 percent. Although the expected value of misfit return is zero, it can be highly variable over time. That variability can be particularly large for a fund sponsor who has retained investment manager teams within the fund's various asset categories that display sizeable style biases relative to their respective asset category benchmarks. Some fund sponsors employ special risk-control strategies to keep this misfit risk within acceptable tolerances.

Investment Managers

In the next level of analysis, to discern the impact of the managers' active management decisions on the change in the Fund's value, macro attribution analysis calculates the value of the Fund as if its beginning value and net external cash flows were invested in the aggregate of the managers' actual portfolios. Again, the weights assigned to the managers' returns to derive the aggregate manager return will come from the policy allocations set by the fund sponsor. A relationship similar to Equation 1.11 describes the return-metric contribution of the Investment Managers strategy:

$$r_{IM} = \sum_{i=1}^{A} \sum_{j=1}^{M} w_i \times w_{ij} \times (r_{Aij} - r_{Bij}) \tag{1.12}$$

where r_{Aij} represents the actual return on the jth manager's portfolio within asset category i and the other variables are as defined previously.

The difference in the Fund's value under the Investment Managers strategy relative to the Benchmarks strategy will depend on whether the managers, in aggregate, exceeded the return on the aggregate benchmark. In the case of the Fund, the aggregate actual return of the managers (calculated using policy weights) was 3.95 percent, as opposed to 3.94 percent return on the aggregate manager investment style benchmark. This modestly positive excess return translates into an incremental increase in the fund's value of $25,580 (= $194,746,106 – $194,720,526) over the value produced under the Benchmarks strategy, for a total value of $194,746,106 under the Investment Managers investment strategy.

It should be emphasized that macro attribution calculates the value added by the Fund's managers based on the assumption that the fund sponsor has invested in each of the managers according to the managers' policy allocations. Of course, the actual allocation to the managers will likely differ from the policy allocations. However, if we wish to correctly isolate the contributions of the various levels of fund sponsor decision making, we must distinguish between those aspects of the Fund's investment results over which the fund sponsor does and does not have control. That is, the fund sponsor sets the allocation of assets to the Fund's managers but has no influence over their investment performance. Conversely, the managers have control over their investment performance, but they do not generally determine the amount of assets placed under their management.

In examining the value added by the Fund's managers, we should assume they were funded at their respective policy allocations and ask the question, "What would the managers have contributed to the Fund's performance if the fund sponsor consistently maintained the stated policy allocations?" However, in examining the contribution of the fund sponsor, it makes sense to calculate the impact of the differences between the managers' actual and policy allocations on the Fund's performance and thus ask the question, "How did the fund sponsor's decisions to deviate from investment manager policy allocations affect the Fund's performance relative to a strategy of consistently maintaining the stated policy allocations?" The analysis performed at the Investment Managers level attempts to answer the former question. The analysis done at the Allocation Effects level begins to answer the latter question.

Allocation Effects

The final macro attribution component is Allocation Effects. In a sense, the Allocation Effects incremental contribution is a reconciling factor—by definition, it is the difference between the Fund's ending value and the value calculated at the Investment Managers level. If the fund sponsor had invested in all of the managers and asset categories precisely at the established policy allocations, then the Allocation Effects investment strategy's contribution would be zero. However, most fund sponsors deviate at least slightly from their policy allocations, thereby producing an allocation effect. The Fund's actual ending value was $194,816,599, which represents a $70,494 increase (= $194,816,599 – $194,746,106) over the value achieved through the Investment Managers investment strategy. By implication, then, MEPA's actual weightings of the asset categories and managers versus the policy weightings contributed positively to the Fund's value in the month of June 20XX.

Micro Attribution Overview

As implied by its name, micro attribution focuses on a much narrower subject than does macro attribution. Instead of examining the performance of a total fund, micro attribution concerns itself with the investment results of individual portfolios relative to designated benchmarks. Thus, let us define the term *account* to mean a specific portfolio invested by a specific investment manager which we will refer to as the "Portfolio." The Portfolio can be formed of various types of securities. Our illustrations will initially be based on a portfolio of U.S. common stocks. We shall address fixed-income attribution later in this section.

Over a given evaluation period, the Portfolio will produce a return that is different from the return on the benchmark. This difference is typically referred to as the manager's value-added or active return. As shown earlier in Equation 1.9, a manager's value added can be expressed as

$$r_v = r_p - r_B$$

Because the return on any portfolio is the weighted sum of the returns on the securities composing the portfolio, Equation 1.9 can be rewritten as

$$r_v = \sum_{i=1}^{n} w_{pi} r_i - \sum_{i=1}^{n} w_{Bi} r_i \tag{1.13}$$

where w_{pi} and w_{Bi} are the proportions of the Portfolio and benchmark, respectively, invested in security i, r_i is the return on security i, and n is the number of securities.[22]

Rearranging the last equation demonstrates that the manager's value added is equal to the difference in weights of the Portfolio and benchmark invested in a security times the return on that security, summed across all n securities in the Portfolio and benchmark:

$$r_v = \sum_{i=1}^{n} [(w_{pi} - w_{Bi}) \times r_i]$$

With further manipulation,[23] it can be shown that

$$r_v = \sum_{i=1}^{n} [(w_{pi} - w_{Bi}) \times (r_i - r_B)] \tag{1.14}$$

where r_B is the return on the Portfolio's benchmark.

Equation 1.14 offers the simplest form of micro performance attribution: a security-by-security attribution analysis. In this analysis, the manager's value added can be seen to come from two sources: the weights assigned to securities in the Portfolio relative to their weights in the benchmark and the returns on the securities relative to the overall return on the benchmark.

There are four cases of relative-to-benchmark weights and returns for security i to consider. Table 1.6 gives those cases and their associated performance impacts versus the benchmark.

TABLE 1.6   Relative-to-Benchmark Weights and Returns

	$w_{pi} - w_{Bi}$	$r_i - r_B$	Performance Impact versus Benchmark
1.	Positive	Positive	Positive
2.	Negative	Positive	Negative
3.	Positive	Negative	Negative
4.	Negative	Negative	Positive

A manager can add value by overweighting (underweighting) securities that perform well (poorly) relative to the benchmark. Conversely, the manager can detract value by overweighting (underweighting) securities that perform poorly (well) relative to the benchmark.

Security-by-security micro attribution generally is unwieldy and typically provides little in the way of useful insights. The large number of securities in a well-diversified portfolio makes the impact of any individual security on portfolio returns largely uninteresting. A more productive form of micro attribution involves allocating the value-added return to various sources of systematic returns.

Underlying most micro attributions is a factor model of returns. A factor model assumes that the return on a security (or portfolio of securities) is sensitive to the changes in various factors. These factors represent common elements with which security returns are correlated. Factors can be defined in a number of ways: They might be sector or industry membership variables; they might be financial variables, such as balance sheet or income statement items; or they might be macroeconomic variables, such as changes in interest rates, inflation, or economic growth.

The market model, introduced previously, relates a security's or portfolio's return to movements of a broad market index, with the exposure to that index represented by the beta of the security. Recall that Equation 1.8 provides one expression of the market model:

$$R_p = a_p + \beta_p R_I + \varepsilon_p$$

Example 1.12 illustrates the calculation of value added (active return) relative to a one-factor model.

EXAMPLE 1.12   Active Return Relative to a One-Factor Model

Assume that the Portfolio has a zero-factor value of 1.0 percent and a beta of 1.2 at the beginning of the evaluation period. During the period, the excess return on the market index was 7 percent. The market model, expressed in Equation 1.8, states that the Portfolio should return 9.4 percent (= 1.0% + 1.2 × 7%). Further, assume that the Portfolio was assigned a custom benchmark with its own market model parameters, a zero-factor value of 2.0 percent and a beta of 0.8, and which thus has an expected return of 7.6 percent (= 2.0% + 0.8 × 7%). If the Portfolio's actual return was 10.9 percent, then the differential return of 3.3 percent could be attributed in part to the Portfolio's differential expected returns. That is, the Portfolio held a zero factor of 1.0 versus the 2.0 of the benchmark, while the Portfolio had a beta of 1.2 versus the benchmark's beta of 0.8. The incremental expected return of the Portfolio versus the benchmark was 1.8 percent [= (1.0% − 2.0%) + (1.2 − 0.8) × 7%]. The remaining 1.5 percent of differential return would be attributed to the investment skill of the manager.

Sector Weighting/Stock Selection Micro Attribution

Many investment managers employ analysts to research securities and portfolio managers to then build portfolios based on that research. With this investment process, managers are interested in an attribution analysis that will disaggregate the performance effects of the analysts' recommendations and the portfolio managers' decisions to over- and underweight economic sectors and industries.

We can define the returns on the Portfolio and its benchmark to be the weighted sums of their respective economic sector returns. Therefore, just as Equation 1.13 expressed the manager's value-added return as the difference between the weighted average return on the securities in the Portfolio and the benchmark, the manager's value-added return can similarly be expressed as the difference between the weighted average return on the economic sectors in the Portfolio and the benchmark:

$$r_v = \sum_{j=1}^{S} w_{pj} r_{pj} - \sum_{j=1}^{S} w_{Bj} r_{Bj} \qquad (1.15)$$

w_{pj} = Portfolio weight of sector j
w_{Bj} = benchmark weight of sector j
r_{pj} = Portfolio return of sector j
r_{Bj} = benchmark return of sector j
S = number of sectors

Continuing with the example of one of MEPA's investment managers, Table 1.7 shows the results of a micro attribution analysis based on partitioning a manager's value added into a part due to skill in sector selection and a part due to skill in security selection. In this example, the return on the Portfolio for a selected one-month period was 1.12 percent. During that same month the benchmark return was 0.69 percent, generating a value added return of 0.43 percent.

Note that this is a holdings-based or "buy-and-hold" attribution. Each sector's contribution to the total allocation and selection effects depends upon the beginning portfolio and benchmark weights in that sector and the constituent securities' returns due to price appreciation and dividend income. The buy-and-hold approach, which disregards the impact of transactions during the evaluation period, has an important practical advantage: Only the holdings and their returns need be input to the attribution system. There is, however, a disadvantage: The account's buy-and-hold return will not equal its time-weighted total return. For that reason, the attribution analysis shown above includes a reconciling item captioned "Trading and Other." In the example shown in Table 1.7, "Trading and Other" is the negative 14 basis point (−0.14 percent) difference between the account's Buy/Hold return of 1.26 percent and the actual portfolio return of 1.12 percent. The imputed "trading and other" factor reflects the net impact of cash flows and security purchases and sales during the evaluation period. In actively managed accounts with high turnover, the "trading and other" factor can be significant. Where this is a concern, transaction-based attribution analysis can be employed.[24]

The value-added return can be segmented into the impact of assigning the assets of the portfolio to various economic sectors and the impact of selecting securities within those economic sectors. Equation 1.15 can be rearranged to form the following relationship:[25]

$$r_v = \underbrace{\sum_{j=1}^{S} (w_{pj} - w_{Bj})(r_{Bj} - r_B)}_{\text{Pure Sector Allocation}} + \underbrace{\sum_{j=1}^{S} (w_{pj} - w_{Bj})(r_{pj} - r_{Bj})}_{\text{Allocation/Selection Interaction}} + \underbrace{\sum_{j=1}^{S} w_{Bj}(r_{pj} - r_{Bj})}_{\text{Within-Sector Selection}} \qquad (1.16)$$

where S is the number of sectors and r_B is the return on the Portfolio's benchmark.

In Equation 1.16, the **Pure Sector Allocation return** equals the difference between the allocation (weight) of the Portfolio to a given sector and the Portfolio's benchmark weight for that sector, times the difference between the sector benchmark's return and the overall Portfolio's benchmark return, summed across all sectors. The pure sector allocation return

TABLE 1.7 Results of a Micro Attribution Analysis

Economic Sectors	Portfolio Weight (%)	Sector Benchmark Weight (%)	Portfolio Return (%)	Sector Benchmark Return (%)	Performance Attribution			
					Pure Sector Allocation	Allocation/ Selection Interaction	Within-Sector Selection	Total Value Added
Basic materials	5.97	5.54	−0.79	−0.67	−0.01	0.00	−0.01	−0.01
Capital goods	7.82	7.99	−3.60	−3.95	0.01	0.00	0.03	0.04
Consumer durables	2.90	2.38	0.46	−0.21	0.00	0.00	0.02	0.01
Consumer nondurables	31.78	34.75	1.92	1.97	−0.04	0.00	−0.02	−0.05
Energy	7.15	6.01	0.37	0.14	−0.01	0.00	0.01	0.01
Financial	22.47	20.91	2.92	2.05	0.02	0.01	0.18	0.22
Technology	12.14	16.02	2.00	−0.30	0.04	−0.09	0.37	0.32
Utilities	8.64	6.40	0.46	−0.37	−0.02	0.02	0.05	0.05
Cash and equivalent	1.13	0.00	0.14		−0.01	0.00	0.00	−0.01
Buy/Hold + Cash	100.00	100.00	1.26	0.69	−0.02	−0.05	0.64	0.57
Trading and Other			−0.14					−0.14
Total Portfolio			1.12	0.69				0.43

assumes that within each sector the manager held the same securities as the benchmark and in the same proportions. Thus, the impact on relative performance is attributed only to the sector-weighting decisions of the manager.

EXAMPLE 1.13   The Pure Sector Allocation Return for Consumer Nondurables

Table 1.7 indicates that at the beginning of the month the Portfolio had a 31.78 percent weight in consumer nondurables, while the benchmark had a 34.75 percent weight. Because the return of the benchmark consumer nondurables sector was 1.97 percent and the return of the overall benchmark was 0.69 percent, the performance impact due to the consumer nondurables sector allocation is -0.04 percent [= (31.78% − 34.75%) × (1.97% − 0.69%)]. That is, the decision to underweight a sector that performed better than the overall benchmark resulted in a negative contribution to the performance of the Portfolio relative to the overall benchmark. The Pure Sector Allocation return is typically the responsibility of the portfolio managers who determine the Portfolio's relative allocations to economic sectors and industries.

The **Within-Sector Selection return** equals the difference between the return on the Portfolio's holdings in a given sector and the return on the corresponding sector benchmark, times the weight of the benchmark in that sector, summed across all sectors. The Within-Sector Selection return implicitly assumes that the manager weights each sector in the Portfolio in the same proportion as in the overall benchmark, although *within the sector* the manager may hold securities in different-from-benchmark weights. Thus, the impact on relative performance is now attributed only to the security selection decisions of the manager.

EXAMPLE 1.14   The Within-Sector Allocation Return for Technology

Table 1.7 shows that the return of the portfolio's technology sector was 2.00 percent, while the return of the benchmark's technology sector was -0.30 percent. Consequently, the performance impact of security selection within the technology sector was +0.37 percent {= 16.02% × [2.00% − (−0.30%)]}, where 16.02 percent is the weight of the benchmark's holdings in the technology sector. During the month, the Portfolio held technology stocks that in total performed better than the aggregate performance of the technology stocks contained in the sector benchmark, thereby contributing positively to the Portfolio's performance relative to the overall benchmark. The Within-Sector Selection impact is often the responsibility of the security analysts. Among the securities that they research, they are expected to identify significantly misvalued securities and recommend appropriate action.

The **Allocation/Selection Interaction return** is a more difficult concept because it involves the joint effect of the portfolio managers' and security analysts' decisions to assign weights to both sectors and individual securities. The Allocation/Selection Interaction equals the difference between the weight of the Portfolio in a given sector and the Portfolio's benchmark for that sector, times the difference between the Portfolio's and the benchmark's returns in that sector, summed across all sectors.

EXAMPLE 1.15   The Allocation/Selection Interaction Return for Technology

Again referring to Table 1.7, we can see that the Portfolio's relative underweight in the Technology sector of -3.88 percent $(= 12.14\% - 16.02\%)$ and the Portfolio's positive relative performance in the Technology sector of 2.30 percent $[= 2.00\% - (-0.30\%)]$ produced an Allocation/Selection Interaction effect of -0.09 percent during the month.

A decision to increase the allocation to a particular security adds not only to the weight in that security but also to the weight of the sector to which the security belongs, unless there is an offsetting adjustment to securities within that sector. Unless the portfolio manager is careful to make offsetting adjustments, security selection decisions can inadvertently drive sector-weighting decisions. In general, the Allocation/Selection Interaction impact will be relatively small if the benchmark is appropriate—that is, one that is devoid of any material systematic biases. Because the Allocation/Selection Interaction impact is often the source of some confusion and is usually the result of security selection decisions, some practitioners consolidate the Allocation/Selection Interaction impact with the Within-Sector Selection impact.

Fundamental Factor Model Micro Attribution

As we have noted, some type of factor model underlies virtually all forms of performance attribution. Economic sectors and industries represent only one potential source of common factor returns. Numerous practitioners and academics (for example, see Sharpe, 1982, and Fama and French, 1992) have investigated other common factor return sources. For example, with respect to common stocks, a company's size, its industry, its growth characteristics, its financial strength, and other factors seem to have an impact on account performance. Often these factors are referred to as fundamental factors. They may be combined with economic sector factors to produce multifactor models that can be used to conduct micro attribution.

As with any form of performance attribution, the exposures of the Portfolio and the benchmark to the factors of the fundamental factor model must be determined at the beginning of the evaluation period. The benchmark could be the risk exposures of a style or custom index, or it could be a set of normal factor exposures that were typical of the manager's portfolio over time. Finally, the performance of each of the factors must be determined.

EXAMPLE 1.16   Fundamental Factor Model Micro Attribution

Table 1.8 provides an example of a fundamental factor model micro attribution analysis where a U.S. growth stock manager invests the Portfolio. The performance attribution example covers a one-month period, and during that time the Portfolio generated a 6.02 percent rate of return, while the normal portfolio and the market index produced returns of 5.85 percent and 6.09 percent, respectively. During this particular month, growth stocks performed less well than the market index, largely explaining why the normal portfolio (representing the manager's investment style) underperformed the return on the market index by −0.24 percent. The performance difference between the Portfolio (6.02 percent) and the normal portfolio (5.85 percent) is a measure of the portfolio manager's investment skill (0.17 percent) or value added.

TABLE 1.8   Micro Attribution Using a Fundamental Factor Model

	Portfolio Exposure	Normal Exposure	Active Exposure	Active Impact	Return
Market Return					6.09%
Normal Portfolio Return					5.85
Cash Timing	2.36	0.00	2.36	−0.13	
Beta Timing	1.02	1.00	0.02	0.04	
Total Market Timing					−0.09
Growth	1.12	0.85	0.27	−0.15	
Size	−0.26	0.35	−0.61	−0.35	
Leverage	−0.33	−0.60	0.27	0.11	
Yield	−0.03	−0.12	−0.09	−0.22	
Total Fundamental Risk Factors				−0.61	
Basic Industry	14.10	15.00	−0.90	0.04	
Consumer	35.61	30.00	5.61	−0.07	
Energy	8.36	5.00	3.36	0.05	
Financials	22.16	20.00	2.16	−0.02	
Technology	17.42	25.00	−7.58	0.16	
Utilities	2.35	5.00	−2.65	−0.01	
Total Economic Sectors					0.15
Specific (unexplained)					0.72
Actual Portfolio Return					6.02%

The micro attribution analysis shown in Table 1.8 attributes the manager's investment skill or value added to four primary sources: (1) market timing, (2) exposures to fundamental factors, (3) exposures to economic sectors, and (4) a specific or unexplained return component. The market-timing component is made up of two performance impacts; one is due to the Portfolio's cash position, and the other relates to the Portfolio's beta. In the example, the combination of these two effects had a negative impact of -0.09 percent. The second primary performance attribute involves the exposures to the fundamental factors. The Portfolio's fundamental factor exposures are contrasted with "normal" fundamental factor exposures, represented by the manager's benchmark.[26] The Portfolio's actual factor exposures versus its "normal" exposures resulted in a negative return impact of -0.61 percent. Similarly, the Portfolio's economic sector allocations are contrasted with the Portfolio's "normal" allocations to produce performance attribution impacts. In this case, the active sector weights had a positive impact of 0.15 percent. Finally, the fundamental factor model was unable to explain a portion of the Portfolio's return; in this case, the Portfolio had a specific or unexplained return of $+0.72$ percent.[27] This specific return that cannot be explained by the factor model is attributed to the investment manager.

Fixed-Income Attribution

The sector weighting/stock selection approach to micro attribution is applicable to fixed-income as well as equity accounts. We mentioned in our remarks on fixed-income style indexes earlier in the chapter that broad fixed-income market indexes may be segregated into their constituent market segments. Accordingly, the sector weighting/stock selection equity attribution analysis can also be adapted for use with fixed-income accounts by substituting market segments such as government bonds, agency and investment-grade corporate credit bonds, high-yield bonds, and mortgage-backed securities, among others, for the economic sectors such as energy, financial, or utilities.

Nonetheless, bonds are unlike stocks, and an approach that merely isolates allocation and selection effects among bond market sectors will be of limited value in analyzing the sources of fixed-income account returns. Useful attribution analysis captures the return impact of the manager's investment decisions, and fixed-income managers weigh variables that differ in important ways from the factors considered by equity portfolio managers. In the interests of mathematical brevity, we will limit our discussion of fixed-income micro performance attribution to a conceptual overview.[28]

Major determinants of fixed-income results are changes in the general level of interest rates, represented by the government (default-free) yield curve, and changes in sector, credit quality, and individual security differentials, or nominal spreads, to the yield curve. As a general rule, fixed-income security prices move in the opposite direction of interest rates: If interest rates fall, bond prices rise, and vice versa. In consequence, fixed-income portfolios tend to have higher rates of return in periods of falling interest rates and, conversely, lower rates of return in periods of rising interest rates. Consider the example displayed in Figure 1.2, where the U.S. Treasury spot rate yield curve shifted upward across all maturities during the nine-month period ending June 30, 2004, and where the return for the Lehman Brothers U.S. Government Index for the nine-month period was -0.56 percent. Comparing the yield curves for September 30, 2004, and June 30, 2004, we see that in the third quarter of 2004 the change in the U.S. Treasury yield curve was more complex: Short-term rates rose, while the yields on government securities with terms to maturity longer than two years

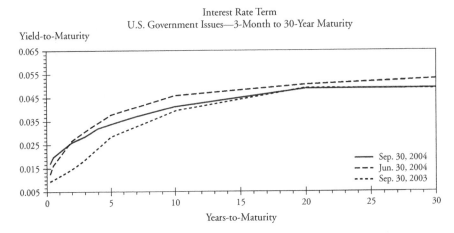

FIGURE 1.2   Interest Rate Term Structure U.S. Government Issue—3-Month to 30-Year Maturity

fell. Reflecting the decline in intermediate and long-term yields, the return on the Lehman Brothers U.S. Government Index for the three-month period was 3.11 percent.

For fixed-income securities that are subject not only to default-free yield-curve movements but also to credit risk, spread changes represent an additional source of interest rate exposure. Companies operating within the same industry face the same business environment, and the prices of the securities they issue have a general tendency to move in the same direction in response to environmental changes. All airlines, for example, are affected by changes in business and leisure travel patterns and the cost of fuel, among other economic factors. In the corporate bond market, such commonalities are reflected in sector spreads, which widen when investors require higher yields in compensation for higher perceived business risk. In addition, rating agencies evaluate the creditworthiness of corporate bond issues, and credit quality spreads vary with changes in the required yields for fixed-income securities of a given rating. Figure 1.3 shows the combined market-based yield effect of the spot rate yield-curve and nominal spread changes for an investor holding AA-rated 10-year industrial bonds. For example, for the nine-month period ending June 30, 2004, increases in the 10-year spot rate and the 10-year AA spread of 0.64 percent and 0.12 percent, respectively, combined to result in a total change of 0.76 percent in the yield of AA-rated 10-year industrial bonds.

Table 1.9 shows the total returns of the Lehman U.S. Government and the Lehman AA Industrials Indexes for the same evaluation periods. The AA Industrials Index modestly underperformed the Government Index in the nine-month period ended June 30, 2004, when the yield curve rose and the nominal spread widened, and significantly outperformed in the subsequent quarter, when the yield curve fell and the nominal spread was essentially unchanged. In addition, of course, the spreads of individual 10-year AA-rated industrial bonds may vary from the average reflected by the sector index, and those differences, too, will be reflected in the actual performance of a specific portfolio.

The impact of interest rate and spread movements on the investment performance of a given portfolio depends upon the nature of the market changes and the interest-sensitive characteristics of the portfolio. We have already seen two types of yield-curve changes: An upward (although nonparallel) shift in the nine-month period ended June 30, 2004, and a twist in the third quarter of 2004 when short-term rates rose and long-term rates fell. Additionally, in both cases, the slope of the yield curve changed. An indicator of the slope

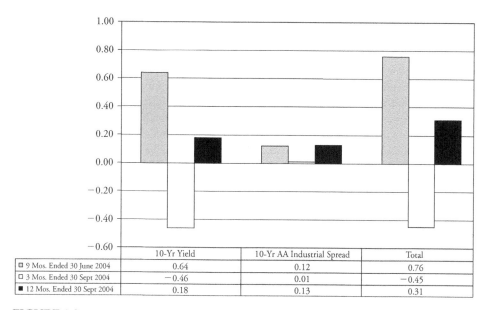

	10-Yr Yield	10-Yr AA Industrial Spread	Total
□ 9 Mos. Ended 30 June 2004	0.64	0.12	0.76
□ 3 Mos. Ended 30 Sept 2004	−0.46	0.01	−0.45
■ 12 Mos. Ended 30 Sept 2004	0.18	0.13	0.31

FIGURE 1.3   Yield Curve and Nominal Spread Changes

TABLE 1.9   Total Returns Data

	Total Returns	
	Lehman U.S. Government Index	Lehman AA Industrials Index
9 months ended June 30, 2004	−0.56%	−0.58%
3 months ended September 30, 2004	3.11%	3.71%
12 months ended September 30, 2004	2.52%	3.11%

is the difference between the 2-year and the 10-year yield-curve rates. The difference was 2.48 percent on September 30, 2003, 1.90 percent on June 30, 2004, and 1.52 percent on September 30, 2004. Thus, over this time frame, the U.S. government spot rate yield curve flattened from one measurement point to the next.

The external interest rate environment is not under the control of the manager; the manager can dictate only the composition of the Portfolio. Subject to the constraints established by the investment mandate and the pertinent policies or guidelines, the manager can adjust the Portfolio's interest-sensitive characteristics in anticipation of forecasted yield-curve and spread changes. Different fixed-income instruments and portfolios will respond diversely to yield-curve movements like those shown above. For example, the resulting adjustment in the valuation of a mortgage-backed portfolio will not be the same as the valuation change of a government bond portfolio. Even portfolios made up of the same types of fixed-income securities (for instance, traditional investment-grade corporate bonds) will have different outcomes, depending upon factors including the maturity, coupon, and option features of their constituent holdings. The manager will modify the Portfolio's interest rate risk profile so as to benefit from expected advantageous movements or to attenuate the return impact of expected adverse changes.

In addition to such interest rate management, other management factors contributing to total portfolio return are the allocation of assets among market segments, economic sectors, and quality grades, and the selection of specific securities within those categories. Trading activity during the evaluation period will also have an impact.

These sources of return are displayed in Figure 1.4.[29] The forward interest rates referred to in this exhibit can be calculated from the points along the spot rate government yield curve at the beginning and the end of the performance evaluation period.

The total return of a fixed-income portfolio can be attributed to the external interest rate effect, on one hand, and the management effect, on the other. The return due to the external interest rate environment is estimated from a term structure analysis of a universe of Treasury securities and can be further separated into the return from the implied forward rates (the expected return) and the difference between the actual realized return and the market implied return from the forward rates (the unexpected return). The overall external interest rate effect represents the performance of a passive, default-free bond portfolio.

The management effect is calculated by a series of repricings and provides information about how the management process affects the portfolio returns. The management effect can be decomposed into four components:

1. **Interest rate management effect.** Indicates how well the manager predicts interest rate changes. To calculate this return, each security in the portfolio is priced as if it were a default-free security. The interest rate management contribution is calculated by subtracting the return of the entire Treasury universe from the aggregate return of these repriced securities. The interest rate management effect can be further broken down into returns due to duration, convexity, and yield-curve shape change, as shown in Table 1.10.

2. **Sector/quality effect.** Measures the manager's ability to select the "right" issuing sector and quality group. The sector/quality return is estimated by repricing each security in the portfolio using the average yield premium in its respective category. A gross return can be then calculated based on this price. The return from the sector/quality effect is calculated by subtracting the external effect and the interest rate management effect from this gross return.

3. **Security selection effect.** Measures how the return of a specific security within its sector relates to the average performance of the sector. The security selection effect for each security is the total return of a security minus all the other components. The portfolio

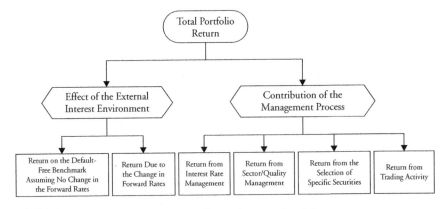

FIGURE 1.4   Sources of the Total Return of a Fixed-Income Portfolio

security selection effect is the market-value weighted average of all the individual security selection effects.

4. **Trading activity.** Captures the effect of sales and purchases of bonds over a given period and is the total portfolio return minus all the other components.

Quantifying the absolute return contributions due to the management effect by means of serial portfolio repricings is data- and computation-intensive, and conducting value-added performance attribution relative to a fixed-income benchmark is still more challenging. Fixed-income investment management organizations often use commercially developed performance measurement and attribution systems. The vendor-provided systems available vary substantially in methodology and level of analytical sophistication, and selecting a system is not a trivial exercise, but most models attempt to isolate and measure the impact of environmental and management factors like those discussed here.

The output of a representative fixed-income attribution system can be demonstrated through a brief illustration. Let us consider the case of the investment officer of the Windsor Foundation, whose consultant has analyzed the performance of two of the foundation's external fixed-income managers, Broughton Asset Management and Matthews Advisors. The consultant has prepared an attribution analysis, shown in Table 1.10, for a particular evaluation period.

TABLE 1.10   Performance Attribution Analysis for Two Fixed-Income Managers for the Windsor Foundation Year Ending December 31, 20XX

	Evaluation Period Returns (%)		
	Broughton Asset Management	Matthews Advisors	Bond Portfolio Benchmark
I. Interest Rate Effect			
1. Expected	0.44	0.44	0.44
2. Unexpected	0.55	0.55	0.55
Subtotal	0.99	0.99	0.99
II. Interest Rate Management Effect			
3. Duration	0.15	−0.13	0.00
4. Convexity	−0.03	−0.06	0.00
5. Yield-Curve Shape Change	0.04	0.13	0.00
Subtotal (options adjusted)	0.16	−0.06	0.00
III. Other Management Effects			
6. Sector/Quality	−0.09	1.15	0.00
7. Bond Selectivity	0.12	−0.08	0.00
8. Transaction Costs	0.00	0.00	0.00
Subtotal	0.03	1.07	0.00
IV. Trading Activity Return	0.10	0.08	0.00
V. Total Return (sum of I, II, III, and IV)	1.28	2.08	0.99

The consultant also included in the analysis the following summary of the investment management strategies of the two firms:

- Broughton Asset Management states that its investment strategy relies on active interest rate management decisions to outperform the benchmark index. Broughton also seeks to identify individual issues that are mispriced.
- Matthews Advisors states that its investment strategy is to enhance portfolio returns by identifying undervalued sectors while maintaining a neutral interest rate exposure relative to the benchmark index. Matthews believes it is not possible to enhance returns through individual bond selection on a consistent basis.

Does the consultant's attribution analysis validate the two firms' self-descriptions of their investment strategies?

In fact, the foundation officer and the consultant can *preliminarily* conclude on the basis of the single year under review that approximately one-half of the incremental return due to Broughton's management process can be attributed to relying on active interest rate management decisions. The total performance contribution for the interest rate management effect—the primary indicator of effective active interest rate management decisions in this analysis—was 16 basis points out of a total of 29 basis points due to the manager's active management process. In addition, the performance contribution for bond selectivity—here, the most direct measure of success in security selection—was 12 basis points. Therefore, nearly all of Broughton's positive performance of 29 basis points (1.28 percent versus 0.99 percent) was a result of its stated strategies of interest rate management (16 basis points) and security selection (12 basis points).

Interestingly, a substantial portion of Matthews' performance results are attributable to the firm's success in identifying undervalued sectors. The positive performance contribution for sector and quality was 1.15 percent, representing a large proportion of Matthews' return relative to the benchmark and indicating success over the evaluation period.

Fixed-income performance attribution is receiving increasing attention from plan sponsors and consultants, but it remains primarily the province of investment managers who have access to the requisite capital market data services as well as the scale of operations to justify the expense and the expertise needed to interpret the results in depth.

PERFORMANCE APPRAISAL

The final phase of the performance evaluation process is performance appraisal. The two preceding phases supplied information indicating how the account performed and quantifying the sources of that performance relative to a designated benchmark. Ultimately, however, fund sponsors are concerned with whether the manager of the account has displayed investment skill and whether the manager is likely to sustain that skill. The goal of performance appraisal is to provide quantitative evidence that the fund sponsor can use to make decisions about whether to retain or modify portions of its investment program.

That said, perhaps no issue elicits more frustration on the part of fund sponsors than the subject of appraising manager investment skill. The problem stems from the inherent uncertainty surrounding the outcome of active management decisions. Even the most talented managers can underperform their benchmarks during any given quarter, year, or even multiyear period due to poor luck. Conversely, ineffective managers at times may make correct decisions and outperform their benchmarks simply by good fortune. We will return to this concept later.

What do we mean by the term *investment skill?* We define **investment skill** as the ability to outperform an appropriate benchmark consistently over time. As discussed previously, a manager's returns in excess of his or her benchmark are commonly referred to as the manager's value-added return or active return. Because no manager is omniscient, every manager's value-added returns, regardless of the manager's skill, will be positive in some periods and negative in others. Nevertheless, a skillful manager should produce a larger value-added return more frequently than his or her less talented peers.

We emphasize that a skillful manager may produce a small value-added return very frequently or a larger value-added return less frequently. It is the magnitude of the value-added returns relative to the variability of value-added returns that determines a manager's skill.

When evaluating managers, many fund sponsors focus solely on the level of value-added returns produced while ignoring value-added return volatility. As a consequence, superior managers may be terminated (or not hired) and inferior managers may be retained (or hired) on the basis of statistically questionable performance data.

Risk-Adjusted Performance Appraisal Measures

Risk-adjusted performance appraisal methods can mitigate the natural fixation on rates of return. There are a number of appraisal measures that explicitly take the volatility of returns into account. A widely accepted principle of investment management theory and practice is that investors are risk averse and therefore require additional expected return to compensate for increased risk. Thus, it is not surprising that measures of performance appraisal compare returns generated by an account manager with the account's corresponding risk. Two types of risk are typically applied to deflate *ex post* returns: the account's market (or systematic) risk, as measured by its beta, and the account's total risk, as measured by its standard deviation.

Three risk-adjusted performance appraisal measures have become widely used: ***ex post*** alpha (also known as **Jensen's alpha**), the **Treynor ratio** (also known as **reward-to-volatility** or excess return to nondiversifiable risk), and the **Sharpe ratio** (also known as **reward-to-variability**). Another measure, **M²**, has also received some acceptance. A thorough discussion of these measures can be found in standard investment texts such as Sharpe, Alexander, and Bailey (1999), but we present a summary here. We consider these measures in their *ex post* (after the fact) form used to appraise a past record of performance.

Ex post Alpha

The *ex post* alpha (also known as the *ex post* Jensen's alpha—see Jensen 1968, 1969) uses the *ex post* Security Market Line (SML) to form a benchmark for performance appraisal purposes. Recall that the capital asset pricing model (CAPM) developed by Sharpe (1966), Lintner (1965), and Mossin (1966), from which the *ex post* SML is derived, assumes that on an *ex ante* (before the fact) basis, expected account returns are a linear function of the risk-free return plus a risk premium that is based on the expected excess return on the market portfolio over the risk-free return, scaled by the amount of systematic risk (beta) assumed by the account. That is, over a single period, the *ex ante* CAPM (SML) is

$$E(R_A) = r_f + \beta_A [E(R_M) - r_f] \qquad (1.17)$$

where

$E(R_A)$ = the expected return on the account, given its beta

r_f = the risk-free rate of return (known constant for the evaluation period)

$E(R_M)$ = the expected return on the market portfolio

β_A = the account's beta or sensitivity to returns on the market portfolio, equal to the ratio of covariance to variance as Cov (R_A, R_M)/Var(R_M)

With data on the actual returns of (1) the account, (2) a proxy for the market portfolio (a market index), and (3) the risk-free rate, we can produce an *ex post* version of the CAPM relationship. Rearranging Equation 1.17, a simple linear regression can estimate the parameters of the following relationship:

$$R_{At} - r_{ft} = \alpha_A + \beta_A(R_{Mt} - r_{ft}) + \varepsilon_t \qquad (1.18)$$

where for period t, R_{At} is the return on the account, r_{ft} is the risk-free return, and R_{Mt} is the return on the market proxy (market index).[30] The term α_A is the intercept of the regression, β_A is the beta of the account relative to the market index, and ε is the random error term of the regression equation. The estimate of the intercept term α_A is the *ex post* alpha. We can interpret *ex post* alpha as the differential return of the account compared to the return required to compensate for the systematic risk assumed by the account during the evaluation period. The level of the manager's demonstrated skill is indicated by the sign and value of the *ex post* alpha. Left unsaid is whether the fund sponsor prefers a manager with a large (positive) but highly variable alpha to one that produces a smaller (positive) but less variable alpha.

Treynor Measure

The Treynor measure (see Treynor 1965) is closely related to the *ex post* alpha. Like the *ex post* alpha, the Treynor measure relates an account's excess returns to the systematic risk assumed by the account. As a result, it too uses the *ex post* SML to form a benchmark, but in a somewhat different manner than the *ex post* alpha. The calculation of the Treynor ratio is

$$T_A = \frac{\bar{R}_A - \bar{r}_f}{\hat{\beta}_A} \qquad (1.19)$$

$\bar{R}_A$ and $\bar{r}_f$ are the average values of each variable over the evaluation period. The Treynor ratio has a relatively simple visual interpretation, given that the beta of the risk-free asset is zero. The Treynor ratio is simply the slope of a line, graphed in the space of mean *ex post* returns and beta, which connects the average risk-free return to the point representing the average return and beta of the account. When viewed alongside the *ex post* SML, the account's benchmark effectively becomes the slope of the *ex post* SML. Thus, a skillful manager will produce returns that result in a slope greater than the slope of the *ex post* SML.

Both the *ex post* alpha and the Treynor measure will always give the same assessment of the existence of investment skill. This correspondence is evident from the fact that any account with a positive *ex post* alpha must plot above the *ex post* SML. Therefore, the slope of a line connecting the risk-free rate to this account must be greater than the slope of the *ex post* SML, the indication of skill under the Treynor ratio.

Sharpe Ratio

Both the *ex post* alpha and Treynor ratio compare excess returns on an account relative to the account's systematic risk. In contrast, the Sharpe ratio (see Sharpe 1966) compares excess returns to the total risk of the account, where total risk is measured by the account's standard deviation of returns. The *ex post* Sharpe ratio is traditionally given by

$$S_A = \frac{\bar{R}_A - \bar{r}_f}{\hat{\sigma}_A} \qquad (1.20)$$

The benchmark in the case of the Sharpe ratio is based on the *ex post* capital market line (CML). The *ex post* CML is plotted in the space of returns and standard deviation of returns and connects the risk-free return and the point representing the mean return on the market index and its estimated standard deviation during the evaluation period. As with the Treynor ratio, a skillful manager will produce returns that place the account above the CML, and hence the slope of the line connecting the risk-free rate and the account will lie above the *ex post* CML. Such a manager is producing more average return relative to the risk-free rate per unit of volatility than is a passive investment in the market index.

M^2

Like the Sharpe ratio, M^2 (see Modigliani and Modigliani 1997) uses standard deviation as the measure of risk and is based on the *ex post* CML. M^2 is the mean incremental return over a market index of a hypothetical portfolio formed by combining the account with borrowing or lending at the risk-free rate so as to match the standard deviation of the market index. M^2 measures what the account would have returned if it had taken on the same total risk as the market index. To produce that benchmark, M^2 scales up or down the excess return of the account over the risk-free rate by a factor equal to the ratio of the market index's standard deviation to the account's standard deviation.

$$M_A^2 = \bar{r}_f + \left(\frac{\bar{R}_A - \bar{r}_f}{\hat{\sigma}_A} \right) \hat{\sigma}_M \tag{1.21}$$

Visually, we can consider a line from the average risk-free rate to the point representing the average return and standard deviation of the account. Extending (or retracing) this line to a point corresponding to the standard deviation of the market index allows us to compare the return on the account to that of the market index at the same level of risk. A skillful manager will generate an M^2 value that exceeds the return on the market index.

M^2 will evaluate the skill of a manager exactly as does the Sharpe ratio. Further, as we discussed, the Jensen's alpha and the Treynor ratio will produce the same conclusions regarding the existence of manager skill. However, it is possible for the Sharpe ratio and M^2 to identify a manager as not skillful, although the *ex post* alpha and the Treynor ratio come to the opposite conclusion. This outcome is most likely to occur in instances where the manager takes on a large amount of nonsystematic risk in the account relative to the account's systematic risk. In that case, one can see by comparing Equations 1.19 and 1.20 that while the numerator remains the same, increased nonsystematic risk will lower the Sharpe ratio but leave the Treynor ratio unaffected. As the market index, by definition, has no nonsystematic risk, the account's performance will look weaker relative to the market index under the Sharpe ratio than under the Treynor ratio (and Jensen's alpha).

Information Ratio

The Sharpe ratio can be used to incorporate both risk-adjusted returns and a benchmark appropriate for the manager of the account under evaluation. In its traditional form, the numerator of the Sharpe ratio is expressed as the returns on the account in excess of the risk-free rate. Similarly, the denominator is expressed as the standard deviation of the difference in returns between the account and the risk-free return. However, by definition, in a single-period context the risk-free rate has no variability, and hence the denominator can be stated as the variability in the account's returns.

Because the Sharpe ratio is based on a differential return, it represents the results of a self-financing strategy. A certain dollar amount can be viewed as being invested in the account, with this long position funded by short-selling the risk-free asset; that is, borrowing at the risk-free rate is assumed to fund the investment in the account. In order to provide a relevant context for performance appraisal using the traditional form, we must identify an appropriate benchmark and compute the Sharpe ratio for that benchmark as well as the account. A higher Sharpe ratio for the account than for the benchmark indicates superior performance.

There is no reason, however, for insisting on appraising performance in the context of borrowing at the risk-free rate to fund the investment in the account. Instead, the Sharpe ratio can be generalized to directly incorporate a benchmark appropriate to the account manager's particular investment style. Equation 1.20 can be rewritten to show the long position in the account is funded by a short position in the benchmark:

$$IR_A = \frac{\bar{R}_A - \bar{R}_B}{\hat{\sigma}_{A-B}} \qquad (1.22)$$

where $\hat{\sigma}_{A-B}$ is the standard deviation of the difference between the returns on the account and the returns on the benchmark. The Sharpe ratio in this form is commonly referred to as the **information ratio,** defined as the excess return of the account over the benchmark relative to the variability of that excess return. The numerator is often referred to as the **active return** on the account, and the denominator is referred to as the account's **active risk**. Thus, from this perspective, the information ratio measures the reward earned by the account manager per incremental unit of risk created by deviating from the benchmark's holdings.

Criticisms of Risk-Adjusted Performance Appraisal Methods

A number of criticisms of risk-adjusted performance measures have surfaced over the years, and we will return to some of those arguments later in the discussion. Perhaps the most prominent criticisms have involved the reliance of the *ex post* alpha and the Treynor ratio on the validity of the CAPM. The CAPM has come under attack for a variety of reasons, most notably the appropriateness of its underlying assumptions and the single-index nature of the model. If assets are valued according to some other equilibrium pricing model, then beta-based performance measures may give inaccurate appraisals.

Critics (for example, Roll 1978) have also pointed to problems raised by the use of surrogates (such as the S&P 500) for the true market portfolio. Roll showed that slight changes in the market portfolio surrogate can yield significantly different performance appraisal answers.

Even those appraisal methods not tied to the CAPM face implementation problems. For example, the use of a market index or custom benchmark in the appraisal of investment performance is open to criticism in that it is difficult in most cases for the account manager to replicate precisely the benchmark's return over time (see French and Henderson 1985). Transaction costs associated with initially creating and then later rebalancing the benchmark, as well as the costs of reinvesting income flows, mean that the benchmark's reported returns overstate the performance that a passive investor in the benchmark could earn.

Stability of the parameters and the estimation error involved in the risk-adjusted appraisal measures is also an issue. Even if the assumptions underlying the appraisal measures hold true, the *ex post* calculations are merely estimates of the true parameters of the actual risk–return relationships. If the estimates are recalculated over another period, they may well show conclusions that conflict with the earlier estimates, even if those relationships are stable over time. Further, that stability cannot be taken for granted; the aggressiveness of the account manager may change rapidly over time in ways that cannot be captured by the estimation procedures.

Quality Control Charts

Conveying the essence of performance appraisal to decision makers is a difficult task. A vast quantity of data needs to be synthesized into a relatively few graphs and tables if information overload is to be avoided. Yet this summary process should not come at the expense of sound data analysis. In particular, it should not preclude a consideration of the statistical and economic significance of the performance results. One effective means of presenting performance appraisal data is through the use of **quality control charts**.

Figure 1.5 presents an example of a quality control chart. It illustrates the performance of an actively managed account versus a selected benchmark. The straight horizontal line emanating from the vertical axis at zero represents the performance of the benchmark. The jagged line is the portfolio's cumulative annualized performance relative to the benchmark (that is, the manager's value-added return). The funnel-shaped lines surrounding the horizontal lines form a confidence band, a statistical concept about which we will have more to say shortly. The confidence band offers a means to evaluate the statistical significance of the account's performance relative to the benchmark.

Underlying the quality control chart's construction are three assumptions concerning the likely distribution of the manager's value-added returns. The primary assumption (and one that we will subsequently test) is referred to as the null hypothesis. The null hypothesis of the quality control chart is that the manager has no investment skill; thus, the expected value-added return is zero. With respect to Figure 1.5, we expect that the manager's value-added return line will coincide with the benchmark line.

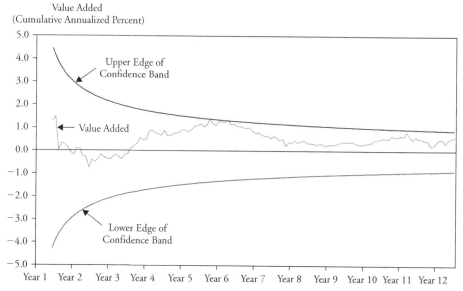

FIGURE 1.5   Quality Control Chart: Cumulative Annualized Value Added Illustrating Manager Performance within Expectations

Of course, at the end of an evaluation period it is highly unlikely that the account's return will precisely equal that of the benchmark. The account's actual return will be either above or below the benchmark's return. The null hypothesis, however, suggests that those *ex post* differences have no directional biases and are entirely due to random chance.

Our second assumption states that the manager's value-added returns are independent from period to period and normally distributed around the expected value of zero. The third assumption is that the manager's investment process does not change from period to period. Among other things, this third assumption implies that the variability of the manager's value-added returns remains constant over time.

Now consider the manager whose investment results are shown in Figure 1.5. Employing the three assumptions described above, we can completely describe the expected distribution of the manager's value-added returns, as illustrated in Figure 1.6. Corresponding to our second assumption of normally distributed value-added returns, the shape of the distribution is the familiar bell-shaped curve. Under our first assumption of no skill (the null hypothesis), the center (or mean) of the distribution is located at 0 percent. Finally, given our third assumption that the manager does not alter his or her investment process over time, we can use the manager's past performance to estimate the dispersion of the value-added return distribution. That dispersion is measured by the standard deviation of the value-added returns, which in this case is an annualized 4.1 percent. We therefore expect that two-thirds of the time, the manager's annual value-added return results will be within ±4.1 percentage points of the zero mean.

Given this information, we can compute a confidence band associated with the expected distribution of the manager's value-added returns. Based on our three assumptions, the **confidence band** indicates the range in which we anticipate that the manager's value-added returns will fall a specified percentage of the time.

In our example, suppose that we wished to determine a confidence band designed to capture 80 percent of the manager's value-added return results. Based on the properties of a normal distribution, we know that 1.28 standard deviations around the mean will capture *ex ante* 80 percent of the possible outcomes associated with a normally distributed random variable. With a 4.1 percent annual standard deviation of value-added returns, the 80 percent confidence band in our example therefore covers a range from approximately −5.2 percent to approximately +5.2 percent around the manager's expected value-added return of zero.

This range, however, corresponds to only one time period: one year from the start of the analysis. To create the confidence band at other points in time, we must transform the

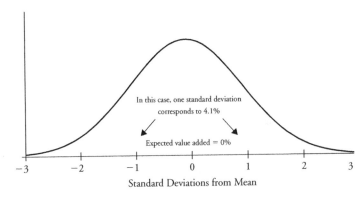

In this case, one standard deviation corresponds to 4.1%

Expected value added = 0%

Standard Deviations from Mean

FIGURE 1.6   Expected Distribution of the Manager's Value Added

standard deviation of the manager's value-added returns to address annualized cumulative value-added returns. This transformation produces the funnel-shaped lines shown in Figure 1.5.

The standard deviation of annualized cumulative value-added returns decreases at a rate equal to the square root of time. As a result, the standard deviation of annualized cumulative value-added returns at two years is $1/\sqrt{2}$ of the one-year value, at three years it is $1/\sqrt{3}$ of the one-year value, and so on. Because the width of the confidence band depends on the standard deviation of value-added returns, as time passes, the confidence band will narrow, converging on the benchmark line.

Intuitively, that convergence means that as we collect more observations on the manager's value-added returns, the cumulative annualized results should lie closer to our expected value of zero. That is, as time passes, it becomes increasingly likely that the manager's random positive- and negative-value-added returns will offset one another. Therefore, the chances that the manager will produce a "large" cumulative annualized value-added return, on either side of the mean, declines over time.

Interpreting the Quality Control Chart

Statistical inference by its nature can be a baffling exercise in double negatives. For example, we do not *accept* the null hypothesis. Rather, lacking evidence to the contrary, we *fail to reject* it. Nevertheless, the equivocal nature of this type of analysis is well suited to the world of investments, where luck often masquerades as skill and skill is frequently overwhelmed by random events.

For example, do the data presented in Figure 1.5 tell us anything about the manager's investment skill? The answer in this case is inconclusive. Over the full period of analysis, the manager has outperformed the benchmark by about 1.0 percent per year. Based on this outcome, we might be tempted to certify the manager as being truly skillful. Before leaping to that conclusion, however, recall that our null hypothesis is that the manager has no skill. What we are really asking is, "Do the manager's performance results warrant rejecting the null hypothesis?" Remember that we assume the manager's value-added returns are normally distributed with a constant annual standard deviation of 4.1 percent. Given those assumptions, under the zero-value-added return null hypothesis, there exists a strong possibility that the manager could possess no skill and yet produce the results shown in Figure 1.5.

The quality control chart analysis provides a likely range of value-added return results for a manager who possesses no skill and who displays a specified level of value-added return variability. For a manager whose investment results are within that range (confidence band), we have no strong statistical evidence to indicate that our initial assumption of no skill is incorrect. Thus we are left with the rather unsatisfying statement, "We cannot reject the null hypothesis that the manager has no skill."

It may be true that the manager in Figure 1.5 has skill and that the 1 percent value-added return was no fluke. Unfortunately, over the limited time that we have to observe the manager, and given the variability of the manager's value-added returns, we cannot classify the manager as unambiguously skillful. Even if the manager could actually produce a 1 percent value-added return over the long run, his or her talents are obscured by the variability of his or her short-run results. That performance "noise" makes it difficult to distinguish his or her talents from those of an unskillful manager.

Now let us consider another manager who generates the value-added return series shown in Figure 1.7. The confidence interval is again designed to capture 80 percent of the potential

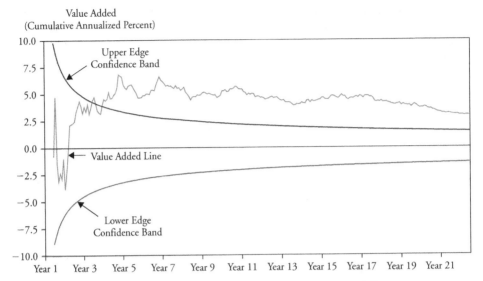

FIGURE 1.7 Quality Control Chart: Cumulative Annualized Value Added Illustrating Manager Performance Significantly Greater than Benchmark

value-added return outcomes for a zero-value-added return manager with a specified level of value-added return variability. In this case, the manager has breached the confidence band on the upside, outperforming the benchmark by about 5 percent per year over the evaluation period. How should we interpret this situation? One view is that the manager has no skill and was simply lucky. After all, there is a 2-in-10 chance that a zero-value added return manager might produce results that lie somewhere outside the confidence band (actually, a 1-in-10 chance of lying above and a 1-in-10 chance of lying below the confidence band).

On the other hand, we could reject the null hypothesis. That is, there is only a 20 percent chance that a zero-value-added return manager would produce results that lie outside the confidence band. Therefore, the occurrence of such an event might indicate that our initial assumption that the manager has no skill is incorrect. Note that our statement would then be, "We reject the null hypothesis that the manager's expected value-added return is zero." By implication, then, we accept a strategy hypothesis that the manager's expected value-added return is not zero.[31]

The quality control chart analysis is similar on the downside. That is, suppose that the manager produces a cumulative negative-value-added return yet lies above the lower edge of the confidence band. In that situation, we should not reject the null hypothesis that the manager's expected value-added return is zero. The manager might be a negative-value-added return investor (that is, be unable to earn back his or her management fees and trading costs). On the other hand, the manager might be skillful and simply be having a poor run of investment luck. In such a case, the relatively small negative-value-added return compared to the variability of that value-added return would make it difficult to reject the null hypothesis.

Conversely, piercing the confidence interval on the downside might lead us to reject the null hypothesis that the manager's expected value-added return is zero. The unstated implication is that the manager is systematically incapable of recapturing the costs of doing business and should be classified as an "underperformer."

THE PRACTICE OF PERFORMANCE EVALUATION

The three components of performance evaluation provide the quantitative inputs required to evaluate the investment skill of an account's manager. However, regardless of the amount of performance data compiled, the process of performance evaluation is fraught with imprecision. Performance evaluation is ultimately a forward-looking decision, and the connection between past performance and future performance is tenuous at best.[32] Indiscriminate use of quantitative data can lead to counterproductive decisions.

As a result, in evaluating investment managers, most fund sponsors follow a procedure that incorporates both quantitative and qualitative elements, with the latter typically receiving more weight than the former. For example, in selecting investment managers, many fund sponsors follow a relatively standard set of procedures. For the sake of exposition, we consider a "typical" fund sponsor. The fund sponsor has a several-person staff that carries out the fund's day-to-day operations. The fund sponsor may retain a consultant to assist in the search for new managers. The staff continually scans the marketplace for promising investment managers. The staff may become aware of a manager through such means as visits from the manager to the staff's office, attendance at various conferences, discussions with peers at other fund sponsor organizations, meetings with consulting firms, and the financial press. The staff maintains files on those managers who have attracted interest, collecting historical return data, portfolio compositions, manager investment process descriptions, and other pertinent data. Upon deciding to hire a new manager, the staff will research its files and select a group of managers for extensive review. This initial cut is an informal decision based on the staff's ongoing survey of the manager marketplace.

The review of the "finalist" group is a much more formal and extensive process. The staff requests that each finalist submit detailed data concerning virtually all aspects of its organization and operations. We broadly group this data into six categories, as shown in Table 1.11.

The staff assigns weights or relative importance to each of these criteria. Table 1.11 shows one possible set of weights. The staff does not apply these criteria and weights in a

TABLE 1.11   Criteria for Manager Selection

Criteria	Importance
Physical	5%
• Organizational structure, size, experience, other resources	
People	25
• Investment professionals, compensation	
Process	30
• Investment philosophy, style, decision making	
Procedures	15
• Benchmarks, trading, quality control	
Performance	20
• Results relative to an appropriate benchmark	
Price	5
• Investment management fees	

mechanical manner. Its ultimate decisions are actually quite subjective. The important point is that the staff considers a broad range of quantitative and qualitative factors in arriving at a selection recommendation. No single factor dominates the decision: Performance data are only one component in the ultimate evaluation decision.

In addition to collecting written information, the staff meets personally with the key decision makers from each of the finalist managers. In those meetings, the staff engages in a broad discussion, the purpose of which is to focus on specific aspects of the managers' operations as highlighted by the selection criteria.

After meeting with all of the finalists, the staff compares notes and selects a manager (or managers) to recommend to the fund sponsor's investment committee, which makes the final decision. The committee members are much more performance-oriented than the staff. Nevertheless, they usually support the staff's well-researched recommendations.

Noisiness of Performance Data

The goal of evaluating prospective or existing managers is to hire or keep the best managers and to eliminate managers likely to produce inferior future results. If past performance were closely tied to future performance, then it would be desirable to rely heavily on past performance in evaluating managers. The problem is that empirical evidence generally does not support such a relationship.

The confusion results from the uncertain, or stochastic, nature of active management. Active managers are highly fallible. While we may expect a superior manager to perform well over any given time period, we will observe that the superior manager's actual performance is quite variable. Even sophisticated investors tend to focus on expected returns and ignore this risk element.

EXAMPLE 1.17   The Influence of Noise on Performance Appraisal

Suppose that we know in advance that a manager is superior and will produce an annual value-added return of 2 percent, on average. The variability of that superior performance is 5 percent per year. Our hypothetical manager has an information ratio of 0.40 (2% ÷ 5%), which by our experience is a high figure. (Hence our assertion that this manager is a superior manager.) Table 1.12 shows the probability of managers outperforming their benchmarks over various evaluation periods, given the information ratios.

TABLE 1.12   Probability of a Manager Outperforming a Benchmark Given Various Levels of Investment Skill

Years	Information Ratio					
	0.20	0.30	0.40	0.67	0.80	1.00
0.5	55.63%	58.40%	61.14%	68.13%	71.42%	76.02%
1.0	57.93	61.79	65.54	74.75	78.81	84.03
3.0	63.81	69.83	75.58	87.59	91.71	95.84
5.0	67.26	74.88	81.45	93.20	96.32	98.73
10.0	73.65	82.86	89.70	98.25	99.43	99.92
20.0	81.70	91.01	96.32	99.86	99.98	99.99

Perhaps surprisingly, Table 1.12 shows that the manager has a one-in-four chance of underperforming the benchmark over a period as long as three years, as seen by the boxed cell in the exhibit. Remember, we have defined this manager in advance to be a superior manager. Other value-added managers with less skill than this one have a greater chance of underperforming their benchmarks over typical evaluation periods.

Most fund sponsors hire more than one manager. Consider a group of 10 superior managers whose investment skills equal those of the manager in Example 1.17 (who has an information ratio of 0.40) and assume independence of decision-making processes. Table 1.13 shows the probability of a given number of this group simultaneously underperforming their benchmarks over a three-year period. As we can see, a fund sponsor using a simple decision rule of firing any manager who underperforms his or her benchmark over a three-year period can expect to follow a busy manager search schedule. Moreover, these probabilities are conservatively low. Few of the fund sponsor's managers will have the investment skill with which we have endowed our hypothetical managers.

In summary, using past performance to evaluate existing managers is statistically problematic. In the long run, superior managers will outperform inferior managers. However, due to the inherent uncertainty of investment management, over typical evaluation periods (three to five years) the odds that superior managers will underperform their benchmarks (and, conversely, that inferior managers will outperform their benchmarks) are disturbingly high. Expensive, incorrect decisions may frequently result from relying on past performance to evaluate investment managers.

Manager Continuation Policy

Frequent manager firings based on recent performance might seem to be merely a waste of a fund sponsor's time if not for the expenses associated with manager transitions. Fired managers'

TABLE 1.13   Probability of Superior Managers Jointly Underperforming Their Benchmarks over a Three-Year Period

Managers Below Benchmark	Probability
0	6.10%
1	19.68
2	28.59
3	24.60
4	13.90
5	5.38
6	1.45
7	0.27
8	0.03
9	0.00
10	0.00

portfolios must be converted to the hired managers' portfolios. This conversion requires buying and selling securities, which in turn involves trading costs. Making assumptions about the cost of trading securities is a tenuous business at best, because many factors influence that cost. For U.S. large-capitalization common stocks, it is reasonable to assume transaction costs of 0.50 percent (one way), and for small company stocks and stocks of companies traded in less liquid markets, those costs can be much higher. A substantial percentage of the fired manager's portfolio may need to be liquidated in the process of moving the assets to a new manager, particularly when the managers' styles are not closely similar. Moreover, this tally of the expenses of converting a manager's portfolio considers only direct monetary costs. For most fund sponsors, replacing managers involves significant time and effort.[33]

In an attempt to reduce the costs of manager turnover yet systematically act on indications of future poor performance, some fund sponsors have adopted formal, written **manager continuation policies** (MCP) to guide their manager evaluations. The purpose of an MCP is severalfold:

- To retain superior managers and to remove inferior managers, preferably before the latter can produce adverse results
- To ensure that relevant nonperformance information is given significant weight in the evaluation process
- To minimize manager turnover
- To develop procedures that will be consistently applied regardless of investment committee and staff changes

An MCP can be viewed as a two-part process. The first part we refer to as **manager monitoring**, while the second part we call **manager review**. Figure 1.8 displays a flow chart description of an MCP.

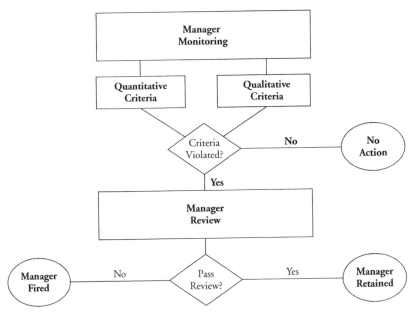

FIGURE 1.8   Manager Continuation Policy

Manager Monitoring

The ongoing phase of an MCP is manager monitoring. The goal of MCP manager monitoring is to identify warning signs of adverse changes in existing managers' organizations. It is a formal, documented procedure that assists fund sponsors in consistently collecting information relevant to evaluating the state of their managers' operations. The key is that the fund sponsor regularly asks the same important questions, both in written correspondence and in face-to-face meetings.

There is no firm set of appropriate manager monitoring criteria. Each fund sponsor must determine for itself the issues that are relevant to its own particular circumstances. Monitoring criteria may even vary from manager to manager. Regardless, the fund sponsor should clearly articulate its established criteria at the time a manager is hired, rather than formulate them later in a haphazard manner.

As part of the manager monitoring process, the fund sponsor periodically receives information from the managers, either in written form or through face-to-face meetings. This information is divided into two parts. The first part covers operational matters, such as personnel changes, account growth, litigation, and so on. The staff should flag significant items and discuss them in a timely manner with the respective managers.

The second part of the responses contains a discussion of the managers' investment strategies, on both a retrospective and a prospective basis. The fund sponsor should instruct the managers to explain their recent investment strategies relative to their respective benchmarks and how those strategies performed. The managers should follow this review with a discussion of their current strategies relative to the benchmark and why they believe that those strategies are appropriate. The goal of these discussions is to assure the fund sponsor that the manager is continuing to pursue a coherent, consistent investment approach. Unsatisfactory manager responses may be interpreted as warning signs that the manager's investment approach may be less well-defined or less consistently implemented than the staff had previously believed.

As part of the manager monitoring process, the staff should regularly collect portfolio return and composition data for a performance attribution analysis. The purpose of such a periodic analysis is to evaluate not how well the managers have performed, but whether that performance has been consistent with the managers' stated investment styles. The staff should address questions arising from this analysis directly to the managers.

Typically, the results of the MCP manager monitoring stage reveal nothing of serious concern. That is, the managers' organizations remain stable, and the managers continue to follow their stated investment approaches regardless of the near-term success or failure of their particular active strategies. While the managers should be able to explain why particular strategies failed, the mere occurrence of isolated periods of poor performance should typically not be a cause for concern, unless the staff finds related nonperformance problems.

Manager Review

Occasionally, manager monitoring may identify an item of sufficient concern to trigger a manager review. For example, a recently successful small manager might experience excessive growth in accounts and assets. Despite discussions with the manager, the staff might be convinced that such growth threatens the manager's ability to produce superior returns in the future. At this point, a formal manager review becomes necessary.

The manager review closely resembles the manager selection process, in both the information considered and the comprehensiveness of the analysis. The staff should review all phases of the manager's operations, just as if the manager were being initially hired. We can view this manager review as a zero-based budgeting process (a budgeting process in which all expenditures must be justified each new period). We want to answer the question, "Would we hire the manager again today?"

As with the initial selection of a manager, the fund sponsor should collect the same comprehensive data and meet face-to-face with the manager in a formal interview setting. The manager's key personnel should attend, with the advance understanding that they must persuade the staff to "rehire" them. On conclusion of the interview, the staff should meet to compare observations, weighing the evaluation criteria in the same manner that it would if it were initially considering the manager. As part of these deliberations, the fund sponsor should also review the information that led to the manager's hiring in the first place.

The primary differences between hiring a new manager and retaining a manager under review are that the fund sponsor once had enough confidence in the manager to entrust a large sum of money to the manager's judgment and that there is a sizable cost associated with firing the manager. Thus, the fund sponsor should address the following questions:

- What has fundamentally changed in the manager's operation?
- Is the change significant?
- What are the likely ramifications of the change?
- Are the costs of firing the manager outweighed by the potential benefits?

Manager Continuation Policy as a Filter

For many reasons, investment skill does not readily lend itself to rigid "good" or "bad" interpretations. For discussion purposes, however, we will arbitrarily divide the investment manager community into three categories: positive-, zero-, and negative-value-added managers. Assume that positive-value-added managers beat their benchmarks (after all fees and expenses) by 2 percent per year, on average. Zero-value-added managers exhibit just enough skill to cover their fees and expenses and thereby match the performance of their benchmarks. Finally, negative-value-added managers lose to their benchmarks by 1 percent per year, on average, due primarily to the impact of fees and expenses.

We have no firm evidence as to how the manager community is apportioned among these three categories, although if we follow the logic of Grossman and Stiglitz (1980) and Sharpe (1994), the zero- and negative-value-added managers must predominate, with the former outnumbering the latter. Nevertheless, we speculate that out of five managers hired, a fund sponsor would be fortunate to hire two positive-value-added managers, two zero-value-added managers, and one negative-value-added manager. Therefore, in aggregate, this successful fund sponsor's managers are expected to outperform their benchmarks by 60 basis points per year, net of all costs [0.6% = (2% × 0.4) + (0% × 0.4) + (−1% × 0.2)].

We can view a MCP as a statistical filter designed to remove negative-value-added managers and retain positive-value-added managers. Zero-value-added managers, much to the consternation of fund sponsors, always present a problem for a MCP, because they are so numerous and because they are statistically difficult to distinguish from positive- and negative-value-added managers.

We begin our MCP analysis with the null hypothesis that the managers under evaluation are at best zero-value-added managers. Then, as with any filter, two types of decision errors may occur:

- **Type I error**—keeping (or hiring) managers with zero value added. (Rejecting the null hypothesis when it is correct.)

- **Type II error**—firing (or not hiring) managers with positive value added. (Not rejecting the null hypothesis when it is incorrect.)

In implementing a MCP, the fund sponsor must determine how fine a filter to construct. A coarse filter will be conducive to Type I errors. For example, a fund sponsor may choose to overlook many violations of its manager monitoring guidelines, with the expectation that most problems experienced by managers are temporary and that they will eventually work themselves out. While this policy will avoid firing some positive-value-added managers, the fund sponsor could have identified in advance some managers who will provide mediocre long-term performance.

Conversely, a fine filter will lead the sponsor to commit more Type II errors. For example, a fund sponsor might apply its manager monitoring guidelines rigidly and automatically fire any manager who loses a key decision maker. While this policy will remove some managers whose operations will be disrupted by personnel turnover, it will also eliminate some managers possibly anticipated to recover from that turnover and to continue with superior results.

Figure 1.9 presents the four possible results from testing the null hypothesis that a manager has no investment skill. Referring back to the quality control chart, if in truth the manager has no skill and we reject the null hypothesis because the manager's value-added returns fall outside of the confidence band (particularly, in this case, on the upside), then we have committed a Type I error. Conversely, if the manager is indeed skillful yet we fail to reject the null hypothesis because the manager's value-added returns fall inside the confidence band, then we have committed a Type II error.

Both Type I and Type II errors are expensive. The art of a MCP is to strike a cost-effective balance between the two that avoids excessive manager turnover yet eliminates managers likely to produce inferior performance in the future. We can control the probabilities of committing Type I and Type II errors by adjusting the width of the confidence band within the quality control chart. For example, suppose that we widened the confidence band to encompass 95 percent of a manager's possible value-added return outcomes. Now it will be less likely than in our earlier examples that a zero-value-added return manager will generate returns that lie outside the confidence band. We thus reduce the chances of a Type I error. However, it will also now be less likely that a truly skillful manager will come to our attention by generating returns that fall outside that manager's confidence band. By continuing not to reject the null hypothesis for such a manager, we commit a Type II error.

Due to the high costs and uncertain benefits of replacing managers, it would seem advisable for fund sponsors to develop manager evaluation procedures that are tolerant toward Type I errors in order to reduce the probability of Type II errors. That is, it may be preferable to endure the discomfort of keeping several unskillful managers to avoid the expense of firing a truly superior manager. However, there is no right answer to this dilemma, and fund

	Reality	
	Value Added = 0	Value Added > 0
Reject	Type I	Correct
Do Not Reject	Correct	Type II

FIGURE 1.9   Null Hypothesis: Manager Has No Skill. Alternative Hypothesis: Manager Is Skillful.

sponsors must undertake their own cost–benefit analyses, weighing the chances of committing one type of error versus the other. The quality control chart approach, however, provides fund sponsors with an objective framework with which to address this issue.

NOTES

1. The evaluation period in this sense can also be called the measurement period.
2. From the fund sponsor's perspective, the account's market value should reflect the impact of all fees and expenses associated with investing the account's assets. Many managers report the return on accounts that they manage without including the effect of various fees and expenses. This practice is often justified based on the fact that fees vary among clients.
3. Note that the account's reported return was lower when the contribution took place at the start of the month than at the end. This result occurs because the account had both a positive return and proportionately more assets to invest over the month when the contribution was received at the beginning as opposed to the end. If the account's return had been negative, then, given the same ending value, a contribution at the beginning of the month would have resulted in a less negative reported return than would have resulted from a contribution that occurred at the end of the month.
4. For a discussion of the use of the MWR as a performance measure for opportunistic investments, see Tierney and Bailey (1997).
5. Nevertheless, for periods beginning January 1, 2010, firms will be required to value portfolios on the date of all large external cash flows to claim compliance with the GIPS standards. In the interim, the GIPS standards admit the use of acceptable daily weighted methods for estimating the time-weighted rate of return. These methods are presented in Chapter 13 of *Managing Investment Portfolios.*
6. Bank Administration Institute (1968, p. 22).
7. The variables used in this section can be interpreted as either rates of return or weights assigned to securities that make up a portfolio.
8. As we have used the term, a benchmark is a means to differentiate managers or fund sponsors who add value through investment insights from those who do not. In this sense, a sponsor's liabilities may also be treated as a type of benchmark. That is, institutional investors such as defined-benefit pension plan sponsors and endowment and foundation executives seek to achieve rates of return enabling them, at a minimum, to meet liabilities as they come due without making greater-than-planned additions to fund assets. (Another way to express this financial objective is to say that institutional investors seek at least to maintain a stated level of fund surplus, defined as the present value of assets less the present value of liabilities.) In terms of asset-liability management, or surplus management, the fund's investment objective may be to achieve a rate of return on assets that meets or exceeds the "return" on liabilities—that is, the percentage change in the present value of the liabilities over the evaluation period. Moreover, because a liability, or a stream of liabilities, may be considered a financial asset held short, it is possible, in principle, to construct a custom index representing the fund's liabilities and to use that index as a benchmark at the level of the total fund.
9. Factor models are discussed in DeFusco, McLeavey, Pinto, and Runkle (2004) as well as in standard investment textbooks such as Sharpe, Alexander, and Bailey (1999).

10. Although the market model has some resemblances to the capital asset pricing model (CAPM), the market model is not an equilibrium model of asset pricing, as is the CAPM. Under a set of specific assumptions, the CAPM states that investors will act in a manner that generates a unique relationship between the beta of a security or portfolio and the return on the market portfolio. Any security or portfolio with the same beta is expected to produce the same return. The market model, on the other hand, is an empirical relationship between the return on a security or portfolio and a particular market index (as opposed to the market portfolio). See Markowitz (1984) for a discussion of this distinction.

11. The ability to track the account's returns is typically measured by the standard deviation of the monthly return differences of the account and the benchmark, called the tracking error.

12. Bailey (1992a) critiques in detail the use of manager universes as benchmarks. Beyond the failure to possess the properties of a valid benchmark and the issue of survivor bias, Bailey also discusses the failure of manager universes to pass tests of benchmark quality. The tests of benchmark quality are summarized in the section titled Tests of Benchmark Quality.

13. The historical beta of the account relative to the benchmark is derived from a regression of the account's past returns on the past returns of the benchmark. The resulting slope of the regression line, termed the beta of the regression, indicates the sensitivity of the account's returns to those of the benchmark. Note that a benchmark may fail this test because the manager holds cash in the account, typically for transaction purposes, while the benchmark may reflect a zero cash position. If the account's beta relative to the benchmark would be 1.0 excluding the positive cash position, the overall beta of the account (including the cash position) will be less than 1.0. As a result, the account will have an unfavorable performance bias in an up market and a favorable bias in a down market. The simple solution is to hold cash in the benchmark at a level reflective of the manager's "neutral" cash position.

14. Risk characteristics refer to factors that systematically affect the returns on many securities. We will return to the issue later in the discussion on performance attribution.

15. Violations of this quality criterion often occur when a benchmark is market capitalization weighted. Because many managers do not utilize a market-capitalization weighting scheme in building their portfolios, the possibility of negative active positions can arise when a capitalization-weighted benchmark is assigned.

16. See Koh, Lee, and Fai (2002).

17. Another approach to determining a rate of return for a long-short portfolio would be to specify the numerator in Equation 1.1 as the profit and/or loss resulting from the particular hedge fund strategy. The denominator could be specified as the asset base over which the strategy applies. This could be defined as the amount of assets at risk and could be approximated by the absolute value of all the long positions plus the absolute value of all the short positions.

18. Rather than using broad market indexes as asset category benchmarks, some fund sponsors and consultants construct asset category benchmarks by weighting the managers' benchmarks in accordance with their policy allocations. Under this approach, using the data given in Table 1.2 and Table 1.3, the blended asset category benchmark for domestic equities would consist of a 65 percent weighting in Large-Cap Growth Index and a 35 percent weighting in Large-Cap Value Index. However, this approach impairs the sponsor's ability to evaluate the impact of "misfit returns" or "style bias" as described later in this chapter.

19. Alternatively, a pension fund might identify the risk-free asset as a portfolio of bonds that best hedges its liabilities.

20. The increment of $575,474 cannot be replicated by multiplying $187,369,405 by 0.31 percent because the $950,000 net contribution (to obtain $187,369,405) was not a single, beginning-of-the-month cash flow.

21. Note: $\sum_{j=1}^{M} w_{ij} = 1$ for all i and $\sum_{i=1}^{A} w_i = 1$

22. For simplicity we assume that the Portfolio's securities are chosen from among the securities in the benchmark. Otherwise n needs to represent the number of securities in the union of the benchmark and the Portfolio.

23. Note that the sum of the security weights in any portfolio must equal 1.0, or, equivalently, $\sum_{i=1}^{n}(w_{pi} - w_{Bi}) = 0$. Because zero multiplied by a constant equals zero, $\sum_{i=1}^{n}(w_{pi} - w_{Bi}) \times r_B = 0$, where r_B is the known return on the benchmark (the constant). Subtracting this expression from the right-hand side of the equation just given yields $r_v = \sum_{i=1}^{n}[(w_{pi} - w_{Bi}) \times (r_i - r_B)]$.

24. See Spaulding (2003). Transaction-based attribution analysis is outside the scope of the present discussion.

25. Equation 1.16 covers performance attribution in the single-period case. Multiperiod performance attribution, while an extension of the single-period approach, involves considerably more complexity. For a discussion of some of the issues involved in multiperiod performance attribution, see Menchero (2004) and Frongello and Bay (2002).

26. Exposure to a fundamental factor in this case is measured in terms of standard deviations from the mean, where the mean is determined by the average value of the particular factor for a group of capitalization-weighted stocks.

27. Although this type of performance attribution analysis provides valuable insights to investment practitioners, there is a serious limitation. It involves the ambiguity of the benchmark. If the benchmark is based solely on a set of exposures to investment risk factors, then the benchmark is ambiguous. That is, we can construct multiple portfolios that have the same risk characteristics, but they will not have the same investment return. For example, many portfolios might have the same beta, but they will have different investment returns. The solution to this limitation is to base the attribution analysis on the risk exposures of an appropriate benchmark portfolio, i.e., a portfolio with specified securities and weights. In this case, the benchmark portfolio will have a specific or unexplained return component. The difference between it and the portfolio's specific return is attributed to the investment manager.

28. A more rigorous treatment of this discussion of fixed-income micro attribution can be found in Fong, Pearson, and Vasicek (1983).

29. Fong, Pearson, and Vasicek (1983).

30. The *ex post* alpha relationship can be expanded to incorporate other sources of risk (for example, the three-factor model developed by Fama and French). See Carhart (1997) for further discussion.

31. Of course, the assumptions underlying the statistical test may not hold. For example, the manager's investment process may have become more aggressive, and hence the variability of his value-added returns may have increased.

32. See Carhart (1997).

33. The costs associated with manager hiring and firing decisions are discussed in Goyal and Wahal (2005).

REFERENCES

Ambachtsheer, Keith. 1986. *Pension Funds and the Bottom Line: Managing the Corporate Pension Fund as a Financial Business*. Homewood, IL: Dow Jones-Irwin.

Bailey, Jeffery V. 1992a. "Are Manager Universes Acceptable Performance Benchmarks?" *Journal of Portfolio Management*. Vol. 18, No. 3: 9–13.

Bailey, Jeffery V. 1992b. "Evaluating Benchmark Quality." *Financial Analysts Journal*. Vol. 48, No. 3: 33–39.

Bank Administration Institute. 1968. *Measuring the Investment Performance of Pension Funds*. Park Ridge, IL: Bank Administration Institute.

Bernstein, Peter L. 2003. "Points of Inflection: Investment Management Tomorrow." *Financial Analysts Journal*. Vol. 59, No. 4: 18–23.

Carhart, Mark M. 1997. "On Persistence in Mutual Fund Performance." *Journal of Finance*. Vol. 51, No. 1: 57–82.

DeFusco, Richard, Dennis McLeavey, Jerald Pinto, and David Runkle. 2004. *Quantitative Methods for Investment Analysis*, 2nd edition. Charlottesville, VA: CFA Institute.

Dietz, Peter. 1966. *Pension Funds: Measuring Investment Performance*. New York: The Free Press.

Ellis, Charles. 1985. *Investment Policy*. Homewood, IL: Dow Jones-Irwin.

Fama, Eugene. 1972. "Components of Investment Performance." *Journal of Finance*. Vol. 27, No. 3: 551–567.

Fama, Eugene, and Kenneth French. 1992. "The Cross-Section of Expected Stock Returns." *Journal of Finance*. Vol. 47, No. 2: 427–465.

Fong, H. Gifford, Charles Pearson, and Oldrich Vasicek. 1983. "Bond Performance: Analyzing Sources of Return." *Journal of Portfolio Management*. Vol. 9, No. 3: 46–50.

French, Dan, and Glenn Henderson, Jr. 1985. "How Well Does Performance Evaluation Perform?" *Journal of Portfolio Management*. Vol. 11, No. 2: 15–18.

Frongello, Andrew, and Scott Bay. 2002. "Linking Single Period Attribution Results." *Journal of Performance Measurement*. Vol. 6, No. 3: 10–22.

Goyal, Amit, and Sunil Wahal. 2005. "The Selection and Termination of Investment Management Firms by Plan Sponsors." Working Paper, Goizueta Business School, Emory University.

Grossman, Sanford, and Joseph Stiglitz. 1980. "On the Impossibility of Informationally Efficient Markets." *American Economic Review*. Vol. 70, No. 3: 393–408.

Jensen, Michael. 1968. "The Performance of Mutual Funds in the Period 1945–1964." *Journal of Finance*. Vol. 23, No. 2: 389–416.

Jensen, Michael. 1969. "Risk, the Pricing of Capital Assets, and the Evaluation of Investment Portfolios." *Journal of Business*. Vol. 42, No. 2: 167–185.

Koh, Francis, David Lee, and Phoon Kok Fai. 2002. "Investing in Hedge Funds: Risk, Return and Pitfalls." Working Paper.

Lintner, John. 1965. "Security Prices, Risk, and Maximal Gains from Diversification." *Journal of Finance*. Vol. 20, No. 4: 587–615.

Markowitz, Harry. 1984. "The Two Beta Trap." *Journal of Portfolio Management*. Vol. 10, No. 1: 12–20.

Menchero, Jose. 2004. "Multiperiod Arithmetic Attribution." *Financial Analysts Journal*. Vol. 60, No. 4: 76–91.

Modigliani, Franco, and Leah Modigliani. 1997. "Risk-Adjusted Performance." *Journal of Portfolio Management*. Vol. 23, No. 2: 45–54.

Mossin, Jan. 1966. "Equilibrium in a Capital Asset Market." *Econometrica*. Vol. 34, No. 4: 768–783.

Roll, Richard. 1978. "Ambiguity When Performance Is Measured by the Security Market Line." *Journal of Finance*. Vol. 33, No. 4: 1051–1069.

Rosenberg, Barr, and Vinay Marathe. 1975. "The Prediction of Investment Risk: Systematic and Residual Risk." *Proceedings of the Seminar on the Analysis of Security Prices*. Center for Research in Security Prices, Graduate School of Business, University of Chicago.

Sharpe, William. 1966. "Mutual Fund Performance." *Journal of Business*. Vol. 39, No. 1: 119–138.

Sharpe, William. 1982. "Factors in New York Stock Exchange Security Returns, 1931–1979." *Journal of Portfolio Management*. Vol. 8, No. 4: 5–19.

Sharpe, William. 1988. "Determining a Fund's Effective Asset Mix." *Investment Management Review*. Vol. 2, No. 6: 59–69.

Sharpe, William. 1992. "Asset Allocation, Management Style and Performance Measurement." *Journal of Portfolio Management*. Vol. 18, No. 2: 7–19.

Sharpe, William. 1994. "The Sharpe Ratio." *Journal of Portfolio Management*. Vol. 21, No. 1: 49–59.

Sharpe, William, Gordon Alexander, and Jeffery V. Bailey. 1999. *Investments*. UpperSaddle River, NJ: Prentice Hall.

Spaulding, David. 2003. "Holdings vs. Transaction-based Attribution, an Overview." *Journal of Performance Measurement*. Vol. 8, No. 1: 52–56.

Tierney, David, and Jeffery V. Bailey. 1997. "Opportunistic Investing." *Journal of Portfolio Management*. Vol. 23, No. 3: 69–78.

Treynor, Jack. 1965. "How to Rate Management of Investment Funds." *Harvard Business Review*. Vol. 43, No. 1: 63–75.

PART II

PERFORMANCE MEASUREMENT

CHAPTER 2

BENCHMARKS AND INVESTMENT MANAGEMENT

Laurence B. Siegel

To highly skilled managers, benchmarks are confining, but to managers without the ability to consistently add alpha and to investors, benchmarks are a boon. In this chapter, the author explores many issues surrounding investment benchmarks and benchmarking and outlines a compromise that might ease the natural tension between active managers who believe they have real skill and bristle at the need to be measured by benchmarks and investors who want a benchmark so they can measure performance.

FOREWORD

Benchmarks determine the performance of investment managers perhaps more than any other influence, including managers' determination to succeed and the resources and skills they bring to this task. We in the industry have largely overlooked this fact, perhaps at our peril. With this outstanding Research Foundation chapter, Laurence Siegel shines a bright light on the role of benchmarks, and he raises critical issues that we can no longer ignore.

Siegel begins by providing historical perspective to the topic, tracing the evolution of benchmarks from their 1884 origin with Charles Henry Dow's average of 11 railroad stocks to their alleged role in the recent stock market bubble. Along the way, he adeptly intertwines the development and application of benchmarks with the development and gradual acceptance of modern portfolio theory. He demonstrates clearly that benchmarks are the practical corollary of the efficient market hypothesis and the capital asset pricing model.

Reprinted from the Research Foundation of CFA Institute (2003).

Siegel focuses much of his efforts on describing the three purposes of benchmarks:

- to function as portfolios for investors who want passive exposure to a particular market segment,
- to serve as performance standards against which to measure the contribution of active managers, and
- to act as proxies for asset classes in the formation of policy portfolios.

Although these purposes may seem self-evident once they are suggested, Siegel delves into a variety of nuances, complexities, and controversies that I suspect most readers will not have considered previously, including the features that distinguish good benchmarks from those that are inadequate.

The message that emerges throughout this chapter is the intense focus that we place on relative performance and the implication of this focus for the allocation of capital resources. For example, the reluctance of managers to depart significantly from benchmarks has the unintended consequence of channeling capital away from securities as they decline in value and toward securities as they grow in value, a practice that some believe contributes to market bubbles. It is within this context that Siegel connects benchmarks to behavioral finance.

The intense focus on benchmarks has another unintended consequence, which I alluded to previously. Together with an inadequate appreciation of within-horizon risk, the concentration on benchmarks leads managers to select securities from a narrower opportunity set than exists naturally in the capital markets—a practice that may harm both providers and users of capital.

These problems demand our attention, and this excellent chapter will help ensure that they get it. The Research Foundation is, therefore, especially pleased to present *Benchmarks and Investment Management*.

Mark Kritzman, CFA
Research Director
The Research Foundation of CFA Institute

PREFACE

In geodetics, a benchmark is a plaque embedded in rock or soil to show the precise latitude, longitude, and altitude of a given location. That the term "benchmark" has been extended, as metaphor, to refer to standards of performance in corporate management and engineering is an intelligent and creative use of language; thus, a 95 percent on-time arrival record might be regarded as a benchmark of good performance for an airline.

But it is in the investment field that benchmarks have acquired a truly special place. Yes, in one sense, they are like benchmarks in corporate management and engineering—that is, benchmarks are paper portfolios constructed for comparison with real portfolios to see whether the latter are being managed effectively. In another sense, however, if the benchmarks are well constructed, they represent much more. They embody the opportunity set of investments in an asset class. The return on the benchmark is the return available from that asset class and from index funds of that asset class. Finally, the benchmark return is also the return (before costs) on the aggregation of all active managers who participate in the asset class. That is a lot of work for a benchmark to do.

Because of the multifaceted role of benchmarks in investing, a clear understanding of the issues surrounding benchmark construction, choice, and use is important. To begin to uncover these issues is the goal of this chapter.

To managers with real skill, benchmarks seem like shackles. "You can't live with them," such managers think, "because they tell you to buy stocks in proportion to the stocks' market capitalizations—which means, all too often, buying the stocks that have become the most overpriced." If active managers don't buy such stocks, they are accused of taking "too much" risk, too much tracking error relative to the benchmark. Such an accusation is ironic because the managers think they are *avoiding* risk by not buying overpriced securities.

To more typical managers, however—those without the ability to consistently add alpha (active return)—benchmarks are a godsend. Such managers, it seems, can't live *without* benchmarks. Benchmarks provide a starting point for portfolio holdings, a list of securities and weights that the manager should or would hold in the absence of a view on any given security. By serving as the starting point, benchmarks are also the control mechanism for active risk. Finally, investing in the benchmark provides the asset-class return, which in rising markets is often enough to satisfy the customer even if no alpha is generated.

Plan sponsors and consultants also can't live without benchmarks. Peter Bernstein has written, "Performance measurers seek benchmarks the way bees seek honey" (2000, p. 1). When charged with the responsibility of measuring something, a manager's natural response is to go out and obtain an objective, widely recognized measuring device. Whatever their flaws, benchmarks serve this role.

There is a tension between managers, who typically believe they have real skill and who bristle at the need to be measured by benchmarks, and investors, whose proper and fitting response is, "I'm from Missouri, and you've got to show me." The tension is natural and is not the fault of benchmarks. It is what happens between the seller and buyer of anything when information is incomplete or costly.

This chapter is an exploration of the many issues surrounding investment benchmarks and benchmarking. The first half of the chapter addresses the questions: What are benchmarks? What are they for? Where did they come from? Where are they going? In "Origins, Uses, and Characteristics of U.S. Equity Benchmarks," I introduce some of the basic issues surrounding benchmarks, with a focus on U.S. equity benchmarks because they are familiar to most readers. "Using Benchmarks to Measure Performance" indicates how benchmarks should be used to measure performance—to isolate the "pure active return" and "pure active risk" that remain after you have adjusted for market and other factor exposures. "Building Portfolios of Managers" takes a brief detour to indicate how the pure active returns and risks of active managers frame an optimization problem that allows the investor to build portfolios of active managers just as he or she would, more conventionally, use similar information to build portfolios of stocks.

"The Evolution of MPT and the Benchmarking Paradigm" opens with a description of the "original paradigm" that governed thinking about investing (and performance measurement) before the great discoveries of the 1950s and 1960s that led to the body of knowledge now generally referred to as modern portfolio theory. I then introduce MPT and make the natural connection between it and benchmarks. The "crisis" in portfolio theory that, arguably, culminated in the stock price bubble of 1998–2000 and the implications of that crisis for benchmarks and benchmarking are the topics of "The 1990s Bubble and the Crisis in MPT." In "Critiques of Benchmarking and a Way Forward," I summarize the critiques of investment benchmarks and outline a compromise that might ease the tension between critics who believe that benchmarks are shackles and those who believe they are an appropriate starting point for portfolio construction, as well as the only acceptable way to measure performance. "The Impact of Benchmarking on Markets and Institutions" discusses the impact of benchmarking on markets and institutions; I describe work that has been done to identify this impact at the micro level (in the pricing of individual securities) and in the macro sphere (in distorting market levels).

The second half of the chapter considers benchmarks as they relate to specific asset classes. "U.S. Equity Style Indexes" focuses on U.S. equity style benchmarks—first, by addressing the history and concepts surrounding them and, second, by indicating how each of the major suites of style benchmarks is constructed and revealing what trade-offs are involved in deciding how to classify stocks into styles. "Fixed-Income Benchmarks" discusses fixed-income benchmarks and makes note of two special issues surrounding them—first, that the duration of the benchmark doesn't necessarily match the duration requirements of any given investor and, second, that lower-quality bonds tend to have large weights in a benchmark. "International Equity Benchmarks" deals with international equity benchmarks from the standpoint of U.S. investors. In "Hedge Fund Benchmarks," I introduce the concept of benchmarks for hedge funds. Funds that hedge are not new, but this old strategy—now revived and converted to the "new new thing"—is increasingly a part of mainstream investors' portfolios and cries out for measurement. "Policy Benchmarks" concludes the chapter by discussing *policy benchmarks*, the indexes-of-indexes used to measure how an investor's whole portfolio is doing.

Some omissions in this chapter may stand out. A chapter on benchmarks might be expected to contain a great deal of data, including construction rules, holdings, performance statistics, and so forth, for various competing benchmarks. Such data presentations tend not only to be voluminous, however, but also quickly become out-of-date, so I keep the data to a minimum and, instead, refer readers to other sources for detail.

Benchmarks for real estate or private equity are not discussed here, and the coverage of fixed-income benchmarks is brief and focused on a few controversial issues; those topics are not my area of comparative advantage. This chapter is not intended to be an encyclopedia.

Finally, I occasionally adopt a personal tone in communicating with the reader. I hope this choice turns out to be helpful without being overdone.

L.B.S.
Wilmette, Illinois
June 2003

ORIGINS, USES, AND CHARACTERISTICS OF U.S. EQUITY BENCHMARKS

The effort to measure the performance of stock markets, as opposed to individual securities, is at least as old as Charles Henry Dow's pioneering average, which he began to calculate in 1884. The first Dow Jones average was simply the average of the prices of 11 railroad stocks. This number was published daily, providing investors with a constantly updated barometer of the market. Maybe the modern mind reads too much into the historical record, but it is tempting to conclude that the construction and popularity of this early market index reflected an awareness that trends in "the market" had a bearing on the prices of individual issues, not just the other way around.[1]

Between 1885 and today, by far the most important innovation in index construction was that made by the Standard Securities Corporation (now Standard & Poor's), which in 1923 constructed the first market-capitalization-weighted index. This index, a composite of 223 securities, later evolved into the S&P 500 Index. Such an index gives each company a weight in proportion to the total market value of that company's outstanding shares. Most of the market indexes in use today, and all those covered in this study, are market-cap weighted. (The Dow Jones Industrial Average, DJIA, in contrast, implicitly weights each company by its per share stock price; other weighting schemes, such as equal weighting, are found in a few other indexes.) The principle of market-cap weighting is so central to modern index construction that I treat it in a separate section.

Today, thousands of market indexes, representing every conceivable country, asset class, and investment style, are available. And although this abundance reflects the explosive growth of the investment industry and suggests a healthy emphasis on quantifying investment results and processes, it also makes differentiation among the many indexes difficult.[2]

Uses of Benchmarks

Over the years, the use of benchmarks has expanded far beyond their original role as a general indicator of market sentiment and direction. They have become central to investment management, with an impact on active management, asset allocation, and performance measurement and reward as well as passive indexing.

"How's the Market?"—Gauge of Sentiment

From the beginning, market indexes have been widely used to answer the question: What is happening in the investment world at this minute? As early users of the DJIA could appreciate, reducing the prices of diverse securities in a market to a single statistic is useful because it reveals the net effect of all factors at work in a market. These factors include not only hopes and fears specific to companies in the index but also broader factors—war, peace, economic expansion, recession, and so forth—that can potentially affect share values. Thus, a frequently updated domestic stock market index gives an indication of how well your home country is thriving at a given point in time.

The use of an index as a sentiment indicator is particularly notable in times of stress, such as when the Allies were faring poorly in World War II (stock indexes were extremely depressed) and when President John F. Kennedy was assassinated (after the large one-day decline, a strong rebound was taken as a sign that national confidence had not been destroyed).

Triple Duty

Market indexes have developed many disparate uses. Because they have market-cap weighting as a characteristic in common, essentially all of the benchmarks of a given market (or market subset) give approximately the same indication of that market's general trends. The principal uses of indexes that motivate us to distinguish one index from another are

- as portfolios (index funds),
- as benchmarks for actively managed funds, and
- as proxies for asset classes in asset allocation.

Practically all benchmarks or indexes are called upon to perform all these tasks, and more. So, when evaluating or trying to understand an index, you must consider the suitability of that index from the point of view of all three of these principal uses.

Portfolios (index funds).   With the growing understanding of portfolio theory, which suggests that beating the market on a risk-adjusted basis is difficult, market-cap-weighted indexes turned out to be preadapted to an important and revolutionary new use—index funds. By simply matching the holdings of a well-constructed index, a portfolio manager can provide the return on the index, minus expenses (which tend to be very low for index funds). In the long run, this asset-class return, rather than value added through stock-selection skill, forms the majority of the gain from investing. Index fund management has become a big business.

An index for which an index fund cannot be constructed is generally not a good index. An example is the Value Line composite, which is calculated by taking the geometric mean of the constituent returns. Because no one can earn this rate of return, the index has limited usefulness. Similarly, equally weighted indexes are flawed as far as indexing is concerned because an index fund designed to track such an index would require constant rebalancing as a result of stock price changes. Also, it would have limited capacity because the smallest stocks in such an index would quickly become scarce as investors bought into the strategy.

Cap-weighted indexes, in contrast, are excellent bases for index funds, as is noted in detail later in this section.

Starting point for active management.   Many active investors—particularly quantitative, active managers of risk-controlled, enhanced-index portfolios—use the contents of an index as their starting point and deviate from index weights according to the degree of conviction they have that a particular stock is more or less attractive than the market as a whole.

Practically all active managers, however—not only those who use the benchmark as a starting point for selecting the portfolio but also traditional active managers—use benchmarks for performance measurement and evaluation and for assessing how much "active risk" they are taking. The investment management consulting industry has cooperated with academics and plan sponsors in making clear the distinction between *policy risk*, the risk that comes from holding the benchmark itself, and *active risk*, the risk that is represented by deviations (resulting from active management) from the benchmark holdings. The section titled Using Benchmarks to Measure Performance covers this distinction, and the section titled Building Portfolios of Managers explores the logical consequences of adopting this way of looking at the world.

As a result of active managers and investors using benchmarks as starting points and measuring tools, the term "risk" has become closely identified with tracking error (deviation from the benchmark). To explore this connection is one of the central purposes of this chapter. At least until the great bear market of 2000–2003, the profound importance of policy risk tended to be neglected as investors focused their attention on active risk—tracking error—as the real risk that needed to be managed in a portfolio. In the section titled Using Benchmarks to Measure Performance, I argue that achieving active return while avoiding active risk is the only goal active managers should pursue *but only after* the greater questions—what policy risks to take and how much of each—have already been decided by the investor.

Asset-class proxies.   Finally, as asset allocation has come to the forefront of the practice of investing, analysts have studied the historical returns and other characteristics of indexes in an attempt to understand the behavior of the asset classes they represent. A benchmark constructed on a consistent basis across time allows you to calculate long-run rates of return and to compare market levels at points widely separated in time.

In addition, investors can use benchmarks to compare the risks of various asset classes and to measure the changes in risk of a given asset class over time, to calculate correlations and gains from diversification among asset classes, and to perform other analyses relevant to determining investment policy.

Performance Measurement, Risk Analysis, and Fee Calculation

One of the pleasing—and possibly unintended—consequences of having a market index available is that it answers the question: Did I beat the market? From the time indexes began to be constructed, the natural human desire to best one's competitors surely must have motivated investors to compare their portfolio returns with index returns. The founding of an organized investment management profession in the 1920s spurred the development of methods to make this comparison more accurate. Today, the modern science of performance measurement, evaluation, and attribution draws on the academic achievements of the 1960s—the capital asset pricing model (CAPM) and related work—in using statistical measures to determine to what extent, and why, a particular portfolio beat or was beaten by a market index.

As noted in the Preface, a "benchmark" in ordinary English is a standard of performance, usually of good or at least acceptable performance, used as a point of comparison. This language has been extended to investment management in a precise way: The benchmark for portfolio performance is the total return on a (usually) cap-weighted index of the securities in the asset class, or subclass, in which the portfolio is intended to be invested. A cap-weighted index is usually used because it is the most workable basis for an index fund of the asset class (or subclass) that could be held as a low-cost, passive alternative to the active strategy being measured. In addition, if the CAPM is correct, a cap-weighted benchmark is efficient, in the sense of having the highest expected return at a given level of risk (volatility).

As a corollary to the use of benchmarks to measure active return, benchmarks are also used to set performance fees—fees that are a proportion of the value added by the active manager beyond the return available from merely buying the benchmark. Clearly, if performance measurement is to be carried out and performance fees are to be set fairly, the benchmark needs to be both well constructed and appropriate to the portfolio being measured.

The story behind the way in which indexes became benchmarks is documented in the section titled The Evolution of MPT and the Benchmarking Paradigm.

Characteristics of a Good Benchmark

For an index to serve as a useful benchmark, it must have certain characteristics, the most important of which is market-cap weighting.

Weighting

For several vitally important reasons, market-cap weighting is the central organizing principle of good index construction. The first and simplest reason is macro consistency: As noted previously, if everyone held a market-cap-weighted index fund and there were no active investors, all stocks would be held with none left over. With other weighting schemes, it is mathematically impossible for all investors to hold the index.

Second, market-cap weighting is the only weighting scheme consistent with a buy-and-hold strategy: The manager of a full-replication fund needs to trade only to reinvest dividends, to keep pace with changes in the index constituents, and to reflect modifications in index weights caused by changes in the constituent companies' numbers of shares outstanding.[3] In contrast, indexes that are not cap weighted require constant rebalancing because of ordinary changes in the prices of stocks.

Third, as explained in the section titled the Evolution of MPT and the Benchmarking Paradigm, according to the CAPM, the cap-weighted market index is the only portfolio of risky assets that is mean–variance efficient. That is, no portfolio can be constructed with the same risk and a higher expected return or with the same expected return and lower risk. If CAPM conditions hold, all investors should hold only this portfolio plus or minus positions in the riskless asset (because each investor must be able to choose his or her desired risk level). Of course, the stringent conditions under which the CAPM was derived don't actually hold, and investors deviate from the index for many valid reasons, including the desire to boost returns through active management. Because of the special place that a cap-weighted index holds in capital market theory, however, such an index is a good baseline.

To represent the shares available for purchase by the public better than a pure market-cap-weighted index can, some index constructors remove closely held and illiquid shares for the purpose of calculating a company's number of shares outstanding. In general, such "float adjustment" increases an index's usefulness as a benchmark, and as the basis for an index fund, because portfolio managers cannot typically buy shares held by founders, directors, employees, other corporations, and governmental bodies.[4] But although float adjustment, which is treated in detail in the discussion of international equity benchmarks, conveys substantial advantages to an index, it should not be considered a prerequisite of a well-constructed benchmark.

Other Characteristics

Ideally, the best choice of an index is one that, simultaneously, is useful as a benchmark for active management, can be used as the basis for index funds, and can provide proxies for asset classes in asset allocation. When selecting an index to use for one or more of these purposes, you must consider all the characteristics of the index and determine the fit with your needs. No benchmark is perfect, so (as with most choices) tradeoffs are involved.

How should you choose among the competing alternatives? In addition to market-cap weighting, which is a literal prerequisite of a good index and which is common to all indexes covered here, at least seven criteria are useful in identifying a good benchmark:

1. completeness,
2. investability,
3. clear, published rules and open governance structure,
4. accurate and complete data,
5. acceptance by investors,
6. availability of crossing opportunities, derivatives, and other tradable products, and
7. low turnover and related transaction costs.

Note that these criteria are best applied when choosing a benchmark for U.S. equities or for a size or style subset of the U.S. equity market; for other asset classes and for international equities, satisfying all these requirements is more difficult. Table 2.1 summarizes the characteristics of the principal broad-cap benchmarks of the U.S. equity market, including the S&P 500 and the Russell 1000 Index (which are often used as broad-cap benchmarks even though they are really large-cap indexes). To provide a framework by which investors can choose a benchmark, Enderle, Pope, and Siegel (2003) rated the benchmarks in Table 2.1 according to each of the seven criteria listed here. U.S. equity style benchmarks are covered in a similar manner in the section titled U.S. Equity Style Indexes, and international equity benchmarks are covered in the section titled International Equity Benchmarks.

TABLE 2.1 Characteristics of Broad-Cap Indexes of the U.S. Equity Market, 31 December 2002 ($ in thousands)

Statistic	Wilshire 5000	Russell 3000	Dow Jones Total Market	S&P 1500	Russell 1000	S&P 500
Capitalization data						
Number of stocks	5,637	2,955	1,579	1,500	991	500
Total market cap ($)	10,160,084,866	8,989,393,568	8,865,970,840	9,135,504,640	8,389,336,332	8,107,401,639
Cap of largest company ($)	276,411,465	241,984,724	242,269,619	276,411,465	241,984,724	276,411,465
Cap of smallest company ($)	48	3,790	61,245	39,165	120,150	279,286
Weighted-average market cap ($)	62,747,682	61,148,735	61,699,861	68,299,843	65,485,068	76,709,263
Fundamental characteristics						
Dividend yield	1.71%	1.82%	1.80%	1.73%	1.84%	1.81%
Beta	1.00	1.00	1.02	0.99	1.01	0.99
Price/book ratio	2.286	2.361	2.38	2.465	2.467	2.559
Price/earnings ratio	23.6	22.7	23.0	22.6	21.9	22.4
Inception date for historical data	January 1971	January 1979	January 1992	January 1995	January 1979	January 1926

Notes: Russell and Dow Jones numbers reflect float-adjusted market cap. Beta is relative to the S&P 500 over the 60 months ended 31 December 2002. S&P 500 data start March 1957 and have been linked by Ibbotson Associates (2003) with a predecessor index, the S&P 90, to form a continuous series from 1926 to the present.

Source: Data from Enderle, Pope, and Siegel (2003).

Trade-Offs in Benchmark Construction and Selection

In this section, I discuss the principal trade-offs involved in building and maintaining broad-cap indexes of the U.S. equity market. Style, fixed-income, and international indexes involve specialized trade-offs, some of which are discussed in the sections that pertain to those asset classes.

Completeness vs. Investability

From a purely theoretical standpoint, the ideal index includes every security in its asset class. No one knows exactly how many stocks are in the United States, but the Wilshire 5000 (so named because it was originally composed of 5,000 stocks) contained 5,637 stocks as of 31 December 2002 and thus included more issues than any other widely distributed U.S. equity index. Many of the small-cap stocks in the Wilshire 5000 are illiquid, however, so investors would have a difficult time trading them. No full-replication index fund has ever been constructed for the Wilshire 5000.[5]

For this reason, a somewhat less broad index is more investable and accessible. By "investable," I mean that the stocks in the index can be bought and sold by a fund manager in sufficient volume that a full-replication index fund or one that is nearly full replication can be constructed without incurring high transaction costs or unusual delays because of illiquidity of index constituents. A particular index is accessible to investors to the extent that the index is the basis for existing index funds and exchange-traded funds (ETFs).[6] Access to the index through derivatives (futures and options) is desirable but less important than access through index funds and ETFs.

The Russell 3000 Index specifically excludes the smallest and most illiquid issues, so all or nearly all of its capitalization can be held efficiently through full replication. This index is the broadest of the well-known, widely distributed indexes that exclude illiquid, hard-to-trade stocks. Narrower U.S. equity indexes that are still considered broad-cap, such as the Dow Jones U.S. Total Market Index and the S&P 1500 Index, are also investable.

The Russell 1000 and S&P 500, which are large-cap indexes, are eminently investable as long as you don't try to buy a stock that has limited float and that has just been selected for the S&P 500 (see the discussion of free-float mismatch in the section titled The Impact of Benchmarking on Markets and Institutions).

Reconstitution Frequency vs. Turnover

Reconstitution—the process of periodically deciding which stocks meet the criteria for inclusion in the index—is a source of turnover (which is costly to investors) because the manager must trade to keep pace with changes in index contents. Because timely reconstitution is what enables an index to accurately track the asset class it is designed to represent, there is a trade-off between such accuracy and trading costs.

Turnover resulting from tracking reconstitution is a major concern for managers of small-cap and style indexes, where companies with a large weight in the index are constantly crossing the size or style boundaries that qualify them for inclusion. For this reason, the constructors of size and style indexes tend to reconstitute them at regular and rather infrequent intervals, such as quarterly or annually.

The lists of holdings of broad-cap indexes are much more stable. Broad-cap indexes tend to experience turnover in their smallest-cap stocks, making turnover less of a problem when measured by the weight in the index of the stocks being traded. So, continuous reconstitution (as is done with the Wilshire 5000 and S&P 500), although not necessarily ideal, is not a terrible burden on investors or managers. Nonetheless, turnover is costly whatever its source or volume, and a cost advantage accrues to indexes that have less of it.

In terms of reconstitution-related turnover and trading costs, indexes that have no fixed limit on the number of stocks and that are all-inclusive in terms of their capitalization range have a small but nontrivial advantage over indexes with a fixed number of stocks. The reason is that an all-inclusive index gains or loses stocks only because of new listings, delistings, and other changes in the identity of the stocks in the market. The holdings list of a fixed-count index, in contrast, typically changes also to reflect the shifts in the capitalization rankings of stocks that occur as their prices fluctuate. Of broad-cap U.S. equity indexes, the only all-inclusive one is the Wilshire 5000; those indexes with a fixed number of stocks include the Russell 3000 and S&P 500. These latter indexes tend to experience higher turnover and, consequently, higher transaction costs. The Dow Jones Total Market is nearly all-inclusive and behaves more like an all-inclusive index than a fixed-count one.

Rebalancing Frequency vs. Turnover

Rebalancing, which is different from reconstitution, is the process of adjusting the weights of stocks in the index for changes in the number of shares outstanding. Taking account of changes in the number of shares outstanding maintains the macro consistency and mean–variance efficiency of the index. A theoretically ideal index would continuously update the number of shares that a company has issued, but a trade-off is involved: The index fund manager must rebalance to reflect these changes, thereby imposing transaction costs on the investor. Thus, index constructors typically decide on a prearranged schedule for updating shares-outstanding data so that changes in the index will be somewhat predictable and index fund managers can decide how to rebalance. Active managers benchmarked to the index also find it useful to be able to predict changes in index contents.

Objective and Transparent Rules vs. Judgment

Some benchmarks are constructed on the basis of rules that are reasonably objective; others are constructed through the use of judgment. The advantage of objective rules is that any investor with access to the rules and the relevant data can predict fairly accurately what stocks will be added to and deleted from the index. This information enables investors to trade in anticipation of (rather than in reaction to) additions and deletions and, in general, to manage the index replication process in an orderly and efficient manner. Active managers also find such information useful.

The use of judgment in selecting stocks or other securities for an index allows the index constructor to achieve certain traits, however, that cannot be achieved through objective rules and that constructors of judgment-based indexes claim are desirable. Standard & Poor's, which uses judgment in selecting stocks for its S&P 500 and other indexes, asserts that its indexes are superior in terms of stability, accurate representation of the industry distribution of the economy, and other attributes. The S&P indexes can achieve these traits specifically because the index construction staff need not act mechanically in selecting and removing stocks and can take conscious steps to construct an index with the desired characteristics.[7]

Thus, the trade-off is between the clarity and predictability of a rule-based index and the flexibility of a judgment-based index.

USING BENCHMARKS TO MEASURE PERFORMANCE

Just about everyone knows that the purpose of active management is to add alpha—extra return relative to a benchmark representing the asset class in which the manager is invested. How should you measure alpha? How should you measure active risk, the risk taken by the active manager in the hope of achieving that alpha? Most importantly, having decided how to measure alpha and active risk, what should you do with the information?

Regression Alpha and Subtraction Alpha

First, recall how the Greek letter α comes into the discussion. It is from the "market model" regression equation of Jensen (1968). The market model is

$$r_i = r_f + \alpha_i + \beta_i(r_m - r_f) + \tilde{\epsilon}, \qquad (2.1)$$

where

r_i = return on security or portfolio i

r_f = riskless rate of return

α_i = unexpected component of return—that is, unexpected if your expectations are formed by the capital asset pricing model (see the section titled The Evolution of MPT and the Benchmarking Paradigm); this alpha may also be regarded as the value added by the manager after adjustment for beta risk

β_i = amount of market risk represented by portfolio i, scaled so that the benchmark or market portfolio has a beta equal to 1.0

r_m = return on the cap-weighted market index

$\tilde{\epsilon}$ = a random error term distributed around zero

In essence, the market model tells you to run a regression with alpha as one of the regression coefficients (results). Specifically, the alpha from Equation 2.1 is the manager's excess return, or value added, after adjusting for the amount of market risk (beta risk) taken. As suggested later, you should adjust for other risks, such as style risks, but in principle, if you use Equation 2.1, you have calculated a risk-adjusted alpha.

Now, a widespread current practice is to calculate alpha as

$$\alpha_i = r_i - r_m. \qquad (2.2)$$

What is wrong with this picture? It contains no adjustment for risk. Suppose, for example, that the portfolio has a higher beta than the benchmark and that the portfolio outperformed the benchmark in a rising market. Wouldn't the investor want to know how much of the extra return was added through market exposure (beta) and how much is "real" alpha, value added? The subtraction alpha that Equation 2.2 provides wrongly attributes the reward for extra beta risk to the manager.[8] The regression alpha from Equation 2.1 is the real alpha, the alpha that controls for beta risk.

Later, I will push even further to "purify" the alpha by adjusting portfolio performance for style exposures (betas) as well as market beta. For now, however, simply note that a regression is required to calculate real alphas.

Dimensions of Active Management

Why should you care about getting as "pure" a measure of manager alpha as possible? Waring and Siegel wrote:

> You can't influence or control the return of your asset allocation policy [the policy for your mix of asset classes and/or style exposures]. The market is going to do what the market is going to do. Other than making a risk level decision—to be more or less aggressive in your [asset allocation]—you're just a passenger. But if you have

skill at security selection (or market timing or sector rotation, any active process), you have some *control* over returns, and this will add value, pure alpha, over and above the return of the policy. The search for such alpha is, arguably, the investor's highest calling. (2003, p. 37)

In addition, Waring and Siegel pointed out that *market exposures* are inherently rewarded. No one would invest in risky markets if the markets didn't offer, *ex ante*, a risk premium over riskless assets. In contrast, *active exposures* are not inherently rewarded. No one should expect active decisions to produce superior returns just because they are active. Active management is a zero-sum game: The returns (before costs) of all active managers in an asset class must sum to the asset-class return, whether the market for securities in that asset class is "efficient" or not.

Waring and Siegel demonstrated that market exposures and pure alpha are separate and separable; these conditions are part of the geometry of the regression used to calculate the alpha. By "separate," I mean that the market, not the manager, determines the market (and style) returns and the market has no influence on pure alpha whatsoever. Similarly, the manager, not the market, determines the pure alpha through his or her skill, or lack of it, and the manager has no influence on the market or style returns whatsoever. By clearly separating the manager's contribution from other factors in this way, you can make well-informed decisions about manager selection and structure—which is why investors seek to measure pure alpha.[9]

Next, Waring and Siegel suggested introducing adjustments for style risk and the measurement of pure active risk. The real dimensions of active management are pure alpha, pure active risk, and costs (which have been ignored up to now)—not the conventional dimensions of style boxes, historical performance horse races, and manager salesmanship. Moreover, as I show in the section titled Building Portfolios of Managers, estimates of pure alpha and of pure active risk can be used to frame a "manager structure optimization" problem (to use the words of Waring, Pirone, Whitney, and Castille 2000) that is incremental to and independent of the more familiar asset-class optimization problem.

Multiple Regression: Adjusting for Style Risk

As researchers since the late 1970s have found, and as I discuss at length in the section titled U.S. Equity Style Indexes, certain factors (usually called "styles") other than the broad market or beta factor help explain the return differences between one stock and another or between one portfolio and another. The most widely recognized style divisions are large company size (capitalization) versus small company size and value stock versus growth stock.[10]

Returns can be adjusted for exposure to style factors in a number of ways. One approach, developed by Fama and French (1993), uses "natural" or unconstrained regression to estimate exposure to style factors. Their three-factor model, the first regression equation in the section titled U.S. Equity Style Indexes is an estimate of the pure alpha or value added by the manager. All other things being equal, natural regression is preferable to constrained regression, but the Fama–French method has the disadvantage that its style factors are amorphous; you cannot obtain index funds offering pure exposure to the factors.

Sharpe (1988, 1992) devised a method that is similar in spirit to the three-factor model, but different mathematically. In using Sharpe's model, the analyst estimates the portfolio of *style index funds* having the "best fit" to the active portfolio being analyzed. The style index funds usually used for this kind of analysis are large-cap value, large-cap growth, small-cap value, and small-cap growth (the "corner portfolios" in a style map). Cash must also be included as a regressor so that the overall level of risk in the best-fit portfolio matches the risk of the portfolio being analyzed. The regression is usually constrained to have a nonnegative (that is, positive or zero) weight for each of the style index funds, and the portfolio may be long or short in cash.[11] An analyst may wish to include other factors—for example, the return on a bond index fund. The alpha from this regression is an estimate of the pure alpha or value added by the manager beyond what could be achieved with a mix of style index funds.

Pure active risk (sometimes denoted by ω, omega) is simply the standard deviation of the pure alpha term. The active manager's information ratio, IR, is given by

$$IR = \frac{\alpha}{\omega} \tag{2.3}$$

and measures the amount of pure active return delivered per unit of active risk taken.

I would argue that the delivery of the information ratio is the only thing active managers should try to achieve: They should seek to maximize their pure alpha per unit of active risk. And the delivery of the information ratio is the only thing for which active managers should be paid an active fee; market and style exposures can be obtained almost for free by the investor using index funds, exchange-traded funds, or derivatives.

Importance of Measuring Pure Alpha and Active Risk

Why is it necessary to measure pure alpha and pure active risk so carefully? For the investor looking backward at history to evaluate a manager's performance, Waring and Siegel wrote:

> [T]hese measures . . . properly separate investment results that are the investor's responsibility from those that are created by the manager. The returns delivered by the capital markets on the particular mix of styles that constitute the manager's custom benchmark are the responsibility of the investor who selected the manager, if only because the investor is the only party in a position to control the market risk exposures across his or her whole portfolio of managers.
>
> Too often, performance evaluation practices confuse the benchmark return and the pure alpha, apportioning credit and blame incorrectly. Even the smartest and most well-intentioned investors are sorely tempted to blame the active manager, rather than themselves, when the manager's asset class delivers a poor policy return (no matter what pure alpha the manager achieved). With the pure active return and risk clearly defined and calculated, these errors need no longer occur. (pp. 38–39)

The future cannot be forecast with anything like the precision achieved in measuring the past. But as I point out in the section titled Building Portfolios of Managers, you need forecasts of manager alphas for building portfolios of managers (the level of selection at which most investors operate) in the portfolio construction or optimization problem, just as you need forecasts of stock-by-stock alphas in building portfolios of stocks. Specifically, the problem of constructing a portfolio of managers requires that you develop forecasts of pure active risk and pure active return for the various managers that you are dealing with already or considering.

In the next section, I turn to framing manager selection as an optimization problem that uses the pure active return and risk defined here as the inputs. I also describe how a portfolio of managers that reflects these principles might look. Once these concepts and methods have been presented, I can return to the discussion of benchmarks.

BUILDING PORTFOLIOS OF MANAGERS

Policy (market and style) risk and active risk are separate and separable. In other words, investors should decide first what policy risks to take and how much of each, and only after that task has been completed should the investor decide how to implement these allocations by selecting a *portfolio of managers*. In this section, manager selection is framed as an optimization problem that uses the pure active return and risk defined in the section titled Using Benchmarks to Measure Performance as the inputs and I describe what such a portfolio of managers might look like. To set the stage, I begin with expected utility and mean–variance optimization.

Expected Utility

One of the first principles of investing is that the investor should seek to maximize expected utility, which is equal to the expected return minus a penalty for risk:

$$E(U_i) = E(r_i) - \lambda_j E(\sigma_i^2), \qquad (2.4)$$

where

$E(U_i)$ = expected incremental utility of portfolio i in the investor's overall portfolio

$E(r_i)$ = expected return of portfolio i

λ_j = risk-aversion parameter for investor j (that is, the rate at which investor j translates risk into a negative return, or disutility; note that this parameter differs from one investor to another)

$E(\sigma_i^2)$ = the expected variance of portfolio i

Now, with so many asset choices, how do you figure out whether each choice provides *incremental* utility—that is, whether the combination of assets selected adds enough expected return to justify the extra risk? In other words, how do you *maximize* expected utility? The answer is through Markowitz mean–variance optimization (MVO). Managers can be considered to be asset choices like any other. Waring and Siegel wrote:

> Building a portfolio of managers is like building a portfolio of anything—it's all about balancing risk and return, trying to find the best trade-off. Optimization is the technology that explicitly calculates these trade-offs in search of the highest-utility portfolio (of anything) for a given investor. (2003, p. 39)

To make optimization useful in a manager-selection framework, you must first invoke the separation principle between policy risk and active risk. The trade-offs involved in asset allocation (that is, in determining the policy mix) are resolved by MVO through use of the utility function in Equation 2.4 with risk-aversion parameter λ specific to the investor; the result is the optimal mix of asset-class exposures for that investor. Next, you can perform a parallel calculation—also involving an optimizer, albeit a special-purpose one—for the managers. In this optimization, you use the expected pure alpha and expected active risk estimates as discussed in the section titled Using Benchmarks to Measure Performance. You also use a utility function for active risk similar in form to Equation 2.4 but expressing the investor's aversion, not to total risk but to the active risk added by a manager. Waring and Siegel noted that for most investors, the active-risk-aversion parameter is several times larger than the policy-risk-aversion parameter.[12] This second step, optimization across manager alphas, is incremental to the first step and preserves the asset mix decided on in the first step. Waring, Pirone, Whitney, and Castille (2000), who provided the full details needed to implement the method, refer to this second step as manager structure optimization (or MSO, in homage to Markowitz's MVO).

Critiques of Optimization

Some investors are reluctant to put optimization into practice because they regard optimizers as error maximizers that cause inaccurate inputs to be translated into potentially even more inaccurate portfolio weights. This criticism has been enunciated by Richard Michaud in several well-known works (see Michaud 1998, 2003; Michaud and Michaud 2003).

The Michaud critique is technically correct: Optimizer inputs, because they are statistical estimates, are necessarily inexact. There is no way to make the precise estimates that would be needed for absolute confidence in the outputs of an optimizer. Mark Kritzman has persuasively argued, however:

> We would be naive if we expected optimization to convert valueless return and risk estimates into efficient portfolios. Rather, we optimize to *preserve* whatever value there is in our . . . estimates when we translate them into portfolios. . . . Optimization is a process that determines the most favorable tradeoff between competing interests. In portfolio management, the competing interests are return enhancement and risk reduction. . . . If we don't optimize, we will fail to translate even valuable inputs into efficient portfolios. Therefore, both good inputs and optimization are necessary . . . but neither by itself is sufficient. (2003, p. 1; formatting modified from the original)

Now, where are these good inputs going to come from when you are building portfolios of managers?

Forecasting Manager Alphas

As Waring and Siegel pointed out, investors make implied forecasts of all their managers' alphas (plus active risk and other parameters) simply by holding whatever manager mix they happen to have. These implied forecasts can be backed out through "reverse optimization." Many investors would be surprised at how large their implied expected alphas for managers are.

Rather than heuristically deciding (say, through a system of filling style boxes) what your manager mix ought to be, you could, instead, explicitly use a special-purpose optimizer to select the manager weights. The required inputs are

- the expected pure alpha and pure active risk for each manager,
- the mix of market and style factors to which each manager is exposed, and
- the return–risk correlation matrix of the factors themselves.[13]

Of these inputs, the tricky one is, of course, the forecast of manager alphas. The discipline required to forecast manager alphas is similar to that required to forecast security alphas for use in a security-level optimizer. The most important caveat is to avoid simply extrapolating past performance into the future; winning managers (or stocks) don't persist with any degree of certainty. You must take into account fundamental and qualitative factors as well as quantitative factors. In the end, you will probably not be fully confident of the forecasts—which is just as it should be. No one makes perfect forecasts. Moreover, manager alpha forecasts don't have to be extraordinarily good to add value (when used in an optimization context); they only have to be more right than wrong.

But without an alpha forecast that represents at least the midpoint estimate of the investor's expectation for the manager, what justification does the investor have for using that manager instead of a mix of index funds representing the same market and style exposures? Alpha forecasts are necessary, if only as a conceptual exercise, to make sure you aren't being unduly swayed by past performance and manager salesmanship. And, having made these alpha forecasts, the investor can take them beyond the conceptual level and actually use them in a manager-level optimizer to build the portfolio. The issue is one of responsibility and accountability: If an investor is going to build a portfolio that includes active managers, that investor should be able to defend the alpha forecasts that are, implicitly or explicitly, embedded in the portfolio's composition. Otherwise, the investor should index.[14]

An Optimized Portfolio of Managers

My earlier discussion of expected utility in the context of manager selection can be summarized as follows: You must expect a manager's alpha to do more than simply be positive. It must be large enough to overcome the loss of utility from the active risk added by the manager. This observation has implications for the issues of whether to use active managers, what kinds of active managers to use, and what their weights should be.

Drawing on expected utility theory, Grinold (1990) and Kahn (2000) demonstrated that the holdings weight of manager i in the investor's total portfolio, h_i, is given by

$$h_i \sim E\left(IR_i \frac{1}{\omega_i} \right),\tag{2.5}$$

where (given that E is the expectational operator) IR_i is the expected information ratio of manager i and ω_i is the expected active risk of manager i—that is, the expected volatility of the manager's pure alpha around a properly established benchmark. In other words, the manager's weight in the portfolio should be proportional to the manager's expected information ratio divided by the manager's active risk or, equivalently (recalling the definition of IR in Equation 2.1), the manager's expected alpha divided by the manager's active risk *squared*.

Thus, if you are going to take active risk, you should seek managers who not only have real skill (a high information ratio) but also exhibit low active risk—for example, enhanced index funds. Traditional medium-risk, long-only active managers would play a lesser role in the portfolio, and concentrated, high-risk, long-only active managers would have the least favored place. The Grinold and Kahn argument also gives a large weight to market-neutral (long–short) equity hedge funds for investors who are allowed to hold such positions.[15]

In summary, constructing a portfolio of managers is like any other portfolio construction problem: It calls for maximizing return while controlling risk, so it is an optimization problem. To solve such a problem, you need forecasts of manager alphas. Making such forecasts is analogous to active equity managers making forecasts for the stocks in their opportunity sets. It is the toughest job in finance, but if you are unable or unwilling to try to make such forecasts, you should simply index.

THE EVOLUTION OF MPT AND THE BENCHMARKING PARADIGM

Before the emergence of modern portfolio theory, the original paradigm for investment management called for portfolio managers to evaluate each investment on its merits and downplayed diversification. This approach gave way to mean–variance optimization and the capital asset pricing model, sometimes grouped together as modern portfolio theory or simply portfolio theory. MPT has, in turn, spawned a "benchmarking" paradigm, one in which benchmarks are used as the starting point for active portfolios and risk is defined as the degree of deviation from the benchmark. In this section, I trace that evolutionary path.

Portfolio Theory as a Scientific Paradigm

In 1962, Thomas Kuhn, the historian of science, characterized scientific revolutions as shifts in *paradigms* (established patterns of thinking) motivated by an accumulation of empirical evidence that the existing theories are not adequate to explain and predict observed phenomena (see Kuhn 1996). According to Kuhn, a crisis point is reached when anomalies (empirical observations that don't fit existing theory) become so troublesome that the need for a new theory is evident, at least to many researchers. The crisis is resolved when a new theory emerges, from the many being tested, that fits observed phenomena, thus eliminating the anomalies. Typically, although not always, the replacement of a strongly established theory by a new one meets with a great deal of resistance from adherents of the old theory. The iconic example is the replacement of the Ptolemaic (geocentric) theory of the solar system by the Copernican (heliocentric) theory in the 16th century.

First published in 1962, Kuhn's book—which, for all practical purposes, gave the word "paradigm" its current place in the English language—is one of the most influential books about science ever written. And it provides a basis for this exploration of benchmarks and benchmarking.

In the original investment paradigm, an investor had to justify each investment on its own merits. This view was largely replaced between about 1964 and 1980 by the body of knowledge loosely known as modern portfolio theory, which relies on capitalization-weighted benchmarks both as the starting point for building actively managed portfolios and as the reference asset for measuring the performance and risk of these portfolios.

A sort of crisis in MPT seemed to arise toward the end of the 1990s bull market, when cap-weighted benchmarks became highly risky because they included securities, at their market weights, that had swollen to huge caps despite having little intrinsic value. This apparent crisis brought to the surface concerns about MPT that had been submerged for a long time. Although no specific theory arose to replace MPT and although (as I argue later) MPT is mostly correct, some recent trends demonstrate that MPT is not fully predictive of investor behavior. The trends include, most notably, the popularity of hedge funds and an emphasis on achieving "absolute returns." Thus, the future of investing may incorporate non-MPT as well as MPT currents of thought.

The Original Paradigm

In the original pre-MPT paradigm, each investment in a portfolio is evaluated separately. The emphasis is on each investment's value, on finding investments that are intrinsically worth more than their current market prices.[16] Not much attention is paid to risk. Portfolio construction disciplines that seek not only to control risk but also to take advantage of the correlation structure of securities are not part of the original paradigm. Other than cash, investors have no "starting point" or "normal" portfolio to which they would retreat if they had no views on any security. The result of this way of thinking about investments is concentrated, and more or less equally weighted, portfolios.

As you will see in detail in a moment, performance measurement is also undeveloped in the original paradigm. Although benchmarks, including some very good ones (e.g., the S&P 90 Index, which is the forerunner of today's S&P 500 Index), existed in the time period when the original paradigm was dominant, the practice of comparing the performance of a particular portfolio with that of a benchmark wasn't widespread. Furthermore, no one knew how to risk-adjust the returns of a portfolio or benchmark so that fair comparisons could be made. That technology required the innovations of MPT.

John Burr Williams' classic 1938 textbook, *The Theory of Investment Value* (see Williams 1956), which introduced the dividend discount model (DDM), is an excellent example of original-paradigm thinking: Williams told investors how to find the *single best* stock and did not recommend (or even really mention) diversification.[17] John Maynard Keynes also thought diversification—"having a small gamble in a large number of different [companies]"—was a "travesty of investment policy" (quoted in Bernstein 1992, p. 48).

Other works of the pre-MPT period do, however, address the idea that investors don't have perfect foresight and thus face risk that can be mitigated by diversification. For example, in his 1949 book *The Intelligent Investor*, Benjamin Graham advised, "Diversification is an established tenet of conservative investment. . . . Even with a margin [of value over price] in the investor's favor, an individual security may work out badly" (see Graham and Zweig 2003, p. 518).

Thus, the investment paradigm that I have termed "original" embodied some common sense as well as some nonsense. It didn't quantify risk or even return (performance), and it paid only passing attention to diversification, but it set the stage for an orderly comparison of security prices with their fundamental values, a discipline still central to the practice of active portfolio management. As noted in the section titled Critiques of Benchmarking and a Way Forward, some of the tenets of the original paradigm are making a comeback as investors question the wisdom of MPT's prescriptions for investor behavior.

The Bad Old Days of No Performance Measurement

Before the capital asset pricing model (CAPM) provided a basis for the quantification of performance relative to a benchmark, investment returns could nevertheless be measured accurately. Fisher (1966), drawing directly on an algorithm created in the 17th century by Sir Isaac Newton and Joseph Raphson, provided a generalized method for calculating internal rates of return, of which the time-weighted rate-of-return calculation now used to measure investment performance is a simple extension.[18] And Cowles (1938) correctly recognized that total return, not price appreciation, is the proper metric of performance.

A retrospective by Jason Zweig, the illustrious financial historian and columnist for *Time* and *Money* magazines, shows, however, that performance measurement—to say nothing of benchmarking and quantitative performance evaluation—was pretty primitive until not long ago. As an example, Zweig noted that even Graham, reflecting on the portfolio managed by his Graham-Newman Corporation in 1936–1956, glided over the problem:

> [Our] portfolio was always well diversified, with more than a hundred different issues represented. In this way [we] did quite well through many years of ups and downs in the general market; [we] averaged about 20 percent per annum on the several millions of capital [that we] had accepted for management, and [our] clients were well pleased with the results. (Graham and Zweig 2003, p. 532)

The clients should have been pleased: From the beginning of 1936 to the end of 1956, the S&P 90, one of the predecessors of the S&P 500, had a total return of only 12.2 percent a year. The casual style in which the information is presented, however, leads me to question whether the return was measured accurately—that is, after taking into account cash flows in and out of the fund, fees, and other factors. The recollection also makes no mention of risk.

Zweig has also recalled:

> I believe it was not until the 1980s that mutual funds were required by the SEC [U.S. Securities and Exchange Commission] to calculate and report a number called "total return." When the SEC proposed that new rule (in the wake of the scandals over GNMA [Government National Mortgage Association] and other "government-plus" bond funds that cannibalized capital in pursuit of current yield), the fund industry met it with howls of execration. The most common refrain was that the investing public would not understand or would misinterpret a single total return figure. Previously, investors had either to calculate the number themselves or rely on services like Wiesenberger, Lipper, or the financial press. The oldest prospectus in my collection, the 1941 prospectus for Investment Company of America, provides a statement of profit and loss, a statement of earned surplus, and a statement of capital surplus, all for three fiscal years, along with a "computation of net asset value," along with a table of all dividends paid over the previous seven or eight years. But total return is not calculated, and performance is not measured against anything of any kind.
>
> By 1970, judging by my Mates Investment Fund prospectus, disclosure had not improved. "Capital changes" had four sub-captions: Net asset value at beginning of period, net realized and unrealized gains (losses), distribution from realized capital gains, net asset value at end of period. Total return is still not calculated, and no benchmark information is provided.[19]

Although precursors to any scientific discovery can usually be found without looking very hard, they are not apparent in the present case. Maybe nothing was happening. Bernstein may have summed up the zeitgeist of the period best by noting:

> Performance measurement was carried out . . . at cocktail parties, dinner parties, bridge games, and the golf course. At these locations, individuals boasted and moaned to one another about what their investment advisors were doing. This lively channel of communication was continuous rather than quarterly, and ignored adjustments for risk, which only made matters worse. Managers who could keep their heads when everyone around them was losing theirs were rare birds indeed. (1994, p. 1)

The Benchmarking Paradigm

Performance measurement, index funds, and "benchmarking" of active funds were made possible by MPT, which emerged in the 1950s and 1960s. The efforts of consultants, index providers, and seekers of "anomalies" or systematic rules to beat the market further enriched this fertile environment.[20]

The Markowitz Revolution

The young Harry Markowitz's University of Chicago Ph.D. dissertation (1952) set the original investment paradigm on its ear. "I was struck with the notion that you should be interested in risk as well as return," he wrote.[21] That a manager or analyst should be "interested" in risk doesn't sound all that revolutionary until you explore the consequences, preferably with mathematical tools.

Markowitz defined the risk of an investment as the period-to-period standard deviation of the investment's return.[22] If you accept that definition, Markowitz's observation leads you to try to build portfolios that maximize the expected return *at each given level of expected standard deviation*. Such portfolios are built by taking advantage of the correlation structure of the available securities—buying more than you otherwise would of a security that has a low (preferably, negative) correlation with the other securities in your portfolio. This complex calculation is best done by use of mean–variance optimization (MVO), an application of quadratic programming developed by Markowitz himself. The resulting portfolio is said to be "efficient," in that no portfolio can be constructed with a higher expected return at the same level of risk (or with the same expected return but a lower level of risk).

What does MVO have to do with benchmarks? Well, if a given portfolio is "optimal" (the most efficient portfolio that can be constructed), then it is a benchmark (in the English language sense) for those who would build portfolios. But because each investor has his or her own unique estimates for the expected returns and standard deviations of securities and for the correlations between them, the "most efficient" portfolio is different for each investor. No objective benchmark emerges from this analysis. Not until the contribution of Sharpe, more than a decade after Markowitz, does one appear.

Sharpe and the CAPM

In pursuit of a general theory of how assets are priced, Sharpe (among several others) noted that if all investors have the *same* expectations of return, risk, and correlation for every security, and if all investors hold efficient portfolios based on these expectations as described by Markowitz, the capitalization-weighted market portfolio itself is mean–variance efficient.[23] The CAPM requires other assumptions—most of them just as unlikely as the supposition that all investors see the same return–risk–correlation picture and use an optimizer—but for elegance, simplicity, and ease of use, the CAPM is difficult to beat, so it has won acceptance despite its reliance on stringent conditions.

If the cap-weighted market portfolio is mean–variance efficient, it is the best portfolio that you can build in the absence of special insight or skill. It should be the benchmark. This principle is strictly true only for portfolios with the same risk as the market, however, because expected return is related to risk. For portfolios with risk levels different from that of the market, an adjustment is necessary.

The CAPM posits that expected return is proportional to that component of risk (called beta) that represents correlation with the market. (By "the market," I mean the cap-weighted market index.) This relationship provides a framework for measuring the performance of portfolios with different risk levels: A portfolio manager adds value (called alpha) if he or she produces, after adjustment for the beta of the portfolio, a return that is greater than the market's return.[24] Table 2.2 presents CAPM performance statistics for a sample of four managers—an index fund, a risk-controlled active (or "enhanced index") fund (BGI Alpha Tilts), a conventional active manager (Fidelity), and a hedge fund (First Eagle). The active managers in the example in Table 2.2 are all successful in the sense of adding alpha; in reality, most managers are not successful.[25]

Thus, the familiar concepts of quantitative performance measurement—with its alphas, betas, tracking errors, and R^2s—are made possible by the CAPM.[26] Some might argue that

TABLE 2.2 Sample CAPM and Related Statistics for Selected Funds for the 60 Months Ending 31 March 2000

Fund	Compound Annual Total Return	Standard Deviation	Sharpe Ratio	CAPM Alpha	Alpha t-statistic	Information Ratio	CAPM Beta	Adjusted R^2
Vanguard 500 Index	26.70%	14.83%	1.348	$-6\,\mathrm{bps}$	-1.44	-0.661	1.001	1.000
BGI Alpha Tilts	27.82	15.06	1.389	70	0.82	0.598	1.009	0.986
Fidelity	26.99	14.45	1.396	191	0.76	0.044	0.912	0.871
First Eagle	27.58	14.36	1.437	488	1.20	0.091	0.786	0.652

Notes: The Sharpe ratio is calculated in excess of the U.S. Treasury bill return. The CAPM alpha and beta, alpha t-statistic, information ratio, and adjusted R^2 are relative to the S&P 500. The negative alpha, alpha t-statistic, and information ratio for the Vanguard 500 Index Fund result from fees and other expenses.

I am making too much of the connection between portfolio theory and benchmarks; after all, performance measurers would seek an objective reference point (in addition to peer group comparisons) even if there were no theory suggesting that the cap-weighted market is a *priori* efficient. And a cap-weighted index, because it requires no rebalancing when security prices change, is a convenient reference point. Portfolio theory, however, provided a powerful impetus to benchmarking: Virtually all investors know they have the option to index at low cost, and they know from their exposure to the basic ideas of portfolio theory that indexing has many desirable properties. Moreover, investors know that if they are going to take active risk (and pay active fees), the decision to do so must be justified by superior performance, which must be measured scientifically.

Performance measurement, however, is not all there is to "benchmarking." Benchmarking is more than constructing market indexes or index funds, and it is more than comparing performance with a properly risk-adjusted (and style-adjusted) market index. The real impact of benchmarking is the pull that benchmarks exert on *active* management through the tools discussed in the next section.

Barr Rosenberg and Factor Models

Cognizant that the market index, or benchmark, is (at least theoretically) the mean–variance-efficient portfolio in the absence of special views on the value of specific securities, any manager might think to build an active portfolio by starting with the benchmark weights, then changing them according to his or her active views. But this is only a conceptual approach, not a scientific discipline. The role of benchmarks in scientifically managing active portfolios was firmly established by Barr Rosenberg, a University of California at Berkeley professor who developed a technique for quantitatively managing active risk (tracking error versus the benchmark). To do so, he integrated two concepts (see Rosenberg 1974; Rosenberg and Marathe 1975):

1. You should optimize active return against active risk just as you optimize policy (market) return against policy risk.[27]

2. Returns on securities are characterized by "extra-market covariance"; that is, security returns are correlated with factors *other* than the market factor. (The market model says that security returns are correlated only with the market factor and are otherwise independent of one another.) As a result, you can model any security as a bundle of factor exposures plus an unexplained risk term. Such a model provides a better estimate of beta for use in the CAPM to determine expected security returns than can be obtained by calculating an ordinary historical regression beta for the security.

Here is the link between the two concepts: To solve the active return–active risk optimization problem at the individual-security level, you need forecasts of return and risk for every security in your opportunity set and you need forecasts of the correlation of every security with every other security. As a result, if the opportunity set is, say, the 3,000 stocks in the Russell 3000, you have $(3{,}000 \times 2{,}999)/2 = 4{,}498{,}500$ correlations to forecast (setting aside, for the moment, the risk and return forecasts). But if you have a model that characterizes each security as a bundle (or vector) of, say, 13 factors—the number of major factors in Rosenberg's best-known U.S. equity model, the Aegis model—then you have to forecast only the correlations of the *factors*, of which there are $(13 \times 12)/2 = 78$, plus the $(3{,}000 \times 13) = 39{,}000$ "loadings" (the degree of exposure of each security to each of the factors). Although 39,078 is still a daunting number, it is a manageable one, at least if you have the requisite software (which, helpfully, is sold by Barra—the company founded by Rosenberg—as well as by several competitors).[28] Most investment managers shortcut the problem further by drastically reducing the number of stocks under consideration.

In other words, the reason you need to build factor models of securities is to reduce the number of estimates needed to solve the active return–active risk optimization problem. Establishing this link and providing the technology to make the forecasts required by the factor model is Rosenberg's unique contribution, and it is this technology that led to the widespread practice of benchmarking—in the sense of managing active portfolios by controlling their degree of departure from cap-weighted benchmarks.

With Barra's or similar tools, the investor can build quantitative active portfolios. The 13 major factors enumerated in Barra's Aegis model are shown in Table 2.3, together with sample factor "loadings" for some stocks and portfolios analyzed by using this factor approach. Factor loadings are expressed as Z-scores—that is, as the number of standard deviations by which a stock's or portfolio's exposure to a given factor differs from the average (or market) exposure to that factor. Table 2.3 indicates that General Motors has a dividend-yield factor exposure of 1.45, which means that General Motors' dividend yield (which is 6.5 percent) is almost one and a half standard deviations larger than the approximately 2 percent dividend yield of the cap-weighted market portfolio.

The Role of Consultants

In the late 1970s and in the 1980s, as the technology for estimating active risk became accessible and as the importance of the new academic theories (the CAPM, efficient markets, and so forth) became widely appreciated, traditional active managers, in addition to "quants" and indexers, began to use this technology. This expansion of the role of quantitative investment analysis was led by the consultant community and resulted in the near universality of benchmarking seen today.

A.G. Becker Funds Evaluation Group was the consulting firm responsible for much of this innovation.[29] In the early 1970s, Becker had an absolute majority of pension fund assets

TABLE 2.3   Barra Risk-Factor Loadings for Two Mutual Funds and Two Stocks,
30 September 2002

	Mutual Funds		Stocks	
Risk Factor	Janus Twenty	Vanguard S&P 500 Index	Intel	General Motors
Market beta (S&P 500)	1.15	1.00	1.68	1.15
Market beta (ALLUS)	1.19	1.03	1.74	1.20
Volatility	0.09	−0.01	1.04	0.22
Momentum	0.08	−0.11	−0.58	−0.03
Size	1.04	0.38	1.07	0.01
Size nonlinearity	0.16	0.11	0.19	0.11
Trading activity	0.01	0.01	0.17	1.25
Growth	0.52	−0.05	−0.49	−0.56
Earnings yield	−0.12	0.03	−0.25	1.56
Value	0.22	−0.05	−0.08	1.71
Earnings variation	0.08	−0.06	−0.20	0.81
Leverage	−0.48	−0.10	−0.68	3.38
Currency sensitivity	0.52	0.00	−0.23	0.20
Dividend yield	−0.31	0.05	−0.53	1.45
Nonestimation universe	0.06	0.02	0.00	0.00

Notes: Factor loadings are relative to the Barra ALLUS (Barra All-U.S.) Index. The "nonestimation universe" factor is 0 if a company is in the Barra estimation universe and 1.0 if it is not. The nonestimation universe factor loading for mutual funds depends on the weight of stocks in the fund that are not in Barra's estimation universe.

Source: Barra.

under consulting advisement, according to a Greenwich Associates survey, but the firm's role was pretty much limited to calculating rates of return on its clients' portfolios as best it could in light of the data limitations. When John O'Brien (one of the founders of Wilshire Associates) joined Becker in the mid-1970s, however, he brought with him Gilbert Beebower, Richard Ennis, and David Booth (among other luminaries), who shared a passionate interest in MPT. The new Becker team introduced CAPM statistics and other practices of MPT to the vast consulting base that Becker already had, setting the stage for the widespread adoption of MPT and the benchmarking paradigm. Becker's base of consulting clients included many investment management firms as well as plan sponsors (pensions, foundations, and endowments), so not only the supply of investment management services but also the demand for services was affected by this new thinking.

    Investment consulting organizations with the capabilities of calculating CAPM statistics, using optimizers to build portfolios, and otherwise implementing MPT ideas proliferated in the 1980s. Today, virtually all investment consulting firms have these capabilities, and small as well as large plan sponsors use these firms' services. Thus, the current large role of "benchmarked" portfolios may be regarded, in part, as an outgrowth of the increasing importance of investment consultants (and academics) in the interplay between investment management firms and their customers.

The Role of Index Providers

A final source of impetus toward the use of benchmarks, both to build index funds and as a starting point for active management, is the commercial index construction industry. When large profits are to be made by selling something, great effort is expended to increase the public's need or desire for it. Licensing fees are the source of profit in the index business. (An index provider, or constructor, collects licensing fees from managers who publicly announce that they are using the index as the basis for a fund or as a benchmark. Of course, various free-rider problems crop up.) Standard & Poor's pioneering role was documented in the Preface, and the emergence of index funds based on the S&P 500 and the rapidly spreading use of that index as a benchmark for active portfolios greatly increased that company's visibility in index provision, in contrast to its traditional role in providing debt ratings. Unfortunately for Standard & Poor's, it did not foresee the importance of index funds and did not position itself to receive large licensing fees.

A contrasting experience was that of the investment management firm Capital International, which introduced international equity benchmarks in 1969 (see the section titled International Equity Benchmarks) and built a successful business around index-associated fees. The consulting world made the next big push. In addition to Wilshire Associates, the Frank Russell Company played a crucial early role in bringing benchmarks to market. Finally, such brokerage firms as Salomon Brothers (now Citigroup) and Lehman Brothers, because they had the only real source of price information in the fixed-income market, became the natural providers of benchmarks in that market. And these firms retain their position as the principal sources of fixed-income benchmarks today.

Conclusion

Cap-weighted market indexes, which represent the theoretically mean–variance-efficient portfolio of securities in a given asset class, have been pressed into duty as performance *benchmarks*. An outgrowth of this transformation of meaning is the benchmarking paradigm, which comprises the following ideas:

- The market portfolio, proxied by a cap-weighted benchmark, is the portfolio with the lowest expected risk in a given asset class (among fully invested portfolios—that is, portfolios with a beta of 1.0 measured relative to the asset class).
- Policy risk and active risk are separate and separable; only when you have arrived at a policy decision (that is, when you have selected asset-class weights) should you implement that decision by selecting asset-class managers.
- Active management can be viewed as taking active bets against a benchmark. In other words, each security in the benchmark can be held at the benchmark weight (which represents no active risk) or at a greater or lesser weight (which represents some active risk). You can also take active risk by holding securities that aren't in the benchmark. Thus, any active portfolio can be understood as an index fund plus a portfolio of long and short positions relative to the benchmark.
- Following this logic, *not* to own the benchmark weight in a security is an active decision that, mathematically, must add to risk. Even if the particular security has little risk or is perceived

as diversifying or removing the risk of other investments in the portfolio, you cannot actually subtract risk by deviating from the benchmark. You can, however, add alpha.

• Active management has only one legitimate role, which is to add expected utility by adding pure alpha minus a penalty for the active risk taken in the effort to add pure alpha (see the section titled Using Benchmarks to Measure Performance). In less technical terms, active managers should try to add pure alpha while controlling the amount of active risk they take.

The idea that the benchmark is the portfolio with the lowest risk among fully invested portfolios in a given asset class is sometimes misunderstood as a claim that "index funds have no risk." No one seriously believes that index funds in risky asset classes have no risk. They have policy risk, which is most of the risk in any investment.

THE 1990s BUBBLE AND THE CRISIS IN MPT

The 1980s and 1990s, which hosted the greatest bull market ever known, were friendly to the new academic and consulting climate that emphasized index funds, actively managed portfolios based on (or "benchmarked to") market-capitalization-weighted indexes, and quantitative control of active risk (or tracking error). With U.S. equity markets rising at an astonishing 20 percent annual rate, your chief risk was being out of the market—or taking active positions that would cause your return to depart from the market return.[30] The volume of assets indexed to, or actively managed but benchmarked to, cap-weighted indexes grew and grew.

Not that all investors and managers were happy with the state of affairs or that portfolios with high active risk did not sometimes earn outsize returns. An article by Clifford, Kroner, and Siegel (2001) revealed that the best-performing portfolio (as measured by the CAPM alpha) over the 20 years and 3 months from January 1980 through March 2000 was Berkshire Hathaway, which had an alpha of 8 percentage points a year and a tracking error against the S&P 500 Index of 22.6 percent.[31] The Driehaus Small Growth Fund, which also had a stellar alpha, had an even larger tracking error. There are a number of other such stories, but not many; in general, because most managers subtract, rather than add, alpha (at least after fees and other costs are considered), the path to riches in the bull market was to stay invested in the equity market and to avoid tracking error. The ready access to technology that enabled managers to measure and control tracking error (and the growing difficulty in adding alpha as markets became more efficient) reinforced this trend.

By the turn of the millennium, when the bull market had run for almost 18 years (with a couple of dramatic interruptions), culminating in a super-boom in technology and other growth issues between 1998 and early 2000, cap-weighted indexes had taken on an odd character. As shown in Table 2.4, only *one* of the top thirty U.S. stocks as ranked by capitalization on 31 March 2000 had a price-to-earnings ratio below 15 (roughly the average historical P/E of the market). Five of the top 30 stocks had a P/E higher than 100, and 9 more had a P/E between 50 and 100. The market capitalization of the 14 largest companies in Table 2.4 with P/Es higher than 50 sums to $3.2 trillion. If these P/Es were ever to be "rationalized"— brought in line with reality—either the companies' earnings would have to grow at extraordinary rates for many years or the capitalization of the market would have to fall by some large fraction of $3.2 trillion.

You know what happened. By 30 September 2002, the capitalization of the 14 largest companies had fallen by $2.5 trillion as part of an overall equity market decline that trimmed more than $6 trillion from total U.S. equity capitalization. The proportion of the loss in

TABLE 2.4   Financial Data for 30 Largest U.S. Stocks by Capitalization, 31 March 2000

Rank	Name	Price per Share	Market Cap (millions)	EPS	Dividends per Share	P/E	Dividend Yield
1	Microsoft	$106.25	$553,016	$1.62	$0	65.8	0%
2	Cisco Systems	77.31	537,796	0.73	0	106.5	0
3	General Electric	155.63	512,833	3.32	1.64	46.9	1.05
4	Intel	131.94	440,935	2.50	0.12	52.8	0.09
5	Exxon Mobil	77.94	271,214	2.95	1.76	26.4	2.26
6	Wal-Mart	56.50	251,636	1.33	0.24	42.5	0.42
7	Oracle	78.06	220,256	0.82	0	95.2	0
8	IBM	118.00	211,664	3.89	0.48	30.3	0.41
9	Citigroup	59.88	200,964	3.31	0.64	18.1	1.07
10	Lucent	61.25	195,233	0.85	0.08	72.1	0.13
11	AT&T	56.31	179,905	2.08	0.88	27.1	1.56
12	Nortel Networks	126.13	177,665	0.33	0.15	382.2	0.12
13	AIG	109.50	169,532	3.36	0.20	32.5	0.18
14	Sun Microsystems	93.69	163,669	1.61	0	58.3	0
15	AOL Time Warner	67.44	153,877	0.36	0	187.3	0
16	Home Depot	64.50	148,502	1.08	0.16	59.7	0.25
17	Merck	62.13	143,917	2.62	1.16	23.7	1.87
18	SBC Communications	42.13	143,199	2.26	0.98	18.6	2.33
19	Pfizer	36.56	140,729	0.92	0.36	39.9	0.98
20	Dell	53.94	138,358	0.73	0	73.9	0
21	EMC	126.00	134,161	1.25	0	100.8	0
22	Texas Instruments	160.00	130,663	2.09	0.17	76.6	0.11
23	Coca-Cola	46.94	116,051	1.31	0.68	35.8	1.45
24	Bristol Myers Squibb	58.00	114,631	1.94	0.98	29.9	1.69
25	Qualcomm	149.31	105,749	3.45	0	43.3	0
26	Motorola	146.00	104,337	2.33	0.48	62.6	0.33
27	Johnson & Johnson	70.25	97,643	3.07	1.12	22.9	1.59
28	Morgan Stanley	82.88	94,219	9.60	0.80	8.6	0.97
29	Yahoo!	171.38	90,226	0.61	0	280.9	0
30	BellSouth	46.88	88,211	2.11	0.76	22.2	1.62

Notes: Earnings, dividends, P/Es, and dividend yields are annualized. Earnings (as reported by Compustat) include "basic" earnings per share (EPS) adjusted to remove (1) the cumulative effect of accounting changes, (2) discontinued operations, (3) extraordinary items, and (4) special items.
Source: Ford Foundation, based on Compustat, Bridge, DAIS, and IDC data.

capitalization that is represented by these few very large, and seemingly very overpriced, companies is remarkable.

After such a fiasco, the benchmarks, index funds, and benchmarked active portfolios became easy targets for critics. Who in their right mind would invest in such overpriced companies—even if, to avoid them, you had to take the "risk" of having large tracking error to a cap-weighted benchmark?

One (possibly too academic) answer is that many people had thought carefully about what the fair prices for technology and other popular growth companies should be and that the prices shown in Table 2.4 are the results of their analysis, as expressed through the supply of and demand for securities. Not many investors were absolutely sure at the time that the market was overpriced or that the cap-weighted benchmark was an *ex ante* inefficient portfolio. Many value managers and tactical asset allocators, to their credit, seemed sure, but they appear to have been a minority.[32]

On 31 March 2000 and for a period of time before and after, the cap-weighted benchmark was not a good portfolio to hold, *ex ante,* and an investor could have arrived at that conclusion through conventional analysis (cash flow or dividend discount models, relative-value or P/E analysis, and so forth). Many—even most—investment professionals could have added alpha simply by betting against the most obviously overvalued companies. But this bubble and its bursting were a once-in-a-generation anomaly. These events are not cause for a general indictment of modern portfolio theory (MPT) and of benchmarks. No sensible person ever said benchmarks were always and everywhere the best portfolios.

The top 30 U.S. equities by capitalization as of 30 September 2002 (that is, after the bear market) are shown in Table 2.5. With the excesses of the bubble era corrected—perhaps more than corrected—it is much less obvious how to avoid overpriced securities or otherwise build a portfolio that is more efficient than the cap-weighted benchmark. Of course, opportunities always exist for astute active managers, but the idea that cap-weighted indexes are fundamentally unsuited for service as portfolios (index funds) or as benchmarks for active management has lost much of its appeal.

Critiques of MPT and Conventional Finance

The bubble gave great encouragement, naturally, to anti-MPT factions, who had been raising sometimes valid critiques but rarely scoring a win in earlier years.[33] The most compelling critique came from behavioral finance, but other criticisms are also noteworthy.

Behavioral Finance

Efficient markets and MPT have been attacked from many angles. What distinguishes the behavioral finance school of thought from other critiques of MPT and benchmarks is that the behaviorists have the beginnings of a real theory and strong evidence for their positions.

Behavioral finance emanates from the observation by Rolf Banz, Sanjoy Basu, and many others (see the section titled U.S. Equity Style Indexes) that the markets contain "anomalies"—Thomas Kuhn's word again—that is, patterns that are not consistent with efficient markets and other tenets of conventional finance and that are, consequently, a challenge to the conventional theories. At the same time that empirical researchers were documenting market anomalies—"small caps beat large caps" and "value beats growth" are the best known—other researchers, with more of a psychological bent, were examining the mistakes made by investors in framing and implementing investment decisions. This group of investigators—led by the

TABLE 2.5   Financial Data for 30 Largest U.S. Stocks by Capitalization, 30 September 2002

Rank	Name	Price per Share	Market Cap (millions)	EPS	Dividends per Share	P/E	Dividend Yield
1	General Electric	$24.65	$245,254	$1.59	$0.73	15.5	2.96%
2	Microsoft	43.74	234,598	1.10	0	39.8	0
3	Wal-Mart	49.24	217,771	1.73	0.28	28.5	0.57
4	Exxon Mobil	31.90	215,562	1.56	0.92	20.4	2.88
5	Pfizer	29.02	179,624	1.47	0.52	19.7	1.79
6	Johnson & Johnson	54.08	160,906	2.21	0.80	24.5	1.47
7	Citigroup	29.65	150,057	2.87	0.70	10.3	2.36
8	AIG	54.70	142,805	2.85	0.18	19.2	0.33
9	Coca-Cola	47.96	119,052	1.77	0.80	27.1	1.67
10	Procter & Gamble	89.38	116,238	3.62	1.52	24.7	1.70
11	Berkshire Hathaway A	73,900.00	113,349	2,729.00	0	27.1	0
12	Merck	45.71	102,828	3.15	1.42	14.5	3.11
13	IBM	58.31	98,796	4.16	0.59	14.0	1.01
14	Bank of America	63.80	95,868	5.65	2.44	11.3	3.82
15	Intel	13.89	92,577	0.58	0.08	23.9	0.58
16	Philip Morris	38.80	82,018	4.69	2.44	8.3	6.29
17	Wells Fargo	48.16	81,812	3.22	1.10	15.0	2.28
18	Cisco Systems	10.48	76,356	0.16	0	65.5	0
19	Verizon	27.44	74,868	3.38	1.54	8.1	5.61
20	Chevron Texaco	69.25	73,964	1.93	2.80	35.9	4.04
21	Viacom B	40.55	71,556	0.81	0	50.1	0
22	SBC Communications	20.10	66,834	2.33	1.07	8.6	5.30
23	PepsiCo	36.95	65,483	1.91	0.60	19.3	1.61
24	Abbott Laboratories	40.40	63,116	2.11	0.92	19.1	2.26
25	Eli Lilly	55.34	62,173	2.49	1.24	22.2	2.24
26	Home Depot	26.10	61,495	1.59	0.20	16.4	0.77
27	Dell	23.51	60,887	0.77	0	30.5	0
28	Fannie Mae	59.54	59,290	6.15	1.32	9.7	2.22
29	Amgen	41.70	53,300	1.34	0	31.1	0
30	UBS AG	41.00	53,099	2.75	0	14.9	0

Note: See notes to Table 2.4.

Source: Ford Foundation, based on Compustat, Bridge, DAIS, and IDC data.

Nobel Prize–winning researcher Daniel Kahneman, the late Amos Tversky, and the writing team of Hersh Shefrin and Meir Statman—produced the literature on behavioral finance that represents the most successful challenge yet to efficient markets and MPT. A full treatment of behavioral finance is in Shefrin (2002).

Among the mistakes made by investors are the following:

- overconfidence in one's own abilities,
- over- or underreaction to new information,
- optimism (pessimists drop out of the game),
- pathological risk aversion (this trait is not inconsistent with optimism, because different investors make different mistakes at different times), and
- "frame dependence"—the difficulty that investors have in separating the verbal or mathematical form of a question, or the setting in which the question is asked, from the true economic content of the question.

In short, investors are not rational economic agents, but human beings with limited cognitive ability and susceptibility to greed, fear, and foolishness who are forced to act in conditions of incomplete information. Welcome to the real world.

Behaviorists have been accused of shaping their theories to fit empirical facts, but they have rarely been charged with having a shortage of facts to support their cause. A great deal of empirical evidence supports the conclusion that the behaviorists are onto something. For example, "experimental economics" techniques (pioneered by Vernon Smith, who shared the 2002 Nobel Prize in Economics with Kahneman) have been used to demonstrate that in laboratory conditions (where, admittedly, the subjects of investigation may not have to live with the real-world consequences of their decisions), investors overreact to certain kinds of information and underreact to others, persistently overestimate their own abilities, and have difficulty avoiding frame dependence.

What behavioral finance implies is that markets cannot really be efficient. Their argument goes beyond acknowledging that some mispriced assets always exist. The bubble of 1998–2000 is evidence that the whole market can become mispriced; technology and Internet stocks were mispriced by large multiples for quite a while.[34] Thus, the bubble gave the behaviorists the push they needed to mount a challenge to conventional finance. And their view is widely accepted, at least in rough outline: Almost no one believes any more that markets are completely efficient.

If behavioral finance paints a true picture of the world, holding benchmarks as portfolios (that is, holding index funds) is not generally a good idea because it is engaging in "herd behavior." Holding the benchmark means holding a disproportionate weight in the most popular companies, which have the highest prices relative to their fundamental values.

What behavioral finance does *not* say is that cap-weighted benchmarks are irrelevant as a basis for measuring performance. Nor does it say how to build a better benchmark. Instead, behavioral finance suggests how to beat the benchmark (primarily but not entirely through value investing). Behavioral finance, moreover, does not overturn Sharpe's "arithmetic of active management"—the observation that the performances of all active managers in an asset class sum to the asset-class return. As a result, practitioners who subscribe to behavioral finance are charged with the same responsibility as any other active manager—beating the cap-weighted benchmark while managing active risk—and they are forced to do so by being smarter, more rational, or more immune to the seductions of greed and fear than their competitors.

Other Critiques of MPT

Other critiques of MPT that are not specifically aimed at benchmarking or the integrity of specific benchmarks but that bear on benchmarks in some way include the following:

- the allegation that MPT is invalid because it is based on unrealistic assumptions,
- the concern that optimizers are "error maximizers" and give unstable or unreliable results,
- the suggestion that standard deviation does not measure the real risk to which investors are averse, and
- the idea that riskier assets do not really have a higher expected rate of return than safe assets.

In the section titled Building Portfolios of Managers, where I suggested that optimization is the right framework for thinking about manager selection and allocation, I introduced one of these criticisms—the "Michaud critique" (see Michaud 1998, 2003; Michaud and Michaud 2003)—and mentioned a response by Kritzman (2003). This section provides a brief description of the other three critiques.

Unrealistic assumptions.   Portfolio theory is not intended to be realistic. Its assumptions—which include, for the CAPM, that all investors have equal and costless access to information and equal ability to process it—do not come close to describing the real world. Such a critique is not fair, however, because no theory is based on entirely realistic assumptions. The purpose of a theoretical model is to simplify reality enough that it can be analyzed, not to replicate reality in its every detail.

The challenge for those who would overturn a given theory is to propose a better theory. Despite great effort, and the promise of great reward to those who can solve the riddle of the markets better than Markowitz, Sharpe, and their fellows, nothing distinctive has emerged. The closest to an alternative theory is behavioral finance, but most of the advocates of behavioral finance do not think they have overturned MPT; their work does not propose a different way to construct benchmarks, nor does it (usually) propose to get rid of them.[35] But behaviorists have enriched the story of modern finance, making it more realistic and less dependent on fanciful assumptions, and they have suggested ways of beating existing benchmarks.

Standard deviation not a perfect measure of risk.   In fact, standard deviation doesn't quite capture the risk to which investors are, or should be, averse.[36] Sortino and Satchell (2001) suggested that semideviation—a measure like standard deviation that takes account only of observations below a target, or investor-specified minimum acceptable return—is a better measure than standard deviation because investors, presumably, aren't averse to good returns (which nevertheless contribute to standard deviation and thus to "risk" as conventionally measured). Other authors have suggested using deviation below the asset's own mean return.[37] Leibowitz and Henriksson (1989) proposed shortfall risk as a measure of the risk to which investors are averse; shortfall risk is the likelihood of a shortfall (expressed as a probability) multiplied by the expected severity of the shortfall should one occur.[38]

If you believe that a particular statistical measure, such as semideviation or shortfall risk, captures risk better than the traditional standard deviation measure does, then use it. Doing so does not affect the decision to use benchmarks or the decision as to which benchmark to use for a given portfolio or asset class. It does, however, affect performance measurement (because you are now defining good performance as alpha minus a penalty for *downside* active risk, or active *shortfall* risk, rather than for omega, active standard deviation; see the section titled Using

Benchmarks to Measure Performance). Many consultants, managers, and plan sponsors already use downside or shortfall measures of risk as well as the conventional standard deviation–based measures to calculate their performance statistics. Moreover, active managers who use quantitative methods to manage their tracking error should use a risk model that captures downside active risk or active shortfall risk if they believe such risk measures to be relevant.

No return premium for riskier assets. A more profound (but, in my view, extremely unpromising) challenge to MPT is the suggestion by Haugen (and others) that risk is not even positively related to expected return. Analyzing work done previously by Fama and French (1992), Haugen wrote:

> Within the largest stocks, those with the highest risk tend to have the lowest returns. The line of the best fit . . . has a negative slope. The same is true for the smallest stocks. High risk, low return. (1995, p. 97)

Behaviorists, who tend to be less radical than Haugen, have offered some support for this challenge to traditional finance. Shefrin, for example, in analyzing stated investor views (rather than past market results), wrote:

> [E]ven though investors may state that in principle, risk and expected return are positively related, in practice they form judgments in which the two are negatively related. (2002, pp. xxx–xxxi)[39]

If risk is unrelated to return on an aggregate level—that is, summing across all investors (or at least across price-setting investors) and looking among as well as within asset classes—the whole edifice of finance crumbles. The structures that fail include not only mean–variance optimization and the CAPM but also the pricing of corporate credit, performance measurement and evaluation, and risk management. That such a radical revision of finance is needed to explain observed phenomena is highly unlikely.

Conclusion

The bubble period of 1998–2000 embodied the crisis (in Kuhn's terminology) in MPT thinking that had been developing over the decades since the theory was first set forth by Markowitz and Sharpe. The crisis was resolved not by the introduction of a new theory that better fit the observed phenomena but, in a compromise, by a growing interest in behavioral considerations and by a better understanding of what MPT, benchmarks, and benchmarking are supposed to accomplish and what their limitations are.

CRITIQUES OF BENCHMARKING AND A WAY FORWARD

In the section titled Using Benchmarks to Measure Performance, I made the strong-form case for benchmarking (although not for indexing—I will never argue that active management is useless). Now, you will hear from the other side, and then I will propose a compromise.

Critiques of Benchmarking

Behavioral finance offers a critique of efficient markets, and thus of indexing, but not of benchmarking in the broader sense of using benchmarks for performance evaluation and active risk management. Other critiques, however, do target benchmarking. "Tracking error is supposed to be as large as possible, only positive," a traditional active manager recently told me. He was only partly kidding. One school of thought in the active management community, especially in the hedge fund world, contends that "real men" don't use cap-weighted market benchmarks as the starting point for portfolio construction.

According to this view, the risk is in buying the benchmark, not in deviating from it. You should be focused on avoiding real risk and on making money or, if you are a conservative investor, on preserving capital. You should not take real risk to avoid apparent risk (or to manage your business risk). This view considers "investing" to consist of analyzing securities and buying those that you believe will go up, not those that are popular with others and that have, therefore, already gone up, which causes them to have a large weight in cap-weighted benchmarks.

This approach is simply pre-MPT thinking with a contrarian cast and a value bias. The portfolios built by the advocates of this point of view are often more or less equally weighted and contain short positions as well as long ones (if, as in a hedge fund, short selling is permitted).

At stress points in the system—the spring of 2000 was one—the critiques of benchmarking resonate with almost everyone, and investors would have been well advised to listen to them that spring, and for a year or so before and after. On average across time, however, prices are at least somewhat related to fundamental value, which places the burden of proof clearly on those who imply, by poking fun at benchmarks, that they can easily beat them—and that they can do so at tolerable levels of active risk.

Critiques of Specific Benchmarks

Some critics of benchmarking are opposed to it not so much in principle, but because of perceived shortcomings in widely used benchmarks. One such potential shortcoming is the decision process used to construct, or "manage," the S&P 500 Index, which is by far the most widely used U.S. equity benchmark. I focus on that issue in this section. Other issues relating to specific benchmarks include inclusion and deletion effects (which are a type of transaction cost) and high levels of turnover concentrated in a short time period. A case in point is the annual 30 June reconstitution of the Russell indexes, producer of "Russell mania." These issues are covered on page 120. Disagreement about how to classify stocks into styles is also a crucial issue in indexing and benchmarking and is treated in the section titled U.S. Equity Style Indexes. In later sections, I discuss the concern that benchmarks in asset classes other than U.S. equity are misleading or poorly constructed.

Is the S&P 500 Managed?

In a kind of mirror image of the critique that the S&P 500 is a poor portfolio to hold because it is stuffed with overpriced stocks, some managers and clients have expressed frustration that the S&P 500 is a difficult index to beat (or to track) because it is "actively managed" through the process by which Standard & Poor's decides what stocks should be in the index at a given time.

My first reaction to this allegation is surprise. Most active managers fail to add any alpha relative to their benchmarks if measured over a long time period. Why should Standard & Poor's be any better at active management than those who practice it with real money?[40] Rattray and Manglani (2003) found, however, that the S&P 500 did, in fact, beat a purely rule-based, passive benchmark (the "top 500" U.S. stocks by capitalization, reranked and rebalanced monthly) by 0.26 percentage points (pps) a year over the 1992–2002 period.[41] The tracking error between the two indexes was a nontrivial 2.08 percent a year. These authors found that the outperformance arose from a value bias (value beat growth in 1992–2002 by a large margin), largely caused by Standard & Poor's unusual requirement that companies have four quarters of profitability to be selected for the index.[42] Because of the profitability requirement and because Standard & Poor's tries to achieve "sector balance," technology stocks were underrepresented in the S&P 500 relative to the Top 500. This technology underrepresentation helped in 2000–2002 more than it hurt in 1998–1999.

Digging further, Rattray and Manglani found that, after they adjusted for the impact of the profitability rule and other fixed rules, the pure stock-selection skill of the S&P 500 committee was *negative*. In other words, Standard & Poor's "discretionary application of the rules" rather than the rules themselves reduced returns by about 0.11 pps annually. This finding is reassuring, especially for anyone who has tried to beat the S&P 500 through active stock selection.

These performance numbers are before adjusting for the S&P 500 inclusion (or reconstitution) effect—that is, the material rise in the price of a stock between the date of the announcement that it will be added to the S&P 500 and the date the stock is actually added to the index. If you assume you could have bought the stocks at the closing price on the day of the announcement—which makes the S&P 500 directly comparable to the Top 500 strategy because the Top 500 was not a real portfolio and had no inclusion effect—the S&P 500 did even better, with a 0.58 pp a year advantage over the Top 500.[43]

The S&P 500, then, is indeed an actively managed portfolio. Before transaction costs, Standard & Poor's has added some alpha. This alpha may or may not be repeatable; it is certainly not statistically significant (the alpha *t*-statistic for 1992–2002 is 0.92). After transaction costs, the alpha is limited to a weak value effect caused by the profitability requirement and perhaps by limits on sector weights. To be safe, you might do better to benchmark your portfolio to a purely rule-based index rather than to the S&P 500.

Is S&P 500 Outperformance a Momentum Effect?

The S&P 500's outperformance could be a momentum effect and could represent evidence that the index is distorting the market. If so, the outperformance would have been concentrated in the up-market years of 1995–1999 and would have reversed during the bear market of 2000–2002. In fact, however, the outperformance was strongest in 2000 and did not vary significantly between up and down markets in general. So, the outperformance is a value, not a momentum, effect. Moreover, Rattray and Manglani's study contains no evidence that indexing to the S&P 500 causes distorted markets.

Reaction

In a trend reflective of the critiques of benchmarking, some of the habits of mind grounded in the original pre-MPT paradigm are making a comeback. The most prominent is the desire to earn an "absolute" return, a return independent of what the markets are doing. How this goal is attainable on any large scale is not clear: The beta of all portfolios must average to one, not zero.[44] On a limited scale, however, investors can hold balanced short and long positions or simply select securities or time the market with the intent of earning a return uncorrelated with either the stock or the bond market. Such investments (which are usually structured as hedge funds) are typically measured against an "absolute return benchmark."

Investing in balanced long–short positions is a legitimate investment strategy. What troubles me is the use of a so-called absolute return benchmark. Typical absolute return benchmarks are "Treasury bills plus 5 percent" or "inflation plus 5 percent" (which often represents the spending goals or requirements of an endowment fund or foundation). But a good benchmark is generally one for which an index fund or tracking portfolio can be constructed. Because no asset other than cash pays an absolute return, very little information can be gained from comparing a portfolio with an absolute return benchmark.

Moreover, I am not optimistic that efforts to earn an absolute return (above that of cash) can succeed, even on a limited scale, more often than would be predicted by chance—although if you did succeed, the rewards would be spectacular.[45] There is a great deal of active risk involved in so-called absolute return investing, and you should be cautious when confronted with a manager who takes the position that "I'm so smart, the usual rules (benchmarks) don't apply to me!" But the current level of interest in absolute return investing is so intense, and the arguments applied by those who advocate it so persuasive on their face, that I devote some attention to this view of the world. And I will argue that one kind of alternative benchmark does make sense for many, if not most, institutions or asset pools—a benchmark that represents the return on the institution's *liabilities*. A focus on liabilities, not on absolute return benchmarks, is the key contribution being made by those who are skeptical of the traditional approach to benchmarking.

A Perspective from Peter Bernstein

Peter Bernstein, the best-selling author of *Against the Gods* (1996) and many other works, is a particularly eloquent advocate of the point of view that you ought to operate in a way that is basically unconstrained by benchmarks, at both the policy and manager levels. Unlike most advocates of benchmark-independent investing, who are merely making self-interested arguments to bolster their case for a large active-risk budget or a fat fee, Bernstein is an independent observer of markets whose views are almost universally respected.[46] His career spans more than half a century. With his permission, this section quotes him at length.[47] After presenting his point of view, I will make suggestions toward a compromise.

Bernstein began by assuming that active management is not a complete waste of time and money:

> I must mention at the outset that the whole structure depends on one overarching assumption—that clients can identify managers capable of generating alphas. (p. 1)[48]

He then argued at length that "traditional benchmarking for active portfolio managers is contrary to the client's best interest" (p. 4) because capitalization-weighted benchmarks are heavily weighted in the currently "hot" stocks and because managers are in a horse race with no well-defined track and a constantly moving finish line. He then defined an investment environment free of traditional benchmarks:

> It must be to the client's best interest to maximize the alphas they are capable of generating. Yet alpha is a relative term, not an absolute one. If we free up the manager from the constraints of the traditional benchmark, how can we discover whether any alpha has been created? How do we make a judgment about a manager's performance?
>
> The answer … is that we cannot make judgments in the traditional manner. The data that emerge from the traditional process are not meaningless—I do not mean to go that far—but they create difficulties for clients because they are constraining. (p. 4)

If you are selecting managers with real skill, the kind to whom (as I said in the Preface) traditional benchmarks are shackles, how should you measure performance? Bernstein wrote:

> I propose that client start at the beginning and move forward. The beginning is the determination of the required return of the total portfolio and the degree of volatility that client can live with in the search for that required return.
>
> When it comes to defining benchmarks, *faute de mieux* the riskless rate itself can serve the purpose, with the active portfolio built up from there. One can go further, however, with the required return falling out of a careful specification of investment objectives. For example, most foundations seek inflation plus 5 percent, pension funds could use as a benchmark an immunized portfolio with zero tracking error to the fund's liability return, endowment funds take spending rates as the key to required returns, and individuals would do well to begin to think of their own objectives in similar kinds of frameworks. (p. 5)

But what does a liability-focused benchmark mean in practice?

> The proper question to ask about an active management organization is not whether it is beating the S&P 500, the Lehman . . . or its peer group. The question should be: How much is this organization contributing to a return in excess of our required return, and at what level of volatility? A manager with bond-like returns but equity-like volatility gets fired; a manager with equity-like returns and bond-like volatility receives an increased allocation. I admit that this keeps the old horse race running, but at least the track and finish line are properly defined. (p. 5)

The consequences of using such a framework for performance measurement, in Bernstein's view, include the following:

- a much looser set of marching orders for managers,
- greater "breadth" in the uses to which a given set of active management skills are put,[49]
- larger allocations to managers who are not afraid to be, in Kritzman's (1998) words, "wrong and alone,"
- greater use of large, multistrategy organizations, and
- greater responsibility on the part of the client's investment officer.

> Bernstein acknowledged that his prescription might result in reduced diversification:
>
> With widened mandates, the possibility exists that all the domestic equity managers will run to [international] investments at the same moment, or all desert one or another subdivisions of the domestic market. (p. 7)

> He had concluded, however, that if implemented sensibly, an investment policy that is focused on seeking return relative to a liability benchmark (or simply an absolute rate of return) and avoiding absolute risk (which he defined as volatility) can "circumvent to the extent possible the dangerous conflicts of interest in traditional arrangements that fester between manager's risk and owner's risk" (p. 7).

Toward a Compromise

How can Bernstein's views be reconciled with the position I took that alpha and active return (measured in relation to a properly selected and constructed benchmark) are the only things that matter? It can't, but as promised, I can outline the structure of a potential compromise. A sponsor's attitude toward active management and managers might be as follows:

- We believe in the abstract that superior managers exist, but we're from Missouri and you'll have to show us. We're going to continue to measure, AND PAY, you (as described in the section titled Building Portfolios of Managers) by "pure" alpha, active risk, and information ratio.
- However, it's rational and potentially fruitful to spend some of our risk budget on managers who are a little different from the crowd, who even may not fit into a single asset class, much less a style. We'll hold them to active return–active risk standards also, and we'll construct a benchmark for them. It could conceivably be a liability-focused benchmark, but more likely, the benchmark will be composed of the returns on the asset class or classes in which we believe the manager is likely to invest.
- At the policy level, we will establish a policy benchmark, but we will not be afraid to stray from it. We're going to compare our own actual asset-class mix with that of the policy benchmark, and we'll calculate our information ratio—pure alpha per unit of tracking error. (Plan sponsors shouldn't be scared of this measurement protocol. The rewards from being right about asset allocation are so generous that any skill in making them will be evident from an information ratio perspective.)
- If we think a traditional active manager's active bets are so unlikely to be successful that we feel we have to hold them to a strict tracking-error constraint, we won't hire them. We will hire managers in whom we have confidence instead, and although we'll measure their tracking error to a sensible benchmark and count that against their risk budgets, we won't constrain them. We'll let the managers do what they want, and we'll let them do their own constraining by being forced to generate information ratio, not just alpha. Thus, although tracking-error constraints are a flawed construct, we are still averse to tracking error. In short, measuring tracking error and rewarding the manager for information ratio is still a good idea.
- We are very much concerned about costs (including manager fees and indirect costs, such as trading costs.). Costs are the one dimension of investment management that can be controlled, so index funds and other low-cost funds have a special place.

If you work through this framework to generate an investment policy, you will wind up with larger-than-traditional weights on index funds, enhanced index funds, and certain types of hedge funds (those that control risk and that deliver pure alpha, not beta masquerading as alpha). You may also make increased use of balanced (including global balanced) funds and tactical asset allocation funds. This framework provides only a small role for traditional active managers benchmarked to a narrowly defined style. Given the huge cluster of resources currently deployed in traditional active management, however, the investor would be derelict to avoid it completely.

No one really knows (yet) how to follow Bernstein's prescription literally. (I lay out further thoughts on it in the discussion of policy benchmarks later in the section titled Policy Benchmarks) What he defines as active risk may be too much influenced by luck to provide a realistic assessment of a manager's skill. Using Bernstein's standard, a large indexed position in the equity market in 1995–1999 would have been scored as a huge active win; if the objective is, say, to earn inflation plus 5 percent, then earning inflation plus 15 percent on a consistent basis for several years should indeed be scored as a win. But without gathering additional information, it is impossible to tell whether investors who had such a position did so because they thought it would earn the highest possible return after adjusting for risk or because all of their peers were doing it.

If the spur was peer pressure, the position was not a win but a stroke of luck (that is, the investor had no skill) and much of the gain from holding it would have unwound by the end of 2002 because the investor, like his or her peers, would have remained invested in the stock market. Real skill must be quantifiable, and if new technologies are needed to measure it in today's supposedly new investment climate, then the search should be on to develop them.

Conclusion

Despite the challenges to benchmarking, and to cap-weighted benchmarks in particular, that have arisen in the past decade, cap-weighted benchmarks will continue to have a special place in investment management and analysis for a simple reason: *You can't design a simple, rule-based, judgment-free portfolio that is demonstrably more efficient than the cap-weighted benchmark.*

Some people have suggested equal-weighted benchmarks, book-value- or earnings-weighted benchmarks, and other types (such as international equity benchmarks that are weighted by gross domestic product by country).[50] But except for equally weighted portfolios, proponents of these alternatives cannot even agree on sensible rules for constructing such benchmarks, much less prove that these portfolios are more efficient than a cap-weighted one (and equally weighted portfolios have very limited capacity).[51] Finally, a theory exists—the capital asset pricing model, with all its flaws—that says cap-weighted benchmarks are efficient. No theory exists—not even a proposed and untested one—that says some other simple, rule-based portfolio is efficient. As a result of all these factors, benchmarking relative to cap-weighted indexes as an important component of a broader performance-measurement discipline (one that also includes comparison with liability-focused benchmarks) is probably here to stay.

THE IMPACT OF BENCHMARKING ON MARKETS AND INSTITUTIONS

Many observers have suggested that indexing and benchmarking have distorting effects on market prices and on the behavior of institutions. (Keep in mind that by "benchmarking," I mean active management that uses a cap-weighted index, or benchmark, as a starting point and that defines active risk as tracking error relative to the benchmark.) In this section, I examine these distortions. The distortions of market pricing that are alleged to accompany indexing and benchmarking may be classified into micro and macro categories. "Micro" distortions generally mean mispricings of one security relative to another; such mispricings tend to be either small but potentially long lasting or potentially large but temporary. These distortions tend to be self-correcting in the long run, but that aspect does not make them trivial. Having to persistently overpay for a class of securities, for example, or having to accept an unfairly low price when selling them, may have a significant effect on an investor's long-term returns.

"Macro" distortions, in contrast, are those that have potentially pervasive and long-lasting effects on market levels or on the level of a significant subset of the market. These distortions emerge because, as noted in the conceptual critique discussed in the section titled The 1990s Bubble and the Crisis in MPT, by holding the benchmark, the investor is doing what everybody else is doing (because the benchmark is the cap-weighted sum of all prices). Thus, indexing and benchmarking are, according to this critique, a form of herd behavior. I explore the consequences of this observation in discussing the impact of benchmarking on institutions, but such an exploration must be more speculative than the treatment of micro distortions because practically no data are available on the macro side.

I also discuss the effect of indexing and of active management (of the kind in which risk is defined as tracking error) on the behavior of such institutions as plan sponsors and their governing committees, investment management firms, consulting firms, and plan beneficiaries.

Market Price Distortions

Observed micro effects on prices include a number of different index reconstitution effects. In addition, free-float mismatch is a micro distortion that has received increasing attention recently.

S&P 500 Index Reconstitution Effect

The first indexers never dreamed that their activities would move market prices, but an "S&P 500 inclusion effect" nevertheless quickly emerged. The inclusion effect is that stocks added to the S&P 500 rise in price dramatically upon announcement of their addition to the index as all the index fund managers try to add the stock to their portfolios at the lowest possible cost. Stocks deleted from the index suffer a corresponding price decline.

Such an effect probably exists with respect to all indexes that have substantial assets under index fund management, although it is presumably smaller for indexes other than the S&P 500. Index funds that track rule-based indexes with predictable constituent changes should have a much less pronounced cost disadvantage from the inclusion effect because investors can act in advance of the changes.

The reason for the inclusion and deletion effects (classified together as a reconstitution effect) is obvious: An increase in the demand for a stock caused by the need for index funds to hold that stock is not met by any change in supply. Thus, the price rises. The market clears when active managers and arbitrageurs, motivated by the desire to sell stocks that have gone up, provide indexers with enough of the stock to enable them to hold it in exactly the index weight.[52] The deletion effect is simply the mirror image of the inclusion effect. The inflexibility of index fund design (a virtue from some points of view) makes reconstitution effects inevitable.

One can interpret reconstitution-related price movements in either of two ways. The price-pressure hypothesis holds that "transitory order imbalance[s] associated with index additions and deletions are the primary source of price movements" (Madhavan 2002, p. 3). The index membership hypothesis holds that index membership itself is a source of value (because of greater liquidity or better information flow), so an inclusion effect is permanent rather than transitory. The two hypotheses are not mutually exclusive; both effects could exist.

The first works that identified the S&P 500 reconstitution effect are Goetzmann and Garry (1986), Harris and Gurel (1986), and Jain (1987). Although somewhat out of date, these studies convey the essence of the effect. Harris and Gurel found excess returns on the announcement day of 3.1 percentage points (pps) for additions and −1.4 pps for deletions, in addition to large trading volumes. They interpreted these results as the effects of transitory price pressure. The Goetzmann–Garry and Jain studies found persistent, long-term stock price declines upon deletion of a stock from the S&P 500. Thus, evidence supporting both the price-pressure and index-membership hypotheses exists.

The implication of these results is that, relative to an idealized situation of no reconstitution effects, the investor overpays for index funds and receives too little. One author's estimate of S&P 500 underperformance as a result of the inclusion/deletion effects in recent years (expressed as an annual rate) is 0.32 pps for 1992–2002 (see the section titled Critiques of Benchmarking and a Way Forward). The amount of underperformance has, of course, been increasing as indexed assets have grown.

After paying the transaction cost caused by the inclusion/deletion effects, an investor in an index fund does, of course, receive the asset-class or style return almost for free, because index funds have low management fees. It is up to the investor to decide if this trade-off is worthwhile.

Smart trading. Some index managers put a great deal of effort into trading disciplines that avoid these reconstitution costs to the greatest extent possible. Such "smart trading" tends to reduce the costs of all transacting, not only costs associated with index reconstitution. Moreover, because firms managing large index funds are *providers* (not just consumers) of liquidity, they may even be able to turn the tables on the arbitrageurs and capture for their investors some of the liquidity premium traditionally received by the "arbs." Managers who are successful at this endeavor can beat the index (by a modest amount) without making any active bets.[53]

Reconstitution effect from active management. Inclusion/deletion effects are probably also caused by benchmark-sensitive management of actively managed portfolios, but these effects cannot be observed separately. As I noted previously, ordinary active managers and self-conscious arbitrageurs provide some of the liquidity needed to effect index funds' reconstitution-related trades and thus profit from the reconstitution. By and large, however, active managers are probably paying, not receiving, reconstitution-related costs. Here is the logic: When a stock is added to an index, the demand from active managers for that stock must increase in roughly the same proportion as the demand from indexers because, on average, the managers will hold the index weight. The reason this effect is not plainly observed is that each manager individually has wide discretion as to whether to hold the stock and how to time the purchase. Moreover, active managers have a strong motivation to avoid paying such unnecessary transaction costs, and now that a reconstitution effect has been identified, at least some active managers have found a way to dodge these costs. Thus, although some of the overall observed reconstitution effect probably comes from active managers' demand, it is muted, and some active managers profit from the effect while others are hurt by it.

Russell Mania

A market microstructure effect that is closely related to but somewhat different in character from the S&P reconstitution effect is what has come to be called "Russell mania." It might seem that the Russell reconstitution, which occurs every 30 June, would be relatively free of price distortions and other technical effects because it is based purely on market capitalization, which is observable by all interested parties in real time. Madhavan found, however:

> Equity returns [arising from the reconstitution of the Russell 3000 and its sub-indexes] are concentrated in time and are much larger in magnitude and in the number of stocks affected than the corresponding effects for S&P 500 index revisions. Specifically, a portfolio long additions and short deletions to the Russell 3000 index (constructed after the determination of new index weights at the end of May) had a mean return over the period 1996–2001 of 15 percent in the month of June. From March–June, the cumulative mean return exceeds 35 percent. (2002, p. 1)

These numbers are *huge*. Understandably, index funds, active managers, hedge funds, brokers, and others find themselves in an annual mania—to capture such returns if they are the liquidity providers and to avoid paying them as a cost if they are the liquidity consumers.

One reason for this large effect is that stocks being added to the Russell 3000 (which embraces 98 percent of U.S. equity market value) are tiny, so they are disproportionately affected by either transitory or permanent changes in demand. An odd institutional artifact, however, makes the Russell effect more complicated and more fun for arbitrageurs. Most large-cap portfolios are indexed or benchmarked to the S&P 500, not the Russell 1000, but a sizable chunk of small-cap portfolios is indexed or benchmarked to the Russell 2000. Thus, when a stock moves from the Russell 1000 to the Russell 2000, because its relative market cap has declined, the demand for the stock *increases.*[54]

Free-Float Mismatch: The "Yahoo! Effect"

The most dramatic S&P 500 inclusion effect in history occurred on 7 December 1999, the day before Yahoo! was added to that index (replacing Laidlaw, the largest school-bus company). On that day, the price of Yahoo! rose by $67.25 per share, or 24 percent, to close at $348, as 66 million shares changed hands. Previously, from the announcement on 30 November 1999 that Yahoo! would be included in the S&P 500 to the inclusion date, investors had run up the stock by 32 percent. This mysterious price levitation was not the result of any special enthusiasm for Yahoo! stock (Yahoo! was just another constituent of the S&P index, and its special merits, whatever they were, were not under consideration that day). The cause was the fact that Yahoo! had been added to the S&P 500 at its full market-cap weight without any adjustment for the free float (the number of shares held by stockholders who were at liberty to sell). Because most shares were held by employees, venture capital firms, and other investors who were restricted from selling, the true supply of Yahoo! shares was only about 10 percent of the full market cap. The result was the radical supply–demand imbalance manifest in the price spike.

The situation was mitigated by the fact that only about 8 percent of the capitalization of the S&P 500 is in index funds linked to the S&P 500. Thus, the demand as well as the supply was limited. If a much larger proportion of the capitalization of the S&P 500 had been in S&P 500 indexed funds, the index fund demand for Yahoo! might not have been met at any price. The market has no precedent for a stock having an infinite price, so, surely, the Micawber rule ("Something will turn up") would have prevailed.[55] Restricted stockholders might have found a way around the restrictions, someone might have issued derivatives acceptable to the index funds, or the funds might have forced Standard & Poor's to drop Yahoo! from the index.

At any rate, the importance of float adjustment, which was previously thought by many to be an unnecessary (or even undesirable) complication in index construction, suddenly became clear. Yahoo! was far from the only stock that was eventually affected; many of the emerging technology companies had little free float because of the need to compensate employees and venture capitalists with restricted stock. Float-adjusted indexes increased in popularity, and Morgan Stanley Capital International converted to a float-adjusted format not long after the Yahoo! episode, although MSCI's action was primarily for other reasons (see the section titled International Equity Benchmarks).

Games Hedge Funds Play

Today, for the first time, much of the market's liquidity is provided by hedge funds— entrepreneurial, risk-seeking, and often highly leveraged institutions that are typically accountable to no one other than their owner/investors. Hedge funds are so named for their original goal of "hedging" or reducing risk, but they more often take risks that investors constrained by traditional benchmarks are loath to accept (see the section titled Hedge Fund Benchmarks). Brokerage houses, the traditional source of liquidity in the stock market, have a smaller role than they once did.

Hedge funds were not established to provide liquidity; they exist to make outsize profits by taking unusual risks. That they do provide liquidity is basically an unintended consequence of their operations (as well as a source of their returns). Index reconstitutions are a major consumer of the liquidity that hedge funds provide.

Thus, investors trading in anticipation of or in reaction to changes in index contents should be aware that, with a high degree of likelihood, they are buying from or selling to a hedge fund that may have better information and possibly greater influence over market prices than the investors do. Careful attention to trading disciplines is a good idea in all situations but especially in index reconstitutions, where demand is predictable and the other side of the trade can be presumed to have put great effort into forecasting it. Active managers as well as index fund managers can benefit from this observation.

Institutional Behavior

In this section, I describe two effects of benchmarking: the play-it-safe impact of benchmarking on active managers and the emergence of index funds as a major force in the market.

The Impact of Benchmarking on Active Managers

The first-order impact of benchmarking on managers (as opposed to markets) is simply to get active managers to take less active risk. Active managers cannot manage active risk if they have never heard of it, as in the original paradigm. Increased awareness from investors, consultants, and managers of the existence and nature of active risk has dramatically reduced the amount of active risk taken; up to 35 percent of the capitalization of U.S. equities is said to be indexed, and probably another 50 percent is managed with an explicit goal of managing active risk while seeking active return. This outcome is exactly as I argued it should be in the section titled Building Portfolios of Managers. A smaller but significant proportion of international equities is indexed or benchmarked, as is a large proportion of fixed-income assets.

But if indexing and benchmarked active management are largely desirable outcomes, they still have a downside. First, as I noted at the outset, for those rare managers with true skill, the concern about active risk leads to impaired courage and, thereby, to lower returns. This result is sometimes described by frustrated managers as being forced to take "real" risk to avoid taking "apparent" risk. Second, probably a more important drawback, the ability to manage a portfolio in a benchmark-sensitive manner has enabled many managers with little or no real skill to deliver only market-like returns but, because of two decades of rising markets, to give their clients the impression that they have added value. And they've been able to charge active fees for this "service." It remains to be seen whether managers who deliver only beta exposures and no alpha (or little alpha per unit of active risk) can maintain their client bases in markets that fluctuate (instead of only going up). I hope not.

In addition, active managers have tightly clustered themselves into styles so that they can be classified into one of the consultants' style boxes. Most consultants and clients do not know how (or do not bother) to run the multivariate regressions described in the section titled Using Benchmarks to Measure Performance; instead, they compare a manager's returns with the single style benchmark that seems to fit best. Thus, a manager has to stay within relatively tight style bounds to be hired by investors acting under their consultants' advice. This practice—which could be called "managing your business risk instead of your portfolio"—has not only restrained the taking of active risk relative to style benchmarks but also discouraged managers from trying to manage broad-cap or core portfolios, to time investments between styles or sectors, or to practice other tactical allocation disciplines—which are as good a way as any to try to add alpha.

The prescription that managers should seek only pure alpha and avoid only pure active risk relative to a properly style-adjusted benchmark does *not* mean that they should "hug" the style benchmarks. If a manager adopts a mix of styles or uses a timing approach to move between styles, the method outlined in the section titled Using Benchmarks to Measure Performance will capture the pure alpha and pure active risk correctly.

Emergence and Popularity of Index Funds

Increased awareness of benchmarks has also led to a vibrant index fund sector. Even proverbially naive individual investors are now more or less universally aware that index funds exist and have low management fees. They allocate to active funds because they think they can beat the index fund, not because they have been exposed only to opportunities for active investment. Index funds (and, to some extent, enhanced index funds, which start with the security weights in the benchmark and then try to add value through risk-controlled active management) now form the core of many, if not most, institutional equity portfolios. This state of affairs must have been a shock and a delight to the pioneers who developed the first index funds only a generation ago, most of whom are still active in the investment management business.

Many observers guess that the move in so short a time from indexing nothing to indexing something like 35 percent of all U.S. equities simply has to have had some effect on market levels and price discovery. I now examine several points of view on this question.

Macro Effects: How Much Indexing Is Too Much?

Ever since indexing started, speculation has occurred about how much indexing is too much. Logically, if everyone indexed all of their assets, no one would be left to price securities. The price-discovery process would disappear, and markets would be completely inefficient. No one seriously suggests that this eventuality can happen, because the potential profits from security analysis would be huge. Ibbotson and Brinson (1987) referred to this idea as the "student's proof of market inefficiency" because, in the experience of finance professors, there is always a bright student in the introductory course who says, "If every investor believed that markets were efficient, the market could not be efficient because no one would analyze securities" (p. 58).[56]

The recent market bubble might have been a hint of what would happen if no one analyzed securities. If no one tried (very hard) to determine the fundamental values of, say, large-cap technology stocks but simply bought them because of their large weights in the benchmark—which is similar to saying that you are buying them because they have gone up—price would become quickly divorced from value.[57]

Taking this observation a bit further and applying it to markets in general, Arnott and Darnell wrote:

> Passive management is the ultimate momentum strategy. Passive investing puts the most money into the largest stocks—not the largest companies, but . . . the stocks that have been the most successful *in the past* and are the most expensive compared to their fundamentals *in the present*. (2003, p. 31; emphasis in original).

In other words, a lot of indexing may have made the market less efficient and (some would argue) made the cap-weighted market benchmark easier to beat through a fundamental valuation approach.

This situation *cannot* go on forever. Active management is still a zero-sum game and, as Arnott and Darnell noted, even the best managers have alphas that slowly regress to zero over very long time periods. Warren Buffett, perhaps the greatest manager ever, earned only a 0.7 information ratio over the past 33 years; his firm's IR was only 0.48 over the 20 years and 3 months ended March 2000. Arnott and Darnell noted that this IR is modest by the standards of plan sponsors looking at managers' three-year track records and self-assessments of their future prospects but "is sufficient to make [Buffett] the world's wealthiest investor (with his co-investors participating almost fully in these gains, contrary to many investment managers)" (p. 32).

Managers cannot win the zero-sum game over long time periods by contrarian investing relative to a cap-weighted benchmark. So, what should the investor do when the bubble is over, when valuation disparities between styles and market sectors are no longer disturbingly large? Arnott and Darnell suggested (surprisingly and, I think, sensibly) a strange new respect for passive investing:

> Consider passive only when active managers have done considerably better than pas- sive managers, lest we enter an up elevator just before it goes down. Consider passive only when a switch to passive will not involve selling our most sensibly priced stocks in order to buy the market's most expensive stocks. (p. 33)

There is not much literature in which researchers try to actually estimate from data the size of the macro effect of indexing. In general, disentangling all the effects at work is too dif- ficult. William Jacques, however, in a 1988 article that superficially sounds like just another "S&P inclusion effect" paper, had the following to say about the consequences in the very long run of membership in that index over the period (1973–1987) when indexing and benchmarking first came to fruition:

> Stocks belonging to the S&P 500 produced approximately 4.0 percent per year of extra return [over 1980–1987], compared with non-index companies with simi- lar characteristics. The phenomenon seems to be accelerating. . . . As active equity managers lost share to index funds, non-S&P 500 stocks were sold to make room for S&P 500 purchases. Not only was buying pressure placed on index members, but selling pressure was exerted in a less liquid sector of the market. (p. 73)

A 4 percent a year cumulative excess return over eight years amounts to almost 37 percent. Jacques' conclusions—that a very large segment of the market became 37 percent more expensive relative to the rest of the market—is qualitatively different from the findings dis- cussed earlier in the section on the S&P inclusion effect and should be regarded as evidence of a macro effect from indexing and benchmarking.

Jacques noted that the cumulative excess return to S&P 500 membership began around 1979, just when the indexing ball got rolling. Regarding benchmarking, Jacques noted that "a more subtle version of buying pressure on the S&P 500 members was generated during the 1980s by closet indexers . . . [namely] those institutional investors who feel compelled to con- struct portfolios whose results will be unlikely to deviate much from the . . . index" (p. 73).

Of course, the view that indexing can cause price distortions on a macro scale is not uni- versally accepted. Rex Sinquefield, an index fund pioneer, enunciated quite a different view. His arguments are heterodox and fascinating:

> If there were a tremendous amount of indexing, it would not necessarily affect the accuracy of prices. As Adam Smith and Friedrich Hayek were quick to point out, we really don't know how the price discovery process works. So to say that indexed

assets won't contribute to price discovery means that one believes price discovery relies specifically on equity analysts. I'm not sure of that at all.

Take, for example, the days before stock markets, when we had goods and services markets around the world for hundreds or thousands of years. Adam Smith and others show that these markets basically work and that civilizations based on free market prices survived, while those that didn't use markets to price goods and services did not survive. We did not have equity analysts back then; we just had people competing in the marketplace providing market pressures to keep prices in line relative to all the alternative consumption and service items that could be bought or sold.

Now taking into consideration stocks and other financial assets in the U.S., there are agents that (regardless of the amount indexed) would always have an interest in keeping prices right or at least in evaluating the prices. Company managements themselves do this when they undertake a "make or buy" decision—should we expand, contract, buy a competitor, should someone buy us, or should we just buy real resources and expand that way? The company's management is comparing the prices of their company, their competitors, and real resources, and this process tends to keep each of these prices in line with the underlying real economic worth of the assets being considered. Market makers, in addition, are always going to have some sense of the valuations of companies. Those are just two sources of price discovery in a highly indexed world.[58]

I suspect that, at the current level of indexing and benchmarking, the macro effect of these practices is sufficient to exacerbate bubbles and crashes considerably. In other words, indexing and benchmarking create price-discovery problems when conditions are extreme.

But modern markets have not experienced many episodes like the bubble of 1998–2000 and the subsequent bear market (the only truly comparable valuations at the peak were in 1929 in the United States and 1989 in Japan). Usually, prices are more sensible. In more ordinary times, indexing and benchmarking probably do not make the market very inefficient. If the momentum strategy argument against indexing is generalizable across time, then value investing should have been a better strategy in the indexing era (say, after 1980) than it was when there were no index funds or almost no assets in index funds. As you will see in the next section, no such pattern emerges. The returns to value and growth investing seesawed back and forth, with value retaining a long-term advantage, in both the pre-indexing and indexing eras.

If the market is inefficient on a large scale because of indexing or some other reason, highly skilled analysts should be able to earn outsize returns at the expense of the less skilled. There is little evidence to indicate that many of them can do so consistently over long periods of time. The market is, at the very least, efficient enough to humble most of us.

U.S. EQUITY STYLE INDEXES

Equity "style" is an elusive and challenging concept.[59] Investors and researchers have long noticed that stock returns tend to cluster (Sharpe 1970; Rosenberg 1974)—in other words, stock returns have factors in common other than the market factor. If they do, a sensible approach is to try to aggregate equities at a level intermediate between the whole market at the macro end and industries and other small groups at the micro end. The construct known as "investment style" is the result of that effort.

Beginning in the late 1970s, researchers noted that two factors—capitalization and valuation—explained a great deal of the cross-section of stock returns. By "capitalization"

I mean the fact that small-cap stocks behave differently from large-cap stocks. By "valuation" I mean that stocks selling for low multiples of earnings, book value, or other related fundamental measures behave differently from those selling for high multiples. The low-multiple stocks are the so-called value stocks, and the high-multiple stocks are the growth stocks (because higher-than-average rates of growth are needed to justify the higher multiples).[60]

Prior to the discovery of the capitalization and valuation effects, the capital asset pricing model (CAPM, see the section titled The Evolution of MPT and the Benchmarking Paradigm) had related the returns on stocks to that on the overall market—that is, to a single factor. And Barr Rosenberg and others had made progress in relating stock returns to multiple factors. The identification of size and valuation—two easily described and easily measured factors—however, enabled consultants and their investor clients to classify stocks, categorize managers, and build style benchmarks in a systematic and meaningful way.

Note the triple duty to which the concept of investment style is put:

1. a way of understanding the characteristics of individual stocks,
2. a way of describing a manager's approach to analyzing securities (thus, value managers would not necessarily buy "value stocks" but might look for attractive valuations anywhere), and
3. a way of building benchmarks—and thus of building index funds, conducting performance evaluation of managers, and managing active portfolios by using the benchmark weights as a starting point.

Because of the importance of size (capitalization) and of value versus growth in explaining stocks' performance, the styles generally identified in current practice are large-cap value, large-cap growth, small-cap value, and small-cap growth. A mid-cap category (divided into value and growth) is also often separated out. Finally, a "core" or "neutral" style (indicating that a stock or portfolio is neither value nor growth) is sometimes broken out.

This classification scheme permeates the investment world and has brought with it a proliferation of style-based funds and benchmarks. Although style as a concept is almost universally accepted, no definition or application of style is universally agreed upon; each index provider constructs style indexes differently. I will discuss how style investing developed and describe how indexes are constructed to measure this market segment.

Multiple Uses of the Style Concept

First, reflect on the three uses to which the value and growth concepts are put: to characterize individual stocks, to describe managers' investment styles, and to build indexes and benchmarks.

Value and Growth Stocks

The fact that stocks differ in their growth prospects, as well as in their valuation multiples, can be used to categorize them. Thus, Microsoft Corporation is typically regarded as a growth stock because it has experienced a 16.8 percent compound annual growth rate of earnings over the past five years; Whirlpool Corporation is a value stock because it has a price-to-earnings ratio (P/E) of 12.

Usually, however, a given stock is considered a value or growth stock because it is in a particular value or growth benchmark. Thus, a "value manager" with no specific views on the stock will hold it at its weight in the value benchmark. Once I've explored how style benchmarks are constructed, it will become clearer why you must be careful when calling a security a "value stock" or "growth stock" simply because it is in a given benchmark.

Value and Growth Managers

Some managers look for stocks selling at prices lower than the book value of their assets or lower even than net working capital; others look for high dividend yields or low P/Es. These managers are the classic "value managers," whose style predates the modern concept of style investing. Their strategy is where the value style got its name.

Classic "growth managers," in contrast, look for companies with the best long-term earnings growth prospects. They are less concerned about paying the lowest possible price.

Traditionally, most managers were neither value nor growth but used elements of both disciplines or ways of looking at the world. This description is still true for many managers today, but the need for managers to be classified as value or growth by consultants (in order to be hired by the consultants' clients) has caused managers to cluster into value and growth camps—mostly by sticking to stocks in their particular style benchmark.

Value and Growth Benchmarks

Finally, the concepts of value and growth are used to define benchmarks. This sense of "investment style" is the principal focus of this section. Typically, but not always, style benchmarks are designed so that a capitalization-weighted combination of them sums to the overall cap-weighted market. To achieve this result, most sets of benchmarks are constructed so that every stock is classified as either growth or value. Alternatively, the capitalization of a stock is split between the two categories; that is, the same stock appears in both the value and growth indexes, with (typically) the capitalization of the stock divided up so that an investor holding both indexes does not get a double weighting in the stock.

A different approach would be to have a third category—core or neutral—in which to put stocks that are neither growth nor value. Because the words "value" and "growth" connote extremes of valuation, the concept of a core or neutral category is intuitively appealing. Unfortunately, none of the index providers whose indexes are reviewed here has a separate core category for which it keeps track of returns and membership.[61] Consequently, many value or growth managers manage tracking error relative to a value or growth benchmark that contains core issues by buying these issues whether they are in keeping with the manager's philosophy and strategy or not.

Also note that the returns on value and growth benchmarks can be interpreted as *factors* (or *betas*), which are used to explain (statistically) the performance of stocks or of groups of stocks and to calculate the "pure alphas" and other performance statistics of managers (see the section titled Using Benchmarks to Measure Performance).

Some Caveats about Style Classification

Stocks classified into the value category are not necessarily underpriced; they may just appear to be. A low stock price may reflect the market's correct assessment of a company's current or future difficulties. A "good deal" can become a "better deal."

Investors should also be careful not to classify a stock as a growth issue simply because some investors or analysts have rosy expectations for the company. Graham and Zweig (2003) cautioned:

> If the definition of a growth stock is a company that will thrive in the future, then that's not a definition at all, but wishful thinking. It's like calling a sports team "the champions" before the season is over. This wishful thinking persists today; among

mutual funds, "growth" portfolios describe their holdings as companies with "above-average growth potential" or "favorable prospects for earnings growth." A better definition might be companies whose net earnings per share have increased by 15 percent for at least five years running. Meeting this definition in the past does not ensure that a company will meet it in the future. (p. 581)

Growth and value benchmarks can have long stretches of exceptionally good or bad relative performance, Growth stocks outperformed value stocks at various times in the 1950s and 1960s; then, value regained the upper hand in the 1970s. More recently, the explosion of growth stocks in the 1990s, consisting mostly of Internet and technology stocks in the market bubble, has given way to a relative advantage for value stocks in recent years. The size of the divergence between returns of different styles is huge, which provides an opportunity to add alpha by changing your allocation to different equity styles. This return variability also shows why diversifying across growth and value segments of the market is important.

Although definitions of growth and value vary from investor to investor, depending on what the investor believes and is trying to achieve, index constructors do not have this luxury. An index must be rigorously and objectively constructed, relatively transparent as to methodology, and at the same time, intuitively appealing. The subjective nature of investment style makes it difficult, if not impossible, for a given index to meet all these criteria. As a result, style index construction methods differ considerably among index providers, so understanding these differences is vital.

Before discussing in detail the various style indexes and the methods used to construct them, I will review some of the research findings and theoretical advances that led to the development of style investing and style benchmarks.

The Evolution of Style Investing

Style investing and style benchmarks lie at the intersection of two threads of investment thinking: (1) traditional portfolio management and (2) quantitative academic research. As mentioned previously, value and growth approaches to security selection existed in the traditional investment management world long before any quantitative style factors were identified. As academics began to discover common statistical factors in stock returns other than the single market factor, they searched for real, or intuitive, factors with which to describe and identify the statistical factors. Value and growth were superbly preadapted to this use.

Traditional Approaches to Portfolio Management

Long before the terms "style," "value," and "growth" became commonplace, investors were already investing in line with these ideas. In 1934, Graham and Dodd argued in their book *Security Analysis* that investors should focus on company fundamentals and financial statement analysis and should buy the stocks of companies trading at less than their intrinsic value. This approach is the essence of value investing. Growth investing became a distinct strategy in the late 1950s and is associated with the work of Philip Fisher (e.g., 1958). It was embodied in the popularity in the early 1970s of the "Nifty Fifty," which were thriving companies (including Eastman Kodak Company, IBM Corporation, and McDonald's Corporation) that steadily rose in price despite lofty valuations. Investors were bidding up the prices in the expectation that earnings would grow even more in the future.

Quantitative Academic Research

The development of the CAPM in the 1960s, as described on page 87, and its popularity in the following decade set researchers to the task of proving it wrong. One way to cast doubt on a theory is to find a persistent "anomaly" or set of facts that is unexplained by the theory. Academic researchers set out to find anomalies and ended up using some of them to develop factor models, define styles, and create style benchmarks.

The size (capitalization) effect. With hundreds of assistant professors looking to make their mark, someone was sure to find something anomalous in the market, but few were expecting anything as dramatic as the finding by Rolf Banz in 1979 that small-cap stocks—stocks with the smaller equity capitalizations (as measured by price times number of shares outstanding)—had a much higher average return than large-cap stocks (see Banz 1981).[62] Gavin Hall of Delaware International Advisers recalled:

> The Banz research covered the years 1936–1975 and, on average, the very smallest stocks on the NYSE (bottom 50) outperformed the very largest (top 50) by just over 100 basis points per month.[63]

Reinganum (1981) independently discovered the same effect.

Even if you do not compare only the very smallest with the very largest stocks, the return difference discovered by Banz and Reinganum was huge when compounded over long time periods—and it was not explained by beta.[64] (If small-cap stocks had higher betas—high enough to explain the higher returns—that fact would take away the mystery or "anomaly" with respect to the CAPM.)

Several explanations for the small-cap effect are possible. First, the market might not be efficient; small-cap stocks might have been underpriced, thus yielding higher returns over the period that Banz and Reinganum studied. Second, small size might be a proxy for some sort of risk that is being priced by the market but that is not measured by beta; if so, then the small-cap effect is the delivery of a risk premium. The second explanation, in other words, says that small size is a risk factor. This risk-factor explanation for the size effect has been more widely accepted since Fama and French clearly advocated it in 1992.

The valuation effect. At roughly the same time as the work of Banz and Reinganum, Basu (1977, 1983) independently discovered that low-P/E stocks have higher returns than high-P/E stocks (again, after adjustment for beta).[65] Using price-to-book-value (P/B) produces much the same result (see Rosenberg, Reid, and Lanstein 1985). Again, either the market is inefficient or P/E is serving as a proxy for some sort of risk not captured by a stock's beta.

Although the reaction of some practitioners to this research was, "Ho hum; underpriced stocks beat overpriced stocks. We knew that," the surprise registered by academic researchers in response to the discovery of the value and size effects is hard to overstate. More than a decade of efficient market and CAPM orthodoxy had convinced most that the cap-weighted market portfolio could not be beaten, at least not with a simple, easy-to-follow decision rule. Yet, here was a collection of properly trained, careful researchers, wielding seemingly accurate data, who claimed that not one but two very profitable such rules existed! These findings created a "crisis" in CAPM thinking from which the theory has never fully recovered. Almost no one today believes that the market is completely efficient or that the CAPM precisely describes the relationship between risk and expected return.

Now that the barn door was open, researchers rushed to discover new factors—new systematic ways to beat the market without taking any added risk (as measured by beta). Most of the factors that were subsequently discovered, however, turned out to be proxies for valuation (or, occasionally, size).

One new factor that looked promising—and that was unrelated to any previously discovered factor—was *momentum* (see Jegadeesh 1990). This discovery was another surprise for efficient market theorists. (I do not cover momentum in this chapter.)

From Factors to Styles

The investment management consulting firms seized on the discovery of the size and valuation effects pretty quickly and began advising clients to achieve maximum diversification by, at first, adding small-cap funds and, later, adding value- and growth-focused funds to their asset mixes. Consultants had already observed that managers' approaches to making investment choices clustered into value and growth categories, and the factors discovered by academics mapped nicely in these categories.

Who was the first to label factor exposures as "styles" is not clear, but by 1988, when Sharpe published his methodology for identifying the factor exposures of a portfolio through regression analysis, the term he used—"returns-based style analysis"—was perfectly well understood by the profession. A more formal write-up by Sharpe in 1992 solidified the use of style analysis in general and of large-cap, small-cap, growth, and value as the choices.

The public understanding of investment styles was greatly aided by Morningstar's decision in the early 1990s to classify mutual funds into the now-familiar three-by-three system of style boxes and to develop the Morningstar style-box "icon," which indicates the style of a given fund. In 1996, Morningstar changed its classification system from a traditional one ("growth," "growth and income," "equity income," and so forth) to one based on the modern conception of styles. As a result of these decisions, mutual funds are now typically named and marketed in ways that explicitly refer to their investment styles.

Sharpe and returns-based style analysis. The work of Basu, Banz, Rosenberg, and others indicated how to rank stocks by size and valuation and, as a result, provided a strong suggestion for how to map stocks into styles. Determining the style of an actively managed portfolio with changing portfolio contents is harder, however, than determining the style of a stock. For this purpose, Sharpe proposed using a type of regression to analyze the historical returns of a portfolio to measure the portfolio's exposures to, say, four well-defined style benchmarks. The return history of the portfolio, he argued, leaves "tracks in the sand" that indicate what style or mix of styles was followed.

One of Sharpe's principal innovations was to emphasize that virtually all portfolios—all portfolios except style index funds—represent a mix of styles. In other words, style is scalar; it is a continuum. As an example, a portfolio that is generally considered to be large-cap growth could be identified as 70 percent large-cap growth, 20 percent large-cap value, 5 percent small-cap growth, and 5 percent small-cap value. These weights may be viewed as the "style betas" of the portfolio, that is, the betas resulting from the regression of the portfolio's returns on those of the style factors. They are the extent to which the portfolio's returns are influenced, or explained, by the return on each of the style benchmarks.

In addition, Sharpe's work enabled a plan sponsor to disentangle a manager's style bets—intended or unintended—from the pure alpha added by the manager. This technology allows sponsors to manage the various risks of the portfolio and to identify managers who actually add alpha relative to a properly style-adjusted benchmark (see the section titled Using Benchmarks to Measure Performance and also Waring and Siegel 2003).

To conduct returns-based style analysis, you need to have well-constructed benchmarks. While other researchers were focusing on P/E, Sharpe decided to focus on P/B as the valuation measure for classifying stocks into styles. Sharpe's choice of P/B has influenced the construction of style benchmarks to this day, and Sharpe's work was one of the motivations for the consulting industry to develop such benchmarks.

An example of Sharpe's returns-based style analysis is in Figure 2.1. The example shows that Fidelity's Magellan Fund was initially exposed in a large degree to small-cap growth but that large-cap value increased in the mid 1990s. Over the whole period, large-cap growth was expanding as an influence on the fund, and by April 2000, it explained most of the fund's return.[66]

Fama and French's three-factor model.   Fama and French (1992, 1993) extended the investigation of the size- and valuation-related anomalies that had been identified more than a decade earlier by backdating the analysis to 1926. Their results, updated to 2003, for large-cap value and growth portfolios are in Figure 2.2. Value beat growth by a large margin over this span, but as Table 2.6 shows, when the data are adjusted for risk by calculation of the Sharpe ratio, the margin is not nearly as large as it looks.

Note from Table 2.6 that the Fama–French large-cap value index was riskier, statistically, than the growth index. This outcome is somewhat surprising, in that value stocks seem safer because of their lower multiples and because value indexes have been less volatile in the experience of investors living today. In the Great Depression of the 1930s, however, the value index fell twice as far as the growth index (in the logarithmic sense; the 90 percent decline in value left the investor with half as much money as the 80 percent decline in growth). This event

Exposure to Style Benchmark (%)

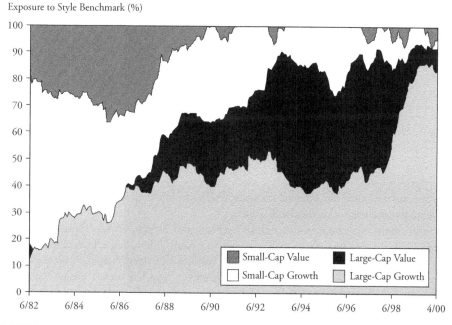

FIGURE 2.1   Returns-Based Style Analysis: Fidelity Magellan Fund, June 1982–April 2000
Source: Clifford, Kroner, and Siegel (2001).

Growth of $1.00 Invested
30 June 1926 (log scale)

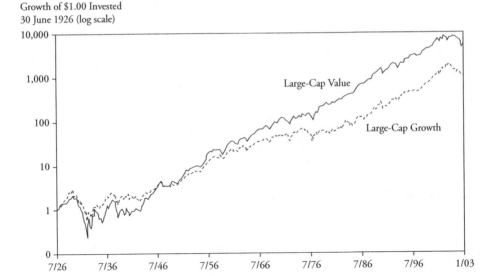

FIGURE 2.2   Cumulative Returns on Fama–French Value and Growth Portfolios, July
1926–January 2003

Source: Kenneth R. French's website, mba.tuck.dartmouth.edu/pages/faculty/ken.french/, which updates
work in Fama and French (1992).

TABLE 2.6   Summary Statistics of Returns on Fama–French Large-Cap Value and
Growth Portfolios, July 1927–January 2003

Statistic	Large-Cap Value	Large-Cap Growth
Compound annual return (%)	11.71	9.48
Arithmetic mean return (%)	14.30	10.92
Annualized standard deviation (%)	25.89	19.08
Sharpe ratio[a]	0.408	0.377

[a]Calculated in excess of U.S. Treasury bill return.

Source: Calculated by the author using data from French (see note to Figure 2.2).

lends support to Fama and French's contention that the value effect is the delivery of a risk
premium, not evidence of market inefficiency.

Surprisingly, over the period examined by Fama and French, which eventually extended
back to 1924, the size and valuation effects were so powerful that these effects eliminated beta
as an explanatory variable for stock returns. The work of Fama and French was interpreted as
meaning "beta is dead." Over certain periods, however, beta has been a useful explanatory
variable (and the logic of the CAPM, which states that beta is the only explanatory variable,
is too compelling to jettison entirely).[67] As a result, Fama and French adopted a three-factor
approach to explaining and predicting the returns on a given stock:

$$r_i = r_f + \beta_1(r_m - r_f) + \beta_2\,(SMB) + \beta_3\,(HML) + \tilde{\varepsilon}$$

where

r_i	= return on stock or portfolio i
r_f	= riskless rate of return
r_m	= return on the cap-weighted market index
SMB	= "small minus big"; the return on a small-cap portfolio minus the return on a large-cap portfolio
HML	= "high minus low"; return on a high-B/P (i.e., value) portfolio minus the return on a low-B/P (i.e., growth) portfolio
$\beta_1, \beta_2,$ and β_3	= betas (or loading factors) on, respectively, the market factor, *SMB*, and *HML*
$\tilde{\varepsilon}$	= random error term with an expected value of zero

This model can be understood as expectational (i.e., as with the CAPM, you put in the expected value for each right-hand-side variable to arrive at the expected return on stock or portfolio i) or as backward looking (i.e., as with the market model, you run a regression to see what factor exposures best explain the return on stock or portfolio i). Using this model, you can express any stock or portfolio as a mixture of exposures to three factors—beta, size, and valuation.

Although the functional form of the Fama–French model is quite different from that of Sharpe's approach, the content is similar. Both methods strongly validate style as a way of understanding investment performance, and both provide a way to use returns (not holdings) to identify the style of a stock or portfolio. Like Sharpe, Fama and French used book value, not earnings or other variables, to capture the fundamental value of the firm. Although book value is not completely satisfying from an economic point of view, it is less volatile than earnings and provides strong style differentiation (that is, value and growth indexes formed using P/B have very different returns).

An evaluation of Fama–French. Is the value effect really the delivery of a risk premium, implying that all styles are priced fairly? The idea that the value premium is a risk premium seems a little *ad hoc* to me. I suspect that if growth stocks had beaten value stocks historically, or large cap had beaten small cap, someone would have proposed a theory saying that a high growth rate (or large size) is a source of special risk for which investors demand, and in the long run receive, a higher return. Positing a "risk premium" to explain whatever factor delivers a superior return smacks of an attempt to preserve efficient market theory in the face of strong evidence against it.

If, instead, the market is inefficient and the value premium is the manifestation of this inefficiency, then value investing is a better strategy than growth investing. But although the market is probably inefficient, simply overweighting value stocks as a way to consistently earn a superior risk-adjusted return is too easy. Simple rule-based systems for beating the market tend to work only until they're discovered. High-beta stocks beat low-beta stocks until William Sharpe discovered beta in 1964; small-cap stocks beat large-cap ones until Banz and Reinganum discovered the size effect in 1979; and the value premium may yet be subject to the same fate.

Investors are powerfully motivated to exploit and eliminate, not just discover and write papers about, profitable market anomalies. For this reason, although underpaying for assets is a better idea than overpaying, value investing as it is currently defined may not be a winner in the indefinite future. Value investing of some kind will probably be a winner, but value may not be defined as low P/E or low P/B. There has been plenty of time (and plenty of capital at work) to arbitrage away the value–growth disparity as defined by these widely followed factors. The winning combination of stocks in the future is likely to be described by a factor or mix of factors that hasn't been discovered yet.

Another way of expressing this thought is to say that prudent investors, no matter what their stated styles, must do the homework of assessing the fundamental value of a stock and comparing that value with the stock's price. Such a discipline is currently associated more with value investing than with growth investing, but it should pervade all security analysis. If you wait long enough, market prices *always* tend toward fundamental value.

Holdings-based vs. returns-based style analysis.   An alternative method of identifying the style of a portfolio is called "holdings-based style analysis" because it uses the characteristics of the securities in a portfolio at a given time as the basis for estimating the manager's likely future style exposures. Returns-based and holdings-based style analyses have different advantages and disadvantages.[68] Holdings-based analysis is up-to-date as of the time of the analysis, whereas returns-based analysis relies on a moving data window and thus incorporates results from a style that the manager may no longer be following. Holdings-based analysis can also become out-of-date quickly, however, because managers can change holdings at any time.

The main problem with holdings-based style analysis is that it requires up-to-date, security-level data and risk-factor exposure estimates for each security for each fund that is being analyzed. Return data are much easier to obtain. Moreover, if you are trying to estimate the historical "pure alpha" described in the section titled Using Benchmarks to Measure Performance (which I argued is the only historical return measure relevant for forecasting a manager's future alpha), you would need data on the holdings *across* time, which are just about impossible to get. Returns-based style analysis, while possibly less precise, has much less formidable data requirements and inherently incorporates changes in the manager's style over the period for which the alpha is being calculated.

Commercial Style Indexes

After factors that map into styles had been identified, the remaining step was to build style benchmarks. Like other benchmarks, style benchmarks (or indexes) are paper portfolios representing the factors or styles that have constituent lists updated in real time and daily return calculation so that indexers can see what securities to buy and active managers can have a benchmark against which to run a portfolio.

The natural providers of these style indexes were the companies that were already providing other types of indexes. In the mid-1980s, Wilshire Associates and the Frank Russell Company became the first companies to build style indexes. Standard & Poor's (originally in collaboration with Sharpe and with Barra) and Dow Jones and Company also constructed style indexes of the U.S. equity market.[69] In the next section, I discuss the characteristics of these suites of style indexes and assess the trade-offs involved in constructing them.

Index Construction and Trade-Offs

Style and size indexes of U.S. equities differ from one another much more than do the unstylized, broad-cap indexes discussed in the section titled Origins, Uses, and Characteristics of U.S. Equity Benchmarks. As a result, the investor must understand the methods used to construct the various style indexes in order to decide which index to use and to know how to use it. In the next discussions, I describe in detail how four of the leading suites of U.S. equity style indexes are constructed and comment on the merits and demerits of each. Then, I discuss the special trade-offs involved in style index construction. Particular attention should be paid to the factors used to classify stocks into styles; some style indexes use one factor (e.g., P/B)—others use multiple factors.

Size Indexes

This discussion of style index construction begins with size because size indexes are built first; index constructors do not assign growth or value designations to stocks at the broad market level. They first break up the broad market into size-specific indexes and then subdivide the size indexes into style subindexes. This approach is sensible because style factors interact with the size factor. For example, large-cap stocks tend to have higher P/Bs. If style were determined at the broad market level, growth indexes would be biased toward large-cap stocks and value indexes would be even more biased than they are toward small-cap stocks.

Although determining the capitalization of a stock is relatively straightforward (the only controversial aspect being float adjustment), the various index constructors differ on how to divide stocks into large-, mid-, and small-cap categories. Table 2.7 outlines the methodology for each major suite of indexes. (Capitalization statistics and fundamental characteristics for the size indexes and the style indexes are provided later.)

Size indexes also differ in the timing of their reconstitutions, rules for rebalancing because of changing numbers of shares and other corporate actions, rules for deleting stocks and (potentially) replacing them, and many other variables. Before moving on to style indexes, I will briefly touch on the differences between the principal suites of size indexes.

Standard & Poor's.   The S&P 500 Index was originally created as a broad-cap index; only more recently has the S&P 500 been viewed as a large-cap index and the S&P 400 (mid-cap) and S&P 600 (small cap) been added. The S&P indexes are not governed by strict market-cap guidelines and include companies regarded by the S&P index committee as "industry leaders" or "representative companies" regardless of their market cap. For all indexes constructed by Standard & Poor's, inclusion and removal decisions are made by the index committee rather than by formulaic decision rules.

Frank Russell Company.   The Frank Russell Company developed its Top 200 and mid-cap indexes as subsets of the Russell 1000. The company refers to the Russell 1000 as

TABLE 2.7   Size Index Inclusion Criteria

Provider	Large	Mid Cap	Small Cap
S&P	Committee selection of 500 industry-leading companies	Committee selection of 400 companies	Committee selection of 600 companies
Russell	Top 200 companies by market cap at reconstitution date	Next 800 companies (ranked 201 to 1,000 by market cap)	Next 2,000 companies (ranked 1,001 to 3,000 by market cap)
Dow Jones	Top 70 percent of float-adjusted market cap	Next 20 percent of float-adjusted cap (70–90%)	Next 5 percent (90–95%)
Wilshire Style	Top 750 companies by market cap	500 companies ranked 501 to 1,000; combination of large cap and small cap	Next 1,750 after large cap (ranked 751 to 2,500)

"representing large-cap stocks" and uses the trademark "Top 200" to differentiate this specialized index from the Russell 1000, which I am treating as a large- and mid-cap index.

Dow Jones.   Unlike the other index constructors, Dow Jones has implemented buffer rules to reduce turnover within the capitalization indexes. For example, a large-cap company that ranks in the top 75 percent of the capitalization of the market will not be deleted from the large-cap index even though it needs to rank in the top 70 percent to be included in the first place. Similar buffer rules apply to the other capitalization strata.[70]

Wilshire Style.   Wilshire Associates constructs two suites of indexes, called "style" and "target" indexes. The style indexes are calculated "to evaluate the performance of active managers," and the target indexes represent more concentrated portfolios intended to be held as style index funds. Throughout this section, I refer only to the style indexes and use the phrase "Wilshire Style" consistently to clarify that point. The mid-cap Wilshire Style index is not a separate segment of the overall market, but an overlay consisting of the bottom 250 stocks in the large-cap Wilshire Style index plus the top 250 stocks in the small-cap Wilshire Style index.

Creating the Style Indexes

All of the index constructors draw on the research findings discussed earlier in this section, but the four major constructors differ in the way they define their growth and value indexes. The only common threads are that they assign style at the capitalization level and that they use P/Bs as at least part of the input. The indexes differ as to what factors besides P/B, if any, to use and how the factors are used to assign stocks to one category or another. Table 2.8 summarizes their construction rules. The most important differences between the suites of style indexes are as follows.

TABLE 2.8   Style Index Construction Rules

Provider	Exclusive or Split Classification[a]	Value + Growth Indexes Sum to Market	Transparency of Factor Model	Factors
S&P	Exclusive	Yes	Transparent—ranking by one variable	P/B
Russell	Split	Yes	Proprietary (not transparent)	P/B I/B/E/S long-term growth estimate
Dow Jones	Exclusive	No	Proprietary (not transparent)	P/B Projected P/E Projected EPS growth Trailing P/E Trailing EPS growth Dividend yield
Wilshire Style	Exclusive	No	Partly transparent	P/B Projected P/E

[a]Exclusive: 100 percent of the capitalization of each stock is assigned to a single style (value, growth, or in some cases, core). Split: The cap of a stock may be split between value and growth.

Standard & Poor's.   For each capitalization index, S&P uses the rank of the stocks by P/B to split the total cap of that stratum so that 50 percent is in the value index and 50 percent is in the growth index. In other words, each company is classified as "all growth" or "all value" on the basis of its P/B as of the reconstitution day. Because growth companies tend to be larger than value companies, the growth index has fewer stocks than the value index.

Frank Russell Company.   The factors used by Russell are P/B and the I/B/E/S consensus long-term growth average (that is, one accounting ratio and one projection or estimate).[71] The total capitalization of the market is split 50–50, but Russell uses an algorithm to classify each stock into one of three categories—all value, all growth, or split between the two. The result is that 70 percent of stocks are 100 percent growth or value and 30 percent are split. The splits are typically uneven (for example, a stock might be, depending on its P/B and estimated growth rate, 25 percent value and 75 percent growth). Russell does not publish the style algorithm, which was created in 1993.

Russell assigns style at the Russell 1000 level and breaks this index up into large cap and mid cap. The result, because large-cap stocks naturally trade at a higher P/B, is that 55 percent of the Russell Top 200 is classified as growth, whereas only 40 percent of the Russell Midcap is classified this way.

Dow Jones.   Dow Jones uses six factors—P/B, projected and trailing P/E, projected and trailing earnings per share (EPS) growth, and dividend yield. Thus, Dow Jones combines a wide variety of historical and projected data. Like Russell, Dow Jones has a proprietary statistical process to translate the raw data into growth–value splits. Each stock is classified as 100 percent growth, 100 percent value, or neutral. Unlike the other index providers, Dow Jones does not split the total capitalization of the market evenly between growth and value.

Wilshire Style.   For each capitalization index, Wilshire classifies stocks into styles by P/B and projected P/E, with P/B given three times the weight of P/E. The total capitalization of the market is split 50–50, and stocks are classified as either 100 percent growth or 100 percent value.

Capitalization statistics of the principal style indexes are in Table 2.9. The relationship between style and size index construction methods, on the one hand, and the performance of those indexes, on the other hand, could and should be a book in itself and is not covered here. Suffice it to say that the performance differences between different equity indexes purporting to measure the same style or size category tend to be large, whereas the performance differences between most other types of indexes are small.

Trade-Offs in Style Index Construction

Because it is important to understand the fine points of style index construction before selecting and using a suite of indexes, this section provides a detailed discussion of the trade-offs in constructing style indexes.

How many style factors? Simplicity vs. explanatory power.   P/B (or its inverse, B/P) is the one factor that is used, at least in part, by all of the index constructors. Its use is supported by the work of Sharpe (1988, 1992) and Fama and French (1993). Standard & Poor's uses only the P/B to classify stocks. The other index providers use other factors in addition to P/B and use them in a variety of ways.

A small number of style factors achieves the virtues of simplicity and transparency. The only set of indexes constructed by sorting stocks on the basis of one variable is that created

TABLE 2.9   Capitalization Statistics of Principal U.S. Equity Size and Style Indexes, 31 December 2002 ($ in thousands)

Style/Statistic	S&P	Russell[b]	Dow Jones Total Market	Wilshire Style
Large cap				
Number of stocks	500	198	215	743
Market cap of total index ($)	8,107,546,624	6,349,761,024	6,481,344,000	8,850,116,608
Largest-stock cap ($)	276,411,456	241,984,720	242,269,616	276,411,456
Smallest-stock cap ($)	279,286	3,246,933	2,199,620	193,899
Weighted-average market cap ($)	76,711,000	89,776,000	88,190,000	71,479,000
Historical inception date	January 1926[a]	January 1979	December 1991	January 1978
Mid cap				
Number of stocks	400	793	504	497
Market cap of total index ($)	702,908,736	2,040,461,696	1,690,023,168	819,479,872
Largest-stock cap ($)	7,292,344	10,345,811	10,213,473	11,124,001
Smallest-stock cap ($)	132,473	120,150	265,080	144,647
Weighted-average market cap ($)	2,513,000	4,562,000	4,933,000	1,997,000
Historical inception date	February 1981[c]	January 1979	December 1991	January 1978
Small cap				
Number of stocks	600	1,964	859	1,729
Market cap of total index ($)	325,187,456	601,010,432	654,667,392	952,756,416
Largest-stock cap ($)	2,685,695	1,769,077	3,030,933	5,032,104
Smallest-stock cap ($)	39,165	3,790	26,455	13,494
Weighted-average market cap ($)	832,000	628,000	1,246,000	878,000
Historical inception date	March 1984[c]	January 1979	December 1991	January 1978
Large-cap value				
Number of stocks	352	143	113	496
Market cap of total index ($)	4,023,928,320	2,952,911,872	3,494,580,736	4,327,615,488
Largest-stock cap ($)	235,107,696	236,963,808	236,104,992	180,745,248
Smallest-stock cap ($)	279,286	673,222	4,070,547	193,899
Weighted-average market cap ($)	51,645,000	71,860,000	76,045,000	849,000
Historical inception date	January 1975	January 1986	June 1997	January 1978
Mid-cap value				
Number of stocks	241	607	204	243
Market cap of total index ($)	356,468,288	1,187,835,264	752,874,432	393,134,336
Largest-stock cap ($)	4,895,093	10,222,605	10,213,473	3,799,880
Smallest-stock cap ($)	132,473	15,953	318,053	438,214
Weighted-average market cap ($)	2,079,000	4,362,000	4,988,000	1,850,000
Historical inception date	June 1991[c]	January 1986	June 1997	January 1978

TABLE 2.9   (*Continued*)

Style/Statistic	S&P	Russell[b]	Dow Jones Total Market	Wilshire Style
Small-cap value				
Number of stocks	390	1,325	295	890
Market cap of total index ($)	163,973,888	307,850,816	251,129,552	459,626,496
Largest-stock cap ($)	1,602,840	1,358,273	2,265,744	5,032,104
Smallest-stock cap ($)	39,165	2,031	26,455	13,494
Weighted-average market cap ($)	613,000	609,000	1,263,000	874,000[d]
Historical inception date	January 1994[c]	January 1979	June 1997	January 1978
Large-cap growth				
Number of stocks	500	198	215	743
Market cap of total index ($)	8,107,546,624	6,349,761,024	6,481,344,000	8,850,116,608
Largest-stock cap ($)	276,411,456	241,984,720	242,269,616	276,411,456
Smallest-stock cap ($)	279,286	3,246,933	2,199,620	193,899
Weighted-average market cap ($)	76,711,000	89,776,000	88,190,000	71,479,000
Historical inception date	January 1975	January 1986	June 1997	January 1978
Mid-cap growth				
Number of stocks	159	454	189	254
Market cap of total index ($)	346,440,672	852,627,008	600,589,504	426,346,080
Largest-stock cap ($)	7,292,344	10,345,811	9,966,566	11,124,001
Smallest-stock cap ($)	334,565	13,402	347,146	144,647
Weighted-average market cap ($)	2,959,000	4,840,000	4,983,000	2,132,000
Historical inception date	June 1991[c]	January 1986	June 1997	January 1978
Small-cap growth				
Number of stocks	210	1,278	286	839
Market cap of total index ($)	161,213,376	293,159,456	192,439,200	493,131,040
Largest-stock cap ($)	2,685,695	1,530,137	3,030,933	3,900,638
Smallest-stock cap ($)	81,995	1,150	45,269	16,684
Weighted-average market cap ($)	1,055,000	648,000	1,202,000	99,362,000
Historical inception date	January 1994[c]	January 1979	June 1997	January 1978

[a]The S&P 500 data start March 1957 and have been linked by Ibbotson Associates (2003) with a predecessor index, the S&P 90, to form a continuous series from 1926 to the present.

[b]The Russell large-cap index described here is the Top 200. The Russell 1000 (Top 200 plus mid-cap 800) is also sometimes referred to as a large-cap index.

[c]Survival biases are known to affect the historically reconstructed S&P mid-cap and small-cap indexes, including style indexes.

[d]Data as of 30 June 2003.

Source: Pope, Rakvin, and Platt (2003).

by S&P (which does, however, apply judgment in building the size indexes out of which the style subindexes are carved). Any combination of variables introduces a degree of opaqueness. Price, book value, and earnings are public information, so investors and managers can predict with considerable accuracy the results of a sorting of stocks by *either* P/B or P/E. When the P/B and P/E factors are combined, however, as in the Wilshire indexes, the investor would have to know the precise algorithm to correctly predict the results of the index reconstitution (it is not enough to know that P/B has three times the weight of P/E).

All other things being equal, a predictable and transparent style classification system reduces transaction costs. The major reason is that brokers and hedge funds create liquidity in anticipation of style index reconstitutions by buying stocks they think they can sell to index funds and benchmark-sensitive active funds and by shorting stocks they think they can buy from these funds. The ability of brokers and hedge funds to create liquidity in this way—and, correspondingly, the ability of indexers and index-sensitive active managers to keep their transaction costs under control—depends on the simplicity and transparency of the style classification system.

On the one hand, because book value is less volatile than earnings, an index constructed by using only book value and price produces more stable portfolios and thus lower transaction costs upon reconstitution. Moreover, proponents of P/B as the sole factor argue that the price-to-book ratio captures all the relevant information contained in the other factors. If it does, then using additional factors is simply redundant, in addition to subtracting from transparency. Furthermore, projected data (such as expected earnings growth) are subject to interpretation and revision, in contrast to accounting data, which are relatively fixed once the numbers are released. The problems with expected earnings growth are especially severe for small-cap stocks that are covered by few analysts.

On the other hand, it is not clear how book value could be so powerful in explaining the cross-section of stock returns that it wipes out the effect of P/E, growth expectations, and other potential factors. Book value is mostly a historical accident. It is the accounting profession's estimate of the company's value; it reflects what the company paid for its assets, except intangible assets, such as goodwill developed internally, but it includes the goodwill of subsidiary companies acquired by purchase. This "cost basis" is then adjusted downward by depreciation and amortization in a highly stylized and rigid attempt to reflect the economic depreciation that actually befalls (most) assets. Off-balance-sheet items are ignored. Finally, the result is augmented by retained earnings. With book value reflecting such a mélange, it is a wonder it has any explanatory power at all for differentiating value from growth stocks—but it does.

Logically, then, additional factors should provide additional information. Because, for example, "growth" might not be the exact opposite of "value," investors might be especially interested in the incremental explanatory power of factors that have nothing to do with valuation but, instead, reflect historical growth and/or expectations for future growth.

A multifactor approach to equity style classification was pioneered by Rosenberg, Reid, and Lanstein (1985). Although this topic has not attracted much subsequent attention from academics, who have mostly focused on P/B as the single style metric, the various index providers who use multifactor methods have done extensive research to support these methods.

Some analysts claim, in support of a multifactor approach, that P/B does not properly describe certain sectors. For example, companies in the technology sector may have understated book values because of intangible assets that are not capitalized. The result is that technology companies have elevated P/Bs, which classifies most of them as growth whether they should be or not. Including other factors could help overcome problems with P/Bs in describing style.

Completeness vs. style purity.   One generally desirable trait of a set of style indexes is that they sum to the overall broad market index. When they do, investors can build a complete asset-allocation strategy—one that does not exclude important components of the market—by combining various style indexes.

The disadvantage of value and growth indexes that sum to the market is that such indexes are not "style pure." The value index includes many stocks (often with large weights) that are actually style neutral or somewhat "growthy." Similarly, the growth index includes stocks that could be construed as neutral or value stocks. By excluding core or neutral stocks, an index constructor provides a better representation of the universes from which style-focused active managers typically select their stocks. Style-pure indexes also provide better return differentiation for the purpose of measuring historical returns and understanding the behavior of the value and growth styles.

The S&P and Russell style indexes do sum to the market portfolio. This attribute is called "completeness." Subindexes that sum to a broader index are also sometimes called a "spanning set."

The Dow Jones value and growth indexes are not a spanning set because they exclude core or neutral stocks; they are thus more style pure than S&P and Russell style indexes. Dow Jones' neutral classification is not investable because performance and constituent (stock) weights are not calculated for this category. Furthermore, Dow Jones requires that each company have data for at least one projected factor and at least three historical factors (out of the six total factors). If a company fails to meet this requirement, it is removed from the universe entirely. This rule is likely to exclude most initial public offerings. Even if you could purchase the neutral index, the broad market index could not be re-created using Dow Jones style indexes since the IPOs would be missing.

The Wilshire Style value and growth indexes do sum to the size stratum of the market from which they are drawn. The mid-cap index, however, is an overlay consisting of some stocks from the small-cap index and some from the large-cap index. Thus, an investor would not be able to exclude mid-cap stocks from an otherwise broad market strategy by using Wilshire Style indexes. An investor could include mid-caps (without double weighting them), however, simply by buying the large-and small-cap indexes and avoiding the mid-cap overlay.

Morningstar, the leading provider of mutual fund data and ratings to retail investors, has a style classification system in which core is a separate style and the returns and index contents are tracked (see Phillips and Kaplan 2003). Morningstar's system, however, has not yet attracted a meaningful institutional following.

Exclusive vs. split classification.   The question of whether to split a stock's capitalization between value and growth indexes is separate from the completeness or spanning question. Most sets of indexes (S&P, Dow Jones, and Wilshire Style) have a requirement that each stock be classified as 100 percent value or 100 percent growth (or, in the case of Wilshire Style, 100 percent neutral). Alternatively, an index provider could split the capitalization of a stock between growth and value so that the name appears in both the value and growth indexes, as Russell does.

As market prices and fundamental variables change, stocks move between the value and growth categories. Being able to split a stock reflects the fact that many stocks are in transition between the categories, and it reduces turnover, which is costly to investors. (Splitting reduces turnover because stocks close to the value–growth boundary do not have 100 percent of their capitalization jump back and forth from one category to another.) It also expands the selection universe for managers who choose from among the stocks in their style benchmark.

Style indexes created by splitting stocks may be confusing at first, however, because many of the same companies appear in both value and growth indexes. The index constructors who use buffer rules argue that reduction in turnover may be accomplished as effectively by using these rules as by splitting the capitalization of stocks between two different style indexes.

Reconstitution/rebalancing frequency vs. turnover. As noted in the section titled Origins, Uses, and Characteristics of U.S. Equity Benchmarks, reconstitution and rebalancing are sources of turnover, which, in turn, imposes transaction costs on investors. Turnover-related costs in style indexes are particularly sensitive to reconstitution frequency because a company can migrate back and forth between styles. The capitalization splits and buffer rules that are used by some index constructors mitigate this problem.

I now review the reconstitution and rebalancing practices of each major provider. Because the basic (not style) S&P indexes contain a fixed number of stocks and membership is decided by committee, these indexes are essentially reconstituted on an *ad hoc* basis. Any company deleted because of a corporate action (e.g., merger) is replaced by another company selected by the index committee. Additionally, Standard & Poor's may remove companies at the committee's discretion. Standard & Poor's also rebalances its indexes each quarter because of changes in the constituent companies' numbers of shares outstanding. The S&P style indexes are reconstituted semiannually.

The Frank Russell Company reconstitutes its indexes annually and does not replace companies between reconstitutions, so deletions resulting from corporate actions do not result in additional membership changes. Instead, the number of companies in the index shrinks until the next reconstitution date. Russell rebalances the index monthly to reflect changes in the number of shares.

The bulk of Russell's reconstitution of its capitalization, style, and overall indexes is done at the end of each June. Capitalization and style classifications occur only during this time and do not change during the following year.

The predictability and magnitude of the Russell reconstitution attracts a great deal of speculation from index funds and benchmark-sensitive managers attempting to trade ahead of the reconstitution and from brokers and hedge funds taking the other side of the trade. These attempts to profit from the anticipated reconstitution often result in temporary price distortions (see "Russell Mania" in the section titled The Impact of Benchmarking on Markets and Institutions).

Like Russell, Dow Jones adds companies only during the scheduled quarterly reconstitutions of its size and style indexes. Rebalancing because of changes in shares outstanding for index constituents is also done quarterly. The only adjustments made between reconstitutions are those resulting from corporate actions, which causes the number of stocks in the Dow Jones indexes to shrink because deleted companies are not replaced until the next reconstitution.

Wilshire updates its overall universe monthly. The number of shares outstanding for each company is updated, and IPOs are added to the index. The capitalization and style indexes, however, are reconstituted only once a year.

Conclusion

U.S. equity style indexes developed out of the traditional methods that managers historically used to identify desirable stocks. These methods coalesced into "styles" as academic researchers sought, and found, common factors in the stock market. These common factors define the styles that are the basis for the style benchmarks now offered by commercial providers.

The style indexes differ in construction, rules, and level of transparency. Each index constructor has a unique "take" on style, and the resulting construction method has profound implications for index performance, index fund management, active portfolio management, and asset allocation. The differences among returns of different equity styles and capitalizations (sizes) are the most surprising and powerful effects in finance. Investors would do well to consider the issues raised in this section before selecting a specific index for use in asset allocation, benchmarking, or performance measurement.

FIXED-INCOME BENCHMARKS

Fixed-income benchmarks embody a great many complex issues, of which I will touch on only a few of the most important here. After an introductory section on the basics of fixed-income benchmarks, I address two issues: the duration problem and the "bums" problem.[72] These issues arise because fixed-income benchmarks are capitalization weighted and all-inclusive. The duration problem is the fact that the duration of the benchmark comes from issuer preferences and is not necessarily the duration that a given investor should hold. The bums (or deadbeats) problem is that the biggest debtors (whether companies, countries, or other entities) have the largest weights in the benchmark.[73]

I will also comment briefly on the risk posed by the growing weight of the credit (corporate bond) component of leading benchmarks at the same time that corporate bonds themselves have become riskier.

The Complex World of Fixed-Income Benchmarks

Unlike equities, which represent ownership interests in unique businesses and which are notoriously hard to group into meaningful categories, fixed-income assets have closely specified cash flows and other properties that make them easy to classify into distinct groupings. Table 2.10 is an "index map" constructed by Lehman Brothers, a major bond dealer and the source of one of the industry's principal suites of indexes. It shows the particular Lehman benchmark for each main type of bond around the world. Note that these are the gross, not fine, divisions of the bond market; Table 2.11 shows some (not all) of the breakdowns within one of the segments, the Lehman Brothers U.S. Aggregate Bond Index. To provide some perspective on the size of each segment, Table 2.11 also shows the market capitalization of each benchmark. (Note that the benchmarks are "nested," so you cannot add the capitalizations of the benchmarks to arrive at the capitalization of the total market.) Other index providers categorize the fixed-income market along the same lines.

This granularity is made possible by the highly specified nature of a bond contract. The term to maturity, type of issuer, currency in which the bond pays interest and principal, priority of claims on the issuer's assets in case of insolvency, "call" or prepayment provisions, and other characteristics form the basis for an index map. Two bonds with similar characteristics will be in the same category or sub-benchmark and will also have similar returns, although no two bonds are identical. As a result, what academics sometimes call "mapping an asset into characteristic space," which refers to analytically breaking up an asset into its most elemental parts so that its returns and other properties can be accurately understood and forecasted, is not only possible but also relatively easy for bonds.[74] The many highly specific benchmarks enumerated in Table 2.10 and Table 2.11 are the outcome of this mapping. Simply knowing

TABLE 2.10   Lehman Brothers Family of Fixed-Income Indexes

Global	U.S. and Canada	Europe	Asia
Multiverse	U.S. Universal	Pan European Universal	Asian Pacific Aggregate
Global Aggregate	U.S. Aggregate	• Euro	• Japan
• Details	• Govt/Credit	Pan European Aggregate	• Non-Japan
• Ex-JPY	• Government	• Euro-Aggregate	• Australian Dollar
• Ex-JPY ex-Securitized	• Credit	Government	Aggregate
• Ex-USD	Details	Credit	Euro Yen
• Ex-Euro	• Securitized	Details	Asia Credit
Global High Yield	• Flash Report	Securitized	Swaps
Global Treasury	U.S. High Yield	• Sterling Aggregate	Customized
Global Credit	• Details	• Swedish Krona	
Global Securitized	Municipals	Aggregate	
Global Real	Canadian	• Danish Krone	
Capital Securities	Other indexes	Aggregate	
Customized	• Euro Dollar	• Norwegian Krone	
	• Hourly Treasury	Aggregate	
	• Short Treasury	Pan-European High Yield	
	• Bellwethers	• Details	
	• 144A	• Euro	
	• CMBS[a]	• Non-Euro	
	• Private Placement	Swiss Franc Aggregate	
	• Corporate Loan	Danish Mortgages	
	• Swaps	Swaps	
	U.S. Convertibles	• Euro	
	Customized	• Sterling	
		Customized	

[a]Commercial mortgage-backed securities.

Source: Lehman Brothers Global Family of Indices reprinted by permission of Lehman Brothers.

the name of a benchmark provides you with a good clue as to what kinds of bonds are in it, and if you have a working understanding of what duration, credit quality, prepayment provisions, and other characteristics imply for the bond's behavior, you can deduce from the fact that a given bond is in a given benchmark most of what you need to know about that bond. (But I don't want to get carried away. A bond can, for example, have a misleading credit rating, so credit analysts can add value by avoiding overrated bonds and buying underrated ones.)

Also note that in the bond market, a single issuer typically has a number of different bond issues outstanding, with different durations and possibly other characteristics that differ from one bond issue to another. That same issuer, if it is a corporation, typically has only one class of equity shares outstanding. The reason is not only that bonds mature (making multiple issues necessary simply to provide continuous financing for the issuer's activities) but also

TABLE 2.11 Detailed Sector Breakdown of Lehman U.S. Aggregate, 23 April 2003
($ in millions)

Index	Market Cap	Index	Market Cap
U.S. Aggregate[a]		*Noncorporate sectors*	
Aaa	$7,946,126	Sovereign	$123,298
Aa	5,980,626	Intermediate	91,897
A	403,252	Long	31,400
Baa	818,320	Supranational	94,997
1–3 year	743,927	Intermediate	85,804
3–5 year	2,072,759	Long	9,193
5–7 year	2,272,284	Foreign agency	52,248
7–10 year	1,164,223	Intermediate	51,327
10+ year	1,262,647	Long	921
	1,174,213	Foreign local government	57,390
		Intermediate	34,538
Sectors		Long	22,852
Intermediate Aggregate	$6,782,703		
U.S. Govt/Credit	4,833,257	*Securitized*	$3,112,869
Intermediate	3,669,835	CMBS	188,138
Long	1,163,422	ABS[b]	151,641
U.S. Government	2,699,308	Credit card	50,330
Intermediate	2,026,225	Auto	41,325
Long	673,083	Home equity	27,390
1–3 year	984,771	Utility	18,882
U.S. Treasury	1,686,062	Manufacturing housing	13,713
Intermediate	1,129,215	Aaa only	139,785
Long	556,847	MBS fixed rate[c]	2,773,090
Treasury 20+ year	209,712	GNMA[d]	451,510
U.S. Agency	1,013,245	GNMA 15 year	19,021
Intermediate	897,010	GNMA 30 year	432,489
Long	116,236	FHLMC[e]	986,911
U.S. Credit	2,133,949	FHLMC 15 year	286,984
Intermediate	1,643,610	FHLMC 20 year	49,422
Long	490,339	FHLMC 30 year	625,636
Corporate	1,806,016	FHLMC balloon	24,869
Intermediate	1,380,044	FNMA[f]	1,334,669
Long	425,972	FNMA 15 year	328,052
Noncorporate	327,933	FNMA 20 year	40,735
Intermediate	263,566	FNMA 30 year	953,981
Long	64,367	FNMA balloon	11,902
Corporate sectors		*Other sectors*	
Industrial	$912,067	Yankee	$503,900
Intermediate	624,495	Intermediate	393,748
Long	287,572	Long	110,152
Utility	171,753		
Intermediate	129,219		
Long	42,534		
Financial institutions	722,196		
Intermediate	626,330		
Long	95,866		

[a]Rating grades of Moody's Investors Service.
[b]Asset-backed securities.
[c]Mortgage-backed securities.
[d]Government National Mortgage Association.
[e]Federal Home Loan Mortgage Corporation.
[f]Federal National Mortgage Association.

Source: Lehman Brothers.

that issuers try to take advantage of the changing shape of yield curves, quirks in regulations and tax laws, and clientele effects.

For these reasons, bond portfolio management has a very different character from equity portfolio management. There are a great many more bonds than stocks in the market.[75] Although most large-cap U.S. equity portfolios have quite a few stocks in common, bond portfolios with similar goals and attributes may not have any issues in common. And although many practitioners of equity research and portfolio management regard their activity as a mixture of art and science, bond management is mostly science, and individuals with advanced mathematical or scientific training tend to be the best at it.

Capitalization Weighting of Fixed-Income Benchmarks

Cap-weighted benchmarks have become standard for almost all asset classes, including fixed income. This practice originated with equities, for which, according to the capital asset pricing model, such a benchmark is the mean–variance-efficient portfolio if you do not have special insight into the value of any particular security (see the section titled The Evolution of MPT and the Benchmarking Paradigm). Equity benchmarks are also typically all-inclusive, in the sense of containing every security that meets the criteria for inclusion; this practice also has been applied to bonds. Extending these equity-based practices to fixed-income securities makes benchmark construction easy, but it does not necessarily make the benchmark a good investment. First, the theoretical argument that the market portfolio of bonds is efficient is much more tenuous than it is for equities.[76] Second, the most highly indebted companies get the biggest benchmark weights (the bums problem). Cap-weighted, all-inclusive benchmarks are useful for performance evaluation, however, because active management against such a benchmark is a zero-sum game by definition.

All-inclusiveness has consequences for liquidity in the bond markets. In equity markets, the stocks making up the lion's share of any cap-weighted benchmark—even the very broad Wilshire 5000—are fairly liquid. The bond market, however, is almost exclusively a dealer market (that is, the investor must buy the bond from the dealer's inventory and sell the bond back to the dealer). As a result, many issues in an all-inclusive bond benchmark, especially corporate issues, are difficult to trade, and price-pressure effects are substantial. Bond portfolio managers thus find tracking the benchmarks, either through sampling or full replication, to be difficult. A number of bond index funds exist, and they track the indexes well, but a fund must be very large to do so because of the large number of bonds in the benchmark and the large order sizes required to get reasonably good execution.[77]

The Duration Problem

The duration structure of a cap-weighted bond benchmark—that is, the proportions of bonds in short-, intermediate-, and long-term categories—reflects the maturity or duration preferences of issuers, who are seeking to minimize their (apparent) cost of capital.[78] Investors, however, are not trying to minimize their returns (which are the issuers' costs of capital) but to maximize returns. Moreover, an investor usually has specific time-horizon preferences that make one duration more advantageous than another. These preferences do not necessarily match those of issuers in the aggregate, whose preferences are reflected in the benchmark. This concept is expressed in the "preferred habitat theory" in the context of explaining why yield curves behave as they do.[79]

For example, defined-benefit pension plans have long-term nominal liabilities and, therefore, consider long-term bonds to be low-risk investments because the duration of the bonds roughly equals the duration of the liabilities. Because of demand from this clientele, the U.S. Treasury and other issuers need to pay only a modest yield premium for long bonds, despite the much greater volatility of these issues. The other major clientele—investors who are concerned about volatility as well as return and who have no specifically defined nominal liabilities—see long bonds as higher-risk investments and thus tend to find these bonds less attractive, at roughly the same yields, than other issues. Investors in this latter category include individuals, endowments, and foundations.

As a result, there is an optimal solution for each investor, not one optimal solution for all investors. No investor—not even one with no defined time horizon at all—should necessarily hold the benchmark duration. Because the benchmark duration is a historical accident, the optimal portfolio for an investor with no defined time horizon should be set by that investor's risk tolerance rather than by matching the duration of the benchmark.

Put another way, a duration is like a beta. It is a factor exposure. Beta is exposure to the equity market factor; duration is exposure to the interest rate factor. The choice of the duration or beta to hold is an asset-allocation decision. In equities, investors typically, and most efficiently, make such decisions by adjusting up or down the proportion of equities in their overall asset mixes, not by holding low- or high-beta stocks. In fixed income, however, adjusting the duration within the portfolio is much more practical than holding a market-duration portfolio and then "levering" the duration up or down to the desired level using cash or derivatives. Because issuers do not have to pay a great deal of yield or return premium to float long-term issues, given the demand for such issues from pension funds and other investors with long-term liabilities, duration extension does not provide much of a risk premium. This assertion is supported by the data in Table 2.12. In 1976–2002, the Lehman U.S. Aggregate, representing the full spectrum of maturities in the fixed-income market, outperformed the intermediate version of that benchmark by only 0.15 percentage points (pps) a year while taking appreciably more risk; as a result, the Sharpe ratio, which measures the reward per unit of risk taken, is lower for the Aggregate than for the Intermediate Aggregate. Because growth in the mortgage market greatly influenced the performance of the Aggregate in this period, the results from comparing these two indexes might be distorted. To remove the distortion, I compared the results for the Lehman Brothers Government/Credit Bond Index and its intermediate counterpart; these indexes do not include mortgages. Table 2.12 shows the return advantage of the longer-maturity Government/Credit Index to be 0.30 pps a year, still not enough to give it a higher Sharpe ratio than the Intermediate Government/Credit Index. In other words, the slope representing the additional return per unit of duration risk taken is not steep. I found similar results when I broke the 1976–2002 period into subperiods.

Thus, although investors with long-duration liabilities, such as pension funds, should hold long-duration fixed-income portfolios, most other categories of investors should avoid these bonds. Many institutional investors have addressed these concerns by adopting intermediate-duration benchmarks, such as the Lehman Brothers Intermediate Aggregate Bond Index, rather than broad market benchmarks.

The Bums Problem

Because the issuers who manage to go deepest into debt—the biggest bums—have the largest weights in a cap-weighted benchmark, such a benchmark is not likely to be mean–variance efficient. If you are tracking such a benchmark, when someone issues a security, you have to buy it in proportion to its capitalization weight to minimize tracking error to the benchmark, even if the security is only marginally of high enough quality to make it into the benchmark

TABLE 2.12   Summary Statistics for Performance of Leading Fixed-Income Indexes,
January 1976–December 2002

Index	Compound Annual Return	Standard Deviation	Sharpe Ratio[a]
Lehman Intermediate Aggregate	9.19%	5.43%	0.512
Lehman Aggregate	9.34	6.64	0.449
Lehman Intermediate Govt/Credit	9.00	4.96	0.516
Lehman Govt/Credit	9.30	6.59	0.446
T-bills[b]	6.54	0.87	0.000

[a]Calculated with the T-bill return (see next note) as the riskless asset.
[b]U.S. T-bills with an average of 30 days remaining to maturity, from Ibbotson Associates (2003).

Sources: Lehman Brothers; Ibbotson Associates.

and even if the size of the issue, and hence its weight in the benchmark, is inordinately large. Such securities would seem to be the most likely to be downgraded or to default. The bums problem applies to countries in an international sovereign bond benchmark just as it does to corporations in a U.S. bond benchmark.

Although the bums problem is probably best appreciated relative to corporate bonds, the international sovereign bond market provides a more clear-cut example of it (because the data are readily available). Table 2.13 shows the weights of various countries in the non-U.S. component of the Citigroup World Government Bond Index (WGBI) as of early 2003.[80] By far the largest weight in the benchmark is Japan, a country that has been in a 13-year bear market involving multiple recessions (sometimes collectively referred to as a depression). A generation ago (until 1966), Japan was constitutionally forbidden to issue debt and Italy had an outsize weight in the index, at least relative to that country's economy. So, holding the benchmark seems to be a bet on whatever country has most profoundly mismanaged its public finances. This bet sometimes works out well: Italy was a strong performer because it became a developed market between 1966 and today and because "convergence" on the way to the formation of the euro caused yields to decline. But the harmonization of Europe is a once-in-a-lifetime event, maybe once in a millennium. A large position in lira-denominated bonds did not seem prudent in the 1960s, and a 35 percent position in yen-denominated bonds does not seem prudent now.

Credit Market Growth and Volatility

A final issue related to fixed-income benchmarks arises from the recent growth in the size of the credit (corporate bond) market at a time when corporate bonds were individually becoming riskier. The interaction of these two factors has caused broad bond benchmarks (the Lehman Aggregate, Lehman Government/Credit, and so forth) to be riskier today than they were historically.

Table 2.14 shows the changing composition of four such benchmarks. Although the trend over the very long term is the displacement of corporate bonds by mortgage-backed securities (MBS) and asset-backed securities (ABS), which bond managers collectively refer to

TABLE 2.13   Country Weights of Non-U.S.
Component of Citigroup WGBI, 20 February 2003

Country	Weight
Australia	0.4%
Belgium	3.8
Canada	3.0
Denmark	1.2
France	10.2
Germany	11.3
Italy	12.1
Japan	35.1
Netherlands	2.8
Spain	4.6
Sweden	0.8
United Kingdom	8.0
Others	6.8

Source: Citigroup.

TABLE 2.14   Changing Composition of Bond Benchmarks

Index	1976	1986	1991	1996	1997	1998	1999	2000	2001	2002
Lehman Govt/Credit										
Treasury	35%	64%	65%	65%	62%	56%	52%	44%	36%	36%
Agency	17	11	10	9	10	12	14	18	19	20
Credit	46	25	24	26	28	32	34	38	45	44
Lehman Aggregate										
Treasury	32%	48%	45%	45%	43%	38%	33%	27%	22%	21%
Agency	15	8	7	7	7	8	9	11	11	12
MBS/ABS	11	25	31	31	31	32	36	38	39	40
Credit	42	19	17	18	19	22	22	24	27	26
Lehman Intermediate Govt/Credit										
Treasury	56%	69%	69%	67%	65%	56%	50%	39%	32%	31%
Agency	24	15	12	10	10	14	17	21	23	24
Credit	20	16	19	23	25	29	33	40	45	45
Lehman Intermediate Aggregate										
Treasury	51%	48%	41%	42%	39%	33%	27%	21%	17%	16%
Agency	22	10	7	6	6	9	9	11	12	13
MBS/ABS	18	11	12	14	15	17	18	21	24	24
Credit	9	30	40	38	39	41	45	47	46	47

Notes: Data for 2002 are as of 29 June; data for other years are as of 31 December. Columns do not sum to 100 percent because of rounding.

Source: Lehman Brothers. Table data originally appeared in Johnson and Siegel (2003).

Option-Adjusted Yield Spread (bps)

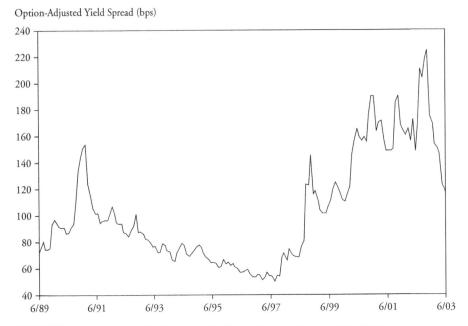

FIGURE 2.3   Yield Spread of Lehman Credit over Treasury Index, 1989–2002

Source: Figure originally appeared in Johnson and Siegel (2003); updated by the author using Lehman Brothers data.

as "mortgages," the more recent trend is a reduction in the size of U.S. Treasury debt and an increase in corporate issues. With $2.2 trillion of the perhaps $5 trillion U.S. corporate bond market having been downgraded in just the two years of 2001 and 2002, the absolute risk in these benchmarks was at or near an all-time high in the fall of 2002, as shown by the yield spread of the Lehman Brothers Credit Bond Index over the Treasury market in Figure 2.3. Although the market then rallied (yield spreads declined), the credit market is still volatile. This is not your father's fixed-income benchmark.

At the same time that corporate bond exposure has made broad fixed-income benchmarks riskier, many fixed-income managers have begun trading bonds like equities—instead of buying and holding them to maturity, as they did a generation ago. This change in behavior is a result of the existence and popularity of cap-weighted fixed-income benchmarks. Increasingly, fixed-income managers regard their job as maximizing active return subject to a penalty for active risk, which is exactly what I suggested in the section titled Using Benchmarks to Measure Performance, that they should be doing. This practice is potentially in conflict, however, with the goals of those fixed-income investors who regard bonds as vehicles for capital preservation, not total return. If you hold bonds as an "anchor to windward"—that is, an investment that preserves its value (and pays a fixed income) while having a low correlation with other assets (such as equities)—maybe you should take less duration risk (and less credit risk) than is found in broad-market bond benchmarks.[81]

Conclusion

Cap-weighted fixed-income benchmarks are a bit of a puzzle. Although they represent the investment opportunities in the asset class, they are unlikely to be an ideal portfolio for any given investor. Nevertheless, active fixed-income management is a zero-sum game relative to a well-constructed cap-weighted benchmark, so performance evaluation can sensibly be conducted by comparing manager returns with benchmark returns—as long as you can simultaneously focus on what the purpose of the fixed-income investment was in the first place.

INTERNATIONAL EQUITY BENCHMARKS

International (that is, non-U.S.) equity benchmarks differ from U.S. equity benchmarks in some distinct ways:[82]

- Float adjustment is much more important for international stocks.
- The convention is to divide international equity markets into developed and emerging categories, and the decision as to which countries belong in which category has consequences for both the benchmarks and the countries' markets.
- An investor/manager must keep track of currencies and construct both local-currency and investor-currency versions of the benchmark.

Expressing benchmark returns in more than one currency is straightforward. Float adjustment and the division of the world into developed and emerging markets, however, are sources of controversy.

The discussion in this section will focus on international equity benchmarks from the viewpoint of U.S. investors. I will also review the trade-offs involved in international equity index construction and touch on the impact of benchmarking in international markets.

Early Development of Indexes

Stock indexes around the world, including the United States, were first typically compiled by newspapers. Examples include the Dow Jones in the United States, the Nikkei in Japan, the DAX in Germany, and the *Financial Times* indexes in the United Kingdom. Such indexes were price-only (not total-return) indexes and were generally not capitalization weighted. Academic or brokerage-affiliated researchers also created stock indexes in some countries.[83] But although stock indexes already existed in a number of countries long before the mid-1960s, the first usable benchmarks were initiated by Nilly Sikorsky of the Capital Group in November 1968.[84] Unlike most inventors who struggle to capitalize on their inventions, the Capital Group's successor company in index construction, Morgan Stanley Capital International (MSCI), became and has remained the dominant provider of international equity indexes.[85]

The Capital Group constructed the MSCI benchmarks to help investors measure active management performance. (Index funds had not been invented yet.) Unlike earlier efforts, the MSCI indexes followed the basic principles of good index construction—market-cap weighting, publication of constituent lists, and historical reconstruction of data so that they would be useful for analyzing asset allocation. These indexes did, however, have one quirk: They sought to capture only 60 percent of the market cap of the countries and sectors they covered. This percentage was small even by the modest standards of the time. MSCI justified this limited capitalization coverage on liquidity grounds and decided that it would be more consistent to have one capitalization coverage standard for all countries rather than cover a larger percentage of capitalization in the more liquid countries, such as the United States and the United Kingdom.

The emergence of international equity indexes of reasonable quality (that is, indexes that were good enough to double as practical benchmarks) meshed nicely with a trend toward internationalization of portfolios that had been developing in the 1970s and that came to the forefront in the 1980s. International portfolios had been available to U.S. investors for a long time, mostly from European managers, such as Robeco. In the late 1970s and early 1980s, however, U.S. investors began to perceive their home country as having inferior economic performance and began more aggressively to seek higher rates of return in booming Japanese, German, and other non-U.S. markets.

U.S. investors in the late 1970s and the 1980s were also influenced by a number of academic studies showing that international investing had delivered a risk premium (Solnik 1974; Bergstrom 1975). Although international stocks had outperformed U.S. stocks in the historical period for which data were available, some investors (and academics) naively interpreted the results of these studies as meaning that international stocks would permanently offer a risk premium in the future. I have always been puzzled by this train of thought: Investors in any country might see investing in countries other than their own as risky. In other words, they might have a "home country bias," so they would require a higher return to entice them to invest in a different country. But that logic works both ways: U.S. investors would require a risk premium to invest in non-U.S. markets and non-U.S. investors would require a premium to invest in the United States. If the markets are roughly the same size (and they are), the two premiums should cancel each other out.[86] Investors should invest internationally for many reasons—for diversification and because the industrial mix of every country is different—but capturing a risk premium is not one of them.

Where there are portfolios, there need to be benchmarks. During this same period, the MSCI EAFE Index was pretty much the only international equity index available, so it became the almost universal standard for international equity benchmarks.[87] It remains so even though EAFE omits Canada, and another index using the same methodology (the MSCI World ex-U.S Index) that includes Canada has been available for quite some time.

Need for Float Adjustment

In the late 1980s, the Japanese equity market entered a super-boom phase that caused the weight of Japan in EAFE to soar to almost 60 percent by the end of 1989. The implications of this development for portfolio management were peculiar. As Japanese stocks took on higher and higher multiples, they became less and less attractive to most fundamentals-oriented active managers. To minimize tracking error to the benchmark, however—and to stay even with the benchmark's performance, which was boosted by its large weight in Japan—portfolio managers had to hold larger and larger Japanese equity positions.

Part of Japan's large weight in EAFE was a result of growth of the country's real economy and was, therefore, justified on fundamental grounds. And part of the large weight was caused by the high multiples that prevailed in the Japanese market. But part of the weight was the result of a large volume of cross-holdings in Japan. In cross-holding, one company owns shares of another, so including the full capitalization of both companies in an index is double counting. In addition, many shares were closely held, so they were unavailable to the public even if they did not represent cross-holdings.

To correct these problems, some managers tried to persuade clients to use either an "EAFE light" benchmark with an artificially reduced weight in Japan or a benchmark weighted by gross domestic product. Free-float adjustment, however, seemed to be a more natural solution.[88]

Salomon–Russell was the first organization (that I know of) to introduce float-adjusted benchmarks. Although the Salomon–Russell (now Citigroup) indexes did not attract a large market share because of the reluctance of sponsors and managers to change benchmarks, the superiority of its methodology was widely recognized. As a result, all the indexes introduced by new providers were float adjusted. Finally, after years of preparation, MSCI converted its indexes to a float-adjusted basis on 31 May 2002. Some details of this conversion and its effect on market prices are discussed later in this section. In the meantime, note the differences in capitalizations and weights between MSCI's full-capitalization and free-float indexes shown in Table 2.15.

TABLE 2.15   Composition of MSCI Float-Adjusted and Full-Cap World Indexes, 30 November 2001

Country	MSCI World Provisional Index (float adjusted, 85% cap coverage)			MSCI World Index (full cap, 60% cap coverage)		
	No. of Companies	Market Cap (millions)	Index Weight	No. of Companies	Market Cap (millions)	Index Weight
Australia	71	$243,658	1.54%	53	$236,243	1.50%
Austria	12	6,580	0.04	15	12,545	0.08
Belgium	17	50,496	0.32	16	70,735	0.45
Canada	86	336,853	2.13	68	340,053	2.16
Denmark	25	45,338	0.29	19	67,676	0.43
Finland	21	143,153	0.91	27	143,997	0.92
France	54	577,055	3.66	50	773,886	4.92
Germany	50	426,671	2.70	45	567,913	3.61
Greece	23	24,711	0.16	23	24,711	0.16
Hong Kong	28	99,401	0.63	28	143,944	0.91
Ireland	14	54,775	0.35	13	48,108	0.31
Italy	42	218,979	1.39	40	312,164	1.98
Japan	322	1,295,698	8.21	274	1,526,191	9.70
Netherlands	25	350,249	2.22	23	386,266	2.46
New Zealand	15	8,047	0.05	11	9,187	0.06
Norway	25	27,141	0.17	21	34,682	0.22
Portugal	10	23,418	0.15	10	37,240	0.24
Singapore	35	45,494	0.29	28	58,947	0.37
Spain	27	206,809	1.31	31	226,677	1.44
Sweden	38	137,015	0.87	34	167,619	1.07
Switzerland	38	467,962	2.97	35	491,214	3.12
United Kingdom	137	1,718,828	10.89	111	1,591,282	10.11
United States	413	9,270,878	58.75	322	8,462,332	53.79
Total	1,528	$15,779,217	100.00%	1,297	$15,733,613	100.00%

Source: MSCI.

When Japanese stocks were rising in the 1980s, managers struggled to stay even with full-cap benchmarks, and as Japanese stocks plunged in the 1990s, they found the full-cap indexes easy to beat. (With all benchmarks now float adjusted and with Japan constituting only 21 percent of EAFE as of March 2003, managers may not find that benchmark as easy to beat in the future.) When a benchmark is either very easy or very difficult for a large proportion of managers to beat, something is probably wrong with the benchmark—not with the theory that says active management is a zero-sum game!

The question of full-capitalization versus float-adjusted benchmarks is still a source of controversy for the U.S. equity market. For international equity benchmarks, however, the question has been resolved. Although the precise nature of the float adjustment varies from provider to provider (see Schoenfeld and Ginis 2002), no international equity benchmark uses full capitalization anymore.

International Equity Indexes Compared

Today, major providers of international equity indexes include MSCI, Citigroup, FTSE, Standard & Poor's, and Dow Jones and Company. Table 2.16 presents the basic characteristics of each index and provides a brief description of how each suite of indexes is constructed. Schoenfeld and Ginis described in detail how each of these indexes is constructed, enumerated the key criteria by which a good international index can be identified, and rated each index according to each of the criteria.

Trade-Offs in Constructing International Indexes

As discussed for the domestic equity indexes, constructing any benchmark involves trade-offs, but the trade-offs differ somewhat from one asset class to another. Trade-offs discussed in this section are specific to international equity benchmarks or have special resonance when a U.S. investor is deciding which international equity benchmark to use (for more, see Schoenfeld and Ginis).

Breadth vs. investability.   International indexes face a direct trade-off between breadth (the number of different stocks in an index) and investability. (An index is investable to the extent that you can readily buy and sell the stocks in it with a minimum of price-pressure effects and other transaction costs.) With international indexes—not only emerging market but also developed country indexes—the illiquidity of the smallest-cap and most closely held stocks is a greater problem than in the United States. Although most indexes exclude the smallest, least liquid securities, when selecting a benchmark you might want to take the extra measure of choosing an index that errs on the side of less breadth and greater liquidity (see Table 2.16 for the number of stocks in each index). For example, the manager of an index fund with substantial cash flows in and out might not want the job of holding all 2,200 stocks in the Dow Jones Global ex-U.S. Index.

Liquidity and crossing opportunities vs. index reconstitution effects.   Indexes that are most popular and most widely used as benchmarks or as the basis for index funds have greater index-level liquidity—that is, liquidity for investors seeking to buy or sell an index fund position or an actively managed position whose contents resemble, at least to some degree, those of the index. Of particular interest to institutional investors are crossing opportunities in such indexes. Crossing is the process by which an investment manager matches its own

TABLE 2.16   Basic Characteristics of Major International Equity Benchmarks, 30 June 2002

Provider	Index	Country Coverage	No. of Securities	No. of Countries	Target Market Cap by Country (%)	Historical Inception Date
MSCI	All Country World Index ex-U.S.	Integrated	1,799	48	85	Jan 1988
MSCI	World ex-U.S.	Developed markets	1,101	22	85	Jan 1970
MSCI	EAFE	Developed markets	1,021	21	85	Jan 1970
FTSE	All-World ex-U.S.	Integrated	1,815	48	85–90	Jan 1994
FTSE	World Developed ex-North America	Developed markets	1,294	21	85–90	Jan 1994
Citigroup	Broad Market Index Global ex-U.S.	Integrated	4,875	49	95	Jul 1989
Citigroup	Primary Markets Index—Europe Pacific	Developed markets	663	21	95	Jul 1989
Citigroup	Global 1200 ex-U.S.	Modified integrated[a]	700	30	70 (by region)	Oct 1989
Dow Jones	Global ex-U.S.	Modified integrated[a]	2,200	33	70 (by region)	Jan 1992

Note: "Integrated" indexes include developed and emerging markets.
[a]Includes advanced emerging markets.

Sources: Schoenfeld and Ginis (2002) and data collected by the author.

clients' buy and sell orders without using a broker and without incurring the transaction costs associated with brokerage. Crossing avoids transaction costs except for a small fee paid to the investment management firm doing the crossing.

Program trades, sometimes called portfolio trades, are another way that investors can buy or sell indexed or "benchmarked" positions. Program trades involve a broker bidding on the right to buy or sell a whole portfolio at an agreed-on price. A popular and liquid benchmark results in a lower bid from the broker because the broker's own costs are lower for such a benchmark.

Popular indexes—domestic and international—suffer, however, from index reconstitution (inclusion and deletion) effects. These effects, which I noted in the section titled Critiques of Benchmarking and a Way Forward, consist of upward price pressure on stocks chosen for inclusion in an index and downward price pressure on stocks taken out of the index. The size of the effect on a portfolio manager is, logically, proportional to the amount of assets indexed or benchmarked to the particular index. Reconstitution effects are detrimental to performance, although the underperformance does not show up in conventional performance evaluation as a negative alpha because the reconstitution effect affects the benchmark as well as the investor's actual portfolio.

Indexes with more index-level liquidity and crossing opportunities may have poorer performance because of reconstitution effects. Of the developed country equity indexes, MSCI EAFE provides by far the most opportunity to investors seeking to cross trades or otherwise take advantage of index-level liquidity, and it is also the most likely to suffer from reconstitution effects because it is the most popular index.[89]

Precise float adjustment vs. transaction costs from rebalancing. As noted, float adjustment for international equity indexes is no longer a matter of controversy. All the indexes are float adjusted in one way or another. In international markets, however, where float adjustment has a large effect on the constituent weights, the exact method of adjustment makes a difference. Indexes that make precise float adjustments and that revise these adjustments frequently impose higher transaction costs on those benchmarking against them than indexes that use float bands or broad categories. Float bands are categories of, say, 15–25 percent, 25–50 percent, 50–75 percent, and 75–100 percent, in which the percentage represents the portion of a company's full capitalization that the index constructors regard as freely floating. Citigroup makes precise float adjustments, whereas MSCI and FTSE use bands. Float bands make sense because transaction costs are a real loss to the investor; what is to be gained by replicating the float of the market exactly is not as clear.

Objectivity and transparency vs. judgment. Objective and clearly stated rules for index construction convey as large an advantage to international equity indexes as to U.S. indexes. They enable both index funds and active managers to predict what will be in the benchmark and, as a result, to trade more effectively in anticipation of changes in benchmark contents. They also make benchmarks easier to understand and to use as proxies for asset classes in asset allocation.

From this perspective, MSCI's judgment-based method for constructing EAFE and its other indexes is difficult to defend (as is S&P's use of an index committee to construct the S&P 500). When MSCI's indexes contained (by design) only 60 percent of the capitalization of each country and sector, however, it had little choice but to use judgment to select the companies. An odd result of this situation was that the MSCI U.S. index did not contain Ford Motor Company because General Motors Corporation accounted for more than 60 percent of the U.S. automotive sector and "crowded out" the other U.S. auto companies, even mega-cap Ford. Thus, a manager using the MSCI U.S. index as a benchmark would have incurred tracking error simply by holding Ford at its market-cap weight. Now that MSCI's indexes capture 85 percent of capitalization, MSCI's use of judgment to pick the stocks has less impact on index contents.

The advantages of benchmarking to a widely accepted index, such as EAFE or the S&P 500, include ease of communication and a high degree of index-level liquidity, which may overcome the disadvantages associated with using a judgment-based index.

Style/Size Indexes

The size and value–growth distinctions are as important for international equities as they are in the U.S. market.[90] Of the index constructors shown in Table 2.16, MSCI and Citigroup calculate style and size subindexes. The MSCI indexes, in particular, also have a substantial back history, which is helpful for understanding and comparing style effects in various countries. These effects are at least as dramatic outside the U.S. market as within it.

An understanding of the specific construction methods of the subindexes is important before attempting to use them as benchmarks or buying index funds based on them. Describing them is beyond the scope of this paper, but you can find information on international style indexes in Schoenfeld and Ginis.

Classification of Countries as Developed or Emerging

The division of non-U.S. markets into developed and emerging categories dates back to 1981 when Antoine van Agtmael, an investment manager at the World Bank, referred (in a flash of marketing brilliance) to what were then called third-world or developing countries as emerging markets (Thomas 1999). Mark Mobius of the Franklin Templeton (then, simply Templeton) organization was among the other managers who quickly capitalized on the trend to invest in countries, such as the Asian tigers, Mexico, Brazil, and (later) the formerly communist countries of Central and Eastern Europe, that were not in any established equity benchmark.[91] The emergence of China as a capitalist society in the 1990s reinforced the level of interest in (although not the performance of) emerging markets, and Russia and India are now having an impact. With the rising interest of institutional investors in the emerging markets came the need for benchmarks, so a number of index providers stepped up to the plate to provide them.

The first emerging market benchmarks were provided by the International Finance Corporation (IFC) and Baring Securities (now ING Barings). Soon afterward, MSCI and Citigroup constructed emerging market indexes. MSCI's Emerging Markets Free Index (EMF) gained an early popular lead, just as MSCI's EAFE had for developed markets. (The "free" in EMF refers not to free float but to the ability of investors from outside a given country to transact freely in that country's market. Such freedom includes the unrestricted exchange of currencies and movement of capital across borders.)

Today, the leading providers of emerging market benchmarks are the same as the leading providers of developed market benchmarks identified in Table 2.16. The Barings indexes have been folded into the FTSE, and the IFC indexes have been folded into the Standard & Poor's series of indexes. All of the providers shown in Table 2.16 also constructed integrated (that is, developed + emerging markets) indexes.

Boundary between Developed and Emerging Markets

When an index constructor decides that a country is going to be in the developed category or the emerging category, that decision has consequences for the characteristics of the benchmark and, potentially, for the country itself. First, the index constructor may be undecided about where to put the country because the country's market capitalization is large relative to an emerging market index. For example, South Korea's equity market is in the MSCI EMF and other emerging market indexes, but its market is quite well developed and has a capitalization of $100.7 billion, equal to 19.9 percent of the EMF. Thus, the decision to include or exclude Korea in the EMF had a real impact on the average company size and average level of country development in that index. As a constituent of EAFE (which it is scheduled to become), Korea will be a small rather than a huge player.

For the country, being in a developed index is highly desirable because far more assets are committed to developed than to emerging markets. For example, Korean companies would rather have a small weight in EAFE than a large weight in the EMF. This preference reflects the fact that when a country graduates from MSCI's emerging markets indexes to EAFE, as Portugal, Greece, Ireland, and many other countries have done and as Korea may do soon, a new source of capital becomes available to that country's companies. Inclusion in a broadly followed index of developed countries, in itself, makes a country more developed.

Acceptance of Integrated Indexes

There is no compelling reason why international managers should segregate themselves into developed and emerging markets specialists or why clients should establish separate allocations to these categories of markets. A historical reason is the desire of clients (investors) to reassure themselves that they are not taking undue risk. They pursued this goal by investing only in developed markets believed to have transparent accounting rules, liquid exchanges, and stable currencies. Investors also sought to avoid capital-control risk by holding only developed market securities. Today, however, the largest companies in the emerging markets are traded on the New York Stock Exchange and are thus free of capital-control risk (as well as subject to the exchange's transparency and liquidity standards). And some of these companies are globally dominant in their industries. Therefore, the developed–emerging distinction seems less important than it once was and investment managers increasingly find that the skills used to identify attractive stocks play equally well in developed and emerging economies.

As a result, integrated mandates (mandates for a single manager to invest in all non-U.S. markets, whether developed or emerging) are growing rapidly. Schoenfeld and Ginis reported that 48 percent of all new international mandates in the first half of 2002 were for integrated portfolios, up from 20 percent in 2000 and 13.6 percent in 1999.[92] The benchmark for such mandates is typically the MSCI All Country World Index ex-U.S.

Impact of Benchmarking on International Markets

The impact of inclusion of a stock in a benchmark on that stock's price has been less thoroughly studied in international markets than in the United States. Two recent events, however, offer evidence on the consequences of benchmarking for international markets.

The Odd Case of Malaysia

Up to 1998, Malaysia was a constituent of both the EAFE and EMF indexes because of an odd historical situation. The countries of Singapore and Malaysia were united until 1965, and their stock exchanges developed as a unit in the early 1970s (even after the countries separated politically), when MSCI was contemplating adding a number of countries to the developed market EAFE index. Singapore was clearly a developed country, but no separate MSCI Singapore index existed, only a Singapore/Malaysia index. In a press release, Capital International, which at the time was the constructor of the MSCI indexes, later explained:

> Although the two markets became increasingly independent, the joint MSCI Singapore/Malaysia Index remained a constituent of the EAFE index for the next 20 years (to avoid disruption to the index, and to the markets). In May 1993, the MSCI Singapore/Malaysia index was finally split into two separate indexes. At that time, in view of Malaysia's long history of inclusion in the MSCI EAFE index, it was decided that it would remain, temporarily, in both the [EAFE and EMF] series.[93]

The result was a double-counting situation in which an investor who held one portfolio benchmarked to EAFE and another benchmarked to the EMF would receive a double weight in Malaysia (the only country in the world in this position). As of 2 September 1998, Malaysia represented 0.37 percent of EAFE and 4.40 percent of the EMF.

Then, in the wake of the Asian financial crisis of 1998, Malaysia imposed capital controls, motivating MSCI to remove that country from EAFE as of 30 September 1998. Capital International stated, "In light of the recent developments in Malaysia, it is time to put an end to this transition period."

If Malaysia had been removed from EAFE to avoid double counting at a time when no externally caused turmoil was occurring in the markets, researchers would have had a noteworthy experimental condition. They could have observed how the change in demand from indexing and benchmarking affected the Malaysian stock index relative to the stock indexes of other, roughly comparable countries, such as Thailand and Indonesia. The imposition of capital controls that spurred MSCI to make the index change, however, also ruined the experiment: Investors wanted to flee Malaysian stocks for reasons having nothing to do with their exclusion from EAFE.

Nevertheless, if only to satisfy curiosity, I've compared the returns on Malaysian stocks with stocks and indexes for the relevant period, 1998–2000, as shown in Figure 2.4. Because the decision to remove Malaysia from EAFE was announced on 4 September 1998 and was to take effect on 30 September of the same year, you can see the effects of the decision by looking at returns in September and October 1998. For September 1998, Malaysia did not have the lowest return in Southeast Asia; in October 1998, it had the lowest return in the

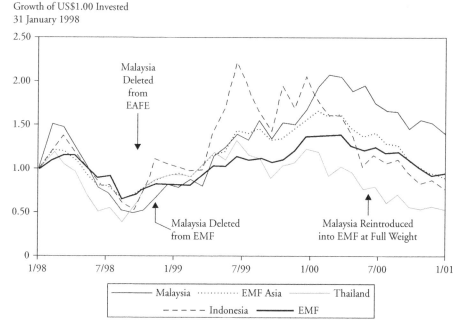

FIGURE 2.4   Cumulative Returns on Malaysian and Other Equity Markets, 1998–2000

Source: MSCI.

region but the return was positive. Thus, without conducting any statistical tests but simply by inspecting the results visually, you can see that the returns for Malaysia appear to have been not much different from those for other countries in the region. Malaysia's returns are also not much different from those for the broad EMF in the period surrounding Malaysia's removal from EAFE.[94]

On 30 November 1998, MSCI also removed Malaysia from the EMF because of the capital controls. When Malaysia was restored to the EMF on 23 May 2000, it had already experienced huge gains (to more than four times the 1998 low in U.S. dollar terms) and was, in fact, at a high that it still has not surpassed.[95] Either investors had been buying Malaysian stocks in anticipation of its reintroduction to the EMF or investors were ignoring Malaysia's absence from it. There was no measurable Malaysian EAFE deletion effect and there was no measurable Malaysian EMF inclusion effect.

The Biggest Index Change Ever

Recognizing that international investors had long held a strong preference for float-adjusted benchmarks and that they had sustained their loyalty to MSCI largely because of the difficulties that sponsors and managers have in switching benchmarks, MSCI converted its indexes to a float-adjusted format in a stepwise process. The process began on 31 May 2001, when the Provisional indexes were introduced. These float-adjusted indexes captured 85 percent of the capitalization of each country and of each country's industrial sectors, and they were designed to run in parallel with the Standard or original indexes for a year. (Recall that the original indexes, which were not float adjusted, captured 60 percent of capitalization by country and sector.) After a year—that is, on 31 May 2002—the Standard indexes were to be discontinued and the Provisional indexes would become the permanent MSCI indexes.

This procedure was designed to allow investors to adjust to the new index construction methods. Both the demand side—index funds and benchmark-sensitive active funds—and the supply side—brokers, hedge funds, and active managers seeking to profit from providing liquidity to the demand side—had plenty of opportunity to observe how the new indexes were constructed and what their constituents would be and to trade in anticipation of the full changeover on 31 May 2002.

Note that the conversion from full capitalization to free float and from 60 percent to 85 percent capitalization coverage affected the MSCI index weight of most of the large- and mid-cap stocks in the world. It was, to borrow the title of a Barclays Global Investors report, "the world's biggest index change ever."[96] Although little of the U.S. equity market is indexed or benchmarked to the MSCI U.S. Index, a large portion of non-U.S. equities are indexed or benchmarked to EAFE or to other MSCI indexes.

One way to measure the success of this effort is by the return differential, or spread, between the Provisional and Standard indexes (both overall and country by country). As liquidity suppliers bought stocks in the Provisional index in the hope of later selling them to indexed or benchmarked investors whose Standard index was about to be abandoned, the Provisional index should have earned an incremental return over the Standard one. In other words, the Provisional-to-Standard spread would be a measure of the transaction costs being paid by investors in the Standard index.

The original forecast was that investors could lose well over 1 percent in performance through transaction costs and/or by not switching benchmarks, Barclays noted.[97] The overall Provisional–Standard spread for the year ended 31 May 2002, however, was only 0.32 percent for the flagship EAFE index. "The World spread finished in negative territory," according to Barclays. Thus, much of the transaction cost that might have been paid was instead avoided through careful planning and a high degree of index transparency.

Results differed, of course, from country to country, and the spreads did not line up cleanly with the amount by which a country gained or lost share in EAFE and other broad indexes. For example, the United Kingdom, the country whose weight in EAFE increased the most as a result of the transition, had a generally strong market (it beat EAFE) and might have also been expected to have a high Provisional–Standard spread (because of a perceived "shortage" of U.K. stocks), but the spread actually turned out to be negative. Japan, the country that lost the most from the transition, had weak markets and might also have been expected to have a negative spread (because of a "glut" of Japanese stocks), but the spread turned out to be close to zero.[98]

Interestingly, in the first half of the transition year, the Provisional–Standard spread dove into negative territory because liquidity providers, reacting to the information in the Provisional with enthusiasm (also known as greed), grossly overestimated the demand for the stocks they were buying, whereas investors on the demand side seemed confused or indifferent. Later in the transition, however, liquidity providers appeared to lose enthusiasm while demand-side investors were coming under increasing pressure to move to the weights in the Provisional indexes. So, the spread turned positive.

The lessons of this episode are not only that investors, managers, and index constructors can cooperate to avoid unnecessary transaction costs but also that markets appear to "work" quite well at the micro level (if the word micro can be used to describe this vast and complex change in an industry-dominant benchmark). They work, that is, to provide liquidity with a reasonable degree of efficiency when it is needed and to make transaction costs, which could have been huge and unpredictable, quite small.

HEDGE FUND BENCHMARKS

The idea that hedge funds need benchmarks (or that their clients need them) is new and surprising.[99] Originally, hedge funds were the preserve of wealthy families. Later, a number of endowments, foundations, and other institutional investors added hedge funds in the belief that managers left to their own devices and freed from the constraints implied by benchmarks would achieve superior performance—perhaps even performance uncorrelated with the overall movements of markets.

Hedge fund investing incorporates several threads, all of which are hostile to benchmarking. One thread is the goal of capital preservation: A strategy intended to avoid losses will also sharply curtail gains when markets are rising if the value added through active management skill is less than exceptional. Short selling (of index futures as well as of securities believed to be overpriced) is a principal strategy in funds managed with such a goal. A second, contrasting thread is the pursuit of high performance: Some investors wish to make as much money as possible, often in highly undiversified and/or leveraged strategies; short selling is also often part of these strategies. With most high-performance strategies, a benchmarking approach would impose a large penalty for taking active risk; it would require a fund's active return to be extraordinary to justify holding the fund. A third thread, woven into the first two, is a belief in pure manager skill, that is, the idea that the essence of active management can be distilled by removing all market influences; thus, traditional asset class benchmarks do not have much relevance to hedge funds.

It is thus a testament to the power of consultants, clients, and the intellectual appeal of performance measurement and evaluation that hedge fund benchmarks emerged at all. Although I doubt that hedge fund managers wanted to be "benchmarked," the desire to measure how managers are doing was too strong for hedge fund managers to resist.[100] As a result, several suites of hedge fund benchmarks—generally consisting of a number of style subcategories as well as an overall index—had been created by early 2003. Among the providers are Zurich Capital Markets (ZCM), CSFB/Tremont (Credit Suisse First Boston/Tremont), Evaluation Associates Capital Markets (EACM), Standard & Poor's, and Morgan Stanley Capital International. This section focuses on the ZCM benchmarks.[101]

Hedge Fund Benchmark Construction

Unlike traditional asset-class benchmarks, for which capitalization weighting is a virtual prerequisite for the index to be acceptable, most hedge fund benchmarks are equally weighted. (CSFB/Tremont is cap weighted, with the assets under management in the funds as the "capitalizations.") With hedge funds, cap weighting makes limited sense: The capitalizations of stocks, bonds, and other primary assets contain economic information because they are the market's appraisal of a business or a stream of cash flows, but the capitalizations of hedge funds themselves contain little information. They reflect only the amount that investors have entrusted to one manager rather than another. After all, hedge funds are portfolios, not companies.[102]

Survivor Bias

Hedge fund indexes typically try to avoid survivor bias by including in the index return the final return for hedge funds that have ceased to exist. Avoiding survivor bias is important because the hedge funds that go out of business, or that simply stop reporting their performance, tend to be those that have poor returns. (A few funds stop reporting because they have become closed to new investment, which usually reflects good performance; they provide a countervailing source of bias.) In practice, avoiding survivor bias is difficult for broadbased indexes that attempt to include all hedge funds because no one knows what hedge funds exist at the current time, much less at all historical points in time. Narrow indexes are less subject to survivor bias, as are indexes that include only large hedge funds.[103]

Rebalancing and Liquidity

Equally weighted benchmarks require frequent rebalancing, of course, to take into account ordinary changes in asset prices (net asset values in the case of hedge funds) and to reflect reconstitution (the addition or deletion of funds in the index). But rebalancing means taking money out of funds that have had the best performance to invest in others. An investor attempting to track one of these benchmarks would probably have difficulty withdrawing money from funds in the first category and might find that some of the funds in the second category were closed to new investment.

Sampling Bias

Because different methods of constructing hedge fund benchmarks result in different portfolios, returns for the same style vary substantially from one index provider to another. A particularly dramatic instance is the difference between ZCM's and EACM's equity long–short return for February 2000. ZCM reported a one-month return of $+20.48$ percent, whereas EACM reported -1.56 percent. In that particular month, growth stocks greatly outperformed value stocks. The ZCM benchmark was known to be growth oriented (that bias has now been eliminated); the EACM benchmark was probably value oriented.

Classifying Hedge Fund Managers into Styles

All suites of hedge fund indexes are segmented by style, but except in the case of ZCM, a manager's self-proclaimed style is used to classify the hedge fund. Instead of relying on the manager, who may have an economic interest in concealing his or her style or varying it over time, ZCM uses a statistical technique called cluster analysis to analyze each manager's historical returns and to classify the managers into styles. Any fund that does not appear to be "style pure" based on the cluster analysis is excluded from ZCM's benchmarks, which makes them exceedingly narrow (60 funds out of a possible 1,100 or so). Standard & Poor's and EACM's indexes, consisting of 40 and 100 funds, respectively, are also narrow.

Classifying hedge funds into styles has been a major source of contention among index constructors, managers, and investors. But a list of principal styles has coalesced over time as the hedge fund industry has become more focused on institutional investors as customers. The principal hedge fund styles are[104]

- convertible arbitrage,
- distressed securities,
- emerging markets,
- equity long–short (long biased),
- equity market neutral,
- fixed-income arbitrage,
- global macro,
- merger and other event arbitrage, and
- short selling only.

Two styles that are structurally different from hedge funds but closely related are managed futures and funds of funds. Managed futures funds are "commodity trading advisors," not hedge funds. Funds of funds differ from hedge funds in that their only portfolio holdings are other hedge funds, not securities.

No index constructor maintains indexes for all of these styles. ZCM maintains six "style pure" style indexes and an aggregate index.

A review of the major suites of hedge fund indexes, along with a summary of the methodology for constructing each of them, is in Amenc and Martellini (2003).

Hedge Fund Factor Exposures

A number of leading researchers have pointed out that hedge fund returns, far from being unrelated to market factors, are well explained by factor exposures. Schneeweis, Kazemi, and Martin (2001) showed that up to 60 percent of the cross-sectional variation in hedge fund style benchmarks is explained by variation in the factors.

These factor exposures are somewhat different from those usually used to explain returns in traditional (long-only) portfolios, which supports the idea that hedge funds are systematically capturing risks (and, potentially, risk premiums or payoffs) that are not captured by traditional investing. Schneeweis et al. identified the following factors as having explanatory power:

- slope of the yield curve (yield difference between 30-year U.S. Treasury bond and three-month U.S. Treasury bill),
- long-term T-bond yield,
- three-month T-bill yield,
- credit spread (yield difference between Baa and Aaa bond yields),
- intramonth standard deviation of daily S&P 500 Index returns,
- S&P 500 total return,
- small-cap (Russell 2000 Index) return,
- Chicago Board Options Exchange (CBOE) Implied Volatility Index (VIX) for options on the S&P 100 Index, and
- intramonth standard deviation of daily Lehman Aggregate Bond Index.[105]

Many of the factors are simply traditional asset-class exposures. Hedge funds, then, are not as much of a mystery as you might think; they are simply investment managers. Because they can sell short and use leverage, however, and because they typically operate free of a traditional asset-class benchmark, their return patterns are generally very different from those of traditional managers, and they need their own specialized benchmarks. Some benchmark constructors argue that the style-specific benchmarks capture the "natural return" of the underlying asset classes or factors and thus that the benchmarks are comparable to traditional asset-class benchmarks. If you accept this proposition, then a given hedge fund would have to add alpha relative to its style-specific benchmark to be considered successful.

Factor analyses show that hedge funds as a group are surprisingly highly correlated with the S&P 500 and sharply negatively correlated with changes in credit spreads. Merger arbitrage and other event-driven strategies are the most "short in volatility"; that is, they are negatively correlated with changes in the CBOE VIX and are thus positioned to gain from decreases in volatility and to lose when volatility increases. By and large, equity long–short funds are also short in volatility. Other categories of hedge funds are volatility neutral on average.

Hedge Fund Index Funds

If hedge funds are simply bets on pure manager skill, an investor has no reason to want an index fund of hedge funds. If hedge funds provide exposure to "priced" market factors that cannot easily be obtained through traditional investments, however, then hedge fund index funds make sense.

Unfortunately, the tracking error between a hedge fund index fund and its index is necessarily large because of the liquidity reasons noted previously. The ZCM index, however, is the basis for a series of "tracking portfolios" (deliberately not called index funds) for each of the style subindexes and for the overall index; the style-tracking portfolios typically have 2.5 percent tracking error relative to the underlying benchmarks (Amenc and Martellini).

Are Hedge Fund Indexes Peer Groups?

Anyone could be forgiven for regarding hedge fund indexes as simply peer groups, not "real" benchmarks. After all, the index constituents are portfolios (managers) and the returns are typically equally weighted, so the index return is the average of the managers' returns—which is a peer group. (In a traditional asset-class benchmark, the constituents are the underlying securities, not a set of managers.) Moreover, if you require a benchmark to be an all-inclusive, macro consistent, and (thus) cap-weighted measure of the asset class or style it is supposed to represent, hedge fund indexes do not meet those criteria.

Traditional benchmarks, however, can also be thought of as peer groups. A cap-weighted equity index (because it is the sum of all prices) represents what everybody else is holding. And if you could construct a "perfect" peer group, the cap-weighted returns of the peer group would sum to the benchmark return—because active management is a zero-sum game. With regard to any kind of market benchmark, as opposed to a so-called absolute return or liability-related benchmark, as described in the section titled Critiques of Benchmarking and a Way Forward, there is really no way out of the critique that a benchmark is a kind of peer group.

POLICY BENCHMARKS

Policy benchmarks are indexes of indexes that represent the intended or normal asset mix of a plan sponsor's or investor's entire portfolio. They are used to determine whether or not, and to what extent, an investor's asset allocation and implementation (manager or security selection) are successful.

Any discussion of policy benchmarks naturally extends somewhat into the territory of investment policy itself: determining who truly owns a given asset pool, assessing its liabilities, and deciding what the asset mix should be, among other topics. My foray into this territory is limited to a few of the more pressing benchmark-related issues.

The first issue is a technical point: I extend the concept of pure alpha from the section titled Using Benchmarks to Measure Performance to the task of performance attribution at the policy or whole-plan level. The discussion then turns to some philosophical and practical issues relating to the use of policy benchmarks. While exploring those issues, I address the possibility (mentioned in previous sections) that the *real* benchmark for investors should be their liability or intended spending.

Performance Attribution at the Policy Level

First, recall from the section titled Using Benchmarks to Measure Performance the definition of the term "active return" as (in contrast to alpha or pure alpha) the return on a portfolio minus the return on a benchmark, without any regression analyses or other adjustments for beta(s).

Brinson, Hood, and Beebower (1986) suggested that to attribute the performance of the overall investment plan as measured against a policy benchmark, you must first isolate the effect of active asset allocation against the policy benchmark, or what the authors called "timing," as follows:

Active return from asset allocation = (Actual asset weights × Asset-class benchmark returns)
− Return on policy benchmark.

Then, you isolate the active return from implementation (manager selection or security selection):

Active return from implementation = (Policy weights × Actual asset-class returns)
− Return on policy benchmark.

These parts—active return from asset allocation, active return from implementation, and the policy benchmark return itself—do not quite add up to the actual return on the portfolio.

There remains a residual, or "plug" number, typically quite small, that may be regarded as coming from the interaction of asset allocation and implementation.

Potentially, a risk misfit can occur between the portfolio and the policy benchmark. If, for example, the actual asset mix was riskier than the policy mix, some of the extra return should be attributed to the higher beta rather than to the pure alpha of the active asset-allocation decisions. The market model (see the section titled The Evolution of MPT and the Benchmarking Paradigm) can be used to turn the Brinson–Hood–Beebower active return from asset allocation into a pure alpha as follows:

$$r_i = r_f + \alpha_i + \beta(r_m - r_f),$$

where

r_i = return given by (Policy weights × Actual asset-class returns)

r_f = riskless rate of return

α_i = pure or regression alpha of the active asset-allocation decisions versus the policy benchmark

β = beta of the return series given by (Policy weights × Actual asset-class returns), scaled so that the beta of the policy benchmark equals 1

r_m = return on the policy benchmark

A similar procedure can be followed for calculating the pure alpha added by implementation. By getting the pure alpha right, you avoid rewarding the wrong kind of behavior (such as inappropriate risk taking) and arrive at a clear measurement of the value added through active management of the asset mix.

Policy Benchmarks in Practice

Capital market theory suggests (if you accept a particularly burdensome set of assumptions) that the optimal portfolio consists of all the wealth in the world leveraged up or down to reflect a given investor's risk tolerance.[106] Most of the world's wealth is tied up in "human capital," in privately held real estate, and in private equity, but the parts that can be accessed by portfolio investors form a vast opportunity set and have been used to compose a number of different "normal portfolios" or prototypical policy benchmarks. The best known is probably Brinson Partners' Multiple Markets Index (MMI), which is constructed from the viewpoint of a U.S. investor and shown in Table 2.17 for July 1991.

Note that this allocation is not truly a "world market wealth portfolio." The weights are rigged so that equities, including venture capital but not real estate, sum to the customary 60 percent of all assets. Many categories of wealth that can be held by portfolio investors, including commodities, various types of real estate (farm land, timber, and non-U.S. real estate), and many types of private equity (buyout firms and energy partnerships), are intentionally left out. The goal of the Brinson MMI was to serve as a template for policy benchmarks, not to measure the return on the wealth of the world.[107]

Pension plan sponsors and other institutional investors in the early days of performance measurement and attribution did not reach the level of complexity represented by the MMI to determine their policy benchmarks. They more typically used something much simpler, such as

Equities	60%
Bonds	35%
Cash	5%

I will argue that the simpler approach is probably better.

TABLE 2.17   Brinson MMI Asset Weights, July 1991

Asset Class	Weight
Equity	
U.S. large capitalization	28%
U.S. small and mid cap	12
Other countries' equity	15
Venture capital	5
Fixed income	
U.S. investment grade	18
U.S. high yield	3
International dollar bonds	2
Nondollar bonds	5
U.S. real estate	12
Cash equivalent	0
Total	100%

Source: Brinson Partners (now part of UBS Asset Management).

Simple vs. Complex Policy Benchmarks

A complex policy benchmark with many asset classes reflects the investment opportunities that exist in the world and, because it is more diversified, is more likely than a simple policy benchmark to maximize the expected return at a given level of risk. Behaviorally, however, a simple benchmark containing U.S. and international equities, bonds, inflation-linked bonds (which behave quite differently from nominal bonds), and cash has many advantages over a complex one:

- Determining the "perfect," mean–variance-efficient benchmark is too much like active management.
- Rebalancing to a complex "world wealth" benchmark that includes illiquid asset classes is costly and impractical.
- Trying to beat your benchmark is a better use of your time than perfecting the benchmark.

These points bear some elaboration. The amount of effort it takes to accomplish a task is not necessarily commensurate with the value of the work accomplished. My experience has been that asset allocation is easy and that security or manager selection is hard. Thus, the traditional 10 percent/90 percent split in effort between policy and implementation is sensible—but not because the rewards are split 10 percent/90 percent. The rewards are split in a proportion more like 40 percent/60 percent (see Ibbotson and Kaplan 2000), and getting 40 percent of the reward for 10 percent of the effort is one of the great gifts that financial markets offer to investors.

As a result, I would not put a team of experts on designing the perfectly diversified and mean–variance-optimized benchmark. Such resource deployment is better suited to active management, to beating the benchmark. In a world with limited resources, an investor should decide on a simple benchmark and spend the bulk of the resources trying to add value.

Thus, a simple approach is probably better than the MMI, although the stock/bond/cash policy benchmark is probably overdoing simplicity; a few more asset classes and a little more thought would convey some benefit.

Automatic Rebalancing vs. Use of Judgment

Some plan sponsors automatically rebalance to their policy benchmarks. The usual rationale given for such behavior is "discipline" or "contrarian investing"—buying when prices (of, say, stocks) are low and selling when they are high. This practice also is not a sound use of resources.

The benchmark is not perfect or magical. It results from an aggregation of good and bad (mostly, mediocre) estimates of expected return, risk, and correlation. Working harder on it or putting more asset classes into it (which requires more estimates) does not make it more perfect or magical. Rebalancing to a perfect portfolio would make sense, but no one knows what a perfect portfolio is.

Why not use judgment, then, to try to improve returns? A plan sponsor who feels qualified to say that this manager is better than that manager or that this stock will go up while another goes down can surely make the judgment that one asset class is more attractive than another on a relative basis at a given point in time. Asset classes are easier to analyze than stocks or managers.

The discipline that appears to result from an automatic rebalancing rule is a red herring. Automatic rebalancing is a way of falling back on fake precision. Institutions with little or no investment capability in their staff can make a sound case for automatic rebalancing, but plan sponsors who take a great deal of investment responsibility in other areas can surely take responsibility for deviating from the asset weights in a policy benchmark.

Importance of Peer Groups

Some investors take the position that they are going to disregard what other institutions are doing and simply pursue their own vision. This attitude ignores what may well be the best thinking on the topic. Some laughable examples of herd behavior in investing may exist, but in general, plan sponsors and asset owners take their responsibilities seriously and are highly capable. These professionals have as their responsibility (basically, their only responsibility) the task of thinking about what asset mix is best for their plan and then implementing it.

Thus, asset-allocation data for a plan sponsor's peer group contain real information—as do data for other peer groups and the comments and suggestions received at industry conferences and through other informal channels. To believe that you should follow your own instincts and dreams rather than respect the conclusions of generally well-informed and well-meaning peers is hubris of the worst kind. You should care greatly what other people think.

This recommendation does not mean you should not vary from the allocations of your peer group if your liability or risk tolerance is different from theirs—that is, if your peer group is improperly constructed or if, for some structural reason, your institution does not have any direct peers. You will get in real trouble, however, by thinking you don't have peers when you do.

Benchmarks and Investment Policy

Any discussion of policy benchmarks naturally drifts into a discussion of policy. In this section, I explore policy issues.[108] The guiding principle comes from Peter Bernstein's suggestion (see the section titled Critiques of Benchmarking and a Way Forward) that the real benchmark for any asset pool is the liability of the fund or, in the absence of a legal liability, the present value of the intended spending out of the fund.[109] This discussion focuses on corporate defined-benefit (DB) pension plans, although the general principles can be applied (directly or indirectly) to any program of investing to pay liabilities or expenses over the long term, including endowments, foundations, and the savings and retirement plans of individuals.

Who Owns the Plan Assets?

At first blush, the law in the United States is unambiguous on the question of what a DB pension plan assets are for. They exist to guarantee that the pension promised to beneficiaries will be paid, and the assets are to be managed for the "exclusive benefit" of those beneficiaries.[110] Superficially, pension managers are exhorted, if not required, to hold the combination of assets with risk and return characteristics that match the pension's liabilities as closely as can be accomplished.

But as everyone knows, few pensions are really managed that way. Most pension liabilities resemble a portfolio of nominal bonds and inflation-linked issues (such as U.S. Treasury Inflation-Indexed Securities, or TIPS) with a small equity component to represent, for instance, the increase over time in real incomes that results from participating in a thriving industry.[111] Most DB pension funds are invested, in contrast, roughly 60–70 percent in equities, with the remainder in fixed income, cash, and sometimes "alternative" (largely equity-like) assets, such as hedge funds and private equity. Where does this mismatch between assets and liabilities come from? Is it good or bad for beneficiaries, for the sponsor, for society?

Until about a generation ago, most pension plans were managed as though they were stand-alone financial institutions with the sole purpose of paying benefits to retirees. As such, they tended to be managed to a close match between assets and liabilities; sometimes they bought bonds, or a mix of bonds and equities, but they bought primarily annuities from insurance companies—which defease (or fund in advance) pension liabilities quite effectively if the pension benefit does not have a cost-of-living adjustment (COLA).[112] In other words, like banks and insurance companies, traditionally managed pension funds took relatively little "gap risk" (the risk that assets will move differently from liabilities). Gap risk can come from a mismatch in the equity beta, nominal interest rate duration, or real interest duration of assets and liabilities or from other sources.[113]

Dominance of Equities

If early U.S. pension plans were managed without taking much gap risk, what changed? First, high inflation rates made keeping up with the pension promise through fixed-income investing difficult. Typical pension contracts are based on "final" pay—that is, the level of pay at or around the time the employee retires. Final pay reflects salary inflation from the time the benefits are earned until the employee retires, which makes the liability sensitive to inflation even in the absence of a postretirement COLA. Second, the Employee Retirement Income Security Act of 1974 and various Financial Accounting Standards Board rulings provided an extremely complex and flexible set of funding and accounting rules for U.S. pensions that allowed sponsors to try to make a profit from their pension plans. At first, the profit could be directly channeled into the sponsor's bank account through pension plan "reversions," or payouts to the sponsor, but these reversions were later taxed so punitively that the profit could only be realized through "contribution holidays." Through these methods, sponsors tried to get the stock market (and other markets) to pay for their employees' retirement benefits for free, or at a deep discount.

Moreover, when the Pension Benefit Guaranty Corporation (PBGC) was set up by the U.S. federal government to guarantee a minimum level of benefits to employees of bankrupt sponsors, sponsors then had a "put option" that enabled them to take more risk without forcing beneficiaries to share in all of it. They could, instead, force the other companies whose pension plans were guaranteed by the PBGC to share in the risk taking.

Treynor (1972), writing pseudonymously as "Walter Bagehot," provided a respectable grounding for the practice of taking risk to earn additional returns for the sponsor. He and many subsequent authors building on his work argued that the pension plan is, in effect, an operating financial subsidiary of the sponsoring corporation, and they composed an "augmented balance sheet" in which pension assets and liabilities were added to, respectively, corporate assets and liabilities to draw the true picture facing shareholders. The pension subsidiary, like any other unit of the company, was said to have the responsibility of helping the sponsor maximize its shareholders' wealth. This maximization could be done, they argued, in the context of providing beneficiaries with a guarantee of benefits by managing the assets properly. If you took additional risk—say, equity risk, which has a return expectation higher than that of the primarily fixed-income mix that most closely matches the liability—the rewards from taking that risk would flow directly to the shareholders without compromising the beneficiaries. If the risk happened not to pay off, additional contributions from the sponsor to the plan would be required to make the beneficiaries whole.[114] This wisdom began to be taught (along with much else about maximizing shareholder value) in business schools in the late 1970s and continues to be taught to this day. But what happened to sponsors who took this advice?

At first, most did extremely well. Two decades of bull markets enabled sponsors to reap large profits from their pension plans, generally by taking long contribution holidays. Some spectacular exceptions occurred, primarily when poor management of the pension plan coincided with bankruptcy of the sponsoring corporation. The PBGC was forced to take over a large number of plans because of insolvency, but the amounts paid represented a small portion of the total dollar value of pension plans overall.[115]

Indeed, the "augmented balance sheet" view of the pension plan works well in rising markets or when companies have no capital constraint (so companies can borrow or can sell equity to meet pension shortfalls). Growing, financially healthy companies can generally operate as if they had no capital constraints, or not enough to make a difference for pension management.

The so-called pension crisis.   Markets go down as well as up, however, and companies go bankrupt or face high capital costs even though they are not bankrupt. In the bear market of 2000–2002, as in previous bear markets, pension surpluses quickly turned to shortfalls, as would be expected when stock prices decline if pension funds are exposed to equities. But this time, bonds also rallied tremendously, with lower interest rates causing pension liabilities to soar (in present value terms) at the same time that asset values were plummeting.

This entirely predictable and avoidable "crisis" did not cause universal distress. Many large companies had no DB plans or had small ones relative to the size of the company and thus were basically unaffected.[116] Severe problems arose only for a modest number of companies—primarily those in the auto, steel, airline, and a few other industries where profit growth had failed to keep pace with pension obligations—but the red flag of risk was raised for all to see. As a result, many companies "terminated" their DB plans (by buying annuities and not accepting further contributions) out of fear that the mysterious risk disease would strike them next. Few companies have started new DB plans in the aftermath of the bear market.

Lessons from the beta mismatch.   What I find surprising is that companies are apparently having such difficulty identifying the true source of their pension funds' apparent riskiness. The source of risk is, of course, the mismatch in beta, real interest rate duration, and inflation duration between the assets and the liabilities. Not only were pension plans "long" in equity beta; they were also "short" in real interest rate duration and "long" in inflation duration after netting out assets and liabilities. This mismatch can be easily fixed. Pension plans can be managed to have little risk. Such a prudent policy, which involves investing in more nominal fixed-income assets and inflation-linked assets (e.g., TIPS), may have a larger apparent cost but not a larger true cost: Companies are already implicitly paying the economic cost of underfunding, with this implied cost showing up as a shrunken share price.

Another way to look at the cost issue is by observing that the cost of making a pension promise is set by the terms of the promise, not by the means of financing it—in other words, the Modigliani and Miller (1958) invariance proposition in a slightly different guise. More precisely, the present value of the promise (liability) is the same no matter what assets are bought in an attempt to defease it. Buying assets with a higher expected return does not raise the present value of the portfolio, as should be obvious to anyone who thinks about it for a second. A dollar of high-risk, high-expected-return assets should have its future cash flows discounted back to the present at a higher rate so that it is worth the same amount as a dollar of low-risk, low-expected-return assets: it's worth a dollar. You cannot change the present value of a portfolio by changing the asset mix.

At any rate, if shareholders want to be long in equity beta, or take any other risk position, they can do it on their own at very low cost through futures or index funds. There is no compelling reason why the companies they invest in should do it for them through their pension plans. I am not saying that sponsors should not take any beta risk, only that they have good reason to rethink how much they take.

To conclude this tale, pension plans should generally be managed to pay the liabilities, not to enrich the company's shareholders. A pension manager could adopt this approach literally by holding the portfolio of assets with the lowest possible tracking error to the "liability benchmark" introduced into the discussion by Bernstein in the section titled Critiques of Benchmarking and a Way Forward. Such a portfolio would consist primarily of nominal and inflation-indexed bonds, with some equities and equity-like securities. Nothing is wrong with trying to earn a higher return than that combination, however, as long as the sponsor fully understands the risk of doing so and is in a position to take that risk without compromising the beneficiaries.

The sponsor who uses a liability benchmark and takes active risk against that benchmark by holding additional equities or other risky assets will be accounting properly for that risk if the sponsor adopts, at a conceptual level, the active risk–active return framework discussed in the section titled Using Benchmarks to Measure Performance. Note that I am using the term "active risk" in a slightly different context than previously. Active risk means deviating from a benchmark, whether by selecting securities or by selecting asset-class weights different from those in the liability or policy benchmark. In other words, if you deviate from the liability benchmark by holding more equities—that is, by taking more beta risk—you are taking active risk. Active risk, in this sense, could also mean taking real interest rate risk or inflation risk relative to the liability benchmark. And each kind of active risk taken, relative to the liability benchmark, must be justified by a defensible expectation of an active return from that risk that is high enough to "pay for" the risk taken—in more technical terms, to add utility after subtracting the appropriate penalty for active risk in Equation 2.4. (Recall that in that equation, the penalty for active risk is the investor's risk aversion parameter, lambda, times the active variance, or square of active standard deviation.)

Public and Nonprofit Plans

So far, the discussion has focused on corporate pension plans, where audited and publicly available balance sheets prevail (I hope!) and the stock price is a living gauge of how well investors think the company is doing at managing the pension plan (as well as its other activities). But the principles outlined apply as well to public and nonprofit plans. Because these types of sponsors may be less sensitive to risks and costs than corporate plans, and because they are not "covered" by security analysts, public and nonprofit sponsors have tended to keep their DB plans in place, but the economic effect of gap risk is the same no matter who the bearer of the risk is. Public and nonprofit plan sponsors should also manage their plans with sensitivity to the liabilities and with an awareness of the cost of taking gap risk, which predictably will have a negative payoff in some time periods.

Individual Investors

Although the problems facing individuals saving for retirement (on their own or through a DC plan) are superficially quite different from those facing a DB plan sponsor, the ultimate goal is similar—namely, to guarantee a lifetime income to the investor.[117] (In the case of the individual, the plan is a one-person plan, so the opportunity to share risk is greatly reduced. One way individuals can share mortality risk is to buy annuities from a commercial provider.) Individuals should manage their personal portfolios as asset/liability portfolios, where the liabilities are the cash flows out of the portfolio (i.e., income) that the investor will require in retirement. Individuals have more flexibility than corporate plan sponsors because individuals can, presumably, live on less income than they were expecting and because excess assets can be spent or bequeathed. In addition, contributions are more flexible (in both directions) for the individual than for the corporate DB sponsor. But the idea of matching a liability benchmark, or trying to beat it by taking various kinds of risk, is the same.

Endowments and Foundations

Endowed institutions typically have no specific liabilities defined independently of their assets; instead, they try to keep their assets whole in real terms (or to achieve growth in the real value of their assets) while spending a relatively fixed percentage of asset value each year. For private foundations, annual spending must at least be equal to 5 percent of asset value; most other types of endowed institutions have more flexibility.

Asset/liability modeling has little to say about the management of these kinds of portfolios. Some institutions manage them as asset-only portfolios and use risk budgets to help establish the asset mix. Although "absolute return benchmarks" (say, inflation plus 5 percent) are sometimes said to represent the goal of an endowment portfolio, such pseudo-benchmarks convey almost no information and should not be used (as noted in the section titled Critiques of Benchmarking and a Way Forward). The management of endowed institution portfolios is a topic of ongoing research.

Two Benchmarks

Realistically, most plan sponsors are not going to hold the portfolio that minimizes tracking error to the liability benchmark. Nominal fixed-income assets and TIPS have yields that are too low for most sponsors to accept. They may not continue to hold their current average of 60–70 percent in equities, but they may hold a mix of asset classes that is quite different from the asset mix that most closely matches the liability benchmark. How should their performance be measured—using two benchmarks?

Yes.

On one side, the investor will be managing in relation to a policy benchmark in the traditional sense. For many types of asset pools, this benchmark should be more conservative and less dominated by equities than has been the practice in the last decade or so, but it will still be a policy benchmark, one that is composed of asset classes that could, if desired, be held passively through index funds. Such an investable benchmark has the measurement power that has been the focus throughout this chapter. Once the proper risk level and the policy benchmark have been determined, the investor must demonstrate that he or she has added pure alpha by deviating from the benchmark while controlling the pure active risk inherent in those deviations. On the other side, the investor will be keeping an eye on a liability-focused benchmark. A benchmark of this kind is less a passive portfolio that you could hold in the absence of active views and more a conceptual reference point for focusing the mind on the real purpose of the asset pool and on the question of whether departing from the asset mix that most closely matches this benchmark is worth the risk (based on the risk aversion the investor has to this particular kind of risk).

The real purpose of the asset pool, of course, is to pay pension benefits, to fund the operations of a foundation or endowed institution, or to provide for the living expenses of an individual saver. By forcing investors to concentrate on the real problem at hand, a liability-focused benchmark can help them with the most crucial problem in investing—taking the right amount and right kind of risk in pursuit of the goal that they are charged with seeking.

ACKNOWLEDGMENTS

This work is dedicated to Connie and to Peter Bernstein.

I want to thank Linda Strumpf of the Ford Foundation for the personal and professional support that made this chapter possible. Linda, and Clinton Stevenson (also of the Ford Foundation), have taught me the plan sponsor's trade over the past eight years and have made innumerable suggestions for improving the chapter's contents and readability. I am also grateful to Mark Kritzman, who suggested the topic of the chapter and provided encouragement and feedback throughout the process of writing it.

This chapter reflects much prior work done jointly with my frequent co-author Barton Waring and also the highly productive, ongoing dialogue in which we openly share results from our separate research interests. He is effectively an unnamed co-author, on active management relative to benchmarks and on building optimal portfolios of managers, respectively; and of the section on asset-allocation policy relative to the liabilities of an investment program. Indeed, the whole chapter benefited from his influence.

Theodore Aronson, Barclay Douglas, Arnold Wood, and Jason Zweig added much wisdom, humor, and encouragement, as well as substantive commentary in interviews and discussions. Elizabeth Hilpman provided a perspective on the investment business and the people who make it work that is an education in itself and that is vigorously reflected here. Finally, in addition to being a great friend, Peter Bernstein has set a standard of quality in writing that all essayists, whether on investment issues or in other fields, would do well to emulate.

I also wish to thank numerous other people who provided suggestions, feedback, interviews, data, and other resources. They include (in alphabetical order) Clifford Asness, Mark Carhart, Thomas Coleman, Donald Galligan, William Goetzmann, Roger Ibbotson, Stephen Johnson, David Kabiller, Paul Kaplan, Susan Ollila, Thomas Philips, Brad Pope, Thomas Schneeweis, Steven Schoenfeld, Rex Sinquefield, Mark Sladkus, and Ronald Surz. Those whom I've forgotten to thank have my apologies in advance.

In addition to these personal acknowledgements, I am grateful to the Research Foundation for financial support for the research and writing of this chapter.

L.B.S.
Wilmette, Illinois
June 2003

NOTES

1. This section initially appeared in a modified form in Enderle, Pope, and Siegel (2002, 2003), which focused not on benchmarks (indexes) in general but on broad-capitalization indexes of equities in the United States. By "broad capitalization," we meant indexes that include stocks of all market sizes—large, medium, and small—as opposed to specialized indexes that measure stocks in only one size category.
2. Throughout this chapter, I use "benchmark" as a synonym for "index" when the index is being used as a point of comparison for actual portfolios.
3. A full-replication fund holds every security in the index in proportion to its index weight; an optimized or sampled fund, which attempts to track an index using a subset of the securities in the index, may require more frequent rebalancing even if the fund is based on a cap-weighted index.
4. Governmental holding of corporate equities is a major consideration in many non-U.S. markets but not in the U.S. market.
5. Because they include a large number of micro-cap stocks, the broadest indexes also suffer from "stale" prices. Stocks that don't trade every day—typically the smallest-cap stocks—are carried at their most recent trade prices, which may not be very recent, or are priced at a broker's bid price or at the average of bid and ask. Other illiquid asset classes for which stale pricing is a problem in index construction are real estate, private equity, some types of corporate and municipal bonds, and the equity markets of some (typically emerging) countries. Stale prices cause the return and risk of a benchmark or portfolio to be misstated. Stale pricing has only a small impact, however, on broad-cap indexes.
6. ETFs are investment funds (typically index funds), shares of which are traded on an exchange like any other stock. Thus, the investor pays and receives the market price, rather than the net asset value (NAV), for a share of an ETF. This characteristic is in contrast to conventional mutual fund shares, which are sold and redeemed by the fund management firm at the NAV. The market price of an ETF tends to remain close to the NAV because of the trading activity of brokers' arbitrage desks and because of the trades executed by the fund management firm itself.
7. The use of judgment to select the S&P 500 has led to the allegation that the S&P 500 is itself an actively managed portfolio and thus should not be used as a benchmark for other active portfolios; the section titled Critiques of Benchmarking and a Way Forward, contains an assessment of this critique.

8. Managers who vary their betas during the measurement period will have an alpha, either positive or negative, but one that should be attributed to tactical asset allocation (market timing) rather than to the security selection for which most managers are hired.

9. Following Waring, Pirone, Whitney, and Castille (2000), I use the term "manager structure" to mean the weights of the various managers in an overall investment program.

10. In addition, some stocks and portfolios are classified as mid-cap (between large and small in capitalization) or "core" (between value and growth), but the estimation of pure alpha will not require these extra wrinkles.

11. If the regression is unconstrained, allowing leveraged or short "positions" in one or more style benchmarks, the "fit" of the regression is better—that is, the regression provides a better model of the manager.

12. Therefore, most investors would rather take policy risk than active risk. This choice makes sense because policy risk is inherently rewarded, on average, over time, whereas active risk is not (because active management is a zero-sum game).

13. You also need the correlation matrix of the active returns of the managers, but this matrix can usually be presumed to be a matrix of zeros (because regression on the market and style factors causes the residuals to be mostly uncorrelated, at least for large-cap U.S. equity managers).

14. Waring and Siegel expressed this concept as follows: "[A]n investor must meet *two conditions* if he or she is to hire active managers. First, one must believe that superior managers really do exist. That's easy, if one accepts that managers differ in their skill levels. Second—this is the hard one—one must believe that he or she can identify which ones will be the winners" (p. 46).

15. Note that the general principle of keeping costs under control is violated with most market-neutral equity hedge funds. I hope that the extraordinarily high fees currently associated with hedge funds will be subject to competitive downward pressure, but pending that development, investors may have to pay such fees to obtain the benefits of this type of fund.

16. Despite the emphasis on value, the growth style in investing is consistent with "original paradigm" thinking, as demonstrated in the excellent writings of Fisher (1958; reprinted 1996). A growth stock is a good value if the present value of its expected future cash flows (dividends plus liquidation price) is greater than its current price.

17. Interestingly, Williams' discovery of the DDM predates by quite a few years the better-known (at least among academics) work of Gordon and Shapiro (1956).

18. According to Fisher (1966), the time-weighted rate of return is the linked internal rate of return, where a portfolio is valued at discrete time intervals and the internal rate of return (IRR) is calculated over the period between two successive valuation times; then, these IRRs are linked (by multiplying together terms consisting of 1 plus the IRR) to produce the time-weighted rate of return. See Fisher (1966), Newton (1664–1671), and Raphson (1690). I thank Ronald J. Surz for pointing out the connection between Fisher's work and the work, more than two and a half centuries earlier, of Newton and Raphson.

19. Personal communication with Jason Zweig.

20. I thank Paul D. Kaplan of Morningstar for his helpful comments on this section.

21. Markowitz noted that investors already behave as though they face risk; they diversify in practice rather than concentrating their holdings on the security perceived to be the best.

22. This definition is itself a source of much controversy. I briefly compare standard deviation with other risk measures in the section titled The 1990s Bubble and the Crisis in MPT.

23. See Sharpe (1964). John Lintner, Jan Mossin, and Jack Treynor discovered the CAPM at about the same time as Sharpe. The story of the derivation of the CAPM is told compellingly in Bernstein (1992).

24. A good general discussion of alpha, beta, and other statistics relevant to performance measurement is in Chapter 7 of Sharpe, Alexander, and Bailey (1995); for a strong discussion of the CAPM, see Chapter 10 of their work.

25. In the section titled Using Benchmarks to Measure Performance, I discussed adjusting portfolio performance for common factors—including style factors—in addition to the market, or beta, when measuring investment performance.

26. Formally, conventional performance measurement relies on the "market model," a backward-looking model with a functional form similar to that of the CAPM but somewhat different in purpose. Specifically, the CAPM seeks to estimate the expected return on an asset or portfolio; the market model seeks to apportion the actual past return between the part arising from market exposure (beta) and the part arising from active bets (alpha). But (and this aspect is rarely pointed out) the market model and the CAPM are not as different as this description makes them sound, because the market model gives accurate measures of the alpha added by the manager only if the CAPM is "true" (that is, if the CAPM gives accurate estimates of the return you should expect from the market or beta component). The method I set forth in the section titled Using Benchmarks to Measure Performance, which measures performance after adjusting for size and valuation as well as beta, relies on a three-factor model of security returns (instead of the CAPM) being "true."

27. I used this insight in the section titled Building Portfolios of Managers in arguing that you should use active return–active risk optimization at the total portfolio level to select managers, but the concept originated with Rosenberg, who carried out this kind of optimization at the security level decades earlier.

28. A good overview of the Barra model is at www.barra.com/research/barrapub/risk_models. asp. Rosenberg is no longer personally associated with Barra.

29. I thank Ronald J. Surz of Performance Presentation Consulting Alliance, who was at one time an executive of Becker, for providing the interview on which this section is based.

30. To be precise, the total return on the S&P 500 Index, including reinvestment of dividends, was 19.75 percent a year, compounded, from 1 September 1982 to 31 March 2000.

31. Although Berkshire Hathaway is structured as an operating company and is traded on the New York Stock Exchange, it is best understood as a portfolio (that is, as an investment manager) and compared with other portfolios (mutual funds, separately managed accounts, and so forth).

32. Among the investment managers who publicly took this position were Robert D. Arnott of First Quadrant, Clifford S. Asness of AQR Capital Management, and Jeremy Grantham of Grantham, Mayo, Van Otterloo, & Company.

33. MPT is sometimes used to describe a wide range of beliefs and practices, but I am defining MPT narrowly to comprise mean–variance optimization, the separation of policy and active risk, and the calculation and management of active risk as defined by the capital asset pricing model and factor models.

34. By "the whole market," I don't mean every single stock; small-cap and value stocks were probably underpriced in the spring of 2000 and later rallied, whereas tech stocks were falling in 2000–2002. I mean that the overall level of broad, cap-weighted market benchmarks was too high.

35. The use of an "absolute return benchmark" or "liability benchmark," discussed in the section titled Critiques of Benchmarking and a Way Forward, is sometimes advocated

by the same people who criticize MPT or who say the market is not efficient. These alternative benchmarks (if you want to call them that) do not, however, fall directly out of the theoretical contributions made by critics of MPT and efficient markets. They are simply alternatives to conventional practice.

36. Markowitz used standard deviation as the measure of risk because it makes the math notably easier than does any other risk measure, not because he thought it was the best measure that could be imagined.

37. Markowitz himself acknowledged (1991) the potential value of semideviation below a target or below the asset's own mean as a measure of risk.

38. By "shortfall" is meant a return below some minimum acceptable return or target.

39. See also Shefrin (2001). Shefrin, like Haugen, was comparing riskier and safer *stocks* (not asset classes).

40. In equities, Standard & Poor's is simply an index constructor, not an asset manager. Standard & Poor's also provides "ratings" (credit assessments) of fixed-income securities.

41. Rattray and Manglani used the same definition of "U.S. stocks" that Standard & Poor's did at each point in time, so their "top 500" sometimes included American Depositary Receipts and sometimes did not. This approach isolates the effect of the S&P decision rules and discretionary calls on the relative returns of the two indexes.

42. Once in the S&P 500, however, companies that become unprofitable are not deleted except under extreme circumstances.

43. I provide more detail on the Standard & Poor's inclusion effect discussion of index price distortions in the section titled The Impact of Benchmarking on Markets and Institutions.

44. If all portfolios were hedge funds, their aggregate beta would also be 1.0.

45. Rewards would be fantastic not only in terms of investment performance but also with regard to the fees that could be collected.

46. By "independent," I mean that he does not, as far as I know, manage any investments for others.

47. All the quotations that follow are from Bernstein's "A Modest Proposal: Portfolio Management Practice for Modern Times" (2000).

48. See also Waring and Siegel (2003).

49. In their Chapter 5, Grinold and Kahn (2000) defined "breadth" as the number of unrelated investment decisions a manager has the freedom to make. They also proposed the following "fundamental law of active management": At a given level of skill, investment performance is proportional to breadth as defined in this way.

50. A definitive examination of the efficiency of equally weighted portfolios is that of Jobson and Korkie (1981). They found that in some conditions, an equally weighted portfolio is as efficient as, or even more efficient than, a cap-weighted one. The small-cap effect, which was powerful in the time period leading up to Jobson and Korkie's work, may at least partly explain this result. If that effect is the correct explanation, their results will not be repeatable.

51. Another line of reasoning about benchmarks is represented by Haugen (1995), who constructed an "efficient index" based on optimization that used estimates of security returns, risks, and correlations derived from fundamental factors. I believe this approach is simply active management: An investor who does not have access to Haugen's specific forecasts cannot determine what the benchmark contents will be.

52. The major categories of arbitrageurs are (1) hedge funds and (2) the proprietary trading desks of brokerage firms.

53. Because the index is calculated on a basis that assumes reconstitution-related costs have been paid, strategies that reduce these costs are seen as adding alpha.

54. The effects of index reconstitutions on international equity prices are discussed in the section titled International Equity Benchmarks. To make sense of the evidence on international reconstitution effects, a reader must first understand in some detail how international equity indexes are constructed, particularly as regards float adjustment and inclusion/deletion of countries.

55. Charles Dickens, *David Copperfield* (1849).

56. On pp. 57–59, Ibbotson and Brinson review other reasons the market cannot be perfectly efficient. See also Grossman and Stiglitz (1980).

57. Now that the bubble is well behind us, it is a good time to look for really strained arguments from finance professors as to why prices during the bubble were actually rational.

58. Personal communication with Rex Sinquefield.

59. Portions of this section also appeared in Pope, Rakvin, and Platt (2003), of which I was a contributing editor. I thank Theodore R. Aronson of Aronson+Johnson+Ortiz, Clifford S. Asness of AQR Capital Management, and Paul D. Kaplan of Morningstar for valuable discussions over the years about value and growth investing and many other topics.

60. When the capitalization and valuation effects were discovered in the late 1970s, they were widely regarded as ways to beat the market. A small-cap and/or value "tilt" to one's portfolio was considered desirable in that it would earn, in expectation, a higher return, even after adjusting for risk. Today, only a minority of analysts would make that claim; they would propose, instead, that style and size categories of the market are (at least on average over time) fairly priced relative to one another, given their inherent risks. I argue briefly in this section that value may be a better long-term strategy than growth, but that is by no means a foregone conclusion.

61. Morningstar, which constructs a suite of style indexes that are not reviewed here, does keep track of returns and constituent (stock) lists for the core category.

62. More detail on the small-cap effect and on the history surrounding its discovery can be found in Clothier, Waring, and Siegel (1998).

63. "Investing in International Small Company Stocks," Institute for Fiduciary Education website: www.ifecorp.com/Papers-PDFs/Hall701.pdf.

64. Some authors have argued that the small-cap effect is smaller, or disappears, if one calculates beta in a way that takes account of infrequent trading and other circumstances peculiar to small-cap stocks. The most recent entry in a large body of literature is Ibbotson, Kaplan, and Peterson (1997).

65. Ball (1978) and others made similar discoveries around the same time.

66. The analysis depicted in Figure 2.1 is based on a rolling 60-month data window; that is, the style exposure shown for each month represents the average style exposure over the five years ending in that month.

67. Beta worked well during the period leading up to the time, in the early 1960s, when Sharpe discovered it, but in the period from 1963 to 1990, the relationship between beta and stock returns was not clear. Instead, Fama and French found that size and book-to-price ratio (B/P, the inverse of P/B) had the greatest power to explain returns. Responding to criticism, they found, by looking at ever longer periods, that the results still held: Size and valuation swamped the effect of beta for 1924–1990. Fama and French showed that B/P is more effective than size at explaining returns and, in fact, when combined with size, renders the other factors (E/P and leverage) redundant.

68. The case for holdings-based style analysis is made by Buetow, Johnson, and Runkle (2000). A number of other authors have made similar arguments.

69. All of these indexes are described in detail later. Additional providers of style indexes for the U.S. equity market, including Morgan Stanley Capital International and Morningstar, are not covered here.

70. For more detail, see Pope, Rakvin, and Platt (2003).

71. I/B/E/S data are now part of the First Call database maintained by Thomson Financial.

72. Issues that are beyond the scope of this chapter include difficulty in tracking bond benchmarks, liquidity and float, reconstitution effects and costs, differences between benchmarks and the criteria for choosing one, and currency hedging for fixed-income international benchmarks.

73. I thank Susan A. Ollila, director of fixed-income investments at the Ford Foundation, for her helpful comments. Steve Johnson and several of his colleagues at INVESCO contributed ideas to this section.

74. Such mapping of equity assets is a goal that generally eludes equity researchers, despite the best efforts of Barra. Researchers have attempted to map stocks into characteristic space by classifying stocks into styles, sectors, and industries. But because each stock represents ownership of a business with a great deal of idiosyncratic (nonmarket) risk and the cash flows from a stock are not well specified in advance, such groupings may contain stocks that are not like one another at all. Two aluminum companies or two insurance companies, for example, may have returns that are mostly unrelated.

75. At least this disparity is true if you count municipal bonds. At any rate, the number of bonds that have a significant impact on the returns of cap-weighted benchmarks is considerably larger than the corresponding number of stocks.

76. Stretching a point, some have argued that if the cap-weighted combination of all risky assets (not only stocks) is mean–variance efficient, as Roll (1977) said, then a cap-weighted portfolio of all outstanding bonds—which is, of course, part of the cap-weighted portfolio of all assets—is the efficient set within the fixed-income asset class. This argument is the theoretical justification for extending cap-weighted benchmarks to asset classes other than equities. For this justification to be valid, however, the assets must represent some sort of wealth in the real economy. Because offsetting claims may exist in the bond market (especially in structured debt and derivatives), which would cause double or multiple counting of wealth, and because controversy continues as to whether government bonds represent wealth (see Barro 1974), to consider the cap-weighted portfolio of bonds to be efficient is theoretically suspect. Each investor, rather than holding the cap-weighted benchmark, should seek the duration and other bond portfolio attributes that fit the investor's needs or liabilities.

77. The observation that large order size is required to get good execution in the bond market is in contrast to the equity market, where large orders tend to be expensive to trade. See Dynkin, Hyman, and Konstantinovsky (2002).

78. I say "apparent" because, according to the Modigliani and Miller (1958) invariance proposition, the cost of capital of a company is set on the asset side of the balance sheet by the risk of the company's projects (business lines), not by the way the projects are financed. The current cost of servicing debt does matter, however, in a world with transaction costs and with differential tax treatment of equity and debt. If you accept these arguments, then the role of the chief financial officer is to minimize the transaction costs and taxes associated with financing the company's operations.

79. See Modigliani and Sutch (1969) and also, for a perspective on market efficiency under preferred habitat conditions, Mishkin (1980).

80. Formerly, this index was maintained by Salomon Smith Barney.
81. Although a given bond pays a fixed income, a bond portfolio (or bond mutual fund) does not because of reinvestment risk and changing portfolio composition. Every once in a while, a reminder to investors of why fixed-income assets are so called is helpful.
82. I thank Mark Sladkus of Morgan Stanley Capital International for providing an interview used in this section, and I thank Steven Schoenfeld of Active Index Advisors for sharing many of the ideas and much of the data in Schoenfeld and Ginis (2002). Schoenfeld was at Barclays Global Investors when he did the work referred to in this section.
83. For an excellent general discussion of global equity returns and indexes and a 101-year historical reconstruction in 16 countries based on returns from various carefully documented sources, see Dimson, Marsh, and Staunton (2002).
84. See Sikorsky (1982). The November 1968 date represents a test launch, and the indexes were backdated to 1959. The eventual MSCI indexes had an initiation and base date of 1 January 1970.
85. Sikorsky is president of Capital International S.A., an operating unit of the Capital Group; MSCI is a joint venture of Morgan Stanley and Capital International and is now controlled by Morgan Stanley.
86. For the two premiums to cancel each other out, U.S. and non-U.S. investors would also need roughly the same amount of aversion to the risk represented by investing in each other's markets.
87. Originally, "EAFE" stood for Europe/Australia/Far East Index. Later, the name was changed to the Europe/Australasia/Far East Index.
88. Free-float weighting does not eliminate distortions caused by high market prices (valuations), as it should not if a cap-weighted benchmark is the goal.
89. Although not specifically discussed previously, this trade-off also applies to the U.S. equity market and should be taken into consideration when selecting a U.S. equity benchmark.
90. For a full discussion of the size effect internationally, see Clothier, Waring, and Siegel (1998).
91. The traditional "Asian tigers" were Hong Kong, South Korea, Singapore, and Taiwan; later, the term was sometimes expanded to include Malaysia, Thailand, and other countries. Mexico was in the original MSCI suite of indexes discussed in Sikorsky (1982). The former communist countries were typically not strangers to equity investing; Hungary, for example, had the world's fourth largest stock exchange in 1900.
92. Schoenfeld and Ginis were citing data from InterSec Research Corporation.
93. This quotation and the next one are from "Malaysia to Be Removed from MSCI EAFE," Capital International press release, 4 September 1998: www.msci.com/pressreleases/archive/pr199809a.html.
94. On a daily basis, the results are quite confusing. The volatile MSCI Malaysia Index actually rose, in U.S. dollars, by 75.0 percent between 1 September and 7 September 1998. By 30 September, it had fallen back to its old low. Currency depreciation was responsible for part of the decline after 7 September but had almost no impact on the 1–7 September advance. The reasons for these dramatic price moves might be a fruitful research topic for those interested in index-inclusion effects (or the effects of capital controls).
95. As of 30 June 2003.
96. Unpublished report, Barclays Global Investors, San Francisco (14 December 2001).

97. This and the following quotation are from "The MSCI Reconstitution: What Happened?" Unpublished report, Barclays Global Investors, San Francisco (2002).

98. I use quotation marks to describe "shortages" and "gluts" in this context because in open markets, supply–demand imbalances (shortages and gluts) exist only at the current price; the imbalance is resolved by a change in price that calls forth additional supply or that removes some of the excess supply.

99. The author thanks Elizabeth Hilpman of Barlow Partners and Thomas Schneeweis of the Center for International Securities and Derivatives Markets at the University of Massachusetts for helpful comments.

100. Naturally, the creators of hedge fund benchmarks have sought to avoid incorporating the traditional market influences (the stock market, bond market, and so forth) while uncovering new ones with greater potential relevance.

101. ZCM has constructed not only hedge fund indexes but also an actual portfolio, called the "Benchmark Series," that is intended to track the index. To avoid confusion, I use the term "benchmark" in the sense in which it is used in the rest of this chapter—a synonym for "index" when the index is being used as a point of comparison for actual portfolios. I do not follow ZCM's use of the name "Benchmark Series," in *contrast* to the index itself.

102. Only if you envision hedge funds as operating companies (in, say, the trading and arbitrage business) does the net capital of a hedge fund represent capitalization (wealth) in the sense that we think of stocks and bonds as wealth. Even then, a hedge fund's net capital position is not a *market* price for the trading business (because it is not arrived at in an arm's-length, continuous-auction market). Its net capital position is the equivalent of a book value.

103. For an extensive discussion of survivor bias in hedge fund indexes, see Fung and Hsieh (2002).

104. Note that I have avoided the popular term "relative value" because it is used as a catch-all term. Virtually all long–short strategies, including all of the arbitrage styles as well as equity long–short and equity market-neutral strategies, are based on the concept of relative value. Yet, five providers of hedge fund indexes have a relative-value style index. EACM's relative-value index includes four subindexes (equity long–short, convertible arbitrage, fixed-income arbitrage, and multistrategy).

105. I would add to the factor list the return difference between U.S. value and growth stocks.

106. Roll (1977) indicated why the (unobservable) cap-weighted portfolio of all risky assets in the world, not just the cap-weighted portfolio of all U.S. or all global publicly traded equities, is mean–variance efficient under the conditions of the capital asset pricing model.

107. Ibbotson and Siegel (1983), updated in Ibbotson, Siegel, and Love (1985), made an explicit effort to measure the returns and weights of the global cap-weighted portfolio of all risky assets.

108. The issues discussed in this section will be developed further in an article in progress by the author and M. Barton Waring of Barclays Global Investors. The discussion presented here emerged from the work we have done in preparing to write that article. I thank Mr. Waring for his contribution to it.

109. The return on the "liability benchmark" is thus the rate of change of the present value of the liability or the rate of change in the present value of the intended spending out of the fund.

110. Note that pension funds are needed only because some possibility exists that the sponsor will go bankrupt. If there were no possibility that a plan sponsor could fail to honor its obligations, a pay-as-you-go system (in which benefits are paid out of the company's or other organization's current income) would work perfectly well with no need for advance funding (investing).

111. In addition, some of the idiosyncratic risk in a given company's pension liability cannot be modeled as either fixed income or equity risk; therefore, you cannot do anything about it (other than to make additional contributions to the fund as required).

112. "Insured" plans actually bought annuities for their participants, so the issuing insurance company, not the sponsor, paid benefits to retirees. In contrast, in "trusteed" plans (the modern structure), the sponsor buys annuities, bonds, and other securities and pays benefits to retirees. My comment about annuities defeasing only noninflating liabilities reflects the fact that during the period when the traditional pension management methods described here were prevalent, no inflation-indexed annuities existed.

113. The distinction between nominal and real interest rate duration, which is fully described in Siegel (2003), may be summarized as follows: The price of a T-bond that is fully inflation indexed, such as TIPS, is insensitive to changes in expected inflation because any such change is matched by an equal change in the bond's expected cash flows; the changes in the cash flows and the discount rate cancel each other out, and the price remains unchanged. Thus, TIPS have an inflation duration, or sensitivity of price with respect to changes in expected inflation, of zero. Like nominal bonds, however, TIPS are sensitive (with a negative sign) to changes in the real interest rate. This sensitivity is the real interest rate duration of TIPS. Thus, TIPS have not one but two durations. This logic implies that any set of cash flows—from a nominal bond, a pension liability, and so forth—has these two durations, although for a nominal bond, they are equal and not separately observable (because the effect of a change in a nominal bond's yield on its price is the same whether the change in yield comes from a change in expected inflation or from a change in real interest rates).

114. This strategy, which is the basis for the modern pension system, depends on the company not entering or approaching bankruptcy (because one would not want the required pension contribution, in case risk taking in the pension plan failed to pay off, to tip the company into bankruptcy).

115. Steven A. Kandarian, executive director of the PBGC, stated, "PBGC insures pension benefits worth $1.5 trillion and is responsible for paying current and future benefits to 783,000 people in over 3,000 terminated defined benefit plans. As a result of the recent terminations of several very large plans, PBGC will be responsible for paying benefits to nearly 1 million people in FY 2003. Similarly, benefit payments that exceeded $1.5 billion dollars in FY 2002 will rise to nearly $2.5 billion in FY 2003." But the 783,000 participants receiving current or deferred payments from the PBGC are a tiny minority of the roughly 44 million DB plan participants whose pensions are insured by that organization. See "Statement of Steven A. Kandarian, Executive Director, Pension Benefit Guaranty Corporation, before the Committee on Finance, United States Senate, March 11, 2003": www.pbgc.gov/news/speeches/Testimony031103.pdf.

116. Their employees were, of course, affected in their defined-contribution (DC) plans by falling stock prices; virtually all companies with no DB plan have a DC plan for their employees.

117. Muralidhar (2001) showed how the similarities between DB and DC plans can be exploited for the purpose of analyzing them and establishing investment policy and social policy.

REFERENCES

Amenc, Noël, and Lionel Martellini. 2003. "The Brave New World of Hedge Fund Indices." Working paper. Available online at www-rcf.usc.edu/~martelli/papers/bnwhfi.pdf.

Arnott, Robert D., and Max Darnell. 2003. "Active versus Passive Management: Framing the Decision." *Journal of Investing*, vol. 12, no. 1 (Spring):31–36.

Asness, Clifford S., Jacques A. Friedman, Robert J. Krail, and John M. Liew. 2000. "Style Timing: Value versus Growth." *Journal of Portfolio Management*, vol. 26, no. 3 (Spring):50–60.

Ball, Ray. 1978. "Anomalies in Relationships between Securities' Yields and Yield-Surrogates." *Journal of Financial Economics*, vol. 6, nos. 2/3 (June):103–126.

Banz, Rolf W. 1981. "The Relationship between Return and Market Value of Common Stocks." *Journal of Financial Economics*, vol. 9, no. 1 (March):3–18.

Barro, Robert J. 1974. "Are Government Bonds Net Wealth?" *Journal of Political Economy*, vol. 82, no. 6 (November/December):1095–1117.

Basu, Sanjoy. 1977. "Investment Performance of Common Stocks in Relation to their Price–Earnings Ratios: A Test of the Efficient Market Hypothesis." *Journal of Finance*, vol. 32, no. 3 (June):663–681.

———. 1983. "The Relationship between Earnings Yield, Market Value, and Return for NYSE Common Stocks: Further Evidence." *Journal of Financial Economics*, vol. 12, no. 1 (June):129–156.

Bergstrom, Gary P. 1975. "A New Route to Higher Return and Lower Risk." *Journal of Portfolio Management*, vol. 2, no. 1 (Autumn):30–38.

Bernstein, Peter L. 1992. *Capital Ideas: The Improbable Origins of Modern Wall Street.* New York: Free Press.

———. 1994. "Measuring the Performance of Performance Measurement." *Economics & Portfolio Strategy.* New York: Peter L. Bernstein, Inc. (1 December).

———. 1996. *Against the Gods: The Remarkable Story of Risk.* New York: John Wiley & Sons.

———. 2000. "A Modest Proposal: Portfolio Management Practice for Modern Times." *Economics & Portfolio Strategy.* New York: Peter L. Bernstein, Inc. (15 April).

Brinson, Gary P., L. Randolph Hood, and Gilbert L. Beebower. 1986. "Determinants of Portfolio Performance." *Financial Analysts Journal*, vol. 42, no. 4 (July/August):39–44. Reprinted in *FAJ*'s 50th Anniversary Issue, vol. 51, no. 1 (January/February 1995): 133–138.

Buetow, Gerald W., Jr., Robert R. Johnson, and David E. Runkle. 2000. "The Inconsistency of Returns-Based Style Analysis." *Journal of Portfolio Management*, vol. 26, no. 3 (Spring):61–77.

Clifford, Scott W., Kenneth F. Kroner, and Laurence B. Siegel. 2001. "In Pursuit of Performance: The Greatest Return Stories Ever Told," *Investment Insights*, vol. 4, no. 1 (August). San Francisco, CA: Barclays Global Investors.

Clothier, Eric, M. Barton Waring, and Laurence B. Siegel. 1998. "Is Small-Cap Investing Worth It? Two Decades of Research on Small-Cap Stocks." *Investment Insights*, vol. 1, no. 5 (December). San Francisco, CA: Barclays Global Investors.

Cowles, Alfred. 1938 (2nd ed. 1939). *Common Stock Indexes: 1871–1937.* Bloomington, IN: Principia.

Dimson, Elroy, Paul Marsh, and Mike Staunton. 2002. *Triumph of the Optimists.* Princeton, NJ: Princeton University Press.

Dynkin, Lev, Jay Hyman, and Vadim Konstantinovsky. 2002. "Sufficient Diversification in Credit Portfolios." *Journal of Portfolio Management*, vol. 29, no. 1 (Fall):89–114.

Enderle, Francis, Brad Pope, and Laurence B. Siegel. 2002. "Broad-Capitalization Indexes of the U.S. Equity Market." *Investment Insights*, vol. 5, no. 2 (May). San Francisco, CA: Barclays Global Investors.

———. 2003. "Broad-Capitalization Indexes of the U.S. Equity Market." *Journal of Investing*, vol. 12, no. 1 (Spring):11–22.

Fama, Eugene F., and Kenneth R. French. 1992. "The Cross-Section of Expected Stock Returns." *Journal of Finance*, vol. 47, no. 2 (June):427–465.

———. 1993. "Common Risk Factors in the Returns on Stocks and Bonds." *Journal of Financial Economics*, vol. 33, no. 1 (February):3–56.

Fisher, Lawrence. 1966. "An Algorithm for Finding Exact Rates of Return." *Journal of Business*, vol. 39, no. 1, part 2 (January):111–118.

Fisher, Philip A. 1958 (Anthology edition 1996). *Common Stocks and Uncommon Profits*. New York: John Wiley & Sons.

Fung, William, and David A. Hsieh. 2002. "Hedge-Fund Benchmarks: Information Content and Biases." *Financial Analysts Journal*, vol. 58, no. 1 (January/February):22–34.

Goetzmann, William N., and Mark Garry. 1986. "Does Delisting from the S&P 500 Affect Stock Price?" *Financial Analysts Journal*, vol. 42, no. 2 (March/April):64–69.

Gordon, Myron J., and Eli Shapiro. 1956. "Capital Equipment Analysis: The Required Rate of Profit." *Management Science*, vol. 3 (October):102–110.

Graham, Benjamin F., and David L. Dodd. 1934 (4th ed. 1972). *Security Analysis*. New York: McGraw-Hill.

Graham, Benjamin, and Jason Zweig. 2003. *The Intelligent Investor*. New York: HarperCollins.

Grinold, Richard C. 1989. "The Fundamental Law of Active Management." *Journal of Portfolio Management*, vol. 15, no. 3 (Spring):30–37.

———. 1990. "The Sponsor's View of Risk." In *Pension Fund Investment Management: A Handbook for Investors and Their Advisors*. Edited by Frank J. Fabozzi. Chicago, IL: Probus.

Grinold, Richard C., and Ronald N. Kahn. 2000. 2nd ed. *Active Portfolio Management*. New York: McGraw-Hill.

Grossman, Sanford J., and Joseph E. Stiglitz. 1980. "On the Impossibility of Informationally Efficient Markets." *American Economic Review*, vol. 70, no. 3 (June):393–408.

Harris, Lawrence, and Eitan Gurel. 1986. "Price and Volume Effects Associated with Changes in the S&P 500 List: New Evidence for the Existence of Price Pressures." *Journal of Finance*, vol. 41, no. 4 (September):815–829.

Haugen, Robert A. 1995. *The New Finance: The Case against Efficient Markets*. Englewood Cliffs, NJ: Prentice-Hall.

Ibbotson Associates. 2003. *Stocks, Bonds, Bills, and Inflation: 2003 Yearbook*. Chicago, IL: Ibbotson Associates (updates work by Roger G. Ibbotson and Rex A. Sinquefield).

Ibbotson, Roger G., and Gary P. Brinson. 1987. *Investment Markets: Gaining the Performance Advantage*. New York: McGraw-Hill.

Ibbotson, Roger G., and Paul D. Kaplan. 2000. "Does Asset Allocation Policy Explain 40, 90, or 100 Percent of Performance?" *Financial Analysts Journal*, vol. 56, no. 1 (January/February):26–33.

Ibbotson, Roger G., and Laurence B. Siegel. 1983. "The World Market Wealth Portfolio." *Journal of Portfolio Management*, vol. 9, no. 2 (Winter):5–17.

Ibbotson, Roger G., Paul D. Kaplan, and James D. Peterson. 1997. "Estimates of Small Stock Betas Are Much Too Low." *Journal of Portfolio Management*, vol. 24, no. 2 (Summer):104–111.

Ibbotson, Roger G., Laurence B. Siegel, and Kathryn S. Love. 1985. "World Wealth: Market Values and Returns." *Journal of Portfolio Management*, vol. 12, no. 1 (Fall):4–23.

Jacques, William E. 1988. "The S&P 500 Membership Anomaly, or Would You Join This Club?" *Financial Analysts Journal*, vol. 44, no. 6 (November/December):73–75.

Jain, Prem C. 1987. "The Effect on Stock Price of Inclusion in or Exclusion from the S&P 500." *Financial Analysts Journal*, vol. 43, no. 1 (January/February):58–65.

Jegadeesh, Narasimhan. 1990. "Evidence of Predictable Behavior of Security Returns." *Journal of Finance*, vol. 45, no. 3 (July):881–898.

Jensen, Michael C. 1968. "Problems in Selection of Security Portfolios: The Performance of Mutual Funds in the Period 1945–1964." *Journal of Finance*, vol. 23, no. 2 (March):389–416.

Jobson, J.D., and Bob Korkie. 1981. "Putting Markowitz Theory to Work." *Journal of Portfolio Management*, vol. 7, no. 4 (Summer):70–74.

Johnson, Stephen M., and Laurence B. Siegel. 2003. "Credit Market Volatility and Change." *Journal of Investing*, vol. 12, no. 1 (Spring):37–46.

Kahn, Ronald N. 2000. "Most Pension Plans Need More Enhanced Indexing." In *Enhanced Indexing: New Strategies and Techniques for Investors*. Edited by Brian R. Bruce. New York: Institutional Investor.

Kritzman, Mark. 1998. "Wrong and Alone." *Economics & Portfolio Strategy*. New York: Peter L. Bernstein, Inc. (15 January).

———. 2003. "Value In—Garbage Out." *Economics & Portfolio Strategy*. New York: Peter L. Bernstein, Inc. (15 January).

Kuhn, Thomas S. 1996. *The Structure of Scientific Revolutions*. 3rd ed. Chicago, IL: University of Chicago Press.

Leibowitz, Martin L., and Roy D. Henriksson. 1989. "Portfolio Optimization with Shortfall Constraints: A Confidence-Limit Approach to Managing Downside Risk." *Financial Analysts Journal*, vol. 45, no. 2 (March/April):34–41.

Lowenstein, Roger. 2001. "Value Vindicated." *SmartMoney* (August).

Madhavan, Ananth. 2002. "Index Reconstitution and Equity Returns." Unpublished manuscript. (Available online at www.itginc.com/research/whitepapers/madhavan/Russell Study.pdf.)

Markowitz, Harry M. 1952. "Portfolio Selection." *Journal of Finance* (March):77–91.

———. 1991. *Portfolio Selection: Efficient Diversification of Investments*. 2nd. ed. Oxford, U.K.: Basil Blackwell.

Michaud, Richard. 2001. *Efficient Asset Management: A Practical Guide to Stock Portfolio Optimization and Asset Allocation*. New York: Oxford University Press. First published in 1998 by Cambridge, MA: Harvard Business School Press.

———. 2003. "An Introduction to Resampled Efficiency." *The Monitor*, Investment Management Consultants Association, vol. 18, no. 1 (January/February):22–23.

Michaud, Richard, and Robert Michaud. 2003. "Resampled Efficiency Issues." (Available online atwww.newfrontieradvisors.com/downloads/pdfs/nfa-written/resampled-efficiency-issues-020103.pdf.)

Mishkin, Frederic. 1980. "Is the Preferred-Habitat Model of the Term Structure Inconsistent with Financial Market Efficiency?" *Journal of Political Economy*, vol. 88, no. 2 (April):406–411.

Modigliani, Franco, and Merton H. Miller. 1958. "The Cost of Capital, Corporation Finance, and the Theory of Investment." *American Economic Review*, vol. 48 (June):261–297.

Modigliani, Franco, and Richard Sutch. 1969. "The Term Structure of Interest Rates: A Re-Examination of the Evidence." *Journal of Money, Credit and Banking*, vol. 1, no. 1 (February):112–120.

Muralidhar, Arun S. 2001. *Innovations in Pension Fund Management*. Stanford, CA: Stanford University Press.

Newton, Isaac. 1664–1671. *De Methodus Fluxionum et Serierum Infinitorum*. London, U.K.

Phillips, Don, and Paul Kaplan. 2003. "What Comes Next? The Case for a New Generation of Indexes." *Journal of Indexes* (First quarter). (Available online at http://indexes .morningstar.com/Index/PDF/WhitePaper1.pdf.)

Pope, Brad, Chad Rakvin, and Gardner Platt. 2003. "Style Indexes of the US Equity Market." *Investment Insights*, vol. 6, no. 3 (July). San Francisco, CA: Barclays Global Investors.

Raphson, Joseph. 1690. *Analysis Aequationum Universalis*. London, U.K.

Rattray, Sandy, and Pravin Manglani. 2003. "Is Standard and Poor's Adding Return by Managing the S&P 500 Index?" Goldman Sachs Derivatives and Trading Research (27 January).

Reinganum, Marc R. 1981. "Misspecification of Capital Asset Pricing: Empirical Anomalies Based on Earnings Yields and Market Values." *Journal of Financial Economics*, vol. 9, no. 1 (March):19–46.

Roll, Richard. 1977. "A Critique of the Asset Pricing Theory's Tests." *Journal of Financial Economics*, vol. 4 (March):129–176.

Rosenberg, Barr. 1974. "Extra-Market Components of Covariance in Security Markets." *Journal of Financial and Quantitative Analysis* (March):263–274.

Rosenberg, Barr, and Vinay Marathe. 1975. "The Prediction of Investment Risk: Systematic and Residual Risk." In *Proceedings of the Seminar on the Analysis of Security Prices*. Chicago, IL: University of Chicago:85–226.

Rosenberg, Barr, Kenneth Reid, and Ronald Lanstein. 1985. "Persuasive Evidence of Market Inefficiency." *Journal of Portfolio Management*, vol. 11 (Spring):9–17.

Schneeweis, Thomas, Hossein Kazemi, and George Martin. 2001. "Understanding Hedge Fund Performance: Research Results and Rules of Thumb for the Institutional Investor." Working paper, Center for International Securities and Derivatives Markets, University of Massachusetts, Amherst (November). (Available online at www.colepartners.com/ downloads/UnderstandingHedgeFundPerformance.pdf.)

Schoenfeld, Steven, and Robert Ginis. 2002. "International Equity Benchmarks for U.S. Investors." *Investment Insights*, vol. 5, no. 4 (November). San Francisco, CA: Barclays Global Investors.

Sharpe, William F. 1964. "Capital Asset Prices: A Theory of Market Equilibrium under Conditions of Risk." *Journal of Finance*, vol. 19, no. 3 (September): 425–442.

———. 1970. *Portfolio Theory and Capital Markets*. Reprint ed. 2000. New York: McGraw-Hill.

———. 1988. "Determining a Fund's Effective Asset Mix." *Investment Management Review*, vol. 2, no. 6 (November/December):59–69.

———. 1992. "Asset Allocation: Management Style and Performance Measurement." *Journal of Portfolio Management*, vol. 18, no. 2 (Winter):7–19.

Sharpe, William F., Gordon J. Alexander, and Jeffery V. Bailey. 1995. *Investments*. 5th ed. Englewood Cliffs, NJ: Prentice-Hall.

Shefrin, Hersh. 2001. "Do Investors Expect Higher Returns from Safer Stocks than from Riskier Stocks?" *Journal of Psychology and Financial Markets*, vol. 2, no. 4 (December):176–181.

———. 2002. *Beyond Greed and Fear*. New York: Oxford University Press.

Siegel, Laurence B. 2003. "TIPS, the Double Duration, and the Pension Plan." Presented at the Barclays Capital Global Inflation-Linked Bond Conference, Key Biscayne, FL (January). A revised version, co-authored with M. Barton Waring, is forthcoming in the *Financial Analysts Journal*.

Siegel, Laurence B., Kenneth F. Kroner, and Scott W. Clifford. 2001. "The Greatest Return Stories Ever Told." *Journal of Investing*, vol. 10, no. 2 (Summer): 91–102.

Sikorsky, Nilly. 1982. "The Origin and Construction of the Capital International Indices." *Columbia Journal of World Business*, vol. 17 (Summer):24–41.

Solnik. Bruno. 1974. "Why Not Diversify Internationally?" *Financial Analysts Journal*, vol. 30, no. 4 (July/August):48–53.

Sortino, Frank A., and Stephen E. Satchell. 2001. *Managing Downside Risk in Financial Markets*. Oxford, U.K.: Butterworth-Heinemann.

Thomas, Landon, Jr. 1999. "Confessions of a Fund Manager." *SmartMoney* (April). (Available online at www.smartmoney.com/10/index.cfm?Story=feature-confessions.)

Treynor, Jack L. (Using pseudonym Walter Bagehot). 1972. "Risk and Reward in Corporate Pension Funds." *Financial Analysts Journal* (January/February):80–84.

Waring, M. Barton, and Laurence B. Siegel. 2003. "The Dimensions of Active Management." *Journal of Portfolio Management*, vol. 29, no. 3 (Spring):35–51. (Available online at www.iijpm.com/common/getArticle.asp?ArticleID=18465.)

Waring, M. Barton, John Pirone, Duane Whitney, and Charles Castille. 2000. "Optimizing Manager Structure and Budgeting Manager Risk." *Journal of Portfolio Management*, vol. 25, no. 3 (Spring):90–104. (Available online at www.iijpm.com/jlevypdfs/2-4.pdf.)

Williams, John Burr. 1956. *The Theory of Investment Value*. Amsterdam, Netherlands: North-Holland. Originally published in 1938 by Cambridge, MA: Harvard University Press.

CHAPTER 3

THE IMPORTANCE OF INDEX SELECTION

Christopher G. Luck, CFA

Although the most commonly used indexes in the United States share some similarities, their differences have recently sharpened, primarily because of the technology boom. No longer can one assume that the standard industry benchmarks serve as good substitutes for each other. Standard & Poor's and Frank Russell Company indexes (the focus of the presentation) differ markedly in their construction parameters: weighting, rebalancing, and reinvestment procedures. Close examination of these parameters reveals that choosing indexes wisely will likely become even more complicated, and more important, in the future.

Although the number of market indexes available is quite large, the most commonly used market indexes in the United States are those created by Standard & Poor's and Frank Russell Company. These indexes have been sliced and diced in an amazing number of ways, including mega cap (S&P 100 Index, Russell Top 200 Index), large cap (S&P 500 Index, Russell 1000 Index), midcap (S&P MidCap 400 Index, Russell Midcap Index), small cap (S&P Small-Cap 600 Index, Russell 2000 Index), and small/midcap (Russell 2500 Index). The most common broad market indexes are the Russell 3000 Index, the S&P SuperComposite 1500 Index, and the Wilshire 5000 Index. Value and growth variants exist for all these indexes as well.

Conventional wisdom holds that the standard domestic equity benchmarks are fairly good substitutes for each other. There is some truth to this belief, but more support is evident for the opposite proposition: The standard domestic equity benchmarks are not good substitutes for each other; in fact, they are in some ways more different than they are similar. In this presentation, I will discuss the characteristics of publicly available indexes, primarily those of S&P and Russell, but I will also include the Wilshire 5000, another widely accepted broad market index.

Reprinted from *AIMR Conference Proceedings: Benchmarks and Attribution Analysis* (June 2001):4–12.

I will look at the changing characteristics of these standard market indexes as well as those of the specialized value and growth indexes. And because concentration levels in the indexes pose particular risks, I will use concentration as a characteristic with which to compare the indexes. I will also discuss managing portfolios to indexes and what implications the differences in the indexes have for active managers.

INDEX METHODOLOGIES

S&P and Russell differ in how they construct their indexes. For example, they do not select stocks for inclusion in the indexes in the same manner. The makeup of the S&P indexes is committee driven; a committee of about nine people decides which companies should enter or be dropped from the indexes. S&P looks for leading companies in leading industries and does not state explicitly that the S&P 500, for example, is a large-cap index by design (even though it is).

In contrast, Russell's indexes are completely formula driven. As such, the management of the Russell indexes is extremely transparent. There are rules to follow, and those rules are followed religiously, although Russell has made changes to its rules over time.

Weighting

S&P indexes are market-cap weighted, whereas Russell's are market-float weighted. Cap weighted is more transparent than float weighted because determining the number of shares outstanding is easier than determining those available for purchase. That is, making float-weighted adjustments for employee stock ownership plans, concentrated holdings, and cross-ownership is a more subjective endeavor than simply determining the number of shares outstanding. In the United States, that distinction is relatively minor, but internationally, a far greater divide exists between the two categories.

Although little difference usually exists between the two methodologies in the U.S. markets, noticeable differences have been apparent at times. Float-weighted adjustments led to the odd occurrence that for about a year (1999), Microsoft Corporation was the largest holding in the S&P 500 while General Electric Company (GE) was the largest holding in the Russell 1000. The float-weighting rules for the Russell indexes required a float adjustment that lowered the total outstanding shares of Microsoft. Thus, the price per share times the number of Microsoft shares outstanding, calculated differently by the two indexes, resulted in Microsoft being a smaller holding in the Russell 1000 than it was in the S&P 500. As of November 2000, GE was the largest holding in both indexes.

Rebalancing

A wide disparity is apparent in how S&P and Russell periodically rebalance their indexes. For active managers, rebalancing presents a serious problem, especially for those who manage to the small-cap indexes. S&P rebalances its indexes continuously. Corporate actions, such as mergers and takeovers, primarily drive the rebalancing in the S&P indexes. Because the S&P indexes contain a fixed number of companies, when one company goes out of business or is acquired, S&P finds a replacement.

S&P can also decide that a particular company simply no longer belongs in an index. At the end of December 2000, for example, several S&P small-cap index names, including Spartan Motors and the Bombay Company, were removed because of their lack of representation. The removal of certain companies for lack of representation has been common in the S&P small-cap index because S&P has been striving to keep the index representative of this segment, but the problem of lack of representation has been occurring more frequently across all the indexes, albeit relatively rarely. For S&P, the idea is to have an "exit strategy" for companies other than that of corporate actions in order to ensure that the indexes broadly represent their respective capitalization segments.

Russell makes all index changes on June 30. On May 31, company capitalizations are used to pick the 1,000, 2,000, and 3,000 largest companies, and on June 30, Russell weights the indexes by the outstanding float. So, the Russell 3000, Russell 2000, and Russell 1000 have 3,000, 2,000, and 1,000 stocks, respectively, on June 30. Company spin-offs and companies that go out of business are not immediately replaced or dropped in response to the event; rather, any resulting changes to the indexes are not made until the following June 30. In fact, at the beginning of November 2000, the Russell 3000, 2000, and 1000 indexes did not contain exactly 3,000, 2,000, and 1,000, stocks, respectively.

Broad Market Indexes

I do not know any clients who use the S&P 1500 as a broad market index. My clients typically choose the Wilshire 3000 or, just as often, the Wilshire 5000—the index that holds almost every company headquartered in the United States and that contains about 7,000 stocks. Unlike the Russell indexes, the Wilshire 5000 is rebalanced monthly.

Value and Growth Indexes

Another point of comparison is that Russell and S&P construct their value and growth indexes differently. I would have to say that the Russell indexes are generally more widely accepted as measures of the value and growth sectors than the S&P indexes.

S&P/Barra

S&P, in cooperation with Barra, has created value and growth indexes based on the S&P 500, S&P MidCap 400, and S&P SmallCap 600. S&P differentiates between value and growth strictly according to a company's book-to-price ratio (B/P), and the indexes are reconstituted twice a year, on June 30 and December 31. On these days, the stocks in the index universe are classified as either value or growth; 50 percent of the total capitalization goes to the value component, and 50 percent goes to the growth component. Although each index does not have an equal number of names, both indexes have equal capitalization, at least on June 30 and December 31. S&P would argue that its base indexes (e.g., the S&P 500) can be reconstituted by simply adding up everything in the growth and value indexes (e.g., S&P 500/Barra Growth Index and S&P 500/Barra Value Index).

Russell

Russell constructs its style indexes by using two criteria for the differentiation between value and growth: B/P (like the S&P/Barra indexes) and I/B/E/S International's forecast earnings-growth measure. The Russell value and growth indexes are reconstituted once a year on June 30, with a nonexclusive style split; 70 percent of the total number of companies in the indexes is exclusively in one index or the other, and the remaining 30 percent is split between the two indexes. Thus, some companies end up in both the Russell 1000 Value Index and the

TABLE 3.1   Number of Names in Indexes as of September 30, 2000

Index	Base Index	Value Index	Growth Index
S&P 500	500	389	111
S&P 400	400	266	134
S&P 600	600	461	179
Russell 1000	978	742	529
Russell Midcap	781	606	403
Russell 2000	1,941	1,253	1,271
Russell 2500	2,427	1,637	1,518
Russell 3000	2,916	na	na
Wilshire 5000	6,793	na	na

na = not applicable

Russell 1000 Growth Index, for example, even though the capitalizations from each index should add up to the overall capitalization in the Russell 1000.

Number of Companies

As Table 3.1 shows, compared with their S&P counterparts, the Russell indexes are more broadly diversified. The Russell value and growth indexes are much larger than those of S&P. As of September 30, 2000, the Russell 1000 consisted of 978 companies. (Remember that the Russell indexes are reconstituted only once a year on June 30 and that Russell does not have an automatic replacement rule for companies in the index that are acquired.) The Russell 1000 Value included 742 companies, and the Russell 1000 Growth included 529, which is indicative of the overlap between the two indexes. The S&P 500, however, had 500 companies in the base index—389 in the value index and 111 in the growth index. Notice that the Wilshire 5000, with 6,793 names, is much broader than the Russell 3000, with 2,916 names. For additional information on these companies' indexes, I suggest visiting their Web sites.[1]

INDEX COMPARISONS

As I stated, the S&P and Russell indexes can be compared along various dimensions— weighting, rebalancing, and composition of subindexes. Other dimensions, including return correlations, tracking error, and turnover, are also useful in distinguishing between the two sets of indexes. Their similarities and differences affect the degree to which an S&P index can be substituted for a Russell index, so I will emphasize that issue. I will also examine the behavior of the two sets of indexes in relation to concentration risk.

Lack of Substitutability

The Russell and S&P indexes can be compared in several areas that highlight their differences and raise the issue of noncomparability. By and large, these differences are readily apparent.

TABLE 3.2   Historical Return Correlations

	Russell 1000	Russell 1000 Value	Russell 1000 Growth
S&P 500	0.9952		
S&P 500 Value		0.9907	
S&P 500 Growth			0.9881
	Russell Midcap	Russell Midcap Value	Russell Midcap Growth
S&P 400	0.9626		
S&P 400 Value		0.9653	
S&P 400 Growth			0.9427
	Russell 2000	Russell 2000 Value	Russell 2000 Growth
S&P 600	0.9721		
S&P 600 Value		0.9735	
S&P 600 Growth			0.9683

Note: Data for Russell 1000 and S&P 500, February 1979–September 2000; data for Russell Midcap and S&P 400, January 1991–September 2000; and data for Russell 2000 and S&P 600, January 1994–September 2000.

Return Correlations

Table 3.2 shows historical return correlations for various S&P and Russell indexes for their common time periods. These time periods are somewhat different for each index, but the large-cap indexes cover the period 1979–2000; the midcap indexes, 1991–2000; and the small-cap indexes, 1994–2000. The data indicate high correlation for these index pairs. For example, the S&P 500 and the Russell 1000 have a correlation of 0.9952. Note that the value indexes are more highly correlated than the growth indexes and that the large-cap indexes are more highly correlated than the small-cap or midcap indexes. But the historical correlation of two other broad market indexes—the Russell 3000 and the Wilshire 5000—is even higher (0.998). Correlation, however, is a relatively simple measure of substitutability. The closer one looks at the indexes, the more obvious the differences become.

Return Regressions

A return regression on each of the index pairs provides further analysis. Table 3.3 shows the alpha and beta coefficients from these regressions over the same time periods as the correlations in Table 3.2. The alpha coefficients for the midcap sector are unusually large. Likewise, the beta coefficients differ from 1 (perfect covariance), which implies that the two indexes have not substantially covaried. Even though the correlation coefficients indicate that these indexes are good substitutes for each other, the beta figures suggest otherwise.

Tracking Error

Table 3.4 gives the tracking error of the index pairs, again over their common time history. Even at the large-cap level (S&P 500 and Russell 1000), the tracking error—almost 1.5 percent a year—is significant. For the large-cap value and growth index pairs, the tracking error is about 2.5 percent, and for the midcap and small-cap pairs, it is even larger (as high as 6.62

TABLE 3.3   Regression Differences: Alpha and Beta

	Russell 1000	Russell 1000 Value	Russell 1000 Growth
S&P 500			
Alpha	−0.16		
Beta	1.006		
S&P 500 Value			
Alpha		0.16	
Beta		0.980	
S&P 500 Growth			
Alpha			−0.04
Beta			1.032
	Russell Midcap	Russell Midcap Value	Russell Midcap Growth
S&P 400			
Alpha	1.33		
Beta	0.858		
S&P 400 Value			
Alpha		0.85	
Beta		0.914	
S&P 400 Growth			
Alpha			1.04
Beta			0.894
	Russell 2000	Russell 2000 Value	Russell 2000 Growth
S&P 600			
Alpha	−0.77		
Beta	1.021		
S&P 600 Value			
Alpha		−0.26	
Beta		1.116	
S&P 600 Growth			
Alpha			−0.06
Beta			0.845

Note: Data for Russell 1000 and S&P 500, February 1979–September 2000; data for Russell Midcap and S&P 400, January 1991–September 2000; and data for Russell 2000 and S&P 600, January 1994–September 2000.

percent). These large tracking-error numbers provide further evidence that these indexes are not good substitutes for each other.

Turnover

Table 3.5 indicates the turnover of the S&P and Russell indexes for the last 10 years and the 12 months ending September 2000. Turnover is clearly a drag on performance. Whether a

TABLE 3.4   Historical Tracking Error (annualized)

	Russell 1000	Russell 1000 Value	Russell 1000 Growth
S&P 500	1.48%		
S&P 500 Value		1.97%	
S&P 500 Growth			2.68%
	Russell Midcap	Russell Midcap Value	Russell Midcap Growth
S&P 400	4.34%		
S&P 400 Value		3.66%	
S&P 400 Growth			6.56%
	Russell 2000	Russell 2000 Value	Russell 2000 Growth
S&P 600	4.33%		
S&P 600 Value		3.81%	
S&P 600 Growth			6.62%

Note: Data for Russell 1000 and S&P 500, February 1979–September 2000; data for Russell Midcap and S&P 400, January 1991–September 2000; and data for Russell 2000 and S&P 600, January 1994–September 2000.

TABLE 3.5   Historical Turnover Levels (annualized)

Large Cap		Midcap		Small Cap	
Index	Turnover	Index	Turnover	Index	Turnover
Since January 1990					
S&P 500	4.5%	S&P 400	16.6%	S&P 600	17.0%
S&P 500 Value	22.7	S&P 400 Value	37.1	S&P 600 Value	42.0
S&P 500 Growth	23.9	S&P 400 Growth	59.5	S&P 600 Growth	52.6
Russell 1000	6.3	Russell Midcap	20.8	Russell 2000	30.3
Russell 1000 Value	16.7	Russell Midcap Value	30.0	Russell 2000 Value	38.9
Russell 1000 Growth	16.1	Russell Midcap Growth	47.3	Russell 2000 Growth	45.4
Trailing 12 months					
S&P 500	12.5	S&P 400	34.5	S&P 600	25.8
S&P 500 Value	26.5	S&P 400 Value	43.4	S&P 600 Value	51.7
S&P 500 Growth	28.9	S&P 400 Growth	89.7	S&P 600 Growth	70.6
Russell 1000	13.3	Russell Midcap	40.2	Russell 2000	35.0
Russell 1000 Value	26.0	Russell Midcap Value	36.2	Russell 2000 Value	44.1
Russell 1000 Growth	30.5	Russell Midcap Growth	74.7	Russell 2000 Growth	52.8

Note: Data through September 2000.

manager manages actively or passively versus a benchmark, the turnover in the indexes affects the turnover in the manager's portfolio. The greater the turnover in the portfolio, the greater the leakage to the brokerage community.

Historically, the larger the stock capitalization, the smaller the amount of turnover in the index. The S&P 500's turnover rate has been 4.5 percent; the Russell 1000's, 6.3 percent. On the midcap side, the S&P 400 has had a turnover rate of 16.6 percent, and the Russell Midcap, 20.8 percent. The higher turnover for midcap and small-cap indexes is predominantly caused by midcap and small-cap stocks growing out of their universes, which forces them into the next index level (e.g., from the small-cap to the midcap index). Such changes have a commensurately larger impact than when, for example, a large-cap stock falls from the large-cap range into the midcap range.

Turnover for the value and growth indexes is much higher than that of the base indexes, which is no surprise because value and growth indexes are using a smaller subset of the universe. Turnover is high in these indexes not only because of capitalization changes but also because stocks migrate across the growth–value divide.

Compared with the data compiled from January 1990, the trailing 12-month figures have increased significantly across the board. The extraordinarily large 12.5 percent turnover for the S&P 500 is probably the result of the technology boom, because the stocks that made it into the index were stocks such as Yahoo!, JDS Uniphase, and other relatively large-cap stocks that were not previously included.

The Russell base indexes exhibit much higher turnover than the S&P base indexes, especially in the small-cap and midcap sectors, but that trend has not appeared in the value and growth indexes. The Russell Midcap Growth Index had 75 percent turnover for the trailing 12-month period. The S&P 400 Growth Index had nearly 90 percent turnover, which is an extraordinarily high turnover to manage a portfolio against. Even the Russell 2000, which is a much broader index than either the Russell Midcap or the S&P 400, has had growth and value turnover levels close to 50 percent. That amount of turnover can be troubling for an indexer who, by definition, must match the index change for change. Active managers, presumably, do not have to replicate the holdings of an index, but having a benchmark with a high level of turnover compounds the turnover levels already encountered with actively managed portfolios. Essentially, managing any portfolio with a high level of turnover is extremely difficult, not the least because of the transaction costs incurred.

The data show that the base S&P indexes have lower turnover than the Russell base indexes, which is primarily a function of S&P's "management" of its indexes. S&P appears to want lower turnover, particularly in the S&P 500, relative to the competition, and with committee-driven rules, S&P can use low turnover as one of its criteria. The key point is that S&P manages its indexes, whereas Russell uses formulas to create and modify its indexes.

For the growth and value sectors, the S&P indexes have higher turnover than the similar Russell indexes. That higher level of turnover is primarily a function of the rebalancing that S&P does twice a year; Russell rebalances only once a year. The turnover difference is also a result of the either/or distinction that S&P imposes on each company. S&P does not allow the same company in more than one index, but Russell does.

Inclusion of Unseasoned Companies

The inclusion of "unseasoned" companies is an increasingly meaningful criterion for analyzing these indexes. This issue was particularly relevant during the initial public offering (IPO) and technology boom of the late 1990s. For about four or five years, the technology sector seemed invincible, and consequently, the number of companies that never reported earnings increased dramatically in the indexes; some indexes even included companies that had reported nothing but negative earnings since going public.

From about 1987 to 1996, whether looking at the S&P 500 or the Russell 1000, the number of companies in the index that never reported positive earnings was small. Starting roughly in 1997, however, the number of such companies rose significantly and was particularly dramatic in the Russell indexes. The reason this phenomenon occurred in the Russell indexes is that the Russell indexes are formula driven. Russell looks at the capitalization of a company, and if the company meets the threshold for a certain index, it enters that index. When, for example, the capitalizations of Amazon.com and priceline.com grew large enough to be included in the top 1,000 companies, they were moved into the Russell 1000. If a company was a growth stock, it also was moved into the growth variant of the index.

S&P has been more conservative about adding such companies to its indexes. Table 3.6 shows the technology orientation of the indexes. The Russell indexes tend to have a slightly higher technology orientation, but interestingly, the difference is not large and is fairly consistent. Russell has been admitting technology-oriented companies more readily than S&P, whereas S&P, with its bias toward seasoned companies, has been including technology-oriented companies more slowly.

The same pattern appears in the midcap and small-cap Russell indexes. Beginning in 1997, Russell's indexes experienced an increase in the number of companies with no reported earnings, especially in the small-cap indexes. For the Russell 2000, 16 percent of its companies never reported positive earnings. For the S&P 600, the number is only 1.5 percent. The technology orientation underscores one key philosophical disparity between the two indexes—the inclusion rate of "unseasoned" companies.

Substitutability

Although the S&P and Russell indexes differ, they have some similarities that make them good substitutes for each other under certain circumstances. The S&P 500 and the Russell 1000, the large-cap indexes, are well correlated and have been good substitutes for each other. They have a strong historical correlation and reasonably low tracking error. The growth and value variations of these two indexes have also been reasonably good substitutes for each other, although to a lesser extent than the base indexes.

TABLE 3.6   Percent of Technology-Oriented Stocks in S&P and Russell Indexes

	Base Index	Value Index	Growth Index
S&P 500	35.9%	14.2%	56.8%
S&P 400	32.9	14.8	48.7
S&P 600	30.9	18.2	46.1
Russell 1000	37.2	13.7	60.4
Russell Midcap	29.1	12.8	55.3
Russell 2000	38.2	10.4	47.7

Notes: Technology orientation based on Barra industry classification, September 30, 2000. Internet industry weight as of September 30, 2000, was 1.8 percent for the S&P 500, 3.4 percent for the Russell 1000, 0.3 percent for the S&P 600, and 3.3 percent for the Russell 2000.

All the large-cap indexes may be better substitutes for each other in the future, because since the technology correction in the market, the difference between the two indexes arising from their technology versus seasoned-company orientations is likely to narrow; in fact, their correlations may well increase. If the market continues to reward new-economy companies relative to the seasoned companies favored by S&P, the degree of substitutability of the two indexes will be altered.

For the small-cap and midcap sectors, the base indexes have not been good substitutes for each other; they have had high relative tracking error. The numbers are even worse for the value and growth indexes, especially for the growth sector. Because of the new-economy orientation—the speculative technology exposure within the Russell indexes—it is unlikely that the S&P and Russell small-cap and midcap indexes will track each other closely, which has strong implications for plan sponsors and anyone managing to these indexes. If one person manages to the S&P 400 and another to the Russell Midcap, they will be managing different portfolios. Similarly, if one person manages to the Russell 2000 and another to the S&P 600, they, too, will potentially produce widely disparate portfolios. These results are even more pronounced for the value and growth indexes.

As for the broad market indexes, the Russell 3000 and the Wilshire 5000 are good substitutes for each other. Although the number of companies in each index differs significantly, the indexes have a historical correlation of 0.998 and a historical tracking error of 1.05 percent. There is no reason to predict that this high degree of correlation will change.

Concentration Risk

Several market analysts claim that the U.S. indexes have become more concentrated, and thus riskier, in recent years. To examine this hypothesis, I chose the seven largest international markets (United Kingdom, Japan, Canada, Germany, France, the Netherlands, and Switzerland) and looked at the primary large-cap index in each market. For each index, I found the top stock and compared it with the top stock in the S&P 500 and Russell 1000. At the end of September 2000, General Electric was the largest stockholding in the S&P 500 and the Russell 1000 with, respectively, a 4.6 percent and 4.5 percent weighting.

Compared with the non-U.S. indexes, the U.S. indexes do not seem concentrated. As of September 30, 2000, the FTSE 100 (United Kingdom) had an 11.0 percent weight in Vodafone Group, the TOPIX (Japan) had 7.7 percent in NTT DoCoMo, the TSE 100 (Canada) had 34 percent in Nortel Networks Corporation, the DAX (Germany) had 13.0 percent in Deutsche Telekom, the CAC 40 (France) had 11.3 percent in France Telecom, the AEX (Netherlands) had 13.8 percent in ING Groep, and the SMI (Switzerland) had 21.2 percent in Novartis. Therefore, merely by looking at the largest stock in each index (a very basic dimension), the U.S. indexes seem well diversified in both absolute and relative contexts.

The top-tier names (in capitalization terms) in the S&P 500 today make up a slightly higher percentage of the total index capitalization than they did in the late 1980s, as shown in Panel A of Figure 3.1. Although the concentration level has jumped modestly in the past several years (currently 24.2 percent for the top 10 names), it is not all that different from the historical norm (20.3 percent for the top 10 names). So, the jump has not been particularly significant relative to historical concentration levels. If I had enough data, I suspect I would find that the low concentration through the 1990s, not the current high concentration, is the exception.

Some of the Russell indexes, in terms of their historical norms, are not particularly concentrated at the present time. Panel B of Figure 3.1 shows that the Russell 1000 has less concentration than that found in the S&P 500. The top 10 names in the Russell 1000

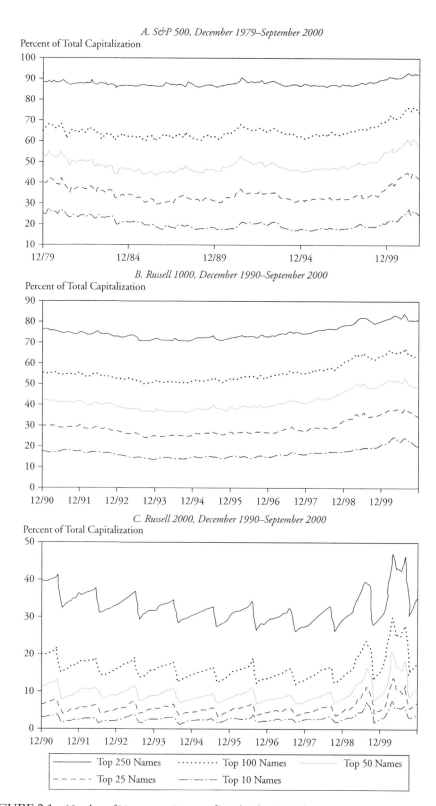

A. S&P 500, December 1979–September 2000

Percent of Total Capitalization

B. Russell 1000, December 1990–September 2000

Percent of Total Capitalization

C. Russell 2000, December 1990–September 2000

Percent of Total Capitalization

| Top 250 Names | Top 100 Names | Top 50 Names |
| Top 25 Names | Top 10 Names | |

FIGURE 3.1   Number of Names as a Percent of Total Index Capitalization

currently make up 20.9 percent of the index, but the historical average for this time period is 16.6 percent. Again, compared with historical norms, the Russell 1000 has a slightly higher concentration at the present time but not significantly so.

The Russell 2000, shown in Panel C of Figure 3.1, yields some interesting results. Because Russell rebalances only once a year, the concentration of stocks in its indexes becomes more pronounced until rebalancing occurs, when the largest-cap stocks in the Russell 2000 are moved to the Russell 1000 and the smallest-cap stocks in the Russell 1000 are moved to the Russell 2000. So, in effect, Russell reduces concentration levels on every rebalance date (June 30). The result is the jagged line shown in Panel C. Historically, the top 250 names composed 33.0 percent of the index; the current figure is 33.7 percent. The biggest difference appeared in the 1998–99 period, when the rebalancing dramatically affected the weights of the holdings. The recent changes in company capitalizations have had a much bigger impact on the Russell 2000 than on the Russell 1000 or S&P 500.

Russell has considered rebalancing twice a year, probably because of the violent concentration swings that have occasionally occurred since 1997. The world has changed, and the amount of change that occurs within a year is much greater now than in the past, a fact that would easily justify more frequent rebalancing. And although the concentration levels in the Russell 2000 are not vastly different from the historical averages, since 1997 the extent of the changes in concentration levels as a result of rebalancing has been significant. These changes have been driven, more or less, by the technology sector.

Summary

Although both sets of indexes are actively managed, their approaches differ. S&P's active-management process consists of a committee deciding which companies to move in and out of the S&P indexes. The active-management decisions for the Russell indexes come from a group of people who establish "rules" for inclusion and exclusion. Russell establishes fairly transparent rules for its indexes, which is to be applauded, but from period to period the rules nevertheless can change. Some of Russell's decisions are proprietary, such as the weightings in growth and value stocks, so its approach is not as transparent as it may seem. In addition, certain biases accompany each of the index sets. Wilshire, by contrast, simply includes the stock of every company headquartered in the United States, so no decision making is involved in creating the Wilshire 5000 Index.

Other points of comparison can be summarized as follows:

- High *turnover* is more evident in the Russell indexes, except for the small-cap growth and value sectors, than in the S&P indexes.
- Russell, to its credit, is much more *transparent* about its methodology than S&P. Transparency is not inherently right or wrong, but more transparency is generally better than less transparency.
- Russell indexes are *broader* than S&P indexes. Russell's midcap and small-cap indexes are particularly well-suited for managers seeking a broad index.
- S&P indexes tend to be more *conservative* than Russell's. S&P indexes have fewer post-IPO names (i.e., more seasoned companies), and this conservatism has created dissimilarities between the indexes.

Finally, although some managers and sponsors combine S&P and Russell indexes, the overlap between the indexes creates a measurement problem. Simply put, combinations of S&P and Russell indexes are not optimal.

MANAGING TO INDEXES

Managers use benchmarks—or indexes—for two reasons: They use them to make asset allocation and style decisions, which is an *ex ante* use of benchmarks, and for performance measurement, an *ex post* use of benchmarks. So, whether making an *ex ante* decision about allocations to a manager or an *ex post* decision about manager performance, an obvious question is whether the index selected is representative of the manager's style. That is, is it the right index to use? If a plan sponsor asks a manager to manage to a benchmark that is not the one the manager normally uses, the sponsor will likely be disappointed in the results, because the manager is being asked to manage a risk budget that differs from the one the manager has historically managed. The point is that the index should be representative of the manager's style.

Another issue is that all of the indexes, on a weighted basis, selected by the sponsor should total to the sponsor's overall fund target. I have seen cases in which a sponsor has S&P 500 mandates as well as Russell mandates, yet ensuring that such combinations add up to a coherent whole at the fund level is difficult.

Some consultants believe indexes cause management difficulties associated with liquidity, turnover, and availability (cap weighting versus float weighting, for example). Such issues can be pronounced in the small-cap and midcap sectors of the marketplace. Therefore, a good question to ask when selecting an index, for both passive and active management, is whether introducing the index will lead to greater management difficulties or higher costs in managing the portfolio. Another good question is whether the selection of the index will affect manager behavior. Certainly, the choice of the index on the passive side will affect manager behavior, but it will also have an impact on behavior on the active side, particularly for structured managers.

Regarding performance measurement, the plan sponsor should ask whether the index provides a meaningful comparison with the manager's actual return and whether the manager could have passively invested in the index.

CONCLUSION

In portfolio management, the choice of the benchmark index is surprisingly important and will become even more important as the economy and market structure evolve. Some of S&P's biases, for example, reflect that it is more conservative than Russell, and if that trend continues, the S&P and Russell indexes will differ more in the future than they will converge.

The philosophical differences between the two sets of indexes have begun to accentuate the significant differences in performance between the two. Sponsors should be cognizant that the index they have chosen may encourage manager behavior that differs from that which caused them to hire the manager in the first place. Sponsors must choose the index that maximizes manager allocation, asset allocation, and performance-measurement decisions.

NOTE

1. See www.russell.com, www.barra.com, www.spglobal.com, and www.wilshire.com.

CHAPTER 4

AFTER-TAX PERFORMANCE EVALUATION

James M. Poterba

Focusing on after-tax returns is a great way to add value and gain competitive advantage in the investment management business. Managers need to understand the factors that affect tax efficiency, to realize that a "one size fits all" performance measure and tax strategy will not work, and to integrate portfolio management with income tax and estate tax planning. Algorithms, such as the "accrual equivalent" tax rate, can help managers educate clients about the various implications of taxes for their portfolios.

The after-tax return associated with a given pretax return may vary considerably among individual tax-paying clients. Portfolio returns from the perspective of pretax reporting or performance management for tax-exempt clients can look very different from returns from the perspective of tax-paying individual investors.

This presentation focuses on the general issue of measuring after-tax performance—how taxes interact with performance management. This focus includes the AIMR Performance Presentation Standards (AIMR-PPS™ standards) and, more generally, the design of broad-based performance evaluation standards. This presentation examines whether an algorithm can be designed and used to tell a particular client the likely after-tax consequences of various portfolio strategies and to compare the after-tax performance of various managers. The presentation also provides an overview of the U.S. income tax environment for high-net-worth households, with particular emphasis on capital gains tax issues. Finally, the presentation reviews three important estate-planning tools that individuals can use to effectively manage estate taxes.

Reprinted from *AIMR Conference Proceedings: Investment Counseling for Private Clients II* (August 2000):58–67.

WHY THE AFTER-TAX FOCUS

A focus on after-tax returns is worthwhile for several reasons. One is that most managers who work with individual clients know that increasingly sophisticated individual investors are demanding analysis of how their taxes are influenced by manager behavior, portfolio selection, and asset allocation. Therefore, managers need to report results in a way that puts taxes into the broader picture.

Another reason is that reducing the tax drag on a portfolio may be an easier way of increasing after-tax returns than searching for additional pretax risk-adjusted returns (alpha). For example, when a manager is liquidating a position, selling highest-cost-basis shares rather than shares with an acquisition price close to the average basis is straightforward and enhances after-tax returns. A manager does not need to be a rocket scientist or need to accurately predict future earnings to follow that strategy. Therefore, a focus on after-tax returns allows recognition that there is some "low-hanging fruit" that many managers can harvest.

Finally, being able to make a coherent presentation on the tax consequences of various investment strategies and management styles can gain a manager an advantage in the competition for client money.

FACTORS AFFECTING TAX EFFICIENCY

Certain key factors influence any portfolio's tax efficiency—that is, the difference between the portfolio's pretax return and its after-tax return for a taxable investor:

- *Portfolio turnover.* Portfolio turnover is clearly one of the key factors affecting tax efficiency, but the notion that high turnover equals bad tax efficiency is a myth. Turnover is like cholesterol: There is good, and there is bad. Good turnover is the harvesting of losses and the early realization of positions that have losses. Bad turnover is the selling of gains and the early triggering of capital gains tax liability. Tax-efficient portfolios should have more of the good and less of the bad turnover.
- *Inflows versus withdrawals.* A second key factor affecting tax efficiency is the pattern of asset inflows and withdrawals. The importance of this factor is particularly clear when examining the after-tax return performance of mutual funds. Consider two funds that are holding identical portfolios at the beginning of a year, and assume that these portfolios have substantial embedded, unrealized capital gains. One of the funds experiences large redemptions; the other experiences inflows during the year. The redeeming fund will have, on average, a higher tax burden for the year. A central issue that the AIMR-PPS Implementation Committee has wrestled with is the extent to which the manager is burdened with the taxes that are realized as a result of withdrawals that are beyond his or her control.
- *Dividend yield versus capital gains.* This factor, as most managers of taxable assets know, is critical. Because dividends are taxed more heavily than realized capital gains for most taxable investors and because unrealized capital gains are taxed even more favorably, a portfolio that generates a high fraction of its returns in the form of dividends will face a higher tax burden than a fund that generates primarily capital gains.

The factors driving tax efficiency are fairly simple, so clients might expect most managers to behave in a tax-efficient manner. But many managers do not. Several hypothetical examples will show how these factors can increase the difference between pretax and after-tax returns.

Mutual Fund Example

Suppose a hypothetical portfolio has the following characteristics:

Beginning-of-period market value	$10.00
Realized long-term capital gains	1.75
Realized short-term capital gains	0.25
Dividend income	0.50
Unrealized capital gains	0.50
Total pretax earnings	3.00

Pretax returns for this portfolio are an impressive 30 percent for the period. Unfortunately, after-tax returns are significantly less. After-tax returns on this fund, for an individual investor in the top U.S. federal marginal income tax bracket, can be calculated as follows:

$$\frac{\$1.75(1.00 - 0.20) + (\$0.25 + \$0.50)(1.00 - 0.396) + \$0.50}{\$10.00} = 23.5\%.$$

The terms $(1.00 - 0.20)$ and $(1.00 - 0.396)$ correspond, respectively, to the *after-tax* value of one dollar of realized long-term capital gains (taxed at 20 percent) and one dollar of realized short-term gains and dividend income, which is taxed at the federal marginal tax rate of 39.6 percent. Published estimates of pretax and after-tax returns on various mutual funds, such as those reported each year in *BusinessWeek*, show just how much of the pretax return can be consumed by taxes. There is typically enormous variation among mutual fund managers in the amount of taxable income they generate for a given amount of pretax return. This variation reflects differences in each of the portfolio attributes described previously in this section.

Given the range of effective tax burdens among mutual funds and the diversity of effective tax rates among private clients, taxable investors should consider after-tax returns when selecting mutual funds.

Client Portfolio with Cash Withdrawals

Cash inflows and withdrawals also influence after-tax portfolio returns. The following example illustrates the measurement of after-tax performance for a client portfolio that has cash withdrawals:

Initial portfolio value	$1,000
Initial unrealized gains	500
Final prewithdrawal portfolio value	1,150
Final postwithdrawal portfolio value	1,100
Total capital appreciation	150
Client cash withdrawal	50
Realized long-term gains	140
Final unrealized gains	510
Cash dividends (distributed)	30

The pretax return on this portfolio is given by

$$\text{Pretax return} = \frac{\begin{array}{l}\text{Dividends}\\+\text{Change in portfolio value}\\+\text{Cash withdrawal}\end{array}}{\text{Initial value}}.$$

In this example, the pretax return is 18 percent. Suppose the general AIMR-PPS algorithm for after-tax performance measurement is used to measure the after-tax returns. This algorithm is as follows:

$$\text{After-tax return} = \frac{\begin{array}{l}\text{Realized long-term gains } (1 - t_{CG})\\+(\text{Realized short-term gains}\\+\text{Dividends}) \, (1 - t_{DIV})\\+\text{Unrealized gains} + \text{Tax-free income}\\+\text{Client withdrawal adjustment factor}\end{array}}{\text{Starting asset value}},$$

where t_{CG} stands for the marginal tax rate on long-term capital gains realizations and t_{DIV} stands for the ordinary income tax rate that applies to dividend income. These tax rates are set at 20 percent and 39.6 percent, respectively.

In this algorithm, the client withdrawal adjustment factor is

$$\frac{t_{CG}(\text{Net withdrawal})(\text{Realized} + \text{Unrealized gains})}{(\text{Final portfolio value} + \text{Net withdrawal})}.$$

When the AIMR-PPS algorithm is used, the aftertax return is significantly less—14.58 percent—than the pretax return of 18 percent. The client withdrawal factor *raises* the reported after-tax return by 6 basis points.

MEASURING AFTER-TAX PERFORMANCE

Differences in investors' income tax rates, and the interplay between investor characteristics and decisions about realizing capital gains, represent major challenges to measuring and evaluating after-tax performance. Therefore, managers need to understand how each investor's federal tax rates and potential estate taxes interact to influence portfolio management decisions. A good starting point for this analysis is the AIMR-PPS algorithm for measuring after-tax performance.

AIMR-PPS Algorithm

According to the AIMR-PPS standards, managers are to use the maximum federal statutory rate for each type of client. So, a manager would use 20 percent as the statutory long-term capital gains rate. But the tax rates clients face actually can vary, even among high-net-worth clients. Therefore, managers may want to customize this rate in the calculation of after-tax return. An investor with large capital loss carryforwards from a failed past investment may face a lower effective capital gains tax rate than someone without such a loss carryforward.

The AIMR-PPS standards also tell managers to exclude state and local taxes. The argument for doing so is that people live in different states. Everyone lives in some state, however, and for people who live in high-tax-burden states—in California (where the top income tax rate is 11 percent), New York (where the rate is 7–8 percent at the state level and more for New York City), and Massachusetts (which used to have a 12 percent tax rate on interest and dividend income)—managers should include the state tax rate in the algorithm so they can report what those taxes do to their clients' returns. Few investors would try to compare the returns on taxable and tax-exempt bond portfolios without recognizing the role of federal and state taxes. Similarly, a manager needs to recognize the role of state and local taxes in after-tax equity portfolio performance.

Individual Federal Tax Rates

Individual investors' federal tax rates vary for several reasons.

Dependence of Taxes on Income, Not Wealth

Some investors have substantial accumulated net worth, but their incomes do not put them in the top end of the income distribution. Managers can get a more systematic handle on this information than from anecdotal client interviews from a database that is collected every three years by the U.S. Federal Reserve Board, which is summarized in the Survey of Consumer Finances. This survey is the best publicly available nonproprietary information on the highest-net-worth part of the U.S. population. In collecting these data, the Fed focuses on households in wealthy communities. The result is a database that includes a nontrivial number of respondents from the segment of the U.S. population with the highest net worth.

The data show that only about a fifth of the households that were in the top 1 percent of the income distribution in 1995 were also in the top 1 percent of the net-worth distribution. In 1995, a family needed an income of about $225,000 to be in the top 1 percent of the income distribution. To be in the top 1 percent of the net-worth group, a family needed about $3 million in total household assets, including retirement accounts.

Whether investment managers' clients have high net worth or high income or both may not be clear. Part of the reason is that many individuals in high-net-worth households are past their prime earning years; they may be retirees whose income is primarily capital income. At the same time, some high-earning younger households may not yet have had time to accumulate substantial assets.

Variation in Income and Asset Values

Taxes also vary because different assets generate different income profiles. People with substantial net worth in real estate or municipal bonds, for example, may have low taxable income relative to others in their net-worth category. Therefore, their tax status may be different from that of others with similar net worth.

Special Circumstances

Finally, individuals' taxes vary because of "specialized tax circumstances." The importance of particular tax conditions, such as tax-planning problems generated by low-cost-basis stock, the alternative minimum tax (AMT), or loss carryforwards, is hard to identify. Nevertheless, such factors generate substantial scope for variations in tax rates.

These issues argue against using a one-size-fits-all performance measure. Managers need to think about a particular client's circumstances. The differences can be accounted for in simple computer programs that allow one to plug in various marginal tax rates as well as underlying information about the realization of gains and the income components of a given pretax return. Once the manager understands the person's marginal federal and state tax rates and other tax complications, the manager can tailor the presentation to those conditions.

Marginal Income Tax Rates

The notion of the "effective marginal tax rate" rather than the "average tax burden" should drive both managers' and clients' behavior. In 1998, the top federal marginal tax rates on interest and dividends were 39.6 percent starting at $271,050 of taxable income, 36 percent starting at $151,750, and 31 percent starting at $99,600. In addition, phase-out rules on deductions can propel top-bracket taxpayers into a tax bracket with a marginal tax rate as high as 41 percent. Managers can get a handle on how the rules on deductions affect a client's marginal tax rate by asking the client to add another $200 of interest income to his or her reported taxable income and then to recompute the taxes. In many cases, this additional income will not change the taxes by 39.6 percent times $200. It will change the taxes by more in some (most!) cases and by less in others. This exercise will give managers an idea of the true marginal tax rate the client faces.

The actual dividend tax rate faced by households with different characteristics is revealing. Table 4.1 is based on a data set that the U.S. Internal Revenue Service (IRS) has released for researchers that includes actual (but anonymous) tax returns for tax year 1994. Note that for households that reported at least $50,000 of dividend and interest income, only about 40 percent were facing tax rates higher than 37 percent. Many people who reported that much in dividend and interest income fell in the 28 percent bracket. In other words, a significant number of households with substantial liquid assets face a marginal tax rate that is lower than the top rate. In the category of households receiving dividends and interest of more than $200,000, about 70 percent faced tax rates of more than 37 percent, whereas nearly 95 percent of those who have high wage and salary income are in the 37–41 percent tax range. There is more variation in the taxes on capital income than on earned income.

TABLE 4.1 Percentage of Households Paying Various Marginal Federal Tax Rates

Marginal Tax Rate	Dividends + Interest >$50,000	Dividends + Interest >$200,000	Wages + Salaries >$500,000
<16 percent	10.0%	10.5%	1.0%
16–29 percent	28.4	13.8	3.5
29–37 percent	22.7	4.1	0.3
37–41 percent	37.7	70.2	94.7
>41 percent	1.3	1.6	0.6
Number of taxpayers	402,800	51,000	76,300

Source: Calculations made using National Bureau of Economic Research TAXSIM model.

Capital Gains Taxes

Taxes on interest and dividends are not a very exciting part of the after-tax portfolio problem. Capital gains are where the action is. Most managers know the tax rules on short-term versus long-term capital gains. The tax rate on short-term capital gains—gains on securities held for less than one year—can go as high as 39.6 percent. Today, the top rate on long-term capital gains is 20 percent; starting in 2005, that rate will come down to 18 percent on assets that have been held for at least five years. The difference between the rates on short-term and long-term gains will be even larger in the future than it is today. The tax-efficient strategy, therefore, when all other aspects of a portfolio are the same, is to realize losses and hold gains until they become long term.

The advantages of generating long-term capital gains relative to other kinds of portfolio income are larger today than they have been in the past. Table 4.2 shows how the Taxpayer Relief Act of 1997 increased the advantages of tax-efficient investing. As recently as 1989, the top marginal tax rate on the highest dividend income and interest income recipients was 28 percent, which was also the top tax rate on capital gains. During the past decade, a zero tax rate differential has widened to a 20 percentage point differential. In the future, the difference between taxes on capital income and long-term capital gains could be as large as 23 percentage points.

This tax environment explains the benefits of tax-efficient portfolio management, but it also raises the issue of tax code risk. The tax system can shift in ways that destroy the advantages of previous tax-efficient behavior. Should investors and managers try to hedge bets on the tax system? Should taxpayers hold some qualified money in a Roth Individual Retirement Account and some in a traditional IRA? The tax treatment of these accounts is different, and one (the Roth) is not affected by future changes in marginal income tax rates. The answer is probably yes, although deciding how to model tax code risk is an unexplored problem.

Unrealized Capital Gains

One of the most difficult problems in measuring after-tax portfolio performance concerns handling unrealized capital gains. The AIMR-PPS standards recommend ignoring potential future taxes on unrealized capital gains. I believe that some positive tax burden should be applied to unrealized gains because they are not untaxed but, rather, carry a contingent future tax liability.

The precise tax burden on unrealized gains depends on client circumstances. First, is the client likely to face substantial "forced realizations"? Such realizations may result from a transaction that sells the client out involuntarily from a position in a low-cost-basis stock or from a substantial consumption demand on the client's part—demand for a new house, a new yacht, or so on. Second, is the client someone who, perhaps because of age, is in a position, from the standpoint of dynastic wealth accumulation, to take advantage of basis step-up at death? Third, is the client going to carry out a gifting strategy that will transfer asset basis to the next generation? If so, the manager should consider carryover basis rather than basis

TABLE 4.2   Top Federal Marginal Tax Rate over Time

Category	1996	1998	2005 (estimate)
Dividends and interest	~41%	~41%	41%
Long-term capital gains	28	20	18

step-up as the likely scenario for assets received by the next generation. These issues can be explored with clients to determine what capital gains tax circumstances apply. They need to be covered in the client's investment plan, not left to the tax planners.

One way to describe the capital gains burden on unrealized gains is with the "accrual equivalent" capital gains tax rate. This concept finds the accrual tax system that gives the client the same total after-tax portfolio value at the end of the "realization period" as the current realization-based system, assuming asset sale at the end of the realization period. The approach is similar to asking what tax rate in New Zealand (which uses an accrual system on capital gains) would give you the same wealth after tax at the end of a given number of years as the 20 percent realization-based tax rate in the United States. The concept is useful to managers in explaining that deferring taxes is not the same as never paying them. It is a way of quantifying the interest-free loan a client is getting from the IRS when the client defers realizing capital gains on a position.

For example, suppose a client buys an asset in Year 0 for $100 and it generates capital gains at 10 percent a year. The asset pays no dividends. If the gains were realized each year and taxed as short-term gains (that is, every 364 days, the manager realized the gains on the position), then the after-tax return each year would be

$$10(1.00 - 0.396) = 6.04\%$$

because the short-term capital gains tax rate is 39.6 percent. After 10 years, no additional taxes would be due and the value would be

$$\$100.00(1.064)^{10} = \$185.96.$$

The value of the portfolio would be greater if the asset were held for 10 years and then the capital gains were realized. Assuming that the asset grew at 10 percent a year for 10 years and that 20 percent of the gains were taxed away in Year 10, the asset's after-tax value in 10 years would be

$$(1.00 - 0.20)[\$100.00(1.10)^{10} - \$100.00] + \$100.00 = \$227.50.$$

The accrual equivalent tax rate depends on the rate of return the asset manager would have had to earn on an after-tax basis year after year to get to the value of $227.50 in 10 years. To find this key bit of information, simply solve the following expression for R, the rate of return:

$$\$100.00(1.00 + R)^{10} = \$227.50.$$

The answer is $R = 8.57\%$. Thus, the accrual equivalent tax rate is

$$\frac{10.00\% - 8.57\%}{10.00\%} = 0.143, \text{ or } 14.30\%.$$

Using the accrual equivalent rate is like comparing the accumulated assets in an IRA with assets that are invested in a taxable account. How can one compare the values of those two investments? One way would be to find the internal rate of return on assets in the IRA that provides the same return as that available, after tax, outside the IRA. The accrual equivalent tax rate is the tax rate that, if it were charged to your account every year on the accruing gains, would give you the same after-tax portfolio value at the end of the planning horizon that you would have had if you had been working under the realization-based system in which you pay taxes only at the end. The 14.3 percent accrual equivalent tax rate can be compared with the other tax rates applicable to the client. Because clients are accustomed to

TABLE 4.3   Accrual Equivalent Return by Holding Period

Holding Period	Return
1 year	8.00%
5 years	8.28
10 years	8.57
20 years	8.98
Until death	10.00

thinking in terms of 39.6 percent as an interest tax burden and 20 percent as the statutory tax burden on long-term realized gains, the 14.3 percent is a comparable measure. It describes what the rate would have to be if every year the assets with unrealized gains were marked to market and taxed on their gains.

The accrual equivalent tax rate provides a flexible tool for analyzing future tax burdens. If the client's tax rate is likely to change in the future, the manager can build that change in to the calculation of an accrual equivalent tax rate. It can also be used to illustrate the value of deferring capital gains realizations over different horizon lengths.

Table 4.3 shows how the accrual equivalent tax rate changes as the holding period increases. If capital gains were realized after one year, the after-tax return would be 8 percent, which implies a 20 percent effective tax burden relative to the pretax 10 percent return. By 20 years, the tax burden is down to about 10 percent. The best outcome, as far as taxes go, is if the asset is held until death, because then the tax liability is extinguished. If this asset generates only capital gains, the accrual equivalent return moves up to the 10 percent pretax return because of basis step-up at death.

The tax return data the IRS receives indicate that in the mid-1990s, the average holding period for corporate stock on which gains were subject to long-term capital gains tax treatment was about 6.5 years. Managers may be able to persuade their clients to hold assets longer by using a similar analysis to that of Table 4.3. This table can also illustrate the important benefits of a low-realization tax-management strategy.

Estate Tax Issues

Table 4.3 shows the potentially substantial tax savings that can flow from holding appreciated assets until death. Is the scenario realistic? Managers need to make some assumptions about the future tax circumstances of clients and about their estate-planning advice to evaluate the chance of basis step-up.

Life expectancy is one factor that applies in judging the likelihood of holding an asset until death. Table 4.4 shows that life expectancy in the United States is quite long, even for people already at advanced ages. These data are based on the entire U.S. population, and the wealthy clients with whom managers deal are likely to live longer than these averages. The exact cause of wealth-related differences in mortality experience is not known, but there is a stark disparity between the mortality rates faced by those in the bottom 20 percent of household income or wealth distribution and those at the top. In short, even if the client is an 85-year-old woman, the client's life expectancy may be 7 years, so whether a basis step-up is just around the corner is hard to judge. Managers, therefore, need to be mindful that the planning horizon, even for older clients, could be substantial.

TABLE 4.4   Life Expectancy at Various Ages, 1994

Age/Sex	Years Expectancy
65-year old	
Man	16.1
Woman	20.0
75-year old	
Man	9.8
Woman	12.8
85-year old	
Man	5.3
Woman	6.9

Source: U.S. Social Security Administration, unpublished tables used in preparing the 1995 Social Security Administration Trustee's Report.

TABLE 4.5   Age Distribution of 1992 Taxable Decedents

Age at Death (years)	Percentage of Tax Returns	Percentage of Estate Value
<50	1.9%	3.1%
50–60	3.1	6.2
60–70	9.9	16.0
70–80	23.4	26.7
>80	61.7	47.9

Source: Martha B. Eller, "Federal Taxation of Wealth Transfers, 1992–1995," *Statistics of Income Bulletin* (Winter 1996–97):8–63.

Most decedents with substantial estates die at quite advanced ages. Table 4.5 shows that in 1992, nearly two-thirds of taxable decedents were in their 80s when they died and more than three-quarters of the value of the estates reported were for decedents who were older than 70.

The estate tax is a large and important tax in relation to other taxes for the small set of taxpayers who are likely to face it. The estate tax will change in the future as a result of a sliding scale of tax thresholds that will phase in between now and 2006. At the moment, an estate must be more than $625,000 to incur federal estate taxes; by 2006, the threshold will be $1 million. Today, marginal estate tax rates start at 37 percent at that $625,000 level and go as high as 60 percent. For a client who is thinking about keeping the assets that he or she has built for the next generation, the estate tax is thus an important part of the tax environment.

Traditional Bequests

Assets can be passed from the wealth accumulator to the next generation in three ways, and the three methods have different tax consequences. The first method, and the one that

TABLE 4.6   Households Making Gifts of at Least $10,000 a Year, 1995

Household Head's Age (years)	Net Worth $1.2 Million to $2.4 Million	Net Worth Greater than $2.4 Million
55–64	12%	29%
65–74	20	30
75+	26	22

Source: Federal Reserve Board, the Survey of Consumer Finances.

receives the most attention, is traditional bequests. Assets are held until the accumulator, or the spouse of the accumulator, dies, and then the assets pass as a bequest to the next generation. Such assets are subject to the estate tax. They receive a basis step-up on any accrued unrealized capital gains, but the heirs face a variety of costs at the time of death, which may involve probate, valuation, and other issues. The costs are likely to be lower for publicly traded securities than for interests in privately held businesses or other less liquid assets.

Tax-Free inter Vivos Gifts

The second way to transfer assets is by carrying out a gifting strategy during the lifetime of the accumulator generation. The allowed annual gifts of $10,000 per recipient per donor avoid the estate tax but do not participate in any step-up in basis, so the capital gains tax liability is not extinguished. In general, high-net-worth clients can have either capital gains tax relief or estate tax relief, but not both. So, for taxpayers who could shift a substantial share of the wealth to the next generation in the form of *inter vivos* gifts, the tax gains from basis step-up are not as great as the simple analysis suggests. Capital gains taxes may be reduced at the cost of higher estate taxes.

For anyone who focuses on tax planning, the data on participation in gifting is remarkable. Table 4.6 shows the percentage of households with householders 55 years old or older that gave assets of $10,000 in support of other households by net worth and by age. (The $10,000 is not $10,000 per child; it is simply giving $10,000 total.) The Survey of Consumer Finances, from which these data are drawn, asks donors about their gifts. It also asks the potential recipients, younger households typically, about the *inter vivos* gift amounts that they received. It turns out that the amount of *inter vivos* giving reported is about twice the amount of *inter vivos* receiving that is reported. No one understands why, but keep it in mind when analyzing these numbers. Table 4.6 indicates that only about a fifth of the households that are headed by somebody over the age of 75 with a net worth of more than $2.5 million are making these kinds of gifts. Whatever the reason, the high-net-worth band is leaving unnecessary tax burdens to their heirs by underusing the *inter vivos* giving option.

Taxable Gifts

The third possibility, which is attractive only for very high-net-worth clients, is to make taxable gifts of more than the untaxed $10,000 per recipient a year. On an after-tax basis, pursuing a taxable gifting strategy is attractive for two reasons. The first is that the effective tax burden on a taxable gift is lower than the effective tax burden on a bequest. Estates and gifts are taxed ostensibly under the same tax rules because we have a unified estate and gift tax in the United States. However, gifts are taxed on a net-of-tax basis, whereas bequests are taxed on a gross basis. The result is that if the estate tax rate facing a potential decedent is T, the tax rate on the gifts is $T/(1 + T)$ instead of T. With a 50 percent statutory tax rate, the tax rate on the gifts (0.5/1.5) effectively becomes a 33 percent rate instead of a 50 percent rate. This consideration is very important, and it is widely underappreciated.

Taxable gifting is greatly preferable to leaving assets to pass through a taxable estate. This is true because of the tax rate difference and because paying the gift tax avoids the later estate and gift tax liability on whatever subsequent appreciation occurs on the assets given away. Appreciation on the assets and income on the assets will accrue to the next generation instead of to the donor generation. The gifting strategy raises, once again, the income tax versus estate tax trade-off. Taxable gifts reduce estate tax burdens, but they preclude taking advantage of capital gains basis step-up at death.

Only a tax lawyer can advise on the trade-offs among estate, gift, and capital gains taxes, but a starting point is that estate and gift tax rates tend to be much higher than the long-term capital gains rate. Estate and gift taxes start at 37 percent and can go as high as 60 percent. So, avoiding the estate tax and paying the capital gains tax at a rate of 18–20 percent along the way is often the preferable strategy.

This issue crystallizes the importance of understanding client-specific circumstances in measuring after-tax results. For example, the trade-off between capital gains and estate/gift taxes is moot for those who are perfectly happy to leave their assets to a charitable foundation; they have a different strategy for reducing estate taxes, a strategy in which the capital gains tax liability is not important. For clients who wish to leave their assets to their children, however, reducing the combination of capital gains taxes and estate taxes is important.

CONCLUSION

Measurement of after-tax portfolio performance is a crucial undertaking for any manager with private clients, and the AIMR-PPS standards are an important systematic effort to bring the industry up to speed in presenting returns on an after-tax basis.

Taxes are complicated, however, for high-net-worth clients. Managers may find that the AIMR-PPS standards are too broad for reporting performance for particular clients. Managers may need to customize the algorithm by client or client group to recognize particular tax circumstances. This customization may involve building in specific tax rates, future tax liabilities, and even intergenerational plans in terms of wealth accumulation and wealth transfers. Tools such as the accrual equivalent tax rate provide managers a straightforward way to explain to clients how important and how valuable deferring capital gains can be. Managers need to think about modeling the client's after-tax returns for various portfolios.

Managers also need to consider the implications of gifting behavior. Apparently, most high-net-worth couples are likely to pass along some assets at the death of the second-to-die spouse, and the estate tax is likely to affect their intergenerational transfers. This practice raises the probability that some assets will face a zero capital gains tax rate (through the basis step-up) and underscores the need to integrate the investment manager into the tax-planning and tax-management picture. In some cases, wealth accumulation must be viewed from the family rather than the individual perspective. Gift giving complicates the problem of measuring marginal tax rates for after-death performance evaluation.

A common misconception is that taxes and investments can be managed separately. But investment managers cannot expect to achieve the best possible after-tax returns if they handle only the portfolio side of a client's affairs and turn over other aspects to tax managers, accountants, or tax planners. These aspects are intertwined. Accountants cannot try to minimize taxes when they are given a pretax return stream as the outcome of what the portfolio manager has done. Two-way communication is necessary if the strategy is to leave the client the largest after-tax wealth possible.

QUESTION AND ANSWER SESSION

Question: How do you benchmark after-tax returns when the accrual equivalent tax rate is used?

Poterba: You have all the mechanics in the basic formula, where a zero tax rate is being applied to the unrealized component of capital gains. The only question is whether to use a positive tax rate. If you want to work with the accrual tax rate, the modification is to put in a 1 minus 10 percent or 1 minus 12 percent tax burden on the unrealized capital gains term. Operationally, after you've run through the calculation for a client and identified the holding period as 20 years, that calculation tells you that the effective accrual capital gains rate on a gain that accrues today is on the order of 10 percentage points. You would assign that rate when you calculated after-tax returns.

Question: Is it reasonable to assume that a client who withdraws 10 percent a year from the assets will have different after-tax performance from a client who adds 10 percent a year to the assets?

Poterba: Yes, the situation is similar to the cost basis of a mutual fund that is getting positive cash flows versus one with negative cash flows. The one with positive flows doesn't have to realize as many gains. A fund with a 10 percent negative cash flow will have to realize gains and will have lower after-tax returns. That outcome is as true for a separately managed account as it is for a mutual fund.

   I would use effective accrual rates to cast light on the effect of withdrawals versus infusions. For example, consider a client who plans to withdraw 10 percent of the portfolio each year. That information tells you that the time horizon or the effective duration for which the money is going to be under management is significantly shorter than for someone who plans to contribute 10 percent of the portfolio value each year until he or she dies. What's driving the difference is that the person who is adding money year after year is getting much longer average interest-free loans on the unrealized capital gains. You would expect to see a substantial difference in the after-tax return performance of those two portfolios.

   Of course, the portfolio manager would be wise to recognize that the strategies and the investments that are optimal for someone who plans to add 10 percent a year will not be the same as the strategies that are optimal for someone who is planning to withdraw 10 percent a year. The trade-offs between the tax savings for low-dividend securities generating capital gains and the potential risks or other costs that arise from tilting the portfolio in that direction will be very different for those two clients.

Question: Is after-tax performance useful or not, then, in measuring manager value?

Poterba: What's the alternative? Is it best to ignore the fact that there were tax consequences associated with realizations and not try to make corrections? Some sort of measurement of after-tax performance makes sense; AIMR introduced the adjustment factor to account for such differences in strategies, but comparability is still not perfect. If you are trying to make comparisons of after-tax performance among managers, what you'd really like to see is the kinds of accounts a manager is running that have withdrawal characteristics like the account you're bringing to the table. The ability to dissect a manager's accounts by client objectives is the sort of information that could be useful, but that sort of detailed performance analysis is virtually impossible.

Question: How does one deal with realized losses that must be carried forward to a future tax year? Are any adjustments made?

Poterba: One thing you can do, in the spirit of the effective accrual tax rate, if a client has a very simple portfolio position with a limited number of managers working with the client and the client realizes a loss that is too large to use up this year (so the losses carry forward) is to ask: What is the discounted present value today of being able to reduce taxable income by $3,000 a year this year, next year, and all along the way until the loss is used up? If the tax rate at which you're deducting those losses is 39.6 percent today and you have $6,000 worth of losses, then you're getting 39.6 percent on the first $3,000 and 39.6 discounted for one period; so, it may be effectively 36 percent on next year's losses in today's dollars.

Simple analysis, however, omits the fact that managers can also modify their behavior with respect to future gain realizations so as to accelerate the use of the loss as a device for sheltering other gains. Therefore, the real issue is how valuable it is to have losses on the books today, given that the client can use these losses to realize some gains tax free and thereby rebalance the portfolio.

Question: What do you do about taking over a portfolio that has large embedded gains when you have been hired to diversify the portfolio (so, the after-tax returns are going to be biased downward)?

Poterba: You need to make some sort of correction in reporting portfolio performance, perhaps group client portfolios that start from similar positions. The issue is reminiscent of the debate that sometimes goes on in the popular press about mutual funds with different amounts of embedded capital gains: If you started tracking two funds today—one a new fund and the other an old fund with substantial embedded capital gains—you would expect the fund with the embedded capital gains to generate more taxable realizations going forward. Comparing the managers would be unfair because they start from different positions.

Question: At what net worth should you suggest to someone that they gift? For example, is $1.2 million enough assets for a 70-year-old couple that may face nursing home costs?

Poterba: The most likely explanation for the low level of taxable gifting, at least among those with net worth below, say, $3 million, is the fear of substantial expenses sometime before the end of their lives. Nursing homes probably loom largest in those anxieties. In most case, those expenses do not, however, make a substantial dent in high-net-worth household assets. Something like 20 percent of 70-year-olds will go into a nursing home at some point before death—the percentage is higher for women than for men. Most stays in nursing homes are relatively short, although most of the dollars spent on nursing home care are spent for the small subset of very long-term stays. Most of these households retain substantial assets at the time of death of the surviving spouse. The reason I focused on the $2.5 million net-worth category is that in that range, potential nursing home bills will not draw down most of the accumulated assets.

One could probably build a simple Monte Carlo simulation to get a handle on the risk of nursing home need versus tax savings. For example, you could find out the rough odds of various expenditures and then point out the trade-off between, say, a 5 percent chance of needing to pay an expense and the saving of 40 percent in terms of the difference between the estate tax and the capital gains tax.

CHAPTER 5

TAXABLE BENCHMARKS: THE COMPLEXITY INCREASES

Lee N. Price, CFA

After-tax benchmarks must adhere to standard benchmark rules while incorporating tax-related concerns (such as income tax rates), but a big hurdle in establishing appropriate benchmarks is choosing which tax rate to use. An after-tax benchmark can best be constructed by using a combination of three levels of approximation as well as a shadow portfolio that allows for adjustments in cash flows and calculations of portfolio-specific cost bases.

Of those who manage taxable portfolios or represent taxable clients, only a small percentage report after-tax returns. One of the reasons managers give for not calculating after-tax returns is the lack of generally available after-tax benchmarks. After addressing the issue of benchmarks in general, I will explain how to calculate after-tax returns according to AIMR-PPS™ standards; the same rules apply to calculating after-tax benchmarks. I will then discuss three levels of approximation for the calculation of after-tax benchmark returns and potential combinations of these approaches.

STANDARD BENCHMARK RULES

A number of well-established principles exist for creating benchmarks. A benchmark should be (1) appropriate to the manager's asset class and investment strategy, (2) unambiguous, (3) specified in advance, (4) investable, and (5) measurable. When constructing an after-tax

Reprinted from *AIMR Conference Proceedings: Investment Counseling for Private Clients III* (August 2001):54–64.

benchmark, a sixth rule is also applicable: (6) subject to the same (or similar) tax considerations as those of the clients whose portfolios are being evaluated against the benchmark. Obviously, an after-tax benchmark must have the same or similar tax considerations as those of the accounts that are being managed, but that does not mean that the benchmark should not also be unambiguous and specified in advance and, most important, appropriate to the manager's investment strategy.

The problem with after-tax benchmarks is that no single after-tax performance number is applicable to all users of the benchmark. One size does not fit all. Whereas pretax benchmark users can expect to have a single number for benchmark performance, after-tax benchmark users should never expect a single value. The S&P 500 Index's pretax return in 1999 was 21.04 percent, according to Ibbotson Associates. But managers who want to compare their results with an after-tax benchmark must recognize the complications involved. The benchmark has to take into account not only the different tax rates of clients but also the variation in capital gain taxes depending on the client's starting cost basis.

A nuclear decommissioning trust with a 20 percent flat tax rate on capital gains should have a different after-tax benchmark from that of an individual with a 46 percent total state and federal tax rate. Equally important is the fact that the after-tax benchmark return depends on the inception date of the portfolio. If the account began in 1998, the 1999 after-tax return will reflect only a minimal amount of capital gains. If the account began in 1989, however, then the 1999 after-tax benchmark return will have a much larger capital gains component generated by every stock sold. The account will reflect 10 years of compounded gains built into the portfolio return, and when the manager sells the stocks, the manager will realize a much larger capital gain than that of the account that had been open for only one year. Consequently, after-tax benchmark returns for any given year tend to be smaller than those for longer holding periods.

AIMR AFTER-TAX STANDARDS

The initial task of the Taxable Portfolios Subcommittee of the AIMR Performance Presentation Standards Implementation Committee, which I chaired when it was formed in 1994, was to evaluate the various ways of computing after-tax returns. We considered everything from cash basis (using only custodian-computed, tax-related cash flows) to full liquidation, partial liquidation, and a present value methodology that would account for the potential tax liability of future portfolio liquidation in current dollars. The committee decided that the realized-basis method was the only acceptable way to report after-tax performance.

Advantages of Realized Basis

In the committee's view, the most important advantage of reporting after-tax returns using realized-basis accounting (which the U.S. SEC now calls "preliquidation") is that implied taxes are linked directly, and in the same period, to the taxable event giving rise to them. Regardless of when taxes are actually paid, the realized-basis method forces the manager to be aware of the tax impact of portfolio trading and security selection. This is true of both taxes on dividend and interest income and of capital gain taxes on security sales. A second important advantage is that after-tax performance computed in this manner will be completely in sync with pretax performance calculated according to the AIMR-PPS standards. All of the same rules regarding interest and dividend income accrual apply in the after-tax arena as well.

Disadvantages of Realized Basis

The biggest disadvantage of using the realized-basis methodology is that it requires complicated accounting—accurate tax lots, calculation of accrued interest, and accretion of OID discounts/premiums—and a great deal of precision. Many investment managers lack the necessary capabilities in their computer systems, even though some software vendors have been working hard to solve that problem.

Another disadvantage of this approach is that it slightly understates performance for all assets by charging taxes before they are actually due.

AIMR-PPS Standards

For before-tax performance, calculations are generally done according to a balance-sheet approach. The balance-sheet approach means that the manager uses the asset values at the end and the beginning of the period and adjusts for both the income received and the cash flows (positive and negative) during the period; the calculation is basically the difference between ending and beginning asset values divided by the average asset value for the period:

$$\text{Pretax performance} = \frac{\text{Ending market value} - \text{Cash flows} - \text{Beginning market value}}{\text{Beginning market value} + \text{Weighted cash flows}}.$$

This method works well for pretax performance calculations but not for the analysis of tax implications.

A completely analogous method, using exactly the same numbers, is an approach based on investment flows. The manager looks at the flow activity during the period rather than focusing on the ending and beginning asset values. The manager can divide the return, in terms of flow, among the various sources of return to the portfolio—realized gains, unrealized gains, and income—and then apply the appropriate tax rate to each type of flow. The denominator is the same as in the pretax calculation—the average assets for the period:

$$\text{After-tax performance} = \frac{\text{Unrealized gains} + \text{Realized gains}(1 - t) + \text{Income}(1 - t)}{\text{Beginning market value} + \text{Weighted cash flows}}.$$

With this methodology, the after-tax implication is clearer because no taxes are incurred on the unrealized gains during the period. This equation is a simplification because realized gains and income are taxed at different rates depending on holding period and type of income, but it is useful for conceptualizing the process. An easier way to calculate the same result is: After-tax performance equals pretax performance minus the tax burden, where the tax burden is as follows:

$$\text{Tax burden} = \frac{(\text{Realized gains} \times \text{Capital gains rate}) + (\text{Income} \times \text{Income tax rate})}{\text{Beginning market value} + \text{Weighted cash flows}}.$$

IMPORTANCE OF THE CAPITAL GAIN
REALIZATION RATE

The realization of capital gains plays a vital role in after-tax performance. The driving force behind the impact of taxes on a portfolio is the relative size of realized capital gains and the frequency with which they are realized. Table 5.1 shows the long-term return for a growth portfolio. I assume that the annual capital gain from price appreciation is 7.5 percent, the percentage of gain realized each year is 40.0 percent, the capital gain tax rate is 28.0 percent, the percentage average dividend yield is 2.3 percent, and the client's income tax rate is 39.6 percent with no dividend exclusion. The long-term pretax return based on these assumptions is 9.8 percent (7.5 percent + 2.3 percent), and the after-tax return is 6.8 percent.

Table 5.1 shows that in the beginning, taxes have only a minor impact on the portfolio, but as the performance period lengthens, the after-tax return decreases because the amount of imbedded gains increases. After a holding period of about 20 years, the after-tax return drops to about 6.8 percent and remains constant. So, according to this particular set of assumptions, a 9.8 percent pretax return converts to 6.8 percent after-tax return. When looking at after-tax performance (particularly long-term after-tax performance), the capital gain realization rate (CGRR) is an important concept. The CGRR is not necessarily the turnover rate. The Taxable Portfolios Subcommittee concluded that the measure of the CGRR should be the net gains or losses realized during the period divided by the average of the available gains during the period. The average stock of available capital gains during the period is

1/2 (Stock of unrealized gains at start + Realized gains + Stock of unrealized gains at end).

Although turnover alone is not the measure that defines CGRR, keep in mind that portfolio turnover is not necessarily bad. For example, turnover may include the selling, or turnover, of cash equivalents. This type of turnover does not affect taxes at all because the tax basis is always 100 percent of the market value. Or the manager may have intentionally harvested losses, which increases turnover but reduces the portfolio's net capital gain realization.

The effect of the CGRR on after-tax returns is rather dramatic. Table 5.2 shows the after-tax returns calculated with this same model under slightly different assumptions to illustrate

TABLE 5.1   Implications of Varying the Rate of Realization of Capital Gains

Item	Year 0	Year 1	Year 4	Year 8
Price index (untaxed)	100.0%	107.5%	133.5%	178.3%
Cost basis	100.0	100.0	111.5	141.6
Pretax gain this year	0.0	7.5	9.3	12.1
Pretax value	100.0	107.5	133.6	173.7
Unrealized gain (cumulative)	0.0	7.5	22.1	32.1
Realized gain	0.0	3.0	8.8	12.8
Tax	0.0	0.8	2.5	3.6
After-tax value[a]	100.0	108.0	132.9	172.3
Compound after-tax return		8.0	7.4	7.0

Note: Assume all capital gains taxes paid and dividends received at year-end.
[a]Including dividends after tax.

TABLE 5.2   Effect of CGRR on After-Tax Return for Various Combinations of Appreciation and Dividend Yield

CGRR[a]	Appreciation/Dividend Yield (%)					
	4.0/6.0	5.0/5.0	6.0/4.0	7.5/2.5	8.0/2.0	9.8/0.2
5%	6.9%	7.3%	7.6%	8.2%	8.4%	9.0%
10	6.5	6.8	7.2	7.7	7.9	8.5
20	6.1	6.4	6.7	7.2	7.4	7.9
40	5.7	6.0	6.3	6.8	6.9	7.4
60	5.6	5.9	6.2	6.6	6.7	7.2
80	5.5	5.8	6.1	6.5	6.6	7.1

Note: Assumes a 28 percent tax rate.
[a]Percent of gains realized each year.

the two things an investment manager can control: the CGRR—at the left of the table—and the investment style (namely, dividend yield)—at the top of the table. A manager cannot control the direction or the volatility of the market, but he or she can control the amount of turnover—a proxy for CGRR—in the portfolio. And the manager can control his or her investment style, whether the manager invests in high-dividend-yield stocks or low-dividend-yield stocks, growth versus value, and so on. Table 5.2 uses exactly the same assumptions presented in Table 5.1, with one exception: The portfolio's rate of total pretax return is 10 percent (rather than 9.8 percent) a year for the next 20 years, regardless of how the portfolio is structured. So, based on a completely hypothetical efficient market assumption, the after-tax returns range from about 9 percent for a portfolio with low turnover and a low dividend yield to 5.5 percent for a portfolio with high turnover and a high dividend yield.

CONVERTING A STANDARD PRETAX BENCHMARK

One approach to constructing an after-tax benchmark is to convert a standard pretax benchmark to an after-tax one. Roughly 50–100 pretax benchmarks are used by managers, with 10–15 used widely. The after-tax benchmarks can be converted using various tax rates and investment periods (different inception dates). As I mentioned earlier, even if one adopts the AIMR-PPS standards realized-basis method, there are three levels of approximation in converting a pretax benchmark to an after-tax benchmark, and I will describe those three levels in this section. At the end of this section, I will cover some of the special problems associated with converting a standard pretax benchmark to an after-tax benchmark.

First Level of Approximation

To convert a pretax benchmark into an after-tax benchmark, at the first level of approximation, the manager must begin by splitting the pretax return between the sources of return: for example, dividend income and appreciation—realized and unrealized. (I will use the S&P 500 as an example, and fortunately, Ibbotson has already split the returns for the S&P 500.) For this first level of approximation, the manager must also assume that the pretax benchmark has a fairly constant CGRR. (I will assume that the CGRR is 5.5 percent for the S&P 500.)

Keep in mind that the CGRR can vary widely depending on the index chosen and the number of years used to construct the data. The CGRR could be 25 percent for the Russell 2000 Index or even 50–70 percent for some of the value indexes. And although the S&P's CGRR has averaged 5.5 percent for the past 12 years, the average depends on which years are used to calculate the measure. The manager must also assume a capital gains tax rate (28 percent) and an income tax rate (39.6 percent) for dividends. Finally, the manager must apply the CGRR to the assumed portfolio appreciation and compound the remaining unrealized gains.

The equations for creating an after-tax benchmark for the S&P 500 are as follows:

Price	$= \text{Price}(-1) \times (1 + \text{Appreciation})$
Realized gain	$= \text{CGRR} \times [\text{Price} - \text{Cost}(-1)]$
Cost	$= \text{Cost}(-1) + \text{Realized gain} (1 - \text{Capital gains tax})$ $+ \text{Dividends} (1 - \text{Dividend tax})$
Tax	$= \text{Realized gain} \times \text{Capital gains tax} + \text{Dividends} \times \text{Dividend tax}$
After-tax value	$= \text{After-tax value}(-1) \times (1 + \text{Appreciation} + \text{Dividends} - \text{Tax})$
After-tax return	$= \text{After-tax value}/\text{After-tax value}(-1) - 1.$

Note that the realized gains and dividends are both calculated as a percentage of Price(-1).

To start the calculation, the manager must have a beginning price, and then he or she increments that beginning price by 1 plus the portfolio appreciation. Next, the manager calculates the potential realized gain, which is the difference between the price at the end of the period and the cost basis. The cost footnoted minus 1 is for the previous period (which is rolled forward each period). The manager multiplies the potential amount of realized gains by the CGRR, and the cost is incremented to reflect the reinvestment of proceeds, but only arithmetically. The U.S. IRS does not allow managers to compound the cost basis, so the manager calculates the cost using the cost of the previous period plus the realized gains from security sales in the current period times the quantity (1 minus the capital gains tax paid) plus the dividends received in the current period times the quantity (1 minus the income tax paid on the dividends). And then finally, the manager can calculate an after-tax return, which is computed on a running basis divided by the previous period's value. The methodology is straightforward and, most importantly, is sensitive to the manager's assumed CGRR and assumed tax rates.

Table 5.3 shows the results of calculating after-tax performance according to the above methodology. For this example, I used the performance of the S&P 500 for the past 10 years. The table shows the pretax return for the S&P 500 for each of the years for 1990 to 1999 and the after-tax performance for each of the same years. Beginning in 1991, more than one after-tax performance number exists for each year because the starting year for the calculation (for the cost) varies. For example, if the portfolio's inception date was 1989 and the market was down 3.2 percent (pretax) in 1990, the after-tax return was a negative 4.4 percent, which may seem odd. Even though the portfolio was just started in 1989 and should not have realized many gains on average in 1990, thus creating only a minimal capital gain tax liability, the average dividend earned on the S&P 500 in 1990 was high. Thus, the income tax liability alone would have had a significant tax impact on the portfolio. Because of the high dividend tax rate assumed in this analysis, the income taxes paid exceeded the net effect of realizing losses, assuming a 5.5 percent portfolio turnover rate. As the holding period increases, the

TABLE 5.3   S&P 500 After-Tax Return for 1990–1999 as a Function of Starting Year

Item	1990	1991	1992	1993	1994	1995	1996	1997	1998	1999
Pretax[a]	−3.17%	30.55%	7.67%	9.99%	1.31%	37.43%	23.07%	33.36%	28.58%	21.04%
Starting year for after-tax return										
1989	−4.43	28.35	6.05	8.46	−0.07	35.13	20.96	31.14	26.43	19.08
1990		28.21	5.94	8.36	−0.17	35.04	20.89	31.08	26.38	19.04
1991			6.22	8.62	0.08	35.28	21.08	31.24	26.51	19.14
1992				8.66	0.11	35.32	21.11	31.27	26.52	19.16
1993					0.19	35.39	21.16	31.31	26.56	19.19
1994						35.34	21.13	31.28	26.54	19.17
1995							21.48	31.58	26.76	19.35
1996								31.81	26.94	19.49
1997									27.27	19.75
1998										20.05

[a]S&P 500 pretax return.

after-tax numbers are always lower than the pretax numbers, and they get lower and lower the longer the investor holds the portfolio, even with a relatively low 5.5 percent CGRR.

This effect is most noticeable in Table 5.3 for the 1999 period. For a portfolio started in 1998, the after-tax return was down about 1 percent—20.05 percent versus the pretax return of 21.04 percent. But if that portfolio had been started in 1989, the after-tax return would have been 19.08 percent.

Table 5.4 highlights the difference between the pretax and after-tax returns for the S&P 500. The one-year difference between pretax and after-tax returns is roughly between 1.0 percent and 2.3 percent, with a 1.75 percent average reduction across the 10 sample years (1990–1999). But for portfolios with a holding period of three years, the difference in the pretax and after-tax return is roughly 1.25–2.1 percent, and by six years, the range is 1.9–2.3 percent. By the time the investor has had the portfolio nine years, the difference is consistently above 2 percent.

The significant cumulative effect of taxes on portfolio returns explains the reason for the SEC's proposal that mutual funds be required to report after-tax returns to their clients. Table 5.5 shows some of the cumulative differences (for portfolios with holding periods of up to 10 years) in pretax and after-tax returns for the years 1995–1999. Again, the difference is negligible in the first year, just 1–2 percent. But at 5 years, the difference accumulates to 19 percent on average, and at 10 years, the cumulative difference is about 77 percent. In other words, the cumulative 10 year pretax return for the S&P 500 in 1999 was about 300 percent, whereas the cumulative after-tax return was about 225 percent, for an approximate difference of 75 percent, which is a fairly striking number. This large cumulative difference is obviously why the SEC is concerned about taxable investors investing in mutual funds to provide for their retirement years. Their realized return will be much lower than what is reported to them on a pretax basis.

TABLE 5.4   S&P 500 Example: Difference between Pretax and After-Tax Returns

Year	1990	1991	1992	1993	1994	1995	1996	1997	1998	1999
1989	1.26%	2.20%	1.62%	1.53%	1.38%	2.30%	2.11%	2.22%	2.15%	1.96%
1990		2.34	1.73	1.63	1.48	2.39	2.18	2.28	2.20	2.00
1991			1.45	1.37	1.23	2.15	1.99	2.12	2.07	1.90
1992				1.33	1.20	2.11	1.96	2.09	2.06	1.88
1993					1.12	2.04	1.91	2.05	2.02	1.85
1994						2.09	1.94	2.08	2.04	1.87
1995							1.59	1.78	1.82	1.69
1996								1.55	1.64	1.55
1997									1.31	1.29
1998										0.99

TABLE 5.5   S&P 500 Example: Cumulative Difference between Pretax and After-Tax Returns

Starting Date	1995	1996	1997	1998	1999
1989	17.92%	26.07	39.87%	57.77%	77.43%
1990	16.84	25.04	38.85	56.87	76.78
1991	8.66	13.77	22.37	33.91	47.01
1992	5.93	10.19	17.32	27.09	38.37
1993	3.59	7.00	12.70	20.69	30.11
1994	2.09	5.20	10.34	17.69	26.51
1995		1.59	4.28	8.41	13.60
1996			1.55	4.16	7.63
1997				1.31	3.22
1998					0.99

Second Level of Approximation

The second level of approximation entails the same general concept as in the first level, but rather than make the assumption that the CGRR is constant every year, the manager must go further and determine the actual CGRR of the index for each period. Historically, companies were dropped from the S&P 500 if their market capitalization shrank or if they declared bankruptcy, events that were usually not likely to create large capital gains. But recently, companies are being dropped because they have been acquired. This heightened merger and acquisition activity has had a noticeable effect on indexes such as the Russell 2000. In addition, the best performers, the ones that rise to the top, often no longer meet the capitalization requirements and are pushed out of the index. Huge capital gains are associated with that kind of turnover.

Looking at the CGRR in detail, not on an average basis but analyzing it year by year, can add a lot of value to the after-tax benchmarking process. The manager has to determine for each year which companies left the index (because of bankruptcies, buyouts, or mergers) and whether the event was taxable. If it was a merger for stock, for example, and the company being dropped from the index was merged in a tax-free exchange with a company already in the same index, then no capital gain tax would be incurred. That kind of turnover does not affect after-tax returns. But if the company being dropped was bought out by a company that was not in the index (perhaps a non-U.S. company), then a manager benchmarked against that index would have to sell that stock and take the capital gain. That is, the manager would have to calculate capital gains based on the actual capital gains realized each period as a function of the tax rate and starting cost basis.

The question then arises as to what happens to after-tax returns as a function of CGRRs. Table 5.6 shows the differential between pretax and after-tax returns for various CGRRs and holding periods. The return differential in Year 1 does not vary greatly as the CGRR varies, but by Year 10, the difference between a CGRR of 5.50 percent (return differential of 1.96 percent) and a CGRR of 30 percent (return differential of 6.54 percent) is substantial. Therefore, calculating an after-tax benchmark using the second level of approximation creates a valuable tool. If the manager assumes a constant CGRR (as in the first level of approximation) when calculating the after-tax returns of the benchmark, the result will be better than not accounting for the tax implications at all, even though it will not be an accurate reflection of what really occurred in the index. If, in fact, the manager's benchmarked index is changing with time (which it is), by incorporating the true CGRR in the after-tax return calculations, the benchmark's after-tax performance numbers will differ from those calculated using the first level of approximation and will more accurately portray reality.

Third Level of Approximation

The third level of approximation involves tracking the actual dividend reinvestment income and reinvesting at the then-current (i.e., at the time of the reinvestment) prices. The manager also rebalances the benchmark portfolio whenever capital action occurs and tracks the new cost basis.

Special Problems

The Dow Jones Industrial Average is probably the most commonly used index by taxable investors. The Dow is price weighted rather than market-cap weighted, which means that

TABLE 5.6   Average Annual Difference in Pretax and After-Tax Returns as a Function of the CGRR: S&P 500 Index

CGRR	Year 1	Year 2	Year 3	Year 4	Year 5	Year 6	Year 7	Year 8	Year 9	Year 10
5.50%	1.50%	1.69%	1.74%	1.84%	1.96%	2.10%	2.08%	2.10%	2.08%	1.96%
10.00	1.71	2.04	2.20	2.39	2.61	2.86	2.92	3.03	3.05	2.93
20.00	2.16	2.79	3.13	3.50	3.90	4.39	4.59	4.88	5.00	4.86
30.00	2.61	3.49	3.96	4.47	5.02	5.73	6.04	6.49	6.70	6.54

every time a corporate action occurs—a stock dividend, a stock split, and so on—the index must be adjusted. For example, if IBM splits two for one, a manager benchmarking against the Dow has to sell half of the IBM shares in the portfolio, regardless of the investment implications. As a result, the manager's portfolio will realize a capital gain, pay capital gain taxes, and reinvest the proceeds in the other 29 stocks in the index. So, an entirely new class of events become taxable events for the price-weighted Dow that would not be considered taxable events for the S&P 500 or most of the other indexes that are constructed according to a market-cap weighting.

Style indexes also have some unique problems, such as when a stock falls in value and drops out of the Russell 1000 Index (a large-cap index) and goes into the Russell 2000 Index (a small-cap index). A manager who is benchmarking against the Russell 1000 would consequently have to sell that stock and realize the gain. In this case, the gain realized may not be large because the stock has dropped in value, but the process applies in the other direction as well. That is, when a stock moves from a small-cap index into a midcap or large-cap index, huge gains might be realized if that stock has to be sold from a small-cap manager's benchmark portfolio.

Fixed-income indexes pose even greater problems for adjustment to an after-tax basis because index providers frequently do not list the securities in the index. Fixed-income indexes tend to be created by percentages of exposure to sectors—a certain percentage of Treasuries, mortgage-backed collateralized bond obligations, corporates, and so on. Thus, managers typically do not know which specific bonds (issuers, coupons, and maturities) are actually in the index. Figuring out this index composition can be difficult, if not impossible. Most fixed-income performance, however, comes from income rather than appreciation, so fixed-income indexes do not usually have the problem of accumulating unrealized capital gains, unless there has been a long period of declining interest rates.

SHADOW PORTFOLIOS

Converting a standard pretax benchmark is one way to construct an after-tax benchmark. A more precise methodology, however, is to create a shadow portfolio that varies according to the client. In other words, the shadow portfolio pays the same *pro rata* capital gain taxes for withdrawals as the actual portfolio. And every time the client gives the manager more money, the shadow portfolio brings that money in at the cost basis at that time.

Clients have different cash flows, and the shadow portfolios (i.e., the benchmarks) will be different for each client. Table 5.7 shows a shadow portfolio of the S&P 500 for a single year. The starting point at the end of 1998 is 100, and then the various monthly returns are shown. Table 5.7 shows a single withdrawal (half of the initial value, which is admittedly an extreme example) by the client at the end of 1999. This withdrawal causes the pretax return (21.02 percent) to drop significantly (to 15.75 percent) as a result of the capital gains tax paid on the capital gains realized from the security sales—security sales that were needed to generate the proceeds for the distribution requirement (withdrawal).

Table 5.8 shows the impact on the after-tax return for the period (1999) if the withdrawal had been made in each month of the year—January, February, and so on. The return for the "No cash flows" row is the same, 20.20 percent, as in the standard benchmark conversion approach. The benchmark return using a shadow portfolio and a 50 percent withdrawal in January, however, is 16.7 percent. So, this withdrawal makes a big difference in the after-tax return, but the impact of the withdrawal varies by month. If the withdrawal had been

TABLE 5.7   S&P 500 Example Shadow Portfolio

Date	Inflow Value	Cost Basis	Out-flow	Tax Rates Dividends	Capital Gains	Benchmark Rates Pretax Return Price	Pretax Return Income	Capital Gains Realization	Returns Pretax	After Tax
12/98	100	100		39.60%	28.00%	5.64%	0.12%	0.46%	5.76%	5.71%
01/99				39.60	28.00	4.10	0.08	0.46	4.18	4.14
02/99				39.60	28.00	−3.23	0.12	0.46	−3.11	−3.17
03/99				39.60	28.00	3.88	0.12	0.46	4.00	3.94
04/99				39.60	28.00	3.79	0.08	0.46	3.87	3.82
05/99				39.60	28.00	−2.50	0.14	0.46	−2.36	−2.43
06/99				39.60	28.00	5.44	0.11	0.46	5.55	5.49
07/99				39.60	28.00	−3.20	0.08	0.46	−3.12	−3.17
08/99				39.60	28.00	−0.63	0.13	0.46	−0.50	−0.57
09/99				39.60	28.00	−2.86	0.11	0.46	−2.75	−2.81
10/99				39.60	28.00	6.25	0.07	0.46	6.32	6.28
11/99				39.60	28.00	1.91	0.13	0.46	2.04	1.97
12/ 99			50	39.60	28.00	5.78	0.11	0.46	5.89	1.90
Total									21.02	15.75

Note: Model from David Stein, Parametric Portfolio Associates.

TABLE 5.8   S&P 500 Example for 1999 with 50 Percent Withdrawal in Various Months

No cash flows	20.20%
January	16.73
February	18.36
March	17.53
April	16.87
May	17.32
June	16.47
July	17.01
August	17.12
September	17.71
October	16.66
November	16.38
December	15.75

made in February, the return would have been 18.4 percent; if it had been made in May, 17.3 percent. Because the index price varies, the benchmark, which is the S&P 500 in this case, also varies as a function of when the withdrawal is made.

CONCLUSION

Constructing after-tax benchmarks is not easy, which is why I have been involved in the AIMR-sponsored effort to create a standardized methodology. Perhaps the most important aspect of constructing an after-tax benchmark is starting with the correct pretax index. The next step is to carry out the first level of approximation—splitting the appreciation and income return sources because of different tax rates and then applying a constant CGRR. The second level of approximation—calculating the after-tax returns with the appropriate CGRR each year—yields an even more accurate view. And finally, a combination of these approximations, plus adjusting for significant cash flows through a shadow portfolio to calculate a portfolio-specific cost basis, produces the most detailed and accurate after-tax benchmark.

QUESTION AND ANSWER SESSION

Question: How would limits on the deductibility of capital losses factor into after-tax benchmarks and portfolio returns?

Price: That question was raised when the Taxable Portfolios Subcommittee first met. Our conclusion then, which has been reiterated in the revised AIMR-PPS standards that will be coming out soon,[1] was that most investors have more than one basket of investments. As a result, we assumed that all losses could be used, although we knew that would not be true in every situation.

These after-tax performance numbers are not a substitute for reported accounting records. We were not trying to create 1099s or any number that would be going to the government. What we were trying to do was look at the investment manager's added value after taxes to see whether the manager was taking his or her losses, which is generally a good thing to do.

For example, if you added a new client in January 2000 and took losses during the year, your after-tax performance was probably higher than your pretax performance for 2000, based on the performance of the S&P 500. If that same account was started in 1995, however, this would not be the case. The huge run up in the S&P 500 would have been reflected in your client's account; even though you took losses in 2000 and benefited from them, you probably also incurred a fair amount of taxable capital gains in the account.

Question: Can exchange-traded funds (ETFs) serve as a proxy for after-tax benchmarks?

Price: Various types of after-tax benchmarks have been proposed. For some mutual funds, such as those based on the S&P 500, you can determine the dividend and appreciation proportions and use that data to construct an after-tax benchmark. In fact, you can get an actual 1099 if you happen to own that mutual fund and appropriately allocate the short-term and long-term gains and so on. Other methodologies, such as using ETFs or options, also exist. These methods are not wrong; their approximations are just different from the ones suggested here.

A big problem with creating after-tax benchmarks for mutual funds or ETFs is the timing issue, or the percentage of unrealized gains in the benchmark or portfolio.

Suppose you were marketing to private clients and wanted an after-tax performance composite. The Taxable Portfolios Subcommittee brought up the point that when creating groups of after-tax portfolios, putting all 50 of your taxable clients together wouldn't necessarily make sense, because some might have started with you last year and others 20 years ago. As a result, the percentage of unrealized, or embedded, capital gains in the portfolios would differ dramatically. But that is what a mutual fund in effect is doing when it reports after-tax performance. Its numbers will also be dramatically affected by net cash inflows or outflows, which may reduce or increase the realization of capital gains.

One solution for managers of individual accounts is to calculate after-tax returns by starting year (those from 20 years ago, those from 15 years ago, etc.), but the result might be only one or two portfolios for each composite, which doesn't make sense and is not helpful to prospective clients. Another way to group those accounts is by percentage of unrealized gains in the portfolios. That same methodology applies to benchmarks. Grouping several different starting years for the S&P 500 and then developing benchmarks that are presented as a percentage of book to value would be easier than having separate benchmarks for every month of every year going back *ad nauseam.*

Question: If a benchmark should be created for each starting year, should you also calculate a separate benchmark for each client?

Price: Back in 1995 (roughly), the Subcommittee recommended that managers create separate composites not for each client but for each type of client. Qualified nuclear decommissioning trusts, for example, have a flat 20 percent tax rate. You can combine all such accounts in one composite and not include those of individual portfolios or property and casualty insurance companies, which have different tax regimes. If you look at types of clients as opposed to specific tax rates, few types probably exist. You may end up with four or five different types, and for that reason, you may end up with four or five different after-tax benchmark returns by tax rate in addition to the by-year distinction. In order to be consistent with the AIMR-PPS standards, the goal should clearly be to create composites of similar portfolios rather than to benchmark separately for each client. But as noted in my presentation, individual shadow portfolios can also be helpful in the case of significant cash flows, even if only for purposes of communication with a particular client.

Question: Can these approaches be used to create after-tax benchmarks for hedge funds?

Price: Conceptually, these same approaches could be applied to hedge funds, but such leveraged portfolios have the more pressing problem of calculating true pretax performance. A hedge fund may have a long–short strategy and be truly market neutral, but what is the divisor? What are the assets at risk? To say that hedge funds don't have any risk and then divide by zero doesn't make sense. And if the hedge fund is truly market neutral, the definition of assets at risk is unclear. The same problem arises even if the fund is only partially hedged. A subcommittee of AIMR's Investment Performance Council (IPC) is studying this issue and hopes to make recommendations soon.

Question: How do you account for state taxes?

Price: The current AIMR-PPS after-tax reporting standards do not factor in state taxes because the subcommittee wanted to get as close as possible to an "apples-to-apples" comparison between managers. Some members thought including state taxes would just muddy the waters. Instead, the suggestion was made that managers use the maximum federal tax rate appropriate for the type of client under management.

Nevertheless, since that standard was adopted, managers have found that some clients want to factor in their state taxes. But if managers include state taxes for individual clients, they must create two presentations: one that ignores state taxes to comply with the AIMR-PPS standards and one that includes state taxes to meet client needs (the second would be shown as supplemental information). Managers have also found that clients want their actual anticipated federal tax rate to be used, not simply the maximum applicable to their type of investor category.

The new standards, I suspect, will allow managers to report based on whichever tax rates they actually use in making investment decisions for clients. The standards will encourage managers to talk to clients about all applicable tax rates, not just federal and state but local as well. If you happen to live in New York or New Jersey and the local tax rates apply to investment income, for example, then those could also be included. Managers would need to create composites of all the accounts that share roughly the same tax rates and would have to disclose what the tax rates were (the weighted average for their composite), but they could then use the same client calculations for their composites.

I still have mixed feelings on this issue. Something in the area of comparability is lost when different managers use different rates, yet I understand why we were getting the complaints and the practical reasons for the new standards.

Question: Are managers required to report after-tax performance?

Price: Remember that all of the AIMR standards regarding performance, including the AIMR-PPS standards, are optional. Nobody has to be in compliance. Even if you feel that the marketplace, your consultants, or your clients require you to be in compliance with AIMR-PPS standards, you do not have to be compliant with the after-tax standards. They are purely optional; the AIMR-PPS standards merely state that if you intend to claim compliance and show after-tax performance, then you must do so according to the after-tax standards.

The same is not true for mutual funds. In January 2001, the U.S. SEC issued its final decision about a proposal that had been floating around for almost a year. Effective April, 16, 2001, mutual funds must report their after-tax performance. Then, starting October 2001, after-tax performance will have to be included in fund advertisements and sales material; in February 2002, mutual fund prospectuses will also provide the information. For mutual funds, the taxable event is when the fund actually declares the dividend, which happens about once or twice a year. So, calculating after-tax performance for mutual funds will be much less complicated than for separately managed portfolios.

Requiring managers to report after-tax numbers helps make them aware of the tax impact on their portfolios and also helps clients reduce their expectations of what their returns will be for the long term. If clients consider after-tax performance, they will realize that no matter whether they have an index fund, an IRA, or an actively managed portfolio, the actual after-tax returns will be lower than the pretax returns.

Question: Do the after-tax return computations ignore the present value of taxes accrued currently and payable in the future?

Price: The realized basis method does ignore the present value of taxes on capital gains that have not yet been realized. Some managers use alternative methodologies to estimate such taxes, based on assumptions of when stocks may be sold and what the discount rate would be between now and then.

Although I understand such concepts, particularly for use by nuclear decommissioning trusts (which may have fairly well-defined termination dates), the committee recommended against such methodologies because of the huge variability introduced by the timing and discount rate assumptions. We did not feel comfortable in mandating specific numbers, but without such a standard, two different managers with identical after-tax performance on a realized basis could show widely different present value performance.

Question: Isn't the issue of after-tax returns more about forcing the manager to take losses versus just having the losses affect the portfolio market value?

Price: This is certainly one of the issues, and it makes sense to take losses, unless you are worried about a wash sale or immediate stock bounce. But after-tax performance covers a lot more than just taking losses; it is about being tax aware when taking gains and selecting a bias toward growth stocks rather than higher-taxed dividend income stocks.

Question: As an international manager with clients around the world who are subject to different tax rates, what information am I providing to prospects when I create an after-tax composite rate of return?

Price: AIMR recognizes that both the current and expected newly revised after-tax guidelines are U.S.-centric, which is why they have been developed by the Performance Presentation Standards Committee, the North American representative to the IPC, rather than by the global group itself. Other countries have already expressed interest in doing something similar—Canada and Australia in particular—but because tax rates and methodologies vary tremendously around the world, creating a worldwide standard for reporting after-tax performance is unlikely.

NOTE

1. This presentation was given before the redrafted AIMR-PPS standards were approved and released in final form.

CHAPTER 6

OVERCOMING CAP-WEIGHTED BOND BENCHMARK DEFICIENCIES

William L. Nemerever, CFA

Generic bond indices, such as the capitalization-weighted Lehman Brothers Aggregate Bond Index, are not the best benchmarks for most fixed-income portfolios. Cap-weighted indices do not represent the opportunity set offered by the broad fixed-income market. As an alternative to generic benchmarks, straightforward, easily replicable domestic and global bond benchmarks can be constructed using derivatives, particularly interest rate swaps and credit derivatives swaps.

Managers often begin meetings with potential fixed-income clients by asking the question, why do you own bonds? Believe me; it is a real conversation stopper. After the client looks at his shoes for a few minutes, the manager gets the following types of responses: Bonds hedge the interest rate risk in the portfolio, diversify exposure to equity markets, act as a deflation hedge, serve as a source of income and foreign currency exposure (for holders of foreign-currency-denominated bonds), or are an "anchor to windward," whatever that means. All in all, these reasons do not provide much guidance to fixed-income managers who are helping clients set portfolio objectives.

Reprinted from *CFA Institute Conference Proceedings Quarterly* (December 2007):55–66.

DIVERSIFICATION

Diversification and protection against equity market declines is the common wisdom for investing part of a balanced portfolio in the fixed-income market. A historical perspective can shed light on the efficacy of this perception. Figure 6.1 shows for the S&P 500 Index, the Lehman Brothers Aggregate Bond Index (Lehman Aggregate), and the long duration component of the Lehman Aggregate only the negative quarters (from most negative to least negative) from 1980 to 2006. This period captures some severe market declines.

As shown in Figure 6.1, it appears that in a crisis, bonds do indeed move in a way that adds diversification—at least most of the time. The bond returns for the period (the white bars) are largely moving in the right direction (up), away from equity market returns, which are moving down, as indicated by the gray bars. A couple of exceptions are worth noting: In the first quarter of 1980 and third quarter of 1981, the bond markets experienced severe adjustments following the U.S. Federal Reserve Board's policy shift in 1979. The long component of the Lehman Aggregate, shown by the black bars in Figure 6.1, seems to provide even more diversification benefits than the Lehman Aggregate alone. Based on this analysis, duration appears to be a good reason for owning bonds. This relationship is not entirely realistic, however, because it assumes a 100 percent allocation to both bonds and equities, although typical allocations over the period were closer to 60/40 equities/bonds. A more realistic analysis would show that the diversification potential of bonds is certainly not as impressive as Figure 6.1 would lead one to believe. Adding bonds does improve diversification, but not markedly. The stock and bond returns in the first quarter of 1980 and third quarter of 1981 remain steadfastly negative.

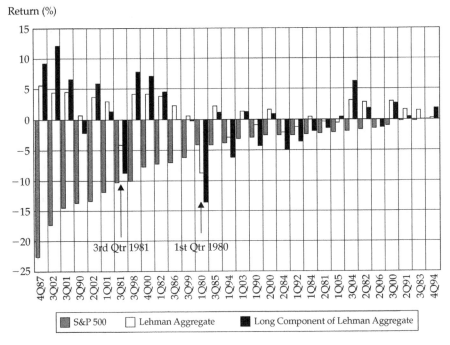

FIGURE 6.1   S&P 500 Negative Quarterly Returns and Associated Returns of the Lehman Aggregate and the Long Component of the Lehman Aggregate, 1980–2006

Many investors today are not enamored with bonds as an investment vehicle and use money that might otherwise be allocated to them primarily to fund alternative investments. The result is a lower portfolio allocation to the fixed-income market. Reflecting this posture, an 80 percent allocation to equities along with a 20 percent allocation first to the Lehman Aggregate and then to the long component of the Lehman Aggregate suggests yet again that the diversification benefits of fixed-income investment remain negligible. This result calls into question clients' claims of owning bonds for diversification purposes. Basically, an allocation to bonds makes clients feel better because they have made an attempt to address the issue of diversification, even if, at the index level, it is not a particularly effective hedge.

A fixed-income index fails to provide diversification in most asset mixes. In other words, typical bond asset-class exposures provide little in the way of equity market diversification. If the goal is to hedge against negative equity returns, neither the duration of the Lehman Aggregate nor that of the long portion of the Lehman Aggregate is sufficient to provide that guarantee—although portfolio durations longer than that of the market are better suited to the task.

Bonds are not an asset class in the way they are currently being used by investors. The available historical return data are based on the returns of bond indices, such as the Lehman Aggregate. But investors use these data to represent the entire fixed-income asset class. Such return histories do not adequately describe the opportunity set offered in today's fixed-income market. Therefore, making a historical bonds-versus-stocks comparison based on an index (e.g., the Lehman Aggregate) does not make sense. The Lehman Aggregate does not represent the range of returns—the opportunity set—that could actually have been realized in the market.

PREVALENCE OF CAP-WEIGHTED BENCHMARKS

Most investors use a capitalization-weighted index as their benchmark because cap-weighted indices are what index creators tend to produce and thus are what the investment community "buys." The result is that the benchmark that the majority of an investor's performance peer group uses is typically the one that the investor is most comfortable adopting.

Consultants also play a role in the prevalence of using cap-weighted indices as benchmarks. Most consultants do not really understand the fixed-income market; they view it as a necessary evil. Therefore, they tend to rely on a published bond index when making their fixed-income asset allocations, and the manager then inherits the index as the portfolio benchmark.

Another reason many investors prefer a broad, cap-weighted index is to stop managers from "cheating" by using beta to create alpha. A simple example of this type of cheating would be a portfolio benchmarked to U.S. government bonds for which the manager buys corporates because he or she has strong corporate credit analysts. This same mindset—not investing outside the benchmark—is present today in equity portfolios when a non-U.S. equity portfolio is prohibited from buying U.S. stocks, even if occasionally doing so would generate a better return than that available within its mandate.

Too many investors confuse the benchmark universe with the investment universe. The two are completely different concepts. The benchmark universe is the performance benchmark against which the manager is measured, and the investment universe is the universe within which the manager has enough skill to add value. This distinction is greater in the fixed-income market because the opportunity set is much less defined than in the equity market.

Just because a security is not in the benchmark does not mean the manager is unreasonable in buying it. Ultimately, the buy decision should be driven by manager skill. This realization gave rise to the core-plus strategy. Essentially, core plus is a way for clients and consultants to give the manager latitude to enter markets outside the mandate, such as high-yield and emerging market debt and currencies, without having to specifically incorporate these markets into the portfolio asset allocation and benchmark. Core plus thus effectively broadens the universe of securities beyond the portfolio benchmark.

WHY MOST BOND BENCHMARKS ARE FLAWED

The number one reason most bond benchmarks are flawed is that they are capitalization weighted. The concept of capitalization weighting is adopted from the equity market, where capitalization is actually a good description of the opportunity set and is a reasonable way to approach investing in the market. But to use capitalization weighting in a bond market index is extremely misleading because a bond manager cannot possibly buy the market. Consider the Canadian bond market. No investor could buy even one of all the bonds in the Canadian bond universe. It is impossible. And even if buying the market were feasible, the composition of the market, and hence the index, would change continuously; the manager would constantly be chasing his shadow. And to complicate matters further, cap-weighted indices focus primarily on the cash bond market and totally ignore the derivatives market.

A number of other problems are associated with cap-weighted indices. For example, they are built using arbitrary rules, such as prohibiting bonds with maturities shorter than one year. Also, although it is one of the broadest bond market indices, the Lehman Aggregate does not include Treasury Inflation-Protected Securities (TIPS), most asset-backed securities (ABS), many commercial mortgage-backed securities (CMBS), bank loans, and floating-rate debt, so its relevance as a benchmark for fixed-income managers is negligible. It is a historical accident that so much asset allocation analysis has been done based on cap-weighted indices.

Another problem is that replicating the benchmark can be very expensive. A look at total return swaps on corporates shows how much this corporate exposure in indices costs investors. Why go to the expense? Why pay to replicate benchmark exposure when the major risks in the benchmark's bonds are relatively straightforward? The most important risks in the bond market often fall outside the index. These risks include term structure risk, credit risk, liquidity risk, optionality risk, and sector risk (but not always in that order).

Another point is that these risks can be captured in a number of ways outside the index. For instance, at Grantham, Mayo, Van Otterloo & Company (GMO), we have Lehman Aggregate and Lehman Global Aggregate mandates for which we do not even buy bonds; we buy swaps, futures, or TBAs (to be announced) in the mortgage market. Soon, a Lehman Aggregate futures contract will be available. Thus, many ways exist to get index exposure without actually buying the bonds in the index.

Most of the return in an index (roughly 95 percent) can be explained by yield-curve moves. Obviously, replicating the broad array of securities in a cap-weighted index is not necessary to capture this return in the index.

Most importantly, however, the index often has little to do with the investor's objectives. Relying on a cap-weighted index means a potential misalignment between the client's needs and the portfolio's benchmark. The manager should find out why the client wants to invest in bonds in the first place, and then go from there.

ANALYSIS OF THREE CAP-WEIGHTED INDICES

I want to pound a wooden stake into the heart of cap-weighted indices so they never see the light of day again. Cap-weighted indices make absolutely no sense in the fixed-income market. With the example of three different indices in three different bond markets—the United States, Switzerland, and Canada—I should be able to make my point clearly.

United States

In the United States, asset-backed securities, a huge and growing part of the domestic bond market, are only a small piece of the most widely used benchmark, the Lehman Aggregate. This minimal representation is mainly caused by the fact that they are floating-rate securities (and, according to the rules of the index, are arbitrarily limited), even though the floating-rate market is one of the largest sectors in the U.S. bond market. Not including floaters means that a huge portion of the bond market is simply ignored.

The cap-weighted nature of the Lehman Aggregate means that its characteristics change over time. The weightings of corporate and mortgage-backed bonds, as well as the benchmark's duration, have shifted dramatically in recent years. For example, over the period from January 1976 to February 2007, corporates have gone from just over 40 percent to just over 20 percent of the index and mortgages have increased dramatically from about 5 percent to about 35 percent. Mortgages quickly surpassed corporates once they were added to what was originally the Lehman Brothers Government/Corporate Bond Index in order to create the Lehman Aggregate. By the mid-1980s, the mortgage composition of the index had outstripped corporates, and it has grown steadily since. In fact, the impetus behind the creation of the Lehman Aggregate was that managers were cheating by buying mortgages when mortgages were not in the benchmark.

Another challenge with a cap-weighted index is shifting interest rate risk. Duration in the Lehman Aggregate has fluctuated significantly over the last 30 years. From January 1975 to February 2007, the duration of the index dropped from just over six years to roughly four and a half years, falling below four years for a while in early 2003. Also noteworthy is that there have been some rather dramatic shifts in duration—of up to 25 percent—in fairly short periods of time. These drivers of portfolio change and rebalancing, if followed simply so that a manager can stay flush with the benchmark, are probably not relevant to the objectives of most investors. Yet, nobody asks any questions. I want to reiterate that managing portfolios in this way is not sensible.

Switzerland

Surprisingly, only 65 percent of the most popular Swiss franc bond index is composed of Swiss-domiciled issuers because the index rules allow any issuer of Swiss franc bonds to be included. This means that if the Ivory Coast, for example, issues debt in Swiss francs, that debt is included in the index solely because it is denominated in Swiss francs. So, the Swiss bond benchmark includes emerging market debt—which makes no sense—simply because it was a convenient way to structure the index.

As is true of the Lehman Aggregate, the duration of the Swiss bond index has changed markedly over time. Over the last nine years, index duration has increased 50 percent, raising the level of interest rate risk in the index from five years in December 1997 to almost eight years in early 2003 and decreasing to seven and a half years in early 2006.

A five- to seven-year duration swing is a massive increase and represents a huge degree of interest rate sensitivity. In this nine-year period are some interesting periodic jumps in duration, and although I cannot say exactly why, I am reasonably sure it is a function of rebalancing the index or of particular bonds falling in or out of government issuance. Swiss government borrowing is certainly not relevant to most clients' investment objectives and definitely not worthy of the transaction costs that would be incurred to chase the resultant duration changes. Once managers are properly motivated, they figure out quickly how to control active risk against the benchmark they are going to be measured against. But let me stress once again, that endgame is not in the client's best interest.

Canada

The Canadian bond index, the DEX Universe Bond Index, is a particularly egregious offender because it has virtually no transparency, is rebalanced daily, and includes a lot of very small issues. The supplier of the index will not disclose its components unless paid to do so. But knowing what is in the index is of little value because it is almost impossible to replicate.

The Canadian index, like its counterparts in the United States and Switzerland, has changed significantly with time. Today, corporate bonds represent 30 percent of the index compared with 10 percent 10 years ago.

HIGH-YIELD SECTOR

An article in the *Financial Times* on 2 April 2007 reported that "three-quarters of loans to junk-rated U.S. companies are now provided by hedge funds and other non-banks, according to a new report on the leveraged loan market" (Beales 2007). Obviously, a large amount of the activity in the high-yield market is not in the traditional marketplace. The majority of the lending to high-yield companies in the United States is done through private placements to hedge funds, other nonbanks, and even some bank lenders.

The *Financial Times* article went on to quote Standard & Poor's, saying that "if the recent steep growth of the leveraged loan market continues, it could overtake the high-yield bond market by 2009." This projection has an impact on the high-yield benchmark in terms of changing market capitalization, sector orientation, and average maturity. Trying to manage against this benchmark leaves a lot to be desired. For example, if telecommunications is a huge borrower in the high-yield market, does it make sense to have a huge telecommunications position in a portfolio just to replicate the active risk in the index? It is doubtful, especially in such a sector as this where cheap money pulls in less-worthy borrowers.

BEYOND CASH BONDS

Today, the fixed-income market is much more than cash bonds. Until the early 1990s, however, the cash bond market was the primary option for fixed-income managers. U.S. Treasury bond futures began trading in the late 1970s, gradually followed by an array of other fixed-income derivatives products, such as mortgage derivatives, which have substantially broadened the fixed-income universe since that time.

The Lehman Aggregate is composed of roughly 3,500 bonds with less than $300 million in outstanding par value. Finding these bonds for a client's portfolio is next to impossible; not only is it a futile endeavor, but it is also totally unnecessary. Many of these bonds are already locked up, for example, in insurance company portfolios, but even if they were not, they are completely irrelevant to most investment-grade fixed-income portfolios. Unlike the purchase of a stock that has very specific exposure to a corporate entity, in the fixed-income market, most of the exposure is to interest rate risk and sector risk with very little risk specific to the particular borrower. Therefore, purchasing a particular issuer or bond in an attempt to replicate the index is counterproductive. Multiple ways are available to get interest rate and sector risk into portfolios.

The derivatives markets are totally ignored in the fixed-income indices, even as their importance has usurped that of the cash markets. The cash markets are relegated to a side-show now; the derivatives markets dwarf them in size. Today, the cash markets trade off of the derivatives markets, not the other way around. Consequently, fixed-income opportunity sets have to include the derivatives markets in order to replicate the average duration in the market. But because derivatives have effectively no market value, they complicate the index business. Index providers simply ignore derivatives and stick with cap-weighted indices that are tractable, even if they are irrelevant.

The dominance of the fixed-income derivatives markets over the cash markets is shown in Figure 6.2. The figure defines the opportunity set by market value outstanding as of 28 February 2007, with the gray bars representing the components of the Lehman Aggregate. Clearly, the Lehman Aggregate does not capture the entire fixed-income market, but neither does it capture the entire cash bond market. Notice that most of the $2 trillion market value outstanding of ABS, which are cash bonds, is not in the Lehman Aggregate.

On the right side of the figure are the bank credit and bank interest rate derivatives. Bank credit derivatives total almost $8 trillion in outstanding notional value, and bank interest rate derivatives have a much larger notional market value at $103.2 trillion. Obviously, a lot of

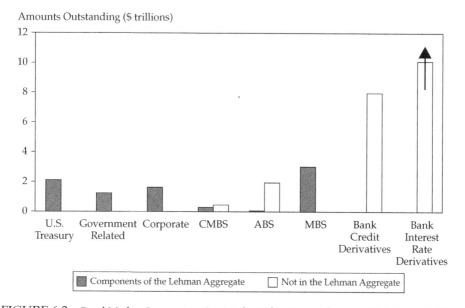

FIGURE 6.2   Bond Market Opportunity Set: Market Value Outstanding as of 28 February 2007

credit exposure is available in derivatives forms, and many investors are buying it over cash bonds. Derivatives have gained popularity because they offer a similar payoff to cash bonds while allowing investors to control interest rate risk.

EMERGING MARKET BOND INDICES

The index industry, which is essentially the dealer community, is way ahead of the rest of the market in trying to establish the more exotic asset classes, such as emerging markets, in fixed-income portfolios. The main dealers involved in this activity are JPMorgan, Merrill Lynch, Citigroup, and Lehman Brothers. Much of the impetus for index design comes from these firms' investment banking groups, who want to sell bonds in Asia in the local currencies because they want to trade the currencies and, recently, local market debt. Because an index is the first step in getting managers to accept a new market as an asset class, the dealer's trading department asks the dealer's index department to create an index for the market(s) in question in the hope that it will jumpstart trading. Three JPMorgan indices are good examples of how these indices are structured—the Global Bond Index–Emerging Markets (GBI-EM), Emerging Markets Bond Index Global (EMBIG) Diversified, and Emerging Local Markets Index Plus (ELMI+).

Keep in mind that these indices are for a market sector that few investors are engaged in—emerging local market bonds. To compound this absurdity, one of the indices, the GBI-EM, has six versions—plain, global, diversified, global diversified, broad, and broad diversified. Each index has its own constituencies and characteristics and, in my opinion, is constructed using strange rules; for example, some indices include all low-income countries and others, only middle-income countries. China and India, the elephants in the room, are huge markets but difficult to access, and because some of the indices include only markets that are easy to access (i.e., those markets without taxes or currency restraints), they ignore China and India. Because these are local currency indices, they all perform differently.

GMO runs a strategy using one of these indices, but there is no compelling reason why one version of the index is better than another. The more exotic the market, the less a benchmark is important. Our main concerns in managing emerging market portfolios are transaction costs and market depth.

GBI-EM

The Global Bond Index–Emerging Markets, rated A– by Standard & Poor's, is a relatively recent index of local-market emerging debt. This is debt issued by poor countries in their local currency. Typically, equity managers do not want to get involved with separately managing currencies, so the more exotic, orphaned currencies become bond managers' tools. Consultants believe that most bond managers have skill in managing currencies, so it seems reasonable to include currencies in the fixed-income opportunity set. Basically, currency exposure is nothing more than a short-term deposit. The extension to a fixed-income classification makes sense.

Table 6.1 illustrates how the index has evolved since its inception in 2003. Some of the countries in the index have had their exposure cut in half over the four-year period; South Africa has gone from 31.1 percent in 2003 to 15 percent in 2006. Turkey and Indonesia, in contrast, have had their exposure in the index increase from no exposure or very little exposure to 5.4 percent and 3.8 percent, respectively. Changes of such magnitude are hard to

TABLE 6.1   GBI-EM Weighting, 2003–2006

Rank	2006 Country	Weight	2005 Country	Weight	2004 Country	Weight	2003 Country	Weight
1	Poland	21.6%	South Africa	20.2%	South Africa	25.8%	South Africa	31.1%
2	Mexico	15.8	Poland	19.1	Poland	19.9	Poland	18.8
3	South Africa	15.0	Mexico	14.8	Mexico	11.6	Mexico	13.7
4	Malaysia	9.9	Malaysia	11.0	Malaysia	9.9	Hungary	9.6
5	Hungary	7.9	Turkey	8.6	Hungary	9.8	Thailand	9.1
6	Thailand	7.8	Hungary	8.2	Thailand	7.6	Malaysia	9.1
7	Czech Republic	6.9	Thailand	6.8	Czech Republic	6.8	Czech Republic	6.4
8	Turkey	5.4	Czech Republic	6.2	Turkey	4.7	Slovakia	1.2
9	Indonesia	3.8	Slovakia	2.0	Slovakia	1.9	Chile	0.5
10	Slovakia	1.9	Indonesia	1.8	Indonesia	1.6	Indonesia	0.5
Total		95.9%		98.6%		99.7%		100.0%

Note: Turkey had 0 percent exposure in 2003.
Sources: JPMorgan and GMO as of 28 February 2007.

ignore in a benchmark, but replication of this exposure in a portfolio is probably not aligned with client objectives.

EMBIG Diversified

The 33 countries in the Emerging Markets Bond Index Global Diversified, rated BB+ by Standard and Poor's, are the countries generally thought of as emerging debt markets. These countries include Russia, Venezuela, Argentina, Mexico, and Brazil. The EMBIG Diversified was created in 1997 after bond managers who were having a hard time beating what was then the most popular emerging bond market index, the JPMorgan Emerging Markets Bond Index Plus (EMBI+), pressed JPMorgan to create a more diversified index. But what was called diversification was actually a suppression of the larger exposures of the bigger countries, such as Brazil, Mexico, and at the time, Argentina. Artificially, some of the market cap in those countries was cut out of the index. At GMO, we do not use this index, but a lot of managers do. The EMBIG Diversified does not represent the entire emerging bond market opportunity set, not only because of the exclusion of a portion of certain countries' market caps but also because it is a cap-weighted index with a set of arbitrary rules for inclusion of assets.

ELMI+

The Emerging Local Markets Index Plus has some strange rules for deriving its index weightings. First, the initial country allocations are derived using a three-year rolling average of exports plus imports, lagged one year. Then, liquidity caps are applied. There is a 10 percent maximum weighting for convertible currencies and a 2 percent maximum weighting for nonconvertible currencies or those with other impediments to investment. The math does not always work, so excess weights have to be reallocated to the noncapped countries.

Like all artificial indices, the ELMI+ does not take into account the costs of rebalancing, which makes replication particularly difficult. Envision the poor manager who is trying to manage against this index, grinding down the return by incurring transaction costs in rebalancing while the index is blissfully sailing along with no transaction costs. Just because an index is an index does not mean it is replicable or replicable at a reasonable price. Although total return swaps are available on many of these indices, they are usually at LIBOR+, which means the manager has to pay extra just to get the index return. This signals drag as well as poor replicability.

Table 6.2 shows the weightings of the top 20 currencies in the index for the years 2003 through 2006. At the top are the most liquid currencies, capped at 10 percent. At the bottom are the currencies limited to a 2 percent weighting. In between the two limited currency groups are the currencies that are not affected by the maximums or minimums. It is a rather tortured group and, like the EMBIG Diversified, does not reflect the market cap, even if that were possible.

NEEDS SHOULD DICTATE THE BENCHMARK

The first step in selecting a fixed-income benchmark is to answer the question, why fixed income? The fixed-income market, as I hope I have illustrated, covers a lot of ground; it ranges from currencies to government bonds, to developing country debt, to high-yield bonds. More often than not, all instruments generically considered bonds are put in one neat

TABLE 6.2 ELMI+ Weighting, 2003–2006

Rank	2006 Country	Weight	2005 Country	Weight	2004 Country	Weight	2003 Country	Weight
1	Hong Kong	10.0%	Hong Kong	10.0%	Hong Kong	10.0%	Hong Kong	10.0%
2	Singapore	10.0	Mexico	10.0	Mexico	10.0	Mexico	10.0
3	Mexico	10.0	Singapore	10.0	Singapore	10.0	Singapore	10.0
4	Poland	8.3	Poland	9.0	Turkey	8.4	Turkey	8.3
5	Turkey	7.8	Turkey	8.8	Poland	8.3	Poland	7.3
6	Czech Republic	6.6	Czech Republic	7.5	Czech Republic	7.4	Czech Republic	7.0
7	Hungary	5.6	Hungary	6.6	Hungary	6.6	Hungary	6.1
8	South Africa	4.8	South Africa	5.4	South Africa	5.6	South Africa	5.7
9	Israel	3.8	Israel	4.7	Israel	5.4	Israel	5.6
10	Chile	2.8	Slovak Republic	3.2	Chile	3.2	Chile	3.5
11	Slovak Republic	2.7	Chile	3.1	Slovak Republic	3.1	Slovak Republic	2.8
12	Romania	2.7	Argentina	2.0	Argentina	2.0	Argentina	2.0
13	China	2.0	Brazil	2.0	Brazil	2.0	Brazil	2.0
14	South Korea	2.0	China	2.0	China	2.0	China	2.0
15	Philippines	2.0	Indonesia	2.0	Colombia	2.0	Colombia	2.0
16	Taiwan	2.0	India	2.0	Indonesia	2.0	Indonesia	2.0
17	Argentina	2.0	South Korea	2.0	India	2.0	India	2.0
18	Brazil	2.0	Philippines	2.0	South Korea	2.0	South Korea	2.0
19	Indonesia	2.0	Russia	2.0	Philippines	2.0	Philippines	2.0
20	India	2.0	Thailand	2.0	Russia	2.0	Russia	2.0
Total		91.2%		96.2%		96.0%		94.1%

Sources: JPMorgan and GMO as of 31 December 2006.

243

box, although they really have nothing in common except an interest rate component. For example, several years ago, high-yield bonds were sometimes managed in the equity group. Clearly, high yield was viewed as having a closer relationship with equity and credit risk than with investment-grade bonds, and they were not placed in the same box.

Many reasons exist for owning bonds, but the main reason, of course, is that they are a source of interest rate exposure. Bonds are also useful for hedging nominal liabilities, diversifying in the event of an equity decline, hedging against deflation, providing exposure to foreign currencies, and producing income. Bonds are good diversifiers of equity exposure only if the duration is long enough, but the duration of most portfolios is too short. Meaningful deflation hedging also requires longer-duration exposure, but a portfolio with a handful of bonds at a five-year duration is not long enough.

Gaining exposure to foreign currencies through a fixed-income portfolio is much simpler than hiring a currency or currency-overlay manager. Short-term foreign currency deposits or foreign-currency-denominated bonds are easily added to a fixed-income portfolio. An allocation to non-U.S. bonds is often made primarily for the foreign currency exposure.

Investors like the income from bonds, although this is a silly, old-fashioned notion. If investors need money, they should just sell an asset. The crux of the matter is that investors prefer not to have to make decisions about selling assets when cash can arrive on a regular basis from bond coupons.

The big tragedy in the fixed-income market is that bonds are not viewed as a source of added value. Broadly, bonds can be a source of alpha and, in fact, a higher quality of alpha than equities. Good bond managers offer higher information ratios, lower fees, and access to a great opportunity set. Many bond managers have significant skill, although it has been hard to see because they are running such low levels of active risk.

ALTERNATIVE BENCHMARKS

Because the popular cap-weighted bond indices are rife with problems, some might be wondering what the benchmark alternatives are. In that vein, I will present a sample U.S. benchmark and a global benchmark, but first, I will relate GMO's experience with creating a liability benchmark.

Liability Benchmark

GMO has been fortunate to get several liability-driven investment (LDI) assignments in Europe, and the process of choosing a benchmark for these assignments has been interesting. One of the actuarial firms that hired us actually suggested the bonds we should buy, country by country, to match its liability stream. Table 6.3 is the liability benchmark that the actuarial firm proposed. We pushed back, citing the expense associated with the approach. Many of the bonds had huge bid–ask spreads. The small amount of sovereign risk diversification they provided did not justify the expense.

Our suggestion was to think in terms of pure interest rate risk. The client agreed, and the benchmark we agreed upon was an index of swaps, as shown in Table 6.4. The alternative and proposed benchmarks have almost identical cash flow patterns, but the alternative benchmark has very low transaction costs. It is also composed of straightforward swap instruments that we can actually buy. As a result, our performance can be measured regularly. The new, straightforward, low-cost benchmark meets the needs of the client because it meets the liability constraint.

TABLE 6.3   Proposed Liability Benchmark

Issuer	Coupon	Maturity	Benchmark Weight
Germany	4.25%	4 Jul 14	0.2%
Germany	3.75	4 Jan 15	0.4
France	5.00	25 Oct 16	0.7
Spain	5.50	30 Jul 17	0.9
Austria	4.65	15 Jan 18	1.0
France	4.25	25 Apr 19	1.1
Italy	4.50	1 Feb 20	1.3
France	3.75	25 Apr 21	1.4
Greece	5.90	22 Oct 22	1.9
France	8.50	25 Apr 23	2.9
Germany	6.25	4 Jan 24	2.8
France	6.00	25 Oct 25	3.2
Italy	7.25	1 Nov 26	4.0
Germany	6.50	4 Jul 27	4.3
Germany	5.625	4 Jan 28	4.2
France	5.50	25 Apr 29	4.4
Germany	6.25	4 Jan 30	5.2
Germany	5.50	4 Jan 31	5.1
France	5.75	25 Oct 32	5.4
Italy	5.75	1 Feb 33	13.7
Germany	4.75	4 Jul 34	12.7
France	4.75	25 Apr 35	12.6
Germany	4.00	4 Jan 37	10.6

TABLE 6.4   Alternative Liability Benchmark:
Lehman Brothers Euro Swap Index Weighting

Swap Maturity (in months)	Benchmark Weight
3	0.7%
12	−0.8
24	−0.1
60	3.4
120	12.1
240	20.5
360	41.3
480	18.0
600	4.9
Total	100.0%

U.S. Bond Benchmark

The primary goal in constructing a fixed-income benchmark is to get enough interest rate exposure. As an example of a clean benchmark, I would suggest an 80 percent weighting in the Lehman 40-Year U.S. Dollar Swaps Index and a 20 percent weighting in the Lehman U.S. Dollar Equal-Weighted Credit Default Swaps Index. The 80 percent weighting in the swaps index pushes duration out long enough to get true diversification against equity market declines. The 20 percent weighting in the credit default swaps (CDS) index provides credit risk. Using the CDS index gives a pure credit risk. The focus is not on single companies but is broadly diversified through an equal-dollar-weighted index.

At GMO, we would use derivatives rather than cash bonds to construct the benchmark. Because the derivatives are not cash intensive, the balance of cash is invested in the JPMorgan U.S. Dollar Cash Index, which earns three-month U.S. dollar LIBOR (London Interbank Offered Rate). The entire benchmarking process is clean, easy, and adaptable to performance measurement. It is replicable and helps investors determine if a manager has skill or not.

Global Bond Benchmark

An example of an alternative global benchmark follows the same approach as the domestic benchmark but is a little more complex. I would suggest an overlay strategy constructed along the following lines:

Derivatives

- 30 percent Lehman 40-Year U.S. Dollar Swaps Index
- 50 percent Lehman 50-Year U.S. Dollar Swaps Index
- 15 percent Lehman U.S. Dollar Equal-Weighted CDS Index
- 5 percent Lehman Eurodollar Equal-Weighted CDS Index

Cash

- 25 percent JP Morgan Three-Month U.S. Dollar Cash Index
- 75 percent JP Morgan Three-Month Swiss Franc Cash Index

This benchmark is for a hypothetical Swiss investor, but euros or other foreign currency can easily be substituted for the Swiss francs. Again, each of the benchmark components is a straightforward, published index that presents no problems with measuring performance. The important point is to be very specific about the risks the client wants to take and use that as the guiding force at the benchmark stage.

CONCLUSION

Always remember to focus on the goal. Determine what purpose fixed-income investments serve in the portfolio in terms of both beta and alpha. If you cannot answer that question, then just buy the Lehman Aggregate and forget about it.

Think beyond the standard benchmarks and do not confuse the opportunity set with the benchmark. A portfolio's benchmark should be driven by its objectives, not the other way around. Just because the Lehman Aggregate has a 25 percent allocation to corporate bonds does not mean the same exposure is appropriate for all portfolios at all times, particularly when corporate spreads are as tight as they are now.

Adopt a strategy that produces alpha along with beta by adding exposures outside the benchmark. Add more active risk. Add duration to ensure that bond alpha diversifies equity alpha. Interest rate and currency markets are excellent sources of uncorrelated fixed-income alpha.

And last but not least, bond managers can and do add value at very reasonable fees.

QUESTION AND ANSWER SESSION

Question: Is it a concern that the most heavily indebted companies are at the top of the cap-weighted index?

Nemerever: Absolutely. A worst-case scenario occurred in 2002 when investors sold investment-grade credits that had defaulted, such as Enron Corporation and WorldCom, with big weights in the Lehman Aggregate. Investors held a lot of those types of bonds because they didn't want benchmark risk. If a company is 8 percent of the Lehman Aggregate, investors naturally want to own a lot of the name. Because heavily weighted companies can definitely run into problems, we prefer equal-weighted benchmarks like the equally weighted CDS index in our proposed U.S. bond benchmark.

Question: Are there any existing derivatives-based corporate bond benchmarks at this point?

Nemerever: Yes, quite a few derivatives-based corporate benchmarks are available. Indices exist for plain swaps, interest rate swaps (in many countries), and CDS. Lehman Brothers has a full range of CDS indices by sector. As benchmarks, CDS indices are a lot cleaner than those using actual bonds because the bonds in the index may not even trade, whereas CDS trade relatively actively.

Question: Is there any situation in which a generic benchmark is appropriate?

Nemerever: Tailor-making a benchmark is usually the best solution, even if it means just picking a generic benchmark whose characteristics are most closely aligned with the client's objectives. Sometimes the best solution is a combination of benchmarks that are congruent with the client's needs. And generic benchmarks with very specific risk exposures can be valuable. But mindlessly defaulting to a generic benchmark like the Lehman Aggregate is a problem because it doesn't represent a real opportunity set.

Question: Would you suggest an alternative to the DEX Universe Bond Index?

Nemerever: A good alternative would be a swaps index to proxy the Canadian bond term structure combined with a CDS index to proxy the corporate exposure. Cash in the index would be invested in Canadian short-term instruments. Basically, this is similar to the benchmark we have proposed for the U.S. market. Using straightforward derivatives swaps avoids the legacy of a lot of small companies in the index. Constructing a derivatives-based benchmark is very easy to do.

Question: Will fixed-income exchange-traded funds (ETFs) become broadly used?

Nemerever: I doubt that ETFs will find a home in institutional portfolios. ETFs are a more complicated asset class in terms of multiple sources of risk compared with fixed-income instruments, whose risk is primarily related to interest rates. Individuals and institutions can get the exposures they need in much more straightforward and less expensive ways than through ETFs.

Question: Are municipal bonds more effective than taxable bonds in diversifying away from equities?

Nemerever: No. As an asset class, municipals have very high transaction costs, and these costs would eat up any diversification benefits. Also, there are no derivatives in the municipal sector. The muni bond future was killed recently, so the market is all cash.

Question: What is your view of the 130/30-type strategies, and would they work in fixed income?

Nemerever: Yes. For a long time, GMO has been running a strategy that is not so much a 130/30 but more long–short. There is nothing magical about the respective long–short percentages—30, 40, or 50 or 100 versus 200. The strategy can be successful, provided the instruments permit you efficiently to go long and short. In our case, we find that interest rate and currency derivatives are very efficient tools for expressing long and short views. The 130/30 concept is packaging. It is a way to move investors out of their shell and toward greater acceptance of and comfort with shorting the market.

Question: If your institutional business is derived from consultants who use traditional benchmarks, how do you grow your business using more appropriate custom benchmarks? Doesn't change have to come from the consulting community or the industry as a whole?

Nemerever: Ultimately, it is an education process. We were successful in our education efforts with our European LDI client. Certainly, if you are in the finals for a Lehman Aggregate benchmark account, you don't want to lambaste the client or consultant on the ins and outs of why it is a bad benchmark. Managing against a generic benchmark doesn't mean a manager can't add value. Any benchmark can be beaten or successfully competed against, but from the client's, sponsor's, and consultant's points of view, choosing the benchmark is an important decision. Essentially, educating clients and consultants about better benchmarks is a long-term process.

Question: How can investors replicate the total return of a specific country in the GBI-EM? Would they use futures, swaps, or cash?

Nemerever: Most of the countries in the GBI-EM have few corporate bonds, but they do have currency forwards, local market interest rate swaps, and sovereign risk credit default swaps. These tools are the most straightforward approach for replicating the index. Typically, we use both interest rate swaps and CDS in these countries and are happy with the results we get.

Question: Would using derivatives instead of bonds add counterparty risk and liquidity risk?

Nemerever: Counterparty risk does have to be monitored, but marking to market and moving collateral help reduce counterparty risk. Derivatives, however, are much more liquid than cash bonds and have much lower transaction costs. Therefore, liquidity is not an issue, and counterparty risk can easily be managed.

Question: For pension funds, what do you recommend as the right benchmark?

Nemerever: First, all the pension plan constituencies—fund manager, actuary, and corporate management—have to decide together how to prioritize the plan's goals. For many plans, the main issue is the matching of liabilities to avoid an income statement effect. But return objectives cannot be ignored, and the two goals are not always consistent. One of the better ways to think about the right benchmark for a given pension plan is to construct a worst-case scenario in terms of the asset/liability mismatch and then try to gauge the company's tolerance for that worst-case scenario. How much asset/

liability mismatch in a worst-case scenario is acceptable? Build the worst-case scenario by starting with interest rates, and move forward from there.

Question: What is the relationship between bond alpha and currency alpha?

Nemerever: Bond alpha and currency alpha are uncorrelated. We have slightly more confidence in currency alpha, so roughly 50 percent of our alpha is from currencies and 40 percent, from bonds. In equities, managers tend to bundle the currency and equity decisions together when they buy a foreign stock and just accept the currency exposure. They are in denial that the two can't be separated. If a manager underweights Japanese stocks, is he negative on the yen? If the manager ignores the currency decision, he effectively shorts the yen as well. Bond alpha and currency alpha are definitely separate, uncorrelated sources of alpha.

REFERENCES

Beales, Richard. 2007. "Hedge Funds Lead US Junk Sector Lending." *Financial Times* (2 April):A1.

CHAPTER 7

YIELD BOGEYS

Brent Ambrose and Arthur Warga

The term "bogey" refers to a target portfolio. In the fixed-income world, it is usually a published index based on some comprehensive list of traded securities. Bogey yields are almost always calculated as the market-value-weighted average of individual component bond yields, but such averages often do a poor job of approximating the actual portfolio yield. Commonly published bogey features such as duration and convexity also are calculated using value-weighted averages, and these measures more nearly approximate the corresponding portfolio values. Thus, the various published bogey characteristics inherently are mismatched. The purpose of this article is to quantify deviations of market-value-weighted bogey yields from actual yield. In some periods, conventionally reported yields have deviated from actual yields by more than 90 basis points.

The bogey for fixed-income portfolios is usually an index published by an investment bank and based on some comprehensive list of traded securities available to a bond fund manager. Portfolio yields are almost always calculated as the market-value-weighted average of the individual component bond yields in the portfolio or bogey. Even though value-weighted yield is known to differ from the true portfolio yield (i.e., internal rate of return), the major published bogeys provide value-weighted figures. This practice has established an accepted procedure for drawing yield comparisons involving market-value weighting. Other bogey features, such as duration and convexity, are commonly published alongside yield, but in their case, value-weighted averages provide correct measures of their corresponding portfolio values. Thus, the measures of yield and of the other characteristics do not necessarily match.

Many periods during the past several years have been characterized by extremely sloped yield curves, and deviations of actual portfolio yields from their value-weighted estimates have reached unprecedented levels. In this study, we quantified the deviations of value-weighted yields from a more accurate measure of portfolio yield based on dollar duration of the bonds.[1]

Reprinted from *Financial Analysts Journal* (September/October 1996):63–68.

Actual portfolio yield for a bogey, or the internal rate of return on the bogey's cash flows, is calculable in principle. In practice, however, the calculation can be an unwieldy exercise because of the great variety of cash flows and cash flow timing involved. A well-known and accurate alternative to value weighting is available that is a close estimate of actual portfolio yield and is simple to calculate. This alternative measure uses an individual bond's dollar duration in place of its market value for weighting.[2]

Anyone involved in making yield comparisons, for example by studying spreads or tracking yields relative to a bogey, should be aware of the large degree to which portfolio yield can be mismeasured if the object of interest is internal rate of return.[3] In some periods, conventionally reported portfolio yields deviate from actual portfolio yields by more than 90 basis points.

APPROXIMATING PORTFOLIO YIELD

Garbade (1988) derived an approximation to portfolio yield based on a first-order Taylor series expansion of the bond pricing equation (present value of yield-discounted cash flows). The resulting approximation for portfolio yield is

$$\text{Portfolio Yield} \approx \frac{\sum_{i=1}^{N} TV_i (D_i^{mod}) Y_i}{\sum_{i=1}^{N} TV_i (D_i^{mod})}, \tag{7.1}$$

where

i	= individual asset subscript
N	= total number of assets
TV_i	= total value of asset i, that is, the number of bonds times the full price of the bond
D_i^{mod}	= the modified duration of asset i
Y_i	= the yield of asset i

As Garbade pointed out, approximating the yield on bond portfolios with value-weighted averages tends to underweight yields on bonds with longer maturities (and hence larger dollar durations). As a result, the conventional approximation tends to understate portfolio yield when the yield curve is positively sloped (and overstate yield when the curve is inverted). Garbade provided an example of a portfolio of equal quantities of two bonds with durations of 1.9 and 5.3 years, respectively, whose portfolio yield is mismeasured by 19 basis points when the value-weighted average yield is used as the portfolio yield. The data were from two Treasury bonds with a settlement date of June 1988.

Since 1988, we have experienced some extremely sloped yield curves. Table 7.1 provides some examples taken from September 1992, when the slope of the yield curve was about as steep as it has been at any time during the past 20 years.[4]

When the two-year Treasury issue (Bond 1) is mixed with a five-year issue (Bond 2), the value-weighted average yield is more than 29 basis points less than the correct yield.[5] When the two-year Treasury issue (Bond 1) is mixed with a seven-year issue (Bond 3), the market-weighted average yield is more than 49 basis points less than the correct yield. The 2-year bond mixed with a 30-year bond results in the conventional yield deviating from the correct yield by almost 130 basis points.

TABLE 7.1   Value-Weighted Average Portfolio Yield versus Dollar-Duration-Weighted Average Portfolio Yield for U.S. Treasury Issues, Quoted on September 30, 1992

Bond	Maturity Date	Quoted Price	Accrued	Coupon	Yield	Duration (years)
1	9/30/94	$100.375	0.0110	4.00	3.805%	1.939
2	9/30/97	100.750	0.0151	5.50	5.327	4.439
3	8/15/99	111.313	1.0217	8.00	5.967	5.457
4	8/15/22	98.469	0.8865	7.25	7.377	12.368

Bond 1 and Bond 2

Duration-Weighted Average Yield	4.863%
Value-Weighted Average Yield	4.567
Difference	0.296

Bond 1 and Bond 3

Duration-Weighted Average Yield	5.442%
Value-Weighted Average Yield	4.947
Difference	0.495

Bond 1 and Bond 4

Duration-Weighted Average Yield	6.881%
Value-Weighted Average Yield	5.582
Difference	1.299

These examples purposely were taken from one of the steepest-sloping yield curves. They illustrate the fact that very misleading results on portfolio yield (internal rate of return) are possible when using the conventional market-value weights. Our primary concern is to quantify the deviations of conventionally reported bogey yields from portfolio internal rate of return. To do so, we reconstructed a bogey from its individual components and used dollar-duration-weighted averages to calculate the yield. The deviations that conventional yields exhibit relative to "dollar-duration" yields are a purely empirical matter. The observed deviations at different points in time are determined by the historical behavior of the yield curve and the distribution (at a point in time) of individual bond durations (and their amount outstanding) present in the bogey or portfolio being scrutinized.

TREASURY YIELD BOGEYS

If the dollar-duration-weighted average is indeed a close approximation to actual portfolio yield, then the slope of the yield curve (measured by the difference in yield on long- and short-term Treasury instruments) should be closely related to the degree to which Equation 7.1 deviates from the conventional market-value-weighted yield. Figure 7.1 illustrates the potential for mismeasuring the yield in the Lehman Brothers Treasury Bond Index.[6] The difference between the yield calculated as in Equation 7.1 and the usual (and published) market-value-weighted yield is plotted along with the slope of the term structure of interest rates

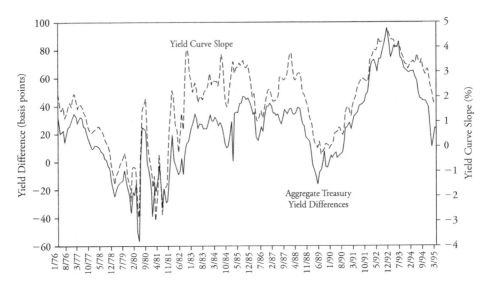

FIGURE 7.1   Treasury Index Yield Differences Compared with Yield Curve Slope, January 1976–March 1995

Note: Yield differences are duration-weighted average yields minus value-weighted average yields.

TABLE 7.2   Dollar-Duration-Weighted Average Yield Minus Market-Value-Weighted Average Yield for Lehman Brothers Treasury Bond Indexes (basis points)

Variable	Mean	Standard Deviation	Maximum	Minimum
Aggregate index	22.85	28.03	94.72	−56.79
Intermediate index	10.85	13.69	37.65	−40.43
Long index	9.51	12.14	48.78	−8.13
Absolute value (aggregate)	29.45			
Absolute value (intermediate)	14.99			
Absolute value (long)	10.47			

(measured as the difference between the bellwether 30-year bond and the bellwether three-month Treasury bill).[7]

The raw correlation between the two series depicted in Figure 7.1 is 92 percent.[8] This correlation keys into the scenarios portfolio managers need to be aware of when judging the ability of conventionally reported yields to provide a measure of actual yield to maturity. The most highly positively or negatively sloped yield curve episodes produce significant differences in the two calculations of portfolio yield. The magnitude of the observed yield calculation differences is similar to that provided in the Table 7.1 examples.

Table 7.2 reports summary statistics for the differences between duration- and value-weighted bond index yields for the Lehman Brothers intermediate, long, and aggregate Treasury bond indexes. Figure 7.2 plots the series.

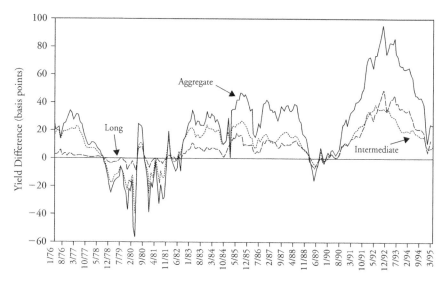

FIGURE 7.2   Treasury Index Yield Differences, January 1976–March 1995

Note: Yield differences are duration-weighted average yields minus value-weighted average yields.

As Table 7.2 and Figure 7.2 show, the intermediate and long indexes have smaller deviations than the aggregate index. This pattern is to be expected because the maturity spectrum of an index is one of the main determinants of the potential for mismeasuring portfolio yield. Regardless, the deviations are large enough so that calculations of spreads of individual bonds from these Treasury bogeys can provide significantly biased measures if the intent is to measure the difference in two internal rates of return.

Corporate bond indexes will suffer from the same yield measurement issues discussed above. Call and other option-like features typical on many corporate issues can greatly complicate the analysis. Option-adjusted spread techniques can be used to address these issues, but rigorous analysis of the problem is outside the scope of this paper. Noncallable corporate issues have recently come to dominate the industrial sector, and so it is of more than academic interest to see empirically how the yield mismeasurement problem has affected industrial bond indexes.

Figure 7.3 shows the differences in yield measurement approaches for aggregate indexes of investment-grade and high-yield industrial noncallable bonds. The period plotted begins in 1991, when industrial bond issuance began to be dominated by noncallable issues. Investment-grade corporate bond yield bogeys were as much as 50 basis points higher when calculated as actual portfolio yield instead of weighted-average yield. Similarly, for the high-yield corporate bond bogey, the differences in yield calculations were as much as 60 basis points.

ARE YIELD BOGEY MISMEASUREMENTS A WASH?

Ultimately, the question of greatest importance is whether the issues we have raised lead to any systematic misjudgments. Clearly, in some periods, reported yield levels are under- or overestimating actual portfolio yields. If an individual bond's spread is being calculated from

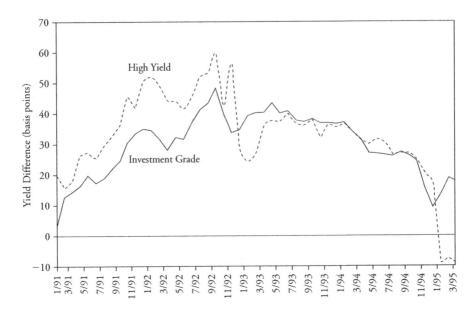

FIGURE 7.3   Industrial Index Yield Differences

Note: Yield differences are duration-weighted average yields minus value-weighted average yields.

an index bogey, then the errors can be large. Often, individual bond spreads are calculated against an individual Treasury bellwether issue, and in this case, no bias will result. For a portfolio, however, when conventional portfolio yields are compared with conventional bogey yields, the spread may not be far from the spread that would have been observed had both portfolio yields been calculated as internal rates of return (i.e., using dollar-duration-weighted averages).

To address this issue, we created a value-weighted portfolio of bellwether Treasury issues and calculated the spread of this portfolio from the Lehman Brothers aggregate Treasury index. The bellwether portfolio represents a monthly rebalanced portfolio of the most liquid issues in the Treasury index.

The spread was calculated in two ways. First, we calculated the "conventional" spread, that is, the spread based on the conventional value-weighted yields of our bellwether and aggregate Treasury portfolios; then, the spread is calculated with the more accurate duration-weighted yields. Figure 7.4 plots the resulting tracking errors. The duration-weighted yield tracking error is systematically below the error based on value-weighted yields.[9] The average tracking errors are −1.3 basis points for the duration-weighted average figure (statistically insignificant) and 10.7 basis points (significant at better than the 1 percent level) for the value-based tracking error.

The analysis based on duration-weighted yields shows that the bellwether portfolio tracks the Treasury bogey closely in the sense that, *on average*, no discernible difference exists. Based on conventional yield measures, the difference in yield exhibited by the bellwether portfolio relative to the Treasury bogey appears to be statistically significant.

Mixing yield measurements for the bogey and a managed portfolio is a recipe for disaster. Tracking errors will appear to be greater than those based separately on either duration-weighted or value-weighted yields. Better to mismeasure both bogey and managed portfolio yields than to correctly measure one and mismeasure the other.[10]

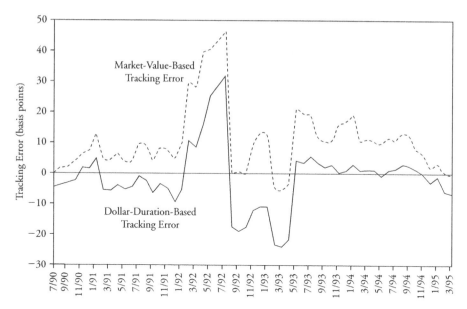

FIGURE 7.4   Duration-Based versus Value-Based Tracking Errors, July 1990–March 1995

CONCLUSION

Conventionally measured portfolio yields on popular index bogeys may be mismeasured relative to actual portfolio yield (internal rate of return) by as much as 50–100 basis points. Furthermore, and as predicted, the degree of deviation in measurement is correlated with the slope of the yield curve. These problems are exacerbated for portfolios covering a broad maturity spectrum, although even intermediate- and long-maturity portfolios can exhibit significant differences in the measurement of portfolio yield.

An example of yield tracking error measured with conventional portfolio yields versus duration-weighted yields shows that different conclusions about the tracking performance of the same portfolio are possible, depending on the measurement technique used.

Anyone involved in making yield comparisons—for example, by studying spreads or tracking yields relative to a bogey—should be aware of the large degree to which portfolio yields and spreads can differ depending on the estimate of yield that is used. Also, based on our analysis, published yield bogeys need to have the conventionally calculated yield (i.e., market-value-weighted) augmented with a more accurate measure of actual portfolio yield.[11]

NOTES

1. By dollar duration, we mean dollar duration multiplied by the par value of a bond present in the portfolio. Similarly, the term "value" in value-weighted represents the bond's full price times par value in the portfolio.
2. Dollar duration refers to a bond's modified Macaulay duration multiplied by the full price of the bond. Equivalently, price value of a basis point weighting (which differs from dollar duration by a scale factor) could be used.

3. The importance of the analysis presented here depends on the purpose for which yields are being used. Yield best measures performance for a horizon equal to the life of the underlying cash flows. An example is bonds that an insurance company declares to be held to maturity (for tax purposes). In some instances, however, market-value-weighted averages of individual bond yields are of more interest than the portfolio yield. As discussed by Ilmanen (1995), one example is in determining near-term expected return (see his footnote 7 on page 9). Ilmanen's article makes the argument (rightly) that total return investors should care more about expected returns than yields. For example, over some investment horizons, the value of convexity may play an important role in expected return, and no yield (measured in any way) can accurately account for this effect.

4. The data used in this study are from the Lehman Brothers Fixed Income Data Base obtained from the Fixed Income Research Program at the University of Wisconsin–Milwaukee. Details of the data base are contained in Warga (1995).

5. We are referring to the dollar-duration-weighted average as the "correct" yield. In this particular example, the exact portfolio yield is not difficult to calculate, and a measure of the accuracy of duration-weighted average yield is established by the fact that the exact portfolio yield deviates from the duration-weighted average by well under half of 1 basis point.

6. The Lehman Brothers Treasury Index includes all U.S. Treasury bonds and notes with a minimum maturity of one year, excluding flower bonds and foreign-targeted issues.

7. Because the Lehman Brothers bellwether series do not begin until 1981, for data from 1973 through 1980, we used the difference between the longest maturity Treasury Bond and a bond with approximately one year to maturity.

8. Even after adjusting the series for their inherent nonstationarity (first differences adequately "whiten" them), the relation is highly significant.

9. On average, by about 12 basis points (statistically significant at better than the 1 percent level).

10. Measurement of historical performance is almost always carried out by examining average total returns, and portfolio *returns* are exactly equal to market-value-weighted averages of the individual bond returns in the portfolio. This note, however, is not a critique of historical performance evaluation methods.

11. The authors wish to thank Antti Ilmanen of Salomon Brothers and Charles Webster of Lehman Brothers for their helpful comments.

REFERENCES

Garbade, K.D. 1988. "Approximating the Yield on a Portfolio of Bonds: Value Weighted Averages versus Value of a Basis Point-Weighted Averages." *Topics in Money and Securities Markets*, no. 41, Bankers Trust Company (September).

Ilmanen, Antti. 1995. "A Framework for Analyzing Yield Curve Trades." *Understanding the Yield Curve: Part 6*, Salomon Brothers.

Warga, Arthur. 1995. "A Fixed-Income Data Base." Working paper, University of Wisconsin–Milwaukee School of Business Administration, Fixed-Income Research Program.

CHAPTER 8

JUMPING ON THE BENCHMARK BANDWAGON

Benchmark Methodologies Are the Subject of Vigorous Debate

Crystal Detamore-Rodman

This article addresses the following key points:

- *There is growing interest in performance attribution to quantify the success of an investment strategy, particularly active management.*
- *Separating "pure alpha" from market exposures paints a better portrait of the manager's skills than some widely used practices.*
- *AIMR's Investment Performance Council (IPC) advocates "tracking error" as a useful measure of portfolio risk.*
- *Because there is no perfect benchmark, tradeoffs are inherent in the selection process.*
- *Absolute return investors often argue that benchmarks are irrelevant.*

The investment management industry has come a long way since the days when the lack of reporting standards gave managers the freedom to market their portfolios in any manner they desired. While the industry has experimented with performance measurement since its infancy, only in recent years have formal standards, such as the AIMR Performance Presentation Standards (AIMR-PPS®) and the Global Investment Performance Standards (GIPS®), helped to reign in unethical reporting practices that gave a distorted view of a manager's performance.

Reprinted from *CFA Magazine* (January/February 2004):54–55.

Today, investors want performance benchmarks that get to the heart of how a return is achieved. In other words, was it manager skill or pure luck that led to the performance outcome? As part of this growing emphasis on quantifying the success of a given investment strategy, consultants and sponsors are demanding more sophisticated tools to evaluate managers. Managers, meanwhile, need to be able to explain their performance to clients in an understandable manner.

IS IT APPROPRIATE?

One of the key issues in the benchmarking debate is the "appropriateness" question. "Everyone knows what an index is, and generally they are pretty standard as far as what's presented to clients," says AIMR Vice President of Investment Performance Standards Alecia Licata. "But the appropriateness of benchmarks usually misses the mark." Licata and others routinely cite widespread use of the S&P 500 or FTSE 100 for a multitude of investment styles and strategies as an example of the mismatch between index and manager. "That's where I see abuses," she adds.

John Stannard, CFA, managing director of client communication and support with the Russell Investment Group in Europe, recalls when his firm introduced the Russell 1000 index in 1984. "The industry was slow to embrace the Russell indices at first, but now they hold quite a dominant position in the United States," says Stannard, who is also the former chair of AIMR's Benchmarks and Performance Attribution Subcommittee.

"More and more, investors are moving to specialized benchmarks, and the number of firms considering benchmarks such as the S&P 500 as the only option is declining," he says. "Inertia does play a role, but, over time, investors recognize the value of improved benchmarks. But, the key always is to match the benchmark with both the strategy and the manager's ability and skills."

"A HELL OF A DISCUSSION"

For its part, AIMR offers guidelines for choosing a benchmark for an investment portfolio or composite in its 1998 "Benchmarks and Performance Attribution Subcommittee Report." An appropriate benchmark, in AIMR's view, is a recognized published index, a tailored composite of assets or indexes, or a peer group or "universe" of similar funds or portfolios. It should be objective and investible, representative of the asset class or mandate, developed from publicly available information, acceptable by the manager as the neutral position, and consistent with the underlying investor status.

AIMR, however, doesn't go so far as to prescribe any specific benchmarking method. "It's a hell of a discussion," says James Hollis, CFA, managing director of Cutter Associates Inc. in Duxbury, Mass., USA, who also served on the Benchmarks and Performance Attribution Subcommittee and is now chair of AIMR's Investment Performance Council (IPC). "We were basically concerned with the proper presentation, and in the document we say, 'Benchmarks should be investible, transparent, understandable, these things.' But we didn't go any further than that."

Hollis would like to see AIMR strengthen reporting standards by requiring managers to offer a composite of all accounts managed in a particular strategy to clients. "If I am one of those clients, I should always ask to see a composite of all the accounts to see where I am in that group. Some of us think it should have more visibility within the consulting community and the sponsors than it does."

MEASURING "PURE ALPHA"

There is growing accountability, to be sure, as the investing community clamors to know whether a manager's performance is a fluke or the result of a well-orchestrated strategy. Says Hollis, "There is a whole group who thinks there should be standards for attribution because [it is] the important part of understanding what the manager did and how the manager out-performed that benchmark."

Indeed, learning the ins and outs of performance reporting is increasingly important to consultants and sponsors eager to gauge whether the higher trading costs and management fees associated with active management are warranted. But the industry isn't entirely in lock step regarding how to measure and benchmark active performance. If the purpose of active management is to add alpha, then how do you measure alpha?

Laurence Siegel, director of investment policy research at the Ford Foundation in New York, NY, USA, says that some accepted practices for measuring alpha are inadequate because they contain no adjustment for risk. Siegel says analysis must take into account the fact that managers have no control over certain market conditions, but if that manager has skill at security selection, he or she has some control over returns, which adds value. By separating market exposures and "pure alpha," the calculation will give a clearer picture of the manager's skill, or lack thereof.

However, if the positions a manager takes versus the index "neutral" position are small, or if the portfolio is very diversified, the alpha will not exceed the active management fees. "Investors should encourage their managers to take appropriate levels of risk," Stannard stresses. "Setting fair but realistic targets for both excess return and risk will clear the waters and help avoid unexpected surprises."

TOUGH CHOICES

While AIMR and researchers like Siegel offer parameters for benchmark selection, decision makers still have some tough choices, such as choosing between how broad a benchmark is and its investibility. "For instance, the Wilshire 5000 for equities represents all of the opportunity in the equity asset class, but it's hard to trade in and out of because probably 2,000 of those 5,000 stocks are highly illiquid," Siegel observes.

Not all investment managers have jumped on the benchmark bandwagon, however. A number of practitioners argue that the performance assessment tool isn't relevant to their investment style, with absolute return investors like hedge funds often leading the charge. "Conventional wisdom suggests that in such cases no benchmark applies," says Stannard. "But in fact it does—the neutral position of an absolute return strategy is zero, or maybe a cash return plus some risk premium. One or the other should be considered as the benchmark to measure the success of the strategy. So the industry can and should continue to discuss best practices in the area of benchmarking."

CONSTRUCTING A SYNTHETIC UNIVERSE

While there is a growing consensus that benchmarks serve a critical function in monitoring industry performance, debate over which method best meets that objective continues. Ronald Surz, president of PPCA Inc., an investment technology firm in San Clemente, Calif., USA, supports the use of a scientific peer group.

Instead of calculating a single return that is the combined performance of all the stocks in the benchmark, Surz's PIPOD system, for Popular Index Portfolio Opportunity Distributions, calculates the performance of all the portfolios that could have been formed from stocks in the benchmark. He says one of the primary advantages is that it takes less time to construct this "synthetic universe" than the four to six weeks it takes to assemble a peer group.

Surz got acquainted with the scientific peer group concept after joining A.G. Becker in 1972, where John O'Brien, founder of Wilshire Associates Inc., introduced Modern Portfolio Theory and Capital Asset Pricing Model practices to Becker's consulting practice to gain insights into the risk-reward payoffs. "John thought of the notion of creating scientific universes," recalls Surz, a member of AIMR's IPC.

"We were getting a lot of pressure to sign off on the universes sooner and sooner," says Surz, but because the firm relied on money managers and custodians to send in performance results, it generally took two months to collect the necessary information. "We could synthesize the real world by creating these random portfolios and could do it literally days after the time period, and we didn't really have to wait for all of the live data to come in," he explains.

A necessary component of assembling a scientific universe is recognizing that certain stocks tend to dominate portfolios. "The academics trade equal-weighted portfolios. Active managers tend to hold equal-weighted portfolios and present that as a way to be diversified. If you do that, you create a world where there's as much Penny Stock Inc. as Microsoft," notes Surz. "There's definitely more Microsoft in the hands of the investing public than there is Penny Stock Inc. You need to account for the macro-economic consistency that there is more Microsoft than there is Penny Stock Inc."

A COLLABORATIVE EFFORT

Whatever the benchmark method, the performance measurement process is complicated. And experts agree that choosing a benchmark should be a collaborative effort to help eliminate misinterpretations. "If managers receive a mandate to beat the S&P 500, then that is their benchmark," Siegel says. "They then want to beat a number of different style bets. Each manager has a strategy for trying to beat the S&P 500, and, more often than not, it involves some sort of style bias like value for growth in large cap and small cap, which then distorts the benchmark."

"Because you can replicate that same bet with an index fund, you then face the question of what is the proper benchmark—the S&P 500, which the client asks you to beat, or the value index fund, which is what you're really delivering?" explains Siegel. "The line of communication has to be open between the manager and the client. That's just one example of the tension that takes place between a manager and clients over benchmarks."

PART **III**

PERFORMANCE
ATTRIBUTION

CHAPTER 9

DETERMINANTS OF PORTFOLIO PERFORMANCE

Gary P. Brinson, L. Randolph Hood, CFA, and Gilbert L. Beebower

In order to delineate investment responsibility and measure performance contribution, pension plan sponsors and investment managers need a clear and relevant method of attributing returns to those activities that compose the investment management process—investment policy, market timing, and security selection. The authors provide a simple framework based on a passive, benchmark portfolio representing the plan's long-term asset classes, weighted by their long-term allocations. Returns on this "investment policy" portfolio are compared with the actual returns resulting from the combination of investment policy plus market timing (over- or underweighting within an asset class). Data from 91 large U.S. pension plans over the 1974–1983 period indicate that investment policy dominates investment strategy (market timing and security selection), explaining on average 95.6 percent of the variation in total plan return. The actual mean average total return on the portfolio over the period was 9.01 percent, versus 10.11 percent for the benchmark portfolio. Active management cost the average plan 1.10 percent per year, although its effects on individual plans varied greatly, adding as much as 3.69 percent per year. Although investment strategy can result in significant returns, these are dwarfed by the return contribution from investment policy—the selection of asset classes and their normal weights.

A recent study indicates that more than 80 percent of all corporate pension plans with assets greater than $2 billion have more than 10 managers, and of all plans with assets greater

Reprinted from *Financial Analysts Journal* (July/August 1986):39–44.

than $50 million, less than one-third have only one investment manager.[1] Many funds that employ multiple managers focus their attention solely on the problem of manager selection. Only now are some funds beginning to realize that they must develop a method for delineating responsibility and measuring the performance contribution of those activities that compose the investment management process—investment policy, market timing, and security selection.[2]

The relative importance of policy, timing, and selection can be determined only if we have a clear and relevant method of attributing returns to these factors. This article examines empirically the effects of investment policy, market timing, and security (or manager) selection on total portfolio return. Our goal is to determine, from historical investment data on U.S. corporate pension plans, which investment decisions had the greatest impacts on the magnitude of total return and on the variability of that return.

A FRAMEWORK FOR ANALYSIS

We develop below a framework that can be used to decompose total portfolio returns. Conceptually valid, yet computationally simple, this framework has been used successfully by a variety of institutional pension sponsors, consultants, and investment managers; it is currently being used to attribute performance contributions in actual portfolios.

Performance attribution, while not new, is still an evolving discipline. Early papers on the subject, focusing on risk-adjusted returns, suggested the initial framework but paid little attention to multiple asset performance measurement.[3] Our task is to rank in order of importance the decisions made by investment clients and managers and then to measure the overall importance of these decisions to actual plan performance.

Table 9.1 illustrates the framework for analyzing portfolio returns. Quadrant I represents policy. Here we would place the fund's benchmark return for the period, as determined by its long-term investment policy.

TABLE 9.1   A Simplified Framework for Return Accountability

| | | Selection | |
		Actual	Passive
Timing	Actual	(IV) Actual Portfolio Return	(II) Policy and Timing Return
	Passive	(III) Policy and Security Selection Return	(I) Policy Return (Passive Portfolio Benchmark)

Active Returns Due to:
Timing	II − I
Selection	III − I
Other	IV − III − II + I
Total	IV − I

A plan's benchmark return is a consequence of the *investment policy* adopted by the plan sponsor. Investment policy identifies the long-term asset allocation plan (included asset classes and normal weights) selected to control the overall risk and meet fund objectives. In short, policy identifies the entire plan's normal portfolio.[4] To calculate the policy benchmark return, we need (1) the weights of all asset classes, specified in advance, and (2) the passive (or benchmark) return assigned to each asset class.[5]

Quadrant II represents the return effects of policy and timing. Timing is the strategic under or overweighting of an asset class relative to its normal weight, for purposes of return enhancement and/or risk reduction. Timing is undertaken to achieve incremental returns relative to the policy return.

Quadrant III represents returns due to policy and security selection. Security selection is the active selection of investments *within* an asset class. We define it as the portfolio's actual asset class returns (e.g., actual returns to the segments of common stocks and bonds) in excess of those classes' passive benchmark returns and weighted by the normal total fund asset allocations.

Quadrant IV represents the actual return to the total fund for the period. This is the result of the actual portfolio segment weights and actual segment returns.

Table 9.2 presents the methods for calculating the values for these quadrants. Table 9.3 gives the computational method for determining the *active* returns (those returns due to investment *strategy*).

Our framework clearly differentiates between the effects of investment policy and investment strategy. Investment strategy is shown to be composed of timing, security (or manager) selection, and the effects of a cross-product term. We can calculate the exact effects of policy and strategy using the algebraic measures given.

DATA

To test the framework, we used data from 91 pension plans in the SEI Large Plan Universe. SEI has developed quarterly data for a complete 10-year (40-quarter) period beginning in 1974; this was chosen as the beginning of the period for study.

TABLE 9.2   Computational Requirements for Return Accountability

| | | Selection | |
		Actual	Passive
Timing	Actual	(IV) $\Sigma_i(Wai \cdot Rai)$	(II) $\Sigma_i(Wai \cdot Rpi)$
	Passive	(III) $\Sigma_i(Wpi \cdot Rai)$	(I) $\Sigma_i(Wpi \cdot Rpi)$

Wpi = policy (passive) weight for asset class i
Wai = actual weight for asset class i
Rpi = passive return for asset class i
Rai = active return for asset class i

TABLE 9.3   Calculation of Active Contributions to Total Performance

Return Due to:	Calculated by:	Expected Value
Timing	$\Sigma[(Wai \cdot Rpi) - (Wpi \cdot Rpi)]$	>0
	(Quadrant II – Quadrant I)	
Security selection	$\Sigma[(Wpi \cdot Rai) - (Wpi \cdot Rpi)]$	>0
	(Quadrant III – Quadrant I)	
Other	$\Sigma[(Wai - Wpi)(Rai \cdot Rpi)]$	N/A
	[Quadrant IV – (Quadrant II + Quadrant III + Quadrant I)]	
Total	$\Sigma[(Wai \cdot Rai) - (Wpi \cdot Rpi)]$	>0
	(Quadrant IV – Quadrant I)	

In order to be selected, a plan had to satisfy several criteria. Each plan had to have been a corporate pension trust with investment discretion solely in the hands of the corporation itself (i.e., no employee-designated funds). Large plans were used because only those plans had sufficient return and investment weight information to satisfy our computational needs. Public and multi-employer plans were excluded because legislative, legal, or other constraints could have dramatically altered their asset mixes from what might have obtained.

The sample represents a major portion of the large corporate pension plans of SEI's clients over the 10-year period. The market capitalization of individual plans in the universe ranges from approximately $100 million at the beginning of the study period to well over $3 billion by its end.

Table 9.4 summarizes the data collected from each plan. Normal weights for each asset class for each plan were not available. We thus assumed that the 10-year mean average holding of each asset class was sufficient to approximate the appropriate normal holding.[6] Portfolio segments consisted of common stocks, marketable bonds (fixed income debt with a maturity of at least one year, and excluding private placements and mortgage-backed securities), cash equivalents (fixed income obligations with maturities less than one year), and a miscellaneous category, "other," including convertible securities, international holdings, real estate, venture capital, insurance contracts, mortgage-backed bonds, and private placements.

Because a complete history of the contents of the "other" component is not available for many plans, we elected to exclude this segment from most of the analysis. We instead calculated a common stock/bonds/cash equivalent subportfolio for use in all quadrants *except* the total fund actual return; here we used the actual return as reported (including "other"). We constructed the subportfolio by eliminating the "other" investment weight from each plan in each quarter and calculating new weights and portfolio returns for the components that remained; this had the effect of spreading the "other" weight proportionally across the remaining asset classes. The bottom panel of Table 9.4 gives the weighting information.

Table 9.4 also gives the market indexes used as passive benchmark returns.[7] For common stocks, we used the S&P 500 composite index total return. The S&P comes under frequent attack for not being representative of the U.S. equity market; we nevertheless selected it, for several reasons. First, the S&P is still quoted and used as a benchmark by many plan sponsors;

TABLE 9.4   Summary of Holdings of 91 Large Pension Plans, 1974–1983

Holdings	Average	Minimum	Maximum	Standard Deviation	Policy Benchmark
All holdings					
Common stock	57.5%	32.3%	86.5%	10.9%	S&P 500 Total Return Index (S&P 500)
Bonds	21.4	0.0	43.0	9.0	Shearson Lehman Government/ Corporate Bond Index (SLGC)
Cash equivalents	12.4	1.8	33.1	5.0	30-Day Treasury Bills
Other	8.6	0.0	53.5	8.3	None
Total	100.0%				
Stocks, bonds, and cash only					
Common stock	62.9%	37.9%	89.3%	10.6%	
Bonds	23.4	0.0	51.3	9.4	
Cash equivalents	13.6	2.0	35.0	5.2	
Total	100.0%				

this indicates its continued acceptance. Second, it is one of the few indexes known over the entire study period and actually available for investment by plan sponsors via, for example, index funds. Third, the S&P 500 does not suffer from the lack of liquidity that affects some segments of the broader market indexes. For completeness, however, we recomputed all the calculations performed below using the Wilshire 5000 Capitalization Weighted Total Return Index in place of the S&P; the results were virtually identical.

We chose the Shearson Lehman Government/Corporate Bond Index (SLGC) for the bond component passive index; this is representative of all publicly traded, investment-grade bonds (excluding mortgage-backed securities) with a maturity of at least one year and a minimum par amount outstanding of $1 million. We used the total return on a 30-day Treasury bill for cash equivalents.

RESULTS

To analyze the relative importance of investment policy versus investment strategy, we began by calculating the total returns for each of our 91 portfolios. Table 9.5 repeats the framework outlined in Table 9.1 and provides a mean of 91 annualized compound total 10-year rates of return for each quadrant.

The mean average annualized total return over the 10-year period (Quadrant IV) was 9.01 percent. This is the return to the entire plan portfolio, not just the common stock/bonds/cash equivalents portion of the plan.[8] The average plan lost 66 basis points per year in market timing and lost another 36 basis points per year from security selection. The mean average annualized total return for the normal plan policy (passive index returns and average weighting) for the sample was 10.11 percent (Quadrant I).

Table 9.6 provides more detail on the various effects of active management and investment policy at work. The effect of market timing on the compound annual return of individual plans ranged from +0.25 to −2.68 percent per year over the period. The effect of security selection ranged from +3.60 to −2.90 percent per year. On average, total active management cost the average plan 1.10 percent per year. Its effects on individual plans varied, however, from a low of −4.17 percent per year to a high of +3.69 percent per year—a range of 7.86 percent.

TABLE 9.5   Mean Annualized Returns by Activity, 91 Large Plans, 1974–1983

	Selection	
	Actual	Passive
Timing — Actual	(IV) 9.01%	(II) 9.44%
Timing — Passive	(III) 9.75%	(I) 10.11%

Active Returns Due to:	
Timing	−0.66%
Security selection	−0.36
Other	−0.07
Total active return	−1.10%

TABLE 9.6   Annualized 10-Year Returns of 91 Large Plans, 1974–1983

Total Returns	Average Return	Minimum Return	Maximum Return	Standard Deviation
Portfolio returns				
Policy	10.11%	9.47%	10.57%	0.22%
Policy and timing	9.44	7.25	10.34	0.52
Policy and selection	9.75	7.17	13.31	1.33
Actual portfolio	9.01	5.85	13.40	1.43
Active returns				
Timing only	−0.66%	−2.68%	0.25%	0.49%
Security selection only	−0.36	−2.90	3.60	1.36
Other	−0.07	−1.17	2.57	0.45
Total active return	−1.10%	−4.17%*	3.69%*	1.45%*

* Not additive.

Active management (and therefore its control) is clearly important. But how important is it relative to investment policy itself? The relative magnitudes indicate that investment policy provides the larger portion of return. This is not surprising in itself, and most would not disagree that the "value added" from active management is small (though important) relative to asset class returns as a whole. However, what does this imply? It implies that it is the normal asset class weights and the passive asset classes themselves that provide the bulk of return to a portfolio.

Note that the range of outcomes and standard deviations of policy returns is small, reflecting the historical tendency of similar (large, corporate) plans to gravitate toward the same policy mix. We would expect that, over time, as plan sponsors dedicate more resources to the policy allocation decision, we would see less of a tendency to cluster asset mix policy according to "peer imitation" or "conventional" investment postures.

RETURN VARIATION

The ability of investment policy to dictate actual plan return requires further analysis. Table 9.7 examines the relative amount of variance contributed by each quadrant to the return to the total portfolio. It thus addresses directly the relative importance of the decisions affecting total return.

The figures here represent the average amounts of variance of total portfolio return explained by each of the quadrants. They were calculated by regressing each plan's actual total return (Quadrant IV) against, in turn, its calculated common stocks/bonds/cash equivalents investment policy return (Quadrant I), policy and timing return (Quadrant II), and policy and selection return (Quadrant III). The value in each quadrant thus has 91 regression equations behind it, and the number shown is the average of 91 unadjusted *R*-squared measures of the regressions.[9]

The results are striking. Naturally, the total plan performance explains 100 percent of itself (Quadrant IV). But the investment policy return in Quadrant I (normal weights and market index returns) explained on average fully 93.6 percent of the total variation in actual plan

TABLE 9.7   Percentage of Total Return Variation Explained by Investment Activity, Average of 91 Plans, 1973–1985

	Selection: Actual	Selection: Passive
Timing: Actual	(IV) 100.0%	(II) 95.3%
Timing: Passive	(III) 97.8%	(I) 93.6%

Variance Explained

	Average	Minimum	Maximum	Standard Deviation
Policy	93.6%	75.5%	98.6%	4.4%
Policy and timing	95.3	78.7	98.7	2.9
Policy and selection	97.8	80.6	99.8	3.1

return; in particular plans it explained no less than 75.5 percent and up to 98.6 percent of total return variation. Returns due to policy and timing added modestly to the explained variance (95.3 percent), as did policy and security selection (97.8 percent). Tables 9.6 and 9.7 clearly show that total return to a plan is dominated by investment policy decisions. Active management, while important, describes far less of a plan's returns than investment policy.

IMPLICATIONS

Design of a portfolio involves at least four steps:

- deciding which asset classes to include and which to exclude from the portfolio;
- deciding upon the normal, or long-term, weights for each of the asset classes allowed in the portfolio;
- strategically altering the investment mix weights away from normal in an attempt to capture excess returns from short-term fluctuations in asset class prices (market timing); and
- selecting individual securities within an asset class to achieve superior returns relative to that asset class (security selection).

The first two decisions aré properly part of investment policy; the last two reside in the sphere of investment strategy. Because of its relative importance, investment policy should be addressed carefully and systematically by investors.

Future attempts to quantify the importance of investment management decisions to portfolio performance would benefit from an examination of the integration of investment policy and investment strategy. An explicit delineation and recognition of the links between investment policy and investment strategy would help to clarify further the role of both activities in the investment process. A simple and accurate, yet complete and measurable, representation of the investment decision-making process would further our understanding of the importance of the various components of investment activity and, we hope, lead to a concise and integrated framework of investment responsibility.

NOTES

1. SEI Corporation, *Number of Managers by Plan Size* (Wayne, Pennsylvania, 1985):1.
2. See W.R. Good, "Accountability for Pension Performance," *Financial Analysts Journal* (January/February 1984):39–42.
3. Early works include E.F. Fama, "Components of Investment Performance," *The Journal of Finance* (June 1972):551–567, and M.C. Jensen, "The Performance of Mutual Funds in the Period 1945–1964," *The Journal of Finance* (May 1968):389–416. Some more recent works have clearly forged ahead. As an excellent example, see J.L. Farrell, Jr., *Guide to Portfolio Management* (New York: McGraw-Hill, 1983):321–339.
4. For a clear treatment of policy versus strategy, see D.A. Love, "Editorial Viewpoint," *Financial Analysts Journal* (March/April 1977):22. For a discussion of normal portfolios, see A. Rudd and H.K. Clasing, Jr., *Modern Portfolio Theory* (Homewood, Ill.: Dow Jones–Irwin, 1982):71–72.

5. We say "specified" even though the actual weights may not be known in advance; this accounts for those who wish to use portfolio insurance techniques. In our view, these techniques are more ones of active asset allocation (market timing) than investment policy. We view investment policy as having an indefinite time horizon, as opposed to a specific, though extendable, one.

   Throughout this article we will use the words "normal," "benchmark," and "passive" interchangeably. For a detailed description on how an investment policy can be derived, see G.P. Brinson, J.J. Diermeier, and G.G. Schlarbaum, "A Composite Portfolio Benchmark for Pension Plans," *Financial Analysts Journal* (March/April, 1986):15–24.

6. While this is clearly a simplification, we are unable to address more accurately the problem of normal weights. Since 10 years covers several business cycles, and since the average standard deviation of asset class holdings for common stocks and bonds is not high relative to the average amounts held, this is probably not a serious problem in the analysis.

7. Data for benchmark returns were provided by R.G. Ibbotson & Associates (Chicago, Ill.) and Shearson/Lehman American Express (New York).

8. We also calculated the stock/bonds/cash equivalents return series and, in all of the analysis that follows, also used that calculated return wherever we used the actual fund return; results were similar in all cases.

9. By "unadjusted," we mean that the R-squared measures are not adjusted for degrees of freedom; thus, for our three simple regression models, the R-squared represents a square of the correlation coefficient and represents the amount of variance of total return explained in excess of the average. While the average of the quarterly total returns may not be predictable, it is nonetheless of interest *ex post* and, in essence, can be specified by the passive portfolio that, when established, becomes the relevant benchmark for any further comparison.

CHAPTER 10

DETERMINANTS OF PORTFOLIO PERFORMANCE II: AN UPDATE

Gary P. Brinson, Brian D. Singer, CFA,
and Gilbert L. Beebower

This article presents a framework for determining the contributions of different aspects of the investment management process—asset allocation policy, active asset allocation, and security selection—to the total return of investment portfolios. Data from 82 large pension plans indicate that asset allocation policy, however determined, is the overwhelmingly dominant contributor to total return. Active investment decisions by plan sponsors and managers did little on average to improve performance over the 10-year period December 1977 to December 1987. The performance attribution framework is also extended to account for actual and synthetic cash holdings within asset classes.

In "Determinants of Portfolio Performance," published in this journal in 1986, we documented the overwhelming contribution of asset allocation policy to the return performance of a sample of 91 large pension plans.[1] That earlier article developed a systematic framework for the attribution of returns to different types of active investment decisions.

This article, also focusing on **return attribution,** updates the results of the previous study and confirms our original conclusions. Specifically, data from 82 large pension plans over the 1977–1987 period indicate that **investment policy** explained, on average, 91.5 percent of the variation in quarterly total plan returns. In addition, this article provides an expanded performance attribution framework that accounts not only for security selection

Reprinted from *Financial Analysts Journal* (May/June 1991):40–48.

and **active asset allocation,** but also for changes in portfolio risk characteristics attributable to risk positioning within individual asset classes.

Neither this article nor its predecessor attempts to evaluate the efficacy of investment policies. Rather, the concentration is on the overwhelming impact of policy—however established—and the incremental effect of active investment strategies.[2]

FRAMEWORK

Our earlier article outlined a framework for dissecting total plan returns into three components— asset allocation policy, active asset allocation, and security selection. The distinction between asset allocation policy and active asset allocation needs to be delineated. Asset allocation policy involves the establishment of *normal* asset class weights and is an integral part of investment policy. Active asset allocation is the process of managing asset class weights *relative to the normal weights* over time; its aim is to enhance the managed portfolio's risk/return tradeoff. This distinction is material to understanding the importance of investment policy relative to active management.

Figure 10.1 illustrates the framework for reporting and analyzing portfolio returns. Quadrant I indicates the total return provided by the investment policy adopted by the plan sponsor. The policy "portfolio" thus represents a constant, normal allocation to passive asset classes. Investment policy, then, identifies the plan's normal portfolio composition. Calculating the policy return involves applying the normal weights of each investable asset class to the respective passive returns.

Quadrants II and III shift the focus to active management. Quadrant II reports the return attributable to a portfolio reflecting both policy and active asset allocation. Whether active allocation involves anticipating price moves (market timing) or reacting to market disequilibria (fundamental analysis), it results in the under- or overweighting of asset classes relative to the normal weights identified by policy.[3] The aim of active allocation is to enhance the return and/or reduce the risk of the portfolio relative to its policy benchmark. The policy and

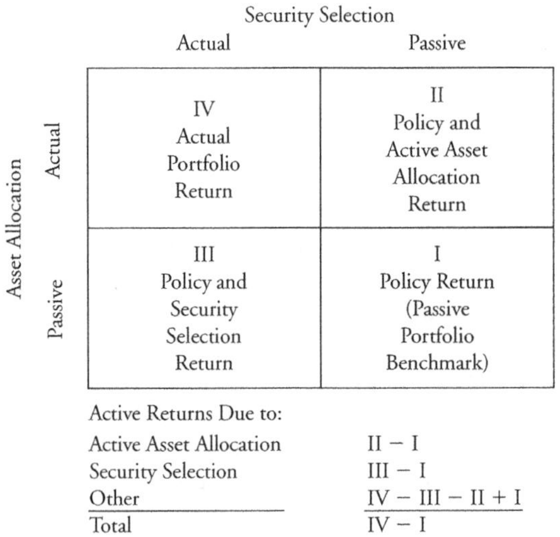

	Security Selection	
	Actual	Passive
Asset Allocation — Actual	IV Actual Portfolio Return	II Policy and Active Asset Allocation Return
Asset Allocation — Passive	III Policy and Security Selection Return	I Policy Return (Passive Portfolio Benchmark)

Active Returns Due to:	
Active Asset Allocation	II − I
Security Selection	III − I
Other	IV − III − II + I
Total	IV − I

FIGURE 10.1   A Simplified Framework for Return Accountability

Glossary

Return Attribution: The process of attributing actual portfolio return to those investment management activities that contribute to the return—investment policy, active asset allocation, and security selection.

Investment Policy: Specification of the plan sponsor's objectives, constraints, and requirements, including identification of the normal asset allocation mix.

Active Asset Allocation: Temporarily deviating from the policy asset mix in order to benefit from a state of capital market disequilibrium with respect to the investment fundamentals underlying the policy mix.

Coefficients of Determination: The percentage of variability in one random variable that is accounted for by another random variable. The more familiar R^2, indicating the variability of the dependent variable accounted for by a regression model, is identical to the coefficient of determination for univariate regressions.

Risk Positioning: The active allocation out of non-cash assets into cash equivalents at the asset allocation level and the holding of cash within an asset class portfolio.

External Risk Positioning: The allocation into and out of cash-equivalent assets. The term "external" refers to positioning at the asset class level. As segregating the cash component at the asset class level is a rather common aspect of active asset allocation performance attribution, "external risk positioning" is used in a broader sense to mean active asset allocation.

Internal Risk Positioning: The establishment of a position in actual or synthetic cash, typically to control beta or duration risk, within an asset class. The term "internal" refers to positioning within an asset class.

---

active asset allocation return is computed by applying the actual asset class weights to their respective passive benchmark returns.

Quadrant III presents the returns to a portfolio attributable to policy and security selection. Security selection involves active investment decisions concerning the securities within each asset class. This framework specifies that the return from policy and security selection is obtained by applying the normal asset class weights to the actual active returns achieved in each asset class.

Finally, Quadrant IV represents the actual return realized by the plan over the period of performance evaluation. This is the result of the plan's actual asset class weights interacting with the actual asset class returns.

Figure 10.2 summarizes the calculations required to determine the returns for Quadrants I, II, and III. Table 10.1 provides the computational methodology for determining the sources of active returns. The active contribution to total performance is composed of active asset allocation, security selection, and the effects of a cross-product term that measures the interaction of the security selection and active asset allocation decisions.

Data

Attributing returns to the various aspects of the investment process according to this framework requires historical data on portfolio composition (weights), actual investment results, and returns to the appropriate benchmarks. SEI Corporation provided 10 years of quarterly

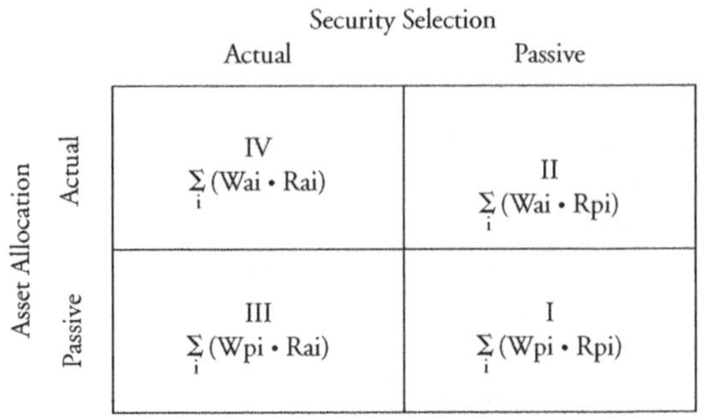

Security Selection

	Actual	Passive

FIGURE 10.2   Computational Requirements for Return Accountability*

*Wpi = policy weight for asset class i; Wai = actual weight for asset class i; Rpi = passive return for asset class i; Rai = actual return for asset class i.

TABLE 10.1   Calculation of Active Contributions to Total Performance

Return Due to		Calculated By
Active Asset Allocation	$\sum_i$	$[(Wai * Rpi) - (Wpi * Rpi)]$ (Quadrant II − Quadrant I)
Security Selection	$\sum_i$	$[(Wpi * Rai) - (Wpi * Rpi)]$ (Quadrant III − Quadrant I)
Other	$\sum_i$	$[(Wai - Wpi)(Rai - Rpi)]$ [Quadrant IV − (Quadrant II + Quadrant III) + Quadrant I]
Total	$\sum_i$	$[(Wai * Rai) - (Wpi * Rpi)]$ (Quadrant IV − Quadrant I)

data, from December 1977 to December 1987, for 82 pension plans in their Large Plan Universe. The seven series available for each plan were four asset-class-weight series for equity, bonds, cash equivalents, and "other" and three quarterly rate-of-return series for the total plan and its associated equity and bond components. The focus of this article is on investment performance, so all returns were expressed gross of management fees.

An analysis of the asset class weights indicates that there was no significant shift in asset class preferences over the period covered by the sample data. Figure 10.3 demonstrates that the average weights of the asset classes for the sample remained remarkably stable over time, despite market trends and volatility. This is somewhat at odds with other surveys showing increased exposure to equities over similar periods.[4]

Because the composition of the "other assets" category was unknown, its weight was allocated to the equity, bond, and cash components in proportion to their respective weights. Table 10.2 shows that this component constituted a relatively small percentage (less than 15 percent) of total plan assets and did not materially affect total plan returns. However, a few plans had extraordinarily large allocations to the "other" category over the period; these

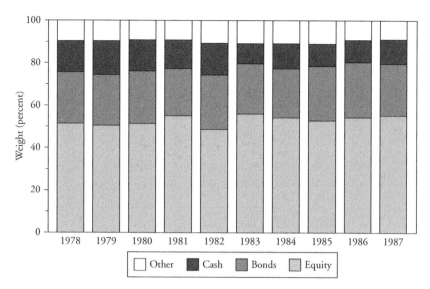

FIGURE 10.3   Average Asset Class Weights, 1977–1987

Source: SEI Corporation.

TABLE 10.2   Analysis of Asset Class Weights, 82 Large Pension Plans, 1977–1987

	Summary of Holdings			
	Average	Maximum	Minimum	Standard Deviation
Equity	53.0%	79.1%	26.0%	10.8%
Bond	24.5%	53.1%	4.0%	10.4%
Cash	12.1%	24.1%	3.0%	4.6%
Other	10.5%	65.4%	0.1%	12.0%
	Summary of Holdings Excluding "Other"			
	Average	Maximum	Minimum	Standard Deviation
Equity	59.6%	83.9%	36.5%	10.5%
Bond	26.9%	54.0%	5.6%	10.2%
Cash	13.6%	24.3%	3.5%	4.9%

"outliers" were omitted from the analysis. None of the sample funds held non-U.S. bonds, and only two held non-U.S. equity. In these cases, the foreign equity was considered part of the equity component, without a material effect on the results.

We defined policy weights for each plan (the normal weights) as the 10-year average of the plan's asset class weights. These funds did not necessarily favor a "typical" mix of assets (such as 60/40 stocks/bonds), although, as Table 10.2 shows, the average mix was very close to 60 percent equity and 40 percent fixed income. Figure 10.4 shows that the observed combinations of equity and bond weights cover almost the whole range of possibilities.

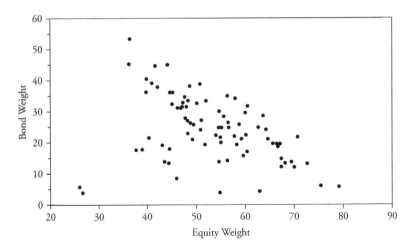

FIGURE 10.4   Average Equity Weight versus Average Bond Weight, 1977–1987

Source: SEI Corporation.

   Some plans showed evidence of a change in policy over the 10 years, either by a clear upward or downward trend in the weight of an asset class or a sudden and apparently permanent shift in the level of the quarterly weights. We attempted to account for this in the analysis. In cases where there appeared to be a policy shift, we divided the 10-year period into two periods—prechange and postchange—and calculated returns based on the policy weights in effect in each period.

RESULTS

In addition to the actual reported return for each plan, we defined three return series—policy, policy and active asset allocation, and policy and security selection. The policy return is the passive portfolio benchmark return, calculated as the sum of the policy weighted passive asset class returns, using the 10-year average asset class weights (as discussed above) and a suitable passive index for each asset class. The S&P 500, the Salomon Broad Investment Grade (BIG) bond index and 30-day Treasury bills were used as the passive indexes for the equity, bond, and cash components, respectively.

   The policy and active asset allocation return is calculated using the actual active weights and the appropriate passive index returns. The policy and security selection return is calculated using the policy weights and the actual active returns. We repeated each analysis using a broader market index than the S&P 500; the results were virtually identical.

   The overall effect of active management by plan sponsors or investment managers was negligible. This confirms the findings of our earlier study. Figure 10.5 and Table 10.3 show that the average portfolio underperformed its policy benchmark by eight basis points a year.

   Individual effects varied widely, from a 3.4 percent per annum underperformance to a 6.7 percent per annum overperformance. The incremental return to active management had a standard deviation of 1.7 percent. Clearly the contribution of active management is not statistically different from zero (that is, it is most likely attributable to chance). While active asset allocation contributed a net underperformance of 26 basis points, and security selection contributed a gain of 26 basis points, neither figure is statistically different from zero.

Security Selection

		Actual	Passive
Asset Allocation	Actual	IV 13.41%	II 13.23%
	Passive	III 13.75%	I 13.49%

Active Returns Due to:

Active Asset Allocation	−0.26%
Security Selection	+0.26%
Other	−0.07%
Total	−0.08%

FIGURE 10.5   Mean Annualized Returns by Activity, 82 Large Pension Plans, 1977–1987

TABLE 10.3   Annualized Returns and Risk by Activity, 1977–1987

	Average Return	Average Risk	Return Minimum	Return Maximum	X-Sec. Std. Dev.
Portfolio					
Policy	13.49	11.42	12.43	14.56	0.49
Policy and Active A/A	13.23	11.56	11.26	15.09	0.68
Policy and Selection	13.75	13.75	10.52	19.32	1.66
Actual Portfolio	13.41	11.65	10.34	19.95	1.75
Active Return Components					
Active A/A Only	−0.26		−1.81	0.86	0.47
Selection Only	+0.26		−3.32	6.12	1.52
Other	−0.07		−3.50	1.33	0.80
Total Active Return	−0.08		−3.43	6.73	1.67

Active management not only had no measurable impact on returns, but (in the absence of a proxy for the variability of the respective pension liabilities), it appears to have increased risk by a small margin (Figure 10.6 and Table 10.3). Given the higher risk level of the policy and security selection portfolio, it is evident that security selection contributed to actual plan risk. Active asset allocation appears to have had a negligible impact on risk relative to the benchmark policy. The imperfect correlation between the performances of the policy and allocation and the policy and security selection portfolios mitigated some of the increased risk.

None of these observations detracts from the finding that the choice of investment policy dominates the risk/return posture of the plan. It is obvious that the overwhelming factor in determining the basic, long-term return achieved per unit of risk was investment policy.

Because active asset allocation is the process of managing asset class weights relative to the normal weights, active management is conditional on the investment policy. Thus active returns are conditionally distributed on the policy return distribution. This dominance is also

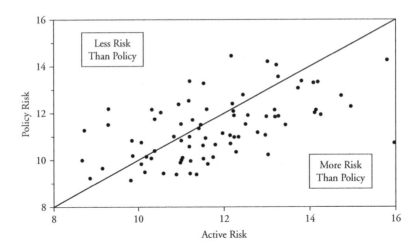

FIGURE 10.6   Policy Risk versus Active Risk, 1977–1987

Source: SEI Corporation.

demonstrated by the **coefficients of determination** for policy, policy and active asset allocation, policy and security selection, and active returns.

The coefficient of determination is the square of the correlation coefficient between two jointly distributed random variables. It is used to describe the amount of variability in one variable that can be accounted for by another variable. In this instance, we are concerned with the percentage of variability in actual returns that is accounted for by policy, by policy and active asset allocation, and by policy and security selection.

Figure 10.7 shows that, on average, policy returns accounted for 91.5 percent of the variance of actual returns. Being conditionally distributed on the policy returns, active asset allocation and security selection combined could have accounted for only a small residual portion of the variance of actual returns. In fact, policy and active asset allocation combined accounted for 93.3 percent and policy and security selection combined accounted for about 96.1 percent. Again, the dominance of investment policy is clear.[5]

Although each level of risk was associated with a range of plan returns, active returns generally increased with plan risk. Figure 10.8 shows that, for a given risk level, the difference in performance between the best and the worst plans was as much as 3 percent annually. The two plans with extraordinarily low risk had higher allocations to the "other asset" class—perhaps real estate, given the low volatility. Three other plans had unusually strong returns, with each showing extraordinary returns from both stock and bond components over the entire 10 years.

There are several possible explanations for these irregularities. First, the analysis did not account for the liability exposure of each plan. The inclusion of a liability proxy might shift these performance statistics. Second, the use of 10-year average weights for the passive benchmark may have created an inefficient benchmark. While the impact was probably not great, some bias was introduced.

It is difficult, given these data, to determine conclusively which asset classes generated good or bad relative performance. It should be noted, however, that 76 of the 82 equity funds under performed the S&P 500 on an equity-only basis. A complete 10-year bond performance was not available for several funds because their bond weights were zero for several

Security Selection

	Actual	Passive

Asset Allocation

	Actual	Passive
	IV 100.0%	II 93.3%
	III 96.1%	I 91.5%

	Average	Minimum	Maximum	Std. Dev.
Policy	91.5%	67.7%	98.2%	6.6%
Policy and Allocation	93.3%	69.4%	98.3%	5.2%
Policy and Selection	96.1%	76.2%	99.8%	5.2%

FIGURE 10.7   Percentage of Variation Explained, 1977–1987

quarters. For the 70 cases with complete bond histories, almost two-thirds outperformed the passive bond benchmark. Of those plans that underperformed their policy benchmarks, over 75 percent underperformed in the bond component. As one would expect, the median cash manager outperformed the 30-day T-bill index.

Limitations

Our analysis lacks some precision because of performance data limitations. First, as noted, the composition of the "other asset" category was unknown; in many cases, however, this category constituted only a small percentage of the total portfolio. Second, policy portfolios were inferred from the long-term average asset class weights, and there is no assurance that they reliably represent the actual benchmarks. In terms of assessing the importance of the benchmark to investment returns, however, this is probably not a serious problem. Adjusting for apparent shifts in policy weights had very little effect on the analysis. In fact, using a simple 60/40 stock/bond mix as a passive benchmark for all the funds resulted in virtually the same *average* results as indicated in Figure 10.8. Given the average portfolio composition in Table 10.2, this is not too surprising.

Finally, we do not know the actual number of different money managers used by these 82 pension plans. While it is highly unlikely that the data represent only a few managers, the study does reflect the performance of individual managers, not necessarily pension fund performance in general. Furthermore, we know nothing about the styles of the managers or their use of futures and options. Some almost certainly altered internal risk positions by hedging during the last quarter of 1987; this is indicated by the positive equity returns at a time when the market as a whole was down by almost 25 percent. The issue of hedging, and the broader issue of **risk positioning,** is treated in more depth below.

INTERNAL VERSUS EXTERNAL RISK POSITIONING

Besides shifting asset class weights—i.e., **external risk positioning**—a manager or sponsor can change exposure to an asset class within a portfolio component—**internal risk positioning**.

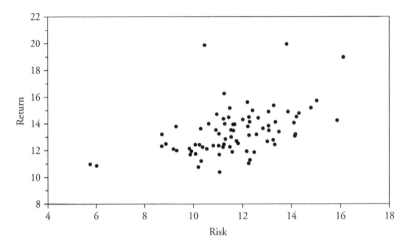

FIGURE 10.8   *Average Return versus Average Plan Risk, 1977–1987*

Source: SEI Corporation.

TABLE 10.4   Attribution of Internal and External Risk Positioning

	Equation (10.1)	Equation (10.3)
Security Selection	$(R_a - R_p)W_p$	$(R_s - R_p)W_p$
Risk Positioning	$(W_a - W_p)(R_p - R)$	$(W_a - W_p)(R_p - R) + c(R_h - R_p)W_a$
External	$(W_a - W_p)(R_p - R)$	$(W_a - W_p)(R_p - R)$
Internal	0	$c(R_h - R_p)W_p$
Cross Product	0	$c(W_a - W_p)(R_h - R_p)$
Cross Product	$(W_a - W_p)(R_a - R_p)$	$[(1 - c)W_a - W_p](R_s - R_p)$

Internal methods include altering the component's beta or duration by using long or short futures positions, carrying cash or hedging the currency component. Looking at any single risk-positioning activity, external or internal, will not give a complete or accurate measure of the active portfolio management effect.

The performance-attribution framework outlined above defines the extra return, E, to a multi-asset portfolio attributable to a particular asset class as

$$E = (R_a - R_p)W_p + (W_a - W_p)(R_p - R) + (W_a - W_p)(R_a - R_p), \qquad (10.1)$$

where

W_p = the normal weight of the asset class,
W_a = the actual weight,
R_p = the total passive return on the asset class index,
R_a = the total active return on the asset class, and
R = the total portfolio benchmark return.

The first term on the right-hand side of Equation (10.1) defines the contribution of security selection and the second gives the portion attributable to external risk positioning (active asset allocation). The third term isolates the interaction of security selection and allocation.

Within this definition of return, the contribution of risk positioning is limited to changes in the weights of asset classes.

This is an unnecessary constraint. We can subdivide the actual active return on each asset class into a pure selection component, R_s—indicating the equity-only return—and a component that isolates the effect of internal risk positioning, R_h—indicating the actual or synthetic cash return:

$$R_a = (1 - c)R_s + cR_h, \qquad (10.2)$$

where c equals the proportion of the fund held in cash. Inserting Equation (10.2) into Equation (10.1) provides a framework for determining the effect of asset class performance, in terms of both security selection and explicit internal risk activity, on the extra return of the entire portfolio:

$$E = (R_s - R_p)W_p + [(W_a - W_p)(R_p - R) + c(R_h - R_p)W_a] \\ + [(1 - c)W_a - W_p] (R_s - R_p). \qquad (10.3)$$

Table 10.4 compares Equations (10.1) and (10.3), showing the contribution to the extra return of a multi-asset portfolio from security selection, active asset allocation (external risk positioning), and internal risk positioning. The effect of internal risk positioning indicated in the table is equal to the difference between the return on the cash position and the return on the asset class index ($R_h - R_p$), adjusted by the implied weight of the risk-adjusted position in the total index (cW_p).

With neither internal nor external risk positioning, the contribution of the asset class manager to the extra return on the total portfolio is given by the extra return from selection only. That is, setting R_a equal to R_s, W_a equal to W_p, and c equal to zero in Equation (10.3) gives

$$E_s = W_p(R_s - R_p). \qquad (10.4)$$

The decision to risk-position internally within the asset class alters this result, and the contribution to relative performance becomes

$$E_h = W_p(R_a - R_p). \qquad (10.5)$$

Subtracting Equation (10.4) from Equation (10.5) gives the total effect of the internal hedging decision being imposed on preexisting selection performance:

$$E_h - E_s = W_p(R_a - R_s) = c(R_h - R_p)W_p - c(R_s - R_p)W_p. \qquad (10.6)$$

The second term is the portion of the cross-product term introduced by the explicit decision to hedge the asset holdings. That is, the first term isolates the pure effect of the hedge and the second measures the effect of the interaction of the hedge and the results of the selection strategy.

Equation (10.6) shows that even if the hedge does protect the fund from an adverse return on the asset class (i.e., $R_h > R_p$), the net effect might be negative. If selection within the fund is also successful (i.e., $R_s > R_p$), the second term in Equation (10.6) could be larger than the first. The more effective the selection process, the less attractive internal hedging is.

Rearranging terms in Equation (10.6) shows that the total effect of the hedge on the performance of the total portfolio is equal to

$$c(R_h - R_s)W_p.$$

If R_s exceeds R_h, an internal hedge will detract from performance of both the fund and a multi-asset portfolio, even when the return on cash exceeds the return on the index ($R_h > R_p$).

Our data do not allow us to go into a detailed analysis of performance attribution. A general proxy for the amount of internal risk positioning, however, could be the beta of the active returns with respect to a passive benchmark. As data become available, it would be useful to explore further the impact of internal risk positioning on performance attribution.

CONCLUSION

For our sample of pension plans, active investment decisions by plan sponsors and managers, both in terms of selection and timing, did little to improve performance over the 10-year period from December 1977 to December 1987. Although individual results varied widely, in general it was difficult to find positive explanatory relations between performance and investment behavior. For example, extra returns seemed to be unrelated to the level of active management. Moreover, it seemed to be harder for managers to outperform equity benchmarks than bond and cash benchmarks; many more plans had positive contributions from the bond and cash portions of their portfolios.

A more detailed history of portfolio compositions would help to specify better the contributions of investment decisions to overall performance. In particular, the extent of internal risk positioning used by managers could significantly alter attributions.[6]

NOTES

1. G.P. Brinson, L.R. Hood, and G.L. Beebower, "Determinants of Portfolio Performance," *Financial Analysts Journal,* July/August 1986.
2. C.R. Hensel, D.D. Ezra, and J.H. Ilkiw ("The Value of Asset Allocation Decisions," *Russell Research Commentaries,* March 1990) provide alternative support for the conclusion that the policy decision dominates other aspects of the investment process. They offer a useful extension of this methodology for evaluating policy allocations.
3. G.P. Brinson, "Asset Allocation vs. Market Timing," *Investment Management Review,* September–October 1988.
4. D. Gallagher, "The Sixty-four Billion Dollar Question," *Global Investor,* June 1988.
5. One potential drawback to the use of correlation coefficients arises from the fact that the return series may not be normally distributed. In fact, an actively managed portfolio is likely to have a chi-square component. This arises from the fact that the return to an actively managed portfolio is the product of normally distributed weights and normally distributed returns. The product of two normally distributed random variables follows the chi-square distribution. A discussion of this phenomenon appears in P.H. Dybvig and S.A. Ross, "Differential Information and Performance Measurement Using a Security Market Line," *Journal of Finance,* June 1985.
6. We thank Matthew R. Smith for his valuable assistance in the preparation of this article.

CHAPTER 11

DETERMINANTS OF PORTFOLIO PERFORMANCE— 20 YEARS LATER

L. Randolph Hood, CFA

It might be one of the most quoted numbers in applied finance: 93.6 percent. Ironically, it is also often misquoted or taken out of context. Just where did this number come from, and what does it really imply for portfolio management? Also, importantly, what does it not imply?

In the early 1980s, Gary Brinson and I were wondering why our institutional pension clients spent so much time and effort in manager searches and so little time in reviewing their asset allocation policies. It was not as if all our clients had identical risk tolerances, liability streams, and funding policies. In discussions with the clients, we discovered that they had a firm belief that manager selection was important (and it is) because they could quantify the benefits of superior management. They could not, however, or perhaps did not wish to, quantify the contributory effects of their allocation policies on the returns to their funds. Explicit policies can be embarrassing because they facilitate measurement of the success or failure of liability funding and the implementation of investment programs. That is, poor outcomes resulting from asset allocation policies are difficult to blame on investment managers.

Our clients considered liability valuation the province of actuaries, and liabilities were far too complicated and esoteric to analyze or to use in making policy decisions. Nevertheless, we firmly believed that investment policy was the heart of the investment planning process. (And somewhat after the fact, the funding debacle of 2001–2003 illustrates allocation's importance. Over that period, plan sponsors lost billions of dollars for their shareholders—despite tremendous efforts devoted to manager selection. The culprit was asset allocation policies that were developed without adequate consideration of the *range* of possible outcomes or the behavior of the liabilities.) So, convinced as we were in the 1980s of the importance of

Reprinted from *Financial Analysts Journal* (September/October 2005):6–8.

allocation policy, and with the assistance of Gilbert Beebower at SEI Corporation, who had the relevant data, we set out to explore the effects of asset allocation policy on plan returns.

Our main finding was that, on average, 93.6 percent of the variation of actual quarterly total returns from 1974 to 1983 of a sample of 91 large corporate pension plans could be explained by using proxy return series. The proxy series were calculated by using each plan's average weight over the 40 quarters for equities, bonds, and cash equivalents and by applying passive index returns for those asset classes for each quarter. Simply put, we found that the broad types of asset classes a fund includes in a portfolio and the proportions they represent have a profound effect on the *variability* of returns. These decisions also directly affect the returns themselves, of course, although we did not choose to stress that aspect. We concluded that asset allocation policy is an important component of the management process and deserves careful consideration. We wanted plan sponsors to focus *first* on their liabilities and explicitly consider what they were trying to achieve with their plans. And with our research, we thought the point had been made.

But debates about the article's findings were surprisingly numerous. Criticisms as well as defenses of the approach—and perceptions of the lessons to be learned from the article—have abounded. So, on behalf of my co-authors and myself, I would like to address some of the most prevalent observations and reactions that have been discussed in the last 20 years.

I want to start with one that we believe has not been discussed much at all: Nothing in the original paper suggests that active asset management is not an important activity. It was not the point of our paper, and our goal was not to demonstrate otherwise.

Although by our calculations it is true that the average plan over the time period we studied lost money from security selection and from market timing as we defined the terms, some plans did quite well. In security selection, for example (see Table 6 of the published article), the average plan active return was −0.36 percent a year, but the range of active returns varied from a loss of −2.90 percent to a gain of +3.60 percent a year—a spread of 650 bps. We would suggest that any activity that can avoid the former or attain the latter is very important indeed. Most plan sponsors appear to agree and think that what might be a small expected loss (0.36 percent) is probably worth the cost of trying to outperform.

Other comments about the research have surfaced over time. Some of the early detractors dismissed the work as being applicable solely to our sample, which it was not, because the results have been repeated with other data. Other criticisms revolved around our use of policy portfolios. We believe policy portfolios are useful and, in many ways, necessary. However, we do not believe that they are never to be changed. Naturally, when the goals or circumstances surrounding the management of portfolios change, so should the investment policy. All we would urge is that the policy be specified in advance and be actionable. As we noted in our article, we had to infer policy targets because we did not have the necessary data. If we had possessed the data, however, our results would certainly have been stronger, not weaker: Unless sponsors and managers actively disregard their policies, the policy effects would have been stronger than we measured.

Another comment has been that perhaps analyzing plans as a group rather than individually across time is the important approach. However, we wanted specifically to challenge this concept. We had no reason to believe that a single asset allocation policy could possibly be right for all of our diverse clients or that the mean policy weights for a group of heterogeneous pension plans had much *ex ante* interest.

Some commentators disliked our use of the "other" term, although it was algebraically necessary in our formulation. One interpretation of the term is that it represents the effect of overweighting managers who then reliably outperform their respective benchmarks, and vice versa, which might be of interest today to those pursuing "portable alpha" approaches.

A further criticism involved our use of *variation of portfolio total returns*, not the returns themselves. We do not understand this point as a criticism. Understanding how something varies, in our context, leads to understanding where it will end up. Our policy portfolio return series all had regression coefficients near unity when explaining actual return series, which is not surprising given their construction, so we did not report the regression coefficients because of space constraints. In Table 6, we reported that the average annual return to the average actual portfolio was equal to its policy portfolio return less 110 bps. We thus did describe the total return, albeit indirectly because it was not our main point. At their best, the compound annual total returns of the plans we studied were not, in themselves, interesting. We thought what was interesting was how the returns turned out to be what they were—with policy, timing, and security selection each contributing with varying degrees of importance. An analogy would be driving directions: One can either give a compass heading and a distance, or more helpfully, one can describe the route. The heading and distance information is akin to total return itself (up 9.01 percent); the variance of total return is akin to the directions: Follow the policy portfolio return wherever it leads (remember, it is specified in advance), but subtract 110 bps each year; on average, you will be right, and you can also see how bumpy the ride is along the way!

Conversely, among the work's supporters, zealous marketing has apparently led some to take liberties with the research. For instance, our findings do not support the notion that "asset allocation" funds are somehow inherently superior to single-asset-class funds. The ability to forecast asset class returns is a far different matter from pointing out that the policy weights and returns will have a profound effect on the return variation—and results—of an investment strategy. Our point was solely that, in aggregate, individual asset class policies, with given weights and broad market representation for returns, appear to dominate portfolio return variations and, by extension, the returns themselves. Furthermore, this conclusion was meant to be descriptive, not prescriptive, of the process we observed.

Looking back, we would not have guessed that a six-page article would be the focal point of a 20-year discussion. The consensus, however, appears to have settled in to agree with us that investment policy will be very important in subsequent results and in describing those results. Of course, other factors (such as active management and cost control) also have roles, and important roles, to play. Our message today remains the same as before: Carefully consider what goal you are trying to achieve, how important it is to achieve it, and how much risk you are willing to tolerate in pursuing it. Then, create a policy portfolio that reflects that goal and your risk tolerance for the probable outcomes—because executing that policy will have a dominant effect on your success. And then, get to work.

CHAPTER 12

EQUITY PORTFOLIO CHARACTERISTICS IN PERFORMANCE ANALYSIS

Stephen C. Gaudette, CFA, and Philip Lawton, CFA, CIPM

". . . when you can measure what you are speaking about, and express it in numbers, you know something about it; but when you cannot measure it, when you cannot express it in numbers, your knowledge is of a meagre and unsatisfactory kind. . . ."
Lord Kelvin, PLA, vol. 1, "Electrical Units of Measurement", 1883-05-03.

Unlike equity analysts, investment performance practitioners are rarely called upon to examine issuers' financial statements or to calculate security-level characteristics. Rather, their role is typically to evaluate system-generated portfolio characteristics in comparison with benchmark characteristics. This chapter addresses input data and portfolio-level characteristic calculation issues, surveys and illustrates the types of characteristics, and examines three principal uses of portfolio characteristics analysis—identifying possible shifts in investment strategy, conducting holdings-based style analysis, and determining the sources of portfolio returns.

The investment management process is composed of integrated activities that combine the client's objectives, constraints, and preferences with the portfolio manager's capital market expectations. (See Figure 12.1.) Portfolio managers make investment decisions under conditions of uncertainty; performance analysts quantify the results of those decisions, providing feedback on the execution of investment strategies in the light of actual outcomes. Portfolio managers can use this information to evaluate their security selection and portfolio construction processes, and their clients can use it as one element in an ongoing endeavor to monitor the manager's organization and to appraise the manager's performance.

Reprinted from CFA Institute (2007).

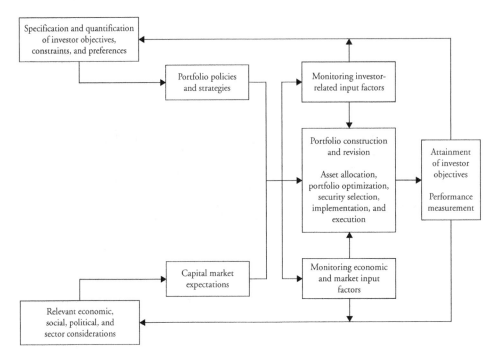

FIGURE 12.1   The Portfolio Construction, Monitoring, and Revision Process

Source: John L. Maginn, Donald L. Tuttle, Dennis W. McLeavey, and Jerald E. Pinto, "The Portfolio Management Process and the Investment Policy Statement," Chapter 1 in John L. Maginn, Donald L. Tuttle, Dennis W. McLeavey, and Jerald E. Pinto, eds., *Managing Investment Portfolios: A Dynamic Approach* (CFA Institute, 2007), p. 6.

Managers look at the capital markets and individual securities in different ways reflecting their distinctive competence, portfolio construction process, and investment strategy. Some organizations with forecasting expertise adopt a top-down approach to portfolio construction, selecting securities in line with their expectations for the overall economy and their judgment about the relative attractiveness of specific sectors and industries. Other organizations may stress their stock-picking skills and employ a bottom-up process, selecting the most undervalued securities across all sectors and industries within the client's or the firm's exposure limits. Managers' strategies and clients' guidelines also govern investment decisions. For example, a manager investing on behalf of a risk-averse client may purchase defensive stocks with high dividend yields, while a manager whose client is willing and able to accept market risk may purchase stocks with greater upside price potential. These factors lead to discernible differences among portfolios.

Equity analysts employed by investment management firms that adopt a fundamental approach to valuation often calculate and evaluate the characteristics of their assigned companies and stocks. In this context, characteristics derived from market data and the issuer's financial statements are one kind of input in a comprehensive process whose essential objective is to identify misvalued securities. Consistent with the portfolio's investment strategy and constraints, portfolio managers may act on the equity analysts' recommendations by purchasing undervalued stocks and selling overvalued stocks.

Unlike equity analysts, investment performance practitioners are rarely if ever called upon to examine issuers' financial statements or to calculate security-level characteristics.

Rather, their role is typically to evaluate system-generated portfolio characteristics in comparison with benchmark characteristics. As explained below, portfolio characteristics are the weighted averages of the characteristics of the securities held in the portfolio. Holdings data are provided by the portfolio accounting system, and calculated security-level characteristics are typically received electronically from external capital market data service providers. Performance analysts then analyze and interpret these data to address specific issues. In order to interpret the data, however, performance analysts must understand how they are prepared.

The following sections will summarize some useful techniques for examining an equity portfolio's composition and relating the portfolio's characteristics to its performance. In the next section, we introduce three principal uses of portfolio characteristics analysis—identifying possible shifts in investment strategy, conducting holdings-based style analysis, and determining the sources of portfolio returns.[1] We then address input data and portfolio-level characteristic calculation issues, survey and illustrate the types of characteristics, and present portfolio monitoring, style analysis, and characteristic- or factor-based attribution in more detail. We close with remarks on the limitations of portfolio characteristics analysis.

USES OF PORTFOLIO CHARACTERISTICS

Macroeconomic, social, political, and other external influences can be expected to alter the revenues and expenses of companies and therefore their profitability. In many cases, companies with similar exposures to external factors will respond similarly to changes in their operating environment. For example, unrest in oil-producing regions may raise the political risk premium by influencing the outlook for future supplies of petroleum products. The impact on current fuel prices may be favorable for oil companies, which benefit from rising revenues, and unfavorable for airlines, which suffer from rising expenses. Investors' expectations of profit changes in the oil and airline industries will result in new security valuations, directly affecting returns. Similarly, an increase in interest rates may be auspicious for lending companies and detrimental to borrowers. Investors' revised estimates of the future earnings of banks, insurance companies, utilities, and other companies with significant interest rate exposures will trigger market adjustments affecting security returns.

Like many athletes, many investment managers believe that their competitive performance improves when they focus on their strengths. Consequently, some investment organizations and most equity portfolio managers adopt strategies centered on particular types of stocks. Since common external influences—including, of course, other investors' expectations—can have a large impact on the performance of groups of securities, it is informative to identify and monitor security characteristics that may affect valuations.

From the client's or the consultant's perspective, periodic comparisons between portfolio and benchmark characteristics may disclose possible deviations from the manager's stated investment strategy or discipline. For example, a sector rotator would not be expected to have a large positive active position in financials when the firm anticipates accelerating inflation. Investors who are attentive to portfolio characteristics are well-positioned to engage their managers in informative dialogue; it may turn out, after all, that the manager has valid reasons for overweighting financial stocks.

Beyond economic sector and industry classifications, other factors commonly used to characterize a domestic equity portfolio are the size of the stocks in which the manager invests and the issuing companies' growth or value traits. As explained below, comparing the market capitalization and value–growth characteristics of an investment portfolio to those of a valid benchmark at a point in time may help identify how the active manager has attempted to outperform the benchmark or how the manager is positioning the portfolio for expected market conditions. Moreover, periodic comparisons over time may help identify style drift or, alternately, confirm that the manager is adhering to the agreed-upon style or strategy mandate.

Finally, in addition to using portfolio characteristics for the purposes of manager monitoring and style analysis, performance analysts can view them as sources of return or, more rigorously, as risk factors with which security returns are correlated. Attribution analysis based upon portfolio characteristics or fundamental factor exposures can illuminate investment results and lead to constructive dialogue about the intended and unintended consequences of the manager's security selection and portfolio construction processes.

DATA AND CALCULATION ISSUES

Portfolio characteristics—the market value-weighted characteristics of the individual non-cash securities held in the portfolio at a point in time—can be meaningfully presented only if reasonably complete and consistent security-level data are available.

Despite the tremendous growth in capital market data services, the performance analyst cannot be assured of complete coverage for all portfolios. Data may be missing for numerous securities, especially if the portfolio is invested in relatively illiquid issues such as micro-cap or emerging market stocks. In practice, the simplest solution for missing data points is to report the weighted average characteristic values of the securities for which data are available along with the percentage of the portfolio's total market value captured by each characteristic. For instance, if a portfolio is valued at £12,548,960 but dividend yields are available only for portfolio holdings that add up to £8,068,981, then the best practice is to indicate that the average dividend yield is based upon 64.3 percent of the portfolio's total market value.

Organizations that attempt to improve security-level coverage by subscribing to several market data services should be alert to potential methodological differences among their providers. For example, the earnings of companies that issue common stock are used in calculating certain characteristics such as price-to-earnings ratios and the growth in earnings per share. One market data service provider may report earnings as shown in the issuer's income statement, while another may make adjustments to eliminate extraordinary, non-recurring, and/or non-cash items. The performance analyst should be aware of such differences; although they generally will not invalidate portfolio characteristics analyses, they may reduce their reliability.

Another issue that arises when calculating portfolio characteristics is the validity of calculated means if potential outliers are observed among the constituent stocks. For example, a portfolio containing 40 stocks is found to have an average five-year earnings per share growth rate of 34.5 percent. However, one of the holdings has a reported historical growth rate of 500 percent; the other 39 have historical growth rates ranging from 12.4 to 38.7. There are several possible reasons for the exceptionally high five-year EPS growth rate reported for the one stock. The company may have had a small positive starting value such as $0.01, or the growth rate as given by the characteristic provider may simply be erroneous. In a production environment, the performance analyst typically does not have the time to examine the company's financial statements and independently validate the data. How should the apparent outlier be handled?

One approach, of course, is to include all the data points, reporting the mean of 34.5 percent. Another approach is to exclude data points that fall outside a tolerance range. For instance, in a normal distribution the range defined as ±2.33 standard deviations

TABLE 12.1   Five-Year EPS Growth Percent

Rank	Arithmetic	Tolerance Range	Trimmed	Winsorized
1	500.0	—	—	38.7
2	38.7	38.7	38.7	38.7
3	38.1	38.1	38.1	38.1
...	...	...	...	...
38	13.6	13.6	13.6	13.6
39	12.9	12.9	12.9	12.9
40	12.4	12.4	—	12.9
Sum	1380.3	880.3	867.9	919.5
N	40	39	38	40
Mean	34.5	22.6	22.8	23.0

around the mean excludes approximately the largest one percent and smallest one percent of observations. In the example shown, the standard deviation is 75.9 percent, so including only the observations falling within 2.33 standard deviations of the mean excludes the 500-percent observation. A third approach is to calculate a trimmed mean that excludes a certain percentage of the largest and smallest data points. In this example, excluding the top and bottom data points in an ordered list results in a trimmed mean of 22.8 percent. A fourth approach is to calculate a winsorized mean, which involves a reassignment of the values of extreme observations. For example, for a 99 percent winsorized mean, the top 0.5 percent of values would be set equal to the value of the observation at the cut-off point for the top 0.5 percent group; similarly, the lowest 0.5 percent of values would assume the value of the observation at their cut-off point. For simplicity, in the case of the 40-stock portfolio described above, Table 12.1 shows the winsorized mean growth rate is 23.0 based on re-assigning the values of the largest observation and the smallest observation in the sample. Table 12.1 also illustrates the other methods discussed above.

Portfolio characteristics are usually calculated as the weighted mean of the observations, where the weight applied to each observation is the fraction of the portfolio's value invested in the holding associated with that observation. However, the weighted harmonic mean may be the most appropriate representation of an average rate or ratio. If the ratio of an individual holding is represented by X_i, the expression for the weighted harmonic mean of the ratio is

$$X_{WH} = \frac{1}{\displaystyle\sum_{i=1}^{n}\left(\frac{w_i}{X_i}\right)} \tag{12.1}$$

where the w_i are portfolio value weights (summing to 1) and $X_i > 0$ for $i = 1, 2,\ldots, n$.

The superiority of weighted harmonic mean estimates over weighted arithmetic mean estimates in this context may be conveyed by an example. Consider a hypothetical portfolio that contains two stocks. One stock has a market capitalization of €700 million and earnings of €70 million, giving it a P/E ratio of 10. The other stock has a market capitalization

TABLE 12.2   P/E Ratio—Weighted Arithmetic and Harmonic Means

	Market Capitalization		Earnings € Million	P/E	Weighted P/E	E/P	Weighted E/P
	€ Million	% of Total					
Stock 1	700	53.85%	70	10	5.38	0.10	0.0538
Stock 2	600	46.15%	3	200	92.31	0.01	0.0023
	1300	100.00%			97.69		0.0562
Weighted Harmonic Mean							17.81

of €600 million and earnings of €3 million, for a P/E ratio of 200. Table 12.2 displays the calculation of the hypothetical portfolio's weighted arithmetic mean P/E and its weighted harmonic mean P/E.

In this example, the weighted harmonic mean of 17.81 is much lower than the weighted arithmetic mean of 97.69. (Note that the harmonic mean inherently gives less weight to higher P/E ratios and more weight to lower P/Es. In general, unless all the observations in a data set have the same value, the harmonic mean is less than the arithmetic mean.) Which is the more accurate value? In fact, the weighted harmonic mean precisely corresponds with the P/E calculated directly by aggregating the companies' market capitalization and earnings: $(700 + 600)/(70 + 3) = 17.81$.

Finally, investment professionals have differences of opinion on the proper treatment of negative ratios. For example, stocks with negative earnings (losses) will have negative P/E ratios.[2] Many consider negative P/Es meaningless and omit them when calculating portfolio averages, while others contend that averaging only the positive P/E ratios falsely overstates the portfolio-level ratio. Whether negative ratios are included in or excluded from the portfolio mean, it is important to treat the benchmark the same way.

Another consideration that a performance analyst must take into account when calculating weighted averages is how to handle short positions. It is inappropriate simply to exclude short positions from the calculation of portfolio-level characteristics, since they are integral to the execution of a long-short strategy. The remaining alternatives are to show net characteristic exposures or to present the components of the net exposure by separately displaying the characteristics of the long and the short portions of the portfolio. Although it may require additional work, the latter method is the more informative because portfolios whose net value is near zero can have distorted weighted average characteristics.

TYPES OF CHARACTERISTICS

Characteristics may generally be classified as belonging to three major groups: macroeconomic characteristics, company fundamental characteristics, and company share-related characteristics.

A company's economic sector and industry membership, already mentioned, is a macroeconomic characteristic. The Global Industry Classification System (GICS®) developed by Standard & Poor's and MSCI Barra is widely used in equity investing and performance measurement. GICS is a four-tier system composed of 10 sectors that are composed, in turn, of 24 industry groups, 67 industries, and 147 sub-industries. For example, the Asset Management & Custody Banks sub-industry belongs to the Capital Markets industry, which belongs to the Diversified Financials industry group, which belongs to the Financials sector. Standard & Poor's and MSCI Barra jointly assign a company to a single GICS sub-industry in accordance with the company's principal business activity.[3] Similar breakdowns are done by other data service providers using the companies' Standard Industry Classification code or the providers' internal classification schemes.

Another macroeconomic characteristic is beta, a linear measure of the sensitivity of a given stock to movements in the overall market under the capital asset pricing model (CAPM). A stock's historical beta may be estimated by taking the ratio of the covariance between the stock's return and the market return to the variance of the market return:

$$\beta_i = \frac{Cov\left(R_i, R_M\right)}{Var\left(R_M\right)} \tag{12.2}$$

where
β_i = the beta of stock i
R_i = the return on stock i
R_M = the return on the market portfolio

A beta greater than 1 indicates greater than average market risk and, according to the CAPM, is expected to earn a higher-than-market return above the risk-free rate. In other words, a stock with a beta greater than 1 has above-average exposure to systematic risk. Its price may be expected to rise more than the market rises and to fall more than the market falls. Conversely, a beta less than 1 indicates less than average market risk and earns a smaller expected excess return.

Company fundamental characteristics include activity, liquidity, solvency, and profitability measures. For example, the ratio of sales to assets is an activity measure. The current ratio, a liquidity measure, compares the obligations that will become payable during the current operating cycle (current liabilities) with the cash that is or will become available to pay them (current assets). The debt-to-equity (D/E) ratio, an indicator of the company's solvency, is the ratio of total debt to total shareholders' equity. Return on equity (ROE) is a critically important profitability measure frequently encountered in portfolio characteristics analyses. It is calculated by dividing average common shareholders' equity into the difference between net income and preferred dividends:

$$ROE = \frac{Net\,Income - Preferred\,Dividends}{Average\,Common\,Shareholder's\,Equity} \tag{12.3}$$

Of particular interest to performance analysts are company share-related characteristics. For example, market capitalization, broadly defined as the number of common stock shares outstanding multiplied by the price of a single share, is a key measure of the company's size that is used in holdings-based style analysis, as explained below.

The price-to-book (P/B) ratio is another valuation measure frequently used to indicate the style of a portfolio. It is calculated by dividing the stock's current market price by the book value per share, where the book value per share is defined as the total common shareholders' equity on the business's balance sheet divided by the number of common stock shares outstanding.

Other ratios that are frequently used to describe the style of the portfolio include the price-to-earnings (P/E) ratio, dividend yield (D/P), and the dividend payout ratio. The trailing P/E ratio, sometimes referred to as the current P/E, is calculated by dividing the current market price of a stock by the most recent four quarters' earnings per share (EPS). The leading P/E ratio, also called the forward P/E or the prospective P/E, is the stock's current price divided by next year's expected earnings; in performance analysis, expected earnings may reflect consensus estimates compiled by market data service providers. For both historical and forward P/E ratios, data providers may have different policies regarding what earnings figures should be used when extraordinary items appear on the income statement. As the next section shows, comparatively high P/B and P/E ratios generally characterize growth stocks, whereas relatively low P/B and P/E ratios typify value stocks.

Dividend yield (D/P) expresses the relationship between a company's distributions to shareholders and the price of its stock, or, from the investor's point of view, between the investment income produced by an asset and the asset's market value. Trailing dividend yield is generally calculated as four times the most recent quarterly per-share dividend divided by the current market price per share. (Note that, unlike the trailing P/E ratio, trailing dividend yield does not look to the historical record for the last four quarters.) The leading dividend yield is calculated as forecasted dividends per share over the next year divided by the current market price per share. The dividend payout ratio equals the percentage of earnings paid out as dividends, that is, dividends divided by net income. Relatively high dividend yields are generally indicators of value stocks, while comparatively low dividend yields are characteristic of growth stocks.

The price-to-sales (P/S) and price-to-cash-flow (P/CF) ratios are also often used by equity analysts in valuation and by performance analysts in portfolio characteristics analysis. The P/S ratio is calculated as price per share divided by annual net sales per share, where net sales is defined as total sales less returns and customer discounts. Annual sales from the company's most recent fiscal year are usually used in the calculation. The P/CF ratio is most frequently calculated using the current price divided by the most recent four quarters' cash flow. Although there are other, more accurate cash flow concepts, in practice data vendors often estimate cash flow by adding non-cash charges back to income. A typical approximation of cash flow per share is EPS plus per-share depreciation, amortization, and, in the case of natural resource companies, depletion.

Other company share-related characteristics include relative strength, typically defined as the ratio of a stock's performance to the performance of an index; liquidity, which is a measure of the number of shares traded relative to the total number of shares outstanding; and volatility, which may be calculated as the annualized standard deviation of an asset's continuously compounded daily returns. Clients and consultants would expect a portfolio containing high-volatility stocks to be adequately diversified and might wish to afford the manager a longer than usual evaluation period.

There are many other characteristics in addition to those mentioned here. Given the wide range of characteristics available, how should the performance analyst select the most meaningful measures?

The answer depends upon the intended use of the portfolio characteristics analysis. When designing standard reports, a mix of macroeconomic, company fundamental, and company share-related characteristics may be most useful to clients. When preparing custom reports, on the other hand, it is sensible to include characteristics that are likely to corroborate or disconfirm that the manager is adhering to the investment strategy. For example, if a manager states that companies' spending on research and development (R & D) is a critical factor in security selection, it is reassuring to see that average R & D spending (for instance, as a percentage of revenues) is higher in the portfolio than in the benchmark. Managers' explanations of their investment philosophy and strategy may indicate which characteristics are most promising. In addition, performance analysis fosters dialogue between clients and managers; in this context, the managers themselves may have helpful suggestions about pertinent characteristics based upon their security selection and portfolio construction processes.

MANAGER MONITORING AND STYLE ANALYSIS

Examining portfolio composition, and tracking changes over time, is an essential element in a sound manager monitoring process.[4] In combination with performance attribution, portfolio characteristics analysis can provide valuable insights into the manager's thinking. Comparing the portfolio's sector weights and other pertinent characteristics with those of a valid benchmark at the same point in time enables the client or consultant to see what bets the manager has made. In addition, while tactical adjustments are normal, an apparent trend in portfolio characteristics relative to the benchmark may alert the client or consultant to possible departures from the manager's investment mandate.

Style analysis is a specific type of manager monitoring based upon the characterization of investment strategies in two dimensions: size (small cap, mid-cap, and large cap) and valuation (value, neutral or core, and growth). In a given measurement period, one style may be in favor, generating highly positive returns, while another is out of favor, producing disappointing results. For example, the returns of small-cap growth portfolios, taken as a group, may differ systematically from those of large-cap value portfolios in the same period. Style analysis has two major variations: returns-based and holdings-based.

Returns-based style analysis[5] determines the combination of indexes that best explains the style in which a portfolio is managed. For example, a portfolio might be described as 53.2% large growth, 32.7% small growth, and 14.1% small value. Given the ease with which commercially available returns-based style models can be used, this approach has great practical appeal; the only data the performance analyst need compile is the portfolio's historical return series and those of appropriate indices. In comparison, holdings-based style analysis requires extensive security-level data. In addition, returns-based style analysis graphically displays how the manager's profile has changed over time. It is more effortful to interpret period-to-period comparisons of holdings-based characteristics. However, beyond observing that the manager's effective mix of style-based benchmarks has evolved, the holdings-based approach described below may enable astute clients and consultants to ask the manager appreciably more pointed questions about potentially significant changes in portfolio structure.

In holdings-based style analysis, an equity portfolio's investment strategy may be profiled by observing its size and value–growth characteristics. Rather than merely tracking changes in the portfolio, however, it is essential to compare the portfolio to a valid benchmark in each period, because the general level of market valuations changes over the course of the business cycle (and over longer periods as well). For example, price-to-earnings (P/E) ratios tend to be high and rising when the outlook for earnings improves, as in the early stages of an economic recovery, and low and falling when the outlook worsens.[6]

Size is measured by the stock's market capitalization. Some capital market index providers adjust market cap weights for each issue's floating supply of shares or "free float," the number of shares outstanding that are actually available to investors after excluding such categories as corporate cross-holdings in the same index, large corporate and private holdings, and government positions in partially privatized companies.

A stock's position on the value–growth spectrum may be indicated by its price-to-earnings (P/E) ratio and/or its price-to-book (P/B) ratio, among other factors. Because the market pays a premium for projected earnings increases, growing companies generally have higher P/E and P/B ratios than companies that are considered to have more limited prospects for expansion.

A stock's dividend yield (D/P) and its issuer's dividend payout ratio provide further information. Generally, growth companies have low dividend yields and dividend payout ratios because they retain most of their income to finance future expansion. Mature companies that do not have attractive reinvestment opportunities distribute a greater portion of their earnings to shareholders. Other measures of a company's relative position are its trailing and forecasted growth in per-share earnings.

Index providers typically use multiple factors when assigning companies to value and growth style categories. For example, the methodology employed in the construction of Standard & Poor's U.S. Style indices and the S&P/Citigroup style benchmark series uses three factors to measure growth and four factors to measure value. The growth factors are the five-year EPS growth rate, the five-year sales per share growth rate, and the five-year internal growth rate, defined as the product of ROE and the earnings retention rate. The value factors are B/P, the cash flow-to-price ratio, the sales-to-price ratio, and dividend yield. Standard & Poor's classifies stocks after ranking them according to their scores on the growth and value dimensions.[7] Russell uses a probability algorithm to assign stocks to the growth and value style indexes on the basis of their relative B/P ratios and I/B/E/S forecast long-term growth mean.[8] Complete descriptions of these providers' style index construction methodologies are available on their Web sites.

Table 12.3 displays comparative values of four Russell style indexes. The Russell 1000® indexes are large-cap indexes and the Russell 2000® indexes are small-cap indexes. As expected, the large-cap and small-cap value indexes have lower P/B and P/E ratios, higher dividend yields, and lower earnings growth statistics than the corresponding growth indexes. Similar comparisons may be done within other index families.

TABLE 12.3   Comparative Index Characteristics

Characteristic	Monthly Data from 31 May 2006 through 31 May 2007			
	Russell 1000® Value Index	Russell 1000® Growth Index	Russell 2000® Value Index	Russell 2000® Growth Index
Average Market Cap in Billions ($ - WTD)	115.939	73.622	1.347	1.420
Median Market Cap in Billions	6.033	6.223	0.686	0.677
Price/Book	2.29	4.30	1.94	3.67
Dividend Yield	2.35	1.11	1.75	0.43
P/E Ex-Neg Earnings	14.88	21.44	19.25	23.93
LT Growth Forecast-IBES	9.48%	14.51%	11.22%	18.77%
EPS Growth 5 Years	19.42	22.15	12.64	21.95

Russell Investment Group is the source and owner of the trademarks, service marks, and copyrights related to the Russell Indexes. Russell® is a trademark of Russell Investment Group.

When conducting holdings-based style analysis, it is helpful to be familiar with the methodologies employed by the market data service provider who supplies security-level characteristics for the portfolio as well as by the index provider who assigns individual stocks to style categories according to its own index construction rules. By observing the different characteristics of the portfolio and those of the benchmark, it is possible to go beyond a simple classification of the manager's style and gain a deeper understanding of some of the factors that the manager emphasizes in his security selection process.

ATTRIBUTION ANALYSIS

Viewed as sources of return, portfolio characteristics are also serviceable in performance attribution analysis. Indeed, the classic sector weighting/stock selection attribution model exemplifies characteristic-based attribution analysis.[9] This single-factor model can be used with characteristics in addition to economic sectors. For example, a portfolio's holdings can be sorted by their P/E ratios and grouped into ranges such as "stocks with P/E ratios equal to or less than 5," "stocks with P/E ratios greater than 5 but less than 10," and so forth. It is then a trivial matter to determine the market value weights of each range and to calculate their contributions to absolute return. If stock-level characteristics and capitalization weights are available for the benchmark, the contribution of each P/E range to the portfolio's value-added return—the return in excess of the benchmark—can also be determined.

While the single-factor approach outlined in the preceding paragraph may offer some insight into the manager's performance, its usefulness is limited at best. In a single-factor model, each view of the portfolio excludes, by definition, all other views. For instance, a single-factor attribution analysis using P/E ranges "explains" all, or almost all, of the portfolio's value-added returns—but so does a single-factor attribution analysis by price-to-book (P/B) ratios or by any other characteristic. There is no perspective in which the analyst can simultaneously evaluate the relative return contributions of multiple portfolio characteristics. A single-factor model may also confound the effects on performance of distinct but correlated risk factors. This can lead the analyst to draw a conclusion for the wrong reason. Consider a situation where tax laws are changed to make dividends more attractive to investors. If an attribution is done based on industry, utilities and REITs might appear to have added to performance when in reality it was their propensity to pay high dividends, rather than their industry membership, that contributed to performance.

In addition, a single-factors model is likely to have less explanatory power than a well-specified multifactor model. Indeed, without conducting tests of statistical significance the analyst cannot be assured that the results of a single-factor attribution analysis are valid. A single-factor attribution analysis using the ratio of blue-eyed to brown-eyed employees of portfolio companies will produce economically meaningless results. At a minimum, attribution analyses must be based upon factors that make sense in light of the manager's investment strategy.

Research has shown that multiple factors affect securities' returns. In contrast with single-factor models, multivariate analysis permits examination of individual characteristics' incremental effects and provides a more nuanced picture of risk. Multifactor models for performance attribution can be built using a variety of factors ranging from fundamental factors to macroeconomic, to a combination of the two.

In performance applications, for example, fundamental multifactor models use techniques of statistical analysis to unpack a stock's return, breaking out the contributions from the stock's exposure to underlying elements found to have systematic effects—for example, membership in an economic sector or industry, forecasted beta, market capitalization, the P/E ratio, the P/B ratio, and the issuing company's financial leverage. At the level of individual securities, the general form of a multifactor model can be expressed by a standard regression equation:

$$R_i = a_i + b_{i1}F_1 + b_{i2}F_2 + \cdots + b_{iK}F_K + \varepsilon_i \qquad (12.4)$$

where

R_i = the return to stock i over the regression period

a_i = the intercept of the regression equation

b_{i1} = the sensitivity of the return to stock i to factor 1

F_1 = the average value of factor 1 across all stocks

K = the number of factors in the model

ε_i = an error term that represents the portion of the return to stock i not explained by the factor model

By looking at a broad universe of stocks over an extended period, one can estimate the return associated with the average exposure to each factor. The empirically determined factor returns can then be combined with a specific stock's relative factor exposures to account for the stock's return. The market value-weighted factor exposures of all holdings can be summed to determine the portfolio's aggregate exposure to each factor and, by extension, the portion of the portfolio's return that is attributable to each exposure. Applying the same procedures to the benchmark constituents enables the performance analyst to establish the portfolio's active factor exposures and to quantify their contributions to the manager's value-added return.

A significant advantage of fundamental multifactor attribution analysis over the single factor approach is that the analyst can see the impact of all of the factors in the model simultaneously. This reduces the likelihood of misconstruing one effect for another. For instance, in a single-factor model, because integrated oil stocks have large market capitalizations, an exposure to integrated oil stocks in an industry view might look very much like the exposure to large-capitalization stocks in a size view. By contrast, a fundamental multifactor model that includes industry and size factors distinguishes between the two effects. The most significant disadvantage is that there is an assumption of linearity in the multifactor approach. For example, if large-cap and small-cap stocks perform poorly but mid-cap stocks perform well, the multifactor approach will not properly identify their contributions. As a result, looking at both single and multifactor analyses may give the most meaningful results.

LIMITATIONS OF PORTFOLIO CHARACTERISTICS ANALYSIS

Portfolio characteristics analysis may not be appropriate in all situations, and common sense must determine whether it is suitable. Some investment strategies do not consider fundamental characteristics either explicitly or implicitly. For example, when monitoring a merger arbitrage strategy, it makes more sense to evaluate the manager's ability to anticipate and analyze deals than to examine the characteristics of the stocks held in the portfolio. Similarly, evaluating a portfolio's leverage and dividend yield is unlikely to provide meaningful information about a manager who picks stocks on the basis of technical analysis. Market data and the analyst's time are expensive. Portfolio characteristics analysis should be employed only where it adds value, for instance, by raising questions about the manager's execution of an investment strategy. In employing portfolio characteristics analysis, it is most important to ensure that the evaluation reflects the different steps in the manager's investment process.

NOTES

1. In addition, portfolio characteristics analysis may be used by investment management firms in the construction and maintenance of custom security-based benchmarks, also known as strategy benchmarks. See Jeffery V. Bailey, Thomas M. Richards, and David E. Tierney, "Evaluating Portfolio Performance," Chapter 12 in John L. Maginn, Donald L. Tuttle, Dennis W. McLeavey, and Jerald E. Pinto, eds., *Managing Investment Portfolios: A Dynamic Process,* Third Edition (CFA Institute, 2007), pp. 737–738; and David E. Kuenzi, "Strategy Benchmarks," *Journal of Portfolio Management* (Winter 2003), pp. 46–56.

2. Faced with the task of ranking stocks, equity analysts have several alternatives for handling negative P/E ratios that are not usually available to performance practitioners. In some cases, replacing trailing earnings with normalized earnings or with estimated prospective earnings may produce positive price-to-earnings ratios. In addition, using the earnings yield ratio (E/P) will result in the correct ordering of positive- and negative-P/E stocks by what may be deemed the cost of earnings. See John D. Stowe, Thomas R. Robinson, Jerald E. Pinto, and Dennis W. McLeavey, *Analysis of Equity Investments: Valuation* (CFA Institute, 2002), pp. 188–189.

3. "Global Industry Classification Standard Methodology" (Standard & Poor's, 2006), pp. 5–6.

4. See Russell L. Olson, *The Independent Fiduciary; Investing for Pension Funds and Endowment Funds* (John Wiley & Sons, 1999), pp. 124–125.

5. For an account of the development and interpretation of returns-based style analysis, see Laurence B. Siegel, *Benchmarks and Investment Management* (The Research Foundation of CFA Institute, 2003), pp. 66–73.

6. John P. Calverley, Alan M. Meder, Brian D. Singer, and Renato Staub, "Capital Market Expectations," Chapter 4 in John L. Maginn, Donald L. Tuttle, Dennis W. McLeavey, and Jerald E. Pinto, eds., *Managing Investment Portfolios; A Dynamic Process,* Third Edition (CFA Institute, 2007), pp. 219–220.

7. "S&P U.S. Style Indices: Index Methodology" (Standard & Poor's, 2006), pp. 7–9.

8. "Russell U.S. Equity Indexes: Construction and Methodology" (Russell, 2007), pp. 13–14.

9. Sector weighting/stock selection attribution analysis is presented and explained in Jeffery V. Bailey, Thomas M. Richards, and David E. Tierney, *op. cit.*, pp. 755–759.

CHAPTER 13

MUTUAL FUND PERFORMANCE: DOES FUND SIZE MATTER?

Daniel C. Indro, Christine X. Jiang, Michael Y. Hu, and Wayne Y. Lee

Fund size (net assets under management) affects mutual fund performance. Mutual funds must attain a minimum fund size in order to achieve sufficient returns to justify their costs of acquiring and trading on information. Furthermore, there are diminishing marginal returns to information acquisition and trading, and the marginal returns become negative when the mutual fund exceeds its optimal fund size. In a sample of 683 nonindexed U.S. equity funds over the 1993–95 period, we found that 20 percent of the mutual funds were smaller than the breakeven-cost fund size and 10 percent of the largest funds overinvested in information acquisition and trading. In addition, we found that value funds and blend (value-and-growth) funds have more to gain than growth funds from these information activities.

In the popular press, the September 30, 1997, closing of the world's largest mutual fund, Fidelity Magellan, has been used as a prime example of a fund that became too big to serve its shareholders' best interests. The widely publicized exit of its portfolio manager, Jeff Vinik, came as a surprise because, as the portfolio manager of the Fidelity Contrafund and Fidelity Growth and Income Fund, Vinik had consistently outperformed the industry benchmark, the S&P 500 Index, by a wide margin. A concern over a large upsurge in stock prices in 1995–1996 had led Vinik to sharply cut his fund's equity holdings in favor of long-term U.S. T-bonds, and unfortunately, the continued rise in the stock market caused the fund's return to significantly underperform the S&P 500 (*Economist* 1996). A long-term record of past achievement was apparently insufficient to outbalance a short-term performance deficit.

Reprinted from the *Financial Analysts Journal* (May/June 1999):74–87.

Nocera (1996) ascribed Magellan's failure to the fund's size: "Magellan [was] no longer manageable even for someone with Vinik's talent."

Fund size in general has become worrisome to mutual fund managers. Despite the swelling popularity of mutual funds, Saunders-Egodigwe and Franecki (1998) reported that mutual funds closed their doors to new investors at a record pace in 1998. This phenomenon and the Magellan example raise an interesting question: Does a rise in net assets under management have an adverse impact on a fund's investment performance?[1]

The perception that fund size can impede performance is a valid concern in a financial market where information acquisition and trading are costly and security prices are noisy reflections of intrinsic value. In such a market, the incentive for active management is that the economic gains to information compensate the fund manager for the costs of research and trading (Grossman 1976; Grossman and Stiglitz 1980). Mutual fund managers who efficiently (inefficiently) expend money to acquire and act on information should experience positive (negative) risk-adjusted returns net of expenses. In a contestable market for savings, investors penalize mutual fund managers who underperform as a consequence of overinvestment in information through (net) share redemptions.

The empirical results of prior studies that examined the relationship between risk-adjusted mutual fund returns and the costs of research (the expense ratio) and costs of trading (turnover) that are associated with active investment management are conflicting (Ippolito 1993). On the one hand, Sharpe (1966) observed that mutual funds with higher reward-to-volatility ratios tend to be those with lower expenses. On the other hand, Friend, Blume, and Crockett (1970) reported an insignificant negative correlation between risk-adjusted mutual fund returns and expense ratios and reported a slight positive relationship with turnover. Similarly, Ippolito (1989) found that risk-adjusted mutual fund returns are unrelated to expense ratios and turnover. But Elton, Gruber, Das, and Hlavka (1993) found that risk-adjusted returns exhibit a negative correlation with expense ratios and turnover when the difference in performance between small-capitalization non-S&P 500 stocks and S&P 500 stocks for the time periods covered in these studies were taken into account.

WHY FUND SIZE MATTERS

We believe the contradictory conclusions of prior research stem from a failure to recognize diminishing returns to scale in active investment management. The expense ratio and turnover do not capture all of the transaction costs associated with an active investment strategy. Because diseconomies of scale are associated with the costs of researching and trading on information, the economic value added by active management will, as Perold and Salomon (1991) suggested, depend on having the right amount of assets under management. Furthermore, the fund manager's investment style, we argue, will significantly influence the right amount of assets to have under management.

Growth in the size of net assets initially provides cost advantages because growth increases net returns. That is, because transaction volume is relatively larger for the larger funds, brokerage commissions on the execution of trades for large firms are lower. In addition, the costs of access to data, research services, and support, as well as administrative and overhead expenses, do not rise in direct proportion to fund size.

However, brokerage commissions are only "the tip of the transaction costs iceberg" (Wagner and Edwards 1993, p. 65). With uncontrolled growth in fund size comes cost disadvantages that reduce net returns. First, transaction costs increase because the purchase and sale of large blocks of stock exacerbate the liquidity and informational asymmetry problem for market makers and increase the bid–ask spread. Based on bid and offer quotes from specialists and market makers for different block sizes on a wide cross-section of stocks, Loeb (1983) found that the bid–ask spread increases dramatically with block size. On average, a change in block size from $1 million to $2.5 million increases the bid–ask spread by 170 basis points (bps) for medium-cap stocks and 70 bps for large-cap stocks. Moreover, whereas small block trades can be executed anonymously, large block trades are typically negotiated with intermediaries. A fund manager known to trade on information will incur a higher transaction cost to execute a large block trade than a manager known to follow a passive investment strategy. Because of the adverse market impact, a fund manager may choose to defer a trade or not execute it at all.

Second, the sheer size of a large fund makes it an obvious target for attention. Outsiders carefully examine the fund manager's stock selections for clues and insights into the manager's information and stock selection and/or market-timing strategy. As a consequence, the fund manager's ability to trade without signaling his or her intentions is greatly curtailed.

Third, a large influx of capital causes administrative stress. The organization has to hire new people to accommodate growth, and the portfolio management process may suffer. The problem of coordination intensifies as the number of portfolio managers grows, and the complexity of overseeing a large fund increases as the universe of stocks expands.

Last but not least, the growth in fund size may cause a manager to boost returns by deviating from the fund's stated investment objectives. As R.B. Clelland of R.J. Metcalf Associates pointed out (Herring 1996):

> "Size alone does not hamper money managers; the issue is style. . . . It really boils down to prudent restraints and portfolio diversification." (p. 18)

With increasing size, a fund manager is likely to engage in strategies (e.g., market timing) or invest in assets that would normally not have been chosen because of policy constraints (e.g., a policy limiting change in the value–growth orientation).

The impact of fund size on the net gains to information acquisition and trading will differ by style. The problem of limited investment opportunities as a fund grows can be particularly critical for value funds that specialize in undervalued large-cap stocks and growth funds that specialize in high-growth small-cap stocks.

SAMPLE DESCRIPTION

To examine the effect of fund size and investment style on the cross-sectional pattern of risk and return, we obtained a sample of 683 U.S. actively managed (nonindexed) equity mutual funds from Morningstar's Mutual Funds OnDisc database. For these funds, information on style is available for each year in the 1993–95 period.

Morningstar classifies funds into one of three investment styles on the value–growth spectrum. Depending on the fund manager's investment orientation/philosophy, a fund is categorized as growth oriented, value oriented, or a blend. Growth-oriented managers concentrate on companies whose earnings have the potential to grow faster than the rest of the market (stocks with high P/Es); value-oriented managers focus on undervalued companies that will eventually be recognized by the market (stocks with low price-to-tangible-book-value ratios, P/Bs). Managers who consciously invest in both growth and value stocks are blend-oriented managers.

The combination of the average P/E and P/B of the stocks in a fund's portfolio relative to the S&P 500 creates a composite measure of where each fund stands on the value–growth spectrum.[2] Morningstar assigns funds to one of the three categories on the basis of the sum of the two index (P/E and P/B) values. Funds with a sum of less than 1.75 are considered value funds; funds with combined ratios that are at least 1.75 but no more than 2.25 are considered blend funds; funds with an index sum greater than 2.25 are considered growth funds.

In addition to average P/Es and P/Bs, Morningstar also provides information on the median market capitalization of the companies in a fund's portfolio. Fama and French (1992) found that, collectively, P/E, P/B, and market capitalization explain the cross-sectional variation in equity returns better than beta or residual risk. In this article, beta is described by the fund's systematic risk relative to the S&P 500; residual risk is the fund's idiosyncratic (unsystematic) risk.

Each fund's return, expense ratio, turnover, and net assets for each year in the 1993–95 period are available from Morningstar. Annual fund returns are net of expenses.

Expense ratios and turnover data reflect the explicit transaction costs associated with research and trading on information. Individuals investing in mutual funds are predominantly passive, uninformed investors, and expense ratios are the costs they pay investment managers to become informed. The expense ratio is the portion of the fund's assets paid for operating expenses and management fees, including 12b-1 fees, administrative fees, and other asset-based costs incurred by the fund but excluding brokerage costs.

Turnover, measured by the lesser of purchases or sales (excluding all securities with maturities of less than one year) as a percentage of average monthly assets proxies for the information-induced trading activity of a fund during the year. A low turnover ratio indicates a buy-and-hold strategy; high turnover, a fund's active market-timing and/or stock selection strategy.

Fund size, defined as the natural logarithm of month-end net assets under management, embodies the implicit transaction costs associated with active investment.[3] Implicit transaction costs include the market impact of a large fund's trades on price and of the bid–ask spread, the opportunity costs of not implementing trades, and the costs of being under constant scrutiny, administrative stress, and deviations from style that result from a fund's excessive size.

DESCRIPTIVE STATISTICS

Table 13.1 shows the summary statistics for net assets under management, return, risk, style, and the information cost variables. All variables reported in the table were computed as three-year (1993–95) averages. So, for example, the average net assets amount for the total sample is $843.6 million. On average, value (growth) funds are the largest (smallest), with net assets of $943.5 million ($662.8 million).

Overall, mutual funds achieved a 13.40 percent average arithmetic annual return for the three years, approximately 188 bps lower than the average arithmetic return on the S&P 500 (15.28 percent).[4] Furthermore, note that growth (blend) funds were the best (worst) performers over the 1993–95 period.[5] Because the systematic risk (beta) of growth funds was not much higher than that of the value or blend funds, it is perhaps not surprising that the higher return for growth funds is coupled with a higher unsystematic (residual) risk.

In addition, significant differences are visible in the characteristics of stocks among fund types. Value funds invested in stocks with relatively larger average capitalizations and lower average P/Es and P/Bs than the growth funds. Blend funds invested in stocks whose average

TABLE 13.1 Mutual Fund Summary Statistics

Statistic	Fund Size: Net Assets (millions)	Three-Year Average Return	Morningstar Time-Series Risk Proxies		Morningstar Cross-Sectional Risk Proxies			Cost of Information and Trading Proxy	
			Beta	Residual	P/E	P/B	Median Market Cap (millions)	Expense Ratio	Turnover
All funds: N = 683									
Mean	$843.61	13.40%	0.87	7.09%	22.03×	3.54×	$5,400.31	1.31%	79.77%
Standard deviation	1,869.28	5.36	0.21	4.84	5.36	1.18	4,659.79	0.81	71.50
Median	217.13	13.19	0.88	5.80	20.75	3.43	4,299.00	1.19	60.67
Value: N = 218									
Mean	943.50	12.97	0.83	5.99	17.79	2.51	4,948.30	1.32	62.01
Standard deviation	1,988.86	4.48	0.20	3.60	2.32	0.52	3,726.93	1.07	49.20
Median	202.07	13.21	0.83	5.02	17.72	2.49	4,398.33	1.12	49.50
Blend: N = 272									
Mean	891.84	12.49	0.88	6.01	21.15	3.45	6,774.95	1.23	80.14
Standard deviation	2,072.79	4.64	0.19	3.72	2.22	0.59	5,226.92	0.75	64.46
Median	201.30	12.58	0.90	5.19	20.77	3.50	5,867.17	1.14	62.50
Growth: N = 193									
Mean	662.81	15.15	0.90	9.84	28.07	4.84	3,973.54	1.41	99.30
Standard deviation	1,352.51	6.67	0.26	6.21	5.57	1.09	4,232.37	0.52	93.91
Median	250.17	14.38	0.94	8.51	27.29	4.80	2,365.67	1.30	70.33
F-statistic	1.37	15.52***	6.67***	49.61***	448.10***	497.04***	23.34***	2.98*	14.48**

Note: The *F*-statistic tests whether there are significant differences in column variables across value, blend, and growth investment styles.
*Significant at the 10 percent level.
**Significant at the 5 percent level.
***Significant at the 1 percent level.

P/Es and P/Bs fell somewhere between the average P/Es and P/Bs of the value and growth funds but with capitalizations greater than those in the value and growth funds.

Moreover, as shown by the average expense ratios, the growth funds invested relatively more in research than the value funds and, as shown by the turnover, traded relatively more on information. Investment in research and trading for the blend funds fell in between those for the value and growth funds.[6]

To assess the importance of size on mutual fund performance, we sorted the full sample into 10 groups by size. Each group in the full sample contained an equal number of funds. The classification is shown in Table 13.2, where for each group, we report the three-year average net assets, average annual returns, average expense ratios, and average turnover.

The smallest and largest size groups in the full sample (Size Groups 1 and 10) had average net assets of, respectively, $15.8 million and $5.17 billion. Note that except for Size Group 10, the three-year average returns for the full sample increased monotonically as the size of net assets increased. Overall, fund performance was positively affected by an increase in the size of net assets. In addition, the expense ratio declined with the size of net assets. Turnover, however, did not show a clear pattern with respect to changes in the size of net assets.

We also separated each size group in the full sample into styles and carried out a χ^2 test to establish whether fund size was uniformly distributed within investment styles. As the χ^2-statistics in Table 13.2 indicate, the value and blend funds were uniformly distributed across fund size groups but the growth funds were not. Fewer growth funds were in the large size categories (Groups 9 and 10), and for each size group, growth funds had, in general, smaller net assets than the value and blend funds. In addition, the growth funds showed more variation in performance among size groups than did the value and blend funds, whose three-year average returns were relatively constant across Size Groups 2–10. Furthermore, except for Size Group 1, the growth funds had higher expense ratios than the value and blend funds. For the full sample, however, returns show an improvement (except for Size Group 10) and expense ratios decline when size increases. Finally, observe that the growth funds traded more actively than the value or blend funds. Although turnover for the value funds declined with the size of net assets, no relationship is apparent between turnover and the size of net assets for growth funds.

NET EFFECTS OF FUND SIZE

For the full sample, the effect of the size of a mutual fund's net assets under management on the fund's performance is presented in Table 13.3. We used two methods to adjust returns for risk. In Regression 1, risk was reflected in the fund's systematic (beta) and unsystematic (residual) risk. In Regression 2, we used the average P/E and P/B, as well as median market capitalization of the fund's stocks, to control for cross-sectional risk differences. The transaction cost variables, expense ratio and turnover, proxied for the extent of active management in Regressions 3 and 4. The effect of fund size is contained in Regressions 5 and 6.

Regression 1 shows that systematic and unsystematic risk capture the cross-sectional variation in mutual fund performance. The statistically significant coefficient estimates imply that risk bearing is rewarded. In Regression 2, P/E, P/B, and median market capitalization also proxy for risk. Moreover, the higher R^2 in this regression suggests that, collectively, P/E, P/B, and median market capitalization explain the cross-sectional variation in mutual fund

TABLE 13.2 Distribution of Return, Expense Ratio, and Turnover by Mutual Fund Size

Size Group (range in $ millions)	Number of Funds	Relative Frequency	Net Assets (millions)	Three-Year Return	Expense Ratio	Turnover
All funds						
1. (0 < Size ≤ 33.60)	69	10.10%	$ 15.80	8.94%	2.20%	99.40%
2. (33.60 < Size ≤ 60.10)	68	9.96	46.00	12.43	1.54	88.98
3. (60.10 < Size ≤ 100.90)	68	9.96	79.30	12.45	1.36	69.24
4. (100.90 < Size ≤ 151.70)	68	9.96	124.10	13.01	1.26	77.57
5. (151.70 < Size ≤ 216.80)	68	9.96	182.10	13.72	1.32	70.48
6. (216.80 < Size ≤ 337.20)	69	10.10	271.00	14.37	1.20	76.03
7. (337.20 < Size ≤ 543.20)	68	9.96	437.00	14.85	1.23	94.67
8. (543.20 < Size ≤ 894.30)	69	10.10	711.90	14.96	1.09	79.01
9. (894.30 < Size ≤ 2,146.60)	68	9.96	1,422.00	15.05	0.99	68.06
10. (2,146.60 < Size ≤ 21,020.10)	68	9.96	5,169.50	14.24	0.88	74.02
Value funds						
1	26	11.93	13.60	8.92	2.59	98.88
2	18	8.26	42.20	14.26	1.49	70.91
3	18	8.26	81.60	12.42	1.28	48.44
4	28	12.84	123.80	13.23	1.18	68.62
5	22	10.09	184.40	13.06	1.25	49.98
6	26	11.93	272.00	13.76	1.13	51.97
7	17	7.80	434.90	13.64	1.26	78.31
8	16	7.34	698.80	13.61	1.26	47.35
9	21	9.63	1,506.90	13.63	1.04	54.86
10	26	11.93	5,318.90	14.00	0.77	45.58
χ^2-statistic		8.15				

(*continued*)

TABLE 13.2 (continued)

Size Group (range in $ millions)	Number of Funds	Relative Frequency	Net Assets (millions)	Three-Year Return	Expense Ratio	Turnover
Blend funds						
1	31	11.40%	$ 18.10	9.96%	1.94%	86.99%
2	35	12.87	45.50	10.85	1.42	85.62
3	32	11.76	78.90	11.15	1.24	77.53
4	23	8.46	126.20	12.19	1.17	82.14
5	19	6.99	181.70	13.93	1.29	79.79
6	16	5.88	260.40	13.97	1.22	69.58
7	28	10.29	453.80	12.67	1.12	82.61
8	27	9.93	741.80	13.67	1.03	73.80
9	32	11.46	1,382.50	14.34	0.85	71.13
10	29	10.66	5,186.50	13.87	0.93	87.05
χ^2-statistic		12.34				
Growth funds						
1	12	6.22	14.50	6.31	2.02	132.58
2	15	7.77	51.70	12.92	1.89	118.49
3	18	9.33	78.00	14.77	1.65	75.30
4	17	8.81	121.80	13.76	1.51	86.14
5	27	13.99	180.60	14.10	1.41	80.62
6	27	13.99	276.40	15.19	1.25	103.02
7	23	11.92	418.10	18.41	1.34	121.43
8	26	13.47	688.90	17.13	1.20	103.92
9	15	7.77	1,387.30	18.57	1.21	80.00
10	13	6.74	4,832.60	15.52	0.96	101.87
χ^2-statistic		16.27*				

Note: The χ^2-statistic tests whether fund size was uniformly distributed within investment styles.
*Significant at the 10 percent level.

TABLE 13.3   Return Regressions for All Funds (dependent variable =
Average 1993–95 returns)

Independent Variable	Regression 1	Regression 2	Regression 3	Regression 4	Regression 5	Regression 6
Intercept	10.30*** (0.87)	9.38*** (0.98)	13.38*** (0.88)	12.70*** (0.94)	9.29*** (1.13)	8.31*** (1.20)
Beta	2.22** (0.95)		2.10** (0.88)		1.67** (0.85)	
Residual risk	0.17*** (0.04)		0.21*** (0.04)		0.18*** (0.04)	
P/E		0.11** (0.05)		0.15*** (0.05)		0.17*** (0.05)
P/B		0.62*** (0.23)		0.57*** (0.21)		0.32 (0.21)
Median market capitalization		−0.001** (0.0005)		−0.002*** (0.0004)		−0.0001*** (0.00004)
Expense ratio			−2.43*** (0.24)	−2.45*** (0.23)	−1.30*** (0.28)	−1.40*** (0.27)
Turnover			−0.002 (0.003)	−0.006** (0.003)	−0.001 (0.003)	−0.005* (0.003)
$\ln(NA)$					0.72*** (0.12)	0.69*** (0.12)
$\ln(NA) -$ $[\text{avg.}\ln(NA)]^2$					−0.26*** (0.05)	−0.22*** (0.05)
F-statistic					26.32***	22.73***
Adjusted R^2	0.03	0.06	0.17	0.21	0.23	0.26
N (number)	683	683	683	683	683	683

Notes: Standard errors are in parentheses. The term $\ln(NA)$ is the natural logarithm of the fund's net assets; the term avg.$\ln(NA)$ is the average $\ln(NA)$ across all funds. The F-statistic tests whether the coefficients of $\ln(NA)$ and $\ln[NA - \text{avg.}\ln(NA)]^2$ are jointly equal to zero.
*Significant at the 10 percent level.
**Significant at the 5 percent level.
***Significant at the 1 percent level.

performance better than do the systematic and unsystematic risk variables—a result consistent with the finding of Fama and French.

In Regressions 3 and 4, note that after adjusting for risk, mutual fund returns are negatively correlated with expense ratios. Because returns are net of expenses, the significant negative coefficients here suggest that mutual funds, on average, overinvest in information. Turnover also had a negative impact on return when P/E, P/B, and median market capitalization were used as proxies for risk.[7] The negative correlation between fund return, on the one hand, and expense ratio and turnover, on the other hand, is consistent with the findings of Elton et al. but contradicts the findings of Ippolito (1989).

In Regressions 5 and 6, we considered the impact of the size of net assets on a fund's return from investments in acquiring and trading on information through the linear and quadratic net asset variables—ln(NA) and [ln(NA) − avg.ln(NA)]^2.[8] The positive linear term coefficients in Regressions 5 and 6 imply increasing returns to active management from increases in the size of net assets. The significant negative coefficients of the quadratic term in Regressions 5 and 6, however, reveal a diminishing return to active management from increases in the size of net assets.[9] The joint significance of linear and quadratic net asset variables attested by the F-statistic confirms the belief shared by many practitioners that many funds are bigger than would be optimal.[10] Regressions 5 and 6 indicate, respectively, that an optimal fund would have $946 million and $1.1 billion of net assets.[11]

Table 13.4 shows the net gains to active management as the size of net assets increases. The columns titled "Regression 3" and "Regression 4" show the incremental contribution to return from the explicit costs of, respectively, acquiring and trading on information—that is, the expense ratio and turnover. The incremental contribution, which is negative for all fund size groups, confirms the findings of Elton et al. that active management hurts performance. This finding fails to consider, however, that the efficiency of active management may not be constant for all fund sizes. That is, because of size differences, the contribution of active management to various funds' returns may be different even though the costs of information acquisition and trading are the same.

The columns in Table 13.4 titled "Regression 5" and "Regression 6" report the incremental contribution to return from the cost of acquiring and trading on information when the size of net assets is taken into account. An interesting pattern emerges. Only the two smallest fund size groups continue to show a significant net loss to information activities. A minimum size of net assets apparently exists below which the return is insufficient to justify the cost of an active investment strategy.

In addition, beyond the breakeven size, the net gain to active management increases with the size of net assets. But as the size of net assets increases in Groups 3–9, the magnitude of the net gain is proportionally less with each successive group. The maximum net gain occurs in Size Group 9 with net assets ranging from $894 million to $2.1 billion. This result confirms the optimal size of net assets implied by Regressions 5 and 6 in Table 13.3. The decline in returns reflects the implicit costs associated with higher transaction costs on large purchase/sale orders, administrative stress, deviations from desired investment style, the opportunity costs of not implementing trades, and lack of the freedom to act without signaling intent.

To validate the finding that the efficiency of active management varies among fund sizes, we performed regressions of return against risk and the expense and turnover ratios for three composite groups of funds.[12] The first composite group consisted of funds in Size Groups 1 and 2 (see Table 13.4); the second consisted of funds in Size Groups 3 through 9; and the third consisted of funds in Size Group 10. The cutoffs corresponded to the breakeven and optimal sizes of net assets. The assumption in these regressions was that the efficiency of active management is different in the three composite groups but is the same within each composite group. The estimated regressions are shown in Table 13.5.

The coefficient for the expense ratio is significantly negative for Composite Groups 1 and 3 and insignificant for Composite Group 2 when the P/E, P/B, and median market capitalization were used to proxy for risk. The coefficient for turnover is significantly negative only for Composite Group 1; it is insignificant for Composite Groups 2 and 3. Because of the composition of the groups (given in the note to Table 13.5), Table 13.5 indicates that,

TABLE 13.4   The Impact of Expense Ratio and Turnover on Average Returns by Fund Size

| Size Group | Average Returns Reflecting the Impact of Expense Ratio and Turnover | | Average Returns Reflecting the Impact of Expense Ratio and Turnover Adjusted for Within-Group Variation in Fund Size | |
	Regression 3 (Table 13.3)	Regression 4 (Table 13.3)	Regression 5 (Table 13.3)	Regression 6 (Table 13.3)
1	−5.54%	−5.99%	−3.65%	−3.96%
2	−3.92	−4.31	−0.05	−0.57
	(2.66)***	(2.64)***	(6.80)***	(6.22)***
3	−3.44	−3.75	0.99	0.50
	(2.25)	(2.27)	(8.66)***	(6.89)***
4	−3.21	−3.55	1.65	1.08
	(1.12)	(0.72)	(6.08)***	(4.16)***
5	−3.34	−3.65	1.93	1.36
	(−0.86)	(−0.52)	(2.94)***	(2.37)
6	−3.07	−3.40	2.38	1.79
	(1.82)	(1.33)	(5.01)***	(3.78)***
7	−3.18	−3.58	2.57	1.90
	(−0.66)	(−1.12)	(2.06)	(0.88)
8	−2.80	−3.14	2.89	2.32
	(2.07)	(2.10)	(3.49)***	(3.25)***
9	−2.54	−2.83	3.01	2.55
	(1.56)	(1.70)	(1.31)	(1.95)
10	−2.29	−2.60	2.51	2.23
	(1.76)	(1.15)	(−4.94)***	(−2.72)***

Notes: The regression coefficients in Table 13.3 were used to generate the returns for each fund in Size Groups 1 through 10. The average returns reported in the table are the simple averages of the returns across all the funds within each size group. The average returns based on Regressions 3 and 4 ignore fund size; those based on Regressions 5 and 6 reflect the cross-sectional variation in fund size within each size group. *t*-Statistics (in parentheses) were computed from a two-sample *t*-test for two adjacent size groups. For instance, the first *t*-statistic is for the difference in means between Size Groups 2 and 1. ***Significant at the 1 percent level.

overall, 20 percent of the mutual funds are below the minimum size necessary to achieve breakeven and 10 percent of the largest funds overinvested in research. Furthermore, the negative turnover coefficient for Composite Group 1 indicates a trading inefficiency associated with higher transaction costs for small funds.

FUND SIZE AND INVESTMENT STYLE

To investigate the impact of the expense ratio and turnover on the returns to value, growth, and blend styles, we computed the net gains for each style as in Table 13.4, based on

TABLE 13.5   Return Regressions across Fund Size (Dependent variable = Average 1993–95 return)

Independent Variable	Composite Group 1	Composite Group 2	Composite Group 3	Composite Group 1	Composite Group 2	Composite Group 3
Intercept	14.93***	10.45***	13.73***	17.76***	8.97***	13.44***
	(1.94)	(1.11)	(2.21)	(2.16)	(1.22)	(3.68)
Beta	0.07	2.46***	2.05			
	(2.08)	(1.02)	(2.03)			
Residual risk	0.29	0.17***	−0.07			
	(0.09)	(0.05)	(0.10)			
P/E				0.12	0.23***	0.20
				(0.09)	(0.06)	(0.26)
P/B				−0.75	0.32	0.14
				(0.58)	(0.26)	(0.74)
Median market capitalization				−0.0001	−0.0001**	−0.0002*
				(0.00009)	(0.00005)	(0.0001)
Expense ratio	−2.64***	−0.05	−1.45	−2.61***	−0.57	−2.48*
	(0.30)	(0.53)	(1.41)	(0.31)	(0.52)	(1.42)
Turnover	−0.02***	0.003	0.006	−0.02**	0.001	−0.0007
	(0.005)	(0.004)	(0.007)	(0.005)	(0.003)	(0.008)
F-statistic	26.78***	6.26***	0.70	20.31***	13.03***	1.65
Adjusted R^2	0.43	0.04	−0.02	0.42	0.11	0.05
N	137	478	68	137	478	68

Notes: The risk proxies for the left panel are beta and residual risk; the risk proxies for the right panel are P/E, P/B, and median market capitalization. Standard errors are in parentheses. Composite groups are based on the last two columns of Table 13.4. Composite Group 1 consists of 137 funds in the first two size groups in Table 13.4. Composite Group 2 consists of 478 funds in Size Groups 3–9, and Composite Group 3 contains the 68 funds in Size Group 10.
*Significant at the 10 percent level.
**Significant at the 5 percent level.
***Significant at the 1 percent level.

Regressions 5 and 6 of fund return against risk, expense ratio, turnover ratio, and fund size reported in Table 13.3. Table 13.6 reports the results.

The patterns of net returns when the sample is divided by style are the same as the pattern for the overall sample: Net returns are negative in the two smallest size groups; as fund size increases, net returns turn positive and increase. Also, the marginal net returns to active management become negative as the fund exceeds an optimal size.

Regardless of the risk proxy, the value and blend funds, which have the most portfolio flexibility, experienced the highest average net gains in the study period. The simple average net gains (computed from the average returns of Size Groups 3–10 in Table 13.6) are 2.33 percent for the value funds and 2.32 percent for the blend funds when beta and residual risk were used and 1.89 percent for the value funds and 1.81 percent for the blend funds when P/E, P/B, and median market capitalization were used to proxy for risk. In contrast,

TABLE 13.6   Impact of Expense Ratio and Turnover on Average Returns by Mutual Fund Size across Investment Styles (impact adjusted for within-group variation in fund size)

Size Group	Number of Funds	Return Adjusted for Beta and Residual Risk	Return Adjusted for P/E, P/B, and Median Market Capitalization
Value funds			
1	26	−4.48	−4.79
2	18	−0.09	−0.52
		(4.36)***	(4.14)***
3	18	1.16	0.75
		(7.70)***	(6.96)***
4	28	1.75	1.23
		(4.13)***	(2.80)**
5	22	2.07	1.59
		(2.09)**	(1.93)*
6	26	2.50	2.01
		(2.72)**	(2.31)**
7	17	2.55	1.94
		(0.29)	(−0.35)
8	16	3.00	2.56
		(2.60)**	(2.99)***
9	21	2.94	2.54
		(−0.37)	(−0.11)
10	26	2.63*	2.49
		(−1.89)	(−0.29)
Blend funds			
1	31	−2.85	−3.14
2	35	0.09	−0.39
		(4.08)***	(3.79)***
3	32	1.13	0.62
		(6.26)***	(4.42)***
4	23	1.78	1.20
		(3.80)***	(2.61)**
5	19	1.96	1.36
		(1.05)	(0.71)
6	16	2.35	1.78
		(2.18)**	(1.80)*
7	28	2.74	2.14
		(2.26)**	(1.57)
8	27	2.99	2.56
		(1.83)*	(2.33)**
9	32	3.19	2.73
		(1.69)*	(1.11)
10	29	2.44	2.09
		(−5.07)***	(−3.81)***

(continued)

TABLE 13.6   (*continued*)

Size Group	Number of Funds	Return Adjusted for Beta and Residual Risk	Return Adjusted for P/E, P/B, and Median Market Capitalization
Growth funds			
1	12	−3.88	−4.26
2	15	−0.36	−1.04
		(3.54)***	(2.90)**
3	18	0.59	0.04
		(3.22)***	(2.93)***
4	17	1.30	0.68
		(3.14)***	(2.28)**
5	27	1.80	1.18
		(3.11)***	(2.51)**
6	27	2.30	1.60
		(3.66)***	(2.35)**
7	23	2.38	1.60
		(0.56)	(0.00)
8	26	2.73	2.04
		(2.46)**	(1.94)*
9	15	2.71	2.18
		(−0.10)	(0.60)
10	13	2.40	2.00
		(−1.30)	(−0.62)

Notes: The regression coefficients in Table 13.3 were used to generate the returns for each fund in Size Groups 1 through 10. The average returns reported in the table are the simple averages of the returns across all the funds within each size group. The average returns based on Regressions 3 and 4 ignore fund size; those based on Regressions 5 and 6 reflect the cross-sectional variation in fund size within each size group. *t*-statistics (in parentheses) were computed from a two-sample *t*-test for two adjacent size groups.
*Significant at the 10 percent level.
**Significant at the 5 percent level.
***Significant at the 1 percent level.

growth funds, with the least portfolio flexibility, have the lowest average net gains to active management. The average gain is 2.03 percent when beta and residual risk were used and 1.42 percent when P/E, P/B, and median market capitalization were used to proxy for risk. In other words, the constraint associated with a limited opportunity set affects growth funds more than value or blend funds. The smaller the median market capitalization of stocks in a fund, the lower the volume and supply of available securities. These stocks tend to be scarce and relatively illiquid. So, eventually, a large influx of money forces growth fund managers to either look elsewhere or close their funds.

Table 13.7 examines the impact of investment style on the incremental contribution to return from active management. For each investment style, fund returns were regressed against risk, expense ratio, turnover, and fund size.

Note that value managers tend to overinvest in research when compared with growth managers. This outcome should be expected because Table 13.1 indicates that value fund

TABLE 13.7   Return Regressions by Investment Orientation (Dependent variable = Average 1993–95 return)

Independent Variable	Value	Blend	Growth	Value	Blend	Growth
Intercept	12.21***	12.81***	−0.26	13.44***	7.79***	−1.77
	(1.51)	(1.62)	(3.09)	(2.28)	(3.24)	(3.98)
Beta	3.87**	−0.18	1.82			
	(1.23)	(1.33)	(1.66)			
Residual risk	−0.09	0.49	0.18***			
	(0.07)	(0.69)	(0.07)			
P/E				0.09	0.33***	0.15*
				(0.12)	(0.12)	(0.08)
P/B				0.03	−0.49	0.57
				(0.58)	(0.45)	(0.39)
Median market capitalization				−0.0000	0.0000	−0.0003**
				(0.0000)	(0.0000)	(0.0001)
Expense ratio	−2.31***	−2.07***	2.08**	−2.29***	−2.13***	1.70**
	(0.29)	(0.41)	(0.98)	(0.30)	(0.42)	(0.96)
Turnover	0.010**	−0.006	−0.001	0.008	−0.007*	−0.003
	(0.005)	(0.004)	(0.005)	(0.005)	(0.004)	(0.005)
ln(NA)	0.16	0.54***	1.86***	0.16	0.53***	1.82***
	(0.16)	(0.16)	(0.34)	(0.16)	(0.16)	(0.34)
ln(NA) − [avg.ln(NA)]^2	−0.11*	−0.12*	−0.49***	−0.10*	−0.12*	−0.51***
	(0.06)	(0.07)	(0.12)	(0.06)	(0.07)	(0.12)
F-statistic	13.26***	15.97***	11.36***	17.84***	15.66***	11.92***
Adjusted R^2	0.38	0.25	0.24	0.35	0.27	0.28
N	218	272	193	218	272	193

Notes: The risk proxies for the left panel are beta and residual risk; the risk proxies for the right panel are P/E, P/B, and median market capitalization. Standard errors are in parentheses. The F-statistic tests whether all the coefficients of the independent variables are jointly equal to zero.
*Significant at the 10 percent level.
**Significant at the 5 percent level.
***Significant at the 1 percent level.

managers tend to invest in the relatively large-cap stocks of well-followed companies whereas growth managers tend to invest in the opposite. Furthermore, trading on information is significant and contributes positively to the return for value funds but is not important for growth funds. This outcome is also not surprising; value managers focus on the shares of undervalued companies that the funds expect will eventually be recognized by the market and, once they are correctly priced, will be sold. In contrast, growth managers concentrate on the shares of companies whose earnings have the potential to grow faster than the rest of the market, so these shares should be sold less frequently—only when the prospects for growth

TABLE 13.8   Distribution of Style-Consistent Funds by Investment Orientation

Statistic	Value	Blend	Growth	All Funds
Style-consistent funds				
Frequency	165	139	125	429
Percent	24.2	20.3	18.3	62.8
Row percent	38.5	32.4	29.1	
Column percent	75.7	51.1	64.8	
Style-inconsistent funds				
Frequency	53	133	68	254
Percent	7.8	19.5	9.9	37.2
Row percent	20.9	52.4	26.8	
Column percent	24.3	48.9	35.2	
Total frequency	218	272	193	683
Total percent (rounded)	31.9	39.8	28.3	100.0
χ^2-statistic	31.75***			

Note: The χ^2-statistic tests that funds are uniformly distributed across investment style and style consistency.
***Significant at the 1 percent level.

fall off. The contribution of blend fund managers to performance naturally falls somewhere between those of value and growth managers.

The size of net assets is more important for growth funds than for value or blend funds. As Table 13.7 shows, the coefficients associated with size are larger in magnitude and significance for growth than for the value or blend funds. The optimal size of net assets is $1.4 billion to $1.5 billion for growth funds, compared with $493 million to $510 million for value funds and $1.9 billion to $2.0 billion for blend funds.[13]

FUND SIZE AND STYLE CONSISTENCY

The distribution of style-consistent and style-inconsistent funds by investment style is shown in Table 13.8 and by the three composite fund size groups is shown in Table 13.9. Style-inconsistent funds are those that switched style in any one of the two years in the three-year sample period. We found that the likelihood that a fund is style consistent depends on its investment style. That is, value funds were more style consistent than growth funds; blend funds were the least style consistent. Furthermore, the proportion of style-inconsistent funds was relatively smaller for funds in Size Groups 3–9 than for funds in Size Groups 1, 2, or 10—that is, those with, respectively, the smallest and largest average net assets.

Table 13.10 shows results of an investigation into the impact of style inconsistency on the efficiency of active management across fund sizes. For the three composite groups of

TABLE 13.9   Distribution of Style-Consistent Funds across Fund Size

Statistic	Composite Group 1	Composite Group 2	Composite Group 3	All Funds
Style-consistent funds				
Frequency	76	310	43	429
Percent	11.1	45.4	6.3	62.8
Row percent	17.7	72.3	10.0	
Column percent	55.5	64.9	63.2	
Style-inconsistent funds				
Frequency	61	168	25	254
Percent	8.9	24.6	3.7	37.2
Row percent	24.0	66.1	9.8	
Column percent	44.5	35.2	36.8	
Total frequency	137	478	68	683
Total percent (rounded)	20.0	70.0	10.0	100.0
χ^2-statistic	4.02			

Notes: The χ^2-statistic tests that funds are uniformly distributed across size and style consistency. See Table 13.5 for an explanation of the composition of composite groups.

funds, we regressed returns against risk, the expense ratio, turnover, and a style-inconsistency dummy variable.

No marginal benefit resulted for maintaining style consistency for the 20 percent smallest funds below the minimum size necessary to achieve breakeven or for the 10 percent largest funds that overinvested in research. The negative turnover coefficient for Group 1 still indicates a trading inefficiency associated with high transaction costs. Maintaining style consistency was clearly beneficial for the 70 percent of funds whose sizes were optimal.

CONCLUSION

Prior studies relating mutual fund returns to the cost of acquiring and trading on information failed to recognize that the efficiency of an active investment management strategy depends on the size of net assets under management. The net returns from active management can be significantly different for funds even if their expense ratios and turnover are the same. We found that actively managed mutual funds have to attain a minimum fund size before they achieve returns sufficient to cover their costs for acquiring and trading on information. We also found that there are diminishing marginal returns to information activities and that the marginal returns become negative when a mutual fund exceeds its optimal size. Overall, 70 percent of the funds in our sample invested efficiently in information activities, and this percentage was approximately the same for the different investment styles. We found evidence of trading inefficiency in 20 percent of the funds in our sample because their size was

TABLE 13.10   Return Regressions across Fund Sizes
(Dependent variable = Average 1993–95 return)

Independent Variable	Composite Group 1	Composite Group 2	Composite Group 3	Composite Group 1	Composite Group 2	Composite Group 3
Intercept	14.78*** (1.96)	10.78*** (1.12)	13.89*** (2.22)	17.62*** (2.18)	9.38*** (1.23)	13.07*** (3.70)
Beta	0.05 (2.09)	2.47*** (1.02)	2.06 (2.03)			
Residual risk	0.29 (0.09)	0.17*** (0.04)	−0.08 (0.10)			
P/E				0.11 (0.09)	0.22*** (0.06)	0.22 (0.26)
P/B				−0.74 (0.58)	0.30 (0.26)	0.11 (0.74)
Median market capitalization				−0.0001 (0.00009)	−0.0001** (0.00005)	−0.0002* (0.0001)
Expense ratio	−2.66*** (0.31)	−0.13 (0.53)	−1.41 (1.41)	−2.63*** (0.31)	−0.62 (0.52)	−2.41* (1.42)
Turnover	−0.02*** (0.005)	0.004 (0.004)	0.008 (0.007)	−0.02*** (0.005)	0.002 (0.003)	−0.001 (0.008)
Style inconsistency	0.49 (0.64)	−0.74** (0.33)	−0.64 (0.69)	0.33 (0.66)	−0.59* (0.32)	−0.63 (0.67)
F-statistic	21.48***	6.03***	0.73	16.87***	11.46***	1.51
Adjusted R^2	0.43	0.05	−0.02	0.41	0.11	0.04
N	137	478	68	137	478	68

Notes: Standard errors are in parentheses. See Table 13.5 for an explanation of the composition of the composite groups. The style-inconsistency dummy variable is 0 if the fund was style consistent and 1 if the fund was style inconsistent.
*Significant at the 10 percent level.
**Significant at the 5 percent level.
***Significant at the 1 percent level.

below the minimum to achieve efficiencies and of overinvestment in research in 10 percent of the largest funds in our sample. Finally, we found that blend and value funds experience higher average net gains to information activities than do growth funds.

NOTES

1. *Mutual Funds Magazine* (1997); Edgerton (1997); Herring (1996); and Zweig (1996).
2. Morningstar uses relative rather than absolute ratios to recognize that a P/E value of 15 and a P/B value of 1.5 may be cheap in one market environment but expensive in another.

3. In general, transaction costs associated with price impact, timing costs, and the opportunity costs of not implementing trades are very difficult to measure for institutional fund managers (Wagner and Edwards; Keim and Madhavan 1998). Bogle (1994) suggested multiplying the fund's turnover ratio by 2 and then by 0.6 percent to measure the lower bound of the performance drag attributed to transaction costs.

4. The S&P 500 returns were 9.99 percent, 1.31 percent, and 37.5 percent, respectively, for 1993, 1994, and 1995.

5. Lakonishok, Shleifer, and Vishny (1994) found that value stocks outperform growth stocks. Our Table 13.1 shows that growth funds outperformed value funds in the period studied. The reason for this difference is that Lakonishok et al. examined the returns of the *potential* portfolio of stocks that could have been chosen by the fund; we analyzed the returns from the fund's actual portfolio. The use of a shorter sample period in our analysis may also explain this difference.

6. In related research, we found that investment in research and trading was greater for actively managed funds than for indexed funds; the average expense ratio was 1.31 percent and turnover was 79.77 percent for the actively managed funds, whereas the average expense ratio was 0.41 percent and average turnover was 19.20 percent for the index funds.

7. The reason turnover has a significant coefficient in Regression 4 but not in Regression 3 is probably because a missing risk factor is not completely captured by beta and residual risk.

8. We also modeled the quadratic term as $[\ln(NA)]^2$. The results were virtually unchanged from those presented in Regressions 5 and 6.

9. Because P/E, P/B, and median market capitalization have also been considered to be anomalies, we reran Regression 5 to include these three variables and found our qualitative conclusions were unchanged.

10. See comments by Tricia Rothschild (Morningstar senior analyst) in Saunders-Egodigwe and Franecki. Also see Edgerton; Herring; Nocera; and Zweig.

11. The linear and quadratic terms in the regressions in Table 13.3 reflect the overall benefits and costs of fund size to the fund's average return. If returns are increasing at a diminishing rate with respect to fund size, then we expect the coefficient of the linear term to be positive and the coefficient of the quadratic term to be negative. The optimal fund size is obtained by taking the first derivative of the linear and quadratic terms with respect to fund size. The avg.$\ln(NA)$ is 5.447. The optimal fund size is computed as avg.$\ln(NA) - (\beta_1/2\beta_2)$, where β_1 and β_2 are the coefficients of the linear and quadratic terms, respectively.

12. The sample size limited the number of fund size groups we could consider without sacrificing statistical power.

13. In analyzing more than 25,000 trades of four investment strategies used by his firm, John Bogle (in Rowland 1998) found that trading, timing, and opportunity costs negatively affect the dollar excess returns of the strategies. He concluded that a fund should be closed as soon as its optimal size is reached. A study by Morningstar (in Curtis 1998) confirmed Bogle's conclusion.

REFERENCES

Bogle, J. 1994. *Bogle on Mutual Funds*. Burr Ridge, IL: Irwin Professional Publishing.

Curtis, Carol E. 1998. "Demon Bloat." *Bloomberg Personal Finance* (September/October): 119–123.

Economist. 1996. "Fidelity's Fallen Star." vol. 339, no. 7968 (June 1):67–68.

Edgerton, Jerry. 1997. "As Magellan Closes, the Question Is: Is Your Fund Too Big for Its Britches?" *Money*, vol. 26, no. 10 (October):52.

Elton, Edwin J., Martin J. Gruber, Sanjiv Das, and Matthew Hlavka. 1993. "Efficiency with Costly Information: A Reinterpretation of Evidence from Managed Portfolios." *Review of Financial Studies*, vol. 6, no. 1 (Spring):1–22.

Fama, Eugene F., and Kenneth R. French. 1992. "The Cross-Section of Expected Stock Returns." *Journal of Finance*, vol. 47, no. 2 (June):427–465.

Friend, Irwin, Marshall E. Blume, and John Crockett. 1970. *Mutual Funds and Other Institutional Investors*. New York: McGraw-Hill.

Grossman, Sanford. 1976. "On the Efficiency of Competitive Stock Markets When Traders Have Diverse Information." *Journal of Finance*, vol. 31, no. 2 (June):573–585.

Grossman, Sanford, and Joseph Stiglitz. 1980. "On the Impossibility of Informationally Efficient Markets." *American Economic Review*, vol. 70, no. 3 (June):393–408.

Herring, Jenny L. 1996. "When Does Fund Size Affect Performance?" *Pension Management*, vol. 32, no. 4 (April):18–20.

Ippolito, Richard A. 1989. "Efficiency with Costly Information: A Study of Mutual Fund Performance, 1965–1984." *Quarterly Journal of Economics*, vol. 104, no. 1 (February):1–23.

———. 1993. "On Studies of Mutual Fund Performance, 1962–1991." *Financial Analysts Journal*, vol. 49, no. 1 (January/February):42–50.

Keim, Donald B., and Ananth Madhavan. 1998. "The Cost of Institutional Equity Trades." *Financial Analysts Journal*, vol. 54, no. 4 (July/August):50–69.

Lakonishok, Josef, Andrei Shleifer, and Robert W. Vishny. 1994. "Contrarian Investment, Extrapolation, and Risk." *Journal of Finance*, vol. 49, no. 5 (December):1541–78.

Loeb, Thomas F. 1983. "Trading Cost: The Critical Link between Investment Information and Results." *Financial Analysts Journal*, vol. 39, no. 3 (May/June):39–43.

Mutual Funds Magazine. 1997. "Point/Counterpoint: Does Fund Size Impede Performance?" (February):82–83.

Nocera, Joseph. 1996. "Time to Bail Out of the Magellan Fund?" *Fortune*, vol. 133, no. 5 (March):128–129.

Perold, André, and Robert Salomon. 1991. "The Right Amount of Assets under Management." *Financial Analysts Journal*, vol. 47, no. 3 (May/June):31–39.

Rowland, Mary. 1998. "Get the Air Out." *Bloomberg Personal Finance* (July/August): 115–117.

Saunders-Egodigwe, Laura, and David Franecki. 1998. "Slam: Mutual-Fund Closings Set a Record Pace." *Wall Street Journal* (May 21):C1, C21.

Sharpe, William F. 1966. "Mutual Fund Performance." *Journal of Business*, vol. 39, no. 1 (January):19–38.

Wagner, Wayne H., and Mark Edwards. 1993. "Best Execution." *Financial Analysts Journal*, vol. 49, no. 1 (January/February):65–71.

Zweig, Jason. 1996. "Today's Hottest Funds Are Too Big for Their Britches." *Money*, vol. 25, no. 4 (April):146–157.

CHAPTER 14

MULTIPERIOD ARITHMETIC ATTRIBUTION

José Menchero, CFA

This article presents a set of qualitative characteristics and quantitative properties for arithmetic multiperiod performance attribution. Such characteristics and properties are essential for ensuring a sound and accurate linking of attribution effects over time. A comparison of various linking algorithms within this framework shows that linking algorithms that are not consistent with this set of quantitative properties can exhibit spurious effects that distort the attribution analysis.

Performance attribution is widely used by plan sponsors, consultants, and fund managers for the purpose of measuring and explaining portfolio performance relative to a benchmark. The objective is to quantify the impact that active management decisions have on the relative performance (i.e., active return) over a given interval of time. More specifically, for each decision made for a portfolio, those measuring performance calculate and associate a number, known as the "attribution effect," that quantitatively measures the amount by which the decision affected the relative performance. The attribution effects aggregated together fully account for the relative performance. Such an analysis is extremely powerful for identifying which aspects of an investment strategy have been most responsible for adding or subtracting value, and therefore, the analysis constitutes important feedback for monitoring and evaluating the investment process.

Because attribution effects describe the impact of active management decisions, it is important that the attribution model reflect the decision-making process. Not surprisingly, therefore, many approaches exist for decomposing relative performance. For instance, equity portfolio managers who use a fundamental risk model in their investment strategies may also decompose the relative performance in terms of active exposures to the same underlying risk factors (as discussed by, for example, Grinold and Kahn 2000). The most widely used performance attribution method for equity portfolios, however, is the so-called sector-based

Reprinted from the *Financial Analysts Journal* (July/August 2004):76–91.

approach. This method is sometimes also known as the Brinson model (see Brinson and Fachler 1985; Brinson, Hood, and Beebower 1995) and has gained widespread popularity because of its intuitiveness and transparency. In this model—described in greater detail later—attribution effects are defined that explain the results of sector selection, stock selection, and the simultaneous action of the two (the interaction effect).

Sector-based approaches have also been developed for the more general case of attribution involving multiple currencies as well as currency hedging. For instance, Ankrim and Hensel (1994) described a model that divides the currency effect into a forward premium and a currency surprise and defines the allocation effect in terms of local country returns. Singer and Karnosky (1995), in contrast, introduced an analysis that measures the allocation effect with respect to the "local risk premium" (i.e., excess return above the cash rate) and defines the currency effect to include the currency return (because of exchange rate fluctuations) as well as the cash return.

Fixed-income managers typically use specialized attribution models that incorporate the effects of yield-curve movements. For instance, Lord (1997) introduced an attribution model that decomposes the relative performance into various effects defined with respect to a synthetic duration-matched U.S. T-bond. Campisi (2000) discussed an attribution model that involves fewer effects but nonetheless uses the same concept of a duration-matched Treasury security. Van Breukelen (2000) proposed a substantially different decomposition in which the allocation effect is defined in terms of durations and changes in yield and the currency effect is defined in a fashion similar to that proposed by Singer and Karnosky. In yet another approach, described by Ramaswamy (2001), the performance attribution analysis is accomplished within the context of a fixed-income risk model.

Although these approaches differ substantially in their decomposition of relative performance, they are similar in that all are based on a single-period analysis. As they stand, these models may, therefore, be useful in describing the relative performance for a day, a week, or (for low-turnover portfolios) perhaps even as much as a month. Usually, however, one is interested in describing relative performance over a longer period—say, a quarter or a year. (I refer here to this longer period as the "reporting period.") Thus, these models by themselves are of little use to practitioners because, typically, several portfolio rebalancings will occur during a reporting period. To apply performance attribution to the real world, a multiperiod approach is required. The objective in such an approach is to take the components of relative performance (i.e., attribution effects) and link them over time to explain the sources of active return for the reporting period. The central challenge is to accomplish this goal in a way that fully preserves the fundamental meaning and interpretation of the attribution effects as defined by the single-period decomposition.

Unfortunately, a great deal of confusion and controversy exists over how best to accomplish such linking over multiple periods. A number of papers have appeared since 1999 proposing a variety of methodologies for linking attribution effects across time. To complicate matters, two formulations of performance attribution exist—arithmetic and geometric. The arithmetic formula measures relative performance by a difference, whereas the geometric formula measures it by a ratio. In addition, considerable confusion exists concerning the relationship between arithmetic and geometric attribution. For instance, as the reader will see later, many of the algorithms that appear on the surface to be arithmetic turn out to be, on closer inspection, arithmetic/geometric hybrids.

Until now, practitioners have had no framework within which to understand and compare the various approaches to multiperiod attribution. The aim of this article is to provide such a framework and, in doing so, to elucidate and clarify the principles underlying multi-period performance attribution.

ARITHMETIC VS. GEOMETRIC MEASURES

Performance attribution measures relative performance. Therefore, clearly specifying *how* relative performance is measured in a method is of central importance. This requirement leads naturally to the notion of a relative performance measure, which I will refer to as a relative performance "metric." The metric is specified by the mathematical form of the linking algorithm. Conceptually, however, a metric can be thought of simply as a measuring stick that is used to measure and compare relative performance.

Keep in mind that the arithmetic measure of relative performance is given by a difference, whereas the geometric counterpart is given by a ratio. Specifically, let R_t be the portfolio return for period t, and let $\bar{R}_t$ be the corresponding return for the benchmark. The arithmetic relative performance is then given by

$$R_t - \bar{R}_t \tag{14.1}$$

and the geometric result is given by

$$\frac{1 + R_t}{1 + \bar{R}_t}. \tag{14.2}$$

Understanding and appreciating the differences between these two measures is important. Insight can be gained by stating Expression 2 in percentage terms—that is,

$$\frac{1 + R_t}{1 + \bar{R}_t} - 1 = \frac{R_t - \bar{R}_t}{1 + \bar{R}_t}. \tag{14.3}$$

Thus, the geometric relative performance is equal to the arithmetic value discounted by $1 + \bar{R}_t$. The two measures, therefore, are indeed different and can sometimes lead to seemingly contradictory results. For instance, suppose that Portfolio Manager A obtains a 30 percent return for a period versus 20 percent for Benchmark A. Further suppose that Portfolio Manager B obtains a 9 percent return versus 0 percent for Benchmark B. According to the arithmetic measure, Manager A had superior performance relative to that of Manager B (excess returns of 10 percent versus 9 percent). The geometric measure, however, leads to the opposite conclusion (8.33 percent versus 9 percent).

Some practitioners prefer the geometric measure because it reflects their view that outperforming a benchmark by a fixed amount in a down market is indeed more difficult than doing so in an up market. Nonetheless, the arithmetic measure retains widespread popularity because it is regarded as more intuitive. Keep in mind, however, that both measures are simply *definitions*, so to regard one or the other as either "correct" or "incorrect" is not appropriate. Once a measure is chosen, however, to avoid generating spurious effects and nonintuitive distortions, it is important to apply the measure consistently across multiple periods.

SINGLE-PERIOD SECTOR-BASED DECOMPOSITION

To put the concepts presented here in concrete form, I briefly review the basics of sector-based performance attribution. Assume for the moment a single-period buy-and-hold situation. Portfolio return R_t for the single period t can be written as the weighted-average return over N sectors:

$$R_t = \sum_{i=1}^{N} w_{it} r_{it}, \tag{14.4}$$

where w_{it} and r_{it} are, respectively, the portfolio weights and returns for sector i and period t. The benchmark quantities are denoted by an overbar; thus, the benchmark return is

$$\bar{R}_t = \sum_{i=1}^{N} \bar{w}_{it} \bar{r}_{it}. \tag{14.5}$$

Note that the correct weights to use in Equations 14.4 and 14.5 are the beginning-of-period weights.

The arithmetic active return is thus

$$R_t - \bar{R}_t = \sum_{i=1}^{N} w_{it} r_{it} - \sum_{i=1}^{N} \bar{w}_{it} \bar{r}_{it}. \tag{14.6}$$

This return can be broken down in several ways. A common approach is to identify three sources of active return. The "issue selection" (also known as "stock selection" or "selection effect") is defined in terms of the benchmark sector weights:[1]

$$I_{it} = \bar{w}_{it} (r_{it} - \bar{r}_{it}). \tag{14.7}$$

Issue selection measures how well the portfolio manager selected securities within the sector. As is obvious in Equation 14.7, issue selection depends *only* on the weights and returns within the sector. For example, stock selection in the large-capitalization equity sector does not depend on weights and returns in, say, the mid-cap equity sector.

"Sector selection" (also known as the "allocation effect") is defined as

$$S_{it} = (w_{it} - \bar{w}_{it})(\bar{r}_{it} - \bar{R}_t) \tag{14.8}$$

and measures how well the portfolio manager overweighted the sectors that performed better than the benchmark (or underweighted the underperforming sectors). Observe that sector selection depends *only* on the sector weights and returns and the total benchmark return.

The "interaction effect" is defined strictly in terms of sector weights and returns,

$$U_{it} = (w_{it} - \bar{w}_{it})(r_{it} - \bar{r}_{it}), \tag{14.9}$$

and measures the simultaneous action of the allocation and selection decisions. A positive interaction effect is obtained by overweighting sectors that have positive issue selection (or by underweighting sectors with negative issue selection).

From Equations 14.7–14.9, the active return for a single period can be expressed as

$$R_t - \bar{R}_t = \sum_{i=1}^{N} (I_{it} + S_{it} + U_{it}). \tag{14.10}$$

Equation 14.10 expresses the relative performance as a sum of attribution effects that fully accounts for the active return for the period.

METHODS' CHARACTERISTICS AND PROPERTIES

The following set of qualitative characteristics and quantitative properties are, I believe, essential for carrying out sound and accurate multiperiod attribution. Although the qualitative characteristics are not controversial, stating them explicitly is nevertheless useful because they provide a valuable basis for discussing and comparing the various linking methodologies.

Any multiperiod algorithm (i.e., arithmetic or geometric) should exhibit the following qualitative characteristics:

- *Intuitiveness.* The results of the model should conform to reasonable expectations and not introduce spurious effects into the analysis. For instance, if a fund manager clearly exhibits positive issue selection for a quarter, then the algorithm should generate a positive number—not a negative one.
- *Transparency.* The underlying structure of the algorithm should be easy to ascertain.
- *Robustness.* The algorithm should give sound and accurate results under any set of reasonable market conditions.

Before I address the quantitative properties, consider how relative performance is defined arithmetically and geometrically over multiple periods. Arithmetically, relative performance is simply the difference in compounded returns, $R - \bar{R}$, where

$$1 + R = \prod_{t=1}^{T}(1 + R_t), \tag{14.11a}$$

$$1 + \bar{R} = \prod_{t=1}^{T}(1 + \bar{R}_t), \tag{14.11b}$$

and T is the number of periods. The well-known difficulty in arithmetic attribution is that, because of geometric compounding, the active returns do not add across time; that is,

$$R - \bar{R} \neq \sum_{t=1}^{T}(R_t - \bar{R}_t). \tag{14.12}$$

The implication is that arithmetic attribution effects cannot simply be added together for multiple periods without introducing an unexplained residual.

In contrast, linking geometric relative performance for multiple periods is straightforward via simple multiplication:

$$\frac{1 + R}{1 + \bar{R}} = \left(\frac{1 + R_1}{1 + \bar{R}_1}\right)\left(\frac{1 + R_2}{1 + \bar{R}_2}\right)\cdots\left(\frac{1 + R_T}{1 + \bar{R}_T}\right) = \prod_{t=1}^{T}\left(\frac{1 + R_t}{1 + \bar{R}_t}\right). \tag{14.13}$$

So, by defining relative performance in terms of a ratio, the geometric approach circumvents the linking difficulties associated with multiperiod attribution within the arithmetic formulation. The clean, natural, and rigorous fashion in which multiperiod attribution is accomplished in the geometric framework provides motivation for the following quantitative properties that arithmetic attribution should also satisfy:

- *Absence of residuals.* The geometric model fully accounts for the relative performance without residuals, so the arithmetic linking algorithms should also avoid the introduction of unexplained residuals.

- *Commutativity.* This characteristic means that the attribution analysis should be independent of the ordering of the periods. In other words, simply interchanging two of the periods should not affect the results. Equation 14.11 clearly shows that time-weighted returns are commutative. It follows that relative performance (both arithmetic and geometric) is also commutative. Given that relative performance is independent of the ordering of the periods, it seems both clear and desirable that the *components* of relative performance (i.e., attribution effects) also be independent of the ordering of periods. Attribution methodologies that depend on the ordering of the periods introduce an artificial dimension into performance attribution analysis. Furthermore, if one were to accept the notion that performance attribution somehow should depend on the ordering of the periods, then one would have to conclude that geometric attribution (which is commutative) is fundamentally incorrect. However, as noted earlier, arithmetic and geometric methods should not be considered in terms of "correct" or "incorrect" but simply as two different ways of measuring active return.
- *Metric preservation.* Two periods that have identical relative performance should contribute equally to relative performance when they are linked together. For instance, if the geometric relative performance is 1.03 (i.e., 3 percent) for, say, Periods 1 and 2, then from Equation 14.13, both periods when linked together continue to contribute equally to relative performance. Arithmetically, the same result should also hold. To say that two periods have identical relative performance when viewed independently but contribute differently to the relative performance when linked together is not consistent. It would imply that the measuring stick was either applied inconsistently or was faulty to begin with. The concept of metric preservation should hold at the fund level as well as at the sector level. That is, two decisions that occur in different periods but generate identical amounts of relative performance should, when linked together, contribute equally to total relative performance. Algorithms that fail to ensure this basic condition (or fail to adhere to it as closely as possible) can exhibit inaccuracies because they, in essence, distort the measuring stick from one period to the next.[2]
- *Ability to be fully linked.* Although this property does not follow directly from Equation 14.13, the ability to decompose relative performance at, first, the fund level and, then, down at the sector level (and even to the level of individual securities) is clearly desirable. The attribution effects at each sublevel should exactly aggregate to the result at the higher level.

These quantitative properties are eminently reasonable and form a sound theoretical basis for understanding and accomplishing multiperiod attribution. The reader should be wary of being led astray, however, by subtle theoretical arguments (from this author or any other). The proof of the merit of any linking methodology ultimately rests not on its level of mathematical sophistication (or lack thereof) but, rather, on the sensibility of the results that are produced by the algorithm. Attribution, after all, is intended to be a practical tool for understanding how active management decisions have affected relative performance. If the linking methodology clouds and distorts this picture, then the value of the analysis itself is diminished. The comparison of the various multiperiod arithmetic algorithms that follows uses this framework of properties and characteristics.

ARITHMETIC ALGORITHMS

The various approaches to arithmetic multiperiod attribution can generally be classified into four categories: (1) linking coefficient approaches, (2) compounded notional portfolio methods, (3) recursive models, and (4) *ad hoc* smoothing algorithms.

Linking Coefficient Approaches

As shown by Equation 14.12, active returns cannot be simply added across multiple periods without generating a residual. If the active returns for each period are multiplied by linking coefficients, however, the returns can be added in a residual-free fashion. Intuitively, the linking coefficients should be thought of as scaling factors that incorporate the effects of geometric compounding. In other words, the linking coefficients, β_t, are constructed to satisfy the following equation:

$$R - \bar{R} = \sum_{t=1}^{T} \beta_t (R_t - \bar{R}_t). \tag{14.14}$$

The same linking coefficients are also used to link the attribution effects: Let $\hat{I}_{it}$, $\hat{S}_{it}$, and $\hat{U}_{it}$ be the amount that sector i and period t contribute to, respectively, the *linked* issue selection, sector selection, and interaction effects. These variables are given by

$$\hat{I}_{it} = \beta_t I_{it}, \tag{14.15a}$$

$$\hat{S}_{it} = \beta_t S_{it}, \tag{14.15b}$$

and

$$\hat{U}_{it} = \beta_t U_{it}. \tag{14.15c}$$

Linked issue-selection effect $\hat{I}_i$, sector-selection effect $\hat{S}_i$, and interaction effect $\hat{U}_i$ for sector i are found by simply summing over time, as follows:

$$\hat{I}_i = \sum_t \hat{I}_{it}, \tag{14.16a}$$

$$\hat{S}_i = \sum_t \hat{S}_{it}, \tag{14.16b}$$

and

$$\hat{U}_i = \sum_t \hat{U}_{it}. \tag{14.16c}$$

The active return over multiple periods can thus be written as

$$R - \bar{R} = \sum_{i=1}^{N} (\hat{I}_i + \hat{S}_i + \hat{U}_i). \tag{14.17}$$

The result is a decomposition of active return into attribution effects at the sector level that exactly add up to give the active return. Formally, Equation 14.17 represents the multiperiod equivalent to Equation 14.10.

The challenge in this approach is, of course, to calculate the appropriate values for β_t.

Optimized Approach

In Menchero (2000), I argued that the most accurate way to link arithmetic attribution effects over multiple periods is to minimize the deviation of the linking coefficients about some value A that corresponds to a *natural scaling* from the single-period to the multiperiod active return space. This scaling is purely a consequence of geometric compounding. Thus, the question is, what value of A best satisfies the following relationship:

$$R - \bar{R} \approx A \sum_{t=1}^{T} (R_t - \bar{R}_t). \tag{14.18}$$

I found the value of the scaling by substituting the geometric mean single-period portfolio return, $(1 + R)^{1/T} - 1$, for the actual single-period portfolio return (and similarly for the benchmark). The result is then given by

$$A = \frac{(R - \bar{R})/T}{(1 + R)^{1/T} - (1 + \bar{R})^{1/T}}. \tag{14.19}$$

The interpretation of Equation 14.19 becomes clear if one notes that the numerator represents the mean *multiperiod* active return per period, whereas the denominator represents the mean *single-period* active return per period. The ratio, therefore, gives the mean scaling from the single-period to the multiperiod case. Further motivation and compelling evidence that this result is indeed appropriate for the natural scaling can be found in Appendix 14A.

Note that R and $\bar{R}$ represent the portfolio and benchmark returns for the reporting period and T represents the number of linking periods within the reporting period. For instance, if a portfolio manager is interested in explaining the active return for an entire year and assumes monthly rebalancing, the manager uses $T = 12$ and substitutes the annual portfolio and benchmark returns for, respectively, R and $\bar{R}$. Also, observe that because natural scaling A depends only on R, $\bar{R}$, and T through the simple expression in Equation 14.19, it is easily computed on an ordinary pocket calculator. For the special case in which $R = \bar{R}$, I showed previously (Menchero) that Equation 14.19 has a simple limiting value.

The optimized linking coefficients can be found by minimizing the squared deviations, α_t^2, from natural scaling A, subject to the constraint that there be no residual. I showed in my 2000 paper that these minimal deviations are given by

$$\alpha_t = C(R_t - \bar{R}_t), \tag{14.20}$$

where C is a constant independent of t and is given by

$$C = \frac{R - \bar{R} - A\sum_{j=1}^{T}(R_j - \bar{R}_j)}{\sum_{j=1}^{T}(R_j - \bar{R}_j)^2}. \tag{14.21}$$

Subscript j is a dummy index of summation over time periods.

The optimized linking coefficients are therefore

$$\beta_t^{Opt} = A + \alpha_t = A + C(R_t - \bar{R}_t). \tag{14.22}$$

Because A and C are independent of t, the optimized linking coefficients, β_t^{Opt}, are manifestly metric preserving. In other words, any two periods with the same relative performance will have identical linking coefficients and thus contribute equally to the relative performance over multiple periods. Also, clearly, neither A nor C depends on the ordering of the periods, so the optimized linking algorithm is commutative. Furthermore, because the linking coefficients satisfy Equation 14.14, the algorithm is strictly residual free. Finally, the same optimized linking coefficients apply at the fund, sector, or holdings level. Therefore, the optimized algorithm is fully linkable and the optimized approach to multiperiod attribution satisfies all four of the quantitative properties listed previously.

Having seen the development of the mathematics of the optimized linking algorithm, step back for a moment and consider the interpretation. Deviations α_t were introduced to ensure a residual-free linking algorithm, and for this reason, they should be included as part of the linking coefficients. Conceptually, however, the α_t are typically negligibly small (and, by construction, always minimally small) compared with natural scaling *A*. Thus, the optimized linking algorithm simply corresponds to a uniform "stretching" of the attribution effects by the natural scaling: *Every basis point of relative performance earned in any single period will contribute approximately* A *bps to the overall linked relative performance*. This property is consistent with the principle of metric preservation. Moreover, given that *A* can be quickly computed on a pocket calculator, a linking algorithm that is more intuitive or transparent is difficult to imagine. That is, although the *derivation* of the optimized algorithm may rely on advanced mathematics, the *essence* can be fully characterized in terms of elementary multiplication. Thus, the optimized linking algorithm can be readily understood by any investment professional. Furthermore, the algorithm is robust, yielding accurate results under even the most adverse market conditions. More precisely, the α_t deviations remain small relative to *A* even for extremely large returns.

Logarithmic Method

Cariño (1999) developed a logarithmic linking coefficient approach. The logarithmic linking coefficients β_t^{Log} satisfy Equation 14.14 and are given by

$$\beta_t^{Log} = \frac{k_t}{k}, \tag{14.23}$$

where k_t in the numerator is defined in terms of natural logarithms involving the portfolio and benchmark returns for period *t* as

$$k_t = \frac{\ln(1 + R_t) - \ln(1 + \bar{R}_t)}{R_t - \bar{R}_t}. \tag{14.24}$$

The *k* in the denominator has the same functional form as k_t but is expressed in terms of the linked portfolio and benchmark returns:

$$k = \frac{\ln(1 + R) - \ln(1 + \bar{R})}{R - \bar{R}}. \tag{14.25}$$

The logarithmic approach shares the nice properties of being residual free, commutative, and fully linkable, but it is not metric preserving. This conclusion follows from the simple observation that two periods with identical active returns will not, in general, have the same linking coefficient. For deeper insight into the underlying structure of this method, however, a Taylor series expansion of Equation 14.24 for small returns can be performed. The result is

$$k_t \approx 1 - \frac{1}{2}(R_t + \bar{R}_t). \tag{14.26}$$

The reader will recognize this expression as essentially a *geometric* scaling factor. In other words, periods of high returns will have smaller logarithmic linking coefficients than periods of low returns, thus contributing less to the active return. The logarithmic approach can be thought of, therefore, as measuring relative performance arithmetically at the sector level but scaled at the fund level by an overall factor consistent with geometric attribution. That is, the arithmetic attribution effects are not uniformly stretched but *variably* stretched from one period to the next depending on the level of returns for the period. Thus, in actuality, the logarithmic approach represents a hybrid measure—neither arithmetic nor geometric—of relative performance. In volatile markets, with portfolio and benchmark returns fluctuating up and down, this hybrid measure can lead to distortions in the linked attribution effects, as will be shown later.

Compounded Notional Portfolio Methods

The compounded notional portfolio method provides a commutative and residual-free means to link the attribution effects at the fund level but provides no clear way to link attribution effects at the sector level without the introduction of residuals (i.e., it is not fully linkable). The algorithm is also not metric preserving, as the examples will demonstrate. The motivation behind the method is to recognize that—for a single period—the issue selection aggregates to

$$I_t = \sum_{i=1}^{N} \bar{w}_{it} \, (r_{it} - \bar{r}_{it}) = R_t^* - \bar{R}_t, \tag{14.27}$$

where R_t^* is a notional return obtained by using benchmark sector weights with portfolio sector returns.

Similarly, the aggregate sector selection for a single period is given by

$$S_t = \sum_{i=1}^{N} (w_{it} - \bar{w}_{it})(\bar{r}_{it} - \bar{R}_t) = \tilde{R}_t - \bar{R}_t, \tag{14.28}$$

where $\tilde{R}_t$ is a notional return obtained by using portfolio sector weights with benchmark sector returns.

The aggregate interaction effect for a single period can be expressed in terms of the same notional returns:

$$U_t = \sum_{i=1}^{N} (w_{it} - \bar{w}_{it})(r_{it} - \bar{r}_{it}) = R_t + \bar{R}_t - R_t^* - \tilde{R}_t. \tag{14.29}$$

The sum of the three attribution effects exactly equals the active return for the period:

$$I_t + S_t + U_t = R_t - \bar{R}_t. \tag{14.30}$$

The critical assumption is then made that the linked attribution effects can be expressed in terms of the *compounded* notional returns. In other words, the linked issue selection in this scheme is assumed to be

$$I = R^* - \bar{R} = \prod_{t=1}^{T}(1 + R_t^*) - \prod_{t=1}^{T}(1 + \bar{R}_t). \tag{14.31}$$

Similarly, the linked sector selection in this method is given by

$$S = \tilde{R} - \bar{R} = \prod_{i=1}^{T}(1 + \tilde{R}_t) - \prod_{t=1}^{T}(1 + \bar{R}_t), \tag{14.32}$$

and the linked interaction effect is expressed as

$$U = R + \bar{R} - R^* - \tilde{R}. \tag{14.33}$$

When the three effects are added together, the notional returns again cancel, giving

$$I + S + U = R - \bar{R}. \tag{14.34}$$

That is, the active return *at the fund level* is recovered without an unexplained residual.

Davies and Laker (2001) asserted that the compounded notional portfolio method represents the *exact* solution (at the fund level only) to the problem of linking attribution effects over time. In fact, they referred to the method as "exact multiperiod Brinson attribution."

I will carefully consider this claim later and show that this method does not, in fact, constitute an exact solution to the problem—*even at the fund level.*

Before considering this question, however, I will address another serious limitation of the compounded notional portfolio method. Although the method provides a means to link attribution effects at the fund level, it does not provide a way to link at the sector level (i.e., it is not fully linkable). Kirievsky and Kirievsky (2000) proposed a method for distributing the aggregate attribution effects among the sectors but not in a way that fully eliminates the residual. In other words, the sum of the attribution effects across sectors does not reproduce the aggregate result. Davies and Laker proposed using the compounded notional portfolio method at the aggregate level and then using the logarithmic method to link at the sector level. This approach, of course, produces a residual. They argued that the residual can then be removed by using an *ad hoc* smoothing algorithm. Such smoothing algorithms are unstable, however, and often produce misleading results, as will be shown.

Three Methods Compared

To provide insight into the methodologies presented thus far—the optimized linking coefficient, logarithmic linking coefficient, and compounded notional portfolio methods—some examples will be useful.

Example 1: Consider a portfolio manager who segments the equity market according to large-cap, mid-cap, and small-cap sectors. The manager pursues the following strategy: In the large-cap sector, he uses an active selection strategy (i.e., he is a large-cap stock picker) and a passive allocation strategy (i.e., he is sector neutral in large cap). In the mid-cap and small-cap sectors, he takes the opposite approach and pursues a passive selection strategy (using, for instance, index funds) and an active allocation strategy. Table 14.1 presents weights, returns, and attribution effects for a three-period example that is consistent with this manager's investment strategy. Did the portfolio manager exhibit positive issue selection over the three periods?

TABLE 14.1   Example 1: Weights, Returns, and Attribution Effects

Sector	Port. Weight	Bench. Weight	Port. Return	Bench. Return	Sector Select.	Issue Select.	Interaction Effect	Active Contribution
Period 1								
Large cap	20.00%	20.00%	0.00%	10.00%	0.00%	−2.00%	0.00%	−2.00%
Mid cap	50.00	35.00	18.00	18.00	1.32	0.00	0.00	1.32
Small cap	30.00	45.00	2.00	2.00	1.08	0.00	0.00	1.08
Total	100.00%	100.00%	9.60%	9.20%	2.40%	−2.00%	0.00%	0.40%
Period 2								
Large cap	20.00%	20.00%	6.00%	5.00%	0.00%	0.20%	0.00%	0.20%
Mid cap	40.00	30.00	11.50	11.50	0.23	0.00	0.00	0.23
Small cap	40.00	50.00	9.50	9.50	−0.03	0.00	0.00	−0.03
Total	100.00%	100.00%	9.60%	9.20%	0.20%	0.20%	0.00%	0.40
Period 3								
Large cap	20.00%	20.00%	10.00%	0.00%	0.00%	2.00%	0.00%	2.00%
Mid cap	50.00	30.00	6.50	6.50	−0.54	0.00	0.00	−0.54
Small cap	30.00	50.00	14.50	14.50	−1.06	0.00	0.00	−1.06
Total	100.00%	100.00%	9.60%	9.20%	−1.60%	2.00%	0.00%	0.40%

The first observation is that all of the issue selection came from the large-cap sector; the manager follows a passive strategy in the mid-cap and small-cap sectors. Therefore, to answer whether the manager exhibited positive stock selection in aggregate, attention should be focused on the large-cap sector. The weight in the large-cap sector was fixed at 20 percent for all periods. In Period 1, the portfolio return in the large-cap sector was 0 percent (versus 10 percent for the benchmark), but in Period 3, these returns reversed. Thus, the negative issue selection from Period 1 should exactly cancel the positive issue selection from Period 3. The answer to the question of whether issue selection is positive overall, therefore, lies with Period 2 as the "tiebreaker." In Period 2, the manager added 20 bps of issue selection in the large-cap sector. So, one might guess that the net issue selection over the three periods would be 20 bps. Geometric compounding, however, leads to a natural scaling A in this example of approximately 1.2. Therefore, the 20 bps of issue selection in Period 2 will translate into approximately 24 bps of issue selection over the three periods.

Table 14.2 presents the results for the linked aggregate sector selection, issue selection, and interaction effect calculated by the optimized method, the logarithmic method, and the compounded notional portfolio method. The optimized and logarithmic approaches both give an issue selection of 24 bps, as expected. The compounded notional portfolio method gives 19 bps, which is less than one would expect. Nonetheless, despite a difference of 5 bps between the methods, all approaches give at least reasonable results for issue selection in this particular instance.

Now consider whether or not the compounded notional portfolio method represents the *exact* solution at the fund level, as argued by Davies and Laker. To answer this question, refer again to the example given in Table 14.1. Did the portfolio manager add value through the interaction effect over the three periods?

Recall that the interaction effect measures the simultaneous action of selection and allocation. By the very nature of this manager's investment strategy, therefore, the interaction effect clearly does not add value. The reason is that the strategy involves either passive allocation with active selection (as in large cap) or active allocation with passive selection (as in mid cap and small cap). Indeed, Table 14.1 indicates that the interaction effect is zero in every sector for every period. The manager actively decided every period *not* to add value through the interaction effect. The only meaningful result, therefore, is that the interaction effect must be exactly zero. Table 14.2 shows that the optimized and logarithmic approaches both indeed give zero for the linked interaction effect, as required. The compounded notional portfolio method, however, would suggest that the interaction effect contributed 9 bps to the active return. To claim that 9 bps is somehow the exact answer would be to decouple the active decision (in this case, not to add value through interaction) from the *impact* that the decision had on relative performance. That is, the 9 bps of interaction effect was not caused by any active management decision but, rather, by an artifact of the linking algorithm. This

TABLE 14.2   Example 1: Aggregate Attribution Effects, with Linking, by Three Methodologies

Method	Sector Selection	Issue Selection	Interaction Effect	Active Contribution
Optimized	1.20%	0.24%	0.00%	1.44%
Logarithmic	1.20	0.24	0.00	1.44
Notional portfolio	1.15	0.19	0.09	1.44

simple example shows that the compounded notional portfolio method does not provide an exact solution to multiperiod attribution even at the fund level.

Example 2: Another example will provide further insight into the three methodologies presented thus far. The reader may have noticed in the previous example that the total portfolio and benchmark returns in Table 14.1 were identical every period (i.e., 9.60 percent for the portfolio and 9.20 percent for the benchmark). In this example, this artificial constraint is relaxed.

Table 14.3 presents weights, returns, and attribution effects for another three-period example for the same portfolio manager following the same strategy as in Example 1 but with different results each period. The portfolio continues to outperform the benchmark by 40 bps every period, but now the portfolio returns vary from 0.80 percent in Period 1 to 17.20 percent in Period 3. Again, the question is: Did the portfolio manager exhibit positive issue selection over the three periods?

First, note that all the issue selection again stemmed from the large-cap sector and all the sector selection came from the mid-cap and small-cap sectors. Second, Table 14.3 indicates that the large-cap weights and returns are identical to those given in Table 14.1. Third, recall that issue selection depends only on the weights and returns within the sector. In the multiperiod case, the linked issue selection resulting from the large-cap sector may depend indirectly on the weights and returns in other sectors only insofar as these quantities may affect natural scaling A. In this example, however, the natural scaling is approximately the same as in Example 1 ($A \approx 1.2$). Therefore, the linked issue selection in this example should equal the linked issue selection of the previous example (i.e., 24 bps).

Table 14.4 presents the linked attribution effects for the optimized, logarithmic, and compounded notional portfolio methods for Example 2. The optimized algorithm produces the expected 24 bps of issue selection. In contrast, the logarithmic and compounded notional portfolio methods generate values of issue selection that are not only different from Table 14.2

TABLE 14.3   Example 2: Weights, Returns, and Attribution Effects

Sector	Port. Weight	Bench. Weight	Port. Return	Bench. Return	Sector Select.	Issue Select.	Interaction Effect	Active Contribution
Period 1								
Large cap	20.00%	20.00%	0.00%	10.00%	0.00%	−2.00%	0.00%	−2.00%
Mid cap	50.00	20.00	4.00	4.00	1.08	0.00	0.00	1.08
Small cap	30.00	60.00	−4.00	−4.00	1.32	0.00	0.00	1.32
Total	100.00%	100.00%	0.80%	0.40%	2.40%	−2.00%	0.00%	0.40%
Period 2								
Large cap	20.00%	20.00%	6.00%	5.00%	0.00%	0.20%	0.00%	0.20%
Mid cap	40.00	30.00	14.00	14.00	0.28	0.00	0.00	0.28
Small cap	40.00	50.00	12.00	12.00	−0.08	0.00	0.00	−0.08
Total	100.00%	100.00%	11.60%	11.20%	0.20%	0.20%	0.00%	0.40%
Period 3								
Large cap	20.00%	20.00%	10.00%	0.00%	0.00%	2.00%	0.00%	2.00%
Mid cap	50.00	30.00	16.00	16.00	−0.16	0.00	0.00	−0.16
Small cap	30.00	50.00	24.00	24.00	−1.44	0.00	0.00	−1.44
Total	100.00%	100.00%	17.20%	16.80%	−1.60%	2.00%	0.00%	0.40%

TABLE 14.4   Example 2: Aggregate Attribution Effects, with Linking, by Three Methodologies

Method	Sector Selection	Issue Selection	Interaction Effect	Active Contribution
Optimized	1.20%	0.24%	0.00%	1.44%
Logarithmic	1.57	−0.13	0.00	1.44
Notional portfolio	1.53	−0.18	0.09	1.44

but are, in fact, *negative*. In these methods, therefore, the negative stock-selection outcome is explained not by what occurred within the large-cap sector (which did not change from the previous example) but by what happened in the mid-cap and small-cap sectors. This interpretation is clearly inconsistent with the basic meaning of stock selection, which depends only on decisions made *within* the sector. Furthermore, these distortions are not small. The logarithmic and compounded notional portfolio methods produce issue selections that are 37 bps less than in Example 1. Considering that the active return over three periods is only 144 bps, a 37 bp distortion is significant.

These results can be interpreted within the context of metric preservation. In the optimized algorithm, which is metric preserving, all linking coefficients are equal to 1.200. The linked issue selection in large cap, therefore, is

$$I^{Opt}_{Large} = (1.200 \times -2.00) + (1.200 \times 0.20) + (1.200 \times 2.00) \quad\quad (14.35)$$
$$= 0.24\%.$$

In the optimized approach, the negative issue selection from Period 1 indeed exactly cancels the positive issue selection from Period 3, as one intuitively expects.

In the logarithmic approach, the linking coefficients are given by 1.303, 1.177, and 1.120 for, respectively, Periods 1, 2, and 3. The linked issue selection within this algorithm, therefore, is

$$I^{Log}_{Large} = (1.303 \times -2.00) + (1.177 \times 0.20) + (1.120 \times 2.00) \quad\quad (14.36)$$
$$= -0.13\%.$$

Clearly, in the logarithmic method, the issue-selection results from Periods 1 and 3 no longer cancel because of the difference in linking coefficients. Period 1, which has low returns, had a larger coefficient than Period 3 (with high returns). As a result of this spurious overweighting of Period 1, the net issue selection comes out negative. The source of the distortions is the *variability* of the linking coefficients from one period to the next.

Note also that the optimized coefficients are exactly equal for all three periods in this example because the active returns were equal each period (40 bps). The effect is strict metric preservation even at the component level. In general, however, the active returns will not be identical for all periods, which will lead to slight variations in the optimized linking coefficients from period to period. By construction, however, these coefficients assuredly have the minimum possible deviation from the natural scaling and, therefore, mathematically represent the most accurate residual-free solution.

Recursive Models

Consider now the recursive approaches to linking attribution effects over time. The essence of these approaches is to take the difference in cumulative active return from one period to the next and attribute it to active decisions within the period. Clearly, however, such an approach can lead to serious problems. For instance, suppose that after some period, the cumulative portfolio return is 10 percent and the cumulative benchmark return is 20 percent. Suppose also that over the ensuing period, the portfolio earned a 10 percent return versus 9.5 percent for the benchmark. The cumulative portfolio return is now 21 percent versus 31.4 percent for the benchmark. Thus, the active return actually *deteriorated* from −10 percent to −10.4 percent, even though the portfolio beat the benchmark by 50 bps over the final period. Therefore, although the portfolio manager clearly added value during the final period, recursive methods will spuriously attribute −40 bps to the period. The underlying reason for such a nonintuitive result is that recursive methods violate the second quantitative property; namely, they are not commutative.

In the recursive linking formula described by Mirabelli (2000/2001), a portfolio compounding factor, γ_t, is defined that incorporates portfolio returns up to the previous period:

$$\gamma_t = \prod_{\tau=1}^{t-1}(1 + R_\tau), \tag{14.37}$$

with $\gamma_1 \equiv 1$ for the first period. A similar quantity, $\overline{\gamma}_t$, is defined for the benchmark:

$$\overline{\gamma}_t = \prod_{\tau=1}^{t-1}(1 + \overline{R}_\tau). \tag{14.38}$$

The linked portfolio return may be written as

$$R = \sum_{t=1}^{T} R_t \gamma_t, \tag{14.39}$$

with a similar expression for the benchmark. The active return is, therefore,

$$R - \overline{R} = \sum_{t=1}^{T}(R_t \gamma_t - \overline{R}_t \overline{\gamma}_t), \tag{14.40}$$

which, after some algebra, can be expressed as

$$R - \overline{R} = \sum_{i}\left[\sum_{t=1}^{T} \overline{w}_{it}(r_{it}\gamma_t - \overline{r}_{it}\,\overline{\gamma}_t) + \sum_{t=1}^{T}(w_{it} - \overline{w}_{it})(\overline{r}_{it} - \overline{R}_t)\overline{\gamma}_t \right. \tag{14.41}$$
$$\left. + \sum_{t=1}^{T}(w_{it} - \overline{w}_{it})(r_{it}\gamma_t - \overline{r}_{it}\overline{\gamma}_t) \right].$$

Mirabelli's method is residual free and fully linkable, but it is neither commutative nor metric preserving. The first set of terms in Equation 14.41 is the contribution that sector i and period t make to the linked issue selection within the Mirabelli approach:

$$\hat{I}_{it}^M = \overline{w}_{it}(r_{it}\gamma_t - \overline{r}_{it}\,\overline{\gamma}_t). \tag{14.42}$$

The second set of terms is the contribution to linked sector selection:

$$\hat{S}_{it}^M = (w_{it} - \overline{w}_{it})(\overline{r}_{it} - \overline{R}_t)\overline{\gamma}_t, \tag{14.43}$$

and the final set of terms is the contribution to linked interaction effect:

$$\hat{U}_{it}^M = (w_{it} - \overline{w}_{it})(r_{it}\gamma_t - \overline{r}_{it}\,\overline{\gamma}_t). \tag{14.44}$$

Formally, Equations 14.42–14.44 appear to be the same as their single-period counterparts (Equations 14.7–14.9), but the portfolio and benchmark returns have everywhere been multiplied by their respective compounding factors. The linked issue selection, sector selection, and interaction effect are found by aggregating across time:

$$\hat{I}_i^M = \sum_{t=1}^{T} \hat{I}_{it}^M, \tag{14.45a}$$

$$\hat{S}_i^M = \sum_{t=1}^{T} \hat{S}_{it}^M, \tag{14.45b}$$

$$\hat{U}_i^M = \sum_{t=1}^{T} \hat{U}_{it}^M. \tag{14.45c}$$

The multiperiod relative performance is thus written as

$$R - \bar{R} = \sum_{i=1}^{N} \left(\hat{I}_i^M + \hat{S}_i^M + \hat{U}_i^M \right). \tag{14.46}$$

Formally, Equation 14.46 is thus the same as Equation 14.17, in that the linked active return is decomposed into attribution effects at the sector level. Although the numbers exactly add up to give the active return, the individual components may cease to be independently meaningful because of potentially serious distortions. For instance, this scheme may produce a negative linked issue selection for a sector in which the portfolio outperformed the benchmark each and every period. Mathematically, this nonintuitive result arises from the fact that, even though r_{it} is greater than $\bar{r}_{it}$, it is still possible that $r_{it}\gamma_t$ will be less than $\bar{r}_{it}\bar{\gamma}_t$ if the benchmark cumulative returns exceed those of the portfolio (i.e., if $\bar{\gamma}_t$ is greater than γ_t). Even if $\gamma_t \approx \bar{\gamma}_t$, the method can produce serious distortions because it will significantly overweight (underweight) events in the final periods relative to the initial periods for the case of positive (negative) returns.

Another recursive algorithm was first described by Frongello (2002) and later by Bonafede, Foresti, and Matheos (2002). Frongello's approach has the same properties as Mirabelli's (i.e., it is residual free and fully linkable but neither commutative nor metric preserving), but it distributes the relative performance differently among the attribution effects. The contribution of sector i and period t to the linked issue selection within the Frongello approach is

$$\hat{I}_{it}^F = I_{it}\gamma_t + \bar{R}_t \sum_{k=1}^{t-1} \hat{I}_{ik}^F, \tag{14.47}$$

where γ_t is defined in Equation 14.37 and I_{it} is the familiar single-period issue selection given by Equation 14.7. The linked issue selection is found by aggregating across time:

$$\hat{I}_i^F = \sum_{t=1}^{T} \hat{I}_{it}^F. \tag{14.48}$$

The linked sector selection and interaction effect in the Frongello method are given by expressions equivalent to Equations 14.47 and 14.48 but with I everywhere replaced by, respectively, S and U.

Interpretation of these expressions as meaningful measures of relative performance is problematic. For instance, suppose that a portfolio manager has obtained positive issue selection through $t - 1$ periods and that the benchmark return for period t is negative. Then, Equation 14.47 asserts that, even if the portfolio manager obtains positive issue selection, $I_{it} > 0$, during period t, the issue selection for that period may actually contribute *negatively* to the linked result (i.e., $\hat{I}_{it}^F < 0$). Also, Equation 14.47 indicates that the contribution of sector i and period t to linked issue selection depends directly on the benchmark return for period t.

This effect is spurious, however, because such a dependency has no apparent rationale. In fact, the Frongello linking algorithm could just as easily be expressed in the following form:

$$\hat{I}_{it}^{F*} = I_{it}\bar{\gamma}_t + R_t \sum_{k=1}^{t-1} \hat{I}_{ik}^{F*}. \tag{14.49}$$

Equation 14.49 is residual free but leads to different results from Equation 14.47. Because there is no economic or mathematical reason to prefer one formula over the other, an arbitrary element exists in the Frongello linking algorithm.

Ad Hoc Smoothing Algorithms

The final class of methods considered here eliminates residuals through *ad hoc* smoothing procedures. Although little has been published on the subject, anecdotal evidence suggests that these smoothing algorithms are being used by some practitioners.

The most well-known smoothing algorithm is attributable to Campisi (2002/2003) and was first described in a review written by Spaulding (2002). In the Campisi method, the attribution effects are simply added across time and then, to eliminate the residual, multiplied by a single coefficient, Q, calculated as

$$Q = \frac{R - \bar{R}}{\sum_t (R_t - \bar{R}_t)}. \tag{14.50}$$

This approach may work well in the majority of cases, but it sometimes leads to completely erroneous results, as illustrated in the following simple example. Suppose the portfolio return for Period 1, R_1, is 10 percent and the benchmark return, $\bar{R}_1$, is 5.1 percent, for an active return of 4.9 percent. Now suppose this active return is explained by 6.9 percent from issue selection and -2.0 percent from sector selection. In Period 2, let the portfolio return, R_2, again be 10 percent but let the benchmark return, $\bar{R}_2$, be 15.0 percent, for an active return of -5.0 percent. Let this active return be explained by 2.0 percent from issue selection and -7.0 percent from sector selection. Linked over two periods, the portfolio and benchmark returns are, therefore, $R = 21.0$ percent and $\bar{R} = 20.865$ percent, giving an active return of 13.5 bps.

Before proceeding any further, step back and consider what happened. Clearly, the portfolio manager added value through issue selection and detracted a roughly equal amount through sector selection. If Equation 14.50 is applied, however, the coefficient is given by $Q = -1.35$. Thus, the linked issue selection from the smoothing algorithm is

$$I_{Smooth} = (6.9 + 2.0) \times -1.35$$

$$= -12.015\%. \tag{14.51}$$

Similarly, the linked sector selection would be given by

$$S_{Smooth} = (-2.0 - 7.0) \times -1.35$$

$$= 12.150\%. \tag{14.52}$$

The attribution effects add exactly to 13.5 bps, but they do not accurately reflect what happened. In fact, based on the results of the smoothing algorithm, one would erroneously conclude that the portfolio manager was poor at selection and good at allocation, whereas, in fact, the opposite is true.

This example with simple numbers clearly illustrates how the Campisi smoothing algorithm is subject to extreme distortions and even spurious sign flips. Recently, Campisi

(2002/2003) argued that under realistic conditions, the smoothing algorithm gives results that are indistinguishable from other, more robust algorithms. In Menchero (2003), however, I showed that the Campisi algorithm is subject to spurious sign flips even for perfectly realistic scenarios. Furthermore, as detailed in Appendix 14A, under typical market conditions, the nonintuitive sign flip occurs in approximately 2 percent of cases.

If the optimized algorithm is applied to the example problem, linking coefficients of $\beta_1^{Opt} = 1.124$ and $\beta_2^{Opt} = 1.075$ are obtained. The result is an issue-selection attribution of 9.906 percent and a sector-selection attribution of -9.771 percent. The 13.5 bps are again fully accounted for but in a way that accurately reflects what happened.

Another common smoothing algorithm "compounds" the attribution effects across time. The sum of these compounded attribution effects will not, of course, add up to the active return, but an *ad hoc* coefficient is then applied to eliminate the residual. Unfortunately, this approach can lead to the same severe distortions as in the Campisi smoothing algorithm.

CONCLUSION

This article presented a set of qualitative characteristics and quantitative properties that I believe are essential for ensuring sound and accurate performance attribution analysis over multiple periods. The article examined several published algorithms within this context. Although all the algorithms are consistent with at least some of the desired properties, most violate one or more of the desirable properties. For instance, the logarithmic method for linking arithmetic attribution effects is, in fact, a hybrid approach (it is not metric preserving) that can lead to distortions by using linking coefficients with high variability from period to period. The compounded notional portfolio method also has serious problems and limitations. In light of the various examples of nonintuitive effects obtained by linking notional portfolios (for instance, spurious generation of nonzero attribution effects), this method clearly also exhibits distortions that render it not an exact approach for linking across multiple periods. Recursive methodologies also produce nonintuitive results. The basic difficulty with recursive methods is that they are not commutative. Finally, the article demonstrated that *ad hoc* smoothing algorithms are particularly prone to generating results that completely misrepresent the effects of active management decisions.

Of the methodologies discussed in this study, the only approach consistent with all of the desirable quantitative properties (including metric preservation) is the optimized linking algorithm. It offers the most accurate method for linking attribution effects over multiple periods.

APPENDIX 14A: NATURAL SCALING FROM SINGLE-PERIOD TO MULTIPERIOD CASE

Given that the optimized algorithm will minimize the squared deviation about *any* value of A, a crucial question is whether the value of A given by Equation 14.19 is indeed appropriate. Several considerations argue strongly in favor of the choice of A. The first is the stringent condition that the natural scaling must have the correct limiting values for $T = 1$ and $T \to \infty$, which are denoted, respectively, A_1 and A_∞.

When $T = 1$, only a single period is involved and, therefore, no scaling is needed, so $A_1 = 1$ in this case. Equation 14.19 indeed gives this result when $T = 1$. For $T \to \infty$, an exact expression for the natural scaling can be derived. The equation that describes the scaling relationship is

$$R - \bar{R} = A_\infty \sum_{t=1}^{T} (R_t - \bar{R}_t), \ (T \to \infty). \tag{14.53}$$

We take the limit $T \to \infty$ by keeping the reporting period fixed (e.g., one year) but subdividing it into infinitesimally small subperiods such that the number of subperiods approaches infinity. The portfolio time-weighted return is

$$1 + R = \prod_{t=1}^{T} (1 + R_t). \tag{14.54}$$

Taking the natural logarithm gives

$$\ln(1 + R) = \sum_{t=1}^{T} \ln(1 + R_t). \tag{14.55}$$

Return R over the reporting period will be finite and generally nonzero. Because the subperiods are infinitesimally small, however, it follows that returns R_t must also be infinitesimally small. We expand the natural logarithm for small values by taking the first nonvanishing term in the Taylor series, $\ln(1 + R_t) \approx R_t$. In the limit, $T \to \infty$, so we obtain

$$\ln(1 + R) = \sum_{t=1}^{T} R_t, \ (T \to \infty). \tag{14.56}$$

A similar expression holds for the benchmark,

$$\ln(1 + \bar{R}) = \sum_{t=1}^{T} \bar{R}_t, \ (T \to \infty). \tag{14.57}$$

Subtracting Equation 14.57 from Equation 14.56 produces

$$\ln(1 + R) - \ln(1 + \bar{R}) = \sum_{t=1}^{T} (R_t - \bar{R}_t), \ (T \to \infty). \tag{14.58}$$

Substituting Equation 14.58 into Equation 14.53, we solve for A_∞:

$$A_\infty = \frac{R - \bar{R}}{\ln(1 + R) - \ln(1 + \bar{R})}. \tag{14.59}$$

Now, we need to show that Equation 14.19 approaches this value as $T \to \infty$. Using L'Hospital's rule, we find

$$\lim_{T \to \infty} T[(1 + R)^{1/T} - 1] = \ln(1 + R). \tag{14.60}$$

Substituting Equation 14.60 (and a similar expression involving the benchmark returns) into Equation 14.19, we obtain the desired result:

$$\lim_{T \to \infty} A = \frac{R - \bar{R}}{\ln(1 + R) - \ln(1 + \bar{R})} \tag{14.61}$$

$$= A_\infty.$$

Thus, Equation 14.19 has the correct limiting value for $T \to \infty$ as well as for $T = 1$.

Useful insights can be gained by calculating the logarithmic linking coefficients in the same limit as the subperiods become infinitesimally small. In this case, $k_t \to 1$, so

$$\lim_{T \to \infty} \beta_t^{Log} = \lim_{T \to \infty} \frac{k_t}{k}$$

$$= \frac{1}{k} \tag{14.62}$$

$$= \frac{R - \bar{R}}{\ln(1 + R) - \ln(1 + \bar{R})}.$$

We thus obtain the interesting result that the logarithmic linking coefficients converge to natural scaling A in the limit of infinitesimally short subperiods. This result implies that the logarithmic and the optimized linking algorithms become identical in the limit of infinitesimally small subperiods. In practice, of course, this limit is never reached because the shortest linking subperiod is a day.

Thus far, we have seen that natural scaling gives the correct limiting values for a single period or for an infinite number of subperiods. Now, we consider an intermediate number of subperiods. Extensive numerical simulations have verified that, indeed, A also provides the correct scaling relationship in this case. For instance, let i denote a single numerical simulation involving T subperiods. Let benchmark return $\bar{R}_t^i$ be drawn from a random-number generator with mean of 1.0 percent and standard deviation of 5.8 percent. (These numbers correspond roughly to the historical monthly norm of the S&P 500 Index.) We draw portfolio returns R_t^i also from a random-number generator with the same expected return as the benchmark but now correlated to produce an annualized tracking error of 4.0 percent. We calculate the optimized linking coefficients about a value kA, where k is a parameter and A is the natural scaling given by Equation 14.19. The optimized linking equation for simulation i can be written

$$R^i - \bar{R}^i = \sum_{t=1}^{T} \left[kA^i + \alpha_t^i(k) \right] (R_t^i - \bar{R}_t^i). \tag{14.63}$$

We next define a variable F that depends on parameter k and measures the mean squared deviations as follows:

$$F(k) = \frac{1}{N} \sum_{i=1}^{N} \sum_{t=1}^{T} [\alpha_t^i(k)]^2, \tag{14.64}$$

where N is the number of simulations.

In this simulation study, we let $T = 12$, corresponding to one year. If Equation 14.19 indeed gives the correct scaling, then $F(k)$ should have a minimum about $k = 1$. When parameter k is varied from 0.9 to 1.1 and 100,000 simulations are run for each value, the results for $F(k)$ are as plotted in Figure 14.1. As can be seen, mean squared deviation $F(k)$ does indeed have a minimum at the appropriate value. This result is additional evidence in favor of Equation 14.19.

A similar study has been made to discover whether adding an arbitrary constant q to the natural scaling could lead to a smaller deviation on average. The following simulations were carried out:

$$R^i - \bar{R}^i = \sum_{t=1}^{T} \left[A^i + q + \alpha_t^i(q) \right] (R_t^i - \bar{R}_t^i), \tag{14.65}$$

and the mean squared deviation was calculated as in Equation 14.64. Again, the minimum deviation occurred, on average, about the natural scaling (i.e., $q = 0$).

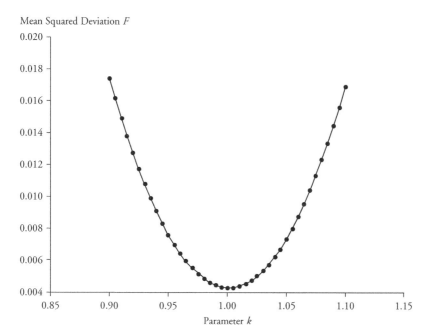

FIGURE 14.1   Mean Squared Deviation F vs. Parameter k

Note: Each data point represents 100,000 numerical simulations.

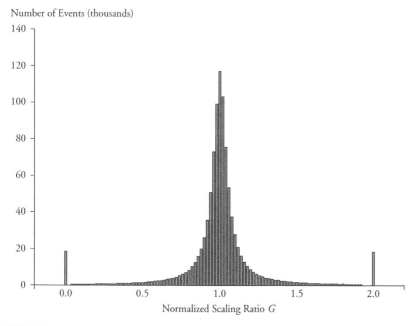

FIGURE 14.2   Histogram of Normalized Scaling Ratio G

Notes: Based on 1,000,000 simulations. Vertical lines at 0.0 and 2.0 represent cumulative number of events to, respectively, left and right of these points.

Consider the natural scaling from yet another perspective. If A represents a true scaling from the single-period active returns to the multiperiod case, then the following normalized scaling ratio,

$$G = \frac{R - \bar{R}}{A \sum_{t=1}^{T} (R_t - \bar{R}_t)}, \tag{14.66}$$

should be distributed about 1.

A set of 1,000,000 simulations was run linking 12 one-month periods (with the same return distributions as those used in Figure 14.1). The value of G was calculated for each simulation, and the resulting frequency distribution is plotted in Figure 14.2. The distribution is clearly centered about 1, with most of the distribution lying between 0.5 and 1.5. This result offers further compelling evidence in favor of Equation 14.19.

Note, however, that nearly 20,000 events (or 2 percent of the distribution) lie to the left of 0. This outcome corresponds to a situation in which, say, the linked active return is positive but the sum of the single-period active returns is negative. Considering that *ad hoc* smoothing algorithms (e.g., the Campisi method) essentially multiply all of the attribution effects by the quantity $Q = AG$, one can see that nearly 2 percent of the time they would reverse the signs of all the attribution effects, thereby rendering the results meaningless. The Campisi smoothing algorithm is an example of a linking methodology that is not robust, and Equations 14.51 and 14.52 provide a vivid illustration of this sort of distortion.

NOTES

1. Another common approach is to define issue selection in terms of portfolio sector weights. In this case, the interaction effect does not appear.
2. Metric preservation is a stricter condition than order independence. That is, all metric-preserving algorithms must be commutative but not all commutative algorithms must be metric preserving.

REFERENCES

Ankrim, E., and C. Hensel. 1994. "Multicurrency Performance Attribution." *Financial Analysts Journal*, vol. 50, no. 2 (March/April):29–35.

Bonafede, J., S. Foresti, and P. Matheos. 2002. "A Multi-Period Linking Algorithm That Has Stood the Test of Time." *Journal of Performance Measurement*, vol. 7, no. 1 (Fall):15–26.

Brinson, G., and N. Fachler. 1985. "Measuring Non-U.S. Equity Portfolio Performance." *Journal of Portfolio Management*, vol. 11, no. 3 (Spring):73–76.

Brinson, G., L. Hood, and G. Beebower. 1995. "Determinants of Portfolio Performance." *Financial Analysts Journal*, vol. 51, no. 1 (January/February):133–138; originally published in vol. 42, no. 4 (July/August 1986):39–44.

Campisi, S. 2000. "Primer on Fixed Income Performance Attribution." *Journal of Performance Measurement*, vol. 4, no. 4 (Summer):14–25.

———. 2002/2003. "While We Expound on Theory, Have We Forgotten Practice?" *Journal of Performance Measurement*, vol. 7, no. 2 (Winter):7–8.

Cariño, D. 1999. "Combining Attribution Effects over Time." *Journal of Performance Measurement*, vol. 3, no. 4 (Summer):5–14.

Davies, O., and D. Laker. 2001. "Multiple-Period Performance Attribution Using the Brinson Model." *Journal of Performance Measurement*, vol. 6, no. 1 (Fall):12–22.

Frongello, A. 2002. "Linking Single Period Attribution Results." *Journal of Performance Measurement*, vol. 6, no. 3 (Spring):10–22.

Grinold, R., and R. Kahn. 2000. *Active Portfolio Management*. New York: McGraw-Hill.

Kirievsky, L., and A. Kirievsky. 2000. "Attribution Analysis: Combining Attribution Effects over Time Made Easy." *Journal of Performance Measurement*, vol. 4, no. 4 (Summer):49–59.

Lord, T. 1997. "The Attribution of Portfolio and Index Returns in Fixed Income." *Journal of Performance Measurement*, vol. 2, no. 1 (Fall):45–57.

Menchero, J. 2000. "An Optimized Approach to Linking Attribution Effects over Time." *Journal of Performance Measurement*, vol. 5, no. 1 (Fall):36–42.

———. 2003. "Linking Differences Do Matter." *Journal of Performance Measurement*, vol. 7, no. 3 (Spring):47–50.

Mirabelli, A. 2000/2001. "The Structure and Visualization of Performance Attribution." *Journal of Performance Measurement*, vol. 5, no. 2 (Winter):55–80.

Ramaswamy, S. 2001. "Fixed Income Portfolio Management: Risk Modeling, Portfolio Construction and Performance Attribution." *Journal of Performance Measurement*, vol. 5, no. 4 (Summer):58–70.

Singer, B., and D. Karnosky. 1995. "The General Framework for Global Investment Management and Performance Attribution." *Journal of Portfolio Management*, vol. 21, no. 2 (Winter):84–92.

Spaulding, D. 2002. "Is Linking Attribution Effects as Hard as It Looks?" *Journal of Performance Measurement*, vol. 6, no. 3 (Spring):32–39.

Van Breukelen, G. 2000. "Fixed Income Attribution." *Journal of Performance Measurement*, vol. 4, no. 4 (Summer):61–68.

CHAPTER 15

OPTIMIZED GEOMETRIC ATTRIBUTION

José Menchero, CFA

To address the problem of geometric performance attribution in a recently proposed framework of qualitative characteristics and quantitative properties, the approach reported here is to solve the problem in a two-step fashion. The first step is to define a set of attribution effects in their "pure" geometric form. Because these pure effects will not aggregate in a residual-free manner, however, the second step is to perturb the geometric attribution effects in such a way that they deviate as little as possible, subject to the constraint that there be no residual, from their pure values. The resulting optimized attribution effects represent the most accurate formulation of geometric attribution.

Attribution analysis is a powerful tool for evaluating the performance of an actively managed portfolio relative to a passive benchmark. The objective is to explain the sources of active return by quantifying the impact of active management decisions. It is accomplished by associating an "attribution effect" with each investment decision. When aggregated, these attribution effects fully account for the active return.

For a single buy-and-hold period (i.e., a period with no transactions), attribution analysis is relatively straightforward. One widely used approach is the sector-based model of Brinson and Fachler (1985). This method, described in greater detail later, decomposes active return into a "selection effect" and an "allocation effect."[1] The selection effect measures the impact of security selection within sectors; the allocation effect measures the effect of overweighting or underweighting the sectors.

The original model (see Brinson and Fachler) is formulated in arithmetic terms. That is, the active return and the attribution effects are given by differences and the attribution effects aggregate additively. The model can, however, be formulated geometrically. One way is to exploit the strong parallel between arithmetic and geometric attribution (Menchero

---

Reprinted from the *Financial Analysts Journal* (July/August 2005):60–69.

2000/2001). In essence, when moving from an arithmetic to a geometric framework, one replaces differences by ratios and replaces addition by multiplication. Hence, in the optimized geometric formulation presented in this article, the active return and the attribution effects are expressed in terms of ratios and the attribution effects aggregate multiplicatively.

Arithmetic and geometric attribution present unique, yet related, challenges. The origin of the challenges is actually the same: Returns are computed *additively* over a single period (as a sum of contributions) but compound *multiplicatively* over multiple periods. As a result, for arithmetic attribution, accurately aggregating effects in a residual-free fashion across time is challenging. For geometric attribution, the situation is reversed: Aggregating across time is simple, but sensibly defining geometric attribution effects that aggregate in a residual-free fashion for a single period is challenging. This point is not widely recognized. In fact, many proponents of geometric attribution mistakenly believe that the geometric approach does not suffer from residuals.

I discussed the problem of multiperiod arithmetic attribution and the optimal way of treating the residual in Menchero (2004). I presented a set of qualitative characteristics and quantitative properties that provide insight into the underlying structure of multiperiod attribution and also ensure the most accurate linking of attribution effects across time. In particular, I introduced the important notion of *metric preservation* in performance attribution. This concept, explored in detail later, is essentially a statement regarding internal consistency. That is, once a metric has been defined to measure active return (or the components of active return), it should be applied consistently across all periods.

SINGLE-PERIOD ATTRIBUTION: REVIEW

For insight into the geometric formulation that follows, a brief review of the basics of sector-based performance attribution will be useful. For a single-period buy-and-hold scenario, the portfolio return for period t, R_p, can be written exactly as the sum of contributions over N sectors,

$$R_t = \sum_{i=1}^{N} w_{it} r_{it}, \qquad (15.1)$$

where w_{it} and r_{it} are, respectively, the portfolio weights and returns for sector i and period t. If the corresponding benchmark quantities are denoted with an overbar, the benchmark return is

$$\bar{R}_t = \sum_{i=1}^{N} \bar{w}_{it} \bar{r}_{it}. \qquad (15.2)$$

The arithmetic active return, after some algebra, can be written as

$$R_t - \bar{R}_t = \sum_{i=1}^{N} w_{it}(r_{it} - \bar{r}_{it}) + \sum_{i=1}^{N} (w_{it} - \bar{w}_{it})(\bar{r}_{it} - \bar{R}_t). \qquad (15.3)$$

The term in the first summation of this equation is the selection effect (also known as "issue selection"),

$$S_{it}^{A} = w_{it}(r_{it} - \bar{r}_{it}), \qquad (15.4)$$

and measures the value added through the security selection decision. The superscript A in Equation 15.4 denotes "arithmetic." If weights are positive (i.e., it is a long-only portfolio), a positive selection effect is obtained by earning a portfolio sector return in excess of the corresponding benchmark sector return. Equation 15.4 clearly shows, and it is important to stress, that selection effect depends *only* on the weights and returns within the sector. Selection effect in, say, the large-capitalization sector does not depend on weights and returns in, say, the mid-cap sector. Keep this important concept in mind when I later consider geometric versions of these attribution effects.

The term in the second summation of Equation 15.3 is the allocation effect (also known as "sector selection"),

$$A_{it}^{A} = (w_{it} - \bar{w}_{it})(\bar{r}_{it} - \bar{R}_{t}), \tag{15.5}$$

and measures the value added through the sector allocation decision. Again, the superscript A denotes "arithmetic." A positive allocation effect is obtained by overweighting outperforming sectors or by underweighting the underperformers. Observe that the allocation effect depends on *only* the sector weights and returns and the total benchmark return. Combining Equations 15.3, 15.4, and 15.5 produces the expression for the active return for a single period:

$$R_{t} - \bar{R}_{t} = \sum_{i=1}^{N}(S_{it}^{A} + A_{it}^{A}). \tag{15.6}$$

Equation 15.6 expresses the relative performance as a sum of attribution effects that exactly aggregates to fully account for the active return for the period.

MULTIPERIOD ATTRIBUTION

The main results of my previous article (Menchero 2004) are also pertinent to the case of geometric attribution. That article presented a set of qualitative characteristics and quantitative properties to ensure sound and accurate linking of attribution effects over multiple periods. Qualitatively, the argument was, any multiperiod algorithm should be intuitive, transparent, and robust.

I also presented a set of quantitative properties that provide an objective framework for comparison of multiperiod algorithms. Those properties also elucidate the underlying structure of multiperiod attribution. Quantitatively, all linking algorithms should be residual free, fully linkable, commutative, and metric preserving:

- *Residual free* means that the attribution effects should fully account for the active return; no "unexplained part" should be left over. This property is desirable for the practical purpose of avoiding the suspicion and unnecessary confusion that are often generated by residuals. The challenge in any multiperiod algorithm is to eliminate the residual without introducing spurious effects.
- *Fully linkable* means that all the attribution effects (including those at the sector level) can be computed over multiple periods and aggregated together in a residual-free fashion. Obviously, it would be undesirable to report residual-free attribution effects at the fund level only to have residuals appear upon drilling down to the sector level. Nevertheless, the reader will see that some linking algorithms suffer from exactly this shortcoming.

- *Commutative* means that the attribution analysis should be independent of the ordering of the periods. Because active return is itself independent of the ordering of the periods, clearly the components of active return (i.e., the attribution effects) should also be independent of the ordering of the periods.
- *Metric preservation*, the fourth property, essentially means that attribution effects should be measured consistently for all periods. Within the arithmetic context, this characteristic can be understood by the simple statement that "every basis point should count equally." For instance, if a manager makes a decision that contributes 1 bp to Period A and another decision that contributes 1 bp to Period B, both decisions add equal value. When linked together over multiple periods, they should contribute equally (or as nearly equally as possible) to the active return. For geometric attribution, the meaning of metric preservation is slightly more subtle than it is in arithmetic attribution. Arithmetically, the distortion arises from multiperiod linking, but in the geometric case, it arises from spurious definitions of the attribution effects for the single period. In other words, metric preservation in the geometric context means that the attribution effects should be defined in a manner consistent with the geometric measure of relative performance.

GEOMETRIC ALGORITHMS

In geometric attribution, the active return is given by a ratio:

$$\frac{1 + R_t}{1 + \bar{R}_t} - 1 = \frac{R_t - \bar{R}_t}{1 + \bar{R}_t}. \tag{15.7}$$

Bacon (2002) argued that geometric active returns are a more appropriate metric than arithmetic returns because they are proportional, convertible, and compoundable:

- *Proportional* in this context means that the active return is given by a ratio, not a difference. The geometric measure of relative performance implies that beating the benchmark by a fixed amount is easier in an up market than in a down market. For instance, outperforming the benchmark by 1 percent when the index is up 10 percent leads to a geometric active return of 91 bps; if the index is down 10 percent, outperforming by 1 percent produces 111 bps. Proportionality is intrinsic to the geometric measure of relative performance.
- *Convertible* means that the reported active return is independent of the base currency. In other words, the geometric active return is the same whether expressed in yen, dollars, euros, or any other currency. In contrast, in reporting arithmetic active returns, small differences can exist for different choices of base currency.
- *Compoundable* simply means that the geometric active return multiplies across time:

$$\frac{1 + R}{1 + \bar{R}} = \prod_t \left(\frac{1 + R_t}{1 + \bar{R}_t} \right). \tag{15.8}$$

This attractive feature of geometric attribution shows nicely the intrinsically commutative nature of multiperiod attribution (i.e., scrambling the order of the periods has no impact on the active return).

Geometric attribution clearly offers some advantages over arithmetic attribution. The primary disadvantage with using geometric attribution is that most people have more difficulty thinking in terms of multiplication and division than thinking in terms of addition and subtraction. Thus, the choice between arithmetic and geometric is regarded largely as a matter of preference. Because some practitioners will undoubtedly use the geometric approach, however, an important question is how best to carry out the analysis—the central topic of this article.

In the following sections, I describe five geometric attribution models in some detail and analyze them within the context of the characteristics and properties discussed previously.

BKT Method

The BKT method is named for its developers, Burnie, Knowles, and Teder (1998), and was elaborated upon later by Bacon. In this scheme, the selection effect is defined as

$$S_{it}^{BKT} = \frac{S_{it}^{A}}{1 + \tilde{R}_t}, \tag{15.9}$$

where S_{it}^{A} is the arithmetic selection effect given by Equation 15.4 and $\tilde{R}_t$ is the notional return involving portfolio sector weights and benchmark sector returns,

$$\tilde{R}_t = \sum_{i=1}^{N} w_{it} \bar{r}_{it}. \tag{15.10}$$

The allocation effect in the BKT approach is given by

$$A_{it}^{BKT} = \frac{A_{it}^{A}}{1 + \tilde{R}_t}, \tag{15.11}$$

where A_{it}^{A} is the arithmetic allocation effect given by Equation 15.5.

Attribution effects combine *additively* in the BKT scheme. Hence, the net selection effect for a single period is

$$1 + S_t^{BKT} = 1 + \sum_{i=1}^{N} S_{it}^{BKT} = \frac{1 + R_t}{1 + \tilde{R}_t}. \tag{15.12}$$

The net allocation effect for the same period is given by

$$1 + A_t^{BKT} = 1 + \sum_{i=1}^{N} A_{it}^{BKT} = \frac{1 + \tilde{R}_t}{1 + \bar{R}_t}. \tag{15.13}$$

Thus,

$$\left(1 + A_t^{BKT}\right)\left(1 + S_t^{BKT}\right) = \frac{1 + R_t}{1 + \bar{R}_t}, \tag{15.14}$$

so the BKT method does not contain an unexplained residual.

Recall that the selection effect for a given sector depends only on weights and returns *within* the sector (see Equation 15.4). The BKT selection effect, given by Equation 15.9, depends explicitly, however, through the notional return, on the weights and returns of *all* sectors. The motivation for introducing the notional return term in the denominator is simply to get the numbers to add up without an unexplained residual. In other words, it is a "plug" that has no grounding in economic or financial principles. Consequently, the BKT selection effect is not consistent with the geometric measure of relative performance; hence, it is not metric preserving. Some of the spurious effects that arise from this definition of selection effect are demonstrated later.

Another problem with the BKT method is that it is not fully linkable. Bacon argued that one of the virtues of geometric attribution is compoundability, but the BKT attribution effects are not compoundable. They can be multiplied across time, of course, but neither the sum nor the product of these "compounded" attribution effects will aggregate to the geometric active return over multiple periods.[2] The reason for this complication is that attribution effects combine additively across sectors in BKT. If they were defined to combine multiplicatively, this difficulty would not arise.

Exponential Method

Cariño (1999) presented another approach to geometric attribution. In this method, the selection effect is given by the exponential

$$1 + S_{it}^{Exp} = \exp(k_t S_{it}^A), \tag{15.15}$$

where S_{it}^A is the familiar arithmetic selection effect given by Equation 15.4 and k_t is defined in terms of natural logarithms,

$$k_t = \frac{\ln(1 + R_t) - \ln(1 + \bar{R}_t)}{R_t - \bar{R}_t}. \tag{15.16}$$

The attribution effects in this exponential approach combine multiplicatively, so the net selection effect for period t is given by

$$1 + S_t^{Exp} = \prod_{i=1}^{N}\left(1 + S_{it}^{Exp}\right) = \exp\left(k_t \sum_i S_{it}^A\right) = \exp[k_t(R_t - \tilde{R}_t)]. \tag{15.17}$$

Similarly, the allocation effect in the exponential scheme is

$$1 + A_{it}^{Exp} = \exp(k_t A_{it}^A), \tag{15.18}$$

where A_{it}^A is the familiar arithmetic allocation effect given by Equation 15.5. The net allocation effect for period t is

$$1 + A_t^{Exp} = \prod_{i=1}^{N}\left(1 + A_{it}^{Exp}\right) = \exp\left(k_t \sum_i A_{it}^A\right) = \exp[k_t(\tilde{R}_t - \bar{R}_t)]. \tag{15.19}$$

The selection effect and the allocation effect multiply to exactly recover the geometric active return:

$$(1 + S_t^{Exp})(1 + A_t^{Exp}) = \exp[k_t(R_t - \bar{R}_t)]$$

$$= \frac{1 + R_t}{1 + \bar{R}_t}, \tag{15.20}$$

so the method leaves no unexplained residual.

This approach begins with the arithmetic attribution effects, then scales them through the factor k_t, and finally, transforms them into a multiplicative form through the exponential. The purpose of introducing k_t is simply to get the arithmetic attribution effects to aggregate without a residual to the geometric active return. Through the factor k_t, the selection effect (Equation 15.15) and the allocation effect (Equation 15.18) depend on the total portfolio return and benchmark return. Because the original definitions, given by Equations 15.4 and 15.5, do not depend on these quantities, the process leads to spurious effects and distortions, as I show later.

Pure Geometric Method

The starting point in both the BKT and the exponential approach is to take the arithmetic attribution effects and adjust them in such a way that they aggregate to the geometric active return. As a result, neither approach can be regarded as truly geometric. Rather, they represent arithmetic/geometric hybrids, which violates metric preservation.

The pure geometric method approaches the challenge differently. Arithmetic attribution effects should not be directly used to compute geometric attribution effects because the two represent intrinsically different measures of relative performance. Trying to "squeeze" arithmetic attribution effects into a "geometric box" leads to inconsistencies.

In the pure geometric approach, the objective is to define attribution effects properly in their geometric form. In particular, the attribution effects should be consistent with the geometric measure of relative performance and free of any spurious dependencies. (Elimination of the residual is a separate problem that I will address later.)

In developing this geometric model, I will follow the main ideas of my 2000/2001 paper—except for a few enhancements. Originally, I defined the "fully geometric" attribution effects to be a product of a "pure" component and a small perturbation that was applied to eliminate the residual. In this section, I focus on only the pure component.

The guiding principle is to exploit the strong parallel between arithmetic and geometric attribution. In essence, sums are replaced by products and differences are replaced by the corresponding ratios. Therefore, the pure geometric selection effect is given by

$$1 + S_{it}^0 = \frac{1 + w_{it}r_{it}}{1 + w_{it}\overline{r}_{it}}, \tag{15.21}$$

where the superscript zero, 0, denotes "pure."

Note that Equation 15.21 depends on the weights and returns within the sector only, so no spurious dependencies arise. It is also defined in a proportional manner; therefore, it is metric preserving. Furthermore, Equation 15.21 is intuitive: If the portfolio sector return is greater than the benchmark sector return, the numerator will be greater than the denominator (assuming positive weights) and the selection effect will be positive.

The pure geometric allocation effect should depend only on portfolio and benchmark sector weights, benchmark sector returns, and total benchmark returns. I originally defined the pure allocation effect by the following ratio:

$$\frac{(1 + w_{it}\overline{r}_{it})(1 + \overline{w}_{it}\overline{R}_t)}{(1 + \overline{w}_{it}\overline{r}_{it})(1 + w_{it}\overline{R}_t)}. \tag{15.22}$$

This definition is consistent with the geometric criteria. It is specified in a proportional manner and does not exhibit any spurious dependencies. Furthermore, the reader can easily verify that overweighting outperforming sectors leads to positive allocation effects, as required.

Although Expression 15.22 is a sound and reasonable definition for the allocation effect, I propose an alternative definition that is simpler and more intuitive:

$$1 + A_{it}^0 = \frac{1 + (w_{it} - \bar{w}_{it})\bar{r}_{it}}{1 + (w_{it} - \bar{w}_{it})\bar{R}_t}. \tag{15.23}$$

The results generated by Equation 15.23 are numerically almost equivalent to those generated by Expression 15.22. Equation 15.23 clearly states that if the portfolio manager overweights an outperforming sector, the numerator will be greater than the denominator and the allocation effect will be positive.

The pure method, however, does create a problem: The pure attribution effects do not exactly aggregate to the geometric active return; that is,

$$\prod_i (1 + S_{it}^0)(1 + A_{it}^0) \neq \frac{1 + R_t}{1 + \bar{R}_t}. \tag{15.24}$$

So, this pure form of geometric attribution is not residual free, and a method of eliminating the residual is needed. The question is how best to eliminate it.

Equations 15.21 and 15.23 represent appropriate "starting points" for carrying out geometric attribution. The central question that remains is how best to eliminate the residual. Here, we will enhance the original methodology of Menchero (2000/2001) in two ways. First, I originally proposed constraining the selection effect and allocation effect to independently aggregate to the BKT results at the fund level, as given by Equations 15.12 and 15.13, respectively. I now regard that constraint as inappropriate and have eliminated it. The rationale will become clear in the example I discuss later. The second enhancement pertains to the distribution of the residual among all the attribution effects. I originally proposed (Menchero 2000/2001) distributing it equally among the attribution effects. However, as pointed out by Carino (2002), this method is not the best choice because it has a disproportionate impact on small attribution effects. To overcome this problem, in this work, I sought to distribute the residual in such a way that the attribution effects would deviate minimally from their pure form while taking special care to ensure that small attribution effects were not disproportionately affected.

ADJUSTED PURE GEOMETRIC METHOD

Carino suggested that the residual be eliminated as follows. The adjusted selection effect is defined as

$$1 + S_{it}^{Adj} = (1 + S_{it}^0)^{\gamma_t}, \tag{15.25}$$

and the allocation effect, as

$$1 + A_{it}^{Adj} = (1 + A_{it}^0)^{\gamma_t}. \tag{15.26}$$

The adjustment factor, γ_t, is given by

$$\gamma_t = \frac{\ln[(1 + R_t)/(1 + \bar{R}_t)]}{\ln\left[\prod_j (1 + S_{jt}^0)(1 + A_{jt}^0)\right]} \tag{15.27}$$

and is a number close to 1. This adjustment indeed eliminates the residual; that is,

$$\prod_i (1 + S_{it}^{Adj})(1 + A_{it}^{Adj}) = \frac{1 + R_t}{1 + \bar{R}_t}. \tag{15.28}$$

Furthermore, small attribution effects are not disproportionately affected. For instance, if an attribution effect is zero in its pure form, the adjusted attribution effect will also be zero.

Careful consideration shows, however, that this approach also is not the best way to eliminate the residual. The optimal solution should, subject to the constraint that there be no residual, perturb the attribution effects as little as possible from their pure values. The adjustment given by Equations 15.25 and 15.26, however, increases or decreases the magnitude of all attribution effects. For instance, suppose that $\gamma_t > 1$. In this case, all positive attribution effects become more positive and all negative effects become more negative. That is, the method produces a cancellation effect in which the perturbations work at cross-purposes. Consequently, each perturbation is larger than necessary—which leads to the next approach.

Optimized Geometric Method

One can eliminate the residual in a manner that deviates minimally from the pure geometric attribution effects. I argue that this optimal adjustment produces the most accurate form of residual-free geometric attribution. The solution, which is derived in Appendix 15A, is found by adapting the optimization procedure from Menchero (2000) to the case of geometric attribution.

The optimized selection effect is given by

$$1 + S_{it}^{Opt} = (1 + S_{it}^0)\Gamma_{it}^S, \tag{15.29}$$

where the perturbation term, Γ_{it}^S, is given by

$$\Gamma_{it}^S = \exp[Q_t \ln^2(1 + S_{it}^0)] \tag{15.30}$$

and Q_t is given by

$$Q_t = \frac{\ln(1 + R_t) - \ln(1 + \bar{R}_t) - \sum_j \ln[(1 + S_{jt}^0)(1 + A_{jt}^0)]}{\sum_j \ln^2\left(1 + S_{jt}^0\right) + \sum_j \ln^2(1 + A_{jt}^0)}. \tag{15.31}$$

The optimized allocation effect is given by a similar expression,

$$1 + A_{it}^{Opt} = (1 + A_{it}^0)\Gamma_{it}^A, \tag{15.32}$$

where

$$\Gamma_{it}^A = \exp[Q_t \ln^2(1 + A_{it}^0)]. \tag{15.33}$$

Note that if the pure effect is equal to zero, the perturbation vanishes. As a result, small attribution effects are not disproportionately affected. Note also that the sign of the perturbation is the same for all attribution effects: If, in aggregate, the attribution effects need to be increased to eliminate the residual, *all* attribution effects will be made more positive. In other words, none of the perturbations work at cross-purposes, which allows the adjustments to be as small as possible.

The Methods Compared

A concrete example will illustrate the effects I have been discussing and allow a comparison of the methods.[3] Consider a portfolio manager who segments the equity market into large-cap, mid-cap, and small-cap sectors. The manager pursues an active stock selection strategy in the large-cap sector. In the mid-cap and small-cap sectors, the manager follows a passive selection strategy (by investing in, for example, index funds or exchange-traded funds).

Table 15.1 shows the weights and returns for a hypothetical three-month period that are consistent with such an investment strategy. The compound portfolio return is 31.84 percent (versus 30.40 percent for the benchmark), which means a geometric active return of 1.10 percent. Did the portfolio manager add value through security selection in this quarter?

First, observe that all the selection effects came from the large-cap sector. Next, note that the portfolio large-cap sector weight was 20 percent at the start of each period. In Month 1, the portfolio earned a return of 0 in the large-cap sector versus a return of 10 percent for the benchmark. In Month 3, these returns reversed. Whether the arithmetic or the geometric measure of relative performance is used, the negative selection effect of Month 1 should exactly cancel the positive selection effect of Month 3. The result leaves Month 2 as the tiebreaker. Because the portfolio outperformed the benchmark in the large-cap sector in Month 2, the selection effect should be positive for the quarter.

Table 15.2 presents month-by-month as well as linked geometric attribution effects for the five methods discussed in this article. Note, first, that all methods except the pure

TABLE 15.1 Weights and Returns for Portfolio and Benchmark for Hypothetical Three-Month Example

Month/Sector	Weight		Return	
	Portfolio	Benchmark	Portfolio	Benchmark
Month 1				
Large cap	20.00%	20.00%	0.00%	10.00%
Mid cap	50.00	20.00	4.00	4.00
Small cap	30.00	60.00	−4.00	−4.00
Total	100.00%	100.00%	0.80%	0.40%
Month 2				
Large cap	20.00%	20.00%	6.00%	5.00%
Mid cap	40.00	30.00	14.00	14.00
Small cap	40.00	50.00	12.00	12.00
Total	100.00%	100.00%	11.60%	11.20%
Month 3				
Large cap	20.00%	20.00%	10.00%	0.00%
Mid cap	50.00	30.00	16.00	16.00
Small cap	30.00	50.00	24.00	24.00
Total	100.00%	100.00%	17.20%	16.80%

TABLE 15.2 Geometric Attribution Effects: Five Methods

	BKT		Exponential		Pure		Adjusted Pure		Optimized	
Sector	Allocation Effect	Selection Effect	Allocation Effect	Selection Effect	Allocation Effect	Selection Effect	Allocation Effect	Selection Effect	Allocation Effect	Selection Effect
Month 1										
Large cap	0.00%	−1.95%	0.00%	−1.97%	0.00%	−1.96%	0.00%	−1.92%	0.00%	−1.97%
Mid cap	1.08	0.00	1.08	0.00	1.08	0.00	1.06	0.00	1.08	0.00
Small cap	1.31	0.00	1.32	0.00	1.32	0.00	1.30	0.00	1.32	0.00
Total	2.39%	−1.95%	2.41%	−1.97%	2.41%	−1.96%	2.37%	−1.92%	2.41%	−1.97%
Aggregate	0.40%		0.40%		0.41%		0.40%		0.40%	
Month 2										
Large cap	0.00%	0.18%	0.00%	0.18%	0.00%	0.20%	0.00%	0.18%	0.00%	0.19%
Mid cap	0.25	0.00	0.25	0.00	0.28	0.00	0.25	0.00	0.26	0.00
Small cap	−0.07	0.00	−0.07	0.00	−0.08	0.00	−0.07	0.00	−0.08	0.00
Total	0.18%	0.18%	0.18%	0.18%	0.20%	0.20%	0.18%	0.18%	0.17%	0.19%
Aggregate	0.36%		0.36%		0.39%		0.36%		0.36%	
Month 3										
Large cap	0.00%	1.74%	0.00%	1.72%	0.00%	2.00%	0.00%	2.11%	0.00%	2.01%
Mid cap	−0.14	0.00	−0.14	0.00	−0.15	0.00	−0.16	0.00	−0.15	0.00
Small cap	−1.23	0.00	−1.22	0.00	−1.49	0.00	−1.57	0.00	−1.48	0.00
Total	−1.37%	1.74%	−1.36%	1.72%	−1.64%	2.00%	−1.73%	2.11%	−1.64%	2.01%
Aggregate	0.34%		0.34%		0.32%		0.34%		0.34%	
Linked										
Large cap	0.00%	−0.06%	0.00%	−0.10%	0.00%	0.20%	0.00%	0.33%	0.00%	0.19%
Mid cap	1.19	0.00	1.20	0.00	1.20	0.00	1.15	0.00	1.18	0.00
Small cap	−0.01	0.00	0.01	0.00	−0.27	0.00	−0.37	0.00	−0.27	0.00
Total	1.17%	−0.06%	1.20%	−0.10%	0.93%	0.20%	0.77%	0.33%	0.91%	0.19%
Aggregate	1.10%		1.10%		1.13%		1.10%		1.10%	

Note: The row labeled "Aggregate" is the product of the total allocation effect and the total selection effect. BKT attribution effects at the sector level were linked by multiplication across time, which led to a small residual at the sector level.

361

approach recover the active return of 110 bps. The pure method, in contrast, reports an active return of 113 bps for a residual of 3 bps over three months.

Next, consider the attribution effects in more detail. In the BKT method, the linked selection effect for the quarter is −6 bps. To understand this nonintuitive result, note that in the BKT method, the selection effects from Month 1 and Month 3 do not cancel (that is, $0.9805 \times 1.0174 = 0.9976$). The combined effect from these two months is thus −24 bps, instead of 0. The reason is that the negative selection effect from Month 1 is weighted more heavily than the effect from Month 3 because the notional return during Month 1 is smaller (2.8 percent) than it is in Month 3 (15.2 percent). In fact, the positive selection effect from Month 2 is not sufficient to drive the overall result positive. Consequently, the result is the spurious effect that the manager exhibited negative selection over the quarter. Note carefully that the reason for the negative selection effect in BKT has nothing to do with security selection decisions in the large-cap sector. Rather, it has to do with the fact that the mid-cap and small-cap sectors performed well in Month 3, thus driving down the positive selection effect in the large-cap sector. Had the mid-cap and small-cap results been down in Month 3, then (as the reader can easily verify) the BKT method would have generated a positive selection effect over the quarter. The nonintuitive result is that a negative selection effect in large-cap is explained by the performance of the mid-cap and small-cap sectors.

The exponential method also produces a negative selection effect (−10 bps) for the quarter, for essentially the same reason. The factor k_t is larger for Month 1 ($k_1 = 0.9940$) than for Month 3 ($k_3 = 0.8547$) because of the smaller returns for Month 1. Consequently, the negative selection effect from Month 1 dominates the positive selection effect from Month 3. Even when the positive selection effect from Month 2 is included, the net result for the quarter is still negative. Again, the result is the nonintuitive interpretation that a negative selection effect in the large-cap sector is explained by the performance of the mid-cap and small-cap sectors.

In the pure geometric approach, the positive selection effect from Month 3 (2.00 percent) cancels the negative effect (−1.96 percent) from Month 1, as one intuitively expects. The net selection effect is thus given exactly by the selection effect from Month 2 (i.e., 20 bps). The pure geometric attribution effects represent the most accurate measure of geometric relative performance. Unfortunately, as discussed, this method is not residual free. The pure geometric active return linked over three months is 113 bps versus the true value of 110 bps, for a residual of 3 bps over three months.

Now consider the adjusted pure geometric method, which eliminates the residual by perturbing the pure attribution effects. The result is indeed residual free, as evidenced by the geometric active return of 110 bps. The perturbations, however, are larger than necessary and hence not optimal. The adjusted pure geometric method leads to a net selection effect of 33 bps, a full 13 bps over the pure value. Most of this difference comes from Month 3, in which the selection effect is 2.11 percent, or 11 bps above the pure value. This adjustment is so large because in Month 3, the true active return is 34 bps versus the pure value of 32 bps. The difference of 2 bps must be distributed among the different attribution effects. In this scheme, however, the negative attribution effects become more negative and the positive become more positive. Hence, in the adjusted method, the negative allocation effect in the small-cap sector goes from a pure value of −1.49 percent to a value of −1.57 percent, whereas the mid-cap sector goes from −0.15 percent to −0.16 percent. To offset these changes *and* eliminate the residual, the adjustment on the positive side must be still larger. To offset the residual of 2 bps for the month, the adjustment is 11 bps on the positive side and 9 bps on the negative side, which is clearly not the optimal adjustment.

In the optimized geometric methodology, the linked selection effect is 19 bps, in almost perfect agreement with the pure value of 20 bps. The selection effects from Month 1 (-1.97 percent) and Month 3 (2.01 percent) almost exactly cancel, unlike the result in all the other methods except the pure method. Also note that the individual attribution effects of the optimized method in every period are in almost exact agreement with the pure results (usually to within 1 bp). For instance, the optimized selection effect for Month 3 in the large-cap sector is within 1 bp of the pure value, whereas the value for the adjusted method differs by 11 bps. This example nicely illustrates the power and accuracy of the optimized geometric algorithm.

In summary, all five methods are commutative, but not all the methods are fully linkable. In some cases, efforts to eliminate the residual give rise to spurious effects and inaccuracies. The way to overcome these difficulties is to first define the attribution effects in their pure geometric (metric-preserving) form and then optimally distribute the residual among the pure effects.

CONCLUSION

I conclude on a somewhat philosophical note. It is not uncommon for analysts schooled in a particular attribution algorithm, such as the BKT or exponential method, to claim that their method represents the exact solution to the problem of multiperiod attribution. This article shows the spurious effects, however, that arise from these methodologies. When presented with such spurious effects, proponents of exact solutions usually explain the effects away with algebra, thereby "proving" that the solution was, after all, exact. I suggest that this turns the task of model building on its head. First and foremost, a model must produce results with a reasonable and intuitive financial interpretation. The interpretation must not be twisted to conform to the mathematics. The mathematics underlying the model must play a subordinate role to the financial meaning. If the math fails to deliver meaningful or reasonable results, the model must be abandoned—or, at least, refined. Thus, developing a good sound model is usually an iterative process.

The approach I took to constructing a model was to first specify the properties and characteristics the model should have. Specifically, I adopted the framework of qualitative characteristics and quantitative properties I set forth in 2004. This step led to definitions of "pure" attribution effects that (1) do not contain any spurious dependencies and (2) are consistent with the geometric measure of relative performance (i.e., are metric preserving). Further guided by the quantitative properties, I required the attribution effects to aggregate multiplicatively, thereby ensuring that the resulting algorithm would be fully linkable. As with all geometric attribution methodologies, the algorithm is automatically independent of the ordering of the periods, so the commutative property is also satisfied. Finally, to satisfy the residual-free condition, I applied an optimization procedure that ensures that the resulting attribution effects deviate as little as possible, subject to the constraint that there be no residual, from the pure effect. Therefore, although I do not claim that optimized geometric attribution is the "exact" solution, I do argue that it is the most accurate.

APPENDIX 15A: DERIVATION OF OPTIMIZED GEOMETRIC ATTRIBUTION

The optimization procedure is analogous to that used in deriving the optimized linking coefficients in arithmetic attribution (Menchero 2000). This analysis begins, therefore, with a brief derivation of the optimized arithmetic linking coefficients.

The residual-free condition is

$$R - \bar{R} = A\sum_t (R_t - \bar{R}_t) + \sum_t \alpha_t (R_t - \bar{R}_t), \tag{15.34}$$

where A is the natural scaling and α_t is a small perturbation.

For convenience, define the quantities

$$H \equiv R - \bar{R} - A\sum_t (R_t - \bar{R}_t) \tag{15.35}$$

and

$$h_t \equiv R_t - \bar{R}_t. \tag{15.36}$$

Then, Equation 15.34 can be rewritten

$$H = \sum_t \alpha_t h_t. \tag{15.37}$$

The optimal solution is found by minimizing the function

$$f = \sum_t \alpha_t^2, \tag{15.38}$$

subject to the constraint of Equation 15.37 (i.e., no residual). The solution can be found by means of Lagrange multipliers and is given by

$$\alpha_t = \frac{H h_t}{\sum_k h_k^2}. \tag{15.39}$$

Now, consider an analogous solution for the case of geometric attribution. For simplicity, the subscript t is suppressed, although the reader should be aware that, in what follows, only a single period is under consideration. For geometric attribution, the residual-free condition is

$$\prod_m (1 + G_m) = \frac{1 + R}{1 + \bar{R}}, \tag{15.40}$$

where G_m is a geometric attribution effect. Note that m represents a composite index denoting both allocation effect and selection effect (thus combining allocation and selection possibilities). Equation 15.40 simply states that multiplying all geometric attribution effects together must give the geometric active return.

An optimized geometric attribution effect should deviate as little as possible from the pure geometric effect. The geometric attribution effect, G_m, is related to the pure effect, denoted G_m^0, through a multiplicative factor, Γ_m:

$$1 + G_m = (1 + G_m^0)\Gamma_m. \tag{15.41}$$

The factor Γ_m should be as close to 1 as possible. Furthermore, in the limit that the pure effect goes to 0, the factor Γ_m should converge to 1 so that small attribution effects are not disproportionately affected, as noted by Cariño (2002). Therefore, the following proposition can be stated for the functional form:

$$\Gamma_m = (1 + \delta_m)^{\ln(1 + G_m^0)}, \tag{15.42}$$

where δ_m is a quantity to be determined. Note that if $G_m^0 = 0$, then $\Gamma_m = 1$, so this functional form guarantees that small attribution effects will not be disproportionately affected.

Substituting Equation 15.41 into Equation 15.40 and taking the natural logarithm produces

$$\ln(1 + R) - \ln(1 + \bar{R}) - \sum_m \ln(1 + G_m^0) = \sum_m \ln(\Gamma_m). \tag{15.43}$$

Now, we define the quantity

$$\hat{H} \equiv \ln(1 + R) - \ln(1 + \bar{R}) - \sum_m \ln(1 + G_m^0), \tag{15.44}$$

which is analogous to Equation 15.35. Combining Equations 15.42, 15.43, and 15.44 results in

$$\begin{aligned} \hat{H} &= \sum_m \ln(\Gamma_m) \\ &= \sum_m \ln(1 + G_m^0)\ln(1 + \delta_m). \end{aligned} \tag{15.45}$$

For convenience, also define

$$\hat{\alpha}_m \equiv \ln(1 + \delta_m) \tag{15.46}$$

and

$$\hat{h}_m \equiv \ln(1 + G_m^0). \tag{15.47}$$

Thus, Equation 15.45 becomes

$$\hat{H} = \sum_m \hat{\alpha}_m \hat{h}_m, \tag{15.48}$$

which is analogous to Equation 15.37. The optimal solution is found by minimizing the function

$$\hat{f} = \sum_m \hat{\alpha}_m^2, \tag{15.49}$$

subject to the constraint of Equation 15.48 (i.e., no residual). The optimal solution is analogous to Equation 15.39,

$$\hat{\alpha}_m = \frac{\hat{H}\hat{h}_m}{\sum_k \hat{h}_k^2}. \tag{15.50}$$

For convenience, define

$$\begin{aligned} Q &= \frac{\hat{H}}{\sum_k \hat{h}_k^2} \\ &\equiv \frac{\ln(1 + R) - \ln(1 + \bar{R}) - \sum_m \ln(1 + G_m^0)}{\sum_k \ln^2(1 + G_k^0)}, \end{aligned} \tag{15.51}$$

which is equivalent to Equation 15.31 in the text. When Equation 15.50 is combined with the definitions for $\hat{\alpha}_m$ (Equation 15.46) and $\hat{h}_m$ (Equation 15.47), the result is

$$\ln(1 + \delta_m) = Q \ln(1 + G_m^0). \tag{15.52}$$

Therefore,

$$1 + \delta_m = (1 + G_m^0)^Q. \tag{15.53}$$

Hence, Equation 15.42 becomes

$$\Gamma_m = (1 + G_m^0)^{Q \ln(1 + G_m^0)}. \tag{15.54}$$

Through the use of standard properties of logarithms and exponentials, Equation 15.54 can be rewritten as

$$\Gamma_m = \exp[Q \ln^2(1 + G_m^0)], \tag{15.55}$$

which is equivalent to Equations 15.30 and 15.33 of the text.

NOTES

1. The Brinson–Fachler approach also breaks out an "interaction effect." Most users do not believe this term reflects the investment process, however, and hence do not isolate it as a separate effect.
2. To express the linked BKT attribution effects in residual-free form, an *ad hoc* smoothing algorithm must be applied.
3. This example is identical to the one in Menchero (2004) for arithmetic attribution except that here, the example is analyzed geometrically.

REFERENCES

Bacon, C. 2002. "Excess Returns—Arithmetic or Geometric?" *Journal of Performance Measurement*, vol. 6, no. 3 (Spring):23–31.

Brinson, G., and N. Fachler. 1985. "Measuring Non-U.S. Equity Portfolio Performance." *Journal of Portfolio Management*, vol. 11, no. 3 (Spring):73–76.

Burnie, J., J. Knowles, and T. Teder. 1998. "Arithmetic and Geometric Attribution." *Journal of Performance Measurement*, vol. 3, no. 1 (Fall):59–68.

Carino, D. 1999. "Combining Attribution Effects over Time." *Journal of Performance Measurement*, vol. 3, no. 4 (Summer):5–14.

———. 2002. "Refinements in Multiperiod Attribution." *Journal of Performance Measurement*, vol. 7, no. 1 (Fall):45–53.

Menchero, J. 2000. "An Optimized Approach to Linking Attribution Effects over Time." *Journal of Performance Measurement*, vol. 5, no. 1 (Fall):36–42.

———. 2000/2001. "A Fully Geometric Approach to Performance Attribution." *Journal of Performance Measurement*, vol. 5, no. 2 (Winter):22–30.

———. 2004. "Multiperiod Arithmetic Attribution." *Financial Analysts Journal*, vol. 60, no. 4 (July/August):76–91.

CHAPTER 16

CUSTOM FACTOR ATTRIBUTION

José Menchero, CFA
Vijay Poduri, CFA

Portfolio analysts often use one set of decision variables for attributing portfolio returns and a different set for attributing risk. This practice obscures the relationship between the sources of risk and return. This article demonstrates how to align the attribution model with the investment process. The attribution methodology can be applied ex ante *or* ex post. *A factor-based investment process illustrates the general framework. Specifically, active return, tracking error, and the information ratio are attributed to a user-defined set of factors that reflect the manager's investment decision-making process. A concrete example with actual market data, a style portfolio, and a parsimonious set of custom factors illustrates how to apply the analysis.*

A common practice in asset management today is to use one model for attributing portfolio returns and to use an entirely different model for attributing risk. For instance, the active return of a portfolio is often decomposed into the allocation and selection effects by using the sector-based Brinson model (Brinson and Fachler 1985). The active risk of that portfolio, however, is typically attributed to a set of factors within a fundamental factor model. This inconsistency obscures the intimate link between the sources of risk and return.

A better approach is to align both the return attribution and risk attribution models to the same underlying investment process. If, for instance, the manager follows a sector-based investment process, then the risk should be attributed to the allocation and selection decision variables. Menchero and Hu (2006) showed how to attribute both *ex ante* and *ex post* tracking error to the allocation and selection decisions of the portfolio manager. Using a consistent framework for attributing both performance and risk provides greater insight into the essential character of the portfolio than is provided by considering each separately.

Reprinted from the *Financial Analysts Journal* (March/April 2008):81–92.

A natural extension of this analysis is to combine return and risk attribution and thereby explain the sources of risk-adjusted performance. This results in an attribution of the *information ratio* (active return divided by tracking error) reflecting the decision variables of the investment process. Menchero (2006/2007) carried out such an analysis for the case of a sector-based investment scheme. He showed that the portfolio information ratio was the weighted average of the component information ratios for each investment decision. The relevant weights, however, are not the investment weights but, rather, the risk weights.

An outstanding issue is how to extend this unified attribution framework to a factor-based investment process. In this article, we show how to attribute performance, risk, and risk-adjusted performance to a user-defined set of custom factors. We stress that we will not use the custom factors for *estimating* risk (this task is reserved for the risk model factors); rather, we present a means of *attributing* risk to the custom factors. With the sources of return and risk cleanly accounted for, we complete the analysis by attribution of the information ratio.

GENERAL ATTRIBUTION

We show here how to attribute performance, risk, and the information ratio to a very general set of investment decisions. Later, we apply this general framework to the special case of an investment process based on a set of custom factors.

Tien, Pfleiderer, Maxim, and Marsh (2005) addressed a related problem. They attributed risk calculated within a statistical factor model to a set of fundamental factors. Although this approach allows the user to attribute risk in a customized fashion, it does not satisfy certain desirable criteria, as we describe later.

Grinold (2006) also considered a similar problem; he attributed performance, risk, and implementation efficiency to a set of return sources. Our approach shares many characteristics with Grinold's. For instance, it is a flexible, unified, and portfolio-centered approach to attribution and it treats *ex ante* and *ex post* quantities in an entirely symmetrical manner. There are also significant differences, however, between the two approaches. For example, whereas Grinold carried out his analysis without explicit mention of a risk model, the risk factors play a central role in our approach. Another significant difference relates to our treatment of risk-adjusted performance attribution; Grinold decomposed the information ratio by using *transfer coefficients* (which measure how efficiently the signal is implemented in the portfolio), whereas we attribute the information ratio within a risk-budgeting framework.

Let m represent an investment decision, and let Q_m be the amount that the decision contributes to portfolio return R. In this article, unless otherwise specified, we use the symbol R to mean either portfolio (i.e., absolute) return or active (i.e., benchmark-relative) return. We consider Q_m a return contribution or an *attribution effect*. Because the attribution model must account for all of the return, we have

$$R = \sum_{m=1}^{M} Q_m, \tag{16.1}$$

where M is the total number of decisions. We emphasize that Q_m represents *any* way of decomposing portfolio return and is thus more general than the simple contribution to absolute return. For instance, Q_m might represent allocation and selection effects within the Brinson model or the contribution to active return arising from factor and idiosyncratic components.

Observe also that Equation 16.1 can be interpreted either *ex ante* or *ex post*. In the *ex ante* sense, Q_m represents the contribution of decision m to portfolio return over the subsequent period; in the *ex post* sense, Q_m represents the realized contribution to portfolio return over some historical interval.

The variance of R is given by

$$\sigma^2(R) = \text{cov}\left(\sum_{m=1}^{M} Q_m, R\right),\tag{16.2}$$

which can be rewritten as

$$\sigma^2(R) = \sum_{m=1}^{M} \text{cov}(Q_m, R).\tag{16.3}$$

Now, expressing the covariance in terms of volatility and correlation, ρ, and dividing out by the portfolio volatility, we have

$$\sigma(R) = \sum_{m=1}^{M} \sigma(Q_m)\rho(Q_m, R).\tag{16.4}$$

This important relationship attributes the risk to the same decision variables that were used to attribute the return in Equation 16.1. Thus, whereas the stand-alone risks, $\sigma(Q_m)$, are not additive, the risk *contributions*, $\sigma(Q_m)\rho(Q_m, R)$, do add up to fully explain the risk of the portfolio. Equation 16.4 is also intuitively appealing; it says that the contribution to risk from an individual position is the product of the *volatility of the contribution* and the *correlation* between the contribution and the portfolio.

Note that Equation 16.4, like Equation 16.1, is also valid in both an *ex ante* and an *ex post* sense. If considered in the *ex ante* case, the volatilities and correlations are based on risk model forecasts; if considered in the *ex post* case, they must be computed from the Q_{mt} and R_t time series over some historical window. If the analysis is performed *ex post*, the asset weights will generally change over time as a result of portfolio rebalancings and price fluctuations. Observe, however, that Equation 16.4 remains an exact *ex post* relationship even if the portfolio is rebalanced.

Although Equation 16.4 is thus of general validity, for purposes of attributing *ex ante* risk, it can be expressed in an even more useful form. *Ex ante* risk is based on a snapshot of portfolio holdings. Hence, the weights are constant and contribution Q_m can be written as the product of a source exposure, x_m, and a source return, g_m:

$$Q_m = x_m g_m.\tag{16.5}$$

Note that the exposure is simply a constant, whereas the return is a random variable. For instance, in the case of selection effect within the Brinson model, x_m would represent the portfolio sector weight and g_m would represent the active return within the sector. In a factor-based performance attribution scheme, x_m would represent the exposure to the factor and g_m would represent the return to the factor.

Substituting Equation 16.5 into Equation 16.4 and extracting the exposure, we obtain

$$\sigma(R) = \sum_{m=1}^{M} x_m \sigma(g_m)\rho(g_m, R).\tag{16.6}$$

This fundamental result formalizes what is already intuitively obvious to most asset managers—namely, that there are three drivers of portfolio risk: (1) the magnitudes of the exposures, x_m, (2) the volatilities of the source returns, $\sigma(g_m)$, and (3) the correlations between the source returns and the rest of the portfolio, $\rho(g_m, R)$. Equation 16.6, therefore, provides a clean, intuitive, and general method for decomposing portfolio risk in a manner that is completely consistent with the corresponding return attribution. Note also that $\sigma(g_m)\rho(g_m, R)$ is the marginal contribution to risk and represents the change in risk for small changes in exposure x_m. In Appendix 16A, we show that for an unconstrained optimized portfolio, the expected return of g_m is proportional to the marginal contribution to risk, with the constant being the information ratio of the portfolio.

Although the attribution framework provided by Equations 16.1–16.6 should be well known in the quantitative finance community, we were unable to locate any references that discussed the results in the full generality expressed here.

Return attribution and risk attribution can be naturally combined to provide risk-adjusted performance attribution. Defining the information ratio, IR, as the active return divided by the tracking error,

$$IR = \frac{R}{\sigma(R)},\tag{16.7}$$

and substituting Equation 16.1 for the numerator, we have

$$IR = \sum_{m=1}^{M} \frac{Q_m}{\sigma(R)}.\tag{16.8}$$

We now multiply and divide each term by the contribution to tracking error given in Equation 16.4 to produce[1]

$$IR = \sum_{m=1}^{M} \left[\frac{\sigma(Q_m)\rho(Q_m, R)}{\sigma(R)} \right]\left[\frac{Q_m}{\sigma(Q_m)\rho(Q_m, R)} \right].\tag{16.9}$$

The first term represents the risk weight of attribution effect Q_m; that is,

$$u_m = \frac{\sigma(Q_m)\rho(Q_m, R)}{\sigma(R)}.\tag{16.10}$$

If we multiply the numerator and denominator of Equation 16.10 by the portfolio risk, we obtain a covariance divided by a variance; hence, we may also interpret u_m as the beta of Q_m relative to the portfolio. The second term in Equation 16.9 represents the component information ratio associated with attribution effect Q_m,

$$IR_m = \frac{Q_m}{\sigma(Q_m)\rho(Q_m, R)}.\tag{16.11}$$

Note that the component information ratio is simply the stand-alone information ratio, $Q_m/\sigma(Q_m)$, magnified by the reciprocal of the correlation. This magnification effect represents the benefit of diversification. The portfolio information ratio can thus be expressed succinctly as a weighted average of the component information ratios:

$$IR = \sum_{m=1}^{M} u_m IR_m.$$ (16.12)

We stress two aspects of Equation 16.12: First, it is valid either *ex ante* or *ex post*, and second, the relevant weights are the *risk* weights, not the investment weights.

   Equations 16.1–16.12 provide the structural foundation for general attribution analysis. In the remainder of this article, we apply this analysis to the case of custom factors.

PERFORMANCE ATTRIBUTION FOR CUSTOM FACTORS

Assume that the true asset returns are generated by a set of K systematic factors, denoted X. Then, the true return-generating process can be written as

$$r_n = \sum_{k=1}^{K} X_{nk} f_k^{(X)} + e_n^{(X)},$$ (16.13)

where

r_n = return to asset n
X_{nk} = asset exposure to factor k
$f_k^{(X)}$ = factor return
$e_n^{(X)}$ = idiosyncratic return

The idiosyncratic returns are taken to be mutually uncorrelated and also uncorrelated with the factor returns. Superscript (X) indicates that the quantity is estimated with respect to the X basis. Because Equation 16.13 represents the true return-generating process, the factors X (assumed known) are the correct ones to include for risk estimation purposes.

   The portfolio return is given by

$$R = \sum_{n=1}^{N} w_n r_n,$$ (16.14)

where N is the number of assets and w_n is portfolio weight.

   Inserting Equation 16.13 into Equation 16.14 leads to

$$R = \sum_{k=1}^{K} X_k^P f_k^{(X)} + \sum_{n=1}^{N} w_n e_n^{(X)},$$ (16.15)

where

$$X_k^P = \sum_{n=1}^{N} w_n X_{nk}$$ (16.16)

is the portfolio exposure to factor k.

   Equation 16.15 attributes portfolio return to a factor component and an idiosyncratic component. Although this approach is perfectly valid, a shortcoming is that the factors typically do not match the investment process of the portfolio manager. In other words, although X represents the "right" factors for risk-forecasting purposes, they are the "wrong" factors for performance attribution purposes.

Let Y denote the custom factors of the portfolio manager. These factors may represent membership in custom groupings, exposures to macroeconomic variables, or expected alpha of stocks. The key point is that they reflect the investment process of the portfolio manager. The decomposition of asset returns with respect to these factors is given by

$$r_n = \sum_{l=1}^{L} Y_{nl} f_l^{(Y)} + e_n^{(Y)}, \qquad (16.17)$$

where

L = total number of custom factors
Y_{nl} = exposure of asset n to custom factor l
$f_l^{(Y)}$ = factor return
$e_n^{(Y)}$ = residual return

Superscript (Y) in this case indicates that the quantities are estimated with respect to the Y basis. Note that we do not assume that $e_n^{(Y)}$ returns are mutually uncorrelated or that $e_n^{(Y)}$ and $f_l^{(Y)}$ are uncorrelated.

Substituting Equation 16.17 into Equation 16.14, we obtain

$$R = \sum_{l=1}^{L} Y_l^P f_l^{(Y)} + \sum_{n=1}^{N} w_n e_n^{(Y)}, \qquad (16.18)$$

where Y_l^P is the portfolio exposure to custom factor l.

Equation 16.18 clearly attributes portfolio return to the factors that drive the investment process. A shortcoming of this approach, however, is that custom factors Y generally will not account for all of the factor risk, which can be fully explained only by risk factors X. Mathematically, we say that the custom factors may not "span the space" of the risk factors. In that case, we would find a gap between the risk model forecast and the factor risk attributable to Y.

A naive attempt to overcome this problem might be to directly include both sets of factors, X and Y, in a single regression,

$$r_n = \sum_{l=1}^{L} Y_{nl} f_l^{(XY)} + \sum_{k=1}^{K} X_{nk} f_k^{(XY)} + e_n^{(XY)}. \qquad (16.19)$$

This combined set of factors would necessarily span the space of the risk factors, but colinearity between X and Y (which could be severe) might confound the interpretations of the factor returns, $f_l^{(XY)}$.

The way out of this conundrum is to include the risk factors but only after orthogonalizing them to the custom factors. Let $\tilde{X}$ denote these residual factors. By construction, the residual factors obey the following condition:

$$\sum_{n=1}^{N} \tilde{X}_{nk} Y_{nl} = 0 \qquad (16.20)$$

for all k and l. The virtue of this approach is twofold: First, $\tilde{X}$ can now be included in the regression without affecting (i.e., confounding) the factor returns in Y, and second, $\tilde{X}$ will capture all of the factor risk left unexplained by Y.

This procedure has strong advantages, but it also comes at a cost; namely, residual factors $\tilde{X}$ now represent original risk factors X plus linear combinations of custom factors Y. If the colinearity between X and Y is small, then the residual factors essentially retain their original meaning. If the colinearity is strong, however, interpretation of the residual factors may not be clear. Nevertheless, even if the residual factors are obscured, the stock exposure to the residual factors will be clearly defined; therefore, the risk arising from the residual factors can be managed.

Decomposing asset returns with respect to the augmented set of factors, we have

$$r_n = \sum_{l=1}^{L} Y_{nl} f_l^{(Y)} + \sum_{k=1}^{K} \tilde{X}_{nk} f_k^{(\tilde{X})} + \tilde{e}_n. \tag{16.21}$$

Note that factor returns $f_l^{(Y)}$ in Equation 16.21 are identical to those in Equation 16.17.

Plugging Equation 16.21 into Equation 16.14 yields

$$R = \sum_{l=1}^{L} Y_l^P f_l^{(Y)} + \sum_{k=1}^{K} \tilde{X}_k^P f_k^{(\tilde{X})} + \sum_{n=1}^{N} w_n \tilde{e}_n, \tag{16.22}$$

which can be conveniently rewritten in compact notation as

$$R = R_Y + R_{\tilde{X}} + R_{\tilde{e}}, \tag{16.23}$$

where

R_Y = return attributable to custom factors
$R_{\tilde{X}}$ = return attributable to residual factors
$R_{\tilde{e}}$ = return from idiosyncratic effects

RISK ATTRIBUTION FOR CUSTOM FACTORS

We focus our attention here on *ex ante* risk, although attributing risk to a set of custom factors can also be carried out *ex post*. We require that our solution satisfy certain criteria. First, the exposures to the custom factors must be intuitive and must aggregate in the usual way (i.e., via Equation 16.16); the manager knows the portfolio exposures to the custom factors, and these must not be altered by the risk attribution scheme. Second, the risk decomposition must not depend on any ordering scheme for the custom factors; such a scheme, ultimately, would be arbitrary and not reflective of the investment process. Third, the portfolio risk must be fully accounted for; that is, there should be no "span gap."

The risk attribution scheme proposed by Tien et al. (2005) is an illustration of a methodology that fails to meet these criteria. For instance, their risk decomposition depends critically on the ordering of the factors, which violates the second criterion. In addition, the factor risk is not fully explained, so the third criterion is also violated.

We obtain our risk decomposition by first applying Equation 16.6 to the return attribution of Equation 16.23. The result is

$$\sigma(R) = \sigma_Y + \sigma_{\tilde{X}} + \sigma_{\tilde{e}}, \tag{16.24}$$

where

$\sigma(R)$ = tracking-error forecast from the risk model

$\sigma_Y = \sigma(R_Y)\rho(R_Y,R)$ = risk attributable to the custom factors

$\sigma_{\tilde{X}} = \sigma(R_{\tilde{X}})\rho(R_{\tilde{X}},R)$ = risk contribution from the residual factors

$\sigma_{\tilde{e}} = \sigma(R_{\tilde{e}})\rho(R_{\tilde{e}},R)$ = risk attributable to the idiosyncratic component

We can drill down into any of these components of risk by application of Equation 16.6 to Equation 16.22. Hence,

$$\sigma_Y = \sum_{l=1}^{L} Y_l^P \sigma\left[f_l^{(Y)} \right] \rho\left[f_l^{(Y)}, R \right] \tag{16.25}$$

decomposes the custom factor risk on a factor-by-factor basis. Similarly,

$$\sigma_{\tilde{X}} = \sum_{k=1}^{K} \tilde{X}_k^P \sigma\left[f_k^{(\tilde{X})} \right] \rho\left[f_k^{(\tilde{X})}, R \right] \tag{16.26}$$

attributes the risk of the residual factors, and finally,

$$\sigma_{\tilde{e}} = \sum_{n=1}^{N} w_n \sigma(\tilde{e}_n)\rho(\tilde{e}_n, R) \tag{16.27}$$

attributes the idiosyncratic risk at the security level. We stress that we used the *ex ante* risk model to compute all of the volatilities and correlations appearing in Equations 16.25–16.27. In Appendix 16B, we provide explicit formulas for these volatilities and correlations.

This risk attribution methodology satisfies our three criteria. First, factor exposures Y_l^P are intuitive and obtained in the usual way (via Equation 16.16). Second, the risk attribution methodology is clearly independent of any ordering of the factors. Finally, as shown in Appendix 16B, this scheme fully accounts for portfolio risk.

RISK-ADJUSTED PERFORMANCE ATTRIBUTION

With return attribution and risk attribution accomplished, the final step is to attribute the risk-adjusted performance, as measured by the information ratio. We begin again at the top level and then drill down. Applying Equation 16.12 to Equation 16.23, we have

$$IR = u_Y IR_Y + u_{\tilde{X}} IR_{\tilde{X}} + u_{\tilde{e}} IR_{\tilde{e}}, \tag{16.28}$$

where $u_Y = [\sigma_Y/\sigma(R)]$ is the risk weight of the custom factors and $IR_Y = (R_Y/\sigma_Y)$ is the component information ratio of the custom factors. The other terms in Equation 16.28 are similarly defined. Drilling down to the factor level, we have

$$IR_Y = \frac{1}{u_Y} \sum_{l=1}^{L} u_l IR_l, \tag{16.29}$$

where u_l is the risk weight of custom factor l and IR_l is the corresponding component information ratio.

We emphasize again that our information ratio decomposition is valid either *ex ante* or *ex post*. If the portfolio is optimized without constraints, then each unit of risk brings the same amount of expected return. In this case, as shown in Appendix 16A, the *ex ante* component information ratios will all be equal to the portfolio information ratio.

The introduction of constraints breaks up this tidy result, of course, and leads to a drop in the *ex ante* portfolio information ratio. One way to study this problem is through the concept of the transfer coefficient, as discussed by Clarke, de Silva, and Thorley (2006) or Grinold (2006). The information ratio decomposition proposed here can give additional insight into the relationship between constraints and implementation efficiency. The basic idea is that constraints give rise to variations in the *ex ante* component information ratios. As a result, parts of the risk budget are allocated to positions that are less than optimal in their risk–return trade-off, which decreases implementation efficiency.

EXAMPLE

Now, we report our use of actual market data in an example that demonstrates how the concepts presented in this article can be applied in practice. The risk model we used is the Barra USE3 model, which contains 13 style factors and 55 industry factors. As our custom factors, we selected the widely adopted Fama–French factors: value versus growth, beta, and size. We standardized these factors to have a mean of 0 and standard deviation of 1. We augmented these three factors with a fourth factor, defined by a column of ones, to represent overall market risk. Whereas the market factor describes the aggregate movement of stocks, the beta factor accounts for *differential* exposure to the market.

We estimated beta by regressing monthly stock returns on the estimation universe returns over a rolling five-year window. The custom size factor was taken verbatim from the Barra USE3 size factor, defined by the log of market capitalization. We defined our custom value factor by a weighted combination of Barra USE3 style factors: 0.40 dividend yield, 0.40 earnings yield, and 0.20 book-to-price ratio. Value stocks were deemed those that scored high along this combination of attributes.

Note that our choice of custom factors introduced three exact colinear relationships between the custom factors and the true risk factors. First, the sum of all industry factors gives the market factor. Second, the Barra size factor is redundant. Third, the custom value factor is defined by an exact linear combination of three Barra style factors. Exact colinearity, if untreated, makes regression impossible. In Appendix 16C, we discuss a method for removing such colinearities via restricted least-squares analysis.

We chose our portfolio/benchmark combination so as to obtain large exposures to the Fama–French factors. Hence, we selected the MSCI US Large Cap Value Index as our portfolio and the MSCI US Small Cap Growth Index as our benchmark. The motivation for selecting this particular combination was not to realistically represent an institutional strategy but to clearly illustrate the concepts in this work. This example was well suited for this purpose because the active risk was largely driven by the Fama–French factors.

For simplicity, we took our analysis period to be a single month, December 2006, although extending the analysis over multiple periods, as in Menchero (2006/2007), would be straightforward. We will combine the *ex ante* risk analysis at the start of the month with the *ex post* return analysis over the month, although we could have also used *ex post* risk analysis (by using realized daily factor returns) or *ex ante* return analysis (by using return forecasts).

In Table 16.1, we present the performance attribution analysis for December 2006. The summary in Panel A shows that the portfolio outperformed its benchmark by 3.14 percent

TABLE 16.1   Performance Attribution Analysis, December 2006

A. Summary view

Source	Portfolio Return	Benchmark Return	Active Return
Custom factors	1.69%	0.24%	1.45%
Residual factors	0.67	−0.55	1.22
Stock specific	0.40	−0.06	0.46
Total	2.76%	−0.37%	3.14%

B. Factor drill-down

Factor	Portfolio Exposure	Benchmark Exposure	Active Exposure	Factor Return	Portfolio Contribution	Benchmark Contribution	Active Contribution
Custom factor							
Market	1.00	1.00	0.00	0.35%	0.35%	0.35%	0.00%
Beta	−0.40	0.04	−0.45	−0.09	0.04	0.00	0.04
Value	1.51	−0.13	1.64	0.79	1.19	−0.10	1.29
Size	3.07	−0.01	3.09	0.04	0.12	0.00	0.12
Total					1.69%	0.24%	1.45%
Residual factor							
Momentum	−0.51	0.22	−0.73	−0.24%	0.12%	−0.05%	0.18%
Yield	0.11	−0.12	0.23	−0.49	−0.05	0.06	−0.11
⋮							
Banks	0.04	−0.01	0.06	0.81	0.04	−0.01	0.05
Biotechnology	0.02	−0.02	0.04	−2.90	−0.07	0.05	−0.12
Total					0.67%	−0.55%	1.22%

C. Stock drill-down

Company	Portfolio Weight	Benchmark Weight	Active Weight	Specific Return	Portfolio Contribution	Benchmark Contribution	Active Contribution
Exxon Mobil	8.08%	0.00%	8.08%	3.24%	0.26%	0.00%	0.26%
General Electric	6.41	0.00	6.41	1.82	0.12	0.00	0.12
Citigroup	4.30	0.00	4.30	7.05	0.30	0.00	0.30
Bank of America	4.26	0.00	4.26	−4.71	−0.20	0.00	−0.20
⋮							
Netflix	0.00	0.16	−0.16	−11.35	0.00	−0.02	0.02
Total	100.00%	100.00%	0.00%		0.40%	−0.06%	0.46%

Notes: Portfolio = MSCI US Large Cap Value; benchmark = MSCI US Small Cap Growth. Totals may not be sums of columns because of rounding.

over the month. Of this amount, 145 bps are attributable to custom factors, 122 bps, to residual factors, and the remaining 46 bps, to idiosyncratic effects.

In Panel B of Table 16.1, we show the drill-down detail for individual factors. Exposures are expressed as standardized *z*-scores. The exposure column multiplied by the factor return gives the return contribution from the factor. For instance, the value factor contributed 129 bps to active return, which was attributable to the large active exposure (1.64) combined with a significant return to the factor (79 bps) over the month. The same analysis holds for residual factors; for economy of space, we report only a handful of residual factors (two styles and two industries).

Panel C of Table 16.1 presents a drill-down to the stock level. Each weight column multiplied by the specific return column gives the contribution to return. For instance, the manager had an active weight of 4.30 percent on Citigroup, which earned a specific return of 7.05 percent, thus contributing 30 bps to active return.

Table 16.1 gives insight into the sources of active return but is silent on the question of risk. In Table 16.2, we decompose the *ex ante* risk in a manner consistent with the return attribution scheme in Table 16.1. In Panel A, we report the sources of portfolio risk, benchmark risk, and tracking error for the analysis date, 30 November 2006. As expected, the custom factors account for virtually all of the active risk in this example. For instance, the total tracking error (active risk) is 11.78 percent, with the custom factors explaining 12.21 percent. The residual factors in this case were diversifying (they reduced tracking error by 54 bps), whereas the specific contribution added 10 bps.

Panel B of Table 16.2 drills down to the factor level. As in Equation 16.6, the three drivers of risk are exposures, stand-alone volatilities, and correlations. The product of these three columns gives the contribution to active risk. Not surprisingly, value and size make greater contributions to overall tracking error than beta, although beta does contribute. The volatility of the active return from custom factors, $\sigma(R_Y)$, is 13.76 percent. The correlation between R_Y and the active return is 0.89, indicating that the custom factors were indeed driving the portfolio returns. Note that these aggregate volatility and correlation numbers were computed as in Appendix 16B and cannot be obtained by aggregating the factor-level values from Table 16.2. The risk contribution from residual factors (-54 bps) can be understood as the volatility, $\sigma(R_{\bar{X}})$, at 6.47 percent, multiplied by the slightly negative correlation, -0.08.

In Panel C of Table 16.2, we show the contribution to specific risk at the stock level. The specific risk is decomposed according to Equation 16.6 (i.e., as the product of three columns—weights, volatilities, and correlations). Although the active weights for some stocks are considerable (e.g., 8.08 percent for Exxon Mobil Corporation) and the specific volatilities can be quite large, the correlations are tiny. As a result, stock-specific risk is generally small. At the aggregate level, we see that the volatility of the specific return, $\sigma(R_{\bar{e}})$, is 1.82 percent and that the correlation of $R_{\bar{e}}$ with the active return is 0.06. These amounts result in a specific contribution of 10 bps to tracking error.

Table 16.3 shows the risk-adjusted attribution analysis for December 2006. Although to draw conclusions based on a single month of observations is ill advised, these results are useful for illustrative purposes. The information contained in Table 16.3 is fully derived from Tables 16.1 and 16.2.

In Panel A of Table 16.3, we present the summary view of the information ratio attribution. The numbers for active return are directly from Table 16.1; the active risk numbers come from Table 16.2 but were divided by $\sqrt{12}$ to restate them on a monthly basis. The component information ratio is simply the contribution to active return divided by the contribution to active risk. For instance, the custom factors contributed 145 bps to active

TABLE 16.2   Risk Attribution Analysis, 30 November 2006

A. Summary view

Source	Portfolio Risk	Benchmark Risk	Active Risk
Custom factors	10.79%	16.40%	12.21%
Residual factors	−0.35	0.26	−0.54
Stock specific	0.11	0.01	0.10
Total	10.55%	16.67%	11.78%

B. Factor drill-down

Factor	Portfolio Exposure	Benchmark Exposure	Active Exposure	Factor Volatility	Active Correlation	Active Risk
Custom factor						
Market	1.00	1.00	0.00	16.06%	−0.77	0.00%
Beta	−0.40	0.04	−0.45	4.17	−0.71	1.32
Value	1.51	−0.13	1.64	4.45	0.57	4.17
Size	3.07	−0.01	3.09	3.15	0.69	6.72
Total				13.76%	0.89	12.21%
Residual factor						
Momentum	−0.51	0.22	−0.73	3.76%	−0.14	0.39%
Yield	0.11	−0.12	0.23	1.84	−0.16	−0.07
$\vdots$						
Banks	0.04	−0.01	0.06	7.80	0.23	0.11
Biotechnology	0.02	−0.02	0.04	15.69	−0.04	−0.02
Total				6.47%	−0.08	−0.54%

C. Stock drill-down

Company	Portfolio Weight	Benchmark Weight	Active Weight	Specific Volatility	Active Correlation	Active Risk
Exxon Mobil	8.08%	0.00%	8.08%	12.60%	0.04	0.04%
General Electric	6.41	0.00	6.41	12.62	0.02	0.02
Citigroup	4.30	0.00	4.30	12.09	0.01	0.00
Bank of America	4.26	0.00	4.26	11.95	0.01	0.01
$\vdots$						
Netflix	0.00	0.16	−0.16	38.74	0.00	0.00
Total	100.00%	100.00%	0.00%	1.82%	0.06	0.10%

Note: See notes to Table 16.1.

TABLE 16.3   Risk-Adjusted Attribution Analysis, December 2006

A. Summary view

Source	Active Return	Active Risk	Risk Weight	Component *IR*	*IR* Contribution
Custom factors	1.45%	3.53%	103.68%	0.41	0.43
Residual factors	1.22	−0.16	−4.56%	−7.87	0.36
Stock specific	0.46	0.03	0.88%	15.46	0.14
Total	3.14%	3.40%	100.00%		0.92

B. Factor drill-down

	Active Return	Active Risk	Risk Weight	Component *IR*	*IR* Contribution
Custom factor					
Market	0.00%	0.00%	0.00%	0.00	0.00
Beta	0.04	0.38	10.82	0.10	0.01
Value	1.29	1.20	34.14	1.07	0.37
Size	0.12	1.94	55.04	0.06	0.04
Total	1.45%	3.53%	100.00%		0.41
Residual factor					
Momentum	0.18%	0.11%	−73.04%	1.56	−1.14
Yield	−0.11	−0.02	12.47	5.79	0.72
$\vdots$					
Banks	0.05	0.03	−19.70	1.59	−0.31
Biotechnology	−0.12	−0.01	4.64	16.84	0.78
Total	1.22%	−0.16%	100.00%		−7.87

Note: Totals may not be sums of columns because of rounding.

return and 353 bps to active risk, resulting in a component information ratio of 0.41. The information ratio contribution is the product of the risk weight and the component information ratio, as in Equation 16.28. The custom factors thus contributed 0.43 to the portfolio information ratio. The component information ratios of the residual factors (−7.87) and the specific-company part (15.46) are very large as a result of the small correlations, as shown in Table 16.2. Note, however, that the large component information ratios tend to be offset by the low risk weights of these contributors. Consequently, the contributions to information ratios for the residual factors (0.36) and the specific contribution (0.14) are reasonable and well behaved.

In Panel B of Table 16.3, we drill down to the factor level to understand the sources of risk-adjusted performance. Most of the information ratio attributed to custom factors (0.41) is ascribable to the value factor (0.37). The size factor, in contrast, delivered little in the way of active return, although it consumed the majority of the risk budget.

Many of the component information ratios for the residual factors may seem strikingly large; for instance, the biotech industry has a component information ratio of 16.84. Again, the cause is the tiny correlation (−0.04), as shown in Table 16.2 (Panel B). In these cases, the risk weights are typically small, so the impact on the portfolio information ratio is limited. For this reason, we do not report component information ratios for the specific contribution at the stock level.

CONCLUSION

Many portfolio managers use a set of custom factors in their investment decision-making processes. These managers want to know how their decisions affect the risk and return characteristics of the portfolio.

We have presented a methodology for attributing active return, tracking error, and the information ratio to a set of custom factors. We directly aligned the attribution methodology to the decision variables of the portfolio manager. Our approach also provides full drill-down capability, so we can explain how each decision contributes to return, risk, and risk-adjusted performance. Our risk attribution scheme produces intuitive exposures to the custom factors, does not impose artificial ordering schemes, and fully accounts for portfolio risk. The methodology can be applied either *ex ante* or *ex post*. For instance, *ex ante* information ratio analysis can provide insights into the relationship between constraints and implementational efficiency; the *ex post* counterpart can be used to provide risk-adjusted attribution analysis.

APPENDIX 16A: OPTIMAL EXPECTED RETURNS

The information ratio is given by Equation 16.7 in the text—that is, return divided by standard deviation of return. In the *ex ante* case, the portfolio return can be decomposed as $\Sigma x_m g_m$, where x_m represents the exposures to the return sources and g_m, the returns to the sources. The tracking error is decomposed according to Equation 16.6 as $\Sigma x_m \sigma(g_m)\rho(g_m, R)$. The optimal portfolio has the maximum information ratio. Hence, setting the partial derivatives to zero, we obtain

$$\frac{\partial}{\partial x_m}\left[\frac{R}{\sigma(R)}\right] = \frac{1}{\sigma(R)}\frac{\partial R}{\partial x_m} - \frac{R}{\sigma^2(R)}\frac{\partial \sigma(R)}{\partial x_m}$$

$$= 0. \tag{16.30}$$

This expression reduces to

$$\frac{g_m}{\sigma(R)} - \frac{R\sigma(g_m)\rho(g_m, R)}{\sigma^2(R)} = 0. \tag{16.31}$$

Solving for the expected returns of the sources, we find

$$g_m = IR[\sigma(g_m)\rho(g_m, R)]. \tag{16.32}$$

The expected return of the source is proportional to the marginal contribution to risk, with the proportionality constant being the portfolio information ratio. Rearranging terms, we obtain

$$\frac{g_m}{\sigma(g_m)\rho(g_m, R)} \equiv IR_m = IR. \tag{16.33}$$

Equation 16.33 states that for an unconstrained optimized portfolio, the component information ratio of each source is equal to the portfolio information ratio.

APPENDIX 16B: FORMULAS FOR VOLATILITIES AND CORRELATIONS

To derive our results, a matrix notation is convenient. The true return-generating process, given by Equation 16.13 in the text, is expressed in matrix form as

$$\mathbf{r} = \mathbf{X}\mathbf{f_X} + \mathbf{e_X}, \tag{16.34}$$

where

$\quad \mathbf{r} \ = N \times 1$ vector of asset returns
$\quad \mathbf{X} = N \times K$ matrix of true factor exposures
$\quad \mathbf{f_X} = K \times 1$ vector of factor returns
$\quad \mathbf{e_X} = N \times 1$ vector of residual returns
The portfolio return is given by

$$R = \mathbf{w}'\mathbf{r}, \tag{16.35}$$

where $\mathbf{w}'$ is the $1 \times N$ vector of portfolio weights.

The asset covariance matrix is

$$\mathbf{V} = \mathbf{X}\mathbf{F}\mathbf{X}' + \boldsymbol{\Delta}, \tag{16.36}$$

where $\mathbf{F}$ is the $K \times K$ factor covariance matrix and $\boldsymbol{\Delta}$ is the diagonal $N \times N$ specific variance matrix.

The risk of the portfolio is given by the usual expression—that is,

$$\sigma(R) = \frac{\mathbf{w}'\mathbf{V}\mathbf{w}}{\sigma(R)}. \tag{16.37}$$

Now, let $\mathbf{Y}$ denote the $N \times L$ matrix of custom factor exposures and let $\tilde{\mathbf{X}}$ denote the $N \times K$ matrix of factor exposures obtained by orthogonalizing true factors $\mathbf{X}$ to custom factors $\mathbf{Y}$. The exposures of the residual factors are given by

$$\tilde{\mathbf{X}} = \mathbf{P_{Y\perp}}\mathbf{X}, \tag{16.38}$$

where $\mathbf{P_{Y\perp}}$ is the projection operator that preserves any component perpendicular to $\mathbf{Y}$ and annihilates any component within the space of $\mathbf{Y}$. This projection operator is defined by

$$\mathbf{P_{Y\perp}} = \mathbf{I}_N - \mathbf{Y}(\mathbf{Y}'\mathbf{Y})^{-1}\mathbf{Y}', \tag{16.39}$$

where $\mathbf{I}_N$ is the $N \times N$ identity matrix.

To verify that the projection operator performs its job as advertised is easy; that is,

$$\begin{aligned} \mathbf{Y}'\tilde{\mathbf{X}} &= \mathbf{Y}'\mathbf{X} - \mathbf{Y}'\mathbf{Y}(\mathbf{Y}'\mathbf{Y})^{-1}\mathbf{Y}'\mathbf{X} \\ &= \mathbf{0}, \end{aligned} \tag{16.40}$$

so $\tilde{\mathbf{X}}$ is, indeed, orthogonal to $\mathbf{Y}$.

Also useful is defining a complementary projection operator, $\mathbf{P_Y}$, which preserves everything within the space of $\mathbf{Y}$ and annihilates all components outside the space:

$$\mathbf{P_Y} = \mathbf{Y}(\mathbf{Y'Y})^{-1}\mathbf{Y'}. \tag{16.41}$$

Note that a projection operator and its complement give the identity matrix:

$$\mathbf{P_Y} + \mathbf{P_{Y\perp}} = \mathbf{I}_N; \tag{16.42}$$

this result is often useful in derivations.

The augmented return structure, given by Equation 16.21 in the text, is expressed in matrix notation as

$$\mathbf{r} = \mathbf{Y}\mathbf{f_Y} + \tilde{\mathbf{X}}\mathbf{f_{\tilde{X}}} + \tilde{\mathbf{e}}, \tag{16.43}$$

where

$\quad \mathbf{f_Y} = L \times 1$ vector of custom factor returns
$\quad \mathbf{f_{\tilde{X}}} = K \times 1$ vector of returns to the residual factors
$\quad \tilde{\mathbf{e}} = N \times 1$ vector of idiosyncratic returns

The factor returns are estimated by ordinary least-squares (OLS) regression as

$$\mathbf{f_Y} = (\mathbf{Y'Y})^{-1}\mathbf{Y'r} \tag{16.44}$$

and, similarly,

$$\mathbf{f_{\tilde{X}}} = (\tilde{\mathbf{X}}'\tilde{\mathbf{X}})^{-1}\tilde{\mathbf{X}}'\mathbf{r}. \tag{16.45}$$

The fact that the OLS solution can be partitioned in this manner (i.e., $\mathbf{f_Y}$ does not depend on $\tilde{\mathbf{X}}$, and $\mathbf{f_{\tilde{X}}}$ does not depend on $\mathbf{Y}$) is a consequence of the orthogonality of $\mathbf{Y}$ and $\tilde{\mathbf{X}}$.

The portfolio return can thus be written as

$$R = R_Y + R_{\tilde{X}} + R_{\tilde{e}}, \tag{16.46}$$

where

$$R_Y = \mathbf{w}'\mathbf{P_Y}\mathbf{r} \tag{16.47}$$

is the return attributable to custom factors,

$$R_{\tilde{X}} = \mathbf{w}'\mathbf{P_{\tilde{X}}}\mathbf{r} \tag{16.48}$$

is the return attributable to residual factors, and

$$R_{\tilde{e}} = \mathbf{w}'(\mathbf{I}_N - \mathbf{P_Y} - \mathbf{P_{\tilde{X}}})\mathbf{r} \tag{16.49}$$

is the purely idiosyncratic return. Note that these three terms (R_Y, $R_{\tilde{X}}$, and $R_{\tilde{e}}$) explain all of the portfolio return.

We can attribute risk to the same return sources contained in Equation 16.46. In other words,

$$\sigma(R) = \sigma_Y + \sigma_{\tilde{X}} + \sigma_{\tilde{e}}, \tag{16.50}$$

where

$$\sigma_Y = \frac{\mathbf{w}'\mathbf{P_Y}\mathbf{Vw}}{\sigma(R)} \tag{16.51}$$

is the risk attributable to custom factors,

$$\sigma_{\tilde{X}} = \frac{\mathbf{w}'\mathbf{P_{\tilde{X}}}\mathbf{Vw}}{\sigma(R)} \tag{16.52}$$

is the risk attributable to residual factors, and

$$\sigma_{\tilde{e}} = \frac{\mathbf{w}'(\mathbf{I}_N - \mathbf{P_Y} - \mathbf{P_{\tilde{X}}})\mathbf{Vw}}{\sigma(R)} \tag{16.53}$$

is the risk attributable to purely idiosyncratic effects. Observe that these three terms (σ_Y, $\sigma_{\tilde{X}}$, and $\sigma_{\tilde{e}}$) fully account for portfolio risk.

The next task is to write explicit expressions for the volatilities and correlations of the factor portfolios. Let $\boldsymbol{\delta}_l$ be an $L \times 1$ vector whose lth component is 1 and whose other components are identically 0. The volatility of the custom factor portfolio is

$$\sigma\left[f_l^{(Y)}\right] = \frac{\boldsymbol{\delta}_l'(\mathbf{Y'Y})^{-1}\mathbf{Y'VY}(\mathbf{Y'Y})^{-1}\boldsymbol{\delta}_l}{\sigma\left[f_l^{(Y)}\right]}, \tag{16.54}$$

and the correlation of the factor portfolio with the overall portfolio is

$$\rho\left[f_l^{(Y)},R\right] = \frac{\boldsymbol{\delta}_l'(\mathbf{Y'Y})^{-1}\mathbf{Y'Vw}}{\sigma\left[f_l^{(Y)}\right]\sigma(R)}. \tag{16.55}$$

The factor marginal contribution to risk is given by the product of volatility $\sigma[f_l^{(Y)}]$ and correlation $\rho[f_l^{(Y)}, R]$ and reduces to

$$\sigma\left[f_l^{(Y)}\right]\rho\left[f_l^{(Y)},R\right] = \frac{\boldsymbol{\delta}_l'(\mathbf{Y'Y})^{-1}\mathbf{Y'Vw}}{\sigma(R)}. \tag{16.56}$$

Meanwhile, the portfolio exposure to custom factor l is

$$Y_l^P = \mathbf{w}'\mathbf{Y}\boldsymbol{\delta}_l. \tag{16.57}$$

Equation 16.25 in the text, therefore, becomes

$$\sum_{l=1}^{L} Y_l^P \sigma\left[f_l^{(Y)}\right]\rho\left[f_l^{(Y)},R\right] = \sum_{l=1}^{L} \frac{\mathbf{w}'\mathbf{Y}\boldsymbol{\delta}_l\boldsymbol{\delta}_l'(\mathbf{Y'Y})^{-1}\mathbf{Y'Vw}}{\sigma(R)}. \tag{16.58}$$

Note, however, that

$$\mathbf{I}_L = \sum_{l=1}^{L} \delta_l \delta_l'$$ (16.59)

is the $L \times L$ identity matrix. Therefore, Equation 16.58 reduces to

$$\sum_{l=1}^{L} Y_l^P \sigma\left[f_l^{(Y)}\right]\rho\left[f_l^{(Y)}, R\right] = \frac{\mathbf{w}'\mathbf{P_Y}\mathbf{V}\mathbf{w}}{\sigma(R)}$$

$$= \sigma_Y,$$ (16.60)

which is Equation 16.25 of the main text.

Similarly, the specific volatility for stock n is

$$\sigma(\tilde{e}_n) = \frac{\delta_n'(\mathbf{I}_N - \mathbf{P_Y} - \mathbf{P_{\tilde{X}}})\mathbf{V}(\mathbf{I}_N - \mathbf{P_Y} - \mathbf{P_{\tilde{X}}})\delta_n}{\sigma(\tilde{e}_n)}$$ (16.61)

and the correlation of this return with the portfolio return is

$$\rho(\tilde{e}_n, R) = \frac{\delta_n'(\mathbf{I}_N - \mathbf{P_Y} - \mathbf{P_{\tilde{X}}})\mathbf{V}\mathbf{w}}{\sigma(\tilde{e}_n)\sigma(R)}.$$ (16.62)

The reader may verify that

$$\sum_{n=1}^{N} w_n \sigma(\tilde{e}_n)\rho(\tilde{e}_n, R) = \frac{\mathbf{w}'(\mathbf{I}_N - \mathbf{P_Y} - \mathbf{P_{\tilde{X}}})\mathbf{V}\mathbf{w}}{\sigma(R)}$$

$$= \sigma_{\tilde{e}},$$ (16.63)

which is Equation 16.27 in the main text.

Although not obvious from Equation 16.61, it can be shown that $\sigma_{\tilde{e}}$ is, in fact, purely idiosyncratic in nature. This fact can be seen by noting $\mathbf{P_{\tilde{X}}}\mathbf{X} = \tilde{\mathbf{X}}$ and $(\mathbf{I}_N - \mathbf{P_Y}) = \mathbf{P_{Y\perp}}$, so $(\mathbf{I}_N - \mathbf{P_Y} - \mathbf{P_{\tilde{X}}})\mathbf{X} = 0$. In contrast, σ_Y and $\sigma_{\tilde{X}}$ will generally contain both a factor component and a specific component.

APPENDIX 16C: REMOVING COLINEARITIES THROUGH RESTRICTED LEAST SQUARES

We attribute returns according to

$$\mathbf{r} = \mathbf{Y}\mathbf{f_Y} + \tilde{\mathbf{X}}\mathbf{f_{\tilde{X}}} + \tilde{\mathbf{e}}.$$ (16.64)

A problem that arises in the implementation of this attribution, however, is that custom factors $\mathbf{Y}$ may be linear combinations of original risk factors $\mathbf{X}$, which induces a linear dependence among orthogonalized factors $\tilde{\mathbf{X}}$. To see this issue, assume that a particular custom factor $\mathbf{y}_l$ is linearly dependent on the risk factors as follows:

$$\mathbf{y}_l = \sum_{j-1}^{J} a_j \mathbf{x}_j.$$ (16.65)

Operating on this equation with the projection operator, $\mathbf{P}_{Y\perp}$, we obtain

$$0 = \sum_{j=1}^{J} a_j \tilde{\mathbf{x}}_j, \tag{16.66}$$

where the left-hand side is zero because $\mathbf{P}_{Y\perp}$ annihilates $\mathbf{y}_l$.

The linear dependence among the orthogonalized factors complicates the problem of estimating the factor returns by regression because matrix $(\tilde{\mathbf{X}}'\tilde{\mathbf{X}})$ is singular. To circumvent this problem, we used Equation 16.66 to impose a constraint on the factor returns,

$$\sum_{j=1}^{J} a_j f_j^{(\tilde{X})} = 0, \tag{16.67}$$

where $f_j^{(\tilde{X})}$ is the jth component of $\mathbf{f}_{\tilde{\mathbf{x}}}$. The returns to the orthogonalized risk factors were then estimated by using restricted least-squares regression, as described by, for example, Ruud (2000).

ACKNOWLEDGMENTS

We would like to thank Lisa Goldberg, Peter Shepard, and Dan Stefek for helpful discussions.

NOTES

1. This decomposition was also discussed by Xiang (2005/2006) within the narrower context of the Brinson model.

REFERENCES

Brinson, G., and N. Fachler. 1985. "Measuring Non-U.S. Equity Portfolio Performance." *Journal of Portfolio Management*, vol. 11, no. 3 (Spring):73–76.

Clarke, R., H. de Silva, and S. Thorley. 2006. "The Fundamental Law of Active Portfolio Management." *Journal of Investment Management*, vol. 4, no. 3 (Third Quarter):54–72.

Grinold, R. 2006. "Attribution." *Journal of Portfolio Management*, vol. 32, no. 2 (Winter):9–22.

Menchero, J. 2006/2007. "Risk-Adjusted Performance Attribution." *Journal of Performance Measurement*, vol. 11, no. 2 (Winter):22–28.

Menchero, J., and J. Hu. 2006. "Portfolio Risk Attribution." *Journal of Performance Measurement*, vol. 10, no. 3 (Spring):22–33.

Ruud, P. 2000. *An Introduction to Classical Econometric Theory*. New York: Oxford University Press.

Tien, D., P. Pfleiderer, R. Maxim, and T. Marsh. 2005. "Decomposing Factor Exposure for Equity Portfolios." In *Linear Factor Models in Finance*. Edited by John Knight and Stephen Satchell. Amsterdam, Netherlands: Elsevier.

Xiang, G. 2005/2006. "Risk Decomposition and Its Use in Portfolio Analysis." *Journal of Performance Measurement*, vol. 10, no. 2 (Winter):26–32.

CHAPTER 17

RETURN, RISK, AND PERFORMANCE ATTRIBUTION

Kevin Terhaar, CFA

To identify sources of manager skill and added value, portfolio managers and analysts must strive for consistency between the investment process and the performance attribution analysis used to evaluate the process. Otherwise, the attribution can yield erroneous results. Three examples explain why consistency is paramount in deciphering risk-adjusted performance and evaluating investment expertise.

In this presentation, I provide three examples to explain why, when evaluating performance, the attribution must be consistent with the investment process, the risk modeling, and all other aspects of the portfolio management process. If they are not consistent, some bizarre, or even erroneous, results can occur. In all three detailed, but fictitious, examples, I ignore currency effects in order to simplify the exposition. I also assume that the returns are continuously compounded, or logarithmic, so that I can aggregate returns through simple addition.

Performance evaluation and attribution should accurately reflect the decision-making process and should operate within the context of relevant and controllable variables. Performance analysis is not helpful if the attribution is to an area that the portfolio manager has no control over. The results should be attributed to those responsible for making the investment decision, and the credit for outperformance and the responsibility for underperformance should be given to whomever it is due.

Evaluating performance is a backward-looking, retrospective process. If a manager wants to measure the outcome of certain investment choices, he uses the historical weights and data on the returns and risks of the portfolio for the evaluation period. Strategy, however, is a forward-looking, or forecasting-based, exercise. Managers set active strategy weights for specific positions in order to garner added value. Therefore, managers accept more risk when they believe the risk–return trade-off is going to be positive. The purpose of performance evaluation

Reprinted from *AIMR Conference Proceedings: Benchmarks and Attribution Analysis* (June 2001):21–27.

is to determine whether the trade-offs made by portfolio managers add value or whether they add risks without adding return.

EXAMPLE 1

This first example illustrates the importance of performance evaluation being consistent with the investment process. Consider an international equity portfolio with a two-country benchmark: 50 percent in France and 50 percent in Germany. For the performance-measurement period, the passive, or index, return for France was 6.0 percent; the German index return was 6.7 percent. Thus, the benchmark return was 6.35 percent.

The portfolio manager took an active bet in both of these countries. She was overweight France, with 53 percent exposure versus 50 percent for the benchmark, and underweight Germany, with 47 percent exposure versus 50 percent for the benchmark. This portfolio manager was thus overweight the poorer performing market and underweight the better performing market, and therefore, an attribution along the country dimension shows that country selection was negative:

$$
\begin{aligned}
\text{Country selection} &= (\text{Active weight of France} \times \text{French market return}) \\
&\quad + (\text{Active weight of Germany} \times \text{German market return}) \\
&= (3\% \times 600 \text{ basis points}) + (-3\% \times 670 \text{ bps}) \\
&= -2 \text{ bps}.
\end{aligned}
$$

The manager had roughly a 2 basis point detraction from return based on her country selection.

Given an actual portfolio return of 6.45 percent, the outperformance was 10 bps. How did the portfolio add 10 bps of value? Country selection had a negative impact of 2 bps, so the plan sponsor (or analyst) could attribute a positive return of 12 bps to security selection. In this case, the stock pickers should be the ones who get the credit for outperformance and receive the big bonuses because they were responsible for the added value.

But what if the plan sponsor considers the breakdown of the benchmark along industry dimensions rather than along country dimensions? The benchmark is weighted 40 percent in autos and 60 percent in semiconductors; the auto industry return was 4.75 percent, which was well below the semiconductor industry return of 7.42 percent. Taking those passive industry weights and multiplying them by the index returns in autos and semiconductors also generates the 6.35 percent return of the benchmark:

$$
40\%(475 \text{ bps}) + 60\%(742 \text{ bps}) = 6.35\%.
$$

The manager's active strategy was to overweight autos by 2 percent and to underweight semiconductors by 2 percent, contrary to the relative returns. As a result, the attribution shows negative industry selection:

$$
\begin{aligned}
\text{Industry selection} &= (\text{Active weight of autos} \times \text{Auto return}) \\
&\quad + (\text{Active weight of semiconductors} \times \text{Semiconductor return}) \\
&= (2\% \times 475 \text{ bps}) + (-2\% \times 742 \text{ bps}) \\
&= -5 \text{ bps}.
\end{aligned}
$$

Recall that the portfolio's actual return was 6.45 percent (i.e., added value of 10 bps). The portfolio lost 5 bps of return because of poor industry selection. Therefore, 15 bps must have

been earned from security selection. This outcome seems to reinforce the fact that the portfolio manager's macrobets were ill chosen, even though the stock pickers did a great job of
adding value.

The problem with such a conclusion is that the portfolio was not managed according
to just a country decision or an industry decision; it was managed along both dimensions
simultaneously. Table 17.1 shows the benchmark weights by industry and country, and Table
17.2 shows the index returns by industry and country. French autos had the lowest return
(4 percent), but French semiconductors had the highest return (8 percent). German semiconductors had a better return than both German and French autos. The manager's bets by
industry and country are given in Table 17.3.

If the benchmark weights from Table 17.1 are applied to the index returns in Table 17.2,
the actual benchmark return of 6.35 percent can be computed (shown in Table 17.2):

$$25\%(400\,\text{bps}) + 25\%(800\,\text{bps}) + 15\%(600\,\text{bps})$$
$$+ 35\%(700\,\text{bps}) = 6.35\%.$$

This decomposition allows the plan sponsor to look at both industry and country dimensions
concurrently, as the portfolio manager did. Remember that the manager was 3 percent overweight in France and 3 percent underweight in Germany, and she was 2 percent overweight
in autos and 2 percent underweight in semiconductors.

The manager's semiconductor and auto bets, or positions, were mostly consistent with
the simultaneous country and industry returns. Within semiconductors, the portfolio was

TABLE 17.1   Benchmark Weights by Industry and Country

Industry	France	Germany	Total
Autos	25%	15%	40%
Semiconductors	25	35	60
Total	50%	50%	100%

TABLE 17.2   Returns by Industry and Country

Industry	France	Germany	Total
Autos	4.00%	6.00%	4.75%
Semiconductors	8.00	7.00	7.42
Combined	6.00	6.70	6.35

TABLE 17.3   Manager's Active Bets: Industry and Country

Industry	France	Germany	Total
Autos	−3%	5%	2%
Semiconductors	6	−8	−2
Total	3%	−3%	

TABLE 17.4   Manager's Active Bets and Index Returns: Industry and Country

Industry	France (active weight × return)		Germany (active weight × return)		Total
Autos	0.22 × 4.0 = 0.88	+	0.20 × 6.0 = 1.20	=	2.08%
Semiconductors	0.31 × 8.0 = 2.48	+	0.27 × 7.0 = 1.89	=	4.37
Total	3.36%	+	3.09%	=	6.45%

overweight France and underweight Germany. Table 17.2 shows that in terms of return, the French semiconductor industry was better performing than the German. Within autos, the portfolio was overweight in Germany and underweight in France, which was also consistent with the returns (higher returns for German autos than French autos). The one area where the portfolio was not consistent with relative returns was within Germany, where autos were overweighted and semiconductors were underweighted. For this period, German semiconductors outperformed German autos. The decision to underweight the outperforming industry hurt the portfolio's performance.

Multiplying the returns in France and Germany in the auto and semiconductor industries by the manager's actual weights, or positions, the plan sponsor can calculate the portfolio's actual return—6.45 percent, as shown in Table 17.4. This analysis indicates that there was no positive security selection; the added value came from joint industry and country strategies. When the attribution is done by industry or country alone, the stock pickers are rewarded for what appears to be positive security selection, and the country and industry analysts are blamed for what appears to be poor country and industry selection. In other words, the first two attributions rewarded the wrong people. The attributions were not consistent with the investment process, which took into consideration both industries and countries when setting strategy.

In this admittedly contrived example, the first two attributions assumed an investment process in which the country and industry selection happened first, followed by the security selection within the industries or countries. But if the portfolio is not managed in such a hierarchical manner, the performance attribution will point to the wrong conclusion. If the portfolio is managed by industry analysts across countries, as this portfolio was, then performance must be evaluated within that framework. An attribution that slices the performance results in ways that are inconsistent with the management process can lead to erroneous results.

EXAMPLE 2

This example examines the decisions of a European equity analyst who is responsible for consumer products companies in a non-U.S. portfolio. The equity analyst's manager is interested in the analyst's stock-picking ability. To get this information, the manager wants to evaluate the analyst's performance solely based on security selection, so he needs to control for market exposure. In other words, he must eliminate any influences that are solely the result of the analyst's market risk exposures. The analyst should not be moving into high-beta stocks simply because her market view is positive; nor should she be moving into low-beta stocks when she believes a market decline is forthcoming if these market "calls" are not hers to make. Consequently, the design of an attribution system or a performance evaluation system should control for, or ignore, any bets an analyst might take in a beta or market dimension.

The attribution system must be designed so that all market effects attributable to beta adjustments are removed. This provision allows the manager to strip out the market effects, leaving only the alpha portion—the superior specific return. The analyst can then be judged on her ability to generate alpha instead of the generation of total value added. The capital asset pricing model (CAPM) states that

$$R_i - R_f = \alpha_i + \beta_{i,m}(R_m - R_f),$$

where

R_i = the return of security i
R_f = the risk-free rate
α_i = alpha (or specific return) for security i
$\beta_{i,m}$ = beta (or systematic risk) for security i relative to market m
R_m = return of the market

In other words, the excess return on any asset in excess of the risk-free rate is equal to alpha plus the stock's systematic excess return. To evaluate whether the analyst has produced any alpha, the systematic return (beta times the market excess return) must be stripped off the total return.

Suppose that one of the stocks the analyst picked was Unilever. The company has dual headquarters and market listings in the Netherlands and in the United Kingdom. For an analyst looking at Unilever, the fundamental characteristics of the company—the cash flows, earnings, dividends, and so on—should be invariant to trading location. And whether the stock trades in Amsterdam in euros or in London in sterling should not have any effect on Unilever's business or its evaluation by the analyst. As a result, the decision to hold Unilever, and the subsequent performance attribution, should be unaffected by the choice of trading location. But it is not.

The analyst can potentially influence the performance evaluation system through the choice of which Unilever shares—London's or the Netherlands'—to hold in the portfolio. When the time comes for the evaluation of security selection, alpha will be calculated by taking out the cost of market impact. The savvy analyst knows that the market baskets of the United Kingdom and the Netherlands differ: Because of their dissimilar compositions, the British and the Dutch equity markets do not always behave in similar ways.

Nonetheless, these two markets can be compared by using 10 years of monthly data and calculating the betas of Unilever in the United Kingdom and the Netherlands against the respective MSCI (local) country indexes. The resulting historical beta in the United Kingdom is 0.8, and in the Netherlands, 0.9. Using these values, the alpha is twice as large in the United Kingdom as in the Netherlands. Thus, if an analyst suspected the return on Unilever to be similar in each market, it would be to the analyst's advantage to pick either the low-beta or the high-beta market, depending on the analyst's expectations for market return. Such a strategy can produce an alpha that magnifies an already good security selection. Thus, betas influence alphas and can produce apparently outstanding security selection ability. Any inconsistencies in measuring risk characteristics of the stock, the portfolio, and the market can affect the outcome of the equity analyst's performance attribution.

In thinking about this example, one might ask whether the local market, either British or Dutch, is in fact the market that should be used in the evaluation of the analyst's performance. The answer is almost certainly no. Because this is a European consumer products analyst, the better choice is likely to be an index of European consumer products companies. This answer logically leads to the next question: Was the decision to overweight Unilever a good one compared with the other European consumer products companies vying for the analyst's recommendation?

Comparing the analyst against an appropriate industry or market index solves one problem but can raise other issues of concern. The performance attribution must account for any responsibility the analyst may have had in determining the overall portfolio's exposure to consumer products companies. If the analyst had input into the degree of exposure of European consumer products companies in the non-U.S. equity portfolio—as opposed to that decision being made at a more senior portfolio management level—then the adjustment of the analyst's selections for beta effects might be exactly the wrong thing to do.

To clarify, consider that exposure to consumer products companies can be added to the portfolio in two ways. One is to increase the allocation or weight of these companies in the overall portfolio. If the portfolio is overweight consumer products companies on the recommendation of the analyst, the resulting performance can *and should* be attributed to the analyst. The other way to add exposure in consumer products companies is to let the analyst put consumer products stocks with high betas into the portfolio. In this situation, stripping out the beta contribution to return in the performance attribution would be incorrect, because the analyst had the mandate to choose high-beta stocks. Clearly, many issues need to be considered when designing an equity performance attribution so that the information culled from the data is correct in light of the specific investment process and responsibility for decision-making in the portfolio.

EXAMPLE 3

This third, and final, example focuses on risk-adjusted performance, specifically on the information ratio. Because two definitions of the information ratio exist, I want to highlight the importance of clarity in communication and terminology. All participants must understand what is contained in the performance evaluation and compliance materials used within their organization, and relevant terms should be precise and well defined.

In this example, I use a balanced benchmark that has the characteristics shown in Table 17.5. The benchmark return was 9.25 percent, and the correlation between equities and bonds was 0.35. Using the correlation, weights, and risk numbers, the benchmark volatility can be calculated as slightly more than 11 percent.

Suppose the manager was underweight in equities and overweight in fixed income in the portfolio, as shown in Table 17.6. Table 17.5 shows the passive return of equities to be 10 percent and the passive return of fixed income to be 7.5 percent; thus, the active strategy adversely affected the return of the portfolio. The actual return in the equity portion of the portfolio was 11 percent—100 bps greater than the passive benchmark return. The equity

TABLE 17.5 Benchmark Characteristics

Asset Class	Weight	Return	Risk
Equity	70%	10.00%	15%
Bonds	30	7.50	5

TABLE 17.6 Portfolio Strategy, Return, and Risk

Asset Class	Weight	Return	Active Risk
Equity	40%	11.00%	3.00%
Bonds	60	8.00	1.00

portfolio had a tracking error (active risk) of 3 percent and earned 100 bps, for a risk–return trade-off of 0.33. Thus, the equity manager added 33 bps of return for every 100 bps of risk taken in that portion of the portfolio.

Fixed-income management also added value. Because the actual return in the bond portfolio was 8 percent, versus 7.5 percent for the benchmark, the fixed-income portion of the portfolio added 50 bps. The tracking error in bonds was 1 percent, so the fixed-income portfolio had a better risk–return trade-off (0.5) than did the equity portfolio. Thus, the information ratio for bonds in this portfolio was 0.5, and for equities, 0.33.

Using the actual equity and fixed-income returns and the allocation information, one can see that the return of the overall portfolio was 9.2 percent. The benchmark return was 9.25 percent, so the portfolio underperformed the benchmark by 5 bps. Even though the portfolio's equity and bond positions did well, the asset allocation strategy of underweighting equities, which outperformed bonds by a wide margin, hurt the portfolio return; however, the under-weighting in equities reduced the total risk of the portfolio. Remember that the correlation between equities and bonds was 0.35 and that equities had three times the risk of fixed income. The benchmark's volatility was 11.1 percent, but the portfolio's total volatility, or absolute risk, was 7.7 percent. The manager thus decreased the return of the portfolio slightly, by 5 bps, while improving the overall risk of the portfolio rather dramatically, which means that the portfolio's Sharpe ratio was much higher than that of the benchmark. The Sharpe ratio is the risk-adjusted excess return of the portfolio, where risk is measured on an absolute basis as opposed to a relative basis (i.e., benchmark).

Additional risk statistics can also be calculated for the portfolio. Although familiarity with betas of individual stocks relative to an equity index is widespread, betas can also be calculated for fixed-income securities relative to a benchmark or for a balanced portfolio against a benchmark portfolio. Beta is simply the price sensitivity of one instrument, or group of instruments, relative to the price sensitivity of another instrument, or group of instruments. With the reduction in overall portfolio risk from 11.1 percent to 7.7 percent, the manager reduced the beta for the portfolio relative to the benchmark from 1.00 to 0.65, which is a significant reduction. In this case, the 0.65 means that for every 1 percent gain (loss) in the benchmark, the manager can expect the portfolio to gain (lose) only 65 bps because of systematic risk.

Referring back to the CAPM equation, one can see that the return on the portfolio is the result of two components: alpha, which is not benchmark related, and beta, which is benchmark related. Thus, in risk terms, the portfolio can have two types of risk. The manager can take bets, or assume risks, relative to the benchmark or take bets, or assume risks, that are unrelated to the benchmark. Tracking error combines both those risks into one number; however, it can be split into two pieces. One piece is the risk that results from having a beta different from 1.00. In the example just described, the risk of underweighting equities and overweighting bonds led to a beta of 0.65. The second part of tracking error is the residual risk, which is related more to security selection or security-specific sources. And just as active risk can be decomposed into benchmark-related and residual components, active return (or value added) can too.

As stated earlier, the main point of this example is to evaluate the information ratio of the portfolio. Remember that the portfolio had 5 bps of negative added value. It also had a tracking error of 4.7 percent and residual risk of 2.7 percent. The information ratio can be calculated two ways. One calculation involves taking the added value, the negative 5 bps, and dividing it by tracking error. This methodology produces an information ratio of −0.01, which indicates that the risk taken by the manager relative to the benchmark went unrewarded.

Alternatively, if the information ratio is calculated using alpha (residual return) and residual risk, the information ratio is high. The alpha for the portfolio was 1.08, and the residual risk was 2.7 percent, which yields an information ratio of 0.40. This information ratio falls between the risk-adjusted return numbers for the equity portion of the portfolio, 0.33, and the bond portion, 0.50.

Risk-related portfolio attribution systems can use either method to calculate an information ratio, and each produces quite different feedback. In this example, the same portfolio generated both a negative information ratio and a positive information ratio. One measure conveys a complete absence of skill, whereas the other indicates good selection ability on the part of the portfolio manager.

Both approaches are valid, but in the world of investment consulting, calculating the information ratio by using the value-added return to tracking error is probably more common than using alpha to residual risk. This preference is because tracking error is the total risk taken relative to the benchmark in the effort to add value, and thus, the measure of added value shows the amount of return the portfolio earned from the risk taken.

CONCLUSION

Performance attribution must measure and be consistent with the relevant variables in investment decision making. If country selection or industry selection is not a relevant decision variable, then performing an attribution on the basis of country or industry variables can produce completely erroneous results. Furthermore, the dimensions along which performance is measured should be controllable. If portfolio managers or analysts cannot control certain aspects of the investment process and have no influence in the original decision, then saddling them with the responsibility for the decision—either penalizing them for a bad outcome or rewarding them for a good outcome—is improper.

Finally, someone must be explicitly accountable for decisions with respect to major sources of risk and return. If a source of risk exists in the portfolio that the portfolio manager has control over—that is, a risk that the manager can increase, minimize, or eliminate (by holding the benchmark)—then the manager needs to be explicitly responsible for that risk and its effect on the portfolio.

QUESTION AND ANSWER SESSION

Question: How common is the problem discussed in Example 1—a mismatch between the benchmark and the actual management process?

Terhaar: Example 1 reflects the changes under way at Brinson Partners. We have seen the global equity markets become more industry focused and less top-down country focused. Our analysts are currently set up to be industry analysts across countries, but if you look at the typical global equity risk and attribution process, it was built as a top-down country model first, so country decisions are given primary importance in both risk modeling and in return attribution. Thus, using that approach to do performance attribution for one of our analysts can give misleading results.

Question: In Example 1, you initially found 10 bps of added value from stock selection, but then it dissipated. Where did it go?

Terhaar: The added value dissipated because of the actual allocations within French and German autos and French and German semiconductors. When I ignored everything except the country decision, it looked like the manager made a poor country decision, given the French and German returns, because she overweighted France and underweighted Germany. When I ignored everything other than the industry decisions, it looked like the manager made a poor decision, given the index returns, on the industry allocation; she overweighted autos and underweighted semiconductors.

There was no currency effect, so if the added value was not from the country or industry decisions, it must have been from stock selection. But when I looked at the combined overweighted French semiconductors, which was the highest return industry in either country, and the underweighted French autos, which was the lowest return industry in either country, I could see that those joint industry and country decisions accounted for all the added value and that stock selection did not add any value.

Question: How can you go from tracking error to residual risk?

Terhaar: Put simply, the answer is $A^2 + B^2 = C^2$. Total tracking error is C^2, and say the benchmark risk is B^2; then, A^2 is the residual risk because it is everything unrelated to the benchmark. By taking the total active risk (tracking error), squaring it, and subtracting the squared benchmark (beta) risk, you get the squared residual risk.

Question: If an analyst adds value by predicting specific country betas, why is that analyst not rewarded?

Terhaar: If it is the analyst's decision to make, then the analyst should be rewarded. But if predicting country betas (or more realistically, making bets on overall market performance) is not the analyst's decision to make, you probably do not want that person taking that risk. If you do not want that person to take that risk, you shouldn't reward him or her for it.

Ultimately, the answer depends on how the portfolio is managed—that is, where the responsibility for the decision lies. Does the responsibility lie with the analyst or with the portfolio manager? If it lies with the portfolio manager, you do not the want the analyst taking that kind of bet. And you do not want to reward the analyst for taking the bet if he or she is not responsible for it; analysts can introduce risks into the portfolio that you have no control over, and you may not realize it until too late.

Question: Is attribution related only to performance measurement, or is it also related to risk management?

Terhaar: Attribution is related to risk management. At Brinson Partners, we have two distinct groups: risk management and performance evaluation. Ultimately, we'd like to have a system that incorporates our views of risk, the portfolio investment process, and the management process so that all three things work together to tell us what we need to know about who makes what decisions and whether they are good or bad decisions. Making the investment process identify the risks you want to take is important, and the performance evaluation can then show whether the risks that were taken were adequately compensated.

CHAPTER 18

GLOBAL ASSET MANAGEMENT AND PERFORMANCE ATTRIBUTION

Denis S. Karnosky

Brian D. Singer, CFA

Introducing currency considerations into portfolio analysis has implications for the manner in which the underlying assets are evaluated. This chapter provides a unified framework for analysis of global asset markets.

FOREWORD

An increased focus on multicurrency investing has heightened the need for a unified framework for analyzing global asset markets. Global investing is more complex than domestic U.S. investing because vastly different currencies and markets are involved. Most existing attribution models are equipped to dissect returns only in single-country markets. When they are used to analyze global markets, therefore, they often prove to be deficient.

In this chapter, Denis Karnosky, Ph.D., and Brian D. Singer, CFA, comprehensively evaluate other attribution frameworks and identify the pitfalls associated with them. They then introduce an analytical framework designed to overcome the deficiencies of existing attribution models.

The authors recognize the need for a utilitarian approach to performance attribution. Thus, while they adhere to a disciplined theoretical approach, they also present a framework that carefully recognizes all components of portfolio performance. The result is a robust and

Reprinted from The Research Foundation of CFA Institute (February 1994).

flexible system that isolates and measures the effects on global portfolios of market allocation, currency management, and security selection. Using the framework will enable the investor to evaluate the separate impacts of each of these key factors. This aspect of the authors' contribution is especially valuable because, in international portfolio management, separate managers are often responsible for the separate functions.

This practical attribution model has strong theoretical underpinnings. The foundation of analysis is the widely accepted axiom that an asset's expected rate of return consists of a real risk-free rate plus a premium to compensate for inflation and a premium to compensate for risk. Recognizing that all investors should demand the same returns to compensate for the risk-free and inflation-premium components, the authors posit that the required future returns from assets will differ only by their respective risk premiums. This approach thus represents an extension of the familiar capital asset pricing model.

Karnosky and Singer continually stress the practical aspects of their attribution model. They begin with the accepted belief that the primary objective of the investor is to maximize the performance of the entire portfolio. In the global setting, this objective can be achieved only if the investor simultaneously pays attention to currency issues and market or country allocations. The fact that different managers may be responsible for currency, market, and security selections intensifies the need for an attribution system capable of isolating returns from each of these components.

Of particular importance in this chapter is the authors' recognition that, for practical purposes, the market and currency variables must be defined in terms that investors can manage if they choose. Application is the primary focus of this system.

The attribution system begins with a recognized single-country attribution model and adds an application that provides a separate calculation for currency attribution. Specifically, a market attribution component of the model isolates all aspects of the total return contribution of active market decisions, independent of all currency effects. Alternatively, a currency attribution component of the model isolates the full effect of currency decisions, accounting for all effects of spot and forward rates in the portfolio. A combination of the two attribution components accounts for the total return of the portfolio.

The usefulness of the attribution model is validated by its ability to accommodate the plethora of instruments—from swaps to futures to other derivatives—that are increasingly used in the management of multicurrency portfolios. The authors assure understanding of the system by a generous use of examples to explain its application.

The Research Foundation is pleased to sponsor this cutting-edge research. Karnosky and Singer have successfully developed and presented a global attribution model that rests on a solid theoretical foundation and provides useful means for measuring the returns attributable to different key return-generating components. Their work adds considerable maturity to an investment topic in its infancy. Global investors should find this model to be an invaluable tool for evaluating portfolio performance and helping achieve investment objectives. Benefits from this work should accrue to investors for many years to come.

John W. Peavy III, CFA

PREFACE

This chapter develops an analytical framework for evaluating global asset markets and uses that framework to construct a performance attribution system that isolates the effects of market allocation, currency management, and security selection on global portfolios. The focus of this presentation is not on deep theoretical issues of asset pricing or optimal investment strategies but, rather, on the issue of developing useful measures of the market and currency components of global asset returns. In adhering to this utilitarian focus, we hope to provide investors and analysts with a general, serviceable framework for analyzing global investment issues.

This work reflects the ongoing efforts within Brinson Partners to address practical issues in the management of global portfolios. The analytical framework and the performance attribution system are integral parts of our investment process, and we believe that open discussion of these tools will enhance general understanding of global investment issues. The analysis provides a consistent framework for all who are involved in the evaluation of investment opportunities, performance, and risks.

This chapter reflects the discussions and research of many Brinson Partners investment managers and analysts, to all of whom we owe a great debt. The presentation benefited particularly from the thoughts and arguments of Gary Brinson, Richard Carr, Khaled Salama, Raymond Chan, and Norman Cumming. Ray Chan was also indispensable in solving the large number of technical issues involved in the performance attribution program. Robert Clarke was instrumental in the early development of the attribution program. We also thank the Research Foundation of the Institute of Chartered Financial Analysts, and AIMR, for their support and encouragement in preparing this chapter.

Denis S. Karnosky, Ph.D.
Brian D. Singer, CFA

INTRODUCTION

The management of currencies has received increasing attention as the perspective of pension plan sponsors and investment managers has become increasingly global. As a result, a great deal of analysis is being devoted to such specific issues as whether the benchmark for a global portfolio should be hedged or unhedged, the existence of an optimal or "universal" hedge ratio, and the merits of currency overlay programs. The ability of the investment community to investigate the issues that are presented by global markets would be enhanced, however, if the investigation could be conducted within a consistent, general framework that accounts for the interaction of global asset returns and currency returns. In particular, such a framework would recognize that introducing currency considerations into portfolio analysis has implications for the manner in which the underlying assets are evaluated.

A general framework for analysis of global markets would help greatly in addressing several of the current issues confronting global investors:

- *Portfolio benchmarks and investment policies.* A unified treatment of markets and currencies would provide a consistent framework for evaluating the manner in which markets and currencies interact in the portfolio. It would also aid in understanding the range of alternatives for managing market versus currency exposures. The potential benefits and pitfalls of currency overlay programs, for example, could be clearly seen in an integrated global framework.
- *Global accounting systems.* As investment portfolios have become increasingly global, the need for accounting systems that can handle multicurrency assets and the range of available derivative instruments has become obvious. Development of these systems has been difficult, however, because of the lack of a consistent framework for treating currency exposures and strategies. Such a framework could also enhance the quality of financial legislation and regulations.

- *A common footing for analyzing markets and currencies.* Currency decisions are often based on short-term considerations, while market selection often involves longer horizons. Treating markets and currencies as separate analytical issues typically results in a view that currency management is, at best, a means of adding value through agile short-term positioning or, more usually, something that should be avoided entirely. In a unified analytical framework, the market and currency analyses could be integrated for identical investment horizons. In particular, a general framework would allow long-term, fundamental currency analysis.
- *Performance attribution.* A framework that distinguishes clearly between market and currency returns would provide the means to evaluate the sources of investment returns and risks, allowing accurate comparisons of performance among portfolios.

The investment community has found global investment issues to be difficult within the context of theoretical frameworks that are commonly applied to analysis of domestic markets, such as the capital asset pricing model (CAPM). This difficulty reflects a view that global markets are somehow different from the domestic U.S. market. The primary objective of this chapter is to provide investors and analysts with a unified framework for analyzing global asset markets. This framework gives academics and practitioners the means to communicate ideas and hypotheses involving multicurrency markets and exchange rates.

The approach that is developed here is well grounded theoretically and practically. On the theoretical level, the foundation of the analysis is the notion that an asset's future return should provide a real risk-free rate plus a premium to cover expected inflation and a risk premium to compensate investors for the uncertainty of future real cash flows. Looking forward, investors should require that all assets provide the same risk-free rate and inflation-premium components. Thus, the required future returns from assets would differ only by their respective risk premiums. The framework provided here extends this basic theoretical model to the global capital market. In effect, global asset returns are distinguished by risk premiums, and the remaining components, the global cash returns, incorporate all currency market considerations.

The analysis presented here draws on the authors' earlier work, a version of which was published (in Japanese) in 1991 (Karnosky, Singer, and Taylor 1991). Several authors have explained the nature of the relationships among assets and exchange rates in global portfolios. They have typically cast the problem in terms of hedged versus unhedged exposures (see, for example, Lee 1987, and Eun and Resnick 1988). The framework in this chapter extends that work and develops the general relationships. This approach reduces the analytical problem to its most basic form, in terms of variables that are common to all global investors. The general framework provides a uniform treatment of global assets and exchange rates. It is universal and identifies the specific market and currency variables that investors can actually manage. It is a basic analytical tool rather than a prescription for formulating and implementing global investment policy.

On the practical level, the framework recognizes that the market and currency variables must be defined in terms that investors can manage if they choose. Also, the framework accommodates the variety of instruments, such as futures, swaps, and other derivative securities, that are increasingly used in the management of multicurrency portfolios. That is, the framework can identify the underlying asset and currency exposures within a portfolio, irrespective of the specific instruments that are used.

Consider, for example, the purchase by a U.S. investor of Japanese equity futures as a means of establishing Japanese market exposure. The return to such a position would be the return on the Nikkei 225 Index less the return on Japanese cash. In other words, the derivative provides an exposure to the Japanese equity market risk premium. If the Japanese equity futures position is not leveraged, however, and the underlying cash is held in U.S. dollars, the position gives market, but not yen, exposure; that is, the Japanese equity position is hedged into U.S. dollars. If the currency strategy called for an unhedged position, purchase of a separate yen-denominated asset is required, involving either converting the cash into yen or entering a yen-denominated forward or currency futures contract. The analytical framework treats this transaction as fundamentally identical to the direct purchase of a Nikkei Index fund, either hedged or unhedged.

The section titled The General Framework develops and explains the general analytical framework for distinguishing between the market and currency returns. The central theme is that market and currency returns must reflect the performance of variables that investors can manage when setting portfolio strategy. That practical consideration leads to the conclusion that active currency management is equivalent in all respects to the management of global cash portfolios. This conclusion, in turn, reduces the market analysis to the evaluation of expected market return premiums—that is, the local currency returns of assets relative to the associated local cash returns.

The section titled Global Performance Attribution uses this framework to develop a method for performance attribution that identifies the effects of market and currency allocation decisions and the returns that are attributable to security selection within each market. Although some progress has been made recently in improving the ability of attribution systems to measure the effect of currency strategies, the prevailing approaches continue to misspecify the effects of market selection either in terms of local currencies or in terms of the base currency of the investor. These approaches give misleading results and provide managers with incentives that can be inconsistent with optimal portfolio strategy.

The section titled Interpretations of Global Performance Attributions applies attribution methodology introduced in the section titled Global Performance Attribution by using the recent experience of actual global equity and bond portfolios for illustration. These portfolios are used to highlight the relevant issues and are also to demonstrate the pitfalls that plague conventional global analytical and attribution frameworks.

A summary of the issues that investors must address in developing global investment strategies and interpreting attribution results is provided in the section titled Global Balanced Portfolios. An actual global balanced portfolio, which involves active management of global equity and bond positions, active currency strategies, and active selection of stocks and fixed-income securities within each market, is the basis for this discussion. This broadly defined portfolio highlights the importance of basing investment analysis on a consistent global framework.

THE GENERAL FRAMEWORK

The primary objective of the investor is to maximize the performance of the entire portfolio. Although the focus of attention in discussions of global markets is often on currency issues, the analytical framework must also account for the market or country allocations so that market and currency strategies can work in concert to achieve optimal joint performance. Optimal market strategy plus optimal currency strategy should produce optimal portfolio performance.

Defining the Market and Currency Variables

Table 18.1 shows that, during the 10 years from December 31, 1982, to December 31, 1992, the Australian equity market generated one of the best continuously compounded annual rates of return (17.04 percent) in local-currency terms of several global equity markets. At the same time, the Australian dollar showed one of the most rapid annual rates of depreciation against the U.S. dollar (−3.53 percent). On the surface, these data might suggest that

TABLE 18.1   Global Equity Returns, December 31, 1982, to December 31, 1992

Market	Local Currency Return	Change in Exchange Rate	Dollar Return	Local-Currency Cash Return
Australia	17.04%	−3.53%	13.51%	13.56%
Canada	8.31	−0.31	8.00	9.73
Germany	11.02	3.84	14.86	6.37
Japan	8.70	6.31	15.01	5.78
United Kingdom	17.12	−0.66	16.46	11.09
United States	14.83	0.00	14.83	9.82
Global index	12.50	1.96	14.46	7.78

Sources: MSCI; the *Financial Times*; and Brinson Partners.

Note: Continuously compounded annual rates of return. The local currency returns for the global equity index reflect the performance of all the markets that are contained in the MSCI World Equity Index. Cash returns are derived from three-month Eurodeposits denominated in the respective currencies.

an investment strategy of overweighting Australian stocks and hedging the resulting currency exposure back into U.S. dollars might have been profitable during this period. In fact, however, the opposite would have been true. Despite the strong performance of the Australian market in local currency returns, underweighting of that market would have enhanced the performance of a global equity portfolio for the period. Overweighting of the Australian dollar would have improved the return of a global equity portfolio that used the Morgan Stanley Capital International (MSCI) World Equity Index as a benchmark.

Obviously, something that is not captured in local currency returns and/or changes in exchange rates was going on in these markets. That other factor was the relative performance of the U.S. and Australian cash markets, the terms under which currency exposures could have been managed. From the perspective of global investment, annual cash returns of 13.56 percent in Australia during the decade were sufficiently greater than those of the United States, and many other cash markets, to overwhelm both the strong returns from the Australian equity market and the general weakness of the Australian dollar.

The role of relative cash returns in currency markets is well understood by foreign exchange managers. Arbitrage pressure assures that differences in term interest rates among countries dominate the forward rates at which currency exposures are exchanged.[1] The ability to borrow and lend in the various Eurodeposit markets assures a close relationship between, for example, three-month forward discounts/premiums and differentials in the associated three-month Eurodeposit rates. Thus, hedging yen into U.S. dollars during a three-month period eliminates exposure to changes in the yen–dollar exchange rate in the period and substitutes a forward return that effectively equals the difference between the current three-month Eurodollar and Euroyen rates.

However, these relative cash market conditions also affect the relative market returns that are actually available to investors. This double effect of cash returns—on both the market and available currency returns—is the key to the general framework for analysis of global markets.

The nature of the relationship between the market and currency returns that are available to global investors can be illustrated with a portfolio of three assets denominated in three currencies. For illustration, this example is the portfolio of a U.S. investor who holds assets that are denominated in dollars, yen, and pounds sterling. The total dollar return, $R_\$$, of this portfolio with no currency hedging would be[2]

$$R_\$ = w_\$ r_\$ + w_£(r_£ + \varepsilon_{\$,£}) + w_¥(r_¥ + \varepsilon_{\$,¥}), \qquad (18.1)$$

where
$\quad R_\$$ = total portfolio return, in U.S. dollars,
$\quad r_i$ = local currency return from country i assets,
$\quad \varepsilon_{\$,i}$ = rate of change of the dollar relative to currency i, and
$\quad w_i$ = weight of each country asset; $\Sigma w_i = 1$.

The unhedged returns from investments in the United Kingdom and Japan are the joint result of the respective local currency returns, r_i, and the rates of change of the associated exchange rates, $\varepsilon_{\$,i}$.

Assume that the investor is comfortable with the market exposures of this portfolio but wants to know whether the total dollar return would be enhanced by altering the currency exposures that result from the market strategy. One alternative would be to hedge the yen and sterling exposure into dollars. In this case, the exchange rate components of the Japanese and U.K. positions would be replaced by the respective forward premiums or discounts, $f_{\$,i}$. The fully hedged return, $HR_\$$, in U.S. dollars, would be

$$HR_\$ = w_\$ r_\$ + w_£(r_£ + f_{\$,£}) + w_¥(r_¥ + f_{\$,¥}). \qquad (18.2)$$

Equations 18.1 and 18.2 illustrate that this currency decision (whether or not to hedge) involves comparison of the returns from forward contracts with exchange rates. That is, the investor would hedge into dollars when the current forward return is greater than the expected percentage change in the exchange rate: $f_{\$,£} > \varepsilon_{\$,£}$ and/or $f_{\$,¥} > \varepsilon_{\$,¥}$.

A close look into the relationship between forward exchange rates and the expected changes in spot exchange rates refines the decision, however. Ignoring the typically small transaction costs, arbitrage activity assures that forward returns are effectively equal to the difference between term interest rates, $f_{j,i} = c_j - c_i$. Thus, the currency decision actually involves comparisons of current interest rate differentials with expected changes in exchange rates. In this example, hedging into dollars is attractive to the investor when the difference between U.S. and foreign term interest rates is greater than the expected rate of change in the associated exchange rates; that is, $(c_\$ - c_£) > \varepsilon_{\$,£}$ and $(c_\$ - c_¥) > \varepsilon_{\$,¥}$. These relationships can be simplified, however, through a slight rearrangement of terms, to $c_\$ > (c_£ + \varepsilon_{\$,£})$ and $c_\$ > (c_¥ + \varepsilon_{\$,¥})$.

Because of the dominance of interest rate differentials in setting forward exchange rates, currency futures prices and currency swaps, the currency decision reduces to a comparison of global cash returns, with all returns expressed in the home currency of the investor.[3] In this example, hedging into the home currency of the investor is a *dollar* strategy that will increase the total returns of the portfolio if and only if the dollar return from Eurodollar deposits is greater than the dollar return from the foreign Eurodeposits.

In fact, the returns that are associated with any currency strategy in any portfolio can be represented by the individual-country Eurodeposit returns converted into the home currency of the investor. This general proposition can be demonstrated by focusing on the Japanese asset and currency components of the portfolio in Equation 18.1 and considering the full set of alternatives for handling the yen exposure. The investor has three basic currency options: a yen strategy, which maintains the unhedged yen position that results from the market strategy (Equation 18.3); a dollar strategy, which hedges yen into the dollar (Equation 18.4); or a sterling strategy, which cross-hedges the yen into a third currency, sterling (Equation 18.5).

The cross-hedge involves the sterling–yen forward premium plus the expected rate of change of the dollar–sterling exchange rate. The dollar returns from applying each of these currency strategies to the Japanese holdings within the portfolio are then

$$R_{\$\yen} = r_\yen + \varepsilon_{\$,\yen} \quad \text{(yen strategy)}, \tag{18.3}$$

$$HR_{\$\yen} = r_\yen + f_{\$,\yen} \quad \text{(dollar strategy)}, \tag{18.4}$$

and

$$CR_{\$\yen} = r_\yen + (f_{\pounds,\yen} + \varepsilon_{\$,\pounds}) \quad \text{(sterling strategy)}, \tag{18.5}$$

where CR is the cross-hedge return.

Substituting the Eurodeposit interest rate differentials, $c_\$ - c_\yen$ and $c_\pounds - c_\yen$, for the respective forward returns ($f_{\$,\yen}$ and $f_{\pounds,\yen}$) in Equations 18.4 and 18.5 and rearranging terms produces

$$R_{\$\yen} = (r_\yen - c_\yen) + (c_\yen + \varepsilon_{\$,\yen}), \tag{18.6}$$

$$HR_{\$\yen} = (r_\yen - c_\yen) + c_\$, \tag{18.7}$$

and

$$CR_{\$\yen} = (r_\yen - c_\yen) + (c_\pounds + \varepsilon_{\$,\pounds}). \tag{18.8}$$

The differences among the dollar returns from the three currency strategies in Equations 18.6, 18.7, and 18.8 are caused entirely by differences in implied Eurodeposit returns, in dollar terms. By definition, therefore, these Eurodeposit returns are the full measure of the pure currency returns associated with each currency strategy. Repeating this exercise for the U.S. and U.K assets in this example would show that these three Eurodeposit terms define the respective currency strategies in each case. Irrespective of the market strategy in this or any dollar-based portfolio:

- The currency return from a dollar strategy is equal to the return from Eurodollar deposits, $c_\$$.
- The currency return from a yen strategy is equal to the dollar return from Euroyen deposits, $c_\yen + \varepsilon_{\$,\yen}$.
- The currency return from a sterling strategy is equal to the dollar return from Eurosterling deposits, $c_\pounds + \varepsilon_{\$,\pounds}$.

Because of the unavoidable impact of interest rate differentials in controlling exchange rate exposures, local Eurodeposit returns are an inseparable component of currency returns. Therefore, as shown in Equations 18.6, 18.7, and 18.8, only the portion of local currency returns in excess of local cash returns, $r_\yen - c_\yen$, remains in each equation as the measure of Japanese asset returns independent of the associated currency strategy. Similar return premiums define the market returns for the U.K. and U.S. assets in the portfolio. This local return premium, not the total local currency return alone, is the unambiguous measure of the pure market return.[4] The implication is that the investment decision facing this hypothetical U.S. investor involves the allocation of funds among market and currency variables that have the following returns:

Market Allocation		Currency Allocation	
Market	Market Return	Currency	Currency Return
United States	$r_\$ - c_\$$	Dollar	$c_\$$
Japan	$r_\yen - c_\yen$	Yen	$c_\yen + \varepsilon_{\$,\yen}$
United Kingdom	$r_\pounds - c_\pounds$	Sterling	$c_\pounds + \varepsilon_{\$,\pounds}$

Three distinct market returns and three distinct currency returns need to be evaluated. The market decision involves evaluating the three return premiums, and the currency decision involves a completely separate allocation among the three cash markets.

All combinations of market and currency strategies for any benchmark and any base currency can be constructed within this framework. Whether an investor decides to manage the currency exposure or not is irrelevant in developing the analytical framework; the portion of portfolio return that is attributable to currency must reflect a return that investors *could* actively manage. The relevant question is: How would the total performance of the portfolio have been affected if the investor had managed the currency exposure differently?

The general definition of the return from a global portfolio, in terms of any base currency, n, can be written in terms of separate market and currency components as[5]

$$R_n = \Sigma[w_i(r_i - c_i) + v_i(k_i - c_i)] + \Sigma\delta_i(c_i + \varepsilon_{n,i}), \tag{18.9}$$

where the general types of returns are

r_i = return from the noncash assets of country i, in local-currency terms,
c_i = return from country i Eurodeposits, in local-currency terms,
k_i = return from country i strategic cash (if held in Eurodeposits, $k_i = c_i$), and
$\varepsilon_{n,i}$ = rate of change in the base currency:currency i exchange rate.

The active decision variables in an unleveraged portfolio are

w_i = weight of country i noncash assets; $0 \leqslant \Sigma w_i = 1$,
v_i = weight of country i cash held as strategic cash; $\Sigma(w_i + v_i) = 1$; in a fully invested portfolio, all $v_i = 0$,
δ_i = weight of currency i; $\delta_i = (w_i + v_i + h_i)$, and $\Sigma\delta_i = 1$, and
h_i = the portion of the portfolio that is converted (hedged or cross-hedged) to currency i; if net short currency positions are prohibited, the following constraint applies: $-(w_i + v_i) \leqslant h_i \leqslant 1$.

In other words, currency strategy is set at the level of the portfolio; the currency exposures are the net result of the market strategy weights, the currencies in which any strategic cash is held, and explicit currency hedging activity. Thus, active currency management can, and often does, involve more than direct hedging or cross-hedging activity. In the end, all that matters is the total currency exposures of the portfolio, regardless of the sources of the exposures. In a balanced portfolio of global stocks, bonds, and cash, this framework also allows the aggregate currency strategy to be evaluated independently of the stock, bond, and cash market decisions. This separation is critical not only for investment analysis but also for performance attribution, as is demonstrated in the section titled Global Performance Attribution.

Equation 18.9 shows that the problem of evaluating an array of alternative currency strategies can be reduced to analysis of a single vector of Eurodeposit returns, evaluated in terms of the base currency of the investor. This single set of cash returns, $c_i + \varepsilon_{n,i}$, contains all the information that is included in the matrix of all possible forward returns versus changes in exchange rates, $\varepsilon_{n,i} - \varepsilon_{n,j}$. Equally important, the returns that are relevant for market or country selection are clearly identified as the respective return premiums—that is, the local asset returns relative to local cash returns, $r_i - c_i$.

In the special case in which maximization of returns is the investment objective, the ranking of the market and currency returns that is given by this approach is identical to that which results from the framework proposed by Lee (1987, p. 73) and others, which is based on hedged returns. The equivalence can be demonstrated by adding and subtracting the return from home country n cash (c_n), assuming a fully invested portfolio, on the right side of Equation 18.9:

$$R_n = \Sigma w_i(r_i - c_i) + \Sigma \delta_i(c_i + \varepsilon_{n,i}) + (c_n - c_n) \qquad (18.9A)$$

Because $\Sigma w_i = \Sigma \delta_i = 1.0$, Equation 18.9A can be rewritten as

$$R_n = w_i[r_i + c_n - c_i] + \Sigma \delta_i[c_i - c_n + \varepsilon_{n,i}] \qquad (18.9B)$$

and

$$R_n = \Sigma w_i[r_i + f_{n,i}] + \Sigma \delta_i[\varepsilon_{n,i} - f_{n,i}]. \qquad (18.9C)$$

The first term on the right of Equation 18.9C is the vector of hedged returns, in terms of the base currency, n. Because the base-currency cash return, c_n, appears as a scalar in each hedged return, it has no effect on the relative order of market returns as given in Equation 18.9. The ranking of hedged returns, $r_i + f_{n,i}$, is identical to that given by the local return premiums, $r_i - c_i$. The second term is the vector of exchange rate versus dollar forward returns. The base-currency cash return also appears as a scalar across the array of currency terms and has no effect on the ranking of the currency terms.

Although these terms can be derived arithmetically from the definition of global returns, they have a strong theoretical foundation. Evaluation of return premiums among global capital markets is an extension of the CAPM, in which risky assets are distinguished by their returns relative to the riskless (cash) asset. With less than full global integration, multiple cash equivalents exist that differ in their currencies of denomination. Because the relevant cash instrument for the U.S. investor, for example, is U.S. cash, the global evaluation process can be thought of as flowing from domestic cash, $c_\$$, to foreign cash, which includes the unavoidable consideration of exchange rates, $c_i + \varepsilon_{\$,i}$, and on to the foreign asset relative to foreign cash, $r_i - c_i$. The first part of that process leads to the currency decision, and the second part encompasses the asset decision. Only in a fully integrated equilibrium environment would comparisons among global cash markets not matter, because exchange rates would then serve a fully transparent price-equilibrating function. That is, full global integration implies an effective single currency.[6]

This framework is applicable to all benchmarks, whether unhedged, hedged, or partially hedged. When the benchmark is unhedged and explicit hedging is prohibited, the market and currency strategies will be identical, because over- or underweighting of any market will necessarily cause an equal over- or underweighting of the associated currency. In effect, strategy is set on the basis of unhedged returns, which are the sum of the market and currency components. Although the investment manager is unable to act on the market and currency components independently, the framework does distinguish between the contribution of market variables and currency variables to the unhedged return from any market. This consideration is particularly important when hedging, even if allowed, is not feasible. Such would be the case with many emerging markets, where no effective instruments for managing currency exposure exist. The investment decision would necessarily involve both market and currency returns.

Keeping "Cash" in Perspective

The framework highlights the significance of cash equivalents, but the distinction between two cash concepts that arise in the framework is important. The first stems from the Eurodeposit rates that dominate the pricing of forward contracts, futures, and swaps that are used in implementing currency strategies. This form of cash enters the analysis, even for portfolios that are fully invested and are holding no explicit strategic cash, because the purchase of any asset—whether equity or fixed income, domestic or foreign—involves implicit exposures to cash and to a return premium over cash. Any decision to hedge involves simply changing the currency denomination of the implicit cash to which the asset's return premium is attached. For example, hedging into U.S. dollars the yen exposure that results from a Japanese equity position involves changing the implicit cash component from Euroyen to Eurodollars. In effect, the Japanese equity return premium is added to the U.S. dollar rather than to the yen Eurodeposit return. Such hedging does not create additional cash; rather, it *substitutes* U.S. dollar cash for non-U.S. cash in the portfolio.

The second cash concept involves holding cash for strategic or operational purposes, which results in a portfolio that is less than fully invested.[7] This cash can be held in any currency and, if held in Eurodeposits, has a return premium of zero. Conceptually, this type of cash represents a market exposure that is no different from equity or fixed-income assets.

The Relationship between Market and Currency Returns

This framework demonstrates that separate currency and market strategies can be implemented within a global portfolio in which a specific currency weight is different from the weight of the associated market.[8] The strategy decisions are interdependent, however, because local Eurodeposit returns affect both expected market and currency returns. Other things being unchanged, an increase in the local Eurodeposit return in a country would increase the attractiveness of that country's currency to all global investors but would also decrease the attractiveness of that country's noncash assets. That is, changes in global cash returns can, independent of current exchange rates and conditions in the underlying asset markets, cause changes in the optimal market and optimal currency strategies.[9]

This link between market and currency returns can be illustrated with an example.[10] Table 18.2 gives three hypothetical situations involving U.S. and Japanese equity markets. The U.S. dollar is the base currency of the investor. The only variables that change among the

TABLE 18.2   Hypothetical Examples

Variable	Case 1	Case 2	Case 3
Yen return on Japanese equity, $r_¥$	14%	14%	14%
Dollar return on U.S. equity, $r_\$$	8	8	8
Change in dollar:yen exchange rate, $\varepsilon_{\$,\,¥}$	−4	−4	−4
Yen return on Euroyen deposits, $c_¥$	9	4	9
Dollar return on Eurodollar deposits, $c_\$$	2	2	4
Return premium			
United States, $r_\$ - c_\$$	6	6	4
Japan, $r_¥ - c_¥$	5	10	5
Eurodeposit returns (in U.S. dollars)			
United States, $c_\$$	2	2	4
Japan, $c_¥ + \varepsilon_{\$,\,¥}$	5	0	5
Optimal market strategy	United States	Japan	Japan
Optimal currency strategy	¥	$	¥
Maximum total return	11%	12%	10%

three cases are the local currency returns from Eurodeposits. For purposes of illustration, the potential behavioral relationships between changes in short-term interest rates and equity returns or exchange rates are ignored.

In all three cases, Japanese equities offer higher returns in both dollar and local-currency (yen) terms. The yen return from Japanese equity is 14 percent, and the yen is expected to depreciate against the dollar at a 4 percent rate, which implies a 10 percent return in dollars. The dollar return on U.S. equity is 8 percent in each case.

Consider Case 1. The four choices are (1) unhedged Japanese equity, generating a 10 percent dollar return; (2) hedged Japanese equity, generating a 7 percent dollar return; (3) U.S. equity, generating an 8 percent dollar return; and (4) U.S. equity reverse-hedged into yen, generating an 11 percent dollar return. Despite the relatively strong performance of Japanese equity in local-currency and dollar terms in this case, the maximum dollar return is produced by a market strategy that invests in U.S. equity. While the yen depreciates, the optimal currency strategy is a "reverse hedge" into yen, which produces an 11 percent dollar return.

The optimal strategy effectively sacrifices the apparently superior Japanese equity return in order to take advantage of an even more attractive situation in global cash markets. The best dollar return is produced by combining the weaker equity market and the weaker currency, in terms of local market and exchange rate returns. No net cash exposure in the portfolio results from this strategy, however, and the portfolio is fully invested in equity.

The key consideration is that although the local currency return of Japanese equity is superior to that of U.S. equity, its performance relative to the local cash return is inferior. In Japan, equity returns a premium of 5 percent over yen cash, while the equity premium is 6 percent in the U.S. market. The dollar return on Eurodollar deposits is only 2 percent, compared with a 5 percent dollar return from Euroyen deposits. Applying the U.S. equity premium of 6 percent to the 5 percent dollar return on Japanese cash gives a total dollar return of 11 percent.

Note that this "extra" return does not result from aggressive management of currencies within the equity portfolio. The additional return is the result of considering a complete set of alternative asset and currency allocations within an unchanged view about exchange rates and equity markets. The information required to achieve the maximum portfolio return is exactly the same as is needed to make the choice between hedging and not hedging, but this framework ensures that the portfolio can make best use of that information.

The simultaneous nature of the market and currency analysis is illustrated by comparing the optimal strategy in Case 1 with the optimal strategies of Cases 2 and 3. In Case 2, lower Euroyen deposit rates reduce the expected yen return from Japanese cash to 4 percent. Although the expected equity and exchange rate returns are unchanged, this lower Japanese cash return implies a portfolio strategy that is the exact opposite of the strategy in Case 1. The optimal portfolio in Case 2 would be fully invested in Japanese equity with a 100 percent hedge into dollars, producing a dollar return of 12 percent.

In Case 2, lower short-term Japanese interest rates imply a larger return premium for Japanese equities, 10 percent versus the 5 percent in Case 1. At this level, the premium over local cash that is offered by Japanese equity is substantially above the 6 percent premium offered by U.S. equity. At the same time, the lower yen return on Japanese cash means that Eurodollar deposits offer the higher dollar return, making exposure to the dollar the better currency strategy.

In Case 3, the narrowed interest spread reflects higher U.S. short-term rates rather than lower Euroyen rates. The expected U.S. cash return of 4 percent produces a U.S. equity return premium of 4 percent. As in Case 2, this situation causes Japan to be a more attractive equity market. In contrast to Case 2, however, the yen is the more attractive currency because Euroyen deposits offer a 5 percent dollar return, compared with a 4 percent return from Eurodollars. The optimal strategy in this case is an unhedged position in Japanese equity, which gives a dollar return of 10 percent.

A given set of local currency and exchange rate returns can yield a variety of optimal portfolio strategies, depending on the situation in global Eurodeposit markets. Not only are returns from alternative currency strategies affected, but changes in cash returns also affect the premiums that are offered by risky assets. To make the market decisions based on returns from either local currency or the base currency and then try to determine the best currency overlay or strategy given those market exposures is, therefore, inappropriate. In all three cases in this illustration, Japanese equity offers the better local currency and unhedged dollar return. Only in Cases 2 and 3, however, is selection of the Japanese market consistent with achieving a maximum portfolio return. Thus, applying a separate currency overlay onto a portfolio in which the market allocations have already been made *on the basis* of *either local currency or unhedged asset returns* can be suboptimal. Only if market selection is based on the evaluation of relative local return premiums can separate market and currency decisions be jointly optimal in all cases.

The Historical Record

The misleading information that is given by local currency and unhedged returns can be seen in recent historical data for the performance of several global markets. Table 18.3 repeats the global equity returns that were shown in Table 18.1 and adds the performance of the associated bond markets. The U.S. dollar returns for each individual market and the indexes are presented on the right. The market and currency components of the dollar returns are presented in both a conventional framework, which focuses on local currency and exchange rate returns, and in terms of local return premiums and cash returns in dollars. The data are shown graphically in Figures 18.1–18.3.

Notice that the conventional framework indicates that changes in exchange rates accounted for only 1.96 percent of the 14.46 percent dollar return from the global equity index and 1.88 percent of the 11.31 percent dollar return from global bonds. The countries included in Table 18.3 experienced significant differences in exchange rate returns, however, ranging from a 6.31 percent rate of appreciation of the yen against the U.S. dollar to a 3.53 percent annual rate of depreciation of the Australian dollar against the U.S. dollar. In fact, although the U.K. and Australian equity and bond markets had particularly strong local currency returns, their respective currencies also showed the largest depreciations against the U.S. dollar. Germany and Japan had the strongest currencies relative to the dollar, but the local currency returns from their equity and bond markets were below the respective indexes.

The upper panels of Figures 18.1 and 18.2 show the local currency returns from each market relative to the local currency returns from the respective global indexes. Figure 18.1 shows that the local currency returns from the Australian, U.K., and U.S. equity markets exceeded the index during this 10-year period. Figure 18.2 shows that the bond markets of these three countries plus Canada provided local currency returns above the index of global bond markets.

The upper panel of Figure 18.3 shows the annual rates of change of each exchange rate relative to the weighted average of the exchange rates for the global equity and bond indexes. Only the mark and the yen exceeded the index.

TABLE 18.3   Global Market Returns, December 31, 1982, to December 31, 1992

Market	Local Currency Return	Dollar Exchange Rate Return	Local-Currency Return Premium	Cash Return in Dollars	Dollar Return
Equity markets					
Australia	17.04%	−3.53%	3.48%	10.32%	13.51%
Canada	8.31	−0.31	−1.43	9.42	8.00
Germany	11.02	3.84	4.65	10.21	14.86
Japan	8.70	6.31	2.92	12.08	15.01
United Kingdom	17.12	−0.66	6.03	10.43	16.46
United States	14.83	0.00	7.01	7.82	14.83
Global equity index	12.50	1.96	4.71	9.74	14.46
Bond markets					
Australia	13.67	−3.53	0.20	10.03	10.22
Canada	11.66	−0.31	1.93	9.42	11.35
Germany	7.35	3.84	0.98	10.21	11.19
Japan	7.06	6.31	1.29	12.08	13.38
United Kingdom	11.23	−0.66	0.14	10.43	10.57
United States	10.22	0.00	2.40	7.82	10.22
Global bond index	9.43	1.88	1.71	9.59	11.31

Sources: MSCI; Salomon Brothers; the Financial Times; and Brinson Partners.

Note: Continuously compounded annual rates of return. The local currency returns for the global equity index are based on the full set of markets that are contained in the MSCI World Equity Index, and the global bond index reflects the performance of the full set of markets contained in the Salomon Brothers World Government Bond Index. Cash returns reflect the performance of the respective three-month Eurodeposits.

As demonstrated, however, the relative local currency and exchange rate returns have no necessary relevance for investment strategy because they do not account for the practical issues involved in the management of currency exposures. The market and currency returns that were actually available to global investors are measured by the local return premiums and the associated cash returns in dollars. In those terms, the global equity index generated an average market return that was 4.71 percent above global cash, and the global bond market produced an average 1.71 percent premium over cash. From this perspective, the United Kingdom and the United States provided above-average equity market returns, as shown in the lower panel of Figure 18.1, and only Canadian and U.S. bond market return premiums were superior to the bond index, as shown in Figure 18.2. The dollar was the poorest performing currency for global investors during the decade, with U.S. cash producing a dollar return of 7.82 percent, compared with index returns of slightly less than 10 percent. In fact, all other currencies in Table 18.3 had returns greater than the cash return, in dollars, from the index. Note that although the Australian dollar showed the largest depreciation against the U.S. dollar among these currencies, the 10.03 percent dollar return from Australian cash was above the market average and was among the highest returns.

Summary

The ability to account consistently for the various factors that influence portfolio performance is critical in investment management. Global portfolios complicate the task by introducing

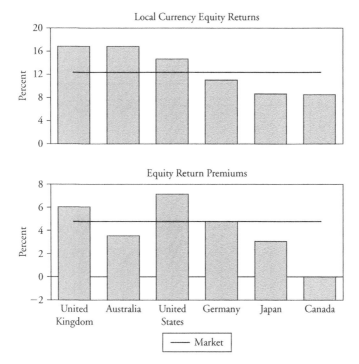

FIGURE 18.1   Global Equity Markets, December 31, 1982, to December 31,1992

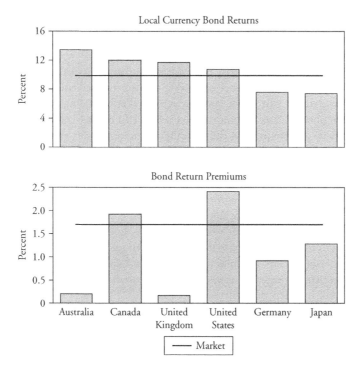

FIGURE 18.2   Global Bond Markets, December 31, 1982, to December 31, 1992

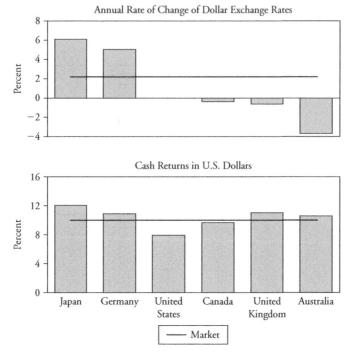

FIGURE 18.3   Global Currency Markets, December 31, 1982, to December 31, 1992

exposures to changes in exchange rates. Recognizing that cash markets are an inseparable part of currency analysis, however, provides the means for handling exchange rate considerations consistently within established asset valuation techniques.

Equally important is the fact that the proper treatment of currencies has implications for the manner in which global asset or market returns are evaluated. Because local cash returns are an inseparable part of the currency returns that can be managed by the investor, the implicit cash portion of asset returns is not relevant to market analysis. Only the return premiums of assets, relative to local cash, distinguish among assets and markets. Failure to exclude local cash from the market returns confounds the market and currency effects and can generate misleading analyses of the market returns that are available to the investor.

Although the range of currency returns is made explicit in the investment process, this framework does not imply that investment managers should manage currency more actively than in the past. Rather, it allows a more informed and consistent treatment of investment alternatives in global portfolios than has been possible. Recasting the global asset management problem into this framework has the merit of both rigor and simplicity. It involves the minimum number of distinct variables that must be evaluated, in terms of risk and return, and allows investment managers to determine optimal market allocations and currency strategies as distinct but interdependent decisions.

The framework for analysis of global asset returns that has been presented in this section gives an unambiguously correct distinction between market and currency returns. It provides, therefore, a consistent, general means for evaluating global investment alternatives in terms of expected market and currency returns. Although investors cannot avoid the risks inherent in acting on uncertain views about future returns, this framework allows the investor's best estimates, however faulty, to be evaluated rationally. Because this analytical approach provides an accurate view of the relative market and currency returns that are perceived by the investor, it also provides the basis for an *ex post* evaluation of resulting investment performance. The next section provides details of a performance attribution system for global portfolios.

GLOBAL PERFORMANCE ATTRIBUTION

This section develops the methodology for global performance attribution that is based on the analytical framework presented in the first section. This attribution approach provides unambiguous measures of the returns that result from market and currency decisions. The method applies to portfolios with unhedged, partially hedged, or hedged benchmarks.

Pitfalls in Performance Attribution

The following example has been constructed with an eye toward highlighting the pitfalls in conventional systems of global performance attribution and the perverse investment incentives that these systems can create.[11] Although this example is hypothetical, similar relative returns are common in the actual performance record of global equity and bond markets, as was shown in Table 18.3.

Table 18.4 provides a set of passive weight and return data for performance evaluation from the perspective of a U.S. investor. These four assets are assumed to represent the market and have equal weights in the market index.

Among these four markets, the U.K. offers the best local currency return, but the pound sterling shows the largest depreciation against the dollar. The German mark (deutsche mark, DM) shows the largest appreciation against the dollar, but the German asset market has the lowest local currency return. The best unhedged dollar return is provided by Japanese securities.

Table 18.5 specifies the total dollar return provided by each of the 16 combinations of market and currency exposures that can be created from the 4 markets and 4 currencies. Unhedged dollar returns are read along the diagonal; hedged dollar returns are in the last column on the right. All other currency strategies involve cross-hedging. The hedged and cross-hedged returns reflect the forward premiums and discounts that are implied by the Eurodeposit rates in Table 18.4. The market/currency combinations that have a dollar return greater than the 8.10 percent dollar return of the equally weighted market index (in Table 18.4) are shown in boldface in Table 18.5.

TABLE 18.4   Global Security Returns

Market	Index Weights	Local Currency Returns	Exchange Rate Returns	U.S. Dollar Returns	Local Eurodeposit Returns
Germany	25.00%	7.00%	1.00%	8.00%	5.00%
United Kingdom	25.00	10.50	−3.00	7.50	11.25
Japan	25.00	9.50	−1.00	8.50	9.00
United States	25.00	8.40	0.00	8.40	7.50
Index	100.00	8.85	−0.75	8.10	8.19

Note: Continuously compounded rates of return.

TABLE 18.5   Dollar Returns from All Combinations of Market and
Currency Strategies

| | Currency Strategy | | | |
Market Strategy	DM	Sterling	Yen	U.S. Dollars
Germany	8.00%	**10.25%**	**10.00%**	**9.50%**
United Kingdom	5.25	7.50	7.25	6.75
Japan	6.50	**8.75**	**8.50**	8.00
United States	6.90	**9.15**	**8.90**	**8.40**

Note: Continuously compounded rates of return. Boldface indicates market/currency combinations that have a dollar return greater than the 8.1 percent dollar return of the equally weighted market index in Table 18.4.

Looking down each column in Table 18.5 reveals that German securities provide the highest dollar returns for each currency strategy. Looking across each row shows that a sterling currency strategy gives the highest dollar return regardless of the market strategy. In terms of maximizing returns, the German market is unambiguously the best market and sterling is unambiguously the best currency exposure. The portfolio that offers the highest dollar return would be invested completely in German securities cross-hedged into sterling. From the data in Table 18.4, the resulting 10.25 percent dollar return of that portfolio reflects the 7 percent DM return from German securities, the 6.25 percent sterling return from selling DM forward into British pounds (11.25 percent Eurosterling return −5.00 percent EuroDM return), and the 3 percent loss from depreciation of sterling against the dollar.

The ranking of market and currency strategies in Table 18.5 is unambiguous. Not only does the German market strategy give the highest dollar return in each column, a U.S. strategy gives the next best return, irrespective of the currency exposure, followed in each case by Japan. Investments in U.K. assets show the lowest return for all currency strategies. Similarly, a yen exposure shows the second highest return in each row, followed in turn by U.S. dollar and DM strategies.

These rankings of market and currency returns are independent of the home currency of the investor. If all returns were converted to yen or marks, for example, the rankings (but not the returns) would be the same as those facing an investor whose base currency is the U.S. dollar.

Because a market strategy of overweighting German securities shows the highest dollar return regardless of the associated currency strategy, the performance attribution system should show a positive contribution from an overweight of the German market. Notice in Table 18.4, however, that German securities have both local currency and unhedged returns that are inferior to the associated index returns. The equally weighted index of local currency returns for these four markets is 8.85 percent, versus 7 percent for Germany; the index of unhedged dollar returns is 8.1 percent, versus 8 percent for Germany. If either local currency or unhedged returns were used as the basis for evaluating alternative market allocations, an overweight of German securities would appear to have detracted from the performance of the portfolio relative to the index. In other words, using either of those returns as the criterion in a global attribution system would have given the investment manager an incentive to avoid the German market, in this example, to the detriment of total portfolio performance.

In fact, judging alternative market strategies on the basis of local currency returns would have given the manager an incentive to invest in U.K. and Japanese securities, which are the only markets in Table 18.4 that gave local currency returns—10.5 percent and 9.5 percent, respectively—that were superior to the 8.85 percent local currency return of the index. Table 18.5 indicates, however, that investment in U.K. securities would have produced the worst dollar return regardless of the associated currency strategy. No currency strategy associated with investment in U.K. securities would have even matched the 8.1 percent dollar return from the passive index. Using unhedged dollar returns as the criterion would have led the manager to invest in the Japanese and U.S. markets. That is, the second and third best markets would have been recommended, while the best choice, Germany, would have again been shunned.

Using the relative attractiveness of markets that is indicated solely by local currency or unhedged returns can lead to nonsensical performance attributions and decisions. Consider, for example, an investor whose policy is to use an investment manager who invests fully in the most attractive market and to use another manager who will apply a currency overlay to gain the best currency exposure. Based on Table 18.4, using local currency returns to evaluate markets would have caused the perceptive market manager to invest the portfolio totally in U.K. securities. Given that market allocation decision, the correct strategy for the overlay manager would have been to do nothing, leaving the sterling position unhedged. Unfortunately, Table 18.5 shows that combination of market and currency strategies producing a 7.5 percent dollar return for the portfolio, 60 basis points less than the passive index.

Which decision, market or currency choice, would then account for the underperformance of the portfolio? Using local currency returns to evaluate the market decision would indicate that the market manager made the correct choice, because U.K. securities offer the highest local currency return, 165 basis points better than the local currency return of the index. The currency decision would also appear to be correct, however, because the currency manager could show that applying any other currency strategy—hedging into dollars or cross-hedging into German marks or yen—would have produced even worse dollar returns. The investor is left with the nonsensical conclusion that both the market and currency managers adopted the best strategies but, nevertheless, the portfolio underperformed the passive benchmark.

The problem has nothing to do with the basic policy decision to use an active currency overlay program. The problem is entirely the result of the misleading information and investment incentives that were given to the market manager by the focus on the local currency returns. As shown previously, development of distinct market and currency returns that allow a separate treatment of market and currency strategies must account for the effect of *cash returns* on both market and currency alternatives.

The analysis in the section titled The General Framework indicated that local-currency return premiums and Eurodeposit returns in base-currency terms give unambiguously correct rankings of the returns from the various market and currency strategies. From the data presented in Table 18.4, the local return premiums and Eurodeposit returns in dollars for each of the four countries are as shown in Table 18.6. The rank of the local return premiums is identical to the rank of returns from the market strategies in Table 18.5, with the German market showing the highest return premium, followed by the United States, Japan, and the United Kingdom, regardless of the currency strategy. Not only are the German and U.S. markets unambiguously the most attractive, but they are also the only markets offering return premiums in excess of the index premium of 0.66 percent. The implication is that the portfolio's return would be enhanced by market strategies that favor German and U.S. assets and underweight the U.K. and Japanese markets.

TABLE 18.6   Global Security Returns

Market	Local Return Premium	Eurodeposit Return in U.S. Dollars	U.S. Dollar Returns
Germany	2.00%	6.00%	8.00%
United Kingdom	−0.75	8.25	7.50
Japan	0.50	8.00	8.50
United States	0.90	7.50	8.40
Index	0.66	7.44	8.10

Note: Continuously compounded rates of return.

The rank of dollar returns from the various Eurodeposit markets is also identical to the rank of dollar returns from the various currency strategies in Table 18.5 regardless of the market strategy. Among the currency alternatives, sterling, yen, and/or dollar cash offer dollar returns above the 7.44 percent Eurodeposit return for the index, in U.S. dollars.

These data would have given the market manager in the prior example the incentive to invest fully in Germany, and the overlay manager would then have converted the resulting German mark exposure into sterling. The total effect would have been a 10.25 percent dollar return for the portfolio, 215 basis points better than the dollar return of the benchmark. Because no other combination of market and currency strategies would have given a better return, the optimal market and currency strategies clearly would have resulted in the optimal portfolio return.

The Global Attribution Framework

Brinson *et al.* (1986, 1991) have presented a framework for separating the total portfolio return into components that are ascribable to active asset allocation strategies and components ascribable to security-selection activity. Active asset allocation reflects the setting of asset class weights within the portfolio relative to the benchmark weights. Security selection involves the specific investment choices within each asset class. Brinson *et al.* applied their framework to a portfolio of domestic assets and measured the portion of extra return that is attributable to the market allocation decisions:

$$\begin{matrix} \text{Market} \\ \text{allocation} \\ \text{return} \end{matrix} = \left(\begin{matrix} \text{Active} \\ \text{market} \\ \text{weight} \end{matrix} - \begin{matrix} \text{Passive} \\ \text{market} \\ \text{weight} \end{matrix} \right) \times \left(\begin{matrix} \text{Passive} \\ \text{market} \\ \text{return} \end{matrix} - \begin{matrix} \text{Index} \\ \text{market} \\ \text{return} \end{matrix} \right).$$

The framework presented in the section titled The General Framework allows this attribution approach to be applied to global portfolios, providing unambiguous measures of the returns that are attributable to market and currency strategies. This application involves only adding a separate calculation for currency attribution, which is identical in concept to the calculation that is used to account for market strategy:

$$\begin{matrix} \text{Currency} \\ \text{allocation} \\ \text{return} \end{matrix} = \left(\begin{matrix} \text{Active} \\ \text{currency} \\ \text{weight} \end{matrix} - \begin{matrix} \text{Passive} \\ \text{currency} \\ \text{weight} \end{matrix} \right) \times \left(\begin{matrix} \text{Passive} \\ \text{currency} \\ \text{return} \end{matrix} - \begin{matrix} \text{Index} \\ \text{currency} \\ \text{return} \end{matrix} \right)$$

Following the Brinson *et al.* approach, Figure 18.4 shows the currency-related decisions in a grid that is separate from, but parallel to, market-related calculations. The market

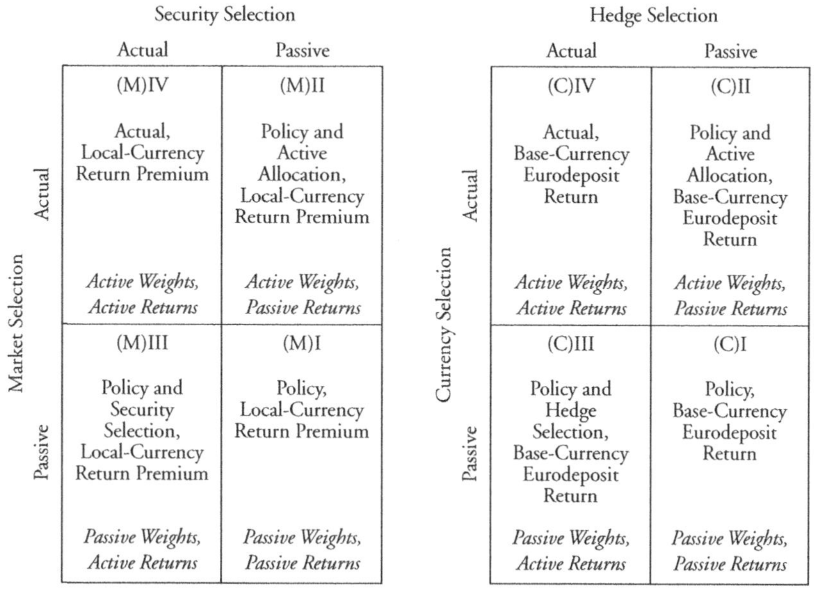

	Security Selection			Hedge Selection	
	Actual	Passive		Actual	Passive

FIGURE 18.4   A Framework for Global Portfolio Return Accountability

attribution grid isolates all aspects of the total return contribution of active market decisions, independent of all exchange rate effects. The currency attribution grid isolates the full effect of currency decisions, accounting for all effects of spot and forward exchange rates in the portfolio. Combining the two grids accounts for the total return of the portfolio. The framework that was presented in the section titled The General Framework yields measures of market and currency returns that can be applied directly to the Brinson *et al.* approach.

- *Market strategy attribution.* The market attribution grid accounts for the return contribution of active decisions across and within asset markets and is based on local-currency return premiums. Quadrant M[arket](I) contains the passive (index) return premium; Quadrant M(IV) gives the active (portfolio) return premium. The difference between Quadrant M(IV) and Quadrant M(I) is the total contribution from all active market decisions, both active market allocation and active security selection within the markets. The contribution from active market allocation only is computed by subtracting the Quadrant M(I) return premium from the Quadrant M(II) return premium. The contribution ascribed to security selection is the difference between Quadrant M(III) and Quadrant M(I).

- *Currency strategy attribution.* The currency attribution follows the same approach. Quadrant C[urrency](I) of the currency attribution grid measures the passive Eurodeposit return for the index, in the base currency of the investor. For an unhedged benchmark, the passive currency weights are the market weights of the benchmark. A fully hedged benchmark would be specified by a 100 percent base-currency allocation with zero allocations to all other currencies. Quadrant C(IV) measures the active (portfolio) Eurodeposit return in base-currency terms. As with market attribution, the contribution of all active currency management is given by the difference between Quadrants C(IV) and C(I). Like the market allocation effect, the total currency effect can be segmented into two active decisions—active currency allocations and active hedge selection. Equation 18.9 showed that currency allocations can result from noncash asset exposures, w_i; strategic cash exposures, v_i; and/or currency hedges, h_i. The difference between Quadrants C(II) and C(I) is the contribution of active currency allocation.

Quadrant C(III) provides the base-currency Eurodeposit return that is achieved through hedge selection only. An example of hedge selection is the return that is achieved by entering forward transactions for a term that is different from the maturity of the normal forward term and also, therefore, different from the benchmark Eurodeposit instrument. The use of a three-month Eurodeposit benchmark defines a three-month currency hedge as the benchmark forward transaction. Any decision to hedge for a term shorter or longer than the benchmark Eurodeposit maturity would then be an active hedge decision. Thus, hedge selection reflects a yield-curve strategy relative to the Eurodeposit benchmark against which performance is measured. The value added by hedge selection, therefore, is the difference between the Eurodeposit returns of Quadrant C(III) and Quadrant C(I).

The portion of the portfolio's added value that can be attributed to each market allocation is thus computed as

$$
\begin{pmatrix} \text{Market} \\ \text{allocation} \\ \text{return} \end{pmatrix} = \begin{pmatrix} \text{Active} \\ \text{market} \\ \text{weight} \end{pmatrix} - \begin{pmatrix} \text{Passive} \\ \text{market} \\ \text{weight} \end{pmatrix} \times \begin{pmatrix} \text{Passive} \\ \text{market} \\ \text{return} \\ \text{premium} \end{pmatrix} - \begin{pmatrix} \text{Index} \\ \text{market} \\ \text{return} \\ \text{premium} \end{pmatrix}
$$

The value added by each specific currency allocation is computed as

$$
\begin{pmatrix} \text{Currency} \\ \text{allocation} \\ \text{return} \end{pmatrix} = \begin{pmatrix} \text{Active} \\ \text{currency} \\ \text{weight} \end{pmatrix} - \begin{pmatrix} \text{Passive} \\ \text{currency} \\ \text{weight} \end{pmatrix} \times \begin{pmatrix} \text{Passive} \\ \text{Eurodeposit} \\ \text{return} \\ \text{in U.S.} \\ \text{dollars} \end{pmatrix} - \begin{pmatrix} \text{Index} \\ \text{Eurodeposit} \\ \text{return} \\ \text{in U.S.} \\ \text{dollars} \end{pmatrix}
$$

The value added by security selection within the various markets is measured as

$$
\begin{pmatrix} \text{Market} \\ \text{security} \\ \text{selection} \end{pmatrix} = \begin{pmatrix} \text{Passive} \\ \text{market} \\ \text{weight} \end{pmatrix} \times \begin{pmatrix} \text{Active} \\ \text{market} \\ \text{return} \\ \text{premium} \end{pmatrix} - \begin{pmatrix} \text{Passive} \\ \text{market} \\ \text{return} \\ \text{premium} \end{pmatrix}
$$

The portion attributable to hedge selection within the various currency exposures is

$$
\begin{pmatrix} \text{Currency} \\ \text{hedge} \\ \text{selection} \end{pmatrix} = \begin{pmatrix} \text{Passive} \\ \text{currency} \\ \text{weight} \end{pmatrix} \times \begin{pmatrix} \text{Active} \\ \text{Eurodeposit} \\ \text{return} \\ \text{in base currency} \end{pmatrix} - \begin{pmatrix} \text{Passive} \\ \text{Eurodeposit} \\ \text{return} \\ \text{in base currency} \end{pmatrix}
$$

Table 18.7 provides a summary of the detailed formulas for determining the contribution of active management to the total performance of a global portfolio.[12] The formulas represent differences in the quadrants defined in Figure 18.4. The active contributions from both market and currency management are composed of active allocation, security/hedge selection, and a cross-product that measures the interaction of the active allocation and selection decisions. Actual portfolio returns and weights are identified by plain lowercase letters, and passive benchmark returns and weights are lowercase letters with bars over them.

From Equation 18.9, the attribution framework treats strategic cash as part of the market allocation decision; the currency exposure that is associated with that cash is incorporated in the currency attribution. Because cash equivalents have passive return premiums at or near zero, any strategic market allocation to cash assets can enhance returns only when the passive return premium provided by the aggregate global benchmark is negative (below the cash-equivalent passive return premium).[13]

A Comparison of Global Attribution Frameworks

Consider a U.S.-dollar-based portfolio with an unhedged benchmark that has been invested in the markets indicated in Table 18.4. Table 18.8 summarizes the active market and currency positions of this portfolio. The portfolio overweights cash and the German market and underweights all other markets. Although the portfolio overweights the German market, it underweights German marks. The opposite is true for the U.K. equity market and sterling. Even though the Japanese market is strategically underweighted, the allocation to the yen is neutral–that is, equal to the benchmark allocation. The yen underweight that results from the market strategy is offset by hedges into yen. The active dollar weight of 10 percent is below that of the index, reflecting the net effect of an underweight of the U.S. market, a small active allocation to U.S. cash, and a forward sale of dollars.

The "Currency Hedging" column indicates the currency hedge positions. This hedging information is incidental, however, because only the net cash allocations, not the sources of currency exposure, are relevant.

Table 18.9 summarizes the passive returns provided by the portfolio benchmark and the actual returns earned by the portfolio. The table indicates that security selection in the U.K., Japanese, and U.S. markets added value, producing local-currency market returns and return premiums in excess of the respective passive country indexes. To simplify the discussion, assume no active hedge management, such as the use of long-term forward contracts or options. Thus, the passive and actual Eurodeposit returns in U.S. dollars are equal.

The chosen portfolio strategy produced a total dollar return of 9.47 percent, 137 basis points above the benchmark.[14] This performance was the joint result of market and currency allocation strategies and security selection within each market.

Conventional global portfolio performance attribution evaluates market selection according to local market returns and currency selection in accordance with exchange rate returns. In that framework, the 8.1 percent U.S. dollar return of the benchmark can be segmented into the local currency return of 8.85 percent and the exchange rate return of −0.75 percent. Table 18.10 provides the results of a performance attribution of this simple portfolio based on the conventional approach.

Recall from Table 18.5 that Germany was the best available market alternative. Thus, overweighting of the German market should have contributed positively to portfolio performance. The conventional attribution indicates, however, that the German market strategy *reduced* the portfolio return by 0.65 percent. In fact, the data in Table 18.10 indicate that the

TABLE 18.7 Summary of Calculations in Global Performance Attribution

Return from	Calculation	Market Quadrant Differences
A. Market attribution Active market selection	$\sum_i \{[w_i - \bar{w}_i][(\bar{r}_i - \bar{c}_i) - RP]\} + \sum_i [(v_i - \bar{v}_i)RP]$	Quadrant M(II) − Quadrant M(I)
Security selection	$\sum_i [\bar{w}_i(r_i - \bar{c}_i) - \bar{w}_i(\bar{r}_i - \bar{c}_i)] + \sum_i [\bar{v}_i(k_i - \bar{c}_i) - \bar{v}_i(\bar{c}_i - \bar{c}_i)]$ $= \sum_i [\bar{w}_i(r_i - \bar{r}_i)] + \sum_i [\bar{v}_i(k_i - \bar{c}_i)]$	Quadrant M(III) − Quadrant M(I)
Market cross-product	$\sum_i \{[w_i - \bar{w}_i][(r_i - \bar{c}_i) - (\bar{r}_i - \bar{c}_i)]\} + \sum_i \{[v_i - \bar{v}_i][(k_i - \bar{c}_i) - (\bar{c}_i - \bar{c}_i)]\}$ $= \sum_i [(w_i - \bar{w}_i)(r_i - \bar{r}_i)] + \sum_i (v_i - \bar{v}_i)(k_i - \bar{c}_i)]$	Quadrant M(IV) − [Quadrant M(II) + Quadrant M(III)] + Quadrant M(I)
Market total	$\sum_i \{[w_i(r - \bar{c}_i) + v_i(k_i - \bar{c}_i)] - [\bar{w}_i(\bar{r}_i - \bar{c}_i)]\}$	Quadrant M(IV) − Quadrant M(I)

B. Currency attribution

Active currency selection	$\displaystyle\sum_i \{[(w_i + v_i + h_i) - (\overline{w}_i + \overline{v}_i + \overline{h}_i)][(\overline{c}_i + \overline{\varepsilon}_i) - c]\}$	Quadrant C(II) − Quadrant C(I)
Hedge selection	$\displaystyle\sum_i \{[(\overline{w}_i + \overline{v}_i + \overline{h}_i)(c_i + \overline{\varepsilon}_i)] - [(\overline{w}_i + \overline{v}_i + \overline{h}_i)(\overline{c}_i + \overline{\varepsilon}_i)]\}$ $\displaystyle= \sum_i [(\overline{w}_i + \overline{v}_i + \overline{h}_i)(c_i - \overline{c}_i)]$	Quadrant C(III) − Quadrant C(I)
Currency cross-product	$\displaystyle\sum_i \{[(w_i + v_i + h_i) - (\overline{w}_i + \overline{v}_i + \overline{h}_i)][(c_i + \overline{\varepsilon}_i) - (\overline{c}_i + \overline{\varepsilon}_i)]\}$ $\displaystyle= \sum_i \{[(w_i + v_i + h_i) - (\overline{w}_i + \overline{v}_i + \overline{h}_i)](c_i - \overline{c}_i)\}$	Quadrant C(IV) − [Quadrant C(II) + Quadrant C(III)] + Quadrant C(I)
Currency total	$\displaystyle\sum_i \{[(w_i + v_i + h_i)(c_i + \overline{\varepsilon}_i)] - [(\overline{w}_i + \overline{v}_i + \overline{h}_i)(\overline{c}_i + \overline{\varepsilon}_i)]\}$	Quadrant C(IV) − Quadrant C(I)

Note: Plain lowercase letters indicate portfolio weights and returns; letters with a bar over them indicate passive benchmark weights and returns.

w_i = weight of country i noncash assets,

v_i = weight of country i strategic cash assets,

h_i = portion of portfolio hedged into (positive) or out of (negative) currency i;

RP = aggregate passive benchmark local-currency return premium,

C = aggregate passive benchmark Eurodeposit return, in base-currency terms,

r_i = return from the noncash assets of country i, in local-currency terms,

c_i = return from country i Eurodeposits, in local-currency terms,

$\overline{\varepsilon}_i$ = rate of change in the base currency–currency i exchange rate, and

k_i = return from actively managed strategic cash in country i, where the passive return is assumed to be the passive return from country i Eurodeposits, $\overline{c}_i$.

TABLE 18.8 Summary of Global Portfolio Strategy

	Market Strategy			Currency Strategy				
Country	Index Weight, $\bar{w}_i$	Active Weight, w_i	Over/Under	Active Market Weight, w_i +	Active Cash Weight, v_i +	Currency Hedge, h_i =	Currency Weight, $w_i + v_i + h_i$	Over/Under
Germany	25.0%	60.0%	35.0%	60.0%	0.0%	−50.0%	10.0%	−15.0%
United Kingdom	25.0	10.0	−15.0	10.0	0.0	45.0	55.0	30.0
Japan	25.0	10.0	−15.0	10.0	0.0	15.0	25.0	0.0
United States	25.0	15.0	−10.0	15.0	5.0	−10.0	10.0	−15.0
Cash	0.0	5.0	5.0	NA	NA	NA	NA	NA
Benchmark/ portfolio	100.0%	100.0%	0.0%	95.0%	5.0%	0.0%	100.0%	0.0%

NA = not applicable.

TABLE 18.9   Summary of Global Portfolio Returns

| | Passive Returns | | | | | Actual Returns | | |
Country	Local Market Return	Local Eurodeposit Return	Exchange Rate Return	Local-Market Return Premium	Eurodeposit Return in U.S. Dollars	Local-Market Return	Local-Market Return Premium	Eurodeposit Return in U.S. Dollars
Germany	7.00%	5.00%	1.00%	2.00%	6.00%	6.80%	1.80%	6.00%
United Kingdom	10.50	11.25	−3.00	−0.75	8.25	12.25	1.00	8.25
Japan	9.50	9.00	−1.00	0.50	8.00	10.50	1.50	8.00
United States	8.40	7.50	0.00	0.90	7.50	9.00	1.50	7.50
U.S. cash	7.50	7.50	0.00	0.00	7.50	8.00	0.50	7.50
Benchmark/ portfolio	8.85	8.19	−0.75	0.66	7.44	8.11	1.58	7.89

Note: Continuously compounded rates of return.

TABLE 18.10 Conventional Value-Added Performance Attribution (percents)

Country	Market Selection	Currency Selection	Security Selection	Total
Germany	−0.65 (0.60 − 0.25)(7.00% − 8.85%)	−0.26 (0.10 − 0.25)[1.00% − (−0.75%)]	−0.12 0.60(6.80% − 7.00%)	−1.03
United Kingdom	−0.25 (0.10 − 0.25)(10.50% − 8.85%)	−0.68 (0.55 − 0.25)[−3.00% − (−0.75%)]	0.18 0.10(12.25% − 10.50%)	−0.75
Japan	−0.10 (0.10 − 0.25)(9.50% − 8.85%)	0.00 (0.25 − 0.25)[− 1.00% − (−0.75%)]	0.10 0.10(10.50% − 9.50%)	0.00
United States	0.05 (0.15 − 0.25)(8.40% − 8.85%)	−0.11 (0.10 − 0.25)(0.00% − (−0.75%)]	0.09 0.15(9.00% − 8.40%)	0.02
U.S. cash	−0.07 (0.05 − 0.00)(7.50% − 8.85%)	NA	0.03 0.05(8.00% − 7.50%)	−0.04
Unexplained	NA	NA	NA	3.16
Total	−1.01	−1.05	0.27	1.37

Note: Continuously compounded rates of return. Totals may not sum because of rounding.

NA = not applicable.

total market strategy reduced returns by 1.01 percent relative to the benchmark, with only the U.S. underweight providing a positive contribution. The total currency strategy is also shown to have reduced returns, by 1.05 percent relative to the benchmark. Again from Table 18.5, U.K. sterling was the best currency alternative, and thus the attribution would be expected to show a positive currency contribution from the sterling overweight. The conventional attribution computes a *negative* contribution, however, of 0.68 percent. Security selection does show a positive effect, a contribution of 0.27 percent extra return.[15] In summary, the incentive provided by the conventional attribution framework would have been to invest in the worst market and the worst currency.

In fact, the superior performance of this portfolio relative to the benchmark is unexplained by the conventional framework, which cannot account for 3.16 percent of the return of the portfolio relative to the benchmark. The magnitude of the unexplained term reflects the effect of hedging marks into sterling and yen. The unexplained portion of the added value attribution can be computed by weighting each Eurodeposit rate with the respective hedge weight: 3.16 percent = [−0.50(5.00 percent) + 0.45(11.25 percent) + 0.15 (9.00 percent) − 0.10(7.50 percent)]. The portfolio maintained a 50 percent hedge out of marks (giving up the local cash return of 5 percent), hedged 45 percent into sterling and 15 percent into yen (gaining the higher local cash returns of 11.25 percent and 9 percent, respectively), and hedged 10 percent out of the dollar (giving up the 7.5 percent cash return).

Use of a currency benchmark that is different from the market benchmark presents a similar and systematic problem of unaccountable performance. A common but extreme example would involve a fully hedged benchmark. In effect, market and currency benchmark differences involve passive forward positions. The conventional attribution framework simply forces these passive forward hedges into the residual. Because the proposed methodology considers currency exposures to be exposures to global cash markets, it accounts for passive forward hedges naturally.

The perverse results of conventional attribution result from focusing on local currency and exchange rate returns while ignoring the interest rate differentials that were actually responsible for a significant portion of the active performance.

The proposed methodology eliminates the unexplained term by accounting for the Eurodeposit returns underlying forward exchange rates as an explicit factor in the currency-selection process and removing that effect from the market-selection process. Table 18.11 provides the results of the proposed attribution procedure according to the formulas provided in Table 18.7.

The contribution from market allocation is indicated to be positive, adding 65 basis points to the portfolio return. The positive effects of the decisions to overweight Germany and underweight the United Kingdom are captured, consistently with the data in Table 18.5. The same observations can be made about the German mark underweight and sterling overweight. The absence of a residual indicates that this system accounts for the effects of all of the decisions that combined to produce the portfolio return of 9.47 percent.

Although the framework is designed to account for currency exposures within global portfolios, perhaps the most interesting results are with regard to the market allocation decision. Correct attribution of the performance contribution of currency allocations places crucial but identifiable constraints on the attribution to market decisions.

The conventional and proposed attribution systems indicate that considering global returns in terms of local currency and exchange rate returns does not provide an adequate basis for market and currency strategy decisions that will jointly produce optimal performance.[16] Existing systems of market and currency performance attribution are potentially perverse in this regard. The proposed attribution system focuses on the return components that provide an accurate distinction between market and currency alternatives.

TABLE 18.11 Proposed Value-Added Performance Attribution (percents)

Country	Market Selection	Currency Selection	Security Selection	Total
Germany	0.47	0.22	−0.12%	0.56%
	(0.60 − 0.25)(2.00% − 0.66%)	(0.10 − 0.25)(6.00% − 7.44%)	0.60(1.80% − 2.00%)	
United Kingdom	0.21	0.24	0.18	0.63
	(0.10 − 0.25)(−0.75% − 0.66%)	(0.55 − 0.25)(8.25% − 7.44%)	0.10(1.00% + 0.75%)	
Japan	0.02	0.00	0.10	0.12
	(0.10 − 0.25)(0.50% − 0.66%)	(0.25 − 0.25)(8.00% − 7.44%)	0.10(1.50% − 0.50%)	
United States	−0.02	−0.01	0.09	0.06
	(0.15 − 0.25)(0.90% − 0.66%)	(0.10 − 0.25)(7.50% − 7.44%)	0.15(1.50% − 0.90%)	
U.S. cash	−0.03	NA	0.03	−0.01
	(0.05 − 0.00)(0.00% − 0.66%)		0.05(0.50% − 0.00%)	
Unexplained	NA	NA	NA	0.00
Total	0.65	0.45	0.27	1.37

Note: Continuously compounded rates of return. Totals may not sum because of rounding.

NA = not applicable.

Summary

This section has presented a general methodology for performance attribution. The approach corrects the remaining problems in the attribution literature by providing unambiguous measures of both market and currency returns in global portfolios. In particular, the attribution shows clearly the dangers inherent in using either local currency or unhedged return in evaluating market returns that are available to investors.

The proposed framework offers several advantages over attribution systems that are currently in use. First, the framework is conceptually valid, which allows a pure segmented evaluation of market and currency decisions according to variables that managers can, in fact, control. Second, it applies to any benchmark currency position, whether unhedged, partially hedged, or fully hedged. Third, it can be applied to portfolios in any base currency. Fourth, by breaking returns into elemental components, it allows attribution for portfolios that use derivatives and synthetics. Finally, and most importantly, it provides the correct incentives to the market and currency managers, thereby assuring that the decisions of each can work in concert to maximize the performance of the portfolio.

This section considered a performance attribution for a single period for a hypothetical portfolio, in order to demonstrate the methodology and to highlight some of the pitfalls of conventional attribution procedures. The sections titled Interpretation of Global Performance Attributions and Global Balanced Portfolios apply the attribution framework to actual global equity, global bond, and global balanced portfolios.

INTERPRETATION OF GLOBAL PERFORMANCE ATTRIBUTIONS

This section contains evaluations of the performance of two global portfolios. It involves a detailed analysis of inputs and a thorough interpretation of the attribution results. To clarify the appropriateness of the proposed performance attribution framework, the results are contrasted with those generated by conventional attribution methods.

A Global Equity Portfolio, 1989

This example considers the performance of a U.S.-dollar-based global equity portfolio during a period when direct hedging in the portfolio was minimal but active currency management was nevertheless significant.

Table 18.12 shows the performance attribution results for the calendar year of 1989. The output is divided into two sections; Part A is a summary of returns attributable to the components of the portfolio return, and Part B presents the detailed data for the specific markets and currencies that were used in the attribution.

The benchmark for this portfolio was the MSCI World Equity (Free) Index. The individual market returns have been adjusted for the withholding taxes that are appropriate for a U.S.-based investor. The base currency was the U.S. dollar. The benchmark total return was 16.97 percent. The portfolio earned a total return of 24.63 percent, producing 7.66 percent of added value through active management.

Of this added value, market selection cost 75 basis points, primarily reflecting a negative contribution from a strategic cash position. Currency selection added 563 basis points, largely through an underweighting of the Japanese yen and overweighting of the U.S. dollar. Stock selection within the various markets contributed 165 basis points. Differences between the exchange rates used by MSCI to compute index returns and those used to value the portfolio

TABLE 18.12   Global Equity Portfolio, 1989 (base currency = U.S. dollar)

A. Portfolio performance summary

MSCI Global Equity Index		16.97%
Market selection	−0.75%	
Currency selection	5.63	
Security selection	1.65	
Exchange rate differences	−0.03	
Intramonth effect	1.16	
Total value added		7.66%
Global equity portfolio		24.63%

B. Attribution of added value (basis points)

Country	Market Selection	Currency Selection	Security Selection	Total
Australia	−8	11	19	22
Austria	−6	−2	0	−8
Belgium	−16	19	2	5
Canada	−8	19	5	16
Denmark	−3	−4	0	−7
Finland	1	−1	0	0
France	−5	−9	20	6
Germany	29	22	6	57
Hong Kong	3	−1	−7	−6
Italy	17	−21	0	−4
Japan	89	297	25	411
Netherlands	14	14	11	39
New Zealand	−34	4	13	−17
Norway	−3	−2	0	−5
Singapore	2	1	−5	−2
Spain	−25	22	19	16
Sweden	−3	−3	0	−7
Switzerland	16	18	−8	26
United Kingdom	21	4	22	47
United States	30	173	43	246
Cash	−185	NA	0	−185
Subtotal	−75	563	165	653
Exchange rate differences				−3
Intramonth effect				116
Total active contribution				766

Note: Totals may not sum because of rounding.

NA = not applicable.

generated a 3–basis-point discrepancy, a transitory valuation factor that is beyond the manager's control. Finally, a residual of 116 basis points reflects primarily the impact of intramonth changes in market and currency allocations. The intramonth residual arises because the specific timing of intramonth changes in strategies was ignored and beginning-of-month weights were used to reflect asset allocations throughout the month. These aggregate contributions reflect the combined effect of active strategies applied among and within individual markets and among currencies.[17]

    Table 18.13 summarizes the average active market and currency strategies for the year. This information is useful for identify[ing] the basic structure of the strategies that produced

TABLE 18.13 Global Equity Portfolio: Average Market and Currency Strategies, 1989 (base currency = U.S. dollar)

	Market-Selection Summary						Currency-Selection Summary			
	Average Market Weight			Return Premium			Average Currency Weight			Eurodeposit Return
Country	Passive	Active	Difference	Passive	Active	Difference	Passive	Active	Difference	in U.S. Dollars (passive)
Australia	1.44%	2.09%	0.65%	0.98%	8.82%	7.85%	1.44%	2.09%	0.65%	9.11%
Austria	0.13	0.00	−0.13	82.16	NA	NA	0.13	0.00	−0.13	12.53
Belgium	0.64	2.14	1.50	3.27	4.31	1.04	0.64	2.14	1.50	13.94
Canada	2.70	3.83	1.13	7.89	10.15	2.26	2.70	3.83	1.13	15.56
Denmark	0.33	0.00	−0.33	26.92	NA	NA	0.33	0.00	−0.33	13.68
Finland	0.05	0.00	−0.05	−1.46	NA	NA	0.05	0.00	−0.05	15.09
France	2.75	2.51	−0.24	19.31	26.15	6.84	2.75	2.51	−0.24	14.25
Germany	2.97	4.94	1.97	30.96	33.31	2.35	2.97	5.10	2.13	11.93
Hong Kong	0.77	0.59	−0.18	−1.48	−12.08	−10.60	0.77	0.59	−0.18	10.01
Italy	1.49	0.00	−1.49	3.29	NA	NA	1.49	0.00	−1.49	15.84
Japan	41.96	14.86	−27.10	11.46	13.66	2.20	41.96	12.77	−29.19	−8.75
Netherlands	1.40	3.00	1.61	21.57	25.67	4.10	1.40	3.01	1.61	12.12
New Zealand	0.16	1.61	1.45	4.01	11.06	7.05	0.16	1.61	1.45	7.43
Norway	0.24	0.00	−0.24	31.46	NA	NA	0.24	0.00	−0.24	11.13
Singapore	0.58	0.33	−0.25	31.13	22.11	−9.02	0.58	0.33	−0.25	8.47
Spain	0.99	2.18	1.19	−6.79	2.71	9.50	0.99	2.18	1.19	17.76
Sweden	0.39	0.00	−0.39	26.92	NA	NA	0.39	0.00	−0.39	10.27
Switzerland	1.14	2.78	1.64	23.36	19.58	−3.78	1.14	3.53	2.38	3.66
United Kingdom	8.26	10.20	1.94	20.31	22.50	2.19	8.26	10.40	2.14	1.66
United States	31.61	35.13	3.52	19.69	21.51	1.82	31.61	49.91	18.30	9.76
Cash	0.00	13.79	13.79	0.00	0.00	0.00	NA	NA	NA	NA
Benchmark/portfolio	100.00%	100.00%	0.00%	15.20%	16.31%	1.11%	100.00%	100.00%	0.00%	1.38%

Note: Totals may not sum because of rounding.
NA = not applicable.

429

the performance shown in Table 18.12. Average weights and returns across multiple valuation periods can be misleading, however, by masking active market and currency changes that occurred during the period. Thus, these summary data should be viewed as only a rough indication of portfolio strategy during the period; they become more tenuous as the attribution horizon lengthens.

The market and currency strategies are specified as deviations from the normal investment policy, as given by the benchmark weights. This specification is a generally accepted interpretation of market strategies but is often not applied to the evaluation of currency strategies. Instead, many incorrectly assume that active currency management is synonymous with currency hedging. This portfolio maintained a significant underweight in Japanese yen relative to the benchmark, however, and a significant overweight in U.S. dollars, even though currency hedging was relatively insignificant. Notice, for example, that the active currency weights are similar to the market strategy weights; an explicit decision was made to accept the currency over- and underweights that resulted from the market strategy. As in the hypothetical portfolio in the section titled Global Performance Attribution a neutral yen strategy would have required hedging into the yen to offset the underweight that was derived from holding a below-benchmark allocation to Japanese equities. In summary, the lack of currency hedging in this portfolio resulted in active currency strategies.

Table 18.14 shows the average hedge positions maintained in this global equity portfolio for the year. The small hedge from yen into U.S. dollars reflects a range forward that was executed with options on futures contracts. As profits (losses) were realized on the option positions, U.S. dollar cash was realized in the margin account and reflected as an increase (decrease) in the portfolio's cash allocation. Other differences between the active market weights and active currency weights reflect strategic allocations to cash in each currency.

The hedges shown in Table 18.14 are provided to aid in the interpretation of the attribution data; they are not necessary for attribution purposes. As Equation 18.9 showed, only the total currency weights in Table 18.13 are relevant.

Interpretation of the market-selection contribution to this portfolio's performance is based on the efficacy of relative return-premium allocations. The return premium of the MSCI World Equity benchmark was an extraordinary 15.2 percent, computed as the weighted-average local-currency total return of each market above the local three-month Eurodeposit return. An active overweight (underweight) in any equity market that had a passive return premium greater (less) than 15.2 percent added value to the global equity portfolio. Conversely, an overweight (underweight) in any market that had a passive return premium less (greater) than the passive benchmark return premium of 15.2 percent detracted from the portfolio's performance. Summing all of the contributions from each individual market strategy shows that the total contribution from market selection was negative 75 basis points.

Table 18.12 suggests that the primary market-selection contribution to portfolio performance came from the allocation to the Japanese market. Table 18.13 shows that a large (27.1 percent) underweight of Japanese equities, which had a passive return premium of 11.46 percent, resulted in this contribution. Although the Japanese return premium was only slightly below that of the benchmark, the magnitude of the underweight produced a large contribution to the differential between portfolio and benchmark total returns.

This added value was more than offset, however, by the effect of a large overweight (13.79 percent) of cash. The passive cash return premium of zero was significantly below that of the benchmark for the portfolio. The benchmark for cash in this portfolio was the return to three-month Eurodeposits. Therefore, and by definition, the passive cash return premium is zero.

TABLE 18.14   The Global Equity Portfolio's
Average Currency Hedges, 1989

Country	Currency Hedges
Australia	0.00%
Austria	0.00
Belgium	0.00
Canada	0.00
Denmark	0.00
Finland	0.00
France	0.00
Germany	0.00
Hong Kong	0.00
Italy	0.00
Japan	−2.57
Netherlands	0.00
New Zealand	0.00
Norway	0.00
Singapore	0.00
Spain	0.00
Sweden	0.00
Switzerland	0.00
United Kingdom	0.00
United States	2.57
Total	0.00%

Although the interpretation of the effect of the total market allocation is relatively straightforward, the interpretation of the individual market contributions can become complicated. In this example, should the Japanese equity underweight be interpreted as a positive contributor to performance? What if the manager had a negative view toward Japan but no strong views on any other markets? Underweighting of Japan requires overweighting of some other markets. To the extent, for example, that this global equity portfolio maintained the cash overweight as a substitute for Japanese equities, would the appropriate interpretation be that the Japanese equity decision, reflecting the combined negative contribution of the cash overweight and positive effect of the Japanese equity underweights, was a hindrance to portfolio performance?

The point is that an underweight of one market requires the overweight of another market. The individual market contributions, even though they are directly calculable, are inseparable portfolio decisions.[18] In the final analysis, at the level of the individual markets, interpretation of performance attribution requires an understanding of the motivation behind each of the active market allocations. Typically, only the investment manager has that information; others should be wary of interpretating attributions to individual markets.

The column of currency-selection contributions in Table 18.12 is based on a comparison of each country's passive three-month Eurodeposit return in U.S. dollars with the 1.38 percent passive U.S.-dollar-denominated three-month Eurodeposit return of the benchmark. The benchmark Eurodeposit return is computed by applying the passive currency (market) weights to the U.S. dollar Eurodeposit returns in each country. The only Eurodeposit return in Table 18.13 that was below that of the benchmark was Japan (−8.75 percent). Thus, a productive portfolio currency strategy would have involved an underweight of the Japanese yen and overweights of any other currency. In fact, this portfolio did maintain its largest currency underweight in yen; although other small underweights existed, each paled in comparison with the yen underweight. The largest currency overweight was in the U.S. dollar.

Keeping in mind the reservations about interpreting individual effects, Table 18.12 indicates that the underweight of yen and the U.S. dollar overweight were largely responsible for the positive effect of currency strategy. Summing the contributions of each active currency decision indicates a total currency-selection contribution of 563 basis points. Even though explicit currency hedging was minimal in this portfolio, active currency selection was the largest contributor to portfolio performance. Currency hedges per se are not the sole indicators of active currency decisions. Net currency over- and underweights relative to the benchmark are active decisions regardless of their source.

Security selection is based on the difference between the active return premium in each country and the passive return premium specified by the benchmark in each country. Because the Eurodeposit returns underlying the active and passive return-premium computations are identical, however, the computation of the returns from security selection using local currency returns is equivalent to using return premiums.[19]

The interpretation of security selection within markets is no different for global than it is for domestic portfolios. Selection of securities in any market that results in above-benchmark performance during the evaluation period adds to the value of the portfolio. As explained in the section titled Global Performance Attribution the cross-product of market- and security-selection decisions is combined into the security-selection effect through the use of active market weights in determining the contribution of security selection to the portfolio. Security selection added value in almost every market in this global equity portfolio.

This example demonstrates that the proposed framework applies to any multicurrency portfolio regardless of whether hedging is used. If hedging is prohibited, however, independent market and currency strategies are not possible. Instead, the market and currency strategies will be identical and the currency effects will become an integral part of the market decision. The combined market allocation effect is identical to the method outlined by Brinson and Fachler (1985). Without authority to hedge, the consideration of exchange rates and short-term interest rates becomes irrelevant and the analysis can be completed in base-currency terms. In that regard, segmentation of market and currency effects as shown in Table 18.12 would indicate the opportunity cost of a policy to restrict hedging.

A Global Bond Portfolio, 1992

Unlike the example global equity portfolio, this attribution example considers the performance of a portfolio for which hedging activity and active currency strategy were significant throughout the evaluation period.

Table 18.15 shows performance attribution results for a global bond portfolio for the 1992 calendar year. The portfolio outperformed the Salomon Brothers World Government Bond Index benchmark's total return of 5.53 percent by 3.56 percent, producing a total return of 9.09

TABLE 18.15   Global Bond Portfolio, 1992 (base currency = U.S. dollar)

A. Portfolio performance summary

Salomon Brothers World Government Bond Index		5.53%
Market selection	0.24%	
Currency selection	3.09	
Security selection	0.48	
Exchange rate differences	−0.16	
Intramonth effect	−0.09	
Total value added		3.56%
Global bond portfolio		9.09%

B. Attribution of added value (basis points)

Country	Market Selection	Currency Selection	Security Selection	Total
Australia	1	5	0	6
Belgium	−7	14	1	9
Canada	39	1	−10	31
Denmark	−14	18	9	14
France	−1	16	−24	−9
Germany	17	33	18	68
Italy	−5	47	0	41
Japan	−23	−16	−14	−53
Netherlands	13	6	7	26
Spain	−5	−28	2	−31
Sweden	−4	23	0	19
Switzerland	1	−3	0	−2
United Kingdom	−10	68	4	62
United States	19	124	53	196
Cash	3	NA	0	3
Subtotal	24	309	48	381
Exchange rate differences				−16
Intramonth effect				−9
Total active contribution				356

Note: Totals may not sum because of rounding.

NA = not applicable.

percent. The portfolio benefited from positive contributions from market, currency, and security selection. Exchange rate differences between the exchange rates within the Salomon Index and those used to value the global bond portfolio reduced the portfolio total return relative to the benchmark by 16 basis points for the year. Finally, the intramonth effect was −0.09 percent.

Table 18.15 shows the contributions from active strategies among and within individual markets and among currencies. The average active market and currency strategies for the year are summarized in Table 18.16. On average, above-normal allocations to markets with return premiums above the 3.77 percent return premium of the benchmark would have added value to the portfolio. Note, however, that market and currency strategies changed significantly during 1992 and, therefore, the summary data can be misleading. Table 18.16 masks the month-to-month market allocations that added to the portfolio total return.

TABLE 18.16 Global Bond Portfolio: Average Market and Currency Strategies, 1992 (base currency = U.S. dollar)

| | Market-Selection Summary | | | | | | Currency-Selection Summary | | | |
| | Average Market Weight | | | Return Premiums | | | Average Currency Weight | | | Eurodeposit Returns in U.S. Dollars (passive) |
Country	Passive	Active	Difference	Passive	Active	Difference	Passive	Active	Difference	
Australia	0.79%	0.00%	−0.79%	2.82%	NA	NA	0.79%	0.00%	−0.79%	−3.25%
Belgium	0.87	0.55	−0.32	−4.07	−3.67	0.41	0.87	0.55	−0.32	3.52
Canada	3.82	5.44	1.62	2.47	3.91	1.44	3.82	7.33	3.51	−2.81
Denmark	1.36	3.44	2.08	−2.53	−1.79	0.74	1.36	0.74	−0.62	4.29
France	6.03	10.41	4.38	0.23	−1.79	−2.02	6.03	5.27	−0.76	3.88
Germany	10.04	16.02	5.98	2.52	3.62	1.10	10.04	6.89	−3.15	3.27
Italy	1.49	0.00	−1.49	−7.04	NA	NA	1.49	0.00	−1.49	−10.87
Japan	18.31	6.50	−11.81	5.60	3.86	−1.75	18.31	8.82	−9.50	5.00
Netherlands	3.89	11.61	7.72	4.63	5.19	0.56	3.89	3.77	−0.13	3.60
Spain	0.35	1.60	1.25	−6.49	−8.49	−2.00	0.35	0.49	0.14	−3.94
Sweden	0.31	0.00	−0.31	−4.36	NA	NA	0.31	0.00	−0.31	−10.63
Switzerland	0.18	0.00	−0.18	2.34	NA	NA	0.18	0.00	−0.18	0.54
United Kingdom	5.67	2.07	−3.60	6.87	5.79	−1.08	5.67	1.38	−4.30	−10.20
United States	46.89	42.43	−4.46	3.00	4.09	1.10	46.89	64.78	17.89	4.09
Cash	0.00	−0.07	−0.07	0.00	0.00	0.00	NA	NA	NA	NA
Total portfolio	100.00%	100.00%	0.00%	3.77%	4.52%	0.75%	100.00%	100.00%	0.00%	1.79%

Note: Totals may not sum because of rounding.
NA = not applicable.

434

Canada is a case in point. Given the relatively low average return premium for the Canadian bond market during the year (2.47 percent versus 3.77 percent for the benchmark), overweighting the Canadian bond market would appear to have been a deterrent to portfolio performance. In fact, however, an overweight early in 1992 and an underweight later in the year captured an early high return premium and avoided poor performance in late 1992. Consequently, the Canadian bond market strategy added 39 basis points to the value of the portfolio. Even though these types of summary data are commonly reported and are useful, they are not a substitute for a comprehensive report of active portfolio strategies and implementation. The *aggregate* effects of market, currency, and security selection, however, are unambiguous.

Among the market allocation decisions, positive contributors included the active over-weighting and then underweighting of Canada, the (essentially) neutral weighting in the beginning of the year followed by a late-year overweighting of Germany, the consistent over-weighting of the Netherlands, and the early neutral weighting then late underweighting of the United States. Consistent underweighting of the Japan and U.K. markets detracted from performance.

A small net short cash position at the year-end valuation date added three basis points to the value of the portfolio. This cash position resulted from small forward-contract losses that generated an unrealizable "negative cash" allocation. Any forward-contract gains outstanding at the time of portfolio valuation would be unrealizable gains reflected as a "positive cash" holding. The previously discussed global equity portfolio attribution had no unrealizable gains or losses because that portfolio's currency hedges were implemented through options on futures. Futures and options on futures are marked to market daily, so gains and losses are realized daily and either reinvested or met through a margin call.

Table 18.17 shows the average hedge positions maintained in this global bond portfolio during the year. The active currency strategy resulted from the bond market allocations combined with these portfolio currency hedges. Even though the portfolio was overweighted in many continental European bond markets, it was underweighted in all of these currencies except the Spanish peseta. Also, hedges into the U.S. dollar totaling 22.34 percent transformed a moderate currency underweight implied by the U.S. bond market strategy into the significant average overweight, 17.89 percent, shown in Table 18.16.

In contrast to the global equity portfolio presented earlier, currency hedges were a means of achieving desired currency strategy in this global bond portfolio. During the year, the magnitudes of these hedges were increased as U.S. dollar cash became increasingly under-valued relative to European cash in U.S. dollar terms. When the Exchange Rate Mechanism stumbled in September 1992, major currency realignments, involving the pound sterling in particular, generated significant portfolio gains relative to the benchmark. The aggregate currency strategy added 309 basis points to the portfolio's return during the year.

Finally, value added through security selection is based on active yield-curve, quality, and sector strategies within the various markets. The active return premiums of the portfolio's U.S. component provided most of the positive security-selection effect. The dominance of the U.S. market's security-selection contribution is a function of that component's superior performance and the large weighting, 42.43 percent, of the active U.S. bond market.

This portfolio example indicates the importance of using the correct attribution framework when large currency hedges are in place. An attribution based on the conventional framework not only gave misleading information on market and currency effects but also resulted in a −173-basis-point residual, over 48 percent of the total added value provided by active portfolio management.

TABLE 18.17   The Global Bond
Portfolio's Average Currency Hedges, 1992

Country	Currency Hedges
Australia	0.00%
Belgium	0.00
Canada	1.89
Denmark	−2.70
France	−5.14
Germany	−9.13
Italy	0.00
Japan	2.31
Netherlands	−7.84
Spain	−1.11
Sweden	0.00
Switzerland	0.00
United Kingdom	−0.69
United States	22.34
Total	−0.07%

The conventional attribution framework creates an incentive to invest in countries with high short-term interest rates and to hedge the resulting currency exposures. This problem can be especially important in attributing added value to emerging markets, which tend to offer high market and cash returns to offset the ravages of relatively high inflation. Conventional attribution frameworks, by overstating the available market returns, would have shown strong market-selection incentives for investing in countries such as Mexico in the early 1980s and Eastern Europe in the early 1990s. Moreover, hedging against the depreciation of the currencies of such countries would also appear advantageous in the conventional framework, whereas in reality, the high cost of hedging that results from high local short-term interest rates would largely offset the apparent benefits.

Summary

Portfolio performance attributions require a framework that parallels the investment decision-making process by allocating responsibility for performance among factors that can be controlled by the investment manager. Currency strategy can be isolated from the market strategy, but only when controllable and separable variables are used to represent each decision. The basic element underlying market decisions and, therefore, market-selection attributions are the return premiums of each market relative to the return premium of the benchmark. The bases for attributions to currency decisions and currency selection are global Eurodeposit returns expressed in the investor's base currency.

Because of the importance of investment policy mandates and the dynamic nature of market and currency allocations, the interpretation of attribution results requires a thorough understanding of the strategies in use during the period in question and the motivation for those strategies.

GLOBAL BALANCED PORTFOLIOS

Broadly based global balanced portfolios that include multicurrency investments in stocks, bonds, and cash are the ultimate test of a global analytical framework. A number of critical issues that are not always evident in the analysis of global equity or global bond portfolios become prominent when equity and bonds are combined in the portfolio. For example, active market and currency strategies are ultimately relevant only at the level of the aggregate portfolio. Bond and equity management are often separated among different managers, however, and the effect on the portfolio of active decisions at the component level may not be evident. Performance attribution that separates the effects of the asset allocation decision—that is, separates the portions of the portfolio that are assigned to various managers—from the effects of the investment expertise of each manager within each specific assignment is clearly necessary.

Currency management in global balanced portfolios can be particularly challenging. Currency exposures are affected by market and currency decisions within the non-U.S.-equity and non-U.S.-bond components as well as by asset allocation decisions that affect the portfolio's exposure to the broad classes of foreign assets. This section addresses these unique issues that arise in the management and performance evaluation of global balanced portfolios.

The Multiple-Asset Problem

A common approach to asset allocation within global balanced portfolios is first to allocate funds among broad U.S.-equity, non-U.S.-equity, U.S.-bond, and non-U.S.-bond asset classes. Subsequent allocations within each of these asset classes reflect relative valuations within the markets of the various countries. While this approach can produce optimal strategies within each asset class, it can lead to unintended and even perverse market and currency strategies for the total global portfolio.

Consider a global balanced portfolio that has normal allocations to U.S. equities of 50 percent, non-U.S. equities of 17 percent, U.S. bonds of 20 percent, non-U.S. bonds of 8 percent, and U.S.-dollar-denominated cash equivalents of 5 percent. Assume that the portfolio strategically underweights global equities and overweights global bonds and cash to provide the following asset-class strategy:

	Normal	*Portfolio*	*Strategy*
U.S. equity	50.0%	25.0%	−25.0%
Non-U.S. equity	17.0	6.0	−11.0
U.S. bonds	20.0	34.0	+14.0
Non-U.S. bonds	8.0	25.0	+17.0
Cash	5.0	10.0	+5.0

The portfolio strategy involves a large non-U.S.-equity underweight and a large non-U.S.-bond overweight. The non-U.S.-equity manager is provided with 6 percent of the aggregate portfolio to manage against a non-U.S.-equity benchmark; the non-U.S.-bond manager is provided with 25 percent of the portfolio to manage against a non-U.S.-bond benchmark.

Both of the non-U.S. managers are charged with and perform in a manner that is consistent with beating their individual benchmarks.

The non-U.S.-equity manager is particularly attracted to the U.K. equity market and allocates 60 percent of the non-U.S.-equity portfolio to that market, roughly twice its weight in a benchmark such as the MSCI Non-U.S. Equity Index. Although the U.K. equity market may outperform the non-U.S.-equity index (in terms of return premiums), the aggregate portfolio may be detrimentally affected by the U.K.-equity-market strategy. To see why, one must view the portfolio in its entirety.

The normal allocation to U.K. equities within the total portfolio is 5.1 percent, which reflects the combined effect of the normal non-U.S.-equity weight of 17 percent and the 30 percent U.K.-equity-market weight within the non-U.S.-equity index. The actual U.K. equity weight at the aggregate portfolio level is obtained by multiplying the actual U.K. allocation of 60 percent within the non-U.S. component by the 6 percent allocation to non-U.S. equities. Even though the equity manager considers the U.K. equity market to be attractive relative to other non-U.S. equities, the actual U.K. weight is only 3.6 percent of the total portfolio, below the normal allocation of 5.1 percent.

The outcome is potentially, but not necessarily, perverse. If the underweighting of the non-U.S.-equity asset class takes into account the relative unattractiveness of non-U.S. equities in general, then the U.K.-equity underweight may be appropriate at the portfolio level even if the U.K. market proves to be the top performing non-U.S. equity market. The key is whether the U.K. equity market offers returns that are superior to the passive return of the total portfolio. The investment process as well as the attribution program must be able to handle the joint asset allocation decision involving the asset-class decision and the market allocation within the asset class.

Now consider the non-U.S.-bond manager's strategy when the U.K. bond market is considered to be unattractive. The non-U.S.-bond manager allocates only 10 percent to U.K. bonds, or about half of the Salomon Brothers Non-U.S. Government Bond Index market capitalization. For an aggregate portfolio, the normal U.K.-bond allocation is 1.6 percent, but the actual allocation is 2.5 percent. Again, both allocations are computed by multiplying the asset-class weights by the market weights within the asset class. Although the non-U.S.-bond manager anticipates underperformance of the U.K. bond market, such a development could detract from overall portfolio performance.

The confluence of decision making at two levels—the asset-class level and the market level—can lead to the unintended market allocations. Unless these decisions are coordinated, the potential for perverse market allocations exists. To the extent that the decisions are separated, performance attribution analysis should provide accurate feedback on the decisions involving both asset allocation and individual market selection.

Currency management is equally complicated. Because global balanced portfolios contain global or non-U.S.-equity and global or non-U.S.-bond components, thinking of currency exposures within each component might seem to be appropriate. Such thinking is misguided at the level of the total portfolio, however, and can produce unintended currency strategies.

For example, relative currency exposures can be eliminated within each component of a global securities portfolio, but the aggregate portfolio may nevertheless incur significant relative currency exposures. This conundrum would arise when currency allocation strategies are set at the asset-class level.

Returning to the actual global balanced portfolio, the allocation strategy overweights non-U.S. bonds by 17 percent and underweights non-U.S. equities by 11 percent. Assume that the weights for the Japanese markets within the equity and the bond components are neutral, equal to the respective asset classes' market capitalizations of 40 percent and 35 percent. In this instance, in the absence of any currency hedging, the yen weights are also neutral within both the non-U.S.-equity and -bond components.

The aggregate portfolio's normal exposure to yen is 9.6 percent, which is the combined normal allocation in the equity and bond components, $0.17(0.40) + 0.08(0.35)$. Even though the relative currency exposure has been eliminated within each component, the actual yen exposure for the entire portfolio is 11.15 percent, an overweight of 1.55 percent. The actual yen allocation is computed by combining the non-U.S.-bond and non-U.S.-equity strategic yen allocations, $0.06(0.40) + 0.25(0.35)$. The entire portfolio is strategically over-weighted in yen even though the actual yen exposure in each of the components is neutral.

The explanation for this counterintuitive outcome is that, through its allocation to the various asset classes, the portfolio is actually buying a small portion of the "equity-based" yen weight and a large portion of the "bond-based" yen weight. Because the overweight of the non-U.S.-bond asset class is significantly greater than the non-U.S.-equity underweight, the portfolio ends up with an above-normal exposure to the yen. Appendix B provides a full accounting of the strategy's interactions and their impact.

Equally glaring is the 6 percent underweight of the U.S. dollar that is implied by this asset allocation strategy in the absence of any hedges into the dollar by the non-U.S.-equity and -bond managers. The normal allocation to non-U.S. assets is 25 percent, but the active allocation strategy has increased the non-U.S. exposure to 31 percent. Such active over- and underweights of the dollar are often the largest active currency allocation decisions in globally diversified pension plans, and although plan sponsors spend a lot of time in setting optimal hedge ratios within the non-U.S. components of their portfolios, such simple active allocations may go managed, even unnoticed.

Global portfolios cannot be managed as a collection of asset classes; they require careful evaluation of interactions among and within asset classes. Nowhere is this necessity so clear as in the management of currencies. Market and currency strategies are often set at the non-U.S.-component level, but the aggregate strategy is all that matters to aggregate portfolio performance.

Currency overlays are one way to deal with the need to set currency strategy at the aggregate portfolio level. Using overlays, however, places specific requirements on the means by which the global assets are to be managed. Because an overlay involves the explicit, and appropriate, separation of market and currency strategies, when overlays are used, the market managers must manage against a return premium or, equivalently, a hedged benchmark. Also, even though these managers may or may not be allowed to hedge currency exposures, their performance must be evaluated in terms of return premiums. If they are measured against a local currency or unhedged benchmark, then as demonstrated in the section titled The General Framework, their decisions could be suboptimal.

A Global Balanced Portfolio

This example addresses several difficulties that arise in performance attribution for actively managed global balanced portfolios. First, the common practice of segmenting portfolios into U.S. equity, non-U.S. equity, U.S. bonds, non-U.S. bonds, and perhaps cash suggests that attributing performance from two perspectives would be useful. One perspective would explicitly recognize that the allocation among asset classes is the primary decision and that selection of markets within asset classes follows. The other approach would assume that, ultimately, performance is determined by specific market over- and underweights, regardless of whether a two-stage decision process is being used.

The second difficulty is the clear need to separate currency strategy from market strategy. To evaluate separate non-U.S.-equity and non-U.S.-bond currency strategies within an aggregate portfolio makes no sense.

Third, a method is needed to present the performance of the non-U.S. components that excludes the contributions of currency management to portfolio performance. This difficulty is particularly relevant in light of the performance presentation standards developed by AIMR for international portfolio carve-outs (AIMR 1993).

Table 18.18 shows performance attribution for an actual global balanced portfolio for the 1992 calendar year. The normal or benchmark weights reflect the Brinson Partners' Global Securities Market Index, which is designed to take into account the risk tolerance of the average U.S. pension plan. On average, the portfolio overweighted U.S. and non-U.S. bonds, underweighted U.S. and non-U.S. equities, and overweighted cash as follows:

	Normal	Active Weights	Strategy
U.S. equity	50.0%	22.0%	−28.0%
Non-U.S. equity	17.0	5.2	−11.8
U.S. bonds	20.0	45.6	+25.6
Non-U.S. bonds	8.0	15.0	+7.0
Cash	5.0	12.2	+7.2

The attribution of total return performance in Table 18.18 indicates positive contributions from market, currency, and security selection. The total value added during the year was 460 basis points above the benchmark return of 4.48 percent. Market allocation accounted for 167 basis points, currency management contributed 123 basis points, and total security selection added 152 basis points. The intramonth effects amounted to only 21 basis points.

Detailed interpretation of the contributions from decisions about individual markets depends, as was discussed in the section titled Global Performance Attribution on the underlying decision-making process that was used in managing this portfolio. The basic market allocation might have been made on a market-by-market basis, as was done in the allocation process for the global equity and bond portfolios in the section titled Global Performance Attribution. Such an approach would imply that the German bond overweight, for example, is as likely to offset explicitly a Japanese equity underweight within the total portfolio as it is to offset an underweight of Japanese bonds within the non-U.S.-bond component, From this perspective, the decision process would have been totally disaggregated, with each individual equity and bond market being treated as a distinct asset class.

On that basis, the U.S. equity underweight clearly detracted from performance, while the U.S. bond overweight clearly added to portfolio value. The cash allocation was a small deterrent to portfolio performance. Clearly also, the Japanese equity underweight made a substantial contribution to the total performance of the portfolio.

Alternatively, the investment decision process might have followed a sequential approach, with the allocation strategy being set across the broad asset classes of U.S. and non-U.S. equity and U.S. and non-U.S. bond markets. Such would be the case, for example, if the portfolio accounted for an entire pension plan's assets and was divided among various managers. From this perspective, the individual market weights would reflect the joint effect of the general asset allocation decision and the subsequent market allocations within each asset class. Thus, the overweight of German bonds would be the result of the general decision to overweight non-U.S. bonds—a decision by the plan sponsor   and/or an explicit decision by

TABLE 18.18   Global Balanced Portfolio: Nontiered Market-Selection Attribution, 1992
(base currency = U.S. dollar)

A. Portfolio performance summary

Global balanced index		4.48%
Market selection	1.67%	
Currency selection	1.23	
Security selection	1.52	
Exchange rate differences	−0.04	
Intrarnonth effect	0.21	
Total value added		4.60%
Global balanced portfolio		9.08%

B. Attribution of added value: Market selection (basis points)

Market	Market Selection	Security Selection
Equity		
United States	−102	112
Australia	1	−1
Austria	1	0
Belgium	0	2
Canada	4	2
Denmark	5	0
Finland	0	0
France	3	−1
Germany	14	0
Hong Kong	−7	0
Italy	5	0
Japan	182	1
Netherlands	1	0
New Zealand	0	−1
Norway	1	0
Singapore	−1	0
Spain	4	0
Sweden	0	0
Switzerland	−6	0
United Kingdom	−11	3
Bond		
United States	56	20
Australia	0	0
Belgium	0	1
Canada	16	3
Denmark	−5	0
France	−2	−2
Germany	6	3
Italy	2	0
Japan	3	1
Netherlands	7	2
Spain	−2	1
Sweden	0	0
Switzerland	0	0
United Kingdom	−2	−1
Cash	−6	7
Subtotal	167	152

(continued)

TABLE 18.18   (*continued*)

C. Attribution of added value: Currency selection (basis points)

Currency	Currency Selection
Australia	3
Austria	0
Belgium	−2
Canada	−5
Denmark	5
Finland	0
France	−1
Germany	21
Hong Kong	0
Italy	11
Japan	−1
Netherlands	6
New Zealand	0
Norway	0
Singapore	0
Spain	3
Sweden	6
Switzerland	3
United Kingdom	52
United States	21
Total	124

Note: Totals may not sum because of rounding.

the non-U.S. -bond manager to overweight the German market within the non-U.S.-bond component. The attribution program should be able to distinguish between these decisions that are made at different levels.

Table 18.19 summarizes the average market strategy weights for this portfolio. The information is divided into three columns: The first shows the broad asset-class weights. The second shows the individual market weights within the non-U.S.-equity and non-U.S.-bond components. The third column shows the individual market allocations as a percentage of the total portfolio. Finally, the table summarizes the average return premiums for the benchmark and the portfolio.

Conceptually, the analysis required to provide information that is relevant for a sequential decision process is simple. The decision to underweight non-U.S. equities can be determined to have added value only if the benchmark return premium offered by non-U.S. equities exceeded the return premium of the global balanced benchmark. The passive non-U.S.-equity return premium was −12.46 percent in 1992, substantially below the benchmark return premium of 1.15 percent. Thus, the non-U.S.-equity asset-class underweight added value.

The subsequent lower level decision to underweight Japan within the non-U. S.-equity component can also be shown to have added value, but the contribution is somewhat less than indicated by the detailed attribution shown in Table 18.18. The Japanese equity return premium of −25.18 percent was below that of the non-U.S.-equity benchmark, while the Japanese equity weight within the non-U.S.-equity component was 24.35 percent, versus the index weight of 41.53 percent. Thus, the Japanese equity underweight within the non-U.S.-equity component added value.

TABLE 18.19 Global Balanced Portfolio: Average Market Strategy, 1992

Market	Passive Weight — Asset Class	Passive Weight — Market within Asset Class	Passive Weight — As Percent of Portfolio	Active Weight — Asset Class	Active Weight — Market within Asset Class	Active Weight — As Percent of Portfolio	Difference — Asset Class	Difference — Market within Asset Class	Difference — As Percent of Portfolio	Market Return Premiums — Passive Return Premium	Market Return Premiums — Active Return Premium	Market Return Premiums — Return Premium Difference
U.S. equity	50.00%		50.00%	22.02%		22.02%	−27.98%		−27.98%	4.70%	11.60%	6.90%
Non-U.S. equity	17.00			5.21			−11.79			NA	NA	NA
Australia		2.71%	0.46		6.45%	0.34		3.73%	−0.13	−12.46	NA	NA
Austria		0.50	0.09		0.00	0.00		−0.50	−0.09	−7.46	10.57	18.03
Belgium		1.22	0.21		3.86	0.20		2.64	−0.01	−13.55	NA	6.46
Canada		4.40	0.75		8.12	0.42		3.72	−0.33	−4.57	1.89	4.84
Denmark		0.77	0.13		0.00	0.00		−0.77	−0.13	−9.37	−4.53	NA
Finland		0.04	0.01		0.00	0.00		−0.04	−0.01	−31.20	NA	NA
France		6.38	1.09		6.64	0.35		0.26	−0.74	−2.93	−3.32	−2.19
Germany		6.88	1.17		9.80	0.51		2.93	−0.66	−1.13	−11.91	1.12
Hong Kong		2.69	0.46		0.54	0.03		−2.15	−0.43	−13.03	17.86	−8.77
Italy		2.12	0.36		2.08	0.11		−0.04	−0.25	26.63	−18.52	−6.30
Japan		41.53	7.06		24.35	1.27		−17.18	−5.79	−12.22	−23.16	2.02
Netherlands		3.16	0.54		4.99	0.26		1.82	−0.28	−25.18	−2.67	−1.59
New Zealand		0.30	0.05		2.67	0.14		2.37	0.09	−1.08	−7.52	−5.57
Norway		0.31	0.05		0.00	0.00		−0.31	−0.05	−1.95	NA	NA
Singapore		1.32	0.22		0.00	0.00		−1.32	−0.22	−14.93	NA	NA
Spain		2.14	0.36		3.97	0.21		1.83	−0.16	4.04	−18.30	−0.09
Sweden		0.96	0.16		0.00	0.00		−0.96	−0.16	−18.21	NA	NA
Switzerland		3.57	0.61		2.73	0.14		−0.84	−0.46	17.16	16.44	−0.72
United kingdom		18.98	3.23		23.76	1.24		4.78	−1.99%	7.52	10.70	3.18
Subtotal		100.00%			100.00%			0.00%				

(continued)

TABLE 18.19 *(continued)*

Market	Passive Weight			Active Weight			Difference			Market Return Premiums		
	Asset Class	Market within Asset Class	As Percent of Portfolio	Asset Class	Market within Asset Class	As Percent of Portfolio	Asset Class	Market within Asset Class	As Percent of Portfolio	Passive Return Premium	Active Return Premium	Return Premium Difference
U.S. bond	20.00		20.00	45.62		45.62	25.62		25.62	3.43	3.87	0.44
Non-U.S. bond	8.00			14.95			6.95			4.06	NA	NA
Australia		1.50	0.12		0.00	0.00		-1.50	-0.12	2.82	NA	NA
Belgium		1.49	0.12		1.38	0.21		-0.11	0.09	-4.07	-3.06	1.01
Canada		7.25	0.58		8.82	1.32		1.57	0.74	2.47	2.44	-0.03
Denmark		2.56	0.20		4.13	0.62		1.57	0.41	-2.53	-2.35	0.18
France		11.39	0.91		17.03	2.55		5.63	1.63	0.23	-0.36	-0.59
Germany		18.97	1.52		25.01	3.74		6.04	2.22	2.52	3.19	0.67
Italy		2.55	0.20		0.00	0.00		-2.55	-0.20	-7.04	NA	NA
Japan		34.67	2.77		19.11	2.86		-15.56	0.08	5.60	5.93	0.33
Netherlands		7.36	0.59		17.71	2.65		10.35	2.06	4.63	5.56	0.93
Spain		0.60	0.05		1.84	0.28		1.24	0.23	-6.49	-5.73	0.76
Sweden		0.54	0.04		0.00	0.00		-0.54	-0.04	-4.36	NA	NA
Switzerland		0.35	0.03		0.00	0.00		-0.35	-0.03	2.34	NA	NA
United Kingdom		10.75	0.86		4.97	0.74		-5.78	-0.12	6.87	3.50	-3.37
Subtotal		100.00%			100.00	100.00%		0.00%				
Cash	5.00		5.00	12.22		12.22	7.22		7.22	-0.59	0.00	0.59
Total	100.00%		100.00%	100.00%		100.00%	0.00%		0.00%	1.15%	NA	NA

Note: Totals may not sum because of rounding.

NA = not applicable.

The questions are:

- How much value was added by the underweight of the non-U.S.-equity asset class?
- How much value was added by underweighting Japan within the non-U.S.-equity asset class?

Table 18.20 gives the performance attribution for a sequential or tiered decision-making process in allocating among markets. Notice that the total market allocation effect (+167 basis points) is unchanged from Table 18.18. Only the sources of that added return are altered.

Table 18.20 indicates that the allocation among asset classes dominated the market-selection contribution. Active asset allocations among U.S. and non-U.S. equities and U.S.

TABLE 18.20   Global Balanced Portfolio: Tiered Market-Selection Attribution, 1992
(base currency = U.S. dollar)

A. Portfolio performance summary

Global balanced index		4.48%
Market selection	1.67%	
Currency selection	1.24	
Security selection	1.52	
Exchange rate differences	−0.04	
Intramonth effect	0.21	
Total value added		4.60%
Global balanced portfolio		9.08%

B. Attribution of added value: Market selection (basis points)

Market	Total	=	Asset Class	+	Market
Equity					
United States	−102		−102		NA
Non-U.S.	196		170		NA
Australia					1
Austria					0
Belgium					1
Canada					1
Denmark					1
Finland					0
France					1
Germany					3
Hong Kong					−3
Italy					0
Japan					17
Netherlands					1
New Zealand					1
Norway					0
Singapore					−1
Spain					0
Sweden					−1
Switzerland					−1
United Kingdom					6
Total					27

(*continued*)

TABLE 18.20   (*continued*)

B. Attribution of added value: Market selection (basis points)

Market	Total	=	Asset Class	+	Market
Bond					
United States	57		57		NA
Non-U.S.	22		21		NA
Australia					0
Belgium					0
Canada					12
Denmark					−2
France					−3
Germany					−1
Italy					0
Japan					−4
Netherlands					1
Spain					−2
Sweden					−1
Switzerland					0
United Kingdom					−2
Total					1
Cash	−6		−6		NA
Total	167	=	140	+	27

Note: Totals may not sum because of rounding and compounding at aggregate, rather than market, level.

NA = not applicable.

and non-U.S. bonds added 140 basis points to portfolio value. Market selection within the non-U.S.-equity component accounted for 27 basis points, and non-U.S.-bond market selection added 1 basis point.

Notice that in Table 18.20 the underweight of Japan within the non-U. S.-equity component added only 17 basis points to aggregate portfolio performance, compared with the 182-basis-point contribution that was indicated in Table 18.18. The difference reflects the alternative decision process that might have been used. Under a sequential process, the higher-level asset allocation decision to underweight the non-U.S.-equity asset class would account for the bulk of the Japanese equity underweight. That decision would actually account for 165 of the 182-basis-point effect shown in Table 18.18. The subsequent decision to underweight the Japanese market further within the non-U.S.-equity component added the remaining 17 basis points. Excluding the large Japanese equity underweight, the other market selections within the non-U.S.-equity component added 10 basis points to total portfolio return.

Similar analysis is appropriate for the non-U.S.-bond component of the portfolio. With a sequential decision process, the attribution shown in Table 18.20 is relevant; it indicates that the overweighting of the non-U.S.-bond asset class accounted for almost all of the market-selection contribution from this component. As in the case of non-U.S. equities, the relatively small allocation to the asset class does not give the non-U.S.-bond manager much latitude to add value through individual market selection.

The level of tiering need not start or stop at the non-U.S. level. In this portfolio, the underweight of Japan in the non-U.S.-equity component dictated an overweight in all other non-U.S. equity markets. A proportional overweight of all the other non-U.S. equity markets would have added 16 basis points to performance. In actuality, however, active market selection within those markets cost 6 basis points, resulting in the 10-basis-point contribution.

Ankrim (1992) provided a crude method for expanding the added value that is attributed to a single market allocation decision to account for the associated impact of that decision on all other market weights. The tiering approach discussed here is conceptually similar to that methodology, but tiering permits a focus on market decisions independent of currency decisions and increases flexibility by increasing the extent to which the tiers can be expanded.

The currency returns and the average strategy for the global balanced portfolio are shown in Table 18.21. The currency strategy in this portfolio was set at the portfolio level. That is, the

TABLE 18.21   Global Balanced Portfolio: Average Currency Strategy, 1992

| Country | Currency Weight | | | Eurodeposit Return | | |
	Passive	Active	Difference	Local-Currency Cash Return	Dollar Exchange Rate Return	Cash Return in U.S. Dollars
Australia	0.58%	0.10%	−0.48%	6.90%	−9.49%	−3.25%
Austria	0.09	0.00	−0.09	10.08	−5.93	3.56
Belgium	0.33	0.37	0.04	10.14	−6.02	3.52
Canada	1.33	2.52	1.20	6.86	−9.04	−2.81
Denmark	0.34	0.18	−0.16	10.78	−5.86	4.29
Finland	0.01	0.00	−0.01	14.10	−20.94	−9.79
France	2.00	2.01	0.02	10.75	−6.20	3.88
Germany	2.69	2.52	−0.16	10.25	−6.33	3.27
Hong Kong	0.46	0.03	−0.43	3.91	0.48	4.42
Italy	0.57	0.12	−0.45	14.29	−22.02	−10.87
Japan	9.83	5.05	−4.78	4.91	0.08	5.00
Netherlands	1.13	1.37	0.24	10.27	−6.05	3.60
New Zealand	0.05	0.14	0.09	6.55	−4.87	1.36
Norway	0.05	0.00	−0.05	11.84	−13.77	−3.56
Singapore	0.22	0.00	−0.22	3.45	−1.25	2.15
Spain	0.41	0.18	−0.23	13.79	−15.58	−3.94
Sweden	0.21	0.00	−0.21	14.03	−21.63	−10.63
Switzerland	0.63	0.14	−0.50	8.74	−7.54	0.54
United Kingdom	4.09	1.08	−3.01	10.97	−19.08	−10.20
United States	75.00	84.19	9.19	4.09	0.00	4.09
Benchmark total	100.00%	100.00%	0.00%	5.06%	−1.65%	3.31%

Note: Totals may not sum because of rounding.

desired currency exposures were set relative to the normal weights of each currency in the total portfolio. Thus, direct hedging activity was used only when the currency exposures that resulted from the combined equity, bond, and cash market decisions were different from the desired strategic currency weights for the entire portfolio. No hedging was done within the non-U.S. -equity or -bond components: Based on Equation 18.9 in the section titled The General Framework, only the net currency exposures at the total portfolio level are relevant for performance; the sources of the exposures are meaningless.

Implementation can become a tricky issue, however, when multiple managers are involved in managing non-U.S. components within a portfolio. One approach would allow the individual managers to set currency strategies within the components and then have a separate currency overlay program achieve the desired aggregate currency exposures. In that case, currency decisions would be made at both the aggregate portfolio level and within the components of the portfolio. As with the sequential market strategies discussed previously, this approach creates a special problem for the performance attribution system, namely, to isolate the effects of the separate currency decisions.

This problem can be avoided by holding the non-U.S.-asset managers accountable for their market-selection activity only and managing the assets against a return premium or fully hedged benchmark. The market managers would not actually have to hedge their currency positions, because the currency exposures resulting from the market allocation decisions would be the responsibility of the currency manager at the aggregate portfolio level. The market managers would be accountable only for the portion of their returns that resulted from market selection, as measured by the return premiums.

Security selection for a global balanced portfolio is no different from what it is for purely domestic portfolios or the global equity and bond portfolios that were evaluated in the section titled Interpretation of Global Performance Attributions. In the portfolio analyzed in this section, security selection within all markets contributed 152 basis points to total portfolio performance. Added value within either the non-U.S.-equity or non-U.S.-bond component can be determined by summing across all markets within each component. Non-U.S.-equity security selection added 4 basis points, and non-U.S. bonds added 9 basis points.

Carve-Out Performance

What if a manager or consultant wants information on the performance of one of the asset classes within a global balanced portfolio? For the U.S. equity and U.S. bond components, this information is a straightforward display of the performance of domestic components. All deviations between component portfolio and benchmark performance are attributable to security selection.

When currency is managed at the aggregate level, the carve-out performance of the non-U.S. components of a global balanced portfolio must exclude the impact of currency management. Why? Because currency strategies exist only at the portfolio level and have no relevance within either non-U.S. component.[20] A global balanced portfolio contains no equity currencies or bond currencies. Therefore, the non-U.S. component of the portfolio returns should reflect only the value added by market- and security-selection decisions. The asset-class benchmark and the returns for the global balanced portfolio, in U.S. dollars, for calendar 1992 were as follows:

U.S.-equity benchmark	8.98%
U.S. -equity portfolio component	16.16

Non-U.S.-equity benchmark	−11.99
Non-U.S.-equity portfolio component (excluding currency management)	−5.93
U.S.-bond benchmark	7.66
U.S.-bond portfolio component	8.12
Non-U.S.-bond benchmark	4.77
Non-U.S.-bond portfolio component (excluding currency management)	5.42

Although these returns are derived from monthly computations, annual data from Tables 18.19 and 18.20 can be used to demonstrate how the returns are calculated. The non-U.S.-equity manager's subbenchmark is the MSCI Non-U.S. Equity (Free) Index adjusted for the withholding taxes of a U.S.-based investor. The benchmark U.S. dollar return was −11.99 percent in 1992. The non-U.S.-equity manager's performance, reflecting only market and security selections, was computed from the following formula:

$$
\text{Component return} = \text{Benchmark return} + \frac{\left(\begin{array}{c}\text{Component market} + \text{Component security} \\ \text{selection} \qquad\qquad \text{selection}\end{array}\right)}{\text{Active component weight}}
$$

Using the average summary data for the year,

$$
\text{Non-U.S.-equity component return} = -0.1199 + \frac{(0.0027 + 0.0004)}{0.0521}
$$
$$
= -6.04 \text{ percent.}
$$

Compounded monthly returns would generate the −5.93 percent return.

The non-U.S.-bond component return, given a non-U.S.-bond benchmark return (in U.S. dollars) of 4.98 percent, is

$$
\text{Non-U.S.-bond component return} = 0.0477 + \frac{(0.0001 + 0.0009)}{0.1495}
$$
$$
= 5.44 \text{ percent.}
$$

Again, compounded monthly returns would generate the 5.42 percent return presented.

These non-U.S.-component returns are the U.S. dollar returns that would have been achieved if each non-U.S.-component portfolio manager made only market- and security-selection decisions and if the currency strategy were held neutral to the benchmark. In other words, currency strategies are assumed not to have occurred and, therefore, not to have affected the components' performance.

If clients, consultants, and the managers themselves want information on total component returns, these considerations are crucial. They also provide a means of presenting carve-out performance in accordance with the objectives of the 1993 AIMR performance presentation standards.

CONCLUSION

Currency issues make the management of global portfolios more complex, but not necessarily more difficult than managing domestic portfolios. Particular care is needed when the portfolio uses separate managers for the U.S. and non-U.S. asset classes as well as for currency management.

The global asset evaluation and attribution framework presented in the first two sections of this chapter provide a robust and flexible system for handling these complexities. The framework offers plan sponsors, investment managers, and consultants an accurate means for determining and attributing returns to market, currency, and security selections regardless of the decision process that is used in the management of the aggregate portfolio.

As an extension of the familiar CAPM, the framework calls for evaluation of all global asset returns in terms of local-currency return premiums. All currency considerations are based on cash returns—typically, Eurodeposit returns—expressed in the base currency of the investor. Recognizing the variables that are actually controllable by investors leads to the conclusion that implementing active currency strategy involves nothing more than global cash management.

The framework for analysis of global asset returns presented in the section titled The General Framework is comprehensive but simple. It allows a clear distinction to be made between the market and currency returns that are available to investors and provides a direct method of treating market and currency strategy options consistently in the investor's decision-making process. The framework is general, applicable to any base currency and any currency benchmark. It is also flexible, in that it handles all types of derivative instruments that might be used in the management of a global portfolio.

A rigorous global performance attribution system can be a powerful tool for investment management by providing a means for critical review of the decision process. Isolation of the effects of market, currency, and security strategies supplies valuable information about the sources of investment returns. The attribution framework presented in the section titled Global Performance Attribution provides a comprehensive and flexible foundation for such analysis.

The sections titled Interpretation of Global Performance Attributions and Global Balanced Portfolios used actual global portfolios to demonstrate the application of the analytical framework to the task of performance attribution for global portfolios. The attribution system identified unambiguously the contributions of aggregate market and currency strategy to portfolio returns. The examples also highlighted, however, the care that must be taken in interpreting the market and currency effects on a country-by-country basis. The general decision process used in the management of the aggregate portfolio significantly influences the manner in which the components of the market and currency effects are presented.

Global balanced portfolios provide the strongest test of the global investment process. The typical sequential approach of first allocating among broad asset classes such as non-U.S. equities and bonds and then selecting markets within these asset classes can lead to unintended and possibly perverse exposures for the aggregate portfolio. The decision process must recognize the implications of such a layered allocation process, and the performance attribution system must be able to account for the effects of each layer of decisions.

The attribution framework that has been presented here can be structured to provide information at all levels of decision making and reveal their ultimate contributions to aggregate portfolio performance. That flexibility applies to the setting of both market and currency strategies for global portfolios.

APPENDIX 18A

The general definition of the return from a portfolio of global assets for an investor with a base currency n can be derived by considering the base-currency return from investments in country i. Equation 18.10 specifies this return in terms of each of the potential returns and strategy weights:

$$R_{n,i} = w_i r_i + v_i k_i + (w_i + v_i)\varepsilon_{n,i} + \sum_j h_{i,f}(f_{i,j} + \varepsilon_{n,i} - \varepsilon_{n,j}). \quad (18.10)$$

Five general types of returns can be involved in such a global portfolio:

$R_{n,i}$ = return from all assets, including cash, of country i, in terms of the base currency, n,

r_i = return from the noncash assets of country i, in local-currency terms,

k_i = return from the explicitly held cash assets of country i, in local-currency terms,

c_i = return from country i Eurodeposits, in local-currency terms,

$\varepsilon_{n,i}$ = rate of change in the base currency:currency i exchange rate, and

$f_{i,j}$ = forward premium of currency j in terms of currency i; $f_{i,j} = c_i - c_j$.

The active decision variables are

w_i = weight of country i noncash assets; $0 \le \Sigma w_i \le 1$,

v_i = weight of country i cash that is held as strategic cash; in a fully invested portfolio, all $v_i = 0$, and

$h_{i,j}$ = portion of the portfolio that is hedged (or cross-hedged) to currency i from currency j; $-(w_i + v_i) \le h_i \le 1$ for portfolios that prohibit net short currency positions.

Substituting for $f_{i,j}$ in Equation 18.10 and rearranging terms gives

$$R_{n,i} = w_i(r_i - c_i) + v_i(k_i - c_i) + (w_i + v_i)(c_i + \varepsilon_{n,i}) \quad (18.11)$$
$$+ \sum_j h_{i,j}(c_i - c_j + \varepsilon_{n,i} - \varepsilon_{n,j}).$$

Because $\sum_j h_{i,j} = h_i$,

$$R_{n,i} = w_i(r_i - c_i) + v_i(k_i - c_i) + (w_i + v_i + h_i)(c_i + \varepsilon_{n,i}) - \sum_j h_{i,j}(c_j + \varepsilon_{n,j}). \quad (18.12)$$

The last term in Equation 18.12 reflects the currency exposures that are eliminated in favor of currency i.

Because the hedge weights, h_i, must sum to zero, the summation across all i gives the total portfolio return as

$$R_n = \Sigma[w_i(r_i - c_i) + v_i(k_i - c_i)] + \Sigma[(w_i + v_i + h_i)(c_i + \varepsilon_{n,i})]. \quad (18.13)$$

The exposure to changes in exchange rates is the net effect of three strategic decisions: (1) The market decision to invest in the noncash assets of the various countries, as reflected in the w_i weights; (2) a decision to hold some portion of the portfolio in cash, which could be denominated in any currency and is reflected in the v_i weights; and (3) decisions to buy and sell currency exposures forward, as reflected in the hedge weights, h_i. In this form, the emphasis is on the portfolio's total exposure to each currency rather than on the specific sources of that exposure. In the absence of differential transaction costs, the means by which currency exposure enters the portfolio is irrelevant.

Thus, the base-currency return from a global portfolio (Equation 18.9) can be written in terms of separate market and currency components as

$$R_n = \Sigma[w_i(r_i - c_i) + v_i(k_i - c_i)] + \Sigma\delta_i(c_i + \varepsilon_{n,i}), \quad (18.14)$$

where

$$\delta_i = w_i + v_i + h_i$$

and

$$\Sigma(w_i + v_i + h_i) = \Sigma\delta_i$$
$$= 1.$$

APPENDIX 18B

The following formulas account for the potential perversity of strategy interactions:

Let $\bar{\delta}_i$ = benchmark currency i weight in the portfolio,

$\bar{w}_e$ = benchmark non-U.S.-equity asset-class weight,

$\bar{w}_b$ = benchmark non-U.S.-bond asset-class weight,

$\bar{\delta}_{ei}$ = benchmark currency i weight in the non-U.S.-equity component,

$\bar{\delta}_{bi}$ = benchmark currency i weight in the non-U.S.-bond component,

δ_i = actual currency i weight in the portfolio,

w_e = actual non-U.S.-equity asset-class weight,

w_b = actual non-U.S.-bond asset-class weight,

δ_{ei} = actual market and currency i weight in the non-U.S.-equity component,

δ_{bi} = actual market and currency i weight in the non-U.S.-bond component.

Let each of the actual market weights equal the benchmark weight plus an active strategy, $w_e = \bar{w}_e + \Delta w_e$. Thus, the actual weight in currency i is

$$\delta_i = (\bar{w}_e \bar{\delta}_{ei} + \Delta \bar{w}_e \bar{\delta}_{ei} + \bar{w}_e \Delta \bar{\delta}_{ei} + \Delta \bar{w}_e \Delta \bar{\delta}_{ei})$$
$$+ (\bar{w}_b \bar{\delta}_{bi} + \Delta \bar{w}_b \bar{\delta}_{bi} + \bar{w}_b \Delta \bar{\delta}_{bi} + \Delta \bar{w}_b \Delta \bar{\delta}_{bi}) \qquad (18.15)$$

Setting the actual weight of currency i equal to its normal weight in both the equity and bond components implies

$$\Delta \bar{\delta}_{ei} = \Delta \bar{\delta}_{bi} = 0.0 \text{ percent.}$$

Thus, Equation 18.15 can be rewritten as

$$\delta_i = (\bar{w}_e \bar{\delta}_{ei} + \bar{w}_b \bar{\delta}_{bi}) + \Delta \bar{w}_e \bar{\delta}_{ei} + \Delta \bar{w}_b \bar{\delta}_{bi}. \qquad (18.16)$$

Equivalently,

$$\delta_i = \bar{\delta}_i + \Delta \bar{w}_e \bar{\delta}_{ei} + \Delta \bar{w}_b \bar{\delta}_{bi}.$$

Even with the currency weights set equal to the normal weights within each component, the total portfolio contains a strategic over/underweight of currency i equal to

$$\delta_i - \bar{\delta}_i = \Delta \bar{w}_e \bar{\delta}_{ei} + \Delta \bar{w}_b \bar{\delta}_{bi},$$

which reflects the effect on currency exposure of the asset allocation decision to alter the weights of non-U.S. equities and non-U.S. bonds within the portfolio—i.e., $\Delta \bar{w}_e$ and $\Delta \bar{w}_b$.

According to Equation 18.16, in the example in the section titled Interpretation of Global Performance Attributions, the strategic weight for yen in the portfolio is

$\delta_i = [(0.17)(0.4) + (0.08)(0.35)] + (-0.11)(0.4) + (0.17)(0.35)$

$\delta_i = [(0.068) + (0.028)] + (-0.044) + 0.0595$

$\delta_i = [0.096] - 0.044 + 0.0595$

$\delta_i = 11.15 \text{ percent.}$

The bracketed calculations indicate, as one might expect intuitively, that the strategic yen weight is equal to the benchmark yen weight of 9.6 percent. Intuition fails to recognize the cross-products, however, that arise from the *interaction* of the non-U.S.-equity and non-U.S.-bond strategies and the yen strategy within each component.

NOTES

1. The use of forward currency contracts in this analysis is based on "covered interest parity." This choice does not imply that the additional notion of "uncovered interest parity" is assumed to hold. The analysis contains no suggestion that the current forward rates are unbiased forecasts of the future spot exchange rate. Instead, investors are faced with a choice between the known (and often negative) returns that are given by interest rate differentials in the current forward market and the uncertainty of changes in spot exchange rates that can occur in a given period.

2. Several simplifying assumptions are made throughout the chapter in order to avoid unnecessary complexity in the presentation of the analysis. First, all returns are initially in continuously compounded terms, which allows simple addition and subtraction of terms. This assumption is relaxed later. Second, the investment objective is the maximization of returns, which allows risk considerations to be ignored. Our focus is on identifying the market and currency variables that are relevant to global investment analysis, not on applying those variables to a specific investment process such as mean–variance optimization. Risk considerations are an implementation issue.

3. In practice, forward exchange contracts for a wide range of time periods are available in the market. Determining the optimal maturity of the contract involves analysis of relative yield curves between countries. We assume that the basic forward contract is short term, reflecting differential interest rates on cash equivalents. Extending the term of the contract is thus treated as an active "hedge-selection" decision involving comparisons of total returns from fixed-income securities. Such issues are temporarily ignored, with no loss in generality, and all forward contracts are assumed to reflect differential cash rates. The cash returns, c_i, reflect the total returns from rolling short-term Eurodeposits over the investment horizon of the portfolio.

4. The term "return premium" is used, rather than the more familiar "risk premium," in order to make a subtle distinction in the underlying cash return. "Risk premium" refers to the return above the return of a riskless asset, often assumed to be a short-term U.S. Treasury instrument. Because this analysis reflects the premium over Eurodeposit returns, which can, depending on the typical (normal) forward term, have longer maturities, the term "return premium" is used.

5. The detailed derivation of the general framework, including the full effects of strategic holdings of cash as an active market decision, is presented in Appendix 18A.

6. For a discussion of the CAPM in a global context, see Karnosky (1993).

7. Currency management through forwards, futures, or swaps can result, however, in gains and losses during the terms of the contracts. If these gains (losses) are not offset, they create effective net cash exposures (portfolio leverage).

8. The benchmark portfolio can also be specified with currency weights that differ from the market allocations (Lee 1987). Such is the case with a hedged benchmark, for example, where the weight of the base-currency cash would be 100 percent and all other cash weights would be set to zero. Conceptually, subject only to external restrictions (such as a prohibition against leveraged positions), any combination of market and currency benchmark weights is possible.

9. This analysis is independent of specific theories about the behavioral relationships among the asset and foreign exchange markets. Economic conditions that change short-term interest rates, for example, could also produce changes in asset returns that result in

no change in return premiums. The focus here is on the analytical framework in which particular global capital market theories can be evaluated.

10. As earlier, risk considerations are ignored, with no loss in generality, and the investment objective is to maximize returns. Mean–variance optimization would involve maximizing the objective function, $E[U] = R_n - (1/T)V[R_n]$, where R_n is the expected return as defined in Equation 18.9. The constraint set would include $\Sigma(w_i + v_i + h_i) = \Sigma\delta_i = 1$. Restrictions on currency strategies would be imposed on the hedge weights, h_i, within the currency weights, δ_i. The covariance matrix would span local return premiums and cash returns expressed in base-currency terms.

11. "Conventional" refers to the majority of attribution methods currently in use. Other approaches have recently been proposed, but although they address the problems of accounting for currency, they provide only partial solutions. Typically, the methods for measuring the effects of market selection remain flawed. For example, see Allen (1991) and Ankrim and Hensel (1992).

12. The segmentation of market and currency management ignores a relatively small term that reflects the interaction of these decisions. This term is $(1 + \varepsilon_{\$,i})(r_i - c_i) - [(1 + r_i)/(1 + c_i) - 1]$, where $r_i =$ local currency return for the portfolio, $c_i =$ local currency Eurodeposit return, and $\varepsilon_{\$,i} =$ portfolio exchange rate return. The portion of the attribution residual accounted for by this interaction is $\{[(1 + \varepsilon_{\$,i}(r_i - c_i)] - [(1 + r_i)/(1 + c_i) - 1]\}$, $-\{[(1 + \overline{\varepsilon}_{\$,i}(\overline{r}_i - \overline{c}_i)] - [(1 + \overline{r}_i) / (1 + \overline{c}_i) - 1]\}$ where plain lowercase letters indicate portfolio returns and letters with a bar over them indicate benchmark returns. In continuously compounded terms, the interaction term reduces to $\varepsilon_{\$,i}(r_i - c_i)$, and the residual accounted for by this term is $\varepsilon_{\$,i}(r_i - c_i) - \overline{\varepsilon}_{\$,i}(\overline{r}_i - \overline{c}_i)$.

13. This presentation generally assumes that the passive strategic cash return in any country equals the passive Eurodeposit return. The assumption is a matter of convenience and does not limit the flexibility of the proposed attribution framework. A portfolio could just as easily incorporate a Treasury bill as the strategic cash benchmark in the United States. The result would be a slightly negative strategic cash passive return premium (the T-bill return would be below the Eurodollar return).

14. Equation 18.9 indicated that the portfolio return can be computed by summing the active local-currency return premiums and the active Eurodeposit returns expressed in base-currency terms. The "market return" of this portfolio would be $\Sigma[w_i(r_i - c_i) + v_i (k_i - c_i)]$, or 1.58 percent. The "currency return" would be $\Sigma[(w_i + v_i + h_i)(c_i + \varepsilon_{n,i})]$, or 7.89 percent. Adding these two continuously compounded components of the global portfolio's return provides the total portfolio return of 9.47 percent.

15. In the conventional and proposed attribution systems, we have used a common convention of combining security selection and the market cross-product. The resulting computation involves the actual market weight rather than the passive weight. This procedure is trivial with respect to the comparison of attribution approaches because the security selections and cross-products are identical.

16. Allen (1991) recognized the important impact that forward contracts have on performance attribution. Although his approach accounts for the impact of both passive and active hedge decisions, it does so only at the portfolio level because of the perceived complexity of forward currency transactions. Also, his system confounds market and currency effects by using unhedged returns to measure the effects of market selection. An unhedged market-selection criterion, as we demonstrated in the section titled The General Framework, can lead to suboptimal market decisions and suboptimal portfolio

returns. Ankrim and Hensel (1992) had similar problems in specifying a market effect that is free of currency influences. Like Allen, however, they specified the currency effect correctly.

17. As indicated in the first section, a manager can allocate among currencies and, by using different forward terms, add value through hedge selection. Because active hedge selection was not a major consideration in the management of this portfolio (or the global bond portfolio that follows), we have simplified the attribution by assuming that passive currency hedges were used. Thus, the attribution results have no accounting for active hedge selection.

18. The section titled Global Balanced Portfolios addresses some of the difficulties that arise in interpreting these individual market contributions by establishing a tiered attribution framework.

19. The computations reflect periodic rather than continuously compounded returns; therefore, the differences in return premiums do not quite equal the differences in local currency returns. The discrepancy is small, however, and has no meaningful impact on the interpretation of attribution results.

20. Only if each non-U.S. manager is asked to manage currency exposure separately can currency management be included in the non-U.S. carve-out. Such management would require a currency overlay of the aggregate portfolio, however.

REFERENCES

AIMR. 1993. *Performance Presentation Standards* (Charlottesville, VA.: Association for Investment Management and Research).

Allen, G. C. 1992. "Performance Attribution for Global Equity Portfolios." *The Journal of Portfolio Management* (Fall).

Ankrim, E. M. 1993. "The Japanese Weighting Decision in International Equity Portfolios: Measuring the Impact." *Russell Research Commentary* (June).

Ankrim, E. M., and C. R. Hensel. 1992. "Multicurrency Performance Attribution." *Russell Research Commentary* (November).

Brinson, G. P., and Nimrod Fachler. 1985. "Measuring Non-U.S. Equity Portfolio Performance." *The Journal of Portfolio Management* (Spring).

Brinson, G. P., R. Hood, and G. L. Beebower. 1986. "Determinants of Portfolio Performance." *Financial Analysts Journal* (July/August):39–44.

Brinson, G. P., B. D. Singer, and G. L. Beebower. 1991. "Determinants of Portfolio Performance II: An Update." *Financial Analysts Journal* (May/June):40–48.

Eun, C. S., and B. G. Resnick. 1988. "Exchange Rate Uncertainty, Forward Contracts and International Portfolio Selection." *The Journal of Finance* (March):197–215.

Karnosky, D. S. 1993. "Global Investment in a CAPM Framework." *The CAPM Controversy: Policy and Strategy Implications for Investment Management.* Charlottesville, VA.: Association for Investment Management and Research:56–61.

Karnosky, D. S., B. D. Singer, and J. G. Taylor. 1991. "The General Framework for Global Asset Analysis." *Security Analysts Journal*, vol. 29 (March):42–51.

Lee, A. F. 1987. "International Asset and Currency Allocation." *The Journal of Portfolio Management* (Fall):68–73.

CHAPTER 19

CURRENCY OVERLAY IN PERFORMANCE EVALUATION

Cornelia Paape

The aim of performance evaluation is to make judgments about the success of portfolio managers in asset allocation and security selection for investment portfolios. This article presents a method of performance measurement that uses the interdependence of market management and currency management in terms of allocation processes but allows their separation in terms of selection processes. As a consequence, performance evaluation is more reasonable than in previous approaches and produces the same results whether the investment process starts with market management followed by currency management or vice versa.

Performance evaluation is a valuable tool in analyzing global investment portfolios. Its purpose is to allow judgments about the success of managers in asset allocation and security selection among various markets and currencies. Many research papers dealing with performance evaluation were published in the 1980s and early 1990s (Brinson and Fachler 1985; Brinson, Hood, and Beebower 1986; Hensel, Ezra, and Ilkiw 1991; Brinson, Singer, and Beebower 1991; Ankrim 1992), but none of them dealt with the interaction of global asset returns and currency returns in investment portfolios. Consequently, in the mid-1990s, the previous approaches were revised to focus on currency aspects (Ankrim and Hensel 1994; Singer and Karnosky 1994). That focus is also the approach of this chapter.

The aim is to develop a performance measurement system that improves on earlier approaches in two ways. First, within performance measurement, a mathematically correct method of evaluating return variables is implemented. Second, according to this correct measurement of return premiums (excess returns), new formulas for the attribution variables are derived. As a result, the portfolio evaluation system presented here consists of an established

Reprinted from *Financial Analysts Journal* (March/April 2003):55–68.

method of portfolio decomposition, a new performance measurement approach, and also a new method of attribution analysis.

The first goal of the proposed method is to define mathematically correct formulas for the return and weight variables that are also in line with practical demands. Thus, in the method presented here, all returns are initially calculated in simple (instead of continuously compounded) terms. Overall performance is defined by multiplying market and currency returns rather than by adding them.[1] Furthermore, for reasons of arbitrage, forward currency returns are expressed as the difference between two Eurodeposit returns divided by a discount factor (see, for example, Fischer-Erlach 1995). Because it considers the market management as well as the currency management stage, this kind of performance measurement provides a breakdown of overall performance that suggests return variables defined as return *premiums* (excess returns). Moreover, it reveals that the management stages are interdependent in terms of asset allocation but are separable in terms of security selection.

The second part of the proposed approach pertains to attribution analysis. The idea is to separate the individual contribution of each market and currency decision to overall portfolio excess return. Hence, value added (defined as the portfolio's excess return over a passive benchmark's return) is split among market allocation, currency allocation, security selection, and currency selection decisions. In this approach, once the return and currency premiums are calculated, the derivation of each attribution formula is straightforward. Each attribution measure is based on the return difference of specifically created active and passive portfolios. The returns of these portfolios differ only in the weight or return variable that specifies the allocation or selection decision to be evaluated. Even though the derivation of the attribution variables is thereby still influenced by the order of decisions about market and currency management within the investment process, the interpretation of the variables leads to the same judgments regardless of the order.

In brief, the intent is to develop clear and comprehensible performance attribution variables together with precise performance measurement.

PORTFOLIO DECOMPOSITION AND PERFORMANCE MEASUREMENT

A major difficulty in performance evaluation is that the process of managing a large investment portfolio depends on teamwork, but the task of performance evaluation is to show the success of each team member separately. The first step in solving this problem is to draw a diagram highlighting the relationships. A detailed graph showing the structure of the portfolio can clarify which weight and return variables must be evaluated. Graphs of various portfolio decompositions can show the effect of different performance measurement systems.

A factor leading to complexity in portfolio evaluation is the obvious interdependency of market and currency management in global investment portfolios. Consider the following simple example: a portfolio with four markets (Japan, the United States, the United Kingdom, and "Euroland") and their four currencies (yen, U.S. dollar, pound sterling, and euro) with the base currency of the portfolio being the U.S. dollar. In every country, only one possible investment may be chosen. A decomposition of this portfolio would show all the markets in which the portfolio invested and the resulting currency exposures.

Figure 19.1 shows the conventional decision tree for this four-market/four-currency example. Here, "conventional" refers to the system of measuring market return in local currency by comparing initial and final values of the various securities (simple compounding of

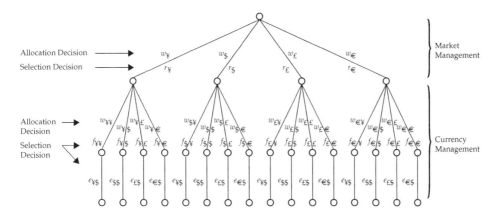

FIGURE 19.1   Investment Alternatives in a Conventional Performance Measurement System

rates of return). Currency rates of return reflect those of forward currency contracts (if hedging or cross-hedging is involved) or exchange rate returns (for unhedged currency). Because only a single period is examined in this example, weight variables retain their initial values. In Figure 19.1, the following variables and relationships are depicted:

i = market currency, with i = ¥, US\$, £, €,

j = hedge currency, with j = ¥, US\$, £, €,

r_i = rate of return in market i measured in local currency,

f_{ij} = rate of return from forward contracts hedging currency i into currency j ($f_{ii} = 0$),

$e_{j\$}$ = rate of change of the U.S. dollar relative to currency j ($e_{\$\$} = 0$),

w_i = weight of market i as a fraction of the total (US\$-based) money value of the portfolio invested in market i, with $w_i \geq 0$, $\Sigma_i w_i = 1$, and

w_{ij} = weight of currency i exchanged into currency j as a fraction of the (local-currency-based) money value of market i, with $w_{ij} \geq 0$, $\Sigma_j w_{ij} = 1$.

This decision tree shows the investment decisions within a conventional performance measurement system—with currency management after market management.

In Figure 19.1, the portion of overall performance that stems from market allocation and security selection decisions (the first layer of nodes in the tree) is measured by the weighted market return. The part that comes from currency management of that particular market's currency is evaluated by the sum of all weighted currency returns gained through hedging that currency exposure (see Appendix 19A for examples of calculating these performance measures and Appendix 19B for the evaluation of overall performance). Currency weight variables, as well as currency return variables, are naturally related to the market choice that produced the currency exposure—shown by the double subscripting of these variables (see the previous notation).

Because the task of performance evaluation is to value market and currency decisions separately, the question is how to isolate these two management stages. In other words, the problem of performance evaluation highlighted in Figure 19.1 is how to judge currency managers after a market manager, acting independently, has made the allocation and selection decisions. For example, suppose the market manager invests in only one market. Instead of 16 possible branches, the currency manager is left with optimizing returns among only 4.

In *Global Asset Management and Performance Attribution*, Singer and Karnosky introduced a performance measurement system that takes this division between market and currency management into consideration.[2] Following their notation, c_i represents the rate of return from local Eurodeposit cash market i. Written in terms of c_i, the rate of return from a currency forward contract, f_{ij}, becomes

$$1 + f_{ij} = \frac{1 + c_j}{1 + c_i}. \tag{19.1}$$

The use of forward currency contracts in this analysis is based on the concept of covered interest rate parity. Equation 19.1 can thus be derived through arbitrage considerations (see Appendix 19C). However, although Singer and Karnosky claimed to have applied covered interest rate parity to define the forward currency return, their result for f_{ij} omitted the denominator $1 + c_i$ in Equation 19.1. This omission caused Singer and Karnosky to achieve an overly simplistic separation.

Singer and Karnosky's proposal to solve complexity in the investment process is not possible, but a separation within asset selection *is* possible and is indicated by the special form of Equation 19.1. The two currencies involved are isolated in, respectively, the numerator and the denominator. This kind of separation helps to define new return variables in the form of premiums (see Appendix 19B for a version of overall portfolio return in terms of premiums), in which c_i reflects rolling short-term Eurodeposits of market i over the investment horizon of the portfolio, μ_i is the market premium for market i, with

$$\mu_i = \frac{r_i - c_i}{1 + c_i}, \tag{19.2}$$

and κ_j is the currency premium for currency j, with

$$\kappa_j = (1 + c_j)(1 + e_{j\$}) - 1. \tag{19.3}$$

Reconstructing the tree with the new variables, μ_i and κ_j, allows for the simpler and more powerful graph of the process shown in Figure 19.2. After moving down any of the available market branches in Figure 19.2, only the same choices present themselves for subsequent currency management. The result is that currency selection (choosing the best value from $\kappa_{\yen}, \ldots, \kappa_{\EUR}$) is now independent of any previous market decision. The currency allocation, however—that is, the allocation of money to the values of $w_{\yen\yen}, \ldots, w_{\EUR\EUR}$—is, as the first subscript indicates, still related to these market decisions.

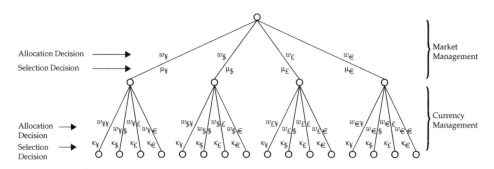

FIGURE 19.2   Investment Alternatives in a New Performance Measurement System

Numerical Example

This section illustrates the differences between the conventional method and the new scheme. Imagine building a "best" portfolio for each of the performance measurement systems, where "best" refers to the investment objective of maximizing overall portfolio return. For completeness, also include a third system that does not differentiate between market and currency returns and is, therefore, based solely on market returns in the base currency. Furthermore, introduce a benchmark portfolio consisting of dollar-equivalent investments in all markets. Now, you can compare the resulting portfolios with the benchmark portfolio and draw conclusions about the various schemes.

For this illustration, Table 19.1 provides some numbers for the four-country/four-currency example introduced in the previous section.[3] Let

r_{ij} = rate of return from currency transfers from currency i to currency j (i,j = ¥, US$, £, €), measured in U.S. dollars; that is,

$$r_{ij} = [(1 + f_{ij})(1 + e_{j\$})] - 1, \qquad (19.4)$$

A_i = optimal portfolio for system i, where i is one of the three systems described,
R^{A_i} = overall return of Portfolio A_i, and
R^B = overall return of benchmark Portfolio B.

The return data in Table 19.1 allow a comparison of the three performance measurement systems introduced in the previous section—the conventional method (System I) shown in Figure 19.1, the new method (System II) shown in Figure 19.2, and the third method (System III) that does not involve explicit currency management. Table 19.2 summarizes the primary features of the three systems.

System I: Conventional Performance Measurement

Assume the portfolio management to be divided into market and currency management. Whereas decisions of the market manager are based on expectations about local-currency market returns, the currency manager's decisions are based on exchange rate returns and forward currency rates of return. Based on the relevant data from Table 19.1, all possible outcomes of the system are shown in Table 19.3.

Because the two management divisions are interdependent, the forming of a return-maximizing portfolio for System I, Portfolio A_I, requires the optimization to be done in two

TABLE 19.1   Example Global Security Returns

Market	Market Return in Local Currency, r_i	Exchange Rate Return in Base Currency, $e_{i\$}$	Eurodeposit Return in Local Currency, c_i
Japan	9.50%	−1.00%	9.00%
United States	8.40	—	7.50
United Kingdom	10.50	−3.00	11.25
Euroland	7.00	1.00	5.00

Source: Singer and Karnosky (1994).

TABLE 19.2   Features of Performance Measurement Systems

System	Market Management	Currency Management
I	Local-currency market returns	Exchange rates of return and forward currency rates of return
II	Local-currency market premiums	Currency premiums
III	Base-currency market returns	—

TABLE 19.3   Performance Measurement with System I

Hedge Currency, j	Market Return in Local Currency, r_i	Currency Return in Base Currency, r_{ij}			
		¥	US$	£	€
Japan (¥)	9.5000%	−1.0000%	−1.3761%	−0.9977%	−2.7064%
United States ($)	8.4000	0.3814	0.0000	0.3837	−1.3488
United Kingdom (£)	10.5000	−3.0022	−3.3708	−3.0000	−4.6742
Euroland (€)	7.0000	2.7714	2.3810	2.7738	1.0000

TABLE 19.4   Portfolio A_I

Portfolio Composition	Market Weight, w_i	Currency Weight, w_{ij}	Market Return in Local Currency, r_i	Currency Return in Base Currency, r_{ij}	Evaluation
Market: United Kingdom	100.00%	—	10.50%	—	$w_£(1 + r_£) = 1.105$
Currency exposure: £	—	100.00%	—	−3.00%	$w_{££}(1 + r_{££}) = 0.970$
Total	100.00%	100.00%	10.50%	−3.00%	$R^{A_I} = 7.185\%$

succeeding steps—market management and currency management. Following Figure 19.1, the first step is to find the branch with the highest return out of the four market branches. Ignoring risk considerations and taking the values given in Table 19.3 as given (that is, assuming the expected ones were realized), then Table 19.3 shows that the best branch is clearly the United Kingdom. The next step is to locate the best value within the four branches beneath the U.K. market (that is, the currency management layer). Again, a look at Table 19.3 reveals that this choice is uniquely British pounds sterling.

The result of the maximization in two separate steps is Portfolio A_I shown in Table 19.4; this portfolio is fully invested in the United Kingdom with unhedged local currency.[4] Notice,

TABLE 19.5   Performance Measurement with System II

Market Currency, i	Market Premium in Local Currency, μ_i	Currency Premium in Base Currency, κ_j	Hedge Currency, j
¥	0.4587%	7.9100%	¥
US$	0.8372	7.5000	$
£	−0.6742	7.9125	£
€	1.9048	6.0500	€

however, that because the second step was optimized under the outcome of the first, the total value, R^{A_1}, can reach the maximal value of the problem only by chance.[5]

System II: New Performance Measurement System

Again, assume the portfolio management to be divided into market and currency management. In contrast to System I, however, decisions about market management are now based on expectations about market premiums, and currency management decisions are based on expectations for currency premiums. Keep in mind that, according to the previous definitions, *market premium* here is the discounted difference between the local-currency market return and the local-currency Eurodeposit return, whereas *currency premium* is any Eurodeposit return in the base currency. The possible outcomes of the system given the data of Table 19.1 are shown in Table 19.5.

Forming a return-maximizing Portfolio A_{II} for System II requires, in this case, optimizing the return within the method shown in Figure 19.2. Again, it is done in two separate optimization steps, but the great advantage is that Step 2 is independent of Step 1.

Based on Table 19.5 data, finding the best value for market management in the first step results in choosing the Euroland premium. A look at Figure 19.2 reveals that the second step, the currency decision, is limited to the four choices beneath the Euroland branch. But regardless of the branch dictated by market management, the four options for currency management remain. Consequently, independent of the outcome of Step 1, the best value for Step 2 is to pick the U.K. currency premium. A portfolio fully invested in the markets of Euroland and using the British cash market for investing would, in this case, hit the target of maximizing overall portfolio performance. The corresponding portfolio, A_{II}, would be as shown in Table 19.6 (for comparison purposes, the values of A_{II} are given in "common" return variables instead of premiums).

The advantage of the new performance measurement system is now obvious. Because currency management was done without restrictions imposed by market management, the maximal possible value of the solution is reached at 9.968 percent, for an improvement in overall performance over the System I portfolio of nearly 40 percent.

System III: Performance Measurement without Currency Management

In this performance measurement system, there is no differentiation between market and currency management. Investment decisions are based only on expectations for market returns

TABLE 19.6   Portfolio A_{II}

Portfolio Composition	Market Weight, w_i	Currency Weight, w_{ij}	Market Return in Local Currency, r_i	Currency Return in Base Currency, r_{ij}	Evaluation
Market: Euroland	100.00%	—	7.000%	—	$w_{\text{€}}(1 + r_{\text{€}}) = 1.07000$
Currency exposure: £	—	100.00%	—	2.774%	$w_{\text{€£}}(1 + r_{\text{€£}}) = 1.02774$
Total	100.00%	100.00%	7.000%	2.774%	$R^{A_{II}} = 9.968\%$

TABLE 19.7   Portfolio A_{III}

Portfolio Composition	Market Weight, w_i	Currency Weight, w_{ij}	Market Return in Local Currency, r_i	Currency Return in Base Currency, r_{ij}	Evaluation
Market: Japan	100.00%	—	9.50%	—	$w_{\text{¥}}(1 + r_{\text{¥}}) = 1.095$
Currency exposure: ¥	—	100.00%	—	−1.00%	$w_{\text{¥}}(1 + r_{\text{¥¥}}) = 0.990$
Total	100.00%	100.00%	9.50%	−1.00%	$R^{A_{III}} = 8.405\%$

in the base currency; currencies remain unhedged. The market returns in the base currency corresponding to Table 19.1 are as follows:

Japan, ¥   = 8.405%
United States, US$ = 8.400%
United Kingdom, £ = 7.185%
Euroland, €   = 8.070%

Because the highest rate of return is found in Japan, a return-optimizing portfolio under System III, Portfolio A_{III}, leads to a 100 percent investment in Japan and the unhedged yen currency. For purposes of comparison, as with Portfolio A_{II}, the market and currency returns are shown separately in Table 19.7.

As with System I, the optimization carried out according to System III is suboptimal.[6]

Benchmark Portfolio

To analyze the performance of the previous portfolios, a benchmark portfolio is needed. The benchmark portfolio consists of a passive market portfolio, dollar invested equally in all possible markets without currency hedging. It is depicted in Table 19.8.

The interesting differences in return (in percentage points) between the active portfolios and the benchmark portfolio (Portfolio B) are summarized in Table 19.9. The superior return of A_{II} is a direct consequence of the advantageous and appropriate separation of tasks as described. Note also that the traditional approach, System I, results in a portfolio that underperforms even the benchmark!

TABLE 19.8   Benchmark Portfolio

Benchmark Composition	Market Weight, w_i	Currency Weight, w_{ij}	Market Return in Local Currency, r_i	Currrency Return in Base Currency, r_{ij}	Evaluation
Market: Japan	25.00%	—	9.50%	—	$w_\yen(1 + r_\yen) = 0.27375$
Currency exposure: ¥	—	100.00%	—	−1.00%	$w_{\yen\yen}(1 + r_{\yen\yen}) = 0.99000$ $0.27375 \times 0.99 = 0.2710125$
Market: U.S.	25.00	—	8.40	—	$w_\$(1 + r_\$) = 0.27100$
Currency exposure: US$	—	100.00	—	0.00	$w_{\$\$}(1 + r_{\$\$}) = 1.00000$ $0.271 \times 1.00 = 0.2710000$
Market: U.K.	25.00	—	10.50	—	$w_\pounds(1 + r_\pounds) = 0.27625$
Currency exposure: £	—	100.00	—	−3.00	$w_{\pounds\pounds}(1 + r_{\pounds\pounds}) = 0.97000$ $0.27625 \times 0.97 = 0.2679625$
Market: Euroland	25.00	—	7.00	—	$w_\euro(1 + r_\euro) = 0.26750$
Currency exposure: €	—	100.00	—	1.00	$w_{\euro\euro}(1 + r_{\euro\euro}) = 1.01000$ $0.26750 \times 1.01 = 0.2701750$
Total	100.00%	100.00%	—	—	$R^B = 8.015\%$

TABLE 19.9   Summary of Portfolio Returns and Excess Returns

Measure	Portfolio A_I	Portfolio A_{II}	Portfolio A_{III}	Portfolio B
Portfolio return	7.185%	9.968%	8.405%	8.015%
Value added (excess return)	−0.830 pps	+1.953 pps	+0.390 pps	—

ATTRIBUTION ANALYSIS

To directly compare returns from an actively managed portfolio, A, with a passive benchmark portfolio, B, this section introduces an allocation variable, α, and a selection variable, σ, for both market management, M, and currency management, C. Without loss of generality, the investment process is divided into market allocation, security selection, currency allocation, and finally, currency selection. To separate out the individual contributions of each of these management decisions for every market i and currency j requires four variables:[7]

$$
\begin{aligned}
\text{Market allocation for market } i &= \alpha_i^M, \\
\text{Security selection for market } i &= \sigma_i^M, \\
\text{Currency allocation for currency } j &= \alpha_j^C, \text{ and} \\
\text{Currency selection for currency } j &= \sigma_j^C.
\end{aligned}
$$

TABLE 19.10   Portfolio Strategies to Isolate Manager Contributions

Attribution Variable	Portfolio	Market Allocation	Security Selection	Currency Allocation	Currency Selection
Market allocation	Active	Active	Passive	Passive	Passive
	Passive	Passive	Passive	Passive	Passive
Security selection	Active	Active	Active	Passive	Passive
	Passive	Active	Passive	Passive	Passive
Currency allocation	Active	Active	Active	Active	Passive
	Passive	Active	Active	Passive	Passive
Currency selection	Active	Active	Active	Active	Active
	Passive	Active	Active	Active	Passive

The derivation of the formulas for these variables is straightforward. Each measure is built by the return difference of two newly created active and passive portfolios. Because the goal is to look at each decision separately, portfolios differ only in one decision—the one to evaluate; everything else is assumed unchanged.

Table 19.10 contains an outline of the created active and passive portfolios of this process. Management stages before the measured decision are seen as actively managed—in recognition of the fact that the investment process is not entirely separable. Decisions thereafter remain as benchmark policy set them.

Market Allocation, α^M

The first decision of active portfolio management is to allocate money to various markets. To measure the effect of deviating from the benchmark's investment policy in market allocation and to suppress the influence of other active portfolio management decisions made thereafter, an active portfolio is created that differs from the benchmark only in market allocation. It consists of the active market allocation strategy, passive security selection, and passive currency strategies. The return to this newly created active portfolio is compared with the return to the benchmark portfolio. The difference is the total excess return that active market allocation added to portfolio value.

Security Selection, σ^M

At this stage, decisions of active market allocation are a given. A new "passive" portfolio is created that implements those decisions but equals the benchmark portfolio in every other strategy. A new active portfolio is built that is in line with the given market allocation and copies active security selection strategies but ignores active currency strategies by choosing the passive, benchmark ones. The difference in return between these two portfolios is the total amount of value added by active security selection.

Currency Allocation, α^C

In this stage, active and passive portfolios take the values of the original active portfolio in market management as given. In terms of currency management, the new passive portfolio equals the benchmark portfolio, whereas the new active portfolio carries out active currency allocation and suppresses the influence of active currency selection by choosing the benchmark values. The return difference between the active and passive portfolios is the measure for currency allocation decisions.

Currency Selection, σ^C

Currency selection is the last step in the management process; therefore, to measure it, all the active decisions made before are taken as given. Active and passive portfolios differ only in currency selection, with the passive strategy choosing the benchmark values and the active strategy using the values of the original active portfolio. Again, the difference between these portfolios represents the total amount added by active currency selection to total portfolio value.

Without any residual term left (therefore, in contrast to many other definitions of these variables), the values of the attribution variables sum to the exact total value added (see Paape 2001):

$$\text{Value added} = R^A - R^B$$
$$= \sum_i (\alpha_i^M + \sigma_i^M) + \sum_j (\alpha_j^C + \sigma_j^C). \tag{19.5}$$

For interpreting attribution variables, note that a positive variable denotes a management decision that created more value than the passive default strategy of the benchmark portfolio. Analogously, a negative variable indicates a decision that led to underperformance of the passive benchmark. Furthermore, because of an adjustment term included in the formula for market allocation variables (see Equation 19.12 in Appendix 19D), this measure has an additional interpretation. Here, the unweighted contribution of a market is compared with the passively weighted average return over all market contributions. If the result is positive, an overweighting of that market (in comparison with the weight of the passive strategy in that market) counts as a good decision and an underweighting is a negative. Accordingly, if the result is negative, an overweighting of that particular market produced underperformance and underweighting produced overperformance.

Numerical Example

Using the attribution variables of the previous section, one can analyze the performance of active Portfolios A_I, A_{II}, and A_{III} by comparing them with the benchmark portfolio.[8] Security selection should be zero for every portfolio because each market had only one security to invest in (see Table 19.1). The currency selection variables are also zero because the given database did not permit selecting between various Eurodeposit returns.[9] In both cases, active portfolio management cannot deviate from the given benchmark policy, which causes the corresponding attribution variables to be zero. Hence, in the following evaluations, only market and currency allocation variables matter.

Analysis of Portfolio A_I

Portfolio A_I was designed to produce a return-maximizing portfolio in the context of a conventional performance measurement system (see Tables 19.3 and 19.4). It was invested in the market with the highest local-currency market return in Table 19.1 (the United Kingdom), and the strategy tried to make the best of using the resulting currency exposure (unhedged British pounds). It failed to beat the benchmark portfolio and produced a total value added, VA, of -0.83 pps (see Table 19.9):

$$VA^{A_I} = R^{A_I} - R^B$$
$$= 7.185\% - 8.015\%$$
$$= -0.830 \text{ pps.}$$

The attribution of VA^{A_I} to market and currency allocation and to security and currency selection is shown in Table 19.11. Because active currency management did not change the given benchmark policy of not hedging at all, the currency allocation variable is zero for all currency markets. Thus, only the market allocation variable is nonzero. Of special significance is the sign of the data for this variable. Because the resulting sign for Portfolio A_I is negative, the conclusion is that portfolio management in this case failed to improve on the outcome for the benchmark portfolio. Table 19.11 shows that the principal reason for Portfolio A_I's poor results is the overweighting in U.K. securities, which performed worse than the overall benchmark performed (see the adjustment term $1 + R^B$ in Appendix 19D). A minor effect was contributed by the underweighting of the other markets, which performed less poorly than the U.K. market in relation to the overall benchmark portfolio.

Analyisis of Portfolio A_{II}

Portfolio A_{II} resulted from creating a return-maximizing portfolio by using the new system (see Table 19.6). It invested in the market with the highest local-currency market premium (Euroland) and the highest currency premium (British pounds) reported in Table 19.5. The highest currency premium reflects the highest cash return possible in the markets. The portfolio was able to outperform the benchmark portfolio by an added value of $+1.953$ pps (see Table 19.9):

$$VA^{A_{II}} = R^{A_{II}} - R^B$$
$$= 9.968\% - 8.015\%$$
$$= +1.953 \text{ pps.}$$

A summary of the attribution variables of Portfolio A_{II} is in Table 19.12. The market allocation variables in the Japanese and the U.S. markets are negative but near zero. Both markets performed better than the overall benchmark return $(1 + R^B)$ but had been underweighted in the active portfolio. To underweight the U.K. market, however, was a good strategy because

TABLE 19.11   Attribution Analysis for Portfolio A_I (in percentage points)

Portfolio A_I	Market Allocation	Security Selection	Currency Allocation	Currency Selection	Sum
Japan	-0.0975	0	0	0	-0.0975
United States	-0.0962	0	0	0	-0.0962
United Kingdom	-0.6225	0	0	0	-0.6225
Euroland	-0.0138	0	0	0	-0.0138
Total	-0.8300	0	0	0	-0.8300

that market performed worse than the overall benchmark did. Finally, the overweighting of the Euroland market can be seen as a positive attribute because Euroland performed better than the benchmark, but this strategy did not have much influence on the portfolio's overall excess return.

The currency allocation variable is zero for all the currency markets except Euroland. The overweighting of the exchange from the euro to the British pound in the active portfolio (active portfolio allocation, 100 percent to the euro; benchmark allocation, 0) and the underweighting of the unhedged position "euro to euro" (the active portfolio's weight, 0; the benchmark, 100 percent) contributed positively to the portfolio's overall excess return.

Analysis of Portfolio A_{III}

Portfolio A_{III} resulted from creating a return-maximizing portfolio without currency management (see Table 19.7 and the base-currency return given in the discussion of System III). It was invested in the market with the highest base-currency market return (Japan, with 8.405 percent) and kept the Japanese yen currency exposure generated by this strategy unhedged.

The portfolio performed well. Table 19.9 shows that it beat the benchmark portfolio by an added value of $+0.39$ pps:

$$
\begin{aligned}
VA^{A_{III}} &= R^{A_{III}} - R^B \\
&= 8.405\% - 8.015\% \\
&= +0.390 \text{ pps.}
\end{aligned}
\tag{19.6}
$$

For a summary of the attribution variables of Portfolio A_{III}, see Table 19.13. All variables except the market allocation variables are zero because the portfolio management did

TABLE 19.12   Attribution Analysis for Portfolio A_{II} (in percentage points)

Portfolio A_{II}	Market Allocation	Security Selection	Currency Allocation	Currency Selection	Sum
Japan	−0.0975	0	0	0	−0.0975
United States	−0.0962	0	0	0	−0.0962
United Kingdom	0.2075	0	0	0	0.2075
Euroland	0.0412	0	1.8980	0	1.9392
Total	0.0550	0	1.8980	0	1.9530

TABLE 19.13   Attribution Analysis for Portfolio A_{III} (in percentage points)

Portfolio A_{III}	Market Allocation	Security Selection	Currency Allocation	Currency Selection	Sum
Japan	+0.2925	0	0	0	+0.2925
United States	−0.0962	0	0	0	−0.0962
United Kingdom	+0.2075	0	0	0	+0.2075
Euroland	−0.0138	0	0	0	−0.0138
Total	+0.3900	0	0	0	+0.3900

not deviate in security selection or currency management from the passive strategy of the benchmark portfolio. Thus, the positive performance of Portfolio A_{III} is all the result of superior market allocation. Specifically, the important factor was the overweighting of the Japanese market and underweighting of the British market; the effects of underweighting the U.S. and Euroland markets were more or less unimportant.

CONCLUSION

For accurate performance evaluation of global portfolios, an understanding of the interdependency of market and currency management is critical. This interdependency affects how to measure the corresponding return variables. Because market returns and currency returns cannot simply be added—they must be multiplied—overall portfolio performance cannot be separated into market returns on the one hand and currency returns on the other. Yet, the interpretation of currency return as return from a forward currency contract, which can be represented as a discounted difference between the term interest rates of the corresponding countries, provides some independence for a part of the investment process, namely, the selection process. In the new system described in this article, therefore, market management is measured by market premiums and currency management is measured by currency premiums. Market premiums represent the discounted difference between the local-market return and the "riskless" return of the same market reflecting the differential interest rates on cash equivalents. Currency premiums, however, are exactly these interest rates—short-term Eurodeposits, measured in the base currency of the analyzed portfolio. Currency management, therefore, becomes simply global cash management.

With this new performance measurement system, appropriate attribution variables can be defined—variables that separate the success of active management decisions (in relation to a benchmark portfolio) into market allocation, security selection, currency allocation, and currency selection.

APPENDIX 19A: PERFORMANCE MEASUREMENT EXAMPLES

The Rate of Return in Market i, r_i

The rate of return for the market is calculated as the ratio of gains or losses of an investment in market i to the initial value of that investment, both measured in local currency. For example, for any country in Euroland ($i = $ €), consider the following data:

Initial Value	One Period of Time	Final Value
€116.94	$(1 + r_\epsilon)$	€123.96

The definition of r_ϵ as the rate of return in Euroland in local currency yields

$$r_\epsilon = \frac{€123.96 - €116.94}{€116.94} \approx 0.0600, \text{or } 6.00\%.$$

Rate of Return from Forward Contracts Hedging Currency i to Currency j, f_{ij}

The rate of return from forward contracts is the rate of return derived from exchanging currency j for one unit of currency i at the actual exchange rate and reexchanging the currencies after one period of time with the help of a forward contract fixed at the beginning of the transaction. Continuing the Euroland example with data taken from the German newspaper *Handelsblatt* for 25 May 2001, we have the following data:

Initial Value	One Period of Time	Final Value
£70.83	$(1 + r_£)(1 + f_{€£})$	£75.18
£1 $\cong$ €1.6510 $\downarrow$		$\uparrow$ €1 $\cong$ £0.6065
€116.94	$1 + r_€$	€123.96

with

$$\frac{£75.18 - £70.83}{£70.83} = \frac{70.83 \times 1.651 \times (1 + r_€) \times 0.6065 - 70.83}{70.83}$$

$$= 1.651 \times (1 + r_€) \times 0.6065 - 1$$

$$= (1 + r_€) \times \left(1 + \frac{0.6065 - 1/1.651}{1/1.651}\right) - 1$$

$$= (1 + r_€)(1 + f_{€£}) - 1$$

$$= 1.06 \times (1 + f_{€£}) - 1$$

$$= 0.0614, \text{ or } 6.14\%,$$

which yields

$$f_{€£} = \frac{0.6065 - 1/1.651}{1/1.651} \approx 0.13\%.$$

Note that £1 $\cong$ €1.651, €1 $\cong$ £1/1.651 $\cong$ £0.6057.

Conversely, to show that Equation 19.1 holds for the forward currency rate of return, consider the Eurodeposit rates of return in euros and pounds for a period of three months—respectively, 4.55 percent a year and 5.1 percent a year ($c_€ = 1.0455^{3/12} - 1$, $c_£ = 1.051^{3/12} - 1$):

$$f_{€£} = \frac{c_£ - c_€}{1 + c_€}$$

$$= \frac{1.051^{1/4} - 1.0455^{1/4}}{1.0455^{1/4}} \approx 0.0013, \text{ or } 0.13\%.$$

Rate of Exchange of the U.S. Dollar Relative to Currency j, $e_{j\$}$

This rate of exchange is derived from exchanging U.S. dollars for one unit of currency j with the actual exchange rate used and reexchanging the currencies after one period of time with the use of the then-current exchange rate between currency j and the U.S. dollar. For the same example:

Initial Value	One Period of Time	Final Value
$100.00	$(1 + r_{\textrm{€}})(1 + f_{\textrm{€£}})(1 + e_{\textrm{£\$}})$	$106.17
$1 \cong £0.7083$ ↓		↑ $£1 \cong \textrm{US}\$1.4122$
£70.83		£75.18
$£1 \cong \textrm{€}1.6510$ ↓		↑ $\textrm{€}1 \cong £0.6065$
€116.94	$1 + r_{\textrm{€}}$	€123.96

with

$$\frac{\$106.17 - \$100}{\$100} = \frac{100 \times 0.7083 \times 1.651 \times (1 + r_{\textrm{€}}) \times 0.6065 \times 1.4122 - 100}{100}$$

$$= 0.7083 \times 1.651 \times (1 + r_{\textrm{€}}) \times 0.6065 \times 1.4122 - 1$$

$$= (1 + r_{\textrm{€}})(1 + f_{\textrm{€£}})\left(1 + \frac{1.4122 - 1/0.7083}{1/0.7083}\right) - 1$$

$$= (1 + r_{\textrm{€}})(1 + f_{\textrm{€£}})(1 + e_{\textrm{£\$}}) - 1$$

$$= 1.06 \times 1.0013 \times (1 + 0.0003) - 1 = 0.0617, \textrm{ or } 6.17\%,$$

which yields

$$e_{\textrm{£\$}} = \frac{1.4122 - 1/0.7083}{1/0.7083} \approx 0.0003, \textrm{or } 0.03\%.$$

Dollar-Weighted Percentage of Original Investment in Market i, w_i

In the same example, if the whole portfolio was initially worth US$1,000, the fraction invested in Euroland is calculated as follows:

$$w_{\textrm{€}} = \frac{\$100}{\$1,000}$$

$$= 0.1.$$

Percentage of the Final Value in Market i Exchanged into Currency j, w_{ij}

This number is the percentage of the final value in market i that was exchanged into currency j. It is weighted in terms of local currency. In the example, the currency of the investment in Euroland was fully cross-hedged to British pounds; therefore,

$$w_{\textrm{€£}} = \frac{\textrm{€}123.96}{\textrm{€}123.96} = 1.0 = 100 \Rightarrow w_{\textrm{€€}} = 0;$$

$$w_{\textrm{€\$}} = 0;$$

$$w_{\textrm{€¥}} = 0.$$

APPENDIX 19B: PORTFOLIO PERFORMANCE

The overall performance of the portfolio is the sum of all end nodes in Figure 19.1. That is, if R is the overall return of the portfolio, then

$$R = \left[\sum_i \sum_j w_i(1 + r_i)w_{ij}(1 + f_{ij})(1 + e_{j\$}) \right] - 1. \tag{19.7}$$

Two points should be made regarding Figure 19.1 and the evaluation of the total rate of return. First, although the individual branches of the tree must be added to get the overall performance of the portfolio, within one branch, market and currency return variables need to be multiplied (Sharpe and Alexander 1990). Market and currency returns here are comparable to returns from different time periods, both derived from the same initial outlay. Second, although continuously compounded rates of return would be computationally easier (rates of return of different time periods need only be added), the discrete nature of the process requires simple compounding for accuracy (otherwise, defining appropriate weight variables becomes difficult).

Rearranging Equation 19.7 using $f_{ij} = (c_j - c_i)/(1 + c_i)$ produces

$$R = \left[\sum_i \sum_j w_i(1 + r_i)w_{ij}\frac{1 + c_j}{1 + c_i}(1 + e_{j\$}) \right] - 1$$

$$= \left[\sum_i w_i\frac{1 + r_i}{1 + c_i}\sum_j w_{ij}(1 + c_j)(1 + e_{j\$}) \right] - 1$$

$$= \left[\sum_i w_i(1 + \mu_i)\sum_j w_{ij}(1 + \kappa_j) \right] - 1. \tag{19.8}$$

APPENDIX 19C: COVERED INTEREST RATE PARITY

The following notation is used for analyzing the strategies:

- h_{ij} = exchange rate between currencies i and j that exchanges one unit of currency i for units of currency j (note: $h_{ij} = 1/h_{ji}$) and
- t_{ij} = forward exchange rate between currencies i and j that allows the exchange of one unit of currency i for units of currency j at a prespecified time in the future (note: $t_{ij} = 1/t_{ji}$).

Now consider the following two strategies:

- *Strategy 1*: Exchange an outlay V_j with current exchange rate h_{ji} to currency i, invest the resulting amount in the Eurodeposit cash market at c_i, and hedge the outcome back to currency j by using forward currency contract t_{ij}.
- *Strategy 2:* Invest an outlay V_j directly in the Eurodeposit cash market at cj.

If the markets are arbitrage free, investing in market i and hedging the currency risk (Strategy 1) and investing directly in market j without currency risk (Strategy 2) must lead to the same result; hence,

$$V_j h_{ji}(1 + c_i)t_{ij} = V_j(1 + c_j). \tag{19.9}$$

Rearranging produces

$$t_{ij} = h_{ij}\left(\frac{1 + c_j}{1 + c_i}\right). \tag{19.10}$$

Finally, defining the rate of return of a forward currency contract, f_{ij}, as the rate of return derived from exchanging currency j for one unit of currency i with the actual exchange rate and reexchanging after one period of time for currency j by using a forward contract fixed at the beginning of the transaction yields (see the numerical example in Appendix 19A)

$$\begin{aligned} f_{ij} &= h_{ji}t_{ij} - 1 \\ &= \frac{t_{ij} - h_{ij}}{h_{ij}} \\ &= \frac{c_j - c_i}{1 + c_i}, \end{aligned} \tag{19.11}$$

which is Equation 19.1 in the text.

APPENDIX 19D: ATTRIBUTION VARIABLES

Market Allocation, α_i^M:

$$\alpha_i^M = (w_i^A - w_i^B)\left\{\left[(1 + \mu_i^B)\sum_{j=1}^{m} w_{ij}^B(1 + \kappa_j^B)\right] - (1 + R^B)\right\}. \tag{19.12}$$

Apart from the adjustment term, $1 + R^B$, Equation 19.12 can be derived from comparison of the following two portfolios:

$$\underbrace{\sum_i w_i^A(1 + \mu_i^B)\sum_j w_{ij}^B(1 + \kappa_j^B)}_{\text{(return of active portfolio)}} - \underbrace{\sum_i w_i^B(1 + \mu_i^B)\sum_j w_{ij}^B(1 + \kappa_j^B)}_{\text{(return of passive portfolio)}}.$$

An interpretation of the adjustment term is provided in the "Attribution Analysis" section.

Security Selection, σ_i^M:

$$\sigma_i^M = w_i^A[(1 + \mu_i^A) - (1 + \mu_i^B)]\left[\sum_{j=1}^{m} w_{ij}^B(1 + \kappa_j^B)\right], \tag{19.13}$$

where the definition is understandable by looking at the difference in returns of the following two portfolios:

$$\sum_i w_i^A(1 + \mu_i^A)\sum_j w_{ij}^B(1 + \kappa_j^B) - \sum_i w_i^A(1 + \mu_i^B)\sum_j w_{ij}^B(1 + \kappa_j^B).$$

(return of active portfolio)   (return of passive portfolio)

Currency Allocation, α_i^C:

$$\alpha_i^C = w_i^A(1 + \mu_i^A)\left[\sum_{j=1}^m (w_{ij}^A - w_{ij}^B)(1 + \kappa_j^B)\right]. \qquad (19.14)$$

Again, scrutiny of the following two special portfolios explains this formula:

$$\sum_i w_i^A(1 + \mu_i^A)\sum_j w_{ij}^A(1 + \kappa_j^B) - \sum_i w_i^A(1 + \mu_i^A)\sum_j w_{ij}^B(1 + \kappa_j^B).$$

(return of active portfolio)   (return of passive portfolio)

Currency Selection, σ_i^C:

$$\sigma_i^C = w_i^A(1 + \mu_i^A)\left[\sum_{j=1}^m w_{ij}^A(1 + \kappa_j^A) - (1 + \kappa_j^B)\right]. \qquad (19.15)$$

And finally, the difference in returns of the following two specially formed portfolios helps to derive this formula:

$$\sum_i w_i^A(1 + \mu_i^A)\sum_j w_{ij}^A(1 + \kappa_j^A) - \sum_i w_i^A(1 + \mu_i^A)\sum_j w_{ij}^A(1 + \kappa_j^B).$$

(return of active portfolio)   (return of passive portfolio)

ACKNOWLEDGMENTS

I gratefully acknowledge partial financial funding by the ca/ris/ma project of Professor Heinz Zimmermann of the University of Basel, Switzerland. For help in writing this article, I thank Angela Haines and Mike Lipkin.

NOTES

1. As in, for example, Sharpe and Alexander (1990).
2. Many other papers have dealt with the currency aspects of international asset allocation. Rudolf (1994) gives a good overview of the literature; see also the works of Merton (1973), Solnik (1974), Adler and Dumas (1983), Solnik (1988), Eun and Resnick (1988), Perold and Schulman (1988), Black (1990), Adler and Prasad (1992), and Drummen and Zimmermann (1992).

3. This example is similar to the example used by Singer and Karnosky.
4. If currency management is considered before market management, the method leads to Portfolio A_{II}, which is discussed later.
5. The mathematical derivation of R^{A_1} is available from the author.
6. A detailed explanation is available from the author.
7. The mathematical formulas are in Appendix 19D.
8. Formulas for calculation of the attribution variables are in Appendix 19D.
9. Eurodeposit returns vary with the maturity of the chosen contract.

REFERENCES

Adler, M., and B. Dumas. 1983. "International Portfolio Choice and Corporation Finance: A Synthesis." *Journal of Finance*, vol. 38, no. 3 (June):925–984.

Adler, M., and B. Prasad. 1992. "On Universal Currency Hedges." *Journal of Financial and Quantitative Analysis*, vol. 27, no. 1 (March):19–38.

Ankrim, E. M. 1992. "Risk-Adjusted Performance Attribution." *Financial Analysts Journal*, vol. 48, no. 2 (March/April):74–82.

Ankrim, E. M., and C. R. Hensel. 1994. "Multicurrency Performance Attribution." *Financial Analysts Journal*, vol. 50, no. 2 (March/April):29–35.

Black, F. 1990. "Equilibrium Exchange Rate Hedging." *Journal of Finance*, vol. 45, no. 3 (July):899–907.

Brinson, G. P., and N. Fachler. 1985. "Measuring Non-U.S. Equity Portfolio Performance." *Journal of Portfolio Management*, vol. 11, no. 3 (Spring):73–76.

Brinson, G. P., R. Hood, and G. L. Beebower. 1986. "Determinants of Portfolio Performance." *Financial Analysts Journal*, vol. 42, no. 4 (July/August):39–44.

Brinson, G. P., B. D. Singer, and G. L. Beebower. 1991. "Determinants of Portfolio Performance II: An Update." *Financial Analysts Journal*, vol. 47, no. 3 (May/June):40–48.

Drummen, M., and H. Zimmermann. 1992. "Portfolioeffekte des Waehrungsrisikos." *Finanzmarkt und Portfolio Management*, vol. 6, no. 1:81–102.

Eun, C. S., and B. G. Resnick. 1988. "Exchange Rate Uncertainty, Forward Contracts, and International Portfolio Selection." *Journal of Finance*, vol. 43, no. 1 (March):197–215.

Fischer-Erlach, P. 1995. "Handel und Kursbildung am Devisenmarkt." 5th ed. Stuttgart, Germany: Kohlhammer.

Hensel, C. R., Don Ezra, and J. H. Ilkiw. 1991. "The Importance of the Asset Allocation Decision." *Financial Analysts Journal*, vol. 47, no. 4 (July/August):65–72.

Merton, R. C. 1973. "An Intertemporal Capital Asset Pricing Model." *Econometrica*, vol. 41, no. 5 (September):867–887.

Paape, C. 1998. "Zur Kreuzproduktproblematik in der Attributions analyse von Investmentfonds." *Finanzmarkt und Portfolio Management*, vol. 12, no. 2:213–220.

———. 2001. "Interne Performance analyse von Investmentfonds." Stuttgart, Germany: Schaeffer-Poeschel Verlag.

Perold, A. F., and E. C. Schulman. 1988. "The Free Lunch in Currency Hedging: Implications for Investment Policy and Performance Standards." *Financial Analysts Journal*, vol. 44, no. 3 (May/June):45–50.

Rudolf, M. 1994. "Algorithms for Portfolio Optimization and Portfolio Insurance." Bern, Switzerland: Paul Haupt.

Sharpe, W. F., and G. J. Alexander. 1990. "Investments." 4th ed. Englewood Cliffs, NJ: Prentice-Hall.

Singer, B. D., and D. S. Karnosky. 1994. *Global Asset Management and Performance Attribution.* Charlottesville, VA: The Research Foundation of the Institute of Chartered Financial Analysts.

―――. 1995. "The General Framework for Global Investment Management and Performance Attribution." *Journal of Portfolio Management*, vol. 21, no. 2 (Winter):84–92.

Solnik, B. H. 1974. "An Equilibrium Model of the International Capital Market." *Journal of Economic Theory*, vol. 8, no. 4 (August):500–524.

―――. 1988. "International Investments." Reading, MA: Addison-Wesley.

PART IV

PERFORMANCE APPRAISAL

CHAPTER 20

ON THE PERFORMANCE OF HEDGE FUNDS

Bing Liang

Empirical evidence indicates that hedge funds differ substantially from traditional investment vehicles, such as mutual funds. Unlike mutual funds, hedge funds follow dynamic trading strategies and have low systematic risk. Hedge funds' special fee structures apparently align managers' incentives with fund performance. Funds with "high watermarks" (under which managers are required to make up previous losses before receiving any incentive fees) significantly outperform those without. Hedge funds provide higher Sharpe ratios than mutual funds, and their performance in the period of January 1992 through December 1996 reflects better manager skills, although hedge fund returns are more volatile. Average hedge fund returns are related positively to incentive fees, fund assets, and the lockup period.

Hedge funds are private investment partnerships in which the general partners make substantial personal investments. These funds are allowed to take both long and short positions, to use leverage and derivatives, to invest in concentrated portfolios, and to move quickly between various markets. Hedge funds usually take large risks on speculative strategies, including leverage bets, program trading, swaps, and arbitrage.

Unlike mutual funds, hedge funds in the United States are not required to register with the U.S. SEC and disclose their asset holdings, primarily because hedge funds are either limited partnerships or offshore corporations.[1] This limited regulatory oversight gives hedge fund managers tremendous flexibility in making investment decisions. Because of the nature of private partnerships, hedge funds are not allowed to advertise to the public. The funds require that 65 percent of all investors be accredited, and the minimum investment requirement is typically $250,000. A lockup period is usually imposed to prevent early redemption.

Hedge funds have special fee structures designed to motivate managers. A management fee is based on asset size, and an incentive fee is established separately to align the manager's interest with the fund's performance. The incentive fee is usually paid only after a hurdle rate

Reprinted from the *Financial Analysts Journal* (July/August 1999):72–85.

has been achieved. A majority of hedge funds also have a "high watermark" provision, under which the manager is required to make up any previous losses before an incentive fee will be paid (i.e., the cumulative returns have to be above the hurdle rate). Furthermore, a manager could "owe" the investors a rebate of fees charged in previous years. All these features give managers better incentives to act in investors' interests than is the case with mutual funds and other traditional investment vehicles.

Hedge fund targets for returns differ from mutual fund targets. Hedge funds are absolute performers; for hurdles, they use some target such as the T-bill rate plus a premium or LIBOR plus a premium. In contrast, mutual funds are relative performers; they use such benchmarks as the S&P 500 Index for equity funds and the Lehman Brothers Aggregate Index for bond funds.

As a result of flexible investment strategies, an effective manager-incentive alignment, sophisticated investors, and limited SEC regulations, hedge funds have gained tremendous popularity. The first hedge fund was established in 1949. By the late 1980s, the number of funds had increased to about 100. Explosive growth in the hedge fund market during the early 1990s, shown in Figure 20.1, has made more than 1,000 funds available to investors today. Moreover, in 1996, to encourage investment in hedge funds, the SEC allowed hedge funds to exceed their previous limit of 100 investors without requiring the kind of registration and disclosure required of mutual funds.[2] The new SEC rules could attract pension funds and other institutional investors to hedge funds.

Despite the popularity of hedge funds, however, and increasing interest in their activities by the banking industry and regulators, there are very few studies in this field (see Fung and Hsieh 1997a; Brown, Goetzmann, and Ibbotson 1999; Ackermann, McEnally, and Ravenscraft 1999). The recent debacle at Long-Term Capital Management LP suggests that empirical studies of hedge funds are needed to educate the public.

The lack of work on hedge funds is a result of the difficulty in accessing private hedge fund data. For the study reported here, I was able to use a large database, consisting of more

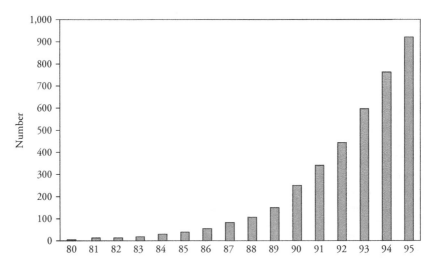

FIGURE 20.1   Growth in Hedge Funds, 1980–1995

Note: 111 funds have missing inception dates.

than 1,000 hedge funds, to investigate the performance, risk, and fee structure of the hedge fund industry. The sample is different from those used in previous studies. An asset-class factor model and mean–variance analysis are used to compare hedge funds with mutual funds. The empirical results reveal several interesting aspects of hedge funds.

DATA AND SAMPLE STATISTICS

The hedge fund data came from Hedge Fund Research, Inc. (HFR), whose database contained information on 1,162 funds with more than $190 billion in total assets under management as of July 1997. The HFR database consists of not only surviving funds but also 108 funds that have disappeared, which mitigates the survivorship bias problem. According to HFR, 16 hedge fund investment strategies exist; their definitions are in Appendix 20A.

Most of the 1,162 funds report returns to their investors on a monthly basis. Therefore, the study required that funds in the sample report returns on a monthly basis. Also required was that funds report returns net of all fees, including incentive fees, management fees, sales/ commission fees, and other fees. The vast majority of funds report returns net of all fees. After deletion of the funds that report returns on a quarterly basis, the funds that report returns with different fees, and the 48 HFR indexes, 921 hedge funds remained in the sample, of which 92 were no longer in operation.

To accurately measure fund performance and risk, the study also required all funds in the three-year sample to have a consecutive monthly return history for January 1994 through December 1996. This requirement reduced the number of funds in the main study to 385. For robustness, I also constructed a five-year sample from January 1992 through December 1996 from the 281 funds that had consecutive monthly returns for that period.

To compare hedge funds with mutual funds, I obtained mutual fund data from Morningstar, Inc. The Morningstar OnDisc database covered 7,746 mutual funds as of December 31, 1996. After the funds with consecutive monthly return histories of less than three years were deleted, 4,776 funds remained in the sample for January 1994 through December 1996.[3] The five-year sample, which contains 2,456 funds, spans the period from January 1992 through December 1996.

Descriptive statistics for the hedge fund sample are in Table 20.1. Hedge fund assets averaged $94 million (median $21 million) in the period, which is smaller than for mutual funds, for which average (median) net fund assets were $306 million ($38 million) as of December 31, 1996. The small asset size of hedge funds reflects the nature of private partnerships and allows hedge fund managers to move quickly among different markets and to invest heavily in concentrated portfolios to take advantage of small pockets of market inefficiency. Note that average firm assets, however, are much higher than average fund assets, which indicates that firms may be managing more than one fund or managed account.

The average and median annual management fees (the fees based on fund size but not fund performance) for hedge funds are a great deal smaller than the average and median annual incentive fees, which are based on annual profits and apply above the hurdle rates.[4] The average and median minimums for investment are substantially above the affordability of most small investors. In addition to the lockup period (average of about three months), Table 20.1 indicates that one-month advance notice is required, on average, for withdrawal.

TABLE 20.1   Hedge Fund Descriptive Statistics, July 1997

Variable	Number of Funds[a]	Mean	Standard Deviation	Median
Fund assets	850	$93.6 million	$329.4 million	$21 million
Firm assets	781	$2.04 billion	$11.03 billion	$181 million
Management fee	839	1.36%	0.8%	1%
Incentive fee	821	16.24%	7.96%	20%
Minimum investment	839	$597,917	$1.2 million	$250,000
Lockup period	749	84 days	164 days	0 day
Advance notice	768	35.12 days	24.94 days	30 days
Additional investment[b]	126	$103,509	$153,122	$100,000

[a]Not all funds reported every descriptive statistic. All 921 hedge funds had monthly returns that were net of all fees; 92 funds were no longer in operation; 48 hedge fund indexes were excluded from the sample.
[b]Subsequent investment in addition to the initial investment.

FUND FEATURES AND PERFORMANCE

Average hedge fund performance was related to some important fund features. First, Panel A of Table 20.2 indicates that most funds are leveraged.[5] Although borrowing gives fund managers more capital to invest and the leveraged funds slightly outperformed the unleveraged funds, the difference in performance was not significant ($t = 0.45$). Further examination by investment strategy revealed that leverage benefited some specific funds, such as convertible arbitrage and merger arbitrage funds. Obviously, leverage increased the volatility of hedge fund returns.

Panel B of Table 20.2 reports that the sample contained more offshore funds than onshore U.S. funds. The reason may be the tax advantages offshore, benefits from fewer regulations enjoyed by offshore funds, globalization in the world financial markets, and/or the growing need for cross-border investments. The offshore funds appear to be more volatile, but the U.S. hedge funds and offshore hedge funds offered similar returns. Funds in the category "Both," which represented an onshore fund with an offshore equivalent, significantly outperformed the onshore-only funds ($t = 3.12$) and the offshore-only funds ($t = 2.82$). These combination funds usually start as onshore-only funds. Then, when the funds perform well, new investors come into the funds, and their assets grow, the managers establish equivalent offshore funds to attract foreign investors. Therefore, combination funds tend to be larger than other funds and the fund managers tend to have more expertise than those of other funds.

Panel C of Table 20.2 reports that the majority of funds have high watermark provisions. This finding indicates that the funds believe investors are generally concerned about recouping past losses, which is consistent with loss-averse behavior in investors. With high watermark provisions, managers collect incentive fees only if they can make up all past losses in such a way that the cumulative returns are above the hurdle rate. This design seems to achieve its purpose: Funds with high watermarks outperformed funds without, and the difference in performance is significant at the 6 percent level.

TABLE 20.2 Hedge Fund Characteristics and Average Monthly Returns, July 1997 (standard deviations in parentheses)

	Number of Funds[a]	Return	Standard Deviation	Minimum	Maximum
A. Leverage					
No	135	1.26%	0.62%	−1.74%	7.78%
Yes	639	1.29	1.02	−4.64	10.00
Difference (yes minus no)		0.03			
		(0.07)			
B. Offshore funds versus onshore funds					
Onshore	208	1.31	1.03	−3.52	6.77
Both[b]	136	1.71	1.29	−3.60	7.24
Offshore	471	1.34	1.54	−4.64	15.42
Difference (offshore minus onshore)		0.03			
		(0.10)			
C. Watermark					
No	169	1.23	1.19	−4.64	5.55
Yes	623	1.43	1.36	−3.60	10.00
Difference (yes minus no)		0.20**			
		(0.11)			
D. Hurdle rate					
No	668	1.40	1.33	−4.64	10.00
Yes	125	1.43	1.83	−2.45	15.42
Difference (yes minus no)		0.03			
		(0.18)			

[a]Not all funds reported every descriptive statistic. All 921 hedge funds had monthly returns that were net of all fees; 92 funds were no longer in operation; 48 hedge fund indexes were excluded from the sample.
[b]An onshore fund with an offshore equivalent.
**Significant at the 6 percent level.

As shown in Panel D of Table 20.2, the majority of the funds did not have hurdle rates.[6] Although the funds with hurdle rates slightly outperformed those without, the return difference is not statistically significant. Unlike the existence of a high watermark provision, the existence of a hurdle rate is apparently not critical for fund performance. Note that the hurdle rate and the high watermark serve different purposes. The hurdle rate is used for collecting incentive fees, whereas the purpose of a high watermark is to assure that past losses are recovered. To that extent, they are independent.[7]

HEDGE FUND PERFORMANCE AND RISK

Cumulative monthly hedge fund returns were calculated on the basis of an equally weighted portfolio for January 1990 through December 1996. These returns are compared with cumulative returns for the S&P 500 in Figure 20.2. Because most of the funds were launched after 1990, the figure captures the majority of hedge funds. As one can see, a $1 investment in the

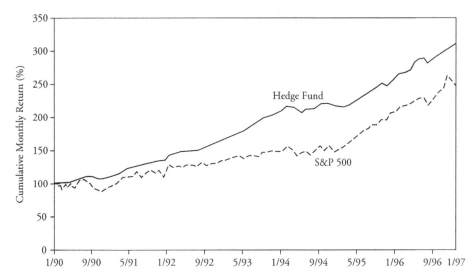

FIGURE 20.2 Cumulative Monthly Returns, January 1990–January 1997

hedge fund portfolio in January 1990 grew to $3.08 and the same investment in the S&P 500 grew to $2.56 by the end of 1996. In terms of total return, hedge funds earned 208 percent, whereas the S&P 500 earned 156 percent. Hedge funds are riskier, however, than the U.S. stock market; the standard deviation of monthly returns was 3.37 percent for the S&P 500 and 4.04 percent for the hedge fund portfolio during this period. Use of leverage, going short, and use of derivatives can increase the volatility of returns for hedge funds. Therefore, risk-adjusted or market-adjusted returns should be examined.

Factor Model Evaluation of Hedge Fund Performance

Hedge funds are exposed to varieties of asset classes through the various strategies the hedge fund managers follow. Examples of these strategies include risk arbitrage, short selling, and market timing. Therefore, instead of using a single-factor model, we adopted an asset-class factor model (Sharpe 1992; Fung and Hsieh 1997a) to evaluate performance and analyze the success of hedge fund styles or strategies. The eight asset classes are as follows: for equity, U.S. equity (the S&P 500), international equity (MSCI World Equity Index), and emerging market equity (MSCI Emerging Market Index); for debt, U.S. debt (Salomon Brothers Government and Corporate Bond Index) and international sovereign debt (the Salomon Brothers World Government Bond Index); for currency, the U.S. Federal Reserve Bank trade-weighted dollar index; for commodities, the gold price; and for cash, the one-month Eurodollar deposit rate.

The asset-class factor model can be expressed as

$$R_t = \alpha + \sum_{k=1}^{8} \beta_k F_{k,t} + \varepsilon_t,$$

where
R_t = the average fund return in month t
α = unexplained return by asset-class factors

β_k = factor loading on the kth factor

$F_{k,t}$ = value of the kth asset-class factor in month t

ε_t = a random error term in month t

Note that some of these factors are highly correlated. For example, the correlation coefficient between the S&P 500 and the MSCI World index is 0.82. To mitigate the potential collinearity problem among factors, I used a stepwise regression procedure to select variables. This approach allowed me to pick up the most relevant factors while avoiding the redundant ones, and it significantly simplified the regression results.

Table 20.3 reports the results of the stepwise regression for the 385 funds with consecutive monthly returns from January 1994 through December 1996. The results indicate that factor loadings are scattered around different asset classes and different strategies. No single asset class dominated in the regression. Although 8 of the 16 hedge funds were heavily invested in U.S. equity, the returns of the other 8 were not significantly correlated with the S&P 500 return. The R^2s of the regressions range from 0.20 to 0.77, which indicates relatively low correlations between hedge fund returns and the standard asset classes. This evidence is consistent with Fung and Hsieh (1997a), who stated that hedge funds follow dynamic trading strategies rather than buy-and-hold strategies.

Convertible arbitrage funds were found to have a factor loading of 0.21 with U.S. government and corporate bonds, which is consistent with the convertible-bond trading strategy of these funds. Distressed securities were found to have a beta of 0.22 with the S&P 500, indicating that these funds are long U.S. stocks. The emerging market funds in the study, with the high factor loading with the emerging market index, also invest heavily in currencies. Funds of funds can be seen to have broad exposure to the world's developed and emerging market equities, currency, commodities, and cash—which results from the funds-of-funds approach of investing in a large variety of hedge funds with various investment strategies. The growth and value funds in the study, as would be expected, had relatively high betas with the U.S. equity market. The results for the macro funds reflect their strategy of following a top-down global approach to investing in world equities, currencies, and commodities. Finally, the large negative beta of the short-selling funds with the S&P 500 reflects the strategy of selling U.S. equities short against broad U.S. market movements. Betas with the S&P 500 in Table 20.3 range from a low of -1.41 to a high of 0.88; the majority are significantly different from zero and below 1.00.[8]

The betas in Table 20.3 suggest two conclusions: First, the low betas with the U.S. equity market indicate that hedge funds are not traditional investment vehicles and are less correlated with the market than traditional vehicles. Second, nonzero betas mean that hedge funds are different from the original "hedge" definition, in which combining long and short positions is designed to neutralize market risk. In general, to make their profits, hedge funds apply dynamic trading strategies and a variety of financial instruments in various markets. Except for the market-neutral strategy, the dynamic trading strategies do not neutralize market risk.

A potential caveat about the regression is necessary. By construction, factor loadings from the regression were assumed to be constant for 36 months, but this assumption conflicts with the dynamic nature of the trading strategies adopted by most hedge funds. For example, if a hedge fund invested in foreign currencies for the first 18 months and then sold those currencies short in the remaining 18 months, the factor loading for currency would show up as close to zero. This phenomenon explains why the fixed-income group did not correlate highly with the bond indexes but did correlate with the currency index.

Following Sharpe, I interpreted the intercept term of the regression as the return not explained by the asset-class factor model. Unexplained returns come from managers' selection skills, which cannot be explained by the style factors from passive portfolios. The unexplained

TABLE 20.3 Stepwise Regression Results for 16 Hedge Fund Strategies

Strategy	Intercept	U.S. Equity	International Equity	Emerging Market Equity	U.S. Debt	International Sovereign Debt	Currency	Commodities	Cash	R^2
Composite	0.68%					0.68**		0.68**		0.23
Convertible arbitrage	−1.14			0.08**	0.21*			0.19**	0.35	0.40
Distressed securities	0.64**	0.22**								0.29
Emerging markets	0.75**		0.12**	0.58**			0.29**			0.77
Fixed income	0.73**						0.15**			0.33
Foreign exchange	0.49					0.76**		0.55*		0.20
Fund of funds	−1.51		0.23**	0.10**			0.31**	0.20**	0.37**	0.67
Growth	−5.22**	0.56**		0.16**	−0.79**				1.13**	0.71
Macro	0.24		0.64**		0.59**		0.72**	0.64**		0.71
Market neutral	−1.56*		0.13**						0.43**	0.27
Market timing	−0.08	0.67**			−0.32*					0.67
Merger arbitrage	0.94**	0.13**						0.14**		0.33
Opportunistic	0.98**	0.29**		0.07		−0.22**		0.16**		0.53
Sector	0.52	0.88**			−0.81**		0.43**	0.31*		0.60
Short selling	1.26*	−1.41**					−0.57*		1.40**	0.48
Value	0.69**	0.46**		0.11**		−0.24**				0.68

Notes: The dependent variable is the average monthly return over 36 months. All 385 hedge funds had 36 consecutive monthly returns from January 1994 through December 1996.

*Significant at the 10 percent level.
**Significant at the 5 percent level.

returns ranged in Table 20.3 from −5.22 percent to 1.26 percent, with a median return of 0.58 percent a month. Positive unexplained returns resulted for 11 out of 16 groups, and 7 hedge fund groups earned significantly positive unexplained returns. Only two groups (growth and market neutral) had significantly negative unexplained returns.

Overall, the low beta values for these hedge fund groups indicate that hedge funds have low systematic risk as a result of combining long and short strategies, concentrating investments in small asset bases, using derivatives, and holding broad asset classes in a variety of markets. In addition, most fund groups displayed positive unexplained returns (statistically significantly positive for seven groups), which provides some evidence of manager skill.

Average Returns on Fund Characteristics

To further examine the determinants of hedge fund returns, I ran a cross-sectional regression of average monthly returns on fund characteristics, such as incentive fees, management fees, and fund assets. The regression equation was

$$\bar{R}_i = \alpha_{0i} + \alpha_{1i}(IFEE) + \alpha_{2i}(MFEE) + \alpha_{3i}[\ln(ASSETS)]$$
$$+ \alpha_{4i}(LOCKUP) + \alpha_{5i}(AGE),$$

where

$\bar{R}_i$	= average monthly return over 36 months for fund i
IFEE	= incentive fee (in percentage)
MFEE	= management fee (in percentage)
$\ln(ASSETS)$	= natural logarithm of fund assets as of July 1997
LOCKUP	= lockup period (in number of days)
AGE	= number of months since fund inception

Table 20.4 reports the regression results. The coefficient for the incentive fee is significantly positive, which suggests that, indeed, a high incentive fee is able to align the manager's incentive with fund performance. In fact, a 1 percent increase in the incentive fee will increase the average monthly return by 1.3 percent. The management fee is not significantly related to performance, which is not surprising because the management fee charged is independent of performance.

TABLE 20.4 Average Fund Returns Regressed on Fund Characteristics

Independent Variable	Parameter Estimate	*t*-Statistic
α_0	−0.772**	−2.621
α_1	0.013**	3.157
α_2	0.030	0.518
α_3	0.090**	5.665
α_4	0.202**	2.243
α_5	−0.020**	−2.062
R^2	0.140	
Adjusted R^2	0.127	

**Significant at the 5 percent level.

The coefficient on ln(*ASSETS*) is significantly positive. Remember that the median fund asset is about $20 million. For most of these hedge funds, the assets have not become too big yet to impede performance. It is suggested that a fund needs a critical mass of $10 million to $20 million to support its operating expenses. The positive coefficient indicates that large funds realize economies of scale. It may also suggest that successful funds attract more money.

The findings reported in Table 20.4 show that the lockup period is critical in determining fund returns. The longer the lockup period, the better the fund performance. Lockup periods can effectively prevent early redemption, reduce cash holdings, and allow managers to focus on relatively long horizons.

Finally, the age of the fund is negatively related to average performance. Long-lived funds did not necessarily outperform young funds during the three-year period studied. One explanation is that managers of young funds work harder than managers of older funds—to build up their reputations and to attract more investors. This finding is consistent with Chevalier and Ellison (1999).

HEDGE FUNDS VERSUS MUTUAL FUNDS

Hedge funds are different from mutual funds. The first difference is the incentive scheme. Mutual fund fees are usually based on fund size independently of performance. For hedge funds, as long as the fund has a hurdle rate and a high watermark, managers will try their best to perform, to collect the incentive fees, and to protect their own investments in the fund. Another difference between hedge funds and mutual funds is that mutual funds are traditional investment vehicles whose returns tend to move together, whereas hedge funds are alternative investment vehicles. Their returns are less correlated with standard asset classes than those of mutual funds, and they can use more flexible investment strategies—such as leverage, derivatives, short selling, and swaps. And hedge fund managers may move quickly among different markets. In addition, hedge funds require a large minimum investment and impose a long lockup period. These differences make hedge funds more likely to outperform mutual funds. Hedge fund returns may be more volatile, however, than mutual fund returns because of leverage, derivatives, short selling, and risky arbitrage.

Efficient Frontiers

As a result of flexible investment strategies and the nontraditional asset classes involved, hedge fund strategies are not highly correlated with each other. Thus, for diversification, investors will benefit more from holding a general hedge fund portfolio than from holding a mutual fund portfolio. The mean–variance-efficient frontiers plotted in Figure 20.3 confirm this argument: The efficient frontier of the hedge funds overwhelmed the efficient frontier for the mutual funds for all feasible standard deviations.[9] For a given standard deviation, investors can do much better by investing in hedge funds than investing in mutual funds. Moreover, given the fact that the hedge fund returns are measured net of all fees, whereas the mutual fund returns are not adjusted for loads, the dominance of hedge funds over mutual funds may be understated in Figure 20.3.[10]

Sharpe's Measure

Another difference between hedge funds and mutual funds is that mutual funds are relative performers that use relative targets, such as the S&P 500, whereas hedge funds are absolute

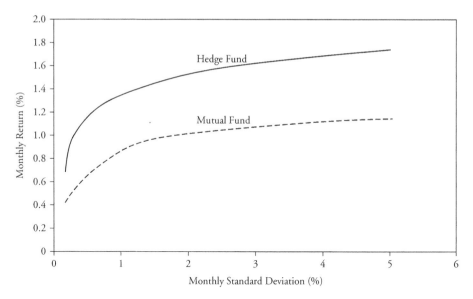

FIGURE 20.3   Efficient Frontiers, 1992–1996

performers that do not use relative benchmarks. So, for example, the U.S. equity market index is not necessarily the right benchmark for hedge funds, and betas and alphas may not be the appropriate measures for risks and profits. To mitigate this problem, I calculated Sharpe ratios.

A comparison of mean returns, risks (standard deviations), and Sharpe ratios for groups of the hedge funds and mutual funds in the study is in Table 20.5. For this analysis, the mutual funds were grouped according to strategies spelled out in the note to Table 20.5. From the three-year sample period (January 1994 through December 1996), the highest Sharpe ratio was found for a hedge fund group—1.11 for the merger arbitrage fund; the next highest was 0.67 for the opportunistic hedge fund. Both funds are arbitrage- and opportunity-seeking funds.

The average Sharpe ratio for the 16 hedge fund groups in the three-year period was 0.36, compared with the average Sharpe ratio of 0.17 for all the mutual fund groups. The difference is significant at the 1 percent level, which indicates that hedge funds, on average, provide better risk-to-reward compensation.

The highest Sharpe ratio for the mutual fund groups in the three-year period was 0.31 for the large-cap/value equity style funds, which is consistent with the literature supporting the advantages of value investing (see Lakonishok, Shleifer, and Vishny 1994). Note that a value style also exists among the hedge fund strategies. The hedge funds following this style earned a Sharpe ratio of 0.45 in the three-year period, which is higher than the ratio for the large-cap/value equity style and than the average Sharpe ratio for all three mutual fund groups following the value style, which was only 0.26. Similar results were found for the growth style: Hedge funds following growth strategies had a Sharpe ratio of 0.38; the three mutual funds carrying out growth strategies had an average Sharpe ratio of only 0.22.

For robustness, I replicated the results for the three-year period by using the five-year period of January 1992 through December 1996. The results from the longer period are very similar to the results of the shorter period. For example, for the five-year sample, the average

TABLE 20.5 Distribution Statistics for Returns of Hedge Funds and Mutual Funds

| | Hedge Funds | | | | | | | Mutual Funds | | | | | |
| | January 1994–December 1996 | | | January 1992–December 1996 | | | | January 1994–December 1996 | | | January 1992–December 1996 | | |
Strategy	Mean	Standard Deviation	Sharpe Ratio	Mean	Standard Deviation	Sharpe Ratio	Strategy	Mean	Standard Deviation	Sharpe Ratio	Mean	Standard Deviation	Sharpe Ratio
Composite	1.06%	3.35%	0.20	1.24%	3.35%	0.27	Bond/stock	0.86%	1.66%	0.28	0.90%	1.40%	0.40
Convertible arbitrage	0.77	1.06	0.36	0.65	0.68	0.45	Large-cap/growth	1.15	2.89	0.26	1.04	2.82	0.25
Distressed securities	0.99	1.16	0.52	1.38	1.54	0.67	Large-cap/value	1.08	2.20	0.31	1.09	2.08	0.36
Emerging markets	0.57	2.96	0.06	1.79	4.62	0.31	Large-cap/blend	1.07	2.38	0.28	1.00	2.23	0.29
Fixed income	0.83	0.71	0.61	0.79	1.32	0.33	Mid-cap/growth	1.08	3.58	0.19	1.12	3.41	0.23
Foreign exchange	0.93	3.44	0.16	0.77	5.16	0.08	Mid-cap/value	0.87	2.16	0.22	1.13	2.06	0.38
Fund of funds	0.60	1.42	0.15	1.00	1.48	0.44	Mid-cap/blend	0.86	2.72	0.17	1.00	2.45	0.27
Growth	1.24	2.21	0.38	1.48	2.62	0.43	Small-cap/growth	1.24	3.96	0.21	1.23	3.86	0.23
Macro	0.97	2.90	0.20	1.55	3.10	0.39	Small-cap/value	1.00	2.31	0.26	1.13	2.39	0.33
Market neutral	0.86	0.92	0.51	0.78	0.88	0.49	Small-cap/blend	1.03	3.00	0.21	1.00	3.06	0.22
Market timing	0.80	2.00	0.20	0.83	1.63	0.30	High/short	0.36	0.58	-0.08	0.39	0.55	0.08

Equity style						
Merger arbitrage	1.13	0.68	1.11	1.07	0.74	0.98
Opportunistic	1.25	1.31	0.67	1.39	1.26	0.83
Sector	1.35	2.79	0.34	1.81	2.66	0.55
Short selling	-0.10	4.91	-0.10	-0.56	5.55	-0.16
Value	1.22	1.84	0.45	1.55	1.83	0.66
Average	0.90	2.10	0.36	1.10	2.40	0.44

Bond style						
High/intermediate	0.47	1.17	0.06	0.50	1.06	0.15
High/long	0.38	1.64	-0.01	0.56	1.52	0.14
Medium/short	0.48	0.60	0.15	0.43	0.41	0.22
Medium/intermediate	0.53	1.22	0.11	0.61	1.13	0.24
Medium/long	0.41	1.57	0.01	0.59	1.47	0.17
Low/intermediate	0.68	1.22	0.24	0.92	1.20	0.48
Low/long	0.65	1.84	0.14	0.67	1.27	0.25
Average	0.79	2.04	0.17	0.85	1.91	0.26

Notes: The mutual fund sample contained nine equity investment styles: large-capitalization/growth, large-cap/value, and large-cap/blend; medium-cap/growth, medium-cap/value, and medium-cap/blend; and small-cap/growth, small-cap/value, and small-cap/blend. The mutual fund sample also contained nine bond investment styles: high-quality/short-term, high-quality/intermediate-term, and high-quality/long-term bonds; medium-quality/short-term, medium-quality/intermediate-term, and medium-quality/long-term bonds; and low-quality/short-term (no data for this category), low-quality/intermediate-term, and low-quality/long-term bonds. The low-quality/short-term strategy had no fund left in the sample that met the requirement for three-year or five-year consecutive monthly returns. One more style classification was needed for the mutual fund groups: funds blending equity and bonds, called here "bond/stock." From January 1994 through December 1996, 385 hedge funds and 4,776 mutual funds with 36 consecutive monthly returns were in the samples; from January 1992 through December 1996, 281 hedge funds and 2,456 mutual funds with 60 consecutive monthly returns were in the samples.

Sharpe ratio for hedge funds is 0.44, much higher than the ratio of 0.26 for mutual funds. This difference between the two Sharpe ratios is significant at the 1 percent level. On average, hedge funds are riskier than mutual funds. Because of the bull market in U.S. equity in 1992–1996, the short-selling hedge funds in this period suffered a monthly loss of 0.56 percent. Relatively speaking, the emerging market hedge funds, the foreign exchange funds, and the short-selling funds had higher standard deviations than the other hedge or mutual funds.

Factor Model Evaluation of Mutual Fund Performance

As for the hedge funds, the stepwise regression was used to extract useful factors for explaining mutual fund returns. The results of regressing the mutual fund strategies against the eight benchmarks are in Table 20.6. In contrast to the results for the hedge funds, four factors were dominant in the mutual fund regressions—emerging market, S&P 500, Eurodollar (cash), and U.S. bond index returns. These four dominant factors explained the majority of mutual fund returns. In fact, 9 out of 18 fund groups had R^2s with these factors above 0.90. Most mutual funds apparently follow buy-and-hold strategies. Therefore, passive portfolios or styles can explain mutual fund returns.

The unexplained returns are negative for all but three mutual fund groups. Ten of eighteen are significantly different from zero, of which only one (the high-quality/short-term bond group) is positive. The largest negative unexplained return was -7.78 percent for the small-cap/growth funds. The median was -1.03 percent a month. This result is in sharp contrast to the corresponding hedge fund results in Table 20.3, for which most of the hedge fund groups earned positive unexplained returns, 7 of 16 were significantly above zero, and the median was 0.58 percent.

In general, mutual funds have higher betas with the markets than do hedge funds. All the mutual fund betas are positive with respect to the S&P 500. The highest beta is for the medium-cap/growth fund and the lowest is for the high-quality/short-term bond funds. Generally, as would be expected, the equity mutual funds (especially growth funds) have higher equity market betas than the bond funds and the bond funds (especially the intermediate-term and long-term bond funds) have higher bond market betas than equity funds.

SURVIVORSHIP BIAS

Grinblatt and Titman (1989), Brown, Goetzmann, Ibbotson, and Ross (1992), Malkiel (1995), and Elton, Gruber, and Blake (1996) indicated that survivorship bias in a mutual fund sample could affect evaluation of funds' performance. The survivorship bias documented in these mutual fund studies is 0.5–1.4 percent a year.

Although the hedge fund sample in this study included both surviving and vanished funds, the sample is not bias free. For example, of 921 funds in the HFR database, only 92 were listed as no longer in operation. That attrition rate is about 10 percent for the period of several years, which is lower than the 4.8 percent average annual attrition rate for mutual funds (see Brown et al., 1992) and the 19 percent annual attrition rate for commodity trading advisors (CTAs) (see Fung and Hsieh 1997b).

The true attrition rate for hedge funds is hard to estimate from our sample because funds that disappeared before HFR started collecting the data would not be included. A reasonable assumption, however, is that annual hedge fund attrition is between that of mutual funds, which are less risky than hedge funds, and CTAs, which are more risky than hedge

TABLE 20.6 Stepwise Regression Results for 19 Mutual Fund Strategies

Strategy	Intercept	U.S. Equity	International Equity	Emerging Market Equity	U.S. Debt	International Sovereign Debt	Currency	Commodities	Cash	R^2
Bond/stock	−1.28%**	0.36**	0.10**	0.03**	0.31**	−0.06			0.26**	0.97
Large-cap/growth	−2.12*	1.00**		0.11**	−0.52**				0.38*	0.91
Large-cap/value	0.00	0.54**	0.20**	0.04**	0.11*		0.06			0.97
Large-cap/blend	−0.99**	0.64**	0.19**	0.06**		−0.07**			0.17**	0.99
Mid-cap/growth	−5.60**	1.12**		0.22**	−1.32**				1.06**	0.78
Mid-cap/value	0.03	0.57**		0.17**						0.89
Mid-cap/blend	−0.07	0.79**		0.25**	−0.51**					0.90
Small-cap/growth	−7.78**	1.08**		0.29**	−1.70**				1.54**	0.70
Small-cap/value	−2.67	0.69**		0.12**	−0.64**				0.55**	0.71
Small-cap/blend	−4.64**	0.88**		0.20**	−1.11**				0.92**	0.72
High/short	0.14**	0.04**		0.02*	0.33**			0.03		0.91
High/intermediate	−0.68**	0.08**	0.05**		0.61**				0.13**	0.97
High/long	−0.20	0.11*			0.87**					0.77
Medium/short	−0.23	0.08**		0.02**	0.25**				0.09**	0.95
Medium/intermediate	−1.06**		0.10**	0.03**	0.68**				0.22**	0.97
Medium/long	−0.18	0.12**			0.83**					0.83
Low/intermediate	−1.62	0.27**					0.15*		0.35*	0.50
Low/long	−2.24**	0.13*		0.19**	0.55**				0.47**	0.83

Notes: The dependent variable is the average monthly return over 36 months. All 4,776 hedge funds had 36 consecutive monthly returns from January 1994 through December 1996.

*Significant at the 10 percent level.
**Significant at the 5 percent level.

funds because they deal purely with derivatives. This assumption would put the survivorship bias for hedge funds between the 0.5 percent a year for mutual funds and the 3.4 percent a year for CTAs (Fung and Hsieh 1997b). In fact, Brown, Goetzmann, and Ibbotson documented a survivorship bias of 2.75 percent a year for offshore hedge funds.

As to the effect of the bias, in the hedge fund sample reported here, the performance difference between all 1,162 funds and 1,054 surviving funds was found to be 0.84 percent, which could underestimate the true bias for the reasons discussed.

Table 20.5 shows that from January 1992 through December 1996, hedge funds outperformed mutual funds by 3 percent a year. I argue that this performance difference cannot be explained by survivorship bias because, as reported in the literature, mutual funds themselves suffer a bias of 0.5–1.4 percent and because the gross returns of mutual funds must be adjusted for a 1.4 percent front-end load and a 0.9 percent back-end load. Even if one assumes a survivorship bias as high as 3 percent for hedge funds, and as low as 0.5 percent for mutual funds and assumes only about a 1.4 percent front-end load, hedge funds still outperformed mutual funds in the five-year period by 2 percent on an annual basis.

Another aspect is the question of bias against successful hedge funds in the HFR database. Successful hedge funds may have little incentive to report fund information to such data vendors as HFR. They may not need to report the fund information in order to attract more investors; they may want to maintain secrecy about their trading strategies and portfolio holdings; or they may choose to close the fund because it has achieved a critical mass in assets as a result of superior performance.[11] This self-selection bias may partially offset the survivorship bias caused by the disappearance of poorly performing funds.

CONCLUSION

A unique hedge fund database, which included vanished as well as operating funds during the sample period, was used to investigate the relationships among hedge fund performance, risk, and fee structures. The empirical evidence revealed several interesting facts about hedge funds.

- Hedge funds have a special fee structure designed to align managers' incentives with the interest of investors. These incentive fees take effect above the hurdle rates. Managers are awarded an average (median) incentive fee of 16.2 percent (20 percent). In most cases, a high watermark is combined with the hurdle rate. Funds with high watermarks provide significantly better returns than funds without them. In short, the incentive fee structure does align manager and investor interests.
- Average hedge fund returns are related to such factors as size of fund assets, lockup period, and fund age. Average monthly returns are related positively to fund assets and presence of a lockup period; they are related negatively to fund age.
- Onshore funds with offshore equivalents outperform onshore-only and offshore-only funds.
- Hedge fund returns have relatively low correlations with the traditional asset classes. Therefore, hedge funds provide diversification opportunities.
- Four benchmarks (emerging market, the S&P 500, Eurodollar, and U.S. bond returns) are importantly related to mutual fund performance, but factor loadings were found to be scattered for hedge funds' performance. On a risk-adjusted basis, most hedge fund groups earn positive unexplained returns, and some of those unexplained returns are statistically significant.

- Finally, on a risk-adjusted basis, the average hedge fund outperformed the average mutual fund in the period January 1992 through December 1996; this performance difference cannot be explained by survivorship bias. Compared with mutual funds as a whole, hedge funds offer higher Sharpe ratios and better manager skills. Hedge funds have lower market betas but higher total risks than their mutual fund peers. The performance superiority of hedge funds is probably attributable to effective incentive schemes, dynamic and flexible trading strategies, and the variety of financial instruments used by hedge funds.

ACKNOWLEDGMENTS

I would like to thank Utpal Bhatacharya, Hemang Desai, Hua He, Inmoo Lee, Ji-Chai Lin, Ranga Narayanan, Ajai Singh, Mike Stutzer, Sam Thomas, Anand Vijh, and seminar participants at the 1998 European Financial Management Association–Financial Management Association Meeting, the 1998 Financial Management Association Meeting, and Case Western Reserve University for useful comments. I am especially obliged to David Hsieh for constructive comments that improved this article substantially. I am grateful also to Hedge Fund Research and Morningstar for providing the data and to Mustafa Atlihan for his excellent research assistance. Finally, I wish to acknowledge the support of a research grant from the Weatherhead School of Management, Case Western Reserve University.

APPENDIX 20A: HEDGE FUND STRATEGIES

Composite: Using one or several strategies to run more than one fund. Returns are calculated across all funds and managed accounts.

Convertible arbitrage: Purchasing a portfolio of convertible securities and hedging a portion of the equity risk by selling short the underlying common stocks.

Distressed securities: Investing in, and maybe selling short, the securities of companies whose stock prices have been affected by reorganization, bankruptcy, distressed sales, and similar corporate restructurings.

Emerging markets: Investing (primarily going long) in corporate securities or the sovereign debt of developing or emerging countries.

Fixed income: Investing in public and private debt instruments (and their derivatives) with fixed rates and maturities.

Foreign exchange: Investing in currency futures or currency interbank products.

Fund of funds: A combination strategy of investing with multiple managers through funds or managed accounts. The aim is to put together a diversified portfolio of managers to significantly lower the risk (volatility) of investing with an individual manager.

Growth: Investing in equity securities of companies exhibiting earnings acceleration, sustainable and rapid revenue growth, and positive relative price strength; portfolios often hedged by short selling and use of options.

Macro: Making leverage bets on anticipated price movements of stock markets, interest rates, foreign exchange, and physical commodities; managers use top-down global approach.

Market neutral: Exploiting pricing inefficiencies between related securities; neutralizing exposure to market risk by combining long and short positions.

Market timing: Allocating assets among investments by switching into investments that appear to be beginning an uptrend and switching out of investments that appear to be beginning a downtrend.

Merger arbitrage: Investing in event-driven situations, such as leveraged buyouts, mergers, and hostile takeovers (also called "risk arbitrage").

Opportunistic: Investing in opportunities created by significant transactional events, such as spin-offs, mergers and acquisitions, bankruptcy reorganizations, recapitalizations, and share buybacks (also called "corporate life cycle" or "event driven" investing).

Sector: Investing in companies in sectors of the economy (e.g., financial institutions or biotechnology). These funds invest both long and short, incorporating one or more of the other strategies, such as value, growth, or opportunistic, and may use options.

Short selling: Selling a security not owned by the seller; a technique used to take advantage of an anticipated price decline.

Value: Investing in securities that are fundamentally undervalued. Value investors generally take a bottom-up approach, whereby fundamental research is performed on individual companies.

NOTES

1. The only government regulator that requires registration of hedge funds, based on the funds' frequent dealings in exchange-traded futures and options, is the Commodities Futures Trading Commission.
2. An investor's net worth, however, must be no less than $5 million.
3. Monthly mutual fund returns are adjusted for management fees, 12b-1 fees, and other costs automatically deducted from fund assets. Returns are not adjusted, however, for front-end load, back-end load, and redemption fees. Hedge fund data and mutual fund data are apparently thus not directly comparable because hedge fund returns are net of all fees, whereas mutual fund returns are not. The hypothesis of this study was, however, that hedge funds can outperform mutual funds. Therefore, if the net returns of hedge funds outperform the gross returns of mutual funds, those results should hold for the net returns of mutual funds. Of course, the gross returns of mutual funds can be adjusted by deducting the corresponding loads to compare them directly with the net returns of hedge funds.
4. The hurdle rate could be zero or some positive number, such as 10 percent, the T-bill rate plus 2 percent, or LIBOR plus some percentage. The hurdle rate can be as high as 100 percent. The highest incentive fee in the sample was 50 percent.
5. The majority of the funds stated simply "yes" or "no" for hurdle rate and leverage. Therefore, I used binary variables instead of numerical variables for these two features. The leverage ratios of hedge funds hardly exceed 5:1. The 50:1 leverage ratio of Long-Term Capital Management was extremely unusual.
6. If a fund specified that it did not have a hurdle rate, a hurdle rate of zero was assumed.
7. For example, assume that a fund has a hurdle rate of 5 percent and an incentive fee of 20 percent. If the annual fund return is 15 percent (after the fees automatically deducted from fund assets) and the fund has no high watermark provision, the manager can collect 20 percent of the 10 percent (15 percent − 5 percent) profits as an incentive fee. If the fund has a high watermark, however, and it lost 10 percent in the previous year, the

manager can collect nothing because (assuming that a 10 percent loss the previous year is the same in dollar amount as a 10 percent profit this year) the 15 percent annual return just covers the 10 percent loss and the 5 percent hurdle rate.

8. Exceptions are the fund specializing in distressed securities and the sector funds. The distressed securities fund group produced a beta of 0.22, not significantly different from zero; the sector fund group produced a beta of 0.88, not significantly different from 1.00.

9. The efficient frontiers were constructed in such a way that short selling was not allowed among hedge fund or mutual fund strategies.

10. Average front-end loads and back-end loads for all mutual funds were, respectively, 1.4 percent and 0.9 percent a year in my mutual fund data. Hedge funds rarely charge these fees.

11. Hedge funds report their information to data vendors voluntarily. They may be encouraged to do so, however, because such reporting can be an important way of providing information and attracting potential investors. The funds are not allowed to advertise to the public.

REFERENCES

Ackermann, C., R. McEnally, and D. Ravenscraft. 1999. "The Performance of Hedge Funds: Risk, Return and Incentives." *Journal of Finance*, vol. 54, no. 2 (June):833–874.

Brown, S.J., W.N. Goetzmann, and R.G. Ibbotson. 1999. "Offshore Hedge Funds: Survival and Performance, 1989–95." *Journal of Business*, vol. 72, no. 1 (January):91–117.

Brown, S.J., W.N. Goetzmann, R.G. Ibbotson, and S.A. Ross. 1992. "Survivorship Bias in Performance Studies." *Review of Financial Studies*, vol. 5, no. 4 (Winter):553–580.

Chevalier, J., and G. Ellison. 1999. "Are Some Mutual Fund Managers Better than Others? Cross-Sectional Patterns in Behavior and Performance." *Journal of Finance*, vol. 54, no. 2 (June):875–899.

Elton, E., M. Gruber, and C. Blake. 1996. "The Persistence of Risk-Adjusted Mutual Fund Performance." *Journal of Business*, vol. 69, no. 2 (April):133–157.

Fung, W., and D.A. Hsieh. 1997a. "Empirical Characteristics of Dynamic Trading Strategies: The Case of Hedge Funds." *Review of Financial Studies*, vol. 10, no. 2 (Summer):275–302.

———. 1997b. "Survivorship Bias and Investment Style in the Returns of CTAs." *Journal of Portfolio Management*, vol. 24, no. 1 (Fall):30–41.

Grinblatt, M., and S. Titman. 1989. "Mutual Fund Performance: An Analysis of Quarterly Portfolio Holdings." *Journal of Business*, vol. 62, no. 3 (July):393–416.

Lakonishok, J., A. Shleifer, and R.W. Vishny. 1994. Contrarian Investment, Extrapolation, and Risk." *Journal of Finance*, vol. 49, no. 5 (December):1541–1578.

Malkiel, B.G. 1995. "Returns from Investing in Equity Mutual Funds, 1971 to 1991." *Journal of Finance*, vol. 50, no. 2 (June):549–572.

Sharpe, W.F. 1992. "Asset Allocation: Management Style and Performance Measurement." *Journal of Portfolio Management*, vol. 18, no. 2 (Winter):7–19.

CHAPTER 21

FUNDS OF HEDGE FUNDS

Performance and Persistence

Stan Beckers

*The funds of hedge funds return profiles can largely be replicated through a judi-
cious combination of some simple directional market exposures. Although funds of
hedge funds do deliver alpha, this alpha is "polluted" with easily replicated betas. A
similar conclusion can be arrived at through a Sharpe style analysis of fund of hedge
fund returns: The largest proportion of the returns is accounted for by the hedge fund
styles. Although the selection returns are small, they do show significant persistence
through time, but no discernable value is added through style rotation.*

Investors want to know what to expect when investing in hedge funds. As is very often the
case, hedge fund investors pay for what they get but do not necessarily get what they pay for.
In this presentation, I will show empirical evidence describing the pros and cons of hedge
fund investing, particularly as seen through the lens of funds of funds.

The analysis is based largely on the fund-of-funds sector because that sector has been
investing in and amassing data on a diversified cross-section of hedge funds for the past
10–15 years. The information is in the public domain; thus, it is easy to access and less sensitive to various biases (survivorship, *ex post* history, self-reporting) that mar the various hedge
fund return databases. One overriding conclusion is that hedge funds, in general, and funds of
funds, in particular, deliver a little bit of alpha and more beta than one might wish for, including both traditional beta and alternative beta. Intelligent investment in hedge funds, therefore, requires an ability to differentiate skill-based alpha returns from the beta returns that
can be accessed more cheaply elsewhere. The question also arises as to whether good historical
alpha delivery has any relevance for the future.

Reprinted from *CFA Institute Conference Proceedings Quarterly* (June 2007):25–33.

I have organized this presentation around various useful steps that will help in understanding and dissecting (fund of hedge) fund returns. I designed a simple, multifactor model to identify fundamental (or beta) factors within fund-of-funds returns. I then detach such factors and determine how much alpha remains. At Barclays Global Investors, we also investigate to what extent these alphas show any persistence through time. Next, I do some traditional Sharpe style analysis and determine how much of the fund-of-hedge-fund returns is attributable to the various hedge fund styles. I then test whether manager selection adds any value beyond style selection and whether this manager selection has persistence. Finally, I conclude with a brief discussion of multistrategy funds and their possible role in the next generation of the hedge fund market.

GROWTH OF FUNDS OF FUNDS

Funds of funds provide investors (typically institutional investors) with a diversified cross-section of hedge funds. Therefore, fund-of-funds returns do not suffer from the problems that are mostly associated with individual hedge fund returns, such as survivorship bias, instant history bias, and self-selection bias. Furthermore, fund-of-funds data provide a reasonably large sample with a history that goes back 15 years or so. In 1990, fewer than 100 funds of funds existed; by 2000, more than 600 had been established; and by 2006, the number of such funds had increased to more than 1,600. Such growth has been driven, at least in part, by institutional investors who favor funds of funds to obtain exposure to the hedge fund world.

ADDED VALUE FROM FUNDS OF FUNDS

Unfortunately, when one looks for the value added by funds of funds, the initial data are not especially encouraging. Using data from Hedge Fund Research (HFR), I have compared the returns of a weighted composite index of hedge funds (HFRI Fund Weighted Composite Index) with a fund-of-funds composite index (HFRI Fund of Funds Composite Index). Comparing the 10 years from 1997 to 2006, I found that the average return for a typical hedge fund was 10.96 percent and the average return for a typical fund of funds was 8.18 percent—a difference of 2.78 percentage points (pps) in favor of the hedge fund index. A large part of this difference is caused by fees, with a typical fund of funds charging 1 and 10 (1 percent of assets and 10 percent of the profits), which accounts for perhaps 2 pps of the difference. Nevertheless, the data from this perspective indicate that funds of funds are not particularly successful at selecting the best performing hedge funds from the broader universe.

When I segmented data from 1991 to 2005 into bottom-quartile, median, and top-quartile performers for both funds of funds and individual hedge funds, I again found that the value-added contribution from the hedge fund selection by funds of funds was not particularly impressive. Only in the bottom quartile did funds of funds outperform the (bottom quartile) index of individual hedge funds—and by no great margin. The median and top-quartile funds of hedge funds, in contrast, significantly underperformed their single hedge fund (median and top quartile) counterparts.

When I looked for value on a risk-adjusted basis, however, the results were more encouraging. The typical fund of funds' median Sharpe ratio was a healthy 1.08, whereas the median for an individual hedge fund was 0.9. Some value was also added, according to the Sharpe ratio, for both the bottom and the top quartiles. Furthermore, the typical Sharpe ratio for long-only exposure to equity and fixed-income markets is roughly 0.4, so achieving a Sharpe ratio of 1.08 explains at least some of the appeal of funds of funds.

From January 1994 to January 2005, the overall average fund-of-funds Sharpe ratio for a trailing 12-month period was 1.33, and the ratio was fairly healthy over the entire period. Even the bottom-quartile funds of funds delivered attractive Sharpe ratios for much of the period. Based simply on their risk-adjusted returns, funds of funds have done a good job.

FUND-OF-FUNDS PERFORMANCE

To determine how well this positive outlook would hold up under more detailed scrutiny, I developed a simple, multifactor model to measure the return characteristics of funds of funds. The model uses eight simple directional market exposures—the fundamental factors—that all institutional investors have in their portfolios to one extent or another. I report for each of these fundamental factors the median, mean, standard deviation, skew, and kurtosis of the monthly returns as well as the percentage of time they are significant. This significance is calculated across all funds of funds using 36-month moving-window regressions, shown in Table 21.1. Interestingly, each of the fundamental variables was negatively skewed and had high kurtosis over the sample period. Later, I will argue that the skewness and kurtosis of hedge fund returns are largely attributable to skewness and kurtosis of these eight traditional betas (or explanatory variables).

TABLE 21.1   Monthly Return Characteristics of Systematic Factors

Explanatory Variable	Percentage of Time Significant	Median	Mean	Standard Deviation	Skew	Kurtosis
Intercept	38.94%					
Russell 1000 Index	19.94	0.93%	0.34%	4.30%	−0.82	1.29
MSCI Emerging Markets Index	10.51	0.42	−0.17	6.87	−1.23	3.97
MSCI World ex U.S. Index	9.65	0.30	0.05	4.22	−0.61	0.63
U.S. small–large[a]	28.94	−0.23	−0.03	3.53	−0.02	3.89
U.S. value–growth[b]	11.45	0.00	−0.09	1.86	−0.82	4.46
Lehman Brothers U.S. Corporate High-Yield Index	23.39	−0.46	−0.36	2.21	−0.01	2.99
Lehman Brothers Global Emerging Markets Index	6.74	0.27	−0.31	4.32	−3.49	26.12
Goldman Sachs Commodity Index	4.80	0.52	0.32	5.74	−0.04	0.36

Source: Based on data in Beckers, Curds, and Weinberger (2006).
[a] Russell 2000–Russell 1000.
[b] Russell 1000 Growth–Russell 1000.

I found that these betas account for approximately 38 percent of the fund-of-hedge-fund return variability. (The overall median adjusted R^2 was 38.90 percent; the overall average adjusted R^2 was 38.14 percent.) Adding in some nontraditional or alternative betas—such as volatility, currency carry, momentum, and liquidity factors—in addition to the eight traditional betas, I found that the R^2 could be increased to 60–65 percent.

Fortunately, after removing the return associated with the traditional betas, some return is still available. Figure 21.1 shows the evolution of typical fund-of-funds alpha. With a 12-month moving window, the overall average alpha is 6.88 percent. The solid line shows the mean return, the dashed line shows the median return, and the shaded area represents the range between the top and bottom quartiles. Alpha has decreased markedly since 2000 and has generally hovered between 0 and 5 percent since the end of 2001. But even the bottom-quartile funds of funds have delivered significantly positive alpha for long periods of time. During the recent past, funds of funds have delivered little negative alpha.

Alpha Performance

After taking out the beta characteristics, I then considered the monthly average return characteristics of alpha and found it to be normally distributed. This result is intuitively reassuring because I would expect that a truly skill-based return should not be anything other than normally distributed. Statistically, it tells me that I have indeed removed most of the sources of skewness and kurtosis that can be attributed to fundamental factors found in beta.

But raw returns lack the context that risk-adjusted returns provide. So, still using the simple multifactor model to decompose the fund-of-hedge-fund returns, I examined the information ratio. The information ratio is the ratio of the alpha divided by the volatility of the alpha. An information ratio of 0.5 would typically position a long-only manager in the top quartile amongst his or her peers. In contrast, from January 1994 to July 2005, the overall

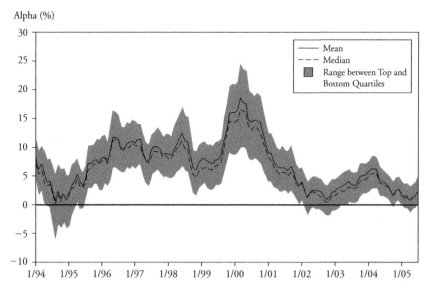

FIGURE 21.1   Evolution of Typical Fund-of-Funds Alpha: Multifactor Model, January 1994–July 2005

Source: Based on data in Beckers, Curds, and Weinberger (2006).

average information ratio for funds of funds was a healthy 1.98—not the top quartile, but the overall average. Even during the past several years, as alpha has declined, the information ratio has remained somewhere between 1.0 and 2.0. Thus, the alpha decline has been accompanied by, and can largely be explained by, a decline in volatility. The cross-sectional dispersion in the market has been fairly low in the recent past, so on a risk-adjusted basis, funds of funds have continued to deliver healthy alphas. Even the bottom-quartile funds of funds have, on average, produced healthy information ratios, which is an encouraging result.

Beta Drag

Unfortunately, the return contribution from the eight fundamental beta factors was, to say the least, disappointing. As I discussed earlier, approximately 38 percent of fund-of-funds return variability is attributable to those fundamental factors. At the same time, exposure to these fundamental factors has actually reduced overall fund-of-funds returns by an average of 92 bps a year. Thus, funds of funds are offering 38 percent of their risk in the form of beta that investors can buy more cheaply elsewhere and that, on average, has detracted from the performance.

Table 21.2 presents this analysis in a simpler, one-factor framework, using the S&P 500 Index as the explanatory variable for fund-of-funds returns. This table differentiates between the exposure of funds of funds to the S&P 500 during months when the S&P 500 was up and the exposure when the S&P 500 was down. As the top row indicates, the beta of funds of funds was 0.07 when the S&P 500 was up and it was 0.19 when the S&P 500 was down. The difference of 0.12 is statistically significant and demonstrates that funds of funds take the wrong risk at the wrong time. They have more exposure to the market when the market goes down and less exposure to the market when the market goes up, thus reinforcing the message that investors should not be purchasing S&P 500 exposure from hedge funds or funds of funds.

To further illustrate the effects of beta on funds of funds, I studied a fund of funds that includes a blue-chip list of 36 hedge fund managers, as shown in Table 21.3. Many of these hedge funds are highly desirable funds that are typically "hard closed" (i.e., they do not take in any more investor money). I tracked the funds' returns from January 2003 through December 2005. Note, however, that I used a slightly different mix of systematic risk factors to analyze these returns—credit exposure, asset-backed exposure, non-U.S. equity,

TABLE 21.2   Median Fund-of-Funds Return and S&P 500 Return in Up and Down Markets, January 1994–July 2005

Measure	Intercept	S&P 500 Up	S&P 500 Down	Up–Down Difference	Adjusted R^2
Excess return	0.61	0.07	0.19	−0.12	25.09%
	(4.42)	(1.56)	(5.53)	(−1.94)	
Common factor return	0.18	0.05	0.2	−0.15	34.13
	(1.61)	(1.45)	(7.13)	(−2.85)	
Specific return	0.43	0.01	−0.01	0.02	−1.10
	(5.25)	(0.59)	(−0.45)	(0.62)	

Source: Based on data in Beckers, Curds, and Weinberger (2006).
Note: t-Statistics are in parentheses.

TABLE 21.3   A Fund of Hedge Funds

Composition

Holding	Weight	Holding	Weight
AlphaGen Capella Fund	3.11%	Moore Global Investments	5.42%
Blue Mountain Credit Alter Fund Ltd.	2.34	Pacific and General Investments Inc.	0.98
Bluecrest Capital International Ltd. Class F USD	1.97	Pharo Arbitrage Fund	3.89
Boyer Allan Pacific Fund Inc.	3.42	Pharo Macro Fund Ltd. Srs 10/05	1.05
Cantillon Europe Ltd. Class B	4.76	PK Japan Class Fund	4.46
Caxton Equity Growth (BVI) Class B	3.06	Plexus Fund Limited	2.30
Creo Asia + Long–Short Equity O/S Feeder	0.62	Rockbay Capital Offshore Fund Ltd.	1.44
D.E. Shaw Oculus International Fund	2.31	Rubicon Global	4.92
Eckhardt Futures (Cayman) Ltd.	1.43	SCP Overseas Fund Ltd.	3.63
Egerton European Dollar Fund	4.30	St. Geoffrey Equity Linked Note	4.80
Eureka (Euro) Fund Limited	2.97	Strategic Value Credit Opp. Fund Ser. A1	0.99
Evolution Fund Ltd. Class M1 Srs	2.00	Sunrise Capital Diversified Ltd.	1.98
Expressway Partners Ltd.	2.15	Tewksbury Investment Fund	3.89
Fairfield Cap Management Japan Fund Class B	2.68	Thales International Fund Limited	2.32
Force Capital Ltd Non-Hot Service 12/05	1.00	The Raptor Global Fund Class B	2.06
Jolly Roger Offshore Fund Ltd. Class C 12/05	1.05	Tomahawk Fund USD Shares	3.52
JWM Global Macro II Fund Ltd. Srs TBA	1.43	Tudor BVI Global Fund Ltd. Class B	7.75
Moore Global Fixed Income	2.32	York European Opp Unit Trust A	1.90

Performance measures, January 2003–December 2005

R^2	76.65%		
Adjusted R^2	70.81		
	Coefficient		t-Statistic
Alpha	−3.86%		−1.322
Credit	0.189		2.188
Asset backed	−0.788		−3.335
Non-U.S. equity	0.343		5.083
U.S. equity	0.007		3.263
Volatility	−0.195		−1.428
Non-U.S. bond	1.149		4.344

Source: BGI Research.

TABLE 21.4 Persistence in Fund-of-Funds Returns

Measure	Correlation	*t*-Statistic	Q1/Q1 Transition Probability
Excess return	3.43	1.74	36.43
Common factor return	12.13	6.19	27.91
Alpha	26.45	13.90	42.33
Sharpe ratio	29.17	15.46	44.65
Common factor ratio	7.80	3.97	23.57
Information ratio	44.07	24.88	49.92

Source: Based on data in Beckers, Curds, and Weinberger (2006).

U.S. equity, volatility, and non-U.S. bond. These six factors, plus alpha, had an adjusted R^2 of 70.81 percent, thereby explaining most of the return variability of this fund of funds. Of greater significance, however, is the fact that the coefficient of the alpha is actually negative by almost 4 percent. This means that the returns generated by the systematic risk factors alone exceeded the returns generated by the hypothetical fund of funds by that amount.

Persistence of Information Ratio

In Table 21.4, I examine the persistence of returns earned by funds of funds. This table presents the correlation between the previous 36-month period and the next 12-month period for excess return, common factor return (which is return attributable to the eight fundamental beta factors used previously), alpha, risk-adjusted Sharpe ratio, risk-adjusted common factor ratio, and risk-adjusted information ratio. The correlations range from a not statistically significant 3.43 for the persistence of excess return to a highly statistically significant 44.07 for the persistence of the information ratio (a *t*-statistic of 25 places its statistical significance well beyond the realm of pure chance). The rightmost column of Table 21.4 (titled "Q1/Q1 Transition Probability") provides the probability that the past provides a reliable indicator of future performance. The "no persistence" threshold is 25 percent; that is, a first-quartile performer in one time period faces no better than a one in four chance of remaining a first-quartile performer. These results indicate that historically successful (top quartile) producers of information ratios have an almost 50 percent chance of continuing to produce a reasonably healthy (top quartile) information ratio in the future.

Persistence drops off for the other measures—slightly for the Sharpe ratio and steeply for excess return. The reason, once again, is the effect of the fundamental beta factors, which hedge funds do not typically have skill in choosing. They dilute a fund's persistence and the predictive value of its historical track record. To the extent possible, therefore, investors should buy only alpha from funds of funds and thus avoid the contaminating factors.

EFFECTS OF STYLE AND MANAGER CHOICE

Figure 21.2 compares the correlations of hedge funds within a given style. In it, I have grouped individual hedge funds within a given HFR style—emerging market, equity, relative

Average Correlation (%)

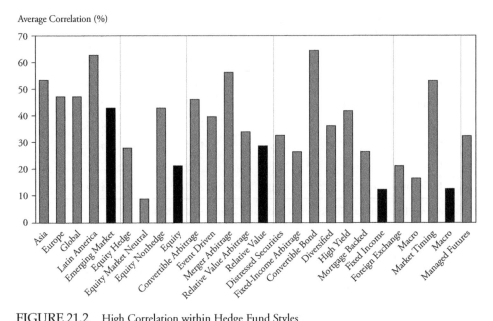

FIGURE 21.2   High Correlation within Hedge Fund Styles

Source: BGI Research.

value, fixed income, macro, and so on—and measured the correlation of the returns within a given bucket. The correlations go as high as 65 percent for hedge funds in the convertible arbitrage category and as low as about 10 percent in the equity market neutral group. A high correlation between the returns within a style bucket means that all those funds are doing much the same thing, which also means that what they are doing is not particularly skillful. Skill is something that is unique, creative, and manager specific. Doing the same thing points to commonality, which, in turn, indicates that investors are paying for something they can probably buy more easily and cheaply elsewhere.

Let us now consider the extent to which fund-of-funds returns can be duplicated in a more or less passive manner using Sharpe's style analysis to determine the optimal weights across the various style indices. The alternative to buying a fund of funds would be to buy the individual style components, such as convertible arbitrage, emerging markets, and so on. How much of fund-of-funds returns is explained by pure style exposure? The fund-of-funds return data for January 1998 to December 2006 show that pure style exposure explains a mean of about 70 percent and a median of about 65 percent of total fund-of-funds returns.

Choosing Managers vs. Style

A large proportion of the fund-of-hedge-fund returns can, therefore, be accounted for by their style exposure. Manager selection within each style, however, plays a relatively minor role. In particular, I looked at the annual mean and median returns of funds of funds from January 1998 through December 2006. The average mean return over that period was 9.81 percent, with 9.28 percent arising from style exposure and only 0.53 percent, or 53 bps, of value being added by manager selection. The average median manager selection return was even worse at a meager 4 bps. Obviously, then, if investors could buy or replicate the various

Return (%)

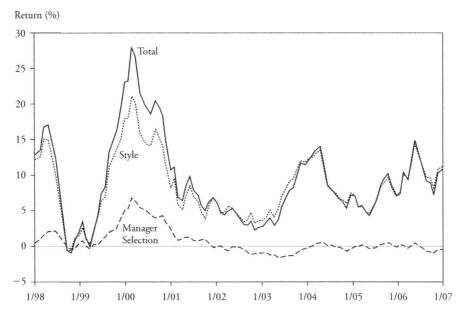

FIGURE 21.3   Twelve-Month Moving-Window Mean Return, January 1998–December 2006

Source: BGI Research.

hedge fund style returns, they could largely duplicate the typical fund-of-hedge-fund return. The procedure would consist of finding the optimal combination of hedge fund style indices that explained the fund-of-hedge-fund returns over the past three years (36 months). The investor would then buy this combination and hold it for the next month. Repeating this process on a monthly basis would have yielded a return that would have been virtually indistinguishable from the average fund-of-hedge-fund return over the past 10 years.

The 12-month moving window of mean returns shown in Figure 21.3 further dramatizes the lack of value added from manager selection, which is represented by the dashed line that creeps along the bottom of the graph. The value added from manager selection has been effectively zero during any 12-month period for the past five years. Value added from manager selection peaked at about 5 percent in 2000–2001, but little value has been added since 2002.

When I examined the interquartile ranges of manager selection, the situation did not improve noticeably. Since January 2002, the top-quartile funds of funds typically added 1–2 percent on an annualized basis from manager selection and the bottom quartile lost 2–4 percent.

The managers of funds of funds argue that such analysis misses the fact that they add value through their style timing. They are able to predict, they argue, when convertible arbitrage will go out of fashion or when fixed-income value managers will hit the jackpot, and they adjust their exposures accordingly throughout the year. To test this argument, I took the annual mean and median style returns and added a third set of returns—cap-weighted style returns—to compare with the previous two sets of returns. To do so, I determined the cap-weighted exposures that each hedge fund style represented within the universe of all hedge funds at the start of each year. I then assumed that the manager bought each style at the start of the year in proportion to its capitalization weight and held that weight constant throughout the year (adjusted for return differentials between the styles as time progresses). The results show that over the 10-year period being tested, had managers held their annual hedge fund style exposures proportional to the capitalization weights, they would have earned a return of 10.57 percent, whereas the mean fund-of-funds style return was 9.28 and the median style return was 9.03 percent. In other words, all evidence points to the fact that the active variation of hedge fund style exposures detracted value from the capitalization-weighted benchmark, implying that the value added from style timing for the typical fund of hedge funds was actually negative.

Value-Added Manager Persistence

Amid my less than glowing findings, I did find a silver lining. Those funds of funds that are better than average at manager selection appear to be able to add value consistently through time. As in my examination of information ratio persistence, I determined the transition probabilities between the top-quartile fund-of-hedge-funds manager selection return over the previous 36-month period and its next 12-month period manager selection return (on a risk-adjusted basis). For the 1997–2005 period, the transition probabilities ranged from 37.33 percent to 48.33 percent, with an overall average of 42.50 percent—all of which are quite healthy percentages. (Recall that 25 percent is the point of no persistence.) My conclusion is that there is some skill within the fund-of-funds community, but it is in manager selection, not in the timing of style choices, keeping in mind though that the absolute magnitude of the manager selection return is low.

PROSPECTS FOR MULTISTRATEGY FUNDS

The typical argument in favor of multistrategy funds is that they provide broad access to various hedge fund styles, as do funds of funds, but that they are much more nimble than funds of funds because they can switch quickly from one style to another. Certainly, the mean and median returns of multistrategy funds (13.24 percent and 11.12 percent, respectively) compare favorably with the comparable mean and median fund-of-funds returns (9.81 percent and 9.05 percent, respectively). But the multistrategy classification has a short history, and it suffers from self-selection bias. All hedge funds classify themselves, and a growing number of funds are calling themselves "multistrategy" funds because that is the classification that is attracting the money. The results for "multistrategy" funds must, therefore, be interpreted with caution. Even so, when I examined the data on style returns, I found no evidence that multistrategy funds are any better at timing styles than are funds of funds.

CONCLUSION

Based on the research and analysis I have done on funds of funds, I would offer the following conclusions.

Funds of funds have large and persistent systematic risk exposures that, on average, have detracted from their performance. Nevertheless, funds of funds have, on average, delivered significant risk-adjusted alpha. Such alpha has been persistent over time, but pure, uncontaminated alpha is difficult to find.

Hedge fund styles account for virtually all the returns earned by funds of funds. At the same time, evidence indicates that neither funds of funds nor multistrategy funds can successfully time the hedge fund styles. Furthermore, manager selection appears to add little value, but for funds of funds that have successfully added value in this manner, there is some evidence of persistence.

Finally, investors should educate themselves about what they are buying because buying beta disguised as alpha is an expensive proposition.

QUESTION AND ANSWER SESSION

Question: Are the data you are using gross of fees or net of fees?

Beckers: They are all net of fees.

Question: Given the nonnormality of hedge fund returns, is it valid to use the Sharpe ratio as a measure of risk?

Beckers: You are right in saying that nonnormality invalidates the use of the Sharpe ratio as a measure of risk-adjusted return. But the alpha component of hedge fund returns is normal. Therefore, the information ratio is appropriate to use, but the Sharpe ratio is not.

Question: What is an appropriate benchmark for funds of funds that does not include other hedge funds?

Beckers: Cash. The only relevant benchmark is cash, both for hedge funds themselves and for funds of funds. Comparing fund-of-funds returns or hedge fund returns with the S&P 500 or any other index is nonsense. To be more specific, if you are buying hedge funds in the hope of buying skill-based or alpha return, then you should compare such skill-based return only with cash. You should expect hedge funds to outperform cash without any significant market exposures.

Question: Are there any significant track records that argue for quant replication over old-fashioned hedge fund investing?

Beckers: One organization, Partners Group in Switzerland, claims to have a one-year track record in hedge fund index replication and to be running about $800 million in this program. But why would anyone want to buy such a product? If a hedge fund index replication engine uses, for example, the S&P 500, the Lehman Brothers Global Aggregate Bond Index, and the difference between the Wilshire 3000 Index and the Wilshire 1000 as building blocks, then it represents nothing more than the combination of things you probably already own. There is nothing magical, as I have just shown, about the way in which hedge funds combine some simple factors. In fact, they are not particularly good at it. So, why replicate a hedge fund index that already has too much beta and not enough alpha?

REFERENCES

Beckers, Stan, Ross Curds, and Simon Weinberger. 2006. "Funds of Hedge Funds Take the Wrong Risks." *Investment Insights*, vol. 9, no. 4 (September).

CHAPTER 22

HEDGE FUND DUE DILIGENCE

Putting Together the Pieces of the Mosaic Helps Reveal Operational Risks

Cynthia Harrington, CFA

This chapter addresses the following key points:
- *Lack of transparency compounds hedge fund risk.*
- *Investors can verify information from manager with independent sources.*
- *First step is evaluating character of the fund manager.*
- *Global regulators are seeking additional disclosure requirements.*

Hedge funds are hot. Offering attractive diversification opportunities, the alternative investments are welcome at more and more investment parties. But because of some wild and destructive past behavior, hedge fund managers are asked to reveal more about their businesses to win investors' confidence. The process involves determining whether the stated performance is real and whether the manager can be trusted to operate his or her business ethically and efficiently.

PAYING CAREFUL ATTENTION

In addition to the high-profile collapses of hedge funds, investors must heed another industry trend. "There's a greater burden on investors today because so many of the good funds are closed," says Majed Muhtaseb, Ph.D., CFA, professor of finance, California State Polytechnic Institute, Pomona, and an independent hedge fund researcher. "That narrows the universe of available funds and removes a good chunk from the top, lowering the average quality."

Reprinted from *CFA Magazine* (May/June 2003):54–55.

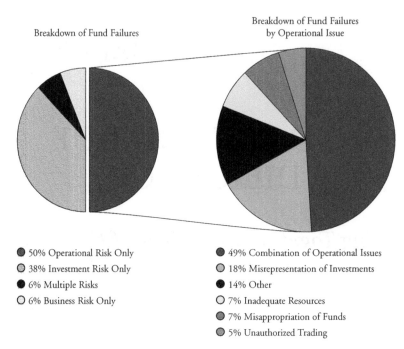

Breakdown of Fund Failures

Breakdown of Fund Failures
by Operational Issue

● 50% Operational Risk Only
◐ 38% Investment Risk Only
● 6% Multiple Risks
○ 6% Business Risk Only

● 49% Combination of Operational Issues
○ 18% Misrepresentation of Investments
● 14% Other
○ 7% Inadequate Resources
● 7% Misappropriation of Funds
◐ 5% Unauthorized Trading

FIGURE 22.1   Understanding and Mitigating Operational Risk in Hedge Fund Investments

Source: Capco, March 2003.

In fact, according to research conducted by Rye, N.Y., USA-based Tremont Advisers, Inc., more than 10 percent of hedge funds closed their doors in 2002 and more than 800 of the 6,000 funds are predicted to close this year. The reasons are varied. Some lost investors and couldn't support their strategies on reduced assets. Some blew up due to fraud or inadequate risk controls. Other managers decided to cash in and retire to their beach homes.

Funds that close at the manager's discretion are less likely to harm investors. In contrast, those that slam the door due to investment losses or operational problems usually create losses for investors. A study conducted by Capco (see Figure 22.1), a global services and technology solutions provider to the financial services industry, suggests that operational problems alone caused more than half of fund failures in the 20 years included in the study. Accordingly, due diligence procedures that can spotlight possible sources of operational risk can save investors plenty.

SHINING A BRIGHT LIGHT

The challenge is that hedge funds are unregulated and seek to keep trading strategies secret. Managers straddle a fine line between the investor's need to know and their need to protect their intellectual capital. While financial statements, monthly performance returns, manager bios, and a description of the trading style are readily handed out to qualified prospective clients, investors want more.

Beyond these easily accessible documents, what investors seek is an independent view of the manager's investment history and operational efficacy. "As a hedge fund administrator, we're getting many more requests for the kind of information we can provide," says Guy Castranova, president of DPM, LLC, a fund administrator based in Somerset, N.J., USA. "Investors and prospective investors in our client firms are concerned about control procedures, risk control, and what the administrative staff provides for the hedge fund."

DPM provides daily investment accounting, financial reporting, multiple broker and trader reconciliation, systems-generated net asset value calculations, risk transparency, and other fund administration services to more than 250 onshore and offshore hedge funds.

Yet, while audited financial statements promise an independent view of a hedge fund, two conditions diminish the effectiveness of the external audit process. The biggest is that audits are annual. The financial condition of a hedge fund could change before the audit work papers are completed, let alone a quarter or two later. The second is the effect of "Enronitis." Confidence in financial statements is down, even if they reflect GAAP or IASB compliance. "Clients get some comfort from audit reports, but really the burden is on the administrator to provide a level of detail needed for due diligence," says Castranova. "However, our experience is that the scope of audits has increased, especially in the OTC world."

Valuing the fund's holdings is a particularly challenging part of the audit. Annual frequency is a problem. Plus, while funds with highly liquid, actively traded positions can be valued with confidence, those holding illiquid assets without a ready market price are less exact. "This is where the auditors are going to spend more of their time," says Castranova. "But the possible response to an error has a great effect on the investor's assets. Investors just have to realize what they own in a fund with illiquid securities."

CREATING A MOSAIC

Mount Lucas Management Corp. is a client firm of administrator DPM. Based in Princeton, N.J., USA, Mount Lucas manages a hedge fund as well as a commodity pool registered with the Commodity Futures Trading Commission. DPM handles all back office functions for all of Mount Lucas' funds. "Prospective clients ask and receive the GAAP audit package," says James Mehling, CFA, Mount Lucas' chief operating officer. "But they also ask for additional years of audited financials, and monthly performance for as far back as they can get it. Then we can set them up to drill down into our financials, the ability of which also comes from DPM."

Fund of funds manager Tremont Advisers starts with the audited financials, then compares numbers between the onshore and the independent reports from administrators for offshore funds, and conducts a strong peer group analysis to verify the reported numbers. "We don't look at just one particular thing, but we create a mosaic that forms the due diligence process," says Barry Colvin, CFA, president and chief investment officer of Tremont.

Colvin's group deepened its ability to monitor fund managers with a tool developed with RiskMetrics Group. The program allows Tremont to track individual managers by size of positions, sector exposure, and amount of leverage, as well as gross exposure to short and long sides of the market. Tremont then brings the analysis to the portfolio level and tracks leverage and amount of gamma. "We can look across the spectrum of risk, see what's going on overall, and make sure each manager is complying with his or her own investment standards," says Colvin. "It gives us an indication of what's going on daily so we don't get caught flat-footed by unexpected changes."

One place investors are unlikely to get independent verification is through the verification of compliance with AIMR-PPS® standards. "First they didn't like the all-cash returns requirement. When that was dropped, we saw some hedge fund managers looking at AIMR compliance," says Matt Forstenhausler, head of investment performance services, Ernst & Young, New York, N.Y., USA, and a member of the Verification Subcommittee of AIMR's Investment Performance Council, "but just when it was safe to get back in the water, the new leveraged guidance statement came out. They're not excited about having to disclose that information."

"Hedge funds would also argue that no two hedge funds are the same, so attempts to standardize disclosures and reporting aren't going to be very successful," adds Forstenhausler. "They're going to provide what investors demand."

The importance of the character of the fund manager is another reason AIMR standards may not be relevant to hedge fund due diligence. "The point is, an investor is going to give this manager his or her money for a year," says Forstenhausler. "If the investor feels the need to verify what the manager is saying, how much does the investor really trust the manager anyway?"

HANDSHAKE BUSINESS

While currently not required to register with the SEC, Mount Lucas Management is one of many hedge fund managers registered as a registered investment adviser. Open for public viewing on the Investment Adviser Registration Depository (IARD) are the standard disclosures about the background of the principals, the percent of the fund owned by principals, the size of the fund, and their types of clients.

Despite the easy look into the fund, investors all come for an on-site visit. "They want to meet the principals, to find out for themselves the personalities and the culture of the firm," says Mehling. "They also want to verify exactly how much the principals committed of their own assets to the fund."

Adding further credence to the consensus that the hedge fund industry is largely a "handshake business," Tremont Advisers relies heavily on personal contact with the managers in their fund of funds. "The quantitative analysis and work are all just tools," says Colvin. "The due diligence and monitoring of work is really done on the qualitative side. We want to investigate the people's backgrounds, their risk exposures, and everything else about them to validate what we've seen and heard."

CHAPTER 23

PUTTING RISK MEASUREMENT IN CONTEXT

Why One Size Does Not Fit All

Cynthia Harrington, CFA

This chapter addresses the following key points:

- *Different risk measures succeed for different applications.*
- *Compensation structures are changing to reward those who meet risk budgets.*
- *Important risk information is often found in a combination of statistics, not a single measure.*

At the core of portfolio management is the desire to limit risk and maximize return. Achieving that lofty goal isn't always so easy, however, largely because risk is difficult to define as well as to measure. But professionals continually try to improve on ways to look at risk in the attempt to avoid it, to manage it, and to talk with clients about it (see Table 23.1).

"The world is becoming more scientific," says Daniel Cashion, CFA, director, BARRA, Inc., in New York, NY, USA. "Looking for the repeatable process of measuring portfolio risk is one of those areas that has improved dramatically over 20 years ago."

With the improved processes comes an awareness that no single risk statistic stands on its own. Some work for some asset classes, some for more than one, and others work best in combinations of more than one. A discussion of the usefulness of risk-adjusted returns must set the individual measurements in their proper contexts.

In fact, when used for certain asset classes, risk measures may have fans yet be decried by others. Mean variance works quite nicely for efficient classes such as large-cap value stocks with no derivatives. But for those with return distributions that don't fall on a beautifully

---

Reprinted from *CFA Magazine* (March/April 2004):44–45.

symmetrical bell curve, those that are lumped to the left or right of mean or have long tails or fat tails, new tools are needed.

MAKING THE GRADE

Primary among the non-normal assets are hedge funds. "When looking at things the least bit complicated, for instance, any manager with an alpha greater than 5 or 6, there's likely something unusual about the return," says Lawrence Pohlman, PhD, director of research for PanAgora Asset Management. "Investors should look at more than a couple of summary statistics in this case."

Pohlman's Boston-based firm manages US$11 billion and promotes strategies that distinguish alpha from beta in overall portfolio management. "Say an event happens three times in the recent past that, on a normal distribution, happened three times every 10,000 years," says Pohlman. "Evaluating the reasons for the increased frequency is an opportunity to do some education on mean standard normal distributions."

Professionals give better grades to some risk measures than others for assets with non-normal distributions. Cashion, for instance, ranks beta a C+ for normally distributed assets but a B+/A for hedge funds. "Because hedge funds look for market neutral exposure, the measure provides greater informational value," he says.

The original risk-adjusted performance statistic gets mixed grades as well. William Sharpe revolutionized the investment world in 1952 with his measure of risk as volatility versus historical returns above the risk-free rate. The Sharpe ratio is easy to use and easy to calculate, so it is in wide use even after 50 years. But for many, it's not enough. "The Sharpe ratio gets a C−," says Cashion. "It can't be applied equally across asset classes. A 0.8 Sharpe on bonds means something different than a 0.8 ratio on equities."

To some, the information ratio (IR) solves this problem. The IR displays the relationship of the returns over a benchmark and the volatility of those returns. "Unlike the Sharpe ratio, the IR means the same thing for bonds and stocks," says Cashion.

To others, the IR falls into the category of the "worst" measures. "Lots of mistakes are made from the use of the IR," says Pohlman.

As with other statistics, the IR's future may not resemble historical data. The IR may also not be useful as a single indicator. "If one manager's IR is 3 and another's is 1, the difference is significant," says Pohlman. "But, I wouldn't count on the difference between a 1.5 and a 2 unless I had lots of other information on the managers."

The other deterrent to usefulness of the IR goes back to hedge funds and the use of derivatives. While options and futures can provide excess returns in certain periods, these managers don't do a great job generating returns versus risk. "Every so often, they get their clocks cleaned," says Pohlman. "Investors have to look beyond one risk measure to see what managers are really doing to produce returns."

LEVERAGING RISK

The IR can work well in conjunction with the technique of risk budgeting. Risk budgets allocate tracking error, or deviance from the benchmark, among the different asset classes. The use of leverage to increase the IR can thus be managed through the risk allocations. "The best IRs come from leveraging up or leveraging down," says Pohlman. "That requires some adjustment to the overall risk budget to allow for greater risk for leveraged managers."

Risk budgeting encompasses the measures effective for normal and for non-normal distributions. Developing the risk budget is a process that ranges from defining the risk to be budgeted to divining a method for calculating the risk, to nailing down the implementation challenges. In the end, the plan sponsor has a method to evaluate return on risk, not return on assets.

The method of managing portfolios also is broad enough to evaluate the interaction of active and passive risks. The latter is the driving force behind the application at the Ontario Teachers' Pension Plan Board (OTPP), North York, Ontario, Canada. "I think we used to do what most people do, and that is to control active risk," says Leo de Bever, senior vice president at OTPP. "But that approach really attacks the wrong problem. Our job is not to beat a benchmark; our job is to pay pensions."

At OTPP, they use historical value at risk (VAR) as the measure of risk. VAR is a technique for estimating the probability of portfolio losses exceeding some specified price, usually within some specific period of time. "We focus the risks on a 1-in-100 times event in individual portfolios, and then aggregate across portfolios," says de Bever. "If we can assume all active programs are uncorrelated, then the aggregate risk is the square of the individual risks."

Individuals manage their portfolios to stay within ranges coded green, yellow, and red. Managers approaching the red zone have some explaining to do. "Even our fundamental bottom-up managers are very quantitative-oriented," says de Bever. "We have to be careful, however, to structure incentives. Managers get a bonus for earning high returns on risk, and we don't want to limit what an individual can earn."

MAXIMIZING VAR

Using VAR to budget risk helps to control risk, but according to de Bever, the process has a larger purpose. "We look across all available strategies and see if any of them are worth looking at," he says. "When we're asking if we want to be in the equity market to the extent we have been, all of a sudden we're having a much more involved discussion than when we used less dynamic methods of allocating resources."

We needed the ways to identify perceived opportunity," says de Bever. "Our focus now is much more on the interaction of active and passive risks."

TABLE 23.1   The Top Risk Measurement Tools

Beta	Relative movement of investment versus a benchmark
Sharpe ratio	Volatility of investment versus historical returns in excess of risk-free rate
Standard deviation	Measure of range of numbers in sample
Excess returns	Difference between actual return and benchmark return
Residual risk	Volatility of excess returns
Information ratio	Excess returns over residual risk
VAR	Probability of portfolio losses exceeding some specified price within specific period of time
Risk budget	Method for tracking the risk per unit of reward

One of the important steps in implementing a risk-budgeting system is the upgrade of the computer and accounting systems. OTPP calculates and evaluates the components of the risk budget daily. The system depends on daily pricing of liquid and illiquid investments, and increased computing power contributes greatly to the effectiveness of all risk measures. "Think about how computers allow the non-normal techniques to become the norm," suggests Cashion.

Whether measuring or modeling or making decisions, there's great uncertainty at the end of all techniques. The tools might be best used as the basis for talking about the specific risks. "First, practitioners and clients have to come to a common ground of understandability and practicality of the tools," says Cashion.

"Imagine if clients asked about how normal returns were for all classes, even large-, mid-, and small-cap value," poses Cashion. "Imagine talking with clients about how small caps and certain sectors and classes are not very well-behaved. Then use the testing on different models to address the problem rather than pretending it doesn't exist."

The search for the perfect measure continues. Several recent developments appear frequently in the academic literature but haven't yet caught on with many investors. Consider the Fouse index, suggested by Bill Fouse of Mellon Capital Management. This index incorporates the investor's utility for a risky outcome, which is the expected return minus some fraction of the risk, where the fraction of risk is an expression of the investor's degree of risk aversion.

Another measure that addresses investor sentiment measures downside risk, or the frequency of negative returns. "We've kicked around the Sortino ratio that measures downside risk for a long time," says Pohlman, "but we've never gotten into it."

New methods will be developed, and current measures' effectiveness will be better known through practice and testing. But, in the end, the measures are just tools. The most sophisticated models will always require human skill and discernment to interpret and apply them.

CHAPTER 24

CONDITIONAL PERFORMANCE EVALUATION, REVISITED

Wayne E. Ferson

Meijun Qian

Traditional performance evaluation assumes that investment styles and economic states remain constant. Conditional performance evaluation, however, compares a fund's returns with the returns of a dynamic strategy that matches the fund's time-varying risk exposures. In this chapter, the authors revisit the main empirical results of the conditional performance evaluation literature using a large, updated sample of mutual funds and expand and refine the treatment of conditioning information. Because conditional performance evaluation uses more information than traditional methods, it has the potential to provide more accurate performance measures—an attractive feature for anyone trying to assess whether a fund's performance arises from manager skill or from chance.

FOREWORD

One of the most difficult challenges for investors is to assess whether a fund's performance arises from a manager's skill or is simply the product of chance. Track records by themselves are typically too short to distinguish skill from chance. Moreover, what shows up as alpha may instead be an artifact of a mis-specified benchmark. The consequences of poor performance evaluation are significant. Investment managers are needlessly fired, and perhaps more often, unjustifiably hired. And the transaction costs associated with this turnover substantially and unnecessarily dilute investor savings.

Reprinted from the Research Foundation of CFA Institute (September 2004).

Another, more subtle, cost of unnecessary turnover exists. If managers operate at different levels of risk, then in the absence of reliable information, switching managers into and out of a portfolio is riskier than maintaining a constant exposure to them. We are thus quite fortunate that Wayne Ferson and Meijun Qian have revisited the critically important topic of conditional performance evaluation.

Unlike the conventional approach to performance evaluation, which assumes that investment styles and economic states remain constant, this methodology compares a fund's returns with the returns of a dynamic strategy that matches the fund's time-varying risk exposures. It thus controls for a variety of biases that might lead an investor to mistakenly shift between managers. And as a nod to the more cynically inclined, conditional performance evaluation prevents managers from gaming less refined performance benchmarks.

Although the methodology is quite sophisticated, Ferson and Qian present the topic in a style that is accessible to practitioners, and they provide sufficient detail to facilitate implementation of their models. Yet, they do not bend to simplicity. Even the most quantitatively advanced scholars will be satisfied with their rigor and their comprehensive review of the extant literature.

Ferson and Qian present a compelling case for conditional performance evaluation, both conceptually and empirically. Managers who are truly confident of their skill should be eager to have it rendered transparent by conditional performance evaluation. And investors should be equally eager to move from a murky system that confounds alpha with shifting economic states to one that shines a light on true skill—or the lack thereof. The Research Foundation is extremely pleased to present *Conditional Performance Evaluation, Revisited*.

Mark Kritzman, CFA
Research Director
The Research Foundation of CFA Institute

PREFACE

Conditional performance evaluation compares a fund's return with the return of a dynamic strategy that attempts to match the fund's risk exposures. The risk exposures are matched as they vary through time by mechanically trading based on easily measured, predetermined variables. A fund's risk exposures and the related market premiums are said to be "conditioned," or allowed to vary over time with the state of the economy as measured by predetermined, public information variables. The performance measures that result are the *conditional alphas*. Our goal in this chapter is to revisit and extend the central empirical findings of the literature on conditional performance evaluation for U.S. equity mutual funds.

The early conditional performance evaluation studies found that controlling for time variation associated with the state of the economy makes the average performance (and also the market-timing ability) of mutual funds look better compared with traditional performance measures (e.g., Ferson and Schadt 1996). Performance net of expenses is mildly negative under traditional models that ignore conditioning but neutral under the conditional models. Ferson and Warther (1996) attributed the difference to predictable patterns of new money flows in and out of mutual funds at the aggregate level. These studies used small samples of mutual funds, subject to survival selection and ending in 1990.

In the present study, we revisit the main empirical results of the conditional performance evaluation literature using a large, updated sample of mutual funds. We assess the robustness of the conditional performance of mutual funds to fresh data that control for survival bias, which is important because survival bias in earlier datasets may have made performance look better than it was. We expand and refine the treatment of conditioning information and expand the list of measures of the state of the economy. Expanding the list of state variables is interesting because the early studies' results were mainly driven by the relationship of returns to an overall market dividend yield and the level of short-term interest rates. Consequently, we want to find out if fund performance responds to other measures of the economic state. We also use the predetermined variables to define discrete states, which helps to avoid statistical problems associated with persistent, lagged regressors.

Our study includes a number of refinements to the conditional performance evaluation methodology. We analyze the performance of funds relative to the funds' characteristics to determine the extent to which the conditional performance of mutual funds can be explained by such factors as fund size, turnover, fee structure, and new money flows. For example, we will answer questions like: Do low-expense-ratio funds have better conditional timing measures than high-expense-ratio funds? (We find that they do.) We also examine the relative performance of funds using cross-sectional regressions, which allows us to isolate the effects of fund style on performance. In addition to a standard market benchmark, we measure conditional performance relative to style-specific benchmarks using an approach similar to that of Sharpe (1992).

We confirm that conditional alphas tend to make funds look better than traditional performance measures in a broader sample of funds that uses fresh data constructed to control survivor-selection bias. Conditional performance, measured at the fund-style-group level, is essentially neutral. On a subsample of balanced and tactical asset allocation funds, we find that conditional timing ability is more likely to be found among the funds with the largest total net assets, the longest track records, and the lowest expense ratios.

Our list of lagged instruments is more inclusive than that of previous studies, thus establishing the robustness of these results to the choice of lagged instruments. The conditional performance analysis reveals patterns in expected performance across fund styles and states of the economy that traditional measures would miss. With our expanded list of instruments, we explore the question of which economic variables are the most informative to condition on. We find that in a list of 11 proxies for the state of the economy, the states of the term structure and interest rates are the most informative about overall fund performance relative to a broad market index. At the level of fund-style groups, we find the strongest evidence for time-varying market betas among the income funds. The variables representing the states of the macroeconomy are found to be informative about shifts in the risk exposure and performance of fund groups, relative to static style-specific benchmarks.

We begin this chapter by reviewing conditional performance evaluation and placing our study in context. We next discuss how we condition on the state of the economy and then introduce the empirical methods and describe the data. We continue by presenting empirical results on the performance of broad fund groups and then summarizing the cross-sectional distribution of individual fund performance. We further study relative performance in relation to fund characteristics as well as market timing. Finally, we review the implications of our findings for practicing investment managers and offer a summary and conclusions.

We hope the reader finds this chapter both intellectually stimulating and useful in a practical environment, and we are grateful to the Research Foundation of CFA Institute for the research support that allowed us to investigate these challenging issues.

CONDITIONAL PERFORMANCE EVALUATION, REVISITED

Traditional measures of risk-adjusted performance for mutual funds compare the average return of a fund with a benchmark designed to control for the fund's average risk. For example, Jensen's (1968) alpha is the difference between the return of a fund and a portfolio constructed from a market index and cash, where the portfolio has the same average market exposure, or beta risk, as the fund. The returns and beta risks are typically measured as averages over the evaluation period, and these averages are taken unconditionally, or without regard to variations in the state of financial markets or the broader economy. One weakness of this approach relates to the likelihood of changes in the state of the economy. For example, if the evaluation period covers a bear market but the period going forward is a bull market, the unconditional performance evaluation may not have much forward-looking value.

REVIEW OF CONDITIONAL PERFORMANCE EVALUATION

In the conditional performance evaluation (CPE) approach, fund managers' risk exposures and the related market premiums are allowed to vary over time with the state of the economy. The state of the economy is measured using predetermined, public information variables. Provided that the analysis period covers both bull and bear markets, one can estimate expected risk and performance in each type of market. Thus, knowing that the current state of the market is a bull market, for example, one can estimate the fund's expected performance given a bull state.

The conditional performance measure, the *conditional alpha*, is the difference between a fund's excess return and that of a strategy that attempts to match the fund's risk dynamics over time by mechanically trading based on the predetermined variables. The idea is a natural generalization of the classical performance measures, which compare a fund's return with a benchmark that carries the same average exposure to risk. In the CPE approach, for example, the risk adjustment for a bull market state may be different from that for a bear market state if the fund's strategy implies different risk exposures in the different states. The conditional alpha can also be estimated conditional on the state, as we will explain later.

Conditional performance evaluation is consistent with a version of semi-strong market efficiency as described by Fama (1970). The idea is that if the market is efficient, a fund manager whose performance can be replicated by mechanically trading on public information is not adding value. In order to add value and generate a positive conditional alpha, a manager should offer a higher return than the mechanical-trading strategy. Although market efficiency motivates the null hypothesis of our tests—that conditional alphas are zero—one need not be a proponent of market efficiency to use CPE. By choosing the lagged variables, it is possible to set the hurdle for superior ability at any desired level of information. Our results show that the choice of lagged variables should matter in practice and provide some practical guidance on the variables to use.

In addition to the lagged state variables, CPE, like any performance evaluation, requires a choice of benchmark portfolios. Traditional measures motivated by the capital asset pricing model [CAPM (Sharpe 1964)] use a broad equity index. Current practice is more likely to use a benchmark representing the fund manager's investment style. We use both types of benchmarks in this chapter. The idea, in any event, is that the portfolio formed from the benchmark should capture an alternative to employing the manager's services. If alpha is positive, the manager adds value relative to the alternative of holding the benchmark portfolio strategy. It is important to recognize, however, the role of costs in this comparison. In most academic studies using the traditional measures and in our analysis using CPE, the benchmark strategy does not pay trading costs. Mutual fund returns, in contrast, are measured net of all expenses and trading costs. Therefore, the measure of value added should be interpreted as an increment to these costs. Roughly speaking, a manager with an alpha of zero has enough ability to cover his or her costs and fees.

Stylized Example

The theoretical appeal of CPE can be illustrated with the following highly stylized numerical example. Assume two equally likely states of the market as reflected in investors' expectations: a bull state and a bear state. In a bull market, assume that the expected return of the S&P 500 Index is 20 percent, and in a bear market, assume it is 10 percent.[1] Take the risk-free return to cash to be 5 percent and assume that all investors share these views—the current state of expected market returns is common knowledge. In this case, if one assumes an efficient market, an investment strategy that uses as its only information the current state will not yield abnormal returns.

Now, imagine a mutual fund that holds the S&P 500 in a bull market and holds cash in a bear market. Consider the performance of this fund based on CPE and Sharpe's CAPM. Conditional on a bull market, the beta of the fund is 1.0, the fund's expected return is 20 percent (equal to the S&P 500), and the fund's conditional alpha is zero.[2] Conditional on a bear market, the fund's beta is zero, the expected return of the fund is the risk-free return (5 percent), and the conditional alpha is, again, zero. A conditional approach to performance evaluation correctly reports an alpha of zero in each state, which is essentially the null hypothesis of a CPE analysis.

By contrast, an unconditional approach to performance evaluation would incorrectly report a nonzero alpha for the hypothetical mutual fund. Without conditioning on the state, the returns of this fund would seem to be highly sensitive to the market return, and the unconditional beta of the fund would be 1.5.[3] The unconditional expected return of the fund would be $0.5(0.20) + 0.5(0.05) = 0.125$. The unconditional expected return of the S&P 500 would be $0.5(0.20) + 0.5(0.10) = 0.15$, and the unconditional alpha of the fund, therefore, would be $(0.125 - 0.05) - 1.5(0.15 - 0.05) = -7.5$ percent.

The unconditional approach leads to the mistaken conclusion that the manager has negative abnormal performance. But the manager's performance does not reflect poor investment choices or wasted resources; it merely reflects common variation over time in the fund's conditional risk exposure and the market premium. In this example, the correlation between the two is positive, meaning that the manager takes more risk when the market premium is higher, which makes the unconditional risk exposure look high. The traditional model, therefore, overadjusts for market risk and assigns the manager a negative alpha. But investors who have access to information about the economic state would not use the inflated risk exposure and would, therefore, not ascribe negative performance to the manager.

Previous Empirical Evidence

The first conditional performance evaluation studies—by Chen and Knez (1996), Ferson and Schadt (1996), and Ferson and Warther (1996)—found that conditioning on the state of the economy is both statistically and economically significant for measuring investment performance. Conditioning also helps control biases in traditional market-timing models. Jagannathan and Korajczyk (1986) and Ferson and Schadt showed that traditional measures of market timing can assign "negative" timing ability to a passive portfolio strategy, and earlier studies had found that measures of timing ability for mutual funds were typically close to zero or negative. Negative timing coefficients make no sense because if funds could time the market but got the direction systematically wrong, investors could profit by taking the opposite position. Ferson and Schadt showed how such a result arises as a statistical bias when funds' betas vary over time with the state of the economy. By using a conditional approach to control for time-varying betas, the bias is removed.

The original studies found that conditioning makes the average performance of mutual funds look better. This result may seem puzzling given that CPE sets a higher information standard for abnormal performance than traditional methods do. But this result can occur, as the stylized example in the previous section suggests. CPE does not penalize a fund for patterns in its risk exposures that are predictable based on public information, even if that predictability may hurt average returns. Early studies suggested that this is the case for U.S. equity funds. Ferson and Warther attributed the higher alphas in the conditional approach to predictable patterns of new money flows in and out of mutual funds. They argued that managers respond passively to new money flows, so their market exposures are lower when more new money flows in. Ferson and Warther also showed that more new money comes in for a typical equity fund when market indicators predict high expected returns. The combined effect lowers the unconditional performance, but not the conditional performance. Such results illustrate the refinements in performance attribution that CPE makes possible in combination with traditional methods.

The original CPE studies used small samples of mutual funds, which were subject to survival selection, ending in 1990. In this study, we use a much larger sample that ends in 2001. Samples limited to survivors are likely to produce biased estimates of performance, as explained by Brown, Goetzmann, Ibbotson, and Ross (1992, 1995); Elton, Gruber, and Blake (1996); and others. If funds that survive have higher new money flows than funds that do not survive, survival screening of the dataset may also affect the relationship between unconditional and conditional performance measures. This hypothesis motivates our use of mutual fund data that avoids survivor-selection bias.

Edelen (1999) considered the effects of new money flows on unconditional measures of performance at the fund level. He argued that flows beyond the manager's control require disadvantageous trades that hurt performance and that discretionary trades should produce better performance. He found that unconditional alphas and timing measures are negatively related to the part of fund turnover that is explained by flows and that performance is positively related to the part of fund turnover that is uncorrelated with flows. He did not, however, examine conditional measures of performance directly. But Rakowski (2003) did find evidence that the volatility of flows hurts fund performance. We thus use a measure of discretionary turnover, following Edelen, in our CPE analysis.

Zheng (1999) and Becker, Ferson, Myers, and Schill (1999) also found that conditional alphas make mutual funds look better than unconditional alphas and that conditional timing models remove spurious negative timing. Christopherson, Ferson, and Glassman (1998) found that the overall distribution of conditional alphas for pension funds is similar to that of the unconditional alphas, unlike the case for mutual funds as found by Ferson and Schadt. Pension funds present a setting where high-frequency flows of new public money are not at issue, and Christopherson, Ferson, and Glassman suggested that these results are consistent with the interpretation of Ferson and Warther. These studies also used limited samples of funds and conditioning variables. No systematic re-examination of these major results has occurred for a large, current database that controls for survival bias. In addition, little analysis has been done on how sensitive conditional performance measures are to the choice of conditioning variables. We provide a detailed analysis of this issue.

Christopherson, Ferson, and Glassman as well as Christopherson, Ferson, and Turner (1999) found that conditional alphas are informative predictors about the cross-section of future performance in samples of pension funds. High-conditional-alpha funds deliver high future returns, and conditional alphas predict future returns better than the traditional, or unconditional, alphas. Del Guercio and Tkac (2002) found that new money flows into pension funds are more responsive than those into mutual funds to "sophisticated" measures of performance, such as Jensen's alpha, but they reported no evidence of fund flows in response to conditional measures of performance.

Most of the conditional performance evaluation of mutual funds has used standard market-wide benchmarks for capturing risk exposure. We refine the approach by also using style-based benchmarks in the performance measurement. Myers (1999) studied the role of investment style and survivorship bias in the evidence for persistence of performance in pension funds. He suggested that much of the persistence in pension fund performance, such as found in Christopherson, Ferson, and Glassman, is related to fund style. These results for pension funds suggest that examining the conditional performance of mutual funds, controlling for style, should be useful. Because performance relative to a peer group receives so much attention in practice and has been found to be a determinant of new money flows into mutual funds (e.g., Sirri and Tufano 1998), comparing and evaluating these alternative approaches should also be interesting.

MEASURING THE STATES OF THE ECONOMY

Previous studies have used a standard set of lagged variables—level of interest rates, yield spread, aggregate market dividend/price or similar ratios, and so on—to measure the state of the economy. For example, Ferson and Warther used a short-term interest rate and a dividend yield, and these are the most important instruments in Ferson and Schadt. In addition, previous studies have modeled the time variation in the CPE measures as linear functions of these variables. For the purposes of checking the robustness and validity of the previous results, we include similar lagged variables. We also expand the list of instruments beyond those of the earlier studies.

We use a list of 11 instruments for the economic state. The first is the level of short-term interest rates, measured as the bid yield to maturity on a 90-day Treasury bill. The second is the term-structure slope, measured as the difference between a five-year and a one-month discount Treasury yield. Term-structure concavity is $y_3 - (y_1 + y_5)/2$, where y_j is a j-year fixed-maturity yield. Interest rate volatility is the monthly standard deviation of three-month Treasury rates, computed from the days within the month.[4] All the interest rate data are from the U.S. Federal Reserve database. Stock market volatility is constructed similarly using daily returns for the S&P 500. Dividend yield is the annual dividend yield of the Center for Research in Security Prices (CRSP) value-weighted stock index. Inflation is the percentage change in the U.S. Consumer Price Index (CPI). Industrial production growth is the monthly growth rate of the seasonally adjusted industrial production index. Short-term corporate illiquidity is the percentage spread of three-month high-grade commercial paper rates over three-month Treasury rates, which follows Gatev and Strahan (2003). Stock market liquidity is the measure from Pastor and Stambaugh (2003), based on price reversals.

Discrete State Approach

In addition to using the lagged variables themselves, we also measure the state of the economy using discrete state variables. These discrete measures may help to resolve some of the potential econometric problems associated with the continuous measures. By using dummy variables to condition performance, we also avoid the linear functional forms assumed by previous studies.

For each state variable, we measure the average abnormal performance, conditional on the state variable being higher than normal, lower than normal, or normal. This approach follows Ferson, Henry, and Kisgen (2003), who used a similar approach to study fixed-income funds in a stochastic discount factor framework. Consider the example where the lagged instrument is the level of a short-term interest rate, r_t. We first convert the rate into a deviation from its recent level, measured as the average value over the last 60 months: $x_t = r_t - (1/60)\Sigma_{j=1,\dots,60} r_{t-j}$. We then use the last 60 months of data to estimate the standard deviation of r_t, $\sigma(r_t)$. The dummy variable $D_{t,hi}$ for a higher-than-normal level of the interest rate is defined as the indicator function: $I\{[x_t/\sigma(x_t)] > 1\}$. Thus, higher than normal is defined as being greater than one standard deviation above the trailing mean. Similarly, the dummy variable $D_{t,lo}$ for a lower-than-normal level of the rate is defined as the indicator function: $I\{[x_t/\sigma(x_t)] < -1\}$. If the data are approximately normally distributed, we should get about two-thirds of the observations in the normal category and one-sixth of the observations each in the high and low categories.

Dummy variables for the other state variables are similarly defined. For example, we measure performance conditional on high versus low market volatility. To construct this series, we use the daily CRSP market index returns within each month to compute a monthly standard deviation. The time series of the monthly standard deviations replaces r_t above, and the dummy variables for high and low volatility are computed in the same fashion.

Summary Statistics

Panel B of Table 24.1 presents summary statistics for the instruments used in constructing the state variable dummies. Many of the instruments are highly persistent series, as can be

TABLE 24.1   Benchmark Returns and Lagged Instruments: Summary Statistics

Series	Mean	Min	Max	Std. Dev.	ρ_1[a]
A. Benchmark returns (January 1973 through December 2000, N = 336)					
90-day bill	0.606	0.19	2.13	0.272	0.7730
One-year bond	0.661	−1.72	5.61	0.630	0.2748
Government bond	0.772	−8.40	15.23	3.051	0.1120
BAA corporate bond	0.819	−10.29	14.27	2.785	0.1930
Broad equity index	1.105	−22.49	16.56	4.618	0.0193
Growth stocks	1.048	−27.45	17.69	5.834	0.1044
Value stocks	1.373	−23.33	25.12	4.639	0.1208
Small-cap stocks	1.279	−29.07	26.73	5.701	0.1643
B. Lagged instruments (December 1967–November 2000)					
Short-term interest rate	6.897	2.785	16.71	2.690	0.9714
Term-structure slope	0.9075	−4.259	5.208	1.331	0.8759
Term-structure concavity	0.09855	−0.6265	0.9035	0.2007	0.7811
Interest rate volatility	0.5980	0.000	1.552	0.2449	0.9121
Stock market volatility	0.03577	0.0001126	0.2512	0.01841	0.4666
Credit spread	1.079	0.5500	2.690	0.4395	0.9639
Dividend yield	3.458	1.450	6.125	1.044	0.9810
Inflation	4.964	−5.412	21.47	3.905	0.5966
Industrial output growth	2.884	−50.96	40.14	9.410	0.3804
Short-term corporate illiquidity	0.07933	−0.09977	1.149	0.1332	0.7382
Stock market liquidity	−0.03129	−0.4689	0.2025	0.05798	0.2100

Note: Returns are monthly rate of return in percent.

[a]ρ_1 is the first-order sample autocorrelation of the series.

seen from their high first-order autocorrelations. For example, the short-term interest rate, credit spread, and dividend yield have autocorrelations in excess of 95 percent. High persistence, however, can create econometric problems as reviewed by Ferson, Sarkissian, and Simin (2003a, 2003b). With persistent variables, finding "spurious" predictability in a given sample is likely because standard statistical analysis suggests the predictability is there but it really is not there when needed, outside the given sample. Our expanded list of instruments includes variables without so much persistence. For example, six of the instruments we introduce in Table 24.1 have first-order autocorrelations less than 0.80. Ferson, Sarkissian, and Simin showed that spurious regression is not a significant issue at these levels of persistence.

In Appendix 24A, Table 24.12 and Table 24.13 report summary statistics for the dummy variable indicators for the various states. The dummy variables are less persistent than the underlying continuous variables from which they are constructed, which reduces concerns about spurious regression biases. For the dummy variables, the largest first-order autocorrelation is 85 percent, and most are much smaller. The lower persistence of the dummy variables is one of their attractive features.

Table 24.13 shows that the state variable dummies are mutually correlated. The highest correlation between the low-state dummies is 83 percent (short-rate level with its volatility). The highest correlation between the high-state dummies is 89 percent (again, short-rate level with its volatility). The other correlations are typically much smaller. For example, the next highest correlations between the dummies are 64 percent and 58 percent; the rest are below 50 percent.

Figure 24.1 presents plots of the lagged state variables and their associated discrete dummy variables. The dummies are shown as positive for a higher-than-normal state, negative for a low state, and zero for a normal state. The graph for the 90-day Treasury bill (short rate) in Panel A shows an overall declining trend in the levels since 1981 but with enough cyclicality that the dummy variables are not simply subperiod indicators for early and late in the sample. At the end of 1989 and in much of 2000, Panel A shows brief periods of high-rate states, and since 1994, it shows long periods of normal rate levels as well. The graph for the slope of the term structure in Panel B reveals a more uniform distribution of shorter-duration high, low, and normal episodes over the sample period. High slopes occur in 1976, 1983–1985, mid-1988, and 1992–1993, interspersed with normal slopes during those periods. Low slopes occur in 1979–1981, 1989–1991, and 1995–1999, also interspersed with normal periods. The graph for concavity in Panel C appears similar to the slope graph. (The dummy variables are scaled as indicated in the titles of the graphs.) When the slope of the term structure is high, it tends to be concave (the two high-state dummies have a correlation of 58 percent), and low slopes tend to be associated with less concavity (the low-state dummies have a correlation of 64 percent). Interest rate volatility, Panel D, displays a decreasing trend since 1982, similar to the interest rate levels. (The dummies for low rates and low volatility have a correlation of 77 percent.) Periods of high interest rate volatility are evident during the 1979–1982 monetary experiment, and periods of low volatility occur during 1985–1988 and 1992–1994.

The first state of the financial market variables in Figure 24.1 is stock market volatility, shown in Panel E. The spike in volatility corresponding to October 1987 is the most prominent feature of the series. Volatility was mostly normal over the 1988–1992 period. The dummies oscillate between low and normal periods during 1984–1986 and 1993–1995, and they oscillate between high and normal periods during 1973–1975, 1980–1983, and 1996–1999. Credit spreads, plotted in Panel F, show a downward drift since 1982, similar to the interest rate level and volatility series. Brief high-spread periods occur in 1975–1976, 1981–1983, and

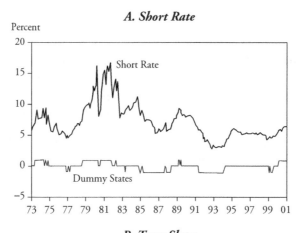

A. Short Rate

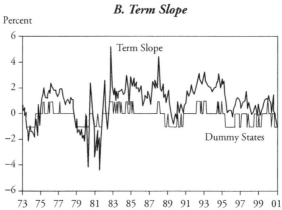

B. Term Slope

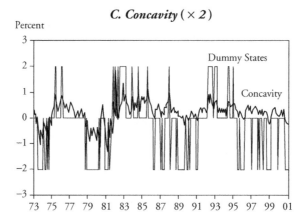

C. Concavity (× 2)

FIGURE 24.1   Lagged State Variables and Their Associated Dummy Variables, 1973–2001

(continued)

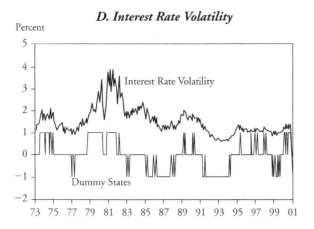

D. Interest Rate Volatility

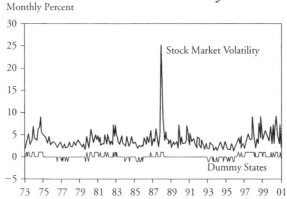

E. Stock Market Volatility

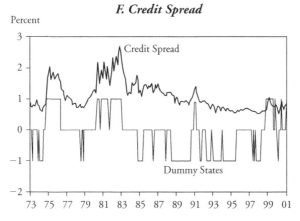

F. Credit Spread

FIGURE 24.1   (*continued*)

(*continued*)

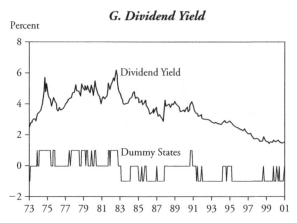

G. Dividend Yield

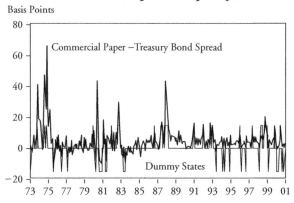

H. Short-Term Corporate Illiquidity (× *15*)

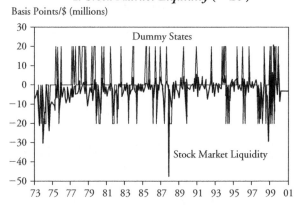

I. Stock Market Liquidity (× *20*)

FIGURE 24.1   (*continued*)

(*continued*)

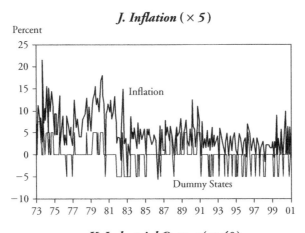

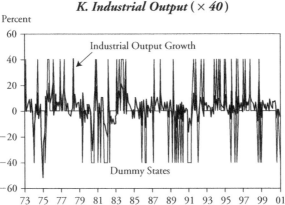

FIGURE 24.1   *(continued)*

since 1999. Much of the period since 1982 is characterized by oscillation between normal and low spreads. Panel G shows the dividend yield, which is the series that appears most likely to be nonstationary. It displays a smooth downward trend since 1982. The dummies indicate mostly high or normal yields during 1973–1982 and mostly low or normal after that. The commercial paper–Treasury spread, our measure of short-term corporate illiquidity shown in Panel H, displays sharp peaks during 1974, 1980, 1983, and 1988. The dummy variables indicate primarily normal or high spreads during 1973–1975 and 1983–1993, with seemingly random patterns over other periods. The stock market liquidity variable, plotted in Panel I, is the most random looking of the financial market indicators, except for a brief period of frequently low liquidity during 1973–1975 and a negative liquidity spike in October 1987.

Finally, Figure 24.1 includes graphs of the state variables for the macro-economy. The inflation rate series, shown in Panel J, looks like a noisier version of the short-term interest rate series, with high, low, and normal states scattered throughout the sample. This similarity makes sense if variation in the short-term rate largely tracks variation in expected inflation, as suggested by Fama (1975). Under this interpretation, the short rate would appear as a smoothed version of the inflation rate. The dummy variables indicate a concentration of low-inflation states during 1982–1988, normal interspersed with low during 1991–1999, and a concentration of high inflation states during 1973–1980. Finally, the industrial output growth rate series, shown in Panel K, appears stationary and largely random. But the dummy variables can pick out business cycle patterns in the growth rate. Frequent high-growth states, although interspersed with normal states, occur during 1983–1984 and 1994–1995. Frequent low-growth states, again interspersed with normal states, occur during 1975, 1981–1982, and 1989–1991. Overall, the state variables track interesting variation in interest rates, financial markets, and the macroeconomy.

EMPIRICAL MODELS

We focus on two versions of conditional performance regressions and two conditional market-timing models, and we compare these with the classical performance measures that they generalize. Three of these conditional models were developed by Ferson and Schadt and one by Christopherson, Ferson, and Glassman. Let $r_{m,t+1}$ be the excess return on a market or benchmark index. For example, it could be the S&P 500, a style index (such as a small-cap growth index), or a vector of excess returns if a multifactor model is used.

Our first model is one proposed by Ferson and Schadt:

$$r_{p,t+1} = \alpha_p + \beta_0 r_{m,t+1} + \beta'(r_{m,t+1} \otimes Z_t) + u_{p,t+1},\tag{24.1}$$

where $r_{p,t+1}$ is the return of the fund in excess of a short-term "cash" instrument, and Z_t is the vector of lagged conditioning variables, in demeaned form. The symbol $\otimes$ denotes the Kronecker product, or element-by-element multiplication when $r_{m,t+1}$ is a single market index. The symbol $u_{p,t+1}$ is the regression error. A special case of Equation 24.1 is the classical CAPM regression, where the terms involving Z_t are omitted. In this case, α_p is Jensen's alpha.

When $r_{m,t+1}$ is the excess return on a broad market index, then Equation 24.1 can be used to estimate a version of the *conditional* CAPM, which says that

$$E(r_{t+1}|Z_t) = \beta(Z_t)\, E(r_{m,t+1}|Z_t),$$

where $\beta(Z_t)$ is the conditional beta and $\alpha_p = 0$ indicates no abnormal performance. The conditional CAPM is examined empirically by Harvey (1989), Shanken (1990), Ferson and Harvey (1991), and Jagannathan and Wang (1996), among others. These authors applied the model to hypothetical, passive portfolios of common stocks. Jagannathan and Wang emphasized that the conditional CAPM can be boiled down to an *unconditional* model—that is, a model for average expected returns with more than one "beta." This interpretation can also be seen in Equation 24.1, where (β_0, β) is a vector of regression coefficients or betas on the multiple factors defined by $(r_{m,t+1}, r_{m,t+1} \otimes Z_t)$.

To see more explicitly how the model in Equation 24.1 arises, consider a market model regression allowing for a time-varying fund beta, $\beta(Z_t)$, that may depend on public information, Z_t:

$$r_{p,t+1} = \alpha_p + \beta(Z_t) r_{m,t+1} + u_{p,t+1}.\tag{24.2}$$

Now, assume that the time-varying beta can be modeled as a linear function: $\beta(Z_t) = \beta_0 + \beta' Z_t$. The coefficient β_0 is the average beta of the fund (because Z is normalized to mean zero), and the term $\beta' Z_t$ captures the time-varying conditional beta. Substituting this expression into Equation 24.2, the result is Equation 24.1. Note that because $E(Z_t) = 0$, it follows that:

$$E[\beta'(r_{m,t+1} \otimes \mathbf{Z_t})] = \text{cov}[\beta(\mathbf{Z_t}), r_{m,t+1}]$$
$$= \text{cov}[\beta(\mathbf{Z_t}), E(r_{m,t+1}|\mathbf{Z_t})], \qquad (24.3)$$

where the second equality follows from representing $r_{m,t+1} = E(r_{m,t+1}|\mathbf{Z_t}) + u_{m,t+1}$, with $\text{cov}[u_{m,t+1}, \beta(\mathbf{Z_t})] = 0$. Thus, the additional factors defined by the interaction term $\beta'(r_{m,t+1} \otimes \mathbf{Z_t})$ in Equation 24.1 arise as a control for common movements in the fund's conditional beta and the conditional expected benchmark return. The conditional alpha, α_p, is measured net of the effects of these risk dynamics.

Christopherson, Ferson, and Glassman proposed a refinement of Equation 24.1 to allow for a time-varying conditional alpha. Our second model is as follows:

$$r_{p,t+1} = \alpha_{p0} + \alpha_p'\mathbf{Z_t} + \beta_0 r_{m,t+1} + \beta'(r_{m,t+1} \otimes \mathbf{Z_t}) + u_{p,t+1}. \qquad (24.4)$$

In this model, $\alpha_{p0} + \alpha_p'\mathbf{Z_t}$ measures the time-varying conditional alpha. This refinement of the model may have more power to detect abnormal performance if performance varies with the state of the economy. For example, if a manager generates positive alpha when the yield curve is steep but negative alpha when it is shallow, the average abnormal performance may be close to zero so that it cannot be detected using Equation 24.1. In such a case, Equation 24.4 would track the time variation in alpha and record it as a nonzero coefficient, α_p, on the instrument for the term-structure slope.

DATA

Our study involves several datasets. This section describes these data, including our sample of mutual fund returns and characteristics.

Benchmark Returns

We use a number of "passive" index returns as benchmarks for the mutual fund performance. Summary statistics for the eight standard indexes are in Panel A of Table 24.1, and their conditional mean returns are presented in Table 24.2. The benchmark indexes cover a range of asset classes with different risks and returns. They include the monthly returns on a "cash" instrument, measured by the 90-day U.S. Treasury bill; a government bond return, measured by the 20-year bond from Ibbotson Associates; a BAA corporate bond index return; a broad equity market index, measured by the CRSP value-weighted market index; a small-cap stock index; and two indexes of stocks grouped according to their lagged book-to-market ratios. The growth index consists of stocks with low book-to-market ratios, and the value index has high book-to-market ratios.[5]

The summary statistics of the benchmark returns, reported in Table 24.1, show the expected result that average return and volatility go together as one moves from cash to government bonds, to corporate bonds, to equities. The cash market returns have significant autocorrelation, at 77 percent, but none of the other autocorrelations are larger than 28 percent.

Over the 1973–2000 period, the value stock index slightly outperformed the small stock index, which, in turn, slightly beat the broad equity index. The growth stock index delivered the lowest equity returns. Growth stocks and small-cap stocks were the most volatile.

TABLE 24.2 Benchmark Return Statistics in Different Economic States, January 1973 through December 2000 (N = 336)

Asset Return	N	90-Day T-Bill		Government Bond		BAA Bond		Broad Equity		Growth		Value		Small Cap	
State	N	Mean	Std. Dev.	Mean	Std. Dev.	Mean	Std. Dev.	Mean	Std. Dev.	Mean	Std. Dev.	Mean	Std. Dev.	Mean	Std. Dev.
A. State of the term structure															
Short-term interest rates															
High	66	0.848	0.0442	0.414	0.442	−0.159	0.470	−0.0647	0.640	−0.213	0.889	0.507	0.662	0.30	0.86
Normal	191	0.585	0.0155	0.831	0.197	1.09	0.187	1.29	0.338	1.22	0.417	1.33	0.340	1.23	0.42
Low	79	0.453	0.0170	0.927	0.374	0.981	0.223	1.65	0.428	1.69	0.505	2.19	0.409	2.21	0.46
Term-structure slope															
High	44	0.555	0.0369	1.93	0.393	2.25	0.374	2.04	0.567	2.25	0.780	2.44	0.555	2.66	0.70
Normal	200	0.573	0.0176	0.706	0.216	0.903	0.182	1.18	0.338	1.17	0.418	1.46	0.335	1.41	0.40
Low	92	0.703	0.0320	0.362	0.326	−0.0466	0.320	0.50	0.477	0.20	0.615	0.68	0.496	0.33	0.63
Term-structure concavity															
High	36	0.659	0.0687	1.68	0.531	2.10	0.520	1.23	0.698	1.21	0.862	2.14	0.658	2.00	0.83
Normal	215	0.562	0.0151	0.633	0.196	0.827	0.172	1.07	0.306	1.02	0.392	1.26	0.319	1.20	0.38
Low	85	0.695	0.0315	0.737	0.367	0.260	0.336	1.14	0.560	1.05	0.689	1.33	0.525	1.17	0.68
Interest rate volatility															
High	68	0.842	0.0447	0.784	0.467	0.181	0.496	0.457	0.683	0.690	0.660	0.293	0.903	0.488	0.854
Normal	193	0.589	0.0147	0.771	0.195	0.973	0.174	1.19	0.329	1.35	0.337	1.17	0.415	1.30	0.417
Low	75	0.436	0.0167	0.764	0.360	1.00	0.239	1.46	0.417	2.04	0.414	1.42	0.477	1.95	0.431
B. State of financial markets															
Stock market volatility															
High	66	0.659	0.0447	1.23	0.428	1.23	0.438	1.45	0.731	1.62	0.968	1.57	0.707	1.81	0.91
Normal	238	0.605	0.0158	0.586	0.189	0.655	0.165	1.04	0.286	0.964	0.352	1.29	0.292	1.13	0.35
Low	32	0.506	0.0390	1.21	0.549	1.19	0.461	0.870	0.497	0.498	0.610	1.61	0.497	1.29	0.56

Credit spread

High	64	0.754	0.0473	0.646	0.413	1.35	0.455	2.33	0.588	2.81	0.724	2.75	0.686	3.24	0.75
Normal	177	0.597	0.0182	0.609	0.238	0.600	0.202	0.656	0.382	0.374	0.478	0.991	0.367	0.679	0.47
Low	95	0.523	0.0190	1.16	0.268	0.869	0.229	1.12	0.347	1.12	0.460	1.16	0.328	1.08	0.41

Dividend yield

High	55	0.820	0.0502	1.66	0.481	1.47	0.568	1.67	0.752	2.03	0.885	2.23	0.732	2.49	0.86
Normal	143	0.655	0.0208	0.542	0.246	0.712	0.228	1.13	0.376	1.11	0.478	1.38	0.400	1.28	0.48
Low	138	0.470	0.0127	0.655	0.247	0.671	0.171	0.849	0.369	0.590	0.480	1.02	0.350	0.79	0.45

Short-term corporate illiquidity

High	36	0.576	0.0474	1.13	0.509	1.47	0.536	2.62	0.924	3.17	1.09	2.49	0.707	3.19	0.83
Normal	275	0.614	0.0165	0.759	0.186	0.775	0.167	0.958	0.264	0.829	0.334	1.34	0.281	1.13	0.35
Low	25	0.566	0.0436	0.403	0.526	0.373	0.441	0.545	1.09	0.407	1.47	0.146	0.969	0.189	1.23

Stock market liquidity

High	46	0.569	0.0372	0.766	0.476	0.889	0.396	1.23	0.566	1.37	0.666	1.14	0.473	1.48	0.56
Normal	250	0.605	0.0159	0.788	0.181	0.860	0.169	1.09	0.298	1.00	0.381	1.46	0.305	1.31	0.38
Low	40	0.653	0.0614	0.682	0.627	0.482	0.563	1.08	0.779	0.967	0.959	1.09	0.775	0.876	0.98

C. State of the macroeconomy

Inflation

High	51	0.707	0.0464	0.626	0.546	0.0357	0.560	0.0986	0.880	−0.477	1.11	0.236	0.873	−0.502	1.11
Normal	231	0.583	0.0166	0.655	0.183	0.803	0.161	1.18	0.286	1.20	0.363	1.37	0.290	1.38	0.35
Low	54	0.609	0.0371	1.41	0.440	1.63	0.348	1.74	0.517	1.82	0.630	2.45	0.480	2.51	0.58

Industrial output growth

High	40	0.560	0.0389	0.433	0.353	0.422	0.326	0.393	0.545	0.185	0.676	1.13	0.492	0.856	0.63
Normal	247	0.595	0.0171	0.738	0.196	0.822	0.176	1.04	0.300	0.889	0.376	1.17	0.298	1.00	0.36
Low	49	0.701	0.0412	1.22	0.500	1.13	0.481	2.03	0.701	2.55	0.911	2.57	0.763	3.01	0.95

Note: Returns are monthly rate of return, in percent.

Previous studies, including Basu (1977), Fama and French (1992), and Lakonishok, Shleifer, and Vishny (1994), have claimed that value strategies, which choose stocks with high book-to-market or earnings-to-price ratios, outperform growth strategies.

Benchmark Returns Conditioned on Economic States

Table 24.2 shows the average return and standard deviation of return for seven of the benchmark indexes conditional on the high, low, and normal values of the economic state dummies. The columns show the various asset returns, from low to high risk as one moves from left to right across the table; the rows correspond to the state variables. The state variables are organized into three groups, with one panel for each group. The first group measures the state of the term structure; the second group measures the state of general financial markets; and the third measures the state of the macroeconomy. In each case, the state variable dummy is used to predict the future returns in real time. For example, the state is defined at the end of January using data prior to the last day of the month, and this information is used to predict the return over the month of February.

Starting with the term-structure state variables in Panel A, we find that the states of the term structure are powerful predictors, not just for fixed-income but also for equity returns. Campbell (1987) and others have observed that term-structure variables could be used to model time variation in expected bond and stock returns. The evidence in Table 24.2 both confirms these claims using more recent data and refines the descriptive relationships using our discrete states. High levels of short-term interest rates predict relatively high and volatile short-term bond returns and low stock returns. A gradual transition occurs between the two cases across the columns as one moves to the longer-term, riskier asset classes. The difference in the broad equity stock return, predicted by low versus high spot rates, is 1.7 percent per month (1.65 percent given low rates and -0.06 percent given high rates) and strongly statistically significant. These results are generally consistent with previous evidence, such as Fama and Schwert (1977) and Ferson (1989), but appear striking in the discrete state design.

A steeply sloped term structure predicts high long-term bond returns and stock returns. The former reflects a failure of the constant-premium version of the expectations hypothesis of the term structure (e.g., Campbell and Shiller 1991). The latter result is consistent with consumption-based model predictions, such as Breeden (1986), which emphasize a positive relationship between the slope of the term structure and expected economic growth and stock returns. Harvey also found that a steep slope predicts high economic growth.

The level and slope seem to be the most informative indicators from the term-structure data about future investment returns, with concavity being less important. This result is not surprising as far as predicting fixed-income returns is concerned, given the evidence in studies such as Litterman and Sheinkman (1988). Table 24.2 shows that higher term-structure concavity predicts higher returns on the longer-term government and BAA corporate bonds but has little predictive power for equity returns. High interest rate volatility states are highly correlated with high interest rate levels; Table 24.13 shows the conditioning dummy variables have correlations between 83 and 89 percent. It is, therefore, not surprising to find that high interest rate volatility is associated with higher and more volatile short-term bond returns and with lower returns on stocks and bonds exposed to default risks.

The variables associated with the state of general financial markets in Panel B of Table 24.2 are also associated with interesting return differences. High credit spreads predict high returns on stocks, consistent with Keim and Stambaugh (1986). High dividend yields predict high returns on stocks and bonds, consistent with Fama and French (1989), but the effect is not statistically significant for the broad equity index or the value stock index. Goyal and Welch (2003) and others have found that the predictive ability of dividend yields is weak in post-1990 data, and the dominant downward trend in yields displayed in Figure 24.1 could be an explanatory factor. The most economically significant predictor among the financial market instruments, judging from the magnitudes of the expected return differences, is the commercial paper–Treasury spread, measuring short-term corporate illiquidity. When the spread is high, all the long-term bonds and stock indexes earn high returns over the next month. For example, the difference in monthly expected returns in high versus low spread states is about 0.70 percentage points (pps) per month for the long-term government bond, 2.1 pps per month for the broad equity index, and an impressive 3 pps per month for the small-cap index. Finally, the stock market liquidity measure predicts no reliable differences in the returns.

The last set of variables measures the state of the macroeconomy. Table 24.2 shows that high inflation is bad news for stocks and corporate bonds. When output growth is abnormally low, it predicts high returns, especially for the riskier assets. In the case of the broad equity index, the difference between the low output state and the high output state is an average return of 1.7 pps per month, while for growth stocks the difference is 2.3 pps per month. The patterns are consistent with the positive relationship between expected economic growth and risky asset returns that most asset-pricing models would predict if economic growth is mean reverting. The intuition is that when the real economy is performing poorly, investors expect it to get better, so expected growth and stock returns are high at such times.[6]

In summary, this section shows that by conditioning on the state of the term structure, general financial markets, and the macroeconomy, predicting differences in the expected returns and volatilities of benchmark asset class returns is possible. Our discrete state approach reveals a number of interesting patterns that have not been exploited by previous studies of conditional fund performance. The discrete variables should also avoid problems with persistent lagged instruments that previous studies were subject to and allow us to check the robustness of CPE results to the choice of state variables.

Mutual Funds

In this study, we use the CRSP mutual fund database, 2001 version, which allows us to expand the coverage of funds to the 1973–2000 period. Ferson and Schadt as well as Ferson and Warther studied the 1968–1990 time period, and the data in Christopherson, Ferson, and Glassman also ended in 1990. Thus, the last 10 years of our study represent an out-of-sample check on the robustness of these earlier findings. The total sample of funds, from which we select a subset, includes all funds for which monthly return data exist in a given month. The number ranges from a low of 146 in January 1962 to a high of 27,289 in June 2001, much larger than the sample of 67 large funds studied by Ferson and Schadt as well as Ferson and Warther. By including funds that do not survive until the end of the sample period, we provide some control of sample-selection bias related to fund survival. We exclude fund years for which the current year is earlier than the reported year in which the fund was organized. This step is done to reduce biases associated with back-filled data. For example, data may be back filled when incubator funds with good track records enter the sample, resulting in a selection bias.[7]

We build two samples of U.S. equity mutual funds. The first is a general sample, which we group by fund style. Styles are defined by their Wiesenberger objective codes, which are available for 1962–2001. These codes are matched with ICDI fund objective codes, available for 1993–2001, and Strategic Insight codes, available starting in 1992. The main style groups are growth, growth and income, income, maximum capital gain, small-cap growth, sector, other aggressive growth, and timing funds. We use the first four groups for comparability with Ferson and Schadt as well as Ferson and Warther, who used the same fund groupings.[8]

The main reason we classify funds by style using the self-reported groups indicated on the CRSP database is for comparability with the earlier CPE studies of mutual funds. A variety of alternative classification schemes, of course, exist. Brown and Goetzmann (1997) developed a returns-based style classification scheme that minimizes the mean within-group sum of squares. Like a conditional performance analysis, their approach allows time variation in funds' conditional betas. They compared their classification scheme with seven other approaches to style classification, including self-reported categories, principal components analysis, and various types of loadings on prespecified factors. They found that their returns-based approach performed relatively well at predicting future fund returns. They also found considerable overlap between the interpretation of their style classifications and the self-reported style groups.[9]

Alternative approaches to fund classification and performance analysis use the reported holdings of the funds. Two versions of this approach exist in the literature. In the first version, the portfolio weights are directly examined to see if they contain information about the future returns of the securities held by the fund. This approach to performance measurement was developed by Grinblatt and Titman (1989). Ferson and Khang (2002) further developed a conditional version of this measure and showed that it has several advantages. In the second version of weight-based approaches, various characteristics of the stocks held by a fund are measured, and using the fund's reported holdings, a characteristics-based style benchmark is constructed. Average performance can be measured as the difference between the fund and benchmark returns. An example of this approach is the style box provided by Morningstar, which is based on the market capitalization, book-to-market, and earnings-to-price ratios of the stocks held by the fund. Daniel, Grinblatt, and Titman (1997) and Wermers (2000) refined and further developed this approach.

Weight-based approaches have advantages and disadvantages compared with the methods used in this chapter. By using more information, weight-based methods may provide more precise performance measures. As Ferson and Khang emphasized, conditional weight-based approaches can avoid biases that arise in returns-based measures as a result of frequent trading by fund managers. But portfolio weights for mutual funds are required to be publicly reported only every six months, while returns are available more frequently. Portfolio weights are subject to "window dressing," whereby end-of-period holdings may not accurately reflect a fund's strategy. Because reported weights are a snapshot, they obviously will not capture dynamic trading strategies that affect returns. Finally, weight-based approaches do not capture actual trading costs as reflected in fund returns.

Funds Grouped by Style

Summary statistics are shown in Table 24.3 for equally weighted portfolios of the mutual funds in each style group. The three largest categories are the growth, growth and income, and income funds. The number of growth funds ranged from 42 in January 1962 to a high of 6,995 in October 2000. The growth and income funds started with 62 and ended with 3,806 over the same period. Income funds started with 20 and ended with 850 over the same period. Data for the other fund groups are available over more limited periods. The maximum capital gain style was discontinued in 1992, and the small-company growth and sector

TABLE 24.3 Mutual Fund Monthly Returns: Summary Statistics

A. Overall equally weighted portfolios

Series	Begin	End	Mean	Min	Max	Std.	$\rho_1{}^a$
Growth	1961	2001	0.9148	−23.41	15.11	4.583	0.1106
Maximum gain	1968	1992	0.8420	−25.53	15.96	5.925	0.1775
Growth and income	1961	2001	0.8843	−16.27	23.19	3.757	0.0707
Income	1961	2001	0.6949	−11.78	9.08	2.320	0.0838
Sector	1988	2001	0.9197	−14.71	10.70	3.686	0.0019
Small-company growth	1989	2001	1.1740	−19.97	15.35	5.207	0.1020
Other aggressive growth	1989	2001	0.9141	−19.38	15.21	4.604	0.0650
Timing	1962	2000	0.8614	−11.90	9.69	2.843	0.0661

B. Means, conditioning on states

Equally Weighted Portfolio of Mutual Funds by Group

	No. Obs.	Growth	Max Cap Gains	Other	Income	Growth and Income	Sector	Small-Company Growth	Timers
State of the term-structure variables									
Short-term rates									
High	66	−0.7709	−0.6995	0.0542	−0.5095	−0.6764	0.1334	0.359	−0.525
Low	79	1.212	1.557	0.8779	0.4729	1.021	0.9296	1.220	0.896
t-Statistic		−2.569	−2.082	−0.3242	−2.803	−2.759	−0.4684	−0.334	−3.056
Term-structure slope									
High	44	1.560	1.862	0.4643	0.4494	1.370	0.5186	0.411	0.388
Low	92	−0.406	−1.388	1.225	−0.0613	−0.2155	0.6936	0.752	−0.264
t-Statistic		2.599	2.775	−0.5412	1.622	2.618	−0.1890	−0.229	1.161
Concavity									
High	36	0.6472	1.126	−0.7201	0.3473	0.5973	−0.2091	−0.749	−0.230
Low	85	0.3810	0.3946	0.9286	0.05392	0.3328	0.9348	1.412	−0.070
t-Statistic		0.3096	0.6082	−1.042	0.7598	0.3742	−1.020	−1.388	−0.290

(*continued*)

541

TABLE 24.3 (continued)

B. Means, conditioning on states

	No. Obs.	Equally Weighted Portfolio of Mutual Funds by Group						Small-Company Growth	Timers
		Growth	Max Cap Gains	Other	Income	Growth and Income	Sector		
Interest rate volatility									
High	68	-0.9893	-1.115	-0.5759	-0.5926	-0.8631	-0.0101	-0.458	-0.367
Low	76	1.315	1.480	0.9985	0.6274	1.172	1.130	1.362	0.644
t-Statistic		**-3.031**	**-2.328**	-0.8939	**-3.474**	**-3.359**	-1.087	-1.148	**-2.164**
State of the financial markets variables									
Stock market volatility									
High	66	0.4649	0.3877	0.9449	0.2780	0.4144	0.6671	0.899	0.272
Low	32	0.2364	-0.2894	1.268	0.5007	0.4070	0.923	1.409	0.909
t-Statistic		0.2580	0.4466	-0.2095	-0.4828	0.0102	-0.2347	-0.319	-1.089
Credit spread									
High	64	1.611	1.659	3.740	0.6488	1.297	3.071	4.245	-0.282
Low	95	0.3523	-0.4880	1.346	0.2194	0.3058	0.9107	1.231	-0.210
t-Statistic		1.791	**2.039**	1.851	1.254	1.720	**2.595**	**2.360**	-0.136
Dividend yield									
High	55	0.6094	1.081	0.000	0.1633	0.466	1.764	1.567	-0.565
Low	138	0.2532	-0.5716	0.000	0.2461	0.303	0.567	0.677	0.790
t-Statistic		0.4177	1.473	0.000	-0.2350	0.238	0.4907	0.2098	**-3.088**

542

	n								
Short-term corporate illiquidity									
High	36	2.139	2.125	3.078	0.7176	1.599	2.496	3.311	0.342
Low	25	0.0627	0.2727	−0.1695	−0.1282	0.0466	0.0029	−0.160	0.587
t-Statistic		1.561	0.7649	1.577	1.274	1.420	1.804	1.691	−0.351
Stock market liquidity									
High	46	0.7608	1.204	0.709	0.112	0.6481	0.617	1.096	0.309
Low	40	0.0866	−1.447	1.988	0.4062	0.2212	2.111	1.741	0.304
t-Statistic		0.6987	1.699	−0.8193	−0.6645	0.5334	−1.287	−0.397	0.009
State of the macroeconomy variables									
Inflation									
High	51	−0.5654	−0.8200	−0.3999	−0.1917	−0.276	−0.1982	−0.477	−0.513
Low	54	1.041	1.695	0.568	0.3842	0.958	0.6780	0.634	0.766
t-Statistic		−1.565	−1.741	−0.5588	−1.343	−1.521	−0.8024	−0.653	**−2.278**
Industrial output growth									
High	40	−0.1757	−0.5759	0.1082	0.1284	0.0153	0.7709	0.231	0.475
Low	49	1.296	2.053	0.2571	0.5288	0.9059	1.320	2.576	−0.478
t-Statistic		−1.591	**−2.274**	−0.0528	−0.7830	−1.184	−0.3601	−1.188	1.522

Notes: The sample periods for the returns are indicated under begin and end. The sample period in Panel B is January 1973–December 2000 (336 observations) or the shorter period beginning when the data are available for a given fund group as indicated in Panel A. The returns are percent per month.
[a] ρ_1 is the first-order sample autocorrelation of the series.

543

series were not usable until 1990 because only a few funds existed prior to that date. For the same reason, the other aggressive growth group was not used until 1992.[10]

The summary statistics in Table 24.3 show that among the groups available beginning in 1961, 1962, or 1968, the growth funds earned the highest average return, while income funds returned the least. The relative volatilities are as expected, with maximum capital gain and growth funds the most volatile, income funds the least volatile, and growth and income funds in between the two. Over the latter part of the sample period, small-company growth funds earned more than sector funds and the other aggressive growth category and also had the highest volatility among those fund groups. The autocorrelations of the equally weighted portfolios of funds vary from less than 1 percent to almost 18 percent. This finding is similar to the passive benchmarks summarized in Table 24.1, except for the higher autocorrelation of the short-term cash return.

We study fund performance in relation to various fund characteristics available in the CRSP database. For example, the characteristics observed at the end of a given calendar year are used to predict relative performance over the next three years in subsequent analysis. Each year the funds are grouped into thirds on the basis of a characteristic at the end of the previous year, and equally weighted portfolios of the funds are formed for the next calendar year. The characteristics are: (1) new cash flow over the past year, defined as $[TNA_t - (1 + R_t)TNA_{t-1}/TNA_{t-1}]$, where TNA is the total net assets of the fund and R_t is the annual return; (2) age of the fund; (3) income passed through to investors in the previous year; (4) capital gains distributions over the past year; (5) reported turnover for the past year; (6) reported total load charges; (7) fund size, measured by total net assets; (8) expense ratio; and (9) lagged annual return over the previous year.

Market-Timing Funds

A broad sample of U.S. equity funds is unlikely to contain many funds that attempt to aggressively time the market. We therefore concentrate our study of conditional market timing on the subsample of funds that are relatively likely to be engaged in market-timing activities as indicated by their declared style.[11] Our group of market-timing funds is dominated by balanced funds but also includes all the funds identified as asset allocation style funds. The initial number of fund years in this sample is 9,626. The number of funds in any given month ranges from a low of 34 in January 1962 to a high of 2,510 in April 2000. As for the broader sample, we exclude fund years for which the current year is earlier than the reported year in which the fund was organized. We find seven such cases.

Summary statistics for an equally weighted portfolio of our market-timing funds are reported in Table 24.3. The average returns and volatility of timing funds are below those of any other group, except the income funds. This result makes sense if the timing funds are out of the market, or holding reduced market exposure, in a substantial fraction of the months.

We form subgroups of the market-timing funds based on the various fund characteristics described previously. Figure 24.2 plots the annual time series of the cutoff values for the fund characteristics that define the upper and lower thirds of the distributions. These figures present a nice illustration of some trends in the mutual fund industry. Because the sample of timing funds is dominated by balanced funds, the figures present a microcosm of how these fund characteristics have evolved over time while abstracting from variation across the fund styles in our broader sample. (We produced similar figures for the growth, income, and sector style groups, and the overall impressions were similar.)

The graph of the fund age breakpoints over time in Panel A of Figure 24.2 illustrates how the large number of new funds entering the sample, starting in the mid-1980s, has

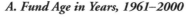

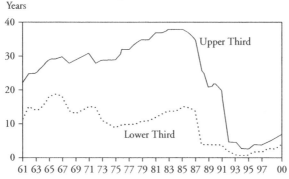

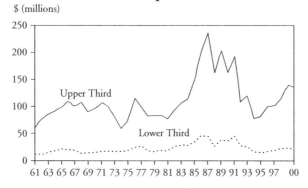

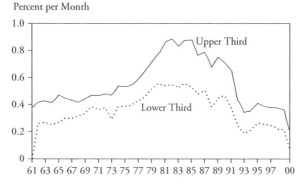

FIGURE 24.2   Annual Time-Series of Cutoff Values for the Fund Characteristics That Define the Upper and Lower Thirds of the Distributions of Market-Timing Funds

(continued)

D. Capital Gains, 1961–2000

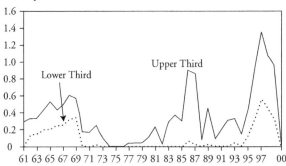

E. Total Loads, 1961–2000

F. Expense Ratios, 1961–2000

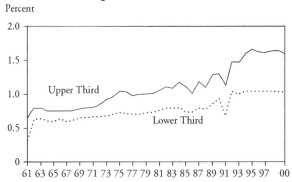

FIGURE 24.2   (*continued*)

(*continued*)

G. Fund Turnover, 1966–2000

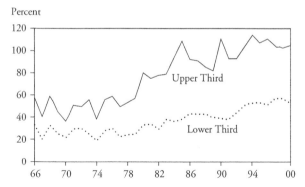

H. Previous Year's New Money Flow, 1963–1999

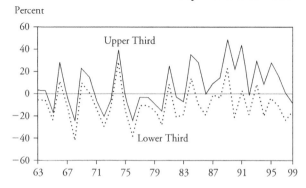

I. Previous Year's Return, 1961–1999

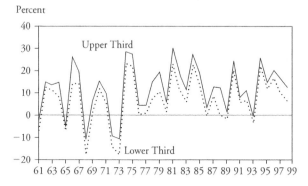

FIGURE 24.2   (*continued*)

driven down the age distribution. The cutoff for the oldest third of the funds peaked at 38 years in 1983–1985, then subsequently fell to a low of only 3 years in 1994–1995. The total net assets per fund, shown in Panel B, has trended up mildly during the sample, with a peak in 1987 and then falling to less than half the peak value by 1994 before resuming a slow upward trend through 1999.

The income return passed through by funds to their shareholders displays an inverted U-shape in Panel C of Figure 24.2 pouring the sample period. The upper-third cutoff for income rose from about 0.4 percent per month in 1961–1962 to just less than 1 percent per month in the high interest rate period ending in 1982–1983 and then fell back to less than 0.4 percent by 1999 as interest rates fell. The capital gains distributions present a different pattern in Panel D. The lower-third cutoff was zero for most of the years between 1970 and 1985. The upper-third cutoff shows peaks in 1968, 1986, and again in 1996–1997. The bull market of the 1990s is clearly evident.

Panel E of Figure 24.2 shows that most funds charged load fees in the 7.5–8.5 percent range during 1961–1967, and funds clustered even more tightly on the maximum 8.5 percent load charge during 1970–1974. Starting in 1975, the lower-third cutoff began to fall, followed by the higher-third cutoff in 1984. By 1978, the lower-third charged no load fees at all, and by the end of the sample, the upper-third cutoff had fallen to 4.75 percent. It is well known that during this period funds began to substitute load charges with 12b-1 fees, and expense ratios have thus risen. The graph of the expense ratios in Panel F shows a clear upward trend over the sample. The upper-third cutoff was 0.65 percent at the beginning of the sample, rising to 1.6 percent by the end. Fund turnover, shown in Panel G, has risen as well, and the spread between low-turnover and high-turnover funds has widened. Until 1979, the upper-third cutoff for turnover hovered near 50 percent per year; then it began to rise, finishing the sample period at more than 100 percent per year.

The final characteristics relate to the flows of new money and the lagged return performance over the preceding year. In Figure 24.2, Panels H and I show that the year-to-year fluctuations in these characteristics are greater than for the other characteristics. New money flows were low during 1975–1980 and relatively high during 1988–1998.

PERFORMANCE OF BROAD FUND GROUPS

In this section, we present an analysis of conditional performance at the level of the fund-style groups. We first examine the fund returns without any risk adjustment, focusing on the conditional behavior across states of the economy. We then use the CAPM for risk adjustment and examine both the unconditional and conditional alphas, which extends the evidence in studies such as Ferson and Schadt. To evaluate the sensitivity of these results to the model for risk, we then replace the market index benchmark of the CAPM with a fund-style-specific benchmark, constructed from the indexes described in Table 24.3. The style-specific benchmarks are constructed using a methodology similar to that of Sharpe (1988, 1992). We then provide a CPE analysis based on the discrete dummy versions of the state variables. By using the discrete state variables in comparison with the continuous versions of the state variables, we conclude this section with an analysis of the time variation in risk exposures at the fund-style-group level.

Panel B of Table 24.3 presents the conditional expected returns of the funds, grouped by style, across the various discrete economic states. For each state variable there are three rows. The first two rows show the expected returns given high and low values of a state variable, and then the third row gives a *t*-statistic for the difference in the conditional means in the high versus low state. The calculations for each group of funds are based on the data for every month in which a return is available for the fund group, starting in January 1973. Like in Table 24.2, the state variables are predetermined, so they could be used to predict the subsequent monthly returns in real time. In many respects, the conditional returns of the funds mirror those of the benchmarks in Table 24.2. But with the shorter sample period available for some of the fund groups, the conditional mean effects do not as often attain statistical significance.

The term-structure state variables seem to be the most powerful predictors of future fund returns. Low short-term interest rates predict high fund returns, and high interest rates predict low returns. The differences in the conditional mean returns given high versus low short-term interest rates are significant, with *t*-statistics larger than 2.0 for five of the eight fund groups, indicated in bold. The expected returns given low interest rates are more than 2 percent per month greater than given high interest rates for the maximum capital gains funds and almost that large for the growth funds. A steep term-structure slope also predicts high subsequent returns for most groups, statistically significant for three of the eight based on the *t*-statistics. The differences are often economically large, at 3.2 percent per month for the maximum capital gains funds and just less than 2 percent for the growth funds. High interest rate volatility is bad news for most fund groups, and the differences are significant for five of the eight fund groups.[12] Finally, term-structure concavity has little predictive ability for fund returns.

The second group of variables captures the general state of financial markets. In this case, we find fewer instances where the conditional expected returns differ significantly across the states. The credit spread indicator produces *t*-statistics larger than 2.0 in three of the eight fund groups, with high spreads predicting high fund returns. The differences exceed 2 percent per month in three cases. Dividend yield, stock market volatility, and market liquidity measures produce no statistically significant effects. But the point estimates under the short-term corporate liquidity variable suggest economic significance, where the high-liquidity states predict higher fund returns for every fund group, with the magnitudes ranging from 0.5 percent to almost 3.5 percent per month across the fund groups.

The final set of state variables reflects the state of the macroeconomy. We find few statistically significant differences in the fund returns across these states. In the case of inflation, the point estimates suggest that low inflation is good news for subsequent fund returns, similar to the long-maturity bonds and passive equity benchmark returns described earlier. But the high volatility of fund returns in high inflation states results in small values of the *t*-statistics that measure the statistical significance of the difference across states. One exception is the case of the timing funds, where the *t*-statistic is 2.3. In the case of industrial output growth, the point estimates suggest that low current growth is good news for subsequent fund returns, again similar to the passive benchmarks, but the *t*-statistic is larger than 2 only in the case of the maximum capital gains funds.

Overall, the conditional mean returns of the funds suggest significant differences predicted by the state of the term structure of interest rates and credit spreads but only statistically weak evidence of conditional mean return differences related to the other state variables. The single state variable with the most predictive ability seems to be the level of the short-term interest rate. Ferson and Schadt found the short-term interest rate to be the most important conditioning variable among the more limited set of variables that they examined, so our evidence supports this finding in fresh data. The next question is whether the differences in conditional returns reflect abnormal performance or if these return differences can be explained by fund risk exposures that vary over time.

Conditional and Unconditional Alphas

Our first set of risk-adjusted performance results, summarized in Table 24.4, uses the equally weighted fund portfolios to examine average performance at the level of the fund-style groups. Although it would be unusual to find significant abnormal performance for entire groups of funds, this section allows us to explore the robustness of the results of previous studies where unconditional and conditional performance was compared for broad fund groups.

We first compare fund performance in conditional and unconditional versions of the CAPM. Panel A of Table 24.4 starts with the unconditional CAPM regression, which is Equation 24.1 without the $(r_{m,t+1} \otimes \mathbf{Z_t})$ term. All of the point estimates of alpha are negative except for the sector funds, but they are small—10 bps per month or less—and are not statistically significant based on the t-statistics, which are denoted t(alpha) in the table. Thus, our sample of funds reproduces the findings of previous studies that found that the unconditional performance of mutual funds tends to be slightly negative. The negative unconditional alphas are of the same order of magnitude as funds' expense ratios, which averaged about 1.2 percent per year over this period according to Figure 24.2. The CAPM betas, as expected, are strongly significant. The betas are sensibly ordered across the fund groups, with small-company growth funds having the largest beta (1.13) and income funds the smallest beta (0.37). The regression model R^2s indicate how much of the volatility of fund returns is associated with fluctuations in the market index. This measure also presents reasonable patterns across the fund groups. For example, the largest regression R^2 is for growth funds, at 92 percent, and the smallest is 58 percent, for the income funds.

Panel B of Table 24.4 presents the Ferson and Schadt regression for the conditional CAPM, as given by Equation 24.1. In this panel, we run the lagged instruments one at a time. The lagged instruments are used in this model to track variation through time in the funds' market betas. We conduct F-tests for the null hypothesis that the additional terms implied by the conditional models may be excluded from the regression. That is, the null hypothesis is that beta is constant over time; the alternative hypothesis is that beta moves as a linear function of the state variable. Only the results for those instruments whose F-tests reject the null hypothesis by producing p-values less than 0.10 are shown. This is a conservative inclusion criterion, and even if no instrument is individually useful, we would expect to find 10 percent of the cases, or 8–9 examples, that meet the inclusion criterion. We find that only 13 of the 88 cases examined meet the criterion.[13] But the cases are not randomly distributed across fund groups; half of them are the income funds. Thus, Table 24.4 suggests that among the various fund groups, income funds are the most likely to shift their stock market betas in response to the state of the economy.

Another pattern that does not appear to be random in Table 24.4 is the frequent presence of the stock market liquidity variable in the regressions with small p-values for the F-statistic. Stock liquidity appears three times, for three fund groups. This finding is interesting because no previous study of funds used a liquidity instrument to condition performance, and we did not find the stock market liquidity variable to be a significant predictor of either the passive benchmark returns or the fund returns. Nevertheless, Panel B suggests that some of the more aggressive fund styles may shift their market betas in response to the state of liquidity in the stock market.

TABLE 24.4 Unconditional and Conditional CAPM Regressions Using Equally Weighted Fund Portfolios

A. Unconditional CAPM regressions

Funds	Alpha	t(Alpha)	Beta	t(Beta)	R^2
Growth	−0.0659	−0.8938	0.974	67.88	0.920
Maximum capital gains	−0.0004	−0.0028	1.118	40.44	0.856
Other	−0.1007	−0.3956	1.101	17.43	0.7078
Income	−0.0126	−0.1514	0.369	11.32	0.5781
Growth and income	−0.0003	−0.0052	0.781	62.21	0.9157
Sector	0.0456	0.3853	0.860	28.88	0.8668
Small-company growth	−0.0255	−0.1060	1.127	21.16	0.7242

B. Conditional CAPM regressions using individual instruments

Funds	Instrument	Alpha	t(Alpha)	Bet0	t(Bet0)	$R^2$1	p-Value
Maximum capital gains	Corporate illiquidity	0.00848	0.05956	1.143	43.22	0.8593	0.021
Income	Interest rates	−0.07219	−0.8688	0.3847	11.37	0.6191	0.000
	Term slope	0.01915	0.2161	0.3631	11.25	0.5843	0.090
	Interest rate volatility	−0.07328	−0.8980	0.3833	11.69	0.6220	0.000
	Credit spread	0.03231	0.4272	0.3798	12.45	0.6458	0.000
	Dividend yield	0.00216	0.0282	0.3827	11.00	0.6436	0.000
	Inflation	−0.04619	−0.5450	0.3803	11.22	0.5890	0.014
Sector	Credit spread	0.04136	0.3481	0.9332	26.77	0.8689	0.066
	Stock liquidity	0.05151	0.4350	0.8541	27.20	0.8689	0.070
Small-company growth	Credit spread	−0.03595	−0.1496	1.304	15.58	0.7305	0.023
	Stock liquidity	−0.01310	−0.05461	1.114	20.57	0.7289	0.060
Other aggressive growth	Stock liquidity	−0.07269	−0.2845	1.101	17.48	0.7136	0.037

C. Conditional CAPM regressions using grouped instruments

Funds	Instrument	Alpha	t(Alpha)	Bet0	t(Bet0)	$R^2$1	p-Value
Income	Term structure	−0.0089	−0.1150	0.8735	10.34	0.6666	0.000
Maximum capital gains	Financial markets	0.0648	0.4247	1.382	8.511	0.8618	0.0409
Growth and income	Financial markets	−0.0722	−0.2458	0.8128	1.456	0.7183	0.0689
Income	Financial markets	0.0102	0.1354	0.8979	10.39	0.6743	0.000
Income	Macroeconomy	−0.0482	−0.5622	0.4371	8.584	0.5893	0.0330

Notes: The sample periods for the returns are January 1973 through December 2000 (336 observations), or a shorter period when indicated by fund availability in Table 24.3. Alphas are the abnormal returns, monthly percent; t(alpha) is a heteroscedasticity-consistent t-statistic. Beta is the CAPM beta, and t(beta) is its t-statistic. R^2 is the coefficient of determination of the regression. In Panels B and C, Bet0 is the average conditional beta, t(bet0) is its t-statistic, $R^2$1 is the regression coefficient of determination, and p-value is the right-tail p-value of the F-statistic for excluding the lagged instrument multiplied by the style index excess return. In Panel C, the instruments are grouped as follows: Term-structure instruments include the interest rate level, slope, convexity, and volatility. The financial markets variables include stock market volatility, credit spread, dividend yield, short-term corporate illiquidity, and stock market liquidity. The macroeconomy variables are inflation and industrial output growth.

551

Ferson and Schadt, using data that ended in 1990, found that conditional alphas tended to make funds look better than unconditional alphas and that conditional alphas were centered around zero. This result is consistent with a market where the typical fund manager has enough ability to cover trading costs and expense ratios once the biases have been removed by conditioning on the public information about the state of the economy. A comparison of Panel A with Panels B and C of Table 24.4 is consistent with this result. Although none of the estimates of alpha is statistically significant, seven of the eight in Panel A are negative, while in the conditional models, about half are positive and half are negative. Thus, the conditional performance is roughly centered at zero.

The original CPE studies used multiple lagged instruments in their regressions, whereas Panel B of Table 24.4 uses only one instrument at a time. In Panel C of Table 24.4, we thus use multiple lagged instruments in the models, where the instruments are grouped as in Table 24.2. The results tend to confirm the impressions from Panel B. (The table reports only the cases where the p-values are less than 10 percent.) Overall, of the 24 cases, 9 of the conditional alpha point estimates are positive and 15 are negative. But in some of these cases, the additional regressors in the conditional models are not significant, and we would expect to get results similar to the unconditional model when the coefficients on the conditional terms are zero. In other words, some of these cases are essentially unconditional alphas. If we restrict our attention to the subset of cases where the p-value of the F-statistics for the conditional terms is less than 0.10, we find 6 of the 24 cases, which is statistically significant.[14] Three of these alphas are positive, and three are negative. This finding confirms two of the main results of the earlier CPE studies: First, the conditioning variables are jointly statistically significant, and second, the conditional alphas are centered around zero.

Because our sample of funds is much broader than that in Ferson and Schadt, Table 24.4 shows that the general flavor of their results on conditional alphas holds in a broader sample of funds constructed to control survivor-selection bias. Our list of lagged instruments is also more inclusive, which shows that the central results are robust to the choice of instruments. Finally, Table 24.4 shows that the main results are robust to including a decade of new data.

Performance against Style-Based Benchmarks

Given the cumulative empirical evidence against the accuracy of the CAPM in describing risk-adjusted required returns, it is increasingly common to evaluate funds relative to benchmark indexes that control for the manager's investment style. This adjustment can be accomplished by using multiple risk factor indexes in place of the market portfolio of the CAPM, as in the arbitrage pricing model (APT, Ross 1976) or the Merton (1973) multifactor asset pricing model. This approach was developed for unconditional fund performance measures by Lehmann and Modest (1987) and Connor and Korajczyk (1986) and applied to style indexes by Carhart (1997). Alternatively, a single index can be constructed from a set of primitive asset class returns, with fund-style-specific weights, and the single index can replace the market return in the CAPM. We use the latter approach. The asset class returns are the passive benchmark returns described in Table 24.1 and whose conditional returns are studied in Table 24.2.

We construct style-matched benchmarks using an approach similar to Sharpe (1988, 1992). The problem is to combine the asset class index returns, denoted by R_i, using a set of portfolio weights, denoted by (w_i), so as to minimize the "tracking error" between the return of the fund or fund-style group in question, denoted by R_p, and the style-matched benchmark portfolio, denoted by $\Sigma_i w_i R_i$. The portfolio weights are required to sum to 1.0

and must be nonnegative, which effectively rules out short positions.[15] We formally state the problem to be solved as

$$\text{Min}_{(wi)} \text{var}(R_p - \Sigma_i w_i R_i), \tag{24.5}$$
$$\text{subject to:}$$
$$\Sigma_i w_i = 1, \ w_i \geq 0 \text{ for all } i,$$

where var($\cdot$) denotes the variance. We solve the problem numerically for each of the fund style groups and derive a set of weights for each group.

In returns-based style analysis as conducted by Sharpe (1988, 1992) and others (and as reviewed recently by Dor, Jagannathan, and Meier), it is common to use the return difference, $R_p - \Sigma_i w_i R_i$, to measure performance. The average difference over an evaluation period is a measure of alpha. The variance of the difference is a measure of tracking error, or active management. But these interpretations are correct only if the style of the fund does not change over the estimation period, as emphasized by Christopherson (1995).[16] Furthermore, this approach assumes that the "beta" of the fund on the style-matched benchmark is constant over time and equal to 1.0. Our approach relaxes the restriction that the beta of the fund on the style-matched benchmark is exactly 1.0. In addition, our conditional models allow the betas to vary over time with the state of the economy.

In Appendix 24A, Table 24.14 presents the style index weights for each asset class (Panel A) and summary statistics for the style-matched benchmark returns that result from applying these weights to the asset class returns (Panel B). Note that although the weights reported in the table do not sum exactly to 1.0 because of rounding errors, we carry many more digits of precision in the actual calculations. In a fair number of cases, the assigned weight is zero (26 out of 64 weights), which indicates that the no-short-selling constraint is binding. The largest weights are for sector funds in growth stocks (78 percent) and small-company growth funds in growth stocks (72 percent), which both make intuitive sense. Other large weights include the weight of growth and income funds on the broad equity index (67 percent) and of timing funds on the one-year government bond return (60 percent). The most concentrated weights are assigned to the sector funds, where the benchmark comprises 78 percent growth stocks and 11 percent each value stocks and long-term government debt. The most disperse set of weights is applied to the maximum capital gains funds, where the benchmark holds six of the eight asset classes and sports five weights in the 4–15 percent range.

The weights applied to the fixed-income asset classes are nontrivial. Timing funds have the highest total fixed-income weight at 82 percent (60 percent in government and 22 percent in corporate bonds) followed somewhat paradoxically by the maximum capital gains funds at 60 percent total fixed income. This finding could indicate a misspecification of the style analysis for maximum capital gains funds. Other cases with large fixed-income weights are income funds (37 percent), other aggressive growth funds (34 percent), growth and income funds (22 percent), and small-company growth funds (28 percent). These large fixed-income weights no doubt reflect the fact that mutual funds hold cash balances in reserve against investor withdrawals.

Panel B of Table 24.14 presents summary statistics for the returns that result when the weights in Panel A are applied to the asset class benchmark returns to construct the style-based benchmark for each fund group. The highest mean return, more than 1 percent per month, is associated with the benchmark for sector funds. This style-based benchmark also has the largest standard deviation of return, more than 5 percent per month. The high mean and high standard deviation reflect the concentration of the sector fund benchmark in growth stocks and its small fixed-income exposure. The lowest mean return and the lowest standard deviation are both associated with the timing-fund benchmark, which earned 0.8 percent per month, with a standard deviation of only 1.4 percent. This result reflects the fact that 82 percent of this benchmark consists of fixed-income securities.

In Appendix 24A, Table 24.15 repeats the performance analysis of Table 24.4, but with the style-based benchmarks replacing the market index of the CAPM. The analysis conducted is otherwise identical to that in Table 24.4. Panel A of Table 24.15, which reports the unconditional regressions, reveals the higher precision that becomes available using style-matched benchmarks. The regression R^2s are higher for seven of the eight fund groups, and they exceed 79 percent in each case except income funds. Using the market index of the CAPM in Table 24.4, we had R^2s as low as 58 percent. Many of the betas are significantly different from 1.0, which supports our approach of not constraining the betas to equal 1.0. The estimated alphas, however, are similar in their overall magnitudes to what we found using the CAPM. Five of the eight are negative. This is weak evidence that the funds look better against their style benchmarks than against the market, where seven of the eight alphas were negative. Because of the greater precision using style benchmarks, we have smaller standard errors, and the absolute values of the t-statistics attached to the alphas are larger than in Table 24.4. Still, no t-statistic for the unconditional alpha of any fund group is larger than 2.0.

Panel B of Table 24.15 presents the regressions estimating the conditional alphas, one instrument at a time. Compared with the model using the market index, we find a larger number of cases where the F-test can reject the hypothesis that the lagged state variables may be excluded from the regression. Using a 10 percent significance level, we find that this null is rejected for 26 of the 88 cases examined; when using a 5 percent level, we find 17 cases. The multiple-comparisons t-statistics for the significance of this finding are 6.11 and 6.16, respectively, at the two significance levels. Thus, we have strong evidence for the statistical significance of conditioning on the state variables when the style benchmarks are used.[17]

The lagged state variables are used here to model time variation in the style index betas. The evidence supports our approach of allowing the betas to vary over time and rejects the restriction that they are always equal to 1.0, as assumed in the traditional returns-based style analysis. This result provides evidence of a form of style drift at the fund group level. That is, funds tend to vary their sensitivity to the average style exposures depending on economic conditions. Income funds and market-timing funds seem most prone to this behavior.

The average conditional alphas remain centered near zero when measured relative to the style benchmarks. In Panel B of Table 24.15 are 12 positive alphas and 14 negative alphas. The only statistically significant conditional alphas are for the timing funds, where the alphas are negative and where four of the six t-statistics are below -2.0. Negative alphas for timing funds are to be expected, according to the analysis of Grant (1977), Jagannathan and Korajczyk, and others, as discussed later in the section on market timing.

Panel C of Table 24.15 summarizes the conditional model regressions when multiple instruments are used, grouped according to the states of the term structure, financial markets, and macroeconomy. Again, we report only the groups where the p-values are below 10 percent. The F-test for the exclusion of the instruments produces p-values this small in 14 of the 24 cases. This result implies a multiple-comparisons t-statistic of 7.9, again producing strong evidence that loadings on the style benchmarks vary with the state of the economy. Interestingly, the state variables related to the macroeconomy produce the most frequent examples of changing loadings, whereas it was the term-structure state variables when the market index of the CAPM was used that showed the most frequent examples of changing loadings. Of the 14 cases where the conditioning variables appear significant, the conditional alphas remain centered near zero, with six of the estimates negative and eight positive. Only two of the *t*-statistics for the alphas are larger than 2.0, which is about what should be expected when 24 cases are examined and the true alphas are zero.

Performance Conditioned on Discrete States

In the unconditional CAPM, we regress the fund excess returns on the market excess return, and the intercept is Jensen's alpha. The conditional model, however, adds interaction terms to the regression. These terms are motivated, as explained earlier, by models in which a fund manager responds linearly to information. The fund's portfolio betas, in particular, are assumed to vary as a linear function of the instruments. But the assumption of linear betas is only an approximation of convenience, and funds may respond nonlinearly to information in practice. For example, the use of derivatives is likely to induce a nonlinear relationship between a fund and the market. But little direct evidence exists in the previous literature on how important beta nonlinearity is for mutual funds. If the true relationship is far from linear, the interactive regressions are likely to be biased and inefficient. If we can measure conditional performance while avoiding the linear beta assumption, we should obtain a more reliable picture of the true performance in cases where nonlinearity is important.

The model of Ferson and Schadt allows only a single conditional alpha and, therefore, only captures the overall average conditional performance.[18] This limitation may obscure conditional performance that depends on the state. For example, some funds may have positive conditional performance in high values of a state variable and negative performance conditional on low states. The returns in Table 24.3 suggest just such a possibility. In this case, by averaging the conditional performances together in a fixed measure, as in Ferson and Schadt, we may produce a neutral measure for the average performance. The desire to measure time-varying conditional performance motivated Christopherson, Ferson, and Glassman to generalize the Ferson and Schadt Equation 24.1 to Equation 24.4, with a time-varying conditional alpha.

This section uses the discrete dummy versions of the lagged state variables to assess performance at the level of the fund groups. We estimate Equation 24.4 where **Z** is the vector of dummy variables corresponding to a given state variable. The vector consists of a constant, the dummy variable indicating a high value of the state variable, and the dummy indicating a low value of the state variable. Using the dummy variable instruments in Equation 24.4, we do not assume that betas respond with any particular functional form. The approach, in this sense, is nonparametric. We simply measure the average conditional beta and the average conditional alpha given that the economy is in one of the three states. We allow both the conditional alphas and betas to vary across the states. We do not model how betas or alphas vary over time within a state. The potential cost of this dummy-variable approach is that it will not capture time variation in alphas or betas that may occur within a regime. For example, if the economy stays in a low interest rate state for an extended period of time, we capture only the average conditional performance given the low rate state but not any time variation in conditional performance during the low interest rate regime.

Table 24.5 presents the conditional alphas based on the discrete state variables. The figures may be compared with those in Panel B of Table 24.3, which gives the conditional returns before risk adjustment. The differences between the two tables are dramatic. In Table 24.3, we found 19 cases where the differences in returns between high and low states produced *t*-statistics larger than 2.0. After adjustment using the conditional CAPM in Table 24.5,

TABLE 24.5 Alphas Conditioned on Discrete State Variables for Equally Weighted Portfolio of Mutual Funds, by Group

Item	No. Obs.	Growth	Maximum Capital Gains	Other Aggressive Growth	Income	Growth and Income	Sector	Small-Company Growth	Timers
A. Term-structure slope									
High	44	0.1963	0.1434	−0.3582	0.1606	0.3259	−0.0447	−0.4531	0.3851
Low	92	−0.2053	−0.0653	−0.1201	0.0253	−0.0538	0.0031	−0.1125	−0.2594
t-Statistic		1.183	0.3352	−0.3176	0.5756	1.202	−0.1489	−0.4181	**3.192**
B. Term-structure concavity									
High	36	0.1261	0.2281	−0.6000	0.1766	0.1566	−0.1149	−0.6229	0.2497
Low	85	−0.0517	0.0683	0.0406	−0.1300	−0.0166	0.0439	0.2778	−0.1936
t-Statistic		0.7776	0.3356	−0.9690	1.265	1.014	−0.4008	−1.161	**2.657**

Notes: Monthly fund group returns in excess of the 90-day T-bill are regressed on a broad equity market excess return and its product with dummy variables for the state of the economy, as in Equation 24.2 of the text. The dummy variables are the same as in Table 24.2. No. obs. is the number of observations for the growth fund sample period, which is January of 1973 through December of 2000 (336 total observations). Other fund groups may have fewer observations, as indicated in Table 24.3. Cases with fewer than 12 nonmissing observations are excluded and shown as 0.000; *t*-statistic is the heteroscedasticity-consistent *t*-statistic for the difference between the high- and low-state conditional alphas. Only states producing an absolute *t*-statistic larger than 2.0 are shown. The units for alpha are percent per month.

we find only two such instances (shown in bold). Only 8 of the 176 conditional alphas examined have *t*-statistics larger than 1.6; among those, five are positive and three are negative. The conditional alphas are also typically small in economic terms compared with the return differences before risk adjustment. In Table 24.3, we found 41 cases where the difference in the conditional mean returns for high- and low-state variables was larger than 1 percent per month, and many were much larger. Only 5 of the 176 conditional alphas examined to construct Table 24.5 are larger than 1 percent in absolute magnitude, and the largest conditional alpha is 1.5 percent per month. The conditional alphas are generally small, and their distribution is centered near zero.

The results of Table 24.5 confirm that the conclusions from the continuous instrument specifications are robust.[19] The strong impression is that the overall conditional performance of the broad fund groups is neutral.

In Appendix 24A, Table 24.16 repeats the analysis of Table 24.5, replacing the market index with the fund-group-specific style benchmarks. Many of the results confirm the findings of Table 24.5. For example, only 9 of the 88 alphas examined in producing the table have absolute *t*-statistics larger than 2.0, and only 3 of the conditional alphas are larger than 1 percent per month. (We only report cases where the absolute *t*-statistic is larger than 2.0.) The conditional alphas are small and centered near zero, indicating that the conditional performance is neutral.

Evaluation of the Time Variation in Risk Exposures

Tables 24.4 and 24.15 present evidence of significant time variation in funds' betas. Betas may vary within an economic regime and also across economic regimes. We now ask how important is time variation across versus within the economic regimes defined by the state

TABLE 24.6   Betas Conditioned on Discrete State Variables for Equally Weighted Portfolio of Mutual Funds, by Group

Item	Growth	Maximum Capital Gains	Other Aggressive Growth	Income	Growth and Income	Sector	Small-Company Growth	Timers
A. State of the term-structure variables								
Term-structure slope								
High	0.9165	1.099	1.577	0.1940	0.7018	1.080	1.658	0.5322
Low	0.9960	1.236	0.992	0.4286	0.8008	0.8159	1.021	0.5941
t-Statistic	−1.157	−1.082	2.230	−3.829	−1.676	2.449	2.219	−1.293
Interest rate volatility								
High	0.9857	1.176	1.082	0.3675	0.7738	0.8629	1.066	0.5838
Low	0.9028	1.015	1.005	0.3567	0.7825	0.8809	1.049	0.5925
t-Statistic	2.217	2.131	0.3510	0.1411	−0.2546	−0.1630	0.0958	−0.2569
B. State of the financial markets variables								
Credit spread								
High	0.9274	1.040	0.9016	0.3217	0.7498	0.7106	0.882	0.5792
Low	0.9776	1.129	1.161	0.4823	0.7939	0.8858	1.143	0.6005
t-Statistic	−0.8497	−0.9571	−1.018	−2.414	−0.9331	−1.585	−0.927	−0.5186
Short-term corporate illiquidity								
High	0.8791	0.958	1.028	0.3068	0.7422	0.7577	1.019	0.5591
Low	0.9653	1.154	0.9905	0.3364	0.7591	0.8118	0.946	0.5176
t-Statistic	−2.428	−2.327	0.1272	−0.3198	−0.3528	−0.2812	0.228	0.9474

Notes: Monthly fund group returns in excess of the 90-day T-bill are regressed on a broad equity market excess return and the products with dummy variables for the state of the economy. The dummy variables are the same as in Table 24.2. The growth fund sample period is January of 1973 through December of 2000 (336 total observations). Other fund groups may have fewer observations, as indicated in Table 24.3. Cases with fewer than 12 nonmissing observations are excluded and shown as 0.000; *t*-statistic is the heteroscedasticity-consistent *t*-statistic for the difference between the high- and low-state conditional betas. Only states producing an absolute *t*-statistic greater than 2.0 are shown.

variables. Using the discrete dummy versions of the state variables in Equation 24.4, we estimate the averages of the conditional betas across the months assigned to the high, low, and normal states. The differences in these betas show how much of the beta variation occurs across the regimes. If the differences across the regimes are small, we conclude that most of the variation through time that we documented earlier occurs within the regimes, most likely at higher frequencies than the long swings depicted by the state variable dummies in Figure 24.1. Such high-frequency beta variation may be induced by the relatively high-frequency flow of monies in and out of mutual funds.[20] Beta variation across the states, in contrast, is more likely related to strategic investment choices by the funds.

Conditional betas are shown in Table 24.6 for the high and low values of the state variables for each fund group, along with a *t*-statistic for the significance of the difference between the high- and low-state conditional betas (with those greater than 2.0 shown in bold). Only states that produced an absolute *t*-statistic larger than 2.0 are shown. The term-structure-slope variable is where most of the action occurs. This variable is associated with significant shifts in betas for four of the seven fund groups. The betas are higher for the pure equity funds and lower for the income funds when the term-structure slope is steeper than when it is shallow. The differences are substantial. For example, the conditional market beta of small-company growth funds is 1.66 when the slope of the term structure is steep and only 1.02 when it is shallow. The income funds' betas average 0.19 given a steep term structure and 0.43 when it is flat. This finding is consistent with the view that equity funds become more aggressive in their market exposure when the term structure is steep, perhaps in anticipation of the higher expected market returns illustrated in Table 24.2 at such times. Although these extreme examples are intriguing, overall only a little evidence exists of shifts in the conditional betas at the fund group level in Table 24.6. About 5 percent of the t-statistics examined in producing the table are larger than 2.0, just as would be expected if beta does not vary across the regimes.

In Appendix 24A, Table 24.17 summarizes the results of replicating Table 24.6 but using the style-specific benchmarks instead of the market index. The results are largely confirmatory. The timing funds seem to show the most significant tendencies to shift betas across the states, producing t-statistics for the hypothesis of no beta shift that exceed 2.0 in 3 of the 11 cases. Overall, however, only 9 of 88 cases present absolute t-statistics larger than 2.0 and no clear patterns exist in the estimates.[21]

In summary, we find that although there is significant time variation in funds' market and style betas, little of this variation is associated with the discrete shifts in the economic states. It seems likely that much of the time variation in beta is related to higher-frequency behavior, perhaps associated with redemptions and new money flows. The broad implications for investors and their advisors relate to strategic asset allocation. Some investors may wish to adjust the risk exposures of their portfolios with respect to the states of the economy. For example, an investor who is more risk averse than average about bad economic times may wish to take less risk when the current state has high volatility or when expected economic performance is poor than at other times during an economic cycle. Our results suggest that such strategies should be implemented by changing the allocation across fund categories. The funds themselves are unlikely to come with such strategic allocations built in, at least at this aggregate level.

INDIVIDUAL FUND PERFORMANCE

Although it may not be surprising to find little evidence of significant performance for entire groups of funds with different styles, the groups may mask significant performance at the fund level. Some funds are likely to perform well and others poorly, even in the same fund group, and the performance of individual funds is of central interest to financial advisors and investors. The next two tables explore the patterns in individual-fund performance.

In Table 24.7 we estimate the performance evaluation regressions for each individual fund with at least 12 months of data available. The instruments are the continuous versions of the lagged variables, grouped as in Panel C of Table 24.4. We summarize the results by recording the fractions of the individual-fund t-statistics that lie between standard critical values for a normal distribution, which is the asymptotic distribution for the t-statistics. The left-most column shows the fraction that would be expected under the null hypothesis of no abnormal performance if the normal distribution provides a good approximation for the t-statistics.

Ferson and Schadt provided an analysis similar to the column labeled "All" in Panels A and B of Table 24.7, where all the individual funds are pooled. Their sample was much smaller (with only 67 funds), and it used data ending in 1990. They found that the distribution of

TABLE 24.7 Cross-Sectional Distribution of *t*-Statistics for Alpha

Item	Null	All	Growth	Maximum Capital Gains	Other Aggressive Growth	Income	Growth and Income	Sector	Small-Company Growth
A. Unconditional alphas									
$t > 2.36$	0.005	0.03	0.02	0.08	0.05	0.02	0.02	0.02	0.05
$2.36 > t > 1.96$	0.02	0.02	0.01	0.04	0.02	0.01	0.02	0.02	0.03
$1.96 > t > 1.65$	0.025	0.02	0.03	0.05	0.02	0.02	0.02	0.04	0.03
$1.65 > t > 0$	0.45	0.38	0.39	0.34	0.39	0.29	0.40	0.54	0.40
$0 > t > -1.65$	0.45	0.40	0.40	0.34	0.41	0.37	0.41	0.32	0.42
$-1.65 > t > -1.96$	0.025	0.03	0.04	0.05	0.03	0.03	0.03	0.01	0.03
$-1.96 > t > -2.36$	0.02	0.03	0.03	0.04	0.02	0.03	0.03	0.01	0.02
$t < -2.36$	0.005	0.09	0.08	0.05	0.05	0.24	0.07	0.03	0.04
B. Alphas conditioned on term structure									
$t > 2.36$	0.005	0.03	0.03	0.09	0.06	0.02	0.02	0.03	0.06
$2.36 > t > 1.96$	0.02	0.02	0.02	0.04	0.02	0.01	0.01	0.03	0.02
$1.96 > t > 1.65$	0.025	0.02	0.02	0.05	0.03	0.01	0.01	0.04	0.03
$1.65 > t > 0$	0.45	0.38	0.39	0.34	0.48	0.24	0.33	0.55	0.50
$0 > t > -1.65$	0.45	0.40	0.40	0.37	0.35	0.40	0.48	0.29	0.35
$-1.65 > t > -1.96$	0.025	0.03	0.04	0.03	0.02	0.03	0.04	0.01	0.01
$-1.96 > t > -2.36$	0.02	0.03	0.04	0.02	0.01	0.03	0.04	0.02	0.01
$t < -2.36$	0.005	0.08	0.07	0.05	0.02	0.25	0.06	0.02	0.01
C. Alphas conditioned on financial markets									
$t > 2.36$	0.005	0.03	0.04	0.07	0.04	0.02	0.03	0.05	0.02
$2.36 > t > 1.96$	0.02	0.01	0.02	0.05	0.01	0.00	0.01	0.01	0.00
$1.96 > t > 1.65$	0.025	0.02	0.02	0.05	0.02	0.01	0.01	0.03	0.02
$1.65 > t > 0$	0.45	0.25	0.27	0.37	0.29	0.15	0.26	0.35	0.29
$0 > t > -1.65$	0.45	0.45	0.43	0.34	0.48	0.45	0.42	0.43	0.53
$-1.65 > t > -1.96$	0.025	0.06	0.05	0.05	0.07	0.06	0.07	0.06	0.07
$-1.96 > t > -2.36$	0.02	0.05	0.06	0.01	0.04	0.05	0.07	0.03	0.04
$t < -2.36$	0.005	0.11	0.10	0.05	0.04	0.25	0.14	0.04	0.02
D. Alphas conditioned on real economy									
$t > 2.36$	0.005	0.03	0.02	0.11	0.05	0.02	0.02	0.02	0.05
$2.36 > t > 1.96$	0.02	0.02	0.02	0.05	0.03	0.01	0.01	0.01	0.02
$1.96 > t > 1.65$	0.025	0.02	0.03	0.03	0.02	0.01	0.02	0.04	0.03
$1.65 > t > 0$	0.45	0.38	0.40	0.34	0.40	0.27	0.39	0.54	0.40
$0 > t > -1.65$	0.45	0.41	0.40	0.35	0.42	0.39	0.43	0.33	0.43
$-1.65 > t > -1.96$	0.025	0.03	0.04	0.03	0.02	0.03	0.03	0.02	0.02
$-1.96 > t > -2.36$	0.02	0.03	0.03	0.04	0.02	0.03	0.03	0.01	0.02
$t < -2.36$	0.005	0.08	0.06	0.05	0.05	0.23	0.06	0.03	0.03

Notes: The time-series Equation 24.1 is estimated for each fund in a style group using the continuous versions of the state variables in the conditional models. Funds with less than 12 observations are excluded. The figures are the fractions of the *t*-statistics located between standard critical values for a normal distribution. The fraction implied by a normal distribution is listed under the heading "Null."

the unconditional alphas was centered slightly to the left of the distribution under the null hypothesis. We find a similar result in Table 24.7. The unconditional performance measures suggest a slightly negative performance distribution. Also similar to Ferson and Schadt, the overall distributions of the t-statistics have fatter tails than a normal distribution. That is, we find more extreme negative and more extreme positive alphas for individual funds than would be observed with a normal distribution.[22]

Ferson and Schadt found that conditional models shift the distribution of individual-fund alphas toward better measured performance. We find no such evidence in Table 24.7. For example, 9 percent of the sample delivers t-statistics for unconditional alpha less than -2.36, while only 0.5 percent is expected if the distribution is normal and centered at zero. Using conditional alphas, we find that the fractions are 8–11 percent, depending on the state variable groups, with no clear shifts in the distributions.

Ferson and Schadt were not able to provide distributions of performance for individual funds within their style groups because of their small sample. With the larger sample in this study, we can examine the conditional performance of individual funds relative to other funds with the same style, thus controlling for performance differences associated with style. Table 24.7 shows that for some fund groups (e.g., maximum capital gains) the conditional alpha distribution looks more favorable than the distribution of unconditional alphas. For other groups (e.g., growth), the conditional alpha distribution is less favorable than the unconditional alpha distribution. Perhaps most striking is the result for income funds, which seem to produce an outsized fraction of low alphas under all versions of the model. Thus, the patterns in individual-fund performance are richer than a pooled analysis can reveal.

In Appendix 24A, Table 24.18 repeats the analysis of Table 24.7 but replaces the market index of the CAPM with the style-specific benchmarks. Therefore, the overall results are similar. The poor conditional performance of the bottom quarter or so of income funds cannot be explained by biases resulting from the use of the broad market index as the benchmark in the CAPM. In practical terms, this analysis suggests that investors and their advisors should be especially careful in their selection of individual income-style funds. Poor risk-adjusted performance is easy to find, and a randomly chosen fund has about a 25 percent chance of significant negative performance.

Although the results in Table 24.7 control for the state of the economy through time-varying betas, those models do not allow the actual performance, measured by the alphas, to vary over time with the economic state. Table 24.5 looked at models where the alphas are conditioned on the discrete state variable indicators taken one at a time, applied to the equally weighted portfolios according to fund-style groups. This approach allows the alphas to vary over time across the various states. Now, we look inside the groups at the performance of individual funds, allowing the conditional alphas to shift over time with the states.

Table 24.8 presents an analysis of the conditional performance of the individual funds using the conditioning dummy variables one at a time. We summarize the results by comparing the individual funds with all other funds in the same style group, again controlling for the performance effects of fund style. Because of the large number of cases to summarize, we simplify the table by reporting only those instances where the distribution of the performance measures' t-statistics depart from the asymptotic distribution under the null hypothesis of no performance. We select those cases using a chi-square test for the hypothesis that the distributions are normal. Similar to Table 24.7, the performance measures are divided into eight bins and the frequency of funds observed in bin i, is f_i, $i = 1,\ldots,8$. The theoretical frequency under the null is g_i, $i = 1,\ldots,8$. The statistic $\chi^2 = \sum_{i=1,\ldots,8} \frac{(f_i - g_i)^2}{g_i}$ is distributed as a chi-square

TABLE 24.8   Distribution of *t*-Statistics for Alphas in High vs. Low Economic States Using a Broad Market Benchmark

Interest Rate Volatility				Dividend Yield			
Income High	Income Low	SCG High	Other AG High	MCG High	Income Low	G&I High	Sector High
0.07	0.08	0.01	0.01	0.26	0.02	0.24	0.40
0.02	0.01	0.00	0.00	0.11	0.01	0.04	0.00
0.01	0.02	0.00	0.01	0.04	0.02	0.03	0.00
0.26	0.25	0.10	0.08	0.37	0.25	0.36	0.30
0.36	0.27	0.40	0.41	0.20	0.27	0.29	0.30
0.02	0.03	0.11	0.10	0.00	0.00	0.01	0.00
0.02	0.04	0.13	0.12	0.00	0.04	0.02	0.00
0.23	0.31	0.25	0.26	0.01	0.41	0.02	0.00

Short-Term Interest Rate		Inflation	Stock Market Volatility	Term Structure Slope	Stock Market Liquidity		
Income High	Income Low	G&I High	Income Low	Income High	SCG Low	Other AG Low	Sector Low
0.06	0.05	0.22	0.10	0.22	0.02	0.04	0.09
0.02	0.02	0.09	0.02	0.05	0.00	0.01	0.02
0.03	0.02	0.09	0.03	0.05	0.00	0.00	0.01
0.39	0.32	0.37	0.31	0.29	0.07	0.12	0.22
0.17	0.27	0.17	0.23	0.21	0.29	0.31	0.36
0.03	0.02	0.01	0.03	0.02	0.07	0.06	0.05
0.04	0.03	0.02	0.03	0.01	0.10	0.08	0.04
0.25	0.26	0.04	0.25	0.15	0.46	0.37	0.22

Notes: MCG = maximum capital gains; SCG = small company growth; Other AG = other aggressive growth; and G&I = growth and income. Alphas and their *t*-statistics are based on the regression Equation 24.4 using the conditioning dummy variables one at a time. High (low) means that the value of the state variable is higher (lower) than one standard deviation from its moving average over the past 60 months. The distributions of the *t*-statistics for alpha are presented in the table for those cases where chi-square tests for departures from a normal distribution produce right-tail *p*-values of 10 percent or less.

with seven degrees of freedom if the null hypothesis is correct (see, for example, Freund 1992, p. 487–488).

One interesting question that this analysis can address is whether the subset of individual funds with good or bad conditional performance generates that performance mainly in particular economic states. For example, we saw that the bottom 20–25 percent of income funds in Table 24.7 turned in highly significant negative alphas. Table 24.8 shows that their poor performance is not concentrated in particular economic regimes. Consider the states defined by the level of interest rates, for example. About 25 percent of the income funds have negative alphas with *t*-statistics larger than 2.36 when interest rates are high, and a similar fraction is found when interest rates are low.

Although the poor conditional performance of income funds cannot be attributed to any particular state of the economy, some interesting cases in Table 24.8 show that the extreme performance of individual funds is concentrated in particular economic states. For example, other aggressive growth funds have a concentration of poor performers when interest rate volatility is high or stock market liquidity is low, and poor performance is relatively rare in this group when interest rate volatility is low. High dividend yield states reveal a large number of individual funds with good performance among the maximum capital gains, growth and income, and sector funds, where none of these funds appears in low dividend yield states. Growth and income funds produce a large number of positive performers when inflation is high but not when inflation is low. Many small-company growth funds perform poorly when interest rate volatility is high or stock market liquidity is low. These patterns in the conditional performance of individual funds are interesting, both from a style allocation and a fund selection perspective. For style allocation, the results suggest that considering the current economic state in setting expectations for individual fund performance is useful depending on the style. For fund selection, the results indicate where poor performance is likely to be harder to avoid and where extra care in fund selection is relatively likely to pay off.

The analysis of Table 24.8 suggests that in several cases the abnormal measured performance of the extreme-performing individual funds in a style group is concentrated in particular economic states. In Appendix 24A, Table 24.19 replicates the analysis of Table 24.8 but replaces the market index benchmark of the CAPM with the fund-style-specific benchmarks. Most of the results just emphasized are robust to this change in the model. These results should be of interest to analysts attempting to pick funds in particular style groups in search of abnormal risk-adjusted returns or in an attempt to avoid poor risk-adjusted performance. The results suggest that certain styles of funds deserve more scrutiny in particular economic states because the likelihood of finding extreme performers may be higher at some times than at other times.

PERFORMANCE AND INDIVIDUAL-FUND CHARACTERISTICS

In this section, we expand our fund-level analysis of performance to include the objective, fund-specific characteristics. We conduct this analysis using cross-sectional regressions, as illustrated by Equation 24.6:

$$\alpha_{it} = \alpha_{0t} + \alpha_{1t}'X_{it-1} + \varepsilon_{it}, \ i = 1,\ldots,N_t. \tag{24.6}$$

At the end of each year, we record the vector of fund characteristics denoted by X_{it-1} for fund i. We use the following 36 months of data to estimate a measure of performance for each fund, denoted by α_{it}. We estimate the cross-sectional regression each year in an attempt to predict fund performance using the lagged fund characteristics.

In each cross-sectional year, we Studentize the fund characteristics, borrowing a technique from quantitative equity models. We subtract the cross-sectional mean from each characteristic and divide by the cross-sectional standard deviation. Thus, the coefficients in Equation 24.6 are interpreted as the percentage increment to alpha associated with a characteristic that is one standard deviation above the mean. For example, for the growth-style funds, the slope coefficient on the characteristic "gains" is about 0.2 percent per month, with a huge t-statistic in the regression predicting unconditional alphas. This result means that, all other things being equal, an individual growth fund that earned capital gains in the top third of all growth funds last year (one standard deviation above the mean) is expected to produce 20 bps per month of extra alpha over the next three years.

The number of observations in a given year, N_t, is the number of funds for which we have the characteristics data at the end of year $t-1$ and for which we also have at least 24 months of return data over the next 36 months to estimate the performance measure.[23] We aggregate the results across years using the methods of Fama and MacBeth (1973), who advocated using the average over time of the cross-sectional regression estimates of α_{1t} to make inferences about the performance differences associated with the characteristics. The standard error for the average coefficient is computed as the standard error of the mean using the time series of the estimated coefficients.[24]

The standard properties of a regression model imply that the analysis using Equation 24.6 automatically focuses on relative fund performance because a regression slope coefficient is invariant to subtracting the sample mean from the dependent variables. We therefore conduct the cross-sectional analysis within fund-style groups, so the coefficients describe individual-fund performance relative to funds with the same style. In our dataset, only three fund-style groups have enough funds to conduct a reasonable cross-sectional analysis, starting with the characteristics in 1972. These are the growth funds, income funds, and growth and income funds. We focus on the growth funds and the income funds here.

One of the interesting fund characteristics is a fund's turnover. Edelen argued that decomposing the cross-section of turnover into two parts is useful. The first component, which we will call "nondiscretionary" turnover, reflects trading in response to flows of new money in or out of the fund. Edelen argued that such nondiscretionary trades may hurt fund performance. The second component is "discretionary" turnover, which reflects the trading that managers conduct not because they are forced to but because they want to. Edelen argued that these are the trades that should enhance performance when managers have skill.

Following Edelen, we use the following cross-sectional regression to decompose a fund's reported turnover each year into discretionary and nondiscretionary components:

$$Turn_{it} = d_{0t} + d_{1t}Flow_{it} + v_{it}, \quad i = 1,\ldots,N_t, \tag{24.7}$$

where d_{0t} and d_{1t} are the regression coefficients and v_{it} is the regression error. The fitted values of the regression for each fund in each year, given by the estimates of $d_{1t}\,Flow_{it}$, measure nondiscretionary turnover; this is the portion of turnover that is explained by the cross-sectional relationship between flow and turnover that year. The intercept plus the residuals of the regression, $d_{0t} + v_{it}$, are used as our estimate of discretionary turnover; this is the portion of turnover that is uncorrelated with fund flow in the cross-section that year.

Table 24.9 summarizes the results of the cross-sectional regression analysis of the individual funds. Panel A presents the results when the unconditional CAPM alpha is the measure of performance. Panel B summarizes the regressions for growth funds using the conditional CAPM alphas as the performance measures, and Panel C summarizes the regressions for the income funds. Panels D, E, and F repeat the analysis substituting the Sharpe style benchmarks for the broad equity index benchmark. We summarize the conditional model results by focusing on the term-structure state variables. The coefficients associated with each characteristic are shown with the Fama–MacBeth t-statistics on the second line.

The regressions suggest a number of interesting patterns. In Panels A and D, older growth funds with a longer track record turn in significantly larger unconditional alphas than younger growth funds, although the magnitude of the difference, at less than 5 bps, is not large. So, a fund that is one standard deviation older than the average fund is expected to generate just less than 5 bps per month of extra alpha over the next three years. The coefficients

TABLE 24.9   Fund Style: Coefficient and t-Statistic for Mutual Fund Characteristic

Group or State Variable	Flow	Age	Total Net Assets	Income	Capital Gains	Discretionary Turnover	Load	Expense	Lagret
A. Performance measured using the unconditional CAPM									
Growth	−6.03	0.046	0.473	−0.150	0.213	−0.0329	0.237	0.135	0.506
t-Statistic	−1.02	3.42	1.52	−1.01	9.66	−1.37	4.31	1.76	9.04
Income	0.707	0.177	0.181	0.215	0.059	0.023	0.127	0.033	−0.0724
	1.06	0.551	1.04	1.34	0.753	1.68	1.97	0.582	−1.86
B. Performance measured using conditional CAPM, growth funds									
Short-rate level	−8.77	0.032	0.453	−0.141	0.195	−0.029	0.224	0.106	0.502
t-Statistic	−1.02	2.32	1.48	−0.947	8.48	−1.24	4.14	1.76	8.48
Term slope	−11.4	0.0405	0.437	−0.175	0.205	−0.0333	0.235	0.119	0.504
t-Statistic	−1.03	3.26	1.55	−0.990	9.37	−1.39	4.29	1.84	8.33
C. Performance measured using conditional CAPM, income funds									
Short-rate level	0.471	0.177	0.182	0.219	0.0565	0.0197	0.107	0.0364	−0.0679
t-Statistic	1.11	0.557	1.01	1.34	0.732	1.33	1.67	0.620	−1.96
Term slope	0.480	0.162	0.176	0.200	0.0574	0.0227	0.121	0.0375	−0.0739
t-Statistic	1.08	0.531	1.02	1.32	0.740	1.66	1.95	0.710	−2.06
D. Performance measured using the unconditional style model									
Growth	−3.64	0.049	0.462	−0.152	0.214	−0.034	0.241	0.135	0.511
t-Statistic	−1.01	3.35	1.50	−1.03	9.74	−1.40	4.54	1.75	8.62
Income	0.838	0.166	0.183	0.207	0.062	0.023	0.127	0.031	−0.072
t-Statistic	1.04	0.529	1.04	1.28	0.762	1.71	1.97	0.558	−1.83
E. Performance measured using the conditional style model, growth funds									
Short-rate level	−1.88	0.033	0.461	−0.109	0.196	−0.029	0.228	0.106	0.506
t-Statistic	−0.981	2.31	1.47	−0.966	8.83	−1.14	4.32	1.70	8.20
Term slope	−10.6	0.044	0.421	−0.181	0.21	−0.034	0.240	0.116	0.510
t-Statistic	−1.03	3.23	1.55	−1.03	9.66	−1.39	4.61	1.77	8.12
F. Performance measured using conditional style model, income funds									
Short-rate level	1.01	0.166	0.183	0.217	0.060	0.020	0.113	0.028	−0.070
t-Statistic	1.05	0.539	1.01	1.25	0.740	1.45	1.67	0.519	−1.98
Term slope	0.034	0.159	0.181	0.174	0.062	0.022	0.125	0.033	−0.075
t-Statistic	0.793	0.533	1.04	1.26	0.767	1.70	1.97	0.668	−2.04

Notes: Cross-sectional regressions of abnormal performance measures on lagged fund characteristics. Characteristics are measured each year from 1972–1997, and future returns for the subsequent 36 months are used to estimate the measures of performance. The regressions are aggregated across years using the methods of Fama and MacBeth (1973), adjusting for overlapping data in the standard errors. The units of the average coefficients are percent per month.

also suggest that funds with large total net assets have higher alphas than small funds and that higher load fees are associated with higher unconditional alphas. All of these results are robust to the choice of the benchmark index.

The result for fund loads is consistent with earlier findings from Ippolito (1989), who observed that load funds offer higher average returns than no load funds. Our regressions show that this result extends to conditional measures of performance, at least for growth funds. Among income funds, however, the predictive power of loads for individual fund alpha is diminished. The coefficient is about half the size, and the *t*-statistic is less than 2.0. Of course, some funds may substitute load fees, which are not reflected in the measured returns, for 12b-1 fees, which are taken out of the returns as part of the expense ratio. In practice, it would be important to consider the cost of the load fee in relation to the investor's horizon when using these results to guide fund selection decisions.

The strongest results for the unconditional alphas relate to the capital gains and total returns of a fund over the previous year. Both gains and lagged return (lagret) have large positive coefficients (20–50 bps per month) and *t*-statistics larger than 9.0 in the growth fund regressions, but in the income funds, neither effect is significant. This finding may be interpreted in terms of "momentum" in stock returns and funds. Jegadeesh and Titman (1993) described momentum as a cross-sectional pattern in stock returns. Stocks whose relative return was large over the last year or so also tend to have large returns over the next year or so relative to the overall market. Grinblatt, Titman, and Wermers (1995) found a similar pattern in equity fund returns. They found that growth funds, in particular, tend to hold momentum stocks. Ferson and Khang, while examining the holdings of pension funds, also found that growth-style funds tend to hold momentum stocks and that value-style funds tend to be contrarian, concentrating their holdings in those stocks that have recently performed poorly. The regressions in Table 24.9 are consistent with these findings. The large positive coefficients on capital gains and lagret among the growth funds indicate a momentum effect: Growth funds with relatively high returns over the past year tend to have larger unconditional alphas going forward. Income funds, in contrast, display no such momentum. This finding makes sense because income funds are more likely to hold stocks whose prices are low, relative to dividends and cash flow measures. Such a strategy is unlikely to imply momentum.

We estimate the regressions using conditional performance measures in Panels B, C, E, and F. The findings are easy to summarize. Every effect that is significant for the growth funds using unconditional alphas is also observed using the conditional alphas. The signs of the coefficients agree in each of these cases, but the effects are reduced relative to the unconditional case: The coefficients are uniformly closer to zero, and the *t*-statistics are uniformly smaller. The effects of fund age, load fees, and the momentum effects still produce *t*-statistics larger than 2.0. For the income funds, the conditional results are also similar to the unconditional results, and the only case where an absolute *t*-statistic is larger than 2.0 is lagret, where the coefficient is negative. The effects of fund flows, discretionary turnover, and expense ratios are all insignificant.

MARKET TIMING

A classical market-timing model follows from Treynor and Mazuy (1966):

$$r_{p,t+1} = a_p + b_p r_{m,t+1} + \Lambda_p r_{m,t+1}^2 + w_{t+1}, \tag{24.8}$$

where a_p, b_p, and Λ_p are the regression coefficients and w_{t+1} is the regression error. Treynor and Mazuy argued that $\Lambda_p > 0$ indicates market-timing ability. The logic is that a market-timing manager will generate a return that bears a convex relationship to the market: When the market is up, the fund will be up by a disproportionate amount. When the market is down, the fund will be down by a lesser amount. But a convex relationship may arise for a number of other reasons, one of which is common time variation in the fund's beta risk and the expected market risk premium resulting from public information on the state of the economy. Ferson and Schadt proposed a refinement of the Treynor–Mazuy model to handle this situation:

$$r_{pt+1} = a_p + b_p r_{m,t+1} + C_p'(\mathbf{Z_t} r_{m,t+1}) + \Lambda_p r_{m,t+1}^2 + w_{t+1}. \qquad (24.9)$$

In Equation 24.9, the term $C_p'(\mathbf{Z_t} r_{m,t+1})$ controls for common time variation in the market risk premium and the fund's beta, just like it did in Equation 24.1.[25]

In theoretical market-timing models (see Admati, Bhattacharya, Pfleiderer, and Ross 1986, or Becker, Myers, and Schill), the timing coefficient is shown to depend on both the precision of the manager's market-timing signal and the manager's risk aversion. Precision probably varies over time because fund managers are likely to receive information of varying uncertainty about economic conditions at different times. Risk aversion may also vary over time, according to arguments describing mutual fund "tournaments" for new money flows (e.g., Brown, Harlow, and Starks 1996), which may induce managers to take more risks when their performance is lagging and to be more conservative when they want to "lock in" favorable recent performance. Therefore, it seems likely that the timing coefficient that measures the convexity of a fund's conditional relationship to the market is likely to vary over time. We take account of such effects by allowing the timing coefficient to vary over time as a function of the state of the economy. We replace the fixed timing coefficient in Equation 24.9 with $\Lambda_p = \Lambda_{0p} + \Lambda_{1p}'\mathbf{Z_t}$. Substituting this equivalence into Equation 24.9, we derive a new conditional timing model with time-varying performance:

$$r_{pt+1} = a_p + b_p r_{m,t+1} + C_p'(\mathbf{Z_t} r_{m,t+1}) + \Lambda_{0p} r_{m,t+1}^2 + \Lambda_{1p}'(\mathbf{Z_t} r_{m,t+1}^2) + w_{t+1}. \quad (24.10)$$

In this model, the new interaction term $(\mathbf{Z_t} r_{m,t+1}^2)$ captures the variability in the managers' timing ability, if any, over the states of the economy. By examining the significance of the coefficients in Λ_{1p}, we test the null hypothesis that the timing ability is fixed against the alternative hypothesis that timing ability varies with the economic state.

A special case of the model of Equation 24.10 occurs when we use the dummy variable versions of the lagged state variables. In this version of the model, we estimate the average conditional timing coefficient given high, low, and normal values of the state variable. The trade-offs here are similar to what we faced in the estimation of conditional alphas. With the dummy variables, we avoid the functional form assumptions, and so the results are robust to misspecification of the functional forms of time-varying betas or conditional timing coefficients, but we capture variation through time only in the aspects of the model that occur across the regimes defined by the state variables.

Lehmann and Modest, Grinblatt and Titman (1988), Cumby and Glen (1990), Ferson and Schadt, and others estimated Treynor–Mazuy regressions and found a tendency for negative estimates of Λ_p for equity mutual funds in Equation 24.8. Ferson and Schadt found that this result is spurious in that negative Λ_p is also found for a buy-and-hold strategy, while negative Λ_p's are not commonly found in the conditional model of Equation 24.9. These studies used broad samples of U.S. equity funds and did not focus in on those funds most likely to engage in timing behavior. Becker, Myers, and Schill, however, found similar results using a different model in a broad sample of funds, and they found less of a tendency for negative timing coefficients in a subsample focused on market-timing-style mutual funds.[26]

Table 24.10 summarizes the results of estimating the market-timing models, Equations 24.8 and 24.9 on our sample of market-timing funds for the 1973–2000 period. We concentrate on the estimates of the timing coefficients and on the marginal explanatory power

TABLE 24.10 Conditional and Unconditional Market-Timing Models

Fund Characteristics	γ_u	$t(\gamma_u)$	$R^2 0$	
A. Unconditional models				
High age	0.2545	**2.744**	0.9054	
High total net assets	0.3383	**3.730**	0.8851	
Low capital gains	0.4658	**2.102**	0.8176	
Low expense	0.2299	**2.697**	0.8992	
	γ_c	$t(\gamma_c)$	$R^2 1$	p-Value
B. Conditioning on term-structure state variables				
High flow	0.2407	1.888	0.8525	0.0610
Medium flow	0.2007	**2.197**	0.8838	0.2119
High age	0.2629	**3.187**	0.9063	0.6882
High total net assets	0.3541	**3.999**	0.8859	0.8370
High income	0.2423	**2.551**	0.8518	0.1833
Medium capital gains	−0.06412	−0.4409	0.8539	0.0528
Low capital gains	0.5242	**3.261**	0.8241	0.0412
Low turnover	0.3267	**2.053**	0.8748	0.0715
Medium load	0.1941	1.763	0.8586	0.0408
Medium expense	0.1823	1.702	0.8541	0.0374
Low expense	0.2487	**3.176**	0.9004	0.5601
Medium lagret	0.2842	**2.210**	0.8774	0.2155
C. Conditioning on financial market state variables				
High flow	0.1271	0.8113	0.8540	0.03306
Medium flow	0.1198	1.158	0.8881	0.00514
Low flow	−0.05503	−0.3742	0.8972	0.00446
High age	0.1964	**2.126**	0.9090	0.05495
Medium age	−0.08550	−0.6139	0.8641	0.01069
Low age	−0.05436	−0.4814	0.8349	0.2120
High total net assets	0.2158	**2.248**	0.8908	0.01388
Medium total net assets	−0.01504	−0.1193	0.8582	0.07998
High income	0.1341	1.020	0.8564	0.00878
Medium income	0.01187	0.1137	0.8871	0.04133
High capital gains	−0.1691	−1.284	0.9085	0.01484
Low capital gains	0.4060	1.805	0.8291	0.00256
High turnover	−0.08277	−0.6799	0.9020	0.02596
Medium turnover	0.07848	0.6958	0.8691	0.00374
Low turnover	0.3191	**2.041**	0.8774	0.01098
Medium load	0.09496	0.7392	0.8619	0.00462
Low load	−0.09841	−0.9495	0.9096	0.1150
Medium expense	0.1130	0.8715	0.8550	0.03227
Low expense	0.1105	1.323	0.9037	0.02641
Medium lagret	0.1065	0.9001	0.8819	0.00489
D. Conditioning on macroeconomy state variables				
High flow	0.1809	1.447	0.8512	0.04788
Low flow	0.05693	0.3770	0.8965	0.00068
High age	0.2421	**2.769**	0.9061	0.5051
Medium age	0.00622	0.0456	0.8602	0.04548
High total net assets	0.3353	**3.569**	0.8857	0.6458
Low capital gains	0.4637	**2.029**	0.8210	0.1043
High turnover	0.07905	0.6321	0.9001	0.0342
Low expense	0.2255	**2.688**	0.9003	0.3332
High lagret	−0.05452	−0.3298	0.8963	0.0367
Medium lagret	0.2342	**2.378**	0.8802	0.0024

Notes: Monthly returns in excess of the 90-day T-bill return for market-timing funds grouped by characteristics are regressed on a broad equity market excess return, its square, and its products with lagged state variables, with the state variables grouped as in the previous tables. The fund sample period is January 1973 through December 2000 (336 total observations). $R^2 0$ is the regression R^2 for the unconditional model, and $R^2 1$ is the conditional model R^2; p-value is the right-tail p-value of the F-test for the null hypothesis that the conditional model's variables may be excluded from the regression.

of the lagged state variables in the conditional models. The state variables are measured in their continuous forms and grouped according to the states of the term structure, financial market, and macroeconomy. The alphas in these models are difficult to interpret as a measure of abnormal return because the timing term is a squared market return instead of the excess return on an asset. The expected value of the squared term, multiplied by the timing coefficient, is essentially deducted from the alpha, and this expected value has no clean interpretation as a return premium. Although it is possible to modify the timing term in order to interpret the modified alpha as a timing-adjusted excess return (e.g., Glosten and Jagannathan 1994), such modifications rely on highly stylized assumptions. The magnitudes of the timing coefficients in Table 24.10 suggest that such an exercise would offer few new insights, so we avoid the extra complexity here.[27]

The first panel of Table 24.10 presents the unconditional timing coefficients, γ_u; their t-statistics, $t(\gamma_u)$; and the R^2s summarizing the explanatory power of the unconditional timing of Equation 24.8. The next three panels present similar information for the conditional models [with γ_u the unconditional model timing coefficient and $t(\gamma_u)$ its heteroscedasticity consistent t-statistic] along with p-values for the F-test of the significance of the lagged state variables. Panel B uses the continuous versions of the state variables related to the term structure, Panel C uses the continuous financial market state variables, and Panel D uses the state variables for the macroeconomy. Each row of the table summarizes a particular characteristics-based fund portfolio. To save space, we only show those cases where a t-statistic for a timing coefficient is larger than 2.0 or the p-value for the additional conditioning variables is less than 10 percent.

From the p-values of the F-tests, we can draw inferences about the significance of the lagged state variables in the conditional models. The state variables in these models capture variation over time in the funds' market betas that is correlated with the lagged public information. The number of cases, out of 28 possible, where the right-tail p-values are less than 5 percent are 3, 16, and 6, respectively, in the three panels. Except for Panel B, small p-values are found more than would be expected under the null hypothesis that the state variables may be excluded from the model. The multiple-comparisons t-statistics for the three panels are 1.39, 12.66, and 3.98, respectively.[28] We thus find particularly strong evidence of time-varying betas for the market-timing funds in response to the public information represented by the financial market state variables.

Ferson and Schadt as well as Becker, Myers, and Schill found that conditional timing models made funds look better than unconditional models. Table 24.10 provides mixed evidence on this score. In Panel B, which conditions on the term-structure state variables, the point estimates of the timing coefficients appear to confirm their result for our sample. Remarkably, in all 28 cases examined, the conditional timing coefficient is larger than the unconditional coefficient. But in Panels C and D, we do not find the same result, and the differences actually go the other way in all but four or five cases we examined in constructing the table. The most important instruments that were used in the studies of Ferson and Schadt and Becker, Myers, and Schill are related to interest rates, which could reconcile our results with those of the earlier studies.

The t-statistics attached to the timing coefficients allow us to address the question of whether the timing funds have significant market-timing ability. For the unconditional timing models, 4 of the 28 fund groupings produce t-statistics larger than 2.0 (shown in bold). On a multiple-comparisons basis, that result implies a t-statistic of 2.25, more than would be expected if there is no ability. Only 5 of the 28 unconditional coefficients are negative, which is consistent with the results of Becker, Myers, and Schill that negative unconditional timing coefficients are less likely to occur when the sample concentrates on likely market timers. Moving to the conditional timing models, we find 8, 3, and 5 examples in the three panels, respectively, where the *t*-statistics are larger than 2.0 in absolute value, and all of these are positive. The multiple-comparisons *t*-statistics for finding this many large *t*-statistics out of 28 are 5.72, 1.39, and 3.12, respectively. So, evidence exists that some of the market-timing funds may have positive conditional timing ability.

Comparing the timing coefficients across the fund groups with high, medium, and low values of the various characteristics provides further insights into which types of timing funds are more likely to be successful. There are several striking results. The strongest results relate to age and fund size as measured by the total net assets (TNA). Older funds tend to be better timers than medium-aged or young funds. Funds with high TNA at the end of the previous year have larger timing coefficients than smaller funds. Funds with the lowest expense ratios have the largest timing coefficients. Medium-expense-ratio funds do not time as well as low-expense-ratio funds, and high-expense-ratio funds have the smallest timing coefficients. Interestingly, there is some evidence, albeit weaker, that high-load funds may have better market-timing ability. This finding is consistent with the use of load fees as a screening device to penalize investors who trade frequently, which can make it more difficult for the fund to effectively implement its own active trading strategy. Finally, when the previous year's capital gains distribution is small, it predicts better timing performance over the next year.

We checked these findings by ungrouping the lagged state variables, using them one at a time, and confirm that the best conditional timers had the longest track records, the largest TNA, the lowest expense ratios, and the smallest capital gains. We also ran the analysis of Table 24.10 substituting the style-related benchmarks for the market index. In this case, we picked a style benchmark at random for each fund-characteristic group. The main findings are also robust to this experiment.

In Table 24.11, we summarize the results for the market-timing model of Equation 24.10 using the discrete dummy versions of the lagged state variables. In this model, we allow timing ability to vary across the states, and as described earlier, we avoid the assumptions that conditional betas are linear functions and that the timing coefficients have any particular functional form. We estimate the average conditional timing coefficient given high, low, and normal values of the state variable; the table summarizes results for the high and low states using the state variables one at a time. We report the timing coefficients in the high and low states, *t*-statistics for the hypothesis that a coefficient differs from zero, and a *t*-statistic that examines the hypothesis that the timing coefficients are equal in the high and low states for a given group of funds. Each row of the table summarizes a particular characteristic-based fund portfolio. To conserve space, only cases where an absolute *t*-statistic is larger than 2.0 are reported.

Much of the evidence of Table 24.11 remains consistent with neutral conditional timing performance. The fraction of absolute *t*-statistics larger than 2.0 is not significant (given the number of cases examined) when we condition on the level of interest rates, interest rate or stock market volatility, credit spread, or macroeconomy state variables. In some instances, however, we find significant evidence of conditional timing in certain states.

The most striking example of time-varying timing ability is related to the slope of the term structure. In 23 cases out of the 56 examined, the absolute *t*-statistic for the timing coefficient is larger than 2.0 (shown in bold). This result corresponds to a multiple-comparisons *t*-statistic of more than 40.0. Furthermore, all the significant cases occur conditional on a high term-structure slope, and all these coefficients are positive. Thus, we have striking evidence that market-timing funds can deliver significant conditional timing performance when

TABLE 24.11 Conditional Market-Timing Models with Time-Varying Ability

Funds	γ_{hi}	$t(\gamma_{hi})$	γ_{lo}	$t(\gamma_{lo})$	$t(H_0: \gamma_{hi} = \gamma_{lo})$
A. Short-term rates					
Low flow	−0.1676	−0.4355	0.4686	**2.237**	−1.528
High capital gains	−0.2143	−0.6171	0.4650	**2.041**	−1.710
B. Term-structure slope					
All	1.182	**3.832**	0.0329	0.1143	**2.729**
High flow	1.695	**3.233**	0.3195	0.8638	**2.186**
Med flow	1.582	**4.167**	0.2148	0.7416	**2.854**
Low flow	0.7967	1.959	−0.3117	−0.8497	**2.056**
High age	1.340	**3.815**	0.3004	1.164	**2.449**
Med age	1.487	**3.832**	−0.2754	−0.6574	**3.086**
High total net assets	1.785	**5.425**	0.3204	1.301	**3.604**
Med total net assets	1.207	**3.116**	−0.0329	−0.093	**2.383**
Low total net assets	0.7717	**3.068**	0.0917	0.242	1.534
High income	1.522	**3.929**	0.1868	0.6728	**2.858**
Med income	1.201	**3.713**	0.1305	0.4120	**2.413**
High capital gains	0.9923	**2.062**	0.05035	0.1589	1.640
Low capital gains	2.109	**4.062**	0.2036	0.6895	**3.216**
High turnover	1.281	**3.570**	−0.1162	−0.3872	**2.963**
Med turnover	0.8490	**2.622**	0.3057	0.9710	1.216
Low turnover	1.861	**4.012**	0.2168	0.6450	**2.910**
High load	1.259	**2.730**	0.3735	1.053	1.532
Med load	1.467	**3.724**	0.04086	0.1193	**2.765**
Low load	0.7728	**2.761**	−0.1253	−0.4308	**2.238**
High expense	0.8288	**2.667**	0.2276	0.6061	1.250
Med expense	1.356	**3.540**	0.01819	0.04606	**2.457**
Low expense	1.341	**4.125**	0.03097	0.1319	**3.278**
Med lagret	1.633	**5.009**	0.1360	0.4291	**3.403**
Low lagret	2.384	**2.894**	0.02229	0.04121	**2.369**
C. Term-structure concavity					
All	0.6625	1.823	−0.2599	−1.214	**2.230**
High flow	1.038	1.840	−0.3444	−1.221	**2.225**
Med flow	0.9374	**2.248**	−0.3735	−1.538	**2.766**
Low flow	0.4214	1.352	−0.3056	−1.175	**1.836**
High age	0.8543	**2.450**	−0.2219	−1.123	**2.733**
High total net assets	1.103	**2.590**	−0.1790	−1.030	**2.839**
Med total net assets	0.6338	1.625	−0.4484	**−2.004**	**2.452**
Low total net assets	0.2272	0.608	−0.3343	−1.327	**1.268**
High income	0.9737	1.866	−0.3633	−1.641	**2.381**
Med income	0.6060	1.982	−0.2736	−1.427	**2.505**
Low capital gains	1.400	**2.119**	−0.6939	**−2.880**	**3.009**
Low turnover	1.088	**2.471**	−0.2425	−1.021	**2.684**
Med load	0.7075	1.212	−0.5114	**−2.195**	1.961
Low load	0.5145	1.869	−0.3875	−1.664	**2.603**
Med expense	0.7377	1.739	−0.5246	−1.950	**2.552**
Low expense	0.7699	**2.076**	−0.106	−0.8321	**2.276**
Med lagret	1.019	**2.008**	−0.3456	−1.772	**2.536**
Low lagret	1.553	**4.269**	−0.9025	**−2.383**	**4.984**
D. Interest rate volatility					
Low flow	−0.4944	−1.623	0.7279	**2.571**	**−3.062**
Med age	−0.8208	−1.902	0.3038	0.820	**−2.054**
Low income	−0.8510	**−2.165**	0.4999	1.147	**−2.397**
High capital gains	−0.4584	−1.590	0.5799	1.688	**−2.388**

(continued)

TABLE 24.11   (*continued*)

Funds	γ_{hi}	$t(\gamma_{hi})$	γ_{lo}	$t(\gamma_{lo})$	$t(H_0: \gamma_{hi} = \gamma_{lo})$
High turnover	−0.4260	−1.478	0.6181	1.735	**−2.350**
Low load	−0.6713	−2.081	0.4837	1.519	**−2.628**
High expense	−0.6715	−1.358	0.6229	1.562	**−2.102**
Low lagret	−1.205	−1.713	0.9673	1.711	**−2.498**
E. Credit spread					
Low turnover	0.9018	**2.185**	0.8291	1.398	0.1036
F. Dividend yield					
High flow	0.5224	1.105	0.2866	**2.070**	0.4894
Med flow	0.2591	1.550	0.2807	**2.911**	−0.1176
High age	0.3351	1.490	0.2939	**3.238**	0.1749
High total net assets	0.4190	**2.001**	0.3041	**3.002**	0.5038
High income	0.4916	1.885	0.3017	**2.421**	0.6745
Low capital gains	0.1839	0.9878	0.6764	**2.967**	−1.732
Low turnover	0.4682	1.014	0.5137	**3.263**	−0.096
Med load	0.3231	1.191	0.2308	**2.176**	0.3245
Low expense	0.3446	1.756	0.1738	**2.138**	0.8171
G. Short-term corporate illiquidity					
High total net assets	0.2845	**2.850**	0.9434	**2.080**	−1.425
Med income	−0.1544	−1.753	0.8574	**2.116**	**−2.447**
High capital gains	−0.2442	**−2.333**	0.8889	**2.422**	**−2.996**
Med capital gains	−0.4287	**−3.406**	0.2807	0.441	−1.094
Low capital gains	0.6123	**3.157**	0.5893	1.233	0.045
High expense	−0.2380	**−2.364**	0.5407	1.603	**−2.225**
Low lagret	−0.05288	−0.2501	1.242	**2.325**	**−2.241**
H. Stock market liquidity					
All	1.791	**2.112**	0.2677	1.176	1.748
High flow	1.992	**3.336**	−0.0043	−0.015	**3.052**
High age	1.198	**2.303**	0.2636	1.101	1.652
High total net assets	1.864	**2.317**	0.1351	0.6481	**2.096**
Med total net assets	1.369	**2.047**	0.2105	0.5538	1.554
High income	1.458	**2.297**	0.1586	0.4708	1.851
Low capital gains	2.858	**3.558**	0.0456	0.1443	**3.315**
Med turnover	1.551	**2.133**	0.2228	0.7958	1.733
Low turnover	1.757	**2.185**	0.1960	0.5698	1.819
Med load	2.148	**2.640**	0.2211	0.6047	**2.207**
Med expense	1.584	**2.355**	0.1868	0.5280	1.886
Med lagret	1.581	**2.436**	0.4784	1.020	1.427
Low lagret	1.425	1.143	0.0821	0.2556	1.053
I. Inflation					
High total net assets	0.5861	**2.270**	−0.0052	−0.0111	1.113
J. Industrial output growth					
Low flow	0.5323	1.112	−0.6697	**−2.718**	**2.335**
High turnover	0.4275	0.6989	−0.6105	**−2.117**	1.578

Notes: Monthly returns for groups of market-timing funds in excess of the 90-day T-bill return are regressed on a broad equity market excess return, its square, its products with lagged state variables, and the products of the state variables with the squared excess return. The state variables are the dummy variables for high and low economic states. The fund sample period is January 1973 through December 2000 (336 total observations); γ_{hi} is the estimated timing coefficient given a high state, and $t(\gamma_{hi})$ is its heteroscedasticity consistent t-statistic; γ_{lo} is the conditional timing coefficient given a low state, and $t(\gamma_{lo})$ is its t-statistic. The right-hand column presents t-statistic testing the hypothesis that the timing coefficients are equal in the high and low states.

the term-structure slope is steep. In contrast, when the slope is shallow, none of the conditional timing coefficients are significant and about one-quarter of the point estimates are negative. The t-statistics testing the hypothesis that the two conditional timing coefficients are equal strongly rejects the hypothesis, with 19 out of 28 t-statistics examined larger than 2.0 (again shown in bold). The timing funds seem unable to deliver reliable market-timing services when the slope of the term structure is flat. The results conditioning on term-structure concavity are similar, with significant timing performance when the term structure is highly concave. This finding probably reflects, in large part, the high correlation between these two states: When the term structure is steep, the yield curve tends to present more concavity.

We find evidence of time-varying conditional timing ability associated with three other state variables relating to the state of the financial markets: dividend yield, short-term corporate illiquidity, and stock market liquidity. In the case of dividend yield, positive timing ability is found conditional on high yield states. We find 10 cases with absolute t-statistics larger than 2.0 in these states, which out of the 56 cases examined implies a multiple-comparisons t-statistic of 14.3. For stock market liquidity, we find 12 absolute t-statistics larger than 2.0, which implies a multiple-comparisons t-statistic of 18.3. All these coefficients are associated with high-liquidity states, and all are positive. In low-liquidity states, we find no t-statistics larger than 2.0 on the timing coefficients, and 6 of the 28 coefficients examined are less than zero. It makes sense that successful market timing should be more likely when the stock market is highly liquid because market-timing trades may be made at lower cost in highly liquid markets. Finally, we find some time variation in timing ability associated with the states of short-term corporate illiquidity. In 9 of 56 absolute t-statistics we examined, the results are larger than 2.0 (multiple-comparisons t-statistic equals 12.3). Among those coefficients with t-statistics larger than 2.0, we find mostly negative coefficients when illiquidity is high and positive coefficients when the markets are more liquid. Thus, the effects of liquidity in the stock and corporate debt markets seem to operate in a similar fashion.

Finally, the results of Table 24.11 confirm our earlier findings about which types of funds are likely to be the most effective market timers. The model with time-varying timing ability almost always assigns the largest conditional timing coefficients to the funds with the longest track records, the largest total net assets, the lowest expense ratios, or the highest load charges.

IMPLICATIONS FOR PRACTICING FINANCIAL ANALYSTS

CPE is potentially important for several areas of investment management (as well as academic research). For institutions that hire money managers, such as mutual fund companies, pension plan sponsors, university endowments, foundations, and trusts, knowing how well a manager has performed is important. Because CPE uses more information than traditional methods (bringing in additional variables to measure the state of the economy), it has the potential to provide more accurate performance measures. This chapter illustrates versions of conditional performance models that can be easily estimated as multiple regressions. Through the choice of the lagged variables in the regressions, one can set the hurdle for superior ability at any desired level of lagged information. That is, managers have to perform better than a mechanical strategy using the chosen lagged variables to record superior performance. Our results provide practical guidance on the regressions to run and the variables to use.

CPE can provide estimates of performance that depend on the economic state, whereas the traditional alpha ignores information about the state of the economy. If managers' performance is variable depending on the economic state, fund sponsors and investors may wish to allocate resources across funds in light of this information. Investors also need to understand how funds implement their investment policies dynamically over time. How, for example, does a fund's equity, bond, or style exposure change in a time of high interest rates or market volatility? CPE is designed to provide a rich description of funds' portfolio dynamics in relation to the state of the economy. For pension consultants and the other intermediaries that work with fund managers and their ultimate investors, CPE opens up a wealth of new descriptive and analytical tools. One of the goals of this chapter is to motivate the use of CPE in future financial practice.

The empirical findings in this chapter carry implications for practicing financial analysts relative to three main issues. The first has to do with understanding the expected returns and risks of classes of financial assets and how these vary with the state of the economy over market and economic cycles. An understanding of these broad patterns is an important input for the problem of asset allocation. The second issue has to do with patterns in the expected returns and risks of mutual funds with different investment styles and fund characteristics and how these behave over market and economic cycles. An understanding of these patterns is important for investors who may choose to implement a portion of their portfolio strategy using mutual funds. The third issue relates to the risk-adjusted, or abnormal, performance of mutual funds. The evidence here may affect the desirability of mutual funds relative to other investment vehicles, as well as the characteristics of specific funds to be included in a portfolio.

Conditional Behavior of Asset Class Returns

Financial analysts need to be aware of time variation in expected returns and risks for different asset classes, such as we document in this study. We group our measures of the state of the economy according to (1) the term structure or government yield curve, (2) the state of general financial markets, and (3) the macroeconomy. We show that states of the term structure are powerful predictors not just for fixed-income but also for equity returns. High levels of short-term interest rates predict relatively high and volatile short-term bond returns and low stock returns, with a gradual transition as one moves from safer and shorter maturities to riskier and longer-term asset classes. The level and the slope of the term structure seem to be the most informative predictors of return, with the concavity of the yield curve being less important. High interest rate volatility states are highly correlated with high interest rate levels.

We find that among the variables that measure the state of financial markets, high credit spreads predict high subsequent returns on stocks, and high dividend yields predict high returns on both stocks and bonds. The latter effect has weakened in more recent data and should probably be viewed with suspicion in the near future. The weakening of the predictive power of dividend yields has been associated with a trend toward lower yields since the early 1990s. Perhaps, as recent tax law changes encourage higher dividend payouts in the future, the predictive ability of aggregate dividend yields could return. The most economically, if not statistically, significant predictor among the financial market instruments we study may be the commercial paper–Treasury spread, measuring short-term corporate illiquidity. When the spread is high, all the long-term bonds and stock indexes earn high returns over the next month. Moreover, these high-spread states do not seem to be associated with higher return volatility on these securities.

Among the variables measuring the macroeconomy, high inflation is bad news for stocks and longer-term bonds. High inflation levels predict low and also relatively volatile returns on long-term bonds and stocks, and short-term cash positions offer relatively high expected returns when inflation is high. When output growth is abnormally low, it predicts high returns, especially for the riskier assets, and the volatility of these investments is also high at such times.

The evidence that the risks and expected returns to different asset classes vary with the states of the economy seems compelling. But how can a financial analyst use this information in practice? Consider an investment advisor for a high-net-worth client. Some value may be added by simply explaining these expected return patterns to the client, relative to the current state of the economy at the time. (We have found a graphical representation of the figures in Table 24.2 to be especially compelling.) A client may wish to alter the asset allocation, taking on more exposure to currently high expected return asset classes and less exposure to asset classes whose currently expected performance is low. This adjustment must be considered, of course, in the context of the total portfolio risk and investment objectives, as well as the client's aversion to particular kinds of risks. In general, clients whose aversion to a specific risk is below that of the average investor may be advised to more aggressively tune the asset allocation to take advantage of higher conditional returns associated with state variables representing that risk at certain times. And an investor who is more risk averse than average about bad economic times may wish to take less risk when volatility is high or expected economic performance is poor than at other times during an economic cycle.

Conditional Behavior of Mutual Fund Returns

In addition to the patterns for broad asset classes, this chapter documents predictable patterns in the returns of some mutual fund types. Some of the patterns mirror those found for the passive asset class benchmarks. For example, the term-structure state variables seem to be the most powerful predictors of future fund returns. Low short-term interest rates predict high equity fund returns, and high interest rates predict low returns. The differences can be dramatic. The expected returns given low interest rates are more than 2 percent per month greater than given high interest rates for the maximum capital gains funds and almost that large for the growth funds. A steep term-structure slope also predicts high subsequent returns for most equity fund types. The differences are often economically large, at 3.2 percent per month for the maximum capital gains funds and just less than 2 percent per month for the growth funds. High interest rate volatility is bad news for most fund groups, but the differences here are not significant, except perhaps for timing funds.

We find significant time variation in funds' market and style betas. But little of this variation is associated with the discrete dummy variables measuring shifts in the economic states. It seems likely that much of the time variation in beta is related to higher-frequency investment decisions by funds, perhaps associated with redemptions and new money flows. One of the broad implications for investors and their advisors relates to strategic asset allocation, as discussed earlier. Our results suggest that such strategies should be implemented by changing the allocation across fund-style categories because funds themselves are unlikely to come with such strategic allocations built in.

Risk-Adjusted Fund Performance

According to the theoretical model of Berk and Green (2004), we should see fund flows in response to informative signals of manager ability, and these flows should occur until expected future performance is neutral in equilibrium after costs. Where the flows in response to performance signals are insufficient to neutralize future performance, we may find predictable abnormal future performance.

Overall, we find that although unconditional measures of fund performance are slightly negative, the theoretically superior conditional measures tend to be centered near zero. This finding is broadly consistent with equilibrium in the fund management industry, where managers have enough skill to cover their costs and fees on the funds they manage. Investors are left roughly indifferent between a passive position in the asset class and an actively managed fund in the same asset class. Thus, actively managed funds may be viewed as a viable alternative to index funds, exchange-traded funds, and other passive strategies.

Although the overall distribution of conditional performance, based on funds' returns net of trading costs and fees, is centered near zero, the final question is whether funds with particular characteristics may offer higher or lower risk-adjusted returns than a randomly chosen fund. Our analysis of the cross-sectional distribution of fund alphas suggests that this may be the case. We find that the bottom 20–25 percent of income funds turned in highly significant negative conditional alphas, and this poor performance is not concentrated in particular economic regimes. Unfortunately, our cross-sectional analysis of the income funds turns up no simple relationship between performance and fund characteristics. Thus, we can offer no mechanical rules for avoiding the poorly performing subset of income funds in these market states.

We also find that extremely good and bad conditional performance is concentrated in particular economic states. Concentrations of abnormally high and low conditional alpha *t*-statistics are associated with dividend yield states for several fund styles. High dividend yield states reveal large fractions of good performers among the growth, small-company growth, sector, and growth and income funds, but none of these appear in low dividend yield states. Growth and income funds are able to generate a large number of positive performers when inflation is high but not when inflation is low.

Finally, our cross-sectional analysis of alphas provides some interesting results in which individual-level fund characteristics are associated with good conditional performance. We find that old growth funds have larger alphas than young funds. Growth funds tend to follow momentum trading strategies, which feeds through to their alphas. Growth funds with relatively high capital gains and total returns over the past year are expected to have higher alphas over the next year. Such a pattern is not to be found, however, among income funds.

We find that funds with higher load charges are expected to have higher alphas than those with lower load charges. This result extends earlier findings of Ippolito to conditional measures. The coefficients for growth funds are on the order of 20–25 bps for a one standard deviation increase in load charges. For income funds, the effect is smaller (10–13 bps) and is not statistically significant. These results must be evaluated in relation to the load fees themselves. Unlike the expense ratios and trading costs, our fund return data are not measured net of load charges, which represent a separate expense to the investor. Thus, the investor needs to balance the higher load charge against the expected performance. Clearly, an investor with a short investment horizon would not want to pay the load fee. But an investor with a very long horizon may be advised to consider load funds.

Market-Timing Ability

A traditional piece of wisdom among many financial analysts is that attempting to time the market is a fool's game. The temptation is great, because if one could correctly call the peaks and troughs and trade accordingly, the returns would be huge. But the chances of successfully calling market highs and lows are thought to be slim, and in the attempt, one is just as likely to buy too high and sell too low, thus missing out on market returns that a passive investment strategy would capture. In addition, market timing requires costly trades that hurt performance. Much of the "bad press" on the market-timing ability of mutual funds, however, is based on unconditional measures of timing ability that are shown to be biased in studies such as Ferson and Schadt as well as Becker, Myers, and Schill. When conditional timing measures are used, the funds that specialize in this activity do not look as bad. We measure timing ability that is neutral to slightly positive. The timing ability comes at a cost, however, in average return. The market-timing funds in our sample earn lower average returns than any other fund group, except the income funds. We do not think the evidence of timing ability is strong enough to justify a ringing endorsement of market timing funds, but neither does our evidence rule out some exposure to this style of fund in a balanced portfolio.

Our analysis of conditional-market-timing ability provides potentially useful insights into which funds are more likely to be successful timers. We find that the best overall market timers are the largest funds (measured by total net assets) and the funds with the lowest expense ratios. We also find that older funds with a longer track record tend to be better timers. When we allow for time variation in conditional timing ability, we find some striking evidence that market-timing funds are able to time better in some economic states than in others. The best states for successful market timing are when the slope of the term structure is steep, short-term corporate debt markets are relatively liquid, and stock markets are relatively liquid. It makes sense that successful market timing should be more likely when the markets are highly liquid because market-timing trades may be made at lower cost in highly liquid markets. Conversely, market-timing funds seem unable to deliver reliable market-timing services when the slope of the term structure is flat or when the markets are in an illiquid state.

SUMMARY AND CONCLUSIONS

As with all studies based on historical data, describing past relationships is easier than inferring whether the future will look similar to history. In this study, we expand the database of mutual funds to include many new funds in recent years. This approach is both an advantage and a disadvantage. The advantages of a larger sample size are obvious, but new entrants may have different characteristics from more seasoned funds. In this case, the underlying relationships in the data could shift during the sample. As Figures 24.1 and 24.2 illustrate, the characteristics of the population of mutual funds have shifted during the period of our analysis. This finding motivates our use of age as a characteristic in sorting the funds, and we find some differences between the old and young funds in our sample. The unit of analysis in our sample is the fund and not the fund manager, which raises another caveat. The investment style of a fund may change over time with changing managers such that data from a given fund may not represent a consistent style or philosophy across economic and market cycles, which is one motivation for allowing time-varying betas as well as alphas, as we do in this study, that may vary across market and economic cycles. Even so, our analysis presumes enough stationarity in the behavior of funds so that the process generating a fund's return is similar across repeated experiences of, for example, a high or low interest rate or inflationary regime. Thus, it is not obvious that one can safely extrapolate our results into the future.

Subject to these caveats, the results of our study are relevant to fund managers, management companies, financial advisors, and their ultimate clients—the individual investors. The results should also be of interest to researchers studying mutual funds and their investment performance. Fund managers are interested in how they stack up relative to their peers, and our analysis of relative performance addresses this issue directly. Management companies, among other things, care about how different fund styles are expected to perform in different economic states. Our characterization of conditional performance using discrete states should be informative on this issue. Financial advisors who wish to advise clients on asset allocation, fund style, and fund selection should find our results directly relevant. Finally, academics should be interested both in the extent to which the "stylized facts" from earlier studies hold up in a broad and updated sample as well as in the further pursuit of some of the issues raised by the new results of our analysis.

APPENDIX 24A: ADDITIONAL TABLES

Table 24.12 reports summary statistics for the dummy variable indicators for the various states, and Table 24.13 reports the correlations of the high- and low-state dummy variables. Table 24.14 presents the style-specific benchmark weights that we apply to the asset class indexes to generate fund-style-specific benchmark index returns. Tables 24.15–24.19 repeat the analyses of Tables 24.4–24.9, substituting the style-specific benchmark indexes for the broad market index of the CAPM.

TABLE 24.12   Summary Statistics of Discrete Dummy Variable Instruments for Economic States, January 1973 through December 2000 (N = 336)

Series	Mean	Min	Max	Std. Dev.	ρ_1[a]
A. High-state dummies					
Short-term interest rate	0.1964	0.000	1.000	0.3979	0.8333
Term-structure slope	0.1310	0.000	1.000	0.3379	0.3981
Term-structure concavity	0.1071	0.000	1.000	0.3098	0.5641
Interest rate volatility	0.2024	0.000	1.000	0.4024	0.6305
Stock market volatility	0.1964	0.000	1.000	0.3979	0.5090
Credit spread	0.1905	0.000	1.000	0.3933	0.8293
Dividend yield	0.1637	0.000	1.000	0.3705	0.7385
Short-term corporate illiquidity	0.1071	0.000	1.000	0.3098	0.3463
Stock market liquidity	0.1369	0.000	1.000	0.3443	0.0928
Inflation	0.1518	0.000	1.000	0.3593	0.3522
Industrial output growth	0.1190	0.000	1.000	0.3243	0.0064
B. Low-state dummies					
Short-term interest rate	0.2351	0.000	1.000	0.4247	0.8501
Term-structure slope	0.2738	0.000	1.000	0.4466	0.7186
Term-structure concavity	0.2530	0.000	1.000	0.4354	0.5778
Interest rate volatility	0.2232	0.000	1.000	0.4170	0.6769
Stock market volatility	0.0952	0.000	1.000	0.2940	0.2777
Credit spread	0.2827	0.000	1.000	0.4510	0.7493
Dividend yield	0.4107	0.000	1.000	0.4927	0.8185
Short-term corporate illiquidity	0.0744	0.000	1.000	0.2628	0.1355
Stock market liquidity	0.1190	0.000	1.000	0.3243	0.1482
Inflation	0.1607	0.000	1.000	0.3678	0.3154
Industrial output growth	0.1458	0.000	1.000	0.3535	0.3340

[a]ρ_1 is the first-order sample autocorrelation of the series.

TABLE 24.13 Correlations between the Discrete Dummy Variable Instruments for Economic States, January 1973 through December 2000 (N = 336)

	Short-Term Interest Rate	Term-Structure Slope	Term-Structure Concavity	Interest Rate Volatility	Stock Market Volatility	Credit Spread	Dividend Yield	Short-Term Corporate Illiquidity	Stock Market Liquidity	Inflation	Industrial Output Growth
A. High-state dummies											
Short-Term Interest Rate	1.000	−0.170	−0.099	0.888	0.208	0.065	0.206	0.375	−0.089	−0.002	−0.044
Term-Structure Slope	−0.170	1.000	0.579	−0.174	0.008	0.149	−0.053	−0.115	0.130	0.122	−0.001
Term-Structure Concavity	−0.099	0.579	1.000	−0.127	−0.026	0.200	0.081	−0.120	0.140	0.067	−0.026
Interest Rate Volatility	0.888	−0.174	−0.127	1.000	0.198	0.020	0.178	0.344	−0.094	−0.031	−0.071
Stock Market Volatility	0.208	0.008	−0.026	0.198	1.000	0.161	0.065	0.041	0.003	0.265	−0.132
Credit Spread	0.065	0.149	0.200	0.020	0.161	1.000	0.216	−0.057	−0.038	0.175	0.049
Dividend Yield	0.206	−0.053	0.081	0.178	0.065	0.216	1.000	0.149	−0.063	0.055	0.058
Short-Term Corporate Illiquidity	0.375	−0.115	−0.120	0.344	0.041	−0.057	0.149	1.000	−0.079	−0.066	0.0004
Stock Market Liquidity	−0.089	0.130	0.140	−0.094	0.003	−0.038	−0.063	−0.079	1.000	−0.068	−0.040
Inflation	−0.002	0.122	0.067	−0.031	0.265	0.175	0.055	−0.066	−0.068	1.000	0.002
Industrial Output Growth	−0.044	−0.001	−0.026	−0.071	−0.132	0.049	0.058	0.0004	−0.040	0.002	1.000
B. Low-state dummies											
Short-Term Interest Rate	1.000	−0.325	−0.210	0.833	0.179	0.119	0.393	0.082	−0.130	−0.130	−0.052
Term-Structure Slope	−0.325	1.000	0.641	−0.287	−0.086	0.118	−0.092	−0.123	0.106	−0.022	0.186
Term-Structure Concavity	−0.210	0.641	1.000	−0.171	−0.072	0.0005	−0.110	−0.124	0.148	−0.035	0.124
Interest Rate Volatility	0.833	−0.287	−0.171	1.000	0.209	0.114	0.380	0.108	−0.045	−0.074	−0.047
Stock Market Volatility	0.179	−0.086	−0.072	0.209	1.000	0.089	0.080	−0.059	−0.077	−0.092	−0.119
Credit Spread	0.119	0.118	0.0005	0.114	0.089	1.000	0.054	−0.077	−0.110	−0.027	0.035
Dividend Yield	0.393	−0.092	−0.110	0.380	0.080	0.054	1.000	0.129	−0.122	0.040	−0.008
Short-Term Corporate Illiquidity	0.082	−0.123	−0.124	0.108	−0.059	−0.077	0.129	1.000	0.095	−0.031	−0.036
Stock Market Liquidity	−0.130	0.106	0.148	−0.045	−0.077	−0.110	−0.122	0.095	1.000	−0.021	0.030
Inflation	−0.130	−0.022	−0.035	−0.074	−0.092	−0.027	0.040	−0.031	−0.021	1.000	0.106
Industrial Output Growth	−0.052	0.186	0.124	−0.047	−0.119	0.035	−0.008	−0.036	0.030	0.106	1.000

TABLE 24.14   Sharpe Style Benchmarks, January 1973–December 2000 (336 observations)

Asset Class	Growth	Maximum Capital Gains	Other Aggressive Growth	Income	Growth and Income	Sector	Small-Company Growth	Timing
A. Weights for each fund group applied to asset class returns								
90-day T-bill	0.250	0.510	0.000	0.000	0.160	0.000	0.000	0.000
One-year bond	0.000	0.000	0.320	0.240	0.000	0.000	0.210	0.600
Government bond	0.002	0.094	0.000	0.018	0.034	0.110	0.068	0.000
BAA corporate bond	0.008	0.000	0.017	0.110	0.027	0.000	0.000	0.220
Broad equity index	0.480	0.040	0.000	0.480	0.670	0.000	0.000	0.037
Value stocks	0.000	0.130	0.000	0.047	0.001	0.110	0.000	0.140
Growth stocks	0.140	0.150	0.420	0.000	0.000	0.780	0.720	0.000
Small-cap stocks	0.120	0.077	0.250	0.100	0.110	0.000	0.000	0.000

B. Summary statistics for style benchmark returns

Fund Group	Mean	Min	Max	Std. Dev.	ρ_1[a]
Growth	0.9900	−17.87	12.76	3.642	0.06856
Maximum capital gains	0.8599	−9.128	9.129	2.109	0.1098
Other aggressive growth	0.9852	−18.24	14.77	3.869	0.1263
Income	0.9855	−13.95	12.12	3.132	0.06749
Growth and income	1.028	−17.80	12.89	3.728	0.04800
Sector	1.053	−23.13	16.70	5.061	0.1011
Small-company growth	0.9458	−18.91	13.30	4.275	0.09984
Timing	0.8099	−4.444	7.488	1.423	0.1684

Note: The return units are percent per month.
[a] ρ_1 is the first-order sample autocorrelation of the series.

TABLE 24.15   Unconditional and Conditional CAPM Regressions Using Style-Based Benchmarks

Funds		Alpha	t(Alpha)	Beta	t(Beta)	R^2	
A. Unconditional CAPM regressions							
Growth		−0.05873	−0.9109	1.247	65.41	0.9394	
Maximum capital gains		−0.1694	−1.351	2.458	31.56	0.8882	
Other aggressive growth		0.07004	0.7882	1.460	61.58	0.9666	
Income		−0.04146	−0.5188	0.561	12.51	0.6123	
Growth and income		−0.01874	−0.3080	0.968	60.19	0.9165	
Sector		0.1805	1.610	0.761	27.10	0.8892	
Small-company growth		0.09665	0.7126	1.287	40.80	0.9220	
Timers		−0.1201	−1.599	1.841	21.66	0.7900	
	Instrument	Alpha	t(Alpha)	Bet0	t(Bet0)	$R^2 1$	p-Value
B. Conditional CAPM regressions using individual instruments							
Growth	Interest rates	−0.0987	−1.235	0.5906	12.30	0.6499	0.000
Maximum capital gains	Industrial output	−0.1388	−1.082	2.513	52.24	0.8939	0.000
Income	Interest rates	−0.0722	−0.8688	0.3847	11.37	0.6191	0.000
	Term slope	0.0192	0.2161	0.3631	11.25	0.5843	0.090
	Convexity	−0.0185	−0.2253	0.5524	12.52	0.6186	0.068
	Rate volatility	−0.1062	−1.354	0.5879	12.66	0.6528	0.000

(*continued*)

TABLE 24.15   (*continued*)

	Instrument	Alpha	*t*(Alpha)	Bet0	*t*(Bet0)	$R^2$1	*p*-Value
	Credit spread	0.0098	0.1340	0.5880	13.58	0.6782	0.000
	Dividend yield	−0.0198	−0.2729	0.5983	11.93	0.6843	0.000
	Inflation	−0.0783	−0.9565	0.5811	12.05	0.6227	0.012
Sector	Convexity	0.1913	1.728	0.7540	29.16	0.8908	0.094
	Stock liquidity	0.0515	0.4350	0.8541	27.20	0.8689	0.070
	Inflation	0.1573	1.406	0.7332	23.11	0.8908	0.085
Small-company growth	Stock volatility	0.0891	0.6755	1.322	44.96	0.9247	0.003
	Stock liquidity	−0.0131	−0.05461	1.114	20.57	0.7289	0.060
	Dividend yield	0.0809	0.6117	1.389	41.93	0.9246	0.004
	Industrial output	0.0868	0.6530	1.287	44.93	0.9243	0.007
Other aggressive growth	Rate volatility	0.0748	0.8389	1.407	23.19	0.9671	0.087
	Stock volatility	0.0615	0.7118	1.483	61.83	0.9675	0.012
	Inflation	0.0539	0.6375	1.413	26.82	0.9672	0.045
	Industrial output	0.0796	0.8964	1.468	60.94	0.9681	0.001
Timers	Interest rates	−0.1734	−2.387	1.976	23.74	0.8102	0.000
	Term slope	−0.1690	−2.149	1.891	24.92	0.7962	0.008
	Rate volatility	−0.1894	−2.585	1.964	22.67	0.8089	0.000
	Credit spread	−0.0979	−1.349	1.931	22.53	0.8013	0.000
	Dividend yield	−0.1141	−1.612	2.008	24.97	0.8098	0.000
	Inflation	−0.1725	−2.242	1.927	25.59	0.7987	0.001
C. Conditional CAPM regressions using grouped instruments							
Maximum capital gains	Term structure	−0.1707	−1.345	2.375	7.039	0.8930	0.017
Income	Term structure	−0.0349	−0.4662	1.274	10.20	0.6946	0.000
Small-company growth	Term structure	0.2039	1.748	0.7815	4.669	0.8926	0.075
Timers	Term structure	−0.1711	−2.314	2.671	10.95	0.8111	0.001
Growth and income	Financial markets	0.1110	1.173	1.887	10.56	0.9688	0.002
Income	Financial markets	−0.0111	−0.1544	1.378	10.51	0.7114	0.000
Other aggressive growth	Financial markets	0.0965	0.6932	1.320	8.616	0.9260	0.011
Timers	Financial markets	−0.1269	−1.803	2.713	8.817	0.8195	0.000
Maximum capital gains	Macroeconomy	−0.1313	−1.011	2.444	29.45	0.8940	0.001
Growth and income	Macroeconomy	0.0657	0.7664	1.532	33.52	0.9686	0.000
Income	Macroeconomy	−0.0783	−0.9428	0.6591	8.840	0.6227	0.031
Small-company growth	Macroeconomy	0.1524	1.376	0.8149	20.86	0.8919	0.042
Other aggressive growth	Macroeconomy	0.0820	0.6274	1.325	22.09	0.9244	0.019
Timers	Macroeconomy	−0.1673	−2.148	2.105	17.37	0.7998	0.002

Notes: Conditional and unconditional alphas relative to Sharpe style benchmarks, based on versions of Equation 24.1. The sample periods for the returns are January 1973 through December 2000 (336 observations), or a shorter period when indicated by fund availability in Table 24.3. Alphas are the abnormal returns; monthly percent *t*(alpha) is a heteroscedasticity consistent *t*-statistic. Beta is the CAPM beta and *t*(beta) is its *t*-statistic. R^2 is the coefficient of determination of the regression. In Panels B and C, the regression is given by Equation 24.1 of the text, which is run for one instrument at a time. Results for instruments that produce exclusion *F*-test *p*-values less than 0.10 are shown. Bet0 is the average conditional beta, *t*(bet0) is its *t*-statistic, $R^2$1 is the regression coefficient of determination, and *p*-value is the right-tail *p*-value of the *F*-statistic for excluding the lagged instrument multiplied by the style index excess return. In Panel C, the instruments are grouped as follows: Term-structure instruments include the interest rate level, slope, convexity, and volatility. The financial markets variables include stock market volatility, credit spread, dividend yield, short-term corporate illiquidity, and stock market liquidity. The macroeconomy variables are inflation and industrial output growth.

TABLE 24.16 Fund Alphas Relative to Style Indexes, Conditional on Discrete State Variables for Equally Weighted Portfolio of Mutual Funds by Group

	No. Obs.	Growth	Maximum CapitalGains	Other Aggressive Growth	Income	Growth and Income	Sector	Small-Company Growth	Timers
A. State of the term-structure variables									
Short-term rates									
High	66.00	0.0316	0.1265	1.291	−0.1963	−0.019	0.9552	1.629	−0.1693
Low	79.00	0.0259	−0.1856	0.079	0.0158	0.0085	0.3407	0.4703	−0.1548
t-Statistic		0.0255	0.8017	**2.685**	−0.8115	−0.1301	1.014	1.623	−0.0609
Term-structure concavity									
High	36.00	0.0266	−0.4712	−0.0783	0.0441	0.0241	0.2887	0.3070	−0.5405
Low	85.00	−0.0176	−0.0240	0.4062	−0.1012	−0.0052	0.2256	0.5310	0.0435
t-Statistic		0.2377	−1.171	−1.856	0.6259	0.1801	0.1607	−0.4806	**−2.300**
B. State of the financial markets variables									
Dividend yield									
High	55.00	−0.3610	−0.3860	0.000	−0.2303	−0.3021	0.4398	−0.8476	−0.4270
Low	138.0	−0.0513	−0.4014	0.000	0.0596	0.0010	0.1437	0.1159	−0.1992
t-Statistic		−1.005	0.03411	0.000	−1.473	−1.247	**2.252**	**−6.272**	−0.9968
C. State of the macroeconomy variables									
Inflation									
High	51.00	0.2072	0.2298	0.8148	0.0397	0.2652	0.4485	0.7085	−0.0674
Low	54.00	−0.1781	−0.6743	−0.2206	−0.1674	−0.0841	0.1860	0.0116	−0.2849
t-Statistic		**2.889**	**2.875**	**3.651**	0.7203	**2.251**	0.6510	1.304	0.6714

Notes: Monthly fund group returns in excess of the 90-day T-bill are regressed on the excess return of a Sharpe style index for the fund group and its product with dummy variables for the state of the economy, as in Equation 24.2 in the text. The dummy variables are the same as in Table 24.2. No. obs. is the number of observations for the growth fund sample period, which is January of 1973 through December of 2000 (336 total observations). Other fund groups may have fewer observations, as indicated in Table 24.3. Cases with fewer than 12 nonmissing observations are excluded and shown as 0.000; *t*-statistic is the heteroscedasticity-consistent *t*-statistic for the difference between the high and low state conditional alphas (those greater than 2.0 shown in bold). Only states with an absolute *t*-statistic greater than 2.0 are shown. The units for alpha are percent per month.

581

TABLE 24.17 Betas on Style Indexes, Conditional on Discrete State Variables for Equally Weighted Portfolio of Mutual Funds, by Group

	Growth	Maximum Capital Gains	Other Aggressive Growth	Income	Growth and Income	Sector	Small-Company Growth	Timers
A. State of the term-structure variables								
Short-term rates								
High	1.213	2.493	1.474	0.4843	0.9227	0.7012	1.189	1.597
Low	1.233	2.488	1.478	0.4971	0.9871	0.7980	1.408	2.043
t-Statistic	-0.477	0.0428	-0.048	-0.1255	-1.417	-0.8836	-2.279	-2.157
Term-structure slope								
High	1.172	2.544	1.466	0.3210	0.8688	0.6343	1.309	1.711
Low	1.261	2.511	1.409	0.6396	0.9871	0.7607	1.191	1.732
t-Statistic	-1.258	0.1691	0.7976	-3.742	-1.644	-1.445	1.103	-0.0955
Term-structure concavity								
High	1.185	2.460	1.477	0.4373	0.9470	0.7574	1.480	1.760
Low	1.254	2.494	1.468	0.6442	0.9859	0.8344	1.267	1.756
t-Statistic	-1.662	-0.2409	0.1869	-2.132	-0.9609	-0.6073	2.043	0.0150
Interest rate volatility								
High	1.215	2.541	1.451	0.4985	0.9347	0.6648	1.179	1.615
Low	1.275	2.558	1.497	0.5883	1.000	0.8105	1.314	2.172
t-Statistic	-1.641	-0.1413	-0.5566	-0.8193	-1.449	-1.701	-1.551	-2.472
B. State of the financial markets variables								
Credit spread								
High	1.188	2.230	1.367	0.4901	0.9285	0.6337	1.115	1.598
Low	1.277	2.628	1.532	0.7274	0.9808	0.7480	1.343	1.825
t-Statistic	-1.033	-1.503	-1.853	-2.745	-0.8316	-1.365	-1.342	-1.614
Dividend yield								
High	1.234	2.412	0.000	0.4954	0.955	0.7179	1.512	1.680
Low	1.276	2.531	0.000	0.6761	1.001	0.7655	1.277	2.221
t-Statistic	-0.5972	-0.4809	0.000	-1.358	-0.9273	-1.341	5.345	-2.458

Notes: Monthly fund group returns in excess of the 90-day T-bill are regressed on a fund group specific style index excess return and the products with dummy variables for the state of the economy. The dummy variables are the same as in Table 24.2. The growth fund sample period is January of 1973 through December of 2000 (336 total observations). Other fund groups may have fewer observations, as indicated in Table 24.3. Cases with fewer than 12 nonmissing observations are excluded and shown as 0.000; t-statistic is the heteroscedasticity consistent t-statistic for the difference between the high and low state conditional betas (those greater than 2.0 shown in bold). Only states with an absolute t-statistic greater than 2.0 are shown.

TABLE 24.18   Cross-Sectional Distribution of *t*-Statistics for Alphas Using Style Benchmarks

Item	Null	All	Growth	Maximum Capital Gains	Other Aggressive Growth	Income	Growth and Income	Sector	Small-Company Growth
A. Unconditional alphas									
$t > 2.36$	0.005	0.12	0.03	0.05	0.15	0.03	0.02	0.06	0.10
$2.36 > t > 1.96$	0.02	0.04	0.03	0.03	0.06	0.02	0.02	0.07	0.04
$1.96 > t > 1.65$	0.025	0.04	0.03	0.04	0.07	0.03	0.02	0.05	0.05
$1.65 > t > 0$	0.45	0.40	0.44	0.25	0.45	0.32	0.43	0.53	0.49
$0 > t > -1.65$	0.45	0.29	0.35	0.41	0.20	0.33	0.42	0.24	0.26
$-1.65 > t > -1.96$	0.025	0.02	0.03	0.05	0.02	0.02	0.02	0.01	0.01
$-1.96 > t > -2.36$	0.02	0.02	0.02	0.07	0.02	0.03	0.03	0.01	0.02
$t < -2.36$	0.005	0.07	0.06	0.09	0.03	0.22	0.05	0.04	0.03
B. Alphas conditioned on term structure									
$t > 2.36$	0.005	0.13	0.05	0.06	0.14	0.03	0.02	0.09	0.09
$2.36 > t > 1.96$	0.02	0.03	0.03	0.03	0.07	0.01	0.01	0.05	0.03
$1.96 > t > 1.65$	0.025	0.04	0.03	0.02	0.07	0.02	0.02	0.05	0.04
$1.65 > t > 0$	0.45	0.39	0.44	0.25	0.44	0.29	0.38	0.53	0.50
$0 > t > -1.65$	0.45	0.30	0.34	0.42	0.23	0.36	0.45	0.21	0.28
$-1.65 > t > -1.96$	0.025	0.02	0.02	0.05	0.01	0.03	0.04	0.01	0.02
$-1.96 > t > -2.36$	0.02	0.02	0.03	0.03	0.02	0.03	0.03	0.02	0.02
$t < -2.36$	0.005	0.06	0.06	0.14	0.02	0.24	0.05	0.02	0.01
C. Alphas conditioned on financial markets									
$t > 2.36$	0.005	0.12	0.04	0.05	0.08	0.04	0.02	0.06	0.04
$2.36 > t > 1.96$	0.02	0.03	0.02	0.03	0.05	0.01	0.02	0.05	0.02
$1.96 > t > 1.65$	0.025	0.03	0.03	0.04	0.05	0.01	0.02	0.04	0.05
$1.65 > t > 0$	0.45	0.30	0.32	0.29	0.39	0.19	0.31	0.45	0.38
$0 > t > -1.65$	0.45	0.35	0.41	0.41	0.33	0.42	0.41	0.30	0.39
$-1.65 > t > -1.96$	0.025	0.04	0.04	0.05	0.04	0.06	0.05	0.03	0.04
$-1.96 > t > -2.36$	0.02	0.04	0.04	0.05	0.03	0.04	0.06	0.03	0.04
$t < -2.36$	0.005	0.09	0.09	0.08	0.04	0.23	0.11	0.05	0.04
D. Alphas conditioned on real economy									
$t > 2.36$	0.005	0.12	0.03	0.09	0.14	0.03	0.02	0.07	0.10
$2.36 > t > 1.96$	0.02	0.03	0.02	0.03	0.06	0.02	0.01	0.04	0.05
$1.96 > t > 1.65$	0.025	0.04	0.03	0.02	0.08	0.03	0.02	0.06	0.05
$1.65 > t > 0$	0.45	0.40	0.45	0.30	0.43	0.30	0.44	0.51	0.45
$0 > t > -1.65$	0.45	0.30	0.35	0.40	0.22	0.35	0.41	0.25	0.30
$-1.65 > t > -1.96$	0.025	0.02	0.03	0.06	0.02	0.03	0.03	0.01	0.02
$-1.96 > t > -2.36$	0.02	0.02	0.03	0.03	0.02	0.02	0.03	0.01	0.02
$t < -2.36$	0.005	0.06	0.05	0.09	0.02	0.22	0.05	0.04	0.02

Note: This table replicates Table 24.7 but uses the Sharpe style benchmarks to replace the broad market index.

TABLE 24.19   Distribution of *t*-statistics for Alphas in High vs. Low Economic States Using Sharpe Style Benchmarks

Interest Rate Volatility				Dividend Yield				
Income High	Income Low	SCG Low	Sector Low	Growth High	Income Low	SCG High	G&I High	Sector High
0.09	0.07	0.26	0.26	0.30	0.03	0.31	0.27	0.46
0.03	0.02	0.03	0.04	0.02	0.01	0.00	0.02	0.00
0.02	0.02	0.03	0.07	0.01	0.03	0.00	0.02	0.00
0.26	0.23	0.45	0.40	0.29	0.28	0.25	0.32	0.40
0.32	0.31	0.18	0.20	0.31	0.22	0.44	0.29	0.15
0.03	0.03	0.01	0.00	0.01	0.01	0.00	0.03	0.00
0.01	0.03	0.00	0.01	0.03	0.01	0.00	0.02	0.00
0.23	0.30	0.02	0.03	0.03	0.41	0.00	0.03	0.00

Short-Term Interest Rate		Inflation	Stock Market Volatility	Term Structure Slope				Stock Market Liquidity
Income High	Income Low	G&I High	Income Low	Income High	MCG High	SCG High	Other AG High	Sector Low
0.04	0.05	0.22	0.08	0.23	0.02	0.30	0.22	0.14
0.03	0.03	0.12	0.03	0.06	0.03	0.01	0.01	0.05
0.02	0.03	0.10	0.02	0.05	0.00	0.01	0.01	0.03
0.41	0.30	0.37	0.29	0.23	0.12	0.30	0.38	0.29
0.18	0.29	0.14	0.27	0.23	0.46	0.32	0.34	0.24
0.04	0.02	0.01	0.03	0.02	0.08	0.01	0.01	0.03
0.03	0.03	0.02	0.03	0.02	0.07	0.01	0.01	0.03
0.24	0.26	0.02	0.25	0.17	0.23	0.05	0.04	0.19

Notes: MCG = maximum capital gains; SCG = small company growth; Other AG = other aggressive growth; and G&I = growth and income. Alphas and their *t*-statistics are based on the regression Equation 24.4 using the conditioning dummy variables one at a time. High (low) means that the value of the state variable is higher (lower) than one standard deviation from its moving average over the past 60 months. The distributions of the *t*-statistics for alpha are presented in the table for those cases where chi-square tests for departures from a normal distribution produce right-tail *p*-values of 10 percent or less.

NOTES

1. This definition, of course, differs from the conventional definition of a bear market, which some consider to be a 20 percent decline from a previous high.
2. The conditional alpha given a bull state, according to the CAPM, is the fund's excess return over cash minus its conditional beta multiplied by the market excess return over cash, which is equal to $(0.20 - 0.05) - 1(0.20 - 0.05) = 0$.
3. The calculation is as follows. The unconditional beta is $cov(F,M)/var(M)$, where F is the fund return and M is the market return. The numerator is:

$$cov(F,M) = E\{[F - E(F)][M - E(M)]|\text{Bull}\} \times prob(\text{Bull}) +$$
$$E\{[F - E(F)][M - E(M)]|\text{Bear}\} \times prob(\text{Bear})$$
$$= [(0.20 - 0.125)(0.20 - 0.15)] \times 0.5 + [(0.05 - 0.125) \times (0.10 - 0.15)] \times 0.5$$
$$= 0.00375.$$

The denominator is:

$$\text{var}(M) = E\{[M - E(M)]^2|\text{Bull}\} \times \text{prob(Bull)} + E\{[M - E(M)]^2|\text{Bear}\}$$
$$\times \text{prob(Bear)}$$
$$= [(0.20 - 0.15)^2] \times 0.5 + [(0.10 - 0.15)^2] \times 0.5$$
$$= 0.0025.$$

The beta is, therefore, $0.00375/0.0025 = 1.5$. Note that the unconditional beta is not the same as the average conditional beta because the latter is 0.5 in this example.

4. One complication is that the daily three-month spot rates are highly autocorrelated. Because the interest rates refer to overlapping periods longer than one month, the data should follow a moving-average process with more terms than the number of days in the month, which causes a bias in the sample variance. We approximately control this bias by modeling the autocorrelation as a first-order autoregressive, or $AR(1)$, process. Let the $AR(1)$ coefficient be ρ, let the number of daily observations in the month be T, and let $s^2(r)$ be the maximum likelihood estimator of the variance, ignoring the autocorrelation. It is easy to show that the expected value of $s^2(r)$ differs from $\sigma^2(r)$, the true variance. An unbiased estimator, in the sense that its expected value under the $AR(1)$ assumption is $\sigma^2(r)$, may be constructed as: $s_*^2 = s^2(r)/\{1 - (1/T) - (2/T^2)[\rho/(1 - \rho)][T(1 - \rho^{T-1}) - (1 - \rho^{T-1})/(1 - \rho) + (T - 1)\rho^{T-1}]\}$. We use s_*^2 as our estimate of the monthly variance, where T is the number of daily observations in the month and $\rho = 0.99$, the value estimated using all the daily observations in the sample.

5. The broad market, small-cap, value, and growth indexes are courtesy of Kenneth French, via his website at Dartmouth College (mba.tuck.dartmouth.edu/pages/faculty/ken.french/), and are formed from data on CRSP and Compustat.

6. See Chen (1991) for related empirical evidence.

7. Elton, Gruber, and Blake (2001), however, argue that the CRSP database may have other selection biases, so the control for sample-selection bias is not perfect.

8. The CRSP codes that define each style group are the same as in Pastor and Stambaugh (2002) and are as follows: The objective codes from Wiesenberger are denoted by OBJ, those from ICDI are denoted ICDI, and those from Strategic Insight are denoted SI. Small-company growth funds are coded OBJ SCG or SI SCG. Other aggressive growth funds are coded OBJ AGG, ICDI AG or AGG, or SI AGG. Growth funds are coded OBJ G, G-S, S-G, GRO or LTG, or ICDI LG or GRO. Income funds are coded OBJ I, I-S, IEQ, or ING or ICDI IN or ING. Growth and income funds are coded OBJ GCI, G-I, G-I-S, G-S-I, I-G, I-G-S, I-S-G, S-G-I, S-I-G, or GRI, or ICDI GI or GRI. Maximum capital gains funds are coded OBJ MCG. Sector funds are coded OBJ ENR, FIN, HLT, TCH, or UTL, or ICDISF, UT, ENV, FIN, HLT, TEC, UTI, RLE, NTR, or SEC. Timing funds include those whose OBJ code is BAL or AAL, whose POLICY is Bal or Flex, whose ICDI_OBJ code is BL, or whose SI_OBJ code is BAL.

9. Brown and Goetzmann identified eight style categories that they interpreted as growth and income, growth, income, global timing, international, value, glamour, and metal funds.

10. For example, the other aggressive growth group had one to three funds in 1989 but no data during the May 1990–November 1991 period. Panel A of Table 24.3 uses all the available data on these funds.

11. We do not study "market timing" taken to mean trading on stale prices in net asset values, or "later trading"—potentially fraudulent trading after the close of the market. These practices are under legal investigation at some mutual fund companies as this is written.

12. Recall that the level and volatility of interest rates are the two most highly correlated state variable dummies, so we are conditioning on periods with significant overlap in these two cases.

13. It is necessary to account for the multiple comparisons in order to conduct meaningful inferences about this finding. Under the null hypothesis of no predictability in fund betas using the lagged instruments and assuming independent Bernoulli trials, the t-statistic for the significance of finding 13 cases is $(13/88 - 8.8/88)/[(0.10) (0.90)/88]^{1/2} = 1.5$.

14. Under the null hypothesis of no predictability and assuming independent Bernoulli trials, the t-statistic for the significance of finding 6 of 24 p-values less than 0.10 is $(6/24 - 0.10)/[(0.10) (0.90)/24]^{1/2} = 2.45$.

15. Dor, Jagannathan, and Meier (2003) argued that when returns-based style analysis is applied to hedge funds, the restriction against short sales may be relaxed.

16 Sharpe (1992) and Dor, Jagannathan, and Meier use a rolling, 60-month estimation period.

17. These inferences are conditioned on the weights of the style-based indexes in the sense that the standard errors do not incorporate the estimation errors involved in the construction of the style-based indexes. Accounting for this additional sampling variation is likely to lower the t-statistics.

18. The average conditional alpha differs from the unconditional alpha to the extent that the conditional beta differs from the unconditional beta and is correlated with the expected market return (see Christopherson, Ferson, and Glassman).

19. Such studies as Harvey (1989), Ferson and Korajczyk (1995), and Jagannathan and Wang found that conditional versions of the CAPM explain equity portfolio returns better than the traditional model, which ignores conditioning. It remains an interesting topic for future research to explore the performance of conditional CAPMs with nonparametric dummy variables for explaining the cross-section of stock returns.

20. Spiegel, Mamaysky, and Zhang (2003) found that a Kalman filter approach to modeling monthly time variation in mutual fund betas works well, which is consistent with the importance of relatively high-frequency variation.

21. Of course, we may lose some power to detect beta variation by coarsening the states to three discrete regimes and by concentrating on one state variable at a time, compared with the multivariate analysis in Panels C of Tables 24.4 and 24.15. But the strong results in Tables 24.2 and 24.3, which find that expected returns differ across the states, suggest that the loss of power should not be large.

22. The nonnormality, per se, in the distribution of the t-statistics is difficult to interpret. It could reflect the presence of extreme abnormal performers. Alternatively, nonnormality could reflect a sample size too small for the asymptotic distribution to be accurate. See Kosloski, Timmermann, Wermers, and White (2003) for a bootstrap analysis that addresses these issues.

23. This selection criteria may introduce a mild survival-selection bias, which seems unavoidable.

24. Because of the overlapping nature of the data used in constructing the performance estimates, the time series of the regression coefficients inherits a moving average structure of order two, or MA(2). We adjust the standard errors of the coefficients for this effect using Hansen's (1992) consistent covariance matrix estimator.

25. Ferson and Schadt also derived a conditional version of the market-timing model of Merton and Henriksson (1981), which views successful market timing as analogous to producing cheap call options. This model is considerably more complex than the conditional

Treynor–Mazuy model, and they found that it produced very similar results. We therefore do not study conditional Merton–Henriksson models in this chapter.

26. They used balanced and asset allocator style funds, as we do here, but their data from Morningstar suffered from survivor-selection bias.

27. The largest timing coefficients in Table 24.10 are about 0.3. Multiplied by the average squared excess return on the market index, the effect of the timing term is no larger than $(0.0105 - 0.00606)^2 \times 0.3 = 0.0006$ percent. Thus, the intercepts in the timing models are very similar to the alphas in the corresponding models that do not include the squared market term, which were studied earlier. In order to adjust the intercepts to compute a timing-adjusted alpha, it is necessary to multiply the timing coefficient by the expected excess return on a strategy that buys call options on the market portfolio with strike prices indexed to the Treasury rate. Because call options are much riskier than the market index, the expected risk premiums attached to the options should be much larger than the squared market return, and the timing-adjusted alphas could be very different from the intercepts in our regressions.

28. The calculations are as follows: Let x be the number of cases where the p-value is less than 0.05. The multiple-comparisons t-statistic across the 28 cases in each panel is $(x/28 - 0.05)/ (0.05 \times 0.95/28)^{1/2}$.

REFERENCES

Admati, Anat R., Sudipto Bhattacharya, Paul Pfleiderer, and Stephen A. Ross. 1986. "On Timing and Selectivity." *Journal of Finance*, vol. 41, no. 3 (July):715–730.

Basu S. 1977. "Investment Performance of Common Stocks in Relation to Their Price-Earnings Ratios: A Test of the Efficient Market Hypothesis." *Journal of Finance*, vol. 32, no. 3 (June):663–682.

Becker, C., W. Ferson, D. Myers, and M. Schill. 1999. "Conditional Market Timing with Benchmark Investors." *Journal of Financial Economics*, vol. 52, no. 1 (April):119–148.

Berk, Jonathan, and Richard C. Green. 2004. "Mutual Fund Flows and Performance in Rational Markets." *Journal of Political Economy*, vol. 112:1269–1295.

Breeden, Douglas T. 1986. "Consumption, Production, and Interest Rates: A Synthesis." *Journal of Financial Economics*, vol. 16 (May):3–39.

Brown, Stephen J., and William N. Goetzmann. 1997. "Mutual Fund Styles." *Journal of Financial Economics*, vol. 43, no. 3 (March):373–399.

Brown, Keith, Van, Harlow, and Laura Starks. 1996. "Of Tournaments and Temptations: An Analysis of Managerial Incentives in the Mutual Fund Industry." *Journal of Finance*, vol. 51, no. 1 (March):85–110.

Brown, Stephen J., William N. Goetzmann, Roger Ibbotson, and Stephen Ross. 1992. "Survivorship Bias in Performance Studies." *Review of Financial Studies*, vol. 5, no. 4 (Winter):553–580.

———. 1995. "Survival." *Journal of Finance*, vol. 50, no. 3 (July):853–874.

Campbell, J. Y. 1987. "Stock Returns and the Term Structure." *Journal of Financial Economics*, vol. 18, no. 2 (June):373–399.

Campbell, John Y., and Robert Shiller. 1991. "Yield Spreads and Interest Rates Movements: A Bird's Eye View." *Review of Economic Studies*, vol. 58, no.3 (May):495–514.

Carhart, Mark M. 1997. "On the Persistence in Mutual Fund Performance." *Journal of Finance*, vol. 52, no. 1 (March):57–82.

Chen, Nai-Fu. 1991. "Financial Investment Opportunities and the Macro Economy." *Journal of Finance*, vol. 46, no. 2 (June):1467–1484.

Chen, Z., and P. J. Knez. 1996. "Portfolio Performance Measurement: Theory and Applications." *Review of Financial Studies*, vol. 9, no. 2 (Summer):511–556.

Christopherson, Jon A. 1995. "Equity Style Classifications." *Journal of Portfolio Management*, vol. 21, no. 3 (Spring):32–43.

Christopherson, Jon A., Wayne Ferson, and Debra A. Glassman. 1998. "Conditioning Manager Alpha on Economic Information: Another Look at the Persistence of Performance." *Review of Financial Studies*, vol. 11, no. 1 (Spring):111–142.

Christopherson, Jon A., W. Ferson, and Andrew L. Turner. 1999. "Performance Evaluation using Conditional Alphas and Betas." *Journal of Portfolio Management*, vol. 26, no. 1 (Fall):59–72.

Connor, G., and R. A. Korajczyk. 1986. "Performance Measurement with the Arbitrage Pricing Theory: A New Framework for Analysis." *Journal of Financial Economics*, vol. 15, no. 3 (March):373–394.

Cumby, Robert, and Jack Glen. 1990. "Evaluating the Performance of International Mutual Funds." *Journal of Finance*, vol. 45, no. 2 (June):497–521.

Daniel, Kent, Mark Grinblatt, and Sheridan Titman. 1997. "Measuring Mutual Fund Performance with Characteristics-Based Benchmarks." *Journal of Finance*, vol. 53, no. 3 (July):1035–1058.

Del Guercio, Diane, and Paula A. Tkac. 2002. "The Determinants of the Flow of Funds of Managed Portfolios: Mutual Funds vs. Pension Funds." *Journal of Financial and Quantitative Analysis*, vol. 37, no. 4 (December):523–558.

Dor, Arik Ben, Ravi Jagannathan, and Iwan Meier. 2003. "Understanding Mutual Fund and Hedge Fund Styles Using Returns-Based Style Analysis." *Journal of Investment Management*, vol. 1, no. 1 (First Quarter):94–134.

Edelen, Roger M. 1999. "Investor Flows and the Assessed Performance of Open-End Mutual Funds." *Journal of Financial Economics*, vol. 53, no. 3 (September):439–466.

Elton, Edwin J., Martin J. Gruber, and Christopher R. Blake. 1996. "Survivorship Bias and Mutual Fund Performance." *Review of Financial Studies*, vol. 9, no. 4 (Winter):1097–1120.

———. 2001. "A First Look at the Accuracy of the CRSP Mutual Fund Data-base and a Comparison of the CRSP and Morningstar Databases." *Journal of Finance*, vol. 56, no. 6 (December):2415–2430.

Fama, Eugene F. 1970. "Efficient Capital Markets: A Review of Theory and Empirical Work". *Journal of Finance*, vol. 25, no. 2 (May):383–417.

———. 1975. "Short-Term Interest Rates as Predictors of Inflation." *American Economic Review*, vol. 65, no. 3 (June):269–282.

Fama, E., and K. French. 1989. "Business Conditions and Expected Returns on Stocks and Bonds." *Journal of Financial Economics*, vol. 25, no. 1 (November):23–49.

———. 1992. "The Cross-Section of Expected Stock Returns." *Journal of Finance*, vol. 47, no. 2 (June):427–465.

Fama, E., and James D. MacBeth. 1973. "Risk, Return, and Equilibrium: Empirical Tests." *Journal of Political Economy*, vol. 81, no. 3 (May/June):607–636.

Fama, Eugene F., and G. William Schwert. 1977. "Asset Returns and Inflation." *Journal of Financial Economics*, vol. 5, no. 2 (November): 115–146.

Ferson, Wayne E. 1989. "Changes in Expected Security Returns, Risk and the Level of Interest Rates." *Journal of Finance*, vol. 44, no. 5 (December): 1191–1217.

Ferson, Wayne E., and Campbell R. Harvey. 1991. "Sources of Predictability in Portfolio Returns." *Financial Analysts Journal*, vol. 47, no. 3 (May/June):49–56.

Ferson, Wayne E., and Kenneth Khang. 2002. "Conditional Performance Measurement Using Portfolio Weights: Evidence for Pension Funds." *Journal of Financial Economics*, vol. 65, no. 2 (August):249–282.

Ferson, Wayne E., and Robert A. Korajczyk. 1995. "Do Arbitrage Pricing Models Explain the Predictability of Stock Returns?" *Journal of Business*, vol. 68 (July):309–349.

Ferson, W., and Rudi Schadt. 1996. "Measuring Fund Strategy and Performance in Changing Economic Conditions." *Journal of Finance*, vol. 51, no. 2 (June):425–462.

Ferson, W., and Vincent A. Warther. 1996. "Evaluating Fund Performance in a Dynamic Market." *Financial Analysts Journal*, vol. 52, no. 6 (November/December):20–28.

Ferson, W., Tyler Henry, and Darren Kisgen. 2003. "Evaluating Government Bond Fund Performance with Stochastic Discount Factors." Working paper, Boston College.

Ferson, Wayne E., Sergei Sarkissian, and Timothy Simin. 2003a. "Is Stock Return Predictability Spurious?" *Journal of Investment Management*, vol. 1, no. 3:10–19.

———. 2003b. "Spurious Regressions in Financial Economics?" *Journal of Finance*, vol. 58, no. 4 (August):1393–1414.

Freund, John E. 1992. *Mathematical Statistics*. 5th ed. Englewood Cliffs, NJ: Prentice Hall.

Gatev, Evan, and Phillip Strahan. 2003. "Banks' Advantage in Hedging Liquidity Risk: Theory and Evidence from the Commercial Paper Market." Working paper, Boston College.

Glosten, Lawrence, and Ravi Jagannathan. 1994. "A Contingent Claims Approach to Performance Evaluation." *Journal of Empirical Finance*, vol. 1, no. 2 (January): 133–166.

Goyal, Amit, and Ivo Welch. 2003. "Predicting the Equity Premium with Dividend Ratios." *Management Science*, vol. 49, no. 5 (May):639–654.

Grant, D. 1977. "Portfolio Performance and the 'Cost' of Timing Decisions." *Journal of Finance*, vol. 32, no. 3 (June):837–846.

Grinblatt, Mark, and Sheridan Titman. 1988. "The Evaluation of Mutual Fund Performance: An Analysis of Monthly Returns." Working paper, University of California at Los Angeles.

———. 1989. "Mutual Fund Performance: An Analysis of Quarterly Portfolio Holdings." *Journal of Business*, vol. 62, no. 3 (July):393–416.

Grinblatt, Mark, Sheridan Titman, and Russ Wermers. 1995. "Momentum Investment Strategies, Portfolio Performance, and Herding: A Study of Mutual Fund Behavior." *American Economic Review*, vol. 85, no. 5 (December): 1088–1105.

Harvey, Campbell R. 1989. "Time-Varying Conditional Covariance in Tests of Asset Pricing Models." *Journal of Financial Economics*, vol. 24, no. 2:289–318.

Hansen, Bruce E. 1992. "Consistent Covariance Estimation for Dependent Heterogeneous Process." *Econometrica*, vol. 60, no. 4 (July):967–972.

Ippolito, Roger A. 1989. "Efficiency with Costly Information: A Study of Mutual Fund Performance." *Quarterly Journal of Economics*, vol. 104, no. 1 (February):1–23.

Jagannathan, R., and R. Korajczyk. 1986. "Assessing the Market Timing Performance of Managed Portfolios." *Journal of Business*, vol. 59, no. 2 (April):217–236.

Jagannathan, R., and Zhenyu Wang. 1996. "The Conditional CAPM and the Cross Section of Expected Returns." *Journal of Finance*, vol. 51, no. 1 (March):3–53.

Jegadeesh, N., and Sheridan Titman. 1993. "Returns to Buying Winners and Selling Losers: Implications to Stock Market Efficiency." *Journal of Finance*, vol. 48, no. 1 (March):65–91.

Jensen, M. 1968. "The Performance of Mutual Funds in the Period 1945–1964." *Journal of Finance*, vol. 23, no. 2 (May):389–416.

Keim, Donald B., and Robert F. Stambaugh. 1986. "Predicting Returns in Stock and Bond Markets." *Journal of Financial Economics*, vol. 17, no. 2 (December):357–390.

Kosloski, John, Alan Timmermann, Russ Wermers, and Halbert White. 2003. "Can Mutual Fund 'Stars' Really Pick Stocks? New Evidence from a Bootstrap Analysis." Working paper, University of Maryland.

Lakonishok, Josef, Andrei Shleifer, and Robert Vishny. 1994. "Contrarian Investment, Extrapolation, and Risk." *Journal of Finance*, vol. 49, no. 5 (December):1541–1578.

Lehmann, Bruce N., and David M. Modest. 1987. "Mutual Fund Performance Evaluation: A Comparison of Benchmarks and Benchmark Comparisons." *Journal of Finance*, vol. 42, no. 2 (June):233–266.

Litterman, R., and J. Sheinkman. 1988. "Common Factors Affecting Bond Returns." New York: Goldman Sachs, Financial Strategies Group.

Merton, Robert C. 1973. "An Intertemporal Capital Asset Pricing Model." *Econometrica*, vol. 41, no. 5 (September):867–887.

Merton, Robert C., and Roy D. Henriksson. 1981. "On Market Timing and Investment Performance II: Statistical Procedures for Evaluating Forecasting Skills." *Journal of Business*, vol. 54, no. 4 (October):513–534.

Myers, David H. 1999. "The Conditional Performance of Pension Funds." Working paper, Lehigh University.

Pastor, Lubos, and Robert F. Stambaugh. 2002. "Mutual Fund Performance and Seemingly Unrelated Assets." *Journal of Financial Economics*, vol. 63, no. 3 (March):315–349.

———. 2003. "Liquidity Risk and Expected Stock Returns." *Journal of Political Economy*, vol. 111, no. 3:642–685.

Rakowski, David. 2003. "Fund Flow Volatility and Performance." Working paper, Georgia State University.

Ross, S. A. 1976. "The Arbitrage Pricing Theory of Capital Asset Pricing." *Journal of Economic Theory*, vol. 13, no. 2 (December):341–360.

Shanken, Jay. 1990. "Intertemporal Asset Pricing: An Empirical Investigation." *Journal of Econometrics*, vol. 45, nos. 1/2:99–120.

Sharpe, W. F. 1964. "Capital Asset Prices: A Theory of Market Equilibrium under Conditions of Risk." *Journal of Finance*, vol. 19, no. 3 (September):425–442.

———. 1988. "Determining a Fund's Effective Asset Mix." *Investment Management Review* (December):59–69.

———. 1992. "Asset Allocation: Management Style and Performance Measurement," *Journal of Portfolio Management*, vol. 18, no. 2 (Winter):7–19.

Sirri, Erik R., and Peter Tufano. 1998. "Costly Search and Mutual Fund Flows." *Journal of Finance*, vol. 53, no. 3 (October):1589–1622.

Spiegel, Matthew, H. Mamaysky, and H. Zhang. 2003. "Estimating the Dynamics of Mutual Fund Alphas and Betas." Yale ICF Working Paper No. 03–03.

Treynor, Jack, and Kay Mazuy. 1966. "Can Mutual Funds Outguess the Market?" *Harvard Business Review*, vol. 44 (July–August):131–136.

Wermers, Russ. 2000. "Mutual Fund Performance: An Empirical Decomposition into Stock Picking Talent, Style, Transactions Costs and Expenses." *Journal of Finance*, vol. 55, no. 4 (August):1655–1695.

Zheng, Lu. 1999. "Is Money Smart? A Study of Mutual Fund Investors Fund Selection Ability." *Journal of Finance*, vol. 54, no. 3 (June):901–933.

CHAPTER 25

DISTINGUISHING TRUE ALPHA FROM BETA

Laurence B. Siegel

Portfolios can be thought of as being composed of a beta component, which is broad asset class exposure, and an alpha component, which is excess return achieved through active management. If investors are hiring active managers, presumably because they believe these managers have real skill or the ability to deliver alpha, then they ought to be sure that they are paying for true alpha and not beta. These principles are not only applicable to traditional institutional portfolios, such as defined-benefit plans and endowments, but are also relevant for nontraditional portfolios, such as hedge funds.

Will Rogers was, among other things, a legendary investor of his personal assets and the first absolute-return investor. His advice to other investors was to: "Buy some good stock and hold it til it goes up, then sell it. If it don't go up, don't buy it."

He was kidding as usual, but a couple of generations ago many long-only managers talked like that, and they were not kidding. They said: "We are absolute-return investors. We just buy stocks that go up. We do not care what the market is doing." Now, a new crop of people who were not born back then are saying the same thing about hedge funds.

In 1964, long-only investors who imagined themselves to be absolute-return investors were set straight by Bill Sharpe when he showed statistically how to separate the policy risk (which he called "beta") from the active risk (which he called "alpha"). His approach caught on fairly quickly, and 10 or 20 years later, most long-only managers had their tail between their legs and were quoting the alphas they had produced, not their absolute returns that included the market or index component. If their alphas were negative, then the consultants punished them by advising clients to invest with another manager. That kind of benchmarking has added a discipline to the market that it desperately needed. Without benchmarking, investors would wind up paying alpha-type fees, active fees, for the index part of the return. Given

Reprinted from *CFA Institute Conference Proceedings: Challenges and Innovation in Hedge Fund Management* (July 2004):20–29.

some advances in measurement, this practice can also be applied to alternative investments, where the beta exposures are not quite as obvious.

Skill in the investment management industry is a rare commodity. The average market participant may be an intelligent individual, but by definition, this average participant cannot beat the average. And because the average return of all market participants can be achieved at very low cost by buying an index fund, an active manager has to be better than average to add alpha. In other words, many investors are better served by investing in a passively managed index fund than by investing with an active manager and taking the risk that the manager has less skill than average and will thus have a negative alpha.

In this presentation, I will try to make sense of this principle and will focus on the distinction between active or alpha risk, which is the risk taken to beat a benchmark, and policy or beta risk, which is the risk taken by merely investing in the benchmark. I will first discuss some general principles that I call the "dimensions of active management" in reference to an article I coauthored with Barton Waring.[1] Then, I will discuss applying those concepts to alternative investments, such as hedge funds, because that subject is of intense interest to so many people right now. Finally, I will talk about policy implications for pension funds and other investors.

THE DIMENSIONS OF ACTIVE MANAGEMENT

Active management has three dimensions:

- pure active return, which is the value added by the manager (or what should be properly called alpha),
- pure active risk, which is the volatility of the pure active return, and
- costs.

A manager does not have absolute control over all three of these dimensions. A manager does not control return; it comes or it does not, according to how the markets perform. An element of control is associated with active risk. Costs, however, are the dimension that a manager directly controls. If a manager wants to add to his or her return, cutting active management fees would be one way of doing so, but cutting costs will not help if the costs pay for actual alpha being delivered on a consistent basis. That cost is worth the money.

A Portfolio of Betas and a Portfolio of Alphas

When investment performance is considered in the three dimensions of return, risk, and cost, a number of puzzle pieces emerge. The first one is taught in business school, but people tend not to apply it: Policy risk and active risk are separable and should be separated. They should really be thought of as two distinct portfolios. One is a portfolio of betas and consumes 100 percent of the capital. It is a portfolio of exposures to various market risk factors, which can conveniently be thought of as index funds, although the investor might be able to invest in futures or exchange-traded funds (ETFs) or something other than traditional index funds. For simplicity, think of it as 100 percent of capital being consumed through bets on various index funds.

The other portfolio is a self-financing portfolio of alphas. It consumes no capital. Theoretically, an investor should be able to earn alpha anywhere in any asset class through a long–short strategy that does not involve using the investor's own capital. The portfolio of alphas should be designed based on where the investor can best earn alpha or best earn a high information ratio (IR), which is the alpha per unit of active risk taken. That mix of assets should have nothing to do with the mix of assets in the portfolio of betas, which should be structured based on the investor's liabilities.

Investing in this way may not always be practical. But the separation of alpha and beta—what is sometimes called portable alpha—is at least a sound conceptual way of thinking about one's portfolio.

Pure Alpha and Naive Alpha

When measuring alpha, differentiating between pure alpha and naive alpha is important. A lot of investment managers subtract the return of the benchmark from the return of their portfolio and then call the remainder alpha. They have not made an adjustment for beta, so this approach does not demonstrate real alpha. Real alpha must be estimated from a regression. Bill Sharpe's market model regression is similar to the capital asset pricing model (CAPM), so most people call it the CAPM regression. That is the first step.

The next step is to see if any other systematic factors in the returns properly belong to the beta category rather than the alpha category. The factors that generally turn out to be meaningful are the two common style factors known as "value minus growth" and "small cap minus large cap." If a manager adjusts for all these common factors and for the beta of the overall portfolio relative to the market, then he or she has isolated the true alpha, the pure alpha, for which active managers should be paid. All the other exposures belong in the portfolio of betas and should reap index fund-like fees.

Style Boxes

Style boxes do not do a good job of categorizing managers. A growth manager who concentrates in the most rapidly growing companies, or a value manager who is more price conscious than most, will not tend to be close to the center of his or her growth or value style box. Thinking of such managers as fitting into these boxes misrepresents managers and affects the style allocations in a negative way. A much better way of thinking about managers is to use a style map that creates a continuum from growth to value, from large to small cap, from zero beta to some beta higher than 1. In this space, a manager represents a point. In other words, the manager can be anywhere on the continuum in any of these dimensions.

Manager Structure Optimization

Having identified the location of each candidate manager on the style map through style analysis, one can then build a portfolio of managers through optimization. As Barton Waring and I discussed in "The Dimensions of Active Management," building a portfolio of managers is like building a portfolio of anything: It is an optimization problem, although it is a little trickier than conventional optimization because it has two stages. One stage is for the portfolio of betas, and the other is for the portfolio of alphas. We refer to the optimization for the portfolio of alphas as "manager structure optimization." To do that optimization, investors require estimates of expected alphas and expected active risk (or tracking error) for managers in exactly the same way they need estimates of the risk and return of the asset classes for the portfolio of betas.

Estimating Expected Alphas for Managers

Estimating expected alphas for managers can be a struggle; many people do not know how to do it. But these expected alphas are already in their portfolios. Through reverse optimization, one can easily calculate the expected alpha implied by the weight the manager has in the portfolio. So, if people do not think they can estimate expected alphas for managers, surprise—they are already doing it.

Constructing the alpha estimates needed to build an efficient portfolio of managers is, without a doubt, difficult. There is no formula or recipe for estimating expected alphas. Each investor has to come up with a way to estimate those numbers, and a particular investor's approach may not necessarily rely on quantitative methods. If an investor is going to justify holding active managers rather than index funds, however, then the investor should be able to quantify the expectation that the manager will earn alpha. If the investor can do that, then a manager structure optimizer can be used to build an optimal portfolio of managers.

Barclays Global Investors has written software to perform manager structure optimization. I have experimented with the software a little bit, and it gives surprisingly neat results. Although it sounds like a mostly theoretical experiment, it is not. The software produces portfolios of managers that are plausible and not subject to the common critique that optimizers are mostly garbage-in, garbage-out machines; the output is actually useful.

Two Conditions for Selecting Active Managers

As I have said, active management should not be expected to win just because it is active; it is a zero-sum game, with winners counterbalanced by losers (and that is before deducting costs). As a result, an investor has to satisfy two conditions for it to be rational to play the active management game. The first is that the investor has to believe that there are some active managers with real skill who add value other than just by chance. The second condition, which is the tougher one, is that the investor has to believe that he or she can pick these exceptional managers from a large population of managers who are mostly not exceptional.

Those who meet the second condition should indeed hire active managers and might like to know what a portfolio looks like that reflects the principles I have been describing. If an investor is constrained to be long-only, then the portfolio must be constructed from managers on the bottom curve in Figure 25.1 Managers on this curve include index funds, enhanced index funds, and traditional active funds (both concentrated and diversified).

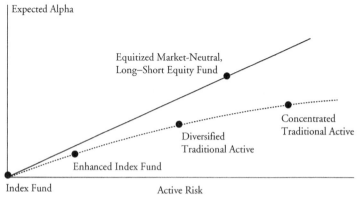

FIGURE 25.1   Impact of the Long-Only Constraint

Note: Expected alpha is conditional on the manager having skill.
Source: Barclays Global Investors.

Manager structure optimization shows that if an investor seeks alpha and is averse to active risk, the weight in traditional active managers—especially those that are concentrated—should be greatly reduced. This result comes about because the no-shorting constraint hurts the IR of traditional, high-active-risk managers more than it does low-active-risk managers, such as enhanced index funds. (With the horizontal axis representing active risk and the vertical axis representing expected alpha, the IR is thus represented by the slope of the line at any given point.)

That the no-shorting constraint hurts higher-active-risk managers more than low-active-risk managers requires some explanation. All managers gather information about overpriced securities, which could be used to sell securities short. If a given manager cannot sell short, the manager can still choose not to own something that is in his or her benchmark. The more securities in the portfolio, the more opportunities to take advantage of the information that would otherwise cause a manager to short a stock. Managers who have a high-active-risk portfolio have far fewer holdings and thus far fewer opportunities to take advantage of any information about overpriced stocks. Thus, the IR is lower for these managers.

Investors who are allowed to sell short can choose from the portfolios on either line in Figure 25.1. If an investor has a high-active-risk budget, the investor's choices might include an equitized market-neutral, long–short hedge fund. Most of the rest of the portfolio would consist of enhanced index funds, with possibly a small allocation to traditional active funds that have particularly high expected alphas. An investor with a high-active-risk budget might not have any pure index funds in his or her optimum portfolio because index funds do not have enough active risk.

At a lower-active-risk budget, an investor who is allowed to sell short would build the portfolio out of index funds and enhanced index funds, plus potentially some of the equitized market-neutral, long–short hedge fund. Such an investor might also hold just a dollop of traditional active managers. Note that this entire analysis has been conducted as if the fees on the long–short and the long-only portfolios were the same. They are not. Investors have to calculate returns after costs, and long–short portfolios are quite aggressively priced these days.

DO HEDGE FUNDS CHARGE ALPHA FEES FOR BETA PERFORMANCE?

My discussion of pure active risk and return can be applied to hedge funds and other alternative investments. Foremost, keep in mind that hedge fund managers are just active managers. There is no magic. The idea that a hedge fund manager is a crazed genius who allows a few of his wealthy friends to invest in the fund if they pay 2 percent of assets and 20 percent of the profit is obsolete. Such fee levels are ridiculous for hedge funds that are large institutional investment organizations. The 2 and 20 fee structure that makes perfect sense for the genius and his friends has been scaled up, without any discounting, to apply to investments in the billions of dollars for prominent hedge funds. The hedge fund fee structure has become little more than a mechanism for transferring wealth from the investor to the manager in a way that is not possible in a traditional, long-only portfolio where the fees and the strategies are more transparent.

Separating Alpha and Beta for Hedge Funds

Putting costs aside for the moment, I will discuss how an investor might apply to hedge funds my earlier comment that the dimensions of active management are pure active return, pure active risk, and costs.

The pure active return is the return left over after adjusting for any beta exposures that exist within the hedge fund. Many investors are used to thinking of beta as exposure to the stock market. But a whole array of other systematic risk factors can also be considered beta.

In a meeting of the Foundation Financial Officers Group in Chicago in October 2003, Clifford Asness said that if a strategy can be written down, in the sense of a recipe that any-one can follow, it is passive and it is beta; anything else is alpha.

Following is a short list of potentially nonobvious beta exposures that are often found in hedge funds:

- value minus growth,
- duration (interest rate risk),
- credit spreads,
- optionality (e.g., being "short volatility"),
- buying merger targets, shorting the acquirers,
- buying convertible bonds, shorting the stock of the issuer,
- borrowing short, lending long when the yield curve is steep (carry trade), and
- borrowing in one currency, lending in another (international carry trade).

Clearly, a lot of market-type exposures are inherent in hedge fund strategies. Although index funds may not exist for these market factors, the systematic strategy can be identified and written down. In principle, investors are paying 2 and 20 for a package deal that includes both true alpha, which is the return above and beyond any returns from these systematic strategies, and a signifi-cant beta component. Getting 2 and 20 for the index part is nice work if a manager can get it.

Clifford Asness said something else very clever at the Chicago meeting: Alpha *becomes* beta over time once the source is discovered and promulgated. What is he talking about? Well, the first person to discover the return potential of value minus growth should be insulted to hear it called a beta factor because that person could have made a huge amount of money and nobody would have been able to determine where it was coming from. But now that everybody knows about it, it is beta. Not only can it be written down; it can be bought at very low cost using index funds or ETFs. Thus, to deserve the 2 and 20 fee structure, the hedge fund must be able to add alpha beyond merely being long in value and short in growth. Hence, alpha became beta over time.

I am not completely comfortable classifying anything that can be written down as beta. I think investors need to be able to "buy" a market factor through long and/or short positions in index funds, ETFs, futures, options, or swaps for it to be beta. Sometimes, investors have to pay alpha-like fees for exotic betas that are not yet available through lower-cost vehicles. I suspect that much of the success and popularity of hedge funds comes from their ability to sell exotic beta rather than from pure alpha as Asness stringently defines it.

Identifying Hedge Fund Betas: A Study

Bridgewater Associates conducted a wonderful study that sought to differentiate alpha from beta for hedge funds. Results for fixed-income arbitrage hedge funds are shown in Figure 25.2.

The dotted line represents six-month rolling returns of an index of fixed-income arbi-trage hedge funds. The solid line is a model that Bridgewater devised that fits the managers' performance pretty closely. The alpha is the area created by geometrically subtracting the dot-ted line from the solid line. Beta is the extent to which the two lines zig and zag together. So, this figure presents a sort of visual returns-based style analysis. The correlation of the model with the managers is 59 percent, which is pretty good considering that the managers typically claim they are absolute-return managers with no beta exposures. The important thing to note about this figure is how little space is between the dotted line and the solid line. In other words, these hedge fund managers produced very little alpha.

The results for emerging market hedge funds are shown in Figure 25.3. For this strategy, the Bridgewater model had a remarkable correlation of 81 percent, which corresponds to an R^2 of 65 percent. That is, 65 percent of the variation in these supposedly beta-free funds was explained by beta factors. Again, there is very little space between the solid line and the dotted line. There is a little alpha, but not very much.

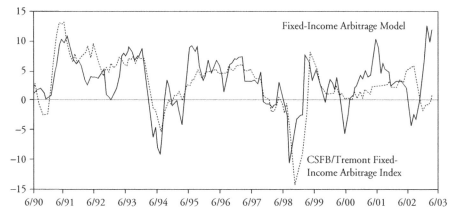

FIGURE 25.2   Fixed-Income Arbitrage Six-Month Rolling Returns, June 1990–June 2003

Note: The fixed-income arbitrage model consists of a 15 percent weight in the Eurodollar over Treasury spread, 5 percent in the emerging market debt spread over comparable-maturity U.S. Treasuries, 35 percent in the U.S. corporate bond spread over Treasuries, and 50 percent in the U.S. mortgage spread over Treasuries.

Source: Based on data from Bridgewater Associates.

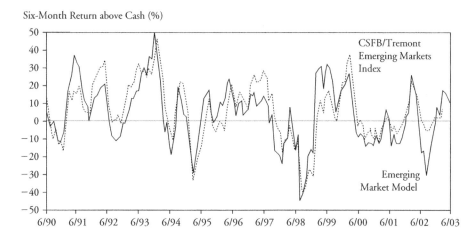

FIGURE 25.3   Emerging Market Six-Month Rolling Returns, June 1990–June 2003

Note: The emerging market model is an equally weighted combination of emerging market debt and emerging market equity indexes.

Source: Based on data from Bridgewater Associates.

Managed futures fund results are shown in Figure 25.4. The model had a correlation of 75 percent and, once again, a very high R^2. The model spends a significant amount of time ahead of the average manager. In this case, it appears that active management subtracted alpha. The model consisted of a series of momentum trades, but one could build an index fund using these trades if so desired, although I do not think any such index funds currently exist.

Six-Month Return above Cash (%)

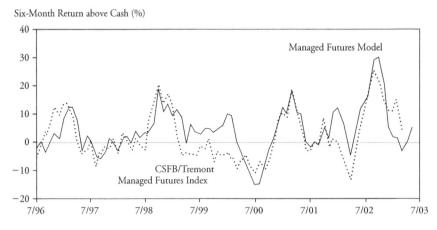

FIGURE 25.4 Managed Futures Six-Month Rolling Returns, July 1996–July 2003

Notes: The managed futures model consists of a "1 × 3 month" momentum strategy in which one buys a given market if the one-month moving average is above the three-month moving average or sells if below. This strategy is followed on an equal-weighted basis across each of the following markets: the euro, yen, U.S. 10-year Treasury bond, S&P 500, and Eurodollar six-month maturity return above cash. *Source:* Based on data from Bridgewater Associates.

Six-Month Return above Cash (%)

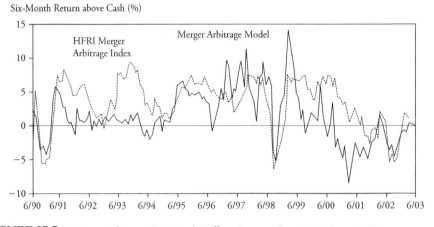

FIGURE 25.5 Merger Arbitrage Six-Month Rolling Returns, June 1990–June 2003

Note: The merger arbitrage model uses the six-month return above cash of the S&P 500, multiplied by a beta (between zero and one) proportional to the number of merger deals available in the market at each point in time. *Source:* Based on data from Bridgewater Associates.

Finally, merger, arbitrage fund results are shown in Figure 25.5. The model was just the return on the S&P 500 Index, with an adjustment made for the number of merger and acquisition deals that were available to invest in. Considering how simple the model is, the tracking between it and the hedge funds' returns is fairly high, with a correlation of 52 percent. But the area between the solid line and the dotted line is substantial. Active managers made a lot more money than would have been achieved by investing in the model.

POLICY IMPLICATIONS FOR PENSION FUNDS AND OTHER INVESTORS

Every pool of assets has been accumulated for some reason. Usually, the assets exist to pay for an actual contracted liability or for a conceptual liability, such as retirement. Fortunately, people are catching on to the idea that the liability is really the ultimate benchmark. If an individual earns a return on his or her accumulated savings that is high enough to maintain his or her lifestyle in retirement, or if a plan sponsor is fully funded relative to its economically determined pension liability, or if the Ford Foundation earns a rate of return high enough to make the grants that it was established to make, then all three have achieved their investment goals.

Foundations

At the Ford Foundation, we have only one problem with that definition of success. Our liability (we are required to pay out annually 5.3 percent of whatever our asset value is at the time) makes us absolute-return investors in principle. But we do not know how to develop an asset allocation policy that has an expected return of 5.3 percent plus the inflation rate (to keep the purchasing power of the portfolio whole). We have to build the policy portfolio out of asset classes that exist. Our estimate for the expected real return on stocks is about 5 percent. Nominal bonds, TIPS (the common name for U.S. Treasury Inflation-Indexed Securities), real estate, cash, and other assets have even lower expected returns. Truly hedged hedge funds, if we held them, would have a zero beta and, for the purpose of calculating their expected return, the benchmark should be the return on cash. Of course, if we thought these funds were going to only earn the cash return, we would not buy them; we would hold cash instead. But any return offered by hedge funds beyond the return on the cash benchmark is alpha, and one should never put alpha into the expected return on a benchmark or policy portfolio. The policy portfolio should consist only of betas, and the production of alpha can then be measured relative to this purely beta-driven benchmark.

So, to answer the question of whether there should be a policy portfolio for an institution with an absolute-return payout requirement, the answer is that we do need one, and it should be built out of assets for which index funds exist. Ours happens to be constructed from indexes of U.S. and international equities, nominal bonds, TIPS, and cash. We can then judge the success of our active asset allocation decisions by reference to this policy portfolio. Of course, we can change the policy portfolio when we believe it is prudent to do so. There is no reason that it should be static, although changing it all the time would tend to blur the distinction between active and policy decisions.

We can also compare our performance with that of a hypothetical asset that returns 5.3 percent plus the inflation rate. But if we decide that we are unable to add alpha, we cannot index the portfolio instead and earn this rate of return. That is why an absolute-return benchmark does not make a lot of sense.

Defined-Benefit Pension Plans

Defined-benefit pension plans have a special set of challenges because the size of the liabilities is set in a process that has nothing to do with the size of the assets. Although a foundation's liabilities are linked to the assets by a simple formula, in a pension plan, the liabilities are set by contracting with the workers without reference to what assets may be available to pay the pension benefits. It is then the sponsor's problem to accumulate enough assets through a mix of pension contributions and investment returns.

To minimize required contributions from the sponsor, many pension plans have adopted very high equity allocations, 70 percent or more. But such an allocation creates a great deal of risk in the pension plan because the pension liabilities look more like a portfolio of nominal bonds and TIPS with only a little in equities. Pension plans should thus consider lowering their equity allocations.

Looked at another way, a pension plan is just a project of the sponsoring corporation. If investing in the S&P 500 is such a great proposition, why not shut down the factory, sell the assets, and just buy shares of the S&P 500 to increase the productivity of the company's capital? The fact that no company ever does that shows companies do not think investing in the S&P 500 is such a great corporate project.

Some people wonder whether a broad shift among pension plans toward a closer match of assets and liabilities would cause the market to decline. If all pension funds decided at once that they needed to sell equities and get to a position that more closely matched their liabilities, who would be buying the equities? The answer is that the investors who hold the shares in these corporations would suddenly find out that they are short in beta because the companies themselves in which they hold stock no longer have a leveraged position in the S&P 500. So, to keep their risk level the same and the reward for taking the risk the same, they would have to buy the equities that the pension funds would be selling. In the short run, any change in the supply and demand for an asset produces volatility. But in the long run, it would not change the overall price level of the market.

Stated another way, if companies that have a bet on the S&P 500 in their pension funds are currently fairly priced and they then unwind this bet, the risk of the companies must go down, but not the expected return, so the stocks will be self-evidently a bargain and investors will buy them.

Defined-Contribution Plans and Individual Investing

The defined-contribution world, which is a subset of individual investing, has been poorly served by the financial system because it sells plan participants high-cost products that produce negative alpha, on average, even before fees. Furthermore, investors do not understand the efficient frontier or how to build an optimal portfolio. Every worker—every airline pilot, every nurse, and every tort lawyer—has gotten roped into the position of being a chief investment officer for his or her own assets.

These workers never asked for this responsibility and have never claimed they were good at it; by and large, they are not. Why not just do it for them? If they could invest in a well-engineered, optimized portfolio consisting mostly of index funds but with some active funds mixed in that are carefully chosen by the sponsor, they would have a lot more money for their retirement and they would be earning it with a lot less risk. In other words, we should be working hard to try to get the principles that I just discussed, which are gaining currency in the world of institutional investing, applied to individuals' investments too.

QUESTION AND ANSWER SESSION

Question: If employees do not require extra compensation for having underfunded pensions, then such underfunded pensions represent free debt. Do employees require such compensation?

Siegel: If employees become involuntary lenders to the company by having a pension plan that is underfunded and thus have to worry about whether they're going to get their pensions, they should in theory be able to negotiate for higher wages because the company is cheating them out of something they have agreed to be paid for. In practice, I don't think that they are able to do anything of the kind.

Generally, companies with underfunded plans are poorly managed in other ways as well. Employees of these companies would often be better off looking for another job. But having given up something without any compensation, the employees should either attempt to negotiate a higher wage or get the company to fully fund the plan, which is a much cheaper solution to the same problem. In fact, it is free. The company doesn't give up anything by fully funding the plan because it owes the money anyway, but the employees get something, which is the reduced risk that they will not be paid their pension.

Question: Are endowments that have invested heavily in hedge funds earning alpha?

Siegel: I think the early adopters earned a lot of alpha. But now that the number of hedge funds has ballooned to 6,000, there is the danger that high compensation schemes have attracted low-skilled people as well as the smartest people. The fees are so high that a lot of "dumb but lucky" managers are going to earn high compensation while the process of weeding out the good from the bad takes place. I'm willing to bet that not nearly as many people will earn alpha from hedge funds going forward.

Question: Is it true that all investors cannot hire index managers because indexing cannot exist without a large component of the market being active?

Siegel: I've been hearing this argument since I was a student. Every time a professor would bring up the efficient market hypothesis, a smart kid in the front row would put up her hand and say that if everybody indexed, the market wouldn't be efficient and prices would be unrelated to value because nobody would be analyzing securities. Roger Ibbotson calls this the "student's proof" of market inefficiency, and it is right.

I don't know whether it takes 10 percent or 80 percent of all investments to be indexed for prices to be unrelated to value. It seems that in every generation there is some kind of bubble or depression where stock prices are unrelated to value, either on the upside or the downside, at least in some industries. We have just been through such a period. So, at the very least, indexing has not made the market self-evidently *more* efficient.

But I think we are very far from a point where indexing is so pervasive that it makes successful active management easy. Most active managers underperform their benchmarks, and you would have done better to invest in an index fund.

Question: What are some of the qualitative elements you should consider when estimating manager alpha and tracking error?

Siegel: We'd look to see whether the historical track record was superior on a properly risk-adjusted basis. But we also want to deal with sensible and reputable people from whom we can learn something. When you talk to a lot of smart people, everybody seems pretty good. But then you have to remember that they're all betting against each other, which is how they're trying to earn alpha. So, you have to look for somebody who is truly superior even in that population.

Thus, I'm looking for somebody who can teach me something original and different, distinguishing himself or herself from the rest of this population that has already been weeded out pretty well.

Question: If the roughly eight defined strategies in Tremont Advisers' hedge fund indexes are different beta strategies, then should we be combining the ones with less than perfectly correlated betas with stocks, bonds, and cash?

Siegel: Yes. That is one of the hidden implications of the principles that I have just explained. Once we've built a portfolio of stocks, bonds, and cash betas, we need to see if we can find some other betas that are not perfectly correlated with these and that have a pay-off. To the extent we can, it raises the efficient frontier.

The hedge fund strategies that I discussed show some pretty strong evidence that they had a payoff over some reasonably long period. So, I would say "yes," but not at any price. Hedge fund investors should be cognizant of high fees, which raise the per-formance hurdle. If there is a way to get exotic beta without paying alpha fees, and if exotic beta and not pure alpha is what you want, you should do so.

Question: How do you incorporate fees into your portfolio optimizations?

Siegel: We would subtract the expected fees from the expected alpha. Note that I said "expected" fees, because the fees are typically conditional on the production of alpha; thus, it is not trivial to estimate them.

Question: Most corporate pension funds and Treasury departments are not abandoning current or even loss-making operations to invest in equities. Is it because they lack an understanding of alpha, of equities, and of the true potential of professional investment management? Or, is it because most executives are personally not successful investors?

Siegel: I think it is because they have a mandate to try to make a go of their auto company, gas company, or software company and not turn their operations into a mutual fund. If they did, shareholders would find another CEO. Shareholders who want to invest in the stock market can do so on their own.

Question: If one accepts the forecast that stocks and bonds will have disappointing returns over the next 20 years, is a long–short strategy a better proxy for equity exposure inclusive of alpha and beta for managing downside drawdowns on an absolute-return basis?

Siegel: There are two things you can do: Live with the low returns, or aggressively add alpha knowing that your chance of succeeding is probably 50 percent. We all want to add alpha, but there should be a backup plan for living with lower returns.

Question: If a manager beats an index by timing weights of high-and low-beta stocks, is that not a source of alpha?

Siegel: Excess return that is created by timing between different beta exposures will show up as alpha in a proper analysis and should be compensated as such.

Question: How predictive is the past record of good managers?

Siegel: It is much less accurate than I would like, but it is not useless. Good performance tends to be predictive for a while because of a momentum effect. If there is a group of stocks that has moved up, all of a sudden everybody wants to buy those stocks. Money then flows into the funds, forcing them to buy more of the same stocks. So, managers can ride that wave a little bit, but that isn't real skill. Fortunately, real skill is also somewhat predictable, but with a wide forecast error.

NOTE

1. M. Barton Waring and Laurence B. Siegel, "The Dimensions of Active Management," *Journal of Portfolio Management* (Spring 2003):35–51.

CHAPTER 26

A PORTFOLIO
PERFORMANCE INDEX

Michael Stutzer

Fund managers may sensibly be averse to earning a time-averaged portfolio return that is less than the average return of some designated benchmark. When a portfolio is expected to earn a higher average return than the benchmark return, the probability that it will not approaches zero asymptotically at a computable exponential decay rate. The probability decay rate is thus proposed here as a new portfolio "performance index." In the widely analyzed special case in which returns are normally distributed, the new performance-index-maximizing portfolio is the same as the popular Sharpe-ratio-maximizing portfolio. The results of the two approaches generally differ, however, because of nonnormal levels of skewness and/or kurtosis in the portfolio attributable to large asymmetrical economic shocks or investments in options and other derivative securities. An illustrative example will show that the new index is easy to implement and, consistent with empirical evidence on portfolio choice, favors investments with positively skewed returns.

Pension and endowment portfolio analysts need a meaningful yet practical way to rank-order feasible portfolios. Perhaps the most widely used measure for this purpose is the Sharpe ratio. The Sharpe ratio of a portfolio is its expected excess return relative to a chosen benchmark (usually the "riskless" rate of interest) divided by the standard deviation of its excess return. When returns are individually and identically normally distributed, risk-averse investors will choose a portfolio that is mean–standard deviation efficient, and Sharpe (1994) summarized the foundational case for using the Sharpe ratio to evaluate (*ex ante*) the growth (i.e., mean) versus security (i.e., standard deviation) trade-off in these portfolios. In practice (*ex post*), a historical time series of portfolio returns minus benchmark returns is used to calculate historical average excess return and historical standard deviation as estimates of the unknown

Reprinted from the *Financial Analysts Journal* (May/June 2000):52–61.

expected excess return and standard deviation. And in practice, portfolios are ranked by the size of this *ex post* Sharpe measure.

But what is to be done when the returns are not normally distributed? The theoretical foundation for the Sharpe measure does not apply when excess returns deviate from the normal because of large absolute values of skewness and/or kurtosis. Such nonnormalities in a portfolio may arise from large asymmetrical economic shocks, investments in options and other derivative securities with inherently asymmetrical returns, limited liability (bankruptcy) effects on asset returns, or other causes.[1] Moreover, a suggestion that has been made for a long time now is that investors value positive skewness of returns (e.g., Kraus and Litzenberger 1976). The Sharpe measure does not consider skewness at all.

ALTERNATIVES TO THE SHARPE RATIO

An alternative performance index should satisfy the following desiderata:

- The index should rank-order portfolios in accord with the Sharpe ratio when returns are normally distributed.
- When returns are not normally distributed, the index should reflect skewness preference while retaining the Sharpe ratio's useful statistical interpretation and ease of implementation.
- The index should be derived from a sound behavioral foundation that is free of unspecified and unknowable parameters and is relevant to many fund managers.

Three general approaches have been used to construct alternative performance indexes: *ad hoc* modifications to the Sharpe ratio, expected utility functions, and expected return relationships implied by perfect financial market equilibrium resulting from investors who maximize expected utility. Each approach has advantages and disadvantages. Accordingly, a single performance index is unlikely to be appropriate for all fund managers.

One way to construct an alternative performance index that retains statistical interpretation and ease of implementation is to modify the Sharpe ratio. Fishburn (1977) noted that "decision makers in investment contexts very frequently associate risk with failure to attain a target return" (p. 117). The Sharpe ratio, however, penalizes return variance and hence penalizes squared deviations from the mean return regardless of whether they are the "bad" deviations below a target return or the "good" deviations above it. To favorably weight positive skewness, one can replace the variance by a statistic that penalizes only the deviations below some cutoff value. Using only those squared deviations produces a semivariance, whose square root has been used as a measure of downside risk (Sortino and van der Meer 1991) to replace standard deviation in the denominator of the Sharpe ratio. Ang and Chua (1979) noted, "Even if return distributions are symmetrical, the semivariance still yields information different from the variance" (p. 363). But they also pointed out that use of semivariance is "in a sense, *ad hoc* because of the absence of a theoretical basis" (p. 363), in violation of the third desideratum.

Another orthodox approach to rank ordering portfolios relies on the expected utility hypothesis. Investors who adhere to the Von Neumann–Morgenstern (1944) behavioral axioms act as if they rank-order the probability distributions of wealth generated by portfolios. Hence, each such investor's chosen portfolio should maximize the expected value of her or his utility function. Skewness preference is embodied in utility functions with positive third derivatives, but even if one ignores the impressive behavioral evidence calling the appropriateness of expected utility theory's behavioral axioms into question (e.g., Machina 1987), fund managers still must make two decisions before they can implement this approach: what utility function to use and what values to assign to the utility function parameters.

In lieu of dealing with the difficulties in making those decisions, a fund manager could start by eliminating portfolios that would never be chosen by any investor with increasing utility (first order stochastically dominated) or with increasing and concave (indicating risk aversion) utility (second order stochastically dominated). The result may not, however, provide much rank ordering of portfolios, in violation of the second desideratum. For example, in a study comparing the performance of 34 mutual funds with the DJIA, Joy and Porter (1974) concluded that, although no fund dominated the DJIA, "28 funds neither dominated the DJIA nor were dominated by it" (p. 31), using second order stochastic dominance.

The fund manager, then, cannot avoid choosing a specific utility function and its parameters. One widely prescribed utility function for managers of long-term funds is the logarithm, advocated centuries ago by Bernoulli as a solution to the St. Petersburg Paradox (for a survey of the log utility literature, see Hakansson and Ziemba 1995). It has several features of interest to pension and endowment managers. First, it has no additional parameters whose values must be specified to produce a rank ordering of portfolios. Second, like maximization of the Sharpe ratio, maximization of expected log utility has a nice statistical interpretation: It is equivalent to maximizing the expected (geometric) growth rate of wealth. Third, it induces a preference for positive skewness. So, it does satisfy the second and third desiderata. The complete emphasis of expected log utility on expected capital growth also appears to be particularly suitable for pension and endowment managers, rather than for investors with shorter horizons. MacLean and Ziemba (1999) emphasized, however, that its use "leads to riskier and less diversified portfolios than most other utility functions" (p. 222). The reason is that it ignores volatility and other higher-order moments of the capital growth rate. A lognormal example of Browne (1999) illustrates the phenomenon: An expected log-maximizing portfolio places an 89 percent weight on stocks when their returns have an 8 percent expected excess return over the risk-free rate and a standard deviation of 30 percent. Yet, there is still a 10 percent probability that the portfolio's wealth will not wind up more than a paltry 10 percent higher than a risk-free investment *after 98 years.*

A third approach to portfolio performance evaluation requires expected utility maximization for *all* investors, rather than only the subset of investors represented by a particular fund manager. Additional assumptions guaranteeing existence of perfect financial market equilibrium result in a predicted relationship between portfolio expected returns and a model-derived measure of risk. Grinblatt and Titman (1995) advocated this third approach. They argued that it

> seems more important to focus on the marginal contributions of a managed portfolio to the risk and expected return of an investor. This necessarily involves adjusting for risk with a marginal risk measure, like beta. (p. 582)

As noted by Leland (1999), "[M]ost practice is firmly rooted in the approach of the capital asset pricing model" (p. 27). He went on to note that superior portfolio performance according to the CAPM is measured by Jensen's alpha (Jensen 1969), which is the portfolio's expected return in excess of the return predicted from the security market line, evaluated at the portfolio's CAPM beta coefficient. Because the CAPM is based on the assumption that all investors care only about the mean and variance of their wealth, it cannot properly adjust for any investor preferences for positive skewness, so Ang and Chua proposed an analogous measure based on the Kraus and Litzenberger three-moment market equilibrium model.

Perhaps the most recent proposal in this vein was made by Leland and is heavily based on the findings of He and Leland (1993). They posited an expected-utility-maximizing, representative-agent exchange model with dynamically complete, frictionless, continuous-time trading possibilities. The key relevant finding was He and Leland's Equation 22, which showed that if the market portfolio's instantaneous rate of return has constant drift and volatility (i.e., if the market portfolio value is lognormally distributed), then the representative agent's utility function must have constant relative risk aversion (CRRA). Leland's proposal uses an equilibrium moment restriction that follows from He and Leland's Equation 22 to derive a performance index that replaces the CAPM beta coefficient in Jensen's alpha with a modified beta that also depends on the market portfolio's drift. In addition to the aforementioned argument of Grinblatt and Titman in favor of indexes of performance based on expected utility maximization with complete markets in equilibrium, the Leland proposal also embodies skewness preference because it is predicated on expected CRRA utility maximization (which has a positive third derivative). Hence, it satisfies the second and third desiderata.

The validity of an index derived via this third approach depends on the accuracy of its equilibrium model's derived relationship between passive portfolio expected returns and the model's measure of risk, because the index evaluates managed portfolio performance relative to this relationship (e.g., Jensen's or Leland's alpha). Unfortunately, these relationships have been shown to be very inaccurate. For example, Campbell, Lo, and MacKinlay (1997) reported that analogous representative-agent, complete-market, equilibrium exchange models using Leland's CRRA utility failed to pass the award-winning asset-pricing statistical tests of Hansen and Singleton (1982).[2] Specifically, Campbell, Lo, and MacKinlay reported that "the over-identifying restrictions of the model are strongly rejected whenever stocks and commercial paper are included together in the system" (p. 314).

Furthermore, the same models suffer from the "equity premium puzzle" discussed by Mehra and Prescott (1985). In a recent survey of the large body of literature surrounding this issue, Kocherlakota (1996) summarized the puzzle as follows: When the CRRA model's measure of risk is used, "stocks are not sufficiently riskier than Treasury bills to explain the spread in their returns" (p. 43). He also noted a "risk-free rate puzzle" implied by this model—that is, even if investors have a coefficient of relative risk aversion high enough to explain the spread between the expected stock return and the risk-free return, the model equilibrium risk-free return must be higher than observed.

Why should the measure of risk in Leland's CRRA representative-agent, complete-market, equilibrium exchange model be used to evaluate managed portfolio performance when analogous models that make those same assumptions cannot correctly predict the expected return of both a stock index portfolio and the risk-free rate?[3] With regard to the Leland model's lognormally distributed market portfolio, he noted that his model implies that the Black–Scholes model should correctly price European options on the market portfolio. In testing this proposition, the commonly adopted proxies for the market portfolio are broad-based stock indexes. Yet, as concluded by Rubinstein (1994) in his presidential address to the American Finance Association, "[T]here has been a very marked and rapid deterioration" (pp. 773–774) since 1986 in the applicability of Black–Scholes to S&P 500 Index options, a finding since confirmed by many others.[4]

In contrast, my proposal combines some advantages that semivariance-type and expected-utility indexes have for a long-horizon portfolio manager, without requiring additional assumptions about the behavior of all other investors and the nature of any resulting financial market equilibrium. Like the semivariance-type indexes, my performance index explicitly incorporates the belief mentioned by Fishburn (i.e., that investors frequently associate risk with failure to attain a target) in an easily interpretable statistical criterion. Specifically, I model a manager who is concerned that the portfolio's discrete-time-averaged, individually and identically distributed (i.i.d) returns will be no greater than the corresponding time-averaged return earned by some benchmark (i.e., the target) that is either specified by the trustee or chosen by the manager. Such benchmarks are pervasive in the investment management industry, and fear of underperformance relative to benchmarks may account for some of the interest in protective put strategies.[5] When the investor holds a portfolio that is *expected* to return more than the benchmark, the probability of missing this time-averaged target return decays to zero as time passes at a computable exponential decay rate. To minimize this probability, the fund manager asks the analyst to find a portfolio that maximizes this decay rate, which is the proposed new portfolio performance index.

Following a summary of the results of Sharpe ratio maximization for the normally distributed case, I develop the alternative behavioral hypothesis and provide a simple, distribution-free approach to estimating the optimal portfolio when excess returns are *not* normally distributed.

SHARPE RATIO MAXIMIZATION

Following Jobson and Korkie's (1982) notation, denote the expected excess returns of the joint normally distributed assets by the vector μ and the covariance matrix of the excess returns by Σ.[6] The Sharpe ratio for any portfolio p with asset proportions w_p summing to 1 (i.e., $w'_p \, \mathbf{e} = 1$, where $\mathbf{e}$ is a vector of 1's) is then

$$\lambda_p = \frac{w'_p \mu}{\sqrt{w'_p \sum w_p}}. \tag{26.1}$$

The tangency portfolio (i.e., the portfolio at the tangency of the capital market line and the risky assets' mean–variance frontier) with weights w_m maximizing the Sharpe ratio is

$$w_m = \frac{\sum^{-1} \mu}{e' \sum^{-1} \mu}, \tag{26.2}$$

which (after a little algebra) can be shown to attain the following maximum attainable value, λ_m, of the Sharpe ratio:

$$\lambda_m \equiv \frac{\mu_m}{\sigma_m}$$

$$= \sqrt{\mu' \sum^{-1} \mu,} \tag{26.3}$$

where σ_m is the standard deviation of the Sharpe-ratio-maximizing portfolio. In the presence of a riskless asset as the benchmark, the tangency portfolio that maximizes the Sharpe ratio is the optimal portfolio of normally distributed risky assets, in the sense that *any* mean–variance-efficient portfolio is a combination of this portfolio and the riskless asset. Thus, Sharpe summarized the case for using the *ex ante* Sharpe ratio to evaluate the relative performance of all risky-asset portfolios. In the CAPM, the portfolio that maximizes the Sharpe ratio is the equilibrium market portfolio of the risky assets.

BEHAVIORAL HYPOTHESIS

Denote a portfolio p's *excess* (i.e., net of a benchmark) rate of return in any time period t by R_{pt}, and denote the time-averaged excess return it earns over T periods by

$$\overline{R_{pT}} \equiv \frac{\sum_{t=1}^{T} R_{pt}}{T}. \tag{26.4}$$

Now, assuming the portfolio has a positive expected excess return, the law of large numbers implies that $\text{prob}\,(\overline{R_{pT}} \leq 0) \to 0$ as $T \to \infty$. In i.i.d. return processes and a wide variety of other return processes, this probability will eventually converge to zero asymptotically at a computable exponential rate I_p; that is,

$$\text{prob}(\overline{R_{pT}} \leq 0) \approx \frac{c}{\sqrt{T}}\,e^{-I_p T}, \tag{26.5}$$

for large T, where c is a constant that depends on the return distribution. Therefore, the behavioral hypothesis is as follows:

> *A fund manager who is averse to receiving a nonpositive time-averaged excess return above some specified benchmark will direct analysts to select a portfolio, m, that makes the probability of such a return occurring decay to zero at the maximum possible rate, I_m.*

Discussion

Pension or endowment fund managers fit the characteristics of the "manager" in this hypothesis. Such funds are often thought to have a "long" investment horizon, but assuming that a pension or endowment fund manager knows the exact horizon length is unreasonable. By contract, the trustees may evaluate the manager's performance over a relatively short time (e.g., five years), but the manager hopes to get the contract renewed. Subsequent evaluations might examine the manager's performance since inception of the relationship rather than only the most recent five-year period. Therefore, assuming that the pension or endowment manager wants to avoid a nonpositive average excess return over the benchmark for much longer than five years is not unreasonable. That is, in computing excess returns, the manager will want to minimize $\text{prob}\,(\overline{R_{pT}} \leq 0)$ over an indefinite time span T that is much longer than the contract interval.

Recent behavior by some actively managed mutual funds is consistent with this hypothesized emphasis on avoiding underperformance, albeit in a more extreme way. A recent article in the *New York Times* documented the practice of "closet indexing," in which supposedly active stock pickers invest heavily in stocks that replicate a benchmark index.[7] The article reported Morningstar research findings that about 40 percent of funds investing in large-capitalization stocks closely track a large-cap index (i.e., regressing their funds' returns on the index returns resulted in an R^2 greater than 90 percent). The article suggested a few reasons for the documented increase in this behavior, including the desire of 401(k) plan sponsors to

> avoid the embarrassment of trying to explain why the large-cap growth fund they selected for the 401(k) is badly trailing the overall market.

This behavior was also attributed to the following managerial motive:

> But because so much of the actively managed fund is tied to an index, it will prob-
> ably not trail the benchmark by much, thus avoiding the huge underperformance—
> say 10 percent or more—that prompts investors to withdraw their money. That is
> good news for the fund company.

The behavioral hypothesis of this article is not a model of closet indexers. The behavioral hypothesis reflects the desire to avoid underperformance of a designated benchmark, but
it emphasizes growth (long-run, time-averaged returns) in excess of the benchmark.
Nevertheless, closet indexing indicates that underperformance of benchmarks is an important concern of many fund managers. The behavioral hypothesis presented here is a model of
fund managers who are willing to trade off some of their extreme concern about underperformance for the possibility of extra growth.

The behavioral hypothesis also differs from conventional minimization of the "probability of ruin," as advocated in the Safety First principle of Roy (1952). In an apt critique of the
expected utility hypothesis, Roy noted:

> In an economic world, disasters may occur if an individual makes a net loss as the
> result of some activity. For large numbers of people some such idea of a *disaster*
> exists, and the principle of Safety First asserts that it is reasonable, and probable in
> practice, that an individual will seek to reduce as far as is possible the chance of such
> a catastrophe occurring. (p. 432)

Unlike the Safety First principle, in the approach presented here, the "disaster level" is
not a fixed minimum value of return or wealth but, rather, a long-run *time-averaged* excess
return, over some benchmark, of zero. One might think that my approach still presumes an
excessively conservative fear of downside risk and that such timid fund managers will never
survive in the harshly competitive world of investment management. But as argued previously, a manager may be fired for choosing an excessively volatile portfolio that has a greater
chance of underperforming the time-averaged return of its benchmark.

Recently, researchers in the rapidly developing field of behavioral finance have proposed
the concept dubbed "loss aversion," which is part of the prospect theory of investor behavior.
As defined in Benartzi and Thaler (1995), loss aversion is the tendency of individuals to be
more sensitive to reductions than to increases in their levels of well-being. Consider the level
of well-being attainable by individuals passively investing in the benchmark, who can thus
ensure an expected excess rate of return of zero. If they are more sensitive to reductions in
this level than to increases, as the hypothesis of loss aversion predicts, they may want fund
managers to behave in accord with the behavioral hypothesis proposed here: Choose a portfolio that minimizes the long-run probability of earning a nonpositive time-averaged excess
return over the benchmark. In this interpretation, the behavioral hypothesis presented here
provides a preference-parameter-free alternative to prospect theory.

The Performance Index

As shown in Bucklew (1990), Cramer's Theorem can be used to provide the following computation of the performance index, I_p, for a portfolio denoted p with return R_p in excess of its
benchmark:

$$I_p = \max_{\theta} - \log E\left(e^{\theta R_p}\right),$$ (26.6)

where θ is a number less than zero and E denotes the expected-value operation. In the important special case of normally distributed portfolio excess returns R_p, Bucklew showed how to compute the performance index (Equation 26.6). The result in this case is that

$$I_p = \frac{1}{2}\lambda_p^2, \tag{26.7}$$

that is, half the squared Sharpe ratio. So, the performance-index-maximizing portfolio (hereafter called "the performance portfolio") is the same as the Sharpe-ratio-maximizing portfolio (hereafter called "the Sharpe portfolio") given in Equation 26.2. It attains the maximum feasible performance index value given by Equations 26.3 and 26.7.

The intuition behind this result is straightforward: A portfolio with a large positive expected excess return has a small chance of producing a finite time series with negative time-averaged excess return. But so does a portfolio with a smaller standard deviation of excess return, for then a bad run of negative excess returns is less likely to drive the time-averaged excess return below zero. Because the Sharpe ratio, λ_p, is the ratio of these two statistics, it will be larger in either case than otherwise.

A hypothesis should be judged mainly by its results rather than by the realism of its assumptions.[8] I have just shown that the rank ordering of feasible normally distributed portfolios implied by the behavioral hypothesis results in the same rank ordering delivered by the Sharpe ratio—the most widely accepted method for evaluating normally distributed portfolios. This result is true even though the behavioral hypothesis *explicitly* stresses minimization of the probability that the riskless rate will not be exceeded, in a way that (the reader can now see) is *implicit* in the Sharpe ratio. More generally, remember that the behavioral hypothesis's minimization of the probability that the time-averaged benchmark will not be exceeded is equivalent to an emphasis on maximizing the probability that the time-averaged benchmark *will* be exceeded. Hence, it does not excessively emphasize security over growth considerations—or at least no more than the Sharpe ratio does.[9]

When excess returns are *not* normally distributed, the performance index I_p is not Equation 26.7. Instead, it will depend on the higher-order cumulants[10] of the nonnormal excess-return distribution (e.g., the function will reflect nonnormal skewness and kurtosis of the excess returns). As illustration, the computation of Equation 26.6 can be quickly rearranged to establish an equivalence to expected constant absolute risk aversion (CARA) utility:

$$-\frac{1}{e^{I_p}} = \max_{-c} E\left(-e^{-cR_p}\right). \tag{26.8}$$

The right side of Equation 26.8 is the CARA expected utility of portfolio R_p with a specific, computable value of its coefficient of risk aversion, c, greater than zero. The left side of Equation 26.8 increases with I_p, so this specific CARA function's rank ordering of portfolios will agree with the performance index's ordering.

Because CARA utility has a positive third derivative, the performance index's ordering will reflect skewness preference, thus satisfying the second desideratum presented in the introduction. The behavioral hypothesis and the CARA-equivalence result provide a behavioral foundation relevant for long-horizon fund managers, thus satisfying the third desideratum.

Although, in general, no explicit computable formula exists for the performance index, its absence is not much of a disadvantage relative to the Sharpe ratio. Uses of the Sharpe ratio still require a time series of past portfolio returns to estimate the portfolio's mean and standard deviation. The next section shows that a time series of past returns also enables straightforward estimation of the performance index, I_p.

FINDING THE OPTIMAL PORTFOLIO: A DISTRIBUTION-FREE APPROACH

Denote a time series of the assets' returns in excess of the chosen benchmark by R_{it}, where $i = 0, \ldots, n$ and $t = 1, \ldots, T$. Then, a portfolio's excess return at t is the weighted average $\sum_{i=0}^{n} w_i R_{it}$. Because the portfolio weight w_0 is equal to $1 - \sum_{i=1}^{n} w_i$, this portfolio excess return at time t may be rewritten as

$$R_{pt} = \sum_{i=1}^{n} w_i (R_{it} - R_{0t}) + R_{0t}. \tag{26.9}$$

So, the estimate for the right side of Equation 26.6 based on historical data is

$$I_p = \max_{\theta} -\log \frac{1}{T} \sum_{t=1}^{T} e^{\theta R_{pt}}. \tag{26.10}$$

Substituting Equation 26.9 into Equation 26.10 shows that the performance portfolio weights are those w that solve

$$I_m = \max_{W_1, \ldots, w_n} \; \max_{\theta} \; -\log \frac{1}{T} \sum_{t=1}^{T} e^{\theta \sum_{i=1}^{n} w_i (R_{it} - R_{0t}) + R_{0t}}. \tag{26.11}$$

The easiest way to solve the numerical maximization problem (Equation 26.11) is by use of the optimizer features of a personal computer spreadsheet. This method generally requires a good initial guess at the solution. To the extent that a normal distribution even roughly approximates the historical return distribution, an estimate of the Sharpe portfolio (Equation 26.2) will be a good initial guess for the portfolio weights; a good initial guess for θ is -1 times that portfolio's mean excess return divided by its variance. Finally, constraints on the portfolio weights (e.g., on short sales) can be imposed through use of the spreadsheet optimizer.

EMPIRICAL EXAMPLE

Following Kroll, Levy, and Markowitz (1984), I chose approximately 20 (23, to be exact) randomly chosen stocks' monthly returns between 1977 and 1997.[11] To investigate the effects of the choice of benchmark on the results, I first examined the zero benchmark (i.e., an under-the-mattress "investment" at an interest rate of zero). The results will later be contrasted to those obtained with a U.S. T-bill benchmark. I used a numerical optimizer to solve Equation 26.11 and to locate the Sharpe portfolio chosen from these 23 stocks. The two portfolios, which (in population) would be the same if returns were normally distributed, are compared in Table 26.1. As expected, the biggest difference in portfolio weights between the Sharpe portfolio and the performance portfolio is in the stock with the highest excess (i.e., nonnormal) skewness, which is stock KMB. Because positive skewness helps avoid the dreaded nonpositive time-averaged excess return, the performance portfolio invests 22 percent of funds in it, whereas the Sharpe portfolio invests only 16 percent. This difference is enough to make KMB the second largest holding in the performance portfolio, but only the fourth largest holding in the Sharpe portfolio. The performance portfolio also gives a lower weight to the stock with the lowest (i.e., most negative) skewness, AT.

TABLE 26.1   Monthly Return Statistics with Benchmark Return of Zero, January 1977–December 1996

Ticker Symbol	μ	σ	Excess Skewness	Excess Kurtosis	Weight in Optimal Portfolio	
					Sharpe Ratio	Performance Index
KU	0.012	0.040	−0.138	0.481	0.34	0.34
BUD	0.017	0.063	0.326	0.649	0.19	0.21
BMY	0.015	0.058	0.056	−0.173	0.17	0.19
KMB	0.017	0.062	**0.868**	3.020	**0.16**	**0.22**
CRS	0.013	0.078	−0.128	1.540	0.12	0.11
CC	0.035	0.126	0.115	1.020	0.12	0.12
AT	0.016	0.060	**−0.217**	0.555	**0.11**	**0.08**
DG	0.028	0.121	0.377	−0.013	0.08	0.09
CPL	0.013	0.050	0.012	0.651	0.07	0.08
NCC	0.014	0.063	−0.162	1.168	0.06	0.04
MUR	0.015	0.090	0.055	0.062	0.04	0.05
ORU	0.011	0.042	0.490	2.683	0.03	0.02
GD	0.019	0.091	0.361	1.320	0.02	0.03
BK	0.018	0.082	0.155	1.100	0.02	0.04
AMD	0.024	0.163	0.260	0.519	0.01	0.00
APD	0.013	0.076	−0.021	0.899	−0.01	−0.01
ALK	0.015	0.105	0.557	1.850	−0.02	−0.05
KOW	0.018	0.113	0.159	0.600	−0.02	−0.02
LTD	0.026	0.129	0.073	0.498	−0.05	−0.05
BCL	0.014	0.076	0.273	2.193	−0.06	−0.10
DCN	0.012	0.080	0.168	0.951	−0.08	−0.11
ACK	0.014	0.088	0.088	0.936	−0.12	−0.12
BAX	0.011	0.073	−0.029	−0.129	−0.15	−0.15

The performance portfolio attained a maximal I_m value of 12.1 percent—higher than the 11.7 percent achieved by the Sharpe portfolio. The implication is that, although the probability of realizing nonpositive time-averaged excess returns decays rapidly for both portfolios, the performance portfolio's probability decays faster (thus, it has a higher level of security). The high degree of risk aversion in the performance portfolio, $c = -\theta = 12.53$, reflects the desire to maximize the probability of outperforming a very conservative benchmark.

Table 26.2 shows the results for the two portfolios when the one-month T-bill return was used as the benchmark. Again, the greatest difference between the performance and Sharpe portfolios is the heavier weight the performance portfolio gives to the most favorably skewed stock, KMB. Because the T-bill benchmark has a positive mean return, the probability of realizing nonpositive time-averaged excess returns is higher in this test. As a result, the

TABLE 26.2   Monthly Return Statistics with a One-Month T-Bill Benchmark, January 1977–December 1996

Ticker Symbol	μ	σ	Excess Skewness	Excess Kurtosis	Weight in Optimal Portfolio	
					Sharpe Ratio	Performance Index
BUD	0.017	0.063	0.326	0.649	0.28	0.30
KMB	**0.017**	**0.062**	**0.868**	**3.020**	**0.27**	**0.32**
CC	0.035	0.126	0.115	1.020	0.23	0.24
BMY	0.015	0.058	0.056	−0.173	0.21	0.24
KU	0.012	0.040	−0.138	0.481	0.21	0.21
AT	0.016	0.060	−0.217	0.555	0.19	0.18
DG	0.028	0.121	0.377	−0.013	0.15	0.17
CPL	0.013	0.050	0.012	0.651	0.14	0.15
CRS	0.013	0.078	−0.128	1.540	0.10	0.10
BK	0.018	0.082	0.155	1.100	0.07	0.09
MUR	0.015	0.090	0.055	0.062	0.03	0.02
GD	0.019	0.091	0.361	1.320	0.02	0.04
AMD	0.024	0.163	0.260	0.519	0.02	0.01
NCC	0.014	0.063	−0.162	1.168	0.01	−0.02
LTD	0.026	0.129	0.073	0.498	−0.03	−0.03
ALK	0.015	0.105	0.557	1.850	−0.05	−0.07
KOW	0.018	0.113	0.159	0.600	−0.05	−0.06
APD	0.013	0.076	−0.021	0.899	−0.06	−0.05
ORU	0.011	0.042	0.490	2.683	−0.07	−0.10
ACK	0.014	0.088	0.088	0.936	−0.12	−0.12
BCL	0.014	0.076	0.273	2.193	−0.13	−0.17
DCN	0.012	0.080	0.168	0.951	−0.18	−0.21
BAX	0.011	0.073	−0.029	−0.129	−0.25	−0.26

maximum attainable performance index value, I_m, drops from 12.1 percent to 6.4 percent when the benchmark is the one-month T-bill return. The performance portfolio's degree of risk aversion also drops, to 6.65, in reflection of the desire to maximize the probability of outperforming a tougher benchmark than before.

CONCLUSIONS

Endowment or pension fund managers may have sensible reasons to be averse to earning a time-averaged portfolio return that is not greater than the average return of some trustee-designated benchmark and, therefore, will choose a portfolio with a positive expected excess return over the benchmark. In that case, the probability that the portfolio will not earn a higher average return than the benchmark approaches zero asymptotically at a computable exponential decay rate. Accordingly, portfolios with high probability decay rates are preferable to portfolios with low probability decay rates. I have thus proposed the probability decay rate as a new portfolio performance index.

The proposed performance index produces the same rank order of normally distributed feasible portfolios as the Sharpe ratio, thus satisfying the first desideratum in the introduction. But returns are not always normally distributed—because of skewness and/or kurtosis attributable to large asymmetrical economic shocks, limited-liability (bankruptcy) effects on asset returns, or strategies involving options and other derivative securities with inherently asymmetrical returns. When excess returns are not normally distributed, the performance index will reflect skewness preference, unlike the Sharpe ratio, but implementation of this index requires the same historical return data and personal computer spreadsheet software that is needed to maximize the Sharpe ratio. Moreover, maximizing the decay rate is equivalent to maximizing expected CARA utility, *with a specific, computable coefficient of risk aversion*. So, the index has a relevant behavioral foundation (with both statistical and expected utility interpretations) that is free of unspecified parameters. Apparently, the new performance index is the only known measure that meets the desiderata. Still, one should acknowledge the judgment of Sortino and Forsey (1996) that for performance measurement, "no one risk measure is the be-all and end-all" (p. 41).[12]

The example of an optimal portfolio formed from 23 randomly selected stocks showed that the performance portfolio did indeed place more weight on assets with positively skewed returns than the Sharpe portfolio did.

ACKNOWLEDGMENTS

Thanks are extended to Tom George and George Chang for their sound advice and assistance. Early conversations with David Tierney were also helpful.

NOTES

1. Maximization of expected quadratic utility "rationalizes" the mean–variance criterion, even when portfolio returns are not normally distributed, but a quadratic utility function is problematic regardless of how its parameter values are chosen. It always has a "bliss" point (i.e., a level of wealth high enough that investors would never want to exceed it), and as noted by Pratt (1964) and others, increases in wealth below the bliss point result in counterintuitively higher aversion to inherent investment risks.
2. He and Leland did not try to explain the level of the risk-free rate, nor did they try to explain the intertemporal spending of their investors, whereas the analogous equilibrium models do.
3. Moreover, changing Leland's lognormal market and CRRA features and permitting continuous consumption will not eliminate the following counterfactual implication of *all* expected-utility-maximizing, representative-agent exchange models with complete markets: All of these models imply that spending by any investor is perfectly correlated with spending by any other investor. Graphs of all investors' intertemporal spending ought to move

up and down in lockstep. They do not. In international asset-pricing models, each country's aggregate consumption should be perfectly correlated with any other's. They are not.

4. Leland did cite empirical evidence that "daily market returns are not lognormal but for longer periods (e.g., three months), returns are quite 'close' to lognormally distributed" (Note 7). This statement does not, however, mitigate the significance of his model's counterfactual implication about Black–Scholes pricing of options on this stock market. For example, the failure might be a result of his assumption of continuous-time, frictionless trading rather than nonlog-normality (but I doubt it).

5. The conventional mean–variance tools cannot properly evaluate the nonnormal, positively skewed returns induced by these strategies, however, so the conventional tools are biased against their adoption.

6. This notation is also in accord with longstanding decrees of the Intra-Fraternity and Pan-Hellenic Councils.

7. October 10, 1999:BU17.

8. Otherwise, the expected utility hypothesis would also have been dismissed long ago.

9. I thank an anonymous referee for motivating this illustration of the behavioral hypothesis's sensibility despite its stress on the probability of underperformance.

10. Coefficients that arise in the series expansion of the logarithm of the moment-generating function.

11. Kroll et al. used 20 randomly chosen stocks. When I made a data request for 20 randomly chosen stocks' monthly returns off the CRSP tapes, 23 were delivered by someone thinking I would be pleased to get the extra data. To prevent even the slightest appearance of data snooping, I used all 23 rather than pare 3 from the set.

12. Finally, should one insist on an index implied by a perfect financial market equilibrium that results when *all* investors behave this way; it is easy to find one by applying Rubinstein's (1973) calculations to this specific CARA utility.

REFERENCES

Ang, J., and J. Chua. 1979. "Composite Measures for the Evaluation of Investment Performance." *Journal of Financial and Quantitative Analysis,* vol. 14, no. 2 (June):361–384.

Benartzi, S., and R. Thaler. 1995. "Myopic Loss Aversion and the Equity Premium Puzzle." *Quarterly Journal of Economics,* vol. 110, no. 1 (February):73–92.

Browne, S. 1999. "The Risk and Rewards of Minimizing Shortfall Probability." *Journal of Portfolio Management,* vol. 25, no. 4 (Summer):76–85.

Bucklew, J.A. 1990. *Large Deviation Techniques in Decision, Simulation, and Estimation.* New York: John Wiley & Sons.

Campbell, J.Y., A.W. Lo, and C.A. MacKinlay. 1997. *The Econometrics of Financial Markets.* Princeton, NJ: Princeton University Press.

Fishburn, P.C. 1977. "Mean-Risk Analysis with Risk Associated with Below-Target Returns." *American Economic Review,* vol. 67, no. 2 (March):116–126.

Grinblatt, M., and S. Titman. 1995. "Performance Evaluation." In *Handbooks in Operations Research and Management Science, 9: Finance.* Edited by R.A. Jarrow, V. Maksimovic, and W.T. Ziemba. Amsterdam: North Holland.

Hakansson, N.H., and W.T. Ziemba. 1995. "Capital Growth Theory." In *Handbooks in Operations Research and Management Science, 9: Finance.* Edited by R.A. Jarrow, V. Maksimovic, and W.T. Ziemba. Amsterdam: North-Holland.

Hansen, L.P., and K.J. Singleton. 1982. "Generalized Instrumental Variables Estimation of Nonlinear Rational Expectations Models." *Econometrica,* vol. 50, no. 5 (September): 1269–86.

He, H., and H. Leland. 1993. "On Equilibrium Asset Price Processes." *Review of Financial Studies,* vol. 6, no. 3 (Fall):593–617.

Jensen, M.C. 1969. "Risk, the Pricing of Capital Assets, and the Evaluation of Investment Portfolios." *Journal of Business,* vol. 42, no. 2 (April):167–247.

Jobson, J.D., and B. Korkie. 1982. "Potential Performance and Tests of Portfolio Efficiency." *Journal of Financial Economics,* vol. 10, no. 4:433–466.

Joy, G.M., and R.B. Porter. 1974. "Stochastic Dominance and Mutual Fund Performance." *Journal of Financial and Quantitative Analysis,* vol. 9, no. 1 (January):25–32.

Kocherlakota, N.R. 1996. "The Equity Premium: It's Still a Puzzle." *Journal of Economic Literature,* vol. 34, no. 1 (March):42–71.

Kraus, A., and R.H. Litzenberger. 1976. "Skewness Preference and the Valuation of Risk Assets." *Journal of Finance,* vol. 31, no. 4 (August):1085–1100.

Kroll, Y., H. Levy, and H. Markowitz. 1984. "Mean–Variance versus Direct Utility Maximization." *Journal of Finance,* vol. 39, no. 1 (February):47–61.

Leland, H. 1999. "Performance Measurement in a Nonsymmetrical World." *Financial Analysts Journal,* vol. 55, no. 1 (January/February):27–35.

Machina, M.J. 1987. "Choice under Uncertainty: Problems Solved and Unsolved." *Economic Perspectives,* vol. 1, no. 1 (Summer):121–154.

MacLean, L.C., and W.T. Ziemba. 1999. "Growth versus Security: Tradeoffs in Dynamic Investment Analysis." *Annals of Operations Research,* vol. 85:93–225.

Mehra, R., and E.C. Prescott. 1985. "The Equity Premium: A Puzzle." *Journal of Monetary Economics,* vol. 15, no. 2 (March):145–161.

Pratt, J. 1964. "Risk Aversion in the Large and Small." *Econometrica,* vol. 32, no. 1–2, (January–April):122–136.

Roy, A.D. 1952. "Safety First and the Holding of Assets." *Econometrica,* vol. 20, no. 3 (May):432–449.

Rubinstein, M. 1973. "The Fundamental Theorem of Parameter-Preference Security Valuation." *Journal of Financial and Quantitative Analysis,* vol. 8, no. 1 (January):61–69.

———. 1994. "Implied Binomial Trees." *Journal of Finance,* vol. 49, no. 3 (July):771–818.

Sharpe, W. 1994. "The Sharpe Ratio." *Journal of Portfolio Management,* vol. 21, no. 1 (Fall):49–58.

Sortino, F.A., and H.J. Forsey. 1996. "On the Use and Misuse of Downside Risk." *Journal of Portfolio Management,* vol. 22, no. 2 (Winter):35–42.

Sortino, F.A., and R. van der Meer. 1991. "Downside Risk." *Journal of Portfolio Management,* vol. 17, no. 4 (Summer):27–31.

Von Neumann, J., and O. Morgenstern. 1944. *Theory of Games and Economic Behavior.* Princeton, NJ: Princeton University Press.

CHAPTER 27

APPROXIMATING THE CONFIDENCE INTERVALS FOR SHARPE STYLE WEIGHTS

Angelo Lobosco and Dan DiBartolomeo

Style analysis is a form of constrained regression that uses a weighted combination of market indexes to replicate, as closely as possible, the historical return pattern of an investment portfolio. The resulting coefficients, called Sharpe style weights, are used to form inferences about a portfolio's behavior and composition. This technique has been widely adopted in the investment industry, despite the fact that no explicit confidence interval measures have been available to describe the results. We derive an approximation for the confidence intervals of these weights and, using Monte Carlo simulation, verify its efficacy. The estimation of these confidence intervals can help practitioners assess the statistical significance of their results and aids in determining which indexes to include in the analysis. It may also encourage the use of daily return data to meaningfully reduce the size of the confidence intervals.

Style analysis, pioneered by William Sharpe (1992), has gained widespread acceptance among investment practitioners. First described by Sharpe (1988) as "effective asset mix analysis," the method is a constrained form of regression analysis used to form inferences about the influences on and composition of investment portfolios, based solely on the historical returns to those investment portfolios. The approach is widely used by investment professionals seeking to understand the composition and investment approach of portfolios for which they have no data on the securities held therein. One of the problems with using the technique is that no explicit measures of the confidence interval on the resultant coefficients, called style weights, have been available.

Reprinted from *Financial Analysts Journal* (July/August 1997):80–85.

A PRIMER ON STYLE ANALYSIS

Style analysis is a way to estimate an asset class factor model. Such a model would take the form

$$R = b_1 F_1 + b_2 F_2 + b_3 F_3 + b_4 F_4 + \cdots + b_n F_n + e, \qquad (27.1)$$

where

    R = time series of returns for a given portfolio
    F_k = time series of returns to factor (asset class) k
    b_k = sensitivity of the portfolio returns to factor k
    e = time series of portfolio residual returns

So far, we have a standard multiple regression equation in which the factors are the independent variables and the return to the portfolio is the dependent variable. In style analysis, we first define the factors as market indexes representing various asset classes or approaches ("styles") of investing. For example, we could select indexes to represent investment in stocks, bonds, and money-market instruments. With our factors so defined, the value of a factor during any time period is merely the return on the market index for the time period in question.

Traditional multiple regression calculations would provide a set of coefficients (b_k, $k = 1,n$) that would estimate how sensitive the return on the subject portfolio is to the returns of the set of market indexes selected as factors. If we hypothesize a causal relationship between the returns on the market indexes and the return on the subject portfolio, we can say that these sensitivity coefficients express the extent to which the returns on the subject portfolio are influenced by returns on the market indexes. Coefficients arising out of the traditional regression process may take on either positive or negative values. Investment practitioners often find it intuitively unappealing that a market index exerted a negative influence on the return on a portfolio. In addition to a frequent lack of intuitive appeal, traditional regression also may exhibit multicollinearity. If the independent variables are highly correlated, as two indexes representing different approaches to investing with the same asset class (say, corporate bonds and Treasury bonds) are likely to be, the reliability of the estimated coefficients in meaningfully describing the underlying true relationship is very much in doubt.

In style analysis, we place two constraints on the range of values that the coefficients (b_k) may take. The first is that the coefficients have only values between 0 and 1. The second constraint is that the sum of the coefficients must equal 1; that is,

$$0 < b_k < 1, \qquad (27.2)$$

and

$$\Sigma_{(k = 1 \text{ to } n)} b_k = 1. \qquad (27.3)$$

In this way, the coefficients have an intuitive interpretation as the weights of the assets within a portfolio and can be conveniently displayed as "slices" in a pie chart. So, style analysis can be thought of as the process of forming a portfolio of indexes that mimics, as closely as possible, the historical performance of a given portfolio. This "mimicking portfolio" is commonly referred to as the Sharpe style index. From the weights ascribed to the various market indexes (known also as Sharpe style weights), we form inferences regarding the behavioral influences on and likely composition of the given portfolio.

By placing these constraints on the values of weights, we also somewhat mitigate the multicollinearity problem of traditional regression. Placing bounds on the weights reduces the likelihood that high correlations between the independent variables will cause the coefficients to "blow up" to unrealistic values. The price we pay for this advantage is that weights that are calculated to be 0 or 1 are not unbiased estimators. A coefficient (weight) on a market index that is calculated to be 0 as derived by traditional regression might have come out negative but is prevented from doing so. Similarly, a value of 1 could have been greater than 1 in a traditional regression.

As in traditional regression, the weights are calculated so as to minimize the sum of the squared differences between the actual dependent variable (the subject portfolio) and the combination of the independent variables (the Sharpe style index). Because of the constraints on the weights, the problem of actually calculating the weights is solved using the technique of quadratic programming. Once the Sharpe style index has been determined, the historical returns on the subject portfolio can be compared with the returns of the Sharpe style index. The portion of the return variability of the subject portfolio that is explained by the Sharpe style index is the R^2 statistic.

Unless we have an index to represent *every possible* asset behavior, it is unrealistic to hope for a perfect fit ($R^2 = 1$ and standard error $= 0$). This statement is true even under the ideal circumstances of knowing exactly the style weights for a given portfolio and set of market indexes.

Empirical style analysis cases calculated in this fashion typically show R^2 values that are only marginally lower than R^2 values derived through traditional unconstrained multiple regression. What style analysis has lacked is a measure of the level of confidence that the individual coefficients (which express the weights in the Sharpe style index) are accurate estimates of the true underlying relationships. Other concerns that surround the use of style analysis are discussed in more detail by Christopherson (1995) and Trzcinka (1995). This article focuses on the issue of establishing confidence intervals for the Sharpe style weights.

The Problem of Linear Combinations

The solution to a style analysis problem is indeterminate if any of the market indexes used as factors can be formed as a linear combination of other indexes. Imagine doing a style analysis of some portfolio using three indexes: A, B, and C. Assume that Index B is formed by combining Indexes A and C in equal proportions. A style analysis that showed the subject portfolio was best mimicked by a portfolio of 30 percent Index A, 40 percent Index B, and 30 percent Index C would be exactly equivalent to a result of 50 percent Index A, 0 percent Index B, and 50 percent Index C, because the 40 percent weight given to Index B can itself be replicated by an equal combination of A and C. In each case, the time series error terms and the R^2 statistic would be identical. *Style analysis can only reliably attribute portfolio returns to the portions of the market index returns that are themselves not attributable to the returns of the other indexes.*

In 1992, Sharpe stated, "Asset class returns should have either low correlations with one another or, in cases in which correlations are high, different standard deviations." This statement is a qualitative description of selecting the market indexes so as to avoid the likelihood that any one index would be a linear combination of others.

Unfortunately, many practitioners fail to heed this warning and routinely select market indexes that are highly correlated and often are *prima facie* likely to be linear combinations of other indexes. For example, intuition might tell us that an index of mid-capitalization stocks is likely to be closely reproduced by a weighted combination of a large-cap stock index and a small-cap stock index. To describe more fully the portfolios under study, practitioners often increase the number and similarity level of the market indexes used in the analysis. Without explicit confidence intervals on the style weights, the damage done to the reliability of the analysis can go undetermined and undetected.

Calculating the Confidence Intervals

In doing a style analysis, we are seeking to identify the "true" underlying relationship between the returns on the subject portfolio and the returns on the market indexes that we choose as factors. Unfortunately, as in any statistical procedure, the best we can hope to do is to estimate the underlying relationship. The style weights that result from performing a style analysis can be thought of as estimates of the true style-weight combination of market indexes. The standard deviation of these estimates is approximated by the following formula:

$$\frac{\sigma_a}{\sigma_{B_i} \times \sqrt{n - k - 1}}, \tag{27.4}$$

where

i = index corresponding to the style weight being estimated
σ_a = standard error of the style analysis
σ_{B_i} = "unexplained Sharpe style index volatility" for index i
n = number of returns used in the style analysis
k = number of market indexes with nonzero style weights

The derivation of this formula and the definition of unexplained Sharpe style index volatility are covered in detail in the appendix. As we might intuitively expect, however, the confidence interval for a style weight of a particular market index

- increases with the standard error of the style analysis,
- decreases with the number of returns used in the style analysis, and
- decreases with the "independence" of that market index from the other market indexes used in the analysis (as represented by the unexplained Sharpe style index volatility).

THE SIMULATION PROCEDURE

To test the efficacy of the measure derived above, we performed Monte Carlo simulations. We first formulated a "portfolio" of return time series that is a known combination of our market indexes. As such, its "true" style weights are known. If we were to perform a style analysis of this portfolio against our market indexes, we would get estimates equal to the true weights. If we were to compare the portfolio returns with the combination of market indexes, we would have a perfect fit, with R^2 equal to 1 and standard error equal to 0.

If we select some arbitrary value, x, for the standard error, we can create a series of simulated error terms by simply taking random draws from a unit normal distribution and multiplying by x. We can then take this series of simulated error terms and add it to the portfolio return time series for which the true style weights are known. Because of the "noise" we will have added to our portfolio return time series, a repeat of the style analysis will yield new weights that are, of course, estimates of the true weights.

By repeating this procedure many hundreds or thousands of times, we obtained the probability distribution for each of the style weights. The mean values of each style weight are approximately equal to the true style weights. We also observed that the standard deviations of the style weights that we used as our confidence-interval measure are very nearly equal to the values predicted by our derived equations. As would be expected, the predicted and simulated style weights' means and confidence interval values converged as the number of iterations increased through the Monte Carlo procedure. In a typical example, a simulation of 10,000 trials produces convergence in the fourth or fifth decimal place.

The predictive formula for the confidence interval on style weights overestimates the standard error if the true style weight is very close to either 0 or 1. In those cases, the constraints truncate the estimated values, making the estimated standard deviation upward biased and biasing the style-weight estimate itself. Quantifying the extent of the bias remains problematic. Except for this truncation effect, we can expect the style weight estimates to be approximately normally distributed, just as in a standard multiple regression, so that a traditional *t*-statistic can be used.

Sample Case

To illustrate how these measures can be calculated in practice, consider the example of the Reich & Tang Equity Fund for the 60-month period from December 12, 1989, through December 31, 1994. We have no special knowledge about the investment style of this fund; we know only that it is a domestic equity mutual fund. For illustrative purposes, assume that the fund has the flexibility to invest in international equities and domestic fixed-income securities. We performed a broad style analysis using the following four indexes: 90-day Treasury bills, the Lehman Aggregate Index, the Russell 3000 Index, and the Morgan Stanley Capital International (MSCI) Europe/Australia/Far East (EAFE) Index.

For the 90-day T-bill index, we determined the Sharpe style index that is composed of the other three indexes. We next calculated the standard deviation of the active return of 90-day T-bills relative to this Sharpe style index (which we called the unexplained Sharpe style index volatility). This procedure was repeated for the remaining indexes, and the results are shown in Table 27.1.

TABLE 27.1   Unexplained Sharpe Style Index Volatility (percent per month)

Index	Unexplained Sharpe Style Index Volatility
90-day Treasury bills	1.01%
Lehman Aggregate	0.85
Russell 3000	2.60
MSCI EAFE	4.59

We then performed a Sharpe style analysis on the Reich & Tang Fund, using these four market indexes to obtain an active standard deviation of 1.28 percent a month for the fund relative to its Sharpe style index. For each index, the standard deviation of its Sharpe style weight can then be expressed as

$$\sigma_{w_i} = 1.28/[(\text{Unexplained Sharpe style index}$$
$$\text{volatility for index } i) \times \sqrt{60 - 3 - 1}\,]$$

because three indexes had nonzero weights. The results of this calculation are shown in Table 27.2 in the row titled Index Group 1.

Now, suppose that we were told in advance that the fund did not invest in fixed-income securities (other than cash). We would then perform the same analysis but excluding the Lehman Aggregate Index. This calculation would produce the results in Table 27.2 shown in the row titled Index Group 2.

We can see the dramatic decrease in the T-bill weight's standard deviation that comes from removing the fixed-income index. This result makes intuitive sense: It is much less

TABLE 27.2 Style Weights and Standard Deviation of Style Weights (standard deviations in parentheses)

	Lehman Aggregate	90-Day Treasury Bills	MSCI EAFE	Domestic Equity Indexes					
				1	2	3	4	5	6
Index Group 1 ($R^2 = 0.868$)	0.0% (20.1)	10.0% (16.9)	2.2% (3.7)	87.8% (6.5)					
Index Group 2 ($R^2 = 0.868$)		10.0 (5.2)	2.2 (3.6)	87.8 (5.7)					
Index Group 3 ($R^2 = 0.872$)		11.6 (5.3)	2.9 (3.6)	70.0 (10.3)	15.5% (7.3)				
Index Group 4 ($R^2 = 0.873$)		9.9 (6.0)	2.7 (3.7)	41.5 (14.4)	30.5 (12.6)	10.0% (14.7)	5.4% (12.3)		
Index Group 5 ($R^2 = 0.872$)		10.1 (6.0)	2.4 (3.8)	29.2 (16.2)	16.3 (13.3)	24.2 (20.7)	17.8 (15.6)	0.0% (14.2)	0.0% (14.4)

Note: Domestic Equity Index Number Assignments

Index Group 1,2	1 = Russell 3000
Index Group 3	1 = Russell 1000
	2 = Russell 2000
Index Group 4	1 = Russell 1000 Value
	2 = Russell 1000 Growth
	3 = Russell 2000 Value
	4 = Russell 2000 Growth
Index Group 5	1 = S&P/BARRA Value
	2 = S&P/BARRA Growth
	3 = Sharpe/BARRA Medium Value
	4 = Sharpe/BARRA Medium Growth
	5 = Sharpe/BARRA Small Value
	6 = Sharpe/BARRA Small Growth

likely for T-bill returns to be replicated only by equities than by a combination of equities and fixed-income securities. *This example illustrates the importance of limiting the number of indexes used for Sharpe style analysis; advance knowledge of a portfolio's investment constraints can be quite valuable in this regard.*

In a style analysis using only the equity and T-bill indexes, we first separated domestic equities into large and small indexes; the corresponding style weights and standard deviations appear in Table 27.2 in the Index Group 3 row. We could also introduce a "growth/value" breakdown (Index Group 4) or further extend the size dimension to include mid-cap equities (Index Group 5).

The standard deviations of the Sharpe style weights for the domestic equity indexes increase with the inclusion of more similar indexes (the weights and standard deviations for the other indexes are relatively unaffected). As expected, the R^2 of the Sharpe style index increases (albeit ever so slightly) with the number of indexes. This result illustrates the need for practitioners to strike a balance between the number of style weights and the likely reliability of each of those weights.

CONCLUSION

Although users of style analysis have used the R^2 statistic as a measure of goodness of fit, no measures for the quality of fit for individual style weights have been available. We derived an expression for the approximate confidence interval on style weights. Through extensive Monte Carlo simulation, we verified that the predicted and simulated values converge.

How can this information—that confidence intervals on style weights can, in fact, be approximated—be of use to practitioners? First, we can make statements about the statistical significance of the results. For example, we can now determine if the differences in the style weights of two different portfolios (analyzed against the same market indexes) are different to a statistically significant extent. In recent years, the potential misclassification of mutual funds into objective categories has received considerable attention in academia, regulatory agencies, and the financial press. Clustering of mutual funds into categories based on their style analysis weights is one technique that has already been used in such studies. The availability of explicit confidence intervals on the style weights should improve the robustness of the results of those efforts.

Another use would be to determine whether differences in style weights for the same portfolio over different time periods are statistically significant. Practitioners often use changes in style weights over time as an indication that a portfolio manager has meaningfully shifted his strategy. Without explicit confidence intervals, apparent shifts in strategy may simply be the result of the level of imprecision in the data and the technique.

The confidence interval measures may also be useful in disallowing certain combinations of market indexes. If the indexes to be used are too similar, the confidence intervals will be unacceptably large. Practitioners can either find other market indexes to represent the range of possible assets and strategies or disallow the use of style analysis for those situations for which this technique is genuinely unsuited.

These measures also may encourage us to use daily return data in our style analysis in order to obtain a meaningful reduction in the confidence intervals of the resulting style weights.

In some coarse sense, this technique is most appropriate for determining a fund's effective asset mix when the market indexes will be used to span a wide range of asset behaviors, but the appropriateness of the technique becomes less certain as we work within a single asset class, using style analysis to analyze finer distinctions in investment-management style.

APPENDIX: APPROXIMATING THE CONFIDENCE INTERVAL FOR SHARPE STYLE WEIGHTS

The return series for the "true" style weight combination of market indexes is defined as

$$S = \sum w_i r_i, \tag{27.5}$$

where

w_i = true style weight of index i
r_i = time series of returns on index i

The values of S and w_i are unknown; we are using Sharpe style analysis to estimate these values. Now, define

$$A = R - S, \tag{27.6}$$

where

R = time series of returns to the subject portfolio

Series A can be thought of as the residual term of a suboptimal constrained regression. Note that the values that compose A are fixed a priori, even though they are unknown to us (because we do not know what the true style weights are). Now, consider the extent to which our estimates for the style weights do not match the true style weights:

$$\omega_i = w_i + \Delta w_i, \tag{27.7}$$

where

ω_i = estimate of the true style weight for index i
Δw_i = amount of error in the estimate of style weight for index i

As in the three-market-index example in the main text, shifting the style weights will not affect the goodness of fit if the market indexes are linear combinations of one another. Therefore, our fitting process must somehow isolate the portion of the market indexes' returns that are independent of the other market indexes used in the analysis. To isolate this independent portion of each index, we define

$$T_i = \sum v_m r_m \ (\text{for } m \neq i), \tag{27.8}$$

and

$$\sum v_m = 1 \ (\text{for } m \neq i), \tag{27.9}$$

where

T_i = returns on the Sharpe style index for market index i analyzed against all market indexes exclusive of i
v_m = style weight on index m
r_m = returns on market index m

In defining the extent to which one market index is a linear combination of the others, the intuitiveness of the explanation is no longer necessary. We thus remove the constraint that the style weights must be in the range of 0 to 1. We can now define

$$B_i = r_i - T_i, \tag{27.10}$$

where

B_i = portion of the returns on index i not attributable to the other market indexes, subject to the constraint in Equation 27.9. In our later example, we refer to the standard deviation of this return series as "unexplained Sharpe style index volatility."

We now have expressions for both the errors in the style weights (Δw_i) and the independent portions of the market index behaviors (B_i). Only through the interaction of these two sets of values can the goodness of fit be varied. It can be shown that the operative process in style analysis is to try to minimize the variance of $R - S - (\Delta w_i B_i)$ or $A - \Delta w_i B_i$. We can set an objective function, Z, to this expression:

$$Z = \text{Var}\,(A - \Delta w_i B_i) \tag{27.11}$$

$$= \sigma_A^2 + \Delta w_i^2 \sigma_{B_i}^2 - 2\Delta w_i \sigma_A \sigma_{B_i} \rho_{AB_i}, \tag{27.12}$$

where

σ = sample standard deviation
ρ = sample correlation coefficient

To solve for the minimum of the variance, we set the derivatives of the variance with respect to the style weights equal to zero:

$$dZ/d\Delta w_i = 2\Delta w_i \sigma_{B_i}^2 - 2\rho_{AB_i} \sigma_A \sigma_{B_i}, \tag{27.13}$$

$$dZ/d\Delta w_i = 0 \ (\text{if and only if } \Delta w_i = \rho_{AB_i} \sigma_A / \sigma_{B_i}). \tag{27.14}$$

Because the standard deviation for ρ is approximately $1/\sqrt{n-2}$, the standard deviation of Δw_i is approximated by

$$\sigma_{\Delta w_i} \cong \sigma_A / (\sigma_{B_i} \times \sqrt{n-2}), \tag{27.15}$$

where

n = number of data points in the return time series

Because we do not know the true style weights, we do not know σ_A. We do know σ_a, however—the standard error of our style analysis computation, where

$$a = R - \sum (w_i + \Delta w_i) r_i. \tag{27.16}$$

Because a has $(n - k)$ degrees of freedom and A has $(n - 1)$ degrees of freedom, we use the relation

$$\sigma_a^2 = \frac{\sigma_A^2 (n-k)}{(n-1)}, \tag{27.17}$$

where

k = number of market indexes with nonzero style weights

Rearranging Equation 27.17 and substituting back into Equation 27.15, we arrive at

$$\sigma_{\Delta w_i} \cong \frac{\sigma_a}{(\sigma_{B_i} \times \sqrt{n - k - 1})}. \qquad (27.18)$$

REFERENCES

Christopherson, John. 1995. "Equity Style Classifications." *Journal of Portfolio Management,* vol. 21, no. 3 (Spring):32–43.

Sharpe, William F. 1988. "Determining a Fund's Effective Asset Mix." *Investment Management Review,* vol. 2, no. 6 (December):59–69.

———. 1992. "Asset Allocation: Management Style and Performance Measurement." *Journal of Portfolio Management,* vol. 18, no. 2 (Winter):7–19.

Trzcinka, Charles. 1995. "Comment on Equity Style Classifications (Christopherson)." *Journal of Portfolio Management,* vol. 21, no. 3 (Spring):44–46.

CHAPTER 28

THE STATISTICS OF
SHARPE RATIOS

Andrew W. Lo

The building blocks of the Sharpe ratio—expected returns and volatilities—are unknown quantities that must be estimated statistically and are, therefore, subject to estimation error. This raises the natural question: How accurately are Sharpe ratios measured? To address this question, I derive explicit expressions for the statistical distribution of the Sharpe ratio using standard asymptotic theory under several sets of assumptions for the return-generating process—independently and identically distributed returns, stationary returns, and with time aggregation. I show that monthly Sharpe ratios cannot be annualized by multiplying by $\sqrt{12}$ except under very special circumstances, and I derive the correct method of conversion in the general case of stationary returns. In an illustrative empirical example of mutual funds and hedge funds, I find that the annual Sharpe ratio for a hedge fund can be overstated by as much as 65 percent because of the presence of serial correlation in monthly returns, and once this serial correlation is properly taken into account, the rankings of hedge funds based on Sharpe ratios can change dramatically.

One of the most commonly cited statistics in financial analysis is the Sharpe ratio, the ratio of the excess expected return of an investment to its return volatility or standard deviation. Originally motivated by mean–variance analysis and the Sharpe-Lintner Capital Asset Pricing Model, the Sharpe ratio is now used in many different contexts, from performance attribution to tests of market efficiency to risk management.[1] Given the Sharpe ratio's widespread use and the myriad interpretations that it has acquired over the years, it is surprising that so little attention has been paid to its statistical properties. Because expected returns and volatilities are quantities that are generally not observable, they must be estimated in some fashion. The inevitable estimation errors that arise imply that the Sharpe ratio is also estimated with error, raising the natural question: How accurately are Sharpe ratios measured?

Reprinted from the *Financial Analysts Journal* (July/August 2002):36–52.

In this chapter, I provide an answer by deriving the statistical distribution of the Sharpe ratio using standard econometric methods under several different sets of assumptions for the statistical behavior of the return series on which the Sharpe ratio is based. Armed with this statistical distribution, I show that confidence intervals, standard errors, and hypothesis tests can be computed for the estimated Sharpe ratio in much the same way that they are computed for regression coefficients, such as portfolio alphas and betas.

The accuracy of Sharpe ratio estimators hinges on the statistical properties of returns, and these properties can vary considerably among portfolios, strategies, and over time. In other words, the Sharpe ratio estimator's statistical properties typically will depend on the investment style of the portfolio being evaluated. At a superficial level, the intuition for this claim is obvious: The performance of more volatile investment strategies is more difficult to gauge than that of less volatile strategies. Therefore, it should come as no surprise that the results derived in this chapter imply that, for example, Sharpe ratios are likely to be more accurately estimated for mutual funds than for hedge funds.

A less intuitive implication is that the time-series properties of investment strategies (e.g., mean reversion, momentum, and other forms of serial correlation) can have a nontrivial impact on the Sharpe ratio estimator itself, especially in computing an annualized Sharpe ratio from monthly data. In particular, the results derived in this chapter show that the common practice of annualizing Sharpe ratios by multiplying monthly estimates by $\sqrt{12}$ is correct only under very special circumstances and that the correct multiplier—which depends on the serial correlation of the portfolio's returns—can yield Sharpe ratios that are considerably smaller (in the case of positive serial correlation) or larger (in the case of negative serial correlation). Therefore, Sharpe ratio estimators must be computed and interpreted in the context of the particular investment style with which a portfolio's returns have been generated.

Let R_t denote the one-period simple return of a portfolio or fund between dates $t-1$ and t and denote by μ and σ^2 its mean and variance:

$$\mu \equiv E(R_t), \tag{28.1a}$$

and

$$\sigma^2 \equiv \text{Var}(R_t). \tag{28.1b}$$

Recall that the Sharpe ratio (SR) is defined as the ratio of the excess expected return to the standard deviation of return:

$$\text{SR} \equiv \frac{\mu - R_f}{\sigma}, \tag{28.2}$$

where the excess expected return is usually computed relative to the risk-free rate, R_f. Because μ and σ are the population moments of the distribution of R_t, they are unobservable and must be estimated using historical data.

Given a sample of historical returns $(R_1, R_2, \ldots, R_T)$, the standard estimators for these moments are the sample mean and variance:

$$\hat{\mu} = \frac{1}{T}\sum_{t=1}^{T} R_t \tag{28.3a}$$

and

$$\hat{\sigma}^2 = \frac{1}{T}\sum_{t-1}^{T} (R_t - \hat{\mu})^2, \tag{28.3b}$$

from which the estimator of the Sharpe ratio ($\widehat{\text{SR}}$) follows immediately:

$$\widehat{\text{SR}} = \frac{\hat{\mu} - R_f}{\hat{\sigma}}. \tag{28.4}$$

Using a set of techniques collectively known as "large-sample" or "asymptotic" statistical theory in which the Central Limit Theorem is applied to estimators such as $\hat{\mu}$ and $\hat{\sigma}^2$, the distribution of $\widehat{\text{SR}}$ and other nonlinear functions of $\hat{\mu}$ and $\hat{\sigma}^2$ can be easily derived.

In the next section, I present the statistical distribution of $\widehat{\text{SR}}$ under the standard assumption that returns are independently and identically distributed (IID). This distribution completely characterizes the statistical behavior of $\widehat{\text{SR}}$ in large samples and allows us to quantify the precision with which $\widehat{\text{SR}}$ estimates SR. But because the IID assumption is extremely restrictive and often violated by financial data, a more general distribution is derived in the "Non-IID Returns" section, one that applies to returns with serial correlation, time-varying conditional volatilities, and many other characteristics of historical financial time series. In the "Time Aggregation" section, I develop explicit expressions for "time-aggregated" Sharpe ratio estimators (e.g., expressions for converting monthly Sharpe ratio estimates to annual estimates) and their distributions. To illustrate the practical relevance of these estimators, I apply them to a sample of monthly mutual fund and hedge fund returns and show that serial correlation has dramatic effects on the annual Sharpe ratios of hedge funds, inflating Sharpe ratios by more than 65 percent in some cases and deflating Sharpe ratios in other cases.

IID RETURNS

To derive a measure of the uncertainty surrounding the estimator $\widehat{\text{SR}}$, we need to specify the statistical properties of R_t because these properties determine the uncertainty surrounding the component estimators $\hat{\mu}$ and $\hat{\sigma}^2$. Although this may seem like a theoretical exercise best left for statisticians—not unlike the specification of the assumptions needed to yield well-behaved estimates from a linear regression— there is often a direct connection between the investment management process of a portfolio and its statistical properties. For example, a change in the portfolio manager's style from a small-cap value orientation to a large-cap growth orientation will typically have an impact on the portfolio's volatility, degree of mean reversion, and market beta. Even for a fixed investment style, a portfolio's characteristics can change over time because of fund inflows and outflows, capacity constraints (e.g., a microcap fund that is close to its market-capitalization limit), liquidity constraints (e.g., an emerging market or private equity fund), and changes in market conditions (e.g., sudden increases or decreases in volatility, shifts in central banking policy, and extraordinary events, such as the default of Russian government bonds in August 1998). Therefore, the investment style and market environment must be kept in mind when formulating the assumptions for the statistical properties of a portfolio's returns.

Perhaps the simplest set of assumptions that we can specify for R_t is that they are independently and identically distributed. This means that the probability distribution of R_t is identical to that of R_s for any two dates t and s and that R_t and R_s are statistically independent for all $t \neq s$. Although these conditions are extreme and empirically implausible—the probability distribution of the monthly return of the S&P 500 Index in October 1987 is likely to differ from the probability distribution of the monthly return of the S&P 500 in December

2000—they provide an excellent starting point for understanding the statistical properties of Sharpe ratios. In the next section, these assumptions will be replaced with a more general set of conditions for returns.

Under the assumption that returns are IID and have finite mean μ and variance σ^2, it is well known that the estimators $\hat{\mu}$ and $\hat{\sigma}^2$ in Equation 28.3 have the following normal distributions in large samples, or "asymptotically," due to the Central Limit Theorem:[2]

$$\sqrt{T}(\hat{\mu} - \mu) \overset{a}{\sim} N(0, \sigma^2), \quad \sqrt{T}(\hat{\sigma}^2 - \sigma^2) \overset{a}{\sim} N(0, 2\sigma^4), \tag{28.5}$$

where $\overset{a}{\sim}$ denotes the fact that this relationship is an asymptotic one [i.e., as T increases without bound, the probability distributions of $\sqrt{T}(\hat{\mu} - \mu)$ and $\sqrt{T}(\hat{\sigma}^2 - \sigma^2)$ approach the normal distribution, with mean zero and variances σ^2 and $2\sigma^4$, respectively]. These asymptotic distributions imply that the estimation error of $\hat{\mu}$ and $\hat{\sigma}^2$ can be approximated by

$$\text{Var}(\hat{\mu}) \overset{a}{=} \frac{\sigma^2}{T}, \quad \text{Var}(\hat{\sigma}^2) \overset{a}{=} \frac{2\sigma^4}{T}, \tag{28.6}$$

where $\overset{a}{=}$ indicates that these relations are based on asymptotic approximations. Note that in Equation 28.6, the variances of both estimators approach zero as T increases, reflecting the fact that the estimation errors become smaller as the sample size grows. An additional property of $\hat{\mu}$ and $\hat{\sigma}$ in the special case of IID returns is that they are statistically independent in large samples, which greatly simplifies our analysis of the statistical properties of functions of these estimators (e.g., the Sharpe ratio).

Now, denote by the function $g(\mu, \sigma^2)$ the Sharpe ratio defined in Equation 28.2; hence, the Sharpe ratio estimator is simply $g(\hat{\mu}, \hat{\sigma}^2) = \widehat{SR}$. When the Sharpe ratio is expressed in this form, it is apparent that the estimation errors in $\hat{\mu}$ and $\hat{\sigma}^2$ will affect $g(\hat{\mu}, \hat{\sigma}^2)$ and that the nature of these effects depends critically on the properties of the function g. Specifically, in the "IID Returns" section of Appendix 28A, I show that the asymptotic distribution of the Sharpe ratio estimator is $\sqrt{T}(\widehat{SR} - SR) \overset{a}{\sim} N(0, V_{IID})$, where the asymptotic variance is given by the following weighted average of the asymptotic variances of $\hat{\mu}$ and $\hat{\sigma}^2$:

$$V_{IID} = \left(\frac{\partial g}{\partial \mu}\right)^2 \sigma^2 + \left(\frac{\partial g}{\partial \sigma^2}\right)^2 2\sigma^4. \tag{28.7}$$

The weights in Equation 28.7 are simply the squared sensitivities of g with respect to μ and σ^2, respectively: The more sensitive g is to a particular parameter, the more influential its asymptotic variance will be in the weighted average. This relationship is reminiscent of the expression for the variance of the weighted sum of two random variables, except that in Equation 28.7 there is no covariance term. This is due to the fact that $\hat{\mu}$ and $\hat{\sigma}^2$ are asymptotically independent, thanks to our simplifying assumption of IID returns. In the next sections, the IID assumption will be replaced by a more general set of conditions on returns, in which case, the covariance between $\hat{\mu}$ and $\hat{\sigma}^2$ will no longer be zero and the corresponding expression for the asymptotic variance of the Sharpe ratio estimator will be somewhat more involved.

The asymptotic variance of $\widehat{SR}$ given in Equation 28.7 can be further simplified by evaluating the sensitivities explicitly—$\partial g/\partial \mu = 1/\sigma$ and $\partial g/\partial \sigma^2 = -(\mu - R_f)/(2\sigma^3)$—and then combining terms to yield

$$V_{IID} = 1 + \frac{(\mu - R_f)^2}{2\sigma^2} = 1 + \frac{1}{2}SR^2. \tag{28.8}$$

Therefore, standard errors (SEs) for the Sharpe ratio estimator $\widehat{\mathrm{SR}}$ can be computed as

$$\mathrm{SE}(\widehat{\mathrm{SR}}) \stackrel{a}{=} \sqrt{\left(1 + \frac{1}{2}\mathrm{SR}^2\right)/T}, \tag{28.9}$$

and this quantity can be estimated by substituting $\widehat{\mathrm{SR}}$ for SR. Confidence intervals for SR can also be constructed from Equation 28.9; for example, the 95 percent confidence interval for SR around the estimator $\widehat{\mathrm{SR}}$ is simply

$$\widehat{\mathrm{SR}} \pm 1.96 \times \sqrt{\left(1 + \frac{1}{2}\widehat{\mathrm{SR}}^2\right)/T}. \tag{28.10}$$

Table 28.1 reports values of Equation 28.9 for various combinations of Sharpe ratios and sample sizes. Observe that for any given sample size T, larger Sharpe ratios imply larger standard errors. For example, in a sample of 60 observations, the standard error of the Sharpe ratio estimator is 0.188 when the true Sharpe ratio is 1.50 but is 0.303 when the true Sharpe ratio is 3.00. This implies that the performance of investments such as hedge funds, for which high Sharpe ratios are one of the primary objectives, will tend to be less precisely estimated. However, as a percentage of the Sharpe ratio, the standard error given by Equation 28.9 does approach a finite limit as SR increases since

$$\frac{\mathrm{SE}\,(\widehat{\mathrm{SR}})}{\mathrm{SR}} = \sqrt{\frac{1 + (1/2)\mathrm{SR}^2}{T\mathrm{SR}^2}} \rightarrow \sqrt{\frac{1}{2T}} \tag{28.11}$$

as SR increases without bound. Therefore, the uncertainty surrounding the IID Sharpe ratio estimator will be approximately the same proportion of the Sharpe ratio for higher Sharpe ratio investments with the same number of observations T.

TABLE 28.1   Asymptotic Standard Errors of Sharpe Ratio Estimators for Combinations of Sharpe Ratio and Sample Size

SR	\multicolumn{8}{c}{Sample Size, T}
	12	24	36	48	60	125	250	500
0.50	0.306	0.217	0.177	0.153	0.137	0.095	0.067	0.047
0.75	0.327	0.231	0.189	0.163	0.146	0.101	0.072	0.051
1.00	0.354	0.250	0.204	0.177	0.158	0.110	0.077	0.055
1.25	0.385	0.272	0.222	0.193	0.172	0.119	0.084	0.060
1.50	0.421	0.298	0.243	0.210	0.188	0.130	0.092	0.065
1.75	0.459	0.325	0.265	0.230	0.205	0.142	0.101	0.071
2.00	0.500	0.354	0.289	0.250	0.224	0.155	0.110	0.077
2.25	0.542	0.384	0.313	0.271	0.243	0.168	0.119	0.084
2.50	0.586	0.415	0.339	0.293	0.262	0.182	0.128	0.091
2.75	0.631	0.446	0.364	0.316	0.282	0.196	0.138	0.098
3.00	0.677	0.479	0.391	0.339	0.303	0.210	0.148	0.105

Note: Returns are assumed to be IID, which implies $V_{IID} = 1 + 1/2\mathrm{SR}^2$.

We can develop further intuition for the impact of estimation errors in $\hat{\mu}$ and $\hat{\sigma}^2$ on the Sharpe ratio by calculating the proportion of asymptotic variance that is attributable to $\hat{\mu}$ versus $\hat{\sigma}^2$. From Equation 28.7, the fraction of V_{IID} due to estimation error in $\hat{\mu}$ versus $\hat{\sigma}^2$ is simply

$$\frac{(\partial g/\partial \mu)^2 \sigma^2}{V_{IID}} = \frac{1}{1 + (1/2)\text{SR}^2} \tag{28.12a}$$

and

$$\frac{(\partial g/\partial \sigma)^2 2\sigma^4}{V_{IID}} = \frac{(1/2)\,\text{SR}^2}{1 + (1/2)\text{SR}^2}. \tag{28.12b}$$

For a small Sharpe ratio, such as 0.25, this proportion—which depends only on the true Sharpe ratio—is 97.0 percent, indicating that most of the variability in the Sharpe ratio estimator is a result of variability in $\hat{\mu}$. However, for higher Sharpe ratios, the reverse is true: For SR = 2.00, only 33.3 percent of the variability of $\widehat{\text{SR}}$ comes from $\hat{\mu}$, and for a Sharpe ratio of 3.00, only 18.2 percent of the estimator error of $\widehat{\text{SR}}$ is attributable to $\hat{\mu}$.

NON-IID RETURNS

Many studies have documented various violations of the assumption of IID returns for financial securities;[3] hence, the results of the previous section may be of limited practical value in certain circumstances. Fortunately, it is possible to derive similar results under more general conditions, conditions that allow for serial correlation, conditional heteroskedasticity, and other forms of dependence and heterogeneity in returns. In particular, if returns satisfy the assumption of "stationarity," then a version of the Central Limit Theorem still applies to most estimators, and the corresponding asymptotic distribution can be derived. The formal definition of stationarity is that the joint probability distribution $F(R_{t_1}, R_{t_2}, \ldots, R_{t_n})$ of an arbitrary collection of returns $R_{t_1}, R_{t_2}, \ldots, R_{t_n}$ does not change if all the dates are incremented by the same number of periods; that is,

$$F(R_{t_1+k}, R_{t_2+k}, \ldots, R_{t_n+k}) = F(R_{t_1}, R_{t_2}, \ldots, R_{t_n}) \tag{28.13}$$

for all k. Such a condition implies that mean μ and variance σ^2 (and all higher moments) are constant over time but otherwise allows for quite a broad set of dynamics for R_t, including serial correlation, dependence on such factors as the market portfolio, time-varying conditional volatilities, jumps, and other empirically relevant phenomena.

Under the assumption of stationarity,[4] a version of the Central Limit Theorem can still be applied to the estimator $\widehat{\text{SR}}$. However, in this case, the expression for the variance of $\widehat{\text{SR}}$ is somewhat more complex because of the possibility of dependence between the components $\hat{\mu}$ and $\hat{\sigma}^2$. In the "Non-IID Returns" section of Appendix 28A, I show that the asymptotic distribution can be derived by using a "robust" estimator—an estimator that is effective under many different sets of assumptions for the statistical properties of returns—to estimate the Sharpe ratio.[5] In particular, I use a *generalized method of moments* (GMM) estimator to estimate $\hat{\mu}$ and $\hat{\sigma}^2$, and the results of Hansen (1982) can be used to obtain the following asymptotic distribution:

$$\sqrt{T}(\widehat{\text{SR}} - \text{SR}) \overset{a}{\sim} N(0, V_{GMM}), \quad V_{GMM} = \frac{\partial g}{\partial \theta} \Sigma \frac{\partial g}{\partial \theta'}, \tag{28.14}$$

where the definitions of $\partial g/\partial\theta$ and Σ and a method for estimating them are given in the second section of Appendix 28A. Therefore, for non-IID returns, the standard error of the Sharpe ratio can be estimated by

$$\mathrm{SE}[\widehat{\mathrm{SR}}] \overset{a}{\cong} \sqrt{\hat{V}_{GMM}/T} \qquad (28.15)$$

and confidence intervals for SR can be constructed in a similar fashion to Equation 28.10.

TIME AGGREGATION

In many applications, it is necessary to convert Sharpe ratio estimates from one frequency to another. For example, a Sharpe ratio estimated from monthly data cannot be directly compared with one estimated from annual data; hence, one statistic must be converted to the same frequency as the other to yield a fair comparison. Moreover, in some cases, it is possible to derive a more precise estimator of an annual quantity by using monthly or daily data and then performing time aggregation instead of estimating the quantity directly using annual data.[6]

In the case of Sharpe ratios, the most common method for performing such time aggregation is to multiply the higher-frequency Sharpe ratio by the square root of the number of periods contained in the lower-frequency holding period (e.g., multiply a monthly estimator by $\sqrt{12}$ to obtain an annual estimator). In this section, I show that this rule of thumb is correct only under the assumption of IID returns. For non-IID returns, an alternative procedure must be used, one that accounts for serial correlation in returns in a very specific manner.

IID Returns

Consider first the case of IID returns. Denote by $R_t(q)$ the following q-period return:

$$R_t(q) \equiv R_t + R_{t-1} + \cdots + R_{t-q+1}, \qquad (28.16)$$

where I have ignored the effects of compounding for computational convenience.[7] Under the IID assumption, the variance of $R_t(q)$ is directly proportional to q; hence, the Sharpe ratio satisfies the simple relationship:

$$\mathrm{SR}(q) = \frac{\mathrm{E}[R_t(q)] - R_f(q)}{\sqrt{Var[R_t(q)]}} = \frac{q(\mu - R_f)}{\sqrt{q}\,\sigma} = \sqrt{q}\,\mathrm{SR}. \qquad (28.17)$$

Despite the fact that the Sharpe ratio may seem to be "unitless" because it is the ratio of two quantities with the same units, it does depend on the timescale with respect to which the numerator and denominator are defined. The reason is that the numerator increases linearly with aggregation value q, whereas the denominator increases as the square root of q under IID returns; hence, the ratio will increase as the square root of q, making a longer-horizon investment seem more attractive. This interpretation is highly misleading and should not be taken at face value. Indeed, the Sharpe ratio is not a complete summary of the risks of a multiperiod investment strategy and should never be used as the sole criterion for making an investment decision.[8]

The asymptotic distribution of $\widehat{\mathrm{SR}}(q)$ follows directly from Equation 28.17 because $\widehat{\mathrm{SR}}(q)$ is proportional to SR:

$$\sqrt{T}[\widehat{\mathrm{SR}}(q) - \sqrt{q}\,\mathrm{SR}] \overset{a}{\sim} N[0, V_{IID}(q)], \quad V_{IID}(q) = qV_{IID} = q\left(1 + \frac{1}{2}\mathrm{SR}^2\right). \quad (28.18)$$

Non-IID Returns

The relationship between SR and SR(q) is somewhat more involved for non-IID returns because the variance of $R_t(q)$ is not just the sum of the variances of component returns but also includes all the covariances. Specifically, under the assumption that returns R_t are stationary,

$$\text{Var}[R_t(q)] = \sum_{i=0}^{q-1} \sum_{j=0}^{q-1} \text{Cov}(R_{t-i}, R_{t-j}) = q\sigma^2 + 2\sigma^2 \sum_{k=1}^{q-1} (q-k)\rho_k, \qquad (28.19)$$

where $\rho_k \equiv \text{Cov}(R_t, R_{t-k})/\text{Var}(R_t)$ is the kth-order autocorrelation of R_t.[9] This yields the following relationship between SR and SR(q):

$$\text{SR}(q) = \eta(q)\text{SR}, \quad \eta(q) \equiv \frac{q}{\sqrt{q + 2\sum_{k=1}^{q-1} (q-k)\rho_k}}. \qquad (28.20)$$

Note that Equation 28.20 reduces to Equation 28.17 if all autocorrelations ρ_k are zero, as in the case of IID returns. However, for non-IID returns, the adjustment factor for time-aggregated Sharpe ratios is generally not $\sqrt{q}$ but a more complicated function of the first $q - 1$ autocorrelations of returns.

Example: First-Order Autoregressive Returns

To develop some intuition for the potential impact of serial correlation on the Sharpe ratio, consider the case in which returns follow a first-order autoregressive process or "AR(1)":

$$R_t = \mu + \rho(R_{t-1} - \mu) + \varepsilon_t, \quad -1 < \rho < 1, \qquad (28.21)$$

where ε_t is IID with mean zero and variance σ_ε^2. In this case, the return in period t can be forecasted to some degree by the return in period $t - 1$ and this "autoregression" leads to serial correlation at all lags. In particular, Equation 28.21 implies that the kth-order auto-correlation coefficient is simply ρ^k; hence, the scale factor in Equation 28.20 be evaluated explicitly as

$$\eta(q) = \sqrt{q} \left[1 + \frac{2\rho}{1-\rho} \left(1 - \frac{1-\rho^q}{q(1-\rho)} \right) \right]^{-1/2}. \qquad (28.22)$$

Table 28.2 presents values of $\eta(q)$ for various values of ρ and q; the row corresponding to $\rho = 0$ percent is the IID case in which the scale factor is simply $\sqrt{q}$. Note that for each holding-period q, positive serial correlation reduces the scale factor below the IID value and negative serial correlation increases it. The reason is that positive serial correlation implies that the variance of multiperiod returns increases faster than holding-period q; hence, the variance of $R_t(q)$ is more than q times the variance of R_t, yielding a larger denominator in the Sharpe ratio than the IID case. For returns with negative serial correlation, the opposite is true: The variance of $R_t(q)$ is less than q times the variance of R_t, yielding a smaller denominator in the Sharpe ratio than the IID case. For returns with significant serial correlation, this effect can be substantial. For example, the annual Sharpe ratio of a portfolio with a monthly first-order autocorrelation of -20 percent is 4.17 times the monthly Sharpe ratio, whereas the scale factor is 3.46 in the IID case and 2.88 when the monthly first-order autocorrelation is 20 percent.

TABLE 28.2   Scale Factors for Time-Aggregated Sharpe Ratios When Returns Follow an AR(1) Process for Various Aggregation Values and First-Order Autocorrelations

	Aggregation Value, q									
ρ (%)	2	3	4	6	12	24	36	48	125	250
90	1.03	1.05	1.07	1.10	1.21	1.41	1.60	1.77	2.67	3.70
80	1.05	1.10	1.14	1.21	1.43	1.81	2.14	2.42	3.79	5.32
70	1.08	1.15	1.21	1.33	1.65	2.19	2.62	3.00	4.75	6.68
60	1.12	1.21	1.30	1.46	1.89	2.55	3.08	3.53	5.63	7.94
50	1.15	1.28	1.39	1.60	2.12	2.91	3.53	4.06	6.49	9.15
40	1.20	1.35	1.49	1.75	2.36	3.27	3.98	4.58	7.35	10.37
30	1.24	1.43	1.60	1.91	2.61	3.65	4.44	5.12	8.23	11.62
20	1.29	1.52	1.73	2.07	2.88	4.04	4.93	5.68	9.14	12.92
10	1.35	1.62	1.86	2.25	3.16	4.45	5.44	6.28	10.12	14.31
0	**1.41**	**1.73**	**2.00**	**2.45**	**3.46**	**4.90**	**6.00**	**6.93**	**11.18**	**15.81**
−10	1.49	1.85	2.16	2.66	3.80	5.39	6.61	7.64	12.35	17.47
−20	1.58	1.99	2.33	2.90	4.17	5.95	7.31	8.45	13.67	19.35
−30	1.69	2.13	2.53	3.17	4.60	6.59	8.10	9.38	15.20	21.52
−40	1.83	2.29	2.75	3.48	5.09	7.34	9.05	10.48	17.01	24.11
−50	2.00	2.45	3.02	3.84	5.69	8.26	10.21	11.84	19.26	27.31
−60	2.24	2.61	3.37	4.30	6.44	9.44	11.70	13.59	22.19	31.50
−70	2.58	2.76	3.86	4.92	7.45	11.05	13.77	16.04	26.33	37.43
−80	3.16	2.89	4.66	5.91	8.96	13.50	16.98	19.88	32.96	47.02
−90	4.47	2.97	6.47	8.09	12.06	18.29	23.32	27.61	46.99	67.65

These patterns are summarized in Figure 28.1, in which $\eta(q)$ is plotted as a function of q for five values of ρ. The middle ($\rho = 0$) curve corresponds to the standard scale factor $\sqrt{q}$, which is the correct factor when the correlation coefficient is zero. The curves above the middle one correspond to positive values of ρ, and those below the middle curve correspond to negative values of ρ. It is apparent that serial correlation has a nontrivial effect on the time aggregation of Sharpe ratios.

The General Case

More generally, using the expression for $\widehat{SR}\,(q)$ in Equation 28.26, we can construct an estimator of SR(q) from estimators of the first $q - 1$ autocorrelations of R_t under the assumption of stationary returns. As in the "Non-IID Return" section, we can use GMM to estimate these autocorrelations as well as their asymptotic joint distribution, which can then be used to derive the following limiting distribution of $\widehat{SR}\,(q)$:

$$\sqrt{T}\,[\widehat{SR}](q) - SR(q) \stackrel{a}{\sim} N[0, V_{GMM}(q)], \quad V_{GMM}(q) = \frac{\partial g}{\partial \theta}\, \boldsymbol{\Sigma}\, \frac{\partial g}{\partial \theta'}, \qquad (28.23)$$

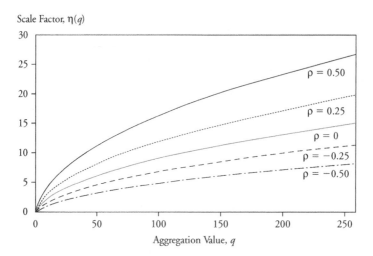

FIGURE 28.1.   Scale Factors of Time-Aggregated Sharpe Ratios When Returns Follow an AR(1) Process: For $\rho = -0.50, -0.25, 0, 0.25,$ and 0.50

where the definitions of $\partial g/\partial\theta$ and Σ and formulas for estimating them are given in the "Time Aggregation" section of Appendix 28A. The standard error of $\widehat{SR}(q)$ is then given by

$$SE[\widehat{SR}(q)] \overset{a}{=} \sqrt{\hat{V}_{GMM}(q)/T} \qquad (28.24)$$

and confidence intervals can be constructed as in Equation 28.10.

Using $\hat{V}_{GMM}(q)$ When Returns Are IID

Although the robust estimator for $SR(q)$ is the appropriate estimator to use when returns are serially correlated or non-IID in other ways, there is a cost: additional estimation error induced by the autocovariance estimator, $\hat{\gamma}_k$, which manifests itself in the asymptotic variance, $\hat{V}_{GMM}(q)$, of $\widehat{SR}(q)$. To develop a sense for the impact of estimation error on $\hat{V}_{GMM}(q)$ consider the robust estimator when returns are, in fact, IID. In that case, $\gamma_k = 0$ for all $k > 0$, but because the robust estimator is a function of estimators $\hat{\gamma}_k$, the estimation errors of the autocovariance estimators will have an impact on $\hat{V}_{GMM}(q)$. In particular, in the "Using $\hat{V}_{GMM}(q)$ When Returns Are IID" section of Appendix 28A, I show that for IID returns, the asymptotic variance of robust estimator $\widehat{SR}(q)$ is given by

$$V_{GMM}(q) = \left[1 - \frac{\upsilon_3 SR}{\sigma^3} + (\upsilon_4 - \sigma^4)\frac{SR^2}{4\sigma^4}\right] + (\sqrt{q}SR)^2 \sum_{j=1}^{q-1}\left(1 - \frac{j}{q}\right)^2, \qquad (28.25)$$

where $\upsilon_3 \equiv E[(R_t - \mu)^3]$ and $\upsilon_4 \equiv E[(R_t - \mu)^4]$ are the return's third and fourth moments, respectively. Now suppose that returns are normally distributed. In that case, $\upsilon_3 = 0$ and $\upsilon_4 = 3\sigma^4$, which implies that

$$V_{GMM}(q) = V_{IID}(q) + (\sqrt{q}SR)^2 \sum_{j=1}^{q-1}\left(1 - \frac{j}{q}\right)^2 \geq V_{IID}(q). \qquad (28.26)$$

The second term on the right side of Equation 28.26 represents the additional estimation error introduced by the estimated autocovariances in the more general estimator given in Equation 28.46 in Appendix 28A. By setting $q = 1$ so that no time aggregation is involved in the Sharpe ratio estimator (hence, no autocovariances enter into the estimator), the expression in Equation 28.26 reduces to the IID case given in Equation 28.18.

The asymptotic relative efficiency of $\widehat{SR}(q)$ can be evaluated explicitly by computing the ratio of $V_{GMM}(q)$ to $V_{IID}(q)$ in the case of IID normal returns:

$$\frac{V_{GMM}(q)}{V_{IID}(q)} = 1 + \frac{2\sum_{j=1}^{q-1}(1 - j/q)^2}{1 + 2/SR^2}, \tag{28.27}$$

and Table 28.3 reports these ratios for various combinations of Sharpe ratios and aggregation values q. Even for small aggregation values, such as $q = 2$, asymptotic variance $V_{GMM}(q)$ is significantly higher than $V_{IID}(q)$—for example, 33 percent higher for a Sharpe ratio of 2.00. As the aggregation value increases, the asymptotic relative efficiency becomes even worse as more estimation error is built into the time-aggregated Sharpe ratio estimator. Even with a monthly Sharpe ratio of only 1.00, the annualized ($q = 12$) robust Sharpe ratio estimator has an asymptotic variance that is 334 percent of $V_{IID}(q)$.

The values in Table 28.3 suggest that, unless there is significant serial correlation in return series R_t, the robust Sharpe ratio estimator should not be used. A useful diagnostic to check for the presence of serial correlation is the Ljung–Box (1978) Q-statistic:

$$Q_{q-1} = T(T + 2)\sum_{k=1}^{q-1}\frac{\hat{\rho}_k^2}{T - k}, \tag{28.28}$$

TABLE 28.3.   Asymptotic Relative Efficiency of Robust Sharpe Ratio Estimator When Returns Are IID

SR	Aggregation Value, q									
	2	3	4	6	12	24	36	48	125	250
0.50	1.06	1.12	1.19	1.34	1.78	2.67	3.56	4.45	10.15	19.41
0.75	1.11	1.24	1.38	1.67	2.54	4.30	6.05	7.81	19.07	37.37
1.00	1.17	1.37	1.58	2.02	3.34	6.00	8.67	11.34	28.45	56.22
1.25	1.22	1.49	1.77	2.34	4.08	7.59	11.09	14.60	37.11	73.66
1.50	1.26	1.59	1.93	2.62	4.72	8.95	13.18	17.42	44.59	88.71
1.75	1.30	1.67	2.06	2.85	5.25	10.08	14.92	19.76	50.81	101.22
2.00	1.33	1.74	2.17	3.04	5.69	11.01	16.34	21.67	55.89	111.45
2.25	1.36	1.80	2.25	3.19	6.04	11.76	17.49	23.23	60.02	119.75
2.50	1.38	1.84	2.33	3.31	6.32	12.37	18.43	24.49	63.38	126.51
2.75	1.40	1.88	2.38	3.42	6.56	12.87	19.20	25.52	66.12	132.02
3.00	1.41	1.91	2.43	3.50	6.75	13.28	19.83	26.37	68.37	136.55

Note: Asymptotic relative efficiency is given by $V_{GMM}(q)/V_{IID}(q)$.

which is asymptotically distributed as χ^2_{q-1} under the null hypothesis of no serial correlation.[10] If Q_{q-1} takes on a large value—for example, if it exceeds the 95 percent critical value of the χ^2_{q-1} distribution—this signals significant serial correlation in returns and suggests that the robust Sharpe ratio, $\widehat{SR}(q)$, should be used instead of $\sqrt{q}\,\widehat{SR}$ for estimating the Sharpe ratio of q-period returns.

AN EMPIRICAL EXAMPLE

To illustrate the potential impact of estimation error and serial correlation in computing Sharpe ratios, I apply the estimators described in the preceding sections to the monthly historical total returns of the 10 largest (as of February 11, 2001) mutual funds from various start dates through June 2000 and 12 hedge funds from various inception dates through December 2000. Monthly total returns for the mutual funds were obtained from the University of Chicago's Center for Research in Security Prices. The 12 hedge funds were selected from the Altvest database to yield a diverse range of annual Sharpe ratios (from 1.00 to 5.00) computed in the standard way ($\sqrt{q}\,\widehat{SR}$, where $\widehat{SR}$ is the Sharpe ratio estimator applied to monthly returns), with the additional requirement that the funds have a minimum five-year history of returns. The names of the hedge funds have been omitted to maintain their privacy, and I will refer to them only by their investment styles (e.g., relative value fund, risk arbitrage fund).[11]

Table 28.4 shows that the 10 mutual funds have little serial correlation in returns, with p-values of Q-statistics ranging from 13.2 percent to 80.2 percent.[12] Indeed, the largest absolute level of autocorrelation among the 10 mutual funds is the 12.4 percent first-order autocorrelation of the Fidelity Magellan Fund. With a risk-free rate of 5/12 percent per month, the monthly Sharpe ratios of the 10 mutual funds range from 0.14 (Growth Fund of America) to 0.32 (Janus Worldwide), with robust standard errors of 0.05 and 0.11, respectively. Because of the lack of serial correlation in the monthly returns of these mutual funds, there is little difference between the IID estimator for the annual Sharpe ratio, $\sqrt{q}\,\widehat{SR}$ (in Table 28.4, $\sqrt{12}\,\widehat{SR}$), and the robust estimator that accounts for serial correlation, $\widehat{SR}(12)$. a For example, even in the case of the Fidelity Magellan Fund, which has the highest first-order autocorrelation among the 10 mutual funds, the difference between a $\sqrt{q}\,\widehat{SR}$ of 0.73 and a $\widehat{SR}(12)$ of 0.66 is not substantial (and certainly not statistically significant). Note that the robust estimator is marginally lower than the IID estimator, indicating the presence of positive serial correlation in the monthly returns of the Magellan Fund. In contrast, for Washington Mutual Investors, the IID estimate of the annual Sharpe ratio is $\sqrt{q}\,\widehat{SR} = 0.60$ but the robust estimate is larger, $\widehat{SR}(12) = 0.65$, because of negative serial correlation in the fund's monthly returns (recall that negative serial correlation implies that the variance of the sum of 12 monthly returns is less than 12 times the variance of monthly returns).

The robust standard errors $SE_3(12)$ with $m = 3$ for $\widehat{SR}(12)$ for the mutual funds range from 0.17 (Janus) to 0.47 (Fidelity Growth and Income) and take on similar values when $m = 6$, which indicates that the robust estimator is reasonably well behaved for this dataset. The magnitudes of the standard errors yield 95 percent confidence intervals for annual Sharpe ratios that do not contain 0 for any of the 10 mutual funds. For example, the 95 percent confidence interval for the Vanguard 500 Index fund is $0.85 \pm (1.96 \times 0.26)$, which is (0.33, 1.36). These results indicate Sharpe ratios for the 10 mutual funds that are statistically different from 0 at the 95 percent confidence level.

TABLE 28.4 Monthly and Annual Sharpe Ratio Estimates for a Sample of Mutual Funds and Hedge Funds

Fund	Start Date	T	$\hat{\mu}$ (%)	$\hat{\sigma}$ (%)	$\hat{\rho}_1$ (%)	$\hat{\rho}_2$ (%)	$\hat{\rho}_3$ (%)	p-Value of Q_{11} (%)	Monthly		Annual			
									$\widehat{SR}$	SE_3	$\sqrt{12}\widehat{SR}$	$\widehat{SR}(12)$	$SE_3(12)$	$SE_6(12)$
Mutual funds														
Vanguard 500 Index	10/76	286	1.30	4.27	−4.0	−6.6	−4.9	64.5	0.21	0.06	**0.72**	**0.85**	0.26	0.25
Fidelity Magellan	1/67	402	1.73	6.23	12.4	−2.3	−0.4	28.6	0.21	0.06	**0.73**	**0.66**	0.20	0.21
Investment Company of America	1/63	450	1.17	4.01	1.8	−3.2	−4.5	80.2	0.19	0.05	**0.65**	**0.71**	0.22	0.22
Janus	3/70	364	1.52	4.75	10.5	−0.0	−3.7	58.1	0.23	0.06	**0.81**	**0.80**	0.17	0.17
Fidelity Contrafund	5/67	397	1.29	4.97	7.4	−2.5	−6.8	58.2	0.18	0.05	**0.61**	**0.67**	0.23	0.23
Washington Mutual Investors	1/63	450	1.13	4.09	−0.1	−7.2	−2.6	22.8	0.17	0.05	**0.60**	**0.65**	0.20	0.20
Janus Worldwide	1/92	102	1.81	4.36	11.4	3.4	−3.8	13.2	0.32	0.11	**1.12**	**1.29**	0.46	0.37
Fidelity Growth and Income	1/86	174	1.54	4.13	5.1	−1.6	−8.2	60.9	0.27	0.09	**0.95**	**1.18**	0.47	0.40
American Century Ultra	12/81	223	1.72	7.11	2.3	3.4	1.4	54.5	0.18	0.07	**0.64**	**0.71**	0.27	0.25
Growth Fund of America	7/64	431	1.18	5.35	8.5	−2.7	−4.1	45.4	0.14	0.05	**0.50**	**0.49**	0.19	0.20

(continued)

TABLE 28.4 (continued)

| | | | | | | | | | Monthly | | | Annual | | |
Fund	Start Date	T	$\hat{\mu}$ (%)	$\hat{\sigma}$ (%)	$\hat{\rho}_1$ (%)	$\hat{\rho}_2$ (%)	$\hat{\rho}_3$ (%)	p-Value of Q_{11} (%)	$\widehat{SR}$	SE_3	$\sqrt{12}\widehat{SR}$	$\widehat{SR}(12)$	$SE_3(12)$	$SE_6(12)$
Hedge funds														
Convertible/option arbitrage	5/92	104	1.63	0.97	42.6	29.0	21.4	0.0	1.26	0.28	**4.35**	**2.99**	1.04	1.11
Relative value	12/92	97	0.66	0.21	25.9	19.2	−2.1	4.5	1.17	0.17	**4.06**	**3.38**	1.16	1.07
Mortgage-backed securities	1/93	96	1.33	0.79	42.0	22.1	16.7	0.1	1.16	0.24	**4.03**	**2.44**	0.53	0.54
High-yield debt	6/94	79	1.30	0.87	33.7	21.8	13.1	5.2	1.02	0.27	**3.54**	**2.25**	0.74	0.72
Risk arbitrage A	7/93	90	1.06	0.69	−4.9	−10.8	6.9	30.6	0.94	0.20	**3.25**	**3.83**	0.87	0.85
Long–short equities	7/89	138	1.18	0.83	−20.2	24.6	8.7	0.1	0.92	0.06	**3.19**	**2.32**	0.35	0.37
Multistrategy A	1/95	72	1.08	0.75	48.9	23.4	3.3	0.3	0.89	0.40	**3.09**	**2.18**	1.14	1.19
Risk arbitrage B	11/94	74	0.90	0.77	−4.9	2.5	−8.3	96.1	0.63	0.14	**2.17**	**2.47**	0.79	0.77
Convertible arbitrage A	9/92	100	1.38	1.60	33.8	30.8	7.9	0.8	0.60	0.18	**2.08**	**1.43**	0.44	0.45
Convertible arbitrage B	7/94	78	0.78	0.62	32.4	9.7	−4.5	23.4	0.60	0.18	**2.06**	**1.67**	0.68	0.62
Multistrategy B	6/89	139	1.34	1.63	49.0	24.6	10.6	0.0	0.57	0.16	**1.96**	**1.17**	0.25	0.25
Fund of funds	10/94	75	1.68	2.29	29.7	21.1	0.9	23.4	0.56	0.19	**1.93**	**1.39**	0.67	0.70

Note: For the mutual fund sample, monthly total returns from various start dates through June 2000; for the hedge fund sample, various start dates through December 2000. The term $\hat{\rho}_k$ denotes the kth autocorrelation coefficient, and Q_{11} denotes the Ljung–Box Q-statistic, which is asymptotically χ^2_{11} under the null hypothesis of no serial correlation. $\widehat{SR}$ denotes the usual Sharpe ratio estimator, $(\hat{\mu} - R_f)/\hat{\sigma}$, which is based on monthly data; R_f is assumed to be 5/12 percent per month; and $\widehat{SR}(12)$ denotes the annual Sharpe ratio estimator that takes into account serial correlation in monthly returns. All standard errors are based on GMM estimators using the Newey–West (1982) procedure with truncation lag $m = 3$ for entries in the SE_3 and $SE_3(12)$ columns and $m = 6$ for entries in the $SE_6(12)$ column.

642

The results for the 12 hedge funds are different in several respects. The mean returns are higher and the standard deviations lower, implying much higher Sharpe ratio estimates for hedge funds than for mutual funds. The monthly Sharpe ratio estimates, $\widehat{SR}$, range from 0.56 ("Fund of funds") to 1.26 ("Convertible/option arbitrage"), in contrast to the range of 0.14 to 0.32 for the 10 mutual funds. However, the serial correlation in hedge fund returns is also much higher. For example, the first-order autocorrelation coefficient ranges from -20.2 percent to 49.0 percent among the 12 hedge funds, whereas the highest first-order autocorrelation is 12.4 percent among the 10 mutual funds. The *p*-values provide a more complete summary of the presence of serial correlation: All but 5 of the 12 hedge funds have *p*-values less than 5 percent, and several are less than 1 percent.

The impact of serial correlation on the annual Sharpe ratios of hedge funds is dramatic. When the IID estimator, $\sqrt{12}\,\widehat{SR}$, is used for the annual Sharpe ratio, the "Convertible/option arbitrage" fund has a Sharpe ratio estimate of 4.35, but when serial correlation is properly taken into account by $\widehat{SR}(12)$, the estimate drops to 2.99, implying that the IID estimator overstates the annual Sharpe ratio by 45 percent. The annual Sharpe ratio estimate for the "Mortgage-backed securities" fund drops from 4.03 to 2.44 when serial correlation is taken into account, implying an overstatement of 65 percent. However, the annual Sharpe ratio estimate for the "Risk arbitrage A" fund *increases* from 3.25 to 3.83 because of negative serial correlation in its monthly returns.

The sharp differences between the annual IID and robust Sharpe ratio estimates underscore the importance of correctly accounting for serial correlation in analyzing the performance of hedge funds. Naively estimating the annual Sharpe ratios by multiplying $\widehat{SR}$ by $\sqrt{12}$ will yield the rank ordering given in the $\widehat{SR}\sqrt{12}$ column of Table 28.4, but once serial correlation is taken into account, the rank ordering changes to 3, 2, 5, 7, 1, 6, 8, 4,10, 9, 12, and 11.

The robust standard errors for the annual robust Sharpe ratio estimates of the 12 hedge funds range from 0.25 to 1.16, which, although larger than those in the mutual fund sample, nevertheless imply 95 percent confidence intervals that generally do not include 0. For example, even in the case of the "Multistrategy B" fund, which has the lowest robust Sharpe ratio estimate (1.17), its 95 percent confidence interval is $1.17 \pm 1.96 \times 0.25$, which is (0.68, 1.66). These statistically significant Sharpe ratios are consistent with previous studies that document the fact that hedge funds do seem to exhibit statistically significant excess returns.[13] The similarity of the standard errors between the $m = 3$ and $m = 6$ cases for the hedge fund sample indicates that the robust estimator is also well behaved in this case, despite the presence of significant serial correlation in monthly returns.

In summary, the empirical examples illustrate the potential impact that serial correlation can have on Sharpe ratio estimates and the importance of properly accounting for departures from the standard IID framework. Robust Sharpe ratio estimators contain significant additional information about the risk-reward trade-offs for active investment products, such as hedge funds; more detailed analysis of the risks and rewards of hedge fund investments is performed in Getmansky, Lo, and Makarov (2002) and Lo (2001).

CONCLUSION

Although the Sharpe ratio has become part of the canon of modern financial analysis, its applications typically do not account for the fact that it is an estimated quantity, subject to estimation errors that can be substantial in some cases. The results presented in this chapter provide one way to gauge the accuracy of these estimators, and it should come as no surprise that the statistical properties of Sharpe ratios depend intimately on the statistical properties of the return series on which they are based. This suggests that a more sophisticated approach to interpreting Sharpe ratios is called for, one that incorporates information about the investment style that generates the returns and the market environment in which those returns are generated. For example, hedge funds have very different return characteristics from the characteristics of mutual funds; hence, the comparison of Sharpe ratios between these two investment vehicles cannot be performed naively. In light of the recent interest in alternative investments by institutional investors—investors that are accustomed to standardized performance attribution measures such as the annualized Sharpe ratio—there is an even greater need to develop statistics that are consistent with a portfolio's investment style.

The empirical example underscores the practical relevance of proper statistical inference for Sharpe ratio estimators. Ignoring the impact of serial correlation in hedge fund returns can yield annualized Sharpe ratios that are overstated by more than 65 percent, understated Sharpe ratios in the case of negatively serially correlated returns, and inconsistent rankings across hedge funds of different styles and objectives. By using the appropriate statistical distribution for quantifying the performance of each return history, the Sharpe ratio can provide a more complete understanding of the risks and rewards of a broad array of investment opportunities.

APPENDIX 28A: ASYMPTOTIC DISTRIBUTIONS OF SHARPE RATIO ESTIMATORS

The first section of this appendix presents results for IID returns, and the second section presents corresponding results for non-IID returns. Results for time-aggregated Sharpe ratios are reported in the third section, and in the final section, the asymptotic variance, $V_{GMM}(q)$, of the time-aggregated robust estimator, $\widehat{SR}(q,)$ is derived for the special case of IID returns.

Throughout the appendix, the following conventions are maintained: (1) All vectors are column vectors unless otherwise indicated; (2) vectors and matrixes are always typeset in boldface (i.e., X and μ are scalars and $\mathbf{X}$ and $\boldsymbol{\mu}$ are vectors or matrixes).

IID Returns

To derive an expression for the asymptotic distribution of $\widehat{SR}$, we must first obtain the asymptotic *joint* distribution of $\hat{\mu}$ and $\hat{\sigma}^2$. Denote by $\hat{\boldsymbol{\theta}}$ the column vector $(\hat{\mu}\ \hat{\sigma}^2)'$ and let $\boldsymbol{\theta}$ denote the corresponding column vector of population values $(\mu\ \sigma^2)'$. If returns are IID, it is a well-known consequence of the Central Limit Theorem that the asymptotic distribution of $\hat{\boldsymbol{\theta}}$ is given by (see White):

$$\sqrt{T}(\hat{\boldsymbol{\theta}} - \boldsymbol{\theta}) \overset{a}{\sim} N(0, \mathbf{V}_\theta), \ \mathbf{V}_\theta \equiv \begin{pmatrix} \sigma^2 & 0 \\ 0 & 2\sigma^4 \end{pmatrix}, \tag{28.29}$$

where the notation $\overset{a}{\sim}$ indicates that this is an asymptotic approximation. Because the Sharpe ratio estimator $\widehat{SR}$ can be written as a function $g(\hat{\boldsymbol{\theta}})$ of $\hat{\boldsymbol{\theta}}$, its asymptotic distribution follows directly from Taylor's theorem or the so-called delta method (see, for example, White):

$$\sqrt{T}[g(\hat{\boldsymbol{\theta}}) - g(\boldsymbol{\theta})] \overset{a}{\sim} N(0, \mathbf{V}_g), \ \mathbf{V}_g \equiv \frac{\partial g}{\partial \boldsymbol{\theta}} \mathbf{V}_\theta \frac{\partial g}{\partial \boldsymbol{\theta}'}. \tag{28.30}$$

In the case of the Sharpe ratio, $g(\cdot)$ is given by Equation 28.2; hence,

$$\frac{\partial g}{\partial \boldsymbol{\theta}'} = \left[\begin{array}{c} 1/\sigma \\ -(\mu - R_f)/(2\sigma^3) \end{array} \right], \tag{28.31}$$

which yields the following asymptotic distribution for $\widehat{\mathrm{SR}}$:

$$\sqrt{T}\,(\widehat{\mathrm{SR}} - \mathrm{SR}) \stackrel{a}{\sim} N(0, V_{IID}), \quad V_{IID} = 1 + \frac{(\mu - R_f)^2}{2\sigma^2} = 1 + \frac{1}{2}\,\mathrm{SR}^2. \tag{28.32}$$

Non-IID Returns

Denote by $\mathbf{X}_t$ the vector of period-t returns and lags $(R_t\ R_{t-1}\ \ldots\ R_{t-q+1})'$ and let $(\mathbf{X}_t)$ be a stochastic process that satisfies the following conditions:

   H1: $\{\mathbf{X}_t\colon t \in (-\infty, \infty)\}$ is stationary and ergodic;

   H2: $\boldsymbol{\theta}_0 \in \boldsymbol{\Theta}$, $\boldsymbol{\Theta}$ is an open subset of $\Re^k$;

   H3: $\forall\, \boldsymbol{\theta} \in \boldsymbol{\Theta}$, $\varphi\,(\cdot, \boldsymbol{\theta})$ and $\varphi_\theta\,(\cdot, \boldsymbol{\theta})$ are Borel measurable and $\varphi_\theta\,\{\mathbf{X}, \cdot\}$ is continuous on $\boldsymbol{\Theta}$ for all $\mathbf{X}$;

   H4: φ_θ is first-moment continuous at $\boldsymbol{\theta}_0$: $\mathrm{E}[\varphi_\theta\,(\mathbf{X}, \cdot)]$ exists, is finite, and is of full rank.

   H5: Let $\varphi_t \equiv \varphi(\mathbf{X}_t\,\boldsymbol{\theta}_0)$

and

$$\mathbf{v}_j \equiv \mathrm{E}[\varphi_0 \mid \varphi_{-1}, \varphi_{-2}, \ldots] - \mathrm{E}[\varphi_0 \mid \varphi_{-j-1}, \varphi_{-j-2}, \ldots]$$

and assume

   (*i*): $\mathrm{E}[\varphi_0\,\varphi_0']$ exists and is finite,

   (*ii*): $\mathbf{v}_j$ converges in mean square to 0, and

   (*iii*): $\displaystyle\sum_{j=0}^{\infty} \mathrm{E}(\mathbf{v}_j'\,\mathbf{v}_j\,)^{1/2}$ is finite,

which implies $\mathrm{E}[\varphi(\mathbf{X}_t, \boldsymbol{\theta}_0)] = 0$.

   H6: Let $\hat{\boldsymbol{\theta}}$ solve $\dfrac{1}{T}\displaystyle\sum_{t=1}^{T}\varphi(\mathbf{X}_t, \boldsymbol{\theta}) = 0$.

Then, Hansen shows that

$$\sqrt{T}\,(\hat{\boldsymbol{\theta}} - \boldsymbol{\theta}_0) \stackrel{a}{\sim} N(0, \mathbf{V}_\theta), \quad \mathbf{V}_\theta \equiv \mathbf{H}^{-1}\boldsymbol{\Sigma}\mathbf{H}^{-1'}, \tag{28.33}$$

where

$$\mathbf{H} \equiv \lim_{T\to\infty} \mathrm{E}\left[\frac{1}{T}\sum_{t=1}^{T}\varphi_\theta(\mathbf{X}_t, \boldsymbol{\theta}_0) \right], \tag{28.34}$$

$$\boldsymbol{\Sigma} \equiv \lim_{T\to\infty} \mathrm{E}\left[\frac{1}{T}\sum_{t=1}^{T}\sum_{s=1}^{T}\varphi(\mathbf{X}_t, \boldsymbol{\theta}_0)\varphi(\mathbf{X}_s, \boldsymbol{\theta}_0)' \right], \tag{28.35}$$

and $\varphi_\theta(R_t, \boldsymbol{\theta})$ denotes the derivative of $\varphi(R_t, \boldsymbol{\theta})$ with respect to $\boldsymbol{\theta}$.[14] Specifically, let $\varphi(R_t, \boldsymbol{\theta})$ denote the following vector function:

$$\varphi(R_t, \boldsymbol{\theta}) \equiv \left[\begin{array}{c} R_t - \mu \\ (R_t - \mu)^2 - \sigma^2 \end{array} \right]. \tag{28.36}$$

The GMM estimator of θ, denoted by $\hat{\theta}$, is given implicitly by the solution to

$$\frac{1}{T} \sum_{t=1}^{T} \varphi(R_t, \theta) = 0, \tag{28.37}$$

which yields the standard estimators $\hat{\mu}$ and $\hat{\sigma}^2$ given in Equation 28.3. For the moment conditions in Equation 28.36, $\mathbf{H}$ is given by:

$$\mathbf{H} \equiv \lim_{T \to \infty} E \left\{ \frac{1}{T} \sum_{t=1}^{T} \begin{bmatrix} -1 & 0 \\ 2(\mu - R_t) & -1 \end{bmatrix} \right\} = -\mathbf{I}. \tag{28.38}$$

Therefore, $\mathbf{V}_\theta = \mathbf{\Sigma}$ and the asymptotic distribution of the Sharpe ratio estimator follows from the delta method as in the first section:

$$\sqrt{T}(\widehat{SR} - SR) \stackrel{a}{\sim} N(0, V_{GMM}), \ V_{GMM} = \frac{\partial g}{\partial \theta} \mathbf{\Sigma} \frac{\partial g}{\partial \theta'}, \tag{28.39}$$

where $\partial g / \partial \theta$ is given in Equation 28.31. An estimator for $\partial g / \partial \theta$ may be obtained by substituting $\hat{\theta}$ into Equation 28.31, and an estimator for $\mathbf{\Sigma}$ may be obtained by using Newey and West's (1987) procedure:

$$\hat{\mathbf{\Sigma}} = \hat{\mathbf{\Omega}}_0 + \sum_{j=1}^{m} \omega(j, m)(\hat{\mathbf{\Omega}}_j + \hat{\mathbf{\Omega}}'_j), \ m \ll T, \tag{28.40}$$

$$\hat{\mathbf{\Omega}}_j \equiv \frac{1}{T} \sum_{t=j+1}^{T} \varphi(R_t, \hat{\theta})\varphi(R_{t-j}, \hat{\theta})', t \tag{28.41}$$

$$\omega(j, m) \equiv 1 - \frac{j}{m+1}, \tag{28.42}$$

and m is the truncation lag, which must satisfy the condition $m/T \to \infty$ as T increases without bound to ensure consistency. An estimator for V_{SR} can then be constructed as

$$\hat{V}_{GMM} = \frac{\partial g(\hat{\theta})}{\partial \theta} \hat{\mathbf{\Sigma}} \frac{\partial g(\hat{\theta})}{\partial \theta'}. \tag{28.43}$$

Time Aggregation

Let $\theta \equiv [\mu \ \sigma^2 \ \gamma_1 \ldots \gamma_{q-1}]'$ denote the vector of parameters to be estimated, where γ_k is the kth-order autocovariance of R_t, and define the following moment conditions:

$$
\begin{aligned}
\varphi_1(\mathbf{X}_t, \theta) &= R_t - \mu \\
\varphi_2(\mathbf{X}_t, \theta) &= (R_t - \mu)^2 - \sigma^2 \\
\varphi_3(\mathbf{X}_t, \theta) &= (R_t - \mu)(R_{t-1} - \mu) - \gamma_1 \\
\varphi_4(\mathbf{X}_t, \theta) &= (R_t - \mu)(R_{t-2} - \mu) - \gamma_2 \\
&\vdots \\
\varphi_{q+1}(\mathbf{X}_t, \theta) &= (R_t - \mu)(R_{t-q+1} - \mu) - \gamma_{q-1} \\
\varphi(\mathbf{X}_t, \theta) &\equiv [\varphi_1 \ \varphi_2 \ \varphi_3 \ldots \varphi_{q+1}]',
\end{aligned} \tag{28.44}
$$

where $\mathbf{X}_t \equiv [R_t\ R_{t-1}\ \ldots\ R_{t-q+1}]'$. The GMM estimator $\hat{\boldsymbol{\theta}}$ is defined by Equation 28.37, which yields the standard estimators $\hat{\mu}$ and $\hat{\sigma}^2$ in Equation 28.3 as well as the standard estimators for the autocovariances:

$$\hat{\gamma}_k = \frac{1}{T} \sum_{t=k+1}^{T} (R_t - \hat{\mu})(R_{t-k} - \hat{\mu}). \tag{28.45}$$

The estimator for the Sharpe ratio then follows directly:

$$\widehat{\mathrm{SR}}(q) = \hat{\eta}(q)\widehat{\mathrm{SR}}, \quad \hat{\eta}(q) \equiv \frac{q}{\sqrt{q + 2\sum_{k=1}^{q-1}(q-k)\hat{\rho}_k}}, \tag{28.46}$$

where

$$\hat{\rho}_k = \frac{\hat{\gamma}_k}{\hat{\sigma}^2}. $$

As in the first two sections of this appendix, the asymptotic distribution of $\widehat{\mathrm{SR}}(q)$ can be obtained by applying the delta method to $g(\hat{\boldsymbol{\theta}})$ where the function $g(\cdot)$ is now given by Equation 28.20. Recall from Equation 28.33 that the asymptotic distribution of the GMM estimator $\hat{\boldsymbol{\theta}}$ is given by

$$\sqrt{T}(\hat{\boldsymbol{\theta}} - \boldsymbol{\theta}) \overset{a}{\sim} N(0, \mathbf{V}_\theta), \mathbf{V}_\theta \equiv \mathbf{H}^{-1}\boldsymbol{\Sigma}\mathbf{H}^{-1}. \tag{28.47}$$

$$\boldsymbol{\Sigma} \equiv \lim_{T \to \infty} \mathrm{E}\left[\frac{1}{T}\sum_{t=1}^{T}\sum_{s=1}^{T}\boldsymbol{\varphi}(\mathbf{X}_t, \boldsymbol{\theta})\boldsymbol{\varphi}(\mathbf{X}_s, \boldsymbol{\theta})'\right]. \tag{28.48}$$

For the moment conditions in Equation 28.44, $\mathbf{H}$ is

$$\mathbf{H} = \lim_{T \to \infty} \mathrm{E}\left\{\frac{1}{T}\sum_{t=1}^{T}\begin{bmatrix} -1 & 0 & 0 & \ldots & 0 \\ 2(\mu - R_t) & -1 & 0 & \ldots & 0 \\ 2\mu - R_t - R_{t-1} & 0 & -1 & \ldots & 0 \\ \vdots & \vdots & \vdots & \ddots & \vdots \\ 2\mu - R_t - R_{t-q+1} & 0 & \ldots & 0 & -1 \end{bmatrix}\right\} = -\mathbf{I}; \tag{28.49}$$

hence, $\mathbf{V}_\theta = \boldsymbol{\Sigma}$. The asymptotic distribution of $\widehat{\mathrm{SR}}(q)$ then follows from the delta method:

$$\sqrt{T}[\widehat{\mathrm{SR}}(q) - \mathrm{SR}(q)] \overset{a}{\sim} N[0, V_{GMM}(q)], \quad V_{GMM}(q) = \frac{\partial g}{\partial \boldsymbol{\theta}}\boldsymbol{\Sigma}\frac{\partial g}{\partial \boldsymbol{\theta}'}, \tag{28.50}$$

where the components of $\partial g/\partial\boldsymbol{\theta}$ are

$$\frac{\partial g}{\partial \mu} = \frac{q}{\sigma\sqrt{q + 2\sum_{k=1}^{q-1}(q-k)\rho_k}}, \tag{28.51}$$

$$\frac{\partial g}{\partial \sigma^2} = -\frac{q^2\mathrm{SR}}{2\sigma^2\left[q + 2\sum_{k=2}^{q-1}(q-k)\rho_k\right]^{3/2}}, \tag{28.52}$$

$$\frac{\partial g}{\partial \gamma_k} = -\frac{q(q-k)\mathrm{SR}}{\sigma^2\left[q + 2\sum_{k=1}^{q-1}(q-k)\rho_k\right]^{3/2}}, k = 1, \ldots, q-1, \tag{28.53}$$

and

$$\frac{\partial g}{\partial \boldsymbol{\theta}} = \left[\frac{\partial g}{\partial \mu} \; \frac{\partial g}{\partial \sigma^2} \; \frac{\partial g}{\partial \gamma_1} \cdots \frac{\partial g}{\partial \gamma_{q-1}} \right]. \tag{28.54}$$

Substituting $\hat{\boldsymbol{\theta}}$ into Equation 28.54, estimating $\boldsymbol{\Sigma}$ according to Equation 28.40, and forming the matrix product $\partial g(\hat{\boldsymbol{\theta}})/\partial \boldsymbol{\theta} \, \hat{\boldsymbol{\Sigma}} \, \partial g(\hat{\boldsymbol{\theta}})/\partial \boldsymbol{\theta}'$ yields an estimator for the asymptotic variance of $\widehat{SR}(q)$.

Using $\widehat{V}_{GMM}(q)$ When Returns Are IID

For IID returns, it is possible to evaluate $\boldsymbol{\Sigma}$ in Equation 28.48 explicitly as

$$\boldsymbol{\Sigma} = \begin{pmatrix} \sigma^2 & v_3 & 0 & 0 & \cdots & 0 \\ v_3 & v_4 - \sigma^4 & 0 & 0 & \cdots & 0 \\ 0 & 0 & \sigma^4 & 0 & \cdots & \vdots \\ 0 & 0 & 0 & \sigma^4 & \cdots & 0 \\ 0 & 0 & \vdots & \vdots & \ddots & \vdots \\ 0 & 0 & 0 & 0 & \cdots & \sigma^4 \end{pmatrix} = \begin{pmatrix} \boldsymbol{\Sigma}_1 & 0 \\ 0 & \boldsymbol{\Sigma}_2 \end{pmatrix}, \tag{28.55}$$

where $v_3 \equiv E[(R_t - \mu)^3]$, $v_4 \equiv E[(R_t - \mu)^4]$, and $\boldsymbol{\Sigma}$ is partitioned into a block-diagonal matrix with a (2×2) matrix $\boldsymbol{\Sigma}_1$ and a diagonal $(q-1) \times (q-1)$ matrix $\boldsymbol{\Sigma}_2 = \sigma^4 \mathbf{I}$ along its diagonal. Because $\gamma_k = 0$ for all $k > 0$, $\partial g/\partial \boldsymbol{\theta}$ simplifies to

$$\frac{\partial g}{\partial \mu} = \frac{\sqrt{q}}{\sigma}, \tag{28.56}$$

$$\frac{\partial g}{\partial \sigma^2} = -\frac{\sqrt{q} SR}{2\sigma^2}, \tag{28.57}$$

$$\frac{\partial g}{\partial \gamma_k} = -\frac{q(q-k)SR}{\sigma^2 q^{3/2}}, k = 1, \ldots, q-1, \tag{28.58}$$

and

$$\frac{\partial g}{\partial \boldsymbol{\theta}} = \left(\frac{\partial g}{\partial \mu} \; \frac{\partial g}{\partial \sigma^2} \; \middle| \; \frac{\partial g}{\partial \gamma_1} \cdots \frac{\partial g}{\partial \gamma_{q-1}} \right) = [\mathbf{a} \; \mathbf{b}], \tag{28.59}$$

where $\partial g/\partial \boldsymbol{\theta}$ is also partitioned to conform to the partitioned matrix $\boldsymbol{\Sigma}$ in Equation 28.55. Therefore, the asymptotic variance of the robust estimator $\widehat{SR}(q)$ is given by

$$\begin{aligned} V_{GMM}(q) &= \frac{\partial g}{\partial \boldsymbol{\theta}} \boldsymbol{\Sigma} \frac{\partial g}{\partial \boldsymbol{\theta}'} = \mathbf{a}\boldsymbol{\Sigma}_1 \mathbf{a}' + \mathbf{b}\boldsymbol{\Sigma}_2 \mathbf{b}' \\ &= q\left[1 - \frac{v_3 SR}{\sigma^3} + (v_4 - \sigma^4)\frac{SR^2}{4\sigma^4} \right] + (\sqrt{q} SR)^2 \sum_{j=1}^{q-1} \left(1 - \frac{j}{q} \right)^2. \end{aligned} \tag{28.60}$$

If R_t is normally distributed, then $\nu_3 = 0$ and $\nu_4 = 3\sigma^4$; hence,

$$
\begin{aligned}
V_{GMM}(q) &= q\left[1 + (3\sigma^4 - \sigma^4)\frac{SR^4}{4\sigma^4}\right] + (\sqrt{q}SR)^2 \sum_{j=1}^{q-1}\left(1 - \frac{j}{q}\right)^2 \\
&= q\left(1 + \frac{1}{2}SR^2\right) + (\sqrt{q}SR)^2 \sum_{j=1}^{q-1}\left(1 - \frac{j}{q}\right)^2 \\
&= V_{IID}(q) + (\sqrt{q}SR)^2 \sum_{j=1}^{q-1}\left(1 - \frac{j}{q}\right)^2 \geq V_{IID}(q).
\end{aligned}
\tag{28.61}
$$

ACKNOWLEDGMENTS

I thank Nicholas Chan, Arnout Eikeboom, Jim Holub, Chris Jakob, Laurel Kenner, Frank Linet, Jon Markman, Victor Niederhoffer, Dan O'Reilly, Bill Sharpe, and Jonathan Taylor for helpful comments and discussion. Research support from AlphaSimplex Group is gratefully acknowledged.

NOTES

1. See Sharpe (1994) for an excellent review of its many applications, as well as some new extensions.
2. The Central Limit Theorem is a remarkable mathematical discovery on which much of modern statistical inference is based. It shows that under certain conditions, the probability distribution of a properly normalized sum of random variables must converge to the standard normal distribution, regardless of how each of the random variables in the sum is distributed. Therefore, using the normal distribution for calculating significance levels and confidence intervals is often an excellent approximation, even if normality does not hold for the particular random variables in question. See White (1984) for a rigorous exposition of the role of the Central Limit Theorem in modern econometrics.
3. See, for example, Lo and MacKinlay (1999) and their citations.
4. Additional regularity conditions are required; see Appendix 28A, Hansen (1982), and White for further discussion.
5. The term "robust" is meant to convey the ability of an estimator to perform well under various sets of assumptions. Another commonly used term for such estimators is "nonparametric," which indicates that an estimator is not based on any parametric assumption, such as normally distributed returns. See Randles and Wolfe (1979) for further discussion of nonparametric estimators and Hansen for the generalized method of moments estimator.
6. See, for example, Campbell, Lo, and MacKinlay (1997, Ch. 9), Lo and MacKinlay (Ch. 4), Merton (1980), and Shiller and Perron (1985).
7. The exact expression is, of course,

$$
R_t(q) \equiv \prod_{j=0}^{q-1}(1 + R_{t-j}) - 1.
$$

For most (but not all) applications, Equation 28.16 is an excellent approximation. Alternatively, if R_t is defined to be the continuously compounded return [i.e., $R_t \equiv \log(P_t/P_{t-1})$, where P_t is the price or net asset value at time t], then Equation 28.16 is exact.

8. See Bodie (1995) and the ensuing debate regarding risks in the long run for further evidence of the inadequacy of the Sharpe ratio—or any other single statistic—for delineating the risk–reward profile of a dynamic investment policy.

9. The kth-order autocorrelation of a time series R_t is defined as the correlation coefficient between R_t and R_{t-k}, which is simply the covariance between R_t and R_{t-k} divided by the square root of the product of the variances of R_t and R_{t-k}. But because the variances of R_t and R_{t-k} are the same under our assumption of stationarity, the denominator of the autocorrelation is simply the variance of R_t.

10. See, for example, Harvey (1981, Ch. 6.2).

11. These are the investment styles reported in the Altvest database; no attempt was made to verify or to classify the hedge funds independently.

12. The p-value of a statistic is defined as the smallest level of significance for which the null hypothesis can be rejected based on the statistic's value. In particular, the p-value of 16.0 percent for the Q-statistic of Washington Mutual Investors in Table 28.4 implies that the null hypothesis of no serial correlation can be rejected only at the 16.0 percent significance level; at any lower level of significance—say, 5 percent—the null hypothesis cannot be rejected. Therefore, smaller p-values indicate stronger evidence against the null hypothesis and larger p-values indicate stronger evidence in favor of the null. Researchers often report p-values instead of test statistics because p-values are easier to interpret. To interpret a test statistic, one must compare it with the critical values of the appropriate distribution. This comparison is performed in computing the p-value. For further discussion of p-values and their interpretation, see, for example, Bickel and Doksum (1977, Ch. 5.2.B).

13. See, for example, Ackermann, McEnally, and Ravenscraft (1999), Brown, Goetzmann, and Ibbotson (1999), Brown, Goetzmann, and Park (2001), Fung and Hsieh (1997a, 1997b, 2000), and Liang (1999, 2000, 2001).

14. See Magnus and Neudecker (1988) for the specific definitions and conventions of vector and matrix derivatives of vector functions.

REFERENCES

Ackermann, C., R. McEnally, and D. Ravenscraft. 1999. "The Performance of Hedge Funds: Risk, Return, and Incentives." *Journal of Finance,* vol. 54, no. 3 (June):833–874.

Bickel, P., and K. Doksum. 1977. *Mathematical Statistics: Basic Ideas and Selected Topics.* San Francisco, CA: Holden-Day.

Bodie, Z. 1995. "On the Risk of Stocks in the Long Run." *Financial Analysts Journal,* vol. 51, no. 3 (May/June):18–22.

Brown, S., W. Goetzmann, and R. Ibbotson. 1999. "Offshore Hedge Funds: Survival and Performance 1989–1995." *Journal of Business,* vol. 72, no. 1 (January):91–118.

Brown, S., W. Goetzmann, and J. Park. 1997. "Careers and Survival: Competition and Risks in the Hedge Fund and CTA Industry." *Journal of Finance,* vol. 56, no. 5 (October): 1869–86.

Campbell, J., A. Lo, and C. MacKinlay. 1997. *The Econometrics of Financial Markets.* Princeton, NJ: Princeton University Press.

Fung, W., and D. Hsieh. 1997a. "Empirical Characteristics of Dynamic Trading Strategies: The Case of Hedge Funds." *Review of Financial Studies,* vol. 10, no. 2 (April):75–302.

———. 1997b. "Investment Style and Survivorship Bias in the Returns of CTAs: The Information Content of Track Records." *Journal of Portfolio Management,* vol. 24, no. 1 (Fall):30–41.

———. 2000. "Performance Characteristics of Hedge Funds and Commodity Funds: Natural versus Spurious Biases." *Journal of Financial and Quantitative Analysis,* vol. 35, no. 3 (September):291–307.

Getmansky, M., A. Lo, and I. Makarov. 2002. "An Econometric Model of Illiquidity and Performance Smoothing in Hedge Fund Returns." Unpublished manuscript, MIT Laboratory for Financial Engineering.

Hansen, L. 1982. "Large Sample Properties of Generalized Method of Moments Estimators." *Econometrica,* vol. 50, no. 4 (July):1029–54.

Harvey, A. 1981. *Time Series Models.* New York: John Wiley & Sons.

Liang, B. 1999. "On the Performance of Hedge Funds." *Financial Analysts Journal,* vol. 55, no. 4 (July/August):72–85.

———. 2000. "Hedge Funds: The Living and the Dead." *Journal of Financial and Quantitative Analysis,* vol. 35, no. 3 (September):309–326.

———. 2001. "Hedge Fund Performance: 1990–1999." *Financial Analysts Journal,* vol. 57, no. 1 (January/February):11–18.

Ljung, G., and G. Box. 1978. "On a Measure of Lack of Fit in Time Series Models." *Biometrika,* vol. 65, no. 1: 297–303.

Lo, A. 2001. "Risk Management for Hedge Funds: Introduction and Overview." *Financial Analysts Journal,* vol. 57, no. 6 (November/December): 16–33.

Lo, A., and C. MacKinlay. 1999. *A Non-Random Walk Down Wall Street.* Princeton, NJ: Princeton University Press.

Magnus, J., and H. Neudecker. 1988. *Matrix Differential Calculus: With Applications in Statistics and Economics.* New York: John Wiley & Sons.

Merton, R. 1980. "On Estimating the Expected Return on the Market: An Exploratory Investigation." *Journal of Financial Economics,* vol. 8, no. 4 (December):323–361.

Newey, W., and K. West. 1987. "A Simple Positive Definite Heteroscedasticity and Autocorrelation Consistent Covariance Matrix." *Econometrica,* vol. 55, no. 3:703–705.

Randles, R., and D. Wolfe. 1979. *Introduction to the Theory of Nonparametric Statistics.* New York: John Wiley & Sons.

Sharpe, W. 1994. "The Sharpe Ratio." *Journal of Portfolio Management,* vol. 21, no. 1 (Fall):49–58.

Shiller, R., and P. Perron. 1985. "Testing the Random Walk Hypothesis: Power versus Frequency of Observation." *Economics Letters,* vol. 18, no. 4:381–386.

White, H. 1984. *Asymptotic Theory for Econometricians.* New York: Academic Press.

CHAPTER 29

RISK-ADJUSTED PERFORMANCE

The Correlation Correction

Arun S. Muralidhar

Current measures of risk-adjusted performance, such as the Sharpe ratio, the information ratio, and the M-2 measure, are insufficient for making decisions on how to rank mutual funds or structure portfolios. This chapter proposes a new measure, called the M-3, that accounts for differences in (1) standard deviations between a portfolio and a benchmark and (2) the correlations of mutual fund portfolios and their benchmarks for an investor's relative-risk target. This technique facilitates port-folio construction to optimally achieve investors' objectives by combining the risk-free asset, the benchmark, and mutual funds. A form of three-fund separation, this para-digm provides optimal mixes of active and passive management based on the ability of fund managers rather than on individual biases about market inefficiency. This chapter provides support for the claim that leverage may not be bad if it is used to structure portfolios to achieve the highest risk-adjusted performance.

The mutual fund industry experienced spectacular asset growth between 1981 and 1998; assets under management grew from \$241 billion to \$5.5 trillion, and the number of funds rose from 665 to 7,314 (Investment Company Institute 1999). As the use of third parties to manage funds has increased, so has the need to measure the performance of these vendors relative not only to their benchmarks but also to their peers. A recent prize-winning article (Sharpe 1998) suggests that existing measures are inadequate and recommends three key pieces of information an investor needs to evaluate fund performance: the fund's likely future exposure to movements in major asset classes, the likely added return above a benchmark, and the fund's risk vis-à-vis the benchmark.

Reprinted with updates from the *Financial Analysts Journal* (September/October 2000):63–71.

The goal of every mutual fund investor is to identify the best performing fund(s) of the many available for any asset class and to ensure that in the future, this fund (or mixture of funds) outperforms the benchmark on a risk-adjusted basis. This chapter provides a methodology for measuring the risk-adjusted performance of a fund that permits effective ranking among peers. In addition, it demonstrates how to create optimal portfolios to appropriately adjust for risk. Finally, it demonstrates how other measures—the information ratio,[1] the Sharpe ratio,[2] and the M-2 measure (described later)—may not appropriately adjust for risk.

THE PROBLEM

This chapter assumes that investors know their desired asset allocation among different asset classes and need to find mutual funds to obtain the highest risk-adjusted return within the asset class.[3] Two fairly recent pieces of research have sought to answer the following related questions: (1) How does one compare the returns of a manager relative to a benchmark on a risk-adjusted basis (Modigliani and Modigliani 1997) with the performance of a manager relative to peers (Muralidhar and U 1997) and (2) how does one distinguish between managerial luck and skill when measured relative to a benchmark (Seigel and Ambarish 1996; Muralidhar 1999b) and how many years of experience are needed to demonstrate the skill of an asset manager with any degree of confidence?

In resolving the first question, Modigliani and Modigliani made an important contribution by showing that to compare a portfolio with a benchmark in terms of basis points of risk-adjusted performance, one must make sure the portfolio and the benchmark have the same standard deviation. Therefore, the authors proposed that the portfolio be leveraged or deleveraged using the risk-free asset: Define σ_i as the standard deviation of returns of portfolio i. If B is the benchmark and the actual portfolio is Portfolio 1, the leverage factor, d, is defined as

$$d = \frac{\sigma_B}{\sigma_1}. \qquad (29.1)$$

This transformation creates a new portfolio, the risk-adjusted portfolio (RAP), whose return, r(RAP), is equal to the leverage factor multiplied by the original return plus 1 minus the leverage factor multiplied by the risk-free rate. Now, define $r(\bullet)$ as the average annualized return of a portfolio. Then, if portfolio F is the riskless asset that has zero standard deviation and is uncorrelated with other portfolios, the risk-adjusted return is

$$r(\text{RAP}) = (d)r(\text{Actual portfolio}) + (1 - d)r(F). \qquad (29.2)$$

The correlation of the original portfolio with the benchmark will be identical to the correlation of the RAP with the benchmark because "leverage or deleverage" using the risk-free rate does not change the correlation characteristics. The correlation will normally be less than unity; if the correlation equals unity, a riskless arbitrage could result.

As shown in Figure 29.1, using this M-2 measure produces four regions:

- portfolios that outperform on both an absolute and a risk-adjusted basis (Region I),
- portfolios that outperform on an absolute basis but underperform on a risk-adjusted basis (Region II),
- portfolios that underperform on both an absolute and a risk-adjusted basis (Region III), and
- portfolios that underperform on an absolute basis but outperform on a risk-adjusted basis (Region IV).

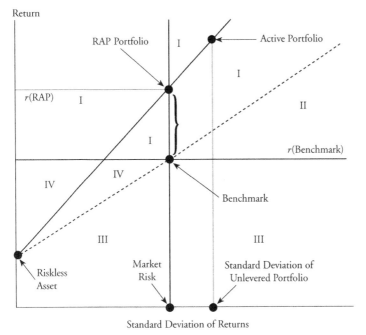

FIGURE 29.1   Risk Adjusting a Portfolio Using the M-2 Measure

Note: The area identified by the brace is the area of correlation risk.

   This M-2 adjustment allows comparison of "apples to apples" because returns from the benchmark and the RAP have the same volatility. In addition, when such an adjustment is made, peer rankings may be reversed.[4] The rankings are identical when the Sharpe ratio measure is used because the principle is similar. The M-2 measure is preferable, however, because it expresses risk-adjusted performance in terms of basis points of outperformance. The new method is also superior to the information ratio because using the IR can lead to incorrect decisions. For example, portfolios in Region IV have a negative IR but a risk-adjusted performance greater than that of the benchmark.

   The M-2 risk adjustment misses one important risk because it defines risk only in terms of variability of returns.[5] Mutual funds generate excess returns through the selection of securities and investment timing, which affects not only the portfolio's standard deviation of returns but also the correlation of the portfolio's returns with the benchmark returns. In effect, because the RAP adjusts the return and standard deviation to be comparable to the benchmark's, managers of RAPs can outperform only by being skillful in taking correlation risk. The M-2 measure does *not* capture correlation risk; hence, using it results in incorrectly ordering portfolios and/or incorrectly evaluating them relative to the benchmark.

   The correlation term is important because once a mutual fund is selected, the returns of the RAP vary around the benchmark performance in every future period, even if the mean returns and standard deviations produced by the fund managers, as well as the correlation of the fund's returns with the benchmark, can be accurately predicted.[6] These portfolios engender tracking error, *TE,* which is defined as the standard deviation of the excess returns over the benchmark returns: If $TE(\bullet)$ is the tracking error of a portfolio vis-à-vis the benchmark and ñ is the correlation between the two, then

$$TE(1) = \sqrt{\sigma_1^2 - 2\rho_{1,B}\sigma_1\sigma_B + \sigma_B^2}. \tag{29.3}$$

If under the RAP, the volatility of the portfolio is set equal to the benchmark, then tracking error, or risk relative to the benchmark of a RAP for Portfolio 1, RAP – 1, is defined as

$$TE(\text{RAP} - 1) = \sigma_B\sqrt{2(1 - \rho_{RAP,B})} = \sigma_B\sqrt{2(1 - \rho_{1,B})}. \tag{29.4}$$

The simple conclusion is that the lower the correlation, the higher the tracking error and hence the greater the future variability of returns of the RAP around the benchmark. Surely, from a pure risk point of view, some managers are skillful at taking correlation risk and some are not—just as some are and some are not skillful at taking risk defined as volatility of returns. The investor will not be indifferent between a low RAP and a high correlation and a slightly higher RAP with a substantially lower correlation. The reason is that the RAP measure gives undue preference to mutual funds with lower correlations because they are the most likely to have the highest RAP, and higher tracking error implies greater variability in returns around the benchmark. Therefore, the investor may reject a portfolio in favor of another purely on the basis of RAP, but if the correlations are different, the comparison is not fair.

LUCK VERSUS SKILL

To resolve the luck-versus-skill question, time and degree of confidence are critical factors as well as the returns and standard deviations of the portfolios and the benchmark and the degree of correlation between the two. The problem is that performance data can contain a lot of noise. And the more volatile the portfolio and the excess return series of a manager, the greater the noise and thus the time needed to resolve this question. Seigel and Ambarish demonstrated the minimum number of data points, or time horizon T, that should be large enough for the skill to emerge from the noise:

$$T > \frac{K^2[TE(1)]^2}{\left\{\left[r(1) - \dfrac{\sigma_1^2}{2}\right] - \left[r(B) - \dfrac{\sigma_B^2}{2}\right]\right\}^2}, \tag{29.5}$$

where K is the number of standard deviations for a given confidence level.

Equation 29.5 suggests that even a 300 basis point (bp) outperformance may require 175 years of data to make a claim with 84 percent confidence that a manager is skillful.[7] Muralidhar (1999b) and Muralidhar and U recognized that T is often given by performance history; hence, they solved instead for the degree of confidence, K.

One interesting result is that when the standard deviation of the portfolio is set equal to the standard deviation of the benchmark, as in the RAP, for a given standard deviation of the benchmark and degree of confidence, the time required becomes a simple function of the correlation parameter and the excess returns; all else being equal, the lower the correlation, the greater the time required.

Here is the conundrum that these propositions yield: From a purely theoretical perspective, the Modigliani adjustment suggests that funds with the highest risk-adjusted outperformance are likely to be those with low correlations (or high tracking errors); the skill-versus-luck measure says that higher tracking error will either lower confidence in the skill of the fund manager or extend the time period needed for evaluation. Therefore, investors should compare returns after adjusting for differences in volatility in returns *and* correlation (tracking error) so that their analyses will be conducted solely with risk-adjusted returns. The easy way to do this comparison is to have a target *TE* that will also define the acceptable time horizon for the investor.[8] Therefore, the correlation measure is an important part of portfolio selection.

CORRELATION-ADJUSTED PORTFOLIO AND THE M-3 MEASURE

The issue investors face is that, because the future is uncertain, they must rely on available data to make projections for the future. Assume that the historical distributions are preserved in the future.[9] The issue is that a three-dimensional problem—the comparisons of returns, standard deviations, and correlations—needs to be synthesized into a simple two-dimensional space of return and risk. In mean–variance space, the riskless asset is portfolio *F* [with returns $r(F)$] and it can be used to leverage or deleverage the desired mutual fund. In tracking-error space, the only portfolio with zero tracking error is the benchmark portfolio, which is perfectly correlated with itself. Therefore, combining active mutual funds with passive benchmarks can be used to alter the overall portfolio's standard deviation and correlation with the benchmark. To create measures of correlation-adjusted performance, the investor needs to invest in the mutual fund, the riskless asset, and the benchmark to ensure that (1) the volatility of this composite is equal to that of the benchmark and (2) the tracking error of this composite is equal to the target tracking error.[10] In the M-2 adjustment, the comparison is made in terms of basis points of outperformance by ensuring that all portfolios have the same variance as that of the benchmark. In three-dimensional space, the investor needs to consider basis points of risk-adjusted performance after ensuring that correlations with the benchmark are also equal; hence, I propose a new measure—the M-3.

THE M-3 MODEL

Assume that the investor is willing to tolerate a certain target annualized tracking error around the benchmark, *TE* (Target), of 300 bps.[11] The investor essentially wants to earn the highest risk-adjusted alpha for a given tracking error and variance of the portfolio. Now, define *a, b,* and $(1 - a - b)$ as the proportions invested in the mutual fund, the benchmark, and the riskless asset. Let CAP be the correlation-adjusted portfolio. The returns of a CAP are then

$$r(\text{CAP}) = (a)r(\text{Mutual fund}) + (b)r(B) + (1 - a - b)r(F). \qquad (29.6a)$$

Furthermore, the investor must hold the appropriate proportions of each to ensure that the final portfolio not only has the target tracking error but also the standard deviation of the benchmark. For a specific mutual fund—say Mutual Fund 1—with a risk-adjusted return $r(\text{CAP}-1)$, Equation 29.6a can be rewritten as

$$r(\text{CAP} - 1) = (a)r(1) + (1 - a - b)r(F) + (b)r(B), \qquad (29.6b)$$

where, to ensure complete risk adjustment, the coefficients of each portfolio represent the optimal weight of that specific portfolio.[12] In addition, the constraint on tracking error creates a unique target correlation between the CAP and the benchmark. This target correlation of the portfolio with that of the benchmark is taken from Equation 29.4:

$$\rho_{T,B} = 1 - \frac{TE(\text{Target})^2}{2\sigma_B^2}. \qquad (29.7)$$

The detailed solution for a, b, and $(1 - a - b)$, given the constraints on variance and tracking error, is provided in Appendix 29A. In summary, for Mutual Fund 1,

$$a = +\sqrt{\frac{\sigma_B^2(1 - \rho_{T,B}^2)}{\sigma_1^2(1 - \rho_{1,B}^2)}} = \frac{\sigma_B}{\sigma_1}\sqrt{\frac{(1 - \rho_{T,B}^2)}{(1 - \rho_{1,B}^2)}} \qquad (29.8)$$

and

$$b = \rho_{T,B} - (a)\frac{\sigma_1}{\sigma_B}\rho_{1,B}. \qquad (29.9)$$

Although b and $(1 - a - b)$ may be greater than or less than zero (negative coefficients being equivalent to shorting the futures contract relating to the benchmark and borrowing at the risk-free rate), a is constrained to being positive because mutual funds cannot be shorted.[13] Notice that if the correlations were not important, a would equal σ_B/σ_1, which is the RAP leverage measure, and b would be zero. Furthermore, allocations to the mutual fund under the M-3 measure will be larger than those under the M-2 only if $\sqrt{(1 - \rho_{T,B}^2)} / (1 - \rho_{1,B}^2) > 1.$

RANKING MUTUAL FUNDS

The discussion in this section revisits the Modigliani–Modigliani analysis. In their 1997 work, the authors compared seven mutual funds on the basis of quarterly data for 10 years ending June 1996. Unfortunately, the correlations of these funds with the S&P 500 Index (the benchmark) were not reported. In this section, I demonstrate how results can be reversed for certain spurious correlations.

Table 29.1 provides the basic data for all seven mutual funds: returns; standard deviations; spurious correlations; RAP leverage factors, d; $r(\text{RAP})$; tracking errors; values for a, b, and $(1 - a - b)$; and $r(\text{CAP})$. Because the lowest $TE(\text{Basic})$ is greater than 300 bps, let us assume the target tracking error is 300 bps, or 3 percent. This tracking error corresponds to a target correlation of 0.91.

Notice the following:

- Portfolios 6 and 7 underperformed on an unadjusted basis but outperformed on a RAP and a CAP basis.
- Portfolios 6 and 7 involved borrowing to generate $r(\text{RAP})$ (i.e., $d > 100$ percent), and Portfolios 5, 6, and 7 involved borrowing for $r(\text{CAP})$ (i.e., $1 - a - b < 0$).

TABLE 29.1   Evaluating the Performance of Modigliani–Modigliani Mutual Funds Using Data from Modigliani–Modigliani, 1997

Fund	Return	Standard Deviation	$\rho_{1,B}$	d	r(RAP)	TE(Basic)	a	b	$(1 - a - b)$	r(CAP)
F	5.50%	0.0%	0.00							
B	14.10	7.2	1.00	100%	14.10%	0.0%				
1	19.70	12.3	0.90	59	13.81	6.6	0.5473	0.0718	0.3810	13.89%
2	16.70	14.0	0.75	51	11.26	9.8	0.3169	0.4511	0.2320	12.93
3	16.00	11.3	0.90	64	12.19	5.8	0.5957	0.0718	0.3325	12.37
4	15.40	8.6	0.75	84	13.78	5.7	0.5158	0.4511	0.0331	14.49
5	13.00	7.5	0.80	96	12.70	4.7	0.6520	0.3698	−0.0219	13.57
6	12.00	4.7	0.55	153	15.45	3.6	0.7475	0.6448	−0.3923	15.90
7	11.30	4.0	0.75	180	15.94	5.0	1.1090	0.4511	−0.5601	15.81

TABLE 29.2   Ranks of Modigliani–Modigliani Funds Produced by Different Methods

Rank	Unadjusted	RAP or Sharpe	CAP
First	1	7	6
Second	2	6	7
Third	3	1	4
Fourth	4	4	1
Fifth	5	5	5
Sixth	6	3	2
Seventh	7	2	3

- Because $\rho_{T,B} > \rho_{1,B}$, allocations to the mutual funds would be significantly lower if the M-3 measure were used rather than the M-2, and for all portfolios, r(CAP) > r(RAP) with $\sigma_i = \sigma_B$.[14] This result suggests that the M-2 measure, by disregarding passive investment in the benchmark to alter portfolio characteristics, may be inadequate.

Table 29.2 provides the rankings of these portfolios when the different methods were used. The interesting conclusion is that for these specific randomly selected correlations, the CAP reverses the RAP ordering. This effect is to be expected for funds with extremely low volatility, because they are less likely than funds with high volatility to be correlated with the benchmark.

Because of the difficulty in obtaining the correlation data for the funds in the Modigliani–Modigliani study, I also obtained monthly data on 10 mutual funds and the S&P 500 for the period September 1989 to August 1999. These funds are ordered by their unadjusted returns in Table 29.3; the relevant details for the calculation of the RAP and the CAP portfolios [assuming a 3 percent target tracking error ($\rho_{T,B} = 0.93$)] are also provided. These funds engendered significant tracking error; therefore, the same calculations are performed for a 7 percent tracking error ($\rho_{T,B} = 0.86$), and the results are in Table 29.4. Table 29.5 provides a simple ranking of the funds by the different methods.

TABLE 29.3   Mutual Fund Performance: 3 Percent *TE*(Target), September 1989–August 1999

Fund	Return	Standard Deviation	ρ	d	r(RAP)	TE (Basic)	TE (RAP)	a	b	(1 − a − b)	r(CAP)	Excess over RAP
F	5.50%	0.00%	0.00									
B	17.09	13.27	1.00	1.00	17.09%							
1	33.24	27.57	0.71	0.48	18.85	20.45%	10.14%	0.15	0.75	0.10	18.43%	−0.42%
2	25.63	24.93	0.77	0.53	16.21	17.02	9.04	0.19	0.71	0.11	17.43	1.22
3	25.04	25.02	0.73	0.53	15.86	17.74	9.68	0.18	0.73	0.09	17.41	1.55
4	24.08	21.33	0.80	0.62	17.06	13.34	8.38	0.23	0.67	0.09	17.65	0.59
5	21.95	21.75	0.59	0.61	15.53	17.52	11.97	0.17	0.81	0.02	17.68	2.14
6	21.90	13.84	0.84	0.96	21.21	7.76	7.57	0.39	0.63	−0.02	19.26	−1.95
7	21.61	14.37	0.83	0.92	20.37	8.13	7.74	0.37	0.64	−0.01	18.91	−1.46
8	20.89	23.06	0.79	0.58	14.36	15.07	8.69	0.21	0.69	0.10	16.70	2.35
9	20.77	14.00	0.89	0.95	19.97	6.53	6.32	0.46	0.54	0.00	18.83	−1.14
10	20.56	14.79	0.92	0.90	19.00	5.74	5.24	0.52	0.44	0.04	18.43	−0.57

TABLE 29.4   Mutual Fund Performance: 7 Percent *TE*(Target), September 1989–August1999

Fund	Return	Standard Deviation	ρ	d	r(RAP)	TE (Basic)	TE (RAP)	a	b	(1 − a − b)	r(CAP)	Excess over RAP
F	5.50%	0.00%	0.00									
B	17.09	13.27	1.00	1.00	17.09%							
1	33.24	27.57	0.71	0.48	18.85	20.45%	10.14%	0.35	0.35	0.30	19.18%	0.33%
2	25.63	24.93	0.77	0.53	16.21	17.02	9.04	0.42	0.25	0.33	16.92	0.71
3	25.04	25.02	0.73	0.53	15.86	17.74	9.68	0.40	0.31	0.29	16.86	1.00
4	24.08	21.33	0.80	0.62	17.06	13.34	8.38	0.53	0.18	0.29	17.41	0.35
5	21.95	21.75	0.59	0.61	15.53	17.52	11.97	0.39	0.49	0.13	17.47	1.94
6	21.90	13.84	0.84	0.96	21.21	7.76	7.57	0.89	0.08	0.03	21.07	−0.14
7	21.61	14.37	0.83	0.92	20.37	8.13	7.74	0.84	0.10	0.05	20.27	−0.10
8	20.89	23.06	0.79	0.58	14.36	15.07	8.69	0.47	0.22	0.31	15.27	0.92
9	20.77	14.00	0.89	0.95	19.97	6.53	6.32	1.04	−0.12	0.07	20.09	0.12
10	20.56	14.79	0.92	0.90	19.00	5.74	5.24	1.18	−0.35	0.17	19.18	0.18

TABLE 29.5   Ranks of 10 Mutual Funds Produced by Different Methods

Rank	Unadjusted	RAP or Sharpe	CAP
First	1	6	6
Second	2	7	7
Third	3	9	9
Fourth	4	10	1
Fifth	5	1	10
Sixth	6	4	5
Seventh	7	2	4
Eighth	8	3	2
Ninth	9	5	3
Tenth	10	8	8

The following conclusions can be drawn from these three tables.

- The unadjusted returns for the mutual funds ranged from an annualized 20.56 percent to 33.24 percent, all of which are greater than the annualized return of the benchmark for the period.
- The standard deviations of all these mutual fund returns were greater than that of the benchmark. These portfolios would be Region I and Region II portfolios in Figure 29.1.
- The correlations of the mutual funds with the benchmark ranged from a low of 0.59 to a high of 0.92. For a target tracking error less than or equal to an annualized 5.2 percent, such correlations imply that $\rho_{T,B} > \rho_{1,B}$.
- Given the performance differences among the funds, the benchmark, and the risk-free asset, the unadjusted returns are higher than $r(\text{RAP})$ or $r(\text{CAP})$.
- RAP leverage is 50–100 percent (i.e., $d < 1$), and on a RAP basis, Funds 2, 3, 4, 5, and 8 underperformed the benchmark.
- The CAP ranking is independent of the target tracking error, but the allocations to the risk-free asset, the benchmark, and the mutual funds are affected. With a 3 percent tracking error target (Table 29.3), borrowing is limited (i.e., less than 2 percent for Funds 6 and 7).
- On a CAP basis, only Fund 8 underperformed the benchmark for a target tracking error of 3 percent (Table 29.3); Funds 2, 3, and 8 underperformed for a target tracking error of 7 percent (Table 29.4). Therefore, for a target tracking error of 3 percent, the allocation to *B*, or indexing, actually improves performance relative to the RAP. For higher tracking-error targets, shorting the benchmark and "leveraging" the mutual funds (e.g., Funds 9 and 10 in Table 29.4) would be optimal.
- Comparison of Tables 29.2 and 29.5 shows that on a CAP basis, the ranking changes from the RAP ranking, but the last columns in Tables 29.3 and 29.4 show no clear dominance between $r(\text{RAP})$ and $r(\text{CAP})$.

Although not reported here, the analysis of luck versus skill favored the CAP measure. This finding would be expected; all mutual fund results are comparable because the only difference among funds that can be used to determine the minimum amount of data to have a certain degree of confidence is $r(\text{CAP}) - r(B)$.

To conclude, as pointed out in Modigliani–Modigliani, the information ratio by itself is not a useful measure of outperformance or useful for ranking portfolios. It is valid only when leverage is not permitted. The M-2 measure is appropriate only for reviewing historical performance; it fails the test on a forward-looking basis or when adding the benchmark can improve the RAP. The M-3 measure provides an accurate measure of risk-adjusted performance by correcting for differences in standard deviations and for differences in correlations. It also ratifies the conclusions in Modigliani–Modigliani that leverage may not always be bad. Furthermore, neither the information ratio nor the Sharpe ratio can indicate how portfolios should be structured to achieve a target tracking error, whereas the M-3 measure provides such guidance.

EXTENSION TO MULTIPLE MUTUAL FUNDS

The average investor rarely chooses only one fund. Therefore, the real problem is to combine the risk-free asset, the benchmark, and multiple funds so as to provide the highest $r(\text{CAP})$. The difficulty here is that, although the correlation of each mutual fund with the benchmark is known, the correlation of a combination of mutual funds with the benchmark is uncertain because it depends on the weight of each fund in the composite. This information is needed to estimate the tracking error of the composite. Appendix 29B specifies the problem and provides the methodology for estimating the correlation of a composite portfolio with a benchmark when the variances and correlation of the individual portfolios with the benchmark are known. As shown in related research, since managers are less than perfectly correlated with each other, unattractive managers on a stand-alone basis may be chosen for their diversification properties and overall risk-adjusted performance can be increased over that of the highest yielding manager. It is also shown that the case for passive management is greatly diminished under this paradigm.[15]

ADJUSTING FOR TIME

When deciding between two competing external managers or investment strategies, investors are faced with a troubling issue: how to compare these options if the two histories are not identical. The industry has had a tendency to drop off excess data to compare the two options, but this discards useful information for the investment option with a longer history. For example, a manager with a lower risk-adjusted performance may have had experience through numerous market cycles as opposed to a manager with an attractive short track record and thereby limited experience. Surely, an investor would not be indifferent between the two options. Utilizing the M-3 measure in (29.6a) and the "Luck vs. Skill" measure in equation (29.5), related research highlights a new performance measure called SHARAD (Skill, History, and Risk-Adjusted Performance). This research demonstrates that new risk-adjusted performance measures make an important contribution to gleaning relevant data from complete histories and could reverse manager rankings based on the skill of a manager.[16]

CAVEATS

In the preceding analysis, the returns, volatilities, and correlations were estimated from a relatively long data series.[17] This technique assumes stability in the distributional characteristics of mutual funds on a forward-looking basis (based either on history or on some ability to predict the future). It will be interesting to see how such techniques perform on an *ex post* basis when they are applied on an *ex ante* basis. Because accurate forecasting of the distribution of either the benchmark or mutual fund returns is difficult, as is forecasting the correlation between the portfolio and the benchmark, techniques that account for uncertainty are needed. Developing such techniques could present problems; these correlations may not be stable over time; thus, a long history would be required before one would be comfortable with a fund. This could result in the exclusion of relatively new funds—something that the luck-or-skill measure would also advocate.

Another caveat is that mutual fund managers engage in two activities to generate excess returns—timing the allocation between risky assets and cash and selecting an optimal portfolio of securities. The M-3 technique does not decouple the two. Therefore, if the M-3 analysis suggests that the manager is not talented at timing, the investor will be undoing the timing decisions by restructuring the portfolio, which will, in turn, raise the cost of managing the portfolio.

Finally, although not explicitly stated, the assumption in M-3 measuring is that the mutual fund returns will be compared on an after-fee basis.

CONCLUSIONS

The Sharpe ratio, the information ratio, and the M-2 measure do not sufficiently assist investors in making the best decisions on ranking mutual funds or structuring portfolios. The critical point is that adjusting for differences in standard deviation between a portfolio and a benchmark is not enough; investors must also adjust for the fact that different correlations imply different relative risks and, possibly, insufficient returns for such risks.

The new M-3 measure is a more comprehensive alternative to these measures. It takes into consideration differences in correlation and the fact that investors have relative-risk targets. Correlations are important for two reasons—as a measure of covariance with other assets for optimal portfolio selection and as a forward-looking risk measure. By exploiting its role as a forward-looking measure of risk, the M-3 measure, which adjusts for standard deviations and correlations, provides rankings of portfolios that are different from the rankings provided by other techniques. The M-3 measure is also attractive as it allows for analyses of portfolios of managers on a risk-adjusted basis. Furthermore, M-3 facilitates portfolio construction to achieve investor objectives by combining an optimal fraction of the risk-free asset, the benchmark, and risky mutual funds. Finally, since rankings based on the M-3 are consistent with rankings based on confidence in skill, the M-3 risk-adjusted performance measure also provides the basis for newer performance measures that also adjust for the experience of the managers. Not only is this paradigm different and a form of three-fund separation, but it also gives investors optimal mixes of active and passive management based not on the investor's views on market efficiency but on the investor's target tracking error and market information.

APPENDIX 29A: DETERMINING a AND b

Consider $r(\text{CAP})$ for Mutual Fund 1,

$$r(\text{CAP} - 1) = (a)r(1) + (1 - a - b)r(F) + (b)r(B). \tag{29.10}$$

The investor wants to select a and b so that

$$\sigma^2_{CAP - 1} = \sigma^2_B \tag{29.11}$$

and

$$TE(\text{CAP}) = TE(\text{Target}), \tag{29.12}$$

which from Equation 29.4 and Equation 29.7 can be rewritten as

$$\rho_{CAP - 1,B} = \rho_{T,B.} \tag{29.13}$$

Expanding Equation 29.11 produces

$$\sigma^2_{CAP-1} = \sigma^2_B = a^2\sigma^2_1 + b^2\sigma^2_B + 2ab\sigma_1\sigma_B\rho_{1,B}. \tag{29.14}$$

Also, the covariance of $r(\text{CAP} - 1)$ and benchmark B is

$$\rho_{CAP - 1,B}\sigma_{CAP - 1}\sigma_B = a\sigma_1\sigma_B\rho_{1,B} + b\sigma^2_B. \tag{29.15}$$

From Equation 29.11 and Equation 29.13, Equation 29.15 can be rewritten as

$$\rho_{T,B}\sigma_B^2 = a\sigma_1\sigma_B\rho_{1,B} + b\sigma_B^2, \tag{29.16}$$

and solving Equation 29.16 produces[18]

$$b = \rho_{T,B} - (a)\frac{\sigma_1}{\sigma_B}\rho_{1,B}. \tag{29.17}$$

Substituting Equation 29.17 in Equation 29.14 results in

$$a^2\sigma_1^2 + \left[\rho_{T,B} - (a)\frac{\sigma_1}{\sigma_B}\rho_{1,B}\right]^2\sigma_B^2 + 2a\left[\rho_{T,B} - (a)\frac{\sigma_1}{\sigma_B}\rho_{1,B}\right]\sigma_1\sigma_B\rho_{1,B} = \sigma_B^2. \tag{29.18}$$

Thus,

$$a = +\sqrt{\frac{\sigma_B^2(1-\rho_{T,B}^2)}{\sigma_1^2(1-\rho_{1,B}^2)}}. \tag{29.19}$$

Assume that a is greater than zero (because one cannot short the mutual fund); however, b may be smaller than zero (if the benchmark is sold short through a futures contract, for example) and $(1 - a - b)$ may be smaller than zero, which would involve borrowing money to invest in the benchmark and/or the mutual fund.

APPENDIX 29B: MULTIPLE MUTUAL FUNDS

Define a portfolio X as the composite of many mutual funds. The problem for the investor is to maximize the following:

$$r(\text{CAP} - X) = (a)r(X) + (1 - a - b)r(F) + (b)r(B), \tag{29.20}$$

subject to a given target tracking error and variance, where

$$r(X) = \sum_i w_i r(i), \tag{29.21}$$

in which w_i is the weight of the ith mutual fund (and their sum is equal to unity) and $r(i)$ is the ith mutual fund's return.

Assume that two mutual funds are defined by standard deviations σ_1 and σ_2 and correlations with the benchmark $\rho_{1,B}$ and $\rho_{2,B}$. Assume that the correlation between these two mutual funds is $\rho_{1,2}$. Assume also that w_1 and w_2 are the respective weights of Mutual Fund 1 and Mutual Fund 2 in portfolio X. Then,

$$\sigma_X^2 = w_1^2\sigma_1^2 + 2w_1w_2\rho_{1,2}\sigma_1\sigma_2 + w_2^2\sigma_2^2 \tag{29.22}$$

and

$$TE(X) = \sigma_X^2 - 2\rho_{X,B}\sigma_X\sigma_B + \sigma_B^2$$
$$= w_1^2\sigma_1^2 + w_2^2\sigma_2^2 + \sigma_B^2$$
$$- 2w_1\rho_{1,B}\sigma_1\sigma_B - 2w_2\rho_{2,B}\sigma_2\sigma_B$$
$$+ 2w_1w_2\rho_{1,2}\sigma_1\sigma_2.$$

(29.23)

Using Equation 29.22 produces

$$TE(X) = \sigma_X^2\sigma_B^2 - 2(w_1\rho_{1,B}\sigma_1 + w_2\rho_{2,B}\sigma_2)\sigma_B.$$

(29.24)

Then, by combining Equation 29.23 and Equation 29.24,

$$\rho_{X,B}\sigma_X = \omega_1\rho_{1,B}\sigma_1 + \omega_2\rho_{2,B}\sigma_2,$$

(29.25)

or alternatively,

$$\rho_{X,B} = \frac{w_1\rho_{1,B}\sigma_1 + w_2\rho_{2,B}\sigma_2}{\sigma_X}.$$

(29.26)

The extension to multiple mutual funds is trivial:

$$\rho_{X,B} = \frac{\sum_i (w_i\rho_{i,B}\sigma_i)}{\sigma_X}.$$

(29.27)

Now, the investor solves for *a*, *b*, and ω_i. Furthermore, the allocation to each mutual fund equals $(a)\omega_i$.

NOTES

1. The ratio of excess returns over the benchmark to the standard deviation of the excess returns.
2. The ratio of excess returns over the risk-free rate to the standard deviation of the portfolio.
3. The methodology to establish the asset allocation for either participants in a defined-contribution plan or administrators of a defined-benefit plan is outlined in Krishnamurthi, Muralidhar, and Van der Wouden (1998).
4. A counterintuitive result of this approach is that if the RAP outperforms the benchmark (with the same standard deviation as the benchmark) and has a correlation less than 1, then if the benchmark was the market portfolio, a portfolio with a beta less than 1 is outperforming the benchmark. Roll (1992) posed such a problem but could not explain the outcome. Counterintuitive results are also derived when the benchmark has negative returns, as in the case of currencies (see Muralidhar 1999b). A purist in regard to the capital asset pricing model will conclude, however, that such a result occurs because the benchmark is not the market portfolio; hence, the results make no comment on market efficiency.

5. In a 1997 paper, Modigliani conducted the same analysis using betas rather than standard deviations.

6. For a different emphasis on correlation, see Muralidhar (1999a).

7. This result is from outperformance engendered through 13.2 percent of tracking error, where the benchmark standard deviation equals 15 percent, the actual standard deviation equals 25 percent, and the correlation between the two is 0.9. If the risk-free rate is 5 percent and the return on the benchmark is 9 percent, however, this portfolio has a r(RAP) of 9.2 percent, or a 20 bp M-2 outperformance.

8. Brennan (1993) considered an unconstrained version of this utility function. My experience with institutional investors has shown, however, that controlling tracking error is a critical objective for pension funds. The implications for asset pricing are considered in Muralidhar (1999a).

9. These assumptions are heroic to say the least. Some forecast must be made of expected outperformance, variability of performance to achieve this outperformance, and correlation between portfolio and benchmark returns. Historical performance is one way of making forecasts, but the M-3 measure is independent of the forecasting technique. In addition, one must believe that markets are inefficient to conduct such analyses.

10. A similar, although less sophisticated, approach to portfolio construction was provided in Muralidhar and Tsumagari (1999).

11. This measure is independent of the level of tracking error, so it is applicable for all tracking-error targets.

12. Equation 29.6b is a form of two-fund separation, except that because the benchmark is a *numeraire* and tracking error is a constraint, three-fund separation follows. See Muralidhar (1999a) and Brennan.

13. In some cases, shorting the benchmark would also be difficult; then, b will need to be constrained to being greater than or equal to zero.

14. This result need not always be true.

15. The extension to multiple portfolios will be developed in forthcoming research. Funds ranked poorly on a stand-alone basis may be attractive on a portfolio basis. See Muralidhar (1999c).

16. See Muralidhar (2002) and Muralidhar (2004). In developing the SHARAD, a very simple utility function is used such that SHARAD is the product of the r(CAP) and the measure of confidence in skill. Other utility functions may place greater emphasis on either the r(CAP) or the confidence in skill.

17. We essentially assumed that static allocations can be made to these mutual funds and benchmarks, whereas in reality, the expected returns, volatilities, and correlations are evolving daily. Therefore, annual rebalancing would seem to be appropriate.

18. This result can also be derived from Appendix 29B by using Equation 29.27.

REFERENCES

Brennan, M. 1993. "Agency and Asset Pricing." Working paper, Anderson Graduate School of Management, Los Angeles, CA (May).

Investment Company Institute. 1999. *Mutual Fund Fact Book*. Washington, DC.

Krishnamurthi, S., A. Muralidhar, and R.J.P. van der Wouden. 1998. "An Asset-Liability Analysis of Retirement Plans." Working paper, The World Bank Investment Management Department, Washington, DC (May).

Markowitz, H. 1959. *Portfolio Selection: Efficient Diversification of Investments.* New York: John Wiley & Sons.

Modigliani, F., and L. Modigliani. 1997. "Risk-Adjusted Performance." *Journal of Portfolio Management,* vol. 23, no. 2 (Winter):45–54.

Modigliani, L. 1997. "Don't Pick Your Managers by Their Alphas." Morgan Stanley Dean Witter U.S. Investment Research (June).

Muralidhar, A. 1999a. "The Death of the CAPM." Unpublished mimeo.

Muralidhar, A. 1999b. "Luck or Skill?" *Investments and Pensions Europe* (September):49–50.

Muralidhar, A. 2001. "Optimal Risk-Adjusted Portfolios with Multiple Managers." *Innovations in Pension Fund Management,* chapter 11, Stanford, CA: Stanford University Press.

Muralidhar, A. 2002. "Skill, History and Risk-Adjusted Performance." *Journal of Performance Measurement* (Fall):53–66.

Muralidhar, A. 2004. "History Matters." *Derivatives Use, Trading, and Regulation,* vol. 10, no. 2:131–148.

Muralidhar, A., and M. Tsumagari. 1999. "A Matter of Style." *Futures and OTC World* (April):8–12.

Muralidhar, A., and K.M. U. 1997. "Establishing a Peer Comparator Universe for an Institutional Investor." *Journal of Pension Plan Investing,* vol. 1, no. 4 (Spring):52–74.

Roll, R. 1992. "A Mean/Variance Analysis of Tracking Error." *Journal of Portfolio Management,* vol. 18, no. 4 (Summer):13–23.

Seigel, L., and R. Ambarish. 1996. "Time Is the Essence." *Risk,* vol. 9, no. 8 (August).

Sharpe, W. 1964. "Capital Asset Prices: A Theory of Market Equilibrium under Conditions of Risk." *Journal of Finance,* vol. 19, no. 3 (September): 425–442.

Sharpe, W. 1998. "Morningstar's Risk-Adjusted Ratings." *Financial Analysts Journal,* vol. 54, no. 4 (July/August):21–33.

The views expressed in this chapter are the author's personal views and are theoretical in nature; they do not represent the views of J.P. Morgan or any of its affiliates.

CHAPTER 30

INDEX CHANGES AND LOSSES TO INDEX FUND INVESTORS

Honghui Chen

Gregory Noronha, CFA

Vijay Singal, CFA

Because of arbitrage around the time of index changes, investors in funds linked to the S&P 500 Index and the Russell 2000 Index lose between $1.0 billion and $2.1 billion a year for the two indices combined. The losses can be higher if benchmarked assets are considered, the pre-reconstitution period is lengthened, or involuntary deletions are taken into account. The losses are an unexpected consequence of the evaluation of index fund managers on the basis of tracking error. Minimization of tracking error, coupled with the predictability and/or pre-announcement of index changes, creates the opportunity for a wealth transfer from index fund investors to arbitrageurs.

"When it comes to choosing your index, don't be too passive."
Oliver Ryan, "Does Your Fund's Index Measure Up?" *Fortune*, 9 August 2004

Modern portfolio theory suggests that holding a well-diversified portfolio of stocks dominates holding a few individual stocks. Because there are thousands of financial securities in the marketplace, however, transaction costs and the burden of monitoring these securities constrain investors from holding a well-diversified portfolio. The advent of the index mutual fund as an investment vehicle afforded investors the opportunity both to diversify at a

Reprinted from the *Financial Analysts Journal* (July/August 2006):31–47.

reasonable cost and to transfer the monitoring function to professional fund managers. Index fund investors expect index fund managers to merely construct a portfolio that mirrors the return and risk of the index at the lowest possible cost. No stock-picking or timing ability is expected. Given that objective, a simple way to constrain the fund manager's propensity to take risk (and, at the same time, evaluate the performance of the fund) is to measure the fund's tracking error—the absolute difference between each month's index return and the fund return summed over the time frame in question.[1] Normally, for large pension fund sponsors, a tracking error in excess of 0.10 percent a year is unacceptable.

Minimizing tracking error would be relatively simple if indexing firms did not periodically change the compositions of the indices.[2] Index changes become necessary when the status or ranking of a company changes because of such major corporate events as bankruptcy, liquidation, delisting, or merger. Index changes may also occur when a company ceases to meet the indexing firm's criteria for inclusion in the index. To help managers alter indexed portfolios concurrently with changes in the index, Standard & Poor's began in October 1989 to announce index changes before implementing them. Changes to the Frank Russell Company indices are also usually known in advance. The prevailing custom is that managers, to minimize tracking error, make changes to their indexed portfolios on the effective date of the change rather than on the day after announcement.

Although foreknowledge of changes may prepare fund managers, it also allows arbitrageurs to play a timing game. Realizing the constraints placed on indexers vis-à-vis tracking error, arbitrageurs buy the stocks to be added to the index when the addition is announced with the expectation of selling the stocks to indexers at a higher price on the effective date. Similarly, upon announcement, arbitrageurs sell short stocks that are to be deleted from the index and expect to repurchase them from indexers at a lower price, or they may buy the deleted stocks on the effective date and hold them for several weeks until prices recover. Several researchers have found evidence of arbitrage activity around changes to the S&P 500 Index (Beneish and Whaley 1996; Chen, Noronha, and Singal 2004; Blume and Edelen 2004). Similar evidence exists for the Russell 2000 Index (Madhavan 2003; Biktimirov, Cowan, and Jordan 2004).

Not surprisingly, arbitrage returns are realized at the expense of index fund investors. In current conditions, index fund investors may be unaware of the loss or consider it minor relative to the alternative of removing managerial constraints.

Any one of the major participants—indexing firms (e.g., Standard & Poor's, Frank Russell Company), index fund managers, or index fund investors themselves—could change the current system to mitigate losses. For example, among index fund managers, The Vanguard Group has been proactive in protecting its investors from indices that are amenable to arbitrage. In spring 2003, Vanguard changed its benchmark for small-cap index funds from the Russell 2000 to the MSCI US Small Cap 1750 Index, a less popular index and, therefore, one less subject to index arbitrage. Gus Sauter, former manager of Vanguard's index fund group and currently chief investment officer at Vanguard, confirmed to Hulbert (2004) that "one of the primary motivations [for the change] was to reduce the ability of traders to exploit those index changes at the expense of index funds."

INDEX CHANGES AND RETURN PATTERNS

We briefly describe the process of indexing and the pattern of returns around index changes for the S&P 500 and Russell 2000.

Indices and Index Changes

Although numerous market indices exist, we focus primarily on the S&P 500 and Russell 2000 for two main reasons. First, these indices are constructed in significantly different ways, which allows us to contrast the impact of changes on index fund investors. Second, the S&P 500 and the Russell 2000 are the most popular indices of U.S. equities with the highest amount of passively indexed assets relative to index value.[3] Thus, investors in these two indices are most affected by index changes.

Index changes may be involuntary or voluntary. Involuntary index changes occur when companies cease to exist publicly because of bankruptcies, liquidations, delistings, leveraged buyouts, or mergers. Voluntary changes occur when constituent companies do not meet the indexing firm's criteria for inclusion. For example, Standard & Poor's deletes a company when it ceases to represent its industry or the industry itself ceases to play a major role in the economy. Frank Russell Company deletes companies from its indices based on market capitalization, stock price, and float (number of shares available to the investing public).

To pick a candidate company for inclusion, Standard & Poor's uses four criteria, which are not always strictly enforced: The company must have sufficient liquidity; company ownership must not be concentrated in a single entity or few entities; the company must be profitable; and the company must be a leader in an important U.S. industry. To keep the number of companies in the S&P 500 constant, additions to the S&P 500 occur throughout the year, usually concurrent with deletions.

In contrast, changes to the Russell 2000 occur at fixed intervals. Since 1990, the index has been reconstituted once a year on the last day of June. Since 2004, additions/changes to the Russell indices have occurred at the close on the last Friday in June. As with the S&P indices, companies that cease to exist are deleted from the Russell indices. Unlike the S&P indices, companies are not contemporaneously added to the Russell indices to replace those deleted until the time of reconstitution. Thus, the number of companies in the Russell 2000 continues to fall from July 1 until the next reconstitution in June the following year.[4] Also, in contrast to companies in the S&P indices, companies that fail to continue to meet the inclusion criteria are not deleted from the Russell indices until the time of reconstitution in June.

On the one hand, although the S&P 500 companies may *not* be the largest companies in the economy or the industry, they are chosen on the basis of their importance to the economy or the industry. On the other hand, additions to the Russell 2000 are based entirely on the company's market cap, subject to the company fulfilling certain conditions related to float and stock price.

The differences in choosing replacements have an effect on index arbitrage. Because changes to the S&P 500 are somewhat subjective and largely unpredictable, arbitrageurs can trade on changes only between the date of announcement of the change and the effective date.[5] Changes to the Russell 2000 provide more attractive arbitrage opportunities for two reasons. First, changes to it are almost fully predictable because they are based primarily on market cap. Indeed, many large investors and financial institutions (e.g., Merrill Lynch, Morgan Stanley, Goldman Sachs) begin to predict changes as early as March. Second, the larger number of changes in small-cap indices (in the Russell 2000, 25 percent of the companies change each year) compared with large-cap indices (in the S&P 500, fewer than 5 percent of the companies turn over each year) gives arbitrageurs more opportunities for timing.

Changes and Returns to the S&P 500

Our initial sample of S&P 500 changes consisted of 303 additions and 303 deletions for the October 1989–December 2002 period. We imposed certain criteria for constructing the

TABLE 30.1   Abnormal Returns around Changes to S&P 500, October 1989–December 2002

Change	Sample Size	Effdate Size[a] (millions)	Anndate CAR	Anndate-to- Effdate CAR	Anndate to Effdate + 20 (CAR20)	Anndate to Effdate + 60 (CAR60)
Additions	263	$8,315	5.12%***	8.37%***	5.95%***	6.36%***
		6,086	0.94***	0.91***	0.69***	0.64***
Deletions	72	498	−8.48***	−14.10***	−4.66	1.52
		310	0.01***	0.04***	0.35**	0.46

Notes: "Effdate" is the effective or implementation date. "Anndate" is the announcement date. "Anndate CAR" is the CAR for the first trading day following the anndate. The "Anndate-to-Effdate CAR" is the CAR from the day following the announcement to the effective date. The first number in each return cell is the mean, and the second number is the proportion of returns that are positive.
[a] The first number is the mean; the second number is the median.
* Significant at the 10 percent level.
** Significant at the 5 percent level.
*** Significant at the 1 percent level.

final sample. First, to focus on a pure-index-change sample devoid of information effects, we excluded companies whose addition to or deletion from the index was caused by a significant contemporaneous event or anticipated likely major corporate event (restructuring, bankruptcy, merger, etc.) based on an inspection of news reports over three months prior to the announcement. Second, we excluded the involuntary deletion of foreign companies in July 2002 as a result of a change in Standard & Poor's policy.[6] The final additions sample consists of 263 companies, and the final deletions sample consists of 72 companies. Although these screens helped generate a clean sample, they may have caused the true impact of index changes on index fund investors to be understated. This and other biases in our estimates are discussed later.

Excess returns—abnormal and cumulative abnormal returns (CARs) measured relative to the S&P 500—for these companies are reported in Table 30.1. The mean abnormal announcement-day return for an addition was 5.12 percent, but the added stock continued to appreciate between announcement and the actual change, accumulating a total abnormal return of 8.37 percent.[7] The results show that there are two components of the abnormal returns from additions—namely, a permanent effect and a temporary effect. The permanent change in the price of added stocks, as reflected in the CAR from the announcement through 60 days after the effective date, provided most of the return (CAR60 = 6.36 percent). The temporary effect, measured by the difference between the CAR from the announcement date up to the effective date and the CAR 60 days after the effective date, was 2.01 percent.

For the deletions sample, the loss upon announcement was a significant 8.48 percent, with an additional loss of 5.62 percent between the announcement date and the effective date. The abnormal return, however, lacks permanence; the negative effect of deletions disappeared completely by 60 days after the effective date. Thus, for deletions, the permanent effect was insignificant but the temporary effect was a large and negative 15.62 percent (−14.10 percent + −1.52 percent).[8]

Changes to the Russell 2000

Because changes to the Russell 2000 can be anticipated, prior research has found an upward price trend in the March–June period for stocks actually added to the index. For example,

TABLE 30.2   Abnormal Returns around Changes to Russell 2000, 1990–2002

Change	Initial Sample	Final Sample	Company Size[a] (millions)	Return		
				June	July	August
Additions	7,259	7,244	$369	3.12%**	−1.70%***	−1.30%**
			253	3.96**	−1.13*	−0.70
Deletions	7,149	4,969	415	−1.19	2.70**	1.56
			90	−4.46***	2.31***	−0.24

Notes: See also the notes to Table 30.1. The first number in each return cell is the abnormal return for the value-weighted portfolio, and the second number is the abnormal return for the equally weighted portfolio.
[a]The first number is the mean; the second number is the median.
* Significant at the 10 percent level.
** Significant at the 5 percent level.
*** Significant at the 1 percent level.

Madhavan (2003) found that additions to the Russell 2000 experience a cumulative return of more than 20 percent in the March–June period, compared with a loss of about 9 percent for deletions during the same period. The companies added to the index lost approximately 7.7 percent in July, suggesting a temporary price pressure similar to that for S&P 500 changes. His sample covered the 1996–2002 period.

We report in Table 30.2 results for a similar process for the Russell 2000 around the time of reconstitution during the 1990–2002 period. Instead of considering the March–June period, however, we considered only the month of June because relying on prior-month returns would have introduced a look-ahead bias (given that changes are not known with certainty until the end of May).[9] Table 30.2 shows clearly that added companies gained in June, as price pressure built in anticipation of buying by index funds upon reconstitution, and then lost in July and August, as the added companies returned to price levels based on their fundamentals. In a symmetrical pattern, deleted companies lost in June and gained in July and August. In summary, the excess returns in June earned by the companies added to the Russell 2000 were surrendered in the two months following the actual addition. Deleted companies, in contrast, lost in June but appreciated by a total of 4.26 percent in July and August.

LOSSES TO INDEX FUND INVESTORS

The previous section made clear that price pressure can occur around the effective date of index additions and deletions. Because indexers and index funds are constrained by tracking-error minimization to trade on the effective date of the change, they must bear most of the losses from index changes. In this section, we estimate these losses. We first estimate the loss based on the temporary price pressure. We compute a more precise estimate later by implementing trading strategies based on price patterns observed in this chapter and other analyses of the effects of index changes.

Approximation

For illustration, we assume that fund managers who are unfettered by tracking-error constraints will trade in accord with the price patterns documented in the previous section. That is, managers will buy additions on the day after their announcement for the S&P 500 and at the end of May for the Russell 2000; they will sell deleted stocks 60 days after the effective date for S&P 500 companies and at the end of August for Russell 2000 companies. Our logic for using different addition and deletion dates for S&P 500 and Russell 2000 changes is based on Greenwood (2004). He found that arbitrageurs realize abnormal returns by waiting until several weeks after the event. In our scenario, fund managers can step into the shoes of the arbitrageurs to capture the abnormal returns by waiting a few weeks after the effective date.

S&P 500

Based on Table 30.1, an average of 20 additions and 6 deletions occurred every year from 1989 through 2002 for the S&P 500. The temporary price effect was 2.01 percent for additions and −15.62 percent for deletions. Because the size of an average company entering the index was $8.3 billion, according to Table 30.1, and the size of an average company dropped from the index was $0.5 billion, the estimated loss to investors is calculated as

$8.3 billion × 20 additions per year @ 2.01% temporary = $3.34 billion.
$0.5 billion × 6 deletions per year @ 15.62% temporary = $0.47 billion.
Combined $3.81 billion (loss) ÷ $10,000 billion (S&P 500 market cap)
   = 0.04% per year.

According to our preliminary calculations, then, the loss to index fund investors was about 4 bps a year. In dollar terms, based on the $1.1 trillion indexed to the S&P 500, the loss to index fund investors was $0.44 billion.

Russell 2000

For 1990–2002, the Russell 2000 experienced an average of 550 additions and 375 deletions per year at the time of reconstitution. The difference in returns was 3.12 percent for additions and 4.26 percent for deletions (calculated as the sum of July and August returns). Per Table 30.2, the average size of the companies added to the index was $369 million and the average size of the companies deleted from the index was $415 million. So, the loss is calculated as[10]

$369 million × 550 additions per year @ 3.12% = $6.33 billion.
$415 billion × 375 deletions per year @ 4.26% = $6.63 billion.
Combined $12.96 billion (loss) ÷ $ 1,000 billion (Russell 2000 market cap)
   = 1.30% per year.

Thus, 1.30 percent was lost by index funds indexed to the Russell 2000. In dollar terms, based on the $43 billion indexed to the Russell 2000, the annual loss to index fund investors was $0.56 billion. This estimate increases to $3.43 billion if all assets benchmarked to the Russell 2000 are considered instead of only passively indexed assets.

More Precise Estimate

To calculate the impact of index changes on an index fund, we constructed trading strategies that took advantage of the known patterns in price changes around the effective date. The effect of the trading strategy was separated from the normal operation of an index fund by overlaying the trading strategy on the index fund, which would normally make all changes on the effective date. For example, in the case of S&P 500 additions, the normal strategy is to buy the added stock on the effective date. Based on our evidence, however, the fund manager should buy the stock on the day after the announcement. Thus, the overlay trading, or incremental trading, strategy entails buying the added stocks at the close on the day after announcement and selling on the effective day. The incremental trading strategy combined with the normal operation gives the desired result.

The abnormal return from the trading strategy is weighted by the size of the added company on the effective date relative to the contemporaneous size of the index to arrive at an estimate of the net effect on the total fund return. Mathematically, the impact of the trading strategy is given by

$$\text{Net impact} = \sum_{i=1}^{C} \frac{FirmSize_i}{IndexSize} \times \left[\left(\prod_t (1 + R_{it}) \right) - \left(\prod_t (1 + R_{mt}) \right) \right], \qquad (30.1)$$

where

$\quad C \;\;=$ number of index changes
$\quad R_{it} \;=$ daily return for stock i on day t
$\quad R_{mt} =$ daily return for the relevant index on day t

S&P 500

For additions to the S&P 500, we constructed a trading strategy in which an added stock was bought on the day after the announcement and sold on the effective day.[11] Essentially, the strategies we used are those that index funds would reasonably pursue in the absence of the focus on tracking-error minimization. We restricted our analysis to added stocks with at least one day between the announcement and effective dates. Results for all added companies by year and for the entire 1989–2002 period are reported in the left half of Table 30.3. The average net impact of added companies in 1989–2002 was 0.101 percent.

Blume and Edelen (2004) proposed an early trading strategy for indexers. They found that if indexers bought on the day after announcement (rather than on the effective day), they would add 19.2 bps per year with no added risk—but with a substantial increase in tracking error. Our numbers are lower for at least two reasons. First, their sample period was 1995 through 2002, a period in which the price impact was larger than in our period. For that same period, our estimate is 15.2 bps. Second, their trading strategy involved trading at the open on the day after announcement, whereas we prescribed trading at the close on the day after announcement.

We followed a different strategy for deleted companies from the one for added companies. Because we had documented a strong negative temporary effect for deleted stocks—an effect that completely reversed three months later (see Table 30.1)—the better overlay strategy for an S&P 500 fund to follow would be to buy at the close of the effective date and sell 60 trading days later when prices had recovered, which is equivalent to the index fund selling the deleted stocks 60 days after deletion instead of on the effective date. We report in the right half of Table 30.3 average risk-adjusted compounded returns and the average relative size of deleted companies on the effective date. Over the 1989–2002 period, the average net impact of deleted companies was 0.022 percent.

Our results imply that a fund indexed to the S&P 500 that bought added stocks following announcement and sold deleted stocks 60 days after the effective date of deletion could earn an additional return of approximately 0.12 percent, or 12 bps, a year. In dollar terms, and given the sizes of the companies, that number translates to $1.32 billion annually.

TABLE 30.3 Impact of S&P 500 Changes, 1989–2002

Period	Additions					Deletions				
	Adds. per Table 30.1	No. of Stocks Used	Abnormal Change in Value from Anndate to Effdate	Size Relative to S&P 500	Net Impact on Index Fund Return	Deles. per Table 30.1	No. of Stocks Used	Abnormal Change in Value from Effdate to Effdate + 60	Size Relative to S&P 500	Net Impact on Index Fund Return
10/89–12/90	14	12	−2.027%	0.051%	−0.012%	1	1	48.017%***	0.000%	0.000%
1991	9	4	7.283	0.157	0.046	1	1	−25.633***	0.001	0.000
1992	6	5	1.436	0.087	0.006	4	4	21.099**	0.001	0.001
1993	6	4	3.028	0.236	0.029	2	2	36.234	0.004	0.004
1994	10	9	3.951	0.250	0.089	6	6	−4.923**	0.048	−0.012
1995	21	19	4.088**	0.128	0.099	9	9	4.934	0.005	0.002
1996	18	16	0.768	0.104	0.013	9	9	3.704	0.007	0.002
1997	23	17	0.250	0.082	0.003	3	3	21.038	0.007	0.005
1998	33	27	4.318*	0.143	0.167	3	3	5.749	0.007	0.001
1999	35	30	21.753***	0.091	0.591	5	5	−8.200	0.007	−0.003
2000	45	39	6.015**	0.116	0.272	19	19	18.357	0.004	0.014
2001	23	18	1.073	0.067	0.013	6	6	15.086	0.008	0.007
2002	20	13	1.273	0.153	0.025	4	4	6.940	0.003	0.001
10/89–12/02	263	213			0.101%**	72	72			0.022%

Notes: Relative size is the ratio of the added stock's market cap on the effective date to the S&P 500 total market cap on the effective date. Net impact on S&P 500 returns was found by first multiplying the abnormal change in value by relative size and then summing across all additions during the year. Reported changes in value from anndate to effdate (raw and adjusted) were weighted by relative size.

* Significant at the 10 percent level.
** Significant at the 5 percent level.
*** Significant at the 1 percent level.

676

Russell 2000

For additions to the Russell 2000, the better strategy is to buy the added stocks at the end of May rather than the end of June. Thus, the incremental strategy consists of buying all added stocks on the last trading day in May and selling them on the last trading day in June. We calculated the net impact in accordance with Equation 30.1.[12] For deletions, the better course is to sell those stocks at the end of August rather than at the end of June. Thus, the incremental strategy consists of buying the deleted stocks at the end of June and selling them at the end of August. The abnormal returns and impacts for this portfolio were computed in a manner similar to that for additions. We report the results in Table 30.4.

Table 30.4 shows that the arithmetic mean abnormal return per year from following both strategies simultaneously was approximately 1.84 percent (0.983 percent for additions and 0.854 percent for deletions). Thus, if a fund indexed to the Russell 2000 had bought additions on 1 June and sold deletions on 31 August of a given year during the 1990–2002 period, it could have earned an abnormal return of about $0.8 billion annually. This estimate increases to $4.86 billion if all assets benchmarked to the Russell 2000 are considered instead of only passively indexed assets.

Biases in Estimation

In estimating losses to index investors from index changes, although we used conservative estimates and conservative methods, our loss estimates are indirect and, therefore, likely to be biased. In this section, we explore the effects on our estimates of two underestimation biases and two overestimation biases.

Underestimation Bias: Price Drift during April and May

Previous work has indicated that stocks likely to be added to and dropped from the Russell 2000 experience price drift in April, May, and June. But our analysis considered only the month of June. Not including the price drift during the earlier months biases the loss estimate downward.

We chose not to include April and May in our calculations because of the uncertainty associated with the changes and the cost of implementing the dynamic trading strategy. Because the final list of changes is based on market capitalizations on the last trading day of May, any earlier time used for ranking will generate an inaccurate list of changes. Suppose a list of additions is generated at the end of March based on market cap.[13] Assume that long positions are taken accordingly. Because stock prices are volatile, rankings on later days could change, generating a different list of probable additions. So, some long positions would need to be closed and new ones created on a continuing basis until the end of May.

In addition to the trading costs of this dynamic trading strategy, a problem is that a potential addition will cease to be an addition only when the stock price falls (relative to other stocks). The implication is that the trading strategy will also incur a loss on the position on top of the additional costs. Losses could be large and could add volatility to the strategy.

The costs associated with a dynamic trading strategy can be controlled by not choosing stocks too close to the breakpoints, but beginning the strategy in March or April would introduce significant uncertainty and ad hoc decision making.

Nevertheless, there are potential gains from starting early. So, not including earlier months probably leads to an underestimate of losses.

TABLE 30.4 Impact of Russell 2000 Changes, 1990–2002

Year	Additions					Deletions			
	30 June Index Market Cap (billions)	Sample Size	June Abnormal Return	Adds. on 30 June Market Cap (billions)	Net Impact on Index Fund Return	Sample Size	July–August Abnormal Return	Deles. End of June Market Cap (billions)	Net Impact on Index Fund Return
1990	$199.16	410	2.717%	$36.95	0.504%	267	3.944%	$39.19	0.776%
1991	218.32	524	3.668	62.20	1.045	419	7.025	38.96	1.254
1992	293.02	575	1.896	89.98	0.582	475	1.756	44.59	0.267
1993	408.32	496	−0.558	110.36	−0.151	406	3.595	71.49	0.629
1994	490.74	608	1.211	151.76	0.375	483	4.126	80.71	0.679
1995	598.51	464	3.202	131.13	0.701	306	4.798	94.19	0.755
1996	807.37	559	0.371	233.99	0.108	385	−0.484	147.91	−0.089
1997	982.89	572	5.659	262.52	1.511	387	4.639	162.45	0.767
1998	1,154.80	586	1.932	314.01	0.525	318	−0.369	230.00	−0.073
1999	1,101.89	567	7.386	311.88	2.090	335	5.329	276.28	1.336
2000	1,269.61	740	13.860	521.07	5.688	414	1.372	366.53	0.396
2001	1,083.29	659	−0.792	274.50	−0.201	410	5.396	291.66	1.453
2002	921.30	484	0.002	171.80	0.000	356	12.354	220.32	2.954
1990–2002					0.983%**				0.854%***

Notes: The abnormal return times the portfolio's market cap on the effective date divided by the Russell 2000 market cap on the effective date is the impact on the index fund's return, where effective date is the last trading day in June. The mean and standard deviation of time-series averages of annual abnormal returns were used for assessing statistical significance.
*Significant at the 10 percent level.
**Significant at the 5 percent level.
***Significant at the 1 percent level.

678

Underestimation Bias: Involuntary Deletions

We sought a pure sample (one devoid of other effects) of index changes so that the loss estimates would be credible. In the process of creating a pure sample, however, many sources of potential losses to index investors may not have been explicitly considered.

One factor we did not consider in our calculations was the effect of involuntary deletions—such as bankruptcies, mergers, liquidations, and spin-offs. Approximately 75 percent of all deletions from the S&P 500 and 25 percent of all deletions from the Russell 2000 are involuntary. Because such deletions typically are accompanied by important company-specific news, we chose to exclude them from our sample to isolate the index effect from the information effect.

Although the actual deletion of companies as a result of major corporate events is involuntary, the timing of deletion from the index is voluntary. Therefore, fund managers can delete a company from the portfolio without waiting for the corporate event (such as a merger) to become effective.[14] As a matter of fact, involuntary deletions are more transparent than voluntary deletions, and they provide additional opportunities for arbitrageurs and fund managers to beat the index. Nonetheless, in many cases, it is difficult to estimate the impact of companies that cease to trade concurrently with the effective date of deletion.

Companies close to bankruptcy provide some noisy information about potential losses because they continue to trade even after the effective date. Pan Am is an example. The announcement of Pan Am's deletion was 8 January 1991 after the close of markets, with 9 January 1991 as the effective date. Its closing price on 8 January 1991 was $0.75. It closed at $0.375 the next day (the effective day) and recovered to close at $0.75 on 10 January 1991. Over the next 60 trading days, its lowest closing price was $0.625, 67 percent above the effective-day closing price. Another example is Carter Hawley Hale Stores. The deletion announcement was made on 11 February 1991, with 12 February 1991 as the effective date. The stock closed at $1.625 on 11 February 1991, fell to $1.125 on the effective date, and recovered to close at $1.375 the following day. Over the next 60 trading days, its lowest closing price was $1.625, 44 percent above the effective-day price. These examples illustrate the potential underestimation of the loss to index fund investors because deletions with confounding events were not included in our sample.

The deletion of foreign companies in July 2002 provides another illustration of companies that continue to trade after deletion. These companies were explicitly excluded from our analysis because the deletions were a one-time event unlikely to be repeated in the future. According to one estimate, however, purchasing the added companies and selling the deleted companies at the open on the day after announcement could have added 0.58 percentage points to an index fund's return relative to the S&P 500 return for 2002.[15]

In addition to constituting a large portion of the changes to the S&P 500, the companies deleted involuntarily are also much larger in size than the companies voluntarily deleted from the index. Thus, exclusion of involuntary deletions from our analysis, although necessary and warranted, introduced a downward bias in the loss estimate.

Overestimation Bias: Mismatched Trades, Transaction Costs, and Volatility

The trading strategies we based on S&P 500 changes and Russell 2000 changes call for buying added companies before the effective date and selling deleted companies after the effective date. Because these trades take place at different times, several issues arise.

The first concern relates to volatility. Do the different positions result in higher risk for the portfolio? As tabulated later, we found the monthly standard deviation of the index fund portfolio with the recommended strategy to be almost the same as that of the S&P 500. The monthly standard deviation of the Russell 2000 fund was marginally higher, 5.363 percent instead of 5.318 percent. These results show no significant increase in risk.[16]

The second concern relates to trading costs. The trading strategies we propose do not actually result in additional trading costs. The added stock is bought only once, and the deleted stock is sold only once, but the trades occur at different times. Therefore, we have no reason to believe that the trading costs are significantly different from those of ordinary indexing.

The third concern relates to availability of investment money. The added companies have to be bought before deleted companies are sold, which requires an additional outlay of funds. One way to circumvent the funding constraint would be to sell short the appropriate index in the cash market—perhaps with exchange-traded funds—and use the short-sale proceeds to buy the added stocks.[17] In addition to easing the funding constraint, short selling might also help align the portfolio with the index, which would reduce overall risk and tracking error.

Another criticism of reliance on mismatched buys and sells is that the design of the strategy is based on limited evidence, especially in the case of the Russell 2000. Greenwood (2004) provided corroborating evidence based on changes in the Nikkei 225, however, that waiting for a few weeks can generate excess returns.

Overestimation Bias: Comparison of S&P 500 and Russell 2000

Although a comparison of these two popular indices is valuable in highlighting the effect of index changes, it gives the impression that, from an investor standpoint, the S&P indices are superior. Such a conclusion is not necessarily valid, however, because the S&P 500 is a large-cap index, whereas the Russell 2000 is a small-cap index. A natural bias arises from the fewer changes that are necessary for a large-cap index and the smaller impact of each index change.

In the case of a small-cap index, a company may be deleted because it becomes too big *or* too small. In contrast, most voluntary deletions from a large-cap index occur only because a company becomes too small. The annual number of changes for the S&P 500 is under 5 percent, whereas the number of changes for the S&P 600 is, at 13 percent, approximately three times as many. Because each index change is a candidate for index arbitrage, fewer changes mean smaller losses for index investors.

The second source of bias is the impact of deletions on the index. Because deletions from a large-cap index occur only from decreased company size, the size of the company being changed is small relative to the index. From Table 30.1 and the discussion, one can see that the relative size of deletions was approximately 0.01 percent of the S&P 500 from October 1989 through December 2002. Deletions from a small-cap index occur for increased and decreased company size, which generally results in a relatively large average company size for voluntary deletions. For the Russell 2000, the average size of a deleted company is about 0.05 percent of index value. Not only is the relative size of deletions five times larger in small-cap indices, but the number of voluntary deletions for a small-cap index as a percentage of total deletions is also larger (about 75 percent) than the number for a large-cap index (25 percent). Note that involuntary deletions are not included in this consideration because of confounding events. Finally, the price impact of large-cap index changes may be smaller because the stocks that belong to a large-cap index have greater liquidity than the stocks in a small-cap index.

Although a comparison between two small-cap indices or two large-cap indices might be preferable, neither the S&P 500 nor the Russell 2000 has a similar-sized index with a comparable level of indexing. Thus, a comparison of the S&P 500 with the Russell 2000 is appropriate and highlights the effects of differences in index construction and index changes. A superficial comparison of indices with similar capitalizations is discussed in the next section.

CORROBORATING EVIDENCE

Our results thus far demonstrate that index fund investors lose when index funds trade on the effective date of index reconstitution, with losses to Russell 2000 investors somewhat greater in percentage terms than those to S&P 500 investors. Another valid question is whether the way in which indices are reconstituted matters. To answer this question, we compared large-cap and small-cap indices from three major indexing firms: Standard & Poor's, Frank Russell Company, and Morgan Stanley Capital International. Although the number of stocks, market cap, and other characteristics of these indices differ, we believe that a comparison is reasonable because all large-cap indices (and small-cap indices) compete for the same customers.

In Table 30.5, we report the main characteristics, annual returns, and associated risks of these indices. The risk and return analysis begins in 1995 because it is the earliest year for which total return data for all indices are available. Panel B shows that the large-cap indices exhibited similar average returns and risk for the 1995–2002 period. The small-cap indices tell a different story. The Russell 2000 earned a lower return than the S&P 600 in all years except 1999 and underperformed the MSCI 1750 in all years. Overall, the average annual return to the Russell 2000 was more than 3 percentage points less than the returns to the other two small-cap indices. At the same time, the risk of the Russell 2000 was not less than that of either the MSCI 1750 or the S&P 600.

In Panel C of Table 30.5, we indicate whether returns were significantly different by computing the fraction of months when the index returns of the S&P and MSCI were higher than the corresponding Russell returns. That is, S&P 500 and MSCI 300 returns were compared with the Russell 1000 return, and the S&P 600 and MSCI 1750 returns were compared with the Russell 2000 return. For the large-cap indices, we found that the fraction of months for which the S&P 500 return was larger than the Russell 1000 return was not significantly different from 0.50.

Comparison of the small-cap indices is more interesting. The S&P 600 had a higher return than the Russell 2000 for 62.5 percent of the months, which is significantly greater than 50 percent. To determine whether the excess return is related to the Russell reconstitution, we examined whether the returns were different around the reconstitution date. Excluding the months from May to August, we found that the S&P 600 outperformed the Russell 2000 only 51.6 percent of the time. It had a higher return than the Russell 2000, however, for 84.4 percent of the time from May to August and 93.8 percent of the time during June and July, both of which are significantly higher than 50 percent.

On the one hand, the differences in returns for the Russell 2000 and S&P 600 indices and the concentration of those differences in the months around reconstitution are consistent with the loss introduced by the arbitrage activity that occurs with predictable index changes in the Russell 2000 and the success of the Russell 2000 as evidenced by the high level of indexing to it. On the other hand, the Russell 1000 does not severely underperform its competing large-cap indices, even with predictable and numerous changes, because the amount of indexing to it is low. Moreover, the subjective nature of index changes in the S&P indices limits the losses from arbitrage for those who index to them, with the result that the popular S&P 500 does not earn returns that are significantly different from other large-cap indices.

TABLE 30.5 Risk and Return of Various Indices

	S&P 500 (large cap)	Russell 1000 (large cap)	MSCI 300 (large cap)	S&P 600 (small cap)	Russell 2000 (small cap)	MSCI 1750 (small cap)
A. *Index characteristics*						
Basis for change	Index committee, unpredictable	Objective and predictable	Objective and predictable	Index committee, unpredictable	Objective and predictable	Objective and predictable
Frequency of change	Anytime, frequent	Once a year	Two times a year	Anytime, frequent	Once a year	Two times a year
Median market cap ($ millions)	9,108	3,789	NA	629	469	NA
Highest market cap ($ millions)	311,066	311,066	NA	4,865	2,064	NA
Lowest market cap ($ millions)	902	489	NA	64	42	NA
Number of changes (%)	4.6 (1977–2002)	15.4 (1983–2000)	NA	12.9 (1995–2002)	27.9 (1990–2002)	21.5 (1999–2002)
B. *Returns and risk by year*						
1995						
Return	37.58	37.77	38.56	29.93	28.45	31.48
Std. dev.	7.83	7.84	7.87	9.48	8.20	8.43
1996						
Return	22.95	22.45	23.18	21.32	16.48	19.02
Std. dev.	11.82	11.62	12.05	10.99	10.67	10.95
1997						
Return	33.36	32.85	34.60	25.58	22.36	24.34
Std. dev.	18.16	17.16	18.16	13.84	12.99	13.26
1998						
Return	28.58	27.02	33.40	–1.30	–2.55	0.58
Std. dev.	20.29	19.96	20.42	21.12	20.15	20.58
1999						
Return	21.04	20.91	22.95	12.41	21.26	21.94
Std. dev.	18.08	17.67	18.67	13.33	14.23	13.88

	(1)	(2)	(3)	(4)	(5)	(6)
2000						
Return	−9.12	−7.79	−13.86	11.80	−3.02	8.67
Std. dev.	22.22	23.16	24.45	26.48	29.89	25.29
2001						
Return	−11.92	−12.45	−13.94	6.53	2.49	3.21
Std. dev.	21.38	21.85	22.59	22.65	23.17	22.66
2002						
Return	−22.06	−21.65	−22.86	−13.50	−20.48	−18.37
Std. dev.	26.04	25.75	26.28	24.67	25.15	23.85
Average for period						
Return	12.55	12.39	12.75	11.60	8.12	11.36
Std. dev.	18.23	18.13	18.81	17.82	18.06	17.36
C. Difference in returns: Fraction of months when the index return was higher than the Russell return (1995–2002)						
All months	0.542	0.542	0.542	0.542	0.625**	0.604*
May–August	0.531	0.563	0.563	0.563	0.844***	0.656
Months other than May–August	0.547	0.531	0.531	0.531	0.516	0.578
June and July	0.563	0.688	0.688	0.688	0.938***	0.750*
Months other than June and July	0.538	0.513	0.513	0.513	0.563	0.575

NA = not available.

Notes: Market caps are as of the end of December 2003. Returns are annual. Daily total return data were obtained from the indexing firms. Standard deviation was calculated for each calendar year based on daily returns.

*Significant at the 10 percent level.

**Significant at the 5 percent level.

***Significant at the 1 percent level.

Sources: Information about market caps for the Russell indices is from Quinn (2004) and for the S&P indices, from Standard & Poor's. Information about the number of changes is from our calculation for the S&P 500; from Gardner, Kondra, and Pritamani (2001) for the Russell 1000; from Table 30.2 for the Russell 2000; from Standard & Poor's for the S&P 600; and from Morgan Stanley Capital International for the MSCI 1750.

The losses from index, particularly small-cap index, changes are well known to mutual fund managers. For example, Vanguard switched to the MSCI 1750 in the spring of 2003 to attenuate losses because of timing by arbitrageurs.

We can conclude from the discussions so far that index fund investors are better served when indexing firms introduce uncertainty into the process of index changes and when indices are not popular. Russell 2000 investors suffer significantly higher losses primarily because of the objective criteria used for its construction. In addition, a reduction in the turnover associated with index changes and possibly a reduction in the length of the pre-announcement period would further limit the ability of arbitrageurs to game index funds.[18]

LIMITATIONS OF TRACKING ERROR

The evidence in the previous section makes it quite clear that index fund investors lose because of the activities of arbitrageurs. These results are consistent with those of Frino, Gallagher, and Oetomo (2005), who found that passive Australian funds would benefit from using less-rigid rebalancing and investment strategies. In this section, we focus on the benefits and costs of the tracking-error constraint.

Tracking Error as a Low-Cost Agency Solution

Given that arbitrageurs can time the index fund managers' moves, why do index fund managers focus on tracking-error minimization and why do investors instruct fund managers to minimize tracking error? A major justification has its roots in the principal–agent problem. When investors delegate investment decision making to fund managers, they accept that these managers' propensity to assume risk to enhance performance may diverge from their own. One way to constrain managerial risk taking is to bind fund managers to an objective of minimizing tracking error against a benchmark. Operationally, a close bind translates to a full index replication strategy, because sampling or enhanced indexing, the other common indexing strategy, is likely to increase tracking error. Thus, tracking error appears to be a simple but effective way of reducing investor–manager conflicts and evaluating performance.

Inadequacy of Tracking-Error Focus

Theoretical arguments suggest that a policy of focusing on tracking error may be suboptimal. Roll (1992) demonstrated that optimizing portfolios with respect to tracking error and its variance is not the same as optimization in a Markowitz mean–variance framework and results in inefficient portfolios. Clarke, Krase, and Statman (1994) went even further to argue that not only is the tracking-error framework of evaluation not grounded in Markowitz mean–variance theory, it is also part of a mental accounting framework related to aversion to regret.

Pope and Yadav (1994) showed that, from the standpoint of usefulness in evaluations, tracking error is subject to estimation bias from negative serial correlation whenever the investment horizon is longer than the data frequency interval used in estimation—which is, presumably, always the case for index fund investors. More recently, Jorion (2003) demonstrated that constraining managers with tracking-error volatility results in their ignoring total portfolio risk and holding inefficient portfolios. Therefore, despite its potential to mitigate an agency problem between investors and index fund managers, the use of tracking-error minimization alone as an evaluative tool may not ultimately be in the best interests of index fund investors.

Nevertheless, the use of tracking error continues to be popular. Index fund managers may be aware of the unattractiveness of prices on the effective date, but Chen, Noronha, and Singal (2004) reported that the trading volume on the effective date is several times the normal daily volume.[19] This finding suggests that index fund managers continue to change their portfolios on the effective date, with a view to minimizing tracking error.

Indeed, if index fund managers did not change their portfolios on the effective date, their tracking errors would be much higher. In Table 30.6, we report estimates of tracking error and standard deviation of tracking error for index funds that followed the strategy we suggested in Tables 30.3 and 30.4. We also compared standard deviations of returns for the index funds with those of the S&P 500 and the Russell 2000.

Not surprisingly, with the implementation of these strategies, the absolute tracking error was 0.15 percent for a fund indexed to the S&P 500 and much higher, at 2.26 percent, for a fund indexed to the Russell 2000. But the higher tracking error was accompanied by additional returns of, respectively, 0.14 percent and 1.87 percent. Equally important is that the standard deviation of the S&P 500 was almost the same as that for the index fund pursuing the strategy we suggest. The yearly results (not reported here) are consistent with the overall average results in Table 30.6, which suggests that managers following the strategies we advocate would not be assuming excessive risk in any given year. The evidence indicates that following the strategies we advocate would have resulted in generally positive alpha without altering risk.

Although principals (index fund investors) would probably welcome higher returns without significantly higher fund volatility, the additional return cannot be earned without increasing tracking error. Thus, the tracking-error focus, while restricting the risk-taking propensities of fund managers, also limits their ability to provide benefit for their principals. Another measure of index fund performance is required. Until a new measure becomes available, however, the prudent approach would be to eschew the use of tracking-error minimization as the only evaluative tool. Positive deviations from the benchmark (positive alpha) should be permitted when not accompanied by increased risk for the fund portfolio, or use of the Sharpe ratio should be extended to index funds. This recommendation is consistent with that of Roll (1992).

TABLE 30.6   Estimated Volatility and Excess Returns for Indexed Funds

Index	Total Index Return	Total Additional Return	Absolute Tracking Error	Std. Dev. of Tracking Error	Std. Dev. of Index	Std. Dev. of Index Fund
S&P 500[a]	11.296%	0.141%***	0.147%	0.025%	4.038%	4.040%
Russell 2000[b]	9.770	1.869***	2.259	0.426	5.318	5.363

Notes: For each day, the index fund return was enhanced by the abnormal returns earned by qualified additions and deletions in Tables 30.3 and 30.4. These daily returns were compounded to the end of the month (year) to obtain the return on the index fund for the month (year). The difference between the annual index fund return and the annual index total return is the "Total Additional Return." The tracking error is the sum of the absolute differences between the monthly index return and the monthly index fund return.
[a]Average of 13.25 years, October 1989–December 2002.
[b]Average for 1990–2002.
*Significant at the 10 percent level.
**Significant at the 5 percent level.
***Significant at the 1 percent level.

IMPROVING INDEX CONSTRUCTION

Arbitrageurs are able to front-run index fund managers and create wealth transfers from index fund investors to themselves when

- index changes are transparent and known sufficiently in advance of the effective date,
- the index is heavily used by passive index funds, *and*
- fund managers are constrained to trade on the effective day by tracking error or other performance metrics.

All three conditions must be met for fund investors to lose from index changes.

We have considered how relaxation of the tracking-error constraint can improve performance. In this section, we discuss other choices that fund managers can make to minimize these losses and ways in which indexing firms can make indices less susceptible to arbitrage.

Silent Indices

According to Gastineau (2002), "A silent index is an index developed and maintained for the use of a single exchange-traded fund or a single traditional mutual fund" (p. 10). The constituents of a silent index would be publicly known, and its construction would be based on a defined set of rules, but unlike a typical index, changes to the index would not be made public until after they were effective.

Construction and creation of silent indices would not necessarily be onerous. Although several silent indices might have the same initial composition, index changes could still be different. For example, if a new stock (like a Google) was to be added to the index, it could be added at various times—spaced by a week among different indices—but would be kept secret. Without prior knowledge of index changes, arbitrageurs could not front-run a fund. Thus, a fund based on silent indices would avoid most of the losses that we have highlighted.

The main concern about silent indices is their lack of transparency. Current U.S. SEC regulations do not allow any index to be silent. All indices must be published, and all changes must be publicly available to all market participants at the same time. Lack of transparency in silent indices would also create marketing issues for the indexing firm because it would introduce uncertainty in the minds of investors. Moreover, creating a silent index might put pressure on indexing firms and fund managers to keep other information—such as the basis for index changes, periodicity of changes, even the type of index—silent so that potential arbitrageurs are unable to predict changes in the index.

Assuming that a silent index could be implemented, it might be the most effective method of neutralizing index arbitrage in the long term. All indices have limitations, but in the short term, a silent index with a slight variation to meet SEC regulations might work best.

Open but Rarely Used Indices

An open index—such as the S&P 500 or Russell 2000—is one with a publicly available list of constituent companies, and changes to its composition are freely available. We define a rarely used index as one to which passive indexing does not exceed 1 percent of the market value of all stocks in the index.[20] Examples are the Russell 1000, MSCI 300, and MSCI 1750. The 1 percent cutoff ensures that the demand created by indexers does not have a significant impact on prices. An examination of the returns of rarely used indices in Table 30.5 shows that such indices do not suffer significant losses because of arbitrage.

An index of this kind has two limitations. First, a fund indexed to any open index is likely to experience some losses because of index arbitrage. Second, when the index becomes popular, fund managers must switch to another index that fits the definition of "open but rarely used." Transition to a new index is costly, however, in terms of managerial time and effort, transaction costs, and realization of taxable capital gains when existing profitable positions are sold and replaced with new stocks.

Adapting Strategy to Popular Indices

With popular indices and minimization of tracking error as an objective, the only way to avoid index arbitrage is by negating transparent index changes that are pre-announced or predictable.

Number of Index Changes

The number of index changes in a given period depends on both the frequency with which changes are made and the criteria driving those changes.[21] A study by Frank Russell Company staffers (Gardner, Kondra, and Pritamani 2001) found that simply changing from annual reconstitution to quarterly reconstitution would have increased the annual number of changes in the Russell 2000 from 546 (27 percent of all companies) to 899 (45 percent of all companies) over the 1983–2000 period—an increase of 65 percent. Because each index change may be associated with an opportunity for index arbitrage, a larger number of changes can translate into a larger loss for index fund investors. But the frequency of index changes can be increased without increasing the number of changes through a judicious choice of other criteria. For example, changes in the S&P 500 are more frequent than changes in the Russell 2000, but the total number of changes as a fraction of the total number of stocks in the S&P 500 is not as large as for the Russell 2000 or the Russell 1000.

Predictability of Index Changes

The second important factor in gaming by arbitrageurs relates to the predictability of index changes. Because subjective criteria are used for changes to S&P indices, predicting which companies will be added to or deleted from the indices is generally difficult.

Because the criteria for changes to the Russell indices (and some other indices) are specified unambiguously, arbitrageurs can easily and accurately predict changes. It would apparently be in the interest of investors if these indexing firms used a random procedure to select some, but not all, of the companies eligible (based on current criteria) for addition or deletion. Introducing limited subjectivity into the selection process would reduce predictability and the turnover associated with index changes every year.

Pre-announcement of Changes

The third factor contributing to losses to index fund investors is the lag between the announcement of a change and its effective date. The lag is of interest only for changes that are unpredictable, as with the S&P 500. Indexing firms claim that the pre-announcements are required to "ease order imbalances" that are likely to result from large transactions initiated by indexers. But the lag does allow arbitrageurs to step in and trade ahead of the indexed funds. This problem has no obvious solution except to minimize the lag to the extent possible.

Summary

A popular index cannot really avoid losses to index funds because of index arbitrage, but the indexing firm can attempt to minimize those losses by reducing the turnover and predictability of changes. Open and popular indices should use an opaque process of index changes without necessarily using any pre-announcement period. If a pre-announcement period is unavoidable, it should be as short as possible. With these characteristics, the major indices would be similar to a silent index.

Recent Changes by the Frank Russell Company

In an attempt to limit arbitrage activities and to make it easier for index funds to manage tracking error, Frank Russell Company has made several changes to the reconstitution process. First, effective in 2004, it changed the reconstitution day from the last trading day in June to the last Friday in June. Second, it posted "provisional" returns for the new index for a two-week period prior to the reconstitution. Third, it used the NASDAQ Closing Cross price for reconstitution to price NASDAQ-listed securities. Finally, it began adding IPOs every quarter instead of only at the time of annual reconstitution.

The change from the last trading day in June to the last Friday in June made managing the reconstitution easier for index fund managers from an operational standpoint. The change has had no effect on index arbitrage. The posting of provisional returns based on the new index is informative but does not change tracking error. Thus, as long as index fund managers are responsible for minimizing tracking error, the posting of provisional returns does not affect their trading at the close on the effective day. The move to quarterly IPO additions has no effect on index arbitrage other than to spread these additions and related index arbitrage to four known dates instead of a single known date.

The use of the NASDAQ Closing Cross is useful for fund managers attempting to exactly match the index. It will probably reduce volatility of prices on the effective day, and it might induce managers to trade at the close instead of throughout the day. It should have no significant effect on index arbitrage, however, because it does not affect the incentives of fund managers.

The Russell 2000 reconstitution in 2004 had a much smaller impact on returns than did reconstitutions in earlier years. Some observers credit this effect to changes instituted by the Frank Russell Company. But based on our analysis, it is premature to suggest that losses to passive fund investors have ceased. Indeed, index arbitrage in 2005 was as significant and pervasive as in earlier years, except 2004. Thus, whether changes to Russell indices' reconstitution have had a significant impact on index arbitrage is not clear.

CONCLUSION

Growth in the popularity of index funds is a testament to portfolio theory and the virtues of diversification. According to Frank Russell Company, about $2,000 billion in assets were benchmarked to major indices as of June 2003—an indication that indices are an important component of the financial landscape.

Investors drawn to the broad diversification and low turnover that characterize index mutual funds no doubt expect the fund portfolios to be invested in the companies constituting the index in the proper proportions at any given time. But fund managers rewarded for performance have an incentive to assume more risk than contracted for by their investors. To address this agency problem, fund managers implicitly or explicitly contract to minimize the size and volatility of tracking error. Accordingly, the performance of index fund managers is usually measured in terms of both the cost of managing the fund and its tracking error.

We showed that index fund investors lose a significant amount because of the predictability and timing of index changes coupled with fund managers' objective of minimizing tracking error. The loss to an investor in the Russell 2000 may be about 130 bps a year and can be as high as 184 bps a year, and S&P 500 investors may lose as much as 12 bps a year. Consistent with this finding, we found that the Russell 2000 underperformed other small-cap indices by more than 3 percentage points a year in the 1995–2002 period, even though comparable indices did not entail greater risk. Moreover, the underperformance was concentrated in months surrounding the annual reconstitution of the index.

No type of index is a perfect solution to index arbitrage. We suggested steps that can be taken by index fund managers, index fund investors, and indexing firms to minimize the losses.

Managers of index funds can minimize losses by not trading on the effective date because the price pressure is the greatest at that time. To provide the necessary flexibility to fund managers, investors should rely on overall risk and return of the portfolio for performance evaluation instead of focusing on tracking error. Indeed, we found that the risk of funds that used the strategies we outlined would not be greater than the risk of the benchmark index, although the return would be higher. Finally, small individual investors can protect themselves by choosing index funds on the basis of not only expenses and loads but also the likelihood of the fund being timed by arbitrageurs.

Indices could be designed to limit front running of index funds. The best long-term solution is a silent index (Gastineau 2002, 2004), but it is not permissible under current SEC regulations. In the short term, investors can look to an open index that is not heavily followed. The limited indexing will curtail gains to index arbitrageurs. But once an open but not heavily used index becomes popular, changing indices can create significant costs for the index fund.

Changes by indexing firms to remove the cause of loss to investors would be the most effective way of protecting fund investors from index arbitrage. Because advance knowledge of changes allows arbitrageurs to time those changes, we recommend that indexing firms reduce the predictability and advance knowledge of index changes as much as possible. In addition, the turnover associated with index changes should be reduced to limit both the opportunity for arbitrage and the transaction costs associated with index changes.

Ultimately, whether any of the alternatives we recommend is an improvement over the status quo is an empirical issue. It is worth exploring different indices and methods of index changes if these methods have the potential to mitigate losses to index fund investors. We hope this chapter spawns more discussion of the alternatives available to index fund investors, index fund managers, and indexing firms for limiting losses because of arbitrageurs.

ACKNOWLEDGMENTS

We thank Sean Collins, Srikant Dash, Gary Gastineau, Mark Hulbert, Greg Kadlec, Hugh Marble, Ken O'Keeffe, Mahesh Pritamani, Gus Sauter, and Chester Spatt for comments on the broad results and implications of this chapter. We thank participants at the SEC; the 2004 Financial Management Association International and Southern Finance Association meetings; and the University of Arkansas, University of Washington at Tacoma, and SUNY Albany for comments and suggestions. In addition, we thank Morgan Stanley Capital

International (and Neil Blundell), Frank Russell Company, Standard & Poor's (and Reid Steadman and Maureen O'Shea), and Quotes Plus (at QP2.com) for providing some of the data used in this chapter. Honghui Chen acknowledges partial financial support from a University of Central Florida summer grant, and Vijay Singal acknowledges partial financial support from a Virginia Tech summer grant.

NOTES

1. Tracking error has no universally accepted definition. Tracking-error calculations may be based on daily returns, monthly returns, quarterly returns, volatility, correlations, and so on. Two common measures, $TE1$ and $TE2$, are as follows (see Ammann and Zimmermann 2001):

$$TE1 = \sqrt{\sum_{k}^{n} (R_{pk} - R_{Bk})^2 / (n - 1)}$$

and

$$TE2 = \sigma(R_p) \sqrt{1 - \rho_{pB}^2},$$

   where R is the return for tracking portfolio p or benchmark portfolio B over n periods, k is an index that goes from 1 to n, and ρ_{pB} is the correlation between returns to the tracking portfolio and the benchmark portfolio. Our definition in the text is one of the simplest.
2. Other important reasons for tracking error and expenses are reinvestment of dividends and cash management to meet investor purchases and redemptions. Fund managers are adept at minimizing the impact of dividends and cash flows by using index futures.
3. We distinguish between "passively indexed" and "benchmarked" in our computations. For example, around $264 billion in assets were benchmarked to the Russell 2000 in 2003 (Smith and Haughton 2003) compared with around $43 billion passively indexed to it during that year (Merrill Lynch 2005). We used the passively indexed estimate in our tests.
4. The exception is that in 2004, Frank Russell Company commenced adding IPOs to the index on a quarterly basis. We consider this change later.
5. Until September 1989, there was no lag between announcement and the actual change to S&P indices. Changes were announced after the close of trading and became effective at the open on the next day.
6. Our sample selection process is similar to that in Chen, Noronha, and Singal (2004).
7. Announcement-day return refers to the return for the trading day following announcement because all announcements are made after the close of markets.
8. This result is similar to those in Chen, Noronha, and Singal (2004) and in Dash (2002), a study conducted by Standard & Poor's.
9. A negative bias was introduced by our excluding the months of March, April, and May because the change list is known with a high degree of confidence as early as March in any year. The probability of addition/deletion for a company on the list is not 1.0, however, which introduces an additional risk factor into a portfolio of additions or deletions formed earlier than 31 May.
10. That the mean size of deleted companies is larger than the mean size of added companies implies that several companies deleted from the Russell 2000 moved up to the

Russell 1000 Index and, similarly, several companies added to the Russell 2000 are those that moved down from the Russell 1000.

11. Because announcements take place after the exchanges have closed, we essentially bought at the closing price on the day after the announcement. Thus, we lost the announcement-day return. This factor helps explain why the numbers in Table 30.3 look considerably different from those in Table 30.1.

12. The net impacts reported were obtained by multiplying the abnormal returns and total market cap of additions or deletions and dividing by the total market cap of the Russell 2000 as of 30 June.

13. The analysis is identical for deletions.

14. We thank a referee for pointing this out.

15. As pointed out previously, trading at the open on the day after announcement can generate additional gains. We thank a referee for providing us with an estimate of loss resulting from the deletion of foreign companies.

16. Year-by-year results are available from the authors.

17. Short-sale proceeds are not usually available for reinvestment, so the actual savings from this strategy might be marginally smaller than those assumed here.

18. One would expect gains to arbitrageurs to dissipate with competition. There may be several explanations of why this does not happen in the case of index reconstitution. First, not all arbitrage opportunities are eliminated by competition. For example, arbitrageurs still profit from merger arbitrage, post-earnings-announcement price drift, and price momentum. Second, in the case of index changes, some market participants—namely, indexers—are focused on tracking-error minimization rather than maximizing profit; hence, they trade at the closing price on the date of reconstitution.

19. Some observers have suggested that the actual trading volume on the effective day is much less than what would be expected if all index fund managers traded on that day. A quick check for all additions to the S&P 500 in the latter half of 2002 revealed, however, that the trading volume is sufficiently large to support all managers trading on that day. The trading volume on the effective date is 9–20 percent of the number of shares outstanding for NYSE stocks and 20–25 percent for NASDAQ stocks (without adjusting the volume for the upward bias in NASDAQ's reported volume). These percentages compare favorably with the ratio of 11.3 percent indexed value to total value for the S&P 500.

20. The 1 percent cutoff is arbitrary and could be lower or higher.

21. As mentioned previously, we assumed that the turnover associated with each index change is the same.

REFERENCES

Ammann, M., and H. Zimmermann. 2001. "Tracking Error and Tactical Asset Allocation." *Financial Analysts Journal*, vol. 57, no. 2 (March/April):32–43.

Beneish, Messod D., and Robert E. Whaley. 1996. "An Anatomy of the 'S&P Game': The Effects of Changing the Rules." *Journal of Finance*, vol. 51, no. 5 (December): 1909–1930.

Biktimirov, Ernest, Arnold Cowan, and Bradford Jordan. 2004. "Do Demand Curves for Small Stocks Slope Down?" *Journal of Financial Research*, vol. 27, no. 2 (June):161–178.

Blume, Marshall, and Roger Edelen. 2004. "S&P 500 Indexers, Tracking Error, and Liquidity: A Complex Answer to Profiting." *Journal of Portfolio Management*, vol. 30, no. 3 (Spring):37–47.

Chen, Honghui, Gregory Noronha, and Vijay Singal. 2004. "The Price Response to S&P 500 Index Additions and Deletions: Evidence of Asymmetry and a New Explanation." *Journal of Finance*, vol. 59, no. 4 (August):1901–1929.

Clarke, Roger, Scott Krase, and Meir Statman. 1994. "Tracking Errors, Regret, and Tactical Asset Allocation." *Journal of Portfolio Management*, vol. 20, no. 3 (Spring):16–24.

Dash, Srikant. 2002. "Price Changes Associated with S&P 500 Deletions: Time Variation and Effect of Size and Share Prices." Standard & Poor's (9 July).

Frino, Alex, David R. Gallagher, and Teddy N. Oetomo. 2005. "The Index Tracking Strategies of Passive and Enhanced Index Equity Funds." *Australian Journal of Management*, vol. 30, no. 1 (June):23–56.

Gardner, Grant, Andra Kondra, and Mahesh Pritamani. 2001. "Russell Indexes: Examining the Frequency of U.S. Reconstitution." Research paper, Frank Russell Company (6 July).

Gastineau, Gary. 2002. "Silence Is Golden." *Journal of Indexes* (2nd Quarter):8–13.

Gastineau, Gary. 2004. "The Benchmark Index ETF Performance Problem." *Journal of Portfolio Management*, vol. 30, no. 2 (Winter):96–103.

Greenwood, Robin. 2004. "Short- and Long-Term Demand for Stocks: Theory and Evidence on the Dynamics of Arbitrage." *Journal of Financial Economics*, vol. 75, no. 3 (March):607–649.

Hulbert, Mark. 2004. "A Quick Path to Profit, in Index Funds." *New York Times* (4 July):26.

Jorion, Philippe. 2003. "Portfolio Optimization and Tracking-Error Constraints." *Financial Analysts Journal*, vol. 59, no. 5 (September/October):70–82.

Madhavan, Ananth. 2003. "The Russell Reconstitution Effect." *Financial Analysts Journal*, vol. 59, no. 4 (July/August):51–64.

Merrill Lynch. 2005. "Equity Derivatives and Indexation" (March).

Pope, Peter, and Pradeep Yadav. 1994. "Discovering Errors in Tracking Error." *Journal of Portfolio Management*, vol. 20, no. 2 (Winter):27–32.

Quinn, Jim. 2004. "U.S. Stock Indexes: Is There a Best Choice?" Research report (April): www.djindexes.com.

Roll, Richard. 1992. "A Mean/Variance Analysis of Tracking Error." *Journal of Portfolio Management*, vol. 18, no. 4 (Summer):12–22.

Ryan, Oliver. 2004. "Does Your Fund's Index Measure Up?" *Fortune* (9 August).

Smith, Matthew, and Eric Haughton. 2003. "US Equity Index Benchmark Usage." Frank Russell Company (30 September):www.russell.com.

CHAPTER 31

INFORMATION RATIOS AND BATTING AVERAGES

Neil Constable

Jeremy Armitage, CFA

The information ratio (IR) and the batting average are two commonly quoted measures of investment success, but these measures have shortcomings: The IR contains no information about higher moments, and the batting average contains only directional information. This chapter demonstrates how the IR and batting average interact and how they can be usefully combined to allow investors to construct a comprehensive picture of the choices they face. The intriguing result is that large batting averages can result in low IRs and, conversely, impressive IRs can be obtained with low batting averages. Furthermore, in choosing between two managers with equivalent IRs, an investor who is averse to blowups should choose the manager with the lower batting average.

The information ratio (IR) is a common measure of the success (or failure) of money managers. Conceptually, it is simply the ratio of excess return (relative to a benchmark) to excess risk of an investment strategy (Sharpe 1966, 1994). Unfortunately, when a fund manager quotes only the IR at the end of some fixed investment horizon, investors in the fund cannot easily ascertain the string of successes and failures that led to the final outcome. Did the manager win or lose most bets? A measure of success that addresses this shortcoming of the IR is the "batting average." It is the percentage of investment decisions that led to a profit. The shortcoming of this measure is that it does not give any information about how much money was made or lost as a result of a particular investment decision.

We demonstrate how the IR and batting average interact, and we also demonstrate how these two measures of success can be usefully combined to allow investors to construct a more comprehensive picture of the choices facing them than either measure alone provides.

Reprinted from the *Financial Analysts Journal* (May/June 2006):24–31.

693

Although the investment strategy used by a particular fund manager cannot be "reverse engineered," we show how one can extract a batting average once an IR is specified. Our batting average indicates how often managers must make independent and profitable investment decisions to obtain their stated IRs. It also provides insight into how much mileage has been obtained from the available information.

The batting average, which is a function of the number of "at bats," will allow us to differentiate among managers who are using different investment strategies because the number of at bats is a good proxy for how often a manager receives information relevant to the implementation of the manager's strategy.

Our results are intended for investors who are faced with choosing from a set of "live" managers when provided with a limited set of performance measures on which to base their decisions. Because the managers analyzed may cease to exist at some point in the future, our results are not necessarily indicative of realized future performance. However, by using our techniques to choose managers who are less prone to occasional large negative returns, investors maximize the probability that they will not be exposed to a failed manager.

All of our analyses explicitly assume that the outcome of each investment decision is independent of all decisions that came before it. Furthermore, we assume that the bets made are always of equal size. The first of these assumptions is in keeping with the analysis that led to Grinold's (1989) "fundamental law of active management," which is another way of viewing some of our results. In the final part of this chapter, we briefly examine the extent to which correlations between investments influence reported batting averages.

THE GAME

To reconstruct the success of a fund manager over the course of an investment horizon, we begin with picturing the fund manager as a batter in a baseball game who steps up to the plate at fixed intervals throughout the duration of the strategy. In this game, if the manager gets a hit (hits the ball and gets on base), then the original investment returns a fixed multiple of itself. If the manager strikes out (fails to get a hit), the capital is reduced by a fixed multiple. The total return is determined by the difference in payoffs for the two outcomes as well as between the number of hits and outs. The batting average is defined as the percentage of at bats that result in a hit.

The problem we are addressing is as follows: What batting average would be required to obtain a particular IR? Or: How much skill as a batter would the fund manager need to produce the same IR as the investment strategy of the fund? The answer is that surprisingly little skill is required—provided the at bats occur frequently enough.

The game can be easily visualized in the form of a binomial tree, as shown in Figure 31.1. At the first node, the investor has the original investment of S. The investment horizon is taken to be one year, during which time N at bats occur at equally spaced intervals. The $N + 1$ nodes in the binomial tree at step N represent all of the possible outcomes for this investment that can be realized at the end of the investment horizon. If an at bat results in a hit, the original capital grows to uS, where u is a number presumably greater than 1. If the manager strikes out, the capital shrinks to dS, where d is a number presumably less than 1. In this way, we construct what is known as a "recombining binomial tree." At the end of the horizon (the last step on the tree), the distribution of the final outcomes can be seen. If the manager obtained a hit p percent of the time, the investor can calculate the expected return and variance resulting from initial investment S. From this information, the investor can construct

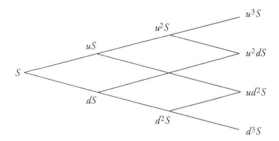

FIGURE 31.1   Standard Three-Step Binomial Tree

the manager's expected IR as it is given by the ratio of expected returns to the standard deviation of those returns. For simplicity, we will use a risk-free world with zero interest rates as the benchmark.

To further understand these ideas, consider the situation where only a single at bat occurs through the entire life of the investment and $d = 1/u$. The result is a one-step tree: The manager gets a hit or is put out. As shown in Appendix 31A, the IR for this game is given by

$$IR = \frac{2p - 1}{2\sqrt{p(1 - p)}},$$

where p is the batting average.

If the IR is known, this equation can be inverted to obtain p. For example, an IR of zero corresponds to a batting average of 50 percent; an IR of infinity corresponds to a batting average of 100 percent. Thus, this equation provides the batting average required to achieve a prespecified IR.

In the case of multiple-step trees, the approach is the same: Construct the expected IR as a function of the probability of getting a hit and the number of at bats; then, given a value of the IR, invert the formula to solve for the batting average.

RESULTS FOR VARIOUS INVESTMENT STRATEGIES

Investment strategies can be distinguished from one another by the frequency with which bets are made. Because most managers act on information as soon as it is available, the number of investment decisions made in a year can be used as a proxy for the frequency with which the manager receives information relevant to the implementation of the strategy. A fund manager who engages in a high-frequency trading strategy, such as statistical arbitrage, cannot be distinguished from a manager who uses strategies based on monthly or quarterly data simply by their respective IRs. As we will demonstrate, managers who act infrequently must have very high batting averages to produce even modest IRs. Conversely, managers who trade often need only moderate success to produce enormous IRs.

In this section, we leave the investment horizon fixed at one year and allow for different strategies by altering the number of steps in the binomial tree. A manager who uses a high-frequency strategy will be represented by a tree with several hundred steps, whereas a manager making only one bet a month will have a tree with only 12 steps. Keeping these elements in mind, we repeat the analysis in the previous section for an N-step binomial tree.

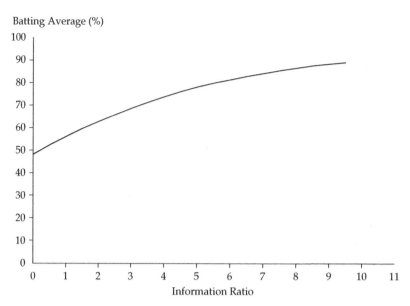

FIGURE 31.2   Plot of Batting Average vs. IR for $N = 52$

The derivation of the IR for this situation, which is more general than the one shown in Figure 31.1, is provided in Appendix 31A.

Symmetrical Upside/Downside Results

Consider the case for which $d = 1/u$, which means that a strike-out followed by a hit results in no change in wealth.[1] In this case, the game is symmetrical, in the sense that hits and strike-outs are on exactly equal footing. (We consider the effect of relaxing this condition later.)

We can numerically implement the inversion of the equation for the IR to solve for the batting average, p, in a reasonably straightforward way (see Appendix 31A). For simplicity (although not efficiency), we use the method of bisections, with the following results.

Figure 31.2 shows the batting average plotted against the desired IR for a fixed number of periods, $N = 52$, with a fixed weekly return of $u = 1.0009$. These conditions correspond to going to bat once a week for one year on an investment with an *annualized* rate of return of 5 percent. The trend clearly indicates the intuitive result that for a fixed number of at bats, obtaining a large IR requires the talents of a very skilled batter.

Now, consider the effect of varying the frequency with which the opportunities to bat occur. Intuitively, if a manager has a winning strategy, that manager will want to get up to the plate as often as possible, although in reality, frequency is clearly limited by the rate at which information arrives. Table 31.1 shows the batting averages (BATs) required to obtain various IRs as a function of the number of attempts made. Note the clear trend in the table indicating that frequent batting significantly reduces the skill level required to obtain a given IR. For small IRs, the batting average is relatively insensitive to the number of at bats. For large IRs, however, the batting average is highly sensitive to the number of at bats. In the extreme case of IR = 4, Table 31.1 shows that a batter who batted only on a quarterly basis would have to get a hit more than 94 percent of the time, whereas a batter who batted daily

TABLE 31.1 Batting Average as a Function of IR and Frequency of at Bats

Input IR	BAT for 4 Steps	BAT for 12 Steps	BAT for 52 Steps	BAT for 252 Steps	BAT for 500 Steps
0.0	50.07%	50.08%	49.92%	49.92%	50.08%
0.5	62.20	57.05	53.35	51.50	51.21
1.0	72.27	63.96	56.75	53.25	52.15
1.5	79.93	69.78	60.28	54.60	53.26
2.0	85.27	75.09	63.28	56.35	54.55
2.5	89.13	79.34	66.43	57.67	55.46
3.0	91.53	82.66	69.13	59.45	56.73
3.5	93.34	85.62	71.91	60.69	57.82
4.0	94.78	87.73	74.17	62.12	58.88

would have to get a hit only 62 percent of the time. Even when we consider a perhaps more realistic example of an IR of 2, the benefits of frequently trading a winning strategy are clear. For the impressive but attainable case of IR = 2, a daily batter would need to get a hit only 56 percent of the time, whereas a quarterly batter would need to get a hit 85 percent of the time. Batting twice a day makes obtaining large IRs even easier.

Asymmetrical Upside/Downside

Now, consider the effects of allowing for hits and outs to be treated asymmetrically (i.e., we remove the constraint of $d = 1/u$). Such results reflect the real-world investment situation, in which upside exposure is not completely offset by downside exposure. An explicit example is when an investor purchases portfolio insurance, which creates a lower bound for the returns on the investment (Lo 2001).

We consider $ud > 1$ and $ud < 1$. The first case is relevant to situations in which hits are compensated to a larger extent than outs are punished, and the second case represents the opposite. Such asymmetrical results can have dramatic effects on the batting average required to obtain a specified IR.

In this analysis, we repeat the previous analysis for an investor whose strategy relies on weekly information and consider the following cases:

- First, $(u, d) = (1.0009, 0.999)$, which corresponds to making an investment with an *annualized* return of 5 percent for wins and -3 percent for losses.
- Second, $(u, d) = (1.0009, 0.998)$, which is equivalent to an investment that returns 5 percent for wins and -7 percent for losses.

The results for investors who bat once a week are presented in Figure 31.3.[2] Clearly, when the positive result from getting a hit exceeds the negative effect of an out ($ud > 1$), the batting average required to obtain impressive IRs falls significantly. In fact, an IR of 1 can be obtained by striking out more than 50 percent of the time! Conversely, when the negative effect of an out exceeds the positive effect of a hit ($ud < 1$), one must have a batting average of approximately 60 percent merely to obtain a positive IR.

Given the seeming ambiguity of the batting average, one might reasonably ask why an investor should care what a fund's batting average is so long as it obtains an acceptable IR.

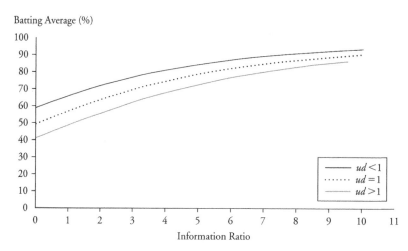

Batting Average (%)

FIGURE 31.3   Batting Average vs. IR for $N = 52$ and Varying u and d

We now address this issue by discussing why good but infrequent batters are not necessarily equivalent to average but frequent batters who achieve the same IR.

GOOD BATTERS ARE SKEWED

Naively, if one considers how much mileage a particular manager gets from available information, then from our findings, a strategy based on monthly information with an IR of 1 should be more impressive than a strategy based on weekly information with a comparable IR. As we now show, this interpretation is somewhat misleading because for a fixed IR, larger batting averages actually imply a greater likelihood of experiencing a blowup.

Consider the results we have presented from the perspective of the distribution of returns generated by following different strategies. To focus the discussion, we will consider two managers. Manager A uses a strategy of writing slightly out-of-the-money binary put options once a week. Manager B follows a strategy of writing deep out-of-the-money binary puts once every month.[3] Both managers have an IR of 1. How does an investor choose which manager to hire?

A writer of a binary put option either keeps the premium charged for the option or pays out a fixed amount. The expected return and standard deviation of this strategy can thus be easily worked out by using the binomial trees of the previous sections. It is relatively straightforward to show that these two managers can have the same IR *if and only if* the binary put options written by Manager A expire in the money 43 percent of the time and those written by Manager B do so 36 percent of the time—in other words, only if Manager A has a batting average of 57 percent and Manager B has a batting average of 64 percent. This situation is entirely analogous to the monthly and weekly strategies in Table 31.1. The two managers have identical risk-adjusted returns, but Manager B is a better batter.

We now come to our main point. Figure 31.4 shows the distribution of returns associated with each. The distribution for Manager A in Panel A is very nearly normal (recall that a normal distribution has zero skewness), whereas Manager B's returns in Panel B have a rather obvious large tail for returns below the mean—that is, negative skewness. Thus, Manager B experiences many more large negative returns than large positive returns. With each manager's

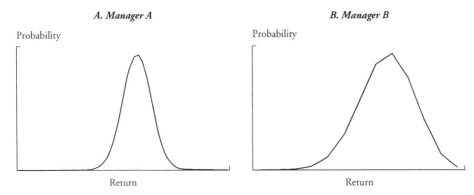

FIGURE 31.4   Return Distributions for Manager A and Manager B

Note:

Moment	Manager A	Manager B
Mean (%)	3.08	1.20
Standard deviation (%)	3.08	1.20
Skewness	−0.04	−0.17
Kurtosis	2.96	2.86

batting average used as input, a short calculation shows that the distribution of returns for Manager A has a skewness of −0.04 and the distribution for Manager B has a skewness of −0.17. In effect, the batting average can be used as a proxy for the skewness present in the returns of one manager relative to another.

The conclusion to be drawn is that, given equivalent IRs, the manager with the larger batting average is more likely to experience a blowup than is the manager with the relatively lower batting average. Therefore, faced with choosing between Manager A and Manager B, an investor who is averse to blowups should choose Manager A, the manager with the lower batting average.

This somewhat counterintuitive result arises from the fact that high batting averages imply more negatively skewed return distributions than the return distributions of low batting averages with the same IR. Because the IR is constructed from only the first two moments of the distribution of expected returns, it cannot reflect information about such higher moments as skewness. In short, expected batting average is a useful proxy for expected skewness.

Consider the applicability of our argument to the common situation in which two managers are writing covered (European) call options. In this strategy, negative skewness will appear in the distributions of both managers because of the optionality embedded in the covered call strategy, but if IRs are equivalent, batting averages will indicate skewness and thus provide additional and *independent* information about the expected performance of the managers.[4]

Finally, consider the distribution of IRs for a set of 375 hedge funds presented in Figure 31.5. The IRs were constructed from return data beginning in January 1994 and ending in December 2003. Note that we rather generously assumed a benchmark return of zero. Interestingly, few funds have an IR higher than 1, and only a handful have an IR beyond 2. Based on these data, we conclude that few hedge funds in this sample have both a high batting average and a high frequency of at bats (because, as demonstrated previously, such a combination

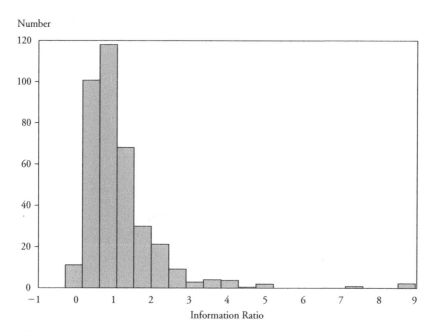

FIGURE 31.5   Distribution of IRs for 375 Hedge Funds, Data for January 1994–December 2003

Source: Data are from the Center for International Securities and Derivatives Markets database, which tracks approximately 2,500 alternative investment vehicles. The CISDM database was formerly owned by Zurich Capital Markets and is currently owned by the University of Massachusetts' Isenberg Center for International Securities and Derivatives Markets.

would lead to a large number of extremely high IRs). Furthermore, our data were not adjusted for survivor bias; that is, our dataset includes only live funds, not those that came into existence and subsequently failed (presumably, because of low or negative IRs). So, the actual number of funds with low IRs is probably much greater than represented in Figure 31.5.

Notice that a large number of funds claim to have IRs of approximately 1. Therefore, the batting average would be particularly useful to an investor who must choose among these funds. The investor could use it to rank them in accordance with the investor's aversion to skewness.

CONCLUSION

Our primary result is intuitive: One should play a winning strategy as often as possible, even if the strategy does not have a high batting average. Strategies based on frequently arriving information produce large risk-adjusted returns with lower batting averages than are required for strategies that can be implemented only infrequently. If the payoffs for winning and losing are symmetrical (a win followed by a loss results in zero return), a winning strategy need only surpass a batting average of 50 percent by a tiny margin to generate spectacular IRs as long as the strategy is implemented frequently.

In the case of asymmetrical payoffs, we found that large batting averages are not at odds with mediocre IRs. Similarly, low batting averages can be consistent with impressive IRs.

Therefore, when the potential upside of taking a particular position is not the same as the downside to which you are exposed, neither the IR nor the batting average is sufficient to gauge performance.

The lesson to be learned is that IRs and batting averages, which are both associated with the success of a manager, are measuring different things. Success is a multidimensional concept, and IRs and batting averages approach it from different directions.

We expanded on these ideas to demonstrate that, whereas the IR is a measure of risk-adjusted returns, the batting average is associated with the skewness of those returns. The IR allows investors to select managers who meet their risk–return needs; the batting average helps an investor discern among those managers based on the investor's aversion to negative skewness. Investors who are averse to blowups should choose managers with relatively low batting averages, even though this finding runs counter to intuition. Such investors should be wary of standard marketing messages that go no further than claiming "our fund outperformed our benchmark in 8 of the last 10 years."

Used together, the IR and the batting average provide orthogonal and complementary information, allowing investors to effectively disentangle the multitude of choices presented to them by the investment community.

APPENDIX 31A: FINDING THE IR FROM THE BATTING AVERAGE

The expected return, $E(r)$, for a one-step binomial tree with $u = 1/d$ is given in a straightforward fashion by the expression

$$E(r)\Delta t = p \ln\left(\frac{uS_0}{S_0}\right) + (1 - p)\ln\left(\frac{S_0}{uS_0}\right),$$

(31.1)

where
    Δt = length of the period in years of the investment horizon
    p = batting average
    $\ln(x)$ = the natural log function
    u = increase in wealth resulting from a hit
    S_0 = original investment
It is also straightforward to show that the variance of these returns is given by

$$\sigma^2 \Delta t = p(1 - p)[\ln(u^2)]^2,$$

(31.2)

where σ is the standard deviation of returns.

The expected IR of this strategy can be constructed by taking the ratio of these equations:

$$IR = \frac{E(r)}{\sigma}$$

$$= \frac{2p - 1}{2\sqrt{\Delta t}\sqrt{p(1 - p)}}.$$

(31.3)

Note the explicit time dependence of this formula for the IR.

For an N-step tree, the expected return for an arbitrary batting average, p, is given by

$$E(r)\Delta t = \sum_{n=0}^{N} \frac{N!}{(N-n)!n!} p^n (1-p)^{N-n} \ln(u^n d^{N-n}),$$

(31.4)

and the variance of these returns is

$$\sigma^2 \Delta t = \sum_{n=0}^{N} \frac{N!}{(N-n)!n!} p^n (1-p)^{N-n} \times [\ln(u^n d^{N-n}) - E(r)]^2,$$

(31.5)

where $N! = N \times (N-1) \times (N-2) \ldots 3 \times 2$ and d is the decrease in wealth resulting from an out.

The N-step IR is then given by

$$IR_N(p) = \frac{E(r)}{\sigma}.$$

(31.6)

As discussed in Sharpe (1994), this expression for IR_N is explicitly time dependent because the mean and standard deviation scale with different powers of Δt. Specifically, IR_N scales as $(\Delta t)^{-1/2}$. If the investment horizon is one year, then $\Delta t = 1$, but in general, it is important to note that the IR is not a static quantity.

Finally, when $u = 1/d$, note that by using the following property of the log function,

$$\ln(x^a) = a \ln(x),$$

one can show that IR_N is completely independent of u.

ACKNOWLEDGMENTS

We would like to thank Mark Kritzman, Paul O'Connell, and Sébastien Page for their comments and advice.

NOTES

1. The case of $d = 1/u$ is often referred to as a Cox–Ross–Rubinstein binomial tree (1979).
2. Although we have presented this analysis for investors who bat once a week, we obtained entirely analogous results for other batting frequencies.
3. A binary put option pays the holder a fixed amount (e.g., $1) if the value of the underlying asset is below the strike price when the option expires; otherwise, it pays nothing.
4. The analysis contains a potential source of ambiguity. The issue here is that of *independent* events. This issue has previously been explored at length in the context of information ratios by Grinold. Independence is of crucial importance in this case as well. In the analysis so far, the outcome of a given at bat was explicitly independent of all of the other at bats. In other words, prior hits or outs had no effect on future success. Such is usually not the case in real investment situations. In many cases, multiple investment deci-

sions are made whose outcomes are correlated. For example, simultaneously investing in software and semiconductors (which are classified as separate industries) could hardly be considered as taking independent bets during the stock market bubble of the late 1990s. In such situations, if both positions are profitable, claiming a batting average of 2 for 2 is somewhat misleading because the correlations make it very likely that either both are hits or both are outs. Counting correlated hits as independent successes will introduce an upward bias in the claimed batting average. To see this, consider batting five consecutive times (e.g., assume long positions in five stocks). After a week, four of the five have made money and all of the positions are closed out. Naively, the implied batting average is 4 for 5, or 80 percent. If three of the stocks that made money are highly correlated, however, the combined position should properly be counted as a single bet. The batting average should, therefore, be 2 for 3, or 67 percent. Of course, this approach assumes perfect correlation, but it demonstrates the point.

REFERENCES

Cox, J., S. Ross, and M. Rubinstein. 1979. "Option Pricing: A Simplified Approach." *Journal of Financial Economics*, vol. 7, no. 3 (September):229–263.

Grinold, R. 1989. "The Fundamental Law of Active Management." *Journal of Portfolio Management*, vol. 15, no. 3 (Spring):30–37.

Lo, Andrew W. 2001. "Risk Management for Hedge Funds: Introduction and Overview." *Financial Analysts Journal*, vol. 57, no. 6 (November/December):16–33.

Sharpe, William F. 1966. "Mutual Fund Performance." *Journal of Business*, vol. 39, no. 1 (January):119–138.

Sharpe, William F. 1994. "The Sharpe Ratio." *Journal of Portfolio Management*, vol. 21, no. 1 (Fall):49–58.

CHAPTER 32

THE INFORMATION RATIO

Thomas H. Goodwin

Despite the widespread use of information ratios to gauge the performance of active money managers, confusion persists over how to calculate an information ratio, how to interpret it, and what constitutes a "good" one. The argument here is that the simplest form and interpretation of the ratio is the most useful for investors. This chapter clarifies the relationship between an information ratio and a t-statistic, compares four methods of annualizing an information ratio, and presents the empirical evidence on the distribution of information ratios by style, which provides a context in which to examine manager performance.

Most money managers routinely report their products' information ratios to investors, and some investors rely heavily on information ratios to hire and fire money managers. The purpose of this chapter is to clear up some of the confusion that exists about information ratios despite their widespread use.

THE RATIO DEFINED

The information ratio is a measure that seeks to summarize in a single number the mean–variance properties of an active portfolio. It builds on the Markowitz mean–variance paradigm, which states that the mean and variance (or mean and standard deviation) of returns are sufficient statistics for characterizing an investment portfolio. Calculation of an information ratio is based on the standard statistical formulas for the mean and standard deviation. If R_{Pt} is the return on an active portfolio in period t and R_{Bt} is the return on a benchmark portfolio or security in period t, then ER_t, the excess return, is the difference:

$$ER_t = R_{Pt} - R_{Bt}. \tag{32.1}$$

$\overline{ER}$ is the arithmetic average of excess returns over the historical period from $t = 1$ through T:

Reprinted from the *Financial Analysts Journal* (July/August 1998):34–43.

$$\overline{ER} = \frac{1}{T} \sum_{t=1}^{T} ER_t ,$$

(32.2)

and $\hat{\sigma}_{ER}$ is the standard deviation of excess returns from the benchmark, or tracking error, for the same period:

$$\hat{\sigma}_{ER} = \sqrt{\frac{1}{T-1} \sum_{t=1}^{T} (ER_t - \overline{ER})^2} .$$

(32.3)

The information ratio based on historical data, IR, is simply the ratio of the return and standard deviation:

$$IR = \frac{\overline{ER}}{\hat{\sigma}_{ER}} .$$

(32.4)

A historical information ratio is easy to calculate using the standard statistical functions in most spreadsheets.

INTERPRETATIONS OF THE RATIO

The information ratio is the average excess return per unit of volatility in excess return. That definition simply puts the statistical formula into words, however, without any indication of what the ratio has to do with information. The first step in gaining some insight into this question is to set up a particular variation of the linear market model:

$$(R_{Pt} - R_{ft}) = \alpha + \beta(R_{Bt} - R_{ft}) + \varepsilon_t,$$

(32.5)

and

$$\mathrm{var}(\varepsilon_t) = \omega^2,$$

where R_{ft} is the hypothetical risk-free rate, usually proxied by the one-month or three-month U.S. T-bill return.

The situation with the most straightforward interpretation is one in which the active manager is confined to the universe of a benchmark index—say, the S&P 500 Index or the Russell 1000 Index—and must maintain the same level of systematic risk as the index. In that case, $\beta = 1$ and

$$(R_{Pt} - R_{ft}) = \alpha + (R_{Bt} - R_{ft}) + \varepsilon_t,$$

(32.6a)

which can be rearranged as

$$
\begin{aligned}
(R_{Pt} - R_{ft}) - (R_{Bt} - R_{ft}) &= (R_{Pt} - R_{Bt}) \\
&= ER_t \\
&= \alpha + \varepsilon_t .
\end{aligned}
$$

(32.6b)

The active manager can add value only by underweighting or overweighting individual securities relative to the benchmark index weights while maintaining the same level of market risk.

Equation 32.6 shows that the excess return over the benchmark is the sum of alpha plus residual risk. The information ratio is then the risk-adjusted alpha:

$$IR = \frac{\overline{ER}}{\hat{\sigma}_{ER}} = \frac{\alpha}{\omega}. \tag{32.7}$$

The under- and overweightings represent the active manager's bets based on the special information, or skill, the manager possesses—hence the name.

In this interpretation, the information ratio measures the quality of the manager's information discounted by the residual risk in the betting process. The information ratio is also known in the finance literature as the "alpha-omega ratio," a term that came from the common textbook habit of using the Greek letters α and ω to represent, respectively, excess return and idiosyncratic risk. Alternative terminology that borrows from engineering calls alpha the "signal" and calls the residual risk "noise," so from an engineering perspective, the information ratio is the signal-to-noise ratio of the active manager. Additional synonyms are "return-to-variability ratio" and "appraisal ratio."

Information Ratios with an Estimated Beta

Some analysts prefer to construct an information ratio from estimating Equation 32.6 by least squares regression. Then, the α of Equation 32.7 becomes the estimated intercept and ω is the standard error of the regression. A common reason for this approach is to avoid rewarding managers for taking on more risk than the benchmark. The rationale is that if the estimated β is greater than 1, the estimated α will be smaller than it would be if β were fixed at 1, which, all else being equal, will decrease the information ratio. However, all else is not equal, because the estimated ω will also be smaller as a result of least squares minimization. Thus, compared with an information ratio with a β fixed at 1, an information ratio with an estimated β greater than 1 can either raise or lower the information ratio of a manager who takes on more than benchmark risk.

If the estimated β is *less* than 1, however, the information ratio will increase, without doubt, because the estimated α will be larger but the estimated ω will be smaller.

So, estimated beta rewards managers who take on less than the benchmark risk with a higher information ratio. In addition, estimated β suffers from a well-established temporal instability, and moving to a multifactor model to enhance stability only raises questions of how many and what factors are appropriate.

In contrast to constructing an information ratio from estimating Equation 32.6 by least squares regression, the simple information ratio presented in Equation 32.4 can be thought of as an *ex post*, model-free measure that is universally applicable and relatively stable over time. The key assumption is that the benchmark roughly matches the systematic risk of the manager, so fixing β at 1 is sensible. Therefore, the simple information ratio is most useful when the benchmark has been carefully chosen to match the style of the manager.

Information Ratios, Information Coefficients, and the Fundamental Law

The information ratio is on center stage in the multifactor-modeling framework of Grinold and Kahn (1995). They proposed a "fundamental law of active management" based on an approximate decomposition of a theoretical maximum information ratio hypothetically achievable by the manager, IR_{max}, into two components—an information coefficient, IC, and the "breadth of the strategy," BR:

$$IR_{max} \approx IC(\sqrt{BR}). \tag{32.8}$$

IR_{max} is an *ex ante* measure based on the residual risk from a multifactor model. IC, the information coefficient, is the correlation between securities' actual returns and the active manager's forecasts of returns on those securities. Grinold and Kahn considered the information coefficient a measure of the manager's skill, or special information. BR, the strategy's breadth, is defined as the number of independent bets taken on forecasts of exceptional returns. Because IR_{max} is an *ex ante* theoretical construct, it has no direct correspondence with the *ex post* information ratio of Equation 32.4 except (roughly) as an upper bound.

Equation 32.8 is a useful expression of the synergy expected from turning the adage "work smarter, not harder" into the well-known variation "work smarter *and* harder." But the concepts have very specific meanings here: "Smarter" means making more-accurate forecasts, and "harder" means covering more securities or forecasting the same securities more frequently.[1]

The maximum information ratio of Equation 32.8 is central to the Grinold–Kahn framework because they claim that the maximum value that can be added by an active manager is proportional to the squared maximum information ratio:

$$\text{Potential added value } = \frac{IR_{max}^2}{4\lambda}, \tag{32.9}$$

where λ is the coefficient of risk aversion of the investor. A manager's IR_{max} determines the manager's potential to add value and is separate from the riskiness of the strategy. So, a manager with an IR_{max} of 0.5 serving a conservative investor with $\lambda = 0.2$ could, at most, deliver 31.25 basis points a year over the benchmark. Conversely, a manager with an IR_{max} of 1.0 serving an aggressive investor with $\lambda = 0.05$ could deliver up to 500 basis points a year over benchmark.

Substituting the fundamental law represented by Equation 32.8 into Equation 32.9 produces the following explicit relationship between skill, effort, risk-taking, and potential added value:

$$\text{Potential added value } \approx \frac{IC^2(BR)}{4\lambda}. \tag{32.10}$$

Because both IR_{max} and BR are difficult (if not impossible) to quantify, the Grinold–Kahn equations (8–10) are of limited operational value, but they do call attention to information ratios and information coefficients estimated from historical data as important indicators of an active manager's abilities. For most investors, an information ratio is more accessible than an information coefficient because information coefficients require detailed security-level forecasts that are usually proprietary to the manager.

THE SHARPE RATIO AND THE INFORMATION RATIO

A statistic that is closely related to the information ratio but predates it is the Sharpe ratio. The original Sharpe ratio, also known as the Sharpe index, was introduced by Sharpe in 1966. This original version was tied to the theory of market equilibrium reflected in the capital asset pricing model. The theory implies the existence of a capital market line connecting the risk-free rate with the "market portfolio." The slope of the capital market line in risk–return space is the *ex ante* Sharpe ratio. Because the market portfolio is unknown, *ex post* performance measurement is based on the actual returns of the portfolio over the risk-free rate:

$$SR = \frac{\overline{R_P} - \overline{R_f}}{\hat{\sigma}_P},$$ (32.11)

where $\hat{\sigma}_P$ is the standard deviation of the active portfolio's returns, sometimes referred to as the "absolute volatility." One well-known portfolio strategy is to pick the active portfolio that maximizes the Sharpe ratio.[2]

The literature on the exact relationship between the Sharpe ratio and the information ratio is confusing, to say the least. Sharpe himself created confusion in a 1994 article in which he asserted that the information ratio is a "generalized Sharpe ratio." This conclusion arises from a view of excess returns as the outcome from a long–short strategy. The original Sharpe ratio is, then, the special case of an information ratio when the risk-free asset is a shorted security; that is, funds are borrowed at the risk-free rate to finance the long portfolio. But that interpretation violates the concept implied by the name of the information ratio. The information ratio is intended to serve as a measure of the special information that an active portfolio reveals through its return. The Sharpe ratio, however, will generally be positive even if the returns to a passive index fund are used for R_P. What special information is contained in a passive index? Logically, the information ratio of any passive benchmark is zero.

An additional source of confusion is contained in the writings of those associated with the BARRA multifactor model. In the paper of Grinold (1989) and the textbook of Rudd and Clasing (1982), the Sharpe ratio is defined as the squared information ratio. The original source of this odd definition can be traced back to Treynor and Black (1973). Moreover, in Grinold and Kahn (1995), the traditional Sharpe ratio defined in Equation 32.11 reappears.

In summary, depending on what source you happen to pick up, you can see the Sharpe ratio defined as the slope of the capital market line, the squared information ratio, or a special case of the information ratio. The definition shown in Equation 32.11 appears to be the most useful for practitioners.

INFORMATION RATIOS AND *t*-STATISTICS

An information ratio is subject to substantial estimation uncertainty, especially when only a short history is available. Quantifying that uncertainty naturally leads to the question of an information ratio's statistical significance. A close connection exists between the statistical significance of excess returns and the statistical significance of an information ratio. Starting with a set of returns in excess of benchmark returns, suppose you wish to find out whether, on average, the set of excess returns is positive and statistically significant. Following standard hypothesis testing, you set up a null hypothesis that the manager's excess returns over benchmark are, on average, zero (or equivalently, less than or equal to zero). The alternative hypothesis is that, on average, the returns are positive. The usual statistical assumption is that the excess returns are normally distributed with a mean and variance that must be estimated.[3] A *t*-statistic is formed as the ratio of average excess return divided by the standard error of the average excess return:

$$t\text{-Statistic} = \frac{\overline{ER}}{\hat{\sigma}_{ER}/\sqrt{T}}.$$ (32.12)

The t-statistic has a t distribution with $T - 1$ degrees of freedom, and standard t-tables can be used to determine the outcome of the hypothesis test. If a t-statistic with, say, 20 degrees of freedom exceeds the 95 percent critical value of 1.725, you can conclude that the manager's excess return is positive, on average, with 95 percent statistical confidence.

The t-statistic of Equation 32.12 has a direct connection to the information ratio because IR is part of the t-statistic:

$$t\text{-Statistic} = \frac{\overline{ER}}{\hat{\sigma}_{ER}/\sqrt{T}} = \frac{IR}{1/\sqrt{T}} = \sqrt{T}\,(IR). \qquad (32.13)$$

You can conduct a hypothesis test directly on the information ratio in which the same critical values of the t-tables apply.

The importance of statistical significance should not be overstated. An IR of 0.5 based on 21 time periods (20 degrees of freedom) will have a t-statistic of 2.29, which exceeds the 95 percent critical value of 1.725, indicating statistical significance. But the same IR of 0.5 based on 9 observations (8 degrees of freedom) will produce a t-statistic of only 1.50, falling short of the 95 percent critical value of 1.860 for 8 degrees of freedom. So, the IR is "significant" in one case and the same IR is "insignificant" in the other case, although they both represent the same value added. All statistical testing does is formalize how confident you can be in the calculated IR based on the length of history you have available.

This testing procedure can be extended to address the question of whether the information ratio exceeds a threshold or hurdle value (which some investors have, in fact, implemented for their hired managers). Suppose an investor has decided that all of its managers should have information ratios significantly in excess of 0.5. The t-statistic then becomes

$$t\text{-Statistic} = \sqrt{T}\,(IR - 0.5), \qquad (32.14)$$

where the same critical values apply. If the calculated t-statistic exceeds the critical value of the t-table for $T - 1$ degrees of freedom, then the manager has beaten the 0.5 hurdle by a statistically significant amount. Note that the caveat on the importance of statistical significance also applies here.

ANNUALIZATION

Information ratios are typically presented in an annualized form, which is intended to facilitate comparison. Annualized information ratios will differ, however, depending on how the returns were annualized. Of the many ways to annualize returns, the four most commonly used methods are considered here. The four methods are formulated for quarterly data to correspond to the data analysis of the next section. Modifications to monthly, weekly, or other data frequencies are straightforward. Throughout this section, the prefix A is used to designate annualized values, IR and ER represent, respectively, the quarterly information ratio and excess return, and subscripts 1 through 4 refer to the method.

1. Using the Arithmetic Mean Excess Return

The most common practice in the industry is to produce annualized statistics by multiplying the quarterly arithmetic mean by 4 and the quarterly tracking error by the square root of 4:

$$\overline{AER_1} = 4(\overline{ER}),\tag{32.15}$$

and

$$\hat{\sigma}_{AER_1} = \sqrt{4}(\hat{\sigma}_{ER}).\tag{32.16}$$

This method produces an annualized information ratio that is exactly twice the quarterly information ratio:

$$AIR_1 = \frac{\overline{AER_1}}{\hat{\sigma}_{AER_1}} = \frac{4(\overline{ER})}{\sqrt{4}(\hat{\sigma}_{ER})} = \sqrt{4}(IR) = 2(IR).\tag{32.17}$$

2. Using the Geometric Mean Excess Return

The geometric mean return is theoretically preferable to an arithmetic mean return because it takes into account the effects of compounding for a buy-and-hold investor. The annualized geometric mean excess return is found by solving[4]

$$\overline{AER_2} = \left[\prod_{t=1}^{T} \left(\frac{1 + R_{Pt}}{1 + R_{Bt}} \right) \right]^{4/T} - 1.\tag{32.18}$$

Typically, the same measure of volatility is used in the denominator of the information ratio as for the arithmetic mean, so

$$AIR_2 = \frac{\overline{AER_2}}{2(\hat{\sigma}_{ER})}.\tag{32.19}$$

3. Using the Continuously Compounded Mean Excess Return

Some analysts argue that working with continuously compounded returns has advantages over working with quarterly compounded returns (see Benninga 1997). The relationship between the two compounded mean returns is

$$
\begin{aligned}
\overline{AER_3} &= \ln{(1 + AER_2)} \\
&= \ln \left[\prod_{t=1}^{T} \left(\frac{1 + R_{Pt}}{1 + R_{Bt}} \right) \right]^{4/T} \\
&= \frac{4}{T} \left[\sum_{t=1}^{T} \ln(1 + R_{Pt}) - \sum_{t=1}^{T} \ln(1 + R_{Bt}) \right].
\end{aligned}\tag{32.20}
$$

Because a continuously compounded return will be lower than either an arithmetic or quarterly compounded return, using in this method the same estimate for volatility as the two previous methods will always produce lower information ratios—in some cases, substantially lower.

A more sensible approach is to calculate a volatility measure based on deviations from the average continuously compounded excess return:

$$\hat{\sigma}_{ER_3} = \sqrt{\frac{1}{T-1} \sum_{t=1}^{T} \left[\ln\left(\frac{1+R_{Pt}}{1+R_{Bt}}\right) - \overline{ER_3} \right]^2}, \tag{32.21}$$

and

$$\overline{ER_3} = \frac{1}{T} \sum_{t=1}^{T} \ln\left(\frac{1+R_{Pt}}{1+R_{Bt}}\right). \tag{32.22}$$

Then, the annualized information ratio is

$$AIR_3 = \frac{\overline{AER_3}}{2(\hat{\sigma}_{ER_3})}. \tag{32.23}$$

4. Using Frequency-Converted Data

Instead of annualizing directly from quarterly data, one can first convert the frequency of the data from quarterly to annual and then calculate the information ratio directly from the now-annual data.

The first step is to convert the frequency of the data from quarterly to annual. The theoretically correct way is to calculate the compound portfolio returns and benchmark returns separately (see Grinold and Kahn 1995). So, for the first year,

$$AR_{P1} = [(1 + R_{P1})(1 + R_{P2})(1 + R_{P3})(1 + R_{P4})] - 1,$$
$$AR_{B1} = [(1 + R_{B1})(1 + R_{B2})(1 + R_{B3})(1 + R_{B4})] - 1,$$

and

$$AER_1 = AR_{P1} - AR_{B1},$$

and for the second year,

$$AR_{P2} = [(1 + R_{P5})(1 + R_{P6})(1 + R_{P7})(1 + R_{P8})] - 1,$$
$$AR_{B2} = [(1 + R_{B5})(1 + R_{B6})(1 + R_{B7})(1 + R_{B8})] - 1,$$

and

$$AER_2 = AR_{P2} - AR_{B2},$$

and so forth. If j indexes the year and t is retained as the quarterly index, the general formula for the frequency-converted annualized excess return is

$$
\begin{aligned}
AER_j &= AR_{Pj} - AR_{Bj} \\
&= \left[\prod_{t=4(j-1)+1}^{4(j-1)+4} (1 + R_{Pt}) \right] - \left[\prod_{t=4(j-1)+1}^{4(j-1)+4} (1 + R_{Bt}) \right],
\end{aligned} \tag{32.24}
$$

with $j = 1,\ldots,(T/4)$.

The information ratio is then calculated on the basis of the annual excess return data:

$$AIR_4 = \frac{\overline{AER_4}}{\hat{\sigma}_{ER_4}}, \tag{32.25}$$

where

$$\overline{AER_4} = \frac{1}{T/4} \sum_{j=1}^{T/4} AER_j, \tag{32.26}$$

and

$$\hat{\sigma}_{AER_4} = \sqrt{\frac{1}{(T/4) - 1} \sum_{j=1}^{T/4} (AER_j - \overline{AER_4})^2}. \tag{32.27}$$

Comparison of the Four Methods.

Any one of these four methods of annualization has some validity, and perhaps a dozen other variations could be explored. An argument can be made that the frequency-conversion method is "best" because it provides the exact information ratio that would be calculated if returns were observed only annually. A practical drawback is that it requires four quarters of data for each year. If you want to update *IR* as new data come in each quarter, you have no easy way to do it.

Either of the compounding methods, AIR_2 and AIR_3, uses theoretically correct returns, but whether the measures of volatility used in the denominators are also theoretically correct is not clear. For example, AIR_2 (see Equation 32.19) uses the geometric mean in the numerator, but the measure of volatility in the denominator is based on deviations from the *arithmetic* mean.

An *IR* based on the arithmetic average returns is the most often used because arithmetic averages are the easiest to calculate and they usually approximate their theoretically superior cousins closely. Also, a transparent relationship exists between the *t*-statistic of Equation 32.13 and the arithmetically annualized *IR* of Equation 32.17 that does not exist for the other annualization methods. A question naturally arises, however, about whether systematic distortions are introduced by using Equation 32.13 instead of one of the other methods.

Given the returns of a particular fund for a particular observation period, can one say anything about whether the annualized information ratios calculated by the four methods will have a particular rank ordering? For example, will the frequency-converted *IR* always be larger than the arithmetic mean *IR*? The answer is that one cannot say anything with mathematical certainty about whether the information ratio found by one method will always be higher or lower than another one. This answer might at first seem counterintuitive, especially when the first method is compared with the second method. Equation 32.17 and Equation 32.19 have the same denominator, but the numerator of Equation 32.17 is based on the arithmetic mean return whereas the numerator of Equation 32.19 is based on the geometric mean return. The geometric mean is always less than the arithmetic mean if there is any volatility in the returns, so intuition would suggest that the solution to Equation 32.19 will always be less than the solution to Equation 32.17 for the same return history. But keep in mind that one method annualizes by multiplying the return by four, whereas the other method takes the return to the fourth power, which removes any consistent ordinal relationship between them. So, the existence of any systematic differences among the annualization methods is an empirical question—which leads to the next section.

EMPIRICAL EVIDENCE ON INFORMATION RATIOS

The empirical study reported here addressed (1) whether the choice among the four methods of annualization matters, (2) the effect of manager style on the distribution of information ratios, and (3) what kinds of information ratios real managers attain. The sample in the study came from the Frank Russell database and consisted of 212 active institutional money managers with quarterly returns spanning the 10 years from first quarter 1986 through fourth quarter 1995. Russell classified the managers in the sample as being in one of six style categories: market-oriented large-capitalization U.S. equities, large-cap value U.S. equities, large-cap growth U.S. equities, small-cap U.S. equities, international EAFE (MSCI's Europe/Australasia/Far East Index) equities, and sector-rotation U.S. bonds. Table 32.1 lists the benchmark indexes associated with the six styles and indicates the number of managers of the sample in each category.

The first question addressed was whether the choice of one of the four methods of annualizing the information ratio made any substantial difference in the overall distributions of the ratios. Surprisingly, extensive analysis produced only one systematic difference among the methods of annualization, namely, that the distribution of frequency-converted *IRs* (see Equation 32.25) had slightly thicker tails; that is, relatively more outliers resulted with this method than with the other methods.[5]

A clear finding of this study is that a manager's information ratio should be judged relative to the manager's style universe. Table 32.2 contains statistics on the distribution of annualized information ratios, and Figure 32.1 contains relative frequency histograms of the data.

TABLE 32.1   Style Benchmarks and Share of Sample

Category	Benchmark Index	Number of Managers
Market-oriented large-cap equity	Russell 1000	48
Large-cap value equity	Russell 1000 Value	35
Large-cap growth equity	Russell 1000 Growth	27
Small-cap equity	Russell 2000	35
International EAFE equity	MSCI EAFE	28
Sector-rotation bonds	Lehman Brothers Aggregate	39

TABLE 32.2   Distribution of Annualized Information Ratios, First Quarter 1986–Fourth Quarter 1995

	Market Oriented	Value	Growth	Small Cap	EAFE	Sector Bonds
N	48	35	27	35	28	39
Maximum ratio	0.74	0.27	0.96	1.03	0.20	1.41
Upper quartile	0.40	0.16	0.34	0.58	0.08	0.48
Median	0.19	0.02	0.23	0.43	0.02	0.30
Lower quartile	−0.20	−0.08	0.11	0.17	−0.06	−0.02
Minimum	−0.68	−0.34	−0.24	−0.05	−0.33	−0.66
Mean	0.11	0.02	0.25	0.41	0.01	0.26
Standard deviation	0.37	0.17	0.26	0.29	0.13	0.39
Portion >1.0	0.0%	0.0%	0.0%	2.9%	0.0%	2.6%
Portion >0.5	12.5%	0.0%	14.8%	40.0%	0.0%	20.5%

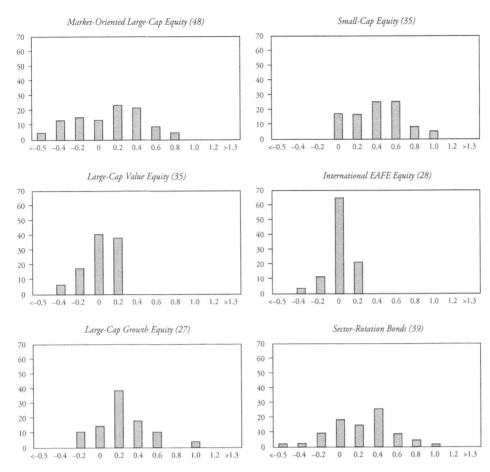

FIGURE 32.1   Relative Frequency Histograms of Information Ratios: Six Styles

Note: Midpoints of ranges. Information ratios are on the *x*-axes; relative frequencies, in percentages, are on the *y*-axes.

These information ratios were all calculated using the arithmetic mean method of annualiza-tion. As can be seen, information ratios for the sample differed dramatically by style. As a group, small-cap managers added the most value over benchmark returns during this period; more than half the managers exceeded 0.4. International managers performed the worst, with not one manager breaking 0.2. Comparing information ratios among styles risks confound-ing manager skill with systematic and cyclical differences among styles.

Another issue is the sensitivity of information ratios to the chosen benchmark. The choice of benchmark is sometimes a matter of intense negotiation between manager and investor, and the benchmarks used here may be inappropriate for some styles. For example, many of the market-oriented managers may have been using the S&P 500 as a bench-mark rather than the Russell 1000. Along similar lines, many small-cap managers have some mid-cap stocks in their portfolios, so the Russell 2500 might have been a more appropriate benchmark for that style universe. Figure 32.2 shows comparisons of relative frequencies for the market-oriented managers when the Russell 1000 was the benchmark and when the S&P 500 was the benchmark (top panel) and the small-cap managers when the Russell 2000 and

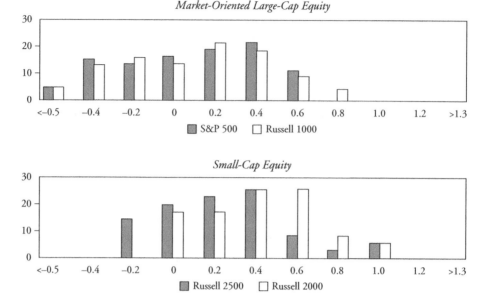

FIGURE 32.2   Relative Frequency Histograms of Information Ratios: Market-Oriented Large-Cap
U.S. Equity Using Two Benchmarks and Small-Cap U.S. Equity Using Two Benchmarks

Note: Midpoints of ranges. Information ratios are on the *x*-axes; relative frequencies, in percentages, are
on the *y*-axes.

the Russell 2500 were the benchmarks (bottom panel). Visual inspection makes clear that, as
a group, market-oriented managers performed worse against the S&P 500 than against the
Russell 1000, and small-cap managers, as a group, performed worse against the Russell 2500
than against the Russell 2000. The average drop in information ratios is 0.03 for market-
oriented and 0.15 for small-cap managers when the alternative benchmarks were used. The
maximum drops are 0.20 and 0.53, respectively. The choice of benchmark clearly matters a
great deal in calculating information ratios and should be thoughtfully considered.

How high must a manager's information ratio be for the manager to be hired, and how
low must it be for a manager to be fired? Grinold and Kahn (1995) asserted that an *IR* of
0.50 is "good," of 0.75 is "very good," and of 1.0 is "exceptional." They also reported that
about 10 percent of all information ratios lie above 1.0. Jacobs and Levy (1996) suggested
that a "good manager might have an *IR* of 0.5 and an exceptional manager might have an *IR*
of 1.0" (p. 11). The authors did not say whether these numbers came from theory, empirical
evidence, or practical experience.

So, the third issue this study addressed was how this experienced group of managers
(a manager had to have at least 10 years of an unbroken return history to be included) measures up to the Grinold–Kahn criteria. Table 32.2 contains statistics on the portions of managers in the right tails of their respective style distributions, which allows an assessment of the
abilities of the managers in the sample. If one accepts the Grinold and Kahn designation of an
"exceptional" money manager as having an information ratio of 1.0 or better, then no managers in four of the styles and fewer than 3 percent of the managers in the other two are exceptional. No one in two of the styles measures up to their designation of a "good" manager (*IR*
> 0.5). Considering that this sample is a data set of 10-year survivors, one would expect any

bias in the distribution to be on the upside, so sustaining a high information ratio over a substantial length of time appears to be a tougher proposition than Grinold and Kahn suggested.

CAVEATS

Investors should keep two warnings in mind when assessing this empirical evidence on information ratios—one related to misusing the ratios to make asset allocation decisions, and the other related to misusing the ratios to make passive versus active decisions. As to the first caveat, the information ratio is not useful for making decisions about how much to allocate to a particular asset class or style. Suppose you calculate that the information ratio of your bond manager is 0.5 and the information ratio of your growth-stock manager is 1.0. Should you shift funds out of bonds and into growth stocks? The answer has to be: not without a lot more information. The information ratio does not contain any information on correlations between asset classes. Furthermore, it does not take into account the risk tolerance of the investor. The information ratio is most useful for measuring the performance of an active manager against an appropriate benchmark. It can be used as a guide to choosing an active manager within a universe of similar asset/style managers, but it is not useful for making asset allocations.

As to the issue of drawing any inferences from the empirical evidence about the passive versus active question, remember that one 10-year past period may tell you nothing about the future. Do the modest-to-poor information ratios of these active value and EAFE managers suggest that investors would be better off going passive in those styles? The answer depends on your assessment of whether style-specific cycles exist. If the opportunities for active managers to add value go through style-specific cycles, then it is entirely possible that value managers will be able to add substantial value over benchmark returns in the future while another style—small-cap managers, for example—is struggling.

CONCLUSION

The information ratio is a powerful tool for assessing the skill of an active manager. It is arguably the best single measure of the mean–variance characteristics of an active portfolio. But investors should never rely exclusively on any single measure. Moreover, as with any statistic based on historical data, a high information ratio in the past is no guarantee of a high one in the future, and vice versa. In addition, the information ratio can be manipulated. Although the choice of annualization method does not make a large difference in most cases, the choice of benchmark does—sometimes dramatically. You should always be cautious in interpreting a published information ratio, and you should discount any that uses an inappropriate benchmark.

NOTES

1. In this interpretation, although working harder garners diminishing returns, being smarter never does.
2. See Ankrim (1992) for the pitfalls of this strategy.
3. Actually, the assumption that excess returns are normally distributed is not necessary. The important requirements are that the population mean and variance of excess returns

exist and that the excess returns be independent. Then, the *average* excess return will be normally distributed (asymptotically) even if the excess returns themselves are not. In practice, an assumption of independence is usually more problematic than an assumption of normality.

4. A simpler approximation is often used:

$$\overline{AER_2} = \left[\prod_{t=1}^{T} (1 + ER_t) \right]^{4/T} - 1 .$$ The result is usually quite close to Equation 32.18.

5. The various methods of annualization can, however, produce some large differences; of the 1,272 pairwise comparisons, the maximum difference was a huge 0.82. The average difference was less than 0.005, however, and the average absolute-value difference was only 0.05.

REFERENCES

Ankrim, Ernest M. 1992. "Risk Tolerance, Sharpe Ratios, and Implied Investor Preferences for Risk." Frank Russell Research Commentary.

Benninga, Simon. 1997. *Financial Modeling*. Cambridge, MA: MIT Press.

Grinold, Richard C. 1989."The Fundamental Law of Active Management." *Journal of Portfolio Management*, vol. 15, no. 3 (Spring):30–37.

Grinold, Richard C., and Ronald N. Kahn. 1992. "Information Analysis." *Journal of Portfolio Management*, vol. 18, no. 3 (Spring): 14–21.

———. 1995. *Active Portfolio Management*. Chicago, IL: Richard D. Irwin.

Jacobs, Bruce I., and Kenneth Levy. 1996. "Residual Risk: How Much Is Too Much?" *Journal of Portfolio Management*, vol. 21, no. 3 (Spring):10–16.

Rudd, Andrew, and Henry Clasing. 1982. *Modern Portfolio Theory*. Homewood, IL: Dow Jones Irwin.

Sharpe, William F. 1966. "Mutual Fund Performance." *Journal of Business*, vol. 39, no. 1, Part II (January):119–38.

———. 1994. "The Sharpe Ratio." *Journal of Portfolio Management*, vol. 21, no. 1 (Fall):49–59.

Treynor, Jack L., and Fischer Black. 1973. "How to Use Security Analysis to Improve Security Selection." *Journal of Business*, vol. 46, no. 1 (January):66–86.

CHAPTER 33

DOES ASSET ALLOCATION POLICY EXPLAIN 40, 90, OR 100 PERCENT OF PERFORMANCE?

Roger G. Ibbotson and Paul D. Kaplan

Disagreement over the importance of asset allocation policy stems from asking different questions. We used balanced mutual fund and pension fund data to answer the three relevant questions. We found that about 90 percent of the variability in returns of a typical fund across time is explained by policy, about 40 percent of the variation of returns among funds is explained by policy, and on average about 100 percent of the return level is explained by the policy return level.

Does asset allocation policy explain 40 percent, 90 percent, or 100 percent of performance? The answer depends on how the question is asked and what an analyst is trying to explain. According to well-known studies by Brinson and colleagues, more than 90 percent of the variability in a typical plan sponsor's performance over time is the result of asset allocation policy.[1] So, if one is trying to explain the variability of returns *over time*, asset allocation is very important.

Unfortunately, the Brinson et al. studies are often misinterpreted and the results applied to questions that the studies never intended to answer. For example, an analyst might want to know how important asset allocation is in explaining the variation of performance *among funds*. Because the Brinson studies did not address this question, the analyst can neither look to them to find the answer nor fault them for not answering it correctly.[2] A different study is required.

Finally, an analyst might want to know what percentage of the *level* of a typical fund's return is ascribable to asset allocation policy. Again, the Brinson studies do not address this question. A different study is needed.

Reprinted from the *Financial Analysts Journal* (January/February 2000):26–33.

Thus, three distinct questions remain about the importance of asset allocation:

1. How much of the variability of returns *across time* is explained by policy (the question Brinson et al. asked)? In other words, how much of a fund's ups and downs do its policy benchmarks explain?
2. How much of the variation in returns *among funds* is explained by differences in policy? In other words, how much of the difference between two funds' performance is a result of their policy difference?
3. What portion of the *return level* is explained by policy return? In other words, what is the ratio of the policy benchmark return to the fund's actual return?

Much of the recent controversy about the importance of asset allocation stems from treating the answer that Brinson et al. provided to Question 1 as an answer to Questions 2 and 3.

The purpose of our study was to ask and answer all three questions. To do this, we examined 10 years of monthly returns to 94 U.S. balanced mutual funds and 5 years of quarterly returns to 58 pension funds. We performed a different analysis for each question.

FRAMEWORK

Our data consisted of the total return for each fund for each period of time (a month or a quarter). The first step in our analysis was to decompose each total return, TR, into two components, policy return and active return, as follows:

$$TR_{i,t} = (1 + PR_{i,t})(1 + AR_{i,t}) - 1,$$

where
  $TR_{i,t}$ = total return of fund i in period t
  $PR_{i,t}$ = policy return of fund i in period t
  $AR_{i,t}$ = active return of fund i in period t

Policy return is the part of the total return that comes from the asset allocation policy. Active return is the remainder. Active return depends on both the manager's ability to actively over- or underweight asset classes and securities relative to the policy and on the magnitude and timing of those bets.

The asset allocation policy of each fund can be represented as a set of asset-class weights that sum to 1. For the pension funds in this study, these weights were known in advance. For the mutual funds, the policy weights were determined by return-based style analysis, which is described in the "Data" section. The policy return of the fund over a given period of time can be computed from the policy weights and returns on asset-class benchmarks as follows:

$$PR_{i,t} = w1_i R1_t + w2_i R2_t + \cdots + wk_i Rk_t - c,$$

where
  $w1_i, w2_i, \ldots, wk_i$ = policy weights of fund i
  $R1_t, R2_t, \ldots, Rk_t$ = returns on the asset classes in period t
  c = approximate cost of replicating the policy mix through indexed mutual funds, as a percentage of assets

Thus, in addition to fund returns, we needed policy weights for each fund and total returns on asset-class benchmarks. Given the total returns to the funds and the estimated policy returns of the funds, we solved for the active returns.

In our time-series analysis, we used the period-by-period returns. In our cross-sectional analysis, we used the compound annual rates of return over the period of analysis. For each fund, we computed the compound annual total return over the entire period as follows:

$$TR_i = \sqrt[N]{(1 + TR_{i,1})(1 + TR_{i,2})\cdots(1 + TR_{i,T})} - 1,$$

where

TR_i = compound annual total return on fund i over the entire period of analysis
$TR_{i,t}$ = total return of fund i in period t
T = number of period returns
N = length of the entire period of analysis, in years

Similarly, we computed the compound annual policy return over the entire period as follows:

$$PR_i = \sqrt[N]{(1 + PR_{i,1})(1 + PR_{i,2})\cdots(1 + PR_{i,T})} - 1,$$

where PR_i is the compound annual policy return on fund i over the entire period of analysis and $PR_{i,t}$ is the policy return to fund i in period t.

DATA

For the mutual fund portion of this study, we used 10 years of monthly returns for 94 U.S. balanced funds. The 94 funds represent all of the balanced funds in the Morningstar universe that had at least 10 years of data ending March 31, 1998. Policy weights for each fund were estimated by performing return-based style analysis over the entire 120-month period.[3] Table 33.1 shows the asset-class benchmarks used and the average fund exposure to each asset class.

TABLE 33.1   Asset Classes and Benchmarks for Balanced Mutual Funds

Asset Class	Benchmark	Average Allocation
Large-cap U.S. stocks	CRSP 1–2 portfolio[a]	37.4%
Small-cap U.S. stocks	CRSP 6–8 portfolio[a]	12.2
Non-U.S. stocks	MSCI Europe/Australasia/Far East Index	2.1
U.S. bonds	Lehman Brothers Aggregate Bond Index	35.2
Cash	30-day U.S. T-bills[b]	13.2

[a]Constructed by CRSP. CRSP excludes unit investment trusts, closed-end funds, real estate investment trusts, Americus trusts, foreign stocks, and American Depositary Receipts from the portfolios. CRSP uses only NYSE firms to determine the size breakpoints for the portfolios. Specifically, CRSP ranks all eligible NYSE stocks by company size (market value of outstanding equity) and then splits them into 10 equally populated groups, or deciles. The largest companies are in Decile 1, and the smallest are in Decile 10. The capitalization for the largest company in each decile serves as the breakpoint for that decile. Breakpoints are rebalanced on the last day of trading in March, June, September, and December. CRSP then assigns NYSE and Amex/Nasdaq companies to the portfolios according to the decile breakpoints. Monthly portfolio returns are market-cap-weighted averages of the individual returns within each of the 10 portfolios. The 1–2 portfolio is the combination of Deciles 1 and 2, and the 6–8 portfolio is the combination of Deciles 6, 7, and 8.
[b]Ibbotson Associates (1998).

In calculating the policy returns for each fund, we assumed that the cost of replicating the policy mix through index mutual funds would be 2 basis points a month (approximately 25 bps annually).

Stevens, Surz, and Wimer (1999) provided the same type of analysis on quarterly returns of 58 pension funds over the five-year 1993–1997 period.[4] We used the *actual* policy weights and asset-class benchmarks of the pension funds, however, rather than estimated policy weights and the same asset-class benchmarks for all funds. In each quarter, the policy weights were known in advance of the realized returns.[5] We report the pension fund results together with our analysis of the mutual fund returns in the next section.

QUESTIONS AND ANSWERS

Now consider the original three questions posed by the study: How much of the variability of return across time is explained by asset allocation policy, how much of the variation among funds is explained by the policy, and what portion of the return level is explained by policy return?

Question #1: Variability across Time

The Brinson et al. studies from 1986 and 1991 answered the question of how much of the variability of fund returns is explained by the variability of policy returns. They calculated the result by regressing each fund's total returns ($TR_{i,t}$ in our notation) against its policy returns ($PR_{i,t}$), reporting the R^2 value for each fund in the study, then examining the average, median, and distribution of these results.

Figure 33.1 illustrates the meaning of the time-series R^2 with the use of a single fund from our sample. In this example, we regressed the 120 monthly returns of a particular mutual fund against the corresponding monthly returns of the fund's estimated policy benchmark. Because most of the points cluster around the fitted regression line, the R^2 is quite high. About 90 percent of the variability of the monthly returns of this fund can be explained by the variability of the fund's policy benchmark.

In the first Brinson et al. study (1986), the authors studied quarterly returns over the 1974–83 period for 91 large U.S. pension funds. The average R^2 was 93.6 percent. In the second Brinson et al. study (1991), they studied quarterly returns over the 1978–87 period for 82 large U.S. pension funds. The average R^2 was 91.5 percent. Based on these results, the authors stated that more than 90 percent of the variability of the average fund's return across time is explained by that fund's policy mix.

The Brinson et al. results show that strategic asset allocation explains much of the variability of pension fund returns because plan sponsors select a long-term strategic target and tend to stick to it. If plan sponsors were more active, the R^2s would be lower.

The results from our analysis of both the mutual fund and the pension data are presented in Table 33.2, together with the Brinson et al. results. Our results confirm the Brinson result that approximately 90 percent of the variability of a fund's return across time is explained by the variability of policy returns. The result in our study for the median mutual fund was 87.6 percent, and the result for the median pension fund was 90.7 percent. The mean results in our study were slightly lower (81.4 percent and 88.0 percent, respectively) because they were skewed by the effect of a few outlier funds. These results are consistent with the notion that pension fund managers as a group are less active than balanced mutual fund managers.

Table 33.3 displays the range of outcomes in our study and shows that the mutual funds were more active than the pension funds. The mutual fund at the 5th percentile of R^2 had only 46.9

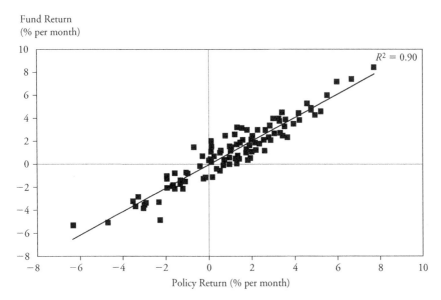

FIGURE 33.1   Time-Series Regression of Monthly Fund Return versus Fund Policy Return: One Mutual Fund, April 1988–March 1998

Note: The sample fund's policy allocations among the general asset classes were 52.4 percent U.S. large-cap stocks, 9.8 percent U.S. small-cap stocks, 3.2 percent non-U.S. stocks, 20.9 percent U.S. bonds, and 13.7 percent cash.

TABLE 33.2   Comparison of Time-Series Regression Studies

Measure	Brinson 1986	Brinson 1991	Mutual Funds	Pension Funds
R^2				
Mean	93.6%	91.5%	81.4%	88.0%
Median	NA	NA	87.6	90.7
Active return[a]				
Mean	−1.10	−0.08	−0.27	−0.44
Median	NA	NA	0.00	0.18

NA = not available.
[a]Active return is expressed as a percentage per year.

percent of the variability of returns explained by the variability of returns of the policy, whereas for the fund at the 95th percentile, the R^2 was 94.1 percent. For the pension funds, the R^2s are in the tighter range of 66.2 percent at the 5th percentile and 97.2 percent at the 95th percentile.

We next considered that the time-series R^2 may be high simply because funds participate in the capital markets in general and not because they follow a specific asset allocation policy. We explored this idea by regressing each mutual fund's total returns against the total returns to a common benchmark (rather than each against the returns to its own policy benchmark). For common benchmarks, we used the S&P 500 Index and the average of all of the policy benchmarks shown in Table 33.1.

TABLE 33.3   Range of Time-Series Regression R^2 Values

Percentile	Mutual Funds	Pension Funds
5	46.9%	66.2%
25	79.8	94.1
50	87.6	90.7
75	91.4	94.7
95	94.1	97.2

TABLE 33.4   Explaining a Mutual Fund's Time Series of Returns Using Different Benchmarks

R^2	S&P 500	Average Policy	Fund's Policy
Mean	75.2%	78.8%	81.4%
Median	81.9	85.2	87.6

The results are shown in Table 33.4. With the S&P 500 as the benchmark for all funds, the average R^2 was more than 75 percent and the median was nearly 82 percent. With the average policy benchmarks across funds as the benchmark, the average R^2 was nearly 79 percent and the median was more than 85 percent. These results are relatively close to those obtained when we used each specific fund's benchmark. Hence, the high R^2 in the time-series regressions result primarily from the funds' participation in the capital markets in general, not from the specific asset allocation policies of each fund. In other words, the results of the Brinson et al. studies and our results presented in Table 33.2 are a case of a rising tide lifting all boats.

Hensel, Ezra, and Ilkiw (1991) made a similar point in their study of the importance of asset allocation policy. In their framework, a naive portfolio had to be chosen as a baseline in order to evaluate the importance of asset allocation policy. They pointed out that in the Brinson et al. studies, the baseline portfolio was 100 percent in cash. In other words, the Brinson studies were written as if the alternative to selecting an asset allocation policy were to avoid risky assets altogether. When we used a more realistic baseline, such as the average policy benchmark across all funds, we found that the specific policies explain far less than half of the remaining time-series variation of the funds' returns.

Question #2: Variation among Funds

To answer the question of how much of the variation in returns among funds is explained by policy differences, one must compare funds with each other through the use of cross-sectional analysis. Many people mistakenly thought the Brinson studies answered this question. If all funds were invested passively under the same asset allocation policy, there would be no variation among funds (yet 100 percent of the variability of returns across time of each fund would be attributable to asset allocation policy). If all funds were invested passively but had a wide range of asset allocation policies, however, all of the variation of returns would be attributable to policy.

To answer the question of how much of the variation in returns among funds is explained by policy differences, we compared each fund return with each other fund's return.

10-Year Compound Annual
Fund Return (%)

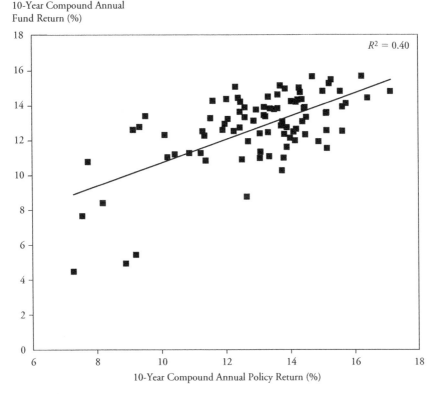

10-Year Compound Annual Policy Return (%)

FIGURE 33.2   Fund versus Policy: 10-Year Compound Annual Return across Funds,
April 1988–March 1998

We carried out a cross-sectional regression of compound annual total returns, TR_i, for the entire period on compound annual policy returns, PR_i, for the entire period. The R^2 statistic of this regression showed that for the mutual funds studied, 40 percent of the return difference was explained by policy and for the pension fund sample, the result was 35 percent.

Figure 33.2 is the plot of the 10-year compound annual total returns against the 10-year compound annual policy returns for the mutual fund sample. This plot demonstrates visually the relationship between policy and total returns. The mutual fund result shows that, because policy explains only 40 percent of the variation of returns across funds, the remaining 60 percent is explained by other factors, such as asset-class timing, style within asset classes, security selection, and fees. For pension funds, the variation of returns among funds that was not explained by policy was ascribable to the same factors and to manager selection.

The cross-sectional R^2 depended on how much the asset allocation policies of funds differed from one another and on how much the funds engaged in active management. To see how much asset allocation policies differed, we examined the cross-sectional distributions of the style weights. Table 33.5 presents the cross-sectional averages, standard deviations, and various percentiles of the style weights of the mutual funds. The last column presents these statistics for the total style allocation to equity. The large standard deviations and spreads between the percentiles indicate large variations in asset allocation policies among the funds.

Given how diverse the asset allocation policies are among these mutual funds, the relatively low R^2 of 40 percent must be the result of a large degree of active management. To

TABLE 33.5   Cross-Sectional Distributions of Balanced Mutual Fund Policy Weights

Measure	Large-Cap U.S. Stocks	Small-Cap U.S. Stocks	Non-U.S. Stocks	U.S. Bonds	Cash	Total Equities
Average	37.4%	12.2%	2.1%	35.2%	13.2%	51.6%
Standard deviation	17.0	7.6	2.3	14.4	15.9	16.0
Percentile						
5	1.2	1.1	0.0	12.8	0.0	23.3
25	29.9	7.1	0.0	26.6	1.0	44.5
50	40.2	11.0	1.5	35.2	7.7	54.5
75	48.8	16.5	3.1	45.1	17.5	62.0
95	56.2	24.8	6.4	56.7	47.3	74.1

see how the degree of active management can affect the cross-sectional R^2, we calculated the cross-sectional R^2 between the 10-year annual returns of the policy benchmarks and the 10-year annual returns of a set of modified fund returns. Each modified fund return was a weighted average of the actual fund return with the return on the policy benchmark so that the degree of active management was adjusted as follows:

$$TR_{i,t}^* = xTR_{i,t} + (1 - x)PR_{i,t},$$

where the value of x sets the level of active management. Setting x equal to 1 gives the sample result. Setting x less than 1 reduces the level of active management below what the funds actually did. Setting x greater than 1 shorts the benchmark and takes a levered position in the fund, thus increasing the level of active management beyond what the funds actually did.

The compound annual return of modified fund returns, TR_i^*, was calculated the same way as the compound annual return of actual fund returns (i.e., as the geometric mean of the modified annual returns).

Figure 33.3 shows the cross-sectional R^2 from regressing the modified compound annual returns on compound annual policy returns for various values of x. At $x = 1$, the cross-sectional R^2 is our original result, 40 percent. If the funds had been half as active ($x = 0.5$), the R^2 would have been much higher, 81 percent. On the other hand, if the funds had been one-and-a-half times as active ($x = 1.5$), the R^2 would have been only 14 percent. Thus, this approach shows how the degree of active management affects the cross-sectional R^2.

Question #3: Return Level

Many people also mistakenly thought the Brinson et al. studies were answering what portion of the return level is explained by asset allocation policy return, with an answer indicating nearly 90 percent. Brinson and his co-authors were not, however, addressing this question. We can address the question by using the Brinson data and the new data from our pension fund and mutual fund studies. We calculated the percentage of fund return explained by policy return for each fund as the ratio of compound annual policy return, PR_i, divided by the compound annual total return, TR_i. This ratio of compound returns is really simply a performance measure. A fund that stayed exactly at its policy mix and invested passively will have a ratio of 1.0, or 100 percent, whereas a fund that outperformed its policy will have a ratio less than 1.0.

Table 33.6 shows the percentage of fund return explained by policy return for the Brinson studies and the two data sets used in this study. On average, policy accounted for a little more

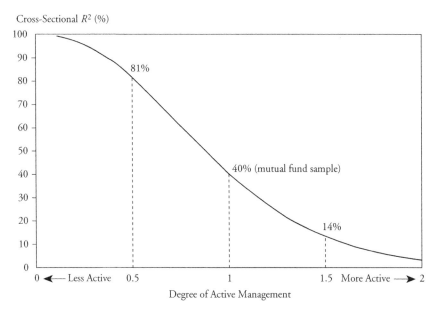

FIGURE 33.3   Degree of Active Management versus Cross-Sectional R^2, April 1988–March 1998

TABLE 33.6   Percentage of Total Return Level Explained by Policy Return

Study	Average	Median
Brinson 1986	112%	NA
Brinson 1991	101	NA
Mutual funds	104	100%
Pension funds	99	99

NA = not available.

than all of total return. The one exception is the pension fund sample in this study, where the mean result was 99 percent. The pension data did not have any expenses subtracted, however, so if we included external manager fees, pension staff costs, and other expenses, the result would probably be close to 100 percent, meaning that no value was added above the benchmark. On average, the pension funds and balanced mutual funds are not adding value above their policy benchmarks because of a combination of timing, security selection, management fees, and expenses. Moreover, results for both groups here may even be better than expected because the timing component might include some benefit from not rebalancing (letting equities run), which would have helped returns in the sample period's nearly continuous U.S. equity bull market.

The range of percentage of fund return explained by policy return is shown in Table 33.7. The mutual funds have a wider range because they are more willing to make timing and selection bets against the benchmark.

These results were anticipated by Sharpe (1991). He pointed out that because the aggregation of all investors is the market, the average performance before costs of all investors must equal the performance of the market. Because costs do not net out across investors, the average investor must be underperforming the market on a cost-adjusted basis. The implication is

TABLE 33.7   Range of Percentage of Total Return Level
Explained by Policy Return

Percentile	Mutual Funds	Pension Funds
5 (best)	82%	86%
25	94	96
50	100	99
75	112	102
95 (worst)	132	113

that, on average, more than 100 percent of the level of fund return would be expected from policy return. Of course, this outcome is not assured for subsamples of the market, such as balanced mutual funds or pension funds.

In our analysis, a fund's policy return measures the performance of the asset classes in which that fund invests. Therefore, based on Sharpe's thesis, we would predict that, on average, a little more than 100 percent of the level of total return would be the result of policy return.[6] Our results confirm this prediction.

This is not to say that active management is useless. An investor who has the ability to select superior managers before committing funds can earn above-average returns. If, as Goetzmann and Ibbotson (1994) suggested, superior performance and inferior performance persist over time, one need only invest in the funds that have outperformed in the past. Nevertheless, the average return across all funds in the market cannot be greater than the return on the market.

CONCLUSION

We sought to answer the question: What part of fund performance is explained by asset allocation policy? If we think of this issue as a multiple-choice question with "40 percent," "90 percent," "100 percent," and "all of the above" as the choices, our analysis shows that asset allocation explains about 90 percent of the variability of a fund's returns *over time* but it explains only about 40 percent of the variation of returns *among funds*. Furthermore, on average across funds, asset allocation policy explains a little more than 100 percent of the *level* of returns. So, because the question can be interpreted in any or all of these ways, the answer is "all of the above."

ACKNOWLEDGMENTS

This chapter grew out of discussions with Ron Surz. We thank Dale Stevens for providing the pension fund data and Mark Wimer of Ibbotson Associates for his able assistance.

NOTES

1. Brinson, Hood, and Beebower (1986); Brinson, Singer, and Beebower (1991).
2. The essence of Jahnke's (1997) critique of the Brinson et al. studies is that they used time-series R^2s to address the question of cross-sectional variability. This critique is unfair because the Brinson studies never addressed the cross-sectional question.

3. Return-based style analysis was first proposed by Sharpe (1992). See Lucas (1998) for a detailed discussion.

4. The results are reported in Stevens, Surz, and Wimer, together with the mutual fund results reported here.

5. The average allocations among the general asset classes used in the pension fund study were 43.7 percent U.S. stocks, 38.0 percent U.S. bonds, 5.0 percent cash, and 13.3 percent other asset classes.

6. We have taken out the cost of indexing from the policy return, so the average underperformance of the fund is less than what Sharpe's analysis would suggest.

REFERENCES

Brinson, Gary P., L. Randolph Hood, and Gilbert L. Beebower. 1986. "Determinants of Portfolio Performance." *Financial Analysts Journal*, vol. 42, no. 4 (July/August):39–48.

Brinson, Gary P., Brian D. Singer, and Gilbert L. Beebower. 1991. "Determinants of Portfolio Performance II: An Update." *Financial Analysts Journal*, vol. 47, no. 3 (May/June):40–48.

Goetzmann, William N., and Roger G. Ibbotson. 1994. "Do Winners Repeat?" *Journal of Portfolio Management*, vol. 20, no. 2 (Winter):9–18.

Hensel, Chris R., D. Don Ezra, and John H. Ilkiw. 1991. "The Importance of the Asset Allocation Decision." *Financial Analysts Journal*, vol. 47, no. 4 (July/August):65–72.

Ibbotson Associates. 1998. *Stocks, Bonds, Bills, and Inflation, 1998 Yearbook*. Chicago, IL: Ibbotson Associates.

Jahnke, William W. 1997. "The Asset Allocation Hoax." *Journal of Financial Planning*, vol. 10, no. 1 (February):109–113.

Lucas, Lori. 1998. "Analyzing Manager Style." In *Pension Investment Handbook, 1998 Supplement*. Edited by Mark W. Riepe and Scott L. Lummer. New York: Panel Publishers.

Sharpe, William F. 1991. "The Arithmetic of Active Management." *Financial Analysts Journal*, vol. 47, no. 1 (January/February):7–9.

———. 1992. "Asset Allocation: Management Style and Performance Measurement." *Journal of Portfolio Management*, vol. 18, no. 2 (Winter):7–19.

Stevens, Dale H., Ronald J. Surz, and Mark E. Wimer. 1999. "The Importance of Investment Policy." *Journal of Investing*, vol. 8, no. 4 (Winter):80–85.

CHAPTER 34

FUND MANAGEMENT CHANGES AND EQUITY STYLE SHIFTS

John G. Gallo and Larry J. Lockwood

We examined changes in performance, risk, and investment style for mutual funds that changed managers during the 1983–1991 period. Results show that funds experiencing a managerial change performed poorly before the change, primarily as a result of inferior security selection. Risk-adjusted performance, on average, improved 200 basis points annually and systematic risk increased significantly after the management change. We also classified funds according to their equity "effective mix" of company sizes and value versus growth. More than 65 percent of the funds experienced a shift in investment style after the management change.

Many institutional portfolios employ multiple domestic (U.S.) equity managers, each representing a particular equity style. Each style is characterized by a unique risk–return pattern, and each style experiences unpredictable cycles in which the style is either penalized or rewarded by the market. As Sharpe (1992) showed, portfolio performance is driven mainly by the portfolio's asset-class allocation. He argued that equity managers should classify equities into asset classes defined according to equity style characteristics, such as market-to-book value and company size. Managers of well-diversified portfolios, therefore, must make optimal allocation decisions among all equity styles to attain the benefits of equity style diversification (Bailey and Arnott 1986).

Institutional plan sponsors obviously want to select equity managers who provide superior performance within each style category. But plan sponsors also want managers who maintain their style throughout an entire market cycle (Logue 1991). Equity managers who stray outside the designated style can be misclassified by investors and expose their overall portfolios to unanticipated style exposure (risk), which reduces the potential benefits of a

Reprinted from *Financial Analysts Journal* (September/October 1999):44–52.

multiple-style strategy. Portfolios that contain misclassified managers fail to attain the desired risk reduction offered by style diversification. DiBartolomeo and Witkowski (1997) reported that 40 percent of mutual funds are misclassified.

We defined four domestic equity styles along value–growth and market-capitalization dimensions.[1] Researchers often use two general approaches to style classification. The classifications are often made on the basis of the fundamental characteristics of portfolio holdings. Managers whose portfolios exhibit similar fundamental characteristics (e.g., betas, P/Es, dividend yields) are placed in the same style group (Christopherson 1995), but this approach is often unduly detailed and expensive (Bailey and Arnott). An alternative approach classifies managers according to exposures to well-recognized risk proxies. Trzcinka (1995) showed that this approach is a simple, effective, and objective equity classification strategy. Finally, Gallo and Lockwood (1997) showed how portfolio risk-adjusted returns are improved by classifying managers on the basis of exposures to large-cap/growth, large-cap/value, small-cap/growth, and small-cap/value indexes.

We examined shifts in performance, risk, and investment style of 69 domestic equity mutual funds that experienced a change in fund management in our sample period. We looked at each fund's returns before and after the management change and discuss here the change in performance, risk profile, and investment style after the management change.

DATA

The analysis covers monthly returns for mutual funds that announced management changes during the 1983–1991 period. To be included in the sample, each fund had to have consecutive monthly returns for a 10-year period during which no more than one management change occurred. One manager had to be in place for the full five-year period before the management change, and the subsequent manager had to be in place for the full five-year period beginning the month following the change (as identified by Morningstar Mutual Funds).[2]

For instance, assume a fund announced a management change in January 1983. To be included in the sample, the management of the fund had to be attributed to only one individual manager for the period January 1978 to December 1982, and the subsequent individual manager had to manage the fund throughout the entire February 1983 to January 1988 period (the period following the management change). Note that for a fund with a management change in December 1991, the subsequent manager would be evaluated for the January 1992 to December 1996 period. Thus, the monthly returns used in the sample spanned the period January 1978 to December 1996.

The sample consists of 69 equity mutual funds.[3] The return series for each fund includes 10 years of monthly observations, excluding the month of management change. All mutual fund and index return data for the period January 1978 to December 1996 were obtained from CDA Investment Technologies.

RESEARCH METHODS

We performed tests to detect changes in performance, risk, and equity style after a change in fund managers. We computed performance and risk measures for each fund in the periods prior to and after the management change. The differences in cross-sectional average fund performance were examined with a t-test.[4]

Performance Measures

Initially, we computed Sharpe's (1966) reward-to-variability measure, *RVAR*, for each fund:

$$RVAR_i = \frac{R_i - R_f}{\sigma_i}, \tag{34.1}$$

where

    R_i = mean monthly return for mutual fund i
    R_f = risk-free rate (the 30-day U.S. T-bill rate)
    σ_i = standard deviation of monthly returns for fund i

We used the $RVAR_i$ to compute the average excess return earned per unit of the fund's total risk.

    We also computed the Jensen alpha for each fund. The alpha equals the difference between the realized mean return for the fund and its risk-adjusted required return determined by the capital asset pricing model. The Jensen alpha is estimated from the following regression:

$$R_{it} - R_{ft} = \alpha_i + \beta_i (R_{Mt} - R_{ft}) + \varepsilon_{it}, \tag{34.2}$$

where for month t,

    R_{it} = return for fund i
    R_{Mt} = return for the market portfolio
    ε = the random error term

We used the Wilshire 5000 Index as the proxy for the market portfolio. A significant positive (negative) α_i indicates superior (inferior) investment performance of the fund.

    We used a dummy variable regression that pooled across the pre- and postchange periods to test for a change in alpha:

$$R_{it} - R_{ft} = \alpha_{1i} + \alpha_{2i}D_{1t} + \beta_{i1} (R_{Mt} - R_{ft}) + \beta_{i2} (R_{Mt} - R_{ft})D_{2t} + \varepsilon_{it}, \tag{34.3}$$

where D_t equaled 1 after the management change month and 0 before the management change month. The prechange alpha is α_1, and the postchange alpha is $\alpha_1 + \alpha_2$. The *t*-statistic for the α_2 estimate was used to test for a change in alpha between pre- and post-management-change periods.

Security Selection and Market Timing

We used the quadratic Treynor–Mazuy (1966) regression model to separate the effects of the sample managers' microforecasting (security-selection) and macroforecasting (market-timing) skills. The Treynor–Mazuy model decomposes the sources of fund performance as follows:

$$R_{it} + R_{ft} = \alpha_i + \lambda_i(R_{Mt} - R_{ft}) + \tau_i(R_{Mt} - R_{ft})^2 + \varepsilon_{it}, \tag{34.4}$$

where α_i represents the security-selection ability of the manager and τ_{i1} indicates the managers' market-timing skill (see also Grinblatt and Titman 1989). Successful market timers will increase (decrease) exposure to a market factor when the market is expected to rise (fall). The quadratic equation is derived by assuming that the fund beta in Equation 34.2 may change in response to the market index. For instance, Equation 34.4 is derived by replacing β_i in Equation 34.2 with $\beta_{it} = \lambda_i + \tau(R_{Mt} - R_{ft})$. A positive (negative) τ_i implies superior (inferior) market-timing skill. A positive (negative) α_i indicates superior (inferior) security-selection ability.

Changes in Risk

We used three measures to examine the impact of management change on fund risk: the standard deviation of monthly returns, σ; beta, β; and error variance, σ_ε^2, which proxy for, respectively, total risk, systematic risk, and unsystematic risk. The fund beta and error variance were derived from Equation 34.2.

An F-test was used to test the equality of pre- and post-management-change total risk. The F-statistic equalled the ratio of the prechange return variance to the postchange return variance and followed an F-distribution with $N_1 - 1$ degrees of freedom in the numerator and $N_2 - 1$ degrees of freedom in the denominator. N_1 and N_2 are, respectively, the number of months (60) in the pre- and postchange periods.

We tested for change in beta using the dummy variable regression, Equation 34.3, that pools across the pre- and post-management-change periods, where D_t equalled 0 before the management change month and 1 after the management change month. The prechange beta was β_1, and the postchange beta was $\beta_1 + \beta_2$. The t-statistic for the β_2 estimate was used to test for a change in beta between the pre- and post-management-change periods.

Finally, we used an F-test to detect changes in fund unsystematic risk. The F-statistic equalled the ratio of the prechange residual variance to the postchange residual variance (from Equation 34.2) and followed an F-distribution with 60 degrees of freedom in both the numerator and the denominator.

Change in Equity Style

We also examined structural shifts in the investment style of each fund by using the effective mix method developed by Sharpe (1992). Sharpe found that equity styles can be determined from mutual funds' sensitivities to the return series on a set of mutually exclusive equity indexes. He argued that the indexes should incorporate market capitalization and value versus growth dimensions. Fama and French also showed that company size and value versus growth factors have been priced in the market. Consequently, we measured the exposure of each fund to large-cap/growth, small-cap/growth, large-cap/value, and small-cap/value indexes. We used the monthly returns to these stock indexes maintained by Wilshire Associates.

We determined the mutual funds' exposures to each style by using the following time-series regression on the five-year prechange excess returns:

$$R_{it} - R_{ft} = a_i + b_{i1}(LCG_t - R_{ft}) + b_{i2}(SCG_t - R_{ft}) \\ + b_{i3}(LCV_t - R_{ft}) + b_{i4}(SCV_t - R_{ft}) + \varepsilon, \qquad (34.5)$$

where LCG, SCG, LCV, and SCV are, respectively, the returns on the large-cap/growth, small-cap/growth, large-cap/value, and small-cap/value Wilshire indexes. The b_i variable is the sensitivity of the excess returns of fund i to the excess returns of the Wilshire indexes.

Following Gallo and Lockwood, we classified each fund as to the investment style for which the fund exposure was highest. We computed Equation 34.5 before and after the management change for each fund, and we examined changes in investment style by comparing classifications before and after the management change. A two-way classification matrix was used to examine style consistency for the entire sample.

Style consistency was also examined with a Chow structural change test. The inputs to the test were derived from Equation 34.2. The F-statistic was computed as

$$\frac{(SSE_\tau - SSE_1 - SSE_2)/K}{(SSE_1 + SSE_2)/(n + m - 2K)}, \qquad (34.6)$$

where
- SSE_τ = error sum of squares over the total period (120 observations)
- SSE_1 = error sum of squares over the prechange period ($n = 60$ observations)
- SSE_2 = error sum of squares over the post-change period ($m = 60$ observations)
- K = number of regression coefficients.[5]

The statistic followed an *F*-distribution with K degrees of freedom in the numerator and $n + m - 2K$ degrees of freedom in the denominator. In the results, a significant *t*-statistic indicates style inconsistency between the prechange and postchange periods.

RESULTS

Management change dates and Jensen alphas for each of the 69 mutual funds are in Table 34.1. The last row presents average results for all 69 mutual funds. Alphas for the period prior to the management change (Pre α) are positive for 20 funds and negative for 49 funds. The percentage of negative alphas (71 percent) is significantly greater than a random event (*t*-statistic = 3.32).[6] The alpha estimates are significantly negative (at the 10 percent level) for 20 funds and significantly positive for only 3 funds. Alphas for the period after the management change (Post α) are positive for 36 funds and negative for 33 funds. The percentage of positive alphas (52 percent) is not significantly different from 50 percent and only 4 of the alphas are significantly negative. Thus, performance generally was below the benchmark prior to the management change and matched the benchmark after the management change.

The Sharpe ratios reflect the results of the Jensen tests.[7] The sample *RVAR*s in the postchange period were considerably higher than in the prechange period ($RVAR_1 = 0.1156$ versus $RVAR_2 = 0.1823$). Individually, 48 (21) funds exhibited higher (lower) *RVAR*s following the management change.

Based on the cross-sectional performance tests, reward-to-variability ratios and alphas improved after the management change. The average *RVAR* improved 57.6 percent and average fund alpha improved more than 100 percent. In fact, the monthly alpha increased 16.58 basis points a month (or 200 bps a year). The *t*-statistics for differences in mean *RVAR* and portfolio alpha were found to be significant (*t*-statistics = 4.36 and 3.65, respectively). Thus, fund performance improved significantly following the management changes. The performance tests suggest that poor performance may have been the catalyst for the management change.

The results of Equation 34.4 (the Treynor–Mazuy multi-index model) are in Table 34.2. The Treynor–Mazuy test decomposes the Jensen alpha and provides insight into the security-selection ability and market-timing skills of fund managers. A positive (negative) alpha indicates superior (inferior) security selection. A positive (negative) τ_i implies superior (inferior) market timing. Individual fund results for the pre- and post-management-change periods are summarized in, respectively, Panels A and B. The cross-sectional average results are in Panel C.

The selection coefficient for the average fund in the pre-management-change period is negative, which suggests that inferior security-selection decisions contributed to the poor performance observed in the prechange period. Individually, 47 funds exhibited negative selection coefficients in the prechange period, of which 20 coefficients were statistically significant. Positive coefficients were found for 22 funds, only 4 of which were significant. Previous studies of mutual funds (for instance, Chang and Lewellen 1984; Lee and Rahman 1990) found, on

TABLE 34.1   Performance Comparisons

Fund	Change Date	Pre α	Post α	$t(\alpha)$
AIM Summitt Investment	January 1988	−0.56**	0.12	2.43**
Affiliated Fund	April 1991	−0.11	0.14	1.27
American Cap Comstock	April 1989	−0.40*	−0.04	1.60
American Cap Enterprise	May 1989	−0.31*	0.03	1.41
American Cap Growth and Income	July 1990	−0.27	0.03	1.20
American Cap Emerging Growth	April 1989	−0.70**	0.47	3.07**
Berger 100	November 1990	0.25	0.13	−0.22
Berger Growth and Income	October 1991	−0.10	−0.07	0.07
Cardinal Fund	January 1991	−0.01	−0.12	−0.63
Colonial Growth Shares	April 1986	−0.17	0.03	0.77
Composite Growth and Income	November 1991	−0.24	0.05	1.44
Dean Witter American Value	January 1987	−0.43*	0.18	2.06**
Dreyfus Appreciation	October 1990	0.16	−0.11	−0.82
Dreyfus Fund	January 1990	0.08	−0.20*	−1.61
Dreyfus Growth Opportunities	June 1990	0.05	−0.34	−1.00
Evergreen Value	March 1991	0.06	0.01	−0.29
FBL Growth	November 1986	−0.54**	−0.26	0.91
Federated American Leaders	January 1990	−0.18	0.08	1.27
Fidelity Trend	June 1987	−0.31*	−0.05	1.01
Financial Industrial	January 1988	−0.41**	−0.10	1.22
Fortis Capital	January 1983	0.75**	−0.12	−2.31**
Fortis Growth	January 1983	1.09**	−0.30	−2.97**
FPA Capital	July 1984	−0.25	−0.09	0.42
Franklin Equity	October 1983	−0.28	0.20	1.39
IDS Discovery	October 1988	−0.86**	0.09	1.95*
IDS Equity Plus	August 1983	0.03	−0.19	−0.77
IDS New Dimensions	March 1991	0.41	−0.07	−1.59
IDS Progressive	April 1991	−0.44	−0.39	0.13
IDS Strategy Equity	June 1989	0.24	0.04	−0.93
Janus Fund	June 1986	0.10	0.33	0.63
Kemper Growth	June 1991	0.34	−0.42*	−2.26**
Kemper Small Cap	January 1987	−0.22	0.13	0.92
Keystone K-2	April 1989	−0.26	0.01	1.01
Keystone S-1	August 1989	−0.19	−0.23*	−0.26
Keystone S-3	September 1987	−0.33*	−0.10	0.99
Lord Abbett Developing Growth	July 1989	−1.21**	−0.11	2.02**
Mass Financial Development	September 1991	−0.20	0.17	1.61
Merrill Lynch Capital	June 1983	0.21	0.29**	0.33
Merrill Lynch Special Value	September 1989	−0.98**	−0.03	1.94*
MFS Value	September 1991	−0.15	0.33	1.55
Mutual Beacon Growth	January 1985	−0.29	0.40*	2.16**
Nationwide Fund	January 1985	−0.06	0.16	1.09
Neuberger Guardian	January 1988	−0.06	0.13	0.89
Neuberger Partners	June 1990	0.02	0.10	0.45
Neuberger Select	January 1988	−0.13	0.11	0.80
Oppenheimer Fund	June 1990	−0.55**	0.02	2.00**
Oppenheimer Special Fund	September 1987	−0.53*	0.20	2.06**

(continued)

TABLE 34.1   (continued)

Fund	Change Date	Pre α	Post α	$t(\alpha)$
Oppenheimer Total Return	February 1990	0.18	0.08	−0.35
Penn Square	March 1986	0.01	−0.04	−0.23
Philadelphia Fund	May 1987	−0.44**	−0.20	0.82
Pilgrim Magna Capital	August 1989	0.13	−0.06	−0.77
Pioneer Fund	January 1986	−0.19	−0.17	0.10
Pioneer II	January 1991	−0.22	0.03	1.17
Prudential Bache Equity B	April 1990	−0.05	0.14	0.85
Putnam Investors	June 1988	−0.33*	−0.01	1.57
Putnam Vista Basic Value	December 1991	−0.02	0.21	0.83
Quest for Value	January 1989	0.00	−0.05	−0.23
Safeco Equity	January 1984	−0.18	−0.07	0.46
Safeco Growth	January 1989	−0.39*	−0.17	0.41
SBS Fundamental Value	November 1990	−0.32	0.26	2.13**
Sentinel Common Stock	January 1985	0.33*	0.05	−1.13
State Street Investment	January 1988	−0.02	−0.12	−0.47
Strong Opportunity	March 1991	0.29	0.22	−0.16
T. Rowe Price Growth	July 1984	−0.53**	−0.05	1.64
T. Rowe Price New Horizon	September 1989	−0.85**	−0.15	1.50
United New Concepts	February 1989	−0.55	0.36	1.83*
USAA Growth	January 1988	−0.50**	−0.03	2.29**
Vanguard World–US Growth	August 1987	−0.09	0.22	1.14
Winthrop Growth and Income	March 1986	0.01	−0.27**	−1.47
Fund average		−0.1640	0.0018	3.65**

Note: The sample period is January 1978 to December 1996. The *t*-statistic in the last column is for the difference between pre- and postchange alphas.
*Significant at the 10 percent level.
**Significant at the 5 percent level.

TABLE 34.2   Security-Selection and Market-Timing Results

Measure	Number of		Number of Significant	
	Positive	Negative	Positive	Negative
A. Frequency of results before management change				
α_{i1}	22	47	4	20
τ_i	32	37	8	11
B. Frequency of results after management change				
α_{i2}	41	28	7	5
τ_i	35	34	15	15
	Before	After	*t*-Statistic	
C. Results for average fund				
α_p	−0.1517	0.0028	2.95**	
τ_p	−0.0001	−0.0005	0.88	

Note: The sample period is January 1978 to December 1996.
**Significant at the 5 percent level.

average, no abnormal security-selection ability. The inferior security selection observed in the prechange period for this sample, therefore, contrasts with prior findings.

For the postchange period, 41 funds have positive security-selection estimates and 28 have negative. The selection estimates in the postchange period are significantly positive for 7 funds and significantly negative for 5 funds. The average estimate in the postchange period is also positive and significantly higher than the estimate in the prechange period. Thus, security-selection ability improved significantly in the postchange period.

Market-timing skills in the prechange period were consistent with skills in the post-change period; we found little difference in the cross-sectional average market-timing coefficients between the periods. The data in Table 34.2 indicate that this sample, on average, displayed neither superior nor inferior market timing in either period, which is consistent with the findings of Coggin, Fabozzi, and Rahman (1993) and Grinblatt and Titman.[8]

Table 34.3 presents the σ, β and σ_ε^2 risk statistics for the 69 funds calculated for the 60-month period preceding the management change and the 60-month period subsequent to the management change. The last row of the table reports average statistics for the 69 funds. On average, total risk fell after a management change, but the findings indicate that systematic risk increased (prechange beta = 0.95; postchange beta = 1.0) while unsystematic risk fell ($\sigma_{\varepsilon 1}^2$ = 1.64 versus $\sigma_{\varepsilon 2}^2$ = 1.5). These findings are consistent with a reversion of systematic risk toward the mean (1.0) after a management change. The change in mean beta is statistically significant (t-statistic = 2.13). As shown in Table 34.1, the increase in mean systematic risk coincides with an increase in mean risk-adjusted performance.

Results of the classification according to investment styles are in Table 34.4. Funds were initially classified on the basis of the highest loading on the Wilshire indexes (from Equation 34.5) for the 60-month period preceding the management change. The funds were then reclassified on the basis of the 60-month period following the management change. Entries down the diagonal of Table 34.4 indicate the number of funds that did not change classification. For example, of the 69 funds, 24 (or 34.8 percent) experienced no change in investment style classification after the management change. The remaining 45 funds (65.2 percent) changed investment style. If the funds had been randomly assigned in the postchange period, the classification accuracy would have been approximately 25 percent (e.g., entries down the diagonal would equal 69/16 on average). The classification accuracy found here (34.8 percent) is thus significantly better than a random selection at the 10 percent level of significance.

Our findings from the effective mix methodology show that classification based on pre-management change is better than a random classification. Clearly, a significant percentage of funds (65.2 percent) changed investment style after the management change, which is consistent with the results of DiBartolomeo and Witkowski. All 12 funds classified as large-cap/growth prior to a management change experienced a shift in style after the management change. Furthermore, 12 of the 19 large-cap funds, 26 of the 35 small-cap/growth funds, and all 3 of the small-cap/value funds experienced a shift in investment style after a change in managers. All of these percentages are statistically significant, so shifts in investment style pervaded all style categories.

Additional evidence of style shifts was provided by the Chow structural changes test, which used the sum of squared errors from Equation 34.5. The Chow test statistic (F = 3.82) indicated that, on average, funds experienced a change in investment style following a change in management. Individually, significant changes in style were found for 51 funds at the 10 percent level (41 at the 5 percent level). Thus, 74 percent of the funds experienced a change in investment style in the post-management-change period.[9]

TABLE 34.3 Risk Comparisons

Fund	Pre σ^2	Post σ^2	$F(\sigma)$	Pre β	Post β	$t(\beta)$	Pre σ_ε^2	Post σ_ε^2	$F(\sigma_\varepsilon^2)$
AIM Summitt Investment	38.32	18.84	2.04**	1.13	1.09	−0.70	3.21	1.31	2.45**
Affliated Fund	23.52	6.25	3.76**	0.87	0.84	−0.57	1.20	0.97	1.24
American Cap Comstock	33.64	13.03	2.57**	1.07	0.95	−2.33**	2.42	0.44	5.50**
American Cap Enterprise	39.94	18.00	2.22**	1.18	1.10	−1.58	2.12	0.92	2.30**
American Cap Growth and Income	35.76	9.99	3.59**	1.09	0.92	−2.68**	3.46	0.34	10.17**
American Cap Emerging Growth	31.88	31.86	1.01	1.03	0.38	3.87**	2.88	5.67	1.97*
Berger 100	35.28	23.62	1.49	0.93	1.36	2.84**	10.08	8.48	1.19
Berger Growth and Income	25.30	8.82	2.87**	0.83	0.91	0.65	6.67	2.66	2.51**
Cardinal Fund	18.58	6.50	2.85**	0.78	0.84	1.11	0.64	1.00	1.56
Colonial Growth Shares	22.09	33.64	1.53	1.06	1.04	−0.33	2.10	1.97	1.07
Composite Growth and Income	15.92	6.76	2.36**	0.73	0.86	2.22**	1.66	0.68	2.44**
Dean Witter American Value	24.40	24.80	1.02	1.07	0.92	−2.44**	3.29	1.98	1.66
Dreyfus Appreciation	34.46	10.63	3.23**	1.01	1.00	−0.14	4.40	1.66	2.65**
Dreyfus Fund	13.10	9.99	1.31	0.69	0.86	4.40**	0.93	0.69	1.35
Dreyfus Growth Opportunities	23.04	19.01	1.21	0.84	1.12	2.92**	4.03	4.63	1.15
Evergreen Value	20.98	5.90	3.55**	0.83	0.82	−0.06	0.72	0.78	1.08
FBL Growth	14.75	18.23	1.23	0.94	0.61	−5.29**	1.37	3.94	2.88**
Federated American Leaders	14.29	12.60	1.13	0.71	0.93	4.41**	1.37	1.25	1.10
Fidelity Trend	25.40	40.83	1.61*	1.11	1.21	1.95*	1.67	1.98	1.19
Financial Industrial	31.81	20.61	1.55*	1.05	1.11	1.13	1.62	2.16	1.33
Fortis Growth	47.47	44.42	1.07	1.25	1.20	−0.51	8.40	4.67	1.80
Fortis Capital Fund	32.38	29.48	1.10	1.04	0.97	−0.95	5.15	3.24	1.59
FPA Capital	14.59	39.56	2.72**	0.74	1.12	5.02**	2.91	5.54	1.90*
Franklin Equity	33.99	36.60	1.08	1.09	1.12	0.45	5.20	2.09	2.49**
IDS Discovery	39.56	28.94	1.37	1.10	1.25	1.29	6.59	7.34	1.11
IDS Equity Plus	22.66	30.47	1.35	0.90	1.03	2.36**	3.30	1.56	2.12*
IDS New Dimensions	30.36	11.36	2.67**	0.95	1.16	2.47**	3.74	1.32	2.83**
IDS Progressive	26.73	6.25	4.28**	0.87	0.74	−1.25	4.48	3.70	1.21
IDS Strategy Equity	14.98	12.89	1.16	0.71	0.87	3.19**	1.48	1.20	1.23

(*continued*)

TABLE 34.3 (*continued*)

Fund	Pre σ^2	Post σ^2	$F(\sigma)$	Pre β	Post β	$t(\beta)$	Pre σ_ε^2	Post σ_ε^2	$F(\sigma_\varepsilon^2)$
Janus Fund	15.29	22.94	1.50	0.82	0.79	−0.35	3.58	4.31	1.20
Kemper Small Cap	27.04	42.77	1.58*	1.14	1.16	0.32	3.22	5.38	1.67
Kemper Growth	33.87	12.82	2.63**	1.02	1.20	1.86*	3.54	2.97	1.19
Keystone K-2	26.01	19.36	1.34	0.94	1.10	2.56**	1.77	2.46	1.39
Keystone S-1	26.21	13.32	1.97**	0.96	0.96	0.00	1.08	0.95	1.14
Keystone S-3	22.85	31.25	1.37	1.11	1.07	−0.98	1.56	1.57	1.01
Lord Abbett Developing Growth	47.61	29.05	1.65*	1.19	1.25	0.48	10.23	7.25	1.41
Mass Financial Development	28.94	12.46	2.32**	0.98	1.19	3.15**	1.52	1.60	1.05
Merrill Lynch Capital	15.84	16.32	1.03	0.75	0.75	0.03	2.75	0.97	2.84**
Merrill Lynch Special Value	33.18	22.85	1.45	1.04	1.05	0.12	5.46	8.23	1.51
MFS Value	35.16	10.69	3.29**	1.07	1.01	−0.62	2.62	2.98	1.14
Mutual Beacon	19.10	12.89	1.48	0.86	0.62	−3.61**	3.22	2.88	1.12
Nationwide Fund	11.09	25.40	2.29**	0.66	0.97	7.33**	1.75	0.78	2.24*
Neuberger Guardian	25.00	18.40	1.36	0.92	1.11	3.70**	1.38	1.52	1.10
Neuberger Partners	17.89	11.70	1.53	0.80	0.95	3.34**	0.61	1.43	2.34**
Neuberger Select	21.82	14.67	1.49	0.83	0.93	1.51	3.03	2.07	1.46
Oppenheimer Total Return	20.52	13.99	1.46	0.84	0.97	1.93*	1.90	2.35	1.23
Oppenheimer Fund	34.57	10.43	3.31**	1.06	0.92	−1.99**	4.04	0.90	4.49**
Oppenheimer Special Fund	17.81	25.40	1.43	0.88	0.94	0.81	4.57	2.70	2.08*
Penn Square	16.81	21.72	1.30	0.93	0.84	−1.89*	1.68	0.84	2.00*
Philadelphia Fund	16.40	19.98	1.22	0.87	0.79	−1.35	1.51	3.42	2.26*
Pilgrim Magna Capital	22.75	13.40	1.70*	0.87	0.95	1.35	1.94	1.44	1.35
Pioneer Fund	29.71	27.56	1.39	1.03	0.95	−1.98**	1.12	1.13	1.01
Pioneer II	29.16	6.05	4.81**	0.97	0.80	−2.88***	1.77	0.84	2.11*
Prudential Bache Equity	29.92	12.25	2.44**	1.05	0.91	−2.46**	1.08	2.07	1.92*
Putnam Investors	32.60	17.72	1.84**	1.07	1.08	0.31	1.72	0.82	2.10*
Putnam Vista Basic Value	27.04	12.04	2.25**	0.98	1.12	1.73*	0.63	3.71	5.89**
Quest for Value	18.32	12.67	1.45	0.78	0.91	2.53**	1.73	1.22	1.42
Safeco Equity	20.07	32.15	1.60*	0.92	1.06	2.82**	2.12	1.47	1.44

Safeco Growth	27.67	39.69	1.44	0.96	1.39	3.68**	2.55	12.19	4.78**
SBS Fundamental Value	25.40	7.51	3.40**	0.89	0.82	−0.91	2.23	1.88	1.19
Sentinel Common Stock	12.60	24.30	1.92**	0.70	0.92	4.37**	2.00	1.56	1.28
State Street Investment	26.94	16.16	1.67*	0.96	1.01	1.01	1.40	1.01	1.39
Strong Opportunity	31.47	9.30	3.37**	0.87	1.00	1.08	9.41	2.01	4.68**
T. Rowe Price Growth	22.28	27.46	1.23	0.95	0.95	−0.01	2.53	2.51	1.01
T. Rowe Price New Horizon	34.69	48.44	1.40	1.28	1.27	−0.03	6.54	6.09	1.07
United New Concepts	33.18	25.30	1.31	0.97	1.16	1.63	7.46	7.08	1.05
USAA Mutual Fund Growth	31.36	12.60	2.49**	0.99	0.90	−1.97*	1.68	0.80	2.10*
Vanguard World–US Growth	19.62	31.81	1.62*	0.97	1.05	1.39	1.81	2.46	1.36
Winthrop Growth and Income	15.29	22.47	1.47	0.90	0.86	−1.02	1.23	0.89	1.38
Fund average	25.92	20.10	4.20**	0.95	1.00	2.13**	3.03	2.65	1.14

Notes: The sample period is January 1978 to December 1996. $F(\sigma)$ is the F-statistic for the difference in pre- and postchange variances of monthly returns; $t(\beta)$ is the t-statistic for the difference between pre- and postchange betas. $F(\sigma_\varepsilon^2)$ is the F-statistic for the difference in pre- and postchange residual variances of monthly returns.

*Significant at the 10 percent level.
**Significant at the 5 percent level.

TABLE 34.4   Style Classification Matrix

Classification before Change	Classification after Change				
	Large-Cap/Growth	Large-Cap/Value	Small-Cap/Growth	Small-Cap/Value	Total
Large-Cap/Growth	0	4	8	0	12
Large-Cap/Value	7	11	1	0	19
Small-Cap/Growth	9	11	13	2	35
Small-Cap/Value	0	2	1	0	3
Total	16	28	23	2	69

CONCLUSIONS

We examined performance, risk, and investment style characteristics of 69 mutual funds that experienced a change in managers during the 1983–1991 period. Risk and performance were compared for the five-year intervals before and after the management change month.

Our findings show that performance, on average, improved after the management change. The average fund's monthly alpha increased 16.58 bps a month (200 bps a year). We also found that, on average, total risk fell but systematic risk increased significantly after the management change. Thus, the results reveal a shift in investment policy on the part of the funds. Beta reverted to the mean. The increase in systematic risk was associated with an increase in risk-adjusted performance, however, as revealed by the higher postperiod alphas.

We also investigated changes in investment style for each fund following the change in managers and found that the majority of funds (65.2 percent) switched style classifications after a change in managers.

These findings have important implications for investors who follow disciplined multiple-style (multiple-manager) strategies. Performance, risk, and investment style may change significantly following a mutual fund's change in managers.

On the one hand, the increase in performance we found would be a positive outcome for investors. On the other hand, the increase in systematic risk and shift in investment style suggest that new managers alter a fund's risk profile. If these changes are unanticipated, investors may be exposed to undesired levels of style risk after a fund manager change, which would reduce the benefits of style diversification. These findings imply that disciplined multiple-style investors should closely monitor funds that experience a change in management.

The results of this study are based entirely on the returns of mutual funds, which behave differently from institutional equity money managers (see Coggin et al.). Thus, our results are applicable only to mutual fund investors. And keep in mind that pension plan sponsors are more likely to employ institutional money managers than mutual funds. Thus, similar tests on institutional money managers would be an interesting extension of this research.

NOTES

1. Value and growth have been delineated by book value to market value (by Sharpe 1992; Fama and French 1992) and by P/E (by Tierney and Winston 1991).

2. We also ran the tests of performance after deleting the first three months after the management change but found no substantive change in our findings.

3. The total sample consisted of equity funds that existed throughout the January 1978 to December 1996 period. By limiting the sample to managers who survived throughout the sample period, we may have introduced survivorship bias into the results. Survivorship bias has been shown to reduce the statistical power of performance evaluation tests (e.g., Brown, Goetzmann, Ibbotson, and Ross 1992). Grinblatt and Titman (1989) showed, however, that the effect of survivorship bias on performance results is likely to be small.

4. We also performed the nonparametric Mann–Whitney test (the *U*-test). The Mann–Whitney test is the nonparametric alternative to the *t*-test used when the normality assumption is not valid. The inferences of the nonparametric test statistics were consistent with those of the parametric measures reported here.

5. To allow for different intercepts between the periods, we used a dummy variable on the intercept in the regression equation (Equation 34.4) estimated over the entire 120-month period. No dummy variable was used in the 60-month subperiod regressions.

6. Relative to the Wilshire 5000, 51 percent of the Morningstar funds in existence during the 1978–1996 period had negative alphas. Thus, the *t*-statistic equals ($p -$ $0.51)/(0.25/69)^{0.05}$, where p is the realized percentage (i.e., equal to 71 percent).

7. Results that are discussed but not presented here are available from the authors.

8. The insignificant timing coefficients provide support for the power of the performance evaluation test (Equation 34.2), because positive market-timing skill implies potential negative bias in the Jensen measure. See Jensen (1972), Admati and Ross (1985), and Grinblatt and Titman.

9. An area of future research would be to compare the observed percentage of style shifts with the percentage of style shifts for a random sample of mutual funds.

REFERENCES

Admati, A., and S. A. Ross. 1985. "Measuring Investment Performance in a Rational Expectations Equilibrium Model." *Journal of Business*, vol. 58, no. 1 (January):1–26.

Bailey, J. V., and R. D. Arnott. 1986. "Cluster Analysis and Manager Selection." *Financial Analysts Journal*, vol. 42, no. 6 (November/December):20–28.

Brown, S. J., W. Goetzmann, R. G. Ibbotson, and S. A. Ross. 1992. "Survivorship Bias in Performance Studies." *Review of Financial Studies*, vol. 5, no. 4 (Winter):553–580.

Chang, E. C., and W. C. Lewellen. 1984. "Market Timing and Mutual Fund Investment Performance." *Journal of Business*, vol. 57, no. 1 (January):57–72.

Christopherson, J. A. 1995. "Equity Style Classifications." *Journal of Portfolio Management*, vol. 21, no. 3 (Spring):32–43.

Coggin, T. D., F. J. Fabozzi, and S. Rahman. 1993. "The Investment Performance of U.S. Equity Pension Fund Managers." *Journal of Finance*, vol. 48, no. 3 (July):1039–1055.

DiBartolomeo, D., and E. Witkowski. 1997. "Mutual Fund Misclassification: Evidence Based on Style Analysis." *Financial Analysts Journal*, vol. 53, no. 5 (September/October):32–43.

Fama, E. F., and K. R. French. 1992. "The Cross-Section of Expected Stock Returns." *Journal of Finance*, vol. 47, no. 2 (June):427–466.

Gallo, J. G., and L. J. Lockwood. 1997. "Benefits of Proper Style Classification for Equity Portfolio Managers." *Journal of Portfolio Management*, vol. 23, no. 3 (Spring):47–56.

Grinblatt, M., and S. Titman. 1989. "Mutual Fund Performance: An Analysis of Quarterly Portfolio Holdings." *Journal of Business*, vol. 62, no. 3 (July):393–416.

Jensen, M. C. 1968. "The Performance of Mutual Funds in the Period 1945–1964." *Journal of Finance*, vol. 23, no. 2 (June):389–416.

———. 1972. "Optimal Utilization of Market Forecasts and the Evaluation of Investment Portfolio Performance." In *Mathematical Methods in Investment and Finance*. Edited by Georgio Szego and Karl Shell. Amsterdam: North Holland.

Lee, C. F., and S. Rahman. 1990. "Market Timing, Selectivity, and Mutual Fund Performance: An Empirical Investigation." *Journal of Business*, vol. 63, no. 2 (April): 261–278.

Logue, D. E. 1991. *Managing Corporate Pension Plans*. Washington, DC: Harper Business.

Sharpe, W. F. 1966. "Mutual Fund Performance." *Journal of Business*, vol. 39, no. 1 (January):119–138.

———. 1992. "Asset Allocation: Management Style and Performance Measurement." *Journal of Portfolio Management*, vol. 18, no. 2 (Winter):7–19.

Tierney, D. E., and K. Winston. 1991. "Using Generic Benchmarks to Present Manager Styles." *Journal of Portfolio Management*, vol. 17, no. 4 (Summer):33–36.

Treynor, J. L., and F. Mazuy. 1966. "Can Mutual Funds Outguess the Market?" *Harvard Business Review*, vol. 44, no. 4:131–136.

Trzcinka, C.A. 1995. "Equity Style Classifications: A Comment." *Journal of Portfolio Management*, vol. 21, no. 3 (Spring):44–46.

CHAPTER 35

MANAGING PERFORMANCE: MONITORING AND TRANSITIONING MANAGERS

Louisa Wright Sellers

The due diligence associated with manager selection is critically important, particularly for the selection of hedge fund managers and managers of taxable portfolios and when transitioning from one manager to another. Thus, the tools and methods used to select managers and monitor the managers' adherence to the style for which they were selected are vital. The crucial elements in a manager's ability to maintain investment style over time are performance, continuity of personnel, conformity to style, and consistency in procedures.

Ashbridge Investment Management originated as the family office for the Grace family, whose wealth was created by Bethlehem Steel Corporation. The Grace family has been through several iterations of managing its wealth, the latest of which began a little more than 20 years ago. This most recent iteration involved a series of decisions by the family that included establishing an investment policy, setting an asset allocation, and hiring outside managers to fulfill the investment mandates. Such an approach does not seem that unusual today; however, for a family to have embarked in this direction 20 years ago is somewhat unique. Although pension plans, endowments, and universities had begun to follow this model, most families at that time were investing primarily in large-cap stocks and municipal bonds.

Reprinted from *AIMR Conference Proceedings: Investment Counseling for Private Clients IV* (August 2002):32–39.

The Grace family's foresight resulted in the organization of Ashbridge Investment Management. At Ashbridge, we now serve about 40 families and clients in addition to the Grace family. The firm's growth has greatly expanded our knowledge base, thus enabling us to increase the number of asset classes and strategies we can make available within our established allocations. We currently allocate to about 60 different managers that span about 25 different asset classes and strategies. The asset classes and strategies we use are domestic and international, long only, and alternative. By alternative, I mean predominately hedged strategies as opposed to private equity and venture capital.

In the course of my presentation, I will touch on a variety of topics, from what it means to monitor managers in general, and hedge fund managers in particular (because hedge fund management is more complex than long-only strategies), to exchange-traded funds (ETFs) and tax-efficient investing.

BACKGROUND

The initial due diligence involved in selecting managers is crucial, but perhaps even more important is the ongoing due diligence of managers once they are selected, particularly in the open architecture model that prevails in the marketplace today. Every investment management firm, no matter whether it is a large investment bank or a trust company, seems to realize that even though a lot of approaches to investing can be successful, no single firm can be an expert in all of them.

Many variations exist for the open architecture model. For Ashbridge, it simply means working as a consultant on behalf of the client and sitting on the client's side of the table. We outsource all custodial and managerial work but retain in-house the setting of policy and the reporting on the outcome of that policy. Our concept of open architecture necessitates extensive discussions between the consultant and the family about the family's long-term and short-term objectives for its wealth. For example, allocating across various investment pockets within the family means establishing asset allocations for family limited partnerships, generation-skipping trusts, charitable trusts, and foundations. The entire plan must be synthesized in a reasonable way.

We set asset allocations for a family's total assets as well as for the individual entities within the family structure and then seek managers to fulfill those allocations. Through our manager selection, we try to create a style, market-capitalization, geographical, and strategy blend that includes hedged strategies to control risk.

SELECTING AN INVESTMENT MANAGER

The initial due diligence on a manager is exhaustive. Typically, the process begins with a database search that has a quantitative focus. A consultant can subscribe to a number of different services that will find thousands of managers around the world. Manager performance is an important factor at this stage, but the performance and the period over which performance is calculated is merely the initial qualifier. We evaluate each manager over a three-year horizon because we want to see how the manager has performed in different markets and how the performance averages out over time.

This screen of the databases provides a subset of managers that is about 20 percent of the original manager universe, which we then evaluate qualitatively. Our qualitative analysis involves fairly rigorous fundamental analysis followed by face-to-face discussions. We rely on one or more face-to-face meetings to solidify what we have learned previously through the quantitative data, telephone conversations, and conference calls. Our goal is to meet the portfolio manager and to ensure adequate access to him or her during our ongoing monitoring of that manager. The chemistry between the portfolio manager and the trader is also an important variable in our decision-making process, especially if their interaction is a key component to the strategy we are using. Furthermore, we want to become acquainted with the analysts at the firm and determine who our primary contact will be; if it is a client services person, we try to find out how knowledgeable that person is about the firm and the execution of the firm's strategy.

Many questions need to be asked throughout the manager-selection process, which can take 6–24 months, depending on the manager and the strategy. We prefer to act slowly and perhaps forgo some return to prepare ourselves for a relationship with a manager. Our goal is to be confident in our decision because we do not want to have to terminate a manager. Certain managers have been working with us for more than 10 years, which demonstrates the importance of doing excellent work at the outset, during the search stage. We believe our efforts will ultimately improve the returns of our clients' portfolios at a reasonable level of risk.

MONITORING AN INVESTMENT MANAGER

The ongoing due diligence of managers we have hired has a slightly different character from the initial due diligence in a manager search, but it nevertheless entails the same quantitative and qualitative criteria used in selecting managers. On an ongoing basis, however, our most important concern is to make sure the manager's strategy is being executed as expected. This oversight builds confidence in the managers we have hired and, in turn, allows us to convey that comfort and confidence to our clients. Furthermore, monitoring managers on an ongoing basis reduces risk by identifying style drift or organizational changes early, before any performance deterioration. We cover four areas in our ongoing due diligence process: performance, continuity, conformity to investment strategy, and consistency of procedures.

Performance

The first variable we review on an ongoing basis is performance. Performance tells the story right up front and clearly sets the tone of the exchange between the consultant and the manager before a conversation even begins. We focus on how the performance looks relative to style benchmarks, peer groups, and the market. Granted, choosing an appropriate performance benchmark is difficult, but for long-only strategies, thanks to the Frank Russell Company, Barra, and other benchmark providers, we have multiple ways to slice and dice almost every manager's portfolio according to market capitalization, style, geography, and sector.

Continuity

We also monitor continuity in personnel. Just as clients seek continuity in their advisors, we seek continuity in the personnel and structure of the manager's organization.

Conformity

Sometimes change is a good thing, but not for a manager given a specific mandate. Therefore, we review conformity to the style or strategy the manager was hired to execute. The manager's strategy is only one piece of a larger policy, so if the manager deviates significantly from his or her initial mandate, that deviation may cause problems.

Consistency

The final variable we monitor is the consistency of various procedures. Specifically, our concern centers on the manager's buy and sell disciplines.

Tools and Practices for Monitoring

To prepare for the monitoring process, we use a rigorous questionnaire that we develop for each manager. A questionnaire for a hedge fund manager, for example, requires that the manager answer as many as 125 questions. The questionnaire is followed by in-depth biographies of the individuals involved with the firm; information on the outside organizations that provide accounting, prime brokerage, and legal services to the manager; a statement about the amount of assets under management at the firm; and an explanation about the way the manager has grown or changed over time. All of the information we gather is gradually streamlined as the ongoing due diligence process is carried out; typically, "ongoing" means a quarterly interview, generally 10–20 days after the end of the calendar quarter. Additionally, we do onsite visits at least once a year.

The quarterly interviews are usually conducted via conference calls. For each call, we generally include a team of individuals with different backgrounds and skill sets to ensure that a wide variety of questions are asked and to broaden the scope of the material we want to cover with the manager. We primarily discuss the manager's most recent performance. If the manager's performance has deviated from his or her benchmark, particularly if it has deviated for the second or third quarter in a row, we view this trend as a problem. Obviously, defending his or her performance is a challenging position for the manager, but defending the manager's performance to the client is equally challenging for us.

Keep in mind that we adopt the role of the intermediary between the manager and the client in order to unearth any relevant issues. Often, the manager's performance turns around. As long as we are satisfied that the underperformance was a result of rational decision making, we will stay with the manager. Recommending to a client that a manager be terminated is not a decision we make lightly. Although a foundation, endowment, or other tax-exempt entity can change managers easily by simply liquidating assets and moving on, as I will discuss in the last section, for taxable clients the decision to change managers is not as simple.

Once we have conducted our quarterly conference calls to each manager, all 60 of them, we record these interviews not only for our own use but also for the benefit of our clients. Each participant in the call records what he or she heard during the manager interview. Although everyone hears the same conversation, each person assigns a slightly different meaning to the same information; we like to compare the varying nuances arising from multiple points of view. Our conference call notes are synthesized to document the call and are then reported to clients as part of a comprehensive reporting package.

Onsite visits are a critical element in the ongoing due diligence process, just as they are in the initial manager search process. We make onsite visits to managers to assess the atmosphere of the firm and the chemistry between the portfolio managers, analysts, and traders.

Monitoring Hedge Funds

Monitoring a hedge fund manager is equivalent, in my view, to turbo-charged monitoring of a long-only manager. An even deeper analysis must be done to understand a hedge fund manager's strategy and the execution of that strategy for a variety of reasons, including the lack of transparency of the portfolio, use of leverage, use of index futures and options, investment in illiquid securities, and tendency of the fund's beta to drift quite high.

A hedge fund's use of leverage and derivatives, combined with the lack of transparency, vastly increases the potential risks in a hedge fund's portfolio. And without sufficient transparency, the ability to satisfactorily assess these risks is seriously impaired. Some of the portfolio risks that concern us are a fund's counterparty risk, regulatory issues that could hamper the fund's strategy, security and credit concentrations, nonmarket security evaluations, currency exposure, and how well hedged the portfolio actually is. Typically, when we conduct a monitoring interview with a hedge fund manager, we ask questions that go far beyond what the manager's top-10 long holdings are. We want to know the manager's gross long and gross short exposures and how those exposures drive the manager to his or her net exposure. We also want to know the manager's top sector and geographical exposures, particularly if the manager is an international manager. Finally, we request that the fund disclose any potential liquidity considerations, especially on the fund's short positions.

Liquidity posed a particular problem a few years ago, when funds were stuffed with hot initial public offering (IPO) issues. Tremendous opportunity existed in 2000 to short many of the IPOs issued in 1998 and 1999, and as the IPO prices dropped, the short squeezes that resulted affected valuations. Most hedge fund managers will not disclose their short positions; they will divulge their sector or country exposure on the short side or the total short exposure in the portfolio, but rarely will they divulge the names of their short stocks. Also, knowing the number of both long and short positions in a portfolio is important. We are most comfortable with long–short equity managers that take a concentrated approach to their long positions and a diversified approach to their short positions. So, to the extent that our hedge fund managers detail their activity over the course of the most recent quarter, we have a sound understanding of the execution of their strategies and, therefore, can apply attribution analysis to their performance analysis—analysis that we find extremely helpful.

At Ashbridge, about 25 percent of our clients' assets is invested in hedged strategies, of which about 40 percent is in trading and arbitrage strategies and 60 percent is in long–short equity. From a tax-efficiency standpoint, most of the fixed-income surrogate strategies will be taxed as short-term gains at approximately a 40 percent rate. Some long–short equity managers, however, depending on their mandate and approach, are able to recognize long-term gains for their clients, which are taxed at a more favorable 20 percent rate. Because so many of these managers invest in their own funds, it is also in their best interest to defer the gain to the extent that the deferral is a good investment decision. In general, hedged strategies may not be tax efficient, but the tax efficiency of funds varies on a case-by-case basis. We thus believe the opportunity exists for tax efficiency in long–short equity funds.

CATALYSTS FOR CHANGING A MANAGER

Several catalysts can lead us to change a manager we have selected. Once we recognize the presence of one of the catalysts, we monitor the manager until we are able to determine whether the situation is temporary or the beginning of a trend. Sustained underperformance relative to the benchmark and to peers over a three- or four-quarter period, inexplicable style drift, departure of key personnel from the organization, acquisition of the investment management firm, and change in the temperament of the portfolio manager—all are possible catalysts for recommending that a manager be dropped.

Catalysts Leading to Change

Inexplicable style drift is a concern because, in all likelihood, a manager is only one of at least six managers of a client's portfolio. Any change in style can wreak havoc on the client's asset allocation policy because a manager's initial mandate is designed to complement the styles and strategies of other managers. Style drift can significantly alter the overall risk–return profile of the client's portfolio, so we need to figure out why the drift is happening.

We also need to understand the implications of personnel changes in a manager's organization. Frequent changes in personnel are no longer unusual, but the impact of such changes on performance can be dramatic. The depth of the team managing the portfolio at the firm—multiple portfolio managers and analysts—can alleviate any problems arising from personnel turnover if the other team members can fill the role of the team member who left the firm. But in a smaller organization (for example, a firm with only five individuals), if the top one or two portfolio managers leave the firm, such a change will likely be a significant problem for the predictability of returns.

On a positive note, consolidation within the financial services industry has become so common that if a manager is acquired, the acquisition does not necessarily have negative consequences. Seven years ago, investors had to question the incentive of the manager when an acquisition occurred. Did the manager want to continue managing money? Were the proper incentives in place for him or her to continue managing aggressively and appropriately for the next three to five years after the acquisition? In the past three years, four or five of our managers have been acquired, but in only two cases did we make a managerial change 6–12 months after the acquisition.

A change in the temperament of a portfolio manager (a phenomenon our research director has deemed "the Ferrari syndrome") also causes us to sit up and take notice. A change in temperament alone is not a concern, but a manager's change in focus is, whether it is a greater desire to acquire "toys" or another type of diversion. It is a delicate issue, but sometimes the questions "How many houses or cars does the manager have?" or "What is happening in the manager's personal life?" must be addressed. Unless a manager's focus is purely on his or her fund, performance results will deviate from expectations.

Our experience has shown that a number of the catalysts that we have identified and that we monitor are bearers of bad tidings in terms of returns. During one of our regular conference calls in the spring of 1999 to a mid-cap growth manager, for instance, we discovered the portfolio manager had changed. The new portfolio manager did not understand the fund's mandate and was taking a barbell approach in his capitalization structure of the portfolio. His strategy was to buy small-cap and large-cap stocks to achieve a mean mid-cap weighting, which was not an appropriate approach within the context of the client's overall portfolio strategy. Our discovery resulted in an immediate transition to a new manager.

Another transition, which took a little longer to play out, occurred after one of our international value managers was acquired by a large firm with a growth orientation. Our understanding after the acquisition was that the manager we had hired would maintain his value bias, but in the course of our quarterly conference calls with the manager, we noticed the returns starting to falter. The stocks being purchased resembled growth stocks, and the value stocks were being sold. We knew from a risk standpoint in the client's overall portfolio that the loss of the value orientation was not acceptable. This change in manager style also coincided with a general shift away from growth and into value outperformance, and that general market shift was equally a problem. This variation from the initial mandate was the signal for us to change managers.

Another catalyst that spurred us to make a manager change had to do with a problem we had with one of our managed futures managers. We use managed futures strategies as an asset class that is truly uncorrelated with fixed-income and equity markets. As with hedged strategies, monitoring these managers, particularly the discretionary traders, is difficult, even though managed futures may have more transparency than hedged strategies. The manager we fired was a discretionary trader. His bets on the directions of various commodities and markets were becoming larger, and he was becoming more leveraged. Not surprisingly, the more positions started going against him, the more he started adding to them. Our response was to terminate our relationship with the manager.

Catalysts Not Leading to Change

For all of the catalysts that prove to be correct in indicating that a change in manager is necessary, just as many never lead to that conclusion. In the case of a large-cap growth manager we have used for an excess of 15 years and a mid-cap value manager we have used for about 5 years, we monitored periods of underperformance that could be rationalized by the managers. Wonderful performance had been achieved prior to this window of underperformance, and during the periods of underperformance, the managers maintained style consistency.

In the case of the growth manager, the manager simply could not justify the high multiples prevalent in 1998 and 1999, and his fund performed poorly relative to its benchmark, the Russell 1000 Growth Index, and its peer groups. Not surprisingly, this manager came into the 2000–2001 window with far less exposure to technology and a far more defensive portfolio, ready to weather the challenges of the past two years. Consequently, this manager has done a fabulous job at capital preservation for our clients, and although convincing clients of the strong points of this manager in 1999 was tough, clients are thrilled now.

Likewise, in the case of the mid-cap value manager, when value managers were tempted in 1999 to find ways to justify buying companies such as America Online and Microsoft Corporation and the more moderately priced technology stocks with lower multiples, this manager simply would not do so. This manager was targeting the cheapest quintile of stocks within his universe, the Russell 1000 Index, when these stocks were dramatically underperforming other market sectors. The manager stuck by his value orientation, and his performance for the 18 months beginning April 2000 has been phenomenal.

Although clients are not always comfortable with the volatility of some of their managers' performance, if a good reason exists to stay the course with a manager through bad times, clients can be substantially rewarded. And from a tax standpoint, remaining with this large-cap growth manager and mid-cap value manager was very much in these clients' best interests.

TRANSFERRING A TAXABLE PORTFOLIO
TO A NEW MANAGER

How do we handle a transition from one manager to another, particularly in the context of working with a new client? A client rarely walks in the door with uninvested cash. Clients usually have a variety of investments they have bought along the way or have a concentrated holding they may or may not have already begun to diversify. In some cases, a client may already be working with a consultant and may have a variety of managers that are too highly correlated or are underperforming. We typically propose an asset allocation that includes the managers we would recommend and try to match the client's current portfolio as closely as we can with some combination of our recommended managers.

When we initially qualify a manager, we want to know that a high degree of the manager's clients are taxable clients and that the manager has acquired a comfort and experience level in working with the taxable investor. We want to be familiar with the tax-savings techniques the manager uses, such as tax-loss harvesting, swapping into similar stocks, or using ETFs to maintain exposure to a sector to avoid the 31-day wash-sale rule. We also seek assurance that the manager has transitioned portfolios in the past into the manager's model portfolio and want to know approximately how long the transition period will be. Ideally, we prefer a two- to three-year period. If the transition drags on any longer, performance will deviate from expectations for too long and the client will become dissatisfied. The family hired the manager with a specific mandate, yet the manager could be handicapped by the portfolio that he or she has to transition, so a balance has to be struck between getting through the transition process quickly and being prudent.

We also want to monitor the performance of that manager during the transition process, even though we understand that the manager's performance may deviate from the performance of his or her typical model portfolio. Consequently, we may adopt less strict performance standards during the migration period to account for divergences in portfolio structure and attribution. Thus, one way of transitioning to a new manager is to start with an existing portfolio, find a manager or managers similar to the existing managers, and allow the new manager to move through the transition steps over a period of time. This type of transition can be done fairly reasonably.

Another transition approach we have used for a client or prospective client with only six or seven managers is to evaluate the portfolio from a tax standpoint to determine where, in a tax-efficient manner, we can raise cash. We then identify losses available to offset gains, sell the selected securities, and invest the proceeds generated with the new managers. Giving managers cash is easy, but analyzing the overall portfolio holdings from a tax perspective is complicated. The process becomes even trickier when the portfolio has a significant embedded gain. Prudence often dictates spacing out the sale of the appreciated securities over a certain period of time and incurring the capital gains tax liability on the sales in different tax years, preferably selling early in the tax year and deferring the tax liability for another 15 months (e.g., sale in January and tax payment in April of the following year). As the appreciated stock is sold, the manager has the opportunity to complement the remaining as-yet-unsold appreciated stock with new stock purchases and also to distinguish and highlight the style he or she has been employed to manage. At the same time, we want that manager to carefully monitor the holdings that are retained. In light of the accounting scandals at Enron Corporation, Global Crossing, and Tyco International, monitoring holdings is as important as monitoring managers, if not more so. And regardless of the tax consequences, if a manager perceives problems in a company, we are inclined to sell the holding. Investment decisions should outweigh pure tax considerations, and we encourage feedback from managers about such issues.

CONCLUSION

Initially selecting a manager is a challenging task, but the hard work pays off in finding superior managers. Equally challenging is the ongoing monitoring of these managers, and perhaps not surprisingly, we use the same quantitative and qualitative criteria to both select and monitor managers. Monitoring managers, however, does require some unique evaluation criteria, and monitoring hedge fund managers in particular, with their lack of transparency, leverage, and high betas, further complicates the process.

Even with careful initial selection of a manager, the monitoring process sometimes reveals changes in a manager's process or firm that require us to terminate the manager in order to maintain the targets that have been set for our clients. But these manager deviations, or catalysts for change, have to be evaluated carefully. Although these catalysts have prompted us to change a manager, they do not always do so. If the deviations occur for a good reason, we will stand by the manager and explain the situation to our clients.

If we are to be good consultants, we must see our roles as questioners, skeptics, and also advocates for managers. At Ashbridge, we value a rigorous approach to our initial due diligence and ongoing monitoring of managers and believe that our efforts will create and sustain the best managerial performance at the most reasonable level of risk for our clients. We feel strongly that asking good questions and constantly seeking better answers are vital aspects of our manager-selection process.

QUESTION AND ANSWER SESSION

Question: Do you recommend passive or active management?

Sellers: In some asset classes, managers can add alpha, and in others, particularly those with underlying indexes that have inherently less turnover, active managers may add less value. A large-cap index fund can play a role in a portfolio and can be complemented by specialist managers in the asset classes that have been proven to be less efficient.

During the past couple of years, so much turnover has occurred within the Russell 2000 Index—with about 500–600 different stocks entering and exiting the index—that the Russell 2000 is probably not a tax-efficient proxy for the small-cap market. Therefore, an active manager for this asset class makes sense. Likewise, although I can't quantify the number of stocks that roll in and out of the MSCI Europe/Australasia/Far East (EAFE) Index on an annual basis, I suspect that number is relatively high. In contrast, only 20–30 names change in the S&P 500 on an annual basis. Because the S&P 500 doesn't have a lot of turnover in its composition each year, it can be a reasonable proxy for the large-cap market; thus, the large-cap market is an asset class that does not typically require active management.

Question: How do you justify your role as an intermediary in terms of the value added to the overall return in your clients' portfolios?

Sellers: Typically, a family turns to a consultant if the amount of assets the family has to give to any single manager is not that great. So, if the consultant can aggregate those assets with those of other investors, the consultant can negotiate lower amounts to invest with a manager for an individual family. Usually, we can also garner lower fees because the manager doesn't have to talk with each of our clients on an ongoing basis—only with us, four times a year.

We add value because we can reduce the manager's fee and help the client achieve superior returns. Our reporting process shows how each manager is performing against his or her appropriate benchmark index, and then we create a blended index for the overall portfolio in which we show the magnitude of manager outperformance over that benchmark of underlying indexes. We can make a compelling case that our managers are adding significant alpha over time. Even in equity markets that have had a relatively flat return for the past three years, our portfolios have been compounding at a rate of 8–10 percent a year. Most of our clients are satisfied with the work we've done because we have created a positively compounding return despite the volatile market.

Question: How much do you emphasize tax efficiency in your manager-selection process?

Sellers: In the long-only strategies, we can select from hundreds of managers, so it boils down to a judgment call. Once we narrow the group to the 20 percent we are interested in, a myriad of factors narrows the group even further. Perhaps the manager is geared more toward institutional investors, or perhaps the manager's fees or minimum account size limit are high. In our dialogue with a manager, if we hear that the manager has high turnover with little consideration of harvesting losses to offset realized gains, we know that this inattention to tax efficiency is not ideal for our clients.

At the same time, if tax efficiency were the only criterion we cared about, we would lose many wonderful managers we've worked with over time that in some years have demonstrated high tax efficiency and in others have taken substantial gains because they felt that was the right thing to do from an investment standpoint.

Question: How truthful are investment management firms about the departure of key individuals? Do you ever confirm the firm's stated reason for the individual's departure with the individual who left the firm?

Sellers: So far, the information we have been given has been truthful. We try to find out where people go after they leave and the reason they left because they can provide key information. This information can tell us a lot about the firm we are presumably staying with, and sometimes, we uncover issues that make us uncomfortable.

Question: What do you look for in your initial due diligence and quarterly interviews with managers?

Sellers: Selecting and then staying with a manager comes down to two key factors—competence and chemistry. In the face-to-face interviews, we hope to determine the synergy between the managers, traders, and analysts. If they have a great deal of enthusiasm and a passion for what they're doing, they will probably do a good job. If an aura of negativity surrounds a manager, it will ultimately spill over into the results achieved in the portfolio.

This aspect of the manager-selection process is more art than science; it cannot be quantified. What comes out of the face-to-face meetings is simply what we observe and how we are treated by the team we are talking to. If the manager has an interest in Ashbridge's client base, what we do, and how we want to work with the manager, that positive attitude will go a long way with us. If we happen to catch someone on a bad day, we're willing to give him or her the benefit of the doubt and come back again, but the confidence we have in a manager is derived from our initial impressions during these interviews.

Question: What does an investment management firm that has been acquired or is no longer independent have to do to avoid getting fired?

Sellers: One of the best examples of this situation is a firm we had worked with for about six years before it was acquired. Right after the announcement was made and the disclosure became public, we received a call from the lead portfolio manager about what had happened so that we would know about it before finding the story in the press.

From our quarterly interviews, we learned the portfolio manager hated the tedium of the paperwork of the takeover. He was clearly annoyed about the takeover getting in the way of his research and his passion for stock picking. He was probably thrilled about the compensation he would receive from the acquisition, but he clearly wanted to be able to focus on managing the portfolio, which was a great sign.

Even better was the fact that when we had an involved conversation with him before our regularly scheduled call, we learned that an abundance of research had been done on a sector of stocks that the manager wanted to add to the portfolio. Sure enough, when the market gave him a buying opportunity, his firm took advantage of it. So, even while this deal was being negotiated, intensive and relevant research was still being done.

Question: With regard to hedge fund manager information, does your firm place any weight on the monetary commitment in the fund from the manager of the fund in terms of the manager's participation?

Sellers: We always prefer to work with managers whose free assets are tied up in the firm and the fund. Such a situation aligns the manager's interests with the interests of our clients.

Question: Significant outperformance by hedge funds seems to be concentrated in the earliest years of a fund's existence. How does this early outperformance influence your decisions?

Sellers: When a portfolio is small, it is easier for managers to execute their ideas. As a fund grows, however, challenges arise. Having said that, we like to see a long track record. We want to see monthly results, and we want to see consistency in those results and the market conditions under which they were achieved.

Rather than act quickly and risk ending up with a poor result, we prefer to miss 6 or 12 months of good performance in order to assure ourselves that this fund is a place that our clients will be happy with for a long time, especially when we are hiring a hedge fund manager. And because of the lockup periods of hedge funds, we have to be especially confident in a manager because our clients will be invested with that manager for at least 12 months and possibly longer. So, hedge funds are no place to be second-guessing those initial decisions.

Question: Is there a particular hedge fund strategy that you would recommend for high-net-worth clients?

Sellers: We think there is much greater opportunity for private clients, for high-net-worth families, to understand a long–short equity strategy than market-neutral pairs trading, for example. Private clients are quite accepting of the idea that there are qualified managers in the industry who can identify companies expected to appreciate in value. And as part of that same process, private clients realize these managers have the ability to identify other companies with deteriorating fundamentals or poor management structures—whatever that catalyst may be—that will drive the stock price down and enable the manager to short the stock profitably.

An important part of our role as an intermediary is educating clients so that they feel comfortable with the strategies we recommend. There is something satisfying about recommending an investment approach to a client that can reduce the client's portfolio risk and have it be one the client can understand.

CHAPTER 36

DOES THE EMPEROR WEAR CLOTHES OR NOT? THE FINAL WORD (OR ALMOST) ON THE PARABLE OF INVESTMENT MANAGEMENT

Philip Halpern, Nancy Calkins, and Tom Ruggels

A goal of many institutional investors is hiring active managers that will consistently beat the market. The question is, how can such managers be identified in advance? This chapter documents one institutional investor's experience with manager selection and offers some thoughts about why successful manager selection is such a challenge.

In the childhood story "The Emperor's New Clothes," the tailor pretends to sew the Emperor a new wardrobe of luxurious clothes. Although the tailor expounds on the beauty and elegance of these clothes, the Emperor looks in the mirror and sees nothing on his body. After days and days of having the clothes properly fitted, the Emperor begins to believe they exist. In the end, the Emperor goes before the people in his new clothes and is embarrassed at believing in what is obviously not there.

   Have plan sponsors, like the Emperor, been tricked by the tailors of the investment management business into believing that active management adds value? Can money managers be

Reprinted from *Financial Analysts Journal* (July/August 1996):9–15.

identified and hired that will consistently beat the market? With regard to ability to add value in public markets, this debate seems to go on and on. Although not totally conclusive, most studies seem to suggest that the answer to the first question is yes and to the second question is no. Yet, whether driven by objective skepticism or personal interest, most investors seem to disagree with these answers.

Three catalysts are responsible for the decision to craft this chapter. First, our own experience with active management has been less than satisfactory. Introspection and internal debate consume much of our time and energy. Sharing our experience with your readership is, in fact, therapeutic.

Second, many of our colleagues at other institutions share our experience. We know this to be true from our professional associations and the conferences we attend. Thus, our own experience is verified.

The final catalyst prompting this analysis was an outstanding chapter published on this subject (Kahn and Rudd 1995). Besides the rigor of the research, this piece is especially appealing because the general findings closely match our own experience. The analysis investigated the persistence of mutual fund performance. Using multiple fund databases, the authors neutralized the impact of "style differences" in order to measure excess returns of equity and fixed-income managers who invest in U.S. securities.

Kahn and Rudd's main conclusions were:

- No persistence of returns can be found among U.S. equity managers.
- Some persistence can be found among U.S. fixed-income managers, but not enough to justify the payment of active-manager fees.

John Bogle, in a complementary chapter (Bogle 1992), concluded that a top fund's performance in one year has borne no systematic relationship to its ranking in the subsequent year. Rankings in subsequent years can be fairly described as "regressing to the mean." Testing over 10-year periods, Bogle deduces that "investing in winners of the past, sheerly in terms of highest relative return, adds no significant value to the selection of the winners of the future." In conclusion, Bogle writes, "Picking *the* winning fund is virtually impossible, because reliance on past performance is of no apparent help." As you might expect, Bogle suggests that "picking *a* winning fund is made easy by selecting a passive all-market index or perhaps by engaging in thorough research and careful analysis."

Although we could cite many other articles, we will add just one more quote, from a Goldman Sachs publication (Hurley et al. 1995): "But as [Table 36.1] shows, few managers consistently outperform the S&P 500. Thus, in the eyes of the plan sponsor, its plan is paying an excessive amount of the upside to the manager while still bearing substantial risk that its investments will achieve sub-par returns."

Drawing upon the implications of these three articles, we present the performance results of our institution's active domestic equity manager pool and internally managed fixed-income portfolio.

Three philosophies underlie the implementation of the portfolio structure:

- When markets are believed to be efficient, investments largely will be managed passively.
- When markets are believed to be inefficient, investments largely will be managed actively.
- Our professionals are good analysts and can make money by developing good policy and strategy, by nimbly spotting niche opportunities, and by hiring exceptional internal and external portfolio managers.

TABLE 36.1   Historical Performance of Managers and Products versus Indexes

		Outperformers	
Asset/Outperformance Period	Benchmark	Managers	Products
Equities	S&P 500 Index		
1 year		44.0%	35.3%
1 and 3 year		33.0	25.2
1, 3, and 5 year		28.3	20.1
Fixed-Income	LBGC Index[a]		
1 year		77.1%	74.6%
1 and 3 year		53.5	41.2
1, 3, and 5 year		43.0	31.3

[a]LBGC = Lehman Brothers Government, Corporate Index data trailing from 12/31/94.

Source: Plan Sponsor Network.

Our institution has investment responsibility for more than $30 billion in pension, insurance, and endowment fund assets. Pension funds are the largest component, totaling nearly $24 billion. Thirty-five percent of the pension fund is allocated to U.S. equities.

EQUITY STRUCTURE

We use external passive and active investment advisors to manage our U.S. equity portfolio. As a result of poor past performance relative to the benchmarks and a new senior management team, the U.S. equity portfolio experienced a complete turnover of investment managers in early 1993. Nearly $6 billion in stocks was redeployed. The new structure, in aggregate, was designed to capture broad market characteristics as measured by the Wilshire 5000 Index.

With the restructuring, approximately 70 percent of the U.S. equity portfolio was allocated to large-capitalization stocks, and the bulk of this amount is invested passively in an S&P 500 Index fund to control costs, reflecting the board's philosophy of using passive management in markets that are generally efficient. Four "enhanced index" managers were hired to invest the remainder of the large-cap portion of the portfolio.

Half of the mid- and small-cap portion of the portfolio is allocated to a passively managed extended markets index fund. Five mid- to small-cap active managers using various investment styles and philosophies were hired to manage the remainder of the portfolio. Each had a mandate to purchase stocks in a particular segment of the market defined by style (value versus growth) and market capitalization range. This split between passive and active management reflects a modest, but not overwhelming, conviction that active managers can add value in the small-cap arena.

The nine active and enhanced index managers were hired through a competitive procurement process. The evaluation criteria used to score the proposals included company background, assets under management, organization, product philosophy and process, performance and attribution, fees, and client services. Performance and attribution were given only a 20 percent

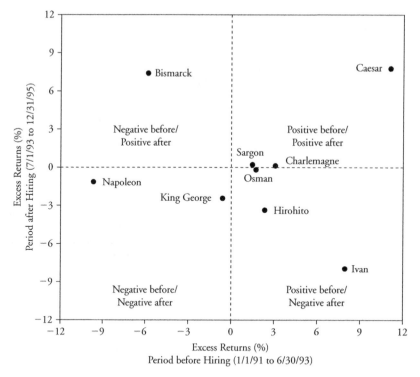

FIGURE 36.1   Equity Manager Performance Records Before and After Hiring

weighting in the scoring process, reflecting skepticism about the power of past performance to predict future performance.

The procurement evaluation team consisted of a well-qualified consultant and investment staff. The board made the final selection of managers from a list of staff- and consultant-approved candidates.

METHODOLOGY

The authors measured the performance of the managers as the annualized excess return (before investment management fees) over mutually agreed-upon style benchmarks. The managers' performance data for the period before hiring (January 1, 1991, to June 30, 1993) are the AIMR composites of each manager's returns for the specified style. The data for the period after hiring (July 1, 1993, through December 31, 1995) are our institution's actual performance. Figure 36.1 plots performance in the period before hiring against that in the period after hiring.

RESULTS

Prior to being hired by the board, six of the nine firms (code-named Caesar, Sargon, Osman, Charlemagne, Hirohito, and Ivan) had positive excess returns ranging from 150 to more than 1,000 basis points above their specified style benchmarks. The underperformance of the remaining three firms (code-named Napoleon, Bismarck, and King George) ranged from 100 to about 1,000 basis points. After being hired by the board, only two of the nine firms (Bismarck and Caesar) demonstrated positive excess returns (each more than 700 basis points above the benchmark); seven managers (Napoleon, Sargon, Osman, Charlemagne, Hirohito, and Ivan) exhibited nearly zero or negative excess returns (as low as 800 basis points below the benchmark) subsequent to the hiring date.

A position in the upper right-hand quadrant of Figure 36.1 indicates that a manager had positive excess returns *both* before and after the hiring date. Out of nine active equity managers, only Caesar prominently holds a position in this quadrant, which indicates persistent, positive returns.

A point in the lower left-hand quadrant denotes persistence of negative excess returns both before and after the hiring. The returns of two managers fall in this quadrant—one (Napoleon) with extremely poor excess returns and the other (King George) with moderately poor excess returns before being hired.

Three managers have shown persistent returns; unfortunately, persistence for two of the three has been negative.

Persistence, negative or positive, clearly is not demonstrated with six of the other managers (Bismarck, Sargon, Osman, Charlemagne, Hirohito, and Ivan). One manager (Bismarck) who experienced negative excess returns prior to being hired achieved positive actual performance against the benchmark with live money. Of the five remaining managers with historically positive excess returns, two (Hirohito and Ivan) experienced negative excess returns and the remaining three (Sargon, Osman, and Charlemagne) provided nearly zero excess returns following their hiring.

Clearly, the study of this active domestic equity manager program demonstrates no general pattern of persistence, which supports the conclusions reached by Kahn and Rudd.

TIME DEPENDENCY

Kahn and Rudd noted that persistent results may be time dependent. In analyzing the performance of our managers, it is clear that the perception of a particular manager's "skill" in managing money is quite dependent on the date that manager was hired. To illustrate this point, consider the case of Bismarck and Ivan, both hired during the second quarter of 1993.

Based upon its outstanding performance since inception, Bismarck is perceived to be one of the board's most skilled managers. During the nine-quarter period ending September 30, 1995, this manager had an annualized excess return of more than 800 basis points above its style benchmark. Conversely, Ivan's annualized performance for this same time period was about 800 basis points *below* its benchmark, leading to the obvious conclusion that this manager is far less skilled at money management than is Bismarck. In fact, Ivan was terminated for its poor performance in the fourth quarter of 1995.

If these managers had been hired five quarters earlier, in March of 1992, however, a far different conclusion might have been drawn. In that event, as of September 30,1995, the performance of these managers, since inception, would look quite similar, with Bismarck having an annualized excess return of about 100 basis points versus its benchmark, only slightly better than Ivan's 80 basis point annualized excess return.

Furthermore, six quarters into the relationship, Ivan, not Bismarck, would have been perceived as clearly the more skilled. At that point in time, Ivan would have returned more than a 2,100 basis point cumulative excess over its benchmark, compared with Bismarck's dismal cumulative return, which was nearly 1,600 basis points *below* its benchmark. In fact, Bismarck, our current star, could well have been terminated for its woeful performance and lack of skill. Ivan, being perceived as a clearly skillful manager, might have been given additional funds with which to underperform during the next eight quarters.

Also, the skill of an investment management firm can be perceived differently by different clients during the same time period. During a recent performance review with one manager, whose performance recently had been extremely strong, we commented that it was pleasant to be discussing such wonderful results. The manager agreed but admitted that other client meetings had been quite *unpleasant*. The difference in experiences was attributable to the fact that one of the firm's other investment products had been underperforming its benchmark significantly. While we were lauding the firm's investment skill, other clients were berating the firm for its ineptitude. Does this firm have skill or not? Or is it more a function of the timing of when a firm is hired that produces the varied (even opposite) judgments?

FIXED-INCOME STRUCTURE

Unlike our U.S. equities, for which outside managers are employed, our fixed-income portfolio is managed in-house. Thus, the expense to run a program is negligible in terms of basis points.

Kahn and Rudd conclude in their study that fixed-income managers can achieve somewhat persistent excess returns. In fact, as Figure 36.2 depicts, our fixed-income returns have been excellent during the three-year period that the same management team has been in

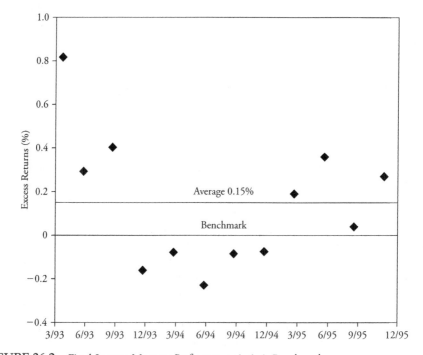

FIGURE 36.2   Fixed-Income Manager Performance vis-á-vis Benchmarks

place. Although underperformance did occur for a few quarters in 1993 and 1994, excess returns averaged about 15 basis points a quarter. Good performance has been achieved with a portfolio fairly neutral in duration to the benchmark: the Lehman Aggregate Index.

Intuitively, we believe that fixed-income managers can outperform a given duration-based index for two reasons:

• Prices are negotiated with the dealer at the time of the trade. Thus, to some extent, an investor is a price maker as well as a price taker.
• Unlike stocks, bonds are usually fixed-term obligations and hence can be substituted more easily. Factor prices (i.e., time-determined pricing of cash flows, pricing of credit risk, and option pricing) determine a larger percentage of the total price of the securities and embody less nonsystematic risk. Security pricing anomalies can be measured more accurately as a result, and arbitrage trading can occur.

INVESTMENT IMPLICATIONS

From the evidence presented on the U.S. equity markets, the logical question becomes whether *identifiable, persistent* factors other than performance (such as style, organizational structure, and personnel) are predictors of future performance. Our staff and the consultant have attempted, with mixed degrees of success, to identify and measure these factors. We believe that the factors are reasonable and the evaluation process sound but that the efficiency of the markets overwhelms the factors' predictive powers.

Our first philosophy has been reinforced: Investments in efficient markets (e.g., S&P 500 companies with large capitalizations that are well covered by Wall Street) should be passively managed. Given our experience, even quasi-active or "enhanced" strategies that take active bets in a rigorous, risk-controlled manner have not added value. Confidence that they will work persistently in the future is low.

Our experience suggests that small- and medium-capitalization stocks may be even more efficiently priced than we had assumed in 1992 and early 1993. Certainly there is no generalized evidence either from Kahn and Rudd or from our experience that managers persistently can add value above their style benchmarks. Quite honestly, we emotionally have not yet given up on active management in this segment of the market, but we are very sober.

Fixed-income markets have some degree of inefficiency, and therefore, arbitrage trading can produce excess returns. This statement is confirmed by both Kahn and Rudd and our in-house bond group, although the results in the Goldman Sachs study are mixed.

CONCLUSIONS

Andrew Rudd suggested in private conversations that some individual equity managers may, in fact, have skill that would not show up in a broad cross-sectional study. That skill may be subtle, either in terms of the persistent value added or in terms of the signals available to observers. The challenge becomes developing a method of correctly identifying any external signals that are emitted and any predictive strength of those signals.

The evidence presented suggests that we have not been totally successful at meeting the challenge of assembling a skillful manager team in aggregate. We can identify three possibilities for this disappointment:

- the criteria used for evaluating managers are not the right determinants;
- the search process fails to provide adequate access to skillful firms; or
- if any firms really do possess persistent skill, they are so few in number that the effort required to find them is greater than the effort we have exerted.

Earlier, we listed the evaluation criteria, in addition to historical performance, we use when conducting manager searches. These criteria are little different from those used by most other institutions and their consultants. If the criteria are wrong, then, how are we to know? The criteria are based on what are believed to be sound economic and psychological principles. We have developed and modified the criteria after many years in the business and after talking to countless managers, consultants, and peers.

With regard to our specific criteria, the most contentious one quite likely is assets under management. As a practical matter, the manager must be of substantial size and possess a sufficient infrastructure to absorb significant incremental assets. The danger is, however, that the successful strategy implementation of small money management firms will no longer work at large sizes.

The industry is full of examples of successful firms becoming unsuccessful when managing a larger asset base. This phenomenon could be because of the difficulty of implementing a strategy in the market with large amounts of money, an increased number of distractions resulting from size (added staff and administration, etc.), or changing business priorities affecting the firm's success (i.e., the firm becomes more conservative in an attempt to maintain its client base).

Another possible explanation is the diseconomies of scale in active portfolio management, explained in Perold and Salomon (1991). In short, the bid–ask spread of a transaction increases as the block size increases, resulting in higher transaction costs as a percentage of the trade. As assets under management increase, so do the block sizes of the firm's trades. The resulting higher transaction costs have a negative impact on performance.

If performance is negatively affected as assets under management increase, a conundrum arises as the money management business matures. The Goldman Sachs study presents compelling evidence that the industry currently suffers from overcapacity. As a result, the authors of that study project that the industry will bifurcate into two groups: 20–25 "large companies" that offer the full spectrum of products and services, and "niche competitors" offering specialty products and services. Today's companies will either commit the resources to expand (or merge) into a large company, find a niche role, or exit the business. Under any scenario, fewer firms will each manage more assets. Therein lies the conundrum: If it is true that an investment management firm's growth can have a negative impact on its performance, it is also true that for most successful firms, such growth is unavoidable. Once discovered, the lesser-known skillful managers quickly rise to prominence as, in order to be fair, consultants share their insights with all their clients. Thus, when a consultant recognizes and recommends the rare odd duckling, many of the consultant's clients quickly select that duckling. Compounding the problem, because this industry has very few secrets, is that knowledge of the manager will be diffused over time to other consultants and clients. By definition, the characteristics of the duckling change as it matures into a duck.

The second possibility for failure lies in the search process itself. Although consultants' manager databases are large and searches are well advertised, the structure of the search process may not always encourage the best managers to bid for the business. The search process, if one of the qualifications is experience with sizable accounts, creates a bias toward large, established firms. Yet, even with the constraints of the search process, a robust sample of more than 100 responses is generally received for major U.S. equity searches. Therefore, we believe that the search process probably does not fully explain the lack of success in finding managers who add value.

A third possibility for failure may be simply that there are very few skillful managers. If so, the institutional investor must ask whether the benefit of discovering those few justifies the effort, given the required resources and the net contribution to a large portfolio. In the real world, plan sponsor staff do not have the required resources to examine thoroughly the subtleties of thousands of investment advisory firms. Consultants, who generally are paid on a retainer basis, also are not motivated to spend lots of money on an exhaustive new manager search.

If we are successful in identifying a team of skillful managers, can the skill and good performance be maintained? The reason for the success could be as simple as anomalies, which can be exploited for a while by skillful managers, become discovered, and later disappear in the marketplace.

A final issue in maintaining a skillful team of managers is distinguishing between bad luck and lack of skill. Once a manager is hired, if it does not exhibit stellar performance, how do we know whether to ride out the wave or cut the manager loose?

During the nearly three-year period our domestic equity program has been in place, we have monitored the managers closely and terminated two of the nine domestic firms for performance-related reasons. Although termination may take place when returns *significantly* underperform the agreed-upon benchmark, it also occurs when the monitoring system identifies changes in strategy, personnel, or organization (i.e., a change in the positive characteristics identified in the initial evaluation). Of our remaining seven managers, one is on the watch list and another was recently removed from probation as a result of deliberate actions the manager took to address perceived danger signals.

Slowly, over time, many large pension funds have shared our experience and have moved toward indexing more domestic equity assets. It seems that when it comes to U.S. equity, the Emperor's wardrobe is mighty bare.

REFERENCES

Bogle, John C. 1992. "Selecting Equity Mutual Funds." *The Journal of Portfolio Management*, vol. 18, no. 2 (Winter):94–100.

Hurley, Mark P., Sharon I. Meers, Ben J. Bornstein, and Neil R. Strumingher. 1995. *The Coming Evolution of the Investment Management Industry: Opportunities and Strategies*, Goldman Sachs Investment Management Industry Group (October).

Kahn, Ronald N., and Andrew Rudd. 1995. "Does Historical Performance Predict Future Performance?" *Financial Analysts Journal*, vol. 51, no. 6 (November/December):43–52.

Perold, André F., and Robert J. Salomon, Jr. 1991. "The Right Amount of Assets under Management." *Financial Analysts Journal*, vol. 47, no. 3 (May/June):31–39.

CHAPTER 37

DOES HISTORICAL PERFORMANCE PREDICT FUTURE PERFORMANCE?

Ronald N. Kahn and Andrew Rudd

An investigation of the persistence of mutual fund performance indicates that investors need more than past performance numbers to pick future winners. In this study, style analysis was used to separate fund total returns into style and selection components. Performance was defined in terms of total returns, selection returns, and information ratios (ratios of selection return to selection risk). For each fund type, two out-of-sample periods were established to investigate persistence of performance from one period to the next using regression analysis and contingency tables. The evidence supported persistence only for fixed-income fund performance. This persistence is beyond any effects of fund fees and expenses or database survivorship bias. Unfortunately, this persistence edge cannot overcome the average underperformance of fixed-income funds resulting from fees and expenses.

Who will be next year's winners? Conventional wisdom in the investment industry is that the first place to look in trying to predict the future performance of mutual funds is past performance. But does it help to know last year's winners? Do winners repeat?

The idea that winners repeat is so obvious and popular, it has spawned an entire mini-industry devoted to documenting past winners. Mutual fund performance reviews regularly appear in publications from *Barrons* to *Business Week* to *Consumer Reports*. Services such as Morningstar and Lipper exist to publish mutual fund rankings. Pension plan consultants closely examine past performance before recommending managers, and successful managers proudly document their past performance. All this activity demonstrates that everyone choosing active managers, from pension plan sponsors to individual investors, is acting as if past performance predicts future performance. But does it?

Reprinted from *Financial Analysts Journal* (November/December 1995):43–52.

In this chapter, we review the history of investigation into this question and then present new results based on the performance of active equity and fixed-income managers of publicly available U.S. mutual funds during the past decade.[1] We also discuss the investment implications of our results.

This study differs from previous studies in its use of "style analysis" to monitor performance,[2] in accounting for the effect of fund expenses and fees,[3] in the use of multiple mutual fund databases, and in the particular historical period investigated.

PREVIOUS RESEARCH

Interest in mutual fund performance has a long history, and many studies have investigated whether mutual funds, on average, outperform the market and whether the performance of the best managers is statistically significant. Those studies, however, do not address the question of persistence of performance. Studies of performance persistence fall into two camps: those that do not find persistence and those that do.

Several studies have shown, based on different asset classes and different time periods, that performance does not persist. Jensen looked at the performance of 115 mutual funds over the 1945–1964 period and found no evidence for persistence.[4] Kritzman reached the same conclusion examining the 32 fixed-income managers retained by AT&T for at least 10 years.[5] Dunn and Theisen found no evidence of persistence in 201 institutional portfolios from 1973 to 1982.[6] Elton, Gruber, and Rentzler showed that performance did not persist for 51 publicly offered commodity funds from 1980 to 1988.[7]

Other studies have found that performance does persist. Grinblatt and Titman found evidence of persistence in 157 mutual funds during the 1975–1984 period.[8] Lehmann and Modest reported similar results looking at 130 mutual funds from 1968 to 1982.[9] In the United Kingdom, Brown and Draper demonstrated evidence for persistence using data on 550 pension managers from 1981 to 1990.[10] Hendricks, Patel, and Zeckhauser documented persistence of performance in 165 equity mutual funds from 1974 to 1988.[11] Recently, Goetzmann and Ibbotson showed evidence for persistence using 728 mutual funds over the 1976–1988 period.[12]

PERFORMANCE MEASURES

Mutual fund performance can be measured in several possible ways, including total or excess returns, risk-adjusted returns (alphas or selection returns), and information ratios (ratios of return to risk). Alphas can be extracted from excess returns through the following regression:

$$r_n(t) = \alpha_n + \beta_n \times r_B(t) + \varepsilon_n(t), \tag{37.1}$$

where $r_n(t)$ is the monthly excess return to the fund in month t, $r_B(t)$ is the monthly excess return to the benchmark, and α_n is the fund's estimated alpha. The information ratio is the annualized ratio of residual return to residual risk. In Equation 37.1, it is the ratio of alpha to the standard deviation of $\varepsilon_n(t)$, annualized.

The past studies of performance persistence have mainly defined performance using total returns or alphas. Lehman and Modest showed that the choice of benchmark can critically influence the resulting estimated alpha.[13] Although the benchmark has a severe impact on individual fund alphas, it has somewhat less influence on fund performance rankings. In the context of arbitrage pricing theory models, Lehman and Modest emphasized the importance of knowing the appropriate risk and return benchmark.

STYLE ANALYSIS

We looked at performance using both selection returns and information ratios. Selection (or style-adjusted) returns credit manager performance relative to a "style" benchmark. Generalizing on Equation 37.1, we estimated selection returns using only the portfolio's returns plus the returns to a set of style indexes; formally,

$$r(t) = \Sigma w_j \times f_j(t) + \psi(t), \tag{37.2}$$

where w_j is the portfolio's weight in style j. These weights define the style benchmark, and $\psi(t)$ is the return in excess of that benchmark. We estimated these weights and the selection returns, $\psi(t)$, using a quadratic program to minimize Var$[\psi(t)]$ subject to the constraints that the weights are positive and sum to l.

For equity funds, the style indexes include the S&P 500/BARRA value and growth indexes, the S&P midcap 400/BARRA value and growth indexes, and the S&P small-cap 600 index,[14] plus a Treasury bill index.

For fixed-income funds, the style indexes include the Lehman Brothers intermediate government bond, long government bond, corporate bond, and mortgage indexes, the Salomon Brothers world government bond index, and a BARRA index of synthetic 30-year Treasury zero-coupon bonds, plus a Treasury bill index.

In contrast to alphas estimated via the unconstrained regression (Equation 37.1), which are uncorrelated (by mathematical construction) with the benchmark, selection returns estimated with constraints on style weights can contain remaining market exposures. The beta of the equity style benchmark is bound by the betas of the lowest and highest index betas. Likewise, the duration of the fixed-income style benchmark is bounded by the durations of the lowest and highest duration indexes. This constraint can cause particular problems for fixed-income funds, which can exhibit durations far in excess of index durations. Hence, we included a 30-year zero-coupon index with a duration of 30 to mitigate this effect. With this index included, we found no correlation between selection returns and duration.

The style weights define the style benchmark as a weighted average of the style indexes. For performance analysis, we estimated this style benchmark at time t, using returns in a 36- to 60-month trailing window (based on data availability), with a 1-month lag. Thus, the style benchmark at time t is based on returns from $[(t - 2)$ to $(t - 1), (t - 3)$ to $(t - 2), \ldots, (t - 61)$ to $(t - 60)]$. The selection return over the period from t to $(t + 1)$ is then the portfolio return over that period minus the style benchmark return. This method for estimating the style benchmark ensures an out-of-sample selection return, and the one-month lag, in principle, allows the manager to know the relevant benchmark before time t.

We believe selection returns as estimated above to be the best estimate currently available (using only returns data) of a "level playing field" on which to compare manager performance. This formulation is an embellishment of Jensen's original idea of controlling for market exposure before analyzing performance.[15] Style analysis controls for several investment styles. Looking forward, the investor chooses an appropriate style benchmark for investment and then selects managers to exceed that benchmark.

In the context of style analysis, the information ratio is the ratio of selection return mean to standard deviation, annualized. If investors wish to maximize the risk-adjusted selection returns defined in the standard mean–variance framework, $\alpha - \lambda \omega^2$, then they will always prefer the highest information ratio managers.[16] Looking forward, after choosing the style benchmark, investors will wish to select the managers with the highest information ratios.

SURVIVORSHIP BIAS

One important issue for all of these studies is survivorship bias. The underlying data on fund performance are not free of survivorship bias, and recently, Brown, Goetzmann, Ibbotson, and Ross showed that survivorship bias can significantly influence the evidence on persistence of performance.[17] This important insight was not recognized in previous work on survivorship bias, which showed only that it was not a significant influence on studies of average mutual fund performance. This new insight has called into question much of the previous work on fund persistence of performance.

THE DATA

We investigated U.S. active equity and fixed-income mutual funds included in both the Micropal and Morningstar databases.[18] In particular, we used all active domestic equity funds included in both databases with data starting in January 1983 but excluded equity index funds. The 300 equity funds in our study included three convertible bond funds. For the fixed-income sample, we included all active taxable domestic bond funds that were in both databases and had data starting in October 1988. We excluded junk bond funds, money market funds, international bond funds, index funds, and preferred stock funds.

To examine fund persistence, the data were separated into equity funds and fixed-income funds and analyzed separately. Separating the funds is clearly important when using standard alpha analysis (Equation 37.1), because their analyses should include very different benchmarks for the two fund types. Even after using style analysis to separate out selection returns, however, equity and fixed-income funds should be analyzed separately because of their differing risk and return levels. Brown et al. have shown that the survivorship bias effect on persistence of performance studies is accentuated by analyzing a group of funds with divergent risk levels.[19] Another reason for separating the two types of funds is that expenses are more important for fixed-income funds.

Because we calculated performance "out-of-sample" using monthly returns, we required an in-sample period of at least 36 months of data to define the style benchmarks. We then divided the remaining data into two out-of-sample periods for the persistence-of-performance study. Table 37.1 lists the periods for the studies.

TABLE 37.1   Study Periods

Asset Category	In-Sample	Period 1	Period 2
Equity	1/83–12/87	1/88–12/90	1/91–12/93
Fixed Income	10/86–9/90	10/90–3/92	4/92–9/93

For each asset category, we tried to define the longest possible analysis period, consistent with the number of funds in the database. Because more equity funds than fixed-income funds had long histories, the equity study extends further back in time. Even though the fixed-income in-sample period starts in October 1986, the sample included funds with data beginning in October 1988. We estimated their style benchmarks using a window that expanded until it included 60 months of data, a technique we believe had no material effect on the results.

We can also characterize these analysis periods along other possibly important dimensions for our study. For example, equity Period 1 corresponds to a time when equity "value" managers outperformed "growth" managers, and Period 2 was a period when growth managers typically outperformed value managers. For the fixed-income study, both periods exhibited steadily falling interest rates.

To ensure data integrity, the study included only funds that appear in both the Micropal and Morningstar databases and for which the data from those two sources lead to substantially similar total returns, selection returns, and information ratios for each fund in each period.[20] Adding these screens for data integrity did not ultimately change the conclusions concerning persistence of performance.

In addition to the returns data in the Micropal and Morningstar databases, we used data on current fees (the expense ratios) contained in the Morningstar database as of November 1994. We used these data to investigate the influence of expenses on persistence of performance.

METHODOLOGY

Our first investigation of persistence used regression analysis, regressing Period 2 performance against Period 1 performance.

$$\text{Performance (2)} = a + b \times \text{Performance (1)} + \varepsilon, \qquad (37.3)$$

where "performance" can be cumulative total returns, cumulative selection returns, or information ratios. Positive estimates of the coefficient b with significant t-statistics are evidence of persistence: Period 1 performance contains useful information for predicting Period 2 performance.

We also used contingency tables to analyze performance persistence. For contingency analysis, we sorted the funds into winners and losers in Period 1 and winners and losers in Period 2. We distinguished winners from losers by ranking fund performance according to the performance measure of interest and defining the top half of the list as winners and the bottom half as losers. If the statistical evidence shows that winners in Period 1 remain winners in Period 2, the case for persistence of performance is proven. The contingency tables show the numbers of funds that were winners in both periods, losers in both periods, winners then losers, and losers then winners.

Because half the funds are winners and half are losers in each period by definition, if performance does not persist, the numbers in each bin should be equal. Evidence for persistence will be (statistically significantly) higher numbers in the diagonal bins (top left and bottom right). To analyze statistical significance, we calculated

$$\chi^2 = \Sigma \, \frac{(O_i - E_i)^2}{E_i},$$

where O_i is the observed number in each bin and E_i is the expected number in each bin. χ^2 follows a chi-square distribution with 1 degree of freedom in the case of a two-by-two table and $(R - 1) \times (C - 1)$ degrees of freedom in an R by C contingency matrix.

EQUITY RESULTS

Figures 37.1 through 37.3 are scatter plots of Period 2 equity fund performance versus Period 1 performance for cumulative total returns, cumulative selection returns, and information ratios respectively. The regression analysis found evidence of persistence at the 95 percent

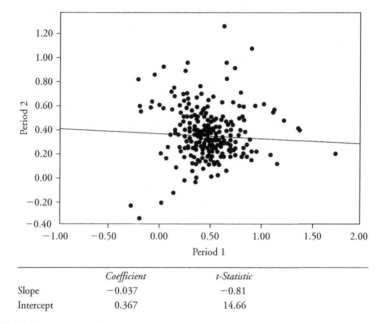

	Coefficient	t-Statistic
Slope	−0.037	−0.81
Intercept	0.367	14.66

FIGURE 37.1   Equity Total Returns

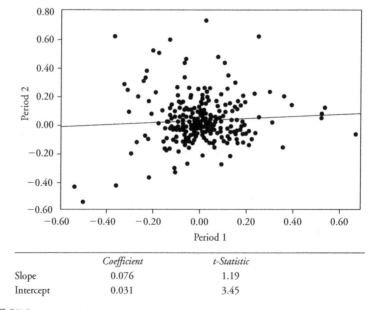

	Coefficient	t-Statistic
Slope	0.076	1.19
Intercept	0.031	3.45

FIGURE 37.2   Equity Selection Returns

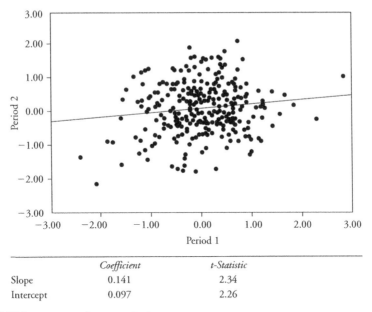

	Coefficient	t-Statistic
Slope	0.141	2.34
Intercept	0.097	2.26

FIGURE 37.3   Equity Information Ratios

confidence level ($t > 2$) only when persistence is defined in terms of information ratios. In this case, the estimated coefficient is 0.141: For a fund with an information ratio of 0.50 in Period 1 (roughly the top quartile), we would expect an information ratio of 0.07 in Period 2 (slightly above the median).

Tables 37.2 through 37.4 are the contingency table information for the total return, selection return, and information ratio data, respectively. Each table displays the number of funds in each bin; the percentages of Period 1 winners and losers that become Period 2 winners and losers; the χ^2 statistic; and the probability, p, that random data could have generated that high a χ^2 statistic.

None of these tables shows evidence of persistence. Table 37.2 shows the rather perverse result that the losers in Period 1 are likely winners in Period 2. Because this table uses total returns data, this apparent mean reversion is probably the result of value outperforming

TABLE 37.2   Total Equity Returns

		Period 2	
		W	L
Period 1	W	62 41.3%	88 58.7%
	L	88 58.7%	62 41.3%
		$\chi^2 = 9.01, p = 0.003$	

TABLE 37.3   Equity Selection Returns

		Period 2	
		W	L
Period 1	W	79 52.7%	71 47.3%
	L	71 47.3%	79 52.7%
		$\chi^2 = 0.85, p = 0.356$	

TABLE 37.4   Equity Information Ratios

		Period 2	
		W	L
Period 1	W	80 53.3%	70 46.7%
	L	70 46.7%	80 53.3%
		$\chi^2 = 1.33, p = 0.248$	

growth in Period 1 and growth outperforming value in Period 2. We focused on selection returns precisely to control for these style effects. We wanted to find out whether funds can consistently outperform appropriate benchmarks.

FIXED-INCOME RESULTS

Figures 37.4 through 37.6 are scatter plots of Period 2 fixed-income fund performance versus Period 1 performance for cumulative total returns, cumulative selection returns, and information ratios, respectively. In contrast to the results for equities, the fixed-income selection returns and information ratios both show evidence of persistence. The t-statistics are large in each case: 4.93 for selection returns and 6.06 for information ratios. For the information ratios, the estimated coefficient is 0.368. So, for a fund with an information ratio of 0.50 in Period 1 (once again roughly top quartile), we would expect an information ratio of 0.18 in Period 2.

Tables 37.5 through 37.7 analyze the same data using contingency analysis. Once again, the fixed-income selection returns and information ratios exhibit persistence of performance. The surprise is that the total returns data show no persistence evidence, because both periods experienced falling interest rates. The long-term funds should have consistently outperformed the short-term funds because rates were falling during this entire period. Evidently, in our database,

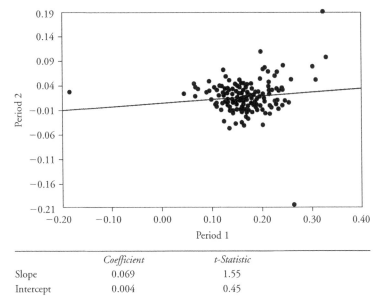

	Coefficient	t-Statistic
Slope	0.069	1.55
Intercept	0.004	0.45

FIGURE 37.4   Fixed-Income Total Returns

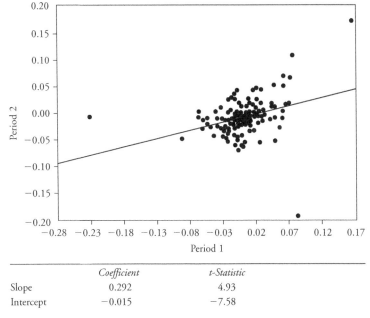

	Coefficient	t-Statistic
Slope	0.292	4.93
Intercept	−0.015	−7.58

FIGURE 37.5   Fixed-Income Selection Returns

the dispersion in fund duration must have been sufficiently small so that other influences masked this expected effect. We did check that the selection returns, with such styles accounted for, exhibited no correlation with fund durations.

The regression analysis and contingency table analysis consistently show significant persistence of fixed-income selection returns and information ratios.

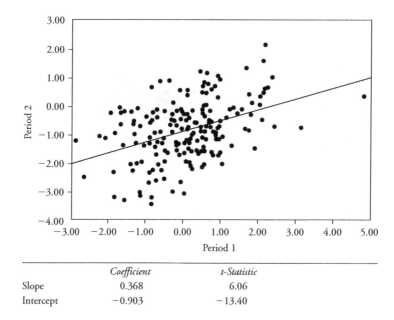

	Coefficient	t-Statistic
Slope	0.368	6.06
Intercept	−0.903	−13.40

FIGURE 37.6   Fixed-Income Information Ratios

TABLE 37.5   Fixed-Income Total Returns

		Period 2	
		W	L
Period 1	W	51	46
		52.6%	47.4%
	L	46	52
		46.9%	53.1%
		$\chi^2 = 0.62, p = 0.431$	

TABLE 37.6   Fixed-Income Selection Returns

		Period 2	
		W	L
Period 1	W	61	36
		62.9%	37.1%
	L	36	62
		36.7%	63.3%
		$\chi^2 = 13.34, p = 0.000$	

TABLE 37.7 Fixed-Income Information Ratios

		Period 2	
		W	L
Period 1	W	59 60.5%	38 39.2%
	L	38 38.8%	60 61.2%

$$\chi^2 = 9.48, p = 0.002$$

ACCOUNTING FOR FEES AND EXPENSES

Our initial analysis of the equity and fixed-income fund returns showed little evidence of persistence among equity fund managers but strong evidence of persistence of selection returns and information ratios among fixed-income fund managers. One possible (and uninteresting) source of persistence could be a strong persistence of strong underperformers, achieved through large fees and expenses. Our results hint at this effect because the persistence appears only for fixed-income funds, which have higher ratios of fees to expected outperformance.

To investigate the influence of fees and expenses on mutual fund performance persistence, we used November 1994 expense ratio data contained in the Morningstar database. The Morningstar expense ratios include all expenses taken directly from the fund's net asset value. The returns data we analyzed are net of these expenses.

To estimate monthly returns *gross* of fees and expenses, we assumed these annual expense ratios to be fixed in time and added (one-twelfth of) them back to each fund's return every month. Then, we reran our persistence studies using these gross return data.

For the equity funds, the gross return data show no evidence of persistence, and even the information ratios, which showed persistence using returns net of fees and expenses, no longer show evidence of persistence based on gross return data. (In this case, the t-statistic drops from 2.34 to 1.10.)

Fees also had a strong influence on information ratios. For the equity funds, using net returns, the mean information ratio is 0.12 with a standard deviation of 0.73 across the 300 funds. Using the gross return data, the mean information ratio rises to 0.36 with a standard deviation of 0.69. On average, managers seem to be capable of producing excellent portfolio returns, but investors do not benefit. The evidence for average outperformance among this group of equity funds mainly disappears when we subtract expenses.

We also saw a strong relationship between net return information ratios and fees. In Period 1, the highest fee fund has the lowest information ratio, and in Period 2, all the highest fee funds are among the lowest decile information ratios. Regressing net return information ratios against expense ratios, this relationship shows up with a t-statistic of -4.77 in Period 1 and -5.74 in Period 2. We also examined average fees for the four groups in Table 37.4. The group of funds labeled as losers in both periods exhibited significantly higher fees than the other three groups, which all exhibited similar fees. Given the lack of reliable persistence elsewhere among equity fund performance, the avoidance of high fees is clearly a defensible strategy.

With regard to fixed-income fund performance, gross of fees, the evidence for persistence remains but the strength diminishes. For fixed-income selection returns, persistence

t-statistics drop from 4.93 to 4.50 and χ^2 statistics drop from 13.34 to 9.48. For fixed-income information ratios, the persistence t-statistics drop from 6.06 to 4.74 and the χ^2 statistics drop from 9.48 to 6.28, all still significant.

The effect of fees and expenses on information ratios is quite dramatic for the fixed-income funds. The mean information ratios move from -0.87, with a standard deviation of 1.00 for net returns across the 195 funds, to a mean of -0.10 with a standard deviation of 0.89 when looking at gross returns. Clearly, the average expenses for fixed-income funds form a much larger fraction of typical risk undertaken than what we observed for equity funds.

According to these numbers, there is no evidence of average over- or underperformance among this group of fixed-income funds gross of fees, but the fees lead to a strong average underperformance when they are netted out. For these fixed-income funds, especially in Period 1, the relationship between net return information ratios and expense ratios is strong; the highest fees correspond to the lowest decile information ratios. The t-statistic for this relationship is -4.56, although it drops to -0.61 in Period 2, when the single highest expense ratio fund is in the top quartile of information ratios. Correspondingly, in Table 37.7, the one group whose fees were significantly above the others were the funds labeled losers in Period 1 and winners in Period 2.

SURVIVORSHIP BIAS

Brown, Goetzmann, Ibbotson, and Ross investigated the influence of survivorship bias on persistence studies.[21] They argued that because of the existence of a distribution of strategies of differing volatilities,[22] even in the absence of any true persistence, survivorship bias will generate the appearance that winners repeat. In effect, managers following high-volatility strategies but with no true skill will either by chance consistently show up as winners or be removed from the business through poor performance. Note that this effect will influence returns more strongly than information ratios.

Brown et al. demonstrated this effect through a Monte Carlo simulation based on a universe of 600 managers with no skill (random returns), a reasonable distribution of active risk levels, and performance studies based on four years of simulated returns. They introduced survivorship bias using a cutoff figure: the percent of funds at the bottom of the performance rankings deleted each year. They then showed how survivorship bias can influence persistence t-statistics and χ^2 statistics as a function of the cutoff. Table 37.8 summarizes results from their paper.

These results call into question our interpretation of the statistical significance of our observed t-statistics and χ^2 statistics. Of course, we do not know an appropriate cutoff number that describes the number of funds going out of business because of poor performance,

TABLE 37.8   Brown et al. Results

Cutoff	Average χ^2	Average t-Statistic
0%	1.04 ($p = 0.308$)	0.0 ($p = 1.000$)
5%	1.64 ($p = 0.200$)	2.0 ($p = 0.0461$)
10%	3.28 ($p = 0.070$)	3.4 ($p = 0.0007$)
20%	7.13 ($p = 0.008$)	4.7 ($p = 0.0000$)

TABLE 37.9   Persistence of Performance Summary

Fund	Statistic	Significance of Persistence	
		Contingency Table	Regression
Equity			
$N = 300$	Total return	No	No
	Total + fee	No	No
	Selection return	No	No
	Selection + fee	No	No
	IR	No	Yes
	IR + fee	No	No
Bond			
$N = 195$	Total return	No	No
	Total + fee	No	No
	Selection return	Yes	Yes
	Selection + fee	Yes	Yes
	IR	Yes	Yes
	IR + fee	Yes	Yes

but it certainly exceeds zero. Roughly speaking, a 20 percent cutoff figure could explain most of our observed results, although a 10 percent cutoff figure could not. Recent work by Brown and Goetzmann showed cutoff figures of roughly 5 percent for common stock funds between 1976 and 1988.[23] Clearly, the best way to resolve the survivorship bias problem is to collect and build databases free of survivorship bias.

SUMMARY OF RESULTS

Table 37.9 summarizes the results on persistence of performance. We found no evidence for persistence of performance among equity mutual funds, but we did find evidence of persistence of fixed-income selection returns and information ratios, even after accounting for expenses.

Overall, we ran 12 tests for persistence of performance, accounting for fees, at the 95 percent confidence level, and 4 of those tests showed positive results.

CONTEXT

How do these empirical findings compare with those of the many similar studies, with a wide variety of conclusions, conducted during the past 25 years? Why do some studies find evidence of persistence and others do not?

This study uses style analysis to separate style returns from selection returns. Studies that look at alphas from regressions of fund returns against S&P 500 returns do not control for fund styles. This omission can generate the appearance of persistence. For example, if value managers, in general, outperform the S&P 500 in both periods, the alpha-based studies will show persistence but the style-based studies will not. Our study examined whether the value managers who outperform a value index in Period 1 also outperform a value index in Period 2. This fundamental difference is one reason why our results may differ from those of other studies.

Other reasons for the discrepancy of results include a variety of effects not sufficiently understood by many of these studies. Survivorship bias is a significant problem and quite difficult to overcome. Also, fees can significantly influence the results, generating persistence of underperformance based on high expenses. Most previous studies have not explicitly investigated the influence of fund expenses on performance persistence.

Equity and fixed-income funds should be separated because they involve very different benchmarks, as well as very different levels of risk and expected return. Combining equity and bond funds together in a persistence study can accentuate survivorship bias problems by greatly broadening the distribution of fund volatilities and can also cause problems when studying persistence of alphas. Fixed-income fund alphas defined relative to an equity benchmark will closely resemble fixed-income total returns because the equity betas of typical fixed-income funds will lie close to zero. Persistence of total returns, however, is not usually of interest.

The integrity of the fund return databases is also an issue for consideration. Relying on two databases and studying only those records beyond question can improve the reliability of the study, even though for this particular study, deleting questionable records did not change the final results.

Finally, of course, these persistence results may be time dependent. Different studies have looked at different time periods. Active managers outperform consistently, however, based on their superior information. As their ideas become widely known, the outperformance disappears. If good ideas do not consistently appear over time but instead arrive episodically, then persistence will be stronger in some periods than in others.

Along these lines, few, if any, of these studies (including ours) distinguish funds from managers. Persistence could be more a property of managers, not funds, even though most funds have a characteristic approach to investing.

INVESTMENT IMPLICATIONS

We found evidence for persistence of fixed-income fund performance and no evidence of persistence of equity fund performance. What are the investment implications of these results?

For equity funds, the implications are simple. With no persistence of selection returns, unless you have another basis for choosing future winners (i.e., your selection criteria include information other than historical performance), the solution is to index, perhaps to a set of style indexes weighted to match your investment objectives. Index funds should achieve at least average performance with low selection risk, low fees, low turnover, and low transaction costs. Because of their low costs, index funds typically perform above the median of all funds with similar styles.

For fixed-income funds, we found significant evidence of persistence of selection returns. Selection of above-average managers based on past performance appears to be possible, but this possibility requires more detailed analysis.

Table 37.5 shows that of the fixed-income funds with above-median selection returns in Period 1, 62.9 percent were above-median funds in Period 2. That percentage sounds like impressive odds for picking Period 2 selection returns. Beyond the winners–losers distinction, however, what returns could these funds achieve? The mean selection return

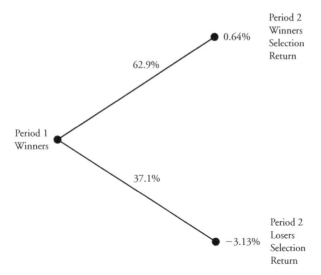

FIGURE 37.7   Expected Period 2 Selection Returns

of the Period 2 winners was 0.64 percent, while the mean selection return of the Period 2 losers was −3.13 percent. In other words, the losers lost much more than the winners won, as Figure 37.7 shows. So, the appropriate use of historical information provides strong odds for beating the median, but unfortunately the median has negative selection return. In this case, Figure 37.7 implies an expected selection return in Period 2 of −0.76 percent for the Period 1 winners, with a standard deviation of 1.82 percent.[24] This result should not be too surprising. Fees and transaction costs imply that average fund returns should underperform benchmarks, and many studies have demonstrated this underperformance.

The investment implications for fixed-income funds, surprisingly, are similar to those for equity funds. Once again, index funds are a very attractive strategy. Presumably, index funds will consistently appear as winners when compared with the funds in this study.

There is also an implication for investors who still wish to choose fixed-income funds based on past selection returns: Choose only one fund. Because the mean selection return is negative, diversifying across funds will simply accentuate that negative return. Assuming normality, by choosing only one winning Period 1 fund, the probability of having a positive Period 2 selection return will be 34 percent. For five equally weighted funds, the probability of positive selection return drops to 17 percent. In this portfolio problem, surprisingly, diversification does not pay.

CONCLUSIONS

We investigated persistence of performance for equity and fixed-income mutual fund managers and found evidence for persistence of fixed-income fund performance, even after controlling for fund style and management fees.

The investment implications for equity and fixed-income fund selection are similar. Given only past performance information, index funds look best for equity and fixed-income investments. Equity index funds make sense because of the absence of persistence in equity fund performance. Fixed-income index funds make sense because, even though performance does persist, the average underperformance of fixed-income funds more than cancels out the benefits of being able to choose above-average funds through persistence alone. Only with information beyond historical performance statistics should investors choose active managers.

NOTES

1. Elsewhere, we have reported preliminary research on the performance of U.S. institutional portfolios. See Ronald N. Kahn and Andrew Rudd, "Practical Applications of Quantitative Theories," presentation at The Financial Planet Symposium, Paris, November 1994.
2. This methodology was originally suggested by Sharpe. See William F. Sharpe, "Asset Allocation: Management Style and Performance Measurement," *The Journal of Portfolio Management*, vol. 18, no. 2 (Winter 1992):7–19.
3. See John C. Bogle, "Selecting Equity Mutual Funds," *The Journal of Portfolio Management*, vol. 18, no. 2 (Winter 1992):94–100. Bogle investigated the impact of expenses and fees but did not use style analysis.
4. M. Jensen, "The Performance of Mutual Funds in the Period 1945–1964," *The Journal of Finance*, vol. 23, no. 2 (May 1968):389–416.
5. Mark Kritzman, "Can Bond Managers Perform Consistently?" *The Journal of Portfolio Management*, vol. 9, no. 4 (Summer 1983):54–56.
6. Patricia C. Dunn and Rolf D. Theisen, "How Consistently Do Active Managers Win?" *The Journal of Portfolio Management*, vol. 9, no. 4 (Summer 1983):47–50.
7. E. Elton, M. Gruber, and J. Rentzler, "The Performance of Publicly Offered Commodity Funds," *Financial Analysts Journal*, vol. 46, no. 4 (July/August 1990):23–30.
8. M. Grinblatt and S. Titman, "The Evaluation of Mutual Fund Performance: An Analysis of Monthly Returns," working paper 13–86, John E. Anderson Graduate School of Management, University of California at Los Angeles (1988).
9. Bruce N. Lehmann and David M. Modest, "Mutual Fund Performance Evaluation: A Comparison of Benchmarks and Benchmark Comparisons," *The Journal of Finance*, vol. 42, no. 2 (June 1987):233–265.
10. G. Brown and P. Draper, "Consistency of U.K. Pension Fund Investment Performance," working paper, University of Strath Clyde Department of Accounting and Finance (1992).
11. Darryll Hendricks, Jayendu Patel, and Richard Zeckhauser, "Hot Hands in Mutual Funds: Short-Run Persistence of Relative Performance, 1974–1988," *The Journal of Finance*, vol. 48, no. 1 (March 1993):93–130.
12. W. N. Goetzmann and Roger Ibbotson, "Do Winners Repeat?" *The Journal of Portfolio Management*, vol. 20, no. 2 (Winter 1994):9–18.
13. See Lehmann and Modest, "Mutual Fund Performance Evaluation."
14. For further reference, see the *S&P 500 1993 Directory*.
15. Jensen, "The Performance of Mutual Funds in the Period 1945–1964."
16. See Richard C. Grinold and Ronald N. Kahn, *Active Portfolio Management* (Chicago: Probus Publishing, 1995), for further justification of this point.

17. Stephen J. Brown, William Goetzmann, Roger G. Ibbotson, and Stephen A. Ross, "Survivorship Bias in Performance Studies," *The Review of Financial Studies,* vol. 5, no. 4 (December 1992): 553–580.

18. The Micropal database is available from Micropal, Inc., 31 Milk Street, Suite 1002, Boston, MA 02109, and the Morningstar database is available from Morningstar, 225 West Wacker Drive, Chicago, IL 60606.

19. Brown, et al., "Survivorship Bias in Performance Studies."

20. We defined "substantially similar" to mean within 2.0 percent for equity total and selection returns, 0.08 for equity information ratios, 0.8 percent for fixed-income total and selection returns, and 0.20 for fixed-income information returns; part of the difference between equity and fixed-income screens was because of differing length periods. These screens reduced the qualifying equity funds from 365 to 300 and the qualifying fixed-income funds from 261 to 195.

21. Brown, et al., "Survivorship Bias in Performance Studies."

22. This problem was part of our motivation for separately analyzing equity funds and fixed-income funds.

23. S. J. Brown and William Goetzmann, "Performance Persistence," New York University, Salomon Center Working Paper Series S-94-28 (September 1994).

24. -0.76 percent $= 0.629 \times 0.64$ percent $+ 0.371 \times -3.13$ percent.

CHAPTER 38

EVALUATING FUND PERFORMANCE IN A DYNAMIC MARKET

Wayne E. Ferson and Vincent A. Warther

Previous studies show that interest rates, dividend yields, and other commonly available variables are useful market indicators, but until now, measures of fund performance have not used the information. This article modifies classical performance measures to take account of well-known market indicators. The conditional performance evaluation approach avoids some of the biases that plague traditional measures. Applied to a sample of mutual funds, the conditional measures make the funds' performance look better.

Standard measures of fund manager performance are known to suffer from a number of problems in practice. Many of the problems reflect the inability of traditional measures to handle the dynamic behavior of returns. An approach called *conditional performance evaluation* addresses this problem.

Traditional approaches to performance measurement are *unconditional*, which means that they use historical average returns to estimate expected performance. For example, an "alpha" may be calculated as the historical average return of a fund in excess of a beta-adjusted historical average for a benchmark portfolio, such as the Standard & Poor's 500 Index. (Sometimes, the beta is simply assumed to equal 1.0.) Unconditional measures do not account for the fact that risk and expected returns may vary with the state of the economy. In particular, traditional performance measures ignore the evidence that expected returns in the stock market are higher at the beginning of an economic recovery, when dividend yields are high and interest rates are low.[1] If the market exposure of a managed portfolio varies predictably with the business cycle but the manager does not have superior forecasting abil-

---

Reprinted from *Financial Analysts Journal* (November/December 1996):20–28.

ity, a traditional approach to performance measurement will confuse the common variation between fund risk and expected market returns with truly superior information and abnormal performance.

The conditional performance evaluation approach we advocate takes the view that a managed portfolio strategy that can be replicated using information readily available to the public should not be judged as having superior information. For example, in a conditional approach, a mechanical market-timing rule using lagged interest rate data does not add value. Only managers who correctly use more information than is generally publicly available are considered to have potentially superior ability. Conditional performance evaluation is, therefore, consistent with a version of market efficiency in the semistrong form sense of Fama (1970).

The beauty of a conditional approach to performance evaluation is that it can accommodate whatever standard of superior information is held to be appropriate by the choice of the *lagged instruments* used to represent the public information. By incorporating a given set of lagged instruments, managers who trade mechanically in response to these variables should be unable to "game" the performance measure. In practice, the trading behavior of managers may overlay complex portfolio dynamics on the underlying assets they trade. The desire to handle such dynamic strategies further motivates a conditional approach. In this article, we illustrate the conditional performance evaluation approach using lagged dividend yields and short-term interest rates as the conditioning information.[2]

A conditional performance evaluation would seem to raise the hurdle on managers seeking abnormal positive performance because it gives them no credit for using readily available variables. We show that a conditional analysis actually makes the performance of a typical mutual fund during the 1970s and 1980s look better. The more-pessimistic results of the traditional measures are attributed to the fact that they ignore common dependencies between mutual fund betas and expected market returns, which are captured by a market dividend yield and a short-term interest rate. This negative correlation seems to reflect higher cash holdings when expected market returns are high, as investors pour new money into mutual funds.

A NUMERICAL EXAMPLE

The appeal of a conditional model for performance evaluation can be illustrated with a numerical example. Assume that investors' expectations reflect two equally likely states of the market—say, a bull state and a bear state. In a bull market, assume that the expected return of the S&P 500 is 20 percent and in a bear market, it is 10 percent. The risk-free return to cash is 5 percent. Assume that all investors share these views—the current state of expected market returns is always common knowledge. An investment strategy using only this information will not, on average, yield abnormal returns and so should have an alpha of zero.

Now, imagine a mutual fund that holds the S&P 500 in a bull market and holds cash in a bear market. Conditional on a bull market, the beta of the fund is 1.0, the fund's expected return is 20 percent, equal to the S&P 500, and the fund's alpha is zero. Conditional on a bear market, the fund's beta is zero, the expected return of the fund is the risk-free return, 5 percent, and the alpha is, again, zero. The conditional approach to performance evaluation correctly reports an alpha of zero.

By contrast, an unconditional approach to performance evaluation incorrectly reports an alpha greater than zero for this hypothetical mutual fund. The unconditional beta of the fund is 0.6.[3] The fund's unconditional expected return is 0.5(0.20) + 0.5(0.05) = 0.125. The unconditional expected return of the S&P 500 is 0.5(0.20) + 0.5(0.10) = 0.15, so the fund's unconditional alpha is therefore (0.125 − 0.05) − 0.6(0.15 − 0.05) = 0.015. The unconditional approach leads to the mistaken conclusion that the manager has positive abnormal performance. The manager's performance, however, does not reflect superior skill or ability; it just reflects the fund's decision to take on more market risk in times when risk is more highly rewarded in the market. Investors, who are assumed to have access to the same information about the economic state, would not be willing to pay the fund management fees to use this common knowledge.

Investors who wish to make optimal portfolio decisions need to avoid the errors that a traditional performance measure is likely to make in classifying portfolio performance. If expectations of future returns and risks vary with publicly available economic information, then conditional expectations should determine the relevant alphas. A conditional performance measure should be a more reliable guide for allocating funds to managers in order to get the highest return for the risk. Relying on the traditional unconditional alphas, however, is likely to produce inferior investment decisions.

DATA

We studied monthly returns for 63 open-end mutual funds from January 1968 to December 1990, a total of 276 observations. The returns include reinvestment of all distributions (e.g., dividends) and are net of expenses, but they disregard load charges and exit fees.

The funds are primarily equity funds, classified by objective as reported in Wiesenberger.[4] The funds are grouped by their stated objectives at a point near the middle of the sample period in 1982. Eight funds are classified as maximum capital gains, 20 are growth-income, 21 are growth funds, and 14 are income funds. Excess returns are measured net of the monthly return of investing in the one-month Treasury bill from Ibbotson & Associates.

Our sample has survivorship biases because it contains only surviving funds. Survivorship bias is expected to make the surviving funds look better than funds as a group (see Grinblatt and Titman 1988; Brown, Goetzmann, Ibbotson, and Ross 1992; and Malkiel 1995). If survivorship bias is important, our estimates of the performance of the mutual funds are too optimistic. We found, however, that the traditional measures suggest poor performance for the funds in our sample and that the performance looks better after controlling for public information variables. Because we used the same sample in both cases, our results are not likely to be driven by survivorship biases.

The S&P 500 was used as the market factor, or benchmark portfolio.[5] To measure the state of the stock market, we used two well-known, traditional market indicators. The lagged level of the one-month Treasury bill yield and the lagged dividend yield of the CRSP value-weighted NYSE and Amex stock indexes are our lagged instruments.[6]

If a particular measure shows simple passive or naive investment strategies to have abnormal performance, it would call into question the quality of that performance measure. We therefore constructed a naive buy-and-hold strategy for comparison that enters 1968 with an arbitrary initial set of weights in four asset classes: 65 percent for large stocks, 13 percent for small stocks, 20 percent for government bonds, and 2 percent for low-grade bonds. The buy-and-hold strategy weights change over time as the relative values of the four asset classes evolve.

TRADITIONAL MEASURES OF PERFORMANCE

A traditional approach to measuring performance is to regress the excess return of a portfolio on the market factor. Assuming that the market beta is constant, the slope coefficient, β, is the market beta, and the intercept, a, is the *unconditional alpha* coefficient, which measures average performance (see Jensen 1968); that is,

$$RP_t = a + \beta\, RM_t + \text{error}, \tag{38.1}$$

where RM is the return of the market benchmark and RP is the return of the fund's portfolio, and both are measured in excess of a short-term bill return.

Performance measures often attempt to distinguish security selection or stock-picking ability from market timing, or the ability to predict market returns. Alpha, typically, reflects both types of ability. Market-timing models represent an attempt to separate these two aspects of performance. Traditional market-timing models, however, have taken the view that *any* information correlated with future market returns is superior information. In other words, they are unconditional models.

A classic market-timing regression is the quadratic regression of Treynor and Mazuy (1966):[7]

$$RP_t = a + \beta\, RM_t + \delta\, RM_t^2 + \text{error}, \tag{38.2}$$

where the coefficient δ measures market-timing ability. The δ coefficient is positive if the manager increases beta when receiving a positive signal about the market. The hypothesis of no timing ability implies that δ is zero.

Table 38.1 shows the results of estimating the traditional unconditional models of performance using our sample of mutual funds. The coefficients are reported for equal-weighted

TABLE 38.1   Unconditional Measures of Performance

Fund Objective	Jensen's Alpha[a]			Market-Timing Model[b]		
	Estimate	t-Ratio	Fraction < 0	Timing Coefficient	t-Ratio	Fraction < 0
Maximum gain	−0.085	−0.59	75.0%	−0.01	−2.64	100.0%
Growth	−0.084	−1.17	81.0	−0.003	−1.70	71.4
Growth/income	−0.065	−1.34	65.0	−0.002	−1.73	65.0
Income	0.024	0.34	42.9	0.004	0.24	50.0
All funds	−0.054	−0.43	66.7	0.0024	0.03	68.3
Buy-and-hold[c]	−0.005	−0.10	—	−0.004	−3.10	—

[a] Jensen's alpha is the average excess return of an equal-weighted portfolio of funds with the stated objective less the beta times the average excess return of the S&P 500 taken over a period from 1968 to 1990, a total of 276 monthly observations. The units are percent per month.

[b] The market-timing models are based on a multiple regression of the funds returns on the excess return of the S&P 500 and its square. The market-timing coefficients are the regression coefficients on the squared term.

[c] The buy-and-hold comparison strategy enters 1968 with the following initial set of weights: 65 percent large stocks, 13 percent small stocks, 20 percent government bonds, and 2 percent low-grade bonds. The buy-and-hold strategy weights change over time as the relative values of the four asset classes evolve.

averages of the funds in each group. Based on the t-statistics for the group averages, only a few coefficients are significant, but two-thirds of the individual fund alphas are negative. Among the maximum-gain funds, 75 percent of the alphas are negative, and among the growth funds, 81 percent of the alphas are negative. Taken at face value, the traditional alphas suggest that too many of these mutual funds do not match the performance of the S&P 500 on a risk-adjusted basis.

The results of the unconditional market-timing model are even more striking. More than two-thirds of the timing coefficients of the individual funds are negative, including more than 70 percent of the growth funds and 100 percent of the maximum-gain funds. The market-timing coefficient of the portfolio of maximum capital gain funds is significant and negative, with a t-statistic of -2.64. These findings are similar to those of previous studies using unconditional models (see, e.g., Henriksson 1984, Chang and Lewellen 1984, Lehmann and Modest 1987, Grinblatt and Titman 1988, and Cumby and Glen 1990).

Taken at face value, the results of Table 38.1 suggest that many funds, especially the more aggressive equity funds, have systematically perverse market-timing abilities. That interpretation, however, is subject to a number of criticisms. First, if the funds actually have superior information about future market moves but systematically get the direction wrong, then astute investors could take the opposite position and profit. A second problem is that market-timing models are known to be distorted if funds are picking stocks or are using leverage, options, or other derivative strategies.

Perhaps the most telling piece of evidence that the traditional market-timing models give false signals about performance is the results for the buy-and-hold strategy. The timing coefficient of the buy-and-hold strategy is significant and negative, with a t-statistic equal to -3.10. Obviously, a buy-and-hold strategy does not involve significant market-timing information. The obvious flaws of the unconditional models provide strong motivation to look to conditional models for improvement.

CONDITIONAL PERFORMANCE EVALUATION

A conditional performance evaluation can be set up using basically the same theoretical assumptions as traditional models. Traditional approaches, however, assume that the consumer of the performance evaluation does not use public information on the economy to form expectations, whereas a conditional approach assumes market efficiency with respect to the particular market indicators. In a conditional market-timing model, the idea is to distinguish market timing based on public information from market-timing information that is truly superior to the public information.

A technical assumption required for our approach is a functional form for the betas or factor sensitivities of a managed portfolio. Time variation in a managed portfolio beta may arise for three distinct reasons. First, the betas of the underlying assets may change over time such that even a passive strategy, such as buy and hold, will experience changes in beta. Second, a manager can actively manipulate the portfolio weights, departing from a buy-and-hold strategy, and thereby create changes in the portfolio beta. Third, a mutual fund may experience net cash inflows or outflows, which the manager does not directly control. If such flows affect the cash holdings of the fund, then beta will fluctuate as the percentage of cash held by the fund fluctuates.

The combined effect of these various factors on the conditional beta is modeled as a "reduced form." As a very simple illustrative model, we use the following linear function, which is a natural extension of traditional models for mutual fund risk (see, e.g., Admati and Ross 1985 and Admati et al. 1986):

$$\beta = b_0 + b_1(D/P) + b_2(TB), \tag{38.3}$$

where (D/P) is the lagged value of the market dividend yield and TB is the lagged value of a short-term Treasury yield. A linear function may be motivated by a Taylor series approximation. A linear function is also attractive because it results in simple regression models that are easy to interpret. Although we use simple linear functions to illustrate the conditional approach, the correct specification of the conditional beta is an empirical issue. The general approach can accommodate other choices for the functional form, so it should be possible to improve upon our example in actual applications.

The conditional model uses the following regression for the managed portfolio return:

$$RP_t = \alpha + b_0 RM_t + b_1[RM_t \times (D/P)_{t-1}] + b_2[RM_t \times (TB)_{t-1}] + \text{error}. \tag{38.4}$$

The conditional model adds two additional predictors to the regression traditionally used to estimate the unconditional alpha. These variables, $[RM_t \times (D/P)_{t-1}]$ and $[RM_t \times (TB)_{t-1}]$, are essentially interaction terms between the return of the S&P 500 benchmark and the lagged values of the market indicators. These interaction terms pick up the movements through time of the conditional betas as they relate to the market indicators. The coefficients b_1 and b_2 measure the response of the conditional betas to the lagged market indicators. The intercept, α, is the conditional alpha, which measures the abnormal performance.

The conditional alpha model of Equation 38.4 may also be interpreted as a multiple factor model, where the market index is the first factor and the product of the market and the lagged market indicators are the additional factors. The additional factors may be interpreted as the returns to dynamic strategies, which hold the market index long, financed by borrowing or selling an equal amount of Treasury bills. The amounts are determined by the values of the market indicators. The dynamic strategies are constructed to replicate the dynamic behavior of the fund's market beta through time. The conditional alpha is the expected difference between a fund's excess return and the excess return to the particular combination of the market index and the dynamic strategies, which replicate the fund's time-varying risk exposure. A manager with a positive conditional alpha is one whose average return is higher than the average return of the combination with the same dynamic beta.

Table 38.2 summarizes the results of estimating the conditional alpha model. The results are quite different from those in Table 38.1. Only 52.4 percent of the funds' conditional alphas are negative overall. The percentage of negative alphas varies among the fund groups from 35.7 percent for the income funds to 62.5 percent for the maximum-gain funds. Unlike the unconditional models, the conditional models do not suggest that the funds routinely underperform the S&P 500 on a risk-adjusted basis. The performance is essentially neutral, as would be expected in an efficient market.

Why do the conditional models produce such a strikingly different impression about alphas than the unconditional models? The statistical reason is that there is common variation through time in the funds' betas and in the expected market return. This variation is captured by the interaction terms in the conditional model. In contrast, the unconditional alpha interprets the common variation as abnormal performance. A comparison of Equations 38.1 and 38.4 shows that the difference between the two measures of alpha is determined by the average values of the interaction terms. These terms measure the covariance between the

TABLE 38.2   Conditional Alphas and Betas

Fund Objective	Conditional Alpha[a]			Conditional Beta[b] $= b_0 + b_1(D/P) + b_2 TB$							Significance Level[c]
	Estimate	*t*-Ratio	Fraction < 0	b_0	$t(b_0)$	b_1	$t(b_1)$	b_2	$t(b_2)$		
Maximum gain	0.063	0.44	62.5%	1.55	10.2 [4.45]	−0.16	−4.13 [−3.24]	0.40	3.37 [2.03]		0.0003
Growth	−0.033	−0.47	57.1	1.22	15.2 [3.65]	−0.06	−2.85 [−0.91]	0.11	1.72 [−1.13]		0.008
Growth/ income	−0.029	−0.57	55.0	1.04	22.0 [2.28]	−0.04	−3.19 [−0.04]	0.01	1.81 [−2.11]		0.008
Income	0.069	0.92	35.7	0.74	8.28 [−1.87]	−0.05	−1.93 [−0.23]	0.01	1.42 [−1.10]		0.049
All funds	0.003	0.01	52.4	1.00	7.39 [2.63]	−0.06	−1.44 [−1.19]	0.01	1.01 [−1.00]		0.146
Buy-and-hold[d]	0.048	0.98	—	0.90	17.1	−0.04	−2.95	0.02	3.67		0.001

[a]The conditional alpha is the intercept in a regression of an equal-weighted portfolio of funds with the stated objective regressed on the excess return of the S&P 500, the product of the S&P 500 with the lagged dividend yield (*D/P*), and the product of the S&P 500 with the lagged one-month Treasury bill yield (*TB*). The sample period is 1968 to 1990, a total of 276 monthly observations. The units are percent per month.

[b]The figures denoted as $t(b)$ are the *t*-ratios for the coefficients. The *t*-ratios in brackets measure the significance of the difference between the coefficients for the fund group and the coefficients for the buy-and-hold strategy. The *t*-ratios that are not in brackets measure the significance of the coefficients relative to zero. All of the *t*-ratios are heteroscedasticity consistent.

[c]The right-tail areas of the *F*-test for the hypothesis that the predetermined market indicators enter the model with zero coefficients. For example, the figure 0.049 shows that the market indicators are significant in the conditional beta model for income funds at the 5 percent significance level.

[d]The buy-and-hold comparison strategy enters 1968 with an initial set of weights: 65 percent large stocks, 13 percent small stocks, 20 percent government bonds, and 2 percent low-grade bonds. The buy-and-hold strategy weights change over time as the relative values of the four asset classes evolve.

conditional beta and the expected value of the market return formed using the lagged instruments. If this covariance is positive (negative), the conditional alpha will be lower (higher) than the unconditional alpha. Therefore, the key to understanding the different results about alpha is the behavior of the conditional betas.

Table 38.2 also records the coefficients of the conditional beta models for the fund groups and their *t*-ratios. For each fund group, the market indicators that allow for time variation in the funds' betas are statistically significant at the 5 percent level or better. The coefficients on the Treasury bill are positive, whereas those on the dividend yield are negative. Both coefficients are statistically significant for most of the groups. Because high dividend yields are a positive market indicator and high short-term interest rates predict low stock returns, the coefficients say that the betas of the funds tend to be negatively correlated with future stock returns. Using the parameters of the model to estimate the correlation between the funds' betas and the expected market return in our sample, the correlation varies between −0.283 and −0.315 among the fund groups.

EXPLAINING BETA CHANGES

Why would mutual fund managers tend to reduce their market betas when public information implies relatively high expected market returns and /or raise them when expected returns are low? Two explanations are considered:

- The betas of the underlying assets change over time, such that even a buy-and-hold strategy has changing betas.
- Fund portfolio weights depart from a buy-and-hold strategy because of flows of cash into the funds or active management behavior.

Table 38.2 provides evidence on the first of these potential explanations. Estimating the conditional betas for the buy-and-hold strategy produces a negative coefficient on the dividend yield and a positive coefficient on the Treasury bill rate, a similar pattern as for the mutual funds. This finding suggests that some of the beta variation is the result of time-varying conditional betas for the underlying assets.[8] Table 38.2 also shows, however, that the coefficients of the funds' betas are significantly different from those of the buy-and-hold strategy for the more aggressive funds. Movements in the betas of the assets held by the mutual funds do not fully explain the patterns of time variation in the betas for mutual funds.

The second explanation for the movements in mutual fund betas involves the flow of money into mutual funds. If money flows into funds when the public perceives expected stock returns to be high and if managers take some time to allocate new money according to their usual investment styles, then the funds would have large cash holdings at such times. Large cash holdings imply low betas. The effects of new money flows on the funds' betas will depend on the magnitudes of the flows, the size of the asset holdings, and the speed with which new monies are invested.

Warther (1995) reported a study of net cash flows for mutual funds. Net cash is defined as new sales (excluding reinvested dividends minus withdrawals, plus net transfers between funds),

TABLE 38.3   Mutual Fund Sales, Conditional Betas, and Market Indicators

Fund Objective	b_0	$t(b_0)$	b_1	$t(b_1)$	b_2	$t(b_2)$
Mutual fund sales and conditional betas[a]						
Maximum gain	0.0003	0.06	−0.5002	−3.72	—	—
Growth	0.0001	0.06	−0.5527	−5.26	—	—
Growth/income	0.0001	0.08	−0.3761	−2.87	—	—
Mutual fund sales and market indicators[b]						
Maximum gain	0.00001	0.00	0.0596	7.04	−0.0039	−1.83
Growth	0.00008	0.16	0.0201	5.91	−0.0012	−1.44
Growth/income	0.00007	0.20	0.0089	3.92	0.0000	0.05

[a] Δ Conditional beta $= b_0 + b_1 \Delta$ Sales. The conditional beta is estimated as the average fitted conditional beta of all funds in the particular category. The sample period is January 1976 through December 1990. Δ denotes first-differencing of the series. Regressions use the Cochrane-Orcutt procedure to correct for autocorrelation in the residuals. t-Statistics for coefficient b are denoted $t(b)$.
[b] Δ Sales $= b_0 + b_1 \Delta(D/P) + b_2 \Delta TB$ D/P is the dividend yield of the S&P 500 lagged one period, and TB is the three-month Treasury bill yield lagged one period.

normalized by the lagged aggregate stock market value. A strong correlation is found between net cash flows and concurrent stock market returns, which suggests a connection between cash flows to funds and expected returns. New money flows are also strongly correlated with the portfolio weight in cash. When inflows are large, cash balances at mutual funds tend to increase. On average, funds invest about 62 cents of each new dollar in the concurrent month; 38 cents goes to increased cash balances.

Table 38.3 offers further evidence of a link between mutual fund inflows and conditional betas. Mutual fund flow data are collected by the Investment Company Institute and include virtually all U.S. mutual funds. Net sales are defined as new sales minus withdrawals, plus the net result of transfers between funds. Reinvested dividends are excluded. Net sales are normalized by dividing by the net asset value of all funds in the category at the end of the previous month. The fund flow data begin in January 1976, so the regressions in Table 38.3 cover the period from January 1976 through December 1990. The top panel presents regressions of changes in conditional betas on changes in net sales for the three stock-fund categories for which fund flow data are available (maximum gain, growth, and growth/income). The conditional betas for each category are from Table 38.2. A significant negative relation exists between changes in sales and changes in the conditional betas. The *t*-statistics range from -2.87 to -5.26; thus, betas tend to decrease when incoming cash flows are higher.

The lower portion of Table 38.3 directly examines the relation between fund inflows and expected market returns. Changes in net sales are regressed on changes in the two lagged market indicators. The coefficients on the dividend yield are highly significant for all three fund categories, with *t*-statistics ranging from 3.92 to 7.04. The coefficients are all positive, indicating that cash inflows into mutual funds increase when dividend yields increase. The finding that high dividend yields signal high expected market returns shows that cash inflows increase when dividend yields indicate high expected returns. Although the coefficients on the Treasury yield do not reach conventional significance levels, they are predominantly negative. Because low bill yields indicate high expected returns, the coefficients are consistent with the story told by the dividend yield coefficients.

Overall, the evidence of Table 38.3 supports the hypothesis that mutual fund flows partly explain the changes in betas over time, which are captured by the lagged market indicators and therefore affect the performance results. Cash flows into funds increase when public expectations of market returns increase, and as a result, cash balances increase and betas decrease. This relationship offers a simple interpretation for the otherwise puzzling result that funds have low market exposure when expected market returns are high.

CONDITIONAL MARKET TIMING

Ferson and Schadt (1996) proposed the following conditional version of the Treynor–Mazuy market-timing regression:

$$RP_t = a + b_0\, RM_t + b_1\, [RM_t \times (D/P)_{t-1}] + b_2\, [RM_t \times (TB)_{t-1}] + \gamma\, RM_t^2 + \text{error},$$

where the coefficients b_1 and b_2, as before, capture the response of the manager's beta to the public information. In the conditional model, any ability to predict the market that can be matched using the public information is not considered to reflect market-timing ability. The coefficient γ measures the sensitivity of the manager's beta to any private market-timing signal, which should be more informative about the future market return than are the dividend yield and interest rate.

TABLE 38.4   Results for the Conditional Market-Timing Model

Fund Objective	Alpha	t-Ratio	Timing Coefficient	t-Ratio	Fraction < 0
Maximum gain	0.101	0.68	−0.002	−0.53	75.0%
Growth	−0.046	−0.60	0.001	0.37	42.9
Growth/income	−0.044	−0.75	0.001	0.38	30.0
Income	−0.001	−0.01	0.004	1.68	35.7
All funds	−0.015	−0.17	0.001	0.33	41.3
Buy-and-hold	0.082	1.68	−0.003	−1.07	—

Table 38.4 presents the results of the conditional market-timing model. The results are very different from those of the unconditional model in Table 38.2. The conditional-timing model produces much more reasonable results. First, the γ coefficients of the buy-and-hold strategy are not statistically significant. This finding is good news for the conditional model because it shows that the model avoids the obvious mistake made by the unconditional model of attributing market timing to a buy-and-hold strategy. In the conditional model, none of the timing coefficients for the fund groups are statistically significant, and the point estimates are positive for every fund group except the maximum-gain funds. Overall, only 41.3 percent of the funds generated negative timing coefficients, much less than in Table 38.2. Therefore, there is no evidence of perverse, negative timing ability in these groups of funds.

CONCLUSIONS

The incorporation of lagged market-indicator variables into the analysis of investment performance, an approach called *conditional performance evaluation,* takes the view that a managed portfolio strategy using only readily available public information does not imply abnormal performance. To illustrate this approach, we used monthly data for 63 mutual funds and lagged dividend yields and Treasury bill yields as the market indicators. There is strong evidence that the funds' market risk exposures change in response to the market indicators. The conditioning information is important, both in statistical and in practical terms.

The traditional, unconditional measures of average performance (Jensen's alpha) are negative more often than positive for the funds, which has been interpreted as inferior performance. Using the conditional models, however, the alphas are centered near zero. The relatively pessimistic results of the traditional measures are attributed to common time variation in the conditional betas and the expected market return. When the common variation is controlled, using the market indicators, the conditional models make the funds' performance during the sample period—the 1970s and 1980s—look better than do the unconditional models. Some of the common variation is explained by new cash flows into mutual funds, which are higher when the indicators predict higher market returns.

Traditional measures of market timing suggest that the typical mutual fund increases its market exposure when stock returns are low. This phenomenon has been interpreted as "perverse" market-timing ability, but this interpretation is implausible because it suggests that one could profit by reversing the funds' timing strategies.

Furthermore, traditional market-timing models are misspecified when applied to naive strategies, and conditional versions of these models are an improvement. Using conditional market-timing models for U.S. equity funds removes the evidence of perverse market timing for the typical fund. These results suggest that incorporating public information variables into the analysis of investment performance is important and should improve upon current practice.[9]

NOTES

1. For evidence that high interest rates are bad news for stocks, see Fama and Schwert (1977); Ferson (1989); and Breen, Glosten, and Jagannathan (1989). For evidence that stock returns are expected to be high when dividend yields are high, see Fama and French (1988) and Campbell and Shiller (1988).
2. For evidence that these variables capture variation in both risk and expected returns, see Ferson and Harvey (1991) and Ferson and Korajczyk (1995).
3. The calculation is as follows. The unconditional beta is $\text{Cov}(F,M)/\text{Var}(M)$, where F is the fund return and M is the market return. The numerator is

$$\text{Cov}(F,M) = E\{[F - E(F)][M - E(M)]\},$$

where $E(\cdot)$ is the unconditional expected value. Thus,

$$\begin{aligned}
\text{Cov}(F,M) &= E\{[F - E(F)][M - E(M)] \mid \text{Bull}\} \times \text{Prob(Bull)} \\
&\quad + E\{[F - E(F)][M - E(M)] \mid \text{Bear}\} \times \text{Prob(Bear)} \\
&= [(0.20 - 0.125)(0.20 - 0.15)] \times 0.5 \\
&\quad + [(0.05 - 0.125)(0.10 - 0.15)] \times 0.5 \\
&= 0.00375.
\end{aligned}$$

The denominator is

$$\begin{aligned}
\text{Var}(M) &= E\{[M - E(M)]^2 \mid \text{Bull}\} \times \text{Prob(Bull)} \\
&\quad + E\{[M - E(M)]^2 \mid \text{Bear}\} \times \text{Prob(Bear)} \\
&= [(0.20 - 0.15)^2] \times 0.5 + [(0.05 - 0.15)^2] \times 0.5 \\
&= 0.00625.
\end{aligned}$$

The beta is, therefore, $0.00375/0.00625 = 0.6$.
4. See Ferson and Schadt (1996), from which much of this chapter was drawn, for details on the fund classification.
5. Ferson and Schadt (1996) also used the CRSP value-weighted market index and a four-factor model with an expanded set of market indicators and obtained results similar to ours.
6. Similar variables have been discussed as stock market indicators since as early as 1920. Pesaran and Timmermann (1995) cited a number of studies from the 1930s to the early 1960s that emphasize stock market predictability based on interest rates, dividend yields, and other cyclical indicators.
7. An alternative model of market timing is developed in Merton and Henriksson (1981). Ferson and Schadt (1996) developed a conditional version of the market-timing model of Merton and Henriksson. They found similar results for this model as for the Treynor–Mazuy model described here.
8. If fund portfolios are concentrated in large stocks, the patterns of beta variation are consistent with time variation in large stock betas, which are shown to be negatively

correlated with expected market returns in the studies by Chan and Chen (1988), Ferson and Harvey (1991), and Jagannathan and Wang (1996).

9. The authors would like to thank the editor, W. V. Harlow, and Ravi Jagannathan, Rene Stulz, and Rudi Schadt for helpful discussions. Ferson acknowledges the financial support of the Pigott-PACCAR professorship at the University of Washington.

REFERENCES

Admati, Anat R., Sudipto Bhattacharya, Stephen A. Ross, Robert E. Verrecchia, and Paul Pfleiderer. 1986. "On Timing and Selectivity." *Journal of Finance,* vol. 41, no. 3 (July):715–730.

Admati, Anat R., and Stephen A. Ross. 1985. "Measuring Investment Performance in a Rational Expectations Equilibrium Model." *Journal of Business,* vol. 58, no. 1 (January): 1–26.

Breen, William, Lawrence Glosten, and Ravi Jagannathan. 1989. "Economic Significance of Predictable Variations in Stock Index Returns." *Journal of Finance,* vol. 44, no. 5 (December):1177–1190.

Brown, Stephen, William Goetzmann, Roger Ibbotson, and Stephen A. Ross. 1992. "Survivorship Bias in Performance Studies." *Review of Financial Studies,* vol. 5, no. 4 (Winter):553–580.

Campbell, John Y., and Robert J. Shiller. 1988. "The Dividend Price Ratio and Expectations of Future Dividends and Discount Factors." *Review of Financial Studies,* vol. 1, no. 1 (Spring):195–228.

Chan, K.C., and Nai-fu Chen. 1988. "An Unconditional Asset-Pricing Test and the Role of Firm Size as an Instrumental Variable for Risk." *Journal of Finance,* vol. 43, no. 2 (June):309–325.

Chang, Eric C, and Wilbur G. Lewellen. 1984. "Market Timing and Mutual Fund Performance." *Journal of Business,* vol. 57, no. 1 (January):57–72.

Cumby, Robert, and Jack Glen. 1990. "Evaluating the Performance of International Mutual Funds." *Journal of Finance,* vol. 45, no. 2 (June):497–521.

Fama, Eugene F. 1970. "Efficient Capital Markets: A Review of Theory and Empirical Work." *Journal of Finance,* vol. 25, no. 2 (May):383–417.

Fama, Eugene F., and Kenneth R. French. 1988. "Dividend Yields and Expected Stock Returns." *Journal of Financial Economics,* vol. 22, no. 1 (October):3–25.

Fama, Eugene F., and G. William Schwert. 1977. "Asset Returns and Inflation." *Journal of Financial Economics,* vol. 5, no. 2 (November):115–146.

Ferson, Wayne E. 1989. "Changes in Expected Security Returns, Risk and the Level of Interest Rates." *Journal of Finance,* vol. 44, no. 5 (December):1191–1217.

Ferson, Wayne E., and Campbell R. Harvey. 1991. "Sources of Predictability in Portfolio Returns." *Financial Analysts Journal,* vol. 47, no. 3 (May/June):49–56.

Ferson, Wayne E., and Robert A. Korajczyk. 1995. "Do Arbitrage Pricing Models Explain the Predictability of Stock Returns?" *Journal of Business,* vol. 68, no. 3 (July):309–349.

Ferson, Wayne E., and Rudi W. Schadt. 1996. "Measuring Fund Strategy and Performance in Changing Economic Conditions." *Journal of Finance,* vol. 51, no. 2 (June):425–462.

Grinblatt, Mark, and Sheridan Titman. 1988. "The Evaluation of Mutual Fund Performance: An Analysis of Monthly Returns." Working paper, University of California at Los Angeles.

Henriksson, Roy D. 1984. "Market Timing and Mutual Fund Performance: An Empirical Investigation." *Journal of Business,* vol. 57, no. 1 (January):73–96.

Jagannathan, Ravi, and Zhenyu Wang. 1996. "The Conditional CAPM and the Cross-Section of Expected Returns." *Journal of Finance,* vol. 51, no. 1 (March):3–54.

Jensen, Michael C. 1968. "The Performance of Mutual Funds in the Period 1945–64." *Journal of Finance,* vol. 23, no. 2 (May):389–446.

Lehmann, Bruce N., and David M. Modest. 1987. "Mutual Fund Performance Evaluation: A Comparison of Benchmarks and Benchmark Comparisons." *Journal of Finance,* vol. 42, no. 2 (June):233–266.

Malkiel, Burton G. 1995. "Returns from Investing in Equity Mutual Funds 1971–91." *Journal of Finance,* vol. 50, no. 2 (June):549–572.

Merton, Robert C, and Roy D. Henriksson. 1981. "On Market Timing and Investment Performance II: Statistical Procedures for Evaluating Forecasting Skills." *Journal of Business,* vol. 54, no. 4 (October):513–534.

Pesaran, M. Hashem, and Allan Timmermann. 1995. "Predictability of Stock Returns: Robustness and Economic Significance." *Journal of Finance,* vol. 50, no. 4 (September):1201–1228.

Treynor, Jack, and Kay Mazuy. 1966. "Can Mutual Funds Outguess the Market?" *Harvard Business Review,* vol. 44, no. 4 (July/August):131–136.

Warther, Vincent A. 1995. "Aggregate Mutual Fund Flows and Security Returns." *Journal of Financial Economics,* vol. 39, no. 2 (October/November):209–236.

CHAPTER 39

INVESTMENT PERFORMANCE APPRAISAL

John P. Meier, CFA

One of the more difficult aspects of managing a portfolio of managers is assessing the underlying manager's performance and deciding whether it is more prudent to keep or terminate the manager. This paper will explore how institutional investors evaluate managers and discuss the appropriate actions to take (or not) on the basis of that evaluation.

Investment officers and consultants overseeing large pension funds, endowments, foundations, or other pools of assets are responsible for directing and monitoring a diversified, multiple-asset class, multiple-manager portfolio. As "managers of managers," they routinely evaluate the success of the overall program as well as the investment firms with specific mandates in the program. One of the most difficult aspects of that job is assessing managers and deciding whether it is more prudent to keep or terminate a manager. This paper will explore how institutional investors evaluate managers and discuss the appropriate actions to take (or not) on the basis of that evaluation.

TOTAL FUND PERSPECTIVE

Managing a portfolio of managers entails answering a number of questions about the investment program and its investment managers. How are the managers performing? What have been the sources of their performance? What are the risks they have taken to achieve that performance? What risks are they currently taking? How could the portfolio have performed if it had been invested with the manager's peers or passively in an index fund? Given the necessary resources, all of this objective information is reasonably easy to determine. The much more

Reprinted from CFA Institute (2008).

difficult part of the job of evaluating an investment program is using all this information to make decisions. Are the managers doing what is expected of them? Can they achieve the desired investment results?

Management of a diversified, multi-manager fund has many similarities to the management of an investment strategy using individual stocks or bonds. However, in the case of a pension or endowment fund, one is not managing the securities, one is managing a portfolio of portfolios. And like the portfolio manager of a stock or bond portfolio, it's the overall strategy that's important, not just the individual names in the portfolio. Holdings within a portfolio have different risk, return, and diversification characteristics that contribute to the success of the overall portfolio and strategy. One must understand and acknowledge the implications of these characteristics when evaluating whether or not one component of the overall portfolio is doing what is expected of it.

It is vitally important for the investment officer and the consultant to have a clear understanding of each manager's investment philosophy, strategy, and decision-making process, including their approaches to security selection and portfolio construction. This knowledge is commonly acquired in the course of due diligence when the manager is first hired. However, professionals who join the staff or start to advise the fund after the portfolio's inception date should make it their business to become familiar with each investment management firm and its role within the overall fund's strategy.

The best way to communicate one's expectations of an investment mandate or strategy, and of the manager who executes it, is through the guidelines set forth in an investment policy statement[1] and incorporated into the contractual agreement between the fund and the investment manager. All strategic parameters including expected normal ranges of portfolio characteristics are typically outlined in the guidelines. Unfortunately many—perhaps most—investment managers view guidelines as impediments to the free exercise of their professional judgment. In this way of thinking, investment managers typically ask for as wide a range of parameters as possible so that their investment decision-making process will be unconstrained by the plan sponsor. However, the fund's overall portfolio is constructed on the basis of expectations about what each investment strategy and manager contributes to the portfolio. The fund's officers and consultants want to ensure that the overall strategy is intact and that the risks being taken with a given mandate are within expectations. In this context, a more constructive view of the guidelines is to consider them as marking points at which the manager is beginning to do things a bit outside the range of normal expectations. At such points, in the interest of both parties, there should be a conversation between the fund and the manager about why the strategy is beginning to deviate from expectations.

Managing a diversified, multiple-asset class, multiple-manager portfolio cannot be a backward-looking process. It must be forward-looking. Nonetheless, investors typically spend a great deal of their time calculating and examining past performance. Indeed, in common practice, past performance is typically a significant factor (perhaps the most significant factor) taken into account when institutional investors decide whether or not to hire, or fire, an investment manager. However, as stated in mutual fund prospectuses and the footnotes of investment managers' presentations, past performance is not a predictor of future performance. Past performance cannot be altered, and it cannot reliably be replicated in future capital market conditions. This does not mean that there is no insight to be gained about an investment manager's prospects from a thorough examination of their investment results. The remainder of this paper will address the question: How can one use past performance to assist the forward-looking management of the portfolio?

PERFORMANCE REPORTS

When called upon to review a fund or a manager in the fund, the investment officer or consultant typically begins by examining the performance measurement report that is prepared for the fund on a regular basis.

In general, the performance measurement report used for fund and manager evaluation is prepared by an organization that is independent from the investment managers, such as the fund's internal performance measurement group, an investment consultant, or the performance measurement department of the fund's custodial bank. The independent calculation and analysis of investment results provides the owner of the assets with a consistent and unbiased view of every manager's performance. Investment managers only get paid if they manage money. Therefore, it is in their financial interest to manage as much money as possible for as long as possible. This is not to say that manager-supplied information will be tainted in any way, but the performance analyst's independence may provide greater assurance that results are evaluated objectively and that potential problems are brought to the surface.

It merits mention that the performance measurement reports prepared by consultants and custodians for plan sponsors and other institutional investors are not GIPS-compliant reports. The GIPS standards apply only to investment firms (and, at this writing, only to investment firms' composite performance presentations for prospective clients, not to performance reports they prepare for existing clients). Consultants, custodians, and other third-party providers may use many of the calculation methodologies prescribed by the Standards, but no claims of GIPS compliance can be made for the reports covering multiple managers and asset classes that we are considering here.

Performance measurement reports for a multi-asset class portfolio like a pension or endowment fund provide performance calculations and analyses not only for individual managers but also, and more importantly, for the total portfolio, asset classes, and potentially groups of managers within an asset class, such as Large Capitalization U.S. Equity managers. Thus, a performance report must be viewed in the context of the overall strategy and each component's role within that strategy.

PERFORMANCE RELATIVE TO THE BENCHMARK

To illustrate the types of analysis employed by investment consultants, let us consider the case of a large-cap U.S. equity manager whose mandate is to manage an enhanced index portfolio. The manager's stated objective is to outperform the portfolio's benchmark by 1 percent per year with a tracking error no greater than 2 percent. Thus, the target information ratio is 0.5 or higher. In addition, most of the risk being taken is expected to come from stock selection, with the remainder from style or industry bets. Given these parameters, the characteristics of the portfolio should closely resemble those of the benchmark, with only small deviations.

This manager uses a quantitative, factor-based approach to rank the attractiveness of large-cap U.S. securities. The ranking process was developed and is conducted by a team of quantitatively oriented security analysts with a respectable long-term track record. To construct the portfolio, the manager uses a constrained optimization process that maintains the portfolio's sector, industry, style, and security weights within fairly tight bands around the corresponding benchmark weights.

TABLE 39.1   U.S. Large-Cap Equity—Enhanced Index
Portfolio, Most Recent Period

			Annualized	
	1 Quarter %	1 Year %	3 Years %	5 Years %
Portfolio	−4.7	0.0	8.3	13.1
Benchmark	−3.2	5.8	9.1	13.4
Excess Returns	−1.5	−5.8	−0.8	−0.3

TABLE 39.2   U.S. Large-Cap Equity—Enhanced Index Portfolio,
One Year Ago

			Annualized	
	1 Quarter %	1 Year %	2 Years %	4 Years %
Portfolio	6.3	15.9	12.7	16.6
Benchmark	7.0	15.5	10.8	15.4
Excess Returns	−0.7	0.4	1.9	1.2

Because the tolerance range for over- and underweighting is limited, performance deviations from the benchmark should be fairly small as well. Given that the manager's investment process has a positive expected annual mean outperformance of 1 percent and a maximum expected tracking error of 2 percent, the probability of underperformance in any given year would be 30 percent. Assuming normal distributions, a one standard deviation event on the negative side, that is, underperformance of 1 percent or more, would be expected to occur about one out of every six years. A two standard deviation event—underperformance of 3 percent or more—would be expected to occur about one out of every 40 years. So expectations about the frequency and magnitude of underperformance have been set.[2]

In view of these expectations, the easiest and most natural way to begin the performance evaluation is to compare the manager's historical returns to those of a valid benchmark. Performance measure reports normally show portfolio and benchmark returns over multiple periods that end with a recent calendar period, such as a month. Typical periods shown are the last month, last quarter, year to date, last year, and annualized multi-year periods such as the past 3 years, past 5 years, and inception to date (the annualized performance of the account from the date of its initial funding). A simplistic analysis of an active investment strategy examines the relative returns and concludes that the manager is succeeding if the portfolio returns are greater than the benchmark returns. However, such an analysis is shortsighted; it overweights recent performance and ignores patterns of returns over time. Table 39.1 displays the performance of the enhanced index relative to the benchmark. Over every time period shown in this limited view, the manager has underperformed the benchmark.

However, Table 39.1 fails to show that the manager's long-term track record is overwhelmed by the short-term underperformance. Consider the same manager's performance prior to the last year. Table 39.2, which covers the first four of the last five years, discloses that the manager's previous record was very positive, outperforming over every period except the last quarter.

Thus, contrary to what one might have supposed on the basis of Table 39.1, the manager hasn't been underperforming for five years. The manager's results have fallen short only

TABLE 39.3   Performance Triangle: Annualized Relative Performance, U.S. Large-Cap Equity—Enhanced Index Portfolio vs. Benchmark

	From Start of Year									
	1	2	3	4	5	6	7	8	9	10
10	0.5%	0.9%	0.7%	0.5%	−0.1%	−0.3%	−0.5%	−0.8%	−2.9%	−5.8%
9	1.2%	1.7%	1.7%	1.6%	1.1%	1.2%	1.5%	1.9%	0.4%	
8	1.3%	1.9%	1.8%	1.8%	1.3%	1.5%	1.9%	3.3%		
7	1.0%	1.7%	1.6%	1.4%	0.6%	0.5%	0.5%			
6	1.1%	1.9%	1.8%	1.7%	0.7%	0.4%				
5	1.2%	2.1%	2.1%	2.0%	0.9%					
4	1.3%	2.7%	2.8%	3.3%						
3	0.4%	2.2%	2.2%							
2	−0.8%	2.3%								
1	−4.0%									

To End of Year

in the most recent measurement periods. This may be taken as a first indication that in-depth analysis, and dialogue with the manager, should focus on identifying changes in the capital markets and/or the investment decision-making process that would account for the recent underperformance.

Some analysts use a performance triangle to examine historical benchmark-relative returns over various intervals. Table 39.3 is a performance triangle for the enhanced index manager. Periods of underperformance are shaded grey, and, as an aid to interpreting the chart, the excess returns for one-year and longer periods that are shown in Tables 39.1 and 39.2 are boxed in Table 39.3.

Reading along the hypotenuse, the performance triangle shows that this manager outperformed the benchmark in 8 of the 10 calendar years. Only those periods longer than one year that are significantly influenced by the manager's substantial underperformance in the first and tenth years show negative excess returns relative to the benchmark.

PEER GROUP COMPARISONS

The enhanced equity index manager's objective is to outperform the benchmark, a suitable large-cap U.S. equity index, so the comparison of the portfolio returns with the benchmark returns is the single most important measure of the manager's success in meeting the fund's expectations. However, comparing managers with their peers in a well-constructed universe also provides a useful context for interpreting investment results. Are managers with similar strategies or styles doing as well (or as poorly)? If the group is performing in synchrony, then the sources of performance differences are more likely to be associated with market conditions than with differences in the managers' investment processes, and vice-versa.

For example, let's assume that another manager, Manager X, is outperforming their benchmark but, in a universe of managers with a similar style, 80 percent of Manager X's

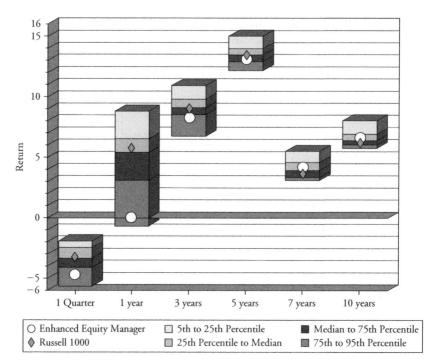

FIGURE 39.1   Manager vs. Universe: Return through December 2007 (not annualized if less than 1 year), U.S. Large-Cap Enhanced Equity Universe
Source: ZephyrStyleAdvisor.

peers have done better. While the fund's investment officer and consultant might be reasonably satisfied, since Manager X is doing what the fund asked of them, they want to know why other managers are achieving more favorable results. A manager universe is not a valid benchmark, for various reasons—for instance, it cannot be purchased—but peer group comparisons may help identify unique features of a manager's investment process or the resulting portfolio characteristics that impaired the firm's performance over the periods in question. Universe comparisons can lead to constructive dialogue if the fund's investment officer or consultant calls upon the manager to articulate the reasons for the firm's performance relative to other managers with a similar investment style.

The universe compiler ranks the performance of all the included managers and determines the returns at specific breakpoints, typically the 5th, 25th, 50th, 75th, and 95th percentiles. Using these data, the typical format for comparing managers to their peers is a "box plot" graph, which locates the returns of the manager and the benchmark relative to the universe breakpoints. In the peer group comparison shown above as Figure 39.1, for example, the one-year return for the median manager (the manager ranked at the 50th percentile) is 5.4%. It is generally considered desirable for a manager's return to rank in the top half of a universe. Figure 39.1 shows that the enhanced equity index manager has generally met the criterion of outperforming the median manager. Most recently, however, especially in the last year, the manager has done worse than the vast majority of large-cap U.S. enhanced equity index managers. This is a further indication that additional analysis is required. Additionally, the quarter and one-year return ranges are abnormally wide for an enhanced index strategy,

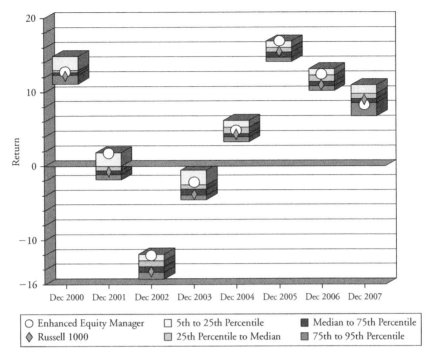

FIGURE 39.2   Manager vs. Universe: Return (36-Month Moving Windows, Computed Yearly), U.S. Large-Cap Enhanced Equity Universe

Source: ZephyrStyleAdvisor.

which provides further evidence that something outside of historical norms is happening within this universe of managers.

One might also look at the consistency of a manager's return ranking over rolling periods. A period of three years is a typical period. Figure 39.2 confirms that the enhanced index manager in our example was consistently ranking in the top half of the Enhanced Equity universe and that the performance difficulties are a recent occurrence.

PORTFOLIO CHARACTERISTICS ANALYSIS

Performance analysis, as described here, attempts to determine whether a manager is doing what is expected of them. A critical part of this analysis is examining the portfolio's characteristics such as the average market capitalization of securities in the portfolio, valuation measures, and industry and sector weightings. Considering the portfolio's characteristics in comparison with the corresponding benchmark characteristics enables the analyst to confirm whether the portfolio reflects the manager's stated investment philosophy and their current investment views. In addition, the comparison may help the analyst discern how the manager is positioning the portfolio for expected market conditions—in other words, to see what bets the manager is taking. Table 39.4 displays pertinent characteristics of the enhanced index manager's portfolio and the benchmark.

TABLE 39.4   Most Recent Quarter, U.S. Large-Cap Equity—Enhanced Index Portfolio vs. Benchmark

	Manager	Russell 1000®
Total Number of Securities	165	—
Total Market Value ($MM)	303.6	—
Average Market Capitalization ($MM)	93,962.9	95,228.7
Median Market Capitalization ($MM)	15,203.2	5,443.3
Dividend Yield	1.81	1.88
P/E	15.04	16.20
Beta	1.12	1.07
Price/Book Ratio	4.73	4.41
Five Year Earnings Growth	26.61	22.88
Return on Equity	24.48	21.56

Russell Investment Group is the source and owner of the trademarks, service marks and copyrights related to the Russell Indexes. Russell® is a trademark of Russell Investment Group.

The results of this analysis are consistent with what would be expected from a large-cap U.S. equity manager with an enhanced index mandate. Given the manager's approach to portfolio construction, which we described as constrained optimization, one would expect the portfolio to exhibit characteristics very similar to those of the benchmark, and that is indeed the case here. Furthermore, knowledge of the manager's investment process would lead one to expect that comparable average capitalization, slightly cheaper valuation characteristics (lower P/E), and slightly higher growth characteristics (higher Earnings Growth and ROE). The portfolio exhibits these characteristics, too. There are no indications that the manager has drifted away from the stated investment process.

In addition to examining portfolio characteristics as of the most recent period to identify the current bets, analysts often look at characteristics over time to see how they much they change and how they may have reacted to different market environments. The graphs contained in Figure 39.3 reflect the use of a factor-based approach to describe the size (market capitalization) and value/growth characteristic history of the portfolio as well as the distribution of those characteristics for the stocks in the portfolio.

Again, we find nothing surprising; the portfolio characteristics are what one would expect from a core, benchmark-like portfolio.

PERFORMANCE ATTRIBUTION

The goal of characteristics analysis is to ascertain whether the portfolio is consistent with the manager's investment philosophy, strategy, and current outlook. However, once we've examined the characteristics of the portfolio and their differences with the benchmark, we will want to know if prior period bets paid off. Performance attribution analysis determines the sources of the difference between the portfolio return and the benchmark return. For equity portfolios, a simple, widely used approach is to attribute the differential or excess return to sector allocation, stock selection, and "trading," using quarterly or monthly buy-and-hold

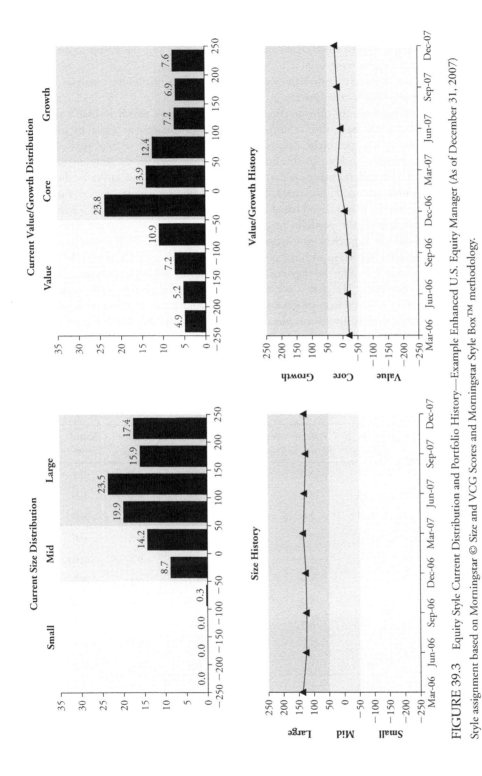

FIGURE 39.3 Equity Style Current Distribution and Portfolio History—Example Enhanced U.S. Equity Manager (As of December 31, 2007)

Style assignment based on Morningstar © Size and VCG Scores and Morningstar Style Box™ methodology.

portfolios and returns. Other more complex approaches use multiple factors, typically includ-ing both industries and other stock characteristics, and are done on a daily basis to minimize the attribution's trading or error term.

Table 39.5 is a simple arithmetic sector/stock selection attribution analysis of the enhanced index portfolio for one quarter.

A single quarter does not provide enough information upon which to base a conclu-sion. Ideally, we would have this information for longer periods to assist in identify-ing and interpreting the persistent determinants of the manager's relative performance. However, the attribution analysis for this quarter shows that, consistently with an enhanced index strategy, the underperformance is not due to sector allocation but rather to the selec-tion of stocks within sectors. Furthermore, the stock selection underperformance is not iso-lated to a single sector; it is a broad-based effect, suggesting the possibility of a systematic cause. Further analysis of the portfolio might include discovering which stock contributed most, either positive or negatively, to a sector's stock selection effect. Such an analysis could provide the basis for a discussion with the investment manager about these stocks. When and why were they purchased? Why did they out- or underperform? What was the manager's reac-tion to their performance? The goal is not merely to identify the manager's past mistakes—recall that managing an investment program is a forward-looking job—but, more importantly, to understand the manager's investment process and to evaluate the skill they bring to it.

TABLE 39.5   Performance Attribution Analysis, U.S. Large-Cap Equity—Enhanced Index Portfolio vs. Benchmark

GICS® Sector	Portfolio		Russell 1000®		Attribution		
	Pct of Begin Mkt Val	Rate of Return %	Pct of Begin Mkt Val	Rate of Return %	Stock Selection	Sector Weighting	Total
Cons Discretionary	11.1	−13.0	10.2	−10.1	−0.3	−0.1	−0.4
Consumer Staples	8.3	3.5	8.8	3.6	0.0	0.0	−0.1
Energy	11.4	2.6	11.3	4.4	−0.2	0.0	−0.2
Financials	19.4	−17.3	19.3	−13.4	−0.8	0.0	−0.8
Health Care	13.1	−5.1	11.4	−0.4	−0.6	0.0	−0.6
Industrials	10.5	−5.5	12.0	−4.1	−0.1	0.0	−0.1
Info Technology	15.0	4.0	15.8	−0.1	0.6	0.0	0.6
Materials	4.5	4.4	3.8	3.2	0.1	0.0	0.1
Telecom Services	2.9	−2.7	3.7	−6.3	0.1	0.0	0.1
Utilities	4	1.0	3.7	6.6	−0.2	0.0	−0.2
	100%	−4.7	100%	−3.2	−1.5	0.0	−1.5

The Global Industry Classification Standard (GICS®) was developed by and is the exclusive property of Morgan Stanley Capital International Inc. and Standard & Poor's. GICS is a service mark of MSCI and S&P and has been licensed for use by CFA Institute.

Russell Investment Group is the source and owner of the trademarks, service marks and copyrights related to the Russell Indexes. Russell® is a trademark of Russell Investment Group.

Columns may not add due to rounding.

RISK ANALYSIS

A performance analysis is not complete until it includes an analysis of the risks taken to achieve that performance. The most relevant risk measures may differ from one strategy or portfolio to another. For typical long-only, public market strategies, total return volatility and tracking error arguably provide the most pertinent information. Accordingly, when evaluating managers, it is a good practice to examine the *ex post* (i.e., realized) volatility for the manager and the benchmark, and the managed portfolio's tracking error (the volatility of the differential returns between the manager and the benchmark). A "snail trail" chart like Figure 39.4 displays information about the general level of volatility of the market over time and shows the volatility of the enhanced equity index portfolio in comparison with that of its benchmark. In this chart, the larger the symbol, the more recent the observation.

Over this seven-year period, the volatility of large-cap U.S. equities has moved quite bit. Over the first three years of analysis, the realized volatility of the market was slightly over 18 percent. However, realized volatilities fell substantially and settled in at about 8 percent for the past five years. Furthermore, in line with expectations, the enhanced equity manager's volatility was the same or slightly higher than that of the market. For some investment strategies or processes, we could see a very different picture.

The graph shown in Figure 39.5 is similar to the graph shown in Figure 39.4 but displays relative returns (portfolio returns in excess of the benchmark return) and relative risk (tracking error). In the graph shown in Figure 39.5, the analyst is primarily interested in the level and consistency of the realized tracking error. In Figure 39.5, the tracking error has been consistent at a level one would expect from an enhanced equity manager over this period, between

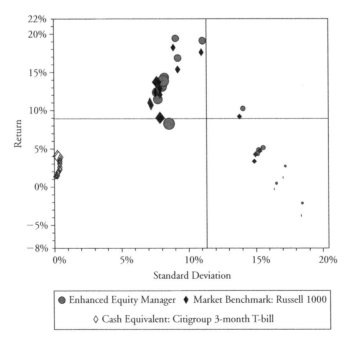

FIGURE 39.4   Manager Risk/Return (36-Month Moving Windows, Computed Quarterly), January 2001–December 2007

Source: ZephyrStyleAdvisor.

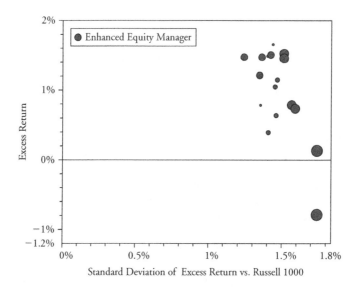

FIGURE 39.5   Annualized Excess Return/Standard Deviation of Excess Return (36-Month Moving Windows, Computed Quarterly) January 2001–December 2007
Source: ZephyrStyleAdvisor.

1.3 percent and 1.7 percent. Here, too, different managers and/or strategies would probably exhibit very different levels of risk. For example, most U.S. fixed income managers would probably have lower risks in the range of 0.5 percent to 1.25 percent, while concentrated equity managers can have a tracking error of 10 percent or greater.

The manager's realized performance should be compared to the performance objectives set for the manager. In the case of the manager we have been examining, the stated objective is to outperform the benchmark by 1 percent per year with a tracking error no greater than 2 percent. Generally, however, if an enhanced equity index manager outperforms by 0.5 to 1.0%, they have done a good job. This manager had achieved the latter result except for the most recent periods. That said, managing the fund is a forward-looking process and the most recent period is a period of significant underperformance. Is that an indicator of future results, or is it just a period of poor performance that all managers, even skilled ones, go through?

That's an extremely difficult question to answer. It requires much more investigation. What are the underlying causes of the underperformance? Is it due to abnormal market conditions or unusual behavior on the part of market participants? Have there been changes to the people and/or the information used in the investment process? How is the manager reacting to the markets and performance? What corrective actions are they taking? We are approaching the point at which we will be adequately equipped by our own analysis to ask the manager what they think and to listen critically to their explanations.

The ultimate investment objective is to achieve superior risk-adjusted returns. Widely used measures of risk-adjusted return are the Sharpe ratio and the information ratio. Preferably, the Sharpe ratio of the portfolio is greater than the Sharpe ratio of the benchmark and the information ratio is positive. The table in Figure 39.6 shows some of the risk statistics for the enhanced equity manager. Unfortunately, over this time period, the manager does

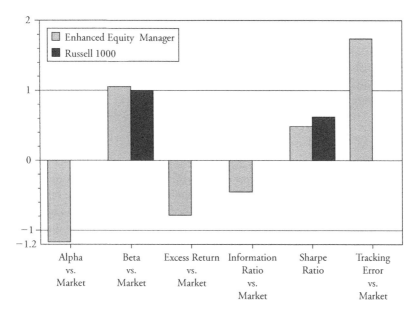

FIGURE 39.6   Risk Statistics (January 2005–December 2007)

Source: ZephyrStyleAdvisor.

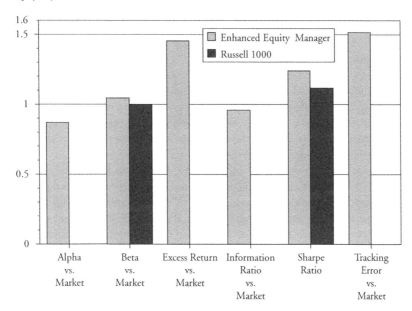

FIGURE 39.7   Risk Statistics (January 2004–December 2006)

Source: ZephyrStyleAdvisor.

not measure up well by either of these calculations. The Sharpe ratio of the portfolio is lower than that of the benchmark, and the information ratio is negative.

One year ago, however, everything looks exceptionally favorable, as illustrated in Figure 39.7.

Once again we are led to ask whether anything happened over the last year, either in the large-cap U.S. equity market or within the investment management firm, that could help explain the significant deterioration in performance.

The *ex post* risk analysis illustrated above could be complemented by a more detailed *ex ante* (i.e., predicted) risk analysis of the latest portfolio. Are the current portfolio's risk exposures consistent with the manager's investment process, objectives, and outlook? Are the sources and levels of risk exhibited by the current portfolio consistent with the strategy's history? *Ex ante* risk analysis is useful in identifying evolutionary shifts or sudden changes in the portfolio's risk posture before they show up in performance.

TAKING ACTION

We have examined the performance and characteristics of a manager in a number of ways. But what does the information tell us, and what actions, if any, should the fund take on the basis of this analysis? How can the investment officer or the consultant judge whether the manager is performing up to expectations? How does one decide whether the manager will provide the future performance results that they are being paid for?

Let us summarize our findings on the enhanced equity manager. Until the last year, everything was going well. Performance was respectable and, importantly, within expectations; there were no exceptionally good results which might imply that unknown risks were being taken in the portfolio. The portfolio's characteristics were in line with those of the benchmark. The realized tracking error of the portfolio was slightly lower than the 2 percent target, but this was a period of exceptionally low market volatility, and realized volatilities for all strategies were coming in lower than expectations. An attribution analysis showed that most of the portfolio's active return was derived from stock selection. The manager was fulfilling their role as an anchor in the portfolio, providing market-like returns, risks and characteristics. No surprises.

And then the last year happened. Performance was deplorable. Over a one-year period, the manager underperformed the benchmark by nearly 6 percent, a 3½ standard deviation event. Assuming a normal distribution, the frequency of such an outcome is once every four millennia! Now that's outside the range of expectations. Other managers investing similarly also had very poor performance, but universe comparisons show that this manager was particularly affected by the market environment.

At this point it is appropriate to call upon the manager to provide insights into their own performance. (Had we called the manager prior to our analysis, we would not have had enough information to evaluate the reasonability of their explanation.) Our questions will focus on changes in market conditions and changes, if any, in the manager's philosophy, organization, strategy, or investment process. In addition to learning how the manager accounts for the recent underperformance, we will seek to understand whether the manager is adjusting the investment process—they may, for instance, have concluded that it is necessary to re-specify their stock valuation model—and how the manager is positioning the portfolio for expected market conditions. This conversation will help the fund decide whether to retain or terminate the manager.

In the case under study here, conversations with the manager confirmed that a massive market liquidity event along with previously unrealized concentration and the popularity of similar strategies caused the enhanced equity manager's excess return models to underperform severely. As a result, the manager described the efforts they were taking in their investment process to mitigate the impact of a similar occurrence in the future. Thus, we have a manager that has severely underperformed but is trying to adapt to the market conditions that led to their underperformance. However, we also have a new understanding of the manager and the risks and rewards of their strategy. Given the change in our expectations about the manager and their strategy, we must re-evaluate their role in the fund's strategy. Depending upon our point of view, we could conclude that the role should remain unchanged or we could conclude that the manager's role in the fund should be reduced or even eliminated.

There are many reasons for which institutional investors terminate managers. Many terminations are fully justified without an analysis of the manager's historical performance. If the entire investment team managing the portfolio leaves their organization, it is reasonable to conclude that in the future the owner of the account is going to receive something different from the firm they originally hired. If the style of the portfolio changes over time, it may not fulfill the role in the plan for which it was originally intended. Unfortunately, a frequent cause of manager terminations is short-term underperformance. This is understandable; it is very difficult to develop future expectations about a manager that are not heavily influenced by their recent unfavorable results. However, an adverse assessment of the manager's prospects may very well turn out to be unproductive.

Nonetheless, the information derived from a sustained analysis of the manager's performance should be used to evaluate whether the characteristics and behavior of the manager's portfolio are consistent with what they have said they would be doing and what the fund expects them to be doing. As long as the manager's strategy is behaving as expected and there are no other changes within the organization, no action is required beyond the day-to-day management of the fund's overall portfolio. However, once a managed portfolio begins to exhibit traits that are outside of expectations, additional due diligence on the manager and their strategy is always necessary. In the end, the decision to retain or to terminate a manager is a matter of professional judgment and should always be supported by factors other than the performance of the manager's portfolio.

NOTES

1. See John L. Maginn, Donald L. Tuttle, Dennis W. McLeavey, and Jerald E. Pinto, "The Portfolio Management Process and the Investment Policy Statement," Chapter 1 in *Managing Investment Portfolios; A Dynamic Process* (CFA Institute, 2007), especially pp. 11–17.
2. These probability statements assume that the mean expected excess return is 1 percent and one standard deviation is 2%. In a normal distribution, the probability that an observation is less than the mean return by ½ standard deviation or more—wiping out the 1% expected outperformance with our assumptions—is 30.85%. The probability that an observation is less than the mean by one standard deviation or more—equal to a portfolio return that is below the benchmark return by 1% or more—is 15.87%. That percentage is very close to 1/6th, implying an event that occurs one out of every six years, assuming the same process generates returns from year to year. The probability that an observation is less than the mean by two standard deviations or more—equal to a portfolio return that is below the benchmark return by 3% or more (1% − 2 × 2% = −3%)—is 2.28%. That percentage is close to 1/40th, implying an event that occurs one out of every 40 years, again under the assumption that the process generating returns does not change.

CHAPTER 40

THINKING OUTSIDE THE BOX: RISK MANAGEMENT FIRMS PUT A CREATIVE SPIN ON COUPLING THEORY WITH PRACTICE

Susan Trammell, CFA

Today, sophisticated analytical tools covering the spectrum of financial instruments are standard equipment among risk managers. Of the small universe of firms offering outsourced risk management services, we surveyed three that, we believe, represent a cross-section of solutions. Most of the tools used by providers are standard in the industry. The methodologies and processes by which each firm integrates theory with practice, however, are proprietary. Underlying the diversity of their solutions is the shared belief that managing risk requires a multidimensional approach.

The risk management industry has evolved beyond a "one-size-fits-all" approach to managing the risk of a portfolio. Today, sophisticated analytical tools covering the spectrum of financial instruments are standard equipment among risk managers. Of the small universe of firms offering outsourced risk management services, we surveyed three that, we believe, represent a cross-section of solutions. In sparest terms, a risk management system is bundled software that quantifies various measures of the risk in a portfolio. How that value is arrived at, however, is as much a matter of rigorous application of risk assessment tools as creative interpretation of the outputs.

All risk managers focus on identifying, measuring, and reporting on the financial risk of portfolios. Some clients, however, need more elaborate services than others. Specific requirements are driven by their portfolios' exposure to different classes of risk, the complexity of

Reprinted from *CFA Magazine* (March/April 2004):32–35.

the positions, and the demands of regulatory compliance, to name only a few of the consid-erations that impact the selection of an outside risk manager.

Most of the tools used by providers are standard in the industry. The methodologies and processes by which each firm integrates theory with practice, however, are proprietary. Underlying the diversity of their solutions is the shared belief that managing risk requires a multidimensional approach.

A SIMPLE REQUEST

It was 1989 and Sir Dennis Weatherstone, the new chairman of JP Morgan, asked that a report be delivered to him every afternoon measuring and explaining the total risk exposure of his firm. Sir Dennis got his reports, and the analytical resources used by the staff were pub-lished online in the RiskMetrics Technical Document. The paper brought together the best practices for assessing financial risk. Since it was freely available, it was widely disseminated and closely examined by academics and the financial community. Constructive criticism led to several revisions as its methods were adopted by banks, asset managers, hedge funds, gov-ernment agencies, and other users.

By 1998, JP Morgan decided that it could no longer meet the call for its risk manage-ment services with in-house resources and spun off the RiskMetrics Group. The founding team of 25, still based in New York, has since grown to a staff of 210. The firm has a presence in seven offices located in the United States, the United Kingdom, Japan, and Singapore. JP Morgan retains a position in the group.

"We employ over 200,000 individual risk factors—equities, fixed income, currencies, volatilities, commodities, spreads, etc.—in our simulations and calculations," explains Gregg Berman, head of Institutional Business at RiskMetrics. "For example, our solutions can help clients better understand the extent to which their positions may be correlated, both within a given asset class as well as across asset classes. It is able to do this because our methodologies are geared toward estimating the idiosyncratic risk between similar positions, in addition to broader market risks."

POWERFUL SOLUTIONS

Berman points out how misestimating correlations can cause banks to overfund or underfund their capital requirements, compelling them to take action. In the first instance, he says, banks with portfolios of similar stocks, bonds, and combinations of both often proxy each position to a general asset class factor. Risk analytics can reveal that a portfolio is more diversified than expected because issuer-specific risks at least partially cancel each other out. Thus, risk analyt-ics may keep a bank from overestimating risk and overfunding capital requirements.

On the other hand, risk measurement tools may reveal underfunding. An asset manager tracking a benchmark sometimes assigns a broad factor to each position. This can lead to a loss of information about the differences in risk between the positions in the portfolio and those in the benchmark. "In this case the tracking error can be much higher then expected," Berman says, "especially if results are tuned to common reporting cycles (such as monthly or quarterly). In such cases, RiskMetrics' ability to update volatilities and correlations on a daily basis become critical."

Risk management systems such as RiskMetrics' pull in data directly from custodians, prime brokers, and other sources. Users can usually classify risks at different levels of aggregation, such as by factor, asset class, strategy, geographic region, and fund manager. The magnitude of theoretical application and computational horsepower that a risk management firm delivers may well be superior to anything that a single client could develop in-house, and certainly more affordable.

ANSWERING THE CALL

Like RiskMetrics, BlackRock Inc.'s external risk management business began in response to external requests. The $294 billion asset management firm was launched in 1988 as a boutique investment manager and was partially spun off in 1999 from PNC Financial Services Group, which retains a majority stake. At first, BlackRock built up an analytic infrastructure to support its own asset management business. Then clients began asking the firm to provide them with certain risk management reports on portfolios managed by others.

"At first, we didn't know how to respond to the requests in a systematic way," recalls Ben Golub, managing director and head of the Portfolio Risk Management Group at BlackRock. "Eventually, we realized there was a bona fide demand for these services, and we began to accommodate it."

A major push came when BlackRock got a call from General Electric to help with Kidder Peabody, an investment banking and brokerage firm that it had acquired. Kidder was going through major financial distress, and its staff was quickly dwindling. GE retained BlackRock to provide consulting and analytics, as well as the hedging for Kidder's positions. BlackRock found itself providing analytical and consulting services unrelated to an asset management assignment, and its outsourcing business took off.

"As the complexity of the markets continued to increase, and as the range of instruments that ended up in fixed-income portfolios became more diverse, the resources required to have a state-of-the-practice infrastructure grew," Golub says. "While BlackRock was a relatively fast growing asset manager, it was unreasonable to assume that its organic asset management business alone could support the costs required to manufacture those analytics." By spreading the cost of development over many clients, providers such as BlackRock are able to stay on top of the game.

Although the concept of offering risk management solutions dates back to the mid-1990s, BlackRock Solutions adopted its name only a few years ago. Today, more than 250 professionals provide risk management reporting on over US$2.3 trillion. BlackRock, a publicly traded company headquartered in New York, has seven other offices in the United States, United Kingdom, Japan, and Hong Kong.

With the external demand for the group's services increasing, Golub, who was co-head of BlackRock Solutions, realigned his responsibilities in 2003 to focus on managing risk for one of its most important clients: the asset management business of BlackRock, Inc.

THE 90/10 RULE

Investor Analytics, LLC, came out of the starting gate in 1999 with the self-appointed mission of getting clients to outsource their risk monitoring and management activities as a way to cut costs and improve service. "There were really a number of driving factors that led us to start the company," says Damian Handzy, managing director and a co-founder. "One of them was the lack of available tools to the portfolio managers and fund-of-funds managers. If you wanted quantitative risk management, you had to build it in-house."

For obvious reason, Handzy explains, that is an inefficient way of doing it. "If you have five firms and each of them is going to build its own solution, 90 percent of the work is overlap. We wanted to build a platform where our clients could get 80 or 90 percent of the functionality they really want by outsourcing it and have the cost savings from the economy of scale that we can pass on to them," he says. "The other 10 percent we can custom-build for them, or they can choose to keep totally proprietary. Call it the 90/10 rule."

Investor Analytics' information processing engines statistically analyze portfolios across major asset classes, focusing on the risk exposure in the portfolios. The results are presented in easy-to-use reports accessible via the Web.

"A European client started with us about a year ago," Handzy recalls. "Within the first two months, the client discovered that the reports coming from the administrator about the portfolio were incomplete and sometimes misleading." In addition, the client had separate risk engines to handle each of its asset classes, making it difficult to understand the firm's risk exposure. As a result of outsourcing risk management to Investor Analytics, Handzy explains, the client gained a better understanding of its holdings and an integrated view of the market risk it was facing.

Investor Analytics, which is based in New York, provides value-added services in three ways. The first, as the earlier example illustrates, is clarity of reporting. The second is the company's proprietary risk tools, which are able to go into what-if/scenario analyses and look at incremental, or marginal, risk. This helps clients to better understand the factors that contribute risk to a portfolio. Handzy describes a typical situation with hedge funds that claim

VAR/EQUITY RISK

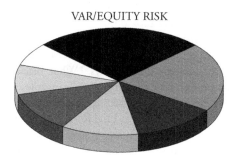

Label	Value	Percent
■ Lodging	2,010	26%
■ Auto parts and Equipment	1,644	21%
■ Office Furnishings	1,029	13%
■ Retail	933	12%
■ Entertainment	924	12%
■ Toys/Games/Hobbies	689	9%
☐ Home Furnishings	586	7%

FIGURE 40.1   Robust risk management solutions can graphically represent the analysis of a portfolio's total risk exposure with clear, intuitive pictures. In the chart shown here, RiskMetrics Group's software has depicted a sample portfolio's value at risk in the form of a pie chart that parses the portfolio's total risk exposure on a sector-by-sector basis.

to have low correlation with the S&P 500. "One of our analyses is an attribution of risk to various factors, one of which could very well be the S&P 500. It essentially tells you how sensitive you are to movements in that fund, instrument, or index."

Finally, clients make Investor Analytics' reports available to their own investors, thereby improving their client services and their own marketing effort.

STRESSING THE DATA

Risk analyses typically start with the standard VAR (value at risk) probability-based measure of loss potential for all the subcategories in a portfolio and then build on that information using processes that challenge less technical managers. Quantifying risk within and across portfolios requires the input of many variables and the flexibility to respond to conditions that are changing constantly. Although the mechanics for applying risk management theory to practice may differ among providers, all offer clients a means of carrying out stress tests, sensitivity analysis, and simulations of possible scenarios.

Stress testing looks at the impact on risk levels of extreme market moves. Particularly since 1998, when credit spreads widened to a degree and for a time span that nearly defied the laws of probability, managers have been alert to the possibility of the virtually impossible.

"If you know the volatilities of your various securities and their correlations, you can calculate VAR," Handzy explains. "How do you figure out the volatilities and correlations? The standard way is to base them on history. But you can also say, 'What if the volatility triples? What if the correlations all go to 1?' That's actually a numerical interpretation of, 'What if we go to war?' or 'What if the market crashes?'

"When a client comes to us and asks for the replay of a scenario, it's typically a historically bad one or a hypothetical 'nightmare'—the crash of 1987, the Fed tightening of 1994, or September 11th. The volatility of stocks in the United States was not 20 percent right after September 11th—it was more like 40 percent. So, the numerical model of replaying September 11th is hiking up the volatility and making the correlations between stocks and bonds what they were in the weeks following September 11th."

New ways of modeling operational risk such as extreme value theory (EVT) have emerged to quantify huge potential losses beyond three confidence levels. Standard measures such as delta factor models are good predictors only of frequent losses that are small. EVT models look at losses above a certain size. The result of combining the two approaches is a more sobering view of the loss exposure in an operation.

SENSITIVITY ANALYSIS AND SIMULATIONS

Sensitivity analysis subjects portfolio data to possible shocks and captures their degree of susceptibility to events. A client bank's balance sheet, for example, will be analyzed for its sensitivity to the different components of interest rate risk. This might be its exposure to repricing risk—caused by changes in interest rates that may make the institution's borrowing more expensive while it holds a portfolio of fixed-income assets—or the option risk embedded in the prepayment features of purchased mortgages.

Says BlackRock's Golub, "There have been a number of instances where clients have had very bad experiences because they didn't appreciate the degree of prepayments and the degree of optionality that was embedded in their position. Or, in attempting to hedge, they may not have matched off the negative convexity of the position properly."

Particularly in the fixed income markets, Golub explained, practitioners focus on the parametric risk measures. "If interest rates move by 100 basis points, what happens? If the two-year spot rate moves by 100 basis points, what happens? What if volatility moves by 10 basis points, or prepayment speeds accelerate by 25 percent? The first component of any risk analysis that we do is to calculate exceedingly precise parametrics, trying to understand the sensitivities of the portfolio to specified events."

Finally, simulations give managers a chance to create a suite of scenarios based on the statistical properties of the markets: volatilities, correlations, and even the history itself of how the markets have performed. "When you develop an entire simulation of potential outcomes, you don't get one valuation change," RiskMetrics' Berman says. "You get a whole suite of changes in valuation."

OUT OF THE BOX . . .

If there is one service descriptor that keeps cropping up among providers, it is transparency. In order for managers to integrate a risk management service effectively into their operations, they need to understand how it works. Gone are the days of black box solutions, where a client handed over its transaction details and then struggled to decipher the risk profile generated by the numbers.

Today's risk management systems work across asset classes, giving an enterprise-wide view of risk. Parametric tools are increasingly client interactive as risk management firms adopt a hosted, application service provider (ASP) model to deliver their services. Reports give clients multiple views of risk matrices whose underlying data is mined, mapped, and three-dimensionally modeled.

Clients have come to expect their outsourced solutions to be flexible and scalable. Methodologies employed throughout system modules should emphasize consistency. Client due diligence on providers should include their long-range plans to keep their applications updated.

Perhaps most importantly, third-party firms act as repositories of information that would be off-limits to any one client. In 2003, RiskMetrics launched Hedge Platform, a risk management service for hedge fund managers. The platform collects data sent in by clients electronically and then aggregates the information so that managers can do stress testing and run other reports. The details of each fund are kept confidential.

. . . AND ONTO THE CUTTING EDGE

Hedge Platform is only one of many service modes that RiskMetrics offers, which encompass market risk and credit risk measurement and reporting, data sets from global providers, financial advisory services to high-net-worth individuals, and research. The firm also recently launched its pioneering CreditGrades methodology, which links credit spreads and equity through a Merton-style process.[1] It allows estimates of issuer-specific credit spread risk on an individual name basis and as part of a correlated portfolio.

BlackRock Solutions gives clients a chance to utilize its services in three ways. The service bureau is able to return the risk of a given set of positions with a customizable reporting suite. Clients can also create their own portfolios and compute certain elements of the risk using the firm's online analytic calculators.

At the high end is the Aladdin suite, an enterprise-wide system that provides all the front, middle, and back office functions required to operate a large fixed-income manager. Many of the techniques used at BlackRock Solutions are the application of ideas published in *Risk Management: Approaches for Fixed Income Markets*, co-authored by Golub, who holds a PhD in finance.

Handzy describes Investor Analytics' risk management platform as a flexible hierarchy that accommodates any portfolio. The firm offers a menu of industry standards approaches to risk measurement, although it can also customize risk analyses that are proprietary to the client. Analytical results are displayed on their screens, and clients can play around with different settings in an interactive mode. Handzy, who holds a doctorate in nuclear physics, recently co-authored a simplified alternative to Monte Carlo simulation.

With the headline-grabbing blowups of several asset management firms in the late 1990s, it is tempting to think that practitioners' focus on risk is a recent phenomenon. Handzy is more philosophical. "It's not that we now know that risk is an important part of investing," he says. "We've always known it. We just forgot it for a while."

NOTE

1. Financial economist Robert Merton developed what is known as a structural model for the pricing of bonds. RiskMetrics uses this class of models in its CreditGrades methodology to relate the equity and spread levels for an issuer given a known debt level.

GLOBAL INVESTMENT PERFORMANCE STANDARDS

CHAPTER 41

GLOBAL INVESTMENT PERFORMANCE STANDARDS

Philip Lawton, CFA, CIPM

W. Bruce Remington, CFA

This chapter covers the accurate calculation and presentation of investment performance results as set forth in Global Investment Performance Standards, a set of standards that has been widely adopted worldwide.

The Global Investment Performance Standards (the GIPS® standards) fulfill an essential role in investment management around the world. They meet the need for consistent, globally accepted standards for investment management firms in calculating and presenting their results to potential clients.

The Standards are based on the ideals of fair representation and full disclosure of an investment management firm's performance history. Firms that claim compliance with the GIPS standards must adhere to rules governing not only rate-of-return calculations but also the way in which returns are displayed in a performance presentation. They are further required to make certain disclosures and are encouraged to make others, assisting the recipient or user in interpreting and evaluating the reported returns. Potential clients are assured that the information shown in a GIPS-compliant performance presentation reasonably reflects the results of the presenting firm's past investment decisions. They are also assured that the returns are calculated and presented on a consistent basis and that they are objectively comparable to those reported by other firms rightfully claiming compliance with the Standards.

Reprinted from *Managing Investment Portfolios: A Dynamic Process*, 3 ed. (John Wiley & Sons, 2007): 783–855.

This chapter comprehensively presents the requirements and recommendations of the 2005 version of the GIPS standards. In addition to presenting the Standards, the chapter explains the rationale and application of specific provisions, with particular attention to implementation issues. "Background of the GIPS Standards" provides background information on the need for the GIPS standards, their history, the role of the Investment Performance Council, and the objectives and key characteristics of the Standards. "Provisions of the GIPS Standards" covers the provisions of the GIPS standards. "Verification" describes verification, and "GIPS Advertising Guidelines" reviews the GIPS Advertising Guidelines enabling firms to claim compliance with the GIPS standards in advertisements that do not accommodate fully compliant performance presentations. "Other Issues" considers other issues relevant to the Standards.

BACKGROUND OF THE GIPS STANDARDS

The GIPS standards, which offer significant advantages to investors and investment management firms, evolved from earlier efforts to improve the reliability of performance information and to standardize calculation methodologies. In this part of the chapter, we will explain the benefits of the GIPS standards, recount their historical development, and introduce the governance body responsible for developing and interpreting the Standards. We will also give an overview of the GIPS standards.

The Need for Global Investment Performance Standards

In their current state, the GIPS standards are so broadly accepted and endorsed in the investment industry that it is worthwhile to recall the reasons they were developed in the first place. The total economic cost of defining, promulgating, interpreting, implementing, updating, monitoring, and validating claims of compliance with these voluntary ethical standards is substantial. Why have investment industry participants seen fit to incur such costs? What are the benefits?

To appreciate the value of industrywide performance presentation standards, consider some of the many ways in which unscrupulous employees might attempt to gather new assets by misrepresenting a firm's historical record in the Standards' absence. In communicating with a prospective client, they could

- Present returns only for the best-performing portfolios as though those returns were fully representative of the firm's expertise in a given strategy or style.
- Base portfolio market values on their own unsubstantiated estimates of asset prices.
- Inflate returns by annualizing partial-period results.
- Select the most favorable measurement period, calculating returns from a low point to a high point.
- Present simulated returns as though they had actually been earned.
- Choose as a benchmark the particular index the selected portfolios have outperformed by the greatest margin during the preferred measurement period.
- Portray the growth of assets in the style or strategy of interest so as to mask the difference between investment returns and client contributions.

- Use the marketing department's expertise in graphic design to underplay unfavorable performance data and direct the prospect's attention to the most persuasive elements of the sales presentation.

Some of the foregoing examples are admittedly egregious abuses. They are not, however, farfetched. In the late 1980s, before performance presentation standards became widely accepted, a groundbreaking committee of the Financial Analysts Federation (a predecessor organization of CFA Institute) reported that investment advisers were "left to their own standards, which have been varied, uneven, and, in many instances, outright irresponsible and dishonest."[1] The investment management industry remains highly competitive, and people whose careers and livelihoods depend on winning new business want to communicate their firm's performance in the most favorable light (as they certainly should). The GIPS standards are ethical criteria designed simply to ensure that the firm's performance history is fairly represented and adequately disclosed. Indeed, employees who are pressured to misrepresent their firm's investment results can and should cite the GIPS standards.

Without established, well-formulated standards for investment performance measurement and presentation, the prospective client's ability to make sound decisions in selecting investment managers would be impaired. Individual investors and their advisers, as well as pension plan sponsors, foundation trustees, and other institutional investors with fiduciary responsibility for asset pools, need reliable information. The GIPS standards give them greater confidence that the returns they are shown fairly represent an investment firm's historical record. The Standards also enable them to make reasonable comparisons among different investment management firms before hiring one of them. Evaluating past returns is only one dimension of the manager selection process, but it is an important one, and the due diligence legally and ethically expected of fiduciaries cannot be satisfied without it.

The Standards' benefits to prospective clients are clear. What, if any, are the benefits to the investment management firms incurring the substantial expenses required to achieve and maintain compliance with the GIPS standards?

There is, first, an incalculable benefit to the investment management industry as a whole. The widespread acceptance of the GIPS standards contributes to the industry's credibility. The GIPS standards reassure investors about compliant firms' veracity in the area of investment performance reporting, which is highly advantageous to an industry built on trust. The development of well-founded, thoughtfully defined performance presentation standards is a great credit not only to the vision of certain professionals and organizations but, above all, to the leadership of the investment management firms that were the early adopters.

The practical benefits to individual firms facing the initial and ongoing expenses of GIPS compliance have increased over time. In some markets, the Standards are so well accepted by plan sponsors and consultants that noncompliance is a serious competitive impediment to a firm's winning new institutional business. Requests for proposals (RFPs) in manager searches routinely ask if the responding firm is in compliance with the GIPS standards and if the firm has been independently verified.[2] In addition, the global recognition the GIPS standards have gained helps the compliant firm to compete in international markets because prospective clients should value the ability to equitably compare its investment performance to that of local GIPS-compliant firms. Compliance with the GIPS standards has appropriately been characterized as the investment management firm's passport to the international marketplace.

Because the GIPS standards reflect best practices in the calculation and presentation of investment performance, firms may also realize internal benefits. In the course of implementing the Standards, they might identify opportunities to strengthen managerial controls. The discipline of reviewing portfolio guidelines and defining, documenting, and adhering to internal policies in support of compliance may generally improve the firm's oversight of investment operations. Similarly, technological enhancements designed to provide valid calculation input data and presentation elements, such as dispersion statistics, may improve the quality of information available to the firm's investment decision makers.

Only investment **firms** may claim compliance with the GIPS standards.[3] Consultants, software houses, or third-party performance measurement providers such as custodians may not claim to be GIPS-compliant. Moreover, investment firms may claim to be compliant only on a firmwide basis (Provision II.0.A.1).[4] GIPS compliance cannot be claimed only for some of an investment firm's products, nor for specific composites.[5] A firm's claim of compliance signifies, among other things, that the firm's performance measurement data inputs, processes, and return calculation methodology conform to the prescribed guidelines and that all of the firm's fee-paying discretionary **portfolios** have been assigned to a **composite.**

The Development of Performance Presentation Standards

Investors have been keeping track of their wealth for as long as capital markets have existed. The industry standards for performance measurement and presentation as we know them today, however, have resulted from developments that began in the late 1960s and gathered speed in the 1990s.

Peter O. Dietz published his seminal work, *Pension Funds: Measuring Investment Performance,* in 1966. The Bank Administration Institute (BAI), a U.S.-based organization serving the financial services industry, subsequently formulated rate-of-return calculation guidelines based on Dietz's work.

In 1980, Wilshire Associates joined with a number of custodial banks to establish the Trust Universe Comparison Service (TUCS), a database of portfolio returns organized for use in peer group comparisons, and the members established standards for computing returns in order to ensure comparability.

The direct lineage of the current Global Investment Performance Standards starts with the voluntary guidelines for the North American marketplace defined by a committee of the Financial Analysts Federation. The Committee for Performance Presentation Standards published a report in the September/October 1987 issue of the *Financial Analysts Journal.* The committee's recommendations notably included using a time-weighted total return calculation; reporting performance before the effects of investment management fees; including cash in portfolio return calculations; reaching agreement with the client in advance on the starting date for performance measurement; selecting a risk- or style-appropriate benchmark for performance comparisons; and constructing and presenting accurate, asset-weighted composites of investment performance. The committee strongly recommended that the Financial Analysts Federation disseminate and attempt to impose performance presentation standards for investment management organizations.[6]

Another milestone was the development of the Association for Investment Management and Research (AIMR) Performance Presentation Standards (AIMR-PPS®). AIMR, founded in January 1990 when the Financial Analysts Federation merged with the Institute of Chartered Financial Analysts, subsequently became CFA Institute. In 1990, as one of its first actions, the AIMR Board of Governors endorsed the AIMR-PPS standards. The Board also established the AIMR Performance Presentation Standards Implementation Committee to review the proposed Standards and to seek industry input prior to formal implementation. The AIMR-PPS standards were implemented, and the first edition of the *AIMR Performance Presentation Standards Handbook* was published in 1993.

Acting independently, the Investment Management Consultants Association (IMCA) also issued performance measurement guidelines in 1993. IMCA endorses the AIMR-PPS standards, which apply to investment firms. Updated in 1998, the IMCA standards complement the AIMR-PPS standards with guidelines for investment consultants in analyzing data obtained from investment managers in the course of manager searches as well as in reporting, monitoring, and analyzing performance results.[7]

In 1995, AIMR formed the Global Performance Presentation Standards Subcommittee, reporting to the Implementation Committee, to address international performance issues and to develop global standards for presenting investment performance. The following year, AIMR revised the AIMR-PPS standards, stipulating new requirements, such as the inclusion of accrued income in bond market values in both the numerator and the denominator of return calculations, and presenting new recommendations, such as the use of temporary accounts for significant cash flows. In 1997, AIMR released the second edition of the *AIMR Performance Presentation Standards Handbook* incorporating these and other changes.

In 1998, after circulating several preliminary drafts among industry participants, the Global PPS Subcommittee released the Global Investment Performance Standards for public comment. The AIMR Board of Governors formally endorsed the GIPS standards early in 1999 and established the Investment Performance Council (IPC) later that year to manage the further development and promulgation of the GIPS standards. (We discuss the IPC's ongoing role below.) In 2001, the AIMR-PPS standards were adopted by the AIMR Board of Governors and the IPC as the U.S. and Canadian Version of GIPS. The first edition of *The Global Investment Performance Standards (GIPS) Handbook* was published in 2002 in a looseleaf format to accommodate changes and additions to the Standards with the passage of time.

By the end of 2004, IPC-endorsed local standards had been adopted—either verbatim in English, or in a straightforward Translation of GIPS, or in a Country Version of GIPS—in 25 countries throughout North America, Europe, Africa, and the Asia Pacific region. (We discuss translations and Country Versions of GIPS in the next section.) In 2005, the IPC issued revised Global Investment Performance Standards funded by CFA Institute and co-sponsored locally by more than 25 other key industry groups. The present chapter is based on the 2005 edition of the GIPS standards, which reflect globally applicable best practices from all regional standards.

Governance of the GIPS Standards

With the release of the GIPS standards in 1999, the Investment Performance Council (IPC) was formed to serve as the committee responsible for maintaining the Standards. It consisted of approximately 36 members from a variety of fields within the global investment industry representing 15 countries. From 1999 to 2006, the IPC focused on its principal goal: to have all countries adopt the GIPS standards as the standard for investment firms seeking to present historical investment performance.

The IPC strongly encouraged countries without an investment performance standard in place to accept the GIPS standards as the local norms, either in English or in a Translation of GIPS (TG).

Due to local regulation or to well-accepted practice, some countries were found to have additional requirements over and above those set forth in the GIPS standards. In these cases, the IPC promoted an approach designated as a "Country Version of GIPS" (CVG). The country would adopt the GIPS standards as their core standards, supplemented by additional provisions as necessary to meet local requirements. If the CVG included any differences that could not be justified on the basis of regulatory stipulations or widely recognized practice, the local sponsor (typically a professional association) was required to provide a transition plan for eliminating the differences within a specified period.

In February 2005, the IPC revised the GIPS standards and created a single global standard for investment performance reporting. The revised Standards grant all CVG-compliant firms reciprocity for periods prior to January 1, 2006, such that their CVG-compliant history will satisfy the GIPS requirement, discussed below, to show at least a five-year track record in performance presentations.

In order to facilitate involvement from all industry stakeholders and provide a necessary conduit for the collaboration of ideas and mutual engagement in the process, the IPC was transformed in 2006 into the GIPS Executive Committee (EC). Consisting of nine members, the EC serves as the effective decision-making authority for the GIPS standards. The EC created four standing subcommittees—the GIPS Council, the Interpretations Subcommittee, the Practitioners/Verifiers Subcommittee, and the Investors/Consultants Subcommittee—to support the work of the EC.

The GIPS Council works directly with all Country Sponsors in the development, promotion, and maintenance of the GIPS standards.

The Interpretations Subcommittee has the responsibility of ensuring the integrity, consistency, and applicability of the GIPS standards by providing guidance to address new issues presented by the global investment industry. Firms claiming compliance with the GIPS standards must also comply with all applicable interpretations and guidance.

The Practitioners/Verifiers Subcommittee is composed of third-party service providers, including verifiers, software developers, and custodians, that assist investment management firms in the implementation and application of the Standards. This Subcommittee provides a forum to discuss the application, implementation, and impact of the Standards. Verification, discussed below, refers to an investment firm's voluntarily engaging an independent third party to test the firm's performance measurement and composite construction procedures in order to validate the firm's claim of compliance with the GIPS standards.

The Investors/Consultants Subcommittee is composed of investors (and those representing investors), regulators, and consultants from the investment industry, including clients, plan sponsors, retail investors, and others, to create a forum for the end user of investment performance information. This subcommittee will be responsible for assisting in the development and direction of the GIPS standards.

Overview of the GIPS Standards

To orient the reader, we present an outline of the Global Investment Performance Standards document in Figure 41.1. Section I, "Introduction," provides extensive information about the Standards. Rather than paraphrasing and commenting on every point made in the Introduction, we will highlight certain concepts in the following paragraphs.

The vision statement in the Introduction to the Global Investment Performance Standards reads, "A global investment performance standard leads to readily accepted presentations of investment performance that (1) present performance results that are readily comparable among investment management firms without regard to geographic location, and (2) facilitate a dialogue between investment managers and their prospective clients about the critical issues of how the manager achieved performance results and determines future investment strategies" (Section I.B.5).

This statement articulates two primary goals of the GIPS standards. First, as we have seen, the establishment and acceptance of global standards enables firms to compete for new

PREFACE: BACKGROUND OF THE GIPS STANDARDS

I. INTRODUCTION
- A. Preamble: Why Is a Global Standard Needed?
- B. Vision Statement
- C. Objectives
- D. Overview
- E. Scope
- F. Compliance
- G. Implementing a Global Standard

II. PROVISIONS OF THE GLOBAL INVESTMENT PERFORMANCE STANDARDS
- 0. Fundamentals of Compliance
- 1. Input Data
- 2. Calculation Methodology
- 3. Composite Construction
- 4. Disclosures
- 5. Presentation and Reporting
- 6. Real Estate
- 7. Private Equity

III. VERIFICATION
- A. Scope and Purpose of Verification
- B. Required Verification Procedures
- C. Detailed Examinations of Investment Performance Presentations

Appendix A: Sample GIPS-Compliant Presentations
Appendix B: Sample List and Description of Composites
Appendix C: GIPS Advertising Guidelines
Appendix D: Private Equity Valuation Principals
Appendix E: GIPS Glossary

FIGURE 41.1 Global Investment Performance Standards
Source: www.cfainstitute.org.

business around the world on an equal footing. This equality expands the marketplace for all investment firms by eliminating barriers to entry.

Second, global standards for performance presentation, including the requirement that a firm show each composite's investment returns alongside the returns of an appropriate benchmark, can lead to an informative discussion about the firm's investment decision-making process. The prospective client might ask, for instance, why the composite outperformed the benchmark in some periods and not in others, inviting the firm's spokespersons to explain past returns and to describe how the investment product is positioned for the future.

It must be stressed in this context that reviewing properly calculated, fully disclosed historical results does not exempt the prospective client from a thorough investigation of the candidate firm's background, resources, and capabilities for the mandate under consideration. Due diligence in selecting an investment manager includes, among many other important elements, examining a firm's regulatory history, the experience and professional credentials of its decision makers, the soundness of its investment philosophy, and the nature of its risk controls. At a minimum, however, the firm's representatives should be able to explain the sources of its past returns reasonably, credibly, and insightfully in light of the firm's investment discipline and the then-prevailing capital market environment.

The Introduction to the GIPS standards also spells out the Standards' objectives (Section I.C). Briefly paraphrased, they are to obtain worldwide acceptance of a common standard for calculating and presenting investment performance fairly, uniformly, and with full disclosure; to ensure accurate and consistent performance data for reporting, record keeping, marketing, and presentation; to promote fair, global competition for all markets without creating barriers to entry for new investment management firms; and to foster the notion of industry self-regulation on a global basis. Performance presentation standards thoughtfully and carefully designed by well-informed industry participants who are committed to the ethical principals of fairness and full disclosure may serve to limit the need for expanded regulatory intervention in this area.

In Section I.D, "Overview," the Introduction also states certain key characteristics of the GIPS standards. Among them is the proposition that the Global Investment Performance Standards are *ethical* standards intended to ensure fair representation and full disclosure of an investment firm's performance history. As ethical standards, they are voluntary. Firms that voluntarily choose to comply with the GIPS standards, however, must apply them with the goal of full disclosure and fair representation. This goal is likely to require more than bare compliance with the minimum requirements—for instance, when specific performance situations arise on which the Standards are silent or open to interpretation. In such cases, disclosures other than those required by the Standards may be necessary, and additional or supplemental information may contribute to a full explanation of the performance.

The GIPS standards apply to investment management firms, not to individuals. (We will return to the definition of the firm for the purpose of compliance with the Standards.) Relying on the integrity of input data, the Standards require firms to use certain calculation and presentation methods and to make certain disclosures. In order to promote fair representations of performance, the GIPS standards require firms to include *all* actual fee-paying, discretionary portfolios in aggregates, known as composites, defined by strategy or investment objective. The GIPS standards further require firms to show history for a minimum of five years, or since inception of the firm or composite if either has existed for less than five years. After presenting at least five years of compliant history, the firm must add annual performance each subsequent year building to a 10-year compliant track record.

The GIPS standards consist of **requirements,** which *must* be followed in order for a firm to claim compliance, and **recommendations,** which are optional but *should* be followed because they represent best practice in performance presentation. When the GIPS standards conflict with local law or regulation, the Standards obligate firms to comply with the local requirements and to make full disclosure of the conflict in the performance presentation. The GIPS standards will continue to evolve as the industry tackles additional aspects of performance measurement and recognizes the implications of new investment technologies, instruments, and strategies. For example, certain recommendations in the current version of the GIPS standards might become requirements in the future.

The Introduction additionally includes remarks on the scope of the Standards (see Section I.E). The Standards apply worldwide: Firms from any country may come into compliance with the Standards, and doing so will facilitate their participation in the investment management industry at home and abroad. Firms previously claiming compliance with an IPC-endorsed Country Version of GIPS are granted reciprocity to claim compliance with the revised GIPS Standards for historical periods prior to January 1, 2006. If the firm previously claimed compliance with a CVG, the firm must at a minimum continue to show the historical CVG-compliant track record up to 10 years, or since inception if the firm has been in existence for fewer than 10 years.

As stated in Section I.F, "Compliance," the effective date of the revised Standards is January 1, 2006. (As we will detail in addressing the provisions of the Standards, certain requirements do not take effect until specified later dates. They should be considered recommendations in the interim.) Firms must meet all the requirements set forth in the GIPS standards to claim compliance with the Standards. There can be no exceptions. Accordingly, firms must take all steps necessary to ensure that they have met all the requirements before claiming compliance with the GIPS standards. The GIPS standards acknowledge the role and value of independent third-party performance measurement and composite construction services.

Finally, Section I.G, "Implementing a Global Standard," recognizes the vital part that local sponsoring organizations play in the effective implementation and ongoing administration of the GIPS standards within their countries. Country sponsors link the GIPS EC and the local markets in which investment managers conduct their business. In addition to supporting the adoption of the Standards, country sponsors will ensure that their country's interests are taken into account as the governing body continues to develop the Standards. The GIPS standards also encourage regulators to recognize the benefit of investment management firms' voluntary compliance with standards representing global best practices, to consider enforcing sanctions on false claims of compliance with the GIPS standards as fraudulent advertising, and to advocate independent verification services.

IMPLEMENTATION (1)

Management Commitment. Senior management's stated commitment to the spirit and objectives of the Standards and steadfast willingness to invest the necessary time and resources are essential for a firm to achieve compliance with the GIPS standards. The implementation effort is most likely to succeed if senior management makes achieving compliance a high priority; communicates the importance of the initiative throughout the firm; oversees the preparation of a comprehensive plan; and establishes an adequate budget, with particular attention to information systems requirements.

The GIPS standards are ethical standards, and compliance is not just another marketing tool. Merely adopting the GIPS standards as a means of passing the initial screening in RFP competitions may lead the firm to take shortcuts that ultimately compromise its application of the Standards.

Some firms may wrongly assume that implementation of the GIPS standards involves "re-crunching" a few numbers and reformatting performance presentation tables. In fact, achieving compliance is a complex, challenging, and potentially expensive undertaking.

A firm must also have a high level of commitment from its investment management, operational, administrative, and sales staffs. Achieving and maintaining compliance with the GIPS standards typically involves an investment firm's Portfolio Accounting, Market Data Services, Information Systems, Portfolio Management, Marketing, and Compliance groups, as well as the Performance Measurement team. It is a complex process for investment management organizations to define and document policies, gather and validate input data, calculate rates of return, construct and maintain meaningful composites, and present investment results wholly in compliance with the GIPS standards. Careful planning with the active participation of diverse organizational units is a critical element of the implementation project.

PROVISIONS OF THE GIPS STANDARDS

We turn now to the specific provisions of the GIPS standards. Section II, "Provisions of the Global Investment Performance Standards," presents firmwide requirements and recommendations in subsections addressing the fundamentals of compliance, input data, calculation methodology, composite construction, disclosures, and presentation and reporting. In addition, the Standards include particular provisions for two asset classes requiring special treatment: real estate and private equity.

Fundamentals of Compliance

Section II.0, "Fundamentals of Compliance," opens with a prime requirement: The GIPS standards must be applied on a firmwide basis (Provision II.0.A.1). That is to say, firms cannot claim to be in compliance with the Standards with regard only to certain asset classes, investment strategies, products, or composites.

To comply with the GIPS standards, a firm must be an investment firm, subsidiary, or division *held out to clients or potential clients as a distinct business entity* (Provision II.0.A.2; emphasis added). The GIPS glossary entry defines a **distinct business entity** as a "unit, division, department, or office that is organizationally and functionally segregated from other units, divisions, departments, or offices and retains discretion over the assets it manages and should have autonomy over the investment decision-making process." Possible criteria for identifying a distinct business entity are the organization being a legal entity, having a distinct market or client type, or using a separate and distinct investment process. The way in which the investment management organization is held out to the public is a key factor in defining the firm. For example, if a unit of a larger company specializes in providing investment management services to private clients, and is marketed as a specialist in meeting the investment needs of high-net-worth individuals and family offices, then that organizational unit might qualify as a "firm" for the purpose of GIPS compliance. Certainly, however, the unit's entitlement to be considered a firm under the GIPS standards could be justified if it additionally were incorporated as a subsidiary and had its own dedicated financial analysts, portfolio managers, and traders located in a separate building or area of the company and reporting through a separate chain of command to the parent organization's senior management.

In view of the complexity of modern organizational structures, it may require judgment to determine if a given unit properly meets the definition of a firm. The decision has immediate and lasting practical consequences, however. Because the GIPS standards apply firmwide, the definition of the firm will determine the extent of the initial implementation and ongoing compliance activities. Furthermore, as we will see, the presentation and reporting requirements of the GIPS standards include displaying the percentage of total firm assets represented by a composite or the amount of total firm assets at the end of each annual period (Provision II.5.A.1.c). **Total firm assets** are all assets (whether or not discretionary or fee-paying) for which a firm has investment management responsibility, including assets managed by subadvisers that the firm has authority to select. The definition of the firm establishes the boundaries for determining total firm assets. In addition, subsequent changes in a firm's organization are not permitted to lead to alteration of historical composite results.

Set forth in Sections II.0.A.1–5, the requirements described above are accompanied by a recommendation in Section II.0.B that firms adopt the broadest, most meaningful definition of the firm. (Recall that the GIPS standards consist of requirements, which must be followed without exception in order for a firm to claim compliance, and recommendations, which are optional but represent best practice in performance presentation.) The Standards recommend that the scope of the definition should encompass all offices operating under the same brand regardless of their geographical location and the actual name of the individual investment management companies. We may observe that defining the firm as broadly as possible reduces the likelihood of confusion among investors and regulators over the intended applicability of a claim of compliance.

IMPLEMENTATION (2)

Defining the Firm. For small investment management boutiques, defining the firm may be a relatively easy task, but it can prove challenging for large firms or subsidiary companies.

Consider the case of a super-regional bank whose trust department consists of two separate and distinct divisions, Personal Trust and Institutional Trust. The personal trust division, called Eastern National Bank Personal Trust Services, offers investment management to private individuals and families. The institutional trust division, called Eastern Institutional Asset Advisors, serves tax-exempt nonprofit organizations including pension funds and charitable foundations; it does not solicit or handle noninstitutional business. Each division has its own investment management team, traders, marketing department, administrative personnel, and accounting department. After a few years of operating in this manner, the institutional investment unit decides to achieve compliance with the GIPS standards, but the personal trust department makes a business decision not to implement the Standards. The institutional investment division may nonetheless be in position to become GIPS-compliant because it holds itself out to customers as a distinct business unit, with its own autonomous investment management, research, trading, and administrative team.

Based on the information provided, the institutional trust division seems to satisfy the conditions for defining itself as a firm for the purpose of compliance with the GIPS standards. Sample language might be, "The firm is defined as Eastern Institutional Asset Advisors, the institutional asset management division of Eastern National Bank."

On the other hand, if both divisions were to use the same investment process, approved security list, style models, etc., and merely divided assets between personal and institutional accounts, then neither division alone could compellingly claim compliance. If the senior investment personnel of the personal trust division had authority to dictate the institutional trust division's investment strategy or tactical asset allocations, or to mandate the investment of institutional clients' funds in specific securities, then the institutional trust division would likely not qualify as a distinct business unit having autonomy over the investment decision-making process and discretion over the assets it manages. If the two divisions were organizationally segregated but shared the same trading desk, the institutional trust division would have to determine whether its decision-making autonomy is compromised by the trading arrangement—if the traders merely fill the portfolio manager's orders, then the institutional trust division arguably remains autonomous, but if the traders actively participate in the identification of misvalued securities, a greater impediment to the autonomy argument would exist.

Defining the firm in such a situation calls for the scrupulous exercise of professional judgment, with due attention to the ethical objectives of the Global Investment Performance Standards.

The "fundamentals of compliance" stipulate that firms must document, in writing, their policies and procedures used in establishing and maintaining compliance with all the applicable requirements of the GIPS standards (Provision II.0.A.6). We will see that in addition to the definition of the firm, the policies and procedures to be documented include but are not limited to the criteria for including portfolios in specific composites; the timing of the inclusion and exclusion of new and terminated portfolios, respectively; the firm's definition of discretion; and the treatment of cash flows. Clearly, such documentation will be useful for employees' future reference. In addition, should the firm elect to have its compliance with the GIPS standards independently verified, the verifiers will ask to see the documents articulating all pertinent policies and procedures.

A firm may claim compliance once it has satisfied all the requirements of the GIPS standards (including those we will present later in this chapter for input data, calculation methodology, composite construction, disclosures, and presentation and reporting). Sections II.0.A.7–10 of the Standards list the requirements for a compliance claim. The firm must use the exact wording of the following compliance statement: "[Name of firm] has prepared and presented this report in compliance with the Global Investment Performance Standards (GIPS®)."[8] As we have already pointed out, no exceptions to the Standards are permitted; the firm cannot represent that it is in compliance with the GIPS standards "except for" anything. Moreover, statements characterizing the calculation methodology used in a composite presentation as being in accordance or in compliance with the GIPS standards are prohibited.[9] Statements referring to the performance of a single, existing client as being "calculated in accordance with the Global Investment Performance Standards" are also prohibited except when a GIPS-compliant firm reports the performance of an individual account to the existing client. Furthermore, managers cannot evade the requirements of composite construction and performance presentation and reporting by showing a prospective client the historical record of a selected existing client and implying in any way that the record meets the GIPS standards.

Sections II.0.A.11–15 of the Standards spell out certain "fundamental responsibilities" of GIPS-compliant firms. First, firms are expected to "make every reasonable effort" to provide all prospective clients with a compliant presentation. In other words, firms cannot choose to whom they want to present GIPS-compliant performance. (The Standards clarify that a firm will have met this requirement if a prospect has received a compliant presentation within the previous 12 months.) In addition, firms must provide a list and description of all composites to any prospective client asking for such information, and they must provide upon request a compliant presentation for any composite listed. Discontinued composites must remain on the list for at least five years after discontinuation.

When a GIPS-compliant firm engages in joint marketing activities with other firms, the compliant firm must be distinguished from the other firms, and the marketing communication must make clear which firm is claiming compliance.

It is also among the compliant firm's fundamental responsibilities to keep abreast of developments in the GIPS standards and to comply with the most recent interpretations and updates, notably including Guidance Statements, in accordance with their effective dates.

Finally, the GIPS standards section devoted to "Fundamentals of Compliance" recommends that firms undertake verification, the review of a firm's performance measurement processes and procedures by an independent, knowledgeable third-party verifier in order to establish that a firm claiming compliance has adhered to the Standards (Sections II.0.B.2–3). The Standards make clear that a single verification report must be issued in respect to the whole firm; verification cannot be carried out for a single composite. (We will return to this point when we discuss Section III of the Global Investment Performance Standards, "Verification.") Firms that have been verified are encouraged to add a disclosure to composite presentations or advertisements concerning this fact. The verification disclosure language should read, "[Name of firm] has been verified for the periods [dates] by [name of verifier]. A copy of the verification report is available upon request."

Input Data

Before turning to time-weighted total return calculations, we will discuss the necessary input data. We observed above that accurate input data are a key characteristic of the GIPS standards. In fact, the Standards rely on the integrity of input data, because correct rates of return obviously cannot be computed from incorrect asset values and transaction records. Accurately calculated results presuppose accurate inputs.

The provisions for input data are laid out in Sections II.1.A (requirements) and II.1.B (recommendations) of the GIPS standards. The first requirement is basic: All data and information necessary to support a firm's performance presentation and to perform the required calculations must be captured and maintained. The need for a firm to obtain the inputs required for compliant rate-of-return calculations and performance presentations is self-evident, although not always easily accomplished. "Maintaining" or storing the data and information, as required by the GIPS standards, is sound business practice, similar to documenting the firm's performance-related policies and procedures. Only if the historical input data have been kept can return calculations be replicated for clients, in the event that questions arise, as well as for regulators and verifiers.

There are three central input data concepts having to do with asset valuations. First, portfolio valuations must be based on **market values,** not cost or book values (Provision II.1.A.2). Second, **trade-date accounting** is required for periods beginning January 1, 2005 (Provision II.1.A.5). Third, **accrual accounting** must be used for fixed-income securities and all other assets that accrue interest income (Provision II.1.A.6). Let us consider each of these provisions in turn.

Because market values reflect the prices at which assets could be sold in the marketplace, they represent in aggregate the portfolio's worth—its fair economic value—as of the valuation date. Cost is pertinent to performance measurement only insofar as it reflects the holding's beginning market value. Book value, an accounting convention, is also irrelevant. (Roughly speaking, a financial asset's book value is its cost adjusted for the accretion of income and the amortization of any discount or premium.) For performance measurement, as opposed to financial or tax accounting, it does not matter whether gains and losses are realized or unrealized.[10] Along with investment income, the significant factors are the magnitude and direction of change in the assets' aggregate market value over the measurement period.

Firms are expected to use the best available information in calculating performance, but valuation sources and methods vary with an asset's liquidity. In the case of frequently traded assets in developed capital markets, values reflecting recent purchase and sale transactions are readily available from recognized commercial pricing services. Valuing illiquid real assets and thinly traded securities such as private equities, however, is more complex. We will consider real estate valuation methods and the GIPS Private Equity Valuation Principals later.

A firm's judicious selection of asset-pricing sources is a key element in achieving the fair representation of investment performance. When consultants and custodial banks providing performance measurement services to institutional clients reconcile the rates of return they calculate with those reported by their clients' investment managers, valuation differences frequently are the primary cause of variances that exceed tolerance ranges. Managers sometimes challenge the custodian's valuations, contending that their daily transactional activity gives them better information about market-clearing prices than the custodian can derive secondhand from commercial market data services. Whatever the merits of this argument in specific cases, the fact remains that ascertaining the most correct asset market values is essential for the fair representation of performance. In the spirit of the GIPS standards, managers should use pricing sources and procedures that reflect objectively established market values consistently. Switching from one source to another so as to improve stated performance at the end of a reporting period is ethically indefensible. Should the firm undertake the verification process, the verifier must determine the firm's policy with regard to the market valuation of investment securities. (See "Required Verification Procedures," Section III.B.1.d.vi.)

The GIPS standards require that firms use trade-date accounting for the purpose of performance measurement for periods beginning January 1, 2005 (Provision II.1.A.5). This requirement is related to the mandatory use of market values. A portfolio manager makes purchase and sale decisions based on current market conditions. (Even holding a security may be considered an investment decision, continuously renewed, to "buy" the security, or equivalently not to sell it and reinvest the proceeds in another security, at the current market value.) The final objective of performance measurement is to quantify the value added by investment management, and the portfolio manager's determinations to buy or hold undervalued securities and to sell overvalued securities reflect her appraisal of those securities' relative attractiveness at the time of her decisions. For the purposes of the GIPS standards, under trade-date accounting the "transaction is reflected in the portfolio on the date of the purchase or sale, and not on the settlement date." Settlement—the actual exchange of a security for cash at the price agreed on when the trade was executed—may take place days later. **Settlement-date accounting** is defined as "recognizing the asset or liability on the date in which the exchange of cash, securities, and paperwork involved in a transaction is completed." If the trade and settlement dates straddle the end date of a performance measurement period, then return comparisons between portfolios that use settlement-date accounting, on one hand, and portfolios that use trade-date accounting, or benchmarks, on the other, may be invalid. The principal behind requiring trade-date accounting is to ensure that no significant lag occurs between a trade's execution and its reflection in the portfolio's performance. For compliance with the GIPS standards, the trade-date accounting requirement is considered to be satisfied provided that transactions are recorded and recognized consistently and within normal market practice, up to three days after trade date.

The GIPS standards also stipulate that accrual accounting must be used for fixed-income securities and all other assets that accrue interest income (Provision II.1.A.6). This provision is also related to the market valuation of assets. When a conventional bond is sold, it will be exchanged for cash in an amount that reflects not only the agreed-upon price of the instrument but also the seller's entitlement to interest earned but not yet paid. Similarly, for GIPS-compliant performance, interest income on an asset that is held must be recognized as it is earned versus when it is received. Accordingly, interest income earned but not yet received must be included in the market value of fixed-income securities and all other assets that accrue interest income. With respect to dividend-paying equities, the GIPS standards recommend that dividends be accrued and reflected in the securities' market values as of the ex-dividend date (Provision II.1.B.1).

In addition to the key valuation-related provisions explained above, the input data requirements of the GIPS standards specify the frequency and timing of portfolio valuations (Provisions II.1.A.3–4). Table 41.1 presents the pertinent requirements.

External cash flows are cash, securities, or assets that enter or exit a portfolio. The GIPS glossary defines external cash flows as "cash, securities, or assets that enter or exit a portfolio." The Standards do not quantify "large" external cash flows; firms are required to define composite-specific amounts or percentages that constitute large external cash flows. Later in this chapter, we examine the significance of cash flows for rate-of-return calculations.

TABLE 41.1   Frequency and Timing of Portfolio Valuations

For Periods . . .	Portfolios Must Be Valued . . .
Prior to January 1, 2001	At least quarterly
Between January 1, 2001, and January 1, 2010	At least monthly
Beginning January 1, 2010	On the date of all large external cash flows
	As of the calendar month-end or the last business day of the month[11]

The Standards additionally require that, for periods beginning January 1, 2006, the firm's composites, and necessarily the portfolios within the composites, must have consistent beginning and ending *annual* valuation dates. Unless the composite is reported on a noncalendar fiscal year, the beginning and ending valuation dates must be at calendar year-end or on the last business day of the year (Provision II.1.A.7).

As a practical matter, the GIPS standards' input data requirements and recommendations have critically important implications for the design of a firm's performance measurement system, including its interface with the firm's portfolio accounting system. Management must be conclusively assured that portfolio valuations are performed properly and that all the data necessary for performance calculations and presentations are captured and maintained.

IMPLEMENTATION (3)

Input Data. Typically, the firm's portfolio accounting system is the primary source of data inputs to the performance measurement system. (The accounting system may itself have automated feeds from other sources, including the trading system for security transactions and external data services for market valuations.) What we may call "performance accounting"—the compilation of data inputs for rate-of-return calculations—differs from financial accounting, however, and the differences must be recognized when designing an interface between the portfolio accounting system and the performance measurement system. For instance, book values and the distinction between realized and unrealized capital gains and losses are necessary for financial accounting but inappropriate or irrelevant for before-tax performance measurement. Convertible and hybrid securities must be treated consistently across time and within composites (Provision II.3.A.6). Investment management fees may require special treatment. A net-of-fee return is defined as the gross return reduced by the **investment management fee.** If investment management fees are paid directly from the client's account, they must be treated as external cash flows for gross-of-fee return calculations; if they are not paid directly from the client's account, they must be attributed to the portfolio and deducted for net-of-fee performance calculations. In order to meet the requirements—and, optimally, the recommendations—of the GIPS standards for input data, calculation methodology, composite construction, and performance presentation and reporting, the firm must comprehensively address these and many other accounting- and system-related issues.

Calculation Methodology: Time-Weighted Total Return

The GIPS standards mandate the use of a total rate of return, called total return for short (Provision II.2.A.1). Total return is the most comprehensive and accurate expression of investment results because it reflects the change in portfolio value during the measurement period, taking into account not only income but also realized and unrealized gains and losses. (Recall from our discussion of input data that, for performance measurement, it does not matter whether gains and losses are transactionally realized. What matters is the change in market value.) In other words, total return captures both the return from investment income and the return from capital gains or losses.

In the simplest case, when no external cash flows (i.e., client-initiated additions to or withdrawals from invested assets) occur during the period, calculating total return is straightforward:

$$r_t = \frac{MV_1 - MV_0}{MV_0} \qquad (41.1)$$

where r_t is the total return for period t, MV_1 is the full market value of the portfolio, including accrued income, at the end of the period; and MV_0 is the portfolio's market value, including accrued income, at the beginning of the period. (Recall that the requirement to include accrued interest income in market values of fixed-income securities appears in Provision II.1.A.6, and the recommendation that accrual accounting should be used for dividends as of the ex-dividend date appears in Provision II.1.B.1.) Equation 41.1 assumes that income received remains in the portfolio and expresses return as the ratio of the change in market value during the period to the market value at the start of the period. Despite its extreme simplicity, the total return formula shown above produces a perfectly accurate representation of investment results in a single period with no external cash flows. As we will see, this formula is also used to calculate subperiod results under the optimal "intraperiod valuation" method when external cash flows occur.

Most portfolios, of course, do have external cash flows. A pension fund, for example, routinely has additions to capital in the form of employer and employee contributions, as well as withdrawals to meet current liabilities. The fund's investment advisers, therefore, expect to see transfers into and out of the portfolios they manage on behalf of the beneficiaries. In evaluating an investment firm, the effect of such contributions and withdrawals should be removed from the return calculation because the timing and amount of external cash flows are typically controlled not by the firm but by the client (in this case, the pension plan sponsor). Because performance measurement attempts to quantify the value added by investment decisions, the GIPS standards require the use of time-weighted rates of return, or approximations to time-weighted rates of return, to eliminate the impact of external cash flows on the return calculation.

Provision II.2.A.2 specifies the use of **time-weighted rates of return** that adjust for external cash flows.[12] At a minimum, for periods beginning January 1, 2005, firms must approximate rates of return that adjust for daily weighted external cash flows, and for periods beginning January 1, 2010, firms must value portfolios on the date of all large external cash flows. (In the interim, Provision II.2.B.3 recommends that firms value portfolios on the date of all large external cash flows.) We will return to the definition of "large" external cash flows below.

The most accurate way to calculate a total return for a measurement period in which external cash flows occur is to value the portfolio whenever an external cash flow occurs, compute a subperiod return, and geometrically chain-link subperiod returns expressed in relative form according to the following formula:

$$r_{twr} = (1 + r_{t,1}) \times (1 + r_{t,2}) \times \ldots \times (1 + r_{t,n}) - 1 \qquad (41.2)$$

where r_{twr} is the time-weighted total return for the entire period and $r_{t,1}$ through $r_{t,n}$ are the subperiod returns. We explicitly point out that Provision II.2.A.2 requires periodic returns to be geometrically linked—that is, converted to relative form $(1 + r)$ and multiplied.

For example, consider a portfolio with a beginning market value of $100,000 as of May 31, 2005, a market value of $109,000 on June 5, 2005 (including a cash contribution of $10,000 received that day), and an ending market value of $110,550 on June 30, 2005. Consider that the first subperiod ends and the second begins on the cash flow date, such that the ending market value for subperiod 1 is $99,000 ($109,000 less the contribution of $10,000) and the beginning market value for Subperiod 2, including the contribution, is $109,000. The portfolio's true time-weighted return using the intraperiod valuation method is 0.41 percent, computed as follows:

$$
\begin{aligned}
r_{t,1} &= \frac{MV_1 - MV_0}{MV_0} = \frac{(109,000 - 10,000) - 100,000}{100,000} \\
&= \frac{99,000 - 100,000}{100,000} = -0.01 \\
r_{t,2} &= \frac{MV_1 - MV_0}{MV_0} = \frac{110,550 - 109,000}{109,000} = 0.0142 \\
r_{twr} &= (1 + r_{t,1}) \times (1 + r_{t,2}) - 1 = [1 + (-0.01)] \times (1 + 0.0142) - 1 \\
&= 1.0041 - 1 = 0.0041 = 0.41\%
\end{aligned}
$$

Geometric linking, as shown here, is correct (and required by the GIPS standards) because returns are compounded and so are not additive but multiplicative.

Assuming the input data are valid, the intraperiod valuation method illustrated above gives truly accurate total returns. The GIPS governance body recognizes, however, that intraperiod portfolio valuations are costly for firms in terms of both the security price data required and the systems capabilities needed to store and process the data. As noted, in the current version of the GIPS standards, portfolio valuations on the date of all large external cash flows is recommended now and will be required for periods beginning January 1, 2010. In the meantime, however, GIPS-compliant firms can use certain approximation methods to compute estimated time-weighted returns.

For periods prior to January 1, 2005, cash flows can be assumed to occur at the midpoint of the measurement period. The Original Dietz method reflects this midpoint assumption:

$$r_{Dietz} = \frac{MV_1 - MV_0 - CF}{MV_0 + (0.5 \times CF)} \qquad (41.3)$$

where CF is the net external cash flow for the period.

Using the same example, the Original Dietz formula gives a return of 0.52 percent:

$$
\begin{aligned}
r_{Dietz} &= \frac{MV_1 - MV_0 - CF}{MV_0 + (0.5 \times CF)} \\
&= \frac{110,550 - 100,000 - 10,000}{100,000 + (0.5 \times 10,000)} = 0.0052 = 0.52\%
\end{aligned}
$$

A time-weighted total return calculation that adjusts for *daily* weighted cash flows is required for periods after January 1, 2005. Examples of acceptable approaches are the Modified

Dietz method and the Modified Internal Rate of Return (Modified IRR) method, both of which weight each cash flow by the proportion of the measurement period it is held in the portfolio.

The formula for estimating the time-weighted rate of return using the Modified Dietz method is

$$r_{ModDietz} = \frac{MV_1 - MV_0 - CF}{MV_0 + \sum(CF_i \times w_i)} \tag{41.4}$$

where $\sum(CF_i \times w_i)$ is the sum of each cash flow multiplied by its weight and $CF = \sum CF_i$. The weight (w_i) is simply the proportion of the measurement period, in days, that each cash flow has been in the portfolio:

$$w_i = \frac{CD - D_i}{CD} \tag{41.5}$$

where CD is the total number of calendar days in the period and D_i is the number of calendar days from the beginning of the period that cash flow CF_i occurs. (Note that this formula assumes that cash flows occur at the end of the day.)[13] In our example, there is a $10,000 contribution on June 5, so $D_i = 5$, and there are 30 days in June, so $CD = 30$. The proportion of the measurement period that the $10,000 is in the portfolio is thus

$$w_i = \frac{CD - D_i}{CD} = \frac{30 - 5}{30} = \frac{25}{30} = 0.83$$

Applying the Modified Dietz formula to the same example gives a return of 0.51 percent:

$$\begin{aligned} r_{ModDietz} &= \frac{MV_1 - MV_0 - CF}{MV_0 + \sum(CF_i \times w_i)} \\ &= \frac{110,550 - 100,000 - 10,000}{100,000 + [10,000 \times (25/30)]} = 0.0051 = 0.51\% \end{aligned}$$

The Modified or Linked IRR method is another estimation approach acceptable prior to January 1, 2010. This method determines the internal rate of return (IRR) for the period, adjusted to take into effect the timing of cash flows. The Modified IRR is the value of r that satisfies the following equation:

$$\text{Ending Market Value} = MV_1 = \sum[CF_i \times (1 + r)^{w_i}] + MV_0(1 + r) \tag{41.6}$$

where the exponent, w_i, is as previously defined the ratio of the amount of time CF_i is in the portfolio to the total time in the measurement period. The equation is solved iteratively by a trial-and-error procedure, settling on the value of r that makes the series of cash flows equal to the ending market value.[14] The Modified IRR method is computationally intensive, but programs are available for solving the equation efficiently. (Some Modified IRR programs use the Modified Dietz return as an initial estimate or seed value.) Applying the Modified IRR method to the simple example used earlier in this section gives a result of 0.51 percent, the same as the rate of return found with the Modified Dietz method.

Bear in mind that approximation methods such as Modified Dietz and Modified IRR will not meet the GIPS standards for periods after January 1, 2010, when firms will be required to value portfolios on the date of all large external cash flows.

Return Calculations: External Cash Flows

In the previous section, different methodologies for calculating a rate of return from a single set of input data gave different answers. To recapitulate:

Inputs:

> Market value on May 31: $100,000
> Cash flow on June 5: +$10,000
> Market value on June 5: $109,000 (after the cash flow)
> Market value on June 30: $110,550

Solutions:

> True time-weighted return: 0.41 percent
> Original Dietz method: 0.52 percent
> Modified Dietz method: 0.51 percent
> Modified IRR method: 0.51 percent

In this particular example, the estimated rates of return given by the Modified Dietz and Modified IRR methods are nearly the same as the estimated return calculated by the Original Dietz method, which assumes that the external cash flow occurred at midmonth. The external cash flow causes the day-weighted estimates (0.51 percent) to vary by 10 basis points from the true time-weighted return (0.41 percent).

To appreciate the potentially distorting impact of external cash flows on estimated time-weighted rates of return, consider Figure 41.2 through 41.4. The exhibits depict a "market index" with a value of 100 as of May 31, and the data below each exhibit represent portfolios with a market value of $100,000 on May 31 and contributions of $10,000 received on June 5 (on the left-hand side) and June 15 (on the right-hand side). In flat and steadily rising or falling markets (illustrated in Figure 41.2 and Figure 41.3), the timing of the cash flows has a relatively modest impact on the accuracy of the estimates. We can observe this phenomenon by comparing the true time-weighted returns with those calculated using the Modified Dietz method. (Note that the Modified Dietz method is mathematically equivalent to the Original Dietz method when the cash flow occurs at the midpoint of the measurement period.) When

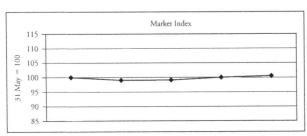

r_{twr}				r_{twr}		
	31-May Market Value	$ 100,000			31-May Market Value	$ 100,000
−1.00%	5-Jun Market Value	$ 99,000		−0.93%	15-Jun Market Value	$ 99,075
	Contribution	$ 10,000			Contribution	$ 10,000
	Total Market Value	$ 109,000			Total Market Value	$ 109,075
1.42%	30-Jun Market Value	$ 110,550		1.35%	30-Jun Market Value	$ 110,550
0.41%	Modified Dietz	0.51%		0.41%	Modified Dietz	0.52%

FIGURE 41.2   Impact of Cash Flows in a Flat Market

Source: Paula Gehr.

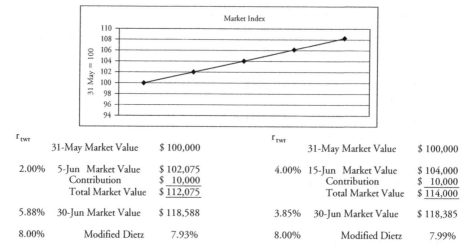

FIGURE 41.3   Impact of Cash Flows in a Steadily Rising Market

Source: Paula Gehr.

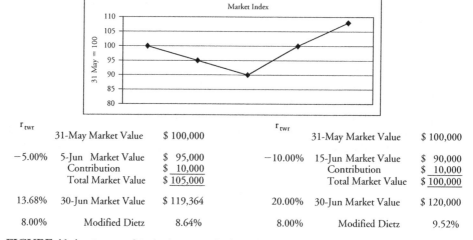

FIGURE 41.4   Impact of Cash Flows in Volatile Market

Source: Paula Gehr.

markets are volatile, however, as illustrated in Figure 41.4, large external cash flows may have a material impact on the accuracy of the estimated return. The reader should work through these examples using the formulas for the true time-weighted return and the Modified Dietz method. The calculations for the first example, on the left-hand side of Figure 41.2, were shown above.

The GIPS standards require firms to formulate and document composite-specific policies for the treatment of external cash flows and to adhere to those policies consistently. (Provision II.2.A.2 reads in pertinent part, "External cash flows must be treated in a consistent manner with the firm's documented, composite-specific policy.") Each policy should describe the firm's methodology for computing time-weighted returns and the firm's assumptions about the timing of capital inflows and outflows. If it is the firm's rule to revalue portfolios on the date of a large external cash flow, as the GIPS standards recommend, then the firm should also state that policy.

As we have previously remarked, the Standards offer no quantitative definition of large external cash flows. Taking into account the liquidity of the market segments or asset classes and the nature of the investment strategy, firms must make their own determinations of significance for each composite. For example, a relatively high percentage of portfolio value might be easily deployed in a developed equity market, while a lower percentage of portfolio value might be deemed the appropriate criterion for a large external cash flow in a comparatively illiquid emerging debt market.

A composite-specific policy may define a "large" external cash flow in terms of an amount or a percentage. Whatever definition a firm adopts, it must document the policy and follow it without exception. For example, if a firm defines a large external cash flow for a specific composite and states that portfolios in that composite are revalued on the date of large external cash flows, then the firm must conform to its own policy. If a portfolio that belongs to the composite in question receives a large external cash flow, as defined, the firm is not at liberty to omit the revaluation on the grounds that the market was not especially volatile during the measurement period. Inconsistent applications of firm policies constitute a breach of the GIPS standards.

IMPLEMENTATION (4)

Return Calculation Policies. The GIPS standards state, "Time-weighted rates of return that adjust for external cash flows must be used. Periodic returns must be geometrically linked. External cash flows must be treated in a consistent manner with the firm's documented, composite-specific policy" (excerpted from Provision II.2.A.2). The Standards also recommend, "Firms should value portfolios on the date of all large external cash flows" (Provision II.2.B.3). The following are examples of internal policy statements addressing these elements.

Portfolio return calculation methodology: "Eastern Institutional Asset Advisors employs the Modified Dietz method to compute portfolio time-weighted rates of return on a monthly basis. Returns for longer measurement periods are computed by geometrically linking the monthly returns."

Large external cash flows: "Eastern Institutional Asset Advisors revalues portfolios that belong to the Large-Cap Domestic Equity composite when capital equal to 10 percent or more of current market value is contributed or withdrawn. Intraperiod portfolio valuations are based on security market values provided by the client's custodian."

Additional Portfolio Return Calculation Standards

The GIPS standards for calculation methodology include further provisions directly affecting portfolio returns. (We will discuss the calculation-related guidelines for composites in a later section.)

The first requirement not previously addressed is that returns from cash and cash equivalents held in portfolios must be included in total return calculations (Provision II.2.A.4). One of the primary purposes of performance measurement is to enable prospective clients and, by extension, their consultants to evaluate an investment management firm's results. Within the constraints established by a client's investment policy statement (IPS), active managers often have discretion to decide what portion of a portfolio's assets to hold in cash or cash equivalents. In other words, the cash allocation decision may be under the manager's control, and thus return calculations must reflect the contribution of the cash and cash equivalents to investment results.

Consider the case of an institutional investor such as a defined-benefit pension plan sponsor. The structure of the sponsor's investment program is, generally, based on an asset allocation or, preferably, an asset/liability study identifying the optimal mix of asset classes to meet the fund's financial objectives at an acceptable level of risk. The sponsor retains investment management firms to invest the fund's assets in specific markets in accordance with the study results. For example, within the domestic equity allocation, the sponsor might hire one firm to invest a certain portion of the fund's assets in small-cap growth stocks and another firm to invest a portion in large-cap value stocks. The sponsor expects the managers to remain fully invested in their mandated market sectors at all times. The sponsor's IPS may, however, allow the managers to hold some amount (e.g., up to 5 percent of portfolio assets) in cash and cash equivalents, if only to accommodate frictional cash thrown off in the process of buying and selling securities. (The client will usually define "cash equivalents," for example, as money market instruments and fixed income securities with less than one year to maturity.) In this case, it is up to the manager to decide how much cash to hold, up to 5 percent of assets.

The total portfolio return will be higher or lower depending on how much cash the manager holds and how the equity and money markets perform relative to one another during the measurement period. A few simple scenarios based on actual historical U.S. market returns will illustrate these points. First, in a rising equity market, cash positions reduce overall portfolio returns; the higher the cash position, the lower the portfolio return. This relationship is illustrated in Table 41.2 in which increasing the cash position (represented here by U.S. Treasury bills) from 1 percent to 5 percent of portfolio assets reduces the portfolio return for a three-month period by 26 basis points (0.26 percent).

In contrast, a higher cash position improves the portfolio return in a falling market. Table 41.3 illustrates this result, whereby increasing the percentage of the portfolio held in cash from 1 percent to 5 percent boosts the three-month portfolio return by 11 basis points (0.11 percent).

TABLE 41.2   Illustration of the Effect of Cash Holdings in Rising Markets

	1% Held in Cash		5% Held in Cash	
	Weight	Return	Weight	Return
Broad U.S. equity market index	99%	6.57%	95%	6.57%
U.S. Treasury bills	1	0.26	5	0.26
Total portfolio	100	6.51	100	6.25

TABLE 41.3   Illustration of the Effect of Cash Holdings in Declining Markets

	1% Held in Cash		5% Held in Cash	
	Weight	Return	Weight	Return
Broad U.S. equity market index	99%	−2.39%	95%	−2.39%
U.S. Treasury bills	1	10.45	5	10.45
Total portfolio	100	−2.36	100	−2.25

Note that cash and cash equivalents must be included in the total return calculation even if the cash is not actually invested by the same person or group. The amount of cash available for short-term investment is more important to overall portfolio results than the money market manager's success in outperforming the short-term market. For the rising and falling equity markets described above, Figure 41.5 illustrates the relative impact of the portfolio manager's increasing the cash allocation from 1 percent to 5 percent and the money market trader's simultaneously achieving excess returns 50 basis points (0.5 percent) higher than Treasury bill returns. The portfolio manager's cash allocation decision has a substantially greater effect on overall portfolio returns than does the money market trader's proficiency in selecting attractive short-term investments.

The GIPS standards further require that returns be calculated after the deduction of actual—not estimated—trading expenses (Provision II.2.A.5). Trading expenses are transaction costs incurred in the purchase or sale of securities, and the performance calculation must include them because these expenses must be paid in order to execute the investment strategy. The GIPS glossary defines **trading expenses** as the costs of buying or selling a security and notes that these costs typically take the form of brokerage commissions or spreads from either internal or external brokers. Commissions are explicit costs, generally a negotiated amount per share of common stock bought or sold, intended to compensate the broker, as the investor's agent, for arranging and settling trades. Bid–ask spreads are the difference between the price at which a dealer, acting for his firm's account, is willing to buy a security from a seller and the price at which he is willing to sell the security to a buyer. From the investor's perspective, the spread is the cost of immediacy or liquidity, and it compensates the dealer for both the cost of operations and the risk of adverse selection (the possibility that a well-informed trader has better information than the dealer has about the fundamental value of a security in the dealer's inventory).[15] Actual trading expenses are necessary input data for GIPS-compliant rate-of-return calculations.

It merits mention in this context that, as the GIPS glossary makes clear, **custody fees** should not be considered direct transaction costs, even when they are charged on a per-transaction basis. Accordingly, they are not to be included among the trading expenses required to be deducted in calculating rates of return.

From a performance measurement perspective, although transaction costs are unavoidably part of executing an investment strategy, they will naturally be higher in a portfolio with

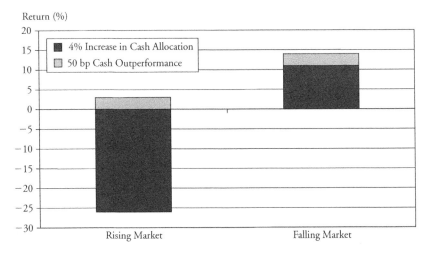

FIGURE 41.5   Impact of Cash on Portfolio Returns

relatively greater turnover. External cash flows, whether inbound or outbound, will occasion a higher-than-normal volume of security transactions, but on an ongoing basis, a manager generally has control over portfolio turnover. A firm's trading capabilities will also affect its level of transaction costs. Although it is not a matter of compliance with the GIPS standards, the investment manager has an ethical and fiduciary responsibility to achieve best execution on behalf of clients. If a client's directed brokerage program requires the firm to channel trades through approved brokers, regular communication with the client is in order.[16]

Returning to the GIPS standards, there are additional requirements when trading expenses cannot be broken out of **bundled fees**, that is, combined fees, which may include any mix of management, transaction, custody, and other administrative charges. The GIPS Glossary cites all-in fees and wrap fees as examples of bundled fees. All-in fee arrangements are common when a single company offers diverse services such as asset management, brokerage, and custody. Wrap fees are specific to an investment product, namely a wrap-fee account (frequently called a separately managed account, or SMA), whereby a sponsoring firm typically engages other firms as subadvisers and service providers. When trading expenses are inextricable, the gross return must be reduced by the entire amount of the bundled fee or by that portion of the bundled fee that includes the direct trading expenses. Specifically, when calculating returns gross of investment management fees, the entire bundled fee or the portion of the bundled fee that includes trading expenses must be deducted. When calculating returns net of investment management fees, the entire bundled fee or the portion(s) of the bundled fee that include the investment management fee and the trading expenses must be deducted. These requirements are presented in Provisions II.2.A.7.a–b, where it is twice reiterated that the use of estimated trading expenses is not permitted.

Finally, it remains to address a recommendation of the GIPS standards pertinent to portfolio return calculations. Standard II.2.B.1 recommends that returns be calculated net of nonreclaimable withholding taxes on dividends, interest, and capital gains. This provision applies to portfolios invested in nondomestic securities. Some countries allow certain kinds of investors to recoup a portion of withholding taxes by filing claims. Withholding taxes subject to reclamation should be accrued until such time as they are actually recovered, and withholding taxes that cannot be recovered should be treated like other transaction costs and deducted from the portfolio before returns are calculated.

Composite Return Calculation Standards

The notion of a composite is central to the GIPS standards. Because composite returns purport to convey the firm's investment results for a given strategy, style, or objective, proper composite construction is essential to achieving the Standards' ethical aims, which are fair representation and full disclosure of the firm's performance.

A composite may be thought of as a combined account composed of similar portfolios in proportion to their weights as a percent of the composite's total assets. Accordingly, the composite return is the asset-weighted average of the returns of all the individual constituent portfolios. In addition to governing the calculation methodology for portfolio returns, the GIPS standards prescribe the asset-weighting methods for composite return calculations.

Standard II.2.A.3 reads, "Composite returns must be calculated by asset-weighting the individual portfolio returns using beginning-of-period values or a method that reflects both beginning-of-period values and external cash flows." Let us explore these methods in an example. Table 41.4 displays the beginning asset market values of four portfolios that, taken together, constitute a composite. The exhibit also shows the external cash flows experienced

TABLE 41.4   A Composite Including Four Portfolios: Weighted External Cash Flows

	Cash Flow Weighting Factor	Portfolio ($ Thousands)				
		A	B	C	D	Total
Beginning assets (May 31)		100.00	97.40	112.94	124.47	434.81
External cash flows:						
June 5	0.83	10.00	15.00			25.00
June 8	0.73				−15.00	−15.00
June 17	0.43		−5.00			−5.00
June 24	0.20				−6.50	−6.50
June 29	0.03		−2.50		−4.00	−6.50
Ending assets (June 30)		110.55	105.20	113.30	100.50	429.55
Beginning assets + Weighted cash flows		108.30	107.63	112.94	112.10	440.97
Percent of total beginning assets		23.00%	22.40%	25.97%	28.63%	100.00%
Percent of total beginning assets + Weighted cash flows		24.56%	24.41%	25.61%	25.42%	100.00%

Note: Weighted cash flows reflect two-decimal-place precision in the weighting factors.

by each portfolio during the month of June. (We have seen Portfolio A before.) For completeness, the exhibit also shows each portfolio's ending market value.

Determining the percentage of total composite assets held in each portfolio at the beginning of the measurement period is straightforward. Portfolio A had a beginning market value of $100,000, and all four portfolios combined had a beginning market value of approximately $435,000, so the percentage held by Portfolio A is 100/434.81 = 0.23 = 23%. As we will show in a moment, under a method reflecting just beginning-of-period values, we can calculate the composite return by multiplying the individual portfolio returns by the percentage of beginning composite assets held in each portfolio and summing the products.

Determining the return impact of portfolios based on beginning assets and weighted external cash flows is a little more complex. The weighting factor, however, is already familiar from our discussion of the Modified Dietz rate-of-return calculation. Each external cash flow is weighted in proportion to percentage of the time it is held in the portfolio during the measurement period. Recall Equation 41.5:

$$w_i = \frac{CD - D_i}{CD}$$

where CD is the total number of calendar days in the period and D_i is the number of calendar days since the beginning of the period when cash flow CF_i occurs. Table 41.4 showed the weighting factor computed to two decimal places with this formula for each of the days in the measurement period (the month of June) on which external cash flows occur that affect any of the portfolios in the composite. The exhibit also showed the weighted external cash flows under the two methods discussed. For the method incorporating weighted external cash flows, the sum of beginning assets and weighted external cash flows, V_p, is calculated as

$$V_P = MV_0 + \Sigma(CF_i \times w_i) \tag{41.7}$$

where MV_0 is the portfolio's beginning market value and $\Sigma(CF_i \times w_i)$ is the sum of each portfolio's weighted external cash inflows and outflows. Note that the right-hand side in Equation 41.7 is the denominator of the Modified Dietz formula (see Equation 41.4).

The composite return is the weighted-average return of the individual portfolios that belong to that composite. Under the "beginning assets" weighting method, the composite return calculation is

$$r_C = \Sigma\left(r_{pi} \times \frac{MV_{0,pi}}{\Sigma MV_{0,pi}}\right) \tag{41.8}$$

where r_C is the composite return, r_{pi} is the return of an individual portfolio i, $MV_{0,pi}$ is the beginning market value of portfolio i, and $\Sigma MV_{0,pi}$ is the total beginning market value of all the individual portfolios in the composite. In other words, the composite return is the sum of the individual portfolio returns weighted in proportion to their respective percentages of aggregate beginning assets.

Under the alternate "beginning assets plus weighted cash flows" method, the return calculation uses the individual portfolios' V_P, computed above, in place of $MV_{0,pi}$:

$$r_C = \Sigma\left(r_{pi} \times \frac{V_{pi}}{\Sigma V_{pi}}\right) \tag{41.9}$$

Table 41.5 supplies each individual portfolio's return for the month of June and presents the composite returns resulting from these two weighting methods.

Under the "beginning assets" weighting method, the composite return shown in Table 41.5 is

$r_C = (0.0051 \times 0.23) + (0.0028 \times 0.224) + (0.0032 \times 0.2597) + (0.0136 \times 0.2863)$
$= 0.0065 = 0.65\%$

Similarly, the composite return under the "beginning assets plus weighted cash flows" method is

$r_C = (0.0051 \times 0.2456) + (0.0028 \times 0.2441) + (0.0032 \times 0.2561) + (0.0136 \times 0.2542)$
$= 0.0062 = 0.62\%$

TABLE 41.5   Composite Returns

	Percent of Beginning Assets	Percent of Beginning Assets + Weighted Cash Flows	Return for Month of June
Portfolio A	23.00%	24.56%	0.51%
Portfolio B	22.40	24.41	0.28
Portfolio C	25.97	25.61	0.32
Portfolio D	28.63	25.42	1.36
	100.00%	100.00%	
Composite Return:			
Based on beginning assets			0.65
Based on beginning assets + Weighted cash flows			0.62

Mathematically astute performance analysts may already have discerned another valid way to compute composite returns under a method that correctly reflects both beginning-of-period values and external cash flows. Beginning assets and intraperiod external cash flows can be summed and, treating the entire composite as though it were a single portfolio, the return can be computed directly with the Modified Dietz formula. Paying attention to the direction of the cash flows, this approach can be illustrated with data from Table 41.7, using Equation 41.4:

$$r_{ModDietz} = \frac{MV_1 - MV_0 - CF}{MV_0 + \sum(CF_i \times w_i)}$$

$$r_C = \frac{429.55 - 434.81 - 25 - (-15) - (-5) - (-6.5) - (-6.5)}{440.97}$$

$$= \frac{2.74}{440.97} = 0.0062 = 0.62\%$$

In the interest of ensuring that firms present composite returns with reasonable accuracy, the GIPS standards specify the required frequency of asset weighting. Provision II.2.A.6 states that for periods beginning January 1, 2006, firms must calculate composite returns by asset weighting the individual portfolio returns at least quarterly. For periods beginning January 1, 2010, composite returns must be calculated by asset weighting the individual portfolio returns at least monthly. In the meantime, Provision II.2.B.2 recommends asset weighting portfolios at least on a monthly basis. The less frequently the asset-weighting exercise is conducted, the greater the likelihood that aggregate composite returns will inaccurately reflect the constituent portfolios' performance. We will encounter this issue again, and illustrate the potential for returns to drift away from mathematically precise computations, when we discuss custom benchmark rebalancing.

Constructing Composites I—Defining Discretion

In order to prevent firms from presenting only their best-performing portfolios to prospective clients, the GIPS standards require that all of the compliant firm's actual fee-paying discretionary portfolios must be included in at least one composite. The first requirement for composite construction reads, "All actual, fee-paying, discretionary portfolios must be included in at least one composite. Although non-fee-paying discretionary portfolios may be included in a composite (with appropriate disclosures), nondiscretionary portfolios are not permitted to be included in a firm's composites" (Provision II.3.A.1).

IMPLEMENTATION (5)

Composite Construction: Portfolio Documentation. The GIPS standards require that all data and information necessary to support a firm's performance presentation must be captured and maintained (Provision II.1.A.1). At the outset of the implementation project, it is useful to develop a complete list of the firm's accounts. The list can then be used to check that all documentation such as investment management contracts, custody agreements, IPSs, and compliance documents are available and up to date. This exercise creates a good opportunity for managers and administrative staff to confirm that portfolios are discretionary and to verify target asset mixes, acceptable asset ranges, account size, tax status, investment restrictions, and other characteristics pertinent to the portfolios' assignment to composites. It is also advisable to conduct a formal review and update of the master account list annually. Doing so will assure that documentation is kept current and that portfolios are assigned to the correct composites, particularly if clients have modified portfolio mandates and constraints during the year. The review will also point out the need for the creation of new composites if a significant number of accounts no longer fit into existing composites or if a new investment strategy is launched.

A key term in this requirement is "discretionary." If an actual, fee-paying portfolio is discretionary, it must be included in at least one composite; if it is not discretionary, it must not be included in any composite. A portfolio is discretionary if the manager is able to implement the intended investment strategy. For example, the manager of a fully discretionary domestic mid-cap value portfolio is free to purchase any stock issued in the investor's home country that meets the pertinent market capitalization and style criteria. The firm might define mid-cap stocks as those whose market capitalization falls within a certain range. Similarly, the firm might define value stocks in terms of their price-to-earnings multiple, price-to-book ratio, dividend yield, or other characteristics intended to distinguish them from growth stocks. In line with best practice, the firm and the client will agree in advance that the portfolio's investment objective is to outperform a specified benchmark that is an appropriate measure of success in the domestic mid-cap market. For instance, the firm might construct a custom benchmark that is acceptable to the client, or the firm and the client might agree to use a commercially available index that mirrors the domestic mid-cap market.

If the client imposes restrictions on the manager's freedom to make investment decisions to buy, hold, and sell securities so as to carry out the investment strategy and achieve the portfolio's financial objectives, then the manager must consider whether the portfolio is in fact discretionary. In general, restrictions that impede the investment process to such an extent that the strategy cannot be implemented as intended may be presumed to render the portfolio nondiscretionary.

Investors commonly set forth investment restrictions in investment policy statements. In addition to articulating the investor's overall financial objectives, an IPS normally expresses a number of constraints intended to limit the investment risks to which the assets are exposed. For example, the IPS may limit an individual equity portfolio's economic sector exposure to a certain percentage of portfolio assets or a certain relationship to the comparable benchmark weight: "No portfolio shall hold more than 15 percent of assets or 125 percent of the corresponding benchmark weight, whichever is greater, in any given sector, such as consumer discretionary stocks or technology stocks." A fixed-income portfolio may be constrained to hold no securities rated below investment grade and to maintain the portfolio's weighted-average duration within a specified range, such as 75 percent to 125 percent of the benchmark duration. These restrictions are intended to preserve the portfolio from a loss in value due to inadequate sector diversification, excessive credit quality risk, or unacceptable levels of interest rate risk.

Clearly, in addition to ensuring that the benchmark is appropriate, investors must be careful to formulate constraints that achieve their intended risk-control objectives without unduly impairing the portfolio manager's ability to act on his professional judgment regarding the relative attractiveness of sectors and securities. In other words, a well-written investment IPS meets the client's need for risk mitigation while respecting the portfolio manager's discretion. The manager is well advised to discuss with the client any restrictions that are incompatible with the intended investment strategy. Upon accepting the investment management assignment, however, the portfolio manager is ethically bound by the client's stated policies. Moreover, investment management agreements often incorporate the IPS, so the portfolio manager may also be legally required to comply with properly communicated client-specified constraints.

In some cases, the client's investment constraints may significantly impinge on the portfolio manager's flexibility. A personal investor might prohibit investment in securities issued by companies operating in industries she considers socially unacceptable, such as alcohol, tobacco, or gaming. A corporate client might prohibit the sale of company stock, or a foundation might similarly ban the sale of "sentimental holdings," securities issued by the company in which its founder made a fortune. Additionally, legal restrictions may apply. For instance, a public fund might be statutorily precluded from investing in nondomestic securities. None of these constraints automatically renders a portfolio nondiscretionary. Rather, in these and other cases, the portfolio manager must determine whether or not he has discretion to execute the investment strategy. It may be appropriate to classify a portfolio as discretionary despite the presence of restrictions (such as the prohibition of alcohol, tobacco, or gaming stocks cited above) and to include it in a composite with other similarly constrained portfolios.

Recognizing that degrees of discretion exist, the firm must consider the interactions among client-directed constraints, the portfolio's strategy or style, and the investment process, notably including the financial instruments employed. For example, a client's investment policy might preclude the use of derivative securities such as futures and options. In this case, the firm must consider whether the restriction is pertinent. To take up the example of the domestic mid-cap stock portfolio again, the fact that the client prohibits the use of derivatives may be irrelevant if the manager simply buys, holds, and sells common stocks. If the use of derivative securities is central to the firm's implementation of the investment mandate, however, then the client's policy may render the portfolio nondiscretionary.

In some cases, the pattern of external cash flows might make a portfolio nondiscretionary. For example, if a client frequently makes large withdrawals, perhaps on a regular schedule, the portfolio manager might have to maintain such a high level of liquidity that she cannot truly implement the investment strategy as she does for other portfolios with a similar stated investment mandate or objective.

IMPLEMENTATION (6)

Defining Discretion. The Standards require that all actual fee-paying discretionary portfolios be included in at least one composite. The key words here are "actual," "fee paying," and "discretionary." Stated in simple terms, every account that meets these criteria has to be included in at least one composite. Because discretion is one of the key variables that determine inclusion in or exclusion from a composite, a firm implementing the GIPS standards must have a clear, written definition of discretion. The "Guidance Statement on Composite Definition" defines discretion as "the ability of the firm to implement its intended strategy," and counsels, "If documented client-imposed restrictions significantly hinder the firm from fully implementing its intended strategy the firm may determine that the portfolio is nondiscretionary." The Guidance Statement, available on the CFA Institute web site, offers a starting point for the firm's internal definition of discretion. The firm's documented policy on discretion should help practitioners judge whether a specific portfolio is discretionary and decide how to handle portfolios deemed wholly or partially nondiscretionary. The firm must consistently apply its definition of discretion.

A client could insist that the manager retain specific holdings that might or might not otherwise be held in a portfolio. For example, the client could direct that legacy holdings with a low cost basis must not be sold due to the adverse tax consequences of realizing large gains. In such cases, retaining the asset in the portfolio may skew performance, and whether the impact is favorable or unfavorable, the outcome would not reflect the results of the manager's actual discretionary investment management. If holding the assets hinders the ability to implement the intended strategy, either the entire portfolio should be considered nondiscretionary and removed from the firm's composites or the individual assets should be moved to a different, nondiscretionary account and the remaining assets for which the manager has full discretion should be retained in (or added to) the composite. Alternately, the firm might include a materiality threshold in its policy, enabling it to consider a portfolio discretionary if the nondiscretionary assets consist of less than a certain percentage of portfolio assets.

Constructing Composites II—Defining Investment Strategies

Defining and constructing meaningful composites is a vital step toward achieving the ideal of fair representation and the goal of providing prospective clients with useful comparative information. Under the GIPS standards, composites must be defined according to similar investment objectives and/or strategies, and the full **composite definition** as documented in the firm's policies and procedures must be made available upon request (Provision II.3.A.2). Well-defined composites will be objectively representative of the firm's products and consistent with the firm's marketing strategy. To promote comparability, it is beneficial for firms to take into account how other firms characterize similar products.

The IPC's "Guidance Statement on Composite Definition" suggests a hierarchy that may be helpful for the firm considering how to define composites. Firms are not required to define their composites according to each level of the suggested hierarchy.

> Investment Mandate
>   Asset Classes
>   Style or Strategy
>   Benchmarks
>   Risk/Return Characteristics

A composite based on the investment mandate bears a summary product or strategy description, such as "Global Equities." This may be an entirely acceptable composite definition as long as no significant strategic differences exist among the portfolios included in the composite. It is a guiding principal of composite definition that firms are not permitted to include portfolios with different investment strategies or objectives in the same composite.

A composite based on the constituent portfolios' asset class, such as "equity" or "fixed income," may also be acceptable; however, asset classes are broadly inclusive, and, because generic descriptions are not very informative, asset class composites should be offered only if they are legitimately and meaningfully representative of the firm's products.

In order to afford investors a better understanding of the nature of a composite, the firm may use an asset-class modifier indicating the composite's investment style or strategy. For example, equity portfolios may be restricted to a specific economic sector such as telecommunications stocks. Stocks issued by corporations competing in the same economic sector are presumably affected more or less the same way by exogenous factors such as changes in raw material prices, consumer demand, or the general level of interest rates.

Equity portfolios might also be actively managed to a defined style. A nine-box style matrix widely used by investment consultants in asset allocation studies and performance evaluations classifies portfolios by capitalization (large cap, mid-cap, and small cap) and by style (value; core, also called neutral, market oriented, or blend; and growth). In addition, some capital market index providers offer capitalization- and style-based indices. Although the construction methodologies for such indices must be carefully considered, they may serve adequately as market-based performance benchmarks for portfolios managed in conformity with these categories. Stocks assigned to one category may move more or less together, and one category may have favorable performance relative to the equity market as a whole while another category underperforms the broad market. For instance, the investment performance of portfolios managed to a small-cap growth strategy may vary considerably from the results achieved by large-cap value portfolios, depending on whether large-cap or small-cap stocks and growth or value stocks are in favor during a given measurement period.

A portfolio may be assigned to one of the style matrix categories based on the money-weighted averages of pertinent characteristics of the portfolio's holdings. For example, a portfolio holding stocks with an average market capitalization of $6 billion along with a relatively high price-to-earnings multiple, a relatively high price-to-book ratio, and a relatively low dividend yield, would likely be identified as a mid-cap growth portfolio. Alternately, the portfolio's monthly or quarterly return history might be regressed against the returns of pertinent capital market indices to determine which style-specific benchmarks best explain the portfolio's performance. Evaluating the comparative merits of these approaches falls outside the scope of this chapter. Suffice it to say that given the widespread acceptance of these categories, a firm may meaningfully and usefully define composites with reference to the capitalization range and the style in which the constituent portfolios are managed.

IMPLEMENTATION (7)

Defining Composites. One of the greatest challenges in implementing the GIPS standards is devising the set of composites that will most meaningfully represent the firm's products. The Standards require each and every actual, fee-paying, discretionary portfolio to be included in at least one composite, and composites to be defined according to similar investment objectives and/or strategies. What appears to be a straightforward exercise—defining composites and assigning portfolios to them—may prove rather difficult in practice.

A useful guideline is to build a set of composites that will accurately represent the firm's distinct investment strategies. With too few composites, a firm risks overlooking significant differences and lumping diverse portfolios together into a single, overly broad composite portfolio subject to a wide dispersion of portfolio returns. With too many composites, in addition to unnecessarily augmenting administrative expense, the firm runs the risk of creating narrowly defined groupings that are too much alike in investment strategy, contain too few accounts or assets to be useful, or compromise client confidentiality.

Assuming that the implementation team has already defined the "firm" and "discretion" and compiled a master list of portfolios, here is a common-sense strategy for reaching agreement on composite definitions.

1. Review the firm's organizational structure and investment process to see if distinctive strategies can be readily identified. For instance, an equity adviser might have units

specializing in one or more active management strategies as well as index fund construction and quantitatively driven enhanced indexing.

2. Review the firm's existing marketing materials, supplemented if possible by marketing materials from competitors and by recently received RFPs. The objective is to determine how the industry defines products similar to those the firm offers.

3. Referring to the hierarchy presented in the "Guidance Statement on Composite Definition," construct a provisional framework using descriptive captions to identify possible composites.

4. Taking into account the clients' investment policies, test how well the firm's actual, fee-paying, discretionary portfolios would fit the provisional framework. The inevitable identification of exceptions—that is, the discovery that portfolios that must be included in some composite do not really fit any—will lead to the redefinition of proposed composites or the creation of new composites. Several iterations may be needed.

5. Review the proposed set of composites for compliance with the Standards.

6. Document the composite definitions in detail, and circulate the definitions for final review by all interested parties within the firm.

Of course, the most effective process for defining composites may differ from one firm to another in view of variables such as organizational structure, culture, and investment strategies, among other factors. Nonetheless, composite definitions have lasting consequences, and it is highly desirable to have a plan for reaching consensus.

Firms may also define composites based on the portfolios' benchmarks, as long as the benchmarks reflect the investment strategy and the firm has no other composites with the same characteristics. This approach is particularly appropriate if the portfolios are limited to holding stocks that are held in the index.

Finally, portfolios sharing distinctive risk/return profiles may reasonably be grouped together. For example, enhanced index funds with benchmark-specific targeted excess returns and tracking error tolerances might fall into natural groups.

Fixed-income composites can likewise be meaningfully and usefully defined in many dimensions. For example, composites might conform to asset classes or market segments such as government debt, mortgage-backed securities, convertible bonds, or high-yield bonds; investment strategies such as fundamental credit analysis, sector rotation, or interest rate anticipation; or investment styles such as indexing or core-plus. However a firm chooses to define the composites representing its investment products, they must be composed of portfolios managed in accordance with similar investment strategies or objectives.

Constructing Composites III—Including and Excluding Portfolios

The GIPS Standards governing composite construction hold that composites must include new portfolios on a timely and consistent basis after the portfolio comes under management unless specifically mandated by the client (Provision II.3.A.3). Firms are required to establish, document, and consistently apply a policy of including new portfolios in the appropriate composites on a timely basis. Preferably, new portfolios should be included as of the beginning of the next full performance measurement period after the firm receives the funds. For example, if a portfolio is funded on May 20 and the firm presents composite returns monthly, optimally the composite should include the new portfolio as of the beginning of June. It may take time to invest the assets of a new portfolio in accordance with the desired investment strategy, however, particularly when the portfolio is funded in kind (that is, with securities other than cash) and the assets have to be redeployed, or when the securities to be purchased are relatively illiquid (e.g., in emerging markets). Accordingly, the Standards give firms some discretion to determine when to add the new portfolio to a composite. In such cases, the firm should establish a policy on a composite-by-composite basis and apply it consistently to all new portfolios. In addition, firms may legitimately defer the inclusion of new portfolios in a composite on the specific instructions of a client. To cite an example, the client may indicate that assets will be deposited over an extended period, delaying the full implementation of the strategy, and the client may further state that returns are not to be calculated until the portfolio has been fully funded.

In addition to winning new business, firms routinely lose relationships. Under the GIPS standards, a firm must include a terminated portfolio in the historical record of the appropriate composite up to the last full measurement period that the portfolio was under management (Provision II.3.A.4). In many cases, the firm loses its discretion over the portfolio upon being notified of a pending termination. The client may instruct the firm to stop buying securities immediately and to commence the liquidation of holdings in preparation for an outbound cash transfer on a specified date. Alternately, the client may halt trading and transfer control of the portfolio to a transition management organization to facilitate moving assets to a new firm. When the firm being terminated thus loses its discretion over the portfolio, it should include the portfolio in the composite through the last full measurement period prior to notification of termination. To use the same example, if a firm that reports performance monthly is informed on May 20 that its management contract is being terminated effective May 31 and is instructed to stop trading forthwith, then the firm should include the portfolio in its composite through April 30. In any event, it is incumbent upon the GIPS-compliant firm to have defined and documented its policies governing the removal of terminated portfolios from composites and, of course, to apply those policies consistently.

IMPLEMENTATION (8)

Adding, Removing, and Switching Portfolios. GIPS-compliant firms must have written policies setting forth when portfolios may be added to or removed from composites. These policies can be either firmwide or composite-specific. For a firm that reports composite performance monthly, a firmwide policy statement could read as follows:

> "All new portfolios funded with cash or securities on or before the 15th day of the month shall be added to the appropriate composite at the beginning of the following month. All new portfolios funded with cash or securities after the 15th day of the month shall be added to the appropriate composite at the beginning of the second month after funding. All portfolios shall be deemed 'nondiscretionary' on the date notice of termination is received and removed from the composite at the end of the month prior to notification. The historical performance record of terminated portfolios shall remain in the appropriate composite."

For a firm that calculates composite performance quarterly and needs more time to implement its investment strategy, the following firmwide policy may be appropriate:

> "All new portfolios funded with cash or securities on or before the 10th day of the last month of the calendar quarter shall be added to the appropriate composite at the beginning of the following quarter. All new portfolios funded with cash or securities after the 10th

day of the last month of the calendar quarter shall be added to the appropriate composite at the beginning of the second quarter after funding. All portfolios shall be deemed 'non-discretionary' on the date notice of termination is received and removed from the composite at the end of the calendar quarter prior to notification. The historical performance record of terminated portfolios shall remain in the appropriate composite."

Policies like the samples above allow firms a reasonable amount of time to implement the strategy without delaying inclusion of the portfolio in the appropriate composite. Each firm should develop a policy that conforms to its own investment process while meeting the GIPS standards' requirement to include portfolios in composites on a timely basis. In many cases, composite-specific policies will be in order.

The firm's policy for adding or removing portfolios should also include language strictly limiting the switching of portfolios from one composite to another. Here is a sample statement for a firmwide policy:

"Portfolios shall not be moved from one composite to another unless the composite is redefined or documented changes in the client's guidelines require restructuring the portfolio in such a way that another composite becomes more appropriate. The portfolio shall be removed from the original composite at the end of the last calendar quarter before the event causing the removal occurred and shall be added to the appropriate new composite at the beginning of the next calendar quarter. The historical performance record of the portfolio shall remain in the appropriate composite."

The GIPS standards also stipulate that portfolios cannot be switched from one composite to another unless documented changes in client guidelines or the redefinition of the composite make it appropriate. The historical record of the portfolio must remain with the appropriate composite (Provision II.3.A.5). This is an important provision; if the Standards permitted firms to transfer portfolios from one composite to another at will, an unethical firm might identify and exploit opportunities to improve the reported performance of selected composites by repopulating them with the portfolios whose investment results were most advantageous during the measurement period.

The Standards spell out the only two conditions under which portfolios can be reassigned. First, a portfolio can be switched from one composite to another if the client revises the guidelines governing the investment of portfolio assets and the guideline changes are documented. For instance, a client might decide to modify the portfolio mandate from mid-cap value to large-cap value, or from domestic equity to global equity, with a corresponding change in the benchmark, while retaining the same investment adviser to restructure and manage the "same" portfolio in accordance with the new strategy. Or perhaps a client might decide to allow the use of derivative securities, previously prohibited, triggering a change in the investment strategy and making it suitable to assign the portfolio to a composite made up of portfolios that use derivatives. Second, a portfolio can be reassigned to another composite if the original composite is redefined in such a way that the portfolio no longer fits it. Generally, if a strategy evolves over time, it is most appropriate to create a new composite; accordingly, the redefinition of an existing composite should be a highly unusual event. (See the related disclosure requirement stated in Provision II.4.A.22, where it is also asserted that the Standards do not permit changes to composites to be applied retroactively.) To repeat, if a portfolio is switched from one composite to another as permitted in these two situations— a pertinent, documented change in the client's investment guidelines or a redefinition of the composite—the historical record of the portfolio must remain in the appropriate composite.

In the event of significant external cash flows, the GIPS standards recommend that firms use **temporary new accounts** rather than temporarily removing portfolios from composites (see Provision II.3.B.2). Firms adopting this direct approach channel incoming cash and securities to a new account that is not included in any composite until the cash has been fully invested in accordance with the intended strategy. The timing of the temporary new account's integration into the existing portfolio and the composite is governed by the firm's general or composite-specific policy on the inclusion of new portfolios. Relatedly, when the client initiates a large capital withdrawal, the firm moves cash and securities in the desired amount to a new account until it liquidates the securities. The transfer is treated as an outflow in calculating the portfolio's time-weighted total return. This theoretically appropriate means of handling large external cash flows is recommended but not required because current technology does not readily allow for the establishment of temporary new accounts. Firms may be compelled to temporarily remove portfolios from composites when large external cash flows occur. We refer the reader to the IPC's "Guidance Statement on the Treatment of Significant Cash Flows" for further information and direction on this practically important topic.

We have said that all actual portfolios that are fee-paying and discretionary must be included in at least one composite, but we have not commented on the meaning of "actual" in this context. The Standards specify that composites must include only assets under management within the defined firm. Firms are not permitted to link simulated or model portfolios with actual performance (Provision II.3.A.8). In the process of developing, testing, and refining new investment strategies, firms frequently construct model portfolios and use historical security prices to simulate their hypothetical performance in past measurement periods. Composites cannot include simulated, backtested, or model portfolios. (The "Guidance Statement on the Use of Supplemental Information" states that model, hypothetical, backtested, or simulated returns can be shown as **supplemental information** but cannot be linked to actual performance returns.) On the other hand, if the firm actually created and managed portfolios with its own seed money, it could include them from inception in appropriate composites (or, more likely, construct new composites reflecting the new strategies), subject to a presentation and reporting requirement related to the inclusion of non-fee-paying portfolios in composites (see Provision II.5.A.7, discussed later). Simply stated, only portfolios in which actual assets are invested, not hypothetical portfolios, can be included in composites.

The GIPS provisions for composite construction additionally address the issue of minimum asset levels. A firm might decide that a particular composite will not include any portfolios whose market value is below a specified level, on the grounds, for instance, that the investment strategy can be fully implemented only for portfolios above a certain size. The Standards rule that if a firm sets a minimum asset level for portfolios to be included in a composite, no portfolios below that asset level can be included in that composite. In other words, the policy, once established, must be followed consistently (Provision II.3.A.9).

The "Guidance Statement on Composite Definition" notes that portfolios may drop below a composite-specific minimum asset level because of client withdrawals or depreciation in market value. If a firm establishes a minimum asset level for a composite, it must document its policies regarding how portfolios will be treated if they fall below the minimum. The Guidance Statement recommends that firms specify in their policies the basis for evaluating portfolios against a composite's minimum asset level (for instance, a firm might use beginning market value, ending market value, or beginning market value plus cash flows, etc.). In order to curtail the movement of portfolios into and out of composites, the Guidance Statement further recommends that firms consider establishing a valuation threshold and a minimum time period for applying the policy. For example, the firm might establish a range of ±5 percent of the minimum asset level and a condition that portfolios must remain above or below the minimum asset level for at least two periods before they are added to or removed from the composite. If a portfolio is removed from a composite, its prior history must remain in the composite. The firm must determine if the portfolio that has been removed meets any other composite definition and include it in the appropriate composite in a timely and consistent manner.

Provision II.3.A.9, mentioned earlier, also stipulates that any changes to a composite-specific minimum asset level cannot be applied retroactively. This requirement can create a problem when capital market movements cause portfolios' market values to fall below the stated minimum. For example, the total market value of the Dow Jones Wilshire 5000 Index reached a high point of approximately $14.75 trillion on March 24, 2000. Over the period March 24, 2000, to September 30, 2002, the index had a return of −45.6 percent, representing a loss of shareholder value in excess of $6.7 trillion. If a firm's composite had a minimum portfolio asset level of $50 million, a portfolio initially valued at $85 million that experienced a comparable decline in market value would no longer qualify for inclusion in the composite. Under the Standards, the portfolio would have to be removed from the composite when its market value fell below the minimum asset level. Although the magnitude of the drop in the broad U.S. equity market during this period was atypical, firms are well advised to consider the risk of having to exclude portfolios from composites with minimum asset levels. The minimum asset level can be changed prospectively, subject to disclosure (see Provision II.4.A.3), but not retroactively.

The Standards also recommend that firms should not market a composite to a prospective client whose assets are less than the composite's minimum asset level (Provision II.3.B.3). It is to be presumed that the firm has sound reasons for establishing a minimum asset level for a given strategy. Accordingly, it would be inappropriate for a firm to solicit funds from a prospect with insufficient investable assets for that particular strategy.

Constructing Composites IV—Carve-Out Segments

The GIPS standards codify the proper treatment of asset class segments "carved out" of portfolios invested in multiple asset classes.

In discussing the requirements surrounding the calculation methodology, we recognized that returns from cash and cash equivalents held in portfolios must be included in total return calculations (Provision II.2.A.4), and we examined the impact of short-term investments on equity portfolio results in "up" and "down" markets. The requirement that cash and cash equivalents be taken into account in portfolio and composite return calculations is based on the fundamental principal of fair representation: A composite that did not include cash would not fairly represent investment performance to a prospective client.

This principal carries over to the inclusion of portfolio segments in composites. Provision II.3.A.7 opens with the declaration that **carve-out** segments *excluding cash* cannot be used to represent a discretionary portfolio and, as such, cannot be included in composite returns. For example, the stock portion alone of a portfolio consisting of stocks, bonds, and cash cannot be included in an equity composite as though it were a stand-alone discretionary portfolio. The provision continues, "When a single asset class is carved out of a multiple asset class portfolio and the returns are presented as part of a single asset composite, cash must be allocated

TABLE 41.6   Allocating Cash to Carve-Out Segments: Data

	Actual Market Value as of May 31	Percent of Beginning Portfolio Market Value	Percent of Beginning Invested Assets	Strategic Target	June Returns
Stocks	44,609	35.0%	36.1%	37.5%	2.50%
Bonds	79,021	62.0	63.9	62.5	1.50%
Subtotal: Invested assets	123,630	97.0	100.0%	100.0%	
Cash	3,824	3.0		0.0	0.45%
Total portfolio assets	127,454	100.0%		100.0%	1.82%

to the carve-out returns in a timely and consistent manner." In the equity segment example, a pro rata portion of the portfolio's cash position must be allotted to the stocks, and the carved-out segment return must take into account both the stocks and the temporary investments reasonably associated with them. Carve-out returns, if used at all, should be representative of the results that would realistically have been achieved in a stand-alone strategy, and as we have seen, that entails recognizing the impact of tactical and frictional cash positions.

The "Guidance Statement on the Treatment of Carve-Outs" describes two acceptable allocation methods for situations in which the carved-out segment is not managed with its own cash. Under the "beginning of period allocation" method, the cash allocation percentage for each portfolio segment is identified at the beginning of the measurement period. Under the "strategic asset allocation" method, the allocation is based on the target strategic asset mix. To see how these methods can be used to determine the cash allocation for the equity segment of a balanced portfolio, consider the data in Table 41.6.

Applying the beginning-of-period allocation method, cash might be allocated to the equity segment in proportion to stocks' percentage of invested assets excluding cash.

$$\text{Equity Allocated Cash}_{\text{Beginning}} = \$3,824 \times \frac{44,609}{123,630} = \$1,380$$

Alternately, using the strategic asset allocation method, the cash position is assumed to be the difference between the portfolio's strategic and actual allocation to equities. In the example presented in Table 41.6, the strategic allocation target for equities is 37.5 percent, and the actual beginning allocation to equities is 35 percent. The difference (2.5 percent of total portfolio assets) is assumed to be held in cash and cash equivalents associated with the equity segment.

$$\text{Equity Allocated Cash}_{\text{Strategic}} = \$127,454 \times (0.375 - 0.35) = \$3,186$$

Table 41.7 displays the results, including the weighted segment returns for the month of June. As this example illustrates, the cash allocation method chosen and the way in which the method is implemented can substantially affect the performance calculation. Under the "beginning of period allocation" method, the equity segment return for the month is 2.44 percent (the simple arithmetic result of having 97 percent of segment assets invested in stocks with a return of 2.5 percent and 3 percent invested in cash with a return of 0.45 percent). Under the "strategic asset allocation" method, the equity segment return for the month is 8 basis points lower (2.36 percent).

TABLE 41.7   Allocation of Cash to Carve-Out Segments: Two Methods

	Beginning-of-Period Allocation		Strategic Asset Allocation	
Stocks	44,609	97.0%	44,609	93.3%
Allocated cash	1,380	3.0	3,186	6.7
Total equity segment assets	45,989	100.0%	47,795	100.0%
Equity segment return		2.44%		2.36%

It is of course illogical to conclude from this one example that the beginning-of-period allocation method will always produce a higher segment return than the strategic asset allocation method. The relative outcomes might be reversed in another case. In any event, the firm must determine which method to employ, document the policy, and apply it consistently, without regard to the *ex post* performance impact in any measurement period. Under the GIPS standards, the allocation of cash to carved-out segments is permitted only until January 1, 2010. From that date forward, carve-out returns cannot be included in single-asset-class composite returns *unless the carve-out is actually managed separately with its own cash balance* (emphasis added; from Provision II.3.A.7). In the interim, the GIPS standards recommend that carve-out returns should not be included in single-asset-class composite returns unless the carve-outs are actually managed separately with their own cash balance (Provision II.3.B.1).

Carve-out segments are also addressed in the provisions for disclosure and for presentation and reporting. For periods prior to January 1, 2010, when a single asset class is carved out of a multiple-asset portfolio and the returns are presented as part of a single-asset composite, firms must disclose the policy used to allocate cash to the carve-out returns (see Provision II.4.A.11). In addition, beginning January 1, 2006, if a composite includes or is formed using single-asset-class carve-outs from multiple-asset-class portfolios, the presentation must include the percentage of the composite that is composed of carve-outs prospectively for each period (see Provision II.5.A.5).

IMPLEMENTATION (9)

Carve-Out Segments. Equilibrium Capital Advisors, a firm specializing in balanced portfolios, maintains a number of multi-class composites constructed according to strategic asset mix ranges. For example, among other multi-class composites, Equilibrium Capital Advisors has a Standard Balanced Account Composite composed of portfolios with a strategic asset allocation target of 50 percent fixed-income and 50 percent equity; a Conservative Balanced Account Composite composed of portfolios with a 65/35 fixed-income/equity strategic mix; and an Aggressive Balanced Account Composite composed of portfolios with a 20/80 fixed-income/equity strategic mix. In order to control transaction expenses by reducing the frequency of portfolio rebalancing, the target mixes are accompanied by 5 percent tolerance ranges. For instance, the Aggressive Balanced Account Composite is permitted to vary from 15/85 to 25/75 fixed-income/equity mixes. The equity segments of all the balanced composites are managed in accordance with a single strategy by the Equity Markets Group under the leadership of John Boyle, and the fixed income segments of the balanced composites as well as all cash and cash equivalent positions are managed by the Fixed Income Markets Group. Boyle wants to create a new equity composite composed of the equity segments of the multi-class portfolios. Can such a composite be constructed in compliance with the GIPS standards?

Provision II.3.B.1 recommends against constructing the composite Boyle requests. The Standard reads, "Carve-out returns should not be included in single-asset-class composite returns unless the carve-outs are actually managed separately with their own cash balance." In the case of Equilibrium Capital Advisors, it appears that the cash generated in the course of equity and fixed-income investment management is pooled, and short-term investing is conducted for the balanced portfolio as a whole. The equity segment is not managed separately with its own cash balance.

Provision II.3.A.7 states that beginning January 1, 2010, carve-out returns cannot be included in single-asset-class composite returns unless the carve-out is actually managed separately with its own cash balance. Until that time, however, the provision allows carve-out segments to be included in single-asset-class composites on the condition that cash is allocated to the carve-out returns in a timely and consistent manner. Accordingly, Equilibrium Capital Advisors can construct and maintain a composite composed of the equity segments of balanced portfolios until January 1, 2010. The firm must decide on an acceptable cash allocation method, document the method, and apply it consistently. The Standards expressly prohibit carve-out segments excluding cash from being included in composite returns. As noted in the text, the cash allocation method must be disclosed (Provision II.4.A.11), and beginning January 1, 2006, the percentage of the composite that is composed of carve-outs must be shown prospectively for each period in GIPS-compliant performance presentations (Provision II.5.A.5).

Disclosure Standards

The GIPS standards advance the ideals of fair representation and full disclosure. We will consider the presentation and reporting provisions shortly. Before doing so, however, we will cite the required and recommended disclosure provisions. The reader will already be familiar with most of these topics from previous sections, so we will discuss each item here only briefly. For ease of exposition, we have grouped the disclosure provisions by subject area.

Several of the provisions concern disclosures related to the GIPS-compliant firm. The definition of the *firm* used to determine the firm's total assets and firmwide compliance is a required disclosure (Provision II.4.A.1). A clear explanation of the way in which the firm is defined enables the prospective client to understand precisely which investment organization (or unit of a larger entity) is presenting results, is claiming compliance, and will be responsible for managing the client's assets if hired. If a firm is redefined, it must disclose the date and reason for the redefinition (Provision II.4.A.21).

Firms are further required to disclose all significant events that help a prospective client interpret the performance record (Provision II.4.A.19). For example, a firm must advise the prospective client if past results in a given strategy were achieved by a star portfolio manager who has left the firm, or if key members of the research team supporting the strategy have resigned. Beginning January 1, 2006, firms must disclose the use of a subadviser or subadvisers and the periods in which one or more subadvisers were used (Provision II.4.A.18).

The availability of a complete list and description of all of the firm's composites is a required disclosure (Provision II.4.A.2). This information enables prospective clients to determine if the composite they have been shown is the most appropriate for their needs and to request any other composites of interest. Note that the list must include not only all of the firm's current composites but also any that have been discontinued within the last five years (see Provision II.0.A.12). GIPS Appendix B provides a sample list and description of composites.

In addition to the foregoing firm-related requirements, the Standards make two recommendations. First, if a parent company contains multiple defined firms, each firm within the parent company is encouraged to disclose a list of the other firms contained within the parent company (Provision II.4.B.1). Second, firms that have been verified (that is, firms whose performance measurement processes and procedures have been reviewed in reference to the GIPS standards by a qualified, independent third party) should add a disclosure to their composite presentation stating that the firm has been verified and clearly indicating the periods the verification covers if not all the periods presented have been subject to firmwide verification (Provision II.4.B.3).

Other disclosure provisions concern rate-of-return calculations and **benchmarks**. Firms must disclose the currency used to express performance (Provision II.4.A.4). Firms must also disclose and describe any known inconsistencies in the exchange rates used among the portfolios within a composite and between the composite and the benchmark (Provision II.4.A.8). Firms must disclose relevant details of the treatment of withholding tax on dividends, interest income, and capital gains. If using indices that are net of taxes, the firm must disclose the tax basis of the benchmark (for example, Luxembourg based or U.S. based) versus that of the composite (Provision II.4.A.7). Firms must also disclose that **additional information** regarding policies for calculating and reporting returns in compliance with the GIPS standards is available upon request (Provision II.4.A.17). To cite obvious examples, GIPS-compliant firms should be prepared to respond to prospective clients' questions about their return calculation methodology, valuation sources, or treatment of large external cash flows. The Standards recommend, but do not require, that firms disclose when a change in a calculation methodology or valuation source results in a material impact on the performance of a composite (Provision II.4.B.2).

Numerous disclosure standards address the topic of fees. Returns must be clearly labeled as gross of fees or net of fees (Provision II.4.A.6). For reference, the GIPS glossary defines the **gross-of-fees return** as the return on assets reduced by any trading expenses incurred during the period and the **net-of-fees return** as the gross-of-fees return reduced by the investment management fee. When presenting gross-of-fees returns, firms must disclose if they deduct any other fees in addition to the direct trading expenses (Provision II.4.A.15). Similarly, when presenting net-of-fees returns, firms must disclose if any other fees are deducted in addition to the direct trading expenses and the investment management fee (Provision II.4.A.16). The firm must also disclose the **fee schedule** appropriate to the presentation (Provision II.4.A.12). As explained in the GIPS glossary, the term "fee schedule" refers to the firm's current investment management fees or bundled fees for a particular presentation. If a composite contains portfolios with bundled fees, firms must disclose the percentage of composite assets that are bundled-fee portfolios for each annual period shown in the performance presentation (Provision II.4.A.13). Firms must also disclose the various types of fees that the bundled fee includes (Provision II.4.A.14).

Some disclosure standards are pertinent to individual composites. Firms must disclose a description of the investment objectives, style, and/or strategy of the composite (Provision II.4.A.20). It is not enough merely to have a broadly indicative name such as "Growth and Income Composite," which might mean one thing to one person and something else to another; the provision requires that prospective clients be given a reasonably informative explanation, however concise, setting forth the composite's salient features. For example, a "Growth and Income Composite" composed of balanced portfolios or "accounts" managed on behalf of individuals might be described in these terms: "The Growth and Income Composite" includes taxable balanced accounts with assets greater than $100,000. The accounts are managed to a strategic asset allocation target of 50 percent fixed income and

50 percent equity within a tactical range of 10 percent. The fixed income segments of the individual accounts are invested in investment-grade instruments including U.S. government and agency securities, corporate bonds, and mortgage-backed securities. The equity segments are invested in large-capitalization common stocks. The benchmark for this strategy is a blended index made up of 50 percent Lehman Aggregate Bond Index and 50 percent Standard & Poor's 500 Stock Index." Appendix B of the GIPS standards includes other examples of **composite descriptions**.

Firms must also disclose the **composite creation date** (Provision II.4.A.24), the date on which the firm first grouped the portfolios to form the composite. This is not necessarily the earliest date for which composite performance is reported. If a firm has redefined a composite, the firm must disclose the date and nature of the change. As previously noted, the Standards do not permit changes to composites to be applied retroactively (Provision II.4.A.22). Similarly, firms must disclose any changes to a composite's name (Provision II.4.A.23).

As we will see when examining the provisions of the GIPS standards related to presentation and reporting, firms must report a measure of the **dispersion** of the returns of the individual portfolios within a composite. There are different ways to convey dispersion. The disclosure standards require firms to disclose which dispersion measure they present (Provision II.4.A.26).

The preceding requirements apply to all composites. Several further requirements apply in certain cases. First, firms must disclose the minimum asset level, if any, below which portfolios are not included in a composite. Firms must also disclose any changes to the minimum asset level (Provision II.4.A.3). Second, for periods prior to January 1, 2010, when a single asset class is carved out of a multiple-asset portfolio and the returns are presented as part of a single-asset composite, firms must disclose the policy used to allocate cash to the carve-out returns (Provision II.4.A.11). Third, firms must disclose if, prior to January 1, 2010, portfolios are not valued as of calendar month-end or the last business day of the month (Provision II.4.A.25).

It is an important, albeit challenging, provision that firms must disclose the presence, use, and extent of leverage or derivatives, if material. The disclosure must include a description of the use, frequency, and characteristics of the instruments sufficient to identify risks (Provision II.4.A.5). As a practical matter, it is admittedly difficult to explain in writing the use of leverage or derivative securities and the attendant risks of their use, especially for the benefit of prospective clients who may not have been exposed previously to complex investment strategies. A clear explanation, however, will help prospective clients interpret the historical performance record and evaluate the additional risk resulting from the use of leverage or derivatives. Adequate disclosure, as required by the GIPS standards, includes a description of the investment characteristics of the financial instruments employed and an explanation of the way in which they are used.

For example, a fixed income manager might use interest rate futures contracts as an efficient and economical means of adjusting the sensitivity of corporate bond portfolios to anticipated changes in the general level of interest rates. The firm might provide the following description of its use of derivatives: "Crystal Capital routinely uses U.S. Treasury bond futures contracts to change the portfolios' modified duration. Because of their call features and credit risk, the corporate bonds held in the portfolio may experience price changes that do not closely match movements in the U.S. Treasury bond futures contracts, resulting in portfolio valuations that differ from the targeted outcome."

Finally, two disclosure provisions pertain to performance presentations. Firms must disclose if the presentation conforms with local laws and regulations that differ from the requirements of the GIPS standards. The manner in which any local laws or regulations conflict with the Standards must also be disclosed (Provision II.4.A.9). For any performance presented for periods prior to January 1, 2000, that does not comply with the GIPS standards, firms must disclose the period and the nature of noncompliance (Provision II.4.A.10.) See also Section I.F.13, "Effective Date," and Provision II.5.A.2, discussed later.

Meeting the objectives of fair representation and full disclosure may call for providing more information than the GIPS standards minimally require. Practitioners are well advised to prepare compliance checklists to ensure that the disclosure requirements and, where feasible, the recommendations of the GIPS standards are met for the firm as a whole and for each composite presented. We turn now to the provisions for presentation and reporting.

Presentation and Reporting Requirements

The ethical ideals of fair representation and full disclosure come to fruition in GIPS-compliant performance presentations. In this section, we will focus on the required elements of performance presentations prepared in accordance with the GIPS standards.

For each composite presented, the Standards require that firms show at least five years of GIPS-compliant performance (less if the firm or composite has been in existence for a shorter period), and that the GIPS-compliant performance record must then be extended each year until 10 years' results have been presented. The core elements of a GIPS-compliant performance presentation additionally include annual returns for all years; the number of portfolios (if six or more), the amount of assets in the composite, and either the percentage of the firm's total assets represented by the composite or the amount of total firm assets at the end of each period; and a measure of dispersion of individual portfolio returns if the composite contains six or more portfolios for the full year. These requirements are set forth in Provisions II.5.A.1.a–d. Some of them are straightforward; others call for more explanation.

Annual returns, required by Provision II.5.A.1.b, are normally presented for calendar years, although they may be presented for other annual periods if the composite is reported on a noncalendar fiscal year.

Provision 5.A.1.d mandates reporting a measure of dispersion of the annual returns earned by individual portfolios belonging to the composite. This important provision is intended to allow users to determine how consistently the firm implemented its strategy across the portfolios in the composite. A wide range of results should prompt the recipient of the performance presentation to inquire about possible causes of the variability of returns to individual portfolios purportedly managed in accordance with the same strategy. It may suggest, among many other possibilities, that the composite is defined too broadly to provide meaningful information.

The dispersion of the annual returns of individual portfolios within a composite can be measured and shown in various ways, and the GIPS glossary mentions several acceptable methods. Let us refer to the data in Table 41.8, showing the beginning market values (in euros) and the annual rates of return earned by the 14 portfolios that were in a German Equity composite for the full year 200X. (Note that only those portfolios in the composite for the entire year are included in the calculation of a dispersion measure.) The portfolios presented in Table 41.8 are arrayed in descending order of returns.

The GIPS glossary defines dispersion as "a measure of the spread of the annual returns of individual portfolios within a composite" and indicates that acceptable measures include high/low, interquartile range, and standard deviation. Using the data in Table 41.8, we will consider each of these measures in turn.

TABLE 41.8   Data for Calculation of Dispersion

Portfolio	Beginning Market Value	200X Return
A	€118,493	2.66%
B	€79,854	2.64
C	€121,562	2.53
D	€86,973	2.49
E	€105,491	2.47
F	€112,075	2.42
G	€98,667	2.38
H	€92,518	2.33
I	€107,768	2.28
J	€96,572	2.21
K	€75,400	2.17
L	€77,384	2.07
M	€31,264	1.96
N	€84,535	1.93

The simplest method of expressing the dispersion is to disclose the highest and lowest annual returns earned by portfolios that were in the composite for the full year. In the case of the German Equity composite, the highest return was 2.66 percent and the lowest was 1.93 percent. (The high/low range—the arithmetic difference between the highest and the lowest return—might also be presented. In this case it was 0.73 percent, or 73 basis points.) The high/low disclosure is easy to understand. It has, however, a potential disadvantage. In any annual period, an outlier—that is, one portfolio with an abnormally high or low return—may be present, resulting in a measure of dispersion that is not entirely representative of the distribution of returns. Although they are more difficult to calculate and to interpret, other measures are statistically superior.

A second measure cited in the GIPS glossary is an interquartile range, the difference between the returns in the first and the third quartiles of the distribution. Quartiles divide the distribution of returns into quarters, such that 25 percent of the observations fall at or above the first quartile and 25 percent fall at or below the third quartile. Thus the interquartile range represents the length of the interval containing the middle 50 percent of the data. In the case of the German Equity composite, the interquartile range is approximately 36 basis points (0.36 percent).[17] Because it does not contain the extreme values, the interquartile range does not risk being skewed by outliers. Prospective clients, however, may be unfamiliar with the interquartile range as a measure of dispersion.

The standard deviation of returns to portfolios in the composite is another acceptable measure of composite dispersion.[18] As applied to composites, standard deviation measures the cross-sectional dispersion of returns to portfolios in the composite. Standard deviation for a composite in which the constituent portfolios are equally weighted is[19]

$$S_c = \sqrt{\frac{\sum_{i=1}^{n}(r_i - \bar{r}_c)^2}{n-1}}$$

(41.10)

where r_i is the return of each individual portfolio, $\bar{r}_c$ is the equal-weighted mean or arithmetic mean return to the portfolios in the composite, and n is, as before, the number of portfolios in the composite. Applying Equation 41.10 to the portfolio data given in Table 41.8, assuming equal weighting, the standard deviation proves to be 23 basis points (0.23 percent). If the individual portfolio returns are normally distributed around the mean return of 2.32 percent, then approximately two-thirds of the portfolios will have returns falling between the mean plus the standard deviation (2.32% + 0.23% = 2.55%) and the mean minus the standard deviation (2.32% − 0.23% = 2.09%).

The standard deviation of portfolio returns is a valid measure of composite dispersion. Most spreadsheet programs include statistical functions to facilitate the calculation, and many prospective clients will have at least a passing acquaintance with the concept of a standard deviation.

Note that the GIPS glossary states that measures of dispersion may include but are not limited to those introduced above (high/low, interquartile range, and standard deviation). A GIPS-compliant firm may prefer another way of expressing composite dispersion. The method chosen should, however, fairly represent the range of returns for each annual period. Recall that firms must disclose the measure of dispersion presented.

We observed in reviewing the disclosure standards that, for any performance presented for periods prior to January 1, 2000, that does not comply with the GIPS standards, the firm must disclose the period of noncompliance and the way in which the presentation fails to comply with the Standards (Provision II.4.A.10). Firms are permitted to link non-GIPS-compliant performance to their compliant history as long as the disclosure requirements are met and only compliant returns are presented for periods after January 1, 2000 (Provision II.5.A.2).

The GIPS provisions for presentation and reporting stipulate that portfolio or composite returns for periods of less than one year must not be annualized (Provision II.5.A.3). Extrapolating partial-year returns by annualizing them would amount in effect to a prediction about investment results for the rest of the year.

The "portability" of past performance is a complex subject, but Provision II.5.A.4 summarizes the explicit conditions under which performance track records of a past firm or affiliation *must* be linked to or used to represent the historical record of a new firm or new affiliation. The conditions are that (1) substantially all the investment decision makers are employed by the new firm, (2) the staff and decision-making process remain intact and independent within the new firm, *and* (3) the new firm has records that document and support the reported performance. The new firm must disclose that the performance results from the past firm are linked to the performance record of the new firm. When a firm combines with an existing firm, there is a further requirement: The performance of composites from both firms can be linked to the ongoing returns only if substantially all the assets from the past firm's composite transfer to the new firm. If a GIPS-compliant firm acquires or is acquired by a noncompliant firm, the firms are allowed one year to bring the noncompliant assets into compliance.

In our discussion of composite construction (Provision II.3.A.7) and required disclosures (Provision II.4.A.11), we mentioned the practice of "carving out" or extracting performance data on a single asset class included in a multiple-asset-class strategy for inclusion in a single-asset-class composite. A related presentation and reporting requirement exists. Under Provision II.5.A.5, beginning January 1, 2006, if a composite includes or is formed using single-asset-class carve-outs from multiple-asset-class portfolios, the presentation must include the percentage of the composite that is composed of carve-outs prospectively for each period. In this context, "prospectively" means from January 1, 2006, onward. The Standards do not require firms to disclose what percentage of the composite was composed of carve-outs for historical periods.

We have previously remarked on the importance of selecting appropriate benchmarks in order to interpret historical results and to conduct meaningful performance evaluations.

We have also made note of certain benchmark-related disclosure requirements (see Provisions II.4.A.7–8). An important presentation and reporting requirement is set forth in Provision II.5.A.6: The total return for the benchmark(s) reflecting the investment strategy or mandate represented by the composite must be presented for each annual period. If no benchmark is presented, the firm must explain why none is shown. In addition, if the firm changes the benchmark used for a given composite, the firm must disclose the date of and the reason for the change.

Provision II.5.A.6 also addresses the use of custom benchmarks. For example, a firm might construct a custom security-based benchmark composed of securities that conform to the firm's investment process and the composite's strategy. Or, as another example, a firm's balanced composite might have a blended benchmark reflecting the strategic asset mix with reference to which the portfolios are managed. The benchmark in this case might be constructed by weighting well-chosen capital market indices with desirable characteristics such as asset class representativeness and investability. The provision states that if the firm uses a custom benchmark or benchmarks, the firm must describe the benchmark creation and rebalancing process.

IMPLEMENTATION (10)

Benchmark Presentation. Eastern Institutional Asset Advisors presents the performance of a Global Balanced Composite. The strategic asset mix of the portfolios in the composite is 50 percent U.S. equity, 10 percent international equity, 35 percent U.S. fixed-income securities, and 5 percent cash. The composite has a blended benchmark composed of capital market indices weighted in accordance with the strategic asset allocation. In compliance with Provision II.5.A.6, Eastern Institutional Asset Advisors places the following disclosure on the Global Balanced Composite's performance presentation:

> *"The benchmark for the Global Balanced Composite is composed of 50 percent S&P 500, 10 percent MSCI EAFE Index, 35 percent Lehman Aggregate Bond Index, and 5 percent U.S. Treasury bills. The benchmark is rebalanced monthly."*

The frequency of benchmark rebalancing can affect the reported returns for an annual period. Table 41.9 displays one calendar year's data for the Global Balanced Composite described in Implementation (10). For the purpose of comparison, the blended benchmark return for the year is calculated first on a monthly and then on a quarterly basis.

In this example, the monthly calculation produces a blended benchmark return of −9.30 percent for the year, while the quarterly calculation (using the same input data) produces a return of −8.98 percent for the year. There is a difference of 32 basis points (0.32 percent) between the full-year benchmark returns under the two rebalancing methods. Once established, the firm must apply its benchmark rebalancing policy consistently, without regard to the *ex post* impact on the composite's relative performance in any annual period.

The final requirement of the GIPS standards for presentation and reporting to be mentioned here addresses the inclusion of non-fee-paying portfolios in composites. We saw when discussing the requirements for composite construction that all actual, fee-paying, discretionary portfolios must be included in at least one composite. Provision II.3.A.1 goes on to state that non-fee-paying discretionary portfolios may be included in a composite (with appropriate

TABLE 41.9   Illustration of Rebalancing Policies

	Domestic Equity Index	International Equity Index	Domestic Corporate Bond Index	Cash Equivalents Index	Blended Benchmark
Blended Benchmark Weights	50%	10%	35%	5%	
			Monthly Rebalancing		
January	−1.46%	−3.96%	0.79%	0.15%	−0.84%
February	−1.93	0.61	0.96	0.13	−0.56
March	3.76	5.56	−1.65	0.15	1.87
April	−6.06	0.76	1.90	0.16	−2.28
May	−0.74	1.65	0.85	0.16	0.10
June	−7.12	−4.41	0.74	0.14	−3.74
July	−7.79	−9.21	1.19	0.15	−4.39
August	0.66	0.00	1.75	0.14	0.95
September	−10.87	−10.43	1.59	0.16	−5.91
October	8.80	4.87	−0.45	0.15	4.74
November	5.89	4.56	−0.02	0.16	3.40
December	−5.87	−2.86	2.08	0.12	−2.49
Linked monthly returns	−22.09%	−13.50%	10.11%	1.78%	→ −9.30%
			Quarterly Rebalancing		
First quarter	0.27%	2.00%	0.08%	0.43%	0.38%
Second quarter	−13.39	−2.09	3.53	0.46	−5.65
Third quarter	−17.27	−18.68	4.60	0.45	−8.87
Fourth quarter	8.45	6.52	1.60	0.43	5.46
Linked quarterly returns	−22.08%	−13.49%	10.11%	1.78%	→ −8.98%

disclosures).[20] For example, in the interest of public service or community relations, a firm might waive the investment management fee on a charitable organization's portfolio, or a firm might use its own or its principals' capital to implement a new investment strategy. In the section of the GIPS standards devoted to presentation and reporting, Provision II.5.A.7 stipulates that if a composite contains any non-fee-paying portfolios, the firm must present, as of the end of each annual period, the percentage of the composite assets represented by the non-fee-paying portfolios.

Appendix A of the GIPS standards contains several sample GIPS-compliant performance presentations. We have reproduced one of them in Table 41.10.

Presentation and Reporting Recommendations

In addition to the requirements explained above, the GIPS standards include recommended practices in presentation and reporting of investment results.

TABLE 41.10   Sample 1 Investment Firm Balanced Composite, January 1, 1995, through December 31, 2004

Year	Gross-of-Fees Return (percent)	Net-of-Fees Return (percent)	Benchmark Return (percent)	Number of Portfolios	Internal Dispersion (percent)	Total Composite Assets (CAD million)	Total Firm Assets (CAD million)
1995	16.0	15.0	14.1	26	4.5	165	236
1996	2.2	1.3	1.8	32	2.0	235	346
1997	22.4	21.5	24.1	38	5.7	344	529
1998	7.1	6.2	6.0	45	2.8	445	695
1999	8.5	7.5	8.0	48	3.1	520	839
2000	−8.0	−8.9	−8.4	49	2.8	505	1,014
2001	−5.9	−6.8	−6.2	52	2.9	499	995
2002	2.4	1.6	2.2	58	3.1	525	1,125
2003	6.7	5.9	6.8	55	3.5	549	1,225
2004	9.4	8.6	9.1	59	2.5	575	1,290

Sample 1 Investment Firm has prepared and presented this report in compliance with the Global Investment Performance Standards (GIPS®).

Notes:

1. Sample 1 Investment Firm is a balanced portfolio investment manager that invests solely in Canadian securities. Sample 1 Investment Firm is defined as an independent investment management firm that is not affiliated with any parent organization. For the periods from 2000 through 2004, Sample 1 Investment Firm has been verified by Verification Services Inc. A copy of the verification report is available upon request. Additional Information regarding the firm's policies and procedures for calculating and reporting performance results is available upon request.

2. The composite includes all nontaxable balanced portfolios with an asset allocation of 30 percent S&P TSX and 70 percent Scotia Canadian Bond Index Fund, which allow up to a 10 percent deviation in asset allocation.

3. The benchmark: 30 percent S&P TSX; 70 percent Scotia Canadian Bond Index Fund rebalanced monthly.

4. Valuations are computed and performance reported in Canadian dollars.

5. Gross-of-fees performance returns are presented before management and custodial fees but after all trading expenses. Returns are presented net of nonreclaimable withholding taxes. Net-of-fees performance returns are calculated by deducting the highest fee of 0.25 percent from the quarterly gross composite return. The management fee schedule is as follows: 1.00 percent on first CAD25M; 0.60 percent thereafter.

6. This composite was created in February 1995. A complete list and description of firm composites is available upon request.

7. For the periods 1995 and 1996, Sample 1 Investment Firm was not in compliance with the GIPS Standards because portfolios were valued annually.

8. Internal dispersion is calculated using the equal weighted standard deviation of all portfolios that were included in the composite for the entire year.

Source: Global Investment Performance Standards, 2005.

Provisions II.5.B.1.a–g recommend that certain items be presented. First, Provision II.5.B.1.a recommends that firms present composite performance gross of investment management and administrative fees and before taxes, except for nonreclaimable withholding taxes. **Administrative fees,** defined as all charges other than trading expenses and investment management fees, could include custody, accounting, consulting, and legal fees, among others. Such fees are typically not under an investment manager's control.

Provision II.5.B.1.b recommends that, in addition to the required annual returns, firms should present cumulative composite and benchmark returns for all periods. Cumulative returns are calculated by geometrically linking historical returns. For instance, using Equation 41.2 and the data given in Table 41.10, we find that the composite's cumulative gross-of-fees return was 74.5 percent and the cumulative benchmark return was 68.8 percent for the 1995 to 2004 period.

The Standards also recommend that annualized composite and benchmark returns be presented for periods greater than 12 months (Provision II.5.B.1.f). As expressed in Equation 41.11, annualized returns are calculated by taking the nth root of chain-linked returns, where n is the number of years in the period.

$$r_{ann} = \sqrt[n]{(1 + r_{t,1}) \times (1 + r_{t,2}) \times \cdots \times (1 + r_{t,N})} - 1 \qquad (41.11)$$

For instance, the sample GIPS-compliant presentation shown above covers the 10-year period 1995 through 2004. Applying Equation 41.11 to the cumulative returns calculated above, we find that the annualized gross-of-fees return for the composite during that 10-year period was approximately 5.73 percent, and the annualized return for the benchmark during the same period was approximately 5.37 percent.

The GIPS standards also recommend that performance presentations include returns for quarterly and/or shorter time periods (Provision II.5.B.1.e). We have already seen, of course, that returns for periods shorter than one year must *not* be annualized.

Recall that the standards require composite returns to be calculated on an asset-weighted basis (Provision II.2.A.3). Provision II.5.B.1.c recommends that firms present equal-weighted mean and median returns for each composite. The equal-weighted mean and the median returns for the composite portfolios may provide useful information to prospective clients, particularly if the required dispersion measure has been calculated on an equal-weighted basis.

The Standards further recommend that firms present composite-level country and sector weightings (Provision II.5.B.1.g). This information may give prospective clients a sense of each composite's diversification.

In addition, the GIPS standards suggest that firms prepare graphs and charts presenting specific information that the Standards require or recommend (Provision II.5.B.1.d). Carefully constructed graphical exhibits can convey information in a way that prospective clients find easy to grasp. Of course, the ethical ideals of fair representation and full disclosure remain in force; firms should design their graphs and charts so as to present information objectively.

We have seen that the Standards require the presentation of a measure of dispersion of portfolio returns across the composite. The GIPS standards also recommend, but do not require, the presentation of relevant composite-level risk measures. Examples of such measures cited in Provision II.5.B.2 include beta, tracking error, modified duration, the information ratio, Sharpe ratio, Treynor ratio, credit ratings, value at risk, and the volatility or variability of composite and benchmark returns over time. (Volatility might be represented by the annualized standard deviation of composite and benchmark returns during the period covered by the performance presentation if it is long enough to provide a statistically valid measure.) A discussion of the definitions, computation, applicability, and limitations of these various indicators of risk falls outside the scope of this chapter. The key point to note is that the GIPS standards advocate offering prospective clients relevant quantitative information they can use to evaluate the riskiness of the investment strategy represented by a composite.

Finally, we saw earlier that for any noncompliant performance presented for periods prior to January 1, 2000, the disclosure standards require firms to disclose the period and the nature of the noncompliance (Provision II.4.A.10). The GIPS standards for presentation and reporting encourage firms that have presented the required five years of compliant historical performance to bring any remaining portion of their historical track record into compliance with the Standards (Provision II.5.B.3). This recommendation does not relieve firms of the requirement to add annual performance on an ongoing basis to build a 10-year compliant track record.

Introduction to the Real Estate and Private Equity Provisions

The GIPS standards codify the treatment to be accorded direct real estate and private equity, two major asset classes with distinctive characteristics. In general, the GIPS standards in force for all other asset classes apply to real estate and private equity as well; however, the Standards stipulate certain exceptions to the main provisions, and set forth additional requirements and recommendations for these asset classes.

The GIPS standards for real estate and private equity override, or replace, specific provisions of the main GIPS standards for valuation. Because these types of investments (as defined below) do not trade in organized exchanges, their market values are not readily obtainable. Accordingly, the GIPS standards prescribe valuation techniques adapted to each of these asset classes. Moreover, the Standards for private equity override specific provisions for calculation methodology, fees, and the presentation and reporting of returns.

The Standards for real estate and private equity also put forward requirements and recommendations in addition to those set forth in the other sections of the Standards. For example, in the area of presentation and reporting, the provisions for real estate require that firms present total return accompanied by the component returns for income and capital appreciation. To cite another example, the provisions for private equity require that, in addition to presenting total composite assets and total firm assets, firms must disclose the total committed capital for the composite.

Real estate and private equity investments can be structured in many different ways. In order to demarcate the scope of the asset class–specific provisions, the GIPS standards specify the types of investments that are *not* considered real estate. Publicly traded real estate securities (such as real estate investment trusts, or REITs), including any listed securities issued by public companies, and commercial mortgage-backed securities (CMBSs), are subject to the general provisions rather than to the real estate provisions of the GIPS standards. Also excluded from the real estate provisions are private debt investments, including commercial and residential loans for which the expected return is solely related to contractual interest rates without any participation in the economic performance of the underlying real estate. If a portfolio holds both real estate and other types of investments that are not considered real estate, then the real estate provisions apply only to the real estate portion of the portfolio, and the carve-out provisions of the GIPS standards must also be brought to bear.

Similarly, the **private equity** provisions pertain to private equity investments other than **open-end** or **evergreen** funds, which allow for ongoing investment and redemptions. Open-end and evergreen funds remain subject to the main GIPS standards.

Real estate investing and private equity investing are highly specialized areas of expertise, and the GIPS standards governing them are necessarily complicated. In the following sections, we will consider principal concepts and major provisions of the pertinent Standards. This discussion is not an exhaustive treatment of these complex topics.

Real Estate Standards

Market values are central to calculating returns on real estate assets, and accordingly the GIPS standards for input data and disclosures include provisions related to valuation procedures.

Firms are not required to determine the market value of real estate assets as frequently as they must value portfolios composed of more-liquid securities in accordance with the general provisions of the GIPS standards. At present, real estate investments must be valued at market value at least once every 12 months and, for periods beginning January 1, 2008, at least quarterly (Provision II.6.A.1). In the absence of transactions, however, managers' estimates of market values may be based on debatable assumptions. Accordingly, the Standards further require firms to have valuations conducted periodically by independent, credentialed experts. Specifically, Provision II.6.A.2 reads in part, "Real estate investments must be valued by an external **professionally designated, certified** or **licensed commercial property valuer/appraiser** at least once every 36 months." In markets where specialists with appropriate credentials are unavailable, the firm must take steps to ensure that it uses only well-qualified valuers or appraisers. Common-sense steps might include considering the appraiser's pertinent experience in the local market with the kind of properties to be independently valued.

The Standards recommend that real estate investments be valued, either internally or by an external appraiser, at least quarterly. (As noted, quarterly valuations will be required for periods beginning January 1, 2008.) They also recommend that real estate investments be valued by an external valuer or appraiser at least once every 12 months (Provisions II.6.B.1–2).

In addition to the other disclosure requirements of the GIPS standards, performance presentations for real estate investments must include disclosures about the methods, sources, and frequency of valuations. Provision II.6.A.3.c requires that firms disclose their valuation methods and procedures for real estate. For example, among other conventional approaches, the firm might capitalize the income generated by a property, using an income capitalization rate imputed or "extracted" from the market based on the net operating income and sale prices of similar properties; or the firm might base the valuation of the subject property directly on the reported sale prices of comparable nearby properties, with adjustments to reflect differences in the properties' location, features, or condition.[21] The real estate standards also require firms to disclose the source of the valuation for each period—that is, whether the valuation is prepared internally, determined by an external valuer, or obtained from a third-party manager (Provision II.6.A.3.e). The firm additionally must disclose the asset-weighted percentage of composite real estate assets valued by an **external valuation** for each period as well as the frequency with which real estate investments are valued by external valuers (Provisions II.6.A.3.f–g).

In an earlier section, we discussed the definition of *discretion* under the main GIPS standards. The GIPS provisions for disclosure associated with real estate performance presentations require firms to provide a description of discretion (Provision II.6.A.3.b). The principals we have already considered in connection with the general standards apply to real estate portfolios, which are considered discretionary if the manager has sole or primary responsibility for major investment decisions. The firm must judge whether client-imposed constraints are so restrictive as to prevent the manager from executing the desired investment strategy, thus rendering a portfolio nondiscretionary. For example, if a client motivated by tax considerations prohibits the manager from selling properties when the manager thinks their value should be realized, or if a client orders that properties be sold at a time when the manager thinks they should be held until prices improve, then the firm may conclude that the portfolio is nondiscretionary.

The Standards also include particular rate-of-return presentation and related disclosure requirements for real estate. **Total return** and its components, income return and capital return, must be presented (Provision II.6.A.4), and the calculation methodology for component returns must be disclosed (Provision II.6.A.3.a). Let us define these terms and explain the calculations.

Total return, income return, and capital return are all calculated based on **capital employed,** computed by adjusting the beginning capital for time-weighted cash flows that occur during the measurement period. Conceptually, we can adjust for weighted cash flows in the same way that we adjust beginning composite assets for external cash flows (see the treatment of Provision II.2.A.3). On the model of Equation 41.7, we can compute capital employed, here designated C_E, as follows:

$$C_E = C_0 + \Sigma(\mathrm{CF}_i \times w_i) \qquad (41.12)$$

where C_0 is the beginning capital.

The **capital return** is calculated by dividing the capital employed (C_E) into the change in market value during the measurement period minus capital expenditures (E_C) plus sale proceeds (S), as shown in Equation 41.13.

$$r_C = \frac{(\mathrm{MV}_1 - \mathrm{MV}_0) - E_C + S}{C_E} \qquad (41.13)$$

The classification of outlays as "capital expenditures" is subject to accounting rules, but capital expenditures may broadly be characterized as costs incurred to acquire and improve real assets. In contrast to costs that are expensed immediately, capital expenditures for long-lived improvements are added to the value of the asset.

The **income return** is calculated by dividing capital employed into investment income accrued during the period (INC_A) minus nonrecoverable expenditures (E_{NR}), interest expense on debt (INT_D), and property taxes (T_P). Nonrecoverable expenditures are items not reimbursed by tenants, such as leasing and financing costs, maintenance, and major repairs. The expression for income return is

$$r_I = \frac{\mathrm{INC}_A - E_{NR} - \mathrm{INT}_D - T_P}{C_E} \qquad (41.14)$$

The single-period total return for real estate, then, is the sum of the component returns:

$$r_T = r_C + r_I \qquad (41.15)$$

As noted, the provisions for disclosure require firms to disclose the calculation methodology for component returns (Provision II.6.A.3.a). In particular, the disclosure must indicate whether the firm calculates component returns in separate series using chain-linked time-weighted rates of return or, alternately, adjusts the returns to make the sum of the income return and the capital return equal to the total return for the periods presented. For example, Table 41.11 displays a composite's income return, capital return, and total return for the four

TABLE 41.11   Real Estate Total Return: An Illustration

	Income Return	Capital Return	Total Return
First quarter	2.15%	−0.52%	1.63%
Second quarter	2.20	0.59	2.79
Third quarter	2.17	0.75	2.92
Fourth quarter	2.10	0.91	3.01
200X	8.90	1.73	10.75

quarters of the year 200X. The full-year returns are calculated by chain-linking the quarterly returns for each series.

With this method, although the income return and the capital return added together equal the total return for each quarter, the component returns for the full year (as they will appear in the performance presentation) do not sum to the total return. The required disclosure on the calculation methodology will explain how the returns were chain linked. Alternatively, if the firm makes an adjustment forcing the component returns taken together to equal the total return, it must disclose that it has done so. Needless to say, the adjustment method must be set forth in the firm's internal documentation.

In addition to requiring that the capital return, income return, and total return of the composite be presented for each period (Provision II.6.A.4), the GIPS standards recommend that the capital and income segments of the appropriate real estate benchmark be presented when the data are available (Provision II.6.B.5).

The GIPS standards for real estate further recommend that firms present the **since-inception internal rate of return** (SI-IRR) for the composite (Provision II.6.B.6). We will encounter SI-IRR again in connection with the standards for private equity, where it is a required element. The internal rate of return is the discount rate that sets an investment's net present value equal to zero; expressed another way, it is the discount rate that equates the present value of an investment's cost with the present value of its benefits. The cost is the capital the client invests; the benefits are the distributions the client receives plus the asset's market value at the end of the measurement period. Mathematically, we calculate the annualized internal rate of return from the value of r that solves the following equation:

$$MV_0 = \frac{CF_1}{(1 + r)^1} + \frac{CF_2}{(1 + r)^2} + \cdots + \frac{MV_N}{(1 + r)^N} \qquad (41.16)$$

where MV_0 represents the initial investment (the beginning market value), the terms CF_1, CF_2, and so on represent interim cash flows, and MV_N represents the ending market value. For simplicity, Equation 41.16 assumes equally spaced end-of-period cash flows. In this equation, r is a subperiod return; when annualized, it is the internal rate of return.

Of course, the investor may make more than one capital contribution. With attention to the direction (the sign) of the cash flows, we can restate the formula for the internal rate of return as follows:

$$\sum_{i=0}^{N} \frac{CF_i}{(1 + r)^i} = 0 \qquad (41.17)$$

where CF_i is the cash flow for the period i and N is the total number of periods. In Equation 41.17, a negative CF_i represents a net cost or outflow to the investor and a positive CF_i represents a net distribution or inflow to the investor; CF_0 and CF_N incorporate MV_0 and MV_N, respectively, in Equation 41.17. This formulation accommodates multiple contributions (cash inflows to the portfolio) and distributions (cash outflows from the portfolio) over the entire inception-to-date timeframe. By setting the sum of the present values of cash inflows and outflows equal to zero, the equation effectively defines r as the discount rate that makes the present value of the cost equal the present value of the benefits.

An example may make the calculation more clear. Let us consider the investment from the perspective of the client who funds the real estate portfolio and receives benefits in the form of cash distributions during the measurement period and ownership of assets valued at market value as of the end of the period. For this example, Table 41.12 shows the timing and

TABLE 41.12   Data for an IRR Calculation

	Date	Quarter	Amount
Initial investment	December 31 Year 0	0	−$150,000
Additional investment	June 30 Year 1	2	−$100,000
Distribution received	March 31 Year 2	5	$12,665
Distribution received	September 30 Year 2	7	$11,130
Ending market value	December 31 Year 2	8	$274,300

amount of the quarterly cash flows. The portfolio's real estate assets are valued as of the end of the second year, so the since-inception performance measurement period is eight quarters.

The client's experience can be expressed graphically, as in Figure 41.6, with the ending market value displayed as a cash flow. Note that in some periods, no cash flows occur.

Using the data in Table 41.12 as inputs to Equation 41.17, we find through an iterative trial-and-error process that the quarterly discount rate r is approximately 2.53 percent. Table 41.13 demonstrates this result. The present value factor applied to each cash flow is $1/(1 + r)^i$, where r is the discount rate and i is the sequential number of the subperiod. For instance, the present value factor applied to the cash distribution of $12,665 received on March 31 of Year 2, the fifth quarter, is

$$\frac{1}{(1 + 0.0253)^5} = 0.88256$$

Table 41.13 shows that 2.53 percent is the quarterly discount rate that sets the sum of the present values of the cash flows from inception through the end of the measurement period equal to zero. The GIPS standards for real estate require us to annualize the since-inception internal rate of return. To annualized a quarterly return, we calculate $(1 + r)^4 - 1$, so the SI-IRR earned in this example is 10.51 percent.

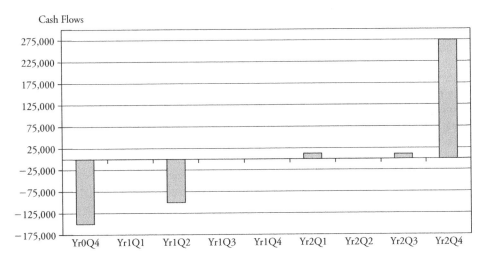

FIGURE 41.6

TABLE 41.13 Demonstration That the Computed IRR Is Correct

Date	Cash Flow	Period	Present Value Factor ($r = 2.53\%$)	Present Value
December 31 Year 0	(150,000)	0	1	(150,000)
June 30 Year 1	(100,000)	2	0.95126	(95,126)
March 31 Year 2	12,665	5	0.88256	11,178
September 30 Year 2	11,130	7	0.83954	9,344
December 31 Year 2	274,300	8	0.81883	224,605
Total (does not equal zero due to rounding)				1

If the SI-IRR is shown, the firm should disclose the time period that is covered as well as the frequency of the cash flows used in the calculation (Provision II.6.B.4). The Standards further recommend that firms use quarterly cash flows at a minimum in calculating the SI-IRR (Provision II.6.B.3). In other words, CF_i should reflect the net cash flow for a period no longer than a quarter.

The GIPS standards also recommend that firms present the annualized since-inception time-weighted rate of return and internal rate of return gross and net of fees. In all cases, the fees should include incentive allocations (i.e., incentive fees). The gross-of-fees and net-of-fees SI-IRRs should be presented on two bases: first, reflecting the composite's ending market value (as shown in the example above), and second, reflecting only realized cash flows—that is, excluding unrealized gains (Provisions II.6.B.7.a–b). The returns mentioned in this paragraph are especially recommended in circumstances in which the investment manager can control the timing of cash contributions to the fund.

Finally, the GIPS standards for real estate suggest that other performance measures may provide additional useful information. Provision II.6.B.7.c advises that the GIPS standards for private equity, discussed below, provide guidance on additional measures such as **investment** and **realization multiples** and ratios based on **paid-in capital.**

Private Equity Standards

The GIPS provisions for private equity use technical terms that may be unfamiliar to the performance measurement generalist. Although simplified for brevity, an overview of the private equity investment process may facilitate understanding of the Standards' requirements and recommendations. Let us take for an example a **venture capital** fund organized as a **limited partnership,** one of many investment structures used in the private equity market. A venture capital firm identifies an emerging industry, develops the fund concept, and secures commitments from investors who pledge to pay in a certain amount of capital over a certain period of time, often three to five years. In this structure, a venture capital firm will serve as **general partner,** and the investors will be **limited partners.** The general partner screens early stage companies' business plans, identifies the most promising enterprises, and conducts in-depth analysis and due diligence on the quality of their management, the legal status of their intellectual property rights, and the prospective demand for their products, among many other factors. The general partner then negotiates deals with the companies that pass scrutiny and places capital calls drawing down the limited partners' committed capital for investment in the portfolio companies. There may be multiple capital calls to meet each company's cash requirements in accordance with the terms of the deal. As the fund matures, the general partner harvests the portfolio companies (for instance, by taking them public) and distributes the proceeds to the limited partners. With this background in mind, let us turn to the GIPS standards for private equity.

Recognizing that valuations of untraded securities are critically based on business assumptions and that practitioners employ a range of valuation methods, the GIPS standards include an exposition of principals to which firms must adhere when estimating the market value of private equities (GIPS Appendix D, "Private Equity Valuation Principals"). Although they appear in an appendix, these principals are integral to the GIPS standards: Provision II.7.A.1 explicitly requires private equity investments to be valued in accordance with them.

The principals obligate firms to ensure that valuations are prepared with integrity and professionalism by individuals with appropriate experience and ability under the direction of senior management and in accordance with documented review procedures. The valuation basis must be divulged as transparently as possible in view of legal and practical constraints; for the latest period presented, the firm must clearly disclose the methodologies and key assumptions used in valuing private equity investments. The valuation basis must be logically cohesive and rigorously applied. At a minimum, valuations must recognize the impact of events that diminish an asset's value. For instance, occurrences such as defaults, legal contests, changes in management, foreign currency devaluations, or substantial deteriorations in market conditions, among many others, may adversely affect an asset's estimated market value. Private equity valuations must be prepared on a consistent and comparable basis from one period to the next; if any change to the valuation basis or method is deemed appropriate, it must be explained and its effect, if material, must be disclosed. Valuations must be prepared at least annually, but quarterly valuations are recommended (see the "Guidelines for Valuation" in GIPS Appendix D and Provision II.7.B.1).

The principals recommend that private equity investments be valued on a fair value basis. **Fair value** represents the amount or price at which an asset could be bought or sold in a current transaction between willing, knowledgeable parties. The GIPS standards set forth a hierarchy or order of fair value methodologies. In this order, the best valuation method looks to a market transaction. For example, if a new round of financing takes place for a closely held company, the arm's-length price at which an external party makes a material investment might provide a sound basis for establishing the current market value of previously issued securities. In the absence of recent market transactions, the next-best method is to use market-based multiples appropriate to the business being valued. For example, the valuation might be based on the current price-to-earnings ratio for comparable publicly traded companies engaged in the same line of business, with an appropriate discount for the limited marketability of the subject company's securities. The least preferred of the three methods in the hierarchy is to calculate the present value of risk-adjusted expected cash flows discounted at the risk-free rate. The risk-free rate is observable, so the discount rate is objectively determinable, but this method is nonetheless critically sensitive to the assumptions underlying the cash flow projections and risk adjustments.

Valuing private equity investments is a challenging assignment even for well-qualified professionals who are informed about the marketplace, knowledgeable about the issuing company's business, trained in financial statement analysis, and experienced in assessing deal structures and terms. This cursory treatment may nonetheless suffice to convey the complexity of the task. We refer the reader to GIPS Appendix D for additional considerations pertaining to the fair valuation of private equity investments.

The GIPS provisions for private equity presentation and reporting require firms to present both the net-of-fees and the gross-of-fees annualized SI-IRR of the composite for each year since inception (Provision II.7.A.20).[22] The calculation methodology provisions for private equity specify that the annualized SI-IRR must be calculated using either daily or monthly cash flows and the end-of-period valuation of the unliquidated holdings remaining in the composite portfolios. Stock **distributions** must be valued at the time of distribution (Provision II.7.A.3).

Net-of-fee returns must be net of **carried interest,** representing the percentage of profits on the fund's investments that general partners receive, as well as investment management fees and **transaction expenses** (Provision II.7.A.4). For **investment advisers,** who (unlike general partners) have no role in the actual management of the portfolio companies held in the fund, *all* returns must be net of underlying partnership and/or fund fees and carried interest, and net-of-fees returns must in addition be net of the investment adviser's own fees, expenses, and carried interest (Provision II.7.A.5).

The GIPS provisions for composite construction require all closed-end private equity investments to be included in a composite defined by strategy and **vintage year** (Provision II.7.A.6). The vintage year, the year that capital is first **drawn down** or called from investors, is useful information for prospective clients who wish to establish the comparability of different composites. The Standards distinguish **direct investments** in assets (for instance, in equity securities issued by a single closely held company) from investments made through partnerships or funds, and they require that partnership and fund investments, direct investments, and open-end private equity investments be in separate composites (Provision II.7.A.7).

Specific disclosure requirements also apply for private equity. Firms must disclose the vintage year of each composite (Provision II.7.A.8) and provide a definition of the composite investment strategy (Provision II.7.A.15). In the private equity arena, the strategy may be, for instance, to make early stage investments in growing companies, to finance turnarounds of distressed companies, or to channel capital to companies operating in a particular geographic area, among other possibilities. Firms must also disclose the total **committed capital** of the composite for the most recent period (Provision II.7.A.11).

As one might expect, there are disclosure requirements pertaining to the valuation of composite assets. For the most recent period, firms must disclose the valuation methodologies employed. In addition, if any change from the prior period occurs in either the valuation basis or the valuation methodology, such a change must be disclosed (Provision II.7.A.12). As noted previously, assets must be valued in accordance with the GIPS Private Equity Valuation Principals. If the presentation complies with any local or regional valuation guidelines in addition to the GIPS principals, firms must disclose which local or regional guidelines they are required to use (Provision II.7.A.13). It must also be disclosed that the firm's valuation review procedures are available upon request (Provision II.7.A.14). Importantly, if a valuation basis other than fair value is used, firms must disclose for the most recent period presented an explanation why fair value is not applicable. Additionally, firms must disclose the number of holdings that are not fair-valued and their carrying value both in absolute amount and relative to the total fund (Provision II.7.A.17). Firms must also disclose the unrealized appreciation or depreciation of the composite for the most recent period (Provision II.7.A.10). This information about the magnitude of unrealized gains or losses will assist prospective clients in evaluating the significance of the estimated end-of-period market values used as inputs to the rate-of-return calculations.

Recall that the GIPS provisions for private equity calculation methodology require firms to use daily or monthly cash flows in computing the SI-IRR. The disclosure provisions require firms to state whether they are using daily or monthly cash flows in the SI-IRR calculation (Provision II.7.A.18).

If benchmark returns are presented, the firm must disclose the calculation methodology used for the benchmark (Provision II.7.A.16). On the other hand, if no benchmark is shown, the presentation must explain why none is provided (see Provision II.7.A.23). Also, the period-end used for a composite must be disclosed if it is not a calendar year-end (Provision II.7.A.19).

Under the general GIPS standards, discontinued composites must remain on the firm's list of composites for at least five years after discontinuation, and firms must provide a compliant presentation upon request for any composite listed (see Provisions II.0.A.12–13). For discontinued private equity composites, the final realization or liquidation date must be stated (Provision II.7.A.9). Disclosing the **final realization date** as well as the vintage date enables prospective clients to determine the time period that the fund existed, for the purpose of comparing one investment with another.

Having reviewed the valuation principals and the requirements for input data, calculation methodology, composite construction, and disclosure, we are in position to address the GIPS provisions for private equity presentation and reporting. We have already noted the requirement that the annualized gross-of-fees and net-of-fees SI-IRRs must be presented for each year since inception (Provision II.7.A.20). A benchmark reflecting the same vintage year and investment strategy may be shown (indeed, if none is shown, firms must justify the omission). If a benchmark is shown, firms must present the cumulative annualized SI-IRR of the benchmark for the same periods that composite performance is presented (Provision II.7.A.23).

Further requirements pertain to the funding status of the composite. For each period presented, firms must report cumulative paid-in capital—that is, the total payments drawn down to date from the capital committed by investors. Paid-in capital may include amounts received by the fund but not yet invested in portfolio companies; the Standards stipulate that firms must also present total current **invested capital** for each period. In addition, firms are required to report cumulative **distributions** paid out to investors in cash or stock for each period presented (Provision II.7.A.21).

Firms must also report certain multiples or ratios for each period presented. One of them is the ratio of **total value** to paid-in capital (TVPI, also called the **investment multiple**). Representing the total return of the investment although not taking time into account, TVPI gives prospective clients information about the value of the composite relative to its cost basis. For the purpose of the TVPI calculation, total value can be determined by adding distributions to date to the end-of-period **residual value** or net asset value of the fund—that is, the market value of assets less accrued investment management fees and carried interest. Firms must also report the ratio of cumulative distributions to paid-in capital (DPI, also called the **realization multiple**); the ratio of **paid-in capital to committed capital (PIC)**; and the ratio of **residual value to paid-in capital (RVPI)**. Listed in Provision II.7.A.22, these required statistics afford prospective clients useful information about the financial history and status of the fund. The provisions for presentation and reporting also recommend, but do not require, that firms report the average holding period of the investments (for example, the portfolio companies in a fund) over the life of the composite (Provision II.7.B.2).

The intricacies of performance presentation in compliance with the GIPS standards for private equity reflect this field's complexity. Of necessity, the introductory treatment given the subject here does not address many nuances or special circumstances that the practitioner may encounter. Further guidance may be found in a paper entitled "Private Equity Provisions for the GIPS Standards" prepared by the Venture Capital and Private Equity Subcommittee of the IPC. This resource is available on the CFA Institute web site.

VERIFICATION

Verification is a review of performance measurement policies, processes, and procedures by an independent third party[23] for the purpose of establishing that a firm claiming compliance has adhered to the GIPS standards. Although verification can be costly and time-consuming, it may offer the firm a competitive marketing advantage by making the claim of compliance more credible. In addition, preparing for and undergoing the verification process may help the firm improve its internal operations. Verification powerfully supports the guiding principals of fair representation and full disclosure of investment performance.

The GIPS standards currently do not require firms to be verified, although verification may become mandatory at some point in the future. Nonetheless, the Standards strongly encourage firms to undergo verification. Section III of the GIPS standards reviews the scope and purpose of verification and sets forth the minimum procedures that verifiers must follow prior to issuing a verification report to the firm. The stated goal of the Investment Performance Council in presenting the verification procedures is to encourage broad acceptance of verification.

IMPLEMENTATION (11)

Selecting a Verification Firm. Verification is a major undertaking, and it is crucial for the investment management firm to choose an independent verifier whose resources match the firm's needs. At the outset of the selection process, the investment management firm approaching verification should consider the scope of its operations and the nature of its products. The requirements of a large investment management organization with a presence in markets around the world will differ from those of a firm operating in only a single country. Similarly, a hedge fund manager, a manager who engages in real estate or private equity investing, a quantitatively oriented manager whose investment strategies rely heavily on the use of derivative securities, or a manager who manages tax-aware portfolios for individuals may have more specialized requirements than a manager who manages funds for tax-exempt institutions such as pension plans and charitable foundations. These factors should be communicated to potential verifiers and reflected in the selection criteria.

Some organizations have standard request-for-proposal templates that can be adapted for specific purposes. The RFP should include a description of the issuing organization and a statement on the scope of the project. Firms investigating verifiers' qualifications might consider initially asking for the following information:

- A description of the verification firm, including its history, ownership, and organizational structure; a description of the performance-related services it offers; and a representative list of verification assignments completed indicating the nature of the investment management firm verified (e.g., "institutional trust division of a regional bank").
- An explanation of the firm's approach to project management, sampling, and testing.
- The roles and professional biographies of the verifiers who will be assigned to this project.
- Client references, including contact details, and information about the number of clients added and lost over some period of time (for instance, the last three years).
- The verification firm's fee schedule.
- A preliminary project plan setting forth the major tasks and estimated timeframes for completion in view of the investment management firm's organizational structure, product line, and clientele.

The reader is also referred to "Suggested Questions to Ask Prospective Verification Firms," a paper published by the IPC. This resource is available on the CFA Institute web site.

In introducing the GIPS standards, we stressed that they must be applied on a firmwide basis (Provision II.0.A.1). The standards for verification state that a verification report can be issued only with respect to the whole firm. In other words, verification cannot be carried out for a single composite (Section III.A.1). After the firm has been verified, as evidenced by a verification report, it may additionally choose to have a detailed Performance Examination conducted on one or more specific composites, but firms are expressly prohibited from stating that a particular composite presentation has been "GIPS verified" (see Section III.C).

The minimum initial period for which verification can be performed is one year of a firm's presented performance. The Standards recommend that verification cover all periods for which the firm claims GIPS compliance (Section III.A.3).

A verification report must confirm that the firm has complied with all the composite construction requirements of the GIPS standards on a firmwide basis and that the firm's processes and procedures are designed to calculate and present performance results in compliance with the GIPS standards. Without such a report from the verifier, the firm cannot state that its claim of compliance with the GIPS standards has been verified (Section III.A.4).

We have seen that a firm that does not meet all the requirements of the GIPS standards may not claim compliance; the firm cannot represent that it is in compliance with the GIPS standards "except for" certain requirements (Provision II.0.A.8). We have seen, too, that firms must document their policies and procedures in writing (Provision II.0.A.6), and they must maintain all data and information necessary to perform the required calculations and to support a performance presentation (Provision II.1.A.1). After conducting the required verification procedures summarized below, however, a verifier may conclude that the firm is not in compliance with these or other requirements of the GIPS standards. In such situations, the verifier must provide a statement to the firm explaining why it cannot issue a verification report (Section III.A.5).

The GIPS standards set forth minimum knowledge-based qualifications for verifiers. Specifically, verifiers must understand all the requirements and recommendations of the GIPS standards, including Guidance Statements and interpretations, and must adhere to any updates and clarifications published by CFA Institute and the IPC (Section III.B.1.b). In addition, verifiers must be knowledgeable about any country-specific laws and regulations that apply to the firm, and they must determine any differences between the GIPS standards and applicable country-specific laws and regulations (Section III.B.1.c).

Required preverification procedures include learning about the firm, the firm's performance-related policies, and the valuation basis for performance calculations. We will consider these requirements in turn.

First, verifiers must obtain selected samples of investment performance reports and other available information to ensure appropriate knowledge of the firm (Section III.B.1.a). This information will enable the verifiers to evaluate the firm's self-definition for the purpose of GIPS compliance.

Second, verifiers must determine the firm's assumptions, policies, and procedures for establishing and maintaining compliance with all applicable requirements of the GIPS standards. Section III.B.1.d enumerates the minimum requirements. Among other items, verifiers must receive the firm's written definition of investment discretion and the guidelines for determining whether accounts are fully discretionary; the firm's list of composite definitions, with written criteria for including accounts in each composite; and the firm's policies regarding the timeframe for including new accounts in and excluding closed accounts from composites. (The section of the GIPS standards devoted to verification uses the term "account" in place of "portfolio.") Verifiers must also determine the firm's policies related to input data, including dividend and interest income accruals and market valuations; portfolio and composite return calculation methodologies, including assumptions on the timing of external cash flows; and the presentation of composite returns. Verifiers must also obtain information on such items as the use of leverage and derivatives, investments in securities or countries that are not included in a composite's benchmark, and the timing of implied taxes on income and realized capital gains if the firm reports performance on an after-tax basis. This list is not exhaustive; indeed, the last item listed in Section III.B.1.d is "any other policies and procedures relevant to performance presentation."

Finally, prior to undertaking verification, verifiers must ensure that they understand the policies and methods used to record valuation information for the purpose of calculating performance. In particular, verifiers must determine that the firm's policy on classifying fund flows (such as interest, dividends, fees, and taxes, as well as contributions and withdrawals) will produce accurate returns in conformity with the GIPS requirements. Verifiers must confirm that the accounting treatment of investment income is appropriate; that tax payments, reclaims, and accruals are handled in a manner consistent with the desired before-tax or after-tax return calculation; that policies governing the recognition of purchases, sales, and the opening and closing of other positions are internally consistent and will produce accurate results; and that the firm's accounting for investments and derivatives is consistent with the GIPS standards. The foregoing requirements are presented in Section III.B.1.e.

IMPLEMENTATION (12)

Preparing for Verification. The investment management firm undertaking verification should gather the following information. The verifiers may use this information to prepare a fee estimate and a project plan, and they will need it in the course of the review.

- Sample performance presentations and marketing materials.
- All of the firm's performance-related policies, such as the firm's definition of discretion; the sources, methods, and review procedures for asset valuations; the time-weighted rate-of-return calculation methodology; the treatment of external cash flows; the computation of composite returns; etc.
- The complete list and description of composites.
- Composite definitions, including benchmarks and written criteria for including accounts.
- A list of all portfolios under management.
- All investment management agreements or contracts, and the clients' investment guidelines.
- A list of all the portfolios that have been in each composite during the verification period, the dates they were in the composites, and documentation supporting any changes to the portfolios in the composites.

The verifiers will also require historical portfolio- and composite-level performance data for sampling and testing. Other information requirements may come to light in the course of the review.

Having summarized the prerequisites for verification (the verifier's qualifications, familiarity with the firm, review of the firm's documented policies, and knowledge of the valuation basis for performance calculations), we turn now to the minimum required verification procedures.

Verifiers must first determine that the firm has been and remains appropriately defined for the purpose of GIPS compliance (Section III.B.2.a). Next, the GIPS standards for verification mandate testing of composite construction. The specific areas to be tested are set forth in Sections III.B.2.b.i–vii. Verifiers must be satisfied that the firm has defined and maintained composites according to reasonable, GIPS-compliant guidelines that have been applied consistently. Verifiers must also confirm that benchmarks are consistent with composite definitions (that is to say, the benchmark chosen for a specific composite appropriately reflects the composite's investment strategy) and that they have been consistently applied over time. Verifiers must be satisfied that the firm's list of composites is complete. In addition, verifiers must determine that all of the firm's actual discretionary fee-paying portfolios are included in at least one composite, that all accounts are included in their respective composites at all times, and that no accounts that belong in a particular composite have been excluded at any time. Verifiers must also be confident that the definition of discretion has been consistently applied over time. Section III.B.2.c requires verifiers to obtain a listing of all the firm's portfolios and to determine that selected accounts have been properly classified as discretionary or nondiscretionary in accordance with the firm's definition of discretion and the account agreements.

Verifiers must obtain a complete list of open and closed accounts for all composites for the years under examination, but they may base their compliance checks on a sample of the firm's accounts. The minimum factors to be considered when selecting sample accounts include the number of composites at the firm, the number of portfolios in each composite, and the nature of the composites. In addition, verifiers must take into account the total assets under management, the internal control structure at the firm, the number of years under examination, the computer applications used in the calculation of performance and the construction and maintenance of composites, and whether the firm uses external performance measurement services. The selection of sample accounts for testing is a critical step in the verification process. If the verifier encounters errors or discovers that the firm's record-keeping is deficient, a larger sample or additional verification procedures may be warranted (Section III.B.2.d).

Verifiers must trace selected accounts from the account agreements to the composites and confirm that the objectives articulated in the account agreement reflect the composite definition. (Verifiers must also determine that all portfolios sharing the same guidelines are included in the same composite.) For selected accounts, verifiers must confirm that the timing of the accounts' initial inclusion in their composites follows the firm's policy for new accounts, and similarly that the timing of the accounts' exclusion from the composite follows the firm's policy for closed accounts. Verifiers must furthermore determine that shifts from one composite to another are consistent with the documented guidelines of the firms' clients (Section III.B.2.e).

Verifiers must also determine whether the firm has computed performance in accordance with the methods and assumptions documented in its policies and disclosed in its presentations. In reaching this determination, verifiers should recalculate rates of return for selected accounts using an acceptable time-weighted rate of return formula as prescribed by the GIPS standards. Verifiers should also use a reasonable sample of composite calculations to test the accuracy of the asset weighting of returns, the geometric chain-linking generating annual rates of return, and the computation of the dispersion measure (Section III.B.2.f).

Verifiers must review a sample of composite presentations to ensure that they include the required information and disclosures (Section III.B.2.g).

Finally, under the GIPS standards, verifiers must maintain sufficient information to support the verification report. In particular, as part of the supporting documentation, verifiers must obtain a representation letter from the firm confirming major policies and any other representations made to the verifier during the examination (Section III.B.2.h).

GIPS ADVERTISING GUIDELINES

A firm may wish to claim that it complies with the GIPS standards in advertisements that do not accommodate fully compliant performance presentations. For instance, space may be limited, or the creative design and marketing message may not call for a performance presentation meeting all the requirements of the GIPS standards. To address this need, the Standards include an appendix expounding ethical standards for the advertisement of performance results. The guidelines are mandatory for firms that include a claim of GIPS compliance in their advertisements. Because the guidelines represent best practices in advertising, however, all firms are encouraged to respect them.

The GIPS Advertising Guidelines do not replace the broader GIPS standards, nor do they in any way exempt firms that claim GIPS compliance from adhering to all the required provisions of the Standards. Moreover, the guidelines do not replace laws and regulations governing performance advertisements. Firms must comply with applicable laws and regulations, and they must disclose any conflicts between the legal or regulatory requirements and the GIPS Advertising Guidelines.

Advertisements include any written or electronic materials addressed to more than one prospective or existing client. Thus "one-on-one" presentations and individual client reports are not considered advertisements. (This rule applies on a relationship basis. Presentations and reports to a single prospective or existing client are not considered advertisements despite the fact that a number of people may be in attendance, such as a board of trustees or the members of an investment committee.) The GIPS Advertising Guidelines pertain to any material disseminated more broadly to retain existing clients or solicit new clients for an adviser.

IMPLEMENTATION (13)

Communicating the GIPS Advertising Guidelines. Applying the GIPS Advertising Guidelines affects the work of marketing and creative staff members who may be unfamiliar with the GIPS standards. The firm's performance practitioners might conduct an educational session or workshop to present the guidelines and discuss implementation with the marketing group, including copywriters and graphic designers, and with the firm's legal or compliance officers. Here are some suggestions for presenting the guidelines and facilitating the discussion:

- Explain that the GIPS standards are ethical standards for fair representation and full disclosure of investment performance.
- Describe in general terms the domains for which Standards have been developed (fundamentals of compliance, input data, calculation methodology, composite construction, disclosures, presentation and reporting, real estate, and private equity, as well as the advertising guidelines).
- Explain how the firm is defined.
- Distribute the firm's list of composites and composite descriptions.
- Explain the relationship between the GIPS standards and the GIPS Advertising Guidelines.
- Explain how advertisements are defined for the purposes of the guidelines.
- Explain the relationship between applicable laws and regulations and the GIPS Advertising Guidelines.
- Present the requirements and recommendations of the advertising guidelines in detail as they apply to

1. Advertisements in which the firm claims compliance with the GIPS standards but does not present performance results.
2. Advertisements in which the firm claims compliance with the GIPS standards and also presents performance.

- Review the sample advertisements provided in Appendix C of the Global Investment Performance Standards.
- Explain how supplemental information can be used to enhance performance presentations. (Consult the IPC's "Guidance Statement on the Use of Supplemental Information," available on the CFA Institute web site.)
- Reach agreement on compliance review procedures for new advertising materials. Because information used in advertisements subject to the guidelines is taken or derived from GIPS-compliant performance presentations, it is advisable for both a legal or compliance officer and a member of the performance measurement group to approve new advertising materials.

All advertisements that state a claim of compliance must include a description of the firm and information about how to obtain a list and description of all the firm's composites or a presentation that complies with the requirements of the GIPS standards (GIPS Advertising Guidelines B.1 and B.2). The required wording of the statement claiming compliance is, "[Name of firm] claims compliance with the Global Investment Performance Standards (GIPS®)" (Guideline B.3). We draw the reader's attention to the difference in wording between the GIPS Advertising Guidelines claim of compliance and the compliance statement that must appear on a fully compliant performance presentation: "[Name of firm] has prepared and presented this report in compliance with the Global Investment Performance Standards (GIPS®)."

All advertisements that not only state a claim of compliance but also present performance results must provide further information, as detailed below, and the relevant information must be taken or derived from a presentation that complies with the requirements of the GIPS standards. The required information includes, among other elements, a description of the strategy of the composite being advertised (Guideline B.4), an indication whether performance is shown gross of fees, net of fees, or both (Guideline B.6), and the currency used to express returns (Guideline B.8). When presenting noncompliant performance information for periods prior to January 1, 2000, in an advertisement, firms must disclose what information does not conform to the GIPS standards, explain the reasons, and identify the periods of noncompliance (Guideline B.10).

Advertisements that state a claim of compliance and present performance must also include period-to-date composite results. Returns for periods less than one year cannot be annualized. In addition to the period-to-date performance, the advertisement must also present either annualized composite returns for the one-year, three-year, and five-year periods ending as of a specified date, or five years of annual composite returns. Whichever option a firm chooses, it must clearly identify the end-of-period date. If the composite has been in existence for a period longer than one year but shorter than five years, the ad must show returns since inception. The annualized or annual returns must be calculated through the same period of time as presented in the corresponding GIPS-compliant presentation (Guideline B.5.a–b).

Advertisements asserting a claim of GIPS compliance must also present the benchmark total return for the same periods as those for which composite performance is presented. The appropriate benchmark, which must be described in the advertisement, is the same benchmark used in the corresponding GIPS-compliant presentation. If no benchmark is presented, the advertisement must disclose the reason why none is shown (Guideline B.7).

Advertisements stating compliance with the GIPS standards and presenting performance must also describe how and to what extent leverage or derivative securities are used if they are actively employed as part of the investment strategy and have a material effect on composite returns (Guideline B.9).

GIPS Appendix C, "GIPS Advertising Guidelines," includes sample advertisements with and without performance information. As the samples illustrate, it takes more space to spell out the requirements than to meet them. The guidelines recommend that firms present supplemental or additional performance information, in a manner consistent with the ethical principals of fair representation and full disclosure, on the conditions that the supplemental information must be clearly labeled as such and displayed with equal or lesser prominence than the required information. When supplemental information is presented for noncompliant periods, the advertisement must identify the periods, disclose what information is not in compliance with the GIPS standards, and explain why it is so. The reader is referred to the IPC's "Guidance Statement on the Use of Supplemental Information" for further direction.

OTHER ISSUES

We have finished reviewing the GIPS standards. In this part of the chapter, we will introduce after-tax performance measurement issues and calculation techniques, and we will comment on ways to keep informed about future developments affecting the application of the GIPS standards.

After-Tax Return Calculation Methodology

The GIPS standards do not require compliant firms to present after-tax returns for composites made up of portfolios managed on a tax-aware basis. Many firms engage in investment management on behalf of taxable institutions, individuals, and family offices, however, and they market tax-aware strategies to prospective clients who wish to evaluate their performance records. The interaction of complex regional tax codes with clients' varied circumstances and objectives not only renders tax-aware investing extremely arduous but also complicates performance measurement for firms subscribing to the ethical principals of fair representation and full disclosure. In this section, we will discuss major issues surrounding after-tax performance evaluation and present fundamental concepts and norms for after-tax return calculations based on standards defined for U.S.-based firms that complied with the former AIMR Performance Presentation Standards (AIMR-PPS). The AIMR-PPS after-tax provisions have been incorporated in the GIPS "Guidance Statement for Country-Specific Taxation Issues." Although country-specific tax regulations vary widely, many of the principals of after-tax performance measurement apply universally.

Let us first consider certain theoretical aspects and practical factors that make valid after-tax performance measurement, analysis, and evaluation problematic.

The timeframe in which estimated tax liabilities are assumed to be realized affects the after-tax rate of return. As we will see, a "preliquidation" calculation method (required under the section of the Guidance Statement for Country-Specific Taxation Issues subtitled "GIPS United States After-Tax Guidance") takes into account only the taxes realized during the measurement period. That is, the before-tax return is reduced by the taxes associated with investment income earned and gains and losses realized during the period. This calculation may understate the tax effect, however, because it does not recognize any tax liability or benefit for unrealized gains and losses embedded in the portfolio's ending market value. Although the securities in the portfolio are subject to future price-driven changes in market value, and the tax-aware portfolio manager will take advantage of opportunities to offset gains with losses and to defer taxes,[24] the preliquidation method entirely disregards the prospective tax effects that may result from the portfolio's currently unrealized capital gains and losses. In other words, the preliquidation method effectively assumes that unrealized capital gains are untaxed.[25]

Another calculation method assumes that all taxes on unrealized gains are immediately payable as of the end of the measurement period. (The Guidance Statement for Country-Specific Taxation Issues permits firms reporting after-tax returns to disclose this "mark-to-liquidation" return as supplemental information.) This method may overstate the tax effect, however, because in addition to disregarding future market value changes affecting the actual tax liability, it neglects the time value of money. Portfolios are generally managed on an ongoing basis, and in the normal course of events, taxable gains and losses will be realized as securities are sold, and the proceeds distributed or reinvested, at an indeterminate pace over the planning horizon.

For analytical purposes, we may derive potentially useful information from estimating the timing and amount of future tax assessments over suitably extended periods.[26] Such estimates of the portfolio's "true economic value," however, necessarily rest on debatable assumptions about future returns, among other parameters, and at present no generally accepted guidelines exist for modeling prospective tax outcomes in a manner that ensures the methodological comparability warranted for performance reporting.[27] After-tax returns uniformly calculated in accordance with the "preliquidation" and "mark-to-liquidation" methods reflect actual before-tax results achieved during the measurement period rather than projected investment experience. Given the known deficiencies of these latter methods, however, the prospective client must interpret after-tax returns with care.

We have seen that the historical cost of securities held in a portfolio is irrelevant to before-tax performance measurement, where assets are valued at market value and no distinction is made between realized and unrealized gains and losses. The taxable "cost basis" of portfolio investments is used, however, in determining tax liabilities for the purpose of after-tax return calculations. In addition, different tax regulations and rates may apply depending on the length of the holding period and the types of securities held. Clients' anticipated tax rates also vary, contingent on such factors as their level of income and the tax jurisdictions to which they belong. As a practical matter, therefore, substantially more extensive input data must be captured and managed to support reasonable after-tax performance calculations.[28]

IMPLEMENTATION (14)

Anticipated Tax Rates. The GIPS standards for U.S. after-tax performance require the consistent use over time and within each composite of either the "anticipated tax rates" or the maximum tax rates applicable to each client. It is recommended that after-tax performance be calculated based on each client's "anticipated tax rates" for investment income and capital gains.

Determined in advance of the performance measurement period, the anticipated tax rates should be the tax rates that an investment manager expects a specific taxable client to face on returns generated during the prospective reporting period for each applicable tax class. The subsequent computation of the client's actual tax liability may be based on rates that prove, after the fact, to differ from the expected rates. The anticipated tax rates are appropriate for performance measurement, however, because they are the rates that guide the tax-aware portfolio manager's investment decisions. In addition, use of the anticipated tax rates enables the firm to use the same after-tax returns when reporting to individual clients and constructing composites.

Different clients will have different anticipated tax rates depending on myriad factors, typically including their income from all sources, their domicile, the types of securities in which they invest, and the details of the tax codes to which they are subject. For instance, an individual who resides in New York City is liable for U.S., New York State, and New York City income taxes, and her anticipated tax rate will differ from that of another individual holding the same assets and earning the same income elsewhere. Depending on the applicable regulations, which vary widely from one jurisdiction or tax regime to another, different rate schedules may apply to different kinds of income (e.g., ordinary income, short-term capital gains, and long-term capital gains) and to different types of securities (e.g., corporate bonds and municipal securities). In addition, taxes paid to one authority may reduce the amount payable to another. For example, income taxes paid at the state and local level may be deductible from the federal tax liability. In this case,

$$\text{Anticipated income tax rate} = \text{Federal tax rate} + [\text{State tax rate} \times (1 - \text{Federal tax rate})] + [\text{Local tax rate} \times (1 - \text{Federal tax rate})]$$

If the applicable federal, state, and local income tax rates for an individual client are estimated to be 22 percent, 5 percent, and 3 percent, respectively, and the state and local taxes are deductible from the federal taxes, then the client's anticipated income tax rate, T_{incr}, is

$$\begin{aligned} T_{incr} &= 0.22 + [0.05 \times (1 - 0.22)] + [0.03 \times (1 - 0.22)] \\ &= 0.22 + 0.039 + 0.023 \\ &= 0.282 = 28.2\% \end{aligned}$$

The client or the investment manager may need to consult with a qualified tax accountant or attorney to determine the anticipated tax rates. The client-specific IPS or guidelines for tax-aware investment mandates should document the agreed-upon anticipated tax rates in sufficient detail to support portfolio management decisions and to facilitate the determination of valid after-tax returns. Of course, the anticipated tax rates should be periodically reviewed and updated to reflect changes in the client's circumstances.

If the client's anticipated tax rate is unknown, the section of the Guidance Statement for Country-Specific Taxation Issues subtitled "GIPS United States After-Tax Guidance" permits the use of the maximum federal tax rate (or the maximum federal, state, and local tax rates) for the specific category of investor.

Not only is calculating after-tax portfolio returns intricate, selecting or devising appropriate performance benchmarks is also difficult. Valid before-tax benchmarks have certain properties. Among other attributes, they are unambiguous, investable, measurable, specified or agreed upon in advance, and consistent with the investment strategy or style of the portfolio or composite. After-tax benchmarks should have all the desirable properties of suitable before-tax benchmarks, and one more: They should additionally reflect the client's tax status.

Financial services firms publish capital market indices representing a wide range of investment strategies and styles. Some providers calculate index returns net of withholding taxes on dividends, but at this writing none have published index returns fully reflecting imputed effects of taxation. Conceptually, given information on the constituent securities or the price and income return components, investment management firms could adjust reported before-tax index results to construct an after-tax benchmark. Adjusting standard before-tax indices is easier said than done, however. The adjustment methodology would have to incorporate the provider's rules for constructing and rebalancing the original index (e.g., whether it is equal weighted, capitalization weighted, or float weighted), the taxable turnover of securities held in the index, and issuers' corporate actions such as stock splits, as well as security-specific dividend and interest payments and price changes. A firm might formulate some simplifying assumptions to lessen the data requirements and reduce the computational intensity introduced by these factors.[29]

Alternatives to modifying standard before-tax indices include using mutual funds or exchange-traded funds as benchmarks, or developing customized shadow portfolios. Mutual funds and exchange-traded funds benchmarked to capital market indices are imperfect benchmarks because they are subject to fees, and their returns may deviate from those of the indices they emulate. The tax liabilities of mutual funds are affected by the portfolio manager's security transactions and by the collective deposit and redemption activities of shareholders. Exchange-traded funds likewise have turnover, but they do not incur taxes as a result of other investors' actions, so they may be better suited as benchmarks for after-tax performance evaluation.

Nonetheless, the investment management firm seeking a valid after-tax benchmark must address the fact that any one particular client's tax experience depends not only on the rates at which her investment income and capital gains are taxed but also the cost basis of the securities and the sequence of cash flows in her portfolio. The firm that uses custom security-based benchmarks for performance evaluation is well positioned to simulate the tax impact of external cash flows on benchmark results. Firms that use standard indices for before-tax performance evaluation can simulate the effect of client-specific cash flows on estimated after-tax benchmark returns by assuming that the benchmark pays proportionately the same capital gains taxes for withdrawals as the actual portfolio and invests contributions at the cost basis of the index at the time the contribution is made.[30] Alternately, firms can use mutual funds or exchange-traded funds to build shadow portfolios in which simulated purchases and sales are triggered by client-initiated cash flows. These approaches, however, are also data and computation intensive. Moreover, a customized shadow portfolio that works well for a single portfolio is unlikely to be useful for a composite made up of multiple client portfolios. Constructing valid benchmarks remains one of the greatest challenges in after-tax performance evaluation.

Let us turn to the mathematics of after-tax portfolio returns. To illustrate the calculations, we will consider a U.S. equity portfolio managed by the Personal Trust Services division of Eastern National Bank for Edward Moriarty, a wealthy individual who has inquired about his portfolio's performance on an after-tax basis. The data in Table 41.14 reflect activity in the Moriarty portfolio for the month of June, when the portfolio's before-tax return calculated in accordance with the Modified Dietz method was 7.19 percent. The anticipated tax rates used in this example are hypothetical. Dividends are assumed to be taxable at the ordinary income tax rate.

The GIPS provisions for U.S. after-tax performance presentation require firms to use a "preliquidation" calculation methodology reflecting the incidence of taxation on a realized basis (GIPS United States After-Tax Guidance, A.1.a). Several preliquidation alternatives were defined to parallel before-tax return calculations conforming to the main standards. The after-tax Modified Dietz method adjusts before-tax returns by reducing the numerator in the amount of realized taxes, reflecting the tax liability or benefit associated with the accrued taxable income and net realized gains or losses that occurred during the measurement period. (As noted above, preliquidation return calculation methods do not consider the tax

TABLE 41.14   Data for an Illustration of After-Tax
Performance Presentation

Market value as of May 31	25,000,000
Withdrawal on June 20	(2,000,000)
Market value as of June 30	24,750,000
Dividend income in June	125,000
Short-term capital gains realized in June	275,000
Long-term capital gains realized in June	2,250,000
Anticipated income tax rate	45.0%
Anticipated short-term capital gains tax rate	25.0%
Anticipated long-term capital gains tax rate	15.0%

implications of unrealized gains.) The tax liability, called "realized taxes" in the GIPS United States After-Tax Guidance, is calculated as follows:

$$T_{\text{real}} = (G_{\text{Lreal}} \times T_{\text{Lcgr}}) + (G_{\text{Sreal}} \times T_{\text{Scgr}}) + (\text{INC}_{\text{tA}} \times T_{\text{incr}}) \qquad (41.18)$$

where T_{real} is "realized taxes," G_{Lreal} is long-term capital gains realized during the period, T_{Lcgr} is the long-term capital gains tax rate, G_{Sreal} is short-term capital gains realized during the period, T_{Scgr} is the short-term capital gains tax rate, INC_{tA} is taxable income accrued during the period, and T_{incr} is the applicable income tax rate. Note that under the GIPS provisions for U.S. after-tax performance presentation, the tax liability or benefit must be recognized in the same period that the taxable event occurs, and taxes on income must be recognized on an accrual basis (GIPS United States After-Tax Guidance A.1.b–c). In addition, all calculations must consistently use either the anticipated tax rate or the maximum tax rate applicable to each client for the period for which the after-tax return is calculated (GIPS United States After-Tax Guidance A.1.e–f).

Adapting Equation 41.4, the preliquidation after-tax Modified Dietz formula can then be represented mathematically as follows:

$$r_{PLATModDietz} = \frac{\text{MV}_1 - \text{MV}_0 - \text{CF} - T_{\text{real}}}{\text{MV}_0 + \sum(\text{CF}_i \times w_i)} \qquad (41.19)$$

where $r_{PLATModDietz}$ is the preliquidation after-tax return, MV_1 is the end-of-period market value, MV_0 is the beginning market value, CF is the sum of external cash flows during the measurement period, T_{real} is the tax liability, and $\sum(\text{CF}_i \times w_i)$ is the sum of each cash flow multiplied by the proportion of the measurement period that each cash flow has been in the portfolio. The calculation of the time-weighting factor w_i is set forth in Equation 41.5. Notice that reducing the numerator by the amount of "realized taxes" is the only change from the modified Dietz formula.

The Moriarty portfolio had only one cash flow during the measurement period, a withdrawal of $2,000,000 that occurred on June 20. The corresponding end-of-day weighting factor is $(30 - 20)/30 = 0.33$. Using Equations 41.18 and 41.19, the after-tax return earned by the Moriarty portfolio in the month of June was 5.29 percent:

$$T_{real} = (2,250,000 \times 0.15) + (275,000 \times 0.25) + (125,000 \times 0.45)$$
$$= 462,500$$

$$r_{PLATModDietz} = \frac{24,750,000 - 25,000,000 - (-2,000,000) - 462,500}{25,000,000 + (-2,000,000 \times 0.33)}$$
$$= 0.0529 = 5.29\%$$

Observe that the preliquidation after-tax return is equivalent to the before-tax return less the return impact of the tax liability:

$$r_{PLATModDietz} = r_{ModDietz} - \frac{T_{real}}{MV_0 + \sum(CF_i \times w_i)} \qquad (41.20)$$

This relationship is borne out in the Moriarty portfolio. The return impact of realized taxes in June precisely accounts for the 1.9 percent difference between the portfolio's before-tax return of 7.19 percent and preliquidation after-tax return of 5.29 percent:

$$\frac{462,500}{25,000,000 + (-2,000,000 \times 0.33)} = 0.019 = 1.9\%$$

The Linked Internal Rate of Return method introduced with Equation 41.6 can also be adapted to calculate the after-tax return on the preliquidation basis. In this case, the ending market value is reduced by the amount of realized taxes, and the after-tax return is the value of r that satisfies the following equation:

$$MV_1 - T_{real} = \sum[CF_i \times (1 + r)^{w_i}] + MV_0(1 + r) \qquad (41.21)$$

The third preliquidation method approved by the GIPS standards for U.S. firms can be used by firms that strike daily market valuations. In this formulation, the preliquidation after-tax return for a single day is the one-day change in market value less the tax liability, expressed as a percentage of the beginning value. (External cash flows are assumed to be captured in the beginning value.) Although daily market valuations are onerous, the after-tax return calculation is straightforward. The formula is

$$r_{PLATdv} = \frac{MV_{ED} - MV_{BD} - T_{real}}{MV_{BD}} \qquad (41.22)$$

where r_{PLATdv} is the preliquidation after-tax return with daily valuations, MV_{ED} is the market value at the end of the day (comparable to MV_1 in earlier return formulas), MV_{BD} is the market value at the beginning of the day (comparable to MV_0), and T_{real} is the tax liability as previously defined. Single-day after-tax returns can then be converted to wealth-relative form $(1 + r)$ and geometrically chain-linked to generate the time-weighted after-tax return for the measurement period.

Among the other requirements of the GIPS provisions for U.S. after-tax calculation methodology, firms must take into account taxes on income and realized capital gains regardless of whether taxes are paid from portfolio assets or from assets held outside the portfolio (GIPS United States After-Tax Guidance A.1.d). The pretax returns for composites that hold tax-exempt securities must be presented without "grossing up" tax-exempt income (GIPS United States After-Tax Guidance A.1.g)—that is, without restating tax-exempt income to a taxable-equivalent basis. Each portfolio in the composite must be given full credit for net realized losses, on the assumption that these losses will be offset by gains at a later date or in the client's other assets (GIPS United States After-Tax Guidance A.1.h).

As indicated above, the pertinent GIPS after-tax standards require U.S. firms that present after-tax returns to calculate them on a preliquidation basis but permitted firms to disclose after-tax returns calculated on a "mark-to-liquidation" basis as supplemental information. The mark-to-liquidation after-tax calculations resemble the preliquidation calculations, but they substitute "liquidation value" for the market value of assets and net cash flows in the return formula. Liquidation value is defined as market value reduced by the tax liability associated with unrealized capital gains in the portfolio. The interpretive guidance in Appendix A of the Guidance Statement for Country-Specific Taxation Issues After-Tax document shows liquidation value used in place of market value in both the numerator and the denominator of the mark-to-liquidation after-tax return formula. Some practitioners hold, however, that using the beginning liquidation value in the denominator may understate the assets at risk and lead to unreasonable results.

We have observed that performance measurement attempts to quantify the value added by a portfolio manager's investment actions. Because managers should not be held accountable for factors beyond their control, the GIPS standards exclude nondiscretionary portfolios from composites and prescribe time-weighted returns to eliminate the impact of external cash flows. Portfolio managers may be compelled to liquidate securities to meet client-directed withdrawals, however, and taxes may be realized as a result of the nondiscretionary asset sales. The GIPS recommendations for after-tax return calculation methodology permits U.S. firms to provide additional supplementary return information with an adjustment to remove the tax effect of nondiscretionary capital gains (GIPS United States After-Tax Guidance B.1.b). In effect, the adjustment adds back the hypothetical realized taxes that were not incurred at the manager's discretion.[31]

To avoid creating a perverse incentive for the portfolio manager to maximize the adjustment credit by selecting highly appreciated assets for sale, the recommended adjustment term reflects the capital gains tax that would be sustained if all the securities in the portfolio were proportionately liquidated. For this purpose, the adjustment term uses a factor called the gain ratio (GR):

$$GR = \frac{G_{real} + G_{unreal}}{MV_1 + CF_{NetOut}} \tag{41.23}$$

where G_{real} is capital gains realized during the period, G_{unreal} is unrealized capital gains held in the portfolio at the end of the period, MV_1 is the ending market value, and CF_{NetOut} is net client withdrawals during the period—that is, withdrawals less investment income and positive cash flows.

The adjustment factor for nondiscretionary realized taxes can then be computed as follows:

$$\text{Adjustment factor} = F = CF_{NetOut} \times T_{cgr} \times GR \tag{41.24}$$

With the adjustment factor in hand, a simple change to the preliquidation Modified Dietz after-tax return calculation (Equation 41.19) removes the effect of nondiscretionary realized taxes:

$$r_{AdjPLATModDietz} = \frac{MV_1 - MV_0 - CF - T_{real} + F}{MV_0 + \Sigma(CF_i \times w_i)} \tag{41.25}$$

Edward Moriarty withdrew $2 million from his portfolio in June. Given that the tax cost basis of the portfolio was $14.25 million at the end of the month, the portfolio's preliquidation after-tax return can be adjusted as shown below to compensate for the nondiscretionary capital gains associated with this withdrawal. Recognizing that both short-term and long-term capital gains were realized during June, we will use a weighted-average capital gains tax rate of 16.1 percent. Note that the net outflow term (CF_{NetOut}) represents the withdrawal less dividend income:

$$GR = \frac{(275,000 + 2,250,000) + (24,750,000 - 14,250,000)}{24,750,000 + (2,000,000 - 125,000)} = 0.4892$$

$$F = (2,000,000 - 125,000) \times 0.161 \times 0.4892 = 147,677$$

$$r_{AdjPLATModDietz} = \frac{24,750,000 - 25,000,000 - (-2,000,000) - 462,500 + 147,677}{25,000,000 + (-2,000,000 \times 0.33)}$$

$$r_{AdjPLATModDietz} = 0.059 = 5.9\%$$

Therefore, in the case of the Moriarty portfolio, the adjustment increases the preliquidation after-tax return for the month of June from 5.29 percent to 5.9 percent, an improvement of 61 basis points (0.61 percent).

There is another situation in which client actions affect after-tax returns (in this case, favorably). The client may instruct a portfolio manager to realize tax losses to offset gains realized either within the portfolio or in other assets held outside the portfolio. For the client, such "tax loss harvesting" reduces his tax liability on net capital gains. This practice is entirely consistent with the fundamental wealth management principal that investors should consider all their assets when making investment decisions. For the portfolio manager who has realized gains or who handles only a portion of the client's assets, however, the nondiscretionary directive to harvest tax losses improves reported after-tax results. One of the disclosure recommendations of the GIPS provisions for U.S. after-tax performance advises firms to disclose the percentage benefit of tax-loss harvesting for the composite if realized losses are greater than realized gains during the period (GIPS United States After-Tax Guidance B.3.b). The recommendation implicitly assumes that tax benefits not used within the portfolio in the measurement period can be used outside the portfolio or in the future. The wealth benefit derived from tax loss harvesting is computed by applying the appropriate capital gains tax rate to the net losses realized in the period; the percentage benefit may be calculated by dividing the money benefit by the simple average assets in the portfolio:

$$\text{Benefit of Tax Loss Harvesting} = B = L_{net} \times T_{cgr} \tag{41.26}$$

where L_{net} designates the amount of net losses (that is, capital losses less capital gains realized during the period) and T_{cgr} designates the applicable capital gains tax rate.

$$\text{Percent Benefit of Tax Loss Harvesting} = \frac{B}{(MV_0 + MV_1)/2} \tag{41.27}$$

where MV_0 is the beginning market value and MV_1 is the ending market value of the portfolio or composite.

With this, we conclude the introduction to after-tax return calculations for individual portfolios. It is evident even from this abbreviated presentation that after-tax performance measurement requires considerable expertise as well as extensive data and powerful technology, particularly when advancing from the portfolio to the composite level. The interpretive guidance accompanying the pertinent GIPS U.S. standards acknowledges that after-tax performance analysis is both a science and an art: "The *'scientific'* aspects are manifested in the discrete requirements and details, while the *'artisanal'* aspects recognize that cash flows, substantial Unrealized Capital Gains, and composite definitions can have a significant impact on after-tax results."[32] Supplemental information, including tax efficiency measures not presented here, can materially assist prospective clients in evaluating a firm's after tax performance record. We refer the practitioner to the fuller treatment given after-tax performance in the GIPS standards and the guidance available on the CFA Institute web site.

Keeping Current with the GIPS Standards

At the beginning of this chapter, we surveyed the evolution of performance presentation standards, marking as particularly noteworthy events the publication of Peter Dietz's work in 1966 and the report of the Financial Analysts Federation's Committee for Performance Presentation Standards in 1987. The Global Investment Performance Standards are now fairly comprehensive and well defined, the integrated product of thoughtful contributions from many academicians and practitioners committed to the ethical ideals of fairness and honesty in reporting investment results. The revised GIPS standards issued in 2005 represent a significant advance in the globalization of performance presentation norms.

Nonetheless, the GIPS standards will continue to evolve over time to address additional aspects of performance presentation. The IPC states that it will continue to develop the GIPS standards so that they maintain their relevance within the changing investment management industry, and it has committed to evaluating the Standards every five years (Provision I.G.24).

Guidance Statements adopted by the IPC or the GIPS EC, as well as interpretations and clarifications published on the CFA Institute web site, apply to all firms that claim compliance with the GIPS standards (Provision II.0.A.15). Practitioners should visit the web site frequently in order to stay informed about requirements and recommended best practices at no cost. CFA Institute and other organizations also offer publications and conduct conferences and workshops designed to help practitioners implement and maintain compliance with the GIPS standards.

NOTES

1. The Committee for Performance Presentation Standards (1987, p. 8).
2. Competence in evaluating compliance with the GIPS standards is a major curriculum element in the Certificate in Investment Performance Measurement (CIPM) program.
3. The GIPS standards refer to the investment management firm claiming compliance as the FIRM. This chapter uses boldface type for terms that are defined in the GIPS glossary (Appendix E of the Global Investment Performance Standards).
4. The GIPS standards have three major sections: I. Introduction; II. Provisions of the Global Investment Performance Standards; and III. Verification. This chapter cites the GIPS standards by giving the major section followed by subsection identifiers.
5. A *composite* is formally defined as an "aggregation of individual portfolios representing a similar investment mandate, objective, or strategy." The construction of composites is discussed in detail on pages 851–863.
6. CPPS (1987, pp. 8–11).

7. For further information, see www.imca.org/standards.

8. The claim of compliance given here may be used only on a fully compliant performance presentation. Different wording for compliance claims in advertisements is stipulated in the GIPS Advertising Guidelines, discussed later in this chapter.

9. It merits repeating that only investment firms can claim to be in compliance with the GIPS standards, and such claims are legitimate only if *all* the requirements have been met. Accordingly, software developers and third-party performance measurement providers may not claim compliance with the Standards.

10. Note, however, that cost or book values and realized gains and losses are pertinent for after-tax performance calculations, discussed later.

11. For periods before 1 January 2010, the Standards recommend but do not require that valuations be done as of calendar month-end or the last business day of the month (Standard II.1.B.3).

12. The GIPS glossary defines a *time-weighted rate of return* as a "calculation that computes period by period returns on an investment and removes the effects of external cash flows, which are generally client driven, and best reflects the firm's ability to manage assets according to a specified strategy or objective."

13. Cash flows can also be assumed to occur at the beginning of the day. In that case, the weight factor is adjusted to add another day to the period of time the cash flow is in the portfolio: $w_i = (CD - D_i + 1)/CD$. It is incumbent upon the firm to establish a policy to weight external cash flows consistently.

14. The Modified IRR method differs from the original internal rate of return method in that the exponent is the proportion of the measurement period that each cash flow is in the portfolio. Therefore, while the original IRR is a money-weighted return, the Modified IRR approximates a time-weighted return.

15. For a comprehensive treatment of these topics, the interested reader is referred to Larry Harris, *Trading and Exchanges; Market Microstructure for Practitioners* (Oxford University Press, 2003).

16. CFA Institute addresses this and many related issues in its "Trade Management Guidelines" and "Soft Dollar Standards," available on the web site at www.cfainstitute. org/standards/ethics.

17. For an explanation how to calculate quartiles, see DeFusco, McLeavey, Pinto, and Runkle (2004, pp. 120–124).

18. The GIPS glossary entry for dispersion indicates that the standard deviation of portfolio returns can be either equal weighted or asset weighted. The presentation here is limited to the equal-weighted calculation.

19. The use of both n and $n - 1$ in the denominator can be supported. If n were used in calculating the standard deviation of returns for the example presented in the text, the result would be 22 basis points (0.22 percent).

20. Nondiscretionary portfolios, however, cannot be included in a firm's composites under the GIPS standards.

21. These and other appraisal techniques are explained in Shilling (2002, Chapters 10 and 11).

22. We introduced the SI-IRR in connection with the GIPS standards for real estate.

23. The "Guidance Statement on Verifier Independence" defines the term *independence* in the context of verification and addresses potential independence issues. It is available on the CFA Institute web site.

24. Existing U.S. tax law also permits the tax cost basis of securities to be "stepped up" to current market value upon the death of the owner, so heirs may avoid taxes on unrealized gains and losses in the portfolio.

25. See Poterba (1999).
26. Stein (1998) proposes a method for estimating a "full cost equivalent" portfolio value.
27. The interpretive guidance in Appendix A of the "Guidance Statement for Country-Specific Taxation Issues" includes an informative treatment of the "true economic value" method in application. See Section I, "Supplemental Return Calculation Methodologies."
28. From an implementation perspective, the input data requirements and after-tax return calculation methodology have significant implications for the development or selection of portfolio accounting and performance measurement systems. See Rogers and Price (2002) and Simpson (2003).
29. Stein, Langstraat, and Narasimhan (1999) suggest a method to approximate after-tax benchmark returns.
30. Price (2001) presents three increasingly accurate levels of approximation in constructing after-tax benchmarks from pretax indices and describes the "shadow portfolio" approach to adjusting indices for client-specific cash flows.
31. Price (1996) presents the logic and implications of this adjustment factor.
32. Guidance Statement for Country-Specific Taxation Issues, Appendix A, "Additional Guidance on United States After-Tax Calculation and Presentation," p. 25.

REFERENCES

Committee for Performance Presentation Standards (CPPS). 1987. "A Report on Setting Performance Presentation Standards." *Financial Analysts Journal.* Vol. 43, No. 5:8.

DeFusco, Richard, Dennis McLeavey, Jerald Pinto, and David Runkle. 2004. *Quantitative Methods for Investment Analysis*, 2nd edition. Charlottesville, VA: CFA Institute.

Dietz, Peter. 1966. *Pension Funds: Measuring Investment Performance.* New York: The Free Press.

Poterba, James. 1999. "Unrealized Capital Gains and the Measurement of After-Tax Portfolio Performance." *Journal of Private Portfolio Management.* Vol. 1, No. 4.

Price, Lee. 1996. "Calculation and Reporting of After-Tax Performance." *Journal of Performance Measurement.* Vol. 1, No. 2.

Price, Lee. 2001. "Taxable Benchmarks: The Complexity Increases." *AIMR Conference Proceedings: Investment Counseling for Private Clients III.* No. 4.

Rogers, Douglas, and Lee Price. 2002. "Challenges with Developing Portfolio Accounting Software for After-Tax Reporting." *Journal of Performance Measurement.* Vol. 6, Technology Supplement.

Shilling, James. 2002. *Real Estate*, 13th edition. Mason, OH: South-Western.

Simpson, John. 2003. "Searching for a System to Meet Your After-Tax Performance Reporting Needs." *Journal of Performance Measurement.* Vol. 7, Performance Presentation Standards Supplement.

Stein, David. 1998. "Measuring and Evaluating Portfolio Performance After Taxes." *Journal of Portfolio Management.* Vol. 24, No. 2.

Stein, David, Brian Langstraat, and Premkumar Narasimhan. 1999. "Reporting After-Tax Returns: A Pragmatic Approach." *Journal of Private Portfolio Management.* Spring.

GLOBAL INVESTMENT PERFORMANCE STANDARDS (GIPS®)

Revised by the Investment Performance Council and adopted by the CFA Institute Board of Governors February 2005

**Created and Funded by CFA Institute
In Conjunction with the Following Local Sponsors:**

Australia — Performance Analyst Group of Australia

Austria — Österreichischen Verreinigung für Finanzanalyse und Asset Management und der Vereinigung Österreichischer Investmentgesellschaften

Belgium — Belgian Association for Pension Institutions

Denmark — The Danish Society of Investment Professionals, The Danish Society of Financial Analysts

France — Société Francaise des Analystes Financiers and Association Francaise de la Gestion Financière

Germany — BVI Bundesverband Investment und Asset Management e.V., Deutsche Vereinigung für Finanzanalyse und Asset Management, and German CFA Society

Hong Kong — The Hong Kong Society of Financial Analysts

Hungary — Hungarian Society of Investment Professionals

Ireland — Irish Association of Investment Managers

Italy — Italian Investment Performance Committee

Japan — The Security Analysts Association of Japan

Luxembourg — Association Luxembourgeoise des Fonds d'Investissement and Association Luxembourgeoise des Gestionnaires de Portefeuilles et Analystes Financiers

Netherlands — Beroepsvereniging van Beleggingsdeskundigen

New Zealand — CFA Society of New Zealand

Norway — The Norwegian Society of Financial Analysts

Poland — Polski Komitet Wyników Inwestycyjnych

Portugal — Associação Portuguesa de Analistas Financeiros

Singapore — Investment Management Association of Singapore

Reprinted from the CFA Institute Centre for Financial Market Integrity (February 2005).

Spain — CFA Spain
South Africa — Investment Management Association of South Africa
Sweden — Swedish Society of Financial Analysts

Switzerland — Swiss Bankers Association
United Kingdom — National Association of Pension Funds Ltd
United States and Canada — CFA Institute

INVESTMENT PERFORMANCE COUNCIL (IPC) 2004–2005

Chair
James E. Hollis III, CFA
Cutter Associates, Inc.
United States

Consultants
Brian Henderson
Hymans Robertson
United Kingdom

Ron Surz
PPCA, Inc.
United States

Derivatives/Performance Measurement
Yoshiaki Akeda
Nomura Funds Research and Technologies
Japan

Bruce J. Feibel, CFA
Eagle Investment Systems
United States

Europe, Middle East, and Africa (EMEA)
Hans-Jörg von Euw
Swisscanto Asset Management Ltd.
Switzerland

Lesley A. Harvey
Ernst & Young
South Africa

Jean-François Hirschel
Societe Generale Asset Management
France

Europe
Stefan Illmer
Credit Suisse Asset Management
Switzerland

Erik Sjöberg
Erik Sjöberg Finanskonsult
Sweden

Individual/Private Investor
Terry Pavlic, CFA
Pavlic Investment Advisors, Inc.
United States

Max Roth
Banque Cantonale Vaudoise
Switzerland

Maria E. Smith-Breslin
Smith Affiliated Capital Corp.
United States

Institutional Investors (1)
David Gamble
United Kingdom

Deborah Reidy
Hewitt & Becketts
Ireland

Institutional Investors (2)
Lynn A. Clark
LA Clark Consulting
Canada

Ehsan Rahman
Washington Metropolitan Area Transit Authority
United States

Insurance
Glenn Solomon
Australia

Todd A. Jankowski, CFA
The Northwestern Mutual Life Company
United States

Japan
Shinichi Kawano
Merrill Lynch Investments Managers Co., Ltd.
Japan

Shigeo Ishigaki
KPMG Japan (KPMG AZSA & Co.)
Japan

Yoh Kuwabara
ChuoAoyama PricewaterhouseCoopers
Japan
Mutual Funds
Alain Ernewein
Stratégie Investissement Performance
France
Neil E. Riddles, CFA
Hansberger Global Investors, Inc.
United States
North America
Karyn D. Vincent, CFA
Vincent Performance Services LLC
United States
Iain W. McAra
JP Morgan Fleming Asset Management
United States
David Spaulding
The Spaulding Group Inc.
United States
Pacific Basin
Louis Boulanger, CFA
New Zealand
Tunku Afwida Malek
Commerce Asset Fund Managers Sdn Bhd
Malaysia

Cheng Chih Sung
Government of Singapore Investment Corporation
Singapore
Venture Capital/Real Estate/Other
Carol Anne Kennedy
Pantheon Ventures Limited
United Kingdom
Paul S. Saint-Pierre
Wall Street Realty Capital
United States
Verification
Carl R. Bacon
Statpro
United Kingdom
Herbert M. Chain
Deloitte & Touche LLP
United States
Louise Spencer
PricewaterhouseCoopers
United Kingdom
CFA Institute Staff
Alecia L. Licata
Cindy S. Kent
Carol A. Lindsey

PREFACE: BACKGROUND OF THE GIPS STANDARDS

Investment practices, regulation, performance measurement, and reporting of performance results have historically varied considerably from country to country. Some countries have established performance calculation and presentation guidelines that are domestically accepted, and others have few standards for presenting investment performance. These practices have limited the comparability of performance results between firms in different countries and have hindered the ability of firms to penetrate markets on a global basis.

CFA Institute (formerly known as the Association for Investment Management and Research or AIMR) recognized the need for a global set of performance presentation standards, and in 1995, it sponsored and funded the Global Investment Performance Standards (GIPS®) Committee to develop a single standard for presenting investment performance. In February 1999, the GIPS committee formalized the GIPS standards and presented them to the AIMR Board of Governors, who formally endorsed them.

Although CFA Institute is funding and administering the activities of the GIPS standards, the success of the Standards is the result of an alliance among experts from a variety of fields within the global investment industry. The following key industry groups have been involved in and contributed significantly to promoting and developing the GIPS standards:

Australia — Performance Analyst Group of Australia
Austria — Österreichischen Verreinigung für Finanzanalyse und Asset Management und der Vereinigung Österreichischer Investmentgesellschaften
Belgium — Belgian Association for Pension Institutions
Denmark — The Danish Society of Investment Professionals, The Danish Society of Financial Analysts

France — Société Francaise des Analystes Financiers and Association Francaise de la Gestion Financière
Germany — BVI Bundesverband Investment und Asset Management e.V., Deutsche Vereinigung für Finanzanalyse und Asset Management, and German CFA Society
Hong Kong — The Hong Kong Society of Financial Analysts
Hungary — Hungarian Society of Investment Professionals

Ireland — Irish Association of Investment Managers
Italy — Italian Investment Performance Committee
Japan — The Security Analysts Association of Japan
Luxembourg — Association Luxembourgeoise des Fonds d'Investissement and Association Luxembourgeoise des Gestionnaires de Portefeuilles et Analystes Financiers
Netherlands — Beroepsvereniging van Beleggingsdeskundigen
New Zealand — CFA Society of New Zealand
Norway — The Norwegian Society of Financial Analysts

Poland — Polski Komitet Wyników Inwestycyjnych
Portugal — Associação Portuguesa de Analistas Financeiros
Singapore — Investment Management Association of Singapore
Spain — CFA Spain
South Africa — Investment Management Association of South Africa
Sweden — Swedish Society of Financial Analysts
Switzerland — Swiss Bankers Association
United Kingdom — National Association of Pension Funds Ltd
United States and Canada — CFA Institute

With the release of the GIPS standards in 1999, the GIPS committee was replaced by the Investment Performance Council (IPC), which serves as the global committee responsible for the Standards. It consists of 36 members from 15 countries. The IPC's members have diverse and in-depth investment experience. They come from firms of all sizes and specialize in mutual funds, private wealth management, insurance, pension funds, private equity and venture capital, real estate, investment consulting services, and performance measurement and verification.

The principal goal of the IPC is to have all countries adopt the GIPS standards as the standard for investment firms seeking to present historical investment performance. The IPC envisions GIPS compliance acting as a "passport" that allows firms to enter the arena of investment management competition on a global basis and to compete on an equal footing. The GIPS passport will level the playing field and promote global competition among investment firms, which will, in turn, provide prospective clients with a greater level of confidence in the integrity of performance presentations as well as the general practices of a compliant firm.

In order to achieve this goal, over the past 5 years, the IPC has used a dual approach convergence strategy to (1) transition the existing local standards to the GIPS standards and (2) evolve the GIPS standards to incorporate local best practices from all regional standards so as to form one improved standard for investment performance calculation and reporting.

The IPC strongly encourages countries without an investment performance standard in place to accept the GIPS standards as the local standard and translate them into the native language when necessary, thus promoting a "translation of GIPS" (TG). However, to effectively transition existing regional standards, the IPC acknowledges that some countries need to adopt certain long-standing requirements in addition to the GIPS standards.

Since 1999, the IPC has promoted the "Country Version of GIPS" (CVG) approach, whereby countries that had existing performance standards could adopt the GIPS standards as the core. This core was only to be supplemented to satisfy local regulatory or legal requirements and well-established practices. Any other differences were to be transitioned out of the CVG so that the CVG would converge with the GIPS standards. The CVG model has facilitated the movement of the industry toward one standard for the calculation and presentation of investment performance.

Today, 25 countries throughout North America, Europe, Africa, and the Asia Pacific Region have adopted the GIPS standards, encouraging investment management firms to follow the Standards when calculating and reporting their performance results. Out of these 25 countries, 9 have an IPC-endorsed CVG (Australia, Canada, Ireland, Italy, Japan, South Africa, Switzerland, United Kingdom, and United States). The remaining IPC-endorsed standards are either translations of GIPS (German, Danish, French, Hungarian, Dutch, Norwegian, Polish, and Spanish) or GIPS (in English).

In addition to improving the original GIPS standards, this version includes new sections to address real estate and private equity investments as well as new provisions to address fees. It also includes guidelines for claiming compliance with the GIPS standards in advertisements and formalizes positions resulting from the development of guidance statements (such as firm definition, composite definition, and portability) and incorporates local best practices for performance measurement and reporting from around the world. A glossary and several examples have been included to assist with the application of the GIPS standards. (Words appearing in CAPITAL letters are defined in the GIPS Glossary in Appendix A5.) The GIPS standards are no longer a minimum worldwide standard. Instead, this version promotes the highest performance measurement and presentation practices and eliminates the need for separate local standards.

We are now entering the second phase of the convergence strategy to the GIPS standards—namely to evolve the GIPS standards to incorporate local best practices from all regional standards. To effectively move toward one globally accepted standard for investment performance calculation and presentation, the IPC strongly encourages countries without an investment performance standard in place to accept the GIPS standards in English or translate them into the local language, adopting a TG approach.

By revising the GIPS standards, it is the IPC's hope that CVGs will no longer be necessary. Instead, all CVG-compliant firms will be granted reciprocity for periods prior to 1 January 2006. Their CVG-compliant history will satisfy the GIPS requirement to show at least a 5-year track record. In this way, firms from all countries will comply with one standard, the GIPS standards, from 1 January 2006 and the industry will achieve convergence of all standards.

I. INTRODUCTION

A. Preamble — Why Is a Global Standard Needed?

1. The financial markets and the investment management industry are becoming increasingly global in nature. Given the variety of financial entities and countries involved, this globalization of the investment process and the exponential growth of assets under management demonstrate the need to standardize the calculation and presentation of investment performance.
2. Prospective clients and investment management firms will benefit from an established standard for investment performance measurement and presentation that is recognized worldwide. Investment practices, regulation, performance measurement, and reporting of performance results vary considerably from country to country. Some countries have guidelines that are widely accepted within their borders, and others have few recognized standards for presenting investment performance.
3. Requiring investment management firms to adhere to performance presentation standards will help assure investors that the performance information is both complete and fairly presented. Investment management firms in countries with minimal presentation

standards will be able to compete for business on an equal footing with investment management firms from countries with more developed standards. Investment management firms from countries with established practices will have more confidence that they are being fairly compared with "local" investment management firms when competing for business in countries that have not previously adopted performance standards.

4. Both prospective and existing clients of investment management firms will benefit from a global investment performance standard by having a greater degree of confidence in the performance numbers presented by the investment management firms. Performance standards that are accepted in all countries enable all investment management firms to measure and present their investment performance so that clients can readily compare investment performance among investment management firms.

B. Vision Statement

5. A global investment performance standard leads to readily accepted presentations of investment performance that (1) present performance results that are readily comparable among investment management firms without regard to geographical location and (2) facilitate a dialogue between investment managers and their prospective clients about the critical issues of how the investment management firm achieved performance results and determines future investment strategies.

C. Objectives

6. To obtain worldwide acceptance of a standard for the calculation and presentation of investment performance in a fair, comparable format that provides full disclosure.
7. To ensure accurate and consistent investment performance data for reporting, record keeping, marketing, and presentations.
8. To promote fair, global competition among investment management firms for all markets without creating barriers to entry for new investment management firms.
9. To foster the notion of industry "self-regulation" on a global basis.

D. Overview

10. The Global Investment Performance Standards ("GIPS standards" or "Standards") have several key characteristics:
    a. For the purpose of claiming compliance with the GIPS standards, investment management FIRMS MUST define an entity that claims compliance ("FIRM"). The FIRM MUST be defined as an investment FIRM, subsidiary, or division held out to clients or potential clients as a DISTINCT BUSINESS ENTITY.
    b. The GIPS standards are ethical standards for investment performance presentation to ensure fair representation and full disclosure of a FIRM's performance.
    c. The GIPS standards REQUIRE FIRMS to include all actual fee-paying, discretionary PORTFOLIOS in COMPOSITES defined according to similar strategy and/or investment objective and REQUIRE FIRMS to initially show GIPS-compliant history for a minimum of five (5) years or since inception of the FIRM or COMPOSITE if in existence less than 5 years. After presenting at least 5 years of compliant history, the FIRM MUST add annual performance each year going forward up to ten (10) years, at a minimum.
    d. The GIPS standards REQUIRE FIRMS to use certain calculation and presentation methods and to make certain disclosures along with the performance record.

e. The GIPS standards rely on the integrity of input data. The accuracy of input data is critical to the accuracy of the performance presentation. For example, BENCHMARKS and COMPOSITES SHOULD be created/selected on an EX ANTE basis, not after the fact.

f. The GIPS standards consist of provisions that FIRMS are REQUIRED to follow in order to claim compliance. FIRMS are encouraged to adopt the RECOMMENDED provisions to achieve best practice in performance presentation.

g. The GIPS standards MUST be applied with the goal of full disclosure and fair representation of investment performance. Meeting the objectives of full disclosure and fair representation will likely require more than compliance with the minimum REQUIREMENTS of the GIPS standards. If an investment FIRM applies the GIPS standards in a performance situation that is not addressed specifically by the Standards or is open to interpretation, disclosures other than those REQUIRED by the GIPS standards may be necessary. To fully explain the performance included in a presentation, FIRMS are encouraged to present all relevant ADDITIONAL INFORMATION and SUPPLEMENTAL INFORMATION.

h. All requirements, clarifications, updated information, and guidance MUST be adhered to when determining a FIRM's claim of compliance and will be made available via the *GIPS Handbook* and the CFA Institute website (www.cfainstitute.org).

i. In cases where applicable local or country-specific law or regulation conflicts with the GIPS standards, the Standards REQUIRE FIRMS to comply with the local law or regulation and make full disclosure of the conflict.

j. The GIPS standards do not address every aspect of performance measurement, valuation, attribution, or coverage of all asset classes. The GIPS standards will evolve over time to address additional aspects of investment performance. Certain RECOMMENDED elements in the GIPS standards may become REQUIREMENTS in the future.

k. Within the GIPS standards are supplemental REAL ESTATE and PRIVATE EQUITY provisions that MUST be applied to these asset classes. (See Sections II.6 and II.7.)

E. Scope

11. *Application of the GIPS Standards:* FIRMS from any country may come into compliance with the GIPS standards. Compliance with the GIPS standards will facilitate a FIRM's participation in the investment management industry on a global level.

12. *Historical Performance Record:*
    a. FIRMS are REQUIRED to present, at a minimum, 5 years of annual investment performance that is compliant with the GIPS standards. If the FIRM or COMPOSITE has been in existence less than 5 years, the FIRM MUST present performance since the inception of the FIRM or COMPOSITE; and
    b. After a FIRM presents 5 years of compliant history, the FIRMS MUST present additional annual performance up to 10 years, at a minimum. For example, after a FIRM presents 5 years of compliant history, the FIRMS MUST add an additional year of performance each year so that after 5 years of claiming compliance, the FIRM presents a 10-year performance record.
    c. FIRMS may link a non-GIPS-compliant performance record to their compliant history so long as no noncompliant performance is presented after 1 January 2000 and the FIRM discloses the periods of noncompliance and explains how the presentation is not in compliance with the GIPS standards.
    d. FIRMS previously claiming compliance with an Investment Performance Council-endorsed Country Version of GIPS (CVG) are granted reciprocity to claim compliance with the GIPS standards for historical periods prior to 1 January 2006.

(See "Background of GIPS Standards" for more details on CVGs). If the FIRM previously claimed compliance with a CVG, at a minimum, the FIRM MUST continue to show the historical CVG-compliant track record up to 10 years (or since inception).

Nothing in this section shall prevent FIRMS from initially presenting more than 5 years of performance results.

F. Compliance

13. *Effective Date:* The GIPS standards were amended by the IPC on 7 December 2004 and adopted by the CFA Institute Board of Governors on 4 February 2005. The effective date of the revised Standards is 1 January 2006. All presentations that include performance results for periods after 31 December 2005 MUST meet all the REQUIREMENTS of the revised GIPS standards. Performance presentations that include results through 31 December 2005 may be prepared in compliance with the 1999 version of the GIPS standards. Early adoption of these revised GIPS standards is encouraged.

14. REQUIREMENTS: FIRMS MUST meet all the REQUIREMENTS set forth in the GIPS standards to claim compliance with the GIPS standards. Although the REQUIREMENTS MUST be met immediately by a FIRM claiming compliance, the following REQUIREMENTS do not go into effect until a future date:

    a. For periods beginning 1 January 2008, REAL ESTATE investments MUST be valued at least quarterly.

    b. For periods beginning 1 January 2010, FIRMS MUST value PORTFOLIOS on the date of all LARGE EXTERNAL CASH FLOWS.

    c. For periods beginning 1 January 2010, FIRMS MUST value PORTFOLIOS as of the calendar month-end or the last business day of the month.

    d. For periods beginning 1 January 2010, COMPOSITE returns MUST be calculated by asset weighting the individual PORTFOLIO returns at least monthly.

    e. For periods beginning 1 January 2010, CARVE-OUT returns are not permitted to be included in single asset class COMPOSITE returns unless the CARVE-OUTS are actually managed separately with their own cash balances.

    Until these future REQUIREMENTS become effective, these provisions SHOULD be considered RECOMMENDATIONS. FIRMS are encouraged to implement these future REQUIREMENTS prior to their effective dates. To ease compliance with the GIPS standards when the future REQUIREMENTS take effect, the industry should immediately begin to design performance software to incorporate these future REQUIREMENTS.

15. *Compliance Check:* FIRMS MUST take all steps necessary to ensure that they have satisfied all the REQUIREMENTS of the GIPS standards before claiming compliance with the GIPS standards. FIRMS are strongly encouraged to perform periodic internal compliance checks and implement adequate business controls on all stages of the investment performance process—from data input to presentation material—to ensure the validity of compliance claims.

16. *Third-Party Performance Measurement and* COMPOSITE *Construction:* The GIPS standards recognize the role of independent third-party performance measurers and the value they can add to the FIRM's performance measurement activities. Where third-party performance measurement is an established practice or is available, FIRMS are encouraged to use this service as it applies to the FIRM. Similarly, where the practice is to allow third parties to construct COMPOSITES for FIRMS, FIRMS can use such COMPOSITES in a GIPS-compliant presentation only if the COMPOSITES meet the REQUIREMENTS of the GIPS standards.

17. *Sample Presentations:* Sample presentations, shown in Appendix A1, provide examples of what a compliant presentation might look like.

G. Implementing a Global Standard

18. In 1999, the Investment Performance Council (IPC) was created and given the responsibility to meet the ongoing needs for maintaining and developing a high-quality global investment performance standard. The IPC provides a practical and effective implementation structure for the GIPS standards and encourages wider public participation in an industry-wide standard.

19. One of the principal objectives of the IPC is for all countries to adopt the GIPS standards as the common method for calculating and presenting investment performance. As of December 2004, more than 25 countries around the world had adopted or were in the process of adopting the GIPS standards. The IPC believes the establishment and acceptance of the GIPS standards are vital steps in facilitating the availability of comparable investment performance history on a global basis. GIPS compliance provides FIRMS with a "passport" and creates a level playing field where all FIRMS can compete on equal footing.

20. The presence of a local sponsoring organization for investment performance standards is essential for their effective implementation and on-going operation within a country. Such country sponsors also provide an important link between the IPC, the governing body for the GIPS standards, and the local markets where investment managers operate.

    The country sponsor, by actively supporting the GIPS standards and the work of the IPC, will ensure that the country's interests can and will be taken into account as the GIPS standards are developed going forward. Compliance with the GIPS standards is voluntary, but support from the local country sponsor will help drive the success of the GIPS standards.

21. The IPC strongly encourages countries without an investment performance standard in place to accept the GIPS standards as the local standard and translate them into the local language when necessary, thus promoting a "translation of GIPS" (TG).

22. Compliance with the GIPS standards will provide FIRMS with a "right of access" to be considered alongside all investment managers, thereby allowing all FIRMS to be evaluated on equal terms.

23. Although the GIPS standards may be translated into many languages, if a discrepancy arises between the different versions of the Standards (e.g., TGs), the English version of GIPS standards is controlling.

24. The IPC will continue to develop the GIPS standards so that they maintain their relevance within the changing investment management industry and has committed to evaluating the Standards every 5 years.

25. The self-regulatory nature of the GIPS standards necessitates a strong commitment to ethical integrity. Self-regulation also assists regulators in exercising their responsibility for ensuring the fair disclosure of information to and within the financial markets in general. Regulators are encouraged to:

    • recognize the benefit of voluntary compliance with standards that represent global best practices,
    • give consideration to adopting a function favored by some regulators, namely to enforce sanctions upon false claims of compliance with the GIPS standards as fraudulent advertising, and
    • recognize and encourage independent verification services.

26. Where existing laws or regulations already impose performance presentation standards, FIRMS are strongly encouraged to comply with the GIPS standards in addition to those local requirements. Compliance with applicable law or regulation does not necessarily lead to compliance with the GIPS standards. When complying with the GIPS standards and local law or regulation, FIRMS MUST disclose any local laws and regulations that conflict with the GIPS standards.

II. PROVISIONS OF THE GLOBAL INVESTMENT PERFORMANCE STANDARDS

The GIPS standards are divided into eight sections that reflect the basic elements involved in presenting performance information: fundamentals of compliance, input data, calculation methodology, COMPOSITE construction, disclosures, presentation and reporting, REAL ESTATE, and PRIVATE EQUITY.

The provisions for each section are divided between REQUIREMENTS, listed first in each section, and RECOMMENDATIONS. FIRMS MUST meet all the REQUIREMENTS to claim compliance with the GIPS standards. FIRMS are strongly encouraged to adopt and implement the RECOMMENDATIONS to ensure that the FIRM fully adheres to the spirit and intent of the GIPS standards. Examples of GIPS-compliant presentations are included as Appendix A1. A Glossary is included as Appendix A5 to serve as a reference and provide brief descriptions of key words and terms in the GIPS standards. Words appearing in CAPITAL letters are defined in the GIPS Glossary.

0. Fundamentals of Compliance: Critical issues that a FIRM MUST consider when claiming compliance with the GIPS standards are defining the FIRM, documenting FIRM policies and procedures, maintaining compliance with updates to the GIPS standards, and properly using the claim of compliance and references to verification. The definition of the FIRM is the foundation for FIRM-wide compliance and creates defined boundaries whereby TOTAL FIRM ASSETS can be determined. Once a FIRM meets all of the REQUIREMENTS of the GIPS standards, it MUST appropriately use the claim of compliance to state compliance with the GIPS standards.

1. Input Data: Consistency of input data is critical to effective compliance with the GIPS standards and establishes the foundation for full, fair, and comparable investment performance presentations.

2. Calculation Methodology: Achieving comparability among FIRMS' performance presentations requires uniformity in methods used to calculate returns. The Standards mandate the use of certain calculation methodologies for both PORTFOLIOS and COMPOSITES. [corrected January 2006]

3. Composite Construction: A COMPOSITE is an aggregation of one or more PORTFOLIOS into a single group that represents a particular investment objective or strategy. The COMPOSITE return is the asset-weighted average of the performance results of all the PORTFOLIOS in the COMPOSITE. Creating meaningful, asset-weighted COMPOSITES is critical to the fair presentation, consistency, and comparability of results over time and among FIRMS.

4. Disclosures: Disclosures allow FIRMS to elaborate on the raw numbers provided in the presentation and give the end user of the presentation the proper context in which to understand the performance results. To comply with the GIPS standards, FIRMS MUST disclose certain information about their performance presentation and policies adopted by the FIRM. Disclosures are to be considered static information that does not normally change from period to period. Although some disclosures are REQUIRED of all FIRMS, others are specific to certain circumstances and thus may not be REQUIRED. No "negative assurance" language is needed for nonapplicable disclosures.

5. Presentation and Reporting: After gathering the input data, calculating returns, constructing the COMPOSITES, and determining the necessary disclosures, the FIRM MUST incorporate this information in presentations based on the REQUIREMENTS set out in the GIPS standards for presenting the investment performance returns. No finite set of provisions can cover all potential situations or anticipate future developments in investment industry structure, technology, products, or practices. When appropriate, FIRMS have the responsibility to include other information not necessarily covered by the Standards in a GIPS-compliant presentation.

6. Real Estate: These provisions apply to all investments where returns are primarily from the holding, trading, development, or management of REAL ESTATE assets. REAL ESTATE includes land, buildings under development, completed buildings, and other structures or improvements held for investment purposes. The provisions apply regardless of the level of control the FIRM has over management of the investment. The provisions apply irrespective of whether a REAL ESTATE asset or investment is producing revenue. They also apply to REAL ESTATE investments with leverage or gearing.

7. Private Equity: These provisions apply to all PRIVATE EQUITY investments other than OPEN-END or EVERGREEN FUNDS (which MUST follow the main GIPS provisions). PRIVATE EQUITY investments MUST be valued according to the GIPS PRIVATE EQUITY Valuation Principles found in Appendix A4. PRIVATE EQUITY refers to investments in nonpublic companies that are in various stages of development and encompasses venture investing, buy-out investing, and mezzanine investing. Fund-of-funds investing as well as secondary investing are also included in PRIVATE EQUITY. Investors typically invest in PRIVATE EQUITY assets either directly or through a fund of funds or LIMITED PARTNERSHIP.

0. Fundamentals of Compliance

0.A Definition of the Firm — Requirements

0.A.1   The GIPS standards must be applied on a FIRM-wide basis.

0.A.2   FIRMS MUST be defined as an investment firm, subsidiary, or division held out to clients or potential clients as a DISTINCT BUSINESS ENTITY.

0.A.3   TOTAL FIRM ASSETS MUST be the aggregate of the MARKET VALUE of all discretionary and nondiscretionary assets under management within the defined FIRM. This includes both fee-paying and non-fee-paying assets.

0.A.4   FIRMS MUST include the performance of assets assigned to a subadvisor in a COMPOSITE provided the FIRM has discretion over the selection of the subadvisor.

0.A.5   Changes in a FIRM's organization are not permitted to lead to alteration of historical COMPOSITE results.

0.B Definition of the Firm — Recommendations

0.B.1   FIRMS are encouraged to adopt the broadest, most meaningful definition of the FIRM. The scope of this definition SHOULD include all geographical (country, regional, etc.) offices operating under the same brand name regardless of the actual name of the individual investment management company.

0.A Document Policies and Procedures — Requirements

0.A.6   FIRMS MUST document, in writing, their policies and procedures used in establishing and maintaining compliance with all the applicable REQUIREMENTS of the GIPS standards.

0.A Claim of Compliance — Requirements

0.A.7   Once a FIRM has met all the REQUIRED elements of the GIPS standards, the FIRM MUST use the following compliance statement to indicate that the FIRM is in compliance with the GIPS standards:

"[Insert name of FIRM] has prepared and presented this report in compliance with the Global Investment Performance Standards (GIPS®)."

0.A.8   If the FIRM does not meet all the REQUIREMENTS of the GIPS standards, the FIRM cannot represent that it is "in compliance with the Global Investment Performance Standards except for . . ."

0.A.9   Statements referring to the calculation methodology used in a COMPOSITE presentation as being "in accordance [or compliance] with the Global Investment Performance Standards" are prohibited.

0.A.10 Statements referring to the performance of a single, existing client as being "calculated in accordance with the Global Investment Performance Standards" are prohibited except when a GIPS-compliant FIRM reports the performance of an individual account to the existing client.

0.A Firm Fundamental Responsibilities — Requirements

0.A.11 FIRMS MUST make every reasonable effort to provide a compliant presentation to all prospective clients. That is, FIRMS cannot choose to whom they want to present compliant performance. (As long as a prospective client has received a compliant presentation within the previous 12 months, the FIRM has met this REQUIREMENT.)

0.A.12 FIRMS MUST provide a COMPOSITE list and COMPOSITE DESCRIPTION to any prospective client that makes such a request (a sample list and COMPOSITE DESCRIPTION are included in Appendix A2). FIRMS MUST list "discontinued" COMPOSITES on the FIRM's list of COMPOSITES for at least 5 years after discontinuation.

0.A.13 FIRMS MUST provide a compliant presentation for any COMPOSITE listed on the FIRM's list and a COMPOSITE DESCRIPTION to any prospective client that makes such a request.

0.A.14 When the FIRM jointly markets with other FIRMS, the FIRM claiming compliance with the GIPS standards MUST be sure that it is clearly defined and separate relative to any other FIRMS being marketed and that it is clear which FIRM is claiming compliance.

0.A.15 FIRMS are encouraged to comply with the RECOMMENDATIONS and MUST comply with all applicable REQUIREMENTS of the GIPS standards, including any updates, reports, guidance statements, interpretations, or clarifications published by CFA Institute and the Investment Performance Council, which will be made available via the CFA Institute website (www.cfainstitute.org) as well as the *GIPS Handbook*.

0.B Verification — Recommendations

0.B.2   FIRMS are encouraged to undertake the verification process, defined as the review of a FIRM's performance measurement processes and procedures by an independent third-party verifier. A single verification report is issued in respect to the whole FIRM; verification cannot be carried out for a single COMPOSITE. The primary purpose of verification is to establish that a FIRM claiming compliance with the GIPS standards has adhered to the Standards.

0.B.3   FIRMS that have been verified are encouraged to add a disclosure to COMPOSITE presentations or advertisements stating that the FIRM has been verified. FIRMS

MUST disclose the periods of verification if the COMPOSITE presentation includes results for periods that have not been subject to FIRM-wide verification. The verification disclosure language SHOULD read:

"[Insert name of FIRM] has been verified for the periods [insert dates] by [name of verifier]. A copy of the verification report is available upon request."

1. Input Data

1.A Input Data — Requirements

1.A.1   All data and information necessary to support a FIRM's performance presentation and to perform the REQUIRED calculations MUST be captured and maintained.

1.A.2   PORTFOLIO valuations MUST be based on MARKET VALUES (not cost basis or book values).

1.A.3   For periods prior to 1 January 2001, PORTFOLIOS MUST be valued at least quarterly. For periods between 1 January 2001 and 1 January 2010, PORTFOLIOS MUST be valued at least monthly. For periods beginning 1 January 2010, FIRMS MUST value PORTFOLIOS on the date of all LARGE EXTERNAL CASH FLOWS.

1.A.4   For periods beginning 1 January 2010, FIRMS MUST value PORTFOLIOS as of the calendar month-end or the last business day of the month.

1.A.5   For periods beginning 1 January 2005, FIRMS MUST use TRADE DATE ACCOUNTING.

1.A.6   ACCRUAL ACCOUNTING MUST be used for fixed-income securities and all other assets that accrue interest income. MARKET VALUES of fixed-income securities MUST include accrued income.

1.A.7   For periods beginning 1 January 2006, COMPOSITES MUST have consistent beginning and ending annual valuation dates. Unless the COMPOSITE is reported on a noncalendar fiscal year, the beginning and ending valuation dates MUST be at calendar year-end (or on the last business day of the year).

1.B Input Data — Recommendations

1.B.1   ACCRUAL ACCOUNTING SHOULD be used for dividends (as of the ex-dividend date).

1.B.2   When presenting NET-OF-FEES RETURNS, FIRMS SHOULD accrue INVESTMENT MANAGEMENT FEES.

1.B.3   Calendar month-end valuations or valuations on the last business day of the month are RECOMMENDED.

2. CALCULATION METHODOLOGY

2.A Calculation Methodology — Requirements

2.A.1   Total return, including realized and unrealized gains and losses plus income, MUST be used. [corrected September 2005]

2.A.2   TIME-WEIGHTED RATES OF RETURN that adjust for EXTERNAL CASH FLOWS MUST be used. Periodic returns MUST be geometrically linked. EXTERNAL CASH FLOWS MUST be treated in a consistent manner with the FIRM's documented, COMPOSITE-specific policy. At a minimum:

a. For periods beginning 1 January 2005, FIRMS MUST use approximated rates of return that adjust for daily-weighted EXTERNAL CASH FLOWS.

　　　b. For periods beginning 1 January 2010, FIRMS MUST value PORTFOLIOS on the
　　　　date of all LARGE EXTERNAL CASH FLOWS.

2.A.3　COMPOSITE returns MUST be calculated by asset weighting the individual PORT-
FOLIO returns using beginning-of-period values or a method that reflects both
beginning-of-period values and EXTERNAL CASH FLOWS.

2.A.4　Returns from cash and cash equivalents held in PORTFOLIOS MUST be included in
TOTAL RETURN calculations.

2.A.5　All returns MUST be calculated after the deduction of the actual TRADING EXPENSES
incurred during the period. Estimated TRADING EXPENSES are not permitted.

2.A.6　For periods beginning 1 January 2006, FIRMS MUST calculate COMPOSITE returns
by asset weighting the individual PORTFOLIO returns at least quarterly. For periods beginning 1 January 2010, COMPOSITE returns MUST be calculated by asset
weighting the individual PORTFOLIO returns at least monthly.

2.A.7　If the actual direct TRADING EXPENSES cannot be identified and segregated from a
BUNDLED FEE:

　　　a. when calculating GROSS-OF-FEES RETURNS, returns MUST be reduced by the
　　　　entire BUNDLED FEE or the portion of the BUNDLED FEE that includes the direct
　　　　TRADING EXPENSES. The use of estimated TRADING EXPENSES is not permitted.

　　　b. when calculating NET-OF-FEES RETURNS, returns MUST be reduced by the entire
　　　　BUNDLED FEE or the portion of the BUNDLED FEE that includes the direct TRAD-
　　　　ING EXPENSES and the INVESTMENT MANAGEMENT FEE. The use of estimated
　　　　TRADING EXPENSES is not permitted.

2.B Calculation Methodology — Recommendations

2.B.1　Returns SHOULD be calculated net of nonreclaimable withholding taxes on dividends,
interest, and capital gains. Reclaimable withholding taxes SHOULD be accrued.

2.B.2　FIRMS SHOULD calculate COMPOSITE returns by asset weighting the member PORT-
FOLIOS at least monthly.

2.B.3　FIRMS SHOULD value PORTFOLIOS on the date of all LARGE EXTERNAL CASH FLOWS.

3. Composite Construction

3.A Composite Construction — Requirements

3.A.1　All actual, fee-paying, discretionary PORTFOLIOS MUST be included in at least one
COMPOSITE. Although non-fee-paying discretionary PORTFOLIOS may be included
in a COMPOSITE (with appropriate disclosures), nondiscretionary PORTFOLIOS are
not permitted to be included in a FIRM'S COMPOSITES.

3.A.2　COMPOSITES MUST be defined according to similar investment objectives and/or
strategies. The full COMPOSITE DEFINITION MUST be made available on request.

3.A.3　COMPOSITES MUST include new PORTFOLIOS on a timely and consistent basis after
the PORTFOLIO comes under management unless specifically mandated by the client.

3.A.4　Terminated PORTFOLIOS MUST be included in the historical returns of the appropriate COMPOSITES up to the last full measurement period that the PORTFOLIO
was under management.

3.A.5　PORTFOLIOS are not permitted to be switched from one COMPOSITE to another
unless documented changes in client guidelines or the redefinition of the COM-
POSITE make it appropriate. The historical record of the PORTFOLIO MUST remain
with the appropriate COMPOSITE.

3.A.6   Convertible and other hybrid securities MUST be treated consistently across time and within COMPOSITES.

3.A.7   CARVE-OUT segments excluding cash are not permitted to be used to represent a discretionary PORTFOLIO and, as such, are not permitted to be included in COMPOSITE returns. When a single asset class is carved out of a multiple asset class PORTFOLIO and the returns are presented as part of a single asset COMPOSITE, cash MUST be allocated to the CARVE-OUT returns in a timely and consistent manner. Beginning 1 January 2010, CARVE-OUT returns are not permitted to be included in single asset class COMPOSITE returns unless the CARVE-OUT is actually managed separately with its own cash balance.

3.A.8   COMPOSITES MUST include only assets under management within the defined FIRM. FIRMS are not permitted to link simulated or model PORTFOLIOS with actual performance.

3.A.9   If a FIRM sets a minimum asset level for PORTFOLIOS to be included in a COMPOSITE, no PORTFOLIOS below that asset level can be included in that COMPOSITE. Any changes to a COMPOSITE-specific minimum asset level are not permitted to be applied retroactively.

3.B Composite Construction — Recommendations

3.B.1   CARVE-OUT returns SHOULD not be included in single asset class COMPOSITE returns unless the CARVE-OUTS are actually managed separately with their own cash balance.

3.B.2   To remove the effect of a significant EXTERNAL CASH FLOW, the use of a TEMPORARY NEW ACCOUNT is RECOMMENDED (as opposed to adjusting the COMPOSITE composition to remove PORTFOLIOS with significant EXTERNAL CASH FLOWS).

3.B.3   FIRMS SHOULD not market a COMPOSITE to a prospective client who has assets less than the COMPOSITE's minimum asset level.

4. DISCLOSURES

4.A Disclosures — Requirements

4.A.1   FIRMS MUST disclose the definition of "FIRM" used to determine the TOTAL FIRM ASSETS and FIRM-wide compliance.

4.A.2   FIRMS MUST disclose the availability of a complete list and description of all of the FIRM'S COMPOSITES.

4.A.3   FIRMS MUST disclose the minimum asset level, if any, below which PORTFOLIOS are not included in a COMPOSITE. FIRMS MUST also disclose any changes to the minimum asset level.

4.A.4   FIRMS MUST disclose the currency used to express performance.

4.A.5   FIRMS MUST disclose the presence, use, and extent of leverage or derivatives (if material), including a sufficient description of the use, frequency, and characteristics of the instruments to identify risks.

4.A.6   FIRMS MUST clearly label returns as GROSS-OF-FEES or NET-OF-FEES.

4.A.7   FIRMS MUST disclose relevant details of the treatment of withholding tax on dividends, interest income, and capital gains. If using indexes that are net-of-taxes, the FIRMS MUST disclose the tax basis of the BENCHMARK (e.g., Luxembourg based or U.S. based) versus that of the COMPOSITE.

4.A.8 FIRMS MUST disclose and describe any known inconsistencies in the exchange rates used among the PORTFOLIOS within a COMPOSITE and between the COMPOSITE and the BENCHMARK.

4.A.9 If the presentation conforms with local laws and regulations that differ from the GIPS REQUIREMENTS, FIRMS MUST disclose this fact and disclose the manner in which the local laws and regulations conflict with the GIPS standards.

4.A.10 For any performance presented for periods prior to 1 January 2000 that does not comply with the GIPS standards, FIRMS MUST disclose the period of non-compliance and how the presentation is not in compliance with the GIPS standards.

4.A.11 For periods prior to 1 January 2010, when a single asset class is carved out of a multiple asset PORTFOLIO and the returns are presented as part of a single asset COMPOSITE, FIRMS MUST disclose the policy used to allocate cash to the CARVE-OUT returns.

4.A.12 FIRMS MUST disclose the FEE SCHEDULE appropriate to the presentation.

4.A.13 If a COMPOSITE contains PORTFOLIOS with BUNDLED FEES, FIRMS MUST disclose for each annual period shown the percentage of COMPOSITE assets that is BUNDLED FEE PORTFOLIOS.

4.A.14 If a COMPOSITE contains PORTFOLIOS with BUNDLED FEES, FIRMS MUST disclose the various types of fees that are included in the BUNDLED FEE.

4.A.15 When presenting GROSS-OF-FEES RETURNS, FIRMS MUST disclose if any other fees are deducted in addition to the direct TRADING EXPENSES.

4.A.16 When presenting NET-OF-FEES RETURNS, FIRMS MUST disclose if any other fees are deducted in addition to the INVESTMENT MANAGEMENT FEE and direct TRADING EXPENSES.

4.A.17 FIRMS MUST disclose that ADDITIONAL INFORMATION regarding policies for calculating and reporting returns is available upon request.

4.A.18 Beginning 1 January 2006, FIRMS MUST disclose the use of a subadvisor(s) and the periods a subadvisor(s) was used.

4.A.19 FIRMS MUST disclose all significant events that would help a prospective client interpret the performance record.

4.A.20 FIRMS MUST disclose the COMPOSITE DESCRIPTION .

4.A.21 If a FIRM is redefined, the FIRM MUST disclose the date and reason for the redefinition.

4.A.22 If a FIRM has redefined a COMPOSITE, the FIRM MUST disclose the date and nature of the change. Changes to COMPOSITES are not permitted to be applied retroactively.

4.A.23 FIRMS MUST disclose any changes to the name of a COMPOSITE.

4.A.24 FIRMS MUST disclose the COMPOSITE CREATION DATE.

4.A.25 FIRMS MUST disclose if, prior to 1 January 2010, calendar month-end PORTFOLIO valuations or valuations on the last business day of the month are not used.

4.A.26 FIRMS MUST disclose which DISPERSION measure is presented.

4.B Disclosures — Recommendations

4.B.1 If a parent company contains multiple defined FIRMS, each FIRM within the parent company is encouraged to disclose a list of the other FIRMS contained within the parent company.

4.B.2 FIRMS SHOULD disclose when a change in a calculation methodology or valuation source results in a material impact on the performance of a COMPOSITE return.

4.B.3   FIRMS that have been verified SHOULD add a disclosure to their COMPOSITE presentation stating that the FIRM has been verified and clearly indicating the periods the verification covers if the COMPOSITE presentation includes results for periods that have not been subject to FIRM-wide verification.

5. Presentation and Reporting

5.A Presentation and Reporting — Requirements

5.A.1   The following items MUST be reported for each COMPOSITE presented:

a. At least 5 years of performance (or a record for the period since FIRM or COMPOSITE inception if the FIRM or COMPOSITE has been in existence less than 5 years) that meets the REQUIREMENTS of the GIPS standards; after presenting 5 years of performance, the FIRMS MUST present additional annual performance up to 10 years. (For example, after a FIRM presents 5 years of compliant history, the FIRMS MUST add an additional year of performance each year so that after 5 years of claiming compliance, the FIRM presents a 10-year performance record.)

b. Annual returns for all years.

c. The number of PORTFOLIOS and amount of assets in the COMPOSITE, and either the percentage of the TOTAL FIRM ASSETS represented by the COMPOSITE or the amount of TOTAL FIRM ASSETS at the end of each annual period. If the COMPOSITE contains 5 PORTFOLIOS or less, the number of PORTFOLIOS is not REQUIRED. [corrected September 2005]

d. A measure of DISPERSION of individual PORTFOLIO returns for each annual period. If the COMPOSITE contains 5 PORTFOLIOS or less for the full year, a measure of DISPERSION is not REQUIRED. [corrected September 2005]

5.A.2   FIRMS may link non-GIPS-compliant returns to their compliant history so long as the FIRMS meet the disclosure REQUIREMENTS for noncompliant performance and only compliant returns are presented for periods after 1 January 2000. (For example, a FIRM that has been in existence since 1995 and that wants to present its entire performance history and claim compliance beginning 1 January 2005 MUST present returns that meet the REQUIREMENTS of the GIPS standards at least from 1 January 2000 and MUST meet the disclosure REQUIREMENTS for any non-compliant history prior to 1 January 2000.)

5.A.3   Returns of PORTFOLIOS and COMPOSITES for periods of less than 1 year are not permitted to be annualized.

5.A.4   a. Performance track records of a past FIRM or affiliation MUST be linked to or used to represent the historical record of a new FIRM or new affiliation if:

i. Substantially all the investment decision makers are employed by the new FIRM (e.g., research department, PORTFOLIO managers, and other relevant staff),

ii. The staff and decision-making process remain intact and independent within the new FIRM, and

iii. The new FIRM has records that document and support the reported performance.

b. The new FIRMS MUST disclose that the performance results from the past FIRM are linked to the performance record of the new FIRM,

c. In addition to 5.A.4.a and 5.A.4.b, when one FIRM joins an existing FIRM, performance of COMPOSITES from both FIRMS MUST be linked to the ongoing returns if substantially all the assets from the past FIRM'S COMPOSITE transfer to the new FIRM.

    d. If a compliant FIRM acquires or is acquired by a noncompliant FIRM, the FIRMS have 1 year to bring the noncompliant assets into compliance.

5.A.5 Beginning 1 January 2006, if a COMPOSITE includes or is formed using single asset class CARVE-OUTS from multiple asset class PORTFOLIOS, the presentation MUST include the percentage of the COMPOSITE that is composed of CARVE-OUTS prospectively for each period.

5.A.6 The total return for the BENCHMARK (or BENCHMARKS) that reflects the investment strategy or mandate represented by the COMPOSITE MUST be presented for each annual period. If no BENCHMARK is presented, the presentation MUST explain why no BENCHMARK is disclosed. If the FIRM changes the BENCHMARK that is used for a given COMPOSITE in the performance presentation, the FIRM MUST disclose both the date and the reasons for the change. If a custom BENCHMARK or combination of multiple BENCHMARKS is used, the FIRM MUST describe the BENCHMARK creation and re-balancing process. [corrected January 2006]

5.A.7 If a COMPOSITE contains any non-fee-paying PORTFOLIOS, the FIRM MUST present, as of the end of each annual period, the percentage of the COMPOSITE assets represented by the non-fee-paying PORTFOLIOS.

5.B Presentation and Reporting — Recommendations

5.B.1 It is RECOMMENDED that FIRMS present the following items:

    a. COMPOSITE returns gross of INVESTMENT MANAGEMENT FEES and ADMINISTRATIVE FEES and before taxes (except for nonreclaimable withholding taxes),

    b. Cumulative returns for COMPOSITE and BENCHMARKS for all periods,

    c. Equal-weighted mean and median returns for each COMPOSITE,

    d. Graphs and charts presenting specific information REQUIRED or RECOMMENDED under the GIPS standards,

    e. Returns for quarterly and/or shorter time periods,

    f. Annualized COMPOSITE and BENCHMARK returns for periods greater than 12 months,

    g. COMPOSITE -level country and sector weightings.

5.B.2 It is RECOMMENDED that FIRMS present relevant COMPOSITE-level risk measures, such as beta, tracking error, modified duration, information ratio, Sharpe ratio, Treynor ratio, credit ratings, value at risk (VaR), and volatility, over time of the COMPOSITE and BENCHMARK. [corrected September 2005]

5.B.3 After presenting the REQUIRED 5 years of compliant historical performance, the FIRM is encouraged to bring any remaining portion of its *historical* track record into compliance with the GIPS standards. (This does not preclude the REQUIREMENT that the FIRM MUST add annual performance to its track record on an *ongoing* basis to build a 10-year track record.)

6. Real Estate

Following are provisions that apply to the calculation and presentation of REAL ESTATE assets. The REAL ESTATE provisions supplement all the REQUIRED and RECOMMENDED element of the GIPS standards (outlined in Section II.0. through Section II.5.), except the REAL ESTATE provisions that override the existing GIPS provisions for valuation: II.6.A.1, II.6.A.2, II.6.B.1, and II.6.B.2. Investment types not considered as REAL ESTATE and, therefore, addressed elsewhere in the general provisions of the GIPS standards include: [corrected January 2006]

- Publicly traded REAL ESTATE securities, including any listed securities issued by public companies,
- Commercial mortgage-backed securities (CMBS),
- Private debt investments, including commercial and residential loans where the expected return is solely related to contractual interest rates without any participation in the economic performance of the underlying REAL ESTATE.

If a PORTFOLIO includes a mix of REAL ESTATE and other investments that are not REAL ESTATE, then these REQUIREMENTS and RECOMMENDATIONS only apply to the REAL ESTATE portion of the PORTFOLIO, and when the FIRM CARVES-OUT the REAL ESTATE portion of the PORTFOLIO, the GIPS CARVE-OUT provisions (see II.3.A.7) MUST also be applied.

6.A Real Estate Input Data — Requirements

6.A.1 REAL ESTATE investments MUST be valued at MARKET VALUE at least once every 12 months. For periods beginning 1 January 2008, REAL ESTATE investments MUST be valued at least quarterly.

6.A.2 REAL ESTATE investments MUST be valued by an external PROFESSIONALLY DESIGNATED, CERTIFIED, OR LICENSED COMMERCIAL PROPERTY VALUER/APPRAISER at least once every 36 months. In markets where neither professionally designated nor appropriately sanctioned valuers or appraisers are available and valuers or appraisers from other countries bearing such credentials do not commonly operate, then the party responsible for engaging such services locally shall take necessary steps to ensure that only well-qualified property valuers are used.

6.B Real Estate Input Data — Recommendations

6.B.1 REAL ESTATE investments SHOULD be valued at least quarterly.

6.B.2 REAL ESTATE investments SHOULD be valued by an external valuer or appraiser at least once every 12 months.

6.B.3 If calculating the INTERNAL RATE OF RETURN, FIRMS SHOULD use quarterly cash flows at a minimum.

6.A Real Estate Disclosures — Requirements

6.A.3 In addition to the other disclosure REQUIREMENTS of the GIPS standards, performance presentations for REAL ESTATE investments MUST disclose:

   a. The calculation methodology for component returns—that is, component returns are (1) calculated separately using chain-linked TIME-WEIGHTED RATES OF RETURN, or (2) adjusted such that the sum of the INCOME RETURN and the CAPITAL RETURN is equal to the TOTAL RETURN, [corrected September 2005]

   b. The FIRM's description of discretion,

   c. The valuation methods and procedures (e.g., discounted cash flow valuation model, capitalized income approach, sales comparison approach, the valuation of debt payable in determining the value of leveraged REAL ESTATE),

d. The range of performance returns for the individual accounts in the COMPOSITE,

e. The source of the valuation (whether valued by an external valuer or INTER-NAL VALUATION or whether values are obtained from a third-party manager) for each period,

f. The percent of total MARKET VALUE of COMPOSITE assets (asset weighted not equally weighted) to total REAL ESTATE assets valued by an EXTERNAL VALUA-TION for each period, and [corrected September 2005]

g. The frequency REAL ESTATE investments are valued by external valuers.

6.B Real Estate Disclosures — Recommendations

6.B.4   If since-inception INTERNAL RATE OF RETURN performance results are shown, the FIRM SHOULD disclose the time period that is covered as well as the frequency of the cash flows used in the calculation.

6.A Real Estate Presentation and Reporting — Requirements

6.A.4   The income and capital appreciation component returns MUST be presented in addition to TOTAL RETURN.

6.B Real Estate Presentation and Reporting — Recommendations

6.B.5   When available, the capital and income segments of the appropriate REAL ESTATE BENCHMARK SHOULD be presented.

6.B.6   It is RECOMMENDED that FIRMS present the since-inception INTERNAL RATE OF RETURN for the COMPOSITE.

6.B.7   It is RECOMMENDED that the following items be presented, especially in those circumstances when the investment manager has the ability to control the timing of investor capital call tranches during the fund's or PORTFOLIO'S initial acquisition period:

a. GROSS- and NET-OF-FEES (including incentive allocations) annualized since inception TIME-WEIGHTED RATE OF RETURN and INTERNAL RATE OF RETURN (terminal value based on ENDING MARKET VALUE net assets of the COMPOSITE) to the last year reported for the COMPOSITE.

b. GROSS- and NET-OF-FEES (including incentive allocations) annualized since inception TIME-WEIGHTED RATE OF RETURN and INTERNAL RATE OF RETURN (based on realized cash flows only, excluding unrealized gains) to the last year reported for the COMPOSITE.

c. In addition, other performance measures may provide additional useful information for both prospective and existing investors. The GIPS PRIVATE EQUITY Provisions (See GIPS standards II.7) provide guidance with regard to such additional measures as investment and REALIZATION MULTIPLES and ratios relating to PAID-IN-CAPITAL.

7. Private Equity

Following are provisions that apply to the calculation and presentation of PRIVATE EQUITY investments other than OPEN-END or EVERGREEN FUNDS (which MUST follow the main GIPS provisions). The PRIVATE EQUITY provisions supplement all the REQUIRED and RECOMMENDED elements of the GIPS standards (outlined in Section II.0. through Section II.5), except these PRIVATE EQUITY provisions that override the existing GIPS provisions for valuation (II.7.A.1

and II.7.B.1), calculation methodology (II.7.A.2 and II.7.A.3), fees (II.7.A.4 and II.7.A.5), and presentation and reporting of returns (II.7.A.20). [corrected January 2006]

7.A Private Equity Input Data — Requirements

    7.A.1 PRIVATE EQUITY investments MUST be valued (preferably quarterly but at least annually) according to the GIPS PRIVATE EQUITY Valuation Principles provided in Appendix A4.

7.B Private Equity Input Data — Recommendations

    7.B.1 PRIVATE EQUITY investments SHOULD be valued quarterly.

7.A Private Equity Calculation Methodology — Requirements

    7.A.2 FIRMS MUST calculate the annualized since-inception INTERNAL RATE OF RETURN (SI-IRR).

    7.A.3 The annualized SI-IRR MUST be calculated using either daily or monthly cash flows and the period-end valuation of the unliquidated remaining holdings. Stock DISTRIBUTIONS MUST be valued at the time of DISTRIBUTION.

    7.A.4 NET-OF-FEES RETURNS MUST be net of INVESTMENT MANAGEMENT FEES, CARRIED INTEREST, and TRANSACTION EXPENSES.

    7.A.5 For INVESTMENT ADVISORS, all returns MUST be net of all underlying partnership and/or fund fees and CARRIED INTEREST. NET-OF-FEES RETURNS MUST, in addition, be net of all the INVESTMENT ADVISOR's fees, expenses, and CARRIED INTEREST.

7.A. Private Equity Composite Construction — Requirements

    7.A.6 All CLOSED-END PRIVATE EQUITY investments, including, but not limited to, fund of funds, partnerships, or DIRECT INVESTMENTS, MUST be included in a COMPOSITE defined by strategy and VINTAGE YEAR.

    7.A.7 Partnership/fund investments, DIRECT INVESTMENTS, and OPEN-END PRIVATE EQUITY investments (e.g., EVERGREEN FUNDS) MUST be in separate COMPOSITES.

7.A. Private Equity Disclosures — Requirements

    7.A.8 FIRMS MUST disclose the VINTAGE YEAR of the COMPOSITE.

    7.A.9 For all closed (discontinued) COMPOSITES, FIRMS MUST disclose the final realization (liquidation) date of the COMPOSITE.

    7.A.10 FIRMS MUST disclose the unrealized appreciation/depreciation of the COMPOSITE for the most recent period.

    7.A.11 FIRMS MUST disclose the total COMMITTED CAPITAL of the COMPOSITE for the most recent period.

    7.A.12 For the most recent period, FIRMS MUST disclose the valuation methodologies used to value their PRIVATE EQUITY investments. If any change occurs in either valuation basis or methodology from the prior period, the change MUST be disclosed.

    7.A.13 If the presentation complies with any local or regional valuation guidelines in addition to the GIPS PRIVATE EQUITY Valuation Principles, FIRMS MUST disclose which local or regional guidelines have been used.

7.A.14 FIRMS MUST document the FIRM's valuation review procedures and disclose that the procedures are available upon request.

7.A.15 FIRMS MUST disclose the definition of the COMPOSITE investment strategy (e.g., early stage, development, buy-outs, generalist, turnaround, mezzanine, geography, middle market, and large transaction).

7.A.16 If a BENCHMARK is used, FIRMS MUST disclose the calculation methodology used for the BENCHMARK.

7.A.17 If a valuation basis other than FAIR VALUE is used to value investments within the COMPOSITE, FIRMS MUST disclose for the most recent period presented their justification for why FAIR VALUE is not applicable. Additionally, FIRMS MUST disclose the following:

    a. The carrying value of non-FAIR-VALUE-basis investments relative to total fund.

    b. The number of holdings valued on a non-FAIR-VALUE basis.

    c. The absolute value of the non-FAIR-VALUE-basis investments.

7.A.18 FIRMS MUST disclose whether they are using daily or monthly cash flows in the SI-IRR calculation.

7.A.19 If a FIRM does not use a calendar year period-end, a disclosure MUST be made indicating the period-end used.

7.A Private Equity Presentation and Reporting — Requirements

7.A.20 FIRMS MUST present both the NET-OF-FEES and GROSS-OF-FEES annualized SI-IRR of the COMPOSITE for each year since inception.

7.A.21 For each period presented, FIRMS MUST report:

    a. PAID-IN CAPITAL to date (cumulative DRAWDOWN),

    b. Total current INVESTED CAPITAL, and

    c. Cumulative DISTRIBUTIONS to date.

7.A.22 For each period presented, FIRMS MUST report the following multiples:

    a. TOTAL VALUE TO PAID-IN CAPITAL (INVESTMENT MULTIPLE or TVPI),

    b. Cumulative DISTRIBUTIONS to PAID-IN CAPITAL (REALIZATION MULTIPLE or DPI),

    c. PAID-IN CAPITAL to COMMITTED CAPITAL (PIC MULTIPLE), and

    d. RESIDUAL VALUE TO PAID-IN CAPITAL (RVPI).

7.A.23 If a BENCHMARK is shown, the cumulative annualized SI-IRR for the BENCH-MARK that reflects the same strategy and VINTAGE YEAR of the COMPOSITE MUST be presented for the same periods for which the COMPOSITE is presented. If no BENCHMARK is shown, the presentation MUST explain why no BENCHMARK) is disclosed.

7.B Private Equity Presentation and Reporting — Recommendations

7.B.2 FIRMS SHOULD present the average holding period of the investments (PORTFOLIO companies) over the life of the COMPOSITE.

III. VERIFICATION

The primary purpose of verification is to establish that a FIRM claiming compliance with the GIPS standards has adhered to the Standards. Verification will also increase the understanding and professionalism of performance measurement teams and consistency of presentation of performance results.

The verification procedures attempt to strike a balance between ensuring the quality, accuracy, and relevance of performance presentations and minimizing the cost to FIRMS of independent review of performance results. FIRMS SHOULD assess the benefits of improved internal processes and procedures, which are as significant as the marketing advantages of verification.

The goal of the IPC in drafting the verification procedures is to encourage broad acceptance of verification.

Verification is strongly encouraged and is expected to become mandatory at a future date. The IPC will re-evaluate all aspects of mandatory verification by 2010 and provide the industry sufficient time to implement any changes.

A. Scope and Purpose of Verification

1. Verification is the review of an investment management FIRM's performance measurement processes and procedures by an independent third-party "verifier." Verification tests:
    a. Whether the FIRM has complied with all the COMPOSITE construction REQUIREMENTS of the GIPS standards on a FIRM-wide basis, and
    b. Whether the FIRM's processes and procedures are designed to calculate and present performance results in compliance with the GIPS standards.

    A single verification report is issued in respect of the whole FIRM; verification cannot be carried out for a single COMPOSITE.
2. Third-party verification brings credibility to the claim of compliance and supports the overall guiding principles of full disclosure and fair representation of investment performance.
3. The initial minimum period for which verification can be performed is 1 year of a FIRM's presented performance. The RECOMMENDED period over which verification is performed is that part of the FIRM's track record for which GIPS compliance is claimed.
4. A verification report must confirm that:
    a. The FIRM has complied with all the COMPOSITE construction REQUIREMENTS of the GIPS standards on a FIRM-wide basis, and
    b. The FIRM's processes and procedures are designed to calculate and present performance results in compliance with the GIPS standards.

Without such a report from the verifier, the FIRM cannot state that its claim of compliance with the GIPS standards has been verified.

5. After performing the verification, the verifier may conclude that the FIRM is not in compliance with the GIPS standards or that the records of the FIRM cannot support a complete verification. In such situations, the verifier must issue a statement to the FIRM clarifying why a verification report was not possible.
6. A principal verifier may accept the work of a local or previous verifier as part of the basis for the principal verifier's opinion.
7. The minimum GIPS verification procedures are described in Section III.B Required Verification Procedures.

B. Required Verification Procedures

The following are the minimum procedures that verifiers must follow when verifying an investment FIRM's compliance with the GIPS standards. Verifiers must follow these procedures prior to issuing a verification report to the FIRM:

1. Pre-verification Procedures
    a. *Knowledge of the FIRM:* Verifiers must obtain selected samples of the FIRM's investment performance reports and other available information regarding the FIRM to ensure appropriate knowledge of the FIRM.
    b. *Knowledge of GIPS Standards:* Verifiers must understand all the REQUIREMENTS and REC-OMMENDATIONS of the GIPS standards, including any updates, reports, guidance statements, interpretations, and clarifications published by CFA Institute and the Investment Performance Council, which will be made available via the CFA Institute website (www. cfainstitute.org) as well as the *GIPS Handbook.* All clarification and update information must be considered when determining a FIRM's claim of compliance.
    c. *Knowledge of the Performance Standards:* Verifiers must be knowledgeable of country-specific laws and regulations applicable to the FIRM and must determine any differences between the GIPS standards and the country-specific laws and regulations.
    d. *Knowledge of FIRM Policies:* Verifiers must determine the FIRM's assumptions and policies for establishing and maintaining compliance with all applicable REQUIREMENTS of the GIPS standards. At a minimum, verifiers must deter mine the following policies and procedures of the FIRM:
        i.   Policy with regard to investment discretion. The verifier must receive from the FIRM, in writing, the FIRM's definition of investment discretion and the FIRM's guidelines for determining whether accounts are fully discretionary;
        ii.   Policy with regard to the definition of COMPOSITES according to investment strategy. The verifier must obtain the FIRM's list of COMPOSITE DEFINITIONS with written criteria for including accounts in each COMPOSITE;
        iii. Policy with regard to the timing of inclusion of new accounts in the COMPOSITES;
        iv.   Policy with regard to timing of exclusion of closed accounts in the COMPOSITES;
        v.   Policy with regard to the accrual of interest and dividend income;
        vi.   Policy with regard to the market valuation of investment securities;
        vii. Method for computing the TIME-WEIGHTED-RATE OF RETURN for the portfolio;
        viii. Assumptions on the timing of capital inflows/outflows;
        ix.   Method for computing COMPOSITE returns;
        x.   Policy with regard to the presentation of COMPOSITE returns;
        xi.   Policies regarding timing of implied taxes due on income and realized capital gains for reporting performance on an after-tax basis;
        xii. Policies regarding use of securities/countries not included in a COMPOSITE's BENCHMARK;
        xiii. Use of leverage and other derivatives; and
        xiv. Any other policies and procedures relevant to performance presentation.
    e. *Knowledge of Valuation Basis for Performance Calculations*: Verifiers must ensure that they understand the methods and policies used to record valuation information for performance calculation purposes. In particular, verifiers must determine that:
        i.   The FIRM's policy on classifying fund flows (e.g., injections, disbursements, dividends, interest, fees, and taxes) is consistent with the desired results and will give rise to accurate returns;
        ii.   The FIRM's accounting treatment of income, interest, and dividend receipts is consistent with cash account and cash accruals definitions;
        iii. The FIRM's treatment of taxes, tax reclaims, and tax accruals is correct and the manner used is consistent with the desired method (i.e., gross- or net-of-tax return);

iv.   The FIRM's policies on recognizing purchases, sales, and the opening and closing of other positions are internally consistent and will produce accurate results; and

v.   The FIRM's accounting for investments and derivatives is consistent with the GIPS standards.

2.   Verification Procedures

   a.   *Definition of the FIRM:* Verifiers must determine that the FIRM is, and has been, appropriately defined.

   b.   *COMPOSITE Construction.* Verifiers must be satisfied that:

   i.   The FIRM has defined and maintained COMPOSITES according to reasonable guidelines in compliance with the GIPS standards;

   ii.   All the FIRM's actual discretionary fee-paying PORTFOLIOS are included in a COMPOSITE;

   iii.   The FIRM's definition of discretion has been consistently applied over time;

   iv.   At all times, all accounts are included in their respective COMPOSITES and no accounts that belong in a particular COMPOSITE have been excluded;

   v.   COMPOSITE BENCHMARKS are consistent with COMPOSITE DEFINITIONS and have been consistently applied over time;

   vi.   The FIRM's guidelines for creating and maintaining COMPOSITES have been consistently applied; and

   vii.   The FIRM's list of COMPOSITES is complete.

   c.   *Nondiscretionary Accounts.* Verifiers must obtain a listing of all FIRM PORTFOLIOS and determine on a sampling basis whether the manager's classification of the account as discretionary or nondiscretionary is appropriate by referring to the account's agreement and the FIRM's written guidelines for determining investment discretion.

   d.   *Sample Account Selection:* Verifiers must obtain a listing of open and closed accounts for all COMPOSITES for the years under examination. Verifiers may check compliance with the GIPS standards using a selected sample of a FIRM's accounts. Verifiers SHOULD consider the following criteria when selecting the sample accounts for examination:

   i.   Number of COMPOSITES at the FIRM;

   ii.   Number of PORTFOLIOS in each COMPOSITE;

   iii.   Nature of the COMPOSITE;

   iv.   Total assets under management;

   v.   Internal control structure at the FIRM (system of checks and balances in place);

   vi   Number of years under examination; and

   vii   Computer applications, software used in the construction and maintenance of COMPOSITES, the use of external performance measurers, and the calculation of performance results.

This list is not all-inclusive and contains only the minimum criteria that SHOULD be used in the selection and evaluation of a sample for testing. For example, one potentially useful approach would be to choose a PORTFOLIO for the study sample that has the largest impact on COMPOSITE performance because of its size or because of extremely good or bad performance. The lack of explicit record keeping or the presence of errors may warrant selecting a larger sample or applying additional verification procedures.

   e.   *Account Review:* For selected accounts, verifiers must determine:

   i.   Whether the timing of the initial inclusion in the COMPOSITE is in accordance with policies of the FIRM;

   ii.   Whether the timing of exclusion from the COMPOSITE is in accordance with policies of the FIRM for closed accounts;

   iii. Whether the objectives set forth in the account agreement are consistent with the manager's COMPOSITE DEFINITION as indicated by the account agreement, PORTFOLIO summary, and COMPOSITE DEFINITION;

   iv. The existence of the accounts by tracing selected accounts from account agreements to the COMPOSITES;

   v. That all PORTFOLIOS sharing the same guidelines are included in the same COMPOSITE; and

   vi. That shifts from one COMPOSITE to another are consistent with the guidelines set forth by the specific account agreement or with documented guidelines of the FIRM's clients.

  f. *Performance Measurement Calculation:* Verifiers must determine whether the FIRM has computed performance in accordance with the policies and assumptions adopted by the FIRM and disclosed in its presentations. In doing so, verifiers SHOULD:

   i. Recalculate rates of return for a sample of accounts in the FIRM using an acceptable return formula as prescribed by the GIPS standards (e.g., TIME-WEIGHTED RATE OF RETURN); and

   ii. Take a reasonable sample of COMPOSITE calculations to assure themselves of the accuracy of the asset weighting of returns, the geometric linking of returns to produce annual rates of returns, and the calculation of the DISPERSION of individual returns around the aggregate COMPOSITE return.

  g. *Disclosures*: Verifiers must review a sample of COMPOSITE presentations to ensure that the presentations include the information and disclosures REQUIRED by the GIPS standards.

 h. *Maintenance of Records*: The verifier must maintain sufficient information to support the verification report. The verifier must obtain a representation letter from the client FIRM confirming major policies and any other specific representations made to the verifier during the examination.

C. Detailed Examinations of Investment Performance Presentations

Separate from a GIPS verification, a FIRM may choose to have a further, more extensive, specifically focused examination (or performance audit) of a specific COMPOSITE presentation.

 FIRMS cannot make any claim that a particular COMPOSITE has been independently examined with respect to the GIPS standards unless the verifier has also followed the GIPS verification procedures set forth in Section III.B. FIRMS cannot state that a particular COMPOSITE presentation has been "GIPS verified" or make any claim to that affect. GIPS verification relates only to FIRM-wide verification. FIRMS can make a claim of verification only after a verifier has issued a GIPS verification report.

 To assert a verification report has been received, a detailed examination of a COMPOSITE presentation is not required. Examinations of this type are unlikely to become a REQUIREMENT of the GIPS standards or become mandatory.

APPENDIX A1—SAMPLE GIPS-COMPLIANT PRESENTATIONS

EXAMPLE 1:

SAMPLE 1 INVESTMENT FIRM BALANCED COMPOSITE 1 JANUARY 1995 THROUGH 31 DECEMBER 2004

Year	Gross-of-Fees Return (percent)	Net-of-Fees Return (percent)	Benchmark Return (percent)	Number of Portfolios	Internal Dispersion (percent)	Total Composite Assets (CAD Million)	Total Firm Assets (CAD Million)
1995	16.0	15.0	14.1	26	4.5	165	236
1996	2.2	1.3	1.8	32	2.0	235	346
1997	22.4	21.5	24.1	38	5.7	344	529
1998	7.1	6.2	6.0	45	2.8	445	695
1999	8.5	7.5	8.0	48	3.1	520	839
2000	−8.0	−8.9	−8.4	49	2.8	505	1014
2001	−5.9	−6.8	−6.2	52	2.9	499	995
2002	2.4	1.6	2.2	58	3.1	525	1125
2003	6.7	5.9	6.8	55	3.5	549	1225
2004	9.4	8.6	9.1	59	2.5	575	1290

Sample 1 Investment Firm has prepared and presented this report in compliance with the Global Investment Performance Standards (GIPS®).

Notes:

1. Sample 1 Investment Firm is a balanced portfolio investment manager that invests solely in Canadian securities. Sample 1 Investment Firm is defined as an independent investment management firm that is not affiliated with any parent organization. For the periods from 2000 through 2004, Sample 1 Investment Firm has been verified by Verification Services Inc. A copy of the verification report is available upon request. Additional information regarding the firm's policies and procedures for calculating and reporting performance results is available upon request.
2. The composite includes all nontaxable balanced portfolios with an asset allocation of 30% S&P TSX and 70% Scotia Canadian Bond Index Fund, which allow up to a 10% deviation in asset allocation.
3. The benchmark: 30% S&P TSX; 70% Scotia Canadian Bond Index Fund rebalanced monthly.
4. Valuations are computed and performance reported in Canadian dollars.
5. Gross-of-fees performance returns are presented before management and custodial fees but after all trading expenses. Returns are presented net of nonreclaimable withholding taxes. Net-of-fees performance returns are calculated by deducting the highest fee of 0.25% from the quarterly gross composite return. The management fee schedule is as follows: 1.00% on first CAD25M; 0.60% thereafter.
6. This composite was created in February 1995. A complete list and description of firm composites is available upon request.
7. For the periods 1995 and 1996, Sample 1 Investment Firm was not in compliance with the GIPS standards because portfolios were valued annually.
8. Internal dispersion is calculated using the equal-weighted standard deviation of all portfolios that were included in the composite for the entire year.

EXAMPLE 2:

SAMPLE 2 ASSET MANAGEMENT COMPANY EQUITIES WORLD BM MSCI
ACTIVE MANDATES DIRECT

	Reporting Currency CHF				Creation Date 01 July 1999	
Period	Total Return (%)	MSCI World (ri) in CHF Benchmark Return (%)	Number of Portfolios	Composite Dispersion (Range)	Total Composite Assets (millions)	Percentage of Firm Assets (%)
2004	18.0	19.6	6	0.2	84.3	<0.1
2003	−35.3	−33.0	8	0.7	126.6	0.1
2002	−16.0	−14.5	8	1.5	233.0	0.2
2001	−13.5	−11.8	7	1.3	202.1	0.2
2000	60.2	46.1	<5	N/A	143.7	0.2
1999	21.3	17.5	<5	N/A	62.8	<0.1
1998	22.5	26.3	<5	N/A	16.1	<0.1

Compliance Statement

Sample 2 Asset Management Company has prepared and presented this report in compliance with the Global Investment Performance Standards (GIPS®).

Definition of the Firm

Sample 2 Asset Management Company is an independent investment management firm established in 1997. Sample 2 Asset Management Company manages a variety of equity, fixed income, and balanced assets for primarily Swiss and European clients. Additional information regarding the firm's policies and procedures for calculating and reporting performance returns is available upon request.

Benchmark

Sources of foreign exchange rates may be different between the composite and the benchmark.

Fees

Performance figures are presented gross of management fees, custodial fees, and withholding taxes but net of all trading expenses.

List of Composites

A complete listing and description of all composites is available on request.

Verification

Sample 2 Asset Management Company has been verified by an independent verifier on an annual basis from 1998 through 2003.

EXAMPLE 3:

SCHEDULE OF PERFORMANCE RESULTS SAMPLE 3 REALTY MANAGEMENT FIRM CORE REAL ESTATE COMPOSITE
January 1,1995, through December 31, 2004

| Year | Gross-of-Fees Returns | | | | Composite Dispersion | NCREIF Property Index Benchmark | Number of Portfolios | Year-End Composite | | | Firm Total Net Assets (USD mil) | Percent of Firm Assets |
	Income Return	Capital Return	TOTAL	Range of Returns				Net Assets (USD mil)	Percent Leveraged	External Valuation		
1995	5.1%	−4.0%	0.8%	0.7–1.0	NA	−5.6%	<5	$ 79	43%	100%	$ 950	8%
1996	5.5%	−0.9%	4.5%	4.0–5.0	NA	−4.3%	<5	$143	49%	100%	$ 989	14%
1997	6.9%	−1.5%	5.3%	5.0–5.4	NA	1.4%	<5	$217	56%	100%	$1,219	18%
1998	8.1%	0.9%	9.1%	8.9–9.7	NA	6.4%	<5	$296	54%	100%	$1,375	22%
1999	8.9%	1.7%	10.8%	9.9–11.0	NA	7.5%	<5	$319	50%	100%	$1,425	22%
2000	9.0%	0.5%	9.6%	9.1–10.9	0.7	10.3%	5	$367	45%	100%	$1,532	24%
2001	9.1%	1.2%	10.5%	10.0–10.7	0.3	13.9%	5	$349	39%	100%	$1,712	20%
2002	7.9%	1.8%	9.9%	9.8–10.5	0.3	16.3%	6	$398	31%	100%	$1,796	22%
2003	8.5%	2.9%	11.5%	10.9–12.0	0.5	11.1%	6	$425	28%	100%	$1,924	22%
2004	8.2%	2.5%	10.8%	9.9–11.8	0.8	12.0%	7	$432	22%	100%	$1,954	22%

Annualized Since Inception Time-Weighted Returns:

7.7% 0.5% 8.0%   6.7%

Annualized Since Inception Internal Rate of Return:

7.8%

Fee Schedule

The standard fixed management fee for accounts with assets under management of up to CHF50 million is 0.35% per annum.

Minimum Account Size

The minimum portfolio size for inclusion in Equities World BM MSCI composite is CHF1 million.

Example 3: Sample 3 Realty Management Firm

DISCLOSURES

Compliance Statement

Sample 3 Realty Management Firm has prepared and presented this report in compliance with the Global Investment Performance Standards (GIPS®).

The Firm

Sample 3 Realty Management Firm (the "Firm"), a subsidiary of ABC Capital, Inc., is a registered investment adviser under the Investment Advisors Act of 1940. The Firm exercises complete discretion over the selection, capitalization, asset management, and disposition of investments in wholly-owned properties and joint ventures. A complete list and description of the Firm's composites is available upon request.

The Composite

The Core Real Estate Composite (the "Composite") comprises all actual fee-paying discretionary portfolios managed by the Firm with a core investment and risk strategy with an income focus having a minimum initial portfolio size of $10 million. Portfolios that initially qualify are excluded later from the composite if their asset size decreases below the minimum requirement due to capital distributions. The Composite was created in 1998. Composite dispersion is measured using an asset-weighted standard deviation of returns of the portfolios.

Valuation

Assets are valued quarterly by the Firm and appraised annually by an independent Member of the Appraisal Institute. Both the internal and external property valuations rely primarily on the application of market discount rates to future projections of free cash flows (unleveraged cash flows) and capitalized terminal values over the expected holding period for each property. Property mortgages, notes, and loans are marked to market using prevailing interest rates for comparable property loans if the terms of existing loans preclude the immediate repayment of such loans. Loan repayment fees, if any, are considered in the projected year of sale.

Calculation of Performance Returns

Returns presented are denominated in United States dollars. Returns are presented net of leverage. Composite returns are calculated on an asset-weighted average basis using beginning-of-period values. Returns include cash and cash equivalents and related interest income. Income return is based on accrual recognition of earned income. Capital expenditures, tenant improvements, and lease commissions are capitalized and included in the cost of the property, are not amortized, and are reconciled through the valuation process and reflected in the capital return component. Income and capital returns may not equal total returns due to chain-linking of quarterly returns. Annual returns are time-weighted rates of return calculated by linking quarterly returns. For the annualized since-inception time-weighted return, terminal value is based on ending market value of net assets of the Composite. For the since-inception internal rate of return, contributions from and distributions to investors since January 1, 1995, and a terminal value equal to the composite's ending market value of net assets as of December 31, 2004, are used. The IRR is calculated using monthly cash flows. Additional information regarding policies for calculating and reporting returns in compliance with the GIPS standards is available upon request.

Investment Management Fees

Some of the portfolios pay incentive fees ranging between 10% and 20% of IRR in excess of established benchmarks. Current annual investment advisory fees are as follows:

> Up to $30 million: 1.6%
> $30–$50 million: 1.3%
> Over $50 million: 1.0%

NCREIF Property Index Benchmark

The National Council of Real Estate Investment Fiduciaries (NCREIF) Property Index benchmark has been taken from published sources. The NCREIF Property Index is unleveraged, includes various real estate property types, excludes cash and other nonproperty related assets and liabilities, income, and expenses. The calculation methodology for the index is not consistent with calculation methodology employed for the Composite because the benchmark computes the total return by adding the income and capital appreciation return on a quarterly basis.

EXAMPLE 4:

SAMPLE 4 PRIVATE EQUITY PARTNERS BUY-OUT COMPOSITE 1 JANUARY 1995 THROUGH 31 DECEMBER 2002

Year	Annualized SI-IRR Gross-of-Fees (%)	Annualized SI-IRR Net-of-Fees (%)	Benchmark Return (%)	Composite Assets (USD$ mil)	Total Firm Assets (USD$ mil)
1995	(7.5)	(11.07)	(9.42)	4.31	357.36
1996	6.2	4.53	2.83	10.04	402.78
1997	13.8	10.10	14.94	14.25	530.51
1998	13.1	9.28	14.22	25.21	613.73
1999	53.2	44.53	37.43	54.00	871.75
2000	40.6	26.47	32.97	24.25	1,153.62
2001	29.9	21.86	27.42	8.25	1,175.69
2002	25.3	17.55	25.24	10.25	1,150.78

Year	Paid-In Capital (USD$ mil)	Invested Capital (USD$ mil)	Cumulative Distributions (USD$ mil)	Investment Multiple (TVPI)	Realization Multiple (DPI)	PIC	RVPI
1995	4.68	4.68	0.00	0.92	0.00	0.19	0.92
1996	9.56	9.56	0.00	1.05	0.00	0.38	1.05
1997	14.54	12.91	2.55	1.16	0.18	0.58	0.98
1998	23.79	22.15	2.55	1.17	0.11	0.95	1.06
1999	25.00	19.08	15.78	2.79	0.63	1.00	2.16
2000	25.00	17.46	27.44	2.07	1.10	1.00	0.97
2001	25.00	14.89	39.10	1.89	1.56	1.00	0.33
2002	25.00	13.73	41.25	2.06	1.65	1.00	0.41

TVPI = Total Value to Paid-In Capital
DPI = Distributed Capital to Paid-In Capital
PIC = Paid-In Capital to Committed Capital
RVPI = Residual Value to Paid-In Capital

Sample 4 Private Equity Partners has prepared and presented this report in compliance with the Global Investment Performance Standards (GIPS®).

Example 4: Sample 4 Private Equity Partners

DISCLOSURES

Sample 4 Private Equity Partners is an independent private equity investment firm, having offices in London, New York, and San Francisco. The Sample 4 Buy-Out Composite invests in private equity buyouts and was created in January 1995.

The Sample 4 Buy-Out Composite complies with the XYZ Venture Capital Association's valuation guidelines. Valuations are prepared by Sample 4's valuations committee and reviewed by an independent advisory board. Sample 4 follows the fair value basis of valuation as recommended in the GIPS Private Equity Valuation Principles. All investments within the Sample 4 Buy-Out Composite are valued either using a most recent transaction or an earnings multiple. Sample 4's valuation review procedures are available upon request.

The GP-BO index is used as the benchmark and is constructed as the QRS index return plus 500 basis points. The benchmark return is calculated using monthly cash flows. There is only one fund in the composite for all time periods, and the dispersion of portfolio returns within the composite, therefore, is zero for all years.

The vintage year of the Sample 4 Buy-Out Fund is 1995, and total committed capital is USD$25 million. The total composite assets (unrealized gains) are USD$10.25 million as of 31 December 2002.

The fund's SI-IRR calculation incorporates monthly cash flows.

The standard fee schedule currently in effect is as follows: 1.00% of assets under management. In addition, there is a 20% incentive fee for all assets. The incentive fee is applied to the value added in excess of fees, expenses, and the return of the GP-BO Index [corrected October 2006].

A complete list of firm composites and composite performance results is available upon request. Additional information regarding the firm's policies and procedures for calculating and reporting performance results is available upon request.

APPENDIX A2—SAMPLE LIST AND DESCRIPTION OF COMPOSITES

Sample Asset Management Firm

List and Description of Composites

The **Small Cap Growth Composite** includes all institutional portfolios invested in U.S. equities with strong earnings and growth characteristics and small capitalizations. The benchmark is the Russell 2000® Growth Index.

The **Large Cap Growth Composite** includes all institutional portfolios invested in U.S. equities with strong earnings and growth characteristics and large capitalizations. The benchmark is the Russell 1000® Growth Index.

The **Core Fixed Income Composite** includes all institutional portfolios invested in fixed securities. Portfolios within the composite will have a duration that is plus or minus 20 percent of the benchmark. The benchmark is the Lehman Brothers Aggregate Bond Index.

The **Intermediate Fixed Income Composite** includes all institutional portfolios invested in fixed securities. Portfolios within the composite will have a duration that is plus or minus 20 percent of the benchmark. The benchmark is the Lehman Brothers Intermediate Aggregate Bond Index.

The **High Yield Fixed Income Composite** includes all institutional portfolios invested in high yield debt securities. The benchmark is the Lehman Brothers U.S. Corporate High Yield Bond Index.

The **Balanced Growth Composite** includes all institutional balanced portfolios that have a 50–70% allocation to growth equities, with a typical allocation between 55–65%. The benchmark is 60% S&P 500® and 40% Lehman Brothers Aggregate Bond Index. Only portfolios greater than $5 million are included in the composite.

Terminated Composites

The **GARP Equity Composite** includes all institutional portfolios invested in growth stocks that are reasonably priced and valued "cheap" compared with their peers. The benchmark is the S&P 500® Index. The composite terminated in November 2003.

The **Small-Mid Cap Growth Composite** includes all institutional portfolios invested in U.S. equities with strong earnings and growth characteristics. The benchmark is the Russell 2500® Growth Index. The composite terminated in February 2004.

APPENDIX A3—GIPS ADVERTISING GUIDELINES

A.   Purpose of the GIPS Advertising Guidelines

The Global Investment Performance Standards provide the investment community with a set of ethical standards for FIRMS to follow when presenting their performance results to potential clients. The Standards serve to provide greater uniformity and comparability among investment managers without regard to geographical location and to facilitate a dialogue between FIRMS and their prospective clients about the critical issues of how the FIRM achieved historical performance results and determines future investment strategies.

The GIPS Advertising Guidelines attempt to serve as industry global best practice for the advertisement of performance results. The GIPS Advertising Guidelines do not replace the GIPS standards nor do they absolve FIRMS from presenting performance presentations that adhere to the REQUIREMENTS of the full GIPS standards. The guidelines only apply to FIRMS that already satisfy all the REQUIREMENTS of the Standards on a FIRM-wide basis and claim compliance with the Standards. FIRMS that claim compliance can choose to advertise that claim using the GIPS Advertising Guidelines.

The guidelines are mandatory for FIRMS that include a claim of compliance with the GIPS Advertising Guidelines in their advertisements. The guidelines are voluntary for FIRMS that do not include a claim of compliance in their advertisements. All FIRMS are encouraged to abide by these ethical guidelines.

Definition of Advertisement

For the purposes of these guidelines, an advertisement includes any materials that are distributed to or designed for use in newspapers, magazines, FIRM brochures, letters, media, or any other written or electronic material addressed to more than one prospective client. Any written material (other than one-on-one presentations and individual client reporting) distributed to maintain existing clients or solicit new clients for an advisor is considered an advertisement.

Relationship of GIPS Advertising Guidelines to Regulatory Requirements

The GIPS Advertising Guidelines are guidelines that promote an ethical framework for advertisements. They do not change the scope of the activities of local regulatory bodies regarding the regulation of advertisements. FIRMS advertising performance results MUST also adhere to all applicable regulatory rules and requirements governing advertisements. FIRMS are encouraged to seek legal or regulatory counsel because it is likely that additional disclosures are REQUIRED. In cases where applicable law or regulation conflicts with the GIPS Advertising Guidelines, the guidelines REQUIRE FIRMS to comply with the law or regulation. FIRMS MUST disclose any conflicts between laws/regulations and the GIPS Advertising Guidelines.

The calculation and advertisement of pooled unitized products, such as mutual funds and open-ended investment companies, are regulated in most markets. These advertising guidelines are not intended to replace the regulations when a FIRM is advertising performance solely for a pooled unitized product. However, should a GIPS-compliant FIRM choose to advertise performance results, the FIRMS MUST apply all applicable laws and regulations as well as the GIPS Advertising Guidelines in order to include a claim of compliance with the GIPS standards.

B. Requirements of the GIPS Advertising Guidelines

All advertisements that include a claim of compliance with the GIPS Advertising Guidelines MUST include the following:

1. A description of the FIRM.
2. How an interested party can obtain a presentation that complies with the REQUIREMENTS of GIPS standards and/or a list and description of all FIRM COMPOSITES.
3. The GIPS Advertising Guidelines compliance statement: [Insert name of firm] claims compliance with the Global Investment Performance Standards (GIPS®).

All advertisements that include a claim of compliance with the GIPS Advertising Guidelines and that present performance results MUST also include the following information (the relevant information MUST be taken/derived from a presentation that adheres to the REQUIREMENTS of the GIPS standards):

4. A description of the strategy of the COMPOSITE being advertised.
5. Period-to-date COMPOSITE performance results in addition to either:
   a. 1-, 3-, and 5-year cumulative annualized COMPOSITE returns with the end-of-period date clearly identified (or annualized period since COMPOSITE inception if inception is greater than 1 and less than 5 years). Periods of less than 1 year are not permitted to be annualized. The annualized returns MUST be calculated through the same period of time as presented in the corresponding compliant presentation; or
   b. 5 years of annual COMPOSITE returns with the end-of-period date clearly identified (or since COMPOSITE inception if inception is less than 5 years). The annual returns MUST be calculated through the same period of time as presented in the corresponding compliant presentation.
6. Whether performance is shown gross and/or net of INVESTMENT MANAGEMENT FEES.
7. The BENCHMARK TOTAL RETURN for the same periods for which the COMPOSITE return is presented and a description of that BENCHMARK. (The appropriate COMPOSITE BENCHMARK return is the same BENCHMARK TOTAL RETURN as presented in the corresponding GIPS-compliant presentation.) If no BENCHMARK is presented, the advertisement MUST disclose why no BENCHMARK is presented.
8. The currency used to express returns.
9. The description of the use and extent of leverage and derivatives if leverage or derivatives are used as an active part of the investment strategy (i.e., not merely for efficient PORTFOLIO management) of the COMPOSITE. Where leverage/derivatives do not have a material effect on returns, no disclosure is REQUIRED.
10. When presenting noncompliant performance information for periods prior to 1 January 2000 in an advertisement, FIRMS MUST disclose the period(s) and which specific information is not compliant as well as provide the reason(s) the information is not in compliance with the GIPS standards.

Additional and Supplemental Information

FIRMS are encouraged to present SUPPLEMENTAL INFORMATION or ADDITIONAL INFORMATION (in addition to the information REQUIRED under the GIPS Advertising Guidelines) provided the SUPPLEMENTAL INFORMATION is clearly labeled as such and shown with equal or lesser prominence than the information REQUIRED under the guidelines. Where such SUPPLEMENTAL INFORMATION is included for noncompliant periods, these periods MUST be disclosed together with an explanation of what information is not compliant and why it is not in compliance with the GIPS standards.

SUPPLEMENTAL and ADDITIONAL INFORMATION is the subject of the "Guidance Statement on the Use of Supplemental Information" and users should refer to that guidance for further clarification on how to disclose such data.

Sample Advertisements

Sample Advertisement without Performance Returns

Sample 4 Investments

Sample 4 Investments is the institutional asset management division of Sample 4 Plc and is a registered investment advisory firm specializing in qualitative, growth-oriented investment management.

Sample 4 Investments claims compliance with the Global Investment Performance Standards (GIPS®).

To receive a complete list and description of Sample 4 Investments' composites and/or a presentation that adheres to the GIPS standards, contact John Doe at (800) 555-1234, or write to Sample 4 Investments, 123 Main Street, Resultland 12345, or e-mail jdoe@sample4investments.com

Sample Advertisement Including Performance Returns (1-, 3-, and 5-year annualized)

Sample 4 Investments: Global Equity Growth Composite Performance				
	Ending 31 Mar 04	Ending 31 Dec 03		
Results shown in US $ before fees	Period to Date (3 mths)	1 Year	3 Years per annum	5 Years per annum
Global Equity Growth	−3.84%	−19.05%	−14.98%	0.42%
MSCI World Index	−4.94%	−19.54%	−16.37%	−1.76%

Sample 4 Investments is the institutional asset management subsidiary of Sample 4 plc and is a registered investment advisor specializing in qualitative, growth-oriented investment management. The Global Equity Growth Composite strategy focuses on earnings, growth of earnings, and key valuation metrics.

Sample 4 Investments claims compliance with the Global Investment Performance Standards (GIPS®).

To receive a complete list and description of Sample 4 Investments' composites and/or a presentation that adheres to the GIPS standards, contact Jean Paul at +12 (034) 5678910, or write Sample 4 Investments, One Plain Street, Resultland 12KJ4, or jpaul@sample4inv.com.re.

OR the firm may present:

Sample Advertisement Including Performance Returns (5 years of annual returns)

Sample 4 Investments: Global Equity Growth Composite Performance						
Results are shown in US $ before fees	Period to Date (3 mths to 31 Mar 04)	31 Dec 2003	31 Dec 2002	31 Dec 2001	31 Dec 2000	31 Dec 1999
Global Equity Growth Composite	−3.84%	−19.05%	−17.05%	−8.47%	31.97%	25.87%
MSCI World index	−4.94%	−19.54%	−16.52%	−12.92%	25.34%	24.80%

Sample 4 Investments is the institutional asset management subsidiary of Sample 4 plc and is a registered investment advisor specializing in qualitative, growth-oriented investment management. The Global Equity Growth Composite strategy focuses on earnings, growth of earnings, and key valuation metrics.

Sample 4 Investments claims compliance with the Global Investment Performance Standards (GIPS®).

To receive a complete list and description of Sample 4 Investments' composites and/or a presentation that adheres to the GIPS standards, contact Jean Paul at +12 (034) 5678910, or write Sample 4 Investments, One Plain Street, Resultland 12KJ4, or jpaul@sample4inv.com.re.

APPENDIX A4—PRIVATE EQUITY VALUATION PRINCIPLES

Introduction

Opinions among INVESTMENT ADVISORS, practitioners, and investors differ regarding the valuation of PRIVATE EQUITY assets. The margin of error for a particular valuation methodology may often be greater than the difference between alternative methodologies. The volatility of asset values is also often high, increasing the perception that a historical valuation was "wrong." Although cash-to-cash returns are the principal metric, PRIVATE EQUITY funds raise capital in part based on unrealized interim returns. The valuation of unrealized assets underpinning these interim returns is critical to this analysis.

Although many points are contested, some common ground exists:

- The PRIVATE EQUITY industry must strive to promote integrity and professionalism in order to improve investor confidence and self-regulation.
- Consistency and comparability are important in reporting to investors, and many aspects of valuation SHOULD be transparent. More information, however, does not always equal greater transparency, and there are legal and practical constraints on the dissemination of information.
- Each PRIVATE EQUITY investment is based on a set of assumptions. It is reasonable for investors to expect interim valuations to reflect factors that, at a minimum, adversely impact these assumptions.
- When a PRIVATE EQUITY asset becomes publicly traded, arguments against interim valuations fall away, although practical considerations may remain where there are restrictions on trading or trading volumes are low.

Beyond these issues are the debates on valuation basis and methodology. The Move toward a FAIR VALUE basis has been gathering momentum in most areas of financial reporting. Particularly for early stage venture investments that may not achieve profitability for a number of years, practical problems remain and the utility of the FAIR VALUE basis must garner greater support before a consensus on detailed guidelines is likely to be possible.

Guidelines for Valuation

The following MUST be applied to all forms of investment vehicles making PRIVATE EQUITY investments. These principles do not apply to OPEN-END or EVERGREEN FUNDS.

1. Valuations MUST be prepared with integrity and professionalism by individuals with appropriate experience and ability under the direction of senior management.
2. FIRMS MUST document their valuation review procedures.
3. FIRMS MUST create as much transparency as deemed possible in relation to the valuation basis used to value fund investments. For the latest period presented, the valuation methodologies used to value PRIVATE EQUITY investments MUST be clearly disclosed, including all key assumptions.
4. The basis of valuation MUST be logically cohesive and applied rigorously. Although a FAIR VALUE basis is RECOMMENDED, all valuations MUST, at a minimum, recognize when assets

have suffered a diminution in value. (Please see the Additional Considerations section for further guidance on diminution circumstances.)

5. Valuations MUST be prepared on a consistent and comparable basis from one reporting period to the next. If any change is deemed appropriate in either valuation basis or method, the change MUST be explained. When such a change gives rise to a material alteration in the valuation of the investments, the effect of the change SHOULD also be disclosed.

6. Valuations MUST be prepared at least annually. (Quarterly valuations are RECOMMENDED.)

FAIR VALUE RECOMMENDATION

It is RECOMMENDED that the FAIR VALUE basis, which is consistent with international financial reporting principles, be used to value PRIVATE EQUITY investments. This valuation SHOULD represent the amount at which an asset could be acquired or sold in a current transaction between willing parties in which the parties each acted knowledgeably, prudently, and without compulsion.

The accuracy with which the value of an individual PRIVATE EQUITY asset can be determined will generally have substantial uncertainty. Consequently, it is RECOMMENDED that a valuation method that involves the least number of estimates is preferred over another method that introduces additional subjective assumptions. However, if the latter method results in more accurate and meaningful valuation, then it SHOULD be used instead of the former method.

Valuation Hierarchy

The following hierarchy of FAIR VALUE methodologies SHOULD be followed when valuing PRIVATE EQUITY investments:

1. *Market Transaction*
   Where a recent independent third-party transaction has occurred involving a material investment as part of a new round of financing or sale of equity, it would provide the most appropriate indication of FAIR VALUE.

2. *Market-Based Multiples*
   In the absence of any such third-party transactions continuing to have relevance, the FAIR VALUE of an investment may be calculated using earnings or other market-based multiples. The particular multiple used SHOULD be appropriate for the business being valued. Market-based multiples include, but are not limited to, the following: price to earnings, enterprise value to EBIT, enterprise value to EBITDA, and so on.

3. *Discounted Expected Future Cash Flows*
   This method SHOULD represent the present value of risk-adjusted expected cash flows, discounted at the risk-free rate.

Additional Considerations

1. Where a third-party transaction has taken place other than at arm's length, or where the new investor's objectives in making the investment are largely strategic in nature (i.e., the new investor was not acting solely as a financial investor), the manager SHOULD consider ignoring the valuation or applying an appropriate discount to it.

2. A material diminution in the value of an investment may result from, among other things, a breach of covenant, failure to service debt, a filing for creditor protection or bankruptcy, major lawsuit (particularly concerning intellectual property rights), or a loss or change of management. Other events may include fraud within the company, a material devaluation in an investment currency that is different from the fund currency, substantial changes in quoted market conditions, or any event resulting in profitability falling significantly below the levels at the time of investment or the company performing substantially and consistently behind plan. Estimating the extent of the diminution in most cases will generally involve both quantitative and qualitative analysis and SHOULD be performed with as much diligence as possible.

3. The FIRM SHOULD have policies in place for informing clients/prospects when a material diminution has taken place within the PORTFOLIO. Waiting until a quarterly update may often not provide the prospective investor with this critical information soon enough to make an informed decision.

4. Within the valuation hierarchy, there will be certain industries where very specific valuation methodologies become applicable. Within the correct industry, either of these methods could be considered the primary valuation methodology in the absence of an applicable third-party transaction. Whenever one of these methods is used, the FIRMS MUST justify the measure as representing the most appropriate and accurate method for calculating a FAIR VALUE.

    a. *Net Assets:* For FIRMS that derive a majority of their value from their underlying assets rather than the company's earnings, this method may be preferred.

    b. *Industry BENCHMARKS:* In particular industries, there are metrics, such as "price per subscriber", that can be used to derive the value of a FIRM. These measures are very specialized to the industries they represent and must not be carried over to more diversified FIRMS.

5. It is RECOMMENDED that valuations be reviewed by a qualified person or entity that is independent from the valuer. Such parties would include third-party experts, an independent advisory board, or a committee independent of the executives responsible for the valuations.

6. As stated in the Valuation Hierarchy section of this document, FAIR VALUE allows for the use of a recent transaction as the primary methodology for valuation. Accordingly, when an investment is first made, this "cost" represents the most recent transaction and, therefore, the FAIR VALUE. In this case, the cost is permitted to be used not because it represents the cost of the investment but, rather, because it represents the value of the most recent transaction.

Cost as a basis of valuation is only permitted when an estimate of FAIR VALUE cannot be reliably determined. Although a FAIR VALUE basis SHOULD always be attempted, the PRIVATE EQUITY Provisions do recognize that there may be situations when a non-FAIR-VALUE basis is necessary. Ultimately, FIRMS must keep in mind that investors make decisions based on FAIR VALUES, not out-of-date historical cost-based measures.

In any case, when a non-FAIR-VALUE basis is used, the FIRM MUST disclose its justification for why a FAIR VALUE basis cannot be applied. In addition, for each COMPOSITE, the FIRM MUST disclose the number of holdings to which a non-FAIR-VALUE basis is applied, the TOTAL VALUE of those holdings, and the value of those holdings as a percentage of the total COMPOSITE/fund assets.

7. Where companies have activities that span more than one sector, making it impractical to find comparable companies or sectors, each earnings stream may be valued independently. Sector average multiples, based on companies of comparable size, can be used where it is not practical or possible to identify a sufficient number of directly comparable companies.

8. The entry multiple(s) for an investment SHOULD only be used as a last resort when comparable quoted companies are not available.

9. All quasi-equity investments SHOULD be valued as equity unless their realizable value can be demonstrated to be other than the equity value.

10. When a PRIVATE EQUITY firm has invested in loan stock and preference shares along-side an equity investment, these instruments SHOULD not generally be valued on the basis of their yield. They SHOULD be valued at cost plus any premium or rolled up interest only to the extent it has fully accrued, less any provision/discount where appropriate.

APPENDIX A5—GIPS GLOSSARY

The following definitions are solely for the purpose of interpreting the GIPS standards.

ACCRUAL ACCOUNTING	The system of recording financial transactions as they come into existence as a legally enforceable claim, rather than when they settle.
ADDITIONAL INFORMATION	Information that is REQUIRED or RECOMMENDED under the GIPS standards and is not considered as "SUPPLEMENTAL INFORMATION" for the purposes of compliance.
ADMINISTRATIVE FEES	All fees other than the TRADING EXPENSES and the INVESTMENT MANAGEMENT FEE. ADMINISTRATIVE FEES include CUSTODY FEES, accounting fees, consulting fees, legal fees, performance measurement fees, or other related fees. These ADMINISTRATIVE FEES are typically outside the control of the investment management FIRM and are not included in either the GROSS-OF-FEES RETURN or the NET-OF-FEES RETURN. However, there are some markets and investment vehicles where ADMINISTRATIVE FEES are controlled by the FIRM. (See the term "BUNDLED FEE.")
BENCHMARK	An independent rate of return (or hurdle rate) forming an objective test of the effective implementation of an investment strategy.
BUNDLED FEE	A fee that combines multiple fees into one "bundled" fee. BUNDLED FEES can include any combination of management, transaction, custody, and other ADMINISTRATIVE FEES. Two specific examples of BUNDLED FEES are the wrap fee and the all-in fee.

	All-In Fee	Due to the universal banking system in some countries, asset management, brokerage, and custody are often part of the same company. This allows banks to offer a variety of choices to customers regarding how the fee will be charged. Customers are offered numerous fee models in which fees may be bundled together or charged separately. All-in fees can include any combination of INVESTMENT MANAGEMENT, TRADING EXPENSES, CUSTODY, and other ADMINISTRATIVE FEES.
	Wrap Fee	Wrap fees are specific to a particular investment product. The U.S. Securities and Exchange Commission (SEC) defines a wrap fee account (now more commonly known as a separately managed account or SMA) as "any advisory program under which a specified fee or fees not based upon transactions in a client's account is charged for INVESTMENT ADVISORY services

(which may include PORTFOLIO management or advice concerning the selection of other investment advisers) and execution of client transactions." A typical separately managed account has a contract or contracts (and fee) involving a sponsor (usually a broker or independent provider) acting as the INVESTMENT ADVISOR, an investment management firm typically as the subadvisor, other services (custody, consulting, reporting, performance, manager selection, monitoring, and execution of trades), distributor, and the client (brokerage customer). Wrap fees can be all-inclusive, asset-based fees (which may include any combination of management, transaction, custody, and other ADMINISTRATIVE FEES).

CAPITAL EMPLOYED (REAL ESTATE)

The denominator of the return expressions, defined as the "weighted-average equity" (weighted-average capital) during the measurement period. CAPITAL EMPLOYED SHOULD not include any income or CAPITAL RETURN accrued during the measurement period. Beginning capital is adjusted by weighting the cash flows (contributions and distributions) that occurred during the period. Cash flows are typically weighted based on the actual days the flows are in or out of the PORTFOLIO. Other weighting methods are acceptable; however, once a methodology is chosen, it SHOULD be consistently applied.

CAPITAL RETURN (REAL ESTATE)

The change in the MARKET VALUE of the REAL ESTATE investments and cash/cash equivalent assets held throughout the measurement period (ENDING MARKET VALUE less beginning MARKET VALUE) adjusted for all capital expenditures (subtracted) and the net proceeds from sales (added). The return is computed as a percentage of the CAPITAL EMPLOYED through the measurement period. Synonyms: capital appreciation return, appreciation return.

CARRIED INTEREST (PRIVATE EQUITY)

The profits that GENERAL PARTNERS earn from the profits of the investments made by the fund (generally 20–25%). Also known as "carry."

CARVE-OUT

A single or multiple asset class segment of a multiple-asset-class PORTFOLIO.

CLOSED-END FUND (PRIVATE EQUITY)

A type of investment fund where the number of investors and the total COMMITTED CAPITAL is fixed and not open for subscriptions and/or redemptions.

COMMITTED CAPITAL (PRIVATE EQUITY)	Pledges of capital to a VENTURE CAPITAL fund. This money is typically not received at once but drawn down over three to five years, starting in the year the fund is formed. Also known as "commitments."
COMPOSITE	Aggregation of individual PORTFOLIOS representing a similar investment mandate, objective, or strategy.
COMPOSITE CREATION DATE	The date when the FIRM first groups the PORTFOLIOS to create a COMPOSITE. The COMPOSITE CREATION DATE is not necessarily the earliest date for which performance is reported for the COMPOSITE. (See the term "COMPOSITE INCEPTION DATE.")
COMPOSITE DEFINITION	Detailed criteria that determine the allocation of portfolios to COMPOSITES. COMPOSITE DEFINITIONS MUST be documented in the FIRM's policies and procedures.
COMPOSITE DESCRIPTION	General information regarding the strategy of the COMPOSITE. A description may be more abbreviated than the COMPOSITE DEFINITION but includes all salient features of the COMPOSITE.
COMPOSITE INCEPTION DATE	The earliest date for which performance is reported for the COMPOSITE. The COMPOSITE INCEPTION DATE is not necessarily the date the PORTFOLIOS are grouped together to create a COMPOSITE. Instead, it is the initial date of the performance record. (See the term "COMPOSITE CREATION DATE.")
CUSTODY FEES	The fees payable to the custodian for the safekeeping of the PORTFOLIO's assets. CUSTODY FEES typically contain an asset-based portion and a transaction-based portion of the fee. The total CUSTODY FEE may also include charges for additional services, including accounting, securities lending, or performance measurement. CUSTODY FEES that are charged per transaction SHOULD be included in the CUSTODY FEE and not included as part of the TRADING EXPENSES.
DIRECT INVESTMENTS (PRIVATE EQUITY)	An investment made directly in VENTURE CAPITAL or PRIVATE EQUITY assets (i.e., not via a partnership or fund).
DISPERSION	A measure of the spread of the annual returns of individual PORTFOLIOS within a COMPOSITE. Measures may include, but are not limited to, high/low, inter-quartile range, and standard deviation (asset weighted or equal weighted).

DISTINCT BUSINESS ENTITY	A unit, division, department, or office that is organizationally and functionally segregated from other units, divisions, departments, or offices and retains discretion over the assets it manages and should have autonomy over the investment decision-making process. Possible criteria that can be used to determine this include • being a legal entity • having a distinct market or client type (e.g., institutional, retail, private client, etc.) • using a separate and distinct investment process [corrected August 2005]
DISTRIBUTION (PRIVATE EQUITY)	Cash or the value of stock disbursed to the LIMITED PARTNERS of a venture fund.
DRAWDOWN (PRIVATE EQUITY)	After the total COMMITTED CAPITAL has been agreed upon between the GENERAL PARTNER and the LIMITED PARTNERS, the actual transfer of funds from the LIMITED PARTNERS' to the GENERAL PARTNERS' control in as many stages as deemed necessary by the GENERAL PARTNER is referred to as the drawdown.
ENDING MARKET VALUE (PRIVATE EQUITY)	The remaining equity that a LIMITED PARTNER has in a fund. Also referred to as net asset value or RESIDUAL VALUE.
EVERGREEN FUND (PRIVATE EQUITY)	An OPEN-END FUND that allows for on-going investment and/or redemption by investors. Some EVERGREEN FUNDS reinvest profits in order to ensure the availability of capital for future investments.
EX-ANTE **EX-POST**	Before the fact. (See the term "EX-POST.") After the fact. (See the term "EX-ANTE.")
EXTERNAL CASH FLOW	Cash, securities, or assets that enter or exit a PORTFOLIO.
EXTERNAL VALUATION (REAL ESTATE)	An EXTERNAL VALUATION is an assessment of MARKET VALUE performed by a third party who is a qualified, PROFESSIONALLY DESIGNATED, CERTIFIED, OR LICENSED COMMERCIAL PROPERTY VALUER/APPRAISER. EXTERNAL VALUATIONS MUST be completed following the valuation standards of the local governing appraisal body.
FAIR VALUE	The amount at which an asset could be acquired or sold in a current transaction between willing parties in which the parties each acted knowledgeably, prudently, and without compulsion.

FEE SCHEDULE	The FIRM's current INVESTMENT MANAGEMENT FEES or BUNDLED FEES for a particular presentation. This schedule is typically listed by asset level ranges and should be appropriate to the particular prospective client. [corrected September 2005]
FINAL REALIZATION DATE (PRIVATE EQUITY)	The date when a COMPOSITE is fully distributed.
FIRM	For purposes of the GIPS standards, the term "FIRM" refers to the entity defined for compliance with the GIPS standards. (See the term "DISTINCT BUSINESS ENTITY.")
GENERAL PARTNER (PRIVATE EQUITY)	(GP) a class of partner in a partnership. The GP retains liability for the actions of the partnership. In the PRIVATE EQUITY world, the GP is the fund manager and the LIMITED PARTNERS (LPs) are the institutional and high-net-worth investors in the partnership. The GP earns a management fee and a percentage of profits. (See the term "CARRIED INTEREST.")
GROSS-OF-FEES RETURN	The return on assets reduced by any TRADING EXPENSES incurred during the period.
GROSS-OF-FEES RETURN (PRIVATE EQUITY)	The return on assets reduced by any TRANSACTION EXPENSES incurred during the period.
INCOME RETURN (REAL ESTATE)	The investment income accrued on all assets (including cash and cash equivalents) during the measurement period net of all nonrecoverable expenditures, interest expense on debt, and property taxes. The return is computed as a percentage of the CAPITAL EMPLOYED through the measurement period.
INTERNAL VALUATION (REAL ESTATE)	An INTERNAL VALUATION is an advisor's or underlying third-party manager's best estimate of MARKET VALUE based on the most current and accurate information available under the circumstances. An INTERNAL VALUATION could include industry practice techniques, such as discounted cash flow, sales comparison, replacement cost, or a review of all significant events (both general market and asset specific) that could have a material impact on the investment. Prudent assumptions and estimates MUST be used, and the process MUST be applied consistently from period to period, except where a change would result in better estimates of MARKET VALUE.

INTERNAL RATE OF RETURN (PRIVATE EQUITY)

(IRR) is the annualized implied discount rate (effective compounded rate) that equates the present value of all the appropriate cash inflows (PAID-IN CAPITAL, such as draw-downs for net investments) associated with an investment with the sum of the present value of all the appropriate cash outflows (such as DISTRIBUTIONS) accruing from it and the present value of the unrealized residual PORTFOLIO (unliquidated holdings). For an interim cumulative return measurement, any IRR depends on the valuation of the residual assets.

INVESTED CAPITAL (PRIVATE EQUITY)

The amount of PAID-IN CAPITAL that has been invested in PORTFOLIO companies.

INVESTMENT ADVISOR (PRIVATE EQUITY)

Any individual or institution that supplies investment advice to clients on a per fee basis. The INVESTMENT ADVISOR inherently has no role in the management of the underlying PORTFOLIO companies of a partnership/fund.

INVESTMENT MANAGEMENT FEE

The fee payable to the investment management FIRM for the on-going management of a PORTFOLIO. INVESTMENT MANAGEMENT FEES are typically asset based (percentage of assets), performance based (based on performance relative to a BENCHMARK), or a combination of the two but may take different forms as well.

INVESTMENT MULTIPLE (TVPI MULTIPLE) (PRIVATE EQUITY)

The ratio of TOTAL VALUE to PAID-IN-CAPITAL. It represents the TOTAL RETURN of the investment to the original investment not taking into consideration the time invested. TOTAL VALUE can be found by adding the RESIDUAL VALUE and distributed capital together.

LARGE EXTERNAL CASH FLOW

The Standards do not contain a specified amount of cash or percentage that is considered to be a LARGE EXTERNAL CASH FLOW. Instead, FIRMS MUST define the COMPOSITE-specific size (amount or percentage) that constitutes a LARGE EXTERNAL CASH FLOW.

LIMITED PARTNER (PRIVATE EQUITY)

(LP) an investor in a LIMITED PARTNERSHIP. The GENERAL PARTNER is liable for the actions of the partnership and the LIMITED PARTNERS are generally protected from legal actions and any losses beyond their original investment. The LIMITED PARTNER receives income, capital gains, and tax benefits.

LIMITED PARTNERSHIP (PRIVATE EQUITY)	The legal structure used by most venture and PRIVATE EQUITY funds. Usually fixed life investment vehicles. The GENERAL PARTNER or management firm manages the partnership using the policy laid down in a partnership agreement. The agreement also covers terms, fees, structures, and other items agreed between the LIMITED PARTNERS and the GENERAL PARTNER.
MARKET VALUE	The current price at which investors buy or sell securities at a given time. [corrected August 2005]
MARKET VALUE (REAL ESTATE)	The most probable price that a property SHOULD bring in a competitive and open market under all conditions requisite to a fair sale, the buyer and seller each acting prudently and knowledgeably, and assuming the price is not affected by undue stimulus. Implicit in this definition is the consummation of a sale as of a specified date and the passing of title from seller to buyer under conditions whereby:

   a. Buyer and seller are typically motivated.
   b. Both parties are well informed or well advised and each acting in what they consider their own best interests.
   c. A reasonable time is allowed for exposure in the open market.
   d. Payment is made in terms of currency or in terms of financial arrangements comparable thereto.
   e. The price represents the normal consideration for the property sold unaffected by special or creative financing or sales concessions granted by anyone associated with the sale.

MUST	A REQUIRED provision for claiming compliance with the GIPS standards. (See the term "REQUIRE.")
NET-OF-FEES RETURN	The GROSS-OF-FEES RETURN reduced by the INVESTMENT MANAGEMENT FEE.
OPEN-END FUND (PRIVATE EQUITY)	A type of investment fund where the number of investors and the total COMMITTED CAPITAL is not fixed (i.e., open for subscriptions and/or redemptions). (See the term "EVERGREEN FUND.")
OPEN MARKET VALUE (REAL ESTATE) [corrected January 2006]	An opinion of the best price at which the sale of an interest in the property would have been completed unconditionally for cash consideration on the date of valuation, assuming: a. a willing seller;

b. that prior to the date of valuation there had been a reasonable period (having regard to the nature of the property and the state of the market) for the proper marketing of the interest, for the agreement of the price and terms, and for the completion of the sale;

c. that the state of the market, level of values, and other circumstances were on any earlier assumed date of Exchange of contracts the same as on the date of valuation;

d. that no account is taken of any additional bid by a prospective purchaser with a special interest; and

e. that both parties to the transaction had acted knowledgeably, prudently, and without compulsion.

PAID-IN CAPITAL (PRIVATE EQUITY)

The amount of COMMITTED CAPITAL a LIMITED PARTNER has actually transferred to a venture fund. Also known as the cumulative DRAWDOWN amount.

PIC MULTIPLE (PRIVATE EQUITY)

The ratio of PAID-IN-CAPITAL to COMMITTED CAPITAL. This ratio gives prospective clients information regarding how much of the total commitments has been drawn down.

PORTFOLIO

An individually managed pool of assets. A PORTFOLIO may be a subportfolio, account, or pooled fund.

PRIVATE EQUITY

PRIVATE EQUITY includes, but is not limited to, organizations devoted to VENTURE CAPITAL, leveraged buyouts, consolidations, mezzanine and distressed debt investments, and a variety of hybrids, such as venture leasing and venture factoring.

PROFESSIONALLY DESIGNATED, CERTIFIED, OR LICENSED COMMERCIAL PROPERTY VALUER/ APPRAISER (REAL ESTATE)

In Europe, Canada, and parts of southeast Asia, the predominant professional designation is that of the Royal Institution of Chartered Surveyors (RICs). In the United States, the professional designation is Member [of the] Appraisal Institute (MAI). In addition, each state regulates REAL ESTATE appraisers, and based on one's experience, body of work, and test results, is then registered, licensed, or certified.

REAL ESTATE

REAL ESTATE investments include

- Wholly owned or partially owned properties,
- Commingled funds, property unit trusts, and insurance company separate accounts,
- Unlisted, private placement securities issued by private REAL ESTATE investment trusts (REITs) and REAL ESTATE operating companies (REOCs), and
- Equity-oriented debt, such as participating mortgage loans or any private interest in a property where some portion of return to the investor at the time of investment is related to the performance of the underlying REAL ESTATE.

REALIZATION MULTIPLE (PRIVATE EQUITY)	The REALIZATION MULTIPLE (DPI) is calculated by dividing the cumulative DISTRIBUTIONS by the PAID-IN-CAPITAL.
RECOMMEND/ RECOMMENDATION	Suggested provision for claiming compliance with the GIPS standards. A RECOMMENDATION is considered to be best practice but is not a REQUIREMENT. (See the term "SHOULD.")
REQUIRE/REQUIREMENT	A provision that MUST be followed for compliance with the GIPS standards. (See the term "MUST.")
RESIDUAL VALUE (PRIVATE EQUITY)	The remaining equity that a LIMITED PARTNER has in the fund. (The value of the investments within the fund.) Also can be referred to as ENDING MARKET VALUE or net asset value.
RESIDUAL VALUE TO PAID-IN-CAPITAL (RVPI) (PRIVATE EQUITY)	RESIDUAL VALUE divided by the PAID-IN-CAPITAL.
SETTLEMENT DATE ACCOUNTING	Recognizing the asset or liability on the date when the exchange of cash, securities, and paperwork involved in a transaction is completed. Impact on performance: Between TRADE DATE and SETTLEMENT DATE, an account does not recognize any change between the price of the transaction and the current MARKET VALUE. Instead, on SETTLEMENT DATE, the total difference between the price of the transaction and the current MARKET VALUE is recognized on that day. (See the term "TRADE DATE ACCOUNTING.")
SHOULD	Encouraged (RECOMMENDED) to follow the RECOMMENDATION of the GIPS standards but not REQUIRED. (See the term "RECOMMEND.")
SUPPLEMENTAL	Any performance-related information included as part of a compliant performance presentation that supplements or enhances the REQUIRED and/or RECOMMENDED disclosure and presentation provisions of the GIPS standards.
TEMPORARY NEW ACCOUNT	A tool that FIRMS can use to remove the effect of significant cash flows on a PORTFOLIO. When a significant cash flow occurs in a portfolio, the FIRM may treat this cash flow as a "TEMPORARY NEW ACCOUNT," allowing the FIRM to implement the mandate of the PORTFOLIO without the impact of the cash flow on the performance of the PORTFOLIO.
TIME-WEIGHTED RATE OF RETURN	Calculation that computes period-by-period returns on an investment and removes the effects of EXTERNAL CASH FLOWS, which are generally client-driven, and best reflects the FIRM's ability to manage assets according to a specified strategy or objective.

TOTAL FIRM ASSETS

TOTAL FIRM ASSETS are all assets for which a FIRM has investment management responsibility. TOTAL FIRM ASSETS include assets managed outside the FIRM (e.g., by subadvisors) for which the FIRM has asset allocation authority.

TOTAL RETURN (REAL ESTATE)

The change in the MARKET VALUE of the PORTFOLIO, adjusted for all capital expenditures (subtracted), net proceeds from sales (added), and investment income accrued (added) during the measurement period expressed as a percentage of the CAPITAL EMPLOYED in the PORTFOLIO over the measurement period.

TOTAL VALUE (PRIVATE EQUITY)

RESIDUAL VALUE of the PORTFOLIO plus distributed capital.

TRADE DATE ACCOUNTING

The transaction is reflected in the PORTFOLIO on the date of the purchase or sale, and not on the SETTLEMENT DATE. Recognizing the asset or liability within at least 3 days of the date the transaction is entered into (Trade Date, T+ 1, T+2 or T+3) all satisfy the TRADE DATE ACCOUNTING REQUIREMENT for purposes of the GIPS standards. (See "SETTLEMENT DATE ACCOUNTING.")

TRADING EXPENSES

The costs of buying or selling a security. These costs typically take the form of brokerage commissions or spreads from either internal or external brokers. CUSTODY FEES charged per transaction SHOULD be considered CUSTODY FEES and not direct transaction costs. Estimated TRADING EXPENSES are not permitted.

TRANSACTION EXPENSES (PRIVATE EQUITY)

Include all legal, financial, advisory, and investment banking fees related to buying, selling, restructuring, and recapitalizing PORTFOLIO companies.

VENTURE CAPITAL (PRIVATE EQUITY)

Risk capital in the form of equity and/or loan capital that is provided by an investment institution to back a business venture that is expected to grow in value.

VINTAGE YEAR (PRIVATE EQUITY)

The year that the VENTURE CAPITAL or PRIVATE EQUITY fund or partnership first draws down or calls capital from its investors.

APPENDIX **B**

CORRECTIONS TO GIPS STANDARDS 2005

Last updated October 31, 2006

Provision	Original	Correction
II. Provisions of the Global Investment Performance Standards (page 6)	2. Calculation Methodology: Achieving comparability among firms' performance presentations REQUIRES . . .	2. Calculation Methodology: Achieving comparability among firms' performance presentations requires . . .
2.A.1	TOTAL RETURN, including realized and unrealized gains and losses plus income, MUST be used.	Total return, including realized and unrealized gains and losses plus income, MUST be used.
5.A.1.c	. . . If the COMPOSITE contains less than 5 PORTFOLIOS, the number of PORTFOLIOS is not REQUIRED.	. . . if the COMPOSITE contains 5 PORTFOLIOS or less, the number of PORTFOLIOS is not REQUIRED.
5.A.1.d	. . . If the COMPOSITE contains less than 5 PORTFOLIOS for the full year, a measure of DISPERSION is not REQUIRED.	. . . If the COMPOSITE contains 5 PORTFOLIOS or less for the full year, a measure of DISPERSION is not REQUIRED.
5.A.6	The TOTAL RETURN for the BENCHMARK (or BENCHMARKS) that reflects . . .	The total return for the BENCHMARK (or BENCHMARKS) that reflects . . .
5.B.2	. . . over time of the COMPOSITE and BENCHMARK returns.	. . . over time of the COMPOSITE and BENCHMARK returns.
6. Real Estate	. . . all the required and recommended elements of the GIPS standards (outlined in Section II.1 through Section II.5.), . . .	. . . all the required and recommended elements of the GIPS standards (outlined in Section II.0 through Section II.5.), . . .

6.A.3.a	. . . (1) calculated separately using chain-linked TIME-WEIGHTED RATE OF RETURN, (2) adjusted such that the sum of THE INCOME RETURN and the CAPITAL RETURN is equal to the TOTAL RETURN, or (3) income cash recognition mode	. . . (1) calculated separately using chain-linked TIME-WEIGHTED RATE OF RETURN, or (2) adjusted such that the sum of THE INCOME RETURN and the CAPITAL RETURN is equal to the TOTAL RETURN, ~~or (3) income cash recognition mode,~~
6.A.3.f	The percent of total MARKET VALUE of COMPOSITE assets (asset weighted not equally weighted) total REAL ESTATE assets valued by an EXTERNAL VALUATION for each period, and	The percent of total MARKET VALUE of COMPOSITE assets (asset weighted not equally weighted) to total REAL ESTATE assets valued by an EXTERNAL VALUATION for each period, and
7. Private Equity	. . . all the required and recommended elements of the GIPS standards (outline in Section ll.l through Section II.5.), . . .	. . . all the required and recommended elements of the GIPS standards (outline in Section II.0 through Section II.5.), . . .
Appendix A Example 4: Private Equity Partners Disclosures	The required fee schedule disclosure is inadvertently omitted.	Include sample disclosure text: The standard fee schedule currently in effect is as follows: 1.00% of assets under management. In addition, there is a 20% incentive fee for all assets. The incentive fee is applied to the value added in excess of fees, expenses, and the return of the GP-BO Index.
Glossary, definition of DISTINCT BUSINESS ENTITY	A unit, division, department, or office that is organizationally and functionally segregated from other units, divisions, departments, or office and retains discretion over the assets it manages and autonomy over the investment decision-making process.	A unit, division, department, or office that is organizationally and functionally segregated from other units, divisions, departments, or office and retains discretion over the assets it manages and should have autonomy over the investment decision-making process.
Glossary, definition of FEE SCHEDULE	. . . This schedule is typically listed by asset level ranges and ~~SHOULD~~ be appropriate to the particular prospective client.	. . . This schedule is typically listed by asset level ranges and ~~MUST~~ should be appropriate to the particular prospective client.
Glossary, definition of MARKET VALUE	The current listed price at which investors buy or sell securities at a given time.	The current ~~listed~~ price at which investors buy or sell securities at a given time.
Glossary, definition of OPEN MARKET VALUE (PRIVATE EQUITY)	Open Market Value ~~(PRIVATE EQUITY)~~	Open Market Value (REAL ESTATE)

ABOUT THE CONTRIBUTORS

Brent Ambrose
Jeffery L. and Cindy M. King Faculty Fellow and Professor of Real Estate, The Smeal College of Business at Pennsylvania State University

Jeremy Armitage, CFA
Managing Director and Head of Research, State Street Global Markets

Jeffery V. Bailey, CFA
Director, Benefits Finance, Target Corporation

Stan Beckers
Managing Director, Barclays Global Investors

Gilbert L. Beebower
Senior Vice President of SEI Corporation

Gary P. Brinson
President of GP Brinson Investments

Nancy Calkins
Chief Investment Officer, San Joaquin County Employees' Retirement Association

Honghui Chen
Assistant Professor of Finance, University of Central Florida

Neil Constable
Portfolio Manager and Quantitative Research Analyst, Grantham, Mayo, Van Otterloo and Co. LLC.

Crystal Detamore-Rodman
Freelance Journalist

Dan DiBartolomeo
President, Northfield Information Services

Wayne E. Ferson
Full Professor and Endowed Chair, Marshall School of Business, University of Southern California and Research Associate, National Bureau of Economic Research

John G. Gallo, CFA
Visiting Associate Professor of Finance, Tippie College of Business, University of Iowa

Stephen C. Gaudette, CFA
Northfield Information Services, Inc.

Thomas H. Goodwin
Director, Portfolio Strategies, Russell Investments

Philip Halpern
Private Equity Investor and CIO of Tellus Asset Management

Cynthia Harrington, CFA
Financial Journalist

L. Randolph Hood, CFA
Chief Investment Officer, ERISA Benefits Plans, The Prudential Insurance Company of America

Michael Y. Hu
Bridgestone Chair in International Business and Professor of Marketing at Kent State University

Roger G. Ibbotson
Professor of Finance at Yale School of Management, Chairman & CIO at Zebra Capital Management, and Founder of Ibbotson Associates, a Morningstar Company

Daniel C. Indro
Associate Professor of Finance, Penn State University, Great Valley School of Graduate Professional Studies

Christine X. Jiang
Professor of Finance, University of Memphis

Ronald N. Kahn
Vice President and Director of Research, BARRA

Paul D. Kaplan, CFA
Vice President, Quantitative Research, Morningstar, Inc.

Denis S. Karnosky
Managing Partner, Head of Asset Allocation and Chairman of the Asset Allocation Committee at Brinson Partners, Inc.

Philip Lawton, CFA, CIPM
Head, CIPM Program, CFA Institute

Wayne Y. Lee
Alice L. Walton Chair in Finance and Executive Director, Garrison Financial Institute

Bing Liang
Professor of Finance, Isenberg School of Management, University of Massachusetts-Amherst

Andrew W. Lo
Harris & Harris Group Professor at the Sloan School of Management, Massachusetts Institute of Technology, Cambridge, and Chief Scientific Officer for AlphaSimplex Group, LLC

Angelo Lobosco, CFA
Vice President, State Street Global Advisors

Larry J. Lockwood, CFA
C.R. Williams Professor of Financial Services, Texas Christian University

Christopher G. Luck, CFA
Partner and Director of Equity Portfolio Management, First Quadrant, LP

John P. Meier, CFA
Managing Director, Strategic Investment Solutions, Inc.

José Menchero, CFA
Executive Director, MSCI Barra

Arun S. Muralidhar
Chairman and CIO of AlphaEngine Global Investment Solutions LLC

William L. Nemerever, CFA
Partner, Grantham, Mayo, Van Otterloo & Company, LLC

Gregory Noronha, CFA
Professor of Finance, Milgard School of Business at the University of Washington

Cornelia Paape
Head of Financial Engineering, IDS GmbH – Analysis and Reporting Services, A company of Allianz, Germany

Vijay Poduri, CFA
Managing Director & Analyst, Charles Schwab Investment Management

Meijun Qian
Assistant Professor, National University of Singapore

W. Bruce Remington, CFA
Vice President and Senior Regional Investment Manager, Wells Fargo Institutional Asset Advisors

Thomas M. Richards, CFA
Nuveen Investment Solutions

Andrew Rudd
Chief Executive Officer, BARRA

Tom Ruggels
Senior Investment Officer, Washington State Investment Board

Louisa Wright Sellers
Founder, Weightman Advisory LLC

Laurence B. Siegel
Director of Research, The Ford Foundation

Vijay Singal, CFA
Head of the Department of Finance and J. Gray Ferguson Professor of Finance, Pamplin College of Business at Virginia Tech

Brian D. Singer, CFA
Independent Investor

Michael Stutzer
Director, Burridge Center for Securities Analysis and Valuation, Leeds School of Business, University of Colorado

Kevin Terhaar, CFA
Managing Principal, Stairway Partners

David E. Tierney
Nuveen HydePark Group

Susan Trammell, CFA
Financial Journalist

Arthur Warga
Judge James A. Elkins Professor of Banking and Finance and Dean, C.T. Bauer College of Business, University of Houston

Vincent A. Warther
Senior Vice President, Compass Lexecon

INDEX

Page references followed by *fig* indicate an illustrated figure; followed by *t* indicate a table.

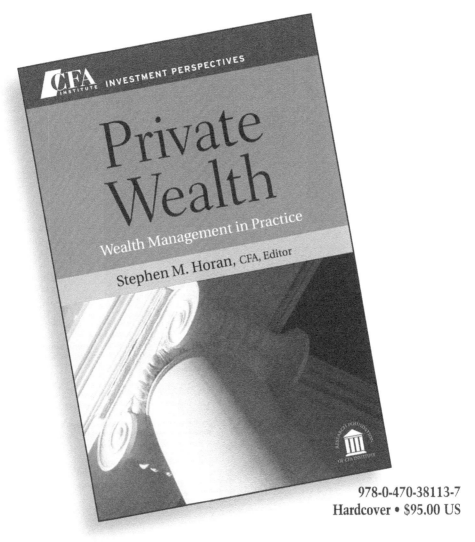

Setting the
industry standard

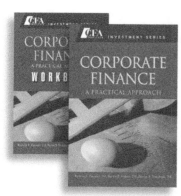

Printed and bound by CPI Group (UK) Ltd, Croydon, CR0 4YY

23/04/2025

14661016-0001